CALENDAR OF NATIONAL LIBRARY MEETINGS

The question mark (?) indicates meeting date or place was *tentative* at the time of compilation—November 1977. Dates are given in the following order: month/day; e.g., 7/1-4 is July 1 through 4.

Note: At the time of compilation, information was not available from American Society of Indexers and Association of Jewish Libraries; The Library Public Relations Council does not hold an annual meeting.

Compiled for the Council of National Library Associations by Caryn S. Katz, Conference and Exhibits Coordinator, Special Libraries Association. Reprinted by courtesy of Special Libraries Association.

	1978	1979	1980
AMERICAN ASSOCIATION OF LAW LIBRARIES	6/25-29 Rochester, New York	7/1-4 San Francisco	6/22-25 St. Louis
AMERICAN LIBRARY ASSOCIATION			
Midwinter	1/22-28 Chicago	1/21-27 Chicago	1/20-26 Chicago
Conference	6/25-7/1 Chicago	6/24-30 Dallas	6/29-7/5 New York City
AMERICAN SOCIETY FOR INFORMATION SCIENCE			
Mid-Year Meeting	5/22-24 Houston		
Conference	11/13-17 New York City	10/14-18 Minneapolis	10/5-10 Anaheim, California
AMERICAN SOCIETY OF INDEXERS: *See Note*			
AMERICAN THEOLOGICAL LIBRARY ASSOCIATION	6/19-24 Latrobe, Pennsylvania	6/??-?? Minneapolis/St. Paul	
ART LIBRARIES SOCIETY OF NORTH AMERICA (ARLIS/NA)	1/20-25 New York	3/??-??	1/??-?? New Orleans
ASSOCIATION OF AMERICAN LIBRARY SCHOOLS	1/20-22 Chicago	1/19-21 Chicago	1/18-20 Chicago
ASSOCIATION OF JEWISH LIBRARIES: *See Note*			
ASSOCIATION OF RESEARCH LIBRARIES	5/4-5 Nashville; 10/25-26 Washington, D.C.	5/10-11 Boston; 10/??-?? Washington, D.C.	10/??-?? Washington, D.C.
CANADIAN LIBRARY ASSOCIATION	6/15-21 Edmonton	6/14-20 Ottawa	6/12-18 Vancouver
CATHOLIC LIBRARY ASSOCIATION	3/27-30 St. Louis	4/16-19 Philadelphia	4/7-10 New Orleans
CHURCH AND SYNAGOGUE LIBRARY ASSOCIATION	6/25-27 Grand Rapids, Michigan	(?) 6/17-19 Richmond, Virginia	(?) 6/15-17 Colorado Springs
COUNCIL OF PLANNING LIBRARIANS	4/28-5/1 Indianapolis		
INFORMATION INDUSTRY ASSOCIATION (IIA)			
Annual Meeting	9/??-??	9-10/??	
National Information Conference and Exposition	4/16-19 Washington, D.C.	4/??-?? Washington, D.C.	4/??-?? Washington, D.C.
National Information Policy	2/21-22 Washington, D.C.		
LIBRARY PUBLIC RELATIONS COUNCIL: *See Note*			
MEDICAL LIBRARY ASSOCIATION	6/10-15 Chicago	6/2-7 Honolulu	6/14-19 Washington, D.C.
MUSIC LIBRARY ASSOCIATION	2/27-3/4 Boston	2/5-10 New Orleans	2/11-16 Washington, D.C.
NATIONAL COMPUTER CONFERENCE	6/5-8 Anaheim, California		
NATIONAL FEDERATION OF ABSTRACTING AND INDEXING SERVICES	3/7-8 Philadelphia	3/6-7 Arlington, Virginia	
SPECIAL LIBRARIES ASSOCIATION			
Winter Meeting	2/1-3 Indianapolis	2/1-3 Tucson	1/30-2/1 San Antonio
Conference	6/11-15 Kansas City	6/10-14 Honolulu	6/8-12 Washington, D.C.
Fall Meeting	11/2-4 New York City	10/11-13 New York City	10/30-11/1 New York City
THEATRE LIBRARY ASSOCIATION			
Conference (one day during ALA)	6/25-7/1 Chicago	6/24-30 Dallas	6/29-7/5 New York City
Fall Meeting	Date of business meeting not set until spring of same year. Usually last Friday in October or first Friday in November.		

AMERICAN LIBRARY ASSOCIATION HIGHLIGHTS AND ORGANIZATION

The American Library Association is the oldest and largest library association in the world. ALA was founded in 1876. The first meeting, organized by Melvil Dewey, was held in Philadelphia, October 4–6, and drew 103 librarians. Since its first meeting, ALA has grown in membership to more than 35,100.

The ALA COUNCIL is the governing body of the Association. It comprises 100 Councilors elected at large and Councilors representing each state, provincial, and territorial chapter. (See Council, ALA, p. 102). Council convenes at two meetings held each year: Midwinter (January) and Annual Conference (summer). The management arm of the Association is the EXECUTIVE BOARD, which comprises the officers of the Association, the immediate Past President, and eight members elected by Council from its membership.

PRESIDENT: Eric Moon, President, Scarecrow Press (June 1977-June 1978)

VICE-PRESIDENT/PRESIDENT-ELECT: Russell Shank

EXECUTIVE DIRECTOR: Robert Wedgeworth

MEMBERSHIP: 30,898 personal members; 4,221 organization members; total (August 31, 1977) 35,119

ANNUAL EXPENDITURES: (August 31, 1977):
General fund	$2,254,561
Publishing	3,353,548
Annual meetings	565,106
	$6,173,215

ANNUAL CONFERENCES: Detroit June 17–23, 1977; Chicago June 25–July 1, 1978; Dallas June 24–30, 1979

The goal of the Association is the promotion of libraries and librarianship to assure the delivery of user-oriented library information service to all. Much of its work is done through ALA Committees.

ACTIVITIES of the Association include:
- Research on library problems
- Development of standards and guidelines
- Accreditation of library education programs
- Clarification of legislative issues
- Vigorous support of intellectual freedom
- Publishing
- Awards
- Leadership in national and international library cooperation

ROUND TABLES are membership units which deal with aspects of librarianship outside the scope of a Division:

- American Library History Round Table 23
- Exhibits Round Table 126
- Federal Librarians Round Table 127
- Government Documents Round Table 139
- Intellectual Freedom Round Table 160
- International Relations Round Table 164
- Junior Members Round Table 165
- Library Research Round Table 180
- Social Responsibilities Round Table 295
- Staff Organizations Round Table 302

ALA OFFICES are headquarters staff units which can address issues that affect the entire profession: Accreditation (14), Intellectual Freedom (155), Service to the Disadvantaged (112), Personnel (223), Research (268), and Legislation (167).

ALA AFFILIATES (1977) covered in text articles are: American Association of Law Libraries (20); American Library Society (24); American Society for Information Science (26); American Theological Library Association (27); Association of Research Libraries (38); Canadian Library Association (80); Catholic Library Association (85); Chinese American Librarians Association (92); Council on Library Technical Assistants (108); Medical Library Association (187); Music Library Association (192); Oral History Association (213); REFORMA (National Associtaion of Spanish-Speaking Librarians) (263); Theatre Library Association (308); and Urban Libraries Council (318).

ALA CHAPTERS are covered under State Reports (pp. 350–416).

ALA UNITS

DIVISIONS of ALA are membership units which provide resources for special knowledge and for advancing knowledge and service through publications and professional programs: The Divisions are:

- American Association of School Librarians 21
- American Library Trustee Association 25
- Association for Library Service to Children 34
- Association of College and Research Libraries 36
- Association of State Library Agencies 42
- Health and Rehabilitative Library Services Division 141
- Information Science and Automation Division 153
- Library Administration Division 172
- Library Education Division 173
- Public Library Association 240
- Reference and Adult Services Division 258
- Resources and Technical Services Division 275
- Young Adult Services Division 333

1978 The ALA Yearbook

A review of
library events 1977
Volume 3 (1978)

American Library Association
Chicago, Illinois

ILLUSTRATION CREDITS

Genealogy and Library Service: xxiv Longin Lonczyna, Jr./courtesy, Latter Day Saints Genealogical Library. xxvi The Newberry Library.

Our Fragile Inheritance: The Challenge of Preserving Library Materials: xxxi Art Plotnik. xxxii, xxxiii Vaghi-Parma. xxxiv *Chicago Sun-Times,* Chuck Kirman. xxxviii Baltimore County Library System. xxxix (t.) Jane Greenfield, Yale University. xlii *American Libraries.*

Library Association Centenary: xliii Cyril Bernard, *Library Association Record.*

Review of the Library Year: 5 Frank Armstrong. 6 Idaho State University, Pocatello. 7 Design Photography, Bob Hitchcock. 9 Northern Illinois University. 19 (t.l.) Nassau Library System; (second l.) Dallas Public Library; (third l.) Topeka Public Library; (b.l.) Akron-Summit County Public Library; (t.r.) Francis X. Feighan, Jr.; (second r.) Houston Public Library; (b.r.) Cincinnati and Hamilton County Public Library. 29 *American Libraries.* 35 ALA. 43 CL Systems, Inc. 45 Dallas Public Library. 59 (r.) Giacomelli Venezie. 60 (r.) Fabian Bachrach. 63 (m.) Kathy Williams; (l.) Art Plotnik. 65 (t.) Art Plotnik; (l.) University of Sussex; (r.) Arthur Swoger. 67 (t.r.) Dementi-Foster. 69 Mississippi Library Commission. 71 (b. & t.) *American Libraries* (m.) © Susan Meiselas: Magnum Dist. Applied Photography Ltd. 74 Chicago Public Library. 75 (t.) Hare Photographs, Inc.; (b.) Chicago Public Library. 76 (t. & r.) Long Beach Public Library; (b.) Omaha Public Library. 80 National Library of Canada. 81 Kathy Williams, CLA Staff. 86 The Children's Book Council, Inc. 87 (t.) *Des Moines Register and Tribune;* (b.) The Children's Book Council, Inc. 88 (t.) Chicago Public Library; (t.r.) Nassau Library System; (r.) Delaware County Public Library. 89 (t.l.) Fred Griffith, *The Commercial Appeal;* (b.l.) Dial Press (r. & margin) George Janoff. 90 (t.) T.Y. Crowell; (b.) Chris Casson, Harper & Row. 91 (top l. & r.) Studio Cole Ltd., from Scribners; (m.) William Bond; (b.) Peter Ferman. 92 (l.) Elliot Fry; (r.) F. Warne Publishers, Ltd. 94 CL Systems, Inc. 95 (t.) Chicago Public Library; (m.) University of Houston; (b.) Dallas Public Library. 98 Milwaukee Public Library. 99 Wyoming State Library. 103 Arkansas Library Association. 109 Oscar Rose Library. 113 (t.) West Virginia Library Commission; (b.) Missouri State Library. 117 Collin Clark, California State Library. 119 Chicago Public Library. 122 Chicago Public Library. 126 PALA. 127 FLIRT. 129 (t.l.) Cinema 5; (lower l.) New Day Films; (t. margin) Phoenix Films, Inc.; (b. margin) Tom Davenport. 130 Phoenix Films, Inc. 131 Marsh Film Enterprises, Inc. 132 Coronet Instructional Media. 133 (l.) West Virginia Library Commission; (r.) Lassau Library System. 135 (t.) Fred Griffith, *The Commercial Appeal;* (b.) Dallas Public Library. 138, 142 Phil Moloitis, Chicago Public Library. 145 IFLA. 148 (r.) Houston Public Library; (margin) CL Systems, Inc. 155 Dallas Public Library. 158 ALA. 189 (l.) IZON Corporation; (r.) Alpine Micrographics. 191 West Virginia Library Commission. 192 *Chicago Sun-Times,* Jim Klepitsch. 197 Houston Public Library. 199 National Library of Medicine. 201 NTIS. 207 (l.) Library of Congress. 208 (r.) Library of Congress. 210 Hess Studios. 211 (m.) Missouri State Library; (r.) Library of Congress. 225 Rothco Cartoons, Inc. 228 Art Plotnik. 237 Marvin M. Greene, *Cleveland Plain Dealer;* (margin) Bruce Wands. 238 Houston Public Library. 242 Michigan Library Association. 243 Public Library of Cincinnati and Hamilton County. 244 ALA. 245 West Virginia Library Commission. 246 ALA. 249 ALA. 250 ALA. 256 Dallas Public Library. 262 Art Plotnik. 267 Joan Roberts. 277 Margaret M. Seylar School. 291 Topeka Public Library. 295 Art Plotnik. 301 Special Libraries Association. 307 *American Libraries.* 308 (t.) Virginia Mulloy; (b.) Mississippi Library Commission. 309 (t.) Christian Steiner; (b.) Rhoda Nathans. 310 Memphis Public Library and Information Center. 311 (t.) Chicago Public Library; (b.) Arkansas Library Association. 312 (l.) Nassau Library System; (r.) West Virginia Library Commission. 318 Universal Serials and Book Exchange. 321 Art Plotnik. 328 R. Haustaerr. 329 (t.l., t.r., m.l.) *New York Times;* (m.r.) Zoe Kamitses; (b.l., b.r.) Dial Press. 330 (t.l.) Bobbie Cormier; (t.r.) Pantheon; (b.l.) Ruth Putter; (m.) Delacorte Press; (b.r.) Ruth Putter. 331 (t.l.) Crown Publishers, Inc.; (b.l.) Thor Publishing Co.

London Correspondent's Report: 343 *The Coleraine Chronicle.* 344 Cyril Bernard. 345 Nottinghamshire County Council. 348 (t.) IAS Cargo Airlines; (b.) George Allen and Unwin Ltd. 349 Phaidon Press Limited

Volume 1 (1976)
Volume 2 (1977)
Volume 3 (1978)

020.62274 American Library Association—Yearbooks
    Library Associations—Yearbooks. Main entry: title
    [Publisher's cataloging].
LC 76-647548
ISBN 0-8389-0261-8

Copyright © 1978 by the American Library Association

All rights reserved. No part of this publication may be reproduced in any form without permission in writing from the publisher, except by a reviewer who may quote brief passages in a review.

Printed in the United States of America.

ALA—PROGRESS AND PROSPECTS

American librarianship is a rich and diverse discipline. Its practitioners apply themselves with equal vigor and commitment to traditional and to novel ventures. In their role as archons of the mechanisms of cultural transfer, they cherish the real image of text on parchment and search for the utility of the virtual image in holograms and cablevision with the same respect.

As the entries in this *Yearbook* attest, the American Library Association mirrors this range of interest. Even more, the Association is dedicated to the sustenance of openness and active outreach that are the hallmarks of American library service in all of its sectors, public and private. Its standards and protocols, its studies and publications, its internal and public programs all strive to improve the performance of librarians and libraries. These are the activities described in the *Yearbook*.

It is impossible to summarize, or even characterize, the events of the world of library service that are reported in the 1978 *Yearbook*. Many things stand out. With the advent of the new administration in the White House we note a hope among librarians for a renewal of federal relationships with library planners. We are on the threshold of a new era of bibliography through the combination of the development of a new cataloging code and the focus at the highest national level on bibliographic networks. A spate of national studies has called attention to the lack of a national information and communications policy. The change of political administrations has slowed deliberations on this vital topic but, we hope, only temporarily. There is obvious progress in expanding the literature of the nation's new social consciousness, and there is a strong movement to enhance the power of human rights in employee-management relationships in libraries. After years of arduous deliberations the nation has a new copyright law that will have an impact on a number of critical aspects of library service. These phenomena and events—and more—are reported in the following pages.

The stresses in the nation's library enterprise, identified in the introductions to previous *Yearbooks*, remain largely unabated. These stresses are principally due to inflation in the economy and the growing power of new communications technology that challenges traditions in library service. Now, however, we look forward to a major national examination of the needs and the delineation of recommendations to meet them. A White House Conference on Library and Information Services is scheduled for 1979, to be preceded by citizens' conferences in each state and territory. Even if the goals of the conferences are long in coming to fulfillment, we should expect benefits from the raising of consciousness among those whom libraries serve—or would serve—of the potential and the plight of libraries. The American Library Association has begun, and will continue, to mobilize its resources in order to enable the profession to work towards the fulfillment of public expectations that should flow from the White House Conference.

The American Library Association is often criticized for allowing its members to spend what appears to be too much time in contemplation of its organizational problems, and on negotiations for place and status in the Association's structure. The activities reported in this *Yearbook* belie that criticism. Much public attention is indeed given to infrastructure and relationships at the conferences and meetings of the Association. But its members are concurrently very hard at work on the substance of librarianship, working inside the organization—in the divisions, sections, committees, round tables, discussion groups, and caucuses—created in the public furor. The two activities are inextricably tied together and the process of creating the products of librarianship is probably well served by the constant attention to the need for change in the structure of the Association—which, after all is said and done, tries only to accommodate to the world in which libraries operate.

RUSSELL SHANK

EDITOR'S INTRODUCTION

The year 1977 saw two significant international milestones. In September the International Federation of Library Associations and Institutions (IFLA) celebrated its 50th anniversary in Brussels with a well-attended meeting held under the patronage of the King of Belgium. It featured a program organized by the American Vice-President, Dr. Robert Vosper of the University of California, Los Angeles. One month later, the Library Association (U.K.) celebrated its centenary in London. During the centenary the American Library Association President, Eric Moon, led a parade of library associations from around the world in extending congratulations and best wishes. Rosamond Kerr has written about the centenary in a feature article for this volume.

Signs of encouragement for library history that emerged during 1977 include the reorganization of the Library of Congress and the first two Pre-White House Conference meetings in the states of Georgia and Pennsylvania. Those events are recorded in various articles within *The ALA Yearbook 1978*, giving evidence of a mood of hope slowly spreading throughout the library world. *The ALA Yearbook 1978* is distinguished by a solid group of feature articles preceding the review of the year.

One of the most controversial issues to surface during 1977 is explored by Peter Watson in *The Dilemma of Fees for Service: Issues and Action for Librarians*. Watson looks at the developing pressure around libraries to charge for services as a way to offset expenses of the new technology and to expand services offered by it. He concludes with his own guidelines to librarians confronting this problem.

Russell Bidlack characterizes the phenomenal growth of interest in genealogy while focusing upon the costly burden which it is placing upon contemporary libraries. His article *Genealogy as it Relates to Library Service* is a rewarding summary of the scope of that new interest, the problem it poses to libraries, and the methods and ways in which libraries are meeting the challenge. In addition, it is a useful guide to the reader on how to approach research on one's own family background. In *Passing Through the Turnstile: A View of Library School Administrations*, Kay Murray examines the question of who decides who is to become a librarian through professional education and, also, how professional schools set policies and standards of admissions. Pamela Darling's *Our Fragile Inheritance: The Challenge of Preserving Library Materials*, is a lucid and fascinating discussion of the growing concern and the growing problems of preserving the irreplaceable treasures of the world's libraries and the modern techniques being employed. She suggests that the Florence floods of 1966 brought about a new awareness of the threat, but that every library collection is steadily undergoing a "quiet disaster" of disintegration from humidity, termites, mold, pollutants, and chemical deterioration, in addition to the more dramatic disasters posed by flood, fire, and theft. Perhaps the strongest appeal for action presented to the library community in recent years, it is an interesting examination of recent developments in preservation and conservation.

In addition to the feature articles, this third volume in the *Yearbook* series provides highlights to such diverse topics as how trustees cope with personnel problems, how some libraries have solved building and remodeling problems on low budgets, a history and outline of the ALA archives, the standardization of international library statistics during the past twenty years, a report on a visit of U.S. librarians to the U.S.S.R., a report on disasters that struck U.S. libraries during 1977, Daniel Boorstin's remarks on the establishment of a Center for the Book at the Library of Congress, highlights on the second edition of the Anglo-American Cataloguing Rules, a copyright bibliography, and a piece on Peter Rabbit, celebrating his 75th anniversary.

Within the A through Z articles there were no major changes in titles this year. We dropped several titles in areas that did not seem to provide enough change to warrant an annual review—furniture, international school librarianship, budgeting and accounting—while we incorporated such titles as interlibrary cooperation into networks. In this year's book we continue an idea which was born with the first volume (1976), that is, to present a unique and comprehensive review of contemporary librarianship focusing upon significant events, activities, and persons. It offers an across-the-board report of every aspect of library and information service: professional, technological, political organizations both in North America and abroad. Its biographical section recognizes librarians who have distinguished themselves during the year; its obituaries mark the passing of distinguished figures in the world of librarianship. In addition, of course, there are the individual state reports as well as reports from Canada and London. Our contributors, who make the work possible, are named with the titles of their articles in the list beginning on page xi.

ROBERT WEDGEWORTH
Editor in Chief

ADVISERS

Warren B. Kuhn, *Chairperson,*
Dean, Library Services, Iowa State University, Ames, Iowa

Lillian Bradshaw, *Director,*
Public Library System, Dallas, Texas

Jack Dalton, *Director,*
Columbia University Library Development Center

William DeJohn, *Director,*
Pacific Northwest Bibliographic Center

Mary V. Gaver, *Director*
of Library Consulting Services, Bro-Dart, Inc.

Warren J. Haas, *Vice-President and University Librarian,*
Columbia University

Edward G. Holley, *Dean,*
School of Library Science, University of North Carolina

Clara Stanton Jones, *Director Emeritus,*
Detroit Public Library System

E. J. Josey, *Chief,*
Bureau of Specialist Library Services, The State Education Department, The New York State Library

Paul Kitchen, *Executive Director,*
Canadian Library Association

Dan Lacy, *Senior Vice-President,*
McGraw-Hill Book Company

John G. Lorenz, *Executive Director,*
Association of Research Libraries

Helen H. Lyman, *Professor Emeritus,*
Library School, University of Wisconsin, Madison

Frank E. McKenna, *Executive Director,*
Special Libraries Association

Keyes D. Metcalf, *Library Consultant,*
Belmont Massachusetts

R. Kathleen Molz, *Professor,*
School of Library Service, Columbia University

Carol Nemeyer, *Associate Librarian for National Programs,*
Library of Congress

LuOuida Vinson Phillips, *Director of Instructional Resources,*
Dallas Independent School District

Alphonse F. Trezza, *Executive Director,*
National Commission on Libraries and Information Science

Helen Welch Tuttle, *Assistant University Librarian for Technical Services, Princeton University Library*

Allen B. Veaner, *University Librarian, University of California, Santa Barbara*

Robert Vosper, *Director,*
Clark Library, University of California, Los Angeles

Leo M. Weins, *President*
H. W. Wilson Company

Virginia P. Whitney, *Professor Emeritus,*
Rutgers University Library

EDITOR IN CHIEF
Robert Wedgeworth

ASSOCIATE EDITOR
Donald E. Stewart

MANAGING EDITOR
Richard Dell

PICTURE EDITOR
Nora Dell

CONTRIBUTING EDITORS
Ruth Tarbox, *Biographies*
Ruth Warncke, *Biographies, Awards and Prizes*

LONDON CORRESPONDENT
Stephanie Mullins, Dorothy Partington

CANADIAN CORRESPONDENT
R. B. Land

PROOFREADERS
Robert Rauch, Harry Sharp

LAYOUT ARTIST
Vladimir Reichl

THE AMERICAN LIBRARY ASSOCIATION

PRESIDENT
Eric Moon

VICE-PRESIDENT/PRESIDENT-ELECT
Russell Shank

TREASURER
William Chait

EXECUTIVE DIRECTOR
Robert Wedgeworth

DEPUTY EXECUTIVE DIRECTOR
Ruth R. Frame

ASSOCIATE EXECUTIVE DIRECTOR FOR PUBLISHING
Donald E. Stewart

ABBREVIATIONS AND ACRONYMS

Following are selected abbreviations and acronyms used in *The ALA Yearbook*. For page references consult the *Index* under full names in this and previous *Yearbook* volumes.

AAAS American Association for the Advancement of Science
AACR Anglo-American Cataloguing Rules
AAEA Appalachian Adult Education Center
AALC Asian American Librarian Caucus
AALL American Association of Law Libraries
AALS Association of American Library Schools
AAP Association of American Publishers
ABA American Booksellers Association
ABLISS Association of British Library and Information Science
ACLD Advisory Council on Library Development
ACNO Advisory Committee of National Organizations
ADPU Association of Public Data Users
AECT Association for Educational Communications and Technology
AFLS Armed Forces Librarians Section
AHEC Area Health Education Councils
AIRS Alliance of Information and Referral Services
ALHRT American Library History Round Table
ALS American Library Society
ALSC Association for Library Service to Children (former CSD)
ALSA Area Library Service Authority
ALTA American Library Trustee Association
AMIGOS Southwestern states network
ANSI American National Standards Institute
ARAC Aerospace Research Application Center
ARL Association of Research Libraries
ARSC Association for Recorded Sound Collections
ASIDIC Association of Information and Dissemination Centers
ASIS American Society for Information Science
ASLA Association of State Library Agencies
ASTED L'Association pour l'avancement des sciences et des techniques de la documentation
ATLA American Theological Library Association
ATS Applications Technology Satellite
BALLOTS Bibliographic Automation of Large Library Operations Using a Time-Sharing System
BARC Bay Area Reference Center
BLLD British Library Lending Division
BNB British National Bibliography
BPA British Publishers' Association
BPDC Book and Periodical Development Council (Canada)
CACUL Canadian Association of College and University Libraries
CAIN Cataloging and Indexing
CALS Canadian Association of Library Schools
CAPL Canadian Association of Public Libraries
CARL Canadian Association of Research Libraries, a section of CACUL
CASLIS Canadian Association of Special Libraries and Information Services
CCTU Committee of Corporate Telephone Users
CE Continuing Education
CETA Comprehensive Employment and Training Act
CIA Computer Industry Association
CELS Continuing Education for Library Staff in the Southwest
CIN Cooperative Information Network
CIP Cataloging in Publication
CISTI Canadian Institute for Scientific and Technical Information
CLA Canadian Library Association

CLA Catholic Library Association
CLASS California Library Authority for Systems and Service
CLENE Continuing Library Education Network and Exchange
CLEP College Level Examination Program
CLIP Coordinated Library Information Program
CLOUT Concerned Librarians Opposing Unprofessional Trends
CLR Council on Library Resources
CLTA Canadian Library Trustees' Association
COA Committee on Accreditation
COLA Cooperation in Library Automation
COLT Council on Library Technical Assistants
COM Computer Output Microform
COMARC Data base from pre-selected sources redistributed through MARC (LC)
CONSER CONversion of SERials
CONTU National Commission on New Technological Uses of Copyrighted Works
COPA Council on Postsecondary Education
COSLA Chief Officers of State Library Agencies
COMCAT Computer Output Microfilm Catalog
CR Classification Research
CRL Center for Research Libraries
CRS Congressional Research Service
CSAA Council of Specialized Accrediting Agencies
CSD Former Children's Service Division; see ALSC
CSLA Canadian School Library Association
CTS Communications Technology Satellite
CUNY City University of New York
DARE International Data Bank for Social Sciences (UNESCO)
DAVI Department of Audiovisual Instruction (of NEA)
DDC Defense Documentation Center
DISC Divisional Interests Special Committee
DLC District Library Center
DLS Division for Library Services
ERIC Educational Resources Information Center
ERT Exhibits Round Table
ESEA Elementary and Secondary Education Act
FID International Federation for Documentation
FIPS International Federation of Information Processing Societies
FLA Federal Librarians Association
FRACHE Federation of Regional Accrediting Commission of Higher Education
GAC Government Advisory Committee
I & R Information and Referral Services
IAML International Association of Music Libraries
IASA International Association of Sound Archives
IASL International Association of School Librarianship
IBBY International Board on Books for Young People
ICBD International Children's Book Day
IDS Interlibrary Delivery System
IFC Intellectual Freedom Committee
IFLA International Federation of Library Associations and Institutions
IIB International Bibliographic Institute
ILLINET Illinois Library and Information Network
ILRA Independent Research Library Association
ISAD Information Science and Automation Division (1977); see LITA
ISBDS International Standard Bibliographic Description for Serials
ISDS International Serials Data System
ISSN International Standard Serial Number
IUC Interuniversity Council
JCET Joint Council on Educational Telecommunications
JMRT Junior Members Round Table
JOLA Journal of Library Automation
JSCAACR Joint Steering Committee for Revision of AACR
LA Library Association (British)
LASER London and South Eastern Library Region
LEOMA Library Education Opportunities for Mid-America
LITA Library Information and Technology Association (1978); former ISAD (1977)
LOEX Library Orientation-Instruction Exchange
LRRT Library Research Round Table
LSCA Library Services and Construction Act

LUTFCUSTIC Librarians United to Fight Costly, Unnecessary Serial Title Changes (RTSD)
MARBI Representation in Machine-Readable Form of Bibliographic Information
MARC Machine-Readable Cataloging
MARS Machine-Assisted Reference Services
MCC Multicounty Cooperatives
MIDLNET Midwest Region Library Network
MLA Music Library Association
MLSA Metropolitan Library Service Agency
MRAP Management Review and Analysis Program (ARL)
NACAC National Ad Hoc Committee Against Censorship
NAL National Agricultural Library
NALGO National Association of Local Government Officials (British)
NASIC Northeast Academic Science Information Center
NCA National Commission on Accrediting
NCES National Center for Education Statistics
NCLIS National Commission on Libraries and Information Science
NCTM National Council of Teachers of Mathematics
NEA National Education Association
NEDCC New England Document Conservation Center
NEH National Endowment for the Humanities
NELB New England Library Board
NELINET New England Library Information Network
NFAIS National Federation of Abstracting and Indexing Services
NIAL National Institute of Arts and Letters
NIEA National Indian Education Association
NLM National Library of Medicine
NMA National Microfilm Association
NMA National Micrographics Association
NPR National Public Radio
NSDP National Serials Data Program
NTIS National Technical Information Service
OAS Organization of American States
OCLC Ohio College Library Center
OECD Organization for Economic Cooperation and Development
OLLR Office of Libraries and Learning Resources
OLPR Office for Library Personnel Resources
OLSD Office for Library Services to the Disadvantaged
OMS Office of University Library Management Studies
OSHA Occupational Safety and Health Agency
OSIS Office of Science Information Service
PALINET Pennsylvania Area Library Network
PASS Program for Achievement of State Standards
PBS Public Broadcasting Service
PISA Public Interest Satellite Association
PNBC Pacific Northwest Bibliographic Center
PRECIS Preserved Context Index System
PP & E Program Planning & Evaluation
PRS Public Relations Section
PSSC Public Service Satellite Consortium
RAILS Reference and Interlibrary Loan Service
RICE Regional Information and Community Exchange
RLG Research Library Group
SCAN Southern California Answering Network
SDI Selective Dissemination of Information
SHARE Shared Area Resources Exchange
SIE Scientific Information Exchange
SLICE Southwestern Library Interstate Cooperative Endeavor
SOLINET Southeastern Library Network
STAR Serial Titles Automated Records
STC Short Title Catalog
TEC Committee for Technical and Comprehensive Education
TESLA Technical Standards for Library Automation
TLA Theatre Library Association
TWXIL TWX Interlibrary Loan Network
USBE Universal Serials and Book Exchange, Inc.
USOE U.S. Office of Education
WESTEX Western Continuing Education Exchange
YASD Young Adult Services Division

CONTENTS

Features

xv **The Dilemma of Fees for Service: Issues and Action for Librarians**
PETER WATSON, Reference Librarian, California State University, Chico

xxiii **Genealogy As It Relates to Library Service**
RUSSELL E. BIDLACK, Dean, School of Library Science, University of Michigan

xxxi **Our Fragile Inheritance: The Challenge of Preserving Library Materials**
PAMELA W. DARLING, Head, Preservation Department, Columbia University Libraries

xliii **1977: The Library Association Centenary**
ROSAMOND KERR, Program Assistant, IFLA UBC Office

xlvii **Passing Through the Turnstile: A View of Library School Admissions**
KAY MURRAY, Associate Professor of Library Science, School of Library Science, University of North Carolina at Chapel Hill

Review of Library Events 1977

2 **Abstracting and Indexing Services**
TONI CARBO BEARMAN, Executive Director, National Federation of Abstracting and Indexing Services

4 **Academic Libraries**
RICHARD D. JOHNSON, Director of Libraries, State University of New York, Oneonta

14 **Accreditation**
LUCILLE WHALEN, Associate Dean, School of Library and Information Science, State University of New York, Albany

18 **Adults, Library Services to**
MARGARET E. MONROE, Professor of Library Science, University of Wisconsin Library School, Madison

20 **American Association of Law Libraries**
AL COCO, President AALL; University of Denver Law Library

21 **American Association of School Librarians**
FRANCES DEAN, Director, Division of Instructional Materials, Montgomery County Public Schools, Maryland

23 **American Library History**
GEORGE S. BOBINSKI, Dean, School of Information and Library Studies, State University of New York at Buffalo

23 **American Library History Round Table**
BUDD L. GAMBEE, University of North Carolina, Chapel Hill

24 **American Library Society**
JOHN B. HARLAN, President, American Library Society

25 **American Library Trustee Association**
DONALD C. EARNSHAW, Trustee, Mid-Continent Public Library, Independence, Missouri

26 **American Society for Information Science**
AUDREY N. GROSCH, Associate Professor, University of Minnesota Libraries, Minneapolis

27 **American Theological Library Association**
JOHN B. TROTTI, Librarian, Union Theological Seminary, Richmond, Virginia

28 **Archives**
ANN MORGAN CAMPBELL, Executive Director, Society of American Archivists, Chicago, Illinois; TIMOTHY WALCH, Society of American Archivists

31 **Armed Forces Libraries**
DIANA C. PROESCHEL, HQDA, Washington, D.C.

32 **Art Libraries**
NANCY JOHN, National Gallery of Art, Washington, D.C.

34 **Association for Library Service to Children**
BARBARA S. MILLER, Coordinator of Children's Services, Louisville Free Public Library, Kentucky

36 **Association of College and Research Libraries**
JULIE A. CARROLL VIRGO, ACRL Executive Secretary

38 **Association of Research Libraries**
SUZANNE O. FRANKIE, Associate Executive Director, ARL

42 **Association of State Library Agencies**
DONALD B. SIMPSON, Executive Director, Bibliographic Center for Research, Denver, Colorado

43 **Automation**
SUSAN K. MARTIN, Head, Library Systems Office, University of California, Berkeley

47 **Awards and Prizes**

55 **Beta Phi Mu**
HOWARD W. WINGER, Graduate Library School, University of Chicago

55 **Bibliographic Processing Centers**
DONALD B. SIMPSON, Executive Director, Bibliographic Center for Research, Denver, Colorado

57 **Bibliography and Indexes**
CHARLES WM. CONAWAY, Assistant Professor of Library Science, School of Library Science, Florida State University

58 **Binding**
DUDLEY A. WEISS, Executive Director, Library Binding Institute, Boston, Massachusetts

59 **Biographies**

69 **Blind and Physically Handicapped, Library Services for the**
FRANK KURT CYLKE, Chief, Division for the Blind and Physically Handicapped, Library of Congress

71 **Bookselling**
ROBERT D. HALE, Hathaway House Bookshop, Wellesley, Massachusetts

72 **Buildings**
RAYMOND M. HOLT, Consultant, Del Mar, California

80 **Canadian Library Association**
PAUL KITCHEN, Executive Director, Canadian Library Association

82 **Cataloging and Classification**
MARY POUND, Publications Coordinator, General Libraries, The University of Texas at Austin

85 **Catholic Library Association**
MATTHEW R. WILT, Executive Director, CLA

86 **Children's Book Council**
JOHN DONOVAN, Executive Director, Children's Book Council, New York

87 **Children's Library Services**
AMY KELLMAN, Head, Children's Department, Carnegie Library of Pittsburgh

89 **Children's Literature**
ZENA SUTHERLAND, Associate Professor of Library Science, University of Chicago

92 **Chinese American Librarians Association**
TZE-CHUNG LI, Professor, Rosary College Graduate School of Library Science

93 **Circulation Systems**
R. PATRICK MALLORY, Director of the Library, New Mexico Institute of Mining and Technology, Socorro, New Mexico

94 **Collection Development**
FREDERICK C. LYNDEN, Assistant University Librarian for Technical Services, Brown University

97 **Community Delivery Services**
RONALD S. KOZLOWSKI, Library Director, Louisville Free Public Library, Kentucky

98 **Continuing Professional Education**
ELIZABETH W. STONE, Professor, The Catholic University of America

xi

101 **CONTU**
ARTHUR J. LEVINE, Executive Director, CONTU, Washington, D.C.

102 **Copyright**
F. E. MC KENNA, Executive Director, Special Libraries Association

107 **Council, ALA**
PAT HARRIS, Assistant to the Executive Director, ALA

108 **Council on Library Technical Assistants**
MARGARET R. BARRON, Cuyahoga Community College, Cleveland, Ohio

109 **Data Bases, Computer-Readable**
MARTHA E. WILLIAMS, Professor, Coordinated Science Laboratory, University of Illinois, Urbana

112 **Disadvantaged, Library Service to**
MONTERIA HIGHTOWER, Supervisor of Branches and Extension, District of Columbia, Public Library System

113 **Education, Library**
A. VENABLE LAWSON, Director, Division of Librarianship, Emory University, Atlanta, Georgia

117 **Ethnic Groups, Library Service to**
   American Indians
CHERYL METOYER, Assistant Professor of Library Science, University of California at Los Angeles
   Asian Americans
VIVIAN KOBAYASHI, Librarian, San Francisco
   Black Americans
JESSIE CARNEY SMITH, University Librarian, Fisk University, Nashville, Tennessee
   Hispanic Americans
YOLANDA J. CUESTA, California State Library, Sacramento
   Italian Americans
CARMINE M. DIODATI, JR., Supervising Librarian, New York Public Library, Wakefield Branch
   Jewish Americans
MAX CELNIK and DAVID ARONOVITCH, Touro College, New York
   Polish Americans
VICTORIA M. GALA, Polish American Librarians Association, Hamtramck, Michigan

126 **Exhibits Round Table**
JANE BURKE, CLSI, Schaumburg, Illinois

127 **Federal Librarians Round Table**
JOAN M. MAIER, Chief, Library Services, National Oceanic and Atmospheric Library, Boulder, Colorado

128 **Films**
WILLIAM SLOAN, Film Librarian, New York Public Library; Editor, *Film Library Quarterly*

130 **Films, Children's**
MARILYN BERG IARUSSO, Assistant Coordinator, Children's Services, New York Public Library

131 **Filmstrips**
DIANA L. SPIRT, Professor, Palmer Graduate Library School, C. W. Post Center, Long Island University

132 **Foundations and Funding Agencies**
FOSTER E. MOHRHARDT, Consultant, Arlington, Virginia

134 **Freedom to Read Foundation**
R. KATHLEEN MOLZ, Professor, School of Library Service, Columbia University

134 **Friends of Libraries**
LAURA SMITH SHELLEY, Director, Northland Public Library, Pittsburgh, Pennsylvania

135 **Gifts, Bequests, Endowments**
CLYDE C. WALTON, Director of Libraries, University of Colorado, Boulder

139 **Government Documents Round Table**
LOIS MILLS, Western Illinois University, Macomb

140 **Government Publications and Depository System**
LEROY C. SCHWARZKOPF, Government Documents Librarian, McKelden Library, University of Maryland

141 **Health and Rehabilitative Library Services**
HARRIS C. MCCLASKEY, Associate Professor, Library School, University of Minnesota, Minneapolis

143 **Health and Rehabilitative Library Services Division**
SUSAN M. HASKIN, LSCA Title I Specialist, Michigan State Library

144 **IFLA**
MARGREET WIJNSTROOM, Secretary-General, IFLA, The Hague, Netherlands

145 **Independent Research Libraries**
LAWRENCE TOWNER, President and Librarian, Newberry Library, Chicago

147 **Information and Referral Centers**
MILES MARTIN, Professor and Chairperson, Department of Library and Information Services, University of Toledo

149 **Information Industry**
PAUL G. ZURKOWSKI, IIA

153 **Information Science and Automation Division**
DONALD P. HAMMER, Executive Secretary, ISAD

154 **Insurance for Libraries**
DONALD L. UNGARELLI, Director of Libraries, C.W. Post Center, Long Island University

155 **Intellectual Freedom**
JUDITH F. KRUG, Director, Office for Intellectual Freedom, ALA

160 **Intellectual Freedom Round Table**
KARL WEINER, Skokie Public Library, Skokie, Illinois

160 **International Board on Books for Young People**
JOHN DONOVAN, Children's Book Council, New York

161 **International Federation for Documentation FID**
KENNETH R. BROWN, Acting Secretary General, FID, The Hague, Netherlands

162 **International Relations**
JANE WILSON, International Relations Officer, ALA

164 **International Relations Round Table**
EDWARD S. MOFFAT, Long Island University, Graduate Library School

165 **Junior Members Round Table**
MARILYN HINSHAW, Coordinator of Extension, Public Library, El Paso, Texas

166 **Labor Groups, Library Service to**
KATHLEEN IMHOFF, Director of Libraries, Chattahoochee Valley Regional Library Systems, Columbus, Georgia

167 **Law and Legislation**
ALEX LADENSON, Legal Counsel, Urban Libraries Council

169 **Law Libraries**
JULIUS J. MARKE, Professor of Law and Law Librarian, New York University School of Law

170 **Libraries and Learning Resources, Office of**
ROBERT KLASSEN, Chief, Program Development, Office of Libraries and Learning Resources, Washington, D.C.

172 **Library Administration Division**
RICHARD L. WATERS, Associate Director, Public Services, Dallas Public Library, Texas

173 **Library Education Division**
ROBERT D. STUEART, Dean and Professor, School of Library Science, Simmons College

175 **Library of Congress**
CHRISTOPHER WRIGHT, Special Assistant to the Librarian, Library of Congress

179 **Library Press**
ELIZABETH PRYSE MITCHELL, Former Assistant Editor, *American Libraries*

180 **Library Research Round Table**
JANE ROBBINS, Louisiana State University

181 **Literacy Programs, Library**
HELEN HUGUENOR LYMAN, Professor Emeritus, Library School, University of Wisconsin-Madison

182 **Management, Library**
ROBERT H. ROHLF, Director, Hennepin County Library, Edina, Minnesota

184 **Measurement and Evaluation**
ELLEN ALTMAN, Graduate Library School, Indiana University, Bloomington

185 **Mediation, Arbitration, and Inquiry**
RUTH R. FRAME, Deputy Director, ALA

186 **Medical Libraries**
ESTELLE BRODMAN, Librarian and Professor of Medical History, Washington University School of Medicine, St. Louis, Missouri

187 **Medical Library Association**
SCOTT ADAMS, Senior Associate, Urban Studies Center, University of Louisville, Kentucky

188 **Micrographics**
HOWARD S. WHITE, Editor, *Library Technology Reports*

190 **Multimedia Materials**
DAPHNE PHILOS, Executive Director, Association of Media Producers, Washington, D.C.

192 **Music Library Association**
GERALDINE OSTROVE, Director, New England Conservatory of Music Libraries, Boston

193 **National Agricultural Library**
RICHARD A. FARLEY, Director, National Agricultural Library

194 **National Commission on Libraries and Information Science**
FREDERICK BURKHARDT, Chairman, NCLIS

197 **National Endowment for the Humanities**
GLORIA WEISSMAN, Assistant to the Deputy Chairman, NEH

198 **National Library of Medicine**
MELVIN S. DAY, Deputy Director, NLM

199 **National Micrographics Association**
O. GORDON BANKS, Executive Director

200 **National Technical Information Service**
TED RYERSON, Special Assistant, Production, NTIS

202 **Networks**
ALPHONSE F. TREZZA, Executive Director, NCLIS

205 **Notable Books**

207 **Obituaries**

213 **Organization of American States**
MARIETTA DANIELS SHEPARD, Chief, Library and Archives Development Program, OAS

214 **Organizations and Associations**

223 **Personnel and Employment: Affirmative Action**
AGNES M. GRIFFEN

227 **Personnel and Employment: Job Market**
MARGARET MYERS, Program Officer, Office for Library Personnel Resources, ALA

229 **Personnel and Employment: Performance Appraisal**
NEAL K. KASKE, Associate Librarian, Library Systems Office, University of California, Berkeley

230 **Personnel and Employment: Staff Development**
DEANNA MARCUM and DUANE E. WEBSTER, Library Manager, Association of Research Libraries, Office of University Library Management Studies

232 **Preservation of Library Materials**
GAY WALKER, Head, Preservation and Preparations Department, Yale University

235 **Public Libraries**
EDWARD N. HOWARD, Director, Vigo County Public Library, Indiana

240 **Public Library Association**
RONALD DUBBERLY, City Librarian, Public Library, Seattle, Washington

242 **Public Relations**
ALICE NORTON, Public Relations Consultant, Ridgefield, Connecticut

246 **Publishing, ALA**
DONALD E. STEWART, Associate Executive Director for Publishing, ALA

249 **Publishing, Book**
RICHARD P. KLEEMAN, Vice-President, AAP, Washington, D.C.

253 **Publishing, Serials**
W.A. (BILL) KATZ, Professor, Library School, State University of New York at Albany

256 **Realia**
TOM BROWNFIELD, Director, Canal Fulton Public Library, Ohio

257 **Recordings, Sound**
GORDON STEVENSON, Associate Professor, State University of New York at Albany

258 **Reference and Adult Services Division**
VIRGINIA BOUCHER, Research and Planning Librarian, University Libraries, University of Colorado, Boulder

260 **Reference Services**
ROBERT BALAY, Head, Reference Department, Yale University Library

263 **REFORMA**
ILIANA SONNTAG, University of Arizona, Tucson

264 **Regional Library Associations**
H. ROBERT MALINOWSKY, Mountain Plains;
MARY P. NELSON, Pacific Northwest;
J.B. HOWELL, Southeastern;
JOHN F. ANDERSON, Southwestern

268 **Research**
BARBARA O. SLANKER, Former Director, Office for Research, ALA

275 **Resources and Technical Services Division**
NORMAN DUDLEY, Assistant University Librarian for Collection Development, UCLA

276 **School Libraries and Media Centers**
D. PHILIP BAKER, Coordinator, Media Programs, Stamford Public Schools, Connecticut

282 **Science Information, Division of**
LEE G. BURCHINAL, Director, DSI, National Science Foundation

283 **Security Systems**
NANCY H. KNIGHT, Freelance Librarian, Springfield, Virginia

285 **Serials**
WILLIAM H. HUFF, Serials Librarian, University of Illinois, Urbana

290 **Social Responsibilities**
E. J. JOSEY, Chief, Bureau of Specialist Library Services, New York State Education Department

295 **Social Responsibilities Round Table**
MARY BIBLO, University of Chicago High School Library

296 **Special Collections**
ROBERT J. ADELSPERGER, Special Collections Librarian and Curator of Rare Books, University of Illinois at Chicago Circle

300 **Special Libraries**
MIRIAM H. TEES, Chief Librarian, The Royal Bank of Canada, Montreal

302 **Staff Organizations Round Table**
FRANCES JONES, State Library Commission, Charleston, West Virginia

303 **Standards**
DEBORAH BODNER (ANSI Z39 Committee, Secretary/Treasurer) and KATHARINE SILVASI (Former Research Assistant, Z39 Committee)

306 **Telecommunication and Public Broadcasting**
FRANK W. NORWOOD, Executive Director, Joint Council on Educational Telecommunications

308 **Theatre Library Association**
RICHARD M. BUCK, Performing Arts Research Center, New York Public Library at Lincoln Center

309 **Toys and Games**
FAITH H. HEKTOEN, Consultant, Connecticut State Library

310 **Trustees**
ROBERT L. FAHERTY, Editor, *Public Library Trustee*

314 **UNESCO**
I. BETTEMBOURG, UNESCO, Paris

317 **Universal Bibliographic Control**
DOROTHY ANDERSON, Director, ROSAMOND KERR, Program Assistant, IFLA UBC Office

317 **Universal Serials and Book Exchange, Inc.**
ALICE D. BALL, Executive Director, USBE

318 **Urban Libraries Council**
RALPH G. NEWMAN, President, Board of Directors, Chicago Public Library

320 **Washington Report**
EILEEN D. COOKE, Director, Washington Office, ALA

321 **Women in Librarianship, Status of**
KATHLEEN WEIBEL, Library School, University of Wisconsin–Madison

324 **Women's National Book Association**
ANN HEIDBREDER EASTMAN, President, WNBA, 1976-78

325 **Young Adult Library Services**
MARY K. CHELTON, Consultant, Young Adult Services, Westchester Library System, New York

328 **Young Adult Literature**
JACK FORMAN, Regional Adult and Young Adult Services Librarian, Eastern Massachusetts Regional Library System

333 **Young Adult Services Division**
ROSEMARY M. YOUNG, Coordinator of Young Adult Services, Denver Public Library, Colorado

Special Reports

30 **The ALA Archives**
MAYNARD BRICHFORD, University Archivist, University of Illinois at Urbana-Champaign

77 **Making Do in Times of Stringency**
RAYMOND M. HOLT, Library Building Consultant

xiii

84 **A Comparison of AACR 1 and 2**
BEN R. TUCKER, The Library of Congress

92 **Peter Rabbit's 75th Anniversary**
ANNE EMERSON, London Contributor

105 **The New U.S. Copyright Law: A Bibliography**
MILDRED VANNORSDALL, Chicago Public Library

163 **Delegation of U.S. Librarians to the U.S.S.R.**

178 **The Center for the Book**
JOHN Y. COLE, The Library of Congress

284 **Disasters**
NANCY H. KNIGHT

313 **Trustees: Personnel Policy**
JEAN M. COLEMAN, Trustee, Dayton and Montgomery County Public Library, Ohio

315 **The Standardization of International Library Statistics: 1853–1977**
FRANK L. SCHICK, Chair, IFLA Committee on Statistics

335 **Canadian Report**
R. BRIAN LAND, Professor of Library Science, Faculty of Library Science, University of Toronto

343 **London Report**
STEPHANIE MULLINS, DOROTHY M. PARTINGTON, London Correspondents

State Reports
350

Alabama. MOZELLE B. CUMMINGS, President, Alabama Library Association

Alaska. NANCY LESH, Public Library, Anchorage, Alaska

Arizona. HELEN M. GOTHBERG, Assistant Professor, Graduate Library School, University of Arizona

Arkansas. KATHERINE STANICK, Executive Secretary, Arkansas Library Association

California. WILLIAM L. EMERSON, Playa Del Ray, California

Colorado. ANNE MARIE FALSONE, Assistant Commissioner, Office of Library Services, Colorado State Library

Connecticut. BARBARA BYRAN, Fairfield University, Connecticut

Delaware. HELEN H. BENNETT, Retired, State Department of Public Instruction, Delaware

District of Columbia. MARY K. FELDMAN, Department of Transportation Library, Washington, D.C.

Florida. BARRATT WILKINS, State Librarian

Georgia. JOHN E. CLEMONS, Assistant Director, Division of Librarianship, Emory University

Hawaii. ROSE MYERS, Librarian, West Oahu College, Honolulu

Idaho. JEANNE GOODRICH, Idaho Falls Public Library

Illinois. JOHN R. COYNE, Executive Secretary, Illinois Library Association

Indiana. EDWARD N. HOWARD, Director, Vigo County Public Library, Terre Haute

Iowa. GAYLE BURDICK, Editor, Iowa Library Association, Des Moines

Kansas. CHARLES BOLLES, Director, Kansas State Library Development Division

Kentucky. BARBARA S. MILLER, Coordinator of Children's Services, Louisville Free Public Library

Louisiana. VIVIAN CAZAYOUX, Associate State Librarian for Library Development, Baton Rouge

Maine. BENITA DAVIS, Bangor, Public Library

Maryland. LANCE C. FINNEY, President, Maryland State Department of Education, Division of Library Development, Baltimore

Massachusetts. ARTHUR J. KISSNER, Fitchburg Public Library, Massachusetts

Michigan. JULE FOSBENDER, Director, Adrian Public Library, Michigan

Minnesota. ALICE WILCOX, Director, University of Minnesota Library, Minneapolis; ANDREA HONEBRINK, Reference Coordinator, MINITEX

Mississippi. GEORGE R. LEWIS, Director of Libraries, Mississippi State University Library

Missouri. MADELINE MATSON, Missouri State Library, Jefferson, Missouri

Montana. EARLE C. THOMPSON, Dean, Library Service, University of Montana, Missoula

Nebraska. VIVIAN A. PETERSON, Concordia Teachers College, Seward, Nebraska

Nevada. ROBIN BARKER, Nevada State Library, Carson City

New Hampshire. KATHLEEN TAYLOR, Director, Peterborough Town Library, New Hampshire

New Jersey. JOHN H. LIVINGSTONE, JR., Monmouth County Library

New Mexico. PAUL A. AGRIESTI, Deputy State Librarian, New Mexico State Library, Santa Fe

New York. MICHAEL G. DE RUVO, School Media Specialist, Roslyn Junior High School, New York

North Carolina. DAVID P. JENSEN, Director of Library Services, School of Library Science, University of North Carolina, Chapel Hill

North Dakota. PATRICIA SCHOMMER, State University Library, Fargo

Ohio. A. CHAPMAN PARSONS, Executive Director, Ohio Library Association

Oklahoma. IRMA R. TOMBERLIN, Professor of Library Science, School of Library Science, University of Oklahoma, Norman

Oregon. KATHERINE G. EATON, University of Oregon, Eugene

Pennsylvania. PAT REDMOND, Chester County Library, Westchester, Pennsylvania; NANCY L. BLUNDON, Executive Secretary, Pennsylvania Library Association

Rhode Island. EMIL A. CIALLELLA, JR., Director, Central Falls Free Public Library, Rhode Island

South Carolina. CARL STONE, Anderson County Library, South Carolina

South Dakota. EMILY K. GUHIN, Alexander Mitchell Public Library, Aberdeen

Tennessee. ROBERT F. PLOTZKE, Director of Library Services, Wayne Williams Public Library, Johnson City

Texas. MARY POUND, Publications Coordinator, General Libraries, University of Texas at Austin

Utah. K. ELIZABETH RUNYON-LANCASTER, University of Utah Libraries, Salt Lake City

Vermont. JOSETTE ANNE BOISSE, Librarian, Spaulding High School, Barre, Vermont

Virginia. WILLIAM L. WHITESIDES, Director of Libraries, Fairfax County Public Library, Springfield, Virginia

Washington. DOROTHY R. CUTLER, Chief, Library Development, Washington State Library, Olympia

West Virginia. LUELLA DYE, Director, Craft Memorial Library, Bluefield, West Virginia

Wisconsin. CHARLES A. BUNGE, Director, Library School, University of Wisconsin, Madison

Wyoming. PAUL B. CORS, University of Wyoming Library, Laramie

Index
417

The Dilemma of Fees for Service: Issues and Action for Librarians

Peter Watson

1977 marked the attainment of a new stage of maturity in the development of machine-assisted reference service in libraries. In physical terms, growth of this sturdy newcomer continued rapidly; but 1977 will be regarded as the year in which the character of this recent arrival was discussed and some assessment was made of what it ought to become as it begins to coexist with its older siblings in the library family. Computerized bibliographic searches are, of course, being performed in a variety of agencies; but if they are to be integrated into library service, that implies that specific values and standards will be brought to bear, that the service will not just be offered, but offered with a certain distinctive character. The awakening realization by librarians that they do have some choices, some parental authority in this matter, and that they need not feel trapped into accepting the service under conditions they instinctively resent was one of the more encouraging events of the library year.

The digital computer is easily the most powerful and sophisticated information-processing machine ever invented, and it therefore comes as no surprise that its employment as an aid to the library's solidly established intellectual services that we know as "Reference" is raising a host of tremendously complicated technical, operational, and philosophical issues. Looking toward the eventual character of these computer-based services in a library setting (specifically, the on-line bibliographic searching now available nationwide from a small group of vendors), librarians face no issue more crucial than that of whether or not to charge the patron directly for all or part of the cost.

An uneasiness had been slowly heating up in the library profession for several years over the matter of charging library users directly for some service provided. For many years the charges were for fringe services such as use of a rental collection, of meeting rooms, and of films or phonograph records, and for academic libraries' services to industry. The charges were generally minimal. They were not true prices based on elaborate cost studies or market analyses; rather, they were innocuous fees of a few cents or dollars to help with the additional or unusual costs associated with that particular service. In the late 1960's, the situation began to change. The overwhelming evidence of increasing personal affluence and the sudden (and still, to some, bewildering) corporate poverty of public service institutions lent impetus to notions of direct user charges at a time when libraries were caught at the high point of two cost curves. Electronic technology and an improved infrastructure of interlibrary cooperation were opening up vistas of wholly new services that thrust the librarian into the long-awaited role of an active information specialist; but these expanded services, in their infancy, were more expensive than they would later be. At the same time, most libraries were in the final phase of their operation with essentially obsolete manual methods of processing their collections for use; and these traditional methods, in their dotage, were more expensive than they had ever been.

It is instructive to remember that, as charges began to be more visible in librarianship, new technology was not the issue. Changing budgetary patterns for public service agencies and changing concepts of what services should be offered by libraries, and to whom, created the underlying pressures.[1] (Compare in the period of 1965-75 the easy organizational acceptance, plus very low unit cost, of photocopying technology in libraries with the considerable organizational strain, plus high unit cost, of information services to business and industry by academic and large metropolitan public libraries.) Thus, now that on-line bibliographic reference service has stepped into the limelight of a professional discussion on how such charges are compatible with library ideals of equality of access to information, it is particularly important that we look past Technology, the perennially available scapegoat, to the issues of social, professional, and organizational philosophy that are raised by the concept of user charges for library service.

COST COMPONENTS

The cost components of mounting an on-line search service have been well identified in the literature. Briefly recapitulated, they are of two kinds. First, there are the direct search costs, which consist of

- the on-line search cost ("connect time");
- the associated telecommunications cost (generally, going through a carrier network such as Tymnet or Telenet is cheaper than direct long-distance dialing); and
- the cost of off-line printing (cheaper for large volumes of output than staying on-line to print it).

Second, there are the indirect costs of starting and sustaining the operation, which consist of

- salaries;
- training costs;
- equipment purchase or rental;
- any physical remodeling (e.g., for partitions and power supply);
- furniture (e.g., file cabinets, bulletin boards, desks, and chairs);
- supplies (including forms, operating manuals, and publicity material); and
- institutional overhead.

To these indirect costs some would add the "opportunity costs" of relinquishing some other task(s) in order to be able to perform this one. It could also be said, however, that such redirection of effort is necessary and beneficial, calling librarians forward into the role of information specialist that they must occupy in the future if the profession is to retain its dynamism. Likewise, the advent of automated bibliographic searching may challenge the library to improve in other areas—especially in the selection, duplication, and circulation of periodicals or in interlibrary borrowing and lending services. Few would be willing, for that reason, to say, "We cannot provide the search service."

Most libraries initiating a service have done so through special grants, usually from the larger agency of which the library is a part. A lesser number have reallocated existing resources in the amount thought necessary to get the activity launched. Most libraries have either charged from the outset of the service or from the expiration of the specially funded trial period and have accepted their responsibility to absorb the indirect costs. Beyond that, however, libraries have in general seen themselves faced with the choice of passing along to the patron the direct search costs or of being forced to eliminate an obviously valuable new service. This describes the middle of the spectrum. There are, of course, a few libraries toward either end, those adding all or part of the indirect costs onto the search costs and those subsidizing all or part of the search cost itself. Preferential pricing (e.g., different rates for undergraduates, graduates, faculty, and local business) has also been adopted as a means of apportioning the total costs more equitably.

Thus many libraries, perhaps by subconscious recollection of the standard commercial practice of introducing new products or services at an enticing discount, and not knowing much about how to present a major innovative service to their public, have taken the one path almost guaranteed to lead to minimum usage at maximum cost. They have first invested all the necessary venture capital, offering the trial service either free or almost free of charge. After the momentum has begun to build as a result of the early publicity, demonstrations, and searches—just at that critical moment 6 to 12 months after the start— they have switched abruptly to a system involving average charges of $30 to $40 per patron. Usage (the true return on the library's investment) plummets and is slow to climb back. The vendors have not failed to notice this and are in fact anxious to join with librarians in optimizing the conditions under which their services are offered in libraries. They are no more going to provide the service free to libraries, however, than a book publisher would donate books or the American Chemical Society its *Chemical Abstracts*.

One of the least constructive elements in the discussion of the question of charging has been reflected in the statement, frequently uttered as a complaint, that most on-line systems, and indeed a fair number of the data bases they utilize, were developed at public expense. This is true enough, but to resent it is unproductive and appears to imply a lack of understanding of the reasons why, in a capitalist state, the private sector is allowed and even encouraged to exploit the fruits of government-stimulated research and development. To oppose the pump-priming role of government on this issue, and not on the hundreds of other research and development programs that have taken this form, is at best inconsistent. There is a sense in which government exists to be taken fair advantage of. Furthermore, because an increasing number of files as well as some of the information retrieval systems that process them have been developed wholly without government sponsorship or funding, specific disagreement with the application of this concept to information work cannot form the basis for any general solution to the charging question. The library profession's response to this particular challenge to its assumptions and operations must be based on firmer foundations.

Frequently overlooked in discussions of these cost factors is an essential distinction between the principle of transactional accounting and the ultimate source of payment for any given transaction. Computers make very easy the recording, billing, and accounting of each transaction; and most computers, being expensive resources, are operated this way. This is not the tyranny of technology but simply an economic choice that we collectively have made about what we want our computers to do. But it has a chilling effect on librarians, who have been used to having the true costs of their activities kept well away from their work desks. Identifying the precise costs of a transaction and billing accordingly are practices of the modern professional world that are undoubtedly on the increase—not even government is immune to such tendencies—and librarians who wear their professionalism easily will not fear them. But this is a quite different issue from the issue of who ultimately should pay for computerized searches.

There is nothing in the transactional nature of computerized accounting that precludes, say, a decision to offer the service at no cost to the user. The latter is policy; the former, mechanics.

SEARCH FOR ANALOGIES

As is natural, an important feature of the discussion to date has been a search for valid analogies. There are plenty ready to be wheeled into action on either side of the issue. Most of them have their value; but so far, to this observer, in no single case is a governing applicability to the question of charging for computer-based information services in libraries compellingly obvious. The analogies frequently involve tacitly different assumptions about what libraries have been, are, and should be and about the true nature of our abstractly concrete, dynamically static, publicly private stock-in-trade—Information. With such a starting point, the route to broad professional agreement is shaping up to be a veritable pilgrim's progress through many dialectical highways and byways. A brief survey of the analogies will help to illuminate the major facets of this discussion.

The first group of analogies is internal —reference is made to other forms of library and information service. The keystone of this group is the analogy with library provision of books and other resources at no direct charge to the patron. This is the powerful central core of modern librarianship, and the analogy quickly links us back to the rise of free public lending libraries in the 19th century as a great instrument of political and social progress. There is thus an easy connection made to questions of First Amendment rights. Freedom of expression is meaningless, it is argued, unless freedom of access to information is also guaranteed. For academic libraries, moral support may also be found in such cases as *Serrano v. Priest* (California, 1971), which established that the quality of public school education in California should not be a function of the wealth of the school district. How then can an educational support service as crucial as high-quality library service be available only to those districts, or individuals, who can afford it? At the very least, educational need is the same regardless of economic standing—perhaps it is even inversely proportional to it.

For several reasons, the analogy does

not work. First, the connection between libraries and what is, after all, a liberal interpretation of the First Amendment, while certainly attractive, is nonetheless ex post facto. Nothing except the desires and self-image of librarians, reinforced by mute social acquiescence, have demanded that libraries be an agency guaranteeing people their First Amendment rights; and much of the impetus and funding for the first free public lending libraries came from private and charitable sources, not from government. The First Amendment also guarantees freedom of movement, but the government does not provide everyone with a bicycle. Second, to the extent that libraries do now perform this function, that role is predicated on an existing array of resources and services. A computerized information retrieval service is significantly different from any of these and may be the harbinger of a needed set of new rules. Placement of computerized services in the same ethical bag as the existing services is the whole question under discussion; if anything, it should be a conclusion, not a premise.

Third, one of these new rules may indeed have to be that the cost of these "add-on" information services, optional and personal as they are, will have to be passed along to the primary beneficiary. Those who stress that information is an economic good or commodity would go further and say that it *ought* to be passed along. Fourth, the economics of library book purchases are so different from those of computerized information retrieval services that any philosophical value of the analogy is undermined. One book, bought and processed at an average cost of, say, $30 is thereafter available in perpetuity, at least in principle; whatever its operational life, it does not become the property of the requester. If it is used on an average of twice a year for 15 years and then never again, the distributed cost is only $1 per usage. A computer-produced bibliographic search, consuming substantial library personnel time in a new function and useful only to the requester in most cases, may cost from $5 to $200.

However, a further interesting point about this analogy is that relatively high book prices, and the consequent unavailability of books to large segments of the population, were indeed the case in the early 19th century; and these factors undoubtedly helped the drive toward the provision of collections for free public loan. But the vital intermediate growth stage, that of the subscription lending library, should not be overlooked, for its political lesson is that a relative handful of people dedicated to the idea did not bring about immediate public funding of lending libraries. The need had to be tested and demonstrated and a case of figures built up before society as a whole accepted the burden of funding it.

Here are some other internal analogies. With computerization in the rest of the library, we don't charge for modernizing our technical processing capabilities, why charge for modernizing our reference service? It is an interesting question, not fully answered by the obvious comment that computerized bibliographic searching is a new service, for it is not so long ago that the reference service we now call traditional was just as new to librarianship. With existing modes of reference service, the on-line versions of the indexes and abstracts are "just another reference tool." They are, in fact, an aid to increased reference staff productivity, rather like the use of a long-distance telephone call to gain an answer for a patron, and thus should not be chargeable. There is merit to the idea of discretionary use by the librarian of the computerized search option, but it is also undeniably true that the major saving in time accrues to the patron, not to the librarian. And this, although our professional responsibility, is only possible within some given fiscal context.

With the concept of a translation service—it is the library's function to make available any foreign-language material a patron needs and with it a dictionary of that language. It is not the library's function actually to make the translation, but if it were, it would no doubt have to be performed for a fee. Similarly, although the library should guarantee access to information resources in computerized form, it should not also have to pay everyone's processing costs, for the service is then open to considerable abuse—the high-minded kind as well as the crass. This rationale can be used for justifying data base purchases (e.g., census tapes) by the library, as well as for on-line bibliographic search facilities. In either case the user is asked to assume the direct cost of the computer time and services necessary for that individual's own request.

Arguments in favor of charging by analogy with other library services already subject to charges are mainly worthless because they beg the whole question being addressed. In addition, as noted above, there appears to be an order-of-magnitude difference between most such services (e.g., photocopying, rental collections, story hours, and the like) and computerized bibliographic searching. This in itself may cast a significant sidelight on the use of the First Amendment to justify completely free searches. Is this a debate about whether or not there should be charges, or is it ultimately about economics—about the acceptable amounts of such charges? If the principle for which librarians stand is equality of access, does that imply no charges whatsoever? Clearly those libraries that have charged in small ways for other services have not thought so. (Haynes MacMullen reminded us at the 1977 Annual Conference meeting of RASD/MARS (Machine-Assisted Reference Section) that not only have libraries charged but they have been positively creative over the years in thinking up new ways to do so.)

With the realization that there are no compelling internal analogies to use as models comes the need to look outside libraries. The library is a public service institution; and, the argument runs, the principles of service and management that govern this class of organizations would govern libraries. Perhaps they would, if everyone could agree what those principles are; but there are several distinct types of public service organization—government agencies; regulated industries such as the power and communications utilities; other public, nonprofit institutions such as local schools and state universities; and private, nonprofit agencies such as private universities, professional societies, and hospitals. Each of these types may follow quite different operating principles; and, if they charge for some service or product, they are likely to be trying to attain quite different ends by doing so. Obviously they may also, as in the case of governmental agencies, employ different approaches within one type. This permits a potentially vast number of analogies to be examined, and among them are tolls for bridge and highway use, on the principle that for certain types of public service it is appropriate for the immediate beneficiary to pay. The very long amortization periods that apply to roads and bridges, however, cannot apply to a computer search transaction, for which there are direct, nondeferrable costs each time the service is used. Among other analogies are municipal zoos, tennis courts, and museums, for example, where the fee is essentially regulatory; opera and symphony concerts, for which heavy public subsidies do not preclude a charge as high as the market will bear, and which cater to special tastes correlated with educational level, none of which implies that such subsidy is unjustified; and subsidized housing and school lunches, the impulse being social justice and the general welfare. Still others are the view in a national park or the resource called "labor"—the comparison is made with information as a nonconsumable resource. Differing rates are charged for telephone calls from private and public telephones, it is argued, in support of the view that it is justified to keep the "essential public service" part of the traffic as cheap as possible, charging a premium for the "privilege" of private, or personalized, facilities. The reader can probably add to these examples.

The chief identifiable theme running through the analogies between libraries and other public service institutions is that for publicly funded libraries to charge for their services constitutes double taxation. Quite apart from the errant semantics of calling bibliographic service charges a "tax," the variety of charging practices already legally sanctioned in public institutions would tend to cast doubt on this assertion, especially since the great majority of libraries charging for computerized bibliographic searches are not charging in their own right. They are merely transferring the service vendor's charge to the user, as they do (more analogies!) with other services to which the library gives house room, such as coin-operated typewriters or pen vending machines. For the double-taxation argument to be tested in the courts, a citizen would presumably have to sue a governmental agency for refusing to provide citizens with free computerized searches in a publicly supported library. If such a suit were successful, many libraries would immediately be forced to discontinue the service, opening the gates to a herd of lawsuits going in the opposite direction—denial of access on the original, direct cost-recovery basis. Fortunately, it is unlikely that the issue will have to be resolved in this lurching fashion.

One further comment that needs to be made is that the current discussion about the functions of public agencies and the use of tax revenues has not been slow to generate talk of reallocating resources on a large social scale. This may be designated the "neutron bomb" argument—it is better for the future of the human species to have libraries properly funded to perform excellent service than it is to spend untold millions of dollars on ever-more-gruesome weapons of war such as the neutron bomb. As a moral position, few would not support this. As a basis for action, it is regrettably irrelevant. Curtailing the production of neutron bombs and increasing the funding of libraries are both laudable aims, but activities directed toward either of them are best kept separate. It would be naive to hope that achieving the first would have any discernible effect on the second. (Compare the illusory Vietnam "peace dividend.") One virtue of this argument, however, is that it emphasizes that the solution to our charging problem must essentially be a political one, even if not quite on the scale suggested by the analogy.

BEGINNING THE CAMPAIGN

There may be analogies yet to be unveiled, but enough have been explored here to support the belief that in fact there are no governing analogies, no previous models, that we can use. The bulk of what is new about this situation outweighs those elements of similarity with past practice; there is ultimately no other entity like information and no other public service organization like the library. We do have power of choice, perhaps in a deeper sense than any of us suspected a year or two ago. On that basis, the collective judgment of ALA, as expressed in the Resolution on Free Access to Information passed by the Council and Membership at Detroit in June 1977 (see Council, ALA) can and should become the opening statement in a very large and protracted public campaign. The library profession wants to see these computerized services offered at no charge to the user in publicly supported libraries. To achieve this, it is obviously necessary to convince government, and the public at large, to make a fundamental commitment to institutionalize the costs.

Considering where we are starting, this is clearly going to take several years of further discussion and inquiry. It will involve many other groups to which the fate of libraries is linked—not just government as manifested by legislatures, but also the National Commission on Libraries and Information Science, education authorities, professional societies, the information service vendors, social and consumer agencies, intellectual freedom groups, voter organizations, and the mass media. Librarians cannot realistically expect to see a general and permanent solution before 1980—a year after the White House Conference on Library and Information Services scheduled for fall 1979. The Conference should provide an excellent forum for highlighting this issue. More likely, however, is a period of about five years for extensive debate, during which will spring up the normal apparatus of committees, special studies, joint conferences, statistical and opinion surveys, and the like. This phase would culminate in some definitive national recommendations (the kind that begin to form a basis for legislation) and would be followed by federal government action in the period from three to five years afterward.

From the librarian's point of view there are reasons to prefer the longer route. If there is a final decision as quickly as one year after the White House Conference, it will undoubtedly be because the present policy of charging the patron, which after all has relatively few ideological defenders, has been allowed to solidify through inaction or through approaches to changing it that are ill conceived. There is no reason why this should be allowed to happen, but without doubt it will take several years to inform, educate, and change the necessary segments of public opinion toward support of the library profession's position. It will be a huge undertaking in which it will be crucial to forge the kind of alliance with information service vendors that the library profession has long had with the conventional publishing industry. Talk of sides, camps, or "them and us" is hereby outdated.

Whatever pathway the discussion takes, we can already see that it must inevitably arrive at a critical crossroads—the federal government will have to decide what kind of a good information is. Resolution of that question—toward which the recent reexaminations of copyright and patents, of freedom of information and the right to privacy, and of telecommunications have setting the direction—should not occur without the vigorous voice of the library community being heard, for it will be as momentous a social decision as the current one about the nature and consumption of energy in the United States. Upon the outcome will depend issues of spectacular scale. For libraries, it is the issue of whether or not ways should be found for the public purse to support public use of a qualitative advance in information access, any individual's benefiting from it being regarded as contributing to the general well-being (the "merit good" theory). For information service vendors and data base producers, the issue is whether the laws of commercial competition can and should apply. Given that there will never be more than a small handful of such vendors, the question will arise whether there should be created a new type of public utility after the pattern that has proved, in the view of many, an efficient solution to the problem of guaranteeing essential power, water, and communications services without government in direct operational control.

WHAT SHOULD LIBRARIANS DO?

In the meantime, what line of development should libraries follow? Since we wish to see the day when on-line searches will be offered at no direct charge to the library user, how do we get from here to there? By refusing at the outset to perform searches until they are made available to all at no direct cost? Hardly. A long-term strategy is needed. As with the development of free public lending libraries, the case must first be actively demonstrated that constraining the individual to pay for what is becoming a vitally necessary technique of access to gigantic amounts of information is ethically wrong, politically unwise, educationally unsound, and economically inefficient. The patterns and effects of fee-based usage have to be revealed through actual experience, undesirable as this chore may be for librarians. Public or institutional funding will then come in the form of a switchover of a machine already in motion—like a moving train being switched down a different track. So we must bear that future objective in mind as we struggle to start our train moving.

First: Any library finding an information need that can efficiently be met by an on-line search service should adopt this method. That is to say, the systems should be utilized or not utilized on their merits as information resources, not on the grounds of one's personal social philosophy, and certainly not withheld on the chance that they may be free to users very soon.

Second: If, after an honest examination of the other uses to which library funds are put, there is no means of supporting the services except to charge, accept that for now, and provide the service to those who will pay. (They are not all millionaires, as some seem to believe. There are plenty of people on average or lower incomes—students, for example—who think enough of the benefits of these services to pay, even though the cost is not trivial.) But try hard to mitigate the charges by adopting preferential pricing and by finding new sources of institutional funding, either directly or by seeking outside grant money, for that is a step in the right direction. It will alert the funding agencies to the problem and begin to guide their responses into channels that support our eventual goal. It will also show that librarians care enough about *both* principles—free access to information and high-quality service to patrons—to begin to make a commitment. One useful tactic in academic environments is to encourage the idea of class searches. A unifed search can be performed for a particular class, perhaps based on the instructor's existing reading list; for this, instructional innovation funds are often eagerly provided.

Third: From the outset put the service on a basis that will maximize the reference librarian's power of decision over when a computerized search is indicated, thus closing the gap between the purely "on-demand" search and the "discretionary" search that is performed more for the librarian's benefit than the user's. Justify as many of the searches as possible on the grounds of increased staff efficiency. Having the librarian prescribe the computerized search probably does not imply that, because we have taken away much of the element of patron choice, we are obligated not to charge (the analogies in this case being doctors and lawyers); but it can be a salient contributory factor as the general theme gathers strength.

Fourth: Keep statistics on the unserved, both individually—by gathering information on those who decline the search after being told about the charges and also as a class—by examining the nature and extent of the population the library is serving.

Fifth: Keep a record of the time and cost to the library of creating and operating an accounting and billing system for individual charging. Sometimes, for example, the library fines window has to be involved, issuing receipts for payment which then become the user's claim check at the reference desk for collecting search output. And keep notes on any other undesirable side effects of such a system (in addition to the general inhibiting of usage). Does it, for example, necessitate payment in advance?

Sixth: Equipped with many copies of the ALA Resolution, begin to build the broad moral and political case for free services. Be willing to spend money on the right type of publicity, for example, or on documents or on special seminars and workshops. Start with the immediate, active clientele; talk to them and give them handouts. To the inert clientele send a mailing, either an information sheet or a short survey questionnaire. To funding agencies present good arguments, starting with those in the Resolution and, when assembled, facts and figures. Draw attention to the hardship cases and the detrimental effects of allowing this to happen. Begin as soon as possible to provide estimates of what it would cost to run the service without individual charges. Elaborate also on the benefits this would confer—socially as a merit good, and also organizationally in good library public relations, less bureaucratic entanglement in accounting and billing, and the freeing of librarians to fulfill their true professional role as information specialists. Find direct or indirect ways to communicate with legislators, local councillors, and other officials. Do this cautiously at first, for their information and the librarians' own. Do not at this stage talk about specific legislation. ALA and many state library associations will be preparing themselves to propose legislation when the time comes.[2]

And finally: Help colleagues to expand the discussion by communicating to them news, findings, and insights.

---

[1] At the 1977 ALA Annual Conference, one participant in the MARS discussion on charging noted that, when the local authorities who fund her library were exposed to the idea of charging for computerized searches, they immediately asked what other library services she had that they could charge for.

[2] The results of The California Library Association's current initiative (March 1977) in proposing legislation to provide public funding will be carefully studied.

Genealogy As It Relates to Library Service

Russell E. Bidlack

"It is not necessary to have in one's veins 'the blood of all the Howards' to secure an interest in our genealogical relations." So observed New York State Librarian Henry A. Homes in 1876 in *Public Libraries in the United States*. Homes went on to note that prior to 1845, the founding date of the New England Historic Genealogical Society, "the whole number of American genealogical histories was not more than thirty." Homes estimated, however, that by 1876 the number of published genealogies in the United States had increased to more than 400. By 1915 the number had grown to 3,000, and today the figure stands at around 25,000.

CURRENT INTEREST

Evidence of the growing interest in genealogical research, which has been variously described as a "current boom" and a "modern passion," is easily documented. Alex Haley, whose *Roots* has been a primary cause of this boom and passion, has enchanted audiences across the country with his description of the "mystical experience" of discovering the deed that transferred ownership of his slave ancestor, Kunta Kinte, and identifying his Aunt Liz (Elizabeth, age six) on a census record in the National Archives. A merit badge in genealogy has been created for the Boy Scouts, while youngsters in scores of elementary and secondary schools are busy identifying great and great-great-grandparents for social studies projects. Milton Rubincom, Past President of the National Genealogical Society, has been interviewed on the "Today" program.

A Black woman from Detroit who traced her ancestry to William Hood of the Continental Army has been "warmly welcomed" to membership in the Daughters of the American Revolution, the same society that once forbade the appearance of Marian Anderson in Constitution Hall.

In Indiana, the Evansville-Vanderburgh School Corporation has received a federal grant under the Elementary and Secondary Education Act IV to promote genealogical study in the elementary grades. Called TRACE (Tracing and Researching Ancestry to Cultivate Esteem), the project will encourage some 4,000 students in the sixth, seventh, and eighth grades to develop personal genealogies.

"Genealogy is no longer stuffy research done by prim little old ladies," observes Sarakay Jordan of the Texas State Library. Even Dagwood Bumstead recently had a brief enthusiasm for genealogy, although his interest waned when, in Blondie's words, the "poor dear . . . shook his family tree and a bunch of nuts fell out." Dagwood's was not a unique experience, although most beginning genealogists find that, once they begin, regardless of black sheep and closet skeletons, the search never ends. After all, the number of one's ancestors doubles with each generation.

On the occasion of the nation's 201st birthday (July 4, 1977) *Newsweek*'s feature article was devoted to "Everybody's Search for Roots." It is noteworthy that this article ended not only with a bibliography but also with a list of 10 key libraries and archival collections for genealogical research. The change that has taken place in the orientation of genealogical research is illustrated by *Newsweek*'s cover—the family photograph was not that of New England Puritans or Virginia aristocrats, but of a 19th-century Italian immigrant family. It was the prediction of Homes in 1876 that, while "family history in the past has had for its object to trace the pedigree of successful families in a simple line of descent," genealogists of the future would study "the affiliations and ramifications of all the descendants of a common ancestor for many generations," noting that such a pursuit would "promote a sense of republican equality."

Equality is indeed being promoted by genealogical research today. Authorities on American hobbies agree that genealogy is now outranked in popularity only by stamp and coin collecting as hundreds of thousands of Americans search for their roots. Unlike stamps and coins, however, ancestors are not bought and sold, nor in the collection and identification of forefathers and forgotten relatives

Genealogy

does one deal with the objects themselves. The sole quest of the genealogist is for information; and with the wealth of source material provided in recent years, not only through traditional print but also through microfilm, Xerox, offset printing, and computerized searching, genealogy has contributed an appropriate share to the information explosion facing libraries.

CHANGING LIBRARY ATTITUDES

Traditionally, the genealogist has not been a welcome patron in American libraries. The Enoch Pratt Free Library's 1950 staff manual for its General Reference Department set forth a rather typical library position of that time. Citing ALA's 1926 *Survey of Libraries in the United States* as showing that "as a general custom the public libraries of the country find it inadvisable to devote any considerable amount of time to genealogical work or to specialize in genealogical departments or collections," it was explained that, "in accordance with this custom, The Enoch Pratt Free Library does not buy books that are narrowly and technically genealogical." It was further noted that, "if genealogical books are purchased by the Pratt Library, it is because they contain a liberal amount of biographical (as contrasted with strictly genealogical) information about important individuals or families in Maryland."

Although they rarely stated it as clearly, most other public libraries followed the same policy on genealogical works as did Enoch Pratt. While the reasons given were usually the high cost of genealogical publications and the small number of patrons interested in the subject, there were unstated factors that were often more compelling. The genealogist of the past had a rather unflattering image among librarians. She, less often he, tended to be elderly or at least middle-aged and usually possessed an imperfect knowledge of and respect for essentials of proper library usage such as the card catalog and the *Readers' Guide*. Genealogists were not considered serious readers in that they never read a book thoroughly—in fact, they often demanded as many as a dozen volumes at a time only to examine the indexes (and complain mightily if an index were wanting). If the stacks were closed, they demanded access because they were never quite sure what it was they wanted, nor did they trust the page to find it. If there were several genealogists in the reading room at one time, they tended to be noisy—they talked out loud as they shared with each other their discoveries and their frustrations. The fact that they often appeared to be hard of hearing added to the aggravation. Furthermore, they never wanted to leave when it was time to close the reading room—there was always one

"Authorities on American hobbies agree that genealogy is now outranked in popularity only by stamp and coin collecting as hundreds of thousands of Americans search for their roots."

more note to take or another index to check.

The prim little old lady, or the elderly gentleman with a cane, was always, of course, a Wasp. While there were a few genealogists who did their research as thoroughly as the serious historian, many seemed to search for ancestors merely to use them as badges to join exclusive societies, such as DAR, the Society of Mayflower Descendants, the National Society of Colonial Dames of America, or the Society of the Cincinnati. Genealogy was often dismissed by librarians as "the sport of Brahmins."

There is another aspect of ancestor hunting that helps to account for the ridicule that has frequently been directed toward the genealogist. "I am a self-made man" was a motto of distinction worn by the American pioneer, suggesting that family origin had played no role in his success. Abraham Lincoln has often been quoted as saying, "I don't know who my grandfather was; I am much more concerned to know what his grandson will be." While letters survive to prove that, at least in his later years, Old Abe had a keen interest in the Lincoln family history, his earlier view suggesting that the study of one's ancestors was contrary to the American tradition tended to prevail. A good part of the general antipathy of Americans toward England following the Revolution was directed against the English aristocracy. If one hates the aristocracy, which depends upon family relationship for its perpetuation, it may follow that one should also shun all study of one's own family ties.

THE NEW RESEARCHERS

During the past two decades there has been a marked change of attitude toward genealogists. The fact that their number has increased accounts in part for this change, but the image of genealogists has been altered as dramatically as their number. No longer is membership in a hereditary patriotic society a major inspiration for genealogical research. The typical genealogist today is searching for the circumstances of history that account for his/her origin and being. Whether an adopted orphan, the descendant of slaves, or the offspring of a Vanderbilt, we are asking, "Who am I?" In her *How to Find Your Own Roots* (1977), Lisa Ray Clewer, after noting that each of us has eight great-grandparents, adds, "And you are the total of all their inherited qualities, and it is through you that these qualities will be passed on." For many Americans, young and old, this thought has become more and more intriguing. It is likewise intriguing for many librarians as they resolve to improve their service to genealogists. "In order to provide better reference and referral service in this area," reports Hardy Franklin, Director of the District of Columbia Public Library, "we have sent a number of our staff members to various workshops and seminars dealing with genealogy, especially Black genealogy."

Noting that "library users now searching for their ancestors are more representative of the general population than formerly," John S. Burgan, Chief of the Enoch Pratt Central Library, characterizes today's genealogists as "members of virtually every ethnic group prominent in the Baltimore population—Black, British, Chinese, German, Greek, Italian, Jewish, Polish—all are found in our current crop of searchers." Burgan adds, "In age they now range from adolescents to the very old; in fact, staff have observed that fairly often teenager and grandparent work as a team in seeking out the family line."

"Interest in genealogy no longer can be considered a private domain for persons of colonial heritage," observes Joe Shubert, New York State Librarian. Shubert has also noted "a sharp increase in the use of genealogy and local history for other scholarly or governmental research purposes, in such areas as social statistics, political science, and property title researches." Celene E. Idema of the Grand Rapids Public Library reports that an Indian claims settlement has prompted many Michiganders with Indian ancestry to search for their roots. "The increase in use of our facility in the last year has been staggering," reports Morgan J. Barclay, Head of Local History and Genealogy in the Toledo-Lucas County Public Library in Ohio. "Many people of Polish and other East European backgrounds seem to be getting involved, along with members of our Afro-American community."

While the celebration of the nation's Bicentennial and the publication and dramatization of *Roots* must be credited with spurring the new enthusiasm for

Local and Family History Reading Room of Chicago's Newberry Library which holds one of the nation's finest genealogical collections.

genealogy, these events were, in the words of Mary K. Meyer, Genealogical Reference Librarian for the Museum and Library of Maryland History, "the catalyst which brought the steady increase in popularity of the subject to full flower." Just as the Civil War can be credited with awakening an early, though limited, interest in family history, the two World Wars abetted that interest mightily. Whenever soldiers invade the land of their forefathers, whether it is the Union soldier in Virginia or the American GI in Germany, an interest is kindled in family history. "What the son wishes to forget, the grandson wishes to remember," observed historian Marcus Lee Hansen two generations ago. Travel at home and abroad frequently sparks an interest in family history, as does becoming acquainted with someone involved in genealogical research. The "genealogical bug" can be easily transmitted from one already smitten to another innocent victim who simply wonders, "From whence did I come?"

MATERIALS AND SOURCES

Another factor in the spreading enthusiasm for genealogy has been the work of the Church of Jesus Christ of Latter-day Saints. The Mormons' amazing effort and financial investment in gathering and preserving family records stems from their belief in the sacred nature of family relationships and their conviction that these relationships are eternal. A sustained drive by the Mormons to microfilm vital records around the world, as well as to acquire copies of all printed genealogical records, has resulted in a collection of some 130,000 volumes and more than 900,000 reels of microfilm. The LDS Genealogical Library in Salt Lake City is the largest such library in the world, and its 265 branches, which are able to borrow a copy of any film in the central library, constitute an impressive library network. Non-Mormons are served without charge in the same manner as Mormons. Thomas E. Daniels, Public Relations Manager for the LDS Genealogy Department, reports that a decade ago the library served about 700 readers per day. By early 1977, that figure had grown to 2,000. Then, according to Daniels, "along came a man named Alex Haley, and things haven't been the same since, now will they ever be.... Those who didn't come to the library wrote letters asking for help at the rate of 4,000 per month. Patronage increased to 3,000 per day, then to over 4,000 a day during the tourist season in August. It has since leveled back to about 3,000 per day."

What is the nature of the research materials sought by the genealogist? While almost any record of human activity becomes a legitimate source for the family historian, at least 95 per cent of our ancestors did not engage in the kind of activity to assure the preservation of their identity in major written records. Instead, their names may have been recorded only when they were born (or baptized), married, bought or sold land, paid their taxes, sued or were sued by a neighbor, joined a church, signed a petition, performed military duty, were noted by the census taker, made their last will and testament, or were the subject of a brief obituary in the weekly newspaper.

The published family history is based on records of this nature, and the fortunate beginner in genealogy may find that the information desired has already been provided. In that instance, the searcher will probably turn to another ancestral line on which no research has been done.

What is the obligation of the library, particularly the public or state library, in providing research materials for the genealogist? The person who first becomes inspired to search for roots needs guidance, and that initial guidance should be available in the library in the form of how-to-do-it guides. The classic work of this sort, written by the former Director of Libraries at the University of Wisconsin, is Gilbert A. Doane's *Searching for Your Ancestors*, 4th ed. (University of Minnesota Press, 1973). George B. Everton's *The How Book for Genealogists*, 6th ed. (Everton Publishers, 1965) and Ethel W. Williams's *Know Your Ancestors: A Guide to Genealogical Research* (Charles E. Tuttle Company, 1960) should also be recommended by librarians as a necessary first step in climbing one's family tree. An excellent pamphlet by Lisa Ray Clewer, *How to Find Your Own Roots*, was published in 1977 by the Great Western Savings and Loan Association of California and is being distributed free to beginning genealogists as well as to libraries. A number of libraries have published their own manuals for the genealogist in which general instructions are incorporated in a description of the particular service provided by the library in question. All beginners' manuals in genealogy urge that one begin the search with one's own relatives, and that family records be exhausted before turning to library and archival sources.

Beyond providing the basic how-to-do-it reference materials, librarians must consider carefully the degree of service that can be provided the genealogist. If a library has assumed responsibility for preserving its community's history, it is, of course, already involved, because local history and genealogy cannot be separated.

A relatively small portion of the sources for genealogical research have actually been published—most are in manuscript form in courthouses, governmental and church archives, and historical collections of one kind or another. Through microfilming projects (such as those of the Mormons) and extensive indexing programs, however, it is now possible to locate these manuscripts in greater and greater number and to arrange to have copies made. Many of these records, such as baptismal, tax, census, and court records, are now being published. Federal census records from 1790 to 1880, one of the vital sources for the genealogist, are available in microfilm from the National Archives, while printed and computerized indexes to those records are appearing in impressive numbers. About 500 periodicals, many in rather ephemeral formats, are currently being published to provide source materials for the genealogist. Most of these specialize in a particular geographical area or an individual family.

County and town histories have always been a primary source for genealogical data. Not only did the Bicentennial bring forth a whole new series of such publications, but also offset printing and public demand have enabled publishers such as the Genealogical Book Company in Baltimore to reprint large numbers of old local histories.

Too often librarians assume that a genealogical collection consists simply of printed family histories, of which, as noted earlier, about 25,000 have been published in the United States. (The first American genealogy, that of the Samuel Stebbins family, was published in Hartford, Connecticut, in 1771.) Usually published in small editions by obscure publishers, each one a labor of love, family histories have always been expensive and difficult for libraries to acquire except as gifts. While several booksellers, such as Goodspeed's Book Shop in Boston and the Charles E. Tuttle Company in Rutland, Vermont, specialize in out-of-print genealogical works, these volumes are quite expensive.

LIBRARY COLLECTIONS

The *Newsweek* feature article on genealogy indicated that "almost every major public library has a genealogy collection." While this is a bit of an exaggeration, acquisition of genealogical materials

Genealogy

and reference service to genealogists is certainly looked upon more favorably today than it was a few years ago.

As in nearly every area of collection building, libraries often choose to specialize in a particular aspect of genealogy, usually based on geographical considerations. The policy of the South Caroliniana Library, as explained by Reference Librarian Eleanor M. Richardson, is typical: "We attempt to acquire all genealogical publications, by gift or purchase, written by South Carolinians or dealing extensively with South Carolina families." Harold R. Jenkins, Kansas City Public Library Director, notes, "We emphasize certain genealogical areas of the United States: Missouri and those parts of the country from which the majority of 19th-century immigrants came to Missouri—Kentucky, Tennessee, Virginia, the Carolinas, the Middle Atlantic States, New England, Ohio, and Pennsylvania."

The primary purpose of a small number of libraries, such as those of the New England Historic Genealogical Society in Boston and of the National Genealogical Society in Washington, D.C., has always been to serve genealogists. There are other libraries that contain rich genealogical collections but for whom this is just one of many services. The Detroit Public Library's Burton Historical Collection, the Newberry Library's Department of Local and Family History, and the New York Public Library's Local History and Genealogy Collection are examples of such specialties. The growing interest in genealogical research has recently prompted a number of libraries to create special collections, the Fort Wayne Public Library being an excellent example. Aided by a special bequest, this library's genealogical collection now approaches 200,000 volumes and exceeds 20,000 rolls of microfilm.

Source materials sought by historians, especially local historians, have equal appeal to genealogists, and while a hearty welcome has not always been extended to genealogists by directors of historical libraries, these researchers often constitute a major portion of their users. Patricia Harpole, Chief of the Reference Department of the Minnesota Historical Society, reports that "genealogy is the most popular research topic for one-half to two-thirds of our patrons." Mary K. Meyer reports that genealogical researchers have increased by 400 per cent during the past 10 years. William J. MacArthur, Jr., Head of the McClung Historical Collection of the Knoxville-Knox County Public Library, reports that "the McClung Collection has a staff of five full-time and one part-time, including two professional librarians and one history Ph.D. Perhaps 80 per cent of the more than 5,000 researchers who use the collection annually are working on genealogy."

Where a library is located near another institution that is well equipped to serve the genealogist, duplication of such service should logically be avoided. The Chicago Public Library has had a long-standing policy of not collecting in this area since the Newberry Library's Local and Family History Collection is recognized as one of the nation's finest genealogical collections. In explanation of the limited nature of the genealogical collection of the Minneapolis Public Library, Doris Northenscold, Chief of Central Library Services, notes that "we are very fortunate to have a branch Mormon library near, and the Minnesota Historical Society, located in St. Paul, does an excellent job of not only serving patrons, but training librarians [in genealogical service]." Nathan A. Josel, Jr., Assistant Director of the Madison Public Library, has written, "Because Madison Public Library is located only six blocks from the Wisconsin State Historical Society, a great deal of pressure to provide genealogical materials and research, normally associated with public libraries during this newly awakened age of awareness in local history and genealogy has been diverted to that great state and national resource."

An earlier reference was made to the hands-off-genealogy policy of the Enoch Pratt Free Library as expressed in 1950, but that policy changed in 1966 when the Peabody Institute Library was merged with Enoch Pratt. Some 10 per cent (20,000 volumes) of the Peabody collection was genealogical, with emphasis on British and eastern United States sources. Today Enoch Pratt's policy reads:

> Publications of [genealogical] societies, associations, and governmental bodies

are generally added to the collection, but individual family histories are added only when adequately indexed. A few privately published individual family histories that are potentially useful are added as gifts.

Handbooks of procedure, reliable guides to genealogical materials, general genealogical encyclopedias, and historical material of value to the genealogical worker are provided. Emphasis is placed on building on existing strengths, e.g., British and mid-Atlantic United States genealogical materials. Serious expansion into new areas may be undertaken with due consideration of the accessibility of the collections of the Maryland Historical Society and the Library of Congress.

By sharing information and experiences, genealogists learn a great deal from each other. They also have a tendency to organize as local groups, usually identifying the group with the library where its members do research. A growing number of librarians are recognizing the constructive role that such a group can play in the promotion of the library. While this support may be directed primarily toward strengthening the library's genealogical resources, it can easily extend to the entire library. "These people tend to represent some of the community's most influential families," Kenneth King, Director of the Mount Clemens Public Library in Michigan, has observed, "and it follows that their pro-library stance can be very helpful." Individuals in such a group often volunteer to assist beginners in genealogical study and may take on indexing projects. They often assume responsibility for responding to mail requests for local genealogical information. The Detroit Society for Genealogical Research, whose headquarters is the Burton Historical Collection of the Detroit Public Library, has published one of the leading genealogical magazines for more than 40 years. The bequest of a member has recently permitted the library to complete its file of the film of the federal census from the National Archives for 1800 through 1880. Patricia Chadwell, Head of the Genealogy Department of the Fort Worth Public Library, reports that "we receive extensive support from a very active local genealogical society which provides us with 140 periodical titles, a number of review copies, and funds to purchase supplies and equipment which cannot be obtained through city funding."

OTHER ASPECTS

State libraries vary greatly in their concern for genealogy. At least half make no attempt whatever to provide service in this area, often because another nearby agency, such as a state historical society, has this responsibility. On the other hand, some state libraries, such as Michigan's, count their genealogical collection as a major strength. The Indiana State Library, for example, has a separate Genealogy Division that, with the library's recent addition, can now accommodate more than 100 readers. On the other hand, the Nevada State Library gave its genealogy collection to the Washoe County Library in Reno 10 years ago and refers genealogical queries there. For many years, the South Carolina State Library, rather than building a genealogical collection, has used a portion of its budget each year to supplement the genealogical acquisitions of the South Caroliniana Library at the University of South Carolina. According to State Librarian Estellene Walker, "Since the South Caroliniana collection is devoted exclusively to Caroliniana materials, most of the resources purchased with State Library funds are related to surrounding states as well as catalogs of major national genealogical libraries."

A number of libraries report a new demand for workshops in genealogy. Lucia Patrick, a consultant for public library services in the Georgia Department of Education, reports that "several public libraries have held or sponsored workshops on how to get started in tracing your family's roots, and a number of high schools and colleges are giving assignments or courses in genealogy." Jean Waggener of the Tennessee State Library notes that, "due to the increased interest in genealogy, our staff is receiving requests to conduct genealogical workshops. We plan to arrange one workshop for Middle Tennessee and one for East Tennessee. On October 15 representatives from each of our research areas conducted a pilot workshop in Paris, Tennessee." Daniel A. Yanchisin, Head of the History and Travel Department of the Memphis-Shelby County Public Library, reports that "for the last four years we have sponsored an annual genealogical workshop. For the five sessions of last year's workshop we had a total attendance of over 600 people." Although the attendance in 1977 dropped to 200, Yanchisin notes that 90 per cent were new patrons.

Most libraries do not offer genealogical works for interlibrary loan, although some state libraries do so within the state. The policy of the Virginia State Library is more generous than most; according to Donald Haynes, "We lend microfilm copies of public records throughout the country to libraries or individual researchers. In recent years we have restricted the lending of printed genealogical volumes to Virginia, because of increasing demands on the collection."

Because genealogy has rarely figured in university curricula, academic librarians have seldom deliberately collected in this area except where they have been responsible for preserving local history or a special collection. Because the study of history has always gained generous support in the building of academic library collections, however, the large university library inadvertently contains a wealth of materials that can aid the family historian since history and genealogy can scarcely be separated. Reference desk assistance to the genealogist is rarely provided by the academic library except for making available some how-to-do-it manuals, such as the Doane volume. An exception may be made for the family historian seeking information regarding an ancestor associated with the institution.

Because the record that a genealogist seeks is often to be found only in distant places, libraries have always received mail requests for assistance in locating local family data. Libraries known for the wealth of their genealogical resources have also regularly received mail requests for even more extensive coverage. In years past when such requests were infrequent, many librarians gave extensively of their time in providing such assistance. With the great upsurge in genealogical research, however, it is now the rare reference librarian who can provide a more than cursory response to such requests. Many have had to resort to form letters of refusal. What is often done, however, is to refer the letter writer to a local genealogical group or to one or more professional genealogists or record searchers who, usually at an hourly fee, will undertake the research. An alphabetical list of reliable persons interested in performing this service is usually preferred to recommending a single person. Like every popular pursuit, genealogy has attracted its full share of charlatans out to make an easy buck. A library must avoid becoming a medium through which such individuals operate.

A concern of many librarians in charge of genealogical collections is that, with the great increase in their use, these materials are being worn out. Gerald J. Parsons, Head of the Local History and Genealogy Department of the Onondaga County Public Library, has observed that "genealogical and local history books are for the most part scarce, rare and very fragile. Consequently, they are hard to obtain, expensive and deteriorating rapidly. We have volumes which have been on the shelves for 70 to 80 years and have lasted quite well; but with the increase in use, many of our books will be completely worn out within the next 20 years."

Thousands of Americans seem suddenly to have awakened to the truth in an old Chinese proverb: "To forget one's ancestors is to be a brook without a source, a tree without a root." Libraries across the country are being affected by and responding to this awakening.

Our Fragile Inheritance: The Challenge of Preserving Library Materials

Pamela W. Darling

Rare books on display at the Royal Library of Belgium, Brussels.

The library has always been thought of as the preserver of civilization's records, experiences, and wisdom. But our understanding of the preservation function has tended to focus on the acquisition and organization of those records, stopping short of the dreary mechanics of storage and maintenance. To be sure, we have concerned ourselves when necessary with shelving and binding and library paste—often spending large sums in the process—but we (most of us) have approached such matters with the same perfunctory interest we give to ordering pencils, or waste baskets, or color tabs to code our catalogs—and we cringe at the stereotype of the librarian as a fussy custodian or caretaker. Only a few among our ranks have had cause to recognize the library's need for a real caretaker, or the importance of sustained professional attention to the physical maintenance of all those things we have acquired and bibliographically controlled with such enthusiasm.

Perhaps it was the Florence flood that turned the tide of awareness. When the waters went down in the Medici library, there was all that mud on paintings and statues—and books. In living black and white, we read about the international horde of volunteers who assembled to help clean up the mess. And when they returned home with their color slides, we learned about the discoveries and inventions spawned by that awful necessity:

Preservation

Water and mud damage due to flooding in Florence, Italy, in 1966 caused losses of priceless books and manuscripts. Volunteers from throughout the world flocked to the National Library to begin the painstaking task of drying and restoring what was salvageable. Many works had not been microfilmed and are lost forever.

how to wash off the mud and dry thousands of books before the mold appears, how to remove the stains, how to reshape the buckled covers and caved spines, how to trace the soggy bibliographic trail that would lead to those unique treasures that really must be restored. Or if *we* didn't learn all that, at least we learned that others had, that there was indeed something to be learned, that our ignorance was a clear and present danger to the survival of our collections. We began to worry.

The Quiet Disaster. It's a curious thing about libraries and disasters—earthquakes, fires, plagues, pestilences, famines. Disaster in a library nearly always means water: floods from fire hoses, floods from bomb or earthquake-damaged pipes, floods from leaky roofs, floods from faulty heating or cooling or plumbing systems, floods from hurricanes and burst dams and downpours. Water, water everywhere: water in the air, humidity swelling pages and bursting bindings, breeding mold, carrying airborne pollutants into paper fibers, activating acid residues in the paper itself, feeding the chemical process of deterioration . . . or the absence of water: dry, brittle pages crumbling at the touch, cracked spines, powdered leather, glue turned to dust.

The hidden disaster creeping through the stacks—all of the stacks—doesn't make headlines the way the fires and floods that strike so dramatically do. The gradual deterioration of thousands of thousands of not-so-ancient volumes, the silent erosion of yesterday's newspapers and scholarly journals, the disintegration of last year's paperbacks—it's not very good newspaper copy, right?

Wrong. "Great books fail the test of time" proclaimed a banner headline in the Philadelphia *Inquirer* last July: "A literary catastrophe that no one can stop is decimating the nation's best libraries as tens of millions of 19th- and 20th- century books destroy themselves because of acids used in their paper. . . ." And as of this writing, the *National Enquirer* (not the most scholarly of journals) has commissioned an article on the same subject. Matthew Arnold and other 19th-century popularizers could scarcely have asked for a more effective press; and their works will certainly be among those to benefit if this spreading of the word among "the masses" helps to generate the broad support essential to the solution of this awesome problem.

Rising Awareness. Preservation seems to be an idea whose time has come; or rather—let us be more precise—the awareness that mankind's collective memory is seriously endangered has become widespread. Unfortunately, awareness of a problem does not automatically implement a solution. Popular recognition of the fragility of our environment has been followed by years of controversy and technological confusion as we have sought to realign dozens of socioeconomic priorities within the framework of a universe no longer viewed as permanent and inexhaustible. In the same way, popular

recognition of the library preservation problem, though not quite so all-embracing in its implications, is being accompanied by painful controversies about what should be preserved and technological confusion over how to do it. We have as yet no coherent national program to protect the environment; and we do not yet have a comprehensive national program to preserve library materials. But the controversies, frustrating as they may be, are a necessary step in moving from awareness to working programs.

How can we hasten this process, as individual professionals within our own libraries and as an organized profession properly concerned with the collective survival of our vast intellectual resources?

Local Responsibilities. On the local level, a surprising amount of physical protection can be provided through the application of some common sense. The physical mistreatment accorded newly received materials in the processing units of practically any library, the careless slamming and dropping and jamming as materials are hauled from return desks to shelves, the debilitating physical strains on unbound materials shelved upright without proper support, or on bound materials forced into too tight shelves or sprawled drunkenly over half-empty ones... an hour's observation of such common phenomena and two minutes of subsequent "research" inside one's own head, followed by a vigorous program of staff and patron consciousness raising, will go a long way toward minimizing the damage caused by poor shelving and handling practices.

THE RIGHT ENVIRONMENT

Beyond these directly people-caused threats to the survival of our collections are those related to the physical environment. Optimal standards for the storage of paper- and film-based records that are subject to regular use call for a steady temperature of 65° F. ± 5°, and relative humidity of 50% ± 5%. (Temperatures in nonuse storage areas may be much lower.) Higher temperatures accelerate deteriorating chemical reactions, and fluctuations in temperature and humidity cause the moisture content to rise and

fall, weakening and ultimately destroying bonds between paper fibers, the stability of glues and inks, and the adhesion of emulsions to film bases. Airborne pollutants, particularly the sulphurous compounds common to urban and industrial areas, penetrate the surfaces of fibrous materials, combining with the natural moisture to form acids that further eat away at the basic structure. All of which means that air-conditioning systems, which provide filtered air at consistent year-round levels of temperature and humidity, are only incidentally beneficial for patrons and staff. People just sweat if it gets too hot; books will die, eaten by mold if it's too humid, crumbled to dust if it's too dry.

Light. Light is another threat. Leave a folded newspaper in a sunny window for a week and then compare the discoloration and embrittlement of the exposed portion with an inside page. Light, especially the ultraviolet end of the spectrum, acts as a catalyst to speed the oxidation reactions within paper or cloth, encouraging it literally to burn up. A library can't very well be kept in total darkness if its contents are ever to be used. But ultraviolet filters should be applied to windows and fluorescent tubes used in reading and stack areas; timed shut-off switches in the aisles of large stack areas buy time for the books as well as saving on electricity; and exhibit cases, especially those displaying precious

Restoration processes at the Newberry Library, Chicago, include soaking individual pages in magnesium bicarbonate to neutralize acids from the papermaking process, a method which necessitates disassembling bound volumes.

documents, must certainly have this protection.

Dirt. Dirt is an obvious enemy. Gritty accumulations on shelves and volumes can lead to abrasion of cover materials and staining of pages. Dust in a film projector or microform reading machine can scratch the film and mar pictures, garble sound tracks, and even obliterate whole lines of text; and once the surface is broken the image may be eaten away from inside. Regular cleaning of books and shelves and equipment is a must for preservation's sake, quite apart from the aesthetic advantage.

Insects. Insects and vermin have proved only an occasional problem for libraries in the temperate climates of North America, but any conditions that might encourage infestation (food in the stacks, warm or dark trash-collecting corners) should be eliminated. Many animal glues and flour-based adhesives used in bookmaking contain insecticides, and newer polyvinyl adhesives apparently do not appeal to four- and six-footed prowlers. But if they appear, waste no time in calling the exterminator. And keep a sharp eye on shipments of material from tropical areas, which may carry both insects and growing mold (mold spores are everywhere, but start growing only when it's warm and damp). Avoid contaminating the rest of the collection until they have been fumigated. Small shipments can be safely protected against bugs by placing the materials, when thoroughly dry, in a sealable plastic garbage can or an unplugged refrigerator with a small dish of moth crystals for a couple of weeks. If large quantities are involved, or if the problem is clearly mold and mildew requiring thymol treatment, expert advice should be sought before proceeding.

Disaster. The nightmare of every librarian is that some disaster will strike the collection while she/he is responsible, and for hundreds of us each year the dreaded dream of fire or flood becomes a reality. Nothing can make it pleasant; but there are ways to reduce the risk of becoming a victim, and ways to control the damage if it happens. John Morris's *Managing the Library Fire Risk* (University of California Office of Insurance and Risk Management, 1975) is an excellent guide to fire prevention in the library, discussing the pros and cons of various detection and extinguishing systems and analyzing several recent library fires, how they might have been prevented or contained, and what salvage methods were employed. Peter Waters's *Procedures for Salvage of Water-Damaged Library Materials* (Library of Congress, 1975) provides lucid step-by-step instructions for rescuing a flooded collection, a list of people who may be contacted for emergency assistance, and sources for emergency supplies and equipment. Both books should be studied by every librarian and the recommendations for prevention and predisaster development of emergency plans scrupulously followed. Better to have wasted a few hours preparing for a catastrophe that never comes than to be responsible for the unnecessary loss of thousands of books to fire or mold.

Maintenance and Housekeeping. There is nothing very remarkable about these precautions, most of which would quickly occur to any sensible person who gives some attention to the questions of maintenance. What is remarkable is that, by and large, librarians have failed to give this kind of attention to the collections in their care, perhaps because physical custodianship has seemed unworthy of professional attention which "ought" to be focused on the intellectual challenges of selection, cataloging, and reference work. But all the intellectual effort we lavish on those information-bearing objects will be for naught if we don't apply ourselves more effectively to the physical care of the objects themselves.

Good housekeeping, then, is the first commandment. Unfortunately, it will not by itself bring a halt to all deterioration nor undo the damage already done. To do that requires, in addition, a judicious combination of programs for binding and rebinding, repair, restoration, replacement, and conversion to other formats.

RETHINKING THE PURPOSE

To develop a context within which to understand and pursue such programs, it is useful to return briefly to a very basic question: what is the purpose of the library? The answer might be phrased in a thousand different ways, but perhaps most would agree that the purpose of the library is to make available to people the information/material they need, when they need it, and in a form they can use. Notice the hedging in the use of the slashed term. Is a novel or the manuscript of *Roots* "information"? Is the population of India or the freezing point of saltwater "material"? Yet both may properly be sought in libraries and as we learn to distinguish more precisely between these two categories, the decisions about what and how to preserve will be much more intelligently made.

Goals and Orientation. Some libraries, or departments within libraries, are almost exclusively devoted to "materials." They are museums of books and written records that, like museums of art, are committed to preserving for the appreciation of mankind through the ages one-of-a-kind objects that physically represent the risings and fallings of cultures and civilization. Other libraries are esentially stockpiles of information, sources of facts, figures, and ideas that may be stored and communicated effectively through a variety of physical objects. Most libraries actually lie somewhere along the spectrum between these two extremes, and thus we must learn to distinguish within our own collections between those things that are valuable as artifacts quite apart from the information they contain and those that are valuable chiefly—or only—for their intellectual contents. For the first group, we are bound to preserve the original object in as nearly a perfect state as we possibly can. For the second, the physical "container" of the information is of little consequence except insofar as it does or does not facilitate the storage and transfer of its contents, and we are thus quite justified in altering or abandoning altogether the original package if the information can be retained in a more usable or permanent form. Consider the following examples.

The issue of a Colonial newspaper that carried the text of the Declaration of Independence is certainly an historic document of great intrinsic value even though its contents are accessible in a hundred million other places. If discovered creased and crumbling in some library basement, it ought to be flattened, deacidified and restored by an expert, mounted or encapsulated to protect against future damage, and placed in a storage or display environment that, while keeping it accessible to the people for whom it has significance, will insure its survival.

A 40-year run of the same Colonial paper might turn up in the same basement in the same condition. To treat its thousands of pages with the same care given to the Declaration issue would cost tens or hundreds of thousands of dollars —and for what? Our understanding of history is unquestionably enriched by being able to view tangible physical tokens

Preservation

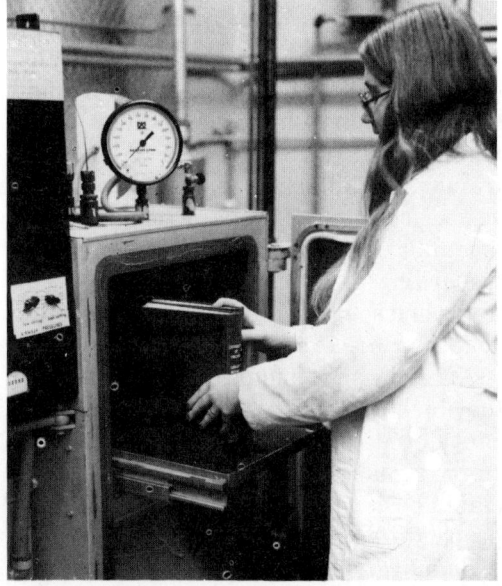

Barrow Laboratory's prototype machine in deacidification can treat bound volumes by forcing a nontoxic gas (morpholene) into books. Since 1976, over 50,000 volumes at the Virginia State Library have been successfully treated to halt the aging process.

of the great and terrible moments of the past. But who has the need or inclination to appreciate every page of every newspaper or journal or collection of sermons or governmental regulations? The 40-year run is valuable as a prime source of historical information. It ought to be reproduced on microfilm, with service copies printed, cataloged, and even indexed to make them readily accessible for historical research. The master negative should be stored under conditions designed to keep it safe for centuries, as an insurance copy and from which to print additional copies for users elsewhere or to replace worn-out service copies. Whatever remains of the original can legitimately be withdrawn from the library's collection (discarded, or sold to those who deal in such "collectibles" if there are enough pieces intact to sell).

As these examples suggest, the significance of the information/material in question must be evaluated in reaching a "preservation decision," to determine whether to focus on the physical object or the intellectual contents. Often this decision is not an automatic one based on the item itself, but a conditioned one relative to the goals of each particular institution. If the remarkable basement hypothesized above were in the library of an oceanographic institute, the discoverer might well decide not to spend a penny on restoring the Declaration issue or in filming the rest, since neither is related to the information needs of the user group. (One trusts, however, that the nearest state archives or historical society would be offered the chance to reclaim these items for posterity.) A research collection devoted to Shakespeare or Dickens might well determine that every edition of its man's works is an artifact of value in tracing the influence of his work on the rest of society, whereas a public or college library would scarcely blink over discarding a worn-out 19th-century edition when so many later editions, in better condition, are available.

After the preliminary determination of the object vs. contents has been made, the range of alternatives—rebind, repair, restore, replace, reproduce—and the associated costs must be reviewed and an appropriate choice made for each item.

Binding/Rebinding. Libraries spend millions of dollars every year on commercial binding and rebinding to support and protect, on the shelf and in use, loose periodical issues and the ever-growing number of paperbacks. Some classes of "currrent-interest-only" materials may not be kept long enough to warrant binding, and certain paperbacks may still be cheaper to replace than to bind. But as a general rule, binding is the best protective measure available for a collection of pages intended to be kept and used; so unbound items should be promptly bound, and previously bound volumes damaged or worn to the point that the pages are no longer completely protected by spine and covers should be rebound.

At present the chief difficulty in binding is the question of standards. "Class A library binding" was widely accepted for many years as the only proper library binding, with standards diligently maintained by most of the industry. Now, however, because of the increasing variety in the kinds of paper and widths of margins and the differences in nature and duration of use, it has become apparent that there is not a single method of binding that is best, or even good, for all kinds of materials. Even as certain disadvantages of "Class A" were being recognized —chiefly in regard to oversewing, which can be very damaging to narrow-margin and brittle-paper items—a number of new materials and methods were being put into use, often without adequate testing to establish how permanent and durable they were. In the face of economic difficulties, some binders sacrificed quality to retain price advantages over other binders, and libraries with reduced or threatened book budgets have been eager to take advantage of cheaper binding possibilities. This propensity has been strengthened by librarians' general lack of knowledge about the technical factors that affect the life and usability of bound materials and their consequent inability to evaluate effectively the numerous possibilities suggested by eager salespeople.

There has been some activity aimed at resolving this situation. The Library Binding Institue (LBI), a trade association with an obvious interest in the matter, supported the 1976 establishment of a book testing laboratory at the Rochester Institute of Technology for evaluating binding materials and methods. The Library of

Congress Binding Office has developed specifications for several styles of binding for different materials in its collections and promises to publish them for use by others. And renewed contacts between LBI and the Preservation Committee of ALA's Resources and Technical Services Division should encourage a cooperative approach to the technical questions and a broader dissemination of accurate information about different binding possibilities. We need standards; but in the meantime, we can apply common sense to evaluating the physical differences among our binders' wares as well as their price tags.

Repair. Whether from the wear and tear of use and abuse, or the self-destructive tendency of the materials themselves, a very large percentage of any collection will eventually start to deteriorate. The sooner remedial action is taken, the less will be needed in most cases.

There is a school of thought that holds that nothing should be touched by anyone but a thoroughly qualified conservator and that other personnel should be trained to not do even minor repairs because they are likely to do them poorly. If there were an abundant supply of thoroughly qualified conservators and if minor repairs were not being done anyway, training or no training, librarians might be able to live with this counsel of perfection. In fact, however, libraries will have to employ some nonexperts in this work for some time to come.

Several library suppliers offer supplies and instruction booklets on repair techniques that are generally suitable for extending the life of heavy-circulation items of little value as objects. Many of these supplies have not been tested adequately for permanence and durability, and although they increase short-term strength, they may decrease long-term stability. For the treatment of materials of greater value as objects, Carolyn Horton's *Cleaning and Preserving Bindings and Related Materials* (ALA Library Technology Program, 2d ed., 1969) gives extended and reliable instructions for organizing and carrying out a manageable rehabilitation program. The choice of supplies and techniques, and the training and skill of staff, are of crucial importance. Much of the work performed by the few professional conservators and restorers in the country is to undo the work of well-intentioned amateurs. In 10 or 15 years we may hope to have a nearly adequate pool of personnel trained in the physical repair and restoration of library materials; and by then the many disagreements over what is or is not safe and proper treatment should be largely settled. Meanwhile, if we must employ nonexperts, the utmost care and discrimination must be exercised in establishing and administering in-house repair programs.

Restoration. When in doubt, don't touch in house. Items of very great value should not be tampered with by the local staff. The services of a professional conservator/restorer should be sought, but for most of us that's easier said than done. For one thing, such work tends to be very expensive because it is a highly skilled handcraft requiring years of training and many hours of painstaking work. For another thing, qualified conservators are hard to find in most places. The American Institute for Conservation of Historic and Artistic Works (AIC 1725 19th Street, N.W., Washington, D.C. 20009) and the Guild of Book Workers (c/o American Institute for Graphic Arts, 1059 Third Avenue, New York, New York 10021) can provide lists of members and fellows. The Library of Congress Preservation Office can help librarians locate book conservators in various parts of the country, and state libraries and archives and major research libraries and rare book collections can often provide references.

But it is a touchy business, because there is as yet little consensus about what constitutes a "qualified conservator," a great deal of professional disagreement about "proper" techniques, and—it must be said—personal jealousy and hostility within the field. AIC, which is primarily an organization of museum conservators but also includes paper and book conservators, has been struggling for some years to develop a certification program; and in the museum area there are now several academic programs providing extensive graduate study combined with apprenticeships to produce skilled practitioners. But no such formal preparation is available in the Western Hemisphere for those concerned with library materials, and it is likely to be several years more before a full-scale program is launched. At the moment, librarians have little

Preservation

choice but to rely on marketplace rumors of reputability until they have developed enough technical sophistication to judge for themselves the work of the experts.

There is another alternative to this *caveat emptor* situation, one that should be considered even by those who couldn't afford a "qualified" conservator if one were to turn up on the doorstep. It's a time-buying device that is variously known as "protective wrapping," "protective encasement," or simply "protection" and involves placing deteriorated items into close-fitting individual containers to hold the pieces together, providing physical support and a measure of protection againt the threatening atmosphere. This does not undo existing damage, of course, but it retards future damage and increases the item's chances of being around to benefit from remedial treatment at some later date. And it does not require much training or, by comparison with full-scale restoration, much money. A wide array of boxes, slipcases, portfolios, and folders made of acid-free materials are available from several suppliers; most come in standard sizes, and some can be ordered from suppliers or binders to fit individual books. The Library of Congress and the library of the American Philosophical Society in Philadelphia will provide easy-to-follow instructions for making custom-fitted containers on the spot. Protection of single sheets—manuscripts, prints, maps, posters—can be done very effectively by enclosing them in a clear envelope of inert polyester film, after which even the most brittle sheet can be safely handled, stored, or displayed. The key feature about these protective devices is their reversibility, a theory of increasing importance within the conservation field as a whole—nothing should be done to preserve or restore cultural objects that cannot easily, and without damaging side effects, be undone should later discoveries provide better ways of preserving them.

No discussion of restoration would be complete without some mention of paper deacidification, the process of neutralizing the destructive acid that is a chief cause of deterioration. Research in this area was begun in earnest two decades ago by the late W.J. Barrow, with the support of the Council on Library Resources (was there any important development in the profession's last 25 years in which Verner Clapp did not play a key role?). Research was continued at the Barrow Research Laboratory until its closing in June 1977, as well as at the Library of Congress and among a few independent researchers. To date there are several patented techniques for neutralizing acid in paper and adding an alkaline buffer to retard future "acidification" from the atmosphere. Some involve immersion of pages in water-based or nonaqueous solutions; some use sprays or transfer from juxtaposed sheets impregnated with a volatile neutralizing agent; some—the most promising for large-scale treatment—use gaseous diffusion processes to penetrate whole books instead of working page by page.

The dream of mass deacidification to stop the "silent erosion" in the stacks has become practically an article of faith among many who have been concerned about preservation in libraries. But to this nonscientist (who would dearly love to become a believer), the causes for scepticism seem to be growing while the promised breakthrough for mass treatment never quite materializes. Is it a question of time for patient research and analysis, luck in hitting on the right solution out of an endless number of possibilities, or ingenuity in transforming small-scale labo-

At Baltimore County's Perry Hall Branch Library, salvageable boxes of books are removed from a water-soaked storage area which flooded in 1971.

ratory equipment into full-size production facilities? Or are we searching for something that isn't there? Even if we find an economical mass deacidification process, it will not solve the preservation problem. Deacidification can reduce the future breakdown of paper fibers by removing a chief cause. It cannot by itself whiten yellowed paper or restore lost strength to embrittled pages or remove stains or mend tattered bindings. Mass deacidification—if it comes—would help to control the size of the problem; it would slow down the erosion of our collections (as would persuading publishers to use acid-free paper in new book production). But it will not relieve us of the professional responsibility to care aggressively and discriminatingly for the materials in our collections.

Replacement/Reproduction. The notion of replacement as a preservation technique would properly scandalize the curators of rare book or manuscript collections, whose materials by definition are irreplaceable. But in most other library situations, replacement has long been accepted as a reasonable approach to the problem of keeping the intellectual content of library materials available when the original package becomes unusable. Most libraries have well-established routines for acquiring new copies of in-print works and for replacing damaged out-of-print works with reprints or new editions. Weeding practices, though they may arise from space pressures, also serve a preservation function by eliminating from the pool of treatment candidates those works whose role within the collection is no longer essential.

Reproduction, or the conversion of content from one physical package to another, is assuming an ever-larger role in this process. The most familiar example is the replacement of bulky, quck-to-disintegrate newspapers with microfilm; but full-size photocopies are not uncommon. Reproductions are also used not to replace but to protect fragile manuscripts and other materials from unnecessary handling. Copies, full-size or microform, can be made available to those users whose work does not require examination of the originals or whose distance from the collection makes direct access impossible.

The conversion process may be performed by the library itself, copying the worn-out index for insertion in a heavily used reference work or microfilming crumbling serials backfiles. But most reproductions are acquired from outside sources, and suppliers—chiefly the micropublishers—are making more and more old material newly available every day. For all that librarians have complained, often with very good reason, about the technical quality, editorial practices, or delivery arrangements for large reprint and microform projects, they can and should be grateful that publishers, macro and micro, have taken on a share of the burden of preserving the intellectual contents of our libraries.

Microforms seem to provoke a lot of strong feelings within libraries from staff and readers alike. This is not the place for extolling the virtues or condemning the inconveniences of the format and its associated equipment (though some interesting theories might be drawn from a comparison of the success of various microform installations with the initial attitudes and expectations of the librarians who did the installing). Whatever the merits of such arguments, the fact is that microforms, alongside books, are in libraries to stay; and more information can be preserved per dollar via microfilming than through

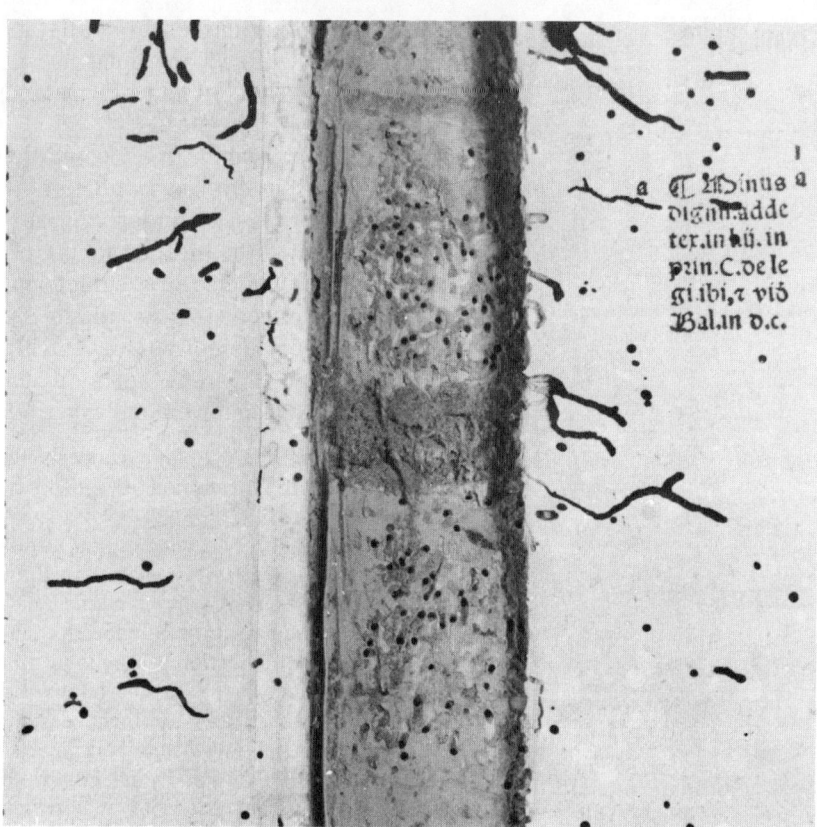

(Above) A casualty of the Powder Post Beetle infestation at the Beinecke Rare Book and Manuscript Library, Yale University, where (below) 30,000 volumes were bagged in plastic and frozen in a custom-made freezer in which they are subjected to temperatures of 20 degrees below zero Farenheit for three days. The technique kills insects, eggs, and larva without injuring the book.

any other technique currently available. Love it or hate it, librarians must use it, and the sooner we accept microforms and get on with the job, the better.

Choosing an Approach. In choosing the "right" alternative for each particular item in a collection, the underlying service responsibilities of the particular institution must be weighed in the decision, along with some good sense about the usefulness of various forms for storing and transferring different sorts of information. Here are some examples:

> Standard-size newspapers are probably most conveniently retained and used in 35mm roll microfilm.
>
> High-reduction COM (Computer-Output Microfiche) is certainly handier than miles of data on a continuous paper printout.
>
> A new edition or full-size reproduction of a reference collection's language dictionary is much to be preferred to the crumbling original or a microform version.
>
> A famous jurist's well-thumbed and annotated copy of *The Federalist Papers* is better put in a protective box or slipcase than either reproduced on paper or film or restored to its original clean-margined state.
>
> A set of environmental study reports heavily used every fall by students in an introductory ecology course had better be sturdily bound, rebound, and replaced with more paper copies if it wears out. The same set in an historical science collection or a research lab's library might best be kept in more durable, space-saving microform since it will be used only for occasional reference.

From this litany of examples, the doctrine of suitable treatment, second only to the first commandment of good housekeeping, should begin to emerge—the choice of the preservation "treatment" must balance the physical characteristics of the original material, the nature of its intellectual contents, and the type of use that a library's clientele can be expected to make of it. A well-articulated collection policy is essential to an effective preservation program, and it should be applied to preservation decisions with the same combination of certain knowledge, hunch playing and ruthlessness that the selection officer must use in sifting through the endless torrent of potential new acquisitions. In fact, in most library situations the final preservation decisions ought to rest in the same hands as the selection decisions, since they represent the two ends of a single process that determines the scope, character, and quality of any collection. Conservators and preservation officers can inform and advise about technical possibilties and carry out the decisions once made; but it is risky to expect of them the broad, in-depth subject knowledge that is the key to developing and maintaining a useful collection.

COOPERATION

There are a variety of cooperative approaches to preservation that strengthen the hand of the individual library or librarian. The least formal, but of enormous potential significance, is the growing "invisible college" of people around the country who are beginning to share preservation problems, information, and experiences with one another. There are a few organizations and institutions that serve as referral points within this informal network: the Library of Congress Preservation Department, the New England Document Conservation Center, the American Institute for Conservation, the Guild of Book Workers, the Council on Library Resources, the Society of American Archivists, the National Conservation Advisory Council, and the Preservation Committees of the Association of Research Libraries and of ALA's Resources and Technical Services Division. But people tend to seek information from "institutions" only if they can't get it from someone they know, and it has been gratifying to note in the past few years a pyramiding of individual contacts. Letters and phone calls crisscross the nation, exchanging information and advice on everything from what to do about new books that fall apart the second time they're circulated to how to establish a preservation program for a large library system. There is, of course, no way to measure the accuracy of the information thus exchanged or the quality of the advice; but in traditional American fashion we are gradually pulling ourselves up by the bootstraps, and the momentum generated by shared concern can't help but improve the general level of professional awareness and sophistication.

Consortium Approaches. Growing out of this shared concern are several types of cooperative activities among libraries. One model is that of the Research Libraries Group (RLG), consisting of Columbia, Harvard, Yale, and the New York Public Library, which has developed a system for designating a "Master RLG Copy" of certain titles. The member holding the Master Copy assumes permanent responsibility for that title, calling on other members to fill gaps in the master set before disposing of duplicates, and insuring that one full set will be available to everyone in the group without each library trying to preserve everything. RLG has also begun a coordinated microfilming program designed to eliminate costly duplicate filming and thus increase the pool of information preserved in this form.

Regional Center. Another model is that of the New England Document Conservation Center, the creation of the New England Library Board. The Center operates a restoration workshop where materials from all eligible libraries within the region can be treated on a nonprofit cost-recovery basis. It also has a mobile fumigation chamber, and the staff is available for consulting on local preservation needs, training, and rescue operations after emergencies. Its move into larger quarters in the fall of 1977 was accompanied by the addition of a preservation microfilming operation.

National Activities. In December 1976, the Council on library Resources (CLR) supported a planning conference at the Library of Congress as a step toward the development of a national preservation program. The conference identified a number of desirable elements in such a program: a national preservation collection (perhaps in cold storage), coordination among microfilming programs, expanded information services, educational programs for preservation administrators and professional conservators, training for conservation technicians, and funding for research. The Library of Congress has subsequently appointed a National Preservation Program Officer, and an advisory committee (again funded by CLR) representing interested groups within the profession will help guide the development of the program.

On the education front, workshops and seminars are springing up practically everywhere. In ALA the Preservation Committee of the Resources and Technical Services Division assembles and distributes information about training programs and resources, and the bandwagon effect is beginning to produce results. Nearly a dozen library schools now offer introductory courses on preservation as a regular part of their curricula. The U.S. Office of Education has funded an intensive four-week institute to prepare practicing librarians for the development and administration of preservation programs in their own libraries, to be conducted at the Columbia University School of Library Service in the summer of 1978. Librarians don't yet know enough collectively to establish full-scale graduate programs in the field, but with the accelerated growth of interest and efforts to develop curricular packages, it shouldn't take many more years.

The literature of the field continues to be widely scattered, from mainstream library periodicals to abstruse scientific journals. A useful introductory bibliography appears as Preservation Leaflet No. 1, in a series distributed free for the asking by the Library of Congress's Preservation Office. At least one state library agency has established a formal clearinghouse for preservation information; and a growing number of large libraries are gathering useful reference collections on the subject, some by design and some as a result of individual staff members' interest, which they are usually happy to share with others.

A SPECIALTY IN SEARCH OF A PHILOSOPHY

Does all this add up to an emerging specialty within the profession? Probably yes, but a specialty still in such an infant state that it is impossible to predict the shape it will have taken 5 to 10 years from now. By then we may have developed techniques that will make today's treatment options appear very primitive indeed; by then we will certainly have a profession better educated as a whole about preservation and a respectable pool of specialist librarians to turn the technical possibilities into actual programs.

By then, too, we may have developed a coherent philosophy of preservation. I have referred facetiously to commandments and doctrines and articles of faith, but at present we have only the barest of intellectual frameworks upon which to build our preservation programs. Clashes among the experts about the "proper" way to do this or that testify not only to the need for continued research, but also

Preservation

to the lack of a common or well-developed philosophy, and it will be slow in coming.

Part of this difficulty may be traced to the fact that most people come to preservation with one of two naturally opposing points of view. On the one hand are the rare book curators, with their museumlike responsibilities for the care of priceless objects. On the other hand are the builders and organizers and administrators of vast general collections. The first group is properly concerned with maintaining the integrity and aesthetic appeal of original materials. The second, appalled by the thought that the entire written record of mankind may be burning up in the stacks, tends to opt for whatever quick and mass solutions come to hand. This genuine conflict of interest has, on occasion, been personalized with charges of philistinism vs. preciousness; but that does nothing to resolve the dilemma. We must forge a philosophy that honors the values of both—that appreciates the significance of objects and the love of books as books, while embracing the usefulness of other media for storing and communicating certain kinds of information.

The scope of the problem that generates this conflict has become truly horrifying in this century, not just because the paper has started to fall apart, but also because there is so much more of it. It is the curse of a literate, technologically marvelous age that we have the capability

"The nightmare of every librarian is that some disaster will strike the collection while she is responsible, and for hundreds of us each year the dreaded dream of fire or flood becomes a reality."

now to record virtually everything anyone discovers or imagines. Nor is it simply an "information" explosion in the utilitarian sense of data or facts; the flow of written and other records from the creative arts is phenomenal (12 new Harlequin romances each month at your favorite newsstand, for one, if crass, example). The level of intellectual production has long since outstripped our ability to absorb the product. Space and budget constraints have brought most libraries to accept the fact that none of us can acquire everything; but we still like to think that, in the aggregate, we can continue to preserve the entire record of our civilization. It may not be true. And if it is not, then we must very quickly decide how to select that portion of the total record that "needs" to be preserved for our own and our distant descendants' sake.

Information fuels our present-day society in an unprecedented fashion. Words about war or peace are more significant events than the battles themselves. Markets rise and fall not because there is a glut or shortage of rice today but because a computer predicts that there may be one 18 months from now. The pen has become dramatically more powerful than the sword, and the library's role in the communication systems that support our world is critical. But to be a successful information supermarket is only part of the job, for we hold on our shelves not just facts, not just information, but the record of humanity's ideas, hopes, and dreams, the key to understanding our world and ourselves, the means whereby we can transform information into knowledge, and knowledge into wisdom.

The challenge that faces us is threefold. We must expand and improve the technical skills for salvaging millions of books and other library materials threatened with physical extinction. We must develop organizational patterns and cooperative systems for employing those skills effectively and economically. And we must hammer out a philosophy to shape these programs, rooted in the dual nature of the library as provider for daily information needs and as a repository of the record of mankind. May we not prove unequal to the task.

1977: The Library Association Centenary

Rosamond Kerr

The 1876 Philadelphia Conference of Librarians might have been invented *pour encourager les autres*. Almost one year later, on October 2, 1877, the International Conference of Librarians began in the lecture theatre of the London Institution, its instigator, E.B. Nicholson, Librarian of the Institution, having been inspired by the American example. After four days of the now traditional round of papers, visits, and receptions, the Conference moved to its final and most significant task—to agree "that a Library Association of the United Kingdom be founded."

ASSOCIATION FOUNDING

One hundred years later the Association, called as if by divine right or perhaps royal prerogative, the Library Association (LA), is still going strong. It celebrated its Centenary in London in October, this time south of the Thames River at the South Bank arts complex, neatly sandwiched between the Houses of Parliament on one side and the National Theatre and St. Paul's Cathedral on the other. History reports that 15 Americans made the trip in 1877. In 1977 there was about a 50 per cent increase in the American delegation, led by the ALA President, Past President, and Executive Director, ALA members having taken the felicitous and fortuitous step of electing a former member of the LA as ALA President in the LA Centenary year.

By British standards it was a large gathering of about 1,100, including day visitors and 170 participants from overseas. Assemblies of the whole library profession are infrequent in the U.K., since the special interest groups of the LA prefer to hold their own annual seminars in the spring of each year.

Eric Moon addressing the association of Assistant Librarians at the Conference.

Overseas VIPs (left to right): Marc Chauveinc (President, Library Association of France); Helene Loukaides (LA Conference Staff); W. D. Linton (President, Library Association of Ireland); Professor R. Vosper (University of California, Honorary Vice-President, LA); Sir Frederick Dainton (President, LA); Ritva Sievanen-Allen (President, Finnish Research Libraries Association); Bob Wedgeworth (Executive Director, ALA); Mrs. Vasper D. Shavit (Israel); Clara Stanton Jones (former President, ALA); unidentified guest; Moostapha Lotun (Mauritius); Bob Hilliard (Secretary, LA); Russell Bowden (Deputy Secretary, LA); N. Ukaonu (Nigeria); Clem Harrison (President, Commonwealth Library Association).

Centennial commemorations are by their nature a time for nostalgia, for looking back and recalling past achievements. Britain's library services, particularly in the public sphere, have always been one of her great accomplishments, and the air of self-congratulation that pervaded the official opening session could be forgiven. A formidable array of dignitaries—including Queen Elizabeth II's cousin, His Royal Highness the Duke of Gloucester, Preben Kirkegaard, the President of the International Federation of Library Associations and Institutions (IFLA); Lord Donaldson, the Minister for the Arts (with special responsibility for libraries); and Lord Eccles, the Chairman of the British Library Board—assembled to pay tribute to the Association and to wish it well in its Centenary year. The Duke of Gloucester, inaugurating the Conference, emphasized the Association's (and hence the profession's) role at home—"I understand that it is the only organization in its field which seeks to bring together and to represent the whole scope of professional activity in librarianship"—and abroad— "The role played by the British profession in international developments, in information systems and information systems development is clearly acknowledged by the presence here today of so many members of the profession from overseas."

Controversial Issue. The euphoria of the opening ceremonies might, however, have been shattered if any of the delegates had been present at the Annual General Meeting of the Association the previous day. The principal motion discussed was an alteration in the Association's Bylaws to permit Chartered Librarians, designated as ALAs (Associates of the Library Association), to remain on the professional register on payment of a minimum subscription of £3 per annum (the estimated cost of processing membership) while enjoying none of the privileges associated with membership— participation in professional meetings organized by the Association and its regional groups, receipt of the Association's journal, the *Library Association Record,* use of the Association's library and information services, voting rights in elections, or representation by the Association and its officers in matters of professional concern. The motion was heavily defeated, with the proviso that the matter should be referred to the Working Party set up to consider the existing membership structure. Despite the patronizing attitude from the platform towards the young Scottish proposers of the motion, which only tended to emphasize the great divide between the London-based establishment and the membership at large, there was recognition that many members were dissatisfied with the services they were getting from headquarters in return for a hefty subscription, ranging upwards on a sliding scale according to salary to £30 per annum.

Qualifications Reviewed. As well as this challenge to the aims of the Association, the Centenary year has also seen a re-evaluation of professional qualifications and of the road to Associateship and Fellowship in the Association. The LA's Working Party on Professional Qualifications reported in 1977 on its assessment of future trends in higher education and how they will affect librarianship and established a firm commitment to an all-graduate profession by the 1980's. Admission to the Register of Chartered Librarians has usually been through the Association's own examinations, for which both graduates and nongraduates were eligible. The expansion of higher education and the establishment in the 1960's of several postgraduate schools of librarianship has led to an increasing number of graduates entering the profession, a situation compounded by the emergence of degree courses in librarianship. Many members, however, were concerned about the abandonment of two-year nongraduate courses leading to the Associateship, since they felt that there was a role to be played by this grade of professional and that present nongraduate Associates would find themselves at a disadvantage. The motion to preserve this alternative path to ALA was carried but, at the request of members present at the Annual General Meeting, was put to a postal vote among the total membership. (The subsequent vote approved the motion by 5,700 votes to 1,036, and the two-year course will continue in principle, although in practice it will be the library schools who will make the final decision.)

It was also obvious that Lord Donaldson's confidence that the current economic stringencies were only temporary, as enunciated at the official opening, was not shared by the membership, when a resolution to campaign against library cuts as "a direct attack on library users, library workers and the service we are providing for the future" was carried. It remains to be seen whether there will be any practical results.

The President's Address. At the official celebrations, the Association remembered some of the giants of the past in a presentation of highlights from the careers of five past Secretaries of the Association—MacAlister, Jast, Pacy, Savage, and McColvin.[1] This nostalgic retrospect was admirably complemented by the President's crystal gazing in his address to the Association. The LA's President in its centenary year is Sir Frederick Dainton, a noted physical chemist with considerable library know-how acquired during his term as Chairman of the National Libraries Committee, which led to the founding of the British Library. He is currently Chairman of the University Grants Committee.

Behind his vision of the "post-industrial society of growing leisure time for the majority," Sir Frederick saw the challenge of what he hoped would be "the learning society." The librarian would need to consider both his role in this society and the new skills he would need to acquire and develop to serve the future citizen: "As education increases public awareness so the professions must accept a greater public interest in how members of a profession select and train their new members; how the professions regulate their own affairs; and so on. . . ." He invited librarians to share a nonlibrarian's confident view that librarians would have a role of increasing importance to play in the post-industrial learning society.

CENTENARY THEMES

At times the Centenary Conference seemed to have been carefully orchestrated around the recurrent theme of "education permanente," "continuing education," or "the learning society," closely intertwined with a vision of man and his libraries at the crossroads looking for appropriate signposts to the future. There were papers with titles such as "The Next Ten Years," "Open Learning and Libraries: Some Implications," "The Library in the Age of Television," and "Signposts." Speaker after speaker from both the academic world and public library service sought to emphasize the role of the library in educating the community, a role heightened by the creation of the Open University, Britain's University of the Air, and the need to meet the demands of increasing leisure time. The speakers emphasized that the librarian and the library user would need to come to terms with the new technologies and new techniques of information access and retrieval. The Post Office's Viewdata system, allowing push-button information in the home via the ubiquitous television set, was on show at the Conference.

Goals Then and Now. The LA may have its roots deeply embedded in dedicated and dignified service to the public, but it also boasts a radical and controversial tradition embodied in the Association of Assistant Librarians, the AAL, which has always represented the younger, dissident element in the profession. Who better to recall the early pioneering days of AAL than Eric Moon, Secretary of the AAL during his first career in England, and now, in his second career, President of ALA. His was a memorable homecoming as, in an address entitled "The State of the Union, Jack," he drew on the example of the increasing social consciousness of ALA with regard to race and sex discrimination and the increasing democratization of ALA that led to both himself and Clara Jones being nominated for President by members at large and beating the official candidates. Moon launched a call to arms for all British librarians in their fight for a more equal, more socially aware, and more democratically run profession. He and many ALA members would find it hard to accept "a procedure by which a small group of senior citizens of the Association retires to a small, closed room, like some medieval Star Chamber, later to emerge and tell you who your next President will be. Not only do you have no voice in the matter; you aren't even offered a choice between two."

The AAL has always attempted to provide a forum for discussion of contemporary issues such as class and race relations and the role of the library in a multiracial and multicultural society, but perhaps it has not taken an active enough role. The message from Moon was clear:

LA Centenary

xlv

"If we do not as organized bodies understand today's world turmoil or the reasons for it, that misunderstanding will be reflected in increasingly irrelevant services in our libraries. If we choose not to participate in the certain massive changes ahead in society—here, in the U.S. and elsewhere—not only we but our libraries will become relegated to the role of bystanders." The standing ovation that greeted Moon was evidence not only of a stimulating, thought-provoking, and entertaining address, but also of a lesson well taken. Let us hope that the mood of revolutionary fervor engendered by Moon will not die a swift death amidst the morass of apathy that bedevils the British library profession.

But activism and militancy have rarely been characteristics of British professional life (except where salaries and conditions of service are concerned), and perhaps British librarians feel that their Association has little relevance to the efficient performance of their jobs. Demands for a more democratic electoral system are also likely to fall on deaf ears in a country that has traditionally had no say in the selection of prime ministers or monarchs. A passing glance at Moon's audience—a collection of his contemporaries and former colleagues—revealed few possible disciples likely to be storming the barricades to elect a Black woman as President. There has, in fact, been only one woman President in the history of the Library Association. Where have all the Assistant (or younger) Librarians gone?

A Summing Up. Although in general the Conference was a time for reexamining the profession and its role in society as it enters its second century, there were also opportunities for the individual groups of the LA to meet to discuss more specialized topics, including UBC, library services for the disadvantaged, children and books, rare book collections in the U.K., and the provision of commercial and business information. The closing session returned to the theme of professional qualifications and discussion on the implications of the Working Party's report. It was, however, rather like closing the stable door after the horse has bolted, since the subject had already been debated at the General Meeting earlier in the week and the proposals on an all-graduate profession rejected in principle.

Overall impressions of the Centenary Conference were favorable. The lack of fragmentation in the Association's structure, with the 14 special interest groups that met during the Conference attempting to organize joint sessions on topics of mutual interest, ensuring the pervasiveness of a feeling of corporate entity and corporate purpose.

But why, at the other end of the scale, the absence of those who will soon be playing a part in running those services, the newly qualified librarians and library school students? Surely there could have been a reduced rate for the whole Conference (apart from the reduced rate for daily attendance)—even IFLA at its 50th Jubilee celebrations in Brussels offered a reduced registration fee to participants under 30—which would not have left the Conference so top-heavy with chief librarians. Rumblings were also heard from representatives of those members, and there are many of them, who are not employed in the public library sector. Admittedly the Association owes its origins and development to the early pioneers in public library service, but there are many other librarians, both academic and specialized, who would have welcomed some acknowledgement and discussion of their problems. The Atkinson Report, advocating the concept of the "self-renewing" academic library (university libraries shall not expand beyond the space available; i.e., if you want to add 10 new books to your stock, you dispose of 10 old books), must be one of the most controversial issues of the day, but it was not mentioned at the Conference.

But perhaps a Centenary Conference is not the time or the place for too much controversy. It is chiefly a time for looking back, looking forward, and above all celebrating. The Conference was, in the words of Lorna Paulin, Chairman of the Working Party on Professional Qualifications and *the* woman President of LA, "a worthy celebration."[2]

REFERENCES
1. For a fuller account of the Association's history, see W.A. Munford, *A History of the Library Association: 1877–1977* (London: Library Association, 1977).
2. The proceedings of the conference were published as *The Library Association Centenary Conference: Proceedings* (London: Library Association, 1977).

Passing Through the Turnstile: A View of Library School Admissions

Kay Murray

The "talent search" for persons entering the profession of librarianship pretty much begins and ends with the process that determines who walks through the doors of our library schools. Who decides to go to library school, why they make such a decision, and how the library school selects students are critical issues to persons interested in libraries and librarianship. The incidence of termination of library education, either for voluntary or involuntary reasons, is so low that it is of negligible importance to this discussion.

WHO AND WHY

Who decides to enter library school and why they do so are questions largely of individual motivation. Library schools in general have not been involved in extensive programs of recruitment, although active recruitment of special target groups is practiced by individual library schools from time to time. Persons in the profession generally attribute their decision to enter library school to one or more of three factors: (1) the influence of an individual in the profession; (2) exposure to the library as a working environment; (3) the belief that librarianship combines readily with other educational and career interests to provide marketable training for employment. Recruitment by library schools, then, is largely passive in nature, with the individual usually initiating the process by requesting information or an application from a library school.

Various studies of library students indicate that they are a rather homogeneous group. Characteristically, they are white middle-class females. They have a B or better grade point average in a liberal arts undergraduate degree program and score relatively high on the verbal portion of the Graduate Record Examination. This description has not altered markedly for many years, although recently the percentage of men entering library school has increased, as has the number holding the master's or doctoral degree.

Historically, library schools have followed closely the patterns and procedures for admission used in other graduate and professional schools. The responsibility for library school admissions may be vested in the entire library school faculty, an admissions committee, the dean, or an admissions officer. Virtually all schools require that one or more applications be submitted, accompanied by grade transcripts and letters of recommendation. Most now require the Graduate Record Examination or the Miller Analogy Test. Some schools may request an interview or require a personal essay from the prospective student. Although entry requirements vary from school to school, a minimum undergraduate grade point average of B and a Graduate Record Examination total of 1,000 is not uncommon.

If one assumes that those persons who are selected for entry into the library profession are going to influence the future shape of librarianship, an examination of the characteristics of those who are admitted to library schools and how they are observed and evaluated in the admissions process is of great importance to librarians and library educators.

RUTGERS STUDY

Phase I of a longitudinal study of persons admitted, rejected, and graduated from the M.L.S. program at the Graduate School of Library Service (GSLS) at Rutgers—the State University has been recently completed. This phase of the larger study analyzes the various data collected from those seeking admission to the library school to determine which application data are most significant in the decision to admit or reject an applicant. (A report of Phase I, containing the complete results and descriptions of the research method and the statistical analysis employed in the study, is being prepared for publication. Subsequent phases will examine the same variables as predictors of the student's academic achievement while in library school and his or her professional development upon graduation.)

Admissions Procedures. Rutgers GSLS is not unlike other library schools, or, for that matter, other graduate and professional schools in the admissions process it follows. The normal pattern proceeds in this manner: (1) a prospective student requests an application; (2) the completed application, along with transcripts of academic work, letters of recommendation, and a personal essay describing why the applicant wants to enter library school, is submitted; (3) members of an admissions committee, comprising faculty, students, and university admission representatives, examine each application; (4) the committee then meets, discusses each applicant, and votes to admit or reject the applicant or to hold the application for further consideration. (The "hold" category is used when application data is incomplete or when an applicant is considered a border line prospective student.) An applicant may also have a personal interview at some point in the process, but this is neither required nor frequent.

Data Study. The objective of Phase I of the Rutgers GSLS study was to determine what admissions data were statistically significant in determining admission or rejection to the library school. Certain categories of variables were analyzed:

(1) Demographic variables.

(2) Educational and work experience variables.

(3) Objective variables—specifically, Graduate Record Examination verbal (GREV) and quantitative (GREQ) scores and percentiles, Test of English as a Foreign Language (TOEFL) scores, and the undergraduate grade point average (UGPA).

(4) Subjective variables—specifically each committee member's assessment of letters of recommendation and of the personal essay.

(5) Other application variables—for example, part-time or full-time status, the intended areas of professional specialization, and pertinent dates.

(6) Committee member variables—specifically, identification of each member of the committee and his or her comments and initial recommendation regarding admission.

(7) Admitting variables—for example, date of enrollment and receipt of financial aid.

(8) Terminating variables—specifically, the date of graduation or withdrawal, the final area of specialization while in library school, and the library school grade point average.

Table 1. Background Variables Related to the Admissions Decision (in percentages)

	Accept	Reject
Overall	70	30
Application Variables:		
Prior Degree—		
Baccalaureate	69	31
Masters	80.3	19.7
Doctorate	100	0
Undergraduate Major—		
Library Science	40	60
Education	58.6	41.4
Applied Science	83.3	16.7
Science	78.2	21.8
Social Science	76.5	23.5
Library Experience	74	26

The data base included all persons who applied to the library school, both those admitted and rejected. This base will permit a comparison between those who were given the opportunity to pursue the profession of librarianship through accepted channels and those who were denied entry. More than 1,300 applicants, spanning a three-year period, were included in the study.

Statistical Analysis. Rutgers GSLS admits 70 per cent of its applicants. A comparison of demographic and educational work experience characteristics of those accepted and those rejected for admission reveal that applicants with prior graduate education have a statistically significant higher rate of acceptance (see Table 1). Undergraduate majors in library science and education have higher rejection percentages, while majors in applied science, science, and social science have higher rates of acceptance. Prior library experience has borderline statistical significance in favor of admission. Non-local residents, except for foreign applicants, have a better chance of being admitted than local residents.

Certain demographic information, collected by most schools on a voluntary basis if at all, was analyzed to the extent that the data were available. The limited data reveal that there is no bias in admission with regard to sex or race—that is, the deviation from the 70-30 percentages of admits to rejects was not statistically significant. Married applicants are slightly favored for admission. The percentage of applicants rejected is higher in the under-25 and in the 36-40 age brackets.

Extensive statistical analysis—including multiple regression analysis, analysis of variance, and discriminant analysis—reveals that, of the more than 50 variables analyzed, only six have any major impact on the decision to admit or reject an applicant:

(1) Three subjective variables— the personal essay (E) and the two letters of recommendation (L1 and L2).

(2) Three objective variables—the GREV, GREQ, and UGPA.

It is not sufficient to identify these as significant variables. It is also important to know how much of the admissions decision-making process is explained by each of them and by certain combinations of the variables—the variance accounted for. These six variables together account for about 47 per cent of the admissions decision. Although this leaves more than 50 per cent of the variance in admissions decisions unaccounted for by any single variable or identifiable combination of variables, statisticians agree that a level of nearly 47 per cent of variance accounted for is very high in a study that has so many variables. Table 2 lists the six variables in the order of rank, with the variable of most significance first, and indicates the contribution that certain logical combinations of variables make to the admissions decision.

There are implications of these results that should be emphasized:

(1) The best combination of three variables is the essay, GREV, and one letter of recommendation. Together they come within 2 per cent of the total variance that can be accounted for.

(2) The personal essay alone is the greatest contributor, accounting for nearly 29 per cent of the variance. This particular variable is generally considered to be the best, although inadequate, indicator of motivation. It is also used, in combination with GREV, to assess communications skills.

(3) Together, the essay and GREV account for nearly 41 per cent of the total variance accounted for.

(4) The addition of a letter of reference contributes another 4 per cent to the explained variance; a second letter of reference makes an insignificant contribution.

(5) The three subjective variables—E, L1, and L2—account for 36 per cent of the variance; the three objective variables—GREV, GREQ, and UGPA—account for 26.5 per cent. (It should be noted that the essay alone accounts for more variance than all three objective variables combined.)

Variables as Predictors. In a related analysis, the performance of these six variables as predictors of admission or rejection was examined. Together they predict the admissions decision at better than the 86 per cent level. In other words, by examining the data collected on the six variables, one can predict accurately 86 per cent of the time whether the admissions committee will accept or reject an applicant (see Table 3). Some variables, however, predict one condition slightly better than another; this accounts for the different percentages recorded in the table. Again, the personal essay is the best predictor; if only the rating of the personal essay is considered, one can predict admission and rejection for 78 per cent of the applicants. An additional fact, not apparent in the table, is that the UGPA accounts for the capability of the objective variables to predict rejection somewhat more consistently than to predict acceptance into the library school at Rutgers.

Although this study reports data from a single school and has special application to that school's efforts to evaluate and improve its own procedures, it has implications for the entire library profession. It has been said that when an organization changes prerequisites for membership it essentially (or eventually) changes its character. The kinds of persons admitted into the profession can be expected to determine the future and nature of librarianship.

Other Factors. Identifying individual variables and the impact each has on the admissions decision certainly provides the library profession with valid data to establish admissions priorities by emphasizing or deemphasizing certain variables. Areas of discrimination in admissions can also be identified and reduc-

Table 2. Variables Influencing Decision to Admit/Reject (in rank order)

Significant Variables		Variance Accounted For (in percentages)
Essay	The Six Significant Variables	46.8
GREV	Essay + GREV	40.6
L#1	Essay + GREV + L#1	44.9
L#2	Essay + L#1 + L#2	36.0
GREQ	GREV + GREQ + UGPA	26.5
UGPA		

ed. There are, however, other factors—economic, professional, and societal trends—that affect library school admissions and therefore the "talent" that enters the profession.

Changing Employment Patterns. The general economic environment and the corresponding job market have caused changes in the employment patterns of persons entering the working world. New graduates find a very competitive market for jobs, but this is especially true for positions in the humanities and in education—fields related to librarianship that have traditionally provided a substantial number of students "crossing over" into librarianship. Hoping to improve their employment opportunities, more students are going directly from undergraduate programs into graduate schools. The compatibility of librarianship with study in other disciplines results in an increasing number of young applicants and of applicants with graduate degrees, persons who might otherwise have entered—at least for a time—other careers.

There is, however, a second economic implication that may well counterbalance the first. There has been, and will continue to be, a sharp reduction in financial aid available to students. At the same time, universities are confronted with rising budgets and are raising their tuitions and fees. In many universities, units that are not essentially "self-supporting" are in danger of elimination. Library schools, along with educational institutions in general, face the possibility of becoming stratified. Applicants will either have to have personal sources of money to attend school or be qualified for the limited financial aid that exists for target groups within society. As was pointed out earlier, these groups have not been the segments of society traditionally represented in librarianship.

The profession itself is undergoing changes as a result of internal pressures. The balance between the jobs available and the librarians available to fill these vacancies has shifted dramatically in a relatively short time. Very few new library positions are being created; at the same time, library school enrollments continue to increase. Whenever economic conditions tighten, services are among the first areas expected to maintain existing budget levels or even to cut back, and libraries are service organizations. Furthermore, the creation of large blocks of new library positions that occurred in past decades has also ended. There are very few new public or academic libraries being established and very little expansion of existing systems being planned. The majority of schools have already been forced by certification and accreditation standards to provide school library and media centers, and many governmental and industrial organizations have already recognized the need for and have established special libraries. Educational institutions, a large "consumer" of librarians, face decreasing enrollments that result in decreasing staff needs as the number of school-age children drops significantly. There is no apparent area in which a wide-ranging expansion of library services will take place in the foreseeable future.

Society's attitudes toward equal opportunity may well have the greatest impact on future admissions into library

Table 3. Variables as Predictors of Admission (in percentages)

	Admit/Reject	Admit	Reject
Total of the six variables	86.4	86.4	86.4
Essay	78.2	78.5	77.4
Essay + GREV + L#1	85.6	84.8	88.2
Essay + L#1 + L#2	82.3	83.0	80.3
GREV + GREQ + UGPA	78.6	78.4	79.3

schools. The implication of two recent events—the Buckley law and the Bakke case—are important. Admissions personnel, sensitive to the possibility of charges of discrimination, are increasingly careful to establish definitive admissions criteria that can be applied equally to all applicants; the rejection of an applicant must be justifiable under the specified criteria. The result is an increasing reliance on objective measures such as GRE and UGPA as admissions criteria. This coincides, however, with two factors that complicate the situation: (1) a growing disenchantment with the GRE and similar tests of intellectual capability as unbiased measures of academic potential, and (2) a period of grade inflation that is causing concern in academic circles. In schools where the number of applicants far exceeds the number of openings, the tendency is to raise the minimum GRE score or UGPA required in an effort to reduce the number of potential candidates to a manageable size.

Motivation Factor. The admissions literature and the Rutgers GSLS study indicate that the assessment of an applicant's motivation to enter the profession has a significant influence upon admission. Determination of motivation is, however, largely subjective in nature, and the subjective criteria—an essay, letters of recommendation, or a personal interview—cannot be translated into specific statements of admissions criteria. An admissions committee or officer may be hard put to justify the rejection of an applicant with adequate grades and GRE scores for lack of motivation as judged from the personal assessment of an essay response or an interview. It is not easy even to justify the selection of one qualified student over another qualified student because one wrote a "better" essay. Further, since an applicant may now examine his or her files and even request that items be removed from them, letters of recommendation—already considered to be of minimum value as a criterion for admission—become even more useless. Again, we find ourselves being pushed to rely more and more heavily on those admissions data that have good discriminant characteristics—the objective variables.

Summary. The number of applications to library school in the next few years may well stay at the current level. A continuing competitive job market and decreasing funds to finance students in graduate study will counterbalance the increasing number of people who feel economic pressures to look for other careers or further education. Unless there are compensating changes in the criteria for admissions and admissions procedures, the people entering our library schools, and ultimately the library profession, are likely to become a more homogeneous group—some might even say "elitist." Those persons with a high GRE, a high UGPA, and money enough to finance their education are going to get the admissions nod. Any deviation from this pattern will have to come from the establishment of special admissions policies or from an active recruitment program for target groups.

The characteristics of those people seeking to enter the profession of librarianship may change, the criteria for admission to library schools may change, the admissions process itself may change. A crucial question is whether the profession will be content to maintain a passive role, responding to such changes in due time; or whether it will take an active role in shaping the policies and procedures that determine who shall enter the profession in order to assure that librarianship remains a profession essential to and influential in shaping our society.

REFERENCES

Robyn M. Dawes, "A Case Study of Graduate Admissions: Application of Three Principles of Human Decision Making," *American Psychologist* (February 1971), pp. 180-88.

Lionel S. Lewis, "On the Genesis of Gray-Flanneled Puritans," *AAUP Bulletin* (Spring 1972), pp. 21-29.

Albert R. Marston, "It's Time to Reconsider the Graduate Record Examination," *American Psychologist* (July 1971), pp. 653-55.

Fred Pfister and Susan N. Roberts, "Study of Exceptions to Regular Admissions Criteria in ALA Accreditated Library Programs" (Tampa: University of South Florida, 1977). A 13-page typed report.

John Mark Tucker, "Library School Admissions and the Liberal Arts," *Journal of Education for Librarianship* (Winter 1975), pp. 183-90.

Warren W. Willingham, "Predicting Success in Graduate Education," *Science* (January 25, 1974), pp. 274-78.

Review of the Library Year

Abstracting and Indexing Services

Abstracting and indexing (A&I) services provide bibliographic aids in the form of references, subject terms, and brief descriptions in order to identify, locate, and obtain access to published or unpublished documents or nonbibliographic sources. The published documents, often referred to as the primary literature, include books, journals, monographic series, plays, newspapers, broadsides, music, and any other form of published works. Unpublished documents are usually technical reports, correspondence, manuscripts, and other material not formally published. Nonbibliographic sources include materials from foundations and other organizations, numeric data, works of art, and other materials not in bibliographic form.

Abstracting services include an abstract or brief summary of each item indexed. Indexing services, including abstracting services, provide data such as author, title, and place of publication to identify uniquely the item indexed so that it can be located. Indexing services usually provide subject access to the document through the use of subject headings, key words, or other subject access points.

In 1977 approximately 2,500 A&I services on all subjects were published.[1] More than 300 of these were available in machine-readable form.[2] Coverage of the primary literature grew approximately 10 per cent over the previous years.[3]

Current trends in A&I services are emerging in seven areas: (1) special current awareness services; (2) increased on-line interactive searching (approximately 90 data bases are now available for on-line searching); (3) changes in formats of primary publications to provide the user with access routes to non-traditional primary sources such as deposited papers, microform publications, audiotapes, videotapes, and computer files; (4) full-text searching to utilize computer-readable records of full documents for purposes other than typesetting, such as fully automatic or machine-aided creation of abstracts (extracts) and of indexes; (5) increased cooperation among A&I services (the report on the National Federation of Abstracting and Indexing Services (NFAIS) Study of Overlap among Fourteen A&I Services was published in 1977 as NFAIS-77/1); (6) expansion of user education programs, which was the most prevalent topic related to A&I in 1977; and (7) progress in standards activities, specifically the publication of the ANSI Z39 bibliographic references standard and the work of the Four-Way Group—Association of Information Dissemination Centers (ASIDIC), European Association of Scientific Information Centers (EUSIDIC), International Council of Scientific Unions Abstracting Board (ICSUAB), and the National Federation of Abstracting and Indexing Services (NFAIS)—on bibliographic descriptions for data bases.

Among the most significant developments in 1977 related to A&I were the publication of the Z39 standard on bibliographic references, the significant growth of educational programs related to on-line searching of data bases, and the establishment of the Copyright Clearance Center. A more detailed review of the 1977 activities appears in the chapter on secondary services and systems in volume 13 of the *Annual Review of Information Science and Technology (ARIST)*.   TONI CARBO BEARMAN

REFERENCES

1. *NFAIS-FID World Inventory of Abstracting and Indexing Services* (to be published in 1978).
2. Martha E. Williams and Sandra H. Rouse, compilers and editors, *Computer-Readable Bibliographic Data Bases; A Directory and Data Sourcebook* (Washington, D.C.: American Society for Information Science (ASIS), 1976).
3. "NFAIS Member Service Statistics," *NFAIS Newsletter* (February 1978).

The Federation has collected statistics of the number of unique items covered by member services since the formation of the Federation in 1958. This table is published regularly and is constantly under revision. With the growth and evolution of abstracting and indexing services over the years, it has become increasingly difficult to present comparative statistical data. In this table, most of the data are presented under the name of the organization producing services, as far as possible. This has caused some change in the way the statistics are presented. Users of previous tables are cautioned not to make comparisons with other data.

This table presents statistical data from 1957 to 1977 for all organizations that were members of the National Federation of Abstracting and Indexing Services in December 1976. The new data in the table were supplied by members during January 1977.

Note: As the table is subject to constant updating and revision, please be sure to quote the date of the table and acknowledge the National Federation of Abstracting and Indexing Services as the source.

National Federation of Abstracting and Indexing Services   **Member Service Statistics (February 1977)**

Full Voting Members	1957	1962	1967	1972	1974	1975	1976	Estimate 1977
American Dental Association	—	—	6,681	7,388	7,200	7,530	7,400	7,600
American Geological Institute	—	—	11,450	42,000	39,733	40,000	45,500	48,000
American Institute of Physics	—	—	—	30,000	33,369	22,504	22,097	22,100
American Mathematical Society[a]	—	—	—	—	—	—	—	—
American Meteorological Society	5,000	12,000	9,000	7,200	7,200	7,200	7,200	7,600
American Petroleum Institute	11,615[b]	21,977	29,151	32,983[c]	40,000	60,000	65,000	66,000
American Psychological Association	9,074	8,776	17,202	24,000	25,558	25,542	24,710	28,500
American Society for Information Science	—	—	—	1,338	—[d]	—[e]	—	—
American Society for Metals	8,219	11,542	23,800	24,400	26,325	30,694	30,294	31,500
BioSciences Information Service	40,061	100,858	125,026	240,006	240,000	240,000	240,000	250,000
Chemical Abstracts Service	102,525	175,138	269,293	379,048	375,663	454,245	458,508	469,883
Center for Applied Linguistics	—	—	—	122	5,901[f]	2,369[f]	2,186[f]	2,000[f]
Documentation Abstracts, Inc.	—	—	1,327	3,618	3,750	4,210	4,325	4,600
Earthquake Engineering Research Center[g]	—	—	—	—	—	—	—	—
Engineering Index, Inc.	26,797	38,120	51,670	83,653	89,393	89,596	88,365	95,000
Exxon Research and Engineering Company[h]	—	—	—	—	—	—	—	—
The Foundation Center[i]	2,500	5,000	9,000	35,800	37,800	38,000	41,000	41,500
Index to Religious Periodical Literature[j]	1,100	2,300	3,241	5,939	5,315	4,300	10,210	12,400
Institute of Electrical and Electronics Engineers	—	—	—	5,473	10,214	10,537	11,300	11,500
Medical Documentation Service[k]	1,500	1,500	1,692	2,500	2,500	2,500	2,500	2,500
National Association of Social Workers	—	—	896	1,068	1,069	1,199	1,215	1,215
Penn State Coal Carbon Data Bases[l]	—	—	—	—	—	—	—	—
Philosophy Documentation Center[m]	—	—	2,000	3,100	4,100	4,200	5,200	5,300
Primate Information Center (Seattle)[n]	—	—	2,219	4,171	4,192	4,397	4,438	4,500
University of Tulsa	—	10,816	15,519	15,502	17,958	18,766	17,396	18,000
Sub Total	**208,391**	**388,027**	**579,167**	**949,309**	**977,240**	**1,067,789**	**1,088,844**	**1,129,698**
United States Government Affiliates								
Defense Documentation Center	21,015	23,897	52,972	36,900	32,335	31,521	26,221	29,000
Energy Research and Development Admin.	14,042	34,149	47,055	60,848	66,236	71,960	150,000[n]	160,000
Library of Congress[o]	—	—	—	—	—	—	—	—
National Aeronautics & Space Admin.	—	—	107,260	81,810	78,511	81,459	81,800	82,000
National Agricultural Library[p]	98,409	94,968	102,198	124,592	114,000	115,762	126,000	126,000
National Institute of Education[q]	—	—	—	—	—	35,396	37,145	39,145
National Library of Medicine[r]	104,517	150,000	165,000	221,000	210,000	225,000	264,000	270,000
National Oceanic and Atmospheric Admin.[s]	876	—	1,224	2,760	2,789	2,394	1,807	2,600
National Technical Information Service	—	—	29,500	54,980	59,001	63,700	90,000	64,260
Water Resources Scientific Information Center	—	—	—	15,000	13,500	12,400	13,200	13,500
Sub Total	**238,859**	**303,014**	**505,209**	**597,890**	**576,372**	**639,592**	**790,173**	**786,505**
Foreign Affiliates								
Centre National de la Recherche Scientifique	148,883	251,274	367,300	470,184	519,754	525,760	510,000	510,000
Commonwealth Scientific and Industrial Research Organization[t]	—	—	—	—	—	—	4,512	4,900
INSPEC	16,452	39,272	71,032	154,074	164,646	161,571	177,965	178,000
International Labour Office	—	—	6,864	4,432	5,800	5,184	5,800	6,000
National Library of Australia	2,500	3,500	4,000	12,500	13,500	13,500	13,000	14,000
United Kingdom Chemical Information Service[u]	—	—	—	—	—	—	—	—
TOTAL	**615,085**	**985,087**	**1,533,572**	**2,188,389**	**2,257,312**	**2,413,396**	**2,590,294**	**2,629,103**

Reprinted with permission of the National Federation of Abstracting and Indexing Services (NFAIS)

a. No longer Federation member as of 1974.
b. Literature (world-wide) only.
c. Augmented patent coverage in cooperative effort with Derwent Services.
d. Clearinghouse ceased operation on December 31, 1973.
e. ERIC/CLIS transferred to Stanford January, 1974. No documents processed.
f. Revised figures represent the addition of 469 citations from the ERIC Clearinghouse on Languages and Linguistics, which began operation at the Center for Applied Linguistics on 1 June 1974. Subsequent CAL figures represent the activity of this clearinghouse, with the exception of 100 citations in 1976.
g. New Federation member as of 1977.
h. EREC believes that the statistics for its in-house abstract bulletins are not parallel to those for other member services. In recent years EREC has shifted extensively to equivalent bulletins published outside, chiefly by the American Petroleum Institute. Internal documents are still computer-based indexed, however.
i. Starting with 1972, these estimates are based on the combined number of records translated into machine readable form relating to private foundation entity data or to the grants that these foundations awarded.
j. Figures before 1976 do not include book reviews. Figures for the years 1960 - 1970 are estimates.

k. Additional abstracts are prepared for client publications. Figures for the years 1957 - 1966 are estimates.
l. Penn State Coal Data Base.

Number of Coal Samples in Data Base

Data Class	1974	1975	1976	1977	1978
1. Primary Numerical Data					
a. Class I	350	560	770	980	1190
b. Class II	70	80	90	100	110
c. Class III	0	140	280	420	560
d. TOTALS	420	780	1140	1500	1860
2. Secondary Numerical Data					
a. Class I	0	—UNDETERMINED—			
b. Class II	0	1000	2000	3000	4000

Data Class
1. Primary Numerical Data
  a. Class I (Coal sample collected by PSU; data generated by PSU).
  b. Class II (Coal sample collected by OCR/ERDA contractors; data generated by PSU).
  c. Class III (Coal sample collected by sub-contractor; data generated by PSU).
2. Secondary Numerical Data
  a. Class I (Data from scientific literature).
  b. Class II (Data from other sources).

m. New Federation member as of 1974.
n. The large increase in 1976 over 1975 is due to the increased scope of interest of ERDA beyond that of the AEC. The 1976 and forward figures are for the ERDA Energy Information Data Base from which a number of abstract journals and other information products are produced.
o. In contrast to most NFAIS members, the Library of Congress qualifies as a center of information services. Its statistics are therefore not relevant to this survey.
p. Figures represent indexing citations published in *Bibliography of Agriculture*. Since 1970, *B of A* produced by commercial publisher from data on CAIN (Cataloging and Indexing) tapes purchased from NAL.
q. New member as of 1975-1976.
r. The indexing backlog was eliminated in 1972. The total of 225,000 articles for 1975 also includes 11,000 Special List items which appeared in Special Bibliographies and the MEDLARS data base but no *Index Medicus*. The projected total of 250,000 articles for 1976 will also include about 12,000 Special List items.
s. 1958 - 1966 figures not available.
t. Statistics for 1957 - 1975 are not available.
u. New member as of 1976. Provides approximately 5% of the total Chemical Abstracts Service input.

Academic Libraries

Two publications—one with a view of the past, the other of the future—gave a broad perspective to academic librarianship in 1977. *Libraries for Teaching, Libraries for Research* (Chicago: ALA, 1977) brought together the separate articles that had appeared in the 1976 issues of *College & Research Libraries*. Originally prepared to honor ALA on its Centennial, the articles provide a reasonably comprehensive view of the century's achievements in the nation's academic and research libraries.

The second publication, *Academic Libraries by the Year 2000* (New York: Bowker, 1977) was a festschrift in honor of Jerrold Orne. Edited by Herbert Poole, this volume contains a series of essays by distinguished American academic librarians on the future prospects for the libraries serving the country's colleges and universities.

LIBRARY MANAGEMENT

MRAP and ALDP. The Management Review and Analysis Program (MRAP), devised by the Office of University Library Management Studies of the Association of Research Libraries (ARL), was developed to assist in improving the management of large academic libraries.

Following its application in a number of institutions, a review of the program was undertaken at Pennsylvania State University, and academic librarians are awaiting publication of the appraisal.

A similar program designed for smaller libraries, the Academic Library Development Program (ALDP), received its first test at North Carolina Central University. P. Grady Morein, project coordinator, and his associates reported on the program in the article "The Academic Library Development Program" in *College & Research Libraries* (January 1977).

In 1977 the Council on Library Resources (CLR) provided grants so that three additional libraries—Carnegie-Mellon University, University of Wisconsin-Parkside, and Drew University—could benefit from this new self-study program.

Financial Support and Budgeting. Several publications and guides have become available to academic libraries as they seek to adjust to reduced levels of financial support. The Systems and Procedures Exchange Center (SPEC) of ARL makes readily available through its series of flyers and kits the experiences of many academic libraries. Several projects for the year were directly related to library budgeting: "Allocation of Resources in Academic Libraries" (SPEC Flyer No. 31, March 1977); "Preparation and Presentation of the Library Budget"(SPEC Flyer No. 32, April 1977); and "The Allocation of Materials Funds in Academic Libraries" (SPEC Flyer No. 36, September 1977).

In its special money issue, *American Libraries* (November 1977) presented C. James Schmidt's very practical point-by-point instructions on "How to Win the Budget Battle on Campus." The proceedings of the 1976 Terre Haute conference on the subject were published in *Library Budgeting: Critical Challenges for the Future* (Ann Arbor: Pierian Press, 1977).

An important financial concern for libraries in institutions that conduct large-scale research programs funded by private or government agencies is the recovery of indirect costs associated with such activities. SPEC Flyer No. 34, issued in July 1977, provides guidelines in summary form for "Determining Indirect Cost Rates in Research Libraries." Miriam A. Drake, in her article "Attribution of Library Costs" in *College & Research Libraries* (November 1977), summarized the various cost accounting methods academic libraries have employed for this purpose.

Library Statistics. Each autumn academic libraries provide statistics on their operations to the National Center for Education Statistics through the Higher Education General Information Survey and the Library General Information Survey, more popularly known under the acronym HEGIS-LIBGIS. In the fall of 1977 libraries were requested for a second time to give the number of reference and directional questions answered in a typical week. Including questions on circulation of library materials, interlibrary loans, and hours of opening, the questionnaire is now more closely directed to gaining information on library use and services.

Another question introduced this year at the request of the National Commission on New Technological Uses of Copyrighted Works (CONTU) concerned the number of photocopies made for patrons or made in lieu of interlibrary loan. The National Agricultural Library and the National Library of Medicine also included questions in the survey on library holdings in the health sciences and agriculture.

Library Employment. Information on positions filled and salaries received by new library school graduates appeared in "Placement & Salaries, 1976: A Year of Adjustment," the *Library Journal* (June 15, 1977) survey article prepared by Carol L. Learmont and Richard L. Darling. Of the placements reported in this series during the decade of the 1960's from 33 to 34 per cent were for positions in college and university libraries. This

See also London and Canadian Correspondents' Reports

figure has declined considerably in the 1970's, and 26.3 per cent of the reported placements in 1976 were in college and university libraries. Based on reports from 443 positions, the average salary for a beginning academic librarian graduating from a U.S. library school in 1976 was $10,804.

Learmont and Darling recognized in their survey that, although jobs may be difficult to find, "there may be more jobs being listed, or, at least, jobs are being advertised more widely." The greater amount of advertising, of course, has resulted from the Equal Opportunity and Affirmative Action programs undertaken by colleges and universities. Rea Christofferson in her report on "The High Cost of Hiring" in *Library Journal* (March 15, 1977) detailed the elaborate procedures required at the University of Georgia to fill a professional library position. At its June 1977 meeting the Board of Directors of the Association of College and Research Libraries (ACRL) approved as its policy the "Guidelines and Procedures for the Screening and Appointment of Academic Librarians." The policy is reported in *College & Research Libraries News* (September 1977).

Unable to secure redress through normal channels of collective bargaining, librarians at Temple University used a different method to seek improved salaries. They filed a class action sex discrimination complaint with the Equal Employment Opportunities Commission against the university, stating that their low salaries are a result of their working in a "woman's occupation."

University of Chicago Automation. Most academic libraries, in one way or another, are involved with computerized operations, whether for accounting purposes, cataloging, acquisitions, or circulation. An important document of the year recording one library's experience was the report in *Library Quarterly* (January 1977) by Charles Payne and his colleagues on "The University of Chicago Library Data Management System." This online system supports all aspects of the library's technical services operations, and other systems, including circulation, are currently under development.

University of California Planning. The University of California published a master plan for the libraries of its nine campuses, describing development scheduled for the

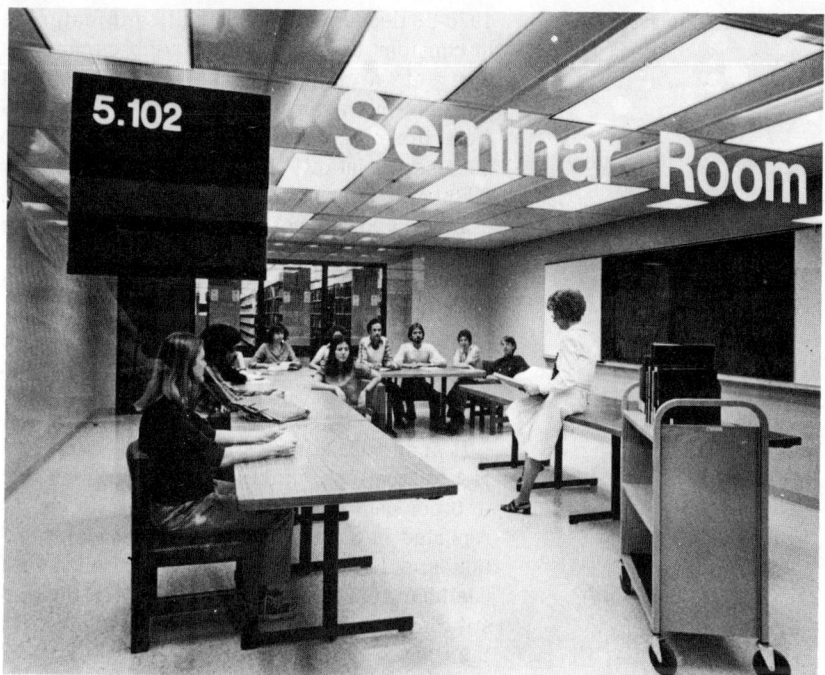

The Perry-Castañeda Library, University of Texas at Austin, opened in 1977. Top, students using one of the seminar rooms.

Center, the library at night.

Bottom, the information desk in the entrance level lobby of the six-level building.

Academic Libraries

1978-88 decade. Its most significant feature is to consider the libraries on each campus as part of a universitywide system linked together by various means. The study came from the office of Stephen R. Salmon, who became Assistant Vice-President for Library Plans and Policies in September. The Institute of Library Research, a part of the university's library schools, was abolished, and all systemwide library automation plans as well as analytical studies of library management problems will now be conducted through Salmon's office.

LIBRARY SECURITY

If academic libraries suffer an annual loss of 1 to 2 per cent of their total collections or 5 to 6 per cent of their current acquisitions, as reported in SPEC Flyer No. 37, "Theft Detection and Prevention in Academic Libraries" (October 1977), replacement costs for each institution can run to thousands of dollars. On the basis of the survey of ARL members reported in the flyer, more than half of the 90 respondent libraries had installed or were installing electronic security systems. Of 30 libraries contacted that had conducted loss studies before and after the installation of such a system, only two reported that they experienced no decline in book losses.

The Idaho State University Library building was dedicated in 1977. Below, a reading area on the second level of the library.

Several new services were established that will be of assistance for rare and more specialized materials. The Society of American Archivists (SAA) established a register of lost or stolen archival materials, and *Bookman's Weekly* began a regular column reporting losses from libraries and book dealers. In addition, SAA announced a consultant service for archival security through which archival repositories can receive assistance in beginning and carrying out their own security programs. Timothy Walch's article on "The Improvement of Library Security" in *College & Research Libraries* (March 1977) reported in detail on the SAA program.

A survey of college students' attitudes toward library book theft at Ohio State University by Allyne Beach and Kaye Gapen, "Library Book Theft: A Case Study" in *College & Research Libraries* (March 1977), presented the disturbing picture of a double standard. Although the students queried believed that book theft is serious, they felt that punishment for it should be confined to the academic realm.

LEGISLATION

Copyright. Each library considered throughout the year how it might best respond to the new copyright law, which became effective January 1, 1978. By November libraries had received the final texts for the various warning signs to post on unsupervised copying machines and at service desks where photocopy requests are received. New interlibrary loan forms were designed to conform to the requirements of the law and related guidelines.

Copyright provided a subject of discussion at most library association meetings during the year. Two special institutes were held on the subject, one at Indiana University in April and a second in December at the University of Pittsburgh.

Interlibrary loan is one of several library services affected by the new legislation. Subsection 108 (g) (2) of the law specifically permits receiving copies through interlibrary loan as long as they are not "in such aggregate quantities as to substitute for a subscription to or purchase of such work." Providing guidelines for this section, CONTU stated that requests each year for photocopies instead of loan are to be limited to five or fewer "copies of an article published in such periodical within five years prior to the date of the request."

Writing from the viewpoint of the small academic library, Patricia Dugan of Utica College demonstrated on the basis of past use that purchasing the journals to stay within the guidelines' limitations would mean an additional expenditure of 6 per cent of the total periodicals budget for her library. She believed implementation of the guidelines "pulls the information rug out from under the one group college libraries exist for—the students." Her article, "The Double Bind: The Environmental Impact of the 1976 Copyright Revision Law," was published in the *Journal of Academic Librarianship* (July 1977).

A contrary view was presented by Richard De Gennaro in his prize-winning article "Copyright, Resource Sharing, and Hard Times: A View from the Field" in *American Libraries* (September 1977). Admittedly writing from the viewpoint of a large university library (Pennsylvania), De Gennaro cited statistics from his library and from Cornell to show that compliance with the guidelines "will not seriously interfere with present interlibrary loan operations and services to users," primarily because photocopying for interlibrary loan represents such a small portion of total library use. De Gennaro did caution librarians not to be unduly timid in working with the new law but "to exercise all the rights and privileges" granted by it. "It is a time for boldness and courage."

The King study of photocopying commissioned by the National Commission on Libraries and Information Science (NCLIS) demonstrated that there would be a relatively low number (500,000 for serials) of items photocopied and possibly subject to royalty payments. The NCLIS study interestingly indicated that, for serials photocopying, academic libraries in 1976 were responsible for some 5,000,000 items copied, third after special libraries (15,000,000) and public libraries (12,000,000).

Title II-C. As reported in the "Academic Libraries" article in the 1977 *ALA Yearbook* a new section, Title II-C, "Strengthening Research Library Resources," was added to the Higher Education Act. This new provision presented the opportunity for aid as well to research libraries not formally linked to institutions of higher education. During 1977 guidelines were prepared for the use of funds so provided, and as the year ended it appeared that there would be an initial appropriation of $5,000,000 for this section.

COOPERATION

OCLC. The most dramatic demonstration of interlibrary cooperation continues to be through the program of the Ohio College Library Center (OCLC). By year's end more than 1,000 libraries located in 46 states and employing more than 1,800 terminals were entering data into and accessing bibliographic records from the central on-line files in Columbus.

With the growth of this major bibliographic network questions were raised as to the con-

The University of Arizona library in Tucson opened in 1977. Left, the information and loan desk of the library.

trol of OCLC and the appropriate form for user representation. With funds provided by CLR, the consulting firm Arthur D. Little, Inc., undertook a study of the center's governance and organization. Norman D. Stevens's article on "Modernizing OCLC's Governance" in *Library Journal* (November 1, 1977) also dealt with the question.

Central Storage and Service Libraries. The Center for Research Libraries (CRL) in Chicago reported during the year the admission of Oklahoma State University as its 100th full insitutional member. Another centralized storage facility in Chicago, the Periodicals Bank of the Associated Colleges of the Midwest (ACM), turned over its resources to the North Suburban Illinois Library System. This system assumed operations of the periodicals bank, adding it to its own previously organized serials access service. Both services will be available on a continuing basis to North Suburban System and ACM members alike, as well as to other libraries wanting to pay an annual fee.

Planning for another regional storage center was under way. The Washington State Cooperative Storage Center is to be in operation in three to four years and will provide fast serials retrieval service to its user libraries.

Although an earlier report from a joint CRL-ARL committee had recommended that CRL be

Academic Libraries

designated as the national periodicals lending library, a change occurred in 1977 with the proposal from NCLIS that a national periodicals center be established at the Library of Congress (LC). As proposed, the new center would be ready for operation in late 1978 or early 1979.

New Cooperative Programs. A grant of $250,000 from the Andrew W. Mellon Foundation will permit four Manhattan libraries to coordinate their operations into a computer-based research library system. The libraries are those of New York University, the New School for Social Research, the Cooper Union for the Advancement of Science and Art, and the Parsons School of Design. The grant will permit preparation of a single computer-based catalog recording the holdings of all four libraries.

Other plans were under way for cooperative endeavors involving academic libraries. The Postsecondary Library Directors of Nebraska unveiled a broad program in their report on "The Nebraska Plan for the Coordination of Postsecondary Educational Libraries." This plan would build upon a limited program of reciprocal borrowing begun in 1974. The Ohio Multitype Interlibrary Cooperation Committee initiated a study that would lead to a statewide resource sharing network to include public, school, academic, and special libraries. In Colorado the state library announced a state network plan calling for a computer-based list of library holdings and recommending that two major resource libraries (Denver Public and University of Colorado) receive special funding to lend their materials to other libraries in the state.

Research Libraries Group. The Research Libraries Group (RLG)—representing Harvard, Yale, Columbia, and New York Public—received a grant of approximately $750,000 from Timothy Mellon of Guilford, Connecticut, to assist the group in the acquisition of computer hardware for its bibliographical system. Previous grants to establish the system had been received on a matching basis from the Carnegie Corporation and the National Endowment for the Humanities.

In 1977 RLG secured direct access to Library of Congress cataloging records by means of terminals located in the Columbia University Libraries and hooked through a computer at the New York Public Library to computers at LC over leased telephone lines. As reported in an RLG newsletter, this event "inaugurates the first computer-to-computer access to LC's bibliographic data" and so opens a "window into LC."

SERVICES

Bibliographic Instruction. The major continuing interest in services to readers during 1977 was an emphasis on formal programs of bibliographic instruction. ARL recognized this interest by issuing an ARL Management Supplement on *Library Use Instruction in Academic and Research Libraries* (Vol. 5, No. 1, September 1977). Organizational recognition was given to this interest through the formation of a Library Instruction Round Table in ALA and a Bibliographic Instruction Section in ACRL.

Additional regional activities in bibliographic instruction flourished. The Bibliographic Instruction Collection in the Simmons College Library became affiliated with the New England Chapter of ACRL and had the benefit of input from that active regional group. The Southeastern Library Association sponsored the establishment of the Southeastern Bibliographic Instruction Clearinghouse at David Lipscomb College in Nashville. The Project Team on Bibliographic Instruction of the Academic Library Association of Ohio published the *Directory of Library Instruction Programs in Ohio Academic Libraries*.

Bibliographic Data Bases. Along with bibliographic instruction, on-line searching of bibliographic data bases provided a major subject for discussion at meetings and for journal articles. For example, three articles in the July 1977 issue of *College & Research Libraries* gave information on British experiences with on-line searching, presented data on terminal costs, and described the data base provided by the National Agricultural Library.

The major question for these new and valuable, yet costly, services was whether users should be requested to pay for them, and the discussion continues. ALA members at the Annual Conference in June 1977, however, affirmed a resolution supporting the principle of free access to all information in libraries.

Grants. The National Endowment for the Humanities (NEH) and CLR announced a total of seven grants under their joint College Library Program, designed to strengthen the library's role in the academic life of its institution. Recipient schools were the University of Evansville, Northwestern University, Saint Olaf College, Ball State University, De Pauw University, the University of Toledo, and the University of Wisconsin-Parkside.

CLR continued for a second year its Library Enhancement Program, provided to give individual librarians the opportunity for a year to develop a project that might improve the role of their library in their college or university. During 1977 awards were made to 13 librarians in the following schools: Beloit College, Colorado College, Georgia Southern College, Georgia State University, Glenville State College, Guilford College, Hampton Institute, Joint University Libraries in Nashville,

Lake Forest College, Tusculum College, the University of Colorado at Colorado Springs, the University of Missouri at Kansas City, and Wayne State University.

Reference Service. A recurring debate in academic libraries concerns the qualifications of individuals giving assistance to readers. Two new studies on the question appeared during 1977. Examining service at the reference desk in the library of the University of Nebraska at Omaha during a sample period, Jeffrey W. St. Clair and Rao Aluri concluded that "carefully trained nonprofessionals at the reference desk can competently answer 80 per cent of these questions." Their article was entitled "Staffing the Reference Desk: Professionals or Nonprofessionals?" and appeared in *Journal of Academic Librarianship* (July 1977). Following the publication of the article, the chairperson of the reference department at the university responded with a statement as to why nonprofessionals have not been employed at that library's reference desk.

Another study by Egill A. Halldorsson and Marjorie E. Murfin on "The Performance of Professionals and Nonprofessionals in the Reference Interview" in *College & Research Libraries* (September 1977) pointed out the superior performance of professionally trained staff at the reference desk.

Circulation. Adoption of various kinds of automated circulation systems continues. Two studies appeared to assist librarians in their selection of an appropriate system: Paula Dranov's *Automated Library Circulation Systems, 1977-78* (White Plains, N.Y.: Knowledge Industry Publications, 1977) and William H. Scholz's "Computer-Based Circulation Systems—A Current Review and Evaluation" in *Library Technology Reports* (May 1977).

In January, Princeton University inaugurated the first academic library application of the 3M automated circulation system, funded under its Andrew W. Mellon Foundation grant. Numerous other academic libraries adopted the system developed by CLSI of Newtonville, Massachusetts. Major installations included the University of Pennsylvania and the University of California, Los Angeles. In the autumn the California State University and Colleges selected CLSI for its libraries and scheduled a six-month trial on the Sacramento campus.

Interlibrary Loan. Although interlibrary loan concerns in 1977 were mainly directed toward the copyright act, librarians also awaited the implementation of the interlibrary loan mode on their OCLC terminals, whereby the terminals would serve as a communications device with other libraries. Unfortunately, the pilot test planned for the system was postponed.

The New England Library Network (NELINET), however, was able to proceed with its own interlibrary loan system funded by a U.S. Office of Education grant. The goal of the project is a regional computerized interlibrary loan system employing the OCLC data base and using the OCLC terminals for communication among members.

Service to the Handicapped. Although libraries have for a long time given attention to visually handicapped readers through the provision of special materials, service to the handicapped in general has new urgency on the nation's campuses with the implementation of Section 504 of the Vocational Rehabilitation Act of 1973. Each campus was required to examine its facilities in order to ensure that barriers to handicapped individuals are removed. An August conference in Ohio on "The Disabled Student on American Campuses" included consideration of the library's role. In October the State University of New York at Albany, through a grant under Title II-B of the Higher Education Act, sponsored an institute on "Library Service to the Adult Handicapped," designed for public and academic librarians.

In his article, "Academic Library Service to Handicapped Students," in the *Journal of Academic Librarianship* (November 1977) William L. Needham drew upon a study conducted in the library at Florida State University. He concluded the article with a useful

Top, Northern Illinois University in De Kalb, Illinois, opened in 1977. Bottom, entrance lobby and glassed-in rooms on the ground level of the library.

Academic Libraries

checklist library administrators could employ in determining the adequacy of their buildings, equipment, materials, services, and staff awareness in working with handicapped students.

RESOURCES

Major Grants and Milestones. The University of Texas observed the addition of its four-millionth volume. In recognition of the occasion the library tower, normally illuminated with white lights, was lit with orange lights, a practice generally reserved for football victories. At the University of Pittsburgh the library was also in the same league as the football team when the chancellor announced that $100,000 from the university's Sugar Bowl proceeds would be allocated for library acquisitions.

The National Endowment for the Humanities presented grants under its Challenge Grant Program to the University of Florida, University of Miami, Case Western Reserve University, Harvard University, New York University, and the University of Rochester. In each case the institution designated at least part of the grant for library acquisitions. Recipient libraries must raise three dollars in new money for each dollar from NEH. Rochester announced that its $333,000 grant was assured by virtue of a $1,000,000 library endowment from the Frank E. Gannett Newspaper Foundation.

The University of Pennsylvania and Smith College libraries were each richer by $1,000,000 through gifts from two of their alumni, Mr. and Mrs. Edmund J. Kahn of Dallas. The University of Southern California announced establishment of a $300,000 endowment to provide library materials for its von KleinSmid World Affairs Library. At Midwestern State University, on the basis of a collection evaluation that stated that $270,000 was required to provide specific needed items, the Texas legislature appropriated $134,000 for the library, to be matched by an equal fund raised through a university campaign. The Colorado School of Mines received a $1,000,000 grant from the Boettcher Foundation to acquire major additions to its library collections.

In Florida the state legislature allocated gross utilities tax money, generally held for school construction, to improve collections and services in the nine state university libraries. This money is to be in addition to regular funding and is projected at $10,000,000 for each of the next five years. The first $10,000,000 was earmarked for library acquisitions only.

Journal Prices. In another of his "call to action" pieces, Richard De Gennaro went after increasing costs for serials in the article "Escalating Journal Prices: Time to Fight Back," published in *American Libraries* (February 1977). Noting that periodical expenditures are taking an increasingly large percentage of the total materials budget for the library, he argued that it is time for libraries to "let the forces of the marketplace take over and create a new environment for the journal and whatever forms will evolve in competition with it."

De Gennaro took particular exception to differential subscription rates for individual and institutional subscribers, and Glenn R. Wittig's study on "Dual Pricing of Periodicals" in *College & Research Libraries* (September 1977) gave specific details on this subject. Wittig showed that, of a sampling of 180 general American journal titles, differential subscription rates were now charged for approximately 15 per cent and that the disparity between the two subscription rates is increasing.

The Pitt Study. The major study released during the year, at least in the discussion it aroused, was the investigation undertaken at the University of Pittsburgh with support from the National Science Foundation. A progress report on the study by Thomas J. Galvin and Allen Kent, "Use of a University Library Collection," appeared in *Library Journal* (November 15, 1977). The basic objective of the study was to determine the extent to which library materials are used and the full cost of such use. Among the results presented was the finding that, in terms of present book selection and acquisition techniques, 40 per cent of the acquired books are not used. A finding on the extent of the nonuse of science and engineering periodicals indicated to the study team that increasing dependence could be placed on resource sharing as well as the removal of back files to low-cost storage areas.

Collection Policies. Following on its work in developing MRAP and ALDP, the Office of University Library Management Studies (OMS) at ARL began a new program. A grant of $110,000 from the Andrew W. Mellon Foundation is being used by OMS to design and test procedures for the analysis of collection acquisition, retention, and preservation policies at university libraries. The initial libraries selected to participate in the program are the Massachusetts Institute of Technology, the University of California at Berkeley, and Arizona State University.

As part of its collection analysis project, OMS undertook in April a survey on "Collection Development Policies" among 69 university libraries, later summarized in SPEC Flyer No. 38, November 1977. Twenty of the reporting libraries indicated their present use of a written collection development policy, and eight more were developing such a document. The major impetus to the preparation of this policy was the hope to distribute limited funds more efficiently and equitably. Limited funds also had a negative impact on such policies. Some librarians reported discounting written guidelines since they were able to purchase only materials required for current teaching and research needs.

Through a separate grant from the Mellon Foundation, Cornell University began its own study to develop a long-term plan for the allocation of resources in the library and for the management of collection growth and costs. A grant under Title II-B of the Higher Education Act to the State University of New York (SUNY) Central Administration permitted that office to undertake a pilot study on collection development among a group of three SUNY libraries and Cornell University through an analysis of OCLC-MARC distribution tapes.

Endangered Manuscript Collections. Academic libraries with collections of manuscripts viewed with alarm the decision of the North Carolina Supreme Court that supported the state's appropriating without reimbursement two pre-Revolutionary documents that a North Carolina dealer had purchased several years earlier at an auction. As summarized in *American Libraries* (October 1977), "the decision places on a private owner of public records the burden of proving that the records were officially removed from public custody and are therefore not subject to replevin (the recovery by the government of any property that has left its custody illegally)." The dealer in this case decided not to appeal the case to the U.S. Supreme Court, and this adverse decision may serve as a precedent for similar actions in other states as well as by the federal government.

Preservation. Academic libraries increasingly are focusing attention on efforts to preserve their collections. Possibly a new spurt of enthusiasm was generated by the December 1976 planning conference for a National Preservation Program at the Library of Congress. During the summer of 1977 the University of California at Santa Cruz held a three-day seminar on conservation practices, and Case Western Reserve University received a federal grant to survey library conservation programs in Ohio. ARL devoted its SPEC Flyer No. 35 (August 1977) to "Preservation of Library Materials." The survey of libraries on which the flyer was based indicated that few libraries possess codified preservation programs but that there is growing recognition of the need for such programs.

Harvard University undertook its own survey among 40 of its library units and discovered, not unexpectedly, the need to upgrade conservation activities. Case Western Reserve University opted to use part of the funds under its NEH Challenge Grant to begin a program of conservation and preservation of library materials, primarily through the provision of appropriate housing and conditions for its various special collections. Yale University received national attention in its fight with bookworms when it subjected 37,000 volumes from its Beinecke Rare Book Library to a deep-freeze treatment in order to kill insects, eggs, and larvae without hurting the volumes themselves.

BIBLIOGRAPHIC CONTROL

As academic librarians awaited the appearance of the second edition of *Anglo-American Cataloguing Rules*, they also discussed the future of their major bibliographic guide, the card catalog. An institute on the "Catalog in the Age of Technological Change," sponsored by ALA's Resources and Technical Services Division and the Information Science and Automation Division, brought forth concerns on the manageability of the card catalog, especially in large research libraries. Speaking at the conference from the viewpoint of one such library (the University of California at Berkeley), Anne Lipow held that "it has become virtually impossible to maintain the catalog as the dynamic finding tool it is meant to be." She looked to the computer-based on-line catalog, which would provide many different approaches to catalog records and thus be a truly user-oriented tool.

Although the on-line catalog has not been adopted as the sole retrieval device, libraries have considered closing their card catalogs and beginning over again. Western Kentucky University announced the closing of its catalog and its replacement by a computer output microform (COM) catalog on microfiche. Instead of the multitray card catalog, there are now 20 microfiche reader stations, to be increased to 58 in the spring of 1978.

As reported in the "Academic Libraries" article in the 1977 *ALA Yearbook*, a pioneer in closing its card catalog was the University of Toronto. Early in 1977 a "mini-evaluation" of the conversion at Toronto from card catalog to COM catalog took place, and initial reports appeared in two articles in the *Journal of Academic Librarianship* for November 1977: "Sometimes Dirty Things Are Seen on the Screen" and Ellen Altman's "Reactions to a COM Catalog."

Two library consortia also announced plans to develop union catalogs of their members' holdings on COM: The Cooperative Libraries in Consortium, a group of eight academic and research libraries in the St. Paul area, and the AMIGOS library network in Texas.

LIBRARY BUILDINGS

Jerrold Orne and Jean O. Gosling's review of "Academic Library Building in 1977" in *Library Journal* (December 1, 1977) indicated

Academic Libraries

a total of 20 academic library projects, of which only six are new libraries. This was a striking change, the authors noted, from 1967 when 73 new libraries were reported. D. Joleen Bock's survey of "Two-Year College LRC Buildings" in *Library Journal* (December 1, 1977) recorded a total of 36 new buildings completed in 1976-77

The largest new library building reported in the Orne-Gosling survey was the Perry-Castañeda Library at the University of Texas. Other major new library buildings for the year included the University of Arizona, Idaho State University, and Northern Illinois University.

Atlanta University Center announced plans for its new central library that will serve the six member institutions, with a scheduled opening for 1979. San Jose State University released plans for its new library building, a library that will rely totally on solar energy.

The University of North Carolina at Chapel Hill announced that it will sell the community's public utilities that it owns and use the funds realized not only to build a new central library on the Chapel Hill campus but also to renovate the Louis Round Wilson Library.

PROFESSIONAL DEVELOPMENT

The Council on Library Resources continued with its several programs to aid in the professional development of academic librarians. It awarded fellowships to 17 librarians (the ninth year for this program). Most of the recipients are from academic libraries. It awarded academic library management internships to five librarians (a program now in its fourth year), and it named four librarians to participate in the second year of its advanced study program.

The Andrew W. Mellon Foundation made a grant for the fourth year of the Academic Library Internship Program for administrators of predominantly black colleges and universities. Six interns were selected for the program.

The State University of New York began a program to recognize its librarians by instituting the Chancellor's Award for Excellence in Librarianship. The first awards of $500 each were made to six SUNY librarians in the spring of 1977.

The New England Academic Librarians' Writing Seminar, funded by a grant from CLR and directed by Norman D. Stevens of the University of Connecticut, began publication of some of its efforts in the *Journal of Academic Librarianship* in September.

In her article on "Publication Activity among Academic Librarians" in *College & Research Libraries* (September 1977), Paula De Simone Watson pointed out that, because so few academic librarians publish, "some academic librarians may have difficulty meeting standards of academic excellence which include publication activity." She recommended the possibility of extending tenure eligibility periods for young professionals or perhaps, as has been done at Ohio State University, to designate research as an assigned responsibility for staff.

Ohio State University also provides another opportunity for publication by its librarians through its publications committee, and a review of its first 12 years was published in Jane L. Nelson's article, "An Academic Library Publications Committee: Twelve Years Later," in *College & Research Libraries* (July 1977).

APPOINTMENTS

Julie A. Carroll Virgo was appointed Executive Secretary of ACRL, succeeding Beverly P. Lynch who became University Librarian at the University of Illinois at Chicago Circle. Richard K. Gardner resigned as editor of *Choice* to assume a teaching post in the library school at the University of California at Los Angeles and was succeeded by Louis A. Sasso.

In November the Board of Directors of the Council on Library Resources announced the election of Warren J. Haas, Vice-President and University Librarian of Columbia University, as President of the Council, succeeding Fred C. Cole, who retired on December 31, 1977.

Three new university librarians were named at campuses of the University of California: Russell Shank at Los Angeles, Allen B. Veaner at Santa Barbara, and David Bishop at San Francisco. Don L. Bosseau assumed the directorship at the University of Hawaii.

In Washington, Merle N. Boylan became library director at the University of Washington and Robert L. Burr at Gonzaga University.

Benjamin C. Glidden became library director at the U.S. Air Force Academy, Clyde C. Walton at the University of Colorado at Boulder, and Milimir Drazic at the University of Houston Victoria campus.

In the Midwest, Willis M. Hubbard was appointed librarian at Stephens College, Philip C. Wei at Carleton College, Stuart A. Stiffler at Cornell College, Harry Boonstra at Hope College, and Ronald D. Frederick at the College of Saint Benedict.

In the East, Alan R. Taylor was appointed director at the University of Rochester, William E. McGrath at the University of Lowell, Norman Jung at the State University College at Old Westbury, New York, W. Stuart Debenham at Colby College, Richard A. Matzek at Nazareth College, and Y.T. Feng at Wellesley College.

In the South, Harry R. Skallerup was named director at Florida Atlantic University, David Lewis Ince at Valdosta State College, James E.

Gaines at Virginia Military Institute, Joanne R. Euster at Loyola University in New Orleans, William J. Kirwan at Western Carolina University, Wilson Luquire at East Carolina University, Thomas Hilton Gunn at Jacksonville University, Eugene W. Huguelet at the University of North Carolina at Wilmington, and John Sheridan at Transylvania University.

RICHARD D. JOHNSON

Preliminary data on college and university libraries for fall 1976 and the academic year 1975–76 were released in November 1977 by the National Center for Education Statistics Department of Health, Education, and Welfare. Data from the survey indicate that:

Books in library collections increased by 4.7 per cent between 1974–75 and 1975–76, but the number of books added during the year declined by 1.2 per cent.

Periodical subscriptions increased by 3.1 per cent in the same period.

Total library expenditures increased by 8.1 per cent between 1974–75 and 1975–76. Expenditures for salaries and wages of library staff increased by 8.6 per cent; expenditures for books by 4.0 per cent; and expenditures for periodicals by 15.4 per cent.

Compensation for library staff (salaries plus fringe benefits) represented 60.6 per cent of total library expenditures in 1975–76. Expenditures for books and periodicals represented 16.3 and 10.9 per cent, respectively.

Although library expenditures as a percentage of educational and general expenditures remained constant at 3.9 per cent, library expenditures per FTE student and library staff per 1,000 FTE students declined slightly.

Full-time-equivalent employment in libraries declined slightly in fall 1976 to 56,732 from 56,836 in fall 1975.

The mean salary of full-time librarians in fall 1976 was $15,300. The mean salary of $17,364 for full-time librarians in public two-year institutions exceeded the mean salary of full-time librarians in other types of institutions.

The mean salary of chief librarians was $18,790 in fall 1976; the mean salary for men was $20,875 and for women, $15,742.

Academic Libraries

Selected data on college and university library collections and expenditures, academic or fiscal years ending in 1975 and 1976, with periodical subscriptions in fall 1975 and 1976: Aggregate United States

Item	Year ending in—1975	1976	Per cent change
	Number		
Collections:			
Periodical subscriptions (fall 1975, 1976)	4,433,743	4,572,822	3.1
Book volumes—			
At end of year	447,059,297	467,957,584	4.7
Added during year	23,242,454	22,966,388	− 1.2
Book titles—			
At end of year	298,596,008	306,373,672	2.6
Added during year	16,063,781	15,613,309	− 2.8
Government documents, end of year	64,472,069	68,960,351	7.0
	Dollars		
Operating expenditures, total	$1,091,783,804	$1,180,004,591	8.1
Salaries and wages (includes salary equivalents of contributed services staff)	526,005,092	571,198,659	8.6
Fringe benefits for staff	66,563,256	78,093,347	17.3
Wages for student assistance (charged to library budget)	61,473,794	66,172,941	7.6
Books	184,707,780	192,108,405	4.0
Periodicals	111,944,895	129,157,617	15.4
Microforms	15,723,587	15,819,180	.6
Binding and rebinding	22,205,776	22,373,005	.8
Other operating expenditures	103,159,624	105,081,437	1.9

Source: National Center for Education Statistics, "Survey of College and University Libraries, Fall 1976 (HEGIS XI)" preliminary data, released November 1977.

Mean and quartile salaries of chief librarians in college and university libraries by institutional control, level and sex: Aggregate United States, Fall 1976

Institutional Level and Sex	Public					Private				
	No. of Librarians	Mean	Quartile 1st	2nd	3rd	No. of Librarians	Mean	Quartile 1st	2nd	3rd
All Institutions	1,100	$21,839	$16,913	$20,505	$26,398	1,092	$15,720	$12,080	$14,595	$18,414
Men	706	23,576	18,410	22,775	28,208	596	17,675	13,479	16,450	20,735
Women	394	18,727	15,000	17,748	22,004	496	13,371	10,748	13,130	15,244
Universities	84	32,565	29,583	32,000	36,521	45	29,203	23,800	28,000	33,000
Men	78	32,808	29,594	31,990	36,632	42	29,458	23,880	28,250	33,200
Women	6	29,395	*	*	*	3	**	**	**	**
Other 4-Year Institutions	391	23,657	19,300	23,400	27,750	909	15,665	12,534	15,000	18,325
Men	304	24,420	19,870	24,407	28,000	501	17,230	13,680	16,500	20,294
Women	87	20,991	17,800	20,000	24,000	408	13,743	11,133	13,500	15,900
2-Year Institutions	625	19,261	15,577	18,156	22,657	138	11,688	9,800	11,819	13,161
Men	324	20,561	16,860	19,782	24,000	53	12,547	10,105	12,060	13,709
Women	301	17,861	14,152	16,880	20,478	85	11,152	8,643	11,666	13,050

*Insufficient data to calculate quartiles
**Data suppressed to preserve the confidentiality of individuals' salaries
Source: These data are from the survey of Salaries of Selected Administrators which was included in the NCES survey of Employees in Institutions of Higher Education, Fall 1976

Number and mean salaries of full-time library staff in college and university libraries, by level of staff, and by control and type of institution: Aggregate United States, Fall 1976

Control and Type of Institution (1)	Library Staff				Mean Salaries (in dollars)		
	Total Number (2)	Librarians (3)	Other Professionals (4)	Non-Professionals (5)	Librarians (6)	Other Professionals (7)	Non-Professionals (8)
All Institutions, Total	51,333	18,601	2,758	29,974	15,300	11,989	7,878
Universities	21,072	7,030	748	13,294	15,556	12,203	7,976
4-Year Institutions With Graduate Students	17,938	6,809	928	10,201	15,144	11,218	7,868
4-Year Institutions Without Graduate Students	4,290	1,956	391	1,943	12,937	9,839	6,722
2-Year Institutions	8,033	2,806	691	4,536	16,688	14,010	8,111
Public, Total	34,485	11,920	1,814	20,751	16,225	12,936	8,190
Universities	13,414	4,467	479	8,468	15,806	12,066	8,074
4-Year Institutions With Graduate Students	12,435	4,535	580	7,320	16,063	11,937	8,334
4-Year Institutions Without Graduate Students	1,103	389	112	602	15,529	12,985	8,003
2-Year Institutions	7,533	2,529	643	4,361	17,364	14,476	8,203
Private, Total	16,848	6,681	944	9,223	13,651	10,170	7,176
Universities	7,658	2,563	269	4,826	15,120	12,447	7,805
4-Year Institutions With Graduate Students	5,503	2,274	348	2,881	13,312	10,019	6,683
4-Year Institutions Without Graduate Students	3,187	1,567	279	1,341	12,294	8,576	6,148
2-Year Institutions	500	277	48	175	10,519	7,767	5,837

Source: National Center for Education Statistics, "Survey of College and University Libraries, Fall 1976 (HEGIS XI)," preliminary data, released November 1977.

Accreditation

The ALA's Committee on Accreditation (COA) completed its work in 1977 of accrediting previously accredited library programs under the 1972 *Standards for Accreditation*, in addition to accrediting ten new programs. Although COA will not begin a new cycle of reaccreditation visits to previously accredited programs until spring 1979, a great deal of work went into improving and strengthening the accreditation process during 1977. A number of specific projects were undertaken for this purpose.

REVISION PROJECTS

Manual Changes. One of the most important of these projects was a painstaking revision of two of the Committee's basic documents: the *Manual of Procedures for Evaluation Visits* and *Self-Study: A Guide to the Process and to the Preparation of a Report for the Committee on Accreditation of the American Library Association*. In the latter, several changes were made in the manner in which information from the schools is to be presented to the Committee, making it easier for the schools to report and also for COA members to interpret the information. Another change in *Self-Study: A Guide* was the addition of questions pertaining to extension/off-campus programs.

More significant changes were made in the *Manual*. These included provision for a school applying for initial accreditation to insist on a site visit even though COA does not believe the program is ready for evaluation; greater flexibility in the size of the visiting team (previously four persons were assigned regardless of the size of the school); provision for obtaining approval by the school of the composition of the team before the individual team members are consulted as to their ability to serve (this procedure places the school in a more favorable position, but it makes the planning of visits, especially when there are several during the same time, somewhat difficult); provision for reaccreditation visits to be made every five to eight years rather than every four to six years; and an addition to the appeals process to include the publication of a report on the appeal at the discretion of the ALA Executive Board.

Surveys and Studies. In order to assist the Committee in making these revisions, two studies were undertaken. One was a survey of the 67 library schools visited under the 1972 standards conducted by Russell E. Bidlack, a member of COA from 1973 to 1977. Each of the schools visited was sent a questionnaire covering all aspects of the accreditation process, from the standards to the Committee's final report. Opinions were sought on 10 broad questions with 38 specific concerns listed as subdivisions of the general questions. Deans and directors of each of the schools were asked that responses be based on opinions of the entire school—faculty, staff, and students— and they were assured that the confidentiality of individual schools would be maintained. Responses, which came from 93 per cent of those receiving the questionnaire, showed that, while there were criticisms and conflicting recommendations, the schools in general believed the accreditation process has been successful. The study was recently published by ALA under the title *The ALA Accreditation Process, 1973-1976* and is available from the ALA for a nominal charge. An article summarizing the study was published in the September 1977 issue of *American Libraries*.

A second study was conducted by John Eastlick, also a former member of COA, who surveyed the chairpersons of the visiting teams. Though a more limited study, it served to corroborate results of the other study and to provide many recommendations for making the site visit more effective.

Another task that the Committee undertook during the year was to develop interpretive or guideline statements for certain phrases. These phrases, used or implied in the standards, had caused difficulty both for the schools in defining them in relation to their programs and for the site visitors and COA members in ascertaining whether a program did indeed meet the standards. Statements were prepared for the following: *extension/off-campus program offerings; a library school's program as a unified whole; goals and objectives; principles and procedures common to all types of libraries* (all taken directly from the standards); and *affirmative action* (related to, but not used in, the standards). These interpretive statements are available from the COA office. It is important to point out that COA interprets but does not make policy; it cannot arbitrarily decide what schools should or should not do. In its decision making, it is bound by the standards that were approved by the ALA Council in June 1972.

Record Preservation. While most of the Committee's work is aimed at developing and maintaining standards for library education, it took steps during the year to put its own house in order. Since, like any other working organization, COA has accumulated through the years many files of records, some decisions had to be made regarding the preservation and use of these records. To this end the Ad Hoc Subcommittee on Archives was appointed. This Subcommittee, attempting to provide for the needs of scholars of library education history and yet to maintain the confidentiality of institutions and individuals when this is necessary, made the following recommendations: (1) that all archival materials up to and including 1948 be deposited in the ALA archives and opened for access to researchers, subject to normal ALA regulations; (2) that COA identify and explore the issues included in the possible future use of its archives and establish guidelines for current retention of material created since 1948; and (3) that funding be sought for microreproduction of the archives after duplicate files have been discarded.

Open Meetings. Again, in an effort to dispel the "secrecy mystique" that has surrounded the work of the Committee, COA held an open meeting during the ALA Annual Conference in Detroit. While most of the discussions held during the regular COA meetings center on individual schools and are therefore subject to confidentiality, it was felt that there were some matters that would be appropriate for open discussion to the benefit of both the Committee members and the attendees. Open meetings are now being planned for future ALA meetings.

COA CONCERNS

COA, while autonomous in carrying out the accreditation process within ALA, is not without some constraints and regulations. In order for the ALA to be on the approved list of accrediting agencies maintained by the U.S. Commissioner of Education, COA must meet the criteria established by the U.S. Office of Education's Division of Eligibility and Agency Evaluation (DEAE). In June two COA members, Russell Bidlack and Lucille Whalen, attended an invitational conference on "The Federal Government's Relationship to the Nationally Recognized Accrediting Agencies" in order to become conversant with some of the problems inherent in this relationship. The conference, sponsored by DEAE and the Commissioner's Advisory Committee on Accreditation and Institutional Eligibility, was held to create improved understanding between the Advisory Committee and the accrediting agencies and to allay the fears of many about the intrusion of the federal government in education. Some of the topics considered were "Confidentiality and Accreditation," "Representation of Public Concerns," and "Improving the Consumer Protection Function of Post-Secondary Education." Discussions at the conference were helpful for the COA representatives in understanding more clearly some of the criteria established by the U.S. Office of Education.

Accrediting Agency Status. In September two COA members and the Accreditation Officer presented the Committee's formal petition for continuance of COA's status as a nationally recognized accrediting agency at a meeting in Washington, D.C. The U.S. Commissioner's Advisory Committee, in response to the petition, recommended that recognition be continued for a period of four years (the maximum allowable), subject to the provision that within one year COA submit a report comply-

Accreditation

ing with three of the criteria relating to "representatives of the public."

In addition to being recognized by the U.S. Commissioner of Education, COA is a member of the Council on Postsecondary Accreditation (COPA), a national nonprofit organization whose major purpose is to support, coordinate, and improve all nongovernmental accrediting activities conducted at the postsecondary level in the United States. It is COPA's responsibility to review, evaluate, and publicly designate through a recognition process reputable and responsible accrediting bodies, to coordinate their accrediting activities, and to reevaluate them periodically to help insure that they maintain acceptable levels of performance. COPA has a review process for its members similar to that of DEAE, and COA is presently preparing its report for this review scheduled for early 1978.

Public Interest. As noted above, one of the aspects of accreditation that is currently of major concern is the matter of protection of the public interest. The public, particularly students, regards accredited status as an indicator of quality education. In response to the demand for information about accredited library education programs, COA publishes and distributes current listings of accredited programs twice yearly. While COA does not rank the programs, each program on the list has been judged to meet the ALA standards. More than 25,000 of these lists are sent each year in answer to requests from libraries of all kinds, from prospective students interested in library education, from librarians, from employers of librarians, from government agencies, and from others making inquiry. As a help to those who wish detailed information on such matters as tuition charges, placement, faculty or curriculum, the listing includes the name, address, and telephone number of the dean or director of each school offering an accredited program.

New Members. At the conclusion of the 1977 ALA Annual Conference, four new members joined the Committee, replacing retiring members Alex Allain, Russell Bidlack, Bernard Fry and Irene Hoadley. Fay Blake, School of Library and Information Studies, University of California, Berkeley; William Eshelman, *Wilson Library Bulletin*; Guy Marco, Library of Congress; and Thomas Watson, University of the South Library were appointed to COA by the ALA Executive Board upon recommendation of the ALA President-Elect, Eric Moon. Continuing members for 1977–78 are Susanna Alexander, Missouri State Library; Charles Churchwell, Brown University Library; Jane Morgan, Detroit Public Library; Bruce Peel, University of Alberta Library; Patricia Pond, Graduate School of Library and Information Sciences, University of Pittsburgh; and Lucille Whalen, School of Library and Information Science, SUNY, Albany, Chair. While there is no formal representation of library organizations or types of libraries on COA, an effort is made to select individuals who can represent not only various aspects of library and information science but also the fields of library practice and library education. Six of the ten Committee members are presently library practitioners.

LUCILLE WHALEN

Acquisitions: see Collection Development

Graduate Library School Programs Accredited by the American Library Association (October 1977)

NORTHEAST

Catholic University of America, *Master of Science in Library Science*[1]
Graduate Department of Library and Information Science, Washington, D.C. 20064. Elizabeth W. Stone, Chair

Clarion State College, *Master of Science in Library Science*
School of Library Media and Information Science, Clarion, Pennsylvania 16214. Elizabeth A. Rupert, Dean

Columbia University, *Master of Science*[1,2]
School of Library Service, New York, New York 10027. Richard L. Darling, Dean

Drexel University, *Master of Science*[2]
Graduate School of Library Science, Philadelphia, Pennsylvania 19104. Guy Garrison, Dean

Long Island University, C. W. Post Center, *Master of Science*[1]
Palmer Graduate Library School, Greenvale, New York 11548. Mohammed M. Aman, Dean

University of Maryland, *Master of Library Science*[2]
College of Library and Information Services, College Park, Maryland 20742. Keith C. Wright, Dean

State University of New York, Albany, *Master of Library Science*
School of Library and Information Science, Albany, New York 12222. Robert S. Burgess, Acting Dean

State University of New York at Buffalo, *Master of Library Science*
School of Information and Library Studies, Buffalo, New York 14260. George S. Bobinski, Dean

State University of New York, College of Arts and Science, Geneseo, *Master of Library Science*[1]
School of Library and Information Science, Geneseo, New York 14454. Ivan L. Kaldor, Dean.

University of Pittsburgh, *Master of Library Science*[1,2]
Graduate School of Library and Information Sciences, Pittsburgh, Pennsylvania 15260. Thomas J. Galvin, Dean

Pratt Institute, *Master of Library Science*[1]
Graduate School of Library and Information Science, Brooklyn, New York 11205. Nasser Sharify, Dean

Queens College, City University of New York, *Master of Library Science*[1]
Department of Library Science, Flushing, New York 11367. Richard J. Hyman, Chairperson

Rutgers University, *Master of Library Service*[1,2]
Graduate School of Library Service, New Brunswick, New Jersey 08903. Thomas H. Mott, Jr., Dean

St. John's University, *Master of Library Science*[1]
Division of Library and Information Science, Jamaica, New York 11439. Antonio Rodriguez-Buckingham, Director

Simmons College, *Master of Science*[2]
School of Library Science, Boston, Massachusetts 02115. Robert D. Stueart, Dean

Southern Connecticut State College, *Master of Science*
Division of Library Science and Instructional Technology, New Haven, Connecticut 06515. Emanuel T. Prostano, Director

Syracuse University, *Master of Science in Library Science*[1,2]
School of Information Studies, Syracuse, New York 13210. Robert S. Taylor, Dean

SOUTHEAST

University of Alabama, *Master of Library Service*
Graduate School of Library Service, University, Alabama 35486. James D. Ramer, Dean

Alabama Agricultural and Mechanical University, *Master of Science in Library Media*[3]
School of Library Media, Normal, Alabama 35762. Dorothy M. Haith, Dean

Atlanta University, *Master of Science in Library Service*[1]
School of Library Service, Atlanta, Georgia 30314. Virginia Lacy Jones, Dean

Emory University, *Master of Arts; Master of Librarianship*[1]
Division of Librarianship, Atlanta, Georgia 30322. A. Venable Lawson, Director

Florida State University, *Master of Science; Master of Arts*[1,2]
School of Library Science, Tallahassee, Florida 32306. Harold Goldstein, Dean

University of Kentucky, *Master of Science in Library Science; Master of Arts*
College of Library Science, Lexington, Kentucky 40506. Timothy W. Sineath, Dean

University of North Carolina, *Master of Science in Library Science*[2]
School of Library Science, Chapel Hill, North Carolina 27514. Edward G. Holley, Dean

North Carolina Central University, *Master of Library Science*
School of Library Science, Durham, North Carolina 27707. Annette L. Phinazee, Dean

George Peabody College for Teachers, *Master of Library Science*[1]
School of Library Science, Nashville, Tennessee 37203. Edwin S. Gleaves, Director

University of South Carolina, *Master of Librarianship*
College of Librarianship, Columbia, South Carolina 29208. F. Williams Summers, Dean

University of South Florida, *Master of Arts*
Graduate Department of Library, Media, and Information Studies, Tampa, Florida 33620. Fred C. Pfister, Chairman

University of Tennessee, Knoxville, *Master of Science in Library Science*
Graduate School of Library and Information Science, Knoxville, Tennessee 37916. Gary R. Purcell, Director

MIDWEST

Case Western Reserve University, *Master of Science in Library Sciencen*[1,2]
School of Library Science, Cleveland, Ohio 44106. Conrad H. Rawski, Dean

University of Chicago, *Master of Arts*[1,2]
Graduate Library School, Chicago, Illinois 60637. Don R. Swanson, Dean

Emporia State University, *Master of Library Science*
School of Library Science, Emporia, Kansas 66801. Sarah R. Reed, Director

University of Illinois, *Master of Science*[1,2]
Graduate School of Library Science, Urbana, Illinois 61801. Herbert Goldhor, Director

Indiana University, *Master of Library Science*[2]
Graduate Library School, Bloomington, Indiana 47401. Bernard M. Fry, Dean

University of Iowa, *Master of Arts*
School of Library Science, Iowa City, Iowa 52242. Frederick Wezeman, Director

Kent State University, *Master of Library Science*[1]
School of Library Science, Kent, Ohio 44242. A. Robert Rogers, Acting Dean

University of Michigan, *Master of Arts in Library Science*[2]
School of Library Science, Ann Arbor, Michigan 48109. Russell E. Bidlack, Dean

University of Minnesota, *Master of Arts*[1,2]
Library School, Minneapolis, Minnesota 55455. Wesley Simonton, Director

University of Missouri, Columbia, *Master of Arts*
School of Library and Informational Science, Columbia, Missouri 65201. Edward P. Miller, Dean

Northern Illinois University, *Master of Arts*
Department of Library Science, DeKalb, Illinois 60115. Lewis F. Stieg, Chairman

Rosary College, *Master of Arts in Library Science*[1]
Graduate School of Library Science, River Forest, Illinois 60305. Sister M. Lauretta McCusker, O.P., Dean

Wayne State University, *Master of Science in Library Science*[1]
Division of Library Science, Detroit, Michigan 48202. Robert E. Booth, Director

Western Michigan University, *Master of Science in Librarianship*[1]
School of Librarianship, Kalamazoo, Michigan 49008. Jean Lowrie, Director

University of Wisconsin-Madison, *Master of Arts*[1,2]
Library School, Madison, Wisconsin 53706. Charles A. Bunge, Director

University of Wisconsin-Milwaukee, *Master of Library Science*
School of Library Science, Milwaukee, Wisconsin 53201. Frederick I. Olson, Acting Dean

SOUTHWEST

University of Arizona, *Master of Library Science*
Graduate Library School, Tucson, Arizona 85721. Donald C. Dickinson, Director

Louisiana State University, *Master of Library Science*
Graduate School of Library Science, Baton Rouge, Louisiana 70803. Donald D. Foos, Dean

North Texas State University, *Master of Library Science*[1,2]
School of Library and Information Sciences, Denton, Texas 76203. Dewey E. Carroll, Dean

University of Texas at Austin, *Master of Library Science*[1,2]
Graduate School of Library Science, Austin, Texas 78712. C. Glenn Sparks, Dean

Texas Woman's University, *Master of Arts; Master of Library Science*[1,2]
School of Library Science, Denton, Texas 76204. Brooke E. Sheldon, Director

WEST

Brigham Young University, *Master of Library Science*
School of Library and Information Sciences, Provo, Utah 84602. Maurice P. Marchant, Director

University of California, Berkeley, *Master of Library Science*[1,2]
School of Library and Information Studies, Berkeley, California 94720. Michael K. Buckland, Dean

University of California, Los Angeles, *Master of Library Science*[1,2]
Graduate School of Library and Information Science, Los Angeles, California 90024. Robert M. Hayes, Dean

University of Denver, *Master of Arts in Librarianship*[1]
Graduate School of Librarianship, Denver, Colorado 80210. Margaret Knox Goggin, Dean

University of Hawaii, *Master of Library Studies*
Graduate School of Library Studies, Honolulu, Hawaii 96822. Ira W. Harris, Dean

University of Oregon, *Master of Library Science*
School of Librarianship, Eugene, Oregon 97403. Marshall D. Wattles, Vice-Provost

University of Southern California, *Master of Science in Library Science*[2]
School of Library Science, University Park, Los Angeles, California 90007. Martha Boaz, Dean

University of Washington, *Master of Librarianship; Master of Law Librarianship*
School of Librarianship, Seattle, Washington 98195. Peter Hiatt, Director

CANADA

University of British Columbia, *Master of Library Science*
School of Librarianship, Vancouver, B.C. V6T 1W5. Roy B. Stokes, Director

Dalhousie University, *Master of Library Service*
School of Library Service, Halifax, Nova Scotia B3H 4H8. Norman Horrocks, Director

McGill University, *Master of Library Science*
Graduate School of Library Science, Montreal, Quebec H3A 1Y1. Vivian Sessions, Director

Université de Montréal, *Maîtrise en bibliothéconomie*
Ecole de bibliothéconomie, Montréal, Québec H3C 3J7. Yves Courrier, Directeur

University of Toronto, *Master of Library Science*[2]
Faculty of Library Science, Toronto, Ontario M5S 1A1. Francess G. Halpenny, Dean

University of Western Ontario, *Master of Library Science*[2]
School of Library and Information Science, London, Ontario N6A 5B9. William J. Cameron, Dean

---

[1] Offers post-Master's specialist or certificate program. (The ALA does not accredit post-Master's specialist or certificate programs.)

[2] Offers program for Doctoral degree. (The ALA does not accredit programs leading to the Doctoral degree.)

[3] Single specliaization program in school library media.

Adults, Library Services to

Adult services in public libraries in the United States in 1977 reflected the growing influence of several forces: grants from the National Endowment for the Arts (NEA) and from the National Endowment for the Humanities (NEH); the rapid expansion of contracts for on-line data base services; research on user needs and information-seeking behavior; steady pressure for planning and evaluation approaches to services; and a fresh, aggressive growth in ALA's Public Library Association (PLA).

Grant Projects. NEH awarded grants to the Houston Public Library and the New Orleans Public Library, designating them as NEH Learning Libraries. Earlier the public libraries of Boston and Chicago had received such grants. Humanities emphasis in public library programming generally tended to include local writers-in-residence; media-designed programs focusing on local history and urban community roots; ethnic cultural festivals, with ethnic foods, activities, and exhibits; and collaboration of libraries with museums and other cultural centers. Small NEA grants stimulated arts shows, art film showings, lectures, and concerts at a variety of culture levels. Following Chicago's leadership, the concept of the cultural center is gaining in acceptability and fuses from time to time with the concept of the learning center spearheaded by Boston and by the Public Library Consortium on Innovation at the Minneapolis Public Library.

The concepts of cultural and learning centers for public library adult services acted in 1977 as a counterbalance to the overwhelming emphasis on information services. Inherent in the context in which these new adult services grow are several social changes: higher levels of public education; the increased size of the educated, leisured, and retired adult population; and changes in social values and life-styles during the last 15 years that recognize leisure and self-actualization as important elements in the quality of life our society seeks. Public library service for leisure (recreation and culture, for example) is now being asked to respond to new concepts that focus on such functions as relaxation, entertainment, and personal growth, all available in a context of free choice and each enjoyed for its own sake. Learning takes its place as one important activity in leisure, and the forms of learning that encourage relaxation, entertainment, and personal growth are becoming important forms of public library adult services. As research on "quality of life" becomes increasingly important in social evaluation, the contributions of adult services in public libraries and in cultural and learning centers will come to demonstrate significant, measurable worth.

Special Publics. Services to special publics continued to receive support during 1977. The role of public libraries in serving the blind has been challenged recently by organizations of the blind that provide a diversity of education and social services. In its study of Massachusetts library service to the blind, however, Warner-Eddison Associates vigorously supported the Library of Congress and public library network of service to the blind and physically handicapped as the most appropriate channel for the distribution of talking books and related library materials. The International Federation of Library Associations (IFLA) took a comparable stand internationally on the issue. New standards for the handicapped were in the process of development as a joint LC-ALA project during 1977. Radio reading services for the blind continued to expand.

Services to the adult new literate received strong support from the publication by ALA of Helen H. Lyman's *Literacy and the Nation's Libraries*. The work draws on her five-year research project on materials for the adult new literate conducted at the University of Wisconsin-Madison Library School. The Adult Literacy and Learning Committee of PLA surveyed publishers' willingness to produce new materials for this group of readers and discovered that the cost of producing such materials is high in contrast with the low demand. Literacy programs in their broadest sense (reading, mathematics, civic competence, and consumer skills) continued in public libraries, with programs on English as a second language receiving strong federal support.

Reports and Studies. As developments in information and referral services have focused on the need for special packaging and active interpretation of information to users on all levels, a similar perception has evolved in discussion of the implications of on-line data base services. The University of Pittsburgh's three-day conference in November 1977 on "The On-line Revolution in Libraries" identified the changing role of the reference librarian (the "intermediary" between the data base and the "end user") from one who locates information to one who reworks information to meet the consumer's needs. Questions about the librarian's role as an intermediary rather than as an educator of users for direct interface with the data base are profound in the implications for changes in the adult services functions of reference librarians.

During 1977 Brenda Dervin and Douglas Zweizig completed the last two phases of their three-phased report on *The Development of Strategies for Dealing with the Information*

Administration: see Management, Library

Aging, Library Service to: see Adults, Library Services to

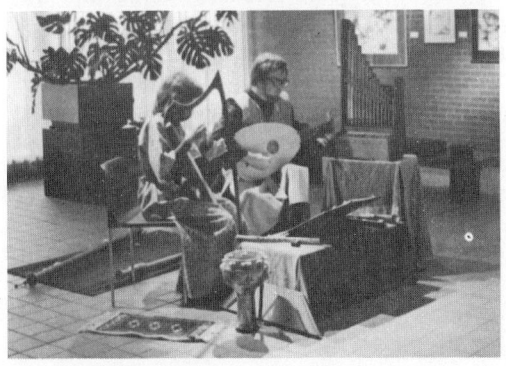

Top left: Job seeking patrons of the Nassau Library System could find employment help at the Hempstead Job Information Center.

Second left: A mime performance at noon in the Dallas Central Library was part of the Community Showcase fine arts series.

Third left: Patrons applaud during one of the four fall special programs designed for retired persons by the Topeka Public Library.

Bottom Left: Two concerts featuring Renaissance and medieval music using period instruments were held in the main Akron-Summit County Library in Ohio.

Top right: Cleveland mayoral candidates Dennis Kucinich (left) and Edward Feighan at one of the four debates sponsored by the Cleveland Public Library and the League of Women Voters.

Second right: It was standing room only at Houston's Central Library when the "Lunch Bunch" weekly series of free entertainment featured Mahal of Houston's Baccahanal School of Belly Dancing.

Bottom right: Cincinnati Public Library's "Hot Off the Presses" program provided new publications to the public immediately after receipt from jobbers without waiting to catalog them first.

Needs of Urban Residents. Phase I had surveyed how citizens articulate their needs, how they see themselves coping, and how they find and use information. Phase II surveyed information practitioners (librarians and social agency staffs) for their view of citizens' articulation of needs, their coping patterns, and their use of information. Contrasts between the findings of Phases I and II set the framework for Phase III—the development and testing of training modules to assist information practitioners in the human communications skills needed for the provision of information. This research project culminated in a tool usable by library staff trainers and library school educators alike. It provides detailed guidance in its use with adult service librarians seeking communications skills in providing information and guidance. The publication of this report in 1977 made the year notable for adult service librarians.

Evaluation of adult services has tended to rely on measurement against "standards" for library collections, staff, and other resources. In 1977 there was some readiness to move into more sophisticated evaluation in terms of library service impacts. Kenneth Shearer's paper in the winter issue of the *PLA Newsletter* on the "social indicator movement" stated the problem. Direct action in Oklahoma was taken in 1977 as Battelle Memorial Laboratories of Columbus, Ohio, launched a statewide evaluation of the effectiveness of libraries in Oklahoma in meeting users' needs.

Professional concern for adult services broadened in 1977, with PLA developing committees and setting priorities in terms of adult services. PLA concentrated on the development of a new statement of mission that focuses on the principles formulated over the years for successful adult services: community involvement in planning, sensitivity to needs created by social change, and activation of the community to the use of library resources. The statement also proposes a fresh, aggressive, and coherent framework for public library development. This statement, issued in 1977, could set the pace for the next decade of public library adult services.

MARGARET E. MONROE

American Association of Law Libraries

The American Association of Law Libraries (AALL) was founded in 1906. According to its constitution, the Association "is established for educational and scientific purposes . . . to promote librarianship, to develop and increase the usefulness of law libraries, to cultivate the science of law librarianship and to foster a spirit of cooperation among the members of the profession." The Association is currently established around 13 regional geographic chapters, each of which has considerable autonomy in its direction and financial management. The seven newly created Special Interest Sections operated successfully during their first year. A proposal for abolishment of overlapping committees was discussed at the midwinter meeting in Atlanta in December 1977.

Activities. In addition to the 39 existing committees, the Committee on Bibliographic Standards was created. It is charged with familiarizing itself with all existing proposed standards relating to micropublications. The Committee will be concerned with establishing standards for volume equivalency of micrographics, audiovisual materials, machine-based systems, and nonbook print. An ad hoc committee to explore the possibility of a formal exchange program between English and Irish Law Librarians and AALL members was also established.

A code of ethics in draft form, as well as a charter for an ethics commission, was presented for discussion at the annual meeting in Toronto by the Ethics Committee. The special Committee on Law Library Network Activities selected Butler Associates of Los Altos, California, as consultants to undertake the law network feasibility and design study for the AALL. The consultants' recommendations were to be reported in December 1977.

The Education Committee conducted two workshops at the Toronto meeting: "Budgeting" and "Canadian and Commonwealth Documents." In addition to regular placement activities, the Placement Committee proposed to offer a Job Exchange as a new service for employers and for librarians.

Publications. *Law Library Journal*, published quarterly by AALL, includes transcripts of the substantive programs of the annual meeting (usually in the November issue) and the proceedings of the business meeting. It also includes reports on statistics for various types of law libraries (collected with the aid of a grant from the Council of Library Resources) and other substantial papers relating to law librarianship. Another Association committee advises the H.W. Wilson Company on indexing and editorial policy for the *Index to Legal Periodicals*, and AALL publishes the *Index to Foreign Legal Periodicals*. The third edition of the AALL's *Biographical Directory* was published in June 1977. The Recruitment Committee has published a new recruitment brochure entitled *Information Brochure* that will be of interest to prospective law librarians. The Audio-Visual Committee published a revised edition of the initial issue of *A/V ALERT* as volume 1, number 1 (Winter 1976-77). The Publications Committee is working on a handbook of law library practice.

Membership. Membership is divided into

several classes with variations in annual dues: institutional, open to any law library ($60 minimum, $30 for each professional staff member); active individual, open to any person connected with a law library, state library, or with a general library having a separately maintained law section ($30); individual associate, for a person not connected with a law library, upon approval by the Membership Committee ($30); institutional associate, for any company or institution other than a law library, upon approval by the Membership Committee ($75); life members, for those retired from active library work (no dues); student, for students in either law or library school ($10). Total membership in 1977, including persons designated as members under institutional membership, was approaching 3,000.

Annual Meeting. The 70th annual meeting of the American Association of Law Libraries was held June 26-30, 1977, at the Sheraton Centre in Toronto, with more than 1,000 registrants in attendance. The meeting was preceded by the Conference of Newer Law Librarians (CONELL) at Toronto and by a week-long institute in Montreal on "Civil Law" for law librarians trained in common law. At the annual meeting, bylaws were revised to permit voting rights and rights of affiliation with Special Interest Sections for student members. The 71st annual meeting is scheduled to be held June 25-28, 1978 at the Holiday Inn and the Americana Hotel in Rochester, New York. Further meeting sites include San Francisco in 1979 and St. Louis in 1980.

AL COCO

AALL Officers

PRESIDENT (June 1977–June 1978):
Alfred J. Coco, Professor of Law and Law Librarian, University of Denver College of Law

VICE-PRESIDENT/PRESIDENT-ELECT:
J. Myron Jacobstein, Professor of Law and Law Librarian, Stanford University Law Library

ADMINISTRATIVE SECRETARY:
Antonette Russo

Headquarters: 53 W. Jackson Blvd. Chicago, Illinois 60614

American Association of School Librarians

The American Association of School Librarians (AASL) is the division of ALA that represents school library media specialists at the national level. AASL offers services and leadership for educators concerned with providing unified quality school media programs as an integral part of the total instructional program. Within elementary and secondary education, media programs begin with a kindergarten child and conclude with a graduating senior, who should be a discriminate user of library media.

State of the Profession. For school library media specialists, the 1960's and early 1970's were a time of growth, federal funds, unlimited career opportunities, and a feeling of optimism. Professionals worked for and believed that a unified media program for every child in the United States was possible, and, in fact, quite probable. By 1977 the impact of declining enrollments, stringent budgets, and pressing social issues such as racism, sexism, and local school developments were forcing AASL to take another look at its structure and programming. A unified media program fully staffed by professional school library media specialists for every child in the United States was, indeed, "a dream deferred."

It is necessary that the profession articulate to the public that the students of 1977 will be users as well as contributors to a vast bank of information by the year 2000. The instructional needs of students and what is required to meet those needs can and must be understood by the taxpaying public. "Back to Basics" is a movement that will be with our profession for some time. The question to be answered is "What are basics?" The 3 R's are certainly basic. Can our profession quarrel with a parent who insists that a child be able to read, write, and compute? As educators, however, we have a responsibility to convey the necessity of three more R's: research skills, retrieval of information, and reevaluation of preconceived ideas and information conveyed by whatever means.

Organizational Structure. For 26 years, the present organization of AASL has proven to be an effective mechanism to address the affairs and needs of school library media specialists. The present structure provides for a Board of Directors, a Supervisors Section, an Affiliate Assembly and 34 committees that represent the diversity and complexity of the school library profession and of the individual members of the Association. In addition, AASL allows access to the much broader field of librarianship through the activities and functions of ALA.

Two offices within ALA that are of prime importance to school library media specialists are the Office for Intellectual Freedom and the Washington Office. It is the Office for Intellectual Freedom that AASL looks to for leadership and guidance on matters concerning intellectual freedom, particularly First Amendment issues. The Washington Office acts as the monitor of Capitol Hill activities and is AASL's direct link to legislative developments. The work of these offices is essential to the varied roles that library media specialists

American Association of School Librarians

assume, whether involved with copyright, Title IV-B of the Elementary and Secondary Education Act, or precedent-setting First Amendment issues.

This structure allows members of our profession to maintain their identity as library media specialists whose primary concern is implementing a media program as an integral part of the total instructional program. Maintaining this identity is especially important at a time when a doubtful taxpaying public and the press do not associate the nebulous term *media* with a library's basic print and nonprint collection. As a result, *media* often implies frills in a school's budget. If school librarianship is to survive the 1970's, it is necessary that the concepts of "library" and "media" be linked in order to define to the general public, school administrators, and legislators that, indeed, libraries do contain information housed in a variety of physical formats. With this in mind, the AASL Board of Directors at the 1977 ALA Midwinter Meeting adopted the following terminology for all official communiqués from the AASL office: *library media center, library media specialist,* and *media program.*

AASL Program for 1977. A Task Force on AASL Goals, Priorities, and Structure for the Future Direction of the Association was established to explore options for the future of AASL as a division within ALA. The Task Force met and then reported to the AASL Board of Directors at the 1977 Midwinter Meeting. This report provided the framework upon which the 1977-78 program was built.

AASL has been responsive to many groups of school library media specialists seeking assistance in the maintenance of staff, standards, and budget. For example, through testimony provided by Alice E. Fite, AASL Executive Secretary, the Hawaiian Association of School Librarians was able to defeat a proposed governmental reclassification which recommended that all school librarians be reassigned under public library regulations and that the classification school librarian be eliminated. In July, Fite delivered testimony to the Board of Education in Philadelphia, calling for a restoration of elementary and secondary school library media specialist positions in the city schools. As a result of her testimony, all of these professional positions were retained for the 1977-78 school year.

In April 1977 the North Central Association met in Chicago. After a comprehensive review of needs within each state represented and after completion of detailed research by the members of the staff, AASL President Peggy L. Pfeiffer testified in opposition to a proposal that would have allowed the substitution of classroom teachers, trained aides, or volunteers for qualified library media specialists. These examples represent multiple successes. There is little reason to doubt that such challenges will be forthcoming in the future. It is reassuring to know, however, that the AASL staff and officers stand ready to protect the professional interests of the field.

Upon examination of AASL's structure, it was apparent that a mechanism was required to provide for the needs of library media specialists serving students who speak English as a second language. An ESOL (English Speakers of Other Languages) Task Force was appointed to study this situation and to make recommendations to the AASL Board of Directors.

The AASL Board of Directors reacted to the ALA Resolution on Racism and Sexism by supporting a preconference entitled "Focus on Change: Sexism Awareness," to be held in Chicago at the 1978 Annual Conference. This program is to be the first in a series of continuing education institutes planned for the members of AASL. The first institute will feature speakers, workshops, and an in-depth review of materials related to sexism awareness training. It is being planned and organized to focus on combating sexism in language, avoiding sexist information sources, maintaining a balanced collection, developing awareness activities for school libraries, and exploring other topics of interest in the promotion of sexism awareness.

In addition, a specific recommendation of the AASL Future Direction Task Force called for AASL publications aimed at current trends and issues in school librarianship. The Ad Hoc AASL Publications Advisory Committee, chaired by Glenn Estes, was appointed to review, analyze, and make determinations for the selection of titles and subjects required in the development of AASL publications; to make recommendations for the processing and ooordination of publishing proposals presented to the AASL Board of Directors from the AASL Program Coordinating Committee; and to develop guidelines and criteria for the style, format, and content of AASL publications.

In March in cooperation with AASL, the National Commission on Libraries and Information Science (NCLIS) established a task force to determine the extent of the involvement of school library media specialists in the total framework of networking within librarianship. Established with a $30,000 grant from NCLIS, the purpose of the task force is to determine the role of the school library media specialist and the school media program in the NCLIS national program. The task force is to review the state of networking in school media programs nationwide and to develop a position paper to clarify, delineate, and describe the role of the school media program within the national program of libraries and information science.

Awards. AASL and the Baker and Taylor Company have established the AASL President's Award. The Award will be given annually to an individual member of the library profession who has made an outstanding national or international contribution to school librarianship and school library development in such areas as service to the organized profession through AASL and related organizations; significant and influential research on school library service; publication of a body of scholarly or theoretical writing contributing to school library development; or planning and implementing a school library media program of such exemplary quality that it has served as a model for others. A committee chaired by Richard Darling of Columbia University was appointed to prepare the guidelines for selection and to serve as a jury for the recipient of the Award.

The 1977 AASL Distinguished Library Service Award for School Administrators was presented to John M. Franco, Superintendent of the City School District in Rochester, New York. The Award was presented at the AASL Honor Luncheon during the Annual Conference in Detroit. The annual citation is presented to a person directly responsible for the administration of a school or group of schools who has made a unique and sustained contribution toward furthering the role of the library and its development in elementary or secondary education.

Los Alamitos (California) Public Schools was the winner of the $5,000 prize in the annual competition recognizing U.S. school systems for achievement in providing exemplary library media programs at the elementary level. The California school district was selected over four other nominees for the School Library Media Program of the Year Award, presented by AASL and Encyclopaedia Britannica. Other school systems nominated for the 1977 award included Brittan School District, Sutter, California; DeKalb County Schools, Decatur, Georgia; Community Unit School District 200, Wheaton, Illinois; and the Portage (Michigan) Public Schools. Each received national finalist citations.

FRANCES DEAN

AASL Officers

PRESIDENT (July 1977-June 1978):
Frances C. Dean, Montgomery County Public Schools, Rockville, Maryland

VICE-PRESIDENT/PRESIDENT-ELECT:
Anna Mary Lowrey, State University of New York, Buffalo

EXECUTIVE SECRETARY:
Alice E. Fite

PROFESSIONAL ASSISTANT:
Babetta Jimpie

Membership (August 31, 1977): 6,181 (4,061 personal and 2,120 organizational)

American Library History

With the end of the ALA Centennial celebrations, American library history activities diminished greatly during 1977. Two 1977 publications were the result of the 1976 ALA Centennial Conference: *Libraries and the Life of the Mind in America: Addresses Delivered at the Centennial Celebration of the American Library Association* and "Audio-cassette Programs from the 1976 Centennial Conference," which include most of the historically oriented programs at the Conference. Both are available through ALA.

There was only one historical celebration during 1977—the 75th anniversary of the Texas Library Association, celebrated April 14-16, 1977, in El Paso. The Dallas Public Library also celebrated its 75th anniversary with the publication of a handsomely illustrated book written by Larry Grove and entitled *Dallas Public Library: The First 75 Years* (Dallas Public Library).

There were a number of other significant publications in American library history during 1977. Included among them were: *Reform and Reaction: The Big City Public Library in American Life* by Rosemary R. Dumont (Greenwood); *The Academic Library Matures*, edited by Richard Johnson (ALA); *Charles Ammi Cutter Library Systematizer*, edited by Francis Miska (Libraries Unlimited); *American Library Development: 1600-1899* by Elizabeth W. Stone (Wilson); and *Women in Librarianship: 1876-1976* by Kathleen M. Weibel and Kathleen M. Heim (Oryx).

The long-awaited *Dictionary of American Library Biography*, edited by George Bobinski, Jesse H. Shera, and Bohdan Wynar (Libraries Unlimited), was published in late 1977. This volume contains 302 scholarly biographies of past American library leaders. More than 200 people made contributions to the dictionary in researching and writing the biographical sketches.

Beginning with the 1977 issues, the *Journal of Library History* was published by the University of Texas Press and edited by Donald G. Davis of the Graduate School of Library Science at the University of Texas. Established in 1966, the journal had been edited by the faculty of Florida State University and its School of Library Science from 1966 through 1976.

GEORGE S. BOBINSKI

American Library History Round Table

The American Library History Round Table (ALHRT) provides a rallying point for the many librarians interested in history—particularly the history of libraries and librarianship. Its members enjoy stimulating contact with others of similar concerns at its meetings, and ample provision is offered to participate in its many committees and activities.

The Round Table's regular programs at ALA Annual Conferences are forums for library historians. At the 1977 program in Detroit, a large audience gathered to hear the presentation of two philosophies of library history by Michael H. Harris, defending the virtues of "revisionist" history, and Edward G. Holley, speaking on behalf of a more traditional viewpoint. A panel, including Peggy Sullivan, Phyllis Dain, and Jesse Shera, provided a commentary on "The Nature and Uses of Library History." The enthusiasm for this topic prompted the taping of the program, and the tapes are available from ALA.

Always seeking to encourage excellence in research in library history, in 1977 the Round Table requested, and ALA approved, the establishment of the American Library History Round Table Award. This $200 prize is to be given for the best unpublished manuscript in library history, judged on the bases of original research and superior style. Selection will be made from among manuscripts submitted by March 1, 1978, to the Award Committee—Haynes McMullen, Chairperson; Wayne A. Wiegand; and Phyllis Dain. The award will be presented at the program meeting of the ALHRT at the ALA Annual Conference in Chicago in June 1978. The recipient will be offered the opportunity to publish the essay in the *Journal of Library History*.

In 1977 the Centenary of the Library Association of Great Britain aroused an interest in library historians second only to that of the Centennial of ALA in 1976. Accordingly, the Executive Board of the Round Table decided to provide grants to assist two of its officers—Donald G. Davis, Chairperson-Elect, and Budd L. Gambee, Chairperson—to attend the Library Association's Centenary Conference in London, October 3-6.

The Centenary Conference proved to be a mixture of professional meetings and elaborate ceremonials. The overriding concern of the Library Association is a proposed revision of the requirements for professional librarians that, if adopted, would by 1986 profoundly upgrade the qualifications for entrance into the profession. Notable ceremonial and social occasions included the Thanksgiving Service in Westminster Abbey, the Lord Mayor's Reception at the Guildhall, the Conference Dinner at the Dorchester Hotel, the Carnegie-Greenaway Medals Luncheon, and the Riverboat Social on the Thames. In accordance with the directive of the ALHRT, the two representatives will give a joint oral report with slides at the Executive Board meeting at the Midwinter Meeting in January 1978, and a written report will appear later in the *Journal of Library History*.

In keeping with this international emphasis, ALHRT has removed the word *American* from phrases in its Constitution that indicated that the Round Table's function was limited to the encouragement of research and publication solely in the field of American library history. For the same reason, the suggestion has been made that the word be removed from the official title of the Round Table.

The ALHRT seeks constantly to enlarge its membership, which stood at 375 for 1977. In this regard the organization is greatly indebted to John F. Harvey of the Membership Promotion Task Force who has master-minded numerous successful recruitment activities. The goal of the Round Table is 400 members for 1978.

During 1977 the Round Table lost through retirement the efficient and seemingly indispensable services of Flora D. Colton, its Staff Liaison at ALA. This position has been filled by Joel Lee, Librarian of the Headquarters Library. — BUDD L. GAMBEE

ALHRT Officers

CHAIRPERSON (July 1977-June 1978):
Budd L. Gambee, University of North Carolina, Chapel Hill

CHAIRPERSON-ELECT:
Donald G. Davis, Jr., University of Texas, Austin

SECRETARY-TREASURER:
Wayne A. Wiegand

Membership (August 31, 1977): 388

American Library Society

The American Library Society (ALS), an international coalition of librarians and others interested in library and information services, was founded in 1970 "to promote the advancement of the library and information sciences; to aid the library and information professions in achieving their goal of providing the best possible in library and information service for the people of the United States of America; and to protect the freedoms of access to information, the press, and speech." In 1977 ALS remained one of the smallest organizations of its kind in the world, and the year was a quiet one for the Society.

The Committee on Ethics, established ad hoc in 1974 to review activity in the field of professional ethics and intellectual freedom and to recommend to the membership ways in which ALS could effectively involve itself, was dissolved in 1977 and succeeded by a standing committee. The new Committee on Ethics has assumed responsibility for revising, updating, and interpreting the "Ethics of Library Service" statement prepared by the ad hoc committee and presented to the ALS membership in 1976 and adopted by acclamation. All members of the ad hoc committee continued to serve on the standing committee for the 1976-78 term: Jay E. Daily of the University of Pittsburgh's Graduate School of Library and Information Sciences, Chairman; William Z. Nasri, also of the library school of Pittsburgh; and the Reverend Chalmers Coe, Minister of the First Congregational Church of Columbus, Ohio.

Publishing continued to be the principal activity of ALS in 1977. *Concerning Libraries*, the quarterly journal, completed its eighth year of publication; the second edition of the *Handbook of the American Library Society* was also published. Plans continued for a series of *Occasional Papers of the American Library Society* despite various delays in the publication of the first number, now tentatively scheduled to appear in mid-1978.

The eighth annual meeting, which was scheduled to be held in Plymouth, Indiana, in August 1977 in conjunction with the dedication of the new Plymouth Public Library building, was cancelled because of delays in construction.

Membership in ALS continues to be open to any individual or organization having a sincere interest in the Society's purposes. Both individual and organizational members receive publications of the Society, but only individual members may vote and hold office. Dues are $1 for individuals and $3 for organizations. The total combined membership was 60 in 1977. — JOHN B. HARLAN

ALS Officers

PRESIDENT (July 1976-July 1978):
John B. Harlan

VICE-PRESIDENT:
Donna B. Harlan, Indiana University at South Bend

SECRETARY/TREASURER:
Kathryn A. Whitman, Indiana University at South Bend

Headquarters: 1705 E. Lakeview Ave., Columbus, Ohio 43224

American Library Trustee Association

Under the leadership of President Maxine Scoville, 1976-77 was a year of soul-searching on the objectives of the American Library Trustee Association (ALTA) and a year of intensive study of the financial position of ALTA within ALA. Scoville reached out for activities and programs that would continue beyond her term in office and initiated close cooperation with the Board of Directors, with the Regional Vice-Presidents, and particularly with Vice-President/President-Elect Donald C. Earnshaw. The President promoted long-range planning for the advancement of the major goal of ALTA—taking full responsibility to serve trustees in carrying out their role as leaders in providing the finest of library services to the people they represent.

One result of the close cooperation carried out by Scoville was improving the financial position of ALTA so that it could be fully self-supporting. This permitted the planning of activities and programs reaching into the future. When Earnshaw became President, he was able to continue programs and obtain the same cooperation with President-Elect Barbara Prentice and Vice-President James Hess. In his inaugural address, "We, Together," Earnshaw expressed his hope that together the trustees could bring about yet greater advances in offering people the finest library service and that ALTA through its Regional Vice-Presidents and its committees could offer publications, counsel, and advice. He accented assistance to the State Associations and to individual trustees, not only through publications and activities but also by reaching out to the other divisions in ALA for areas of cooperation and joint assistance.

New and updated publications began to appear in 1977. They included *Guidelines for Holding a Governor's Conference on Libraries*, 3rd ed., by Minnie-Lou Lynch, and *The Ninth Decade: 1966-76*, by Ruth E. Berg.

Honor Award. Recognition is being given to libraries throughout the country and to public-spirited citizens through a program for honoring library benefactors. The program is administered by the Awards Committee, headed by Charles Reid of New Jersey. Honored in 1976-77 were the following:

The F.W. Symmes Foundation of Greenville, South Carolina, benefactor of Greenville County Library;

The Rosamond Gifford Charitable Corporation of Syracuse, New York, benefactor of North Syracuse Free Library;

T.H. McCasland of Duncan, Oklahoma, benefactor of Duncan Public Library;

The late Viola T. Swetmann, benefactor of Seward Community Library in Seward, Alaska;

The late P.M. Musser and descendants, benefactors of Musser Public Library in Muscatine, Iowa;

The late Sarah Irwin Jones, benefactor of Audubon Regional Library in Clinton, Louisiana;

Ann Smoot of King George, Virginia, benefactor of the Lewis Egerton Smoot Memorial Library in King George.

A member of ALTA presented each award in a local recognition ceremony.

Citations. The 1977 ALA Trustee Citations for distinguished service to library development were presented at the ALA Annual Conference in Detroit. One Citation was awarded to C.E. Campbell Beall of Martinsburg, West Virginia, in recognition of "his pioneering achievements in public library service in West Virginia.... his tenacity and missionary spirit which made possible the new Martinsburg-Berkeley County Public Library.... his success as a member of the West Virginia Library Commission in establishing effective per capita state aid to libraries where none had existed and in promoting state construction grants.... his leadership in organizing West Virginia's First Governor's Conference on Public Library Service; in the creation of a statewide borrower's card honored in public, college and university libraries, and in many other notable innovations."

The Citation presented to Daniel W. Casey of Syracuse, New York, commended him "for distinguished service as organization worker, leader, and spokesperson to libraries at all levels of government and to library trustees; for leadership in increasing funding for and in expansion of libraries in the State of New York.... for energetic promotion, while president of the American Library Trustee Association and a member of the National Commission on Libraries and Information Science, of better financial support for public libraries; and for personifying the commitment of trustees to the unique importance of library service to everyone."

A special Trustee Citation was presented to President Jimmy Carter "for his faithful and valuable service in his first public office as a trustee of the public library serving Sumter County, Georgia, now headquarters of the Lake Blackshear Regional Library; for his leadership as Governor of Georgia in the growth of libraries in that state through inauguration of state-assisted construction, large increases in state aid for library materials, and allocation of contingency funds for county and regional libraries; for his witness as a presidential candidate to the importance of public libraries and their trustees; for his support of the White House Conference on Library and Information Services; and for symbolizing to all the steadfast dedication to service and striving for excellence characteristic of American library trustees."

President Carter responded, "I am deeply honored to receive a special citation from the American Library Association.... My experience as a trustee of the Sumter County, Georgia, Library gave me an invaluable introduction to public service and impressed on me the enormous importance of the free library in our society. I look upon it even now as one of the most cherished and worthwhile experiences of my life."

Programs. ALTA programs during the 1977 ALA Annual Conference included a major presentation entitled "How to Plan and Conduct a Pre-White House State Conference." The ALTA Intellectual Freedom Committee cosponsored a program with the Urban Libraries Council that featured Burton Joseph, a Chicago First Amendment lawyer, and Judith F. Krug, Director of the ALA Office for Intellectual Freedom.

Workshops offered at the 1977 Annual Conference included "America's Millions of Functional Illiterates," "The Care and Feeding of Library Personnel," "Trustees as Image Makers," "The Great Debate: Pros and Cons of Users Fees," "Everything You Have Always Wanted to Know about Library Budgets but Were Afraid to Ask," and a discussion on the National Commission on Libraries and Information Science. DONALD C. EARNSHAW

ALTA Officers

PRESIDENT (July 1977-July 1978):
Donald C. Earnshaw, Lee's Summit, Missouri

FIRST VICE-PRESIDENT/PRESIDENT-ELECT:
Barbara S. Prentice, Tucson, Arizona

EXECUTIVE SECRETARY:
Andrew M. Hansen

Membership (August 31, 1977): 2,088 (1,038 personal and 1,050 organizational)

American Society for Information Science

The primary concern of the American Society for Information Science (ASIS) during 1977 was to strengthen its financial position. To this end, as well as to enhance the Society's publication program, ASIS entered into two major agreements during the year. The Society signed a long-term agreement with John Wiley and Sons, Inc., whereby Wiley will become the publisher of the *Journal of the American Society for Information Science.* ASIS will continue to be responsible for editorial content. ASIS also entered into an agreement with Knowledge Industry Publications, Inc., whereby that organization will serve, for a five-year period, as publisher and distributor of ASIS monographs. These two contracts, coupled with a program of strong financial control implemented by the Society, brought about a drastic improvement of the ASIS financial position.

Meetings. Chicago was the site of the 40th annual meeting of ASIS in September. More than 1,500 attendees and 74 exhibitors were attracted to the conference, the theme of which was "Information Management in the 1980's." The conference focused on the major impacts that technology, government, the economy, and society will have on future information requirements. The keynote address—"Where Is the Payoff?"—was given by Walter Carlson, a corporate marketing consultant for IBM. During the 100 sessions at the conference, seven other organizations conducted their own meetings, including a preconference workshop on the Copyright Clearance Center cosponsored with the American Association of Publishers and the Information Industry Association. The sixth ASIS midyear meeting was held at Syracuse University in May on the theme "The Value of Information."

The Society planned two meetings for 1978. The seventh midyear meeting, chaired by Stephanie Norman, was to be held at Rice University in Houston, May 22-24, on the theme "Management of Information Systems." The 41st annual meeting will be held in New York City, November 13-17. The conference Chairman is Everett Brenner, and the theme will be "The Information Age in Perspective."

Publications. Publications issued in 1977 included the *Journal of the American Society for Information Science,* vol. 28, nos.1-6; *Bulletin of the American Society for Information Science,* vol. 3, nos. 3-6 and vol. 4, nos. 1-2; *Annual Review of Information Science and Technology,* vol. 12 (1977); *Information Management in the 1980's: Proceedings of the ASIS Annual Meetings,* Vol. 14 (1977); and the 1977 update to *Computer-Readable Bibliographic DataBases: A Directory and Data Sourcebook.*

Awards. ASIS presented its 1977 Award of Merit to Allen Kent of the University of Pittsburgh for his many contributions to information science as a researcher, author, and teacher. The Watson Davis Awards—established in commemoration of the Society's founder and given for continuous dedicated services to ASIS—were presented to Simon Newman, Washington, D.C.; Arthur Elias, BIOSIS; Roy D. Tally, Minnesota Department of Education; and Irene Farkas-Conn, Chicago.

AUDREY N. GROSCH

ASIS Officers

PRESIDENT (October 1977—November 1978):
Audrey N. Grosch, University of Minnesota, Minneapolis

PRESIDENT-ELECT:
James M. Cretsos, Merrill Laboratories, Cincinnati

PAST PRESIDENT:
Margaret T. Fischer, Greenwich, Connecticut

TREASURER:
John E. Creps, *Engineering Index.* New York City

MANAGING DIRECTOR:
Samuel B. Beatty

Headquarters: 1155 16th Street, N.W., Washington, D.C. 20036

American Theological Library Association

As an outgrowth of the Religious Books Round Table of ALA and with the impetus of the American Association of Theological Schools (subsequently renamed the Association of Theological Schools in the United States and Canada), the American Theological Library Association (ATLA) was organized in Louisville, Kentucky, in 1947. Its purpose is to bring members into closer working relationships with each other, to support theological and religious librarianship, to improve theological libraries, and to interpret the role of such libraries in theological education.

The Association carries on its work by means of its Board of Directors, which meets regularly in January and in June, and by an annual conference of the Association in June. In addition, there are some 24 work units composed of boards, committees, or ATLA representatives to other groups. The 1977 annual conference was held at the Vancouver School of Theology in British Columbia, June 20-24, 1977. The conference included a presentation on the issue of book conservation by Bob Parliament of the Canadian Conservation Institute; an update on technology in microforms by Susanne Dodson of the University of British Columbia (UBC) Library; a workshop on archives by Richard Bernard of the UBC School of Librarianship; a presentation on library network by Susan K. Martin of the University of California Library; a lecture on "Four Stages in the Development of Jewish Studies" by Jacob Rothschild of the Library School in Jerusalem; and an address by Roy Stokes of the UBC School of Librarianship. The proceedings from the annual conference were to be published in early 1978. The 1978 conference will be held June 19-23 at St. Vincent Seminary in Latrobe, Pennsylvania. The theme for the conference is "Collection Evaluation and Development."

Membership in ATLA is open to all interested parties, but only professionals working in the field at the postbaccalaureate level are eligible for full member status. Only accredited institutions at the postbaccalaureate level are eligible for institutional membership. Personal dues range from $10 to $30, based on salary; and institutional dues range from $30 to $65, based on total operating expenditures. The total of all categories of membership in 1977 was 599.

In addition to the annual *Summary of Proceedings,* the Association publishes the quarterly *Newsletter* under the editorship of Donn Michael Farris of Duke University. The Committee on Publication, under the leadership of Murray Wagner of Bethel Theological Seminary, coordinates such various publications as *Aids to a Theological Library*, No. 1 in the ATLA series published by Scholars Press, and an outstanding monograph and bibliography series published by Scarecrow Press. Forthcoming titles in the monograph and bibliography series are Walter Lowe, *Freud and Recoeur* (No. 9); William Minor, *Creativity in Henry Nelson Wieman* (No. 10); and Norris Magnuson, *Salvation in the Slums* (No. 11).

The Board of Microtext, chaired by Charles Willard of Princeton Theological Seminary, reported two major developments in 1977. One was the introduction of microfiche as the standard format for monographs in the program designed for the conservation of older theological materials and for publication of materials no longer available. The second was the development of the Cooperative Microfilm Project of Religion and Theology (COMPORT). This new structure is designed to enable the Board of Microtext to loan positive copies of titles in its program to participating libraries and to offer titles to its participants at a reduced cost.

The Board of Periodical Indexing has announced a new companion publication to the well-known *Index to Religious Periodical Literature*. The publication is to be known as *Religion Index Two: Multi-Author Works* (RIT-MAW). The current *Index* has the new name *Religion Index One: Periodical* (RIOP) and will continue on its present publication schedule and include the same comprehensive service as offered before. The new *Religion Index Two* is expected to cover the years 1970-75 as its first project. This publication will in many ways be a complement to the publication of an index to *Festschriften* for 1960-69, presently being produced by Betty and Elmer O'Brien of Dayton Theological Seminary.

A new major thrust of ATLA is the creation of the Ad Hoc Committee on Serials Control to implement ATLA participation in the National Program of Serial Control already in progress (CONSER) and to build a single file of theological serial bibliographical records that can be used by ATLA and its membership. Other significant ongoing programs include the Library Materials Exchange Program, the Library Consultation Program, a new Personnel Exchange and Visitation Committee, and committees working on reader services, cataloging and classification, standards of accreditation, and standards for nonprint media.

ATLA officers for 1977-78, elected in June 1977, are president, John B. Trotti, Union Theological Seminary in Virginia; vice-president, Elmer O'Brien, United Theological Seminary; recording secretary, Margaret Whitelock, Princeton Theological Seminary; treasurer, Robert A. Olsen, Jr., Brite Divinity School; and executive secretary, David J. Wartluft, Lutheran Theological Seminary. The headquarters for ATLA is with the Executive Secretary at Lutheran Theological Seminary, 7301 Germantown Avenue, Philadelphia, Pennsylvania 19119. JOHN B. TROTTI

Archives

A number of issues affected archival administration in 1977, but certainly the most significant was the ownership of public papers. The National Study Commission on the Records and Documents of Federal Officials, commonly known as the Public Documents Commission, made its final report to Congress and the White House. The Commission—chaired by former Attorney General Herbert Brownell and composed of representatives from scholarly organizations, the three branches of the government, and the public—heard testimony from numerous archivists and historians and commissioned a number of research reports on all sides of the issue.

Commission Recommendations. The report of the Commission majority recommended that all documentary materials made or received by federal officials in the discharge of their official duties should be recognized as the property of the United States. The Commission suggested that the "tradition of private ownership of public papers had been established because of the failure of the government to provide an alternative. It is time to remedy the situation." The Commission also noted that if its recommendations were adopted the responsibilities of the National Archives and the Archivist of the United States would be greatly increased. The panel recommended that the National Archives be made independent of the General Services Administration and insulated from partisan political influences. The Commission did recognize the need to give federal officials an interval of control over access to materials in order to guarantee that they receive full and frank advice and to encourage them to create and preserve an adequate record of their activities.

Nixon Papers. Legal questions regarding the ownership of the papers of former President Richard Nixon were also addressed in 1977. In a June 28 ruling, the U.S. Supreme Court upheld the constitutionality of the Presidential Recordings and Materials Preservation Act, the law that placed Nixon's papers and tapes in the custody of the National Archives. The Supreme Court, in a vote of seven to two, found that Nixon was a "legitimate class of one," subject to special treatment by Congress because of the possibility that his Presidential papers might otherwise be destroyed. The ruling upheld the 1974 law that directed the General Services Administration (the executive branch agency of which the National Archives is a part) to take possession of the materials, screen them, return those that are personal and private, and determine the conditions of public access to those that are retained. Archival work on the papers has begun. Public access to the papers appears to be far in the future and is expected to be delayed by a series of court actions.

Kissinger Transcripts. A federal district judge ruled in December that 33,000 transcript pages of Henry Kissinger's telephone calls were public property, not private possessions. The documents are presently deposited in the Library of Congress with Kissinger's other papers under access restrictions established by the former Secretary of State. Judge John Lewis Smith, Jr. ordered that the records must be returned to the State Department and made available to the public on the same basis as other government materials.

Other Commissions. Two other federal commissions made final reports in 1977 that have potential implications for the administration of archives. The report of the Privacy Protection Study Commission endorsed guidelines that exclude accessioned federal archives from privacy regulations. A new federal department of administration, which would include the present archival and records management functions of the National Archives and Records Service, was recommended in the final report of the Commission on Federal Paperwork.

Other Issues. Another issue of concern was the identification of important archival projects and programs. A conference on priorities for historical records, cosponsored by the National Endowment for the Humanities and the Society of American Archivists in January 1977, seemed to be prophetic, for throughout the year archivists worked toward the establishment of priorities in a number of critical areas. As in past years, archival projects were generously supported by millions of dollars from a number of foundations, most notably the National Endowment for the Humanities and the National Historical Publications and Records Commission. Identified as areas of high priority by the conference were the intellectual control and the conservation of archives and manuscripts.

Archivists were also concerned about security, and during 1977 they worked for better legal protection. The Security Program of the Society of American Archivists supported this effort by promulgating a model law on library and archives theft and by establishing a security consultant service to assist interested institutions in improving their own security programs.

In a related matter, the replevin (recovery) of archives and manuscripts became an issue of concern in 1977 to manuscript collectors and dealers as well as archivists. The cause of the concern was a North Carolina Supreme Court decision in the case of the *State of North Carolina* v. *B. C. West, Jr.* In suing West, the State of North Carolina sought to recover two 18th-century public documents signed by William Hooper, a signer of the Declaration of Independence. The state alleged that it was the lawful custodian of and had a right to possession of all public records of the state of North Carolina. The defendant admitted possession of the documents, but denied the state's right to them. In June, the North Carolina Supreme Court found in favor of the state, precipitating numerous questions about the thousands of public documents in the possession of private institutions and collectors. Responding to the concerns of the profession, the Society of American Archivists established a select committee to study the issue and establish replevin guidelines.

An equally important issue for archivists in 1977 was professional education and training. The recent rapid growth of the profession has created a demand for better archival education and training programs. In April, the Council of the Society of American Archivists approved basic guidelines for graduate archival education programs. The guidelines stipulate that such programs be offered in accredited colleges or universities with appropriate instructional resources—including established archival programs of their own. Programs should consist of study of at least one year with equal emphasis on instruction in archival theory, laboratory work, and the opportunity for specialized projects through independent study. The profession also began to discuss the merits of a certification program for individual archivists, an issue that will be debated by the profession for some time to come.

Archives

Equipment, demonstrated at the Regional Video V Center of George Washington University Library, will be used to disseminate Vanderbilt University's Television News Archives. The Center was established in 1977 to act as a rental agent and users' center for compiled tapes of TV network newscasts of the last decade.

Genealogy. The growing interest in genealogy had a substantive impact on a great many archival institutions in 1977. The trend was stimulated by the publication of Alex Haley's *Roots* and the television adaptation, which premiered at the National Archives. The search for a personal past sent researchers to all kinds of archival institutions. Perhaps the most popular institution was the National Archives, which was besieged by information requests. In fact, the National Archives branch in San Bruno, California, reported a jump in the number of monthly research permits from an average of 93 per month in 1976 to an extraordinary 391 in March 1977. It was inevitable that commercial interests would capitalize on the popular response to genealogy. Pan American Airlines and Continental Trailways Bus Company arranged travel tours for tracers of family ties, and entertainment seekers in Philadelphia were invited to view the charms of exotic dancer Jeannie Ology, who promised to trace her customers' roots!

ANN MORGAN CAMPBELL
TIMOTHY WALCH

The ALA Archives

The American Library Association is one of the few professional organizations that has archives. In 1973 the Association and the University of Illinois negotiated a three-year agreement for archival services. The agreement was renewed for three additional years in 1976. In 1973-74, the project staff compiled organizational histories for the classification of the records of the Association and trucked 617 cubic feet of the records from the North Pier Terminal Warehouse in Chicago to the University of Illinois in Urbana. The organizational histories provided a basis for archival classification of files according to source rather than subject. In the second and third years of the initial agreement, two half-time graduate research assistants processed 418 cubic feet of records. In four and a half years, 15 library science graduate students from 10 states have arranged, described, and boxed 620 cubic feet of records.

Under a grant from the National Endowment for the Humanities, the staff has achieved automated control over the ALA Archives. Initial conventional descriptive control included Kardex card descriptions of each record series and typed supplementary finding aids, showing the contents of folders in major records series or files. The Archives is now under complete on-line record series control. The PARADIGM data processing program provides a listing of each record series number, title, inclusive dates, volume, type of records, and number of pages of finding aids. Other data bases provide subject coding for the preparation for a subject index and the listing of subject descriptors for each record series. It is possible to "list off" selected record series and descriptor terms. Current printouts and programs can be produced by entering the proper commands at a computer terminal.

The ALA Archives project includes the development of the National Catalog of Sources for the History of Librarianship to improve access to records in other repositories. The staff has obtained data for 225 collections. The same data bases and automated programs will be used as for the ALA Archives. These records will include material relating to the ALA, libraries, library associations, and librarians. The Catalog will be useful in locating files of the ALA Board, Council, and committee members in manuscripts collections.

The Archives is open and available to all researchers completing the user's application form. Only one recordseries requires special permission for its use. Users may photocopy or microfilm records. Control cards are available for 368 record series and 586 pages of supplementary finding aids. Before visiting the Archives, users should telephone 217-333-0798 or send a written outline of their research needs and plans.

The Archives has been used for dissertations and research papers on ALA Library War Service in World War I, the American Library Institute, the Association of College and Research Libraries, descriptive cataloging, the film office, the library school of Hampton Institute, library buildings, national library planning, National Park libraries, and public library development. The Archives was used extensively during 1976 for Centennial publications, an audiovisual history of the ALA, and sketches for the *Dictionary of American Library Biography*. The Archives has also been used for a political science study of international cultural relations, for course papers by library school students, and by authors interested in the history of professionalization and the development of the committee structure of the ALA.

The strengths of the holdings of the American Library Association Archives are in material relating to Annual Conferences, the development of the administrative structure of the Association, war services, statistics, services for children and the foreign born, education for librarianship, accreditation, library extension, public libraries, publishing, the development of standards, public relations, international relations, and school libraries.

The Archives includes processed records from 52 of 75 record groups or administrative offices, ALA Divisions, Round Tables, standing committees, and related units. Gaps in holdings include a general scarcity of records for the 1876-1920 period, the lack of organized files for the executive director from 1920 to 1940, Round Table records, committee files, and photographs. Persons knowing of records that should be in the ALA Archives or reported to the National Catalog of Sources for the History of Librarianship should contact the Archivist, Room 19, Library, University of Illinois, Urbana, Illinois 61801.

The Archives staff has reached potential users through

meetings of the American Library History Round Table and the pages of the *Journal of Library History*. They welcome opportunities to discuss research interests and available sources with potential researchers. Problems relating to the use of the ALA Archives include the need for more and better trained researchers, especially those who have experience in retrospective research methodology and long-term interests in the history of librarianship.

While the ALA Archives has been liberally supported by the American Library Association, Beta Phi Mu, the National Endowment for the Humanities, and the University of Illinois, a need remains for the financial underwriting of archival operations. The Archives requires a continuing level of support to provide suitable staff and space for the growth of the present holdings of 738 cubic feet of archival material, the equivalent of 123 file cabinets. The Archives has been brought from inactive storage in a warehouse to archival control in a research institution. The Association should maintain a permanent, professional archival operation.

MAYNARD BRICHFORD

Armed Forces Libraries

Army Libraries. Army libraries have come a long way from their humble beginnings during the Civil War, when various aid societies, the U.S. Sanitary Commission, and the U.S. Christian Commission provided a variety of books, magazines, and religious tracts to Union soldiers. During 1977 more than 700 libraries worldwide served the educational, informational, and recreational reading needs of Department of the Army personnel. These included 298 libraries providing general service (public, college, and hospital) to military personnel, dependents, and civilians at Army installations and hospitals in the United States and overseas; 53 medical libraries; 102 technical libraries serving scientists, engineers, and other specialists; 22 academic libraries serving the military training schools and colleges, e.g., the U.S. Military Academy and the Army War College; 267 law libraries and other special libraries, e.g., the U.S. Army Military History Institute and the Army Library at the Pentagon. A formal career program insures opportunities for training, development, and assignment for the 500 professional librarians working in the various Army libraries.

As a result of recommendations made by the 1976 Army Library Study, an Army Library Institute was held at Fort Belvoir, Virginia, in 1977, sponsored and funded jointly by Headquarters, Department of the Army, and the U.S. Army Training and Doctrine Command (TRADOC), and be hosted by TRADOC. The intensive five-day program designed to synthesize key managerial and professional skills, with emphasis on practical approaches to management, attracted 153 librarians.

Air Force Libraries. The Air Force provides unified library service under a central point of control through the Air Force Librarian, Air Force Military Personnel Center, Randolph Air Force Base, Texas, to prevent unnecessary duplication of materials and services. The Air Force Library Program during 1977 provided comprehensive service to meet both Air Force official needs and leisure and self-education reading requirements of its personnel.

Three categories of libraries—base, technical, and academic—serve personnel. Base libraries are provided at each major Air Force installation and consist of a single library or library system composed of main, branch and field libraries, and bookmobile service. Technical libraries meet specialized research and development requirements in the Air Force Systems Command, Military Airlift Command, and Air Force Accounting and Finance Center. Air Force Academic Libraries are at the Air University, Air Force Academy, Air Force Institute of Technology, School of Health Care Sciences, Social Actions Training Center, and Keesler Air Force Base Technical Training Center.

Robert Wedgeworth, Executive Director of the American Library Association, was appointed a member of the Air University Board of Visitors, Maxwell AFB; his appointment, announced in 1977 and effective in March 1978, made him the first librarian to serve on the Board.

Navy Libraries. In 1977, the Naval General Library Program served 230 Navy and Marine Corps libraries ashore, including 74 overseas bases, and 522 shipboard libraries. A 10,000-volume ship's library was furnished for the nuclear carrier U.S.S. *Dwight D. Eisenhower*. As part of a program to improve services for personnel afloat, specifications for library furniture and equipment especially adapted for shipboard use and sample layout design plans were under development in 1977 at the Navy Ship Engineering Center in consultation with the General Library Services staff. The Navy's Super 8 general-interest library film program was inaugurated, and a greater library use of other audiovisual media is anticipated. To provide a wide range of collateral support for off-duty education and human resources programs, materials in microform are now being provided.

Some 100 special and technical libraries are administered independently by the organizations they serve. These include technical libraries in the Naval laboratories, medical libraries, and legal libraries. Sometimes included in this group are the academic libraries—the Naval War College Library, the Naval Academy Library, and the Naval Post-Graduate School Library.

The Naval Scientific and Technical libraries are organized in two semi-official groups—CONSATL (Council of Navy Scientific and Technical Libraries) East, and CONSATL West. The Council provides a forum for better formal and informal exchange of professional developments and experiences. Navy technical and academic libraries are moving toward increased participation in library information networks and memberships in consortia.

AFLS. The library organization for all services is the Armed Forces Librarians Section (AFLS) of the Public Library Association, a division of the American Library Association. AFLS is designed to identify new developments in areas of automation, career management, areas of cooperation, and continuing education for federal librarians. Officers who assumed their positions in June 1977 are: Helen McClaughry, President; Louise Nyce, Vice-President/President-Elect; Lee R. McLaughlin, Secretary; and Gerald Cable (resigned November 1977), Navy Representative.   DIANA C. PROESCHEL

Art Libraries

Art libraries are part of a variety of institutions—colleges, universities, museums, galleries, private collections, public libraries, and research institutes. In a few instances they are autonomous collections. The collections include monographs and serials in micro- and macro-formats, in addition to all of the special materials of the visual arts—exhibition catalogs, slides, reproductions, photographs, original works of art, auction catalogs, and a variety of ephemera. Clientele regularly served include researchers from elementary school students through postdoctoral scholars, collectors, artists, publishers, and interested generalists. All art libraries share one basic goal—the documentation of the ever-expanding field of the visual arts.

Broad Spectrum. Art librarians, presumably because they have been buried under the mass of exhibition catalogs and announcements they collect, until recently were relatively unaware of the wide variety of collections and colleagues they had in the United States as well as in other countries. Under the auspices of the Art Section of the Association of College and Research Libraries, American art librarians meet each year at the ALA Annual Conference. There they find, and have found over the past 50 years, strength in the sharing of mutual problems. Other art librarians, particularly those in museums and picture collections, profit from membership in what is now called the Museum, Arts, and Humanities Division of the Special Library Association (SLA) and in SLA's Picture Division. Answers to specialized problems of maintaining and developing museum and picture collections are gained at SLA's annual conference and through other special programs sponsored by SLA chapters during the year.

In 1972, however, a third organization for art librarians came into existence—the Art Libraries Society of North America (ARLIS/NA). Modeled after the Art Libraries Society (ARLIS) in the United Kingdom and Republic of Ireland, ARLIS/NA provides a forum for art librarians to discuss problems and exchange solutions through its annual conference and publication, the *ARLIS/NA Newsletter*. The growth of ARLIS/NA, under the leadership of its founder and Executive Secretary Judith A. Hoffberg, to more than 1,000 institutional and personal members makes ARLIS/NA the largest association of art librarians in the world.

Foreign and Domestic. The combined efforts of ALA, SLA, and ARLIS/NA made 1977 an important year for art libraries in the United States and Canada. In 1977, however it also became clear that the number of art libraries, and therefore art librarians, outside North America was much larger than was previously thought. Librarians from art libraries all over the world were meeting, and two new ARLIS organizations—ARLIS/Sweden and ARLIS/Australia-New Zealand—came into their own. The increase in art library activity made the library community much more aware of the importance of this type of special library.

This importance was emphasized by the participation of American art librarians on the Library of Congress Task Force evaluation and at the International Federation of Library Associations and Institutions (IFLA) conference in Brussels in September 1977. William Walker, Librarian of the National Collection of Fine Arts-National Portrait Gallery Library of the Smithsonian Institution, presented a paper at the Brussels conference in which he proposed that a separate art library subsection in the Special Library Division of IFLA be established. Continued participation in a number of other organizations saw the art library point of view expressed on the Council of National Library Associations, the U.S. IFLA Committee, the Subject Analysis Committee of the Cataloging and Classification Section (CCS) of ALA, the Catalog Code Revision Committee of CCS, and the Board of the College Art Association. Art librarians were also sponsors of the *Repertoire International de la Litterature de l'Art* (RILA), headquartered at the Clark Art Institute in Williamstown, Massachusetts, and participated in special projects and on committees of ALA, SLA, and ARLIS/NA.

Meetings. In late January 1977, ARLIS/NA

held its fifth annual conference in Los Angeles. Programs ranging from conservation to networking, subject headings, and visual resource hardware highlighted the five-day conference. A full report appeared in the *ARLIS/NA Newsletter* (February 1977, pp. 45-62). In June, SLA met in New York City, where it sponsored tours of art library facilities and continued discussions on copyright and problems in visual resource librarianship. Also in June, ALA's Art Section met in Detroit, holding programs on prints and the problem of art theft. Canadian librarians gathered in Montreal at the Canadian Library Association meeting. In Seattle, museum librarians held a session on "Research Facilities in and out of the Museum: Avenues of Cooperation" at the meeting of the American Association of Museums.

In addition, art librarians gathered in nooks and crannies in the United States and Canada through the chapter systems of ARLIS/NA and SLA and within the state and provincial library associations. Workshops on cataloging, collection development, preservation, reference service, and compiling union lists of serials, along with tours and special trips to libraries, took place throughout the year. That the meetings resulted in much more than talk was evidenced by the publications, awards, and other activities during 1977.

Publications. Five issues of the fifth volume of the *ARLIS/NA Newsletter*, under the editorship of Judith A. Hoffberg, appeared during 1977. Along with the useful book review section edited by Robin Kaplan, articles appeared on cataloging, the annual conference, reference assistance in university art libraries, and general news of the art library community in the United States and elsewhere. A special supplement to the April 1977 *Newsletter* contained the *Standards for Staffing Art Libraries*, the culmination of two and a half years of work by an ARLIS/NA committee chaired by William C. Bunce, University of Wisconsin. ARLIS/NA also published a *Guide to Art Resources in Los Angeles*, sponsored by the Southern California Chapter and edited by Joan Hugo. Preliminary and editorial work was completed by Judith Hoffberg and Stanley Hess on the *Directory of Art Libraries and Visual Resource Collections in North America*, which will be published by Neal-Schuman in the spring of 1978.

ARLIS/UK continued to publish the *Art Libraries Journal*. Volume 2 contained articles by American art librarians as well as those in other countries. Philip Pacey of ARLIS/UK edited the *Art Library Manual: A Guide to Resources and Practice* (London and New York: Bowker, in association with ARLIS, 1977), an extremely important collection of articles on art librarianship.

Local chapters of ARLIS/NA produced guides to collections, local newsletters, and checklists of exhibition catalogs. One of the most notable of the year was the checklist of art exhibition catalogs produced by the New York Chapter of ARLIS/NA and the subsequent establishment of a permanent archive of exhibition catalogs at the Fashion Institute of Technology in New York City. Another important local publication was issued by the Museum of Fine Arts in Boston, the *Guide to New England Art Museum Libraries*, by Nancy S. Allen.

Awards. ARLIS/NA had planned to offer two sets of awards during 1977. The first, the Wittenborn Award for a distinguished paper by a library school student on the subject of art librarianship, was not given during the year, however. The ARLIS/NA Art Publishing Awards were granted. The 1977 winners (for books published in 1976) were: David R. Godine, in collaboration with the International Museum of Photography, for general excellence for *The Spirit of Fact: Daguerreotypes of Southworth & Hawes, 1843-1862* by Robert A. Sobieszek and Odette M. Appel (Boston, 1976); Aperture, Inc., a special award for its efforts in support of the field of photography and the uniformly high quality of its publications; and Edward Ruscha, a special award to one "who made books when that seemed an odd thing for an artist to do, and whose style, wit, and energy encouraged other artists to use the inexpensive, self-published book as a form of expression." Honorable mentions went to: Viking Press for *Georgia O'Keeffe*, for the unique insight the book affords into an artist's work; Harry N. Abrams, Inc., for *The Art of the Print: Masterpieces, History, Techniques* by Fritz Eichenberg, for its contribution to the field of prints; and the Sarah Campbell Blaffer Gallery, the University of Houston, for *Edvard Munch* by Peter W. Guenther, for the work's exemplary scholarship.

Special Activities. In the field of cataloging, art librarians continued to raise their cry for more and better cataloging from the Library of Congress. Position papers on subject headings were issued by the ARLIS/NA Cataloging Advisory Committee. The adoption by the Library of Congress of the use of singular media headings resulted from one paper. Continued battle for improvement of descriptive cataloging rules took place at the Catalog Code Revision Committee meetings. A number of important changes will occur in the second edition of the *Anglo-American Cataloguing Rules*, including some restriction of author entry for artists and a clearer, though from the art library perspective not yet ideal, rule for assigning entry under a corporate body. Also during the year, a group of art specialists from the participating libraries in the Research Libraries Group (New York Public Library, Columbia, Harvard, and Yale) formed the

Association for Library Service to Children

group's first task force, which began by examining the needs of art cataloging in general while uniting the cataloging practices of the participating institutions.

> **ARLIS Officers**
>
> CHAIRMAN (February 1977-February 1978):
> **Nancy R. John,** National Gallery of Art, Washington, D.C.
>
> VICE-CHAIRMAN/CHAIRMAN-ELECT:
> **Susan Wyngaard,** University of California, Santa Barbara
>
> SECRETARY:
> **Karen Harvey,** Smith College, Northampton, Massachusetts
>
> TREASURER:
> **D. Sherman Clarke,** University of Pittsburgh
>
> EXECUTIVE SECRETARY:
> **Judith Hoffberg**
>
> Headquarters: P.O. Box 3692, Glendale, California 91201

Standards were of great interest during the year. After the long-awaited publication of the first part of *Standards for Staffing Art Libraries,* work was begun on the second part dealing with standards for staffing visual resource collections. A committee within ARLIS/NA was appointed to begin to solve the second phase of the problem, standards for collection development. A joint statement on professionalism for visual resource curators made by the College Art Association and ARLIS/NA was approved by these two bodies in October.   NANCY JOHN

Association for Library Service to Children

1977 will be remembered in children's library circles as the year in which the Children's Services Division (CSD) became the Association for Library Service to Children (ALSC). The relatively calm ratification of the proposal added validity to the reasons advanced by President Peggy Sullivan. In recommending the change, she asserted that other ALA divisions of the size and prestige of CSD were designated as "associations" and that the term *division* did not accurately describe CSD, with many links to groups outside ALA, or suggest its independence and authority in the field of library service to children. Moreover, the name failed to reflect the division's most important characteristic, its relation to *library service.*

Assessment and Reevaluation. 1977 also was a year of assessment and reevaluation of the activities and programs in which the membership of ALSC is engaged. Concern over continuing budget cuts, job layoffs, and the diminishing job market in the field of library services to children has made librarians increasingly aware that they must find ways to prove that the services and programs they provide are essential library functions. ALSC has strongly encouraged its own committees and has supported educational institutions outside ALA in the development of institutes, programs, and research directed toward finding solutions to this problem. Involvement in questioning the goals, objectives, and procedures universally accepted as desirable practices in the provision of good library service to children inevitably led ALSC to assess the goals, procedures, and achievements of its own programs and activities.

At the 1977 ALA Midwinter Meeting in Washington, D.C., the ALSC Board of Directors requested that a full review be made of the media evaluation activities engaged in by the Association. To implement the Board's instruction, ALSC President Sullivan appointed a Select Media Evaluation Review Committee with Barbara Miller as Chairperson. Following its meeting in the spring of 1977, the Committee made an interim report of its recommendations to the ALSC Board at the ALA Annual Conference in Detroit.

Acting on the Committee's recommendations, the ALSC Board approved submission to members of a bylaws change that would establish a Newbery Award Committee *and* a Caldecott Award Committee (each to be composed of 15 members including the chair). The Board also revised the Newbery and Caldecott Medal terms so that henceforth "any book published in the preceding year shall be eligible to be considered for either or both awards." The Board approved awarding the Laura Ingalls Wilder Medal (previously awarded every five years) every three years, beginning the new cycle in 1980. The Board changed the name of the Book Evaluation Committee to Notable Children's Books Committee and approved closing at least those portions of the Committee meetings at which final votes are taken (discussion sessions remain open). The Board asked that the final meeting of the Committee be an open meeting for distribution of the list of Notable Children's Books and

> **ALSC Officers**
>
> PRESIDENT (July 1977-June 1978):
> **Barbara Miller,** Louisville Public Library, Kentucky
>
> FIRST VICE-PRESIDENT/PRESIDENT-ELECT:
> **Lillian N. Gerhardt,** Editor, *School Library Journal*
>
> SECOND VICE-PRESIDENT:
> **Rosemary Weber,** Graduate School of Library Service, Drexel University
>
> EXECUTIVE SECRETARY:
> **Mary Jane Anderson**
>
> Membership (August 31, 1977): 4,509 (2,823 personal and 1,686 organizational)

presentation of an informal report on the Committee's deliberations and findings. In addition, a number of procedural changes of less magnitude were recommended and accepted by the ALSC Board. A complete account of the Board's major actions appeared in the 1977 fall issue of *Top of the News*.

In order to complete its assignment, the Select Media Evaluation Review Committee met again in November. Its final report was to be ready for ALSC Board consideration at the 1978 ALA Midwinter Meeting in Chicago. In the many letters received from membership about the role of the Association in media evaluation, a large majority of the ALSC membership strongly affirmed support for continued activity in the evaluation of media. This was reassuring to the Review Committee since ALSC is specifically charged by ALA Council with responsibility for evaluation and selection of media for children and improvement of techniques of library service to children.

Projects. A review of the functions, objectives, and procedures of all ALSC committees, initiated by the ALSC Committee on Organization and Bylaws, was completed in 1977. The Committee's task was greatly facilitated by the assistance of ALSC's five priority coordinators, who serve in an advisory capacity to the committees in their priority areas: Child Advocacy; Evaluation of Media; People Power; Social Responsibilities; and Planning, Research, and Development.

In 1977 committee members continued to fulfill the responsibilities of their assignments. The Mildred L. Batchelder Award was not made when the Selection Committee's Chairperson, Karen Hoyle, reported to the ALSC Board that the Committee could not find three books that it felt met the criteria for submission to the membership. Because the Board felt that the terms of the award were not subject to change during the course of the award year, the only option was to report no nominees to the membership.

Other ALSC members were involved in ongoing projects: preparing bibliographies for the Boy Scouts of America; maintaining liaison with other national organizations serving children and, whenever possible, sending representatives to their meetings; selecting and awarding the Newbery and Caldecott Medals; selecting Notable Children's Films of 1975 and Notable Children's Books of 1976; preparing bibliographies for use in conjunction with television viewing; preparing selective bibliographies of prints and posters, toys, and games; selecting the Frederic G. Melcher Scholarship recipient and the four ALSC members who, aided by cash grants from Charles Scribner's Sons, would attend ALA's Annual Conference for the first time; selecting U.S. Children's Books of International Interest for use by teachers and researchers abroad as well as to encourage their translation; and preparing selective bibliographies of foreign children's books for periodic publication in *Booklist*.

Membership. The ALSC Membership Committee is actively involved in recruiting new members and in developing a variety of means to insure their continued interest in Association activities. ALSC members continued their active participation in the U.S. National Section of the International Board on Books for Young People (IBBY), with ALSC Director Zena B. Sutherland currently serving a second term on IBBY's Hans Christian Andersen Award Jury.

New Committees. A Continuing Education Committee was established with the responsibility to invite and receive all proposals for innovative and significant programs outside ALA Annual Conference programming designed to provide continuing education in the field of children's services and to advise the ALSC Board as to whether sponsorship by the Association should be undertaken. The Committee activities will be coordinated through its Chairperson with the activities of the Continuing Library Education Network and Exchange (CLENE). The Joint ALSC and Young Adult Services Division (YASD) *Top of the News* Editorial Committee was established to work cooperatively with the editor to determine overall editorial policy of the jointly supported official journal of ALSC and YASD. A petition of ALSC members for establishment of a Discussion Group of Chairs of Children's Divisions of State and Regional Library Associations was accepted with the provision that their statement of purpose be presented for final approval at the Midwinter Meeting.

Programs. The site of the May Hill Arbuthnot Honor Lecture, sponsored annually by ALSC with the assistance of Scott Foresman and Company, was Boise, Idaho, with Boise State University as ALSC's cosponsor. The lecturer was Shigeo Watanabe, a distinguished Japanese author, translator, and university professor. A symposium on "Research, the Creative Process, and Children's Literature: A Turning Point," sponsored by the University of Washington School of Librarianship with the cooperation of the Committee on National Planning of Special Collections, was presented in Seattle, June 3-4. Prior to ALA's Annual Conference, a spotlight was focused on children's library service by ALA President Clara S. Jones's preconference, "The Changing Role in Children's Work in Public Libraries: Issues and Answers." This preconference, directed by Mary Ploshnick and assisted by a joint ALA planning committee, asked library directors and children's coordinators to explore together the status and goals of children's library services.

ALSC's major Annual Conference program

The CSD became the ALSC in 1977 during the tenure of President Peggy Sullivan, who served also as Chair of the ALA Publishing Committee.

35

was the presentation of "Media Mall," a parent-support program sampler that offered a collage of ongoing and new services to parents of young children. The coordinator of this unique program was Faith H. Hektoen of the Connecticut State Library. The Public Library Association's (PLA) Service to Children Committee presented, in cooperation with ALSC, concurrent one-hour presentations of a program on "Children's Librarians as Administrators and Managers." The topics covered were personnel, grants, evaluation and analysis, and budgets. The ALSC Sexism in Library Materials for Children Discussion Group chose "She Can, He Can ... Sexism in Children's Books" as the subject for its program, which attracted a sizable audience to study and analyze a variety of children's books for sexist traits.

The ALSC Research and Development Committee coordinated the presentation of three research papers about varying aspects of children's services. ALSC's Film Evaluation Committee, with the PLA Audiovisual Committee as cosponsor, arranged a showing of seven films from its list of Notable Films for Chldren. The highlights of the Newbery/Caldecott Awards Dinner were the acceptance speeches of Leo and Diane Dillon, winners of the Caldecott Medal for their illustrations for *Ashanti to Zulu: African Traditions* (Dial) and of Mildred Taylor, winner of the Newbery Medal for her novel *Roll of Thunder, Hear My Cry* (Dial).

Publications. In 1977 publications included the annual brochures *Newbery Medal Books, Caldecott Medal Books,* and *Notable Children's Books.* With the assistance of ALSC, Weston Woods has made available in a limited edition a cassette of the 1977 Caldecott Medal and Newbery Awards acceptance speeches. For the first time, reprints of the speeches, as published in *Top of the News* (Summer 1977), can be obtained from ALSC. The 1977 Research Forum Conference program is also available on cassette tape. A revised edition of the 1975 compilation, a *1977 Directory of Coordinators of Children's Services and Young Adult Coordinators in Public Library Systems Serving at Least 100,000 People,* and a revision of *Resources for Under Achievers in Reading* are completed and are being distributed.

Also available from the ALSC office are *Notable Children's Films—1977,* compiled by the ALSC Film Evaluation Committee; *Non-Sexist Materials for Children,* a list of nonsexist book lists developed by the ALSC Discussion Group on Sexism in Library Materials for Children; a new membership brochure designed and illustrated by Tomie de Paola; *The Library Is My Best Friend,* developed by an ALSC liaison organization, the American Association for Gifted Children, with the assistance of the Library Service to Children with Special Needs Committee to provide guidance in how to work more effectively with gifted children; and the proceedings of the Detroit preconference, the *Changing Role in Children's Work in Public Libraries: Issues and Answers,* which the ALSC office agreed to distribute. BARBARA S. MILLER

Association of College and Research Libraries

The Association of College and Research Libraries (ACRL) has as its ultimate goal the improvement of services to users of academic and research libraries. In order to meet this goal, ACRL's activities are designed to assist librarians as they provide library services and to develop standards and guidelines by which librarians and libraries can measure their performance.

The year 1977 saw several changes in the ACRL Board and staff. On December 31, 1976, Louise Jones Giles, the immediate Past President of ACRL, died in a fire in her home. In recognition of the contributions she had made to librarianship and the loss that was felt by so many, the ALA Minority Scholarship was named the Louise Giles Minority Scholarship. She is sadly missed by the profession and her friends.

The ACRL Executive Secretary, Beverly Lynch, resigned effective January 1, 1977, to become Librarian at the University of Illinois at Chicago Circle. Julie A.C. Virgo, who had been the Director of Education with the Medical Library Association, became the new Executive Secretary on April 4.

Choice. Richard Gardner resigned in June from his position as editor of *Choice* to accept a position on the faculty of the Graduate School of Library and Information Science of the University of California at Los Angeles. Gardner was the founding editor of *Choice* when it began under a grant from the Council on Library Resources in 1963. He continued in the position until 1966 when he left to teach in the School of Library Science at Case Western Reserve University. He returned to *Choice* as editor in 1972. Louis A. Sasso was appointed editor, effective January 2, 1978.

In addition to the change in editors, another set of important changes concerning *Choice* took place during 1977. The Ad Hoc Committee on *Choice,* appointed by the ALA Executive Board and Council, had determined in 1976 that *Choice* was indeed a program of ACRL and not of ALA Publishing Services. In 1977 a series of principles relating to *Choice's* finances were agreed upon by all parties. They dealt with the creation of a separate reserve fund for *Choice,* the development of a plan for the repayment of a *Choice* deficit (which has now been repaid), and an assessment of an overhead charge to be paid to ALA. In a separate action, the ACRL Board voted to assign 10 per cent of the Executive Secretary's salary to the *Choice* budget in order to reflect more closely the actual costs of the magazine.

Conference Programs. More than 20 program sessions were sponsored by ACRL and its various units during the 1977 ALA Annual Conference in Detroit. ACRL's principal program was a speech delivered by Stephen K. Bailey, Acting President of the American Council on Education. Bailey's address, "The Future of College and Research Libraries: A Washington Perspective," was published in the January 1978 issue of *College and Research Libraries.*

The Rare Books and Manuscripts Section held its three-day preconference program in Toronto; participants discussed "Book Selling and Book Buying: Aspects of the Nineteenth Century British and North American Book Trades." Special exhibits were mounted at the Thomas Fisher Rare Book Library at the University of Toronto, at Massey College, at the Osborne and Lillian H. Smith collections of the Toronto Public Libraries, at the E. J. Pratt Library at Victoria University, and at the Art Gallery of Ontario.

ACRL National Conference. The Association of College and Research Libraries is planning its first national conference in Boston, November 8-11, 1978. The conference will focus on the future prospects for academic and research librarianship in the United States and will include a variety of invited and contributed papers at the program meetings. Exhibits, special events such as a reception at the Boston Public Library and an evening at the Boston Museum of Fine Arts, tours to the libraries in the area, and a placement service for library positions will also be a part of the conference.

Internships. Six interns were selected to participate in the fourth year of the intern program for administrators of predominantly Black college and university libraries. The program, funded by a grant from the Andrew W. Mellon Foundation, is intended to accelerate the development of the management ability of librarians in Black colleges and universities by providing them with experience in the administration of strong and progressive academic libraries.

The fourth-year interns are Virgia Brocks-Shedd, Tougaloo College; Alma Dawson, Prairie View A & M University; Doris M Gosier, Fort Valley State College; George M. Martin, Howard University; Millie M. Parker, Paine College; and Jean Frances Williams, Virginia State College.

During the period of the six-month internship, each intern works closely with the director of a major academic library. The host institutions for the fourth year of the program are Mount Holyoke College, Oberlin College, the University of Wisconsin-Milwaukee, and Virginia Commonwealth University. The Mellon Foundation grant provides the salaries, benefits, and approved expenses for each intern, and the host library provides the training. Several workshops for the participants are held.

Rare Books and Manuscripts. The ACRL Board in 1977 took action on two matters affecting librarians who work with rare books and manuscripts. The Board urged the American Library Association to enter into the case of the *State of North Carolina* v. *B.C. West, Jr.,* as fully and as strongly as possible. The case deals with the issue of replevin and is viewed as having a major impact on research collections in the United States. (*See also* Archives.)

In a second action the Board tried to clarify an area of possible conflict between ALA policy (3101.2) and ACRL's "Statement on Access to Original Research Materials in Libraries, Archives, and Manuscript Repositories." ACRL hoped to have added to the ALA policy a statement to the effect that nothing in the ALA policy on confidentiality of library records should be intended to limit the ability of a librarian, archivist, or manuscript curator to inform a researcher in original source materials of parallel research by other persons using the same sources. The only limitation would be that written permission for the use of researchers' names be obtained from each person whose name was to be furnished. The recommendation was to go to the ALA Council for action.

Legislation. The ACRL Committee on Legislation and the Legislative Network continued to be active throughout 1977. It would appear that letters written to congressional representatives by members of the network were instrumental in the passage of legislation favorable to academic and research libraries. The Committee on Legislation developed new language for inclusion in the section "College and Research Libraries" in the new edition of *Federal Legislative Policy of the American Library Association.* On the recommendation of the Committee, the ACRL Board endorsed S. 1328, the Career Education Implementation Act of 1977, with the provision that the role of libraries and librarians in the dissemination of career information be explicitly stated in the text of the Act where appropriate.

The Ad Hoc Committee on the White House Conference and State Library Conferences was appointed to serve as a liaison to agencies involved in the planning of the conferences. The Committee was to represent college and research libraries' interests.

Standards. ACRL is working cooperatively with the Association of Research Libraries to develop standards for university libraries. A joint committee of the two organizations has produced a draft document that is being

Association of Research Libraries

discussed by the members of the two groups. A meeting was held with national higher education associations and regional accrediting bodies to determine how the proposed standards could assist them as they worked with libraries. It is expected that the university library standards will become available towards the end of 1978.

A committee was appointed to review and revise, where necessary, the 1975 *Standards for College Libraries*. The Committee had begun its work at the end of 1977.

Policy Statements. The ACRL Board adopted and made available for distribution policy statements affecting several areas of academic librarianship. Among those approved was the "Statement on the Reproduction of Manuscsripts and Archives for Commercial Purposes." All six available policy statements on manuscripts and archives were issued as a single pamphlet entitled *Guidelines on Manuscripts and Archives*.

"Guidelines for Bibliographic Instruction in Academic Libraries" was developed by the ACRL Bibliographic Instruction Task Force. The Committee on Academic Status proposed, and the Board adopted, "Guidelines and Procedures for the Screening and Appointment of Academic Librarians."

Publications and Activities. Richard Johnson was reappointed as the editor of *College & Research Libraries*, a reflection of the reputation he has established in this responsibility. John Crowley was appointed as the editor of *College & Research Libraries News*. Joe W. Kraus is the new editor of the ACRL *Publications in Librarianship* series.

Two publications relating to the activities of ACRL appeared during the year. *Libraries for Teaching, Libraries for Research: Essays for a Century*, edited by Richard D. Johnson, was published as ACRL *Publications in Librarianship* No. 39. The 1976 issue of *A. B. Bookman's Yearbook*, published at the end of 1977, contained the proceedings of the 1976 Rare Books and Manuscripts Section Preconference on "Maps and Atlases."

ACRL continued to grow throughout the year, and by the end of 1977 there were 30 ACRL committees, 12 sections, 73 section committees, 18 chapters, 15 representatives and affiliates, and 3 discussion groups.

A Continuing Education Committee was established with the charge of developing a continuing education program that would assist ACRL members in their professional growth and thereby benefit them, their libraries, and library users.

The twelfth section within ACRL, the Bibliographic Instruction Section, was established during 1977. Four new groups were granted ACRL chapter status—the Academic and Research Libraries Division of the Maryland Library Association, the Southern California Association of College and Research Libraries, the College and University Libraries Division of the Texas Library Association, and the Virginia Chapter of ACRL. One group, the Cinema Librarians, formed as a discussion group.

JULIE A. CARROLL VIRGO

ACRL Officers

PRESIDENT (July 1977-June 1978):
Eldred R. Smith, University of Minnesota, Minneapolis, Minnesota

VICE-PRESIDENT/PRESIDENT-ELECT:
Evan Ira Farber, Earlham College, Richmond, Indiana

IMMEDIATE PAST PRESIDENT:
Connie R. Dunlap, Duke University, Durham, North Carolina

EXECUTIVE SECRETARY:
Julie A. Carroll Virgo

Membership (August 31, 1977): 8,609
Section Membership (August 31, 1977)

Agriculture and Biological Sciences	1,025
Art	1,175
Law and Political Science	1,169
Slavic and East European	757
Education and Behavorial Sciences	1,499
Asian and African	892
Anthropology	864
Community and Junior College Libraries	1,727
University Libraries	4,192
College Libraries	2,892
Rare Books and Manuscripts	1,674

Association of Research Libraries

At the national level considerable effort was directed in 1977 to passage of the $5,000,000 appropriation for the Higher Education Act Title II-C, Strengthening Research Library Resources. These funds, to be distributed in 1978, are to assist the major research libraries in the United States in making their collections available to other libraries. In 1976 the 105 Association of Research Libraries (ARL) member libraries loaned 2,400,000 items from their collections on interlibrary loan. Because these services involve considerable costs to the lending library, eight ARL libraries reported in 1977 that they no longer could afford to provide these services without compensation and that it would be necessary to charge borrowers for interlibrary loan services until state and federal subsidies became available. The funding of HEA II-C was heralded by the Association as an important first step in gaining the support needed so that research libraries could continue to provide services that extend beyond the boundaries of their institutions.

Other national programs of special interest to ARL in 1977 included the implementation of the revised copyright law. In coordination with other major library associations, ARL prepared and distributed materials and guidelines on the rights and responsibilities of libraries under the new law and represented the interests of research libraries in testimony before the National Commission on New Technological Uses of Copyrighted Works (CONTU). ARL also promoted the establishment of the National Periodicals System. Special ARL task forces continued to work with the National Commission on Libraries and Information Science (NCLIS) and other key agencies in furthering the planning for the establishment and operation of the National Periodicals Library.

The ARL Task Force on Statistics had an extremely productive year in 1977, which resulted in significant expansion of the ARL Salary Survey to include detailed information on average salaries of ARL librarians by position, sex, size and type of institution, and geographical location. In addition, the Task Force used data collected for *ARL Statistics—1976-77* to prepare a special supplementary report explaining the use of regression techniques to analyze the operations of individual libraries and compare them to those of other libraries. The availability in 1978 of machine-readable ARL data collected since 1967 will provide additional capability for analyzing the changing conditions in these research libraries.

The Committee on University Library Standards of ARL and ALA's Association of College and Research Libraries (ACRL), with support from a grant from the Council on Library Resources (CLR), met with representatives from various higher education, scholarly, and professional associations and foundations to review draft standards. It is anticipated that ARL and ACRL members will vote on these standards in late 1978 or early 1979.

The Committee on Access to Manuscripts and Rare Books was concerned with security measures for special collections. Committee members met with representatives of ACRL and the Society of American Archivists to discuss potential cooperative projects.

A significant publication issued in 1977 by the Association was entitled *Thirteen Colonial Americana*, a commemorative volume sampling the variety of products that emerged from the American press during the final 50 years of the American Colonial period. The volume features one publication from each of the 13 colonies. *Thirteen Colonial Americana*, made possible by a grant from the Commonwealth Fund, is a companion volume to the

Association of Research Libraries

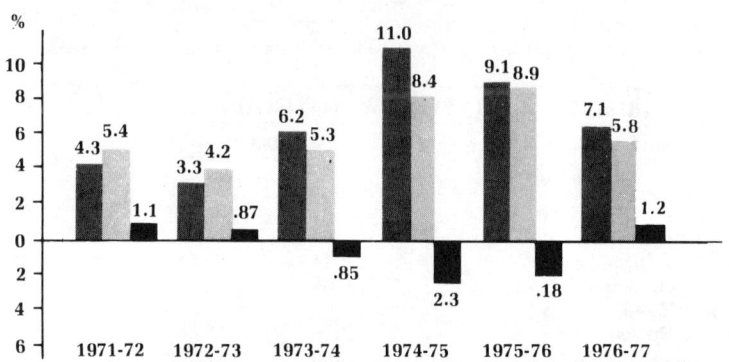

UNIVERSITY LIBRARY SALARIES AND THE COST OF LIVING
(Yearly increases in median salary as compared with increases in the consumer price index)

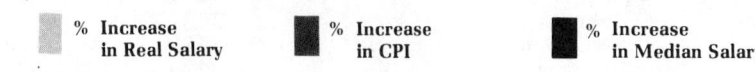

Source: ARL Salary Survey, 1976–77

NUMBER AND AVERAGE SALARIES OF ARL LIBRARIANS, 1976–77

ALL ARL LIBRARIANS

	Position	Number of Staff			Average Salaries		
		Total	Men	Women	Combined	Men	Women
1.	Director	81	73	8	$36,001	$36,191	$34,275
2.	Associate Director	94	71	23	27,965	28,192	27,263
3.	Assistant Director	211	144	67	23,449	23,978	22,313
4.	Medical/Law Head	85	53	32	28,001	28,828	26,630
5.	Branch Head	500	194	306	17,675	18,924	16,884
6.	Subject Specialist	634	318	316	16,258	16,851	15,661
7.	Functional Specialist	260	149	111	17,570	18,316	16,568
8.	Dept. Head: Reference	125	36	89	17,749	18,222	17,558
9.	Cataloging	120	24	96	18,363	18,983	18,208
10.	Acquisition	96	43	53	17,677	18,546	16,972
11.	Serials	77	20	57	16,629	16,331	16,734
12.	Doc./Maps	76	31	45	16,148	15,526	16,576
13.	Circulation	83	37	46	16,212	15,466	16,811
14.	Spec. Clltn.	97	62	35	18,760	20,233	16,151
15.	Other	246	90	156	16,795	17,725	16,258
16.	Other: Over 15 yrs. exper.	456	125	331	16,828	17,662	16,513
17.	10–15 yrs. exper.	473	136	337	15,671	15,920	15,571
18.	5–10 yrs. exper.	894	266	628	14,193	14,497	14,064
19.	Under 5 yrs. exper.	1106	321	785	12,190	12,538	12,048
	Total	5714	2193	3521			

ARL MINORITY LIBRARIANS

		Number of Staff			Average Salaries		
	Position	Total	Men	Women	Combined	Men	Women
1.	Director	3	3	0	*	*	000
2. 3. } Assoc/Asst Dir.		13	7	6	$24,954	$24,337	$25,674
4.	Medical/Law Head	5	5	0	26,859	26,859	000
5.	Branch Head	45	20	25	18,443	19,282	17,771
6.	Subject Specialist	63	34	29	16,704	17,162	16,168
7.	Functional Specialist	23	16	7	17,049	16,741	17,753
8.	Dept. Head: Reference	5	0	5	18,262	000	18,262
9.	Cataloging	10	1	9	18,176	*	18,404
10.	Acquisition	7	0	7	17,413	000	17,413
11.	Serials	5	0	5	17,488	000	17,488
12.	Doc./Maps	2	1	1	*	*	*
13.	Circulation	3	0	3	*	000	*
14.	Spec. Clltn.	7	2	5	15,599	*	15,447
15.	Other	7	2	5	15,354	*	13,499
16.	Other: Over 15 yrs. exper.	40	9	31	16,744	18,708	16,173
17.	10–15 yrs. exper.	62	21	41	15,193	15,339	15,118
18.	5–10 yrs. exper.	85	30	55	14,286	14,458	14,192
19.	Under 5 yrs. exper.	99	25	74	12,639	13,234	12,438
	Total	484	176	308			

*Salary information not published for position when fewer than 4 individuals are involved.

AVERAGE SALARIES BY TYPE OF INSTITUTION

	All Combined (90)		Public (54)		Private and Church-Related (29)	
Position	#	Average Salary	#	Average Salary	#	Average Salary
1. Director	81	$36,001	50	$34,809	24	$36,303
2. Associate Director	94	27,965	48	27,946	33	25,882
3. Assistant Director	211	23,449	121	22,761	70	23,104
4. Medical/Law Head	85	28,001	43	27,317	33	29,298
5. Branch Head	500	17,675	306	17,695	154	16,926
6. Subject Specialist	634	16,258	374	16,114	198	15,849
7. Functional Specialist	260	17,570	150	17,629	83	16,410
8. Dept. Head: Reference	125	17,749	69	17,608	46	17,139
9. Cataloging	120	18,363	60	18,404	50	17,438
10. Acquisition	96	17,677	48	18,087	42	16,606
11. Serials	77	16,629	43	17,444	28	15,190
12. Doc./Maps	76	16,148	48	16,515	22	14,096
13. Circulation	83	16,212	40	16,564	35	14,643
14. Spec. Clltn.	97	18,760	52	19,869	40	17,096
15. Other	246	16,795	117	17,284	100	15,321
16. Other: Over 15 yrs. exper.	456	16,828	289	17,289	135	15,319
17. 10–15 yrs. exper.	473	15,671	296	15,927	136	14,208
18. 5–10 yrs. exper.	894	14,193	564	14,233	238	13,348
19. Under 5 yrs. exper.	1106	12,190	695	12,229	337	11,682

AVERAGE SALARIES BY SIZE OF STAFF

	Staff Over 125 (5)		Staff 75-125 (19)		Staff 50-74 (34)		Staff 1-49 (35)	
Position	#	Salary	#	Salary	#	Salary	#	Salary
1. Director	2	**	12	$41,792	32	$36,113	35	$33,537
2. Associate Director	9	$33,532	20	31,313	37	26,918	28	25,166
3. Assistant Director	19	27,139	50	26,214	76	21,738	66	22,264
4. Medical/Law Head	7	31,285	22	30,529	30	27,153	26	25,956
5. Branch Head	57	18,248	211	18,469	138	17,072	94	16,433
6. Subject Specialist	63	18,116	229	17,537	224	15,322	118	14,559
7. Functional Specialist	24	20,104	103	18,764	81	15,452	52	17,332
8. Dept. Head: Reference	5	19,452	28	20,710	40	18,084	52	15,733
9. Cataloging	7	18,593	32	19,827	43	17,995	38	17,506
10. Acquisition	9	18,254	21	19,021	35	17,144	31	17,201
11. Serials	3	**	15	17,574	27	16,589	32	15,920
12. Doc./Maps	4	**	17	17,488	32	15,538	23	15,249
13. Circulation	6	17,028	21	17,662	29	15,825	27	15,318
14. Spec. Clltn.	2	**	27	19,922	32	18,778	36	17,583
15. Other	11	18,915	77	17,343	81	16,427	77	16,331
16. Other: Over 15 yrs. exper.	49	19,024	171	17,704	146	16,010	90	15,294
17. 10–15 yrs. exper.	70	17,244	160	16,476	151	15,012	92	14,157
18. 5–10 yrs. exper.	105	15,028	280	14,856	330	13,798	179	13,393
19. Under 5 yrs. exper.	126	12,965	303	12,757	427	11,789	250	11,796

**Salary information not published when 4 or fewer individuals are involved.   ( ) Number of ARL libraries included.

Association of Research Libraries

Association's commemorative Bicentennial publication, *76 United Statesiana*. Both volumes were edited by Edward C. Lathem and are examples of exceptionally fine printing, produced by the Stinehour Press in Lunenburg, Vermont.

The Association also received a grant from the H.W. Wilson Foundation to consolidate and update the indexes to the published *Minutes of the ARL Membership Meetings—1932-1977*. The new index will be published in 1978.

The ARL administers the Center for Chinese Research Materials which was founded in May 1968 to reproduce rare and valuable Chinese research materials on 20th-century China and to provide bibliographic services. Funding for this project was made possible with grants from the Ford Foundation, the Andrew W. Mellon Foundation, the National Endowment for the Humanities, and the U.S. Department of State. To date the Center has made available copies of more than 1,400 titles and has sales revenues of $1,000,000.

The ARL also administers the Office of University Library Management Studies (OMS), established in 1970 as a mechanism for addressing some of the management concerns of research libraries. The Office has been funded principally with three grants from CLR. OMS priorities in 1977 included further development of in-house training programs and applications of the Management Review and Analysis Program (MRAP), an assisted self-study procedure on organizational development for libraries. OMS also continued the Systems and Procedure Exchange Center (SPEC), an information clearinghouse on policies and procedures used in academic libraries, and the operation of the Collections Analysis Project, funded by the Mellon Foundation to test procedures for analyzing library collection acquisition, retention, and preservation policies at research libraries.

—SUZANNE O. FRANKIE

ARL Officers

PRESIDENT (October 1977-October 1978): **Edward C. Lathem**, Dartmouth College, Hanover, New Hampshire

VICE-PRESIDENT/PRESIDENT-ELECT: **Ray Franz, Jr.**, University of Virginia, Charlottesville

EXECUTIVE SECRETARY: **John G. Lorenz**

Headquarters: 1527 New Hampshire Ave., N.W., Washington, D.C. 20036

The ARL in 1977
Membership
105 research libraries
94 are university libraries
11 nonuniversity libraries
8 are located in Canada.
Resources
238,000,000 volumes in the collections
9,000,000 volumes added last year
2,700,000 current serials received
35,000 employees
11,000 professional librarians
$626,000,000 operating expenditures

Collections. ARL Members, 1976-77

	Volumes in Library	Volumes Added (net)	Total Microform Units in Library	Current Serials
University Libraries	199,940,530	6,961,651	96,862,544	2,344,217
Nonuniversity Libraries	38,522,474	952,621	9,756,445	400,126
Grand total—All Libraries	238,463,004	7,914,272	106,618,989	2,744,343

Interlibrary Loans. ARL Members, 1976-77

	Loaned			Borrowed		
	Originals	Photocopies	Total	Originals	Photocopies	Total
University Libraries	534,000	971,435	1,647,220	232,800	215,134	496,062
Nonuniversity Libraries	376,140	318,849	715,997	34,776	3,147	49,698
Grand totals	910,140	1,290,284	2,363,217	267,576	218,281	545,760

Personnel

	Professional Staff FTE	Non-professional Staff FTE	Student Assistant FTA	Total Staff FTA
University Libraries	7,148	14,740	5,532	27,420
Nonuniversity Libraries	4,494	2,774	316	7,584
Grand Totals—All ARL Libraries	11,642	17,514	5,848	35,004

Expenditures

	Library Materials	Current Periodicals	Binding	Total Materials and Binding	Total Salaries and Wages	Other Operating Expenditures	Total Library Operating Expenditures
University Libraries	$132,916,809	$58,767,742	$10,470,451	$143,387,214	$261,873,399	$40,452,140	$445,707,987
Nonuniversity Libraries	$12,437,126	$3,973,258	$2,065,985	$14,503,111	$117,115,578	$48,440,048	$180,058,737
Grand totals—All ARL Libraries	$145,353,935	$62,741,000	$12,536,436	$157,890,325	$378,988,977	$88,892,188	$625,766,724

Association of State Library Agencies

Administrative and fiscal concerns were the dominant focus of the Association of State Library Agencies (ASLA) during 1977. Continued emphasis was placed on the development of multitype library cooperative activities in line with the ASLA charge approved by ALA Council in 1972. The ASLA leadership designed and executed a viable financial program for the Association that resulted in a surplus for the first time in many years. Committees and the ASLA Board of Directors were actively engaged in developing new programs as well as establishing two new sections for ASLA. The Association also had a change in Executive Secretaries during the year.

New Division. The dynamism with which ASLA has progressed throughout 1977 has enabled the Association to move ahead significantly in the achievement of its objectives. Strong membership support has engendered substantial success in several major areas. The merger of ASLA with the Health and Rehabilitative Library Services Division (HRLSD) was approved in principle by the ALA Council, which paved the way for the drafting of the concrete terms of the merger. The Association was to present its structural and organizational details, written in concert with HRLSD by the Joint Reorganization Committee with wide representation from both groups, to the ALA Committee on Organization at the 1978 ALA Midwinter Meeting. The new ALA division will have primary responsibility for multitype library cooperatives and specialized services libraries. It will have five sections: (1) Multitype Library Cooperation; (2) State Library Agency; (3) Library Service to the Blind and Physically Handicapped; (4) Library Service to Prisoners; and (5) Library Service to the Impaired Elderly.

Strong programming and vigorous activity by ASLA committees and discussion groups have attracted new members. By the late spring of 1977, ASLA had increased its membership by 48 percent over the previous year. Solid membership promotion by the ASLA Membership Committee, chaired by Shirley C. Mills of West Virginia, and effective membership support by the ASLA office were instrumental in increasing membership.

The 1977 Conference Program Committee, chaired by Bonnie Beth Mitchell of Ohio, presented a dynamic program entitled "Consultant Services: Panacea, First Aid, or Disaster?" that featured Raymond Holt, library consultant from Del Mar, California. Detailing a number of points about obtaining and using the right consultant, Holt concluded that there is no single easy answer to the question. Through an evaluative process, however, seeking and using a productive consultant can provide a bridge to the future and offer guidelines for positive action.

Committee Activities. Other particularly active committees included the State Aid Study Committee, chaired by Patricia Smith of Texas, which planned to survey states concerning their state aid practices; the ASLA Planning Committee, chaired by Lorraine Schaeffer of Florida, which drafted documents related to the creation of ASLA's two new sections and provided material to assist the ASLA/HRLSD Joint Reorganization Committee in its tasks; and, the 1978 Conference Program Committee, chaired by Robert Drescher of Illinois, which was designing a program with contributed papers on the subject of networking as well as a preconference on consultant skills in conjunction with the ASLA Continuing Education Committee, chaired by Charles Bolles of Kansas.

In its drive to meet more fully its authorized charge, ASLA began in 1977 the implementation of two new sections. One, the State Library Agency Section, related directly to the concerns of state library agencies and their personnel. The other, the Multitype Library Cooperation Section, was created in direct response to ASLA's charge dealing with networks, cooperatives, and multitype library systems. Both new sections established executive committees and drafted bylaws that were to be presented to the ASLA Board of Directors at the 1978 ALA Midwinter Meeting.

The 1977 ALA Annual Conference held in Detroit was a busy one for ASLA members and leadership. Plans were begun for an ASLA institute on the nontechnical aspects of planning for networking. The Institute Planning Committee has continued to review the viability and need for such an institute, planning for an early 1979 date. The institute would concentrate on the impact of networking on various aspects of library services as well as the organizational, financial, and political considerations of networking.

ASLA Report. The second edition of the ASLA *Report on Interlibrary Cooperation* moved closer to publication when the ASLA Interlibrary Cooperation Committee, chaired by William DeJohn of Washington, selected a subcommittee, chaired by Beth Hamilton of Illinois, to revise, test, and conduct the survey. While the data gathered will be comparable with the earlier edition, a number of clarifications in terminology and format were made that will make the resulting publication more useful and complete. Release and distribution of the new edition was expected in early 1978.

The major task facing ASLA membership in 1977 was increasing the number of ASLA members. ALA's budgeting policy is to set a limit on budgets based on the actual income of the previous year and to budget only money that can be derived from reasonably secure sources. In its plan for solid, long-term financial footing, ASLA is best served by building a firm base of revenues derived from dues- paying members. While quickly increasing the membership of an organization such as ASLA is not an easy task, the Association had a sound record in 1977 of adding new members.

August 31 marked the last working day of ASLA Executive Secretary Mary R. Power. ASLA acknowledges its debt of gratitude to her for her untiring devotion to ASLA during her two-year tenure. On November 1 Sandra Cooper, formerly of the Louisiana State Library, began her duties as ASLA Executive Secretary, a position shared with HRLSD.

DONALD B. SIMPSON

ASLA Officers

PRESIDENT (July 1977-June 1978):
Donald B. Simpson, Bibliographical Center for Research, Denver

VICE-PRESIDENT/PRESIDENT-ELECT:
Robert R. McClarren, Wheeling, Illinois

EXECUTIVE SECRETARY:
Sandra M. Cooper

Membership (August 31, 1977): 1,236 (381 personal and 855 organizational)

Automation

For the past decade, major events in library automation have focused on the activities of the Library of Congress (LC). The development of the MARC (machine-readable cataloging) format, the MARC distribution service, and the initiation of the COMARC project have kept LC constantly in the public eye. A glance at recent news in library automation, however, indicates clearly that LC's role is changing and that other organizations are providing substantial input into the growth of library automation. It should be noted that this trend parallels a trend taking place within libraries or groups of libraries throughout the country. Deliberately raising their levels of awareness of technology, librarians are stepping in to take an active part in the identification of needs and the specification of requirements for their automated systems. No longer does library automation remain a mysterious element, to be handled by only a few knowledgeable technical experts.

In the long run, this movement of automation initiative from the specialist to the librarian should prove fruitful and beneficial to the profession. In 1977, however, librarians in the field experienced growing pains. No one wanted to be left out of decisions that might have an impact on his or her organization, yet the decision-making process for a large group of people was not only agonizingly slow but was also sometimes economically and administratively intolerable. In addition, the library profession had not yet educated itself to a point where an informed manager could always make informed decisions and deal in a businesslike way with the vendors who supported the automation processes. Paradoxically, vendors themselves complained that librarians came to them to ask their advice.[1] Decision-makers often flocked to an apparently successful system, without regard to their own circumstances or an intent to provide pressure for required services. Some of the year's events were apparently the results of this "semieducation," as well as the natural tendency to buy the product that worked well for the library down the street.

Push button access to millions of published articles is available on 70 business data bases at the Chicago Area Computer Information Center's program sponsored by the Illinois Regional Library Council and the Chicago Public Library.

NATIONAL EVENTS

LC, MARC, COMARC. Although LC's proportion of the 1977 automation news was smaller than in the past, the MARC Development Office, headed by Joseph Price, and the Network Development Office, headed by Henriette Avram, made significant contributions. The MARC Distribution Service expanded its coverage of languages to all Roman alphabet materials,[2] and LC distributed a test tape of federal document materials input by the Government Printing Office in a project intended to test the possibility of including document materials in MARC distribution. The COMARC project, initiated in 1976, continued with batch input from selected libraries to LC of MARC format records for materials not within the scope of the MARC data base. Although some communication problems had been encountered in the early part of the project, these were resolved during the year. COMARC data are successfully but slowly being entered into the MARC distribution cycle.

Automation

By midyear, approximately 24,000 titles had been verified and redistributed by the MARC Editorial Division.

Network Development. In 1976 LC's Network Development Office had established, the Network Advisory Council (NAC), a representative group for the purpose of formulating the design and specifications of a national bibliographic network. A subcommittee of NAC, the Network Technical Architecture Group (NTAG), has been charged with the development of technical specifications for the national network. Vitally interested in the design of a computer-to-computer communications protocol, NTAG has developed several working assumptions about the structure of a network and has designated three groups—the Washington Library Network, Northwestern University Library, and the New York Public Library—to experiment with computer-to-computer links with the Library of Congress for the sharing of bibliographic data.

Several major tasks have been identified by the NAC and were described in a document distributed and discussed at the ALA Annual Conference in Detroit.[3] Among these tasks is the design of a suitable and workable authority control system for a national network. A major study of authority control commissioned to Edwin Buchinski of the National Library of Canada was completed; the study identified approximately 20 areas of concern that will require further investigation in order to implement authority control in a network environment. The LC work on authority control parallels the work being done at the BALLOTS Center at Stanford University, the New York Public Library, the University of Chicago, and Blackwell/North America, among others. Librarians will soon have to find a solution to the problems caused by the lack of authority control. As automated systems become increasingly interdependent, such control will be essential for viable system operation.

Under the aegis of the National Bureau of Standards (NBS), the National Commission on Libraries and Information Science (NCLIS), and the American Library Association, a group of technical experts has worked together since 1976 to design a standard computer-to-computer communications protocol in order to provide the basis for the emerging national network. By the end of 1977, the group had completed its work, although the results had not yet been made public.

CONTU. With the 1976 copyright law to take effect in 1978, the National Commission on New Technological Uses of Copyrighted Works (CONTU) is working on problems identified by the major parties involved in copyright: libraries, publishers, and authors. In addition, two subcommittees of CONTU issued reports and recommendations on the applicability of copyrights to data bases and software.[4,5] Both subcommittees recommended the extension of the new law to include machine-readable data, concluding that the provisions of the law were sufficient to cover both data bases and software. A minority report was issued by author John Hersey, recommending a new mechanism for protection of machine-readable data.[6] Hersey's view was supported by evidence submitted by the Copyright Committee of the Council of National Library Associations.[7]

COOPERATIVE AUTOMATION

Network computer utilities are growing rapidly. The Ohio College Library Center (OCLC) has more than 1,200 customers. The BALLOTS Center grew in one year from one customer to more than 30 shared cataloging customers and more than 100 libraries using the search-only facility. The Washington Library Network (WLN) is implementing its plan for a statewide on-line facility. The experimental connection between the Research Libraries Group (specifically the New York Public Library) and LC became operational during the year. OCLC, which began as an academic library consortium, started to convert the shelflists of a number of Ohio public libraries.

At the same time, libraries were continuing to show concern over the pricing and quality of service provided by network computer utilities. At least two major network organizations were reorganized, modified, or dissolved. CAPTAIN in New Jersey dissolved, and some of its functions were taken over by the Pennsylvania Area Library Network (PALINET).[8] The Southeastern Library Network (SOLINET) withdrew from affiliation with the Southern Regional Education Board (SREB), and SREB retained a consultant to advise it on the nature of its role in library networking. The report, by Butler Associates, recommended that SREB become an independent support agency rather than a production network.[9] The Western Interstate Library Consortium (WILCO) separated from the Western Interstate Commission for Higher Education (WICHE), changed its name to Western Council of State Libraries, and is returning to its original form and function, representing a considerable scaling down of plans and effort for the 17 Western states.

Until 1977, OCLC had been the only real option for libraries wanting to contract for on-line cataloging services. Most libraries have done nothing further than sign a contract with OCLC or one of the regional network organizations. With BALLOTS increasing in size, WLN now operational, and several institutionally developed systems interested in shared operation, more libraries are now looking carefully at the available options. In particular, the Research Libraries Group and the nine-campus University of California requested bids for on-line cataloging and processing systems. The results of the bidding process were not available by the end of 1977, but it is clear that on-line bibliographic systems have moved one step further toward businesslike and responsive operations.

BIBLIOGRAPHIC CONTROL

Since 1975, the CONSER (Conversion of Serials) project has been operated by the Council on Library Resources (CLR), using the OCLC facility to build a data base of serials records for cooperative use. As of 1977, the data base contained approximately 150,000 records, with about 25 per cent of these "authenticated" by either LC or the National Library of Canada. Initial plans called for CLR to turn over the management of the program to LC by late 1977, but failure to obtain funds caused LC to retract its offer. Stepping into the breach, OCLC will devote some of its own resources to maintaining the CONSER program for the immediate future.

In late 1976, OCLC implemented the long-awaited serials check-in system. One hundred and fifty OCLC customers were selected to participate in the pilot test of the check-in module; as of late 1977, no libraries had been added. Although serials check-in is operational, some continue to feel that applications such as serials check-in and circulation are inappropriate for large-scale networking.[10,11]

During the year, OCLC reconstructed its system indexes to provide more rapid access and faster response time. Indications were that by the end of the year this restructuring had succeeded in meeting its objectives. The network was struggling, however, with the problem of retrieving sizable numbers of nondistinctive titles with the search key structure used by the system.[12]

The University of Toronto, active in library automation for nearly 15 years, has now reported widely the development of its on-line processing system—the University of Toronto Library Automation System (UTLAS). Many libraries throughout Canada use the system for processing. The University has also converted the bulk of its catalog to machine-readable form, has closed its card catalog, and makes the catalog available to its patrons in either microfilm or microfiche, with microfiche cumulative supplements. The library spent considerable effort to determine the optimum configuration for its new catalog, and staff members and patrons are apparently pleased with the results, finding few problems in using the microform products.[13]

As reported in *Advanced Technology/ Libraries,* many libraries now have computer output microform (COM) catalogs, or are considering their adoption in the near future.[14] During 1977, the Los Angeles County Public Library, one of the largest public libraries in the country, decided to move from a book catalog to a microform catalog, using the ROM III reader manufactured by Information Design, Inc. At the same time, some librarians are beginning to express doubt that microform catalogs would solve the problems of new technologies and changing cataloging rules. The minicomputer is being viewed as a potential "local catalog," with telecommunications links to regional and national data bases.

CIRCULATION

CL Systems. 1977 was the year of the circulation system. At the ALA Annual Conference in Detroit, seven companies exhibited systems, most of which were either operational or about to become operational in one or more libraries. CL Systems, Inc., the first entrant into the field of on-line minicomputer circulation systems, leads in the number of installations, with more than 100 customers in public and academic libraries. The reorganization of the company in 1976, however, led to a $20,000,000 suit against the company itself, the principals within the company, and Xerox Corporation (a shareholder in the former company) for an alleged conspiracy to defraud by means of the reorganization.

Originally developed for public libraries, CL Systems has been moving in the direction of academic library needs since 1973. Major academic libraries with CLSI systems are the University of Houston, UCLA, the University of California at Davis, the California State University and Colleges System, New York University, and the University of Pennsylvania. The company's efforts to accommodate

Fee-based on-line searching services became a reality at the Dallas Public Library in 1977. Use of the popular CAT system (Community Access Tool) geared to local activities increased 100 per cent over the preceding year.

academic libraries have been less than successful, however. At the end of 1977 several of the customers reported significant periods of downtime, considerably higher installation costs than had been anticipated, and the need to actually increase the size of staff required to run the circulation function.

Other Systems. After an overhaul, the 3M system was selected for the Princeton University Library. This system also encountered difficulties, and at last word had been taken off the market temporarily. Seeing the problems that existed with other commercial circulation systems, some libraries took independent action. The San Jose Public Library contracted with Systems Control, Inc., to design and implement a system for that library's 35 branches. The system was installed in early 1977. At Dallas County Community College, the processing center took its design for a circulation and processing system to DataPhase, a local firm. In early September 1977, the college installed the DataPhase circulation system, and the Tacoma Public Library had contracted to buy the software as a pilot installation for the state of Washington. Before the end of the year, DataPhase had contracted for statewide implementation of the system in public libraries for the state of North Carolina.

Other circulation systems are ULISIS, a Canadian system that has been purchased by the Tucson Public Library; Gaylord (Syracuse), which now has several installations in public libraries; Innovative Systems, the developers of a system for the University of Texas at Dallas, based on a Hewlett Packard 3000 computer; and Cincinnati Electronics, the manufacturers of the circulation terminal used by the University of Chicago Library.

MACHINE-ASSISTED REFERENCE

At the beginning of 1977, the newly formed Bibliographic Retrieval Services (BRS) began offering data base retrieval services, joining the two older companies in the business—System Development Corporation (SDC) and Lockheed Information Systems. Due to BRS's low pricing, Lockheed dropped its rates during the year, and SDC, while leaving its rates untouched, began to place its stress on the quality of the product.

Academic and public libraries have recently become users of these services. With this usage comes a deep concern over charging users for total or partial cost recovery for the service. A large group of librarians feels that it is unconscionable to charge for any kind of service at all in a publicly supported library. The debate continued throughout the year. At the ALA Annual Conference, its Council passed a resolution supporting free access to information but did not condemn cost recovery. Both the Library Institute Planning Committee Institute and the University of Pittsburgh Institute on "The On-Line Revolution" raised considerable debate on the topic. It is clear that the data base proprietors and distributors are not the villains; the use of high technology will inevitably be accompanied by high costs. Librarians will have to learn to phase out older, less essential programs, or be prepared to charge partial or full recovery of direct costs.

COMMERCIAL SERVICES

There were additional events in commercial services that must be included in an account of 1977. Early in the year, Brodart announced an on-line acquisition system for $1,000 monthly. The user would access the Brodart data base, place orders directly through the terminal, and print copies of the orders on a local printer. Later in the year, Brodart and CLSI announced an interface between the Brodart IROS system and the CLSI LIBS 100 system whereby CLSI users could access the IROS system with the CLSI cathode-ray tube (CRT) terminal.

Equipment manufacturers have only recently become aware that the library and information market is a sizable one. A report published recently indicates the availability of CRT and printer terminals with character sets and other features required by libraries.[15] Several different terminals exist and are in use; other manufacturers have indicated a willingness to develop the required equipment.

Conclusion. The year 1977 was an eventful one for library automation. The issue regarding the need for systems specialists in libraries has yet to be resolved; the experiences of 1977 would indicate that benefit would be derived by retaining systems analysts for single libraries or groups of libraries. It is obvious that librarians must begin to pay increasing attention to the problems that exist between the public and private sectors, learn to negotiate contracts properly and specify requirements adequately to meet the needs of their libraries and their users. Librarians are becoming comfortable with new technologies, but they have far to go in learning the correct questions to ask to provide libraries with the best system for the least expenditure.

SUSAN K. MARTIN

REFERENCES

1. Susan K. Martin, "Suddenly This Summer," *Journal of Library Automation* (September 1977), pp. 203-4.
2. "MARC Editorial Division Activities," *LC Information Bulletin* (June 10, 1977), p. 389.
3. Library of Congress, *Toward a National Library and Information Service Network* (Washington, D.C.: Library of Congress, 1977).

4. National Commission on New Technological Uses of Copyrighted Works (CONTU), Subcommittee on Data Bases, *Subcommittee on Data Bases Report and Additional Views* (Washington, D.C.: CONTU, 1977).
5. National Commission on New Technological Uses of Copyrighted Works (CONTU), Subcommittee on Software, *Subcommittee on Software Report and Additional Views* (Washington, D.C.: CONTU, 1977).
6. John Hersey, "Additional Views on Computer Software," in CONTU, *Subcommittee on Software Report and Additional Views* (Washington, D.C.: CONTU, 1977).
7. Council of National Library Associations, Committee on Copyright Practice and Implementation, *A Statement Submitted to the Commission on New Technological Uses of Copyrighted Works*, October 20, 1977.
8. "PALINET to Take Over Where CAPTAIN Left Off," *Advanced Technology/Libraries* (March 1977), p. 3.
9. Brett Butler, *Library Network Development and the Southern Regional Education Board; Final Report* (Stanford, California: Butler Associates, 1976).
10. Richard De Gennaro, "Wanted: A Minicomputer Serials System," *Library Journal* (April 15, 1977), pp. 878-79.
11. Susan K. Martin, "Trends in Library Networking," in Association of Research Libraries (ARL), *Minutes of the Eighty-eighth Meeting, Seattle, May 6-7, 1976* (Washington, D.C.: ARL, 1976).
12. "CONSER Working on Input Problem," *Advanced Technology/Libraries* (June 1977), p. 7.
13. Valentina DeBruin, "Sometimes Dirty Things Are Seen on the Screen," *Journal of Academic Librarianship* (November 1977), pp. 256-66.
14. "Libraries Expand Use of COM Catalogs," *Advanced Technology/Libraries* (February 1977), pp. 1-3.
15. Peter Graham, "Terminals and Printers for Library Use: A Report of a Selection," *Journal of Library Automation* (December 1977).

Awards and Prizes

ALA AWARDS

Through its national awards program, the American Library Association seeks to honor those who have rendered distinguished service to libraries and librarianship. Such recognition is made for individual achievement of a high order in some area of librarianship, for effective participation in library affairs, and for writings and illustrations that enrich our collections. In addition, recognition and assistance are given to individuals and groups selected to conduct special studies, and scholarships are awarded to promising candidates seeking to enter the profession or for advanced study. The juries and committees making the selections are charged with the responsibility of maintaining the high standards established by their predecessors in selecting individuals who have furthered to a notable degree the purposes for which libraries were created.

The following are ALA awards and recipients for the period January 1977 through December 1977. [For 1976 recipients, see the second edition of this *Yearbook* (1977). For a list of all recipients from the first year offered, see the first edition (1976), pages 456-65.]

AWARDS AND CITATIONS

ALA Goal Awards

The J. Morris Jones and Bailey K. Howard—World Book Encyclopedia—ALA Goal Awards (under the jurisdiction of the Executive Board) is an annual grant of $10,000, established in 1960, made by the Field Enterprises Educational Corporation, Inc., to encourage and advance the development of public, academic and/or school library service and librarianship through recognition and support of programs that implement the goals and objectives of ALA.

RECIPIENTS: ALA Public Information Office and ALA National Library Week Committee.

American Association of School Librarians, President's Award

An annual award of $2,000, established in 1977, presented to the individual who has demonstrated excellence and provided an outstanding national or international contribution to school librarianship and school library development. Donated by Baker and Taylor. Administered by the American Association of School Librarians.

(To be awarded in 1978 for the first time.)

American Institute of Architects/ALA/Library Administration Division Award Program

Awards, established in 1962, presented biennially by the American Institute of Architects and the Library Administration Division of ALA to encourage excellence in the architectural design and planning of libraries. Awards are made to all types of libraries. Citations are presented to the winning architectural firms and to libraries; a building plaque is also presented to each library winning an Honor Award. Photographs of the award-winning libraries are displayed at the following ALA Annual Conference.

(To be awarded in 1978.)

American Library History Round Table Essay Award

An award of $200, established in 1977, is presented to the author of an essay that demonstrates excellence in research in library history. Entries should be manuscripts not previously published nor currently under consideration for publication. Essays should combine original historical research on a significant subject of library history. Entries should be organized in a format similar to that of articles published in *The Journal of Library History*. Papers should not exceed 25 typewritten pages. The winner will be offered the privilege of having the winning paper published in a future issue of *The Journal of Library History*. Donated and administered by the ALHRT.

(To be awarded in 1978 for the first time.)

American Library Trustee Association Honor Award

An annual award, a citation, and a plaque, established in 1976, to recognize benefactors to public libraries. The recipient may be a person, institution, agency, or organization. The significance of the gift will be measured from the point of view of the recipient library. Donated and administered by ALTA.

RECIPIENTS: Rosamund Gifford Charitable Corporation, North Syracuse, New York.
Sarah Irwin Jones, Clinton, Louisiana.
T.H. McCasland, Duncan, Oklahoma.
P.M. Musser and descendants, Muscatine, Iowa.
Ann Smoot, King George, Virginia.
Viola T. Swetmann, Seward, Alaska.
F.W. Symmes Foundation, Greenville, South Carolina.

Armed Forces Librarians Achievement Citation

An annual citation, established in 1964, presented to members of the Armed Forces

Librarians Section, Public Library Association, who have made significant contributions to the development of armed forces library service and to organizations encouraging an interest in libraries and reading. Donated and administered by the Armed Forces Librarians Section, Public Library Association.

(Not awarded in 1977.)

(Mildred L.) Batchelder Award

A citation, established in 1966, presented annually to an American publisher for a children's book considered to be the most outstanding of those books originally published in a foreign language in a foreign country, and subsequently published in the United States during the calendar year preceding the appointment of the Mildred L. Batchelder Award Jury. The award will be made annually unless the committee is of the opinion that no book of that particular year is worthy of the award. "Children's book" is to be interpreted as any trade book (including picture books) for children between, and including, the prenursery-age level and the eighth grade. Donated and administered by the Association for Library Service to Children.

RECIPIENT: Atheneum Publishers for *The Leopard* by Cecil Bodke.

Beta Phi Mu Award

An annual award, established in 1972, of $500 and a citation of achievement, presented to a library school faculty member or to an individual for distinguished service to education for librarianship. Donated by Beta Phi Mu, the library science honorary association. Administered by the Library Education Division.

RECIPIENT: Russell E. Bidlack, University of Michigan School of Library Science.

(Randolph) Caldecott Medal

A medal, established in 1937, presented annually to the illustrator of the most distinguished American picture book for children published in the United States in the preceding year. The recipient must be a citizen or resident of the United States. Donated by Daniel Melcher. Administered by the Association for Library Service to Children.

RECIPIENTS: Diane and Leo Dillon, illustrators of *Ashanti to Zulu: African Traditions* by Margaret Musgrove (Dial).

(Francis Joseph) Campbell Citation

A citation and a medal, established in 1965, presented annually to a person who has made an outstanding contribution to the advancement of library service for the blind. This contribution may take the form of an imaginative and constructive program in a particular library; a recognized contribution to the national library program for blind persons; creative participation in library associations or blind organizations that advance reading for the blind; a significant publication or writing in the field; imaginative contribution to library administration, reference, circulation, selections, acquisitions, or technical services; or any activity of recognized importance. Donated and administered by the Section on Library Service to the Blind and Physically Handicapped of HRLSD.

RECIPIENT: Adeline Franzel, New Jersey State Library.

(James Bennett) Childs Award

An engraved plaque, established in 1976, presented to a librarian or other individual for distinguished contributions to documents librarianship. Donated and administered by the Government Documents Round Table.

RECIPIENT: Bernadine A. Hoduski, U.S. Congress, Joint Committee on Printing.

(John Cotton) Dana Public Relations Awards

An annual citation, established in 1942, made to libraries or library organizations of all types submitting materials representing the year's public relations program or a special project terminated during the year. Donated by the H.W. Wilson Company, the awards program is sponsored jointly with the Public Relations Section of the Library Administration Division.

RECIPIENTS: Public Library, Greenville (South Carolina) County Library.

State Library, West Virginia Library Commission.

Cooperating Library System, New York Metropolitan Reference and Research Library Agency.

University Library, University of Utah Library.

School Library, Rocky River (Ohio) High School Library.

Service Library, Clark Air Force Base Library, Philippines.

Dartmouth Medal

A medal, established in 1974, presented to honor achievement in creating reference works outstanding in quality and significance. Creating reference works may include, but need not be limited to, writing, compiling, editing, or publishing books or providing information in other forms for reference use, e.g., a data bank. Bestowal of the award shall normally relate to works that have been published or otherwise made available for the first time during the calendar year preceding the presentation of the award. Donated by Dartmouth College, Hanover, New Hampshire. Administered by the Reference and Adult Services Division.

RECIPIENT: Lester Jesse Cappon, ed., *Atlas of Early American History: The Revolutionary Era, 1760-1790* (Princeton University Press).

(Melvil) Dewey Medal

An engraved medal and a citation, established in 1952, presented annually to an individual or a group for recent creative professional achievement of a high order, particularly in those fields in which Melvil Dewey was actively interested—library management, library training, cataloging and classification, and the tools and techniques of librarianship. Donated by the Forest Press, Inc. Administered by the ALA Awards Committee.

RECIPIENT: Seymour Lubetsky, first editor of *Anglo-American Cataloging Rules*.

Documents to the People Award

A citation of achievement and a cash stipend of $1,000, established in 1976, to be used to promote professional advancement in the field of librarianship presented annually to the individual and/or library, organization, or other appropriate noncommercial group that has most effectively encouraged the use of federal documents in support of library services. Donated by the Congressional Information Service, Inc. Administered by the Government Documents Round Table.

RECIPIENT:

(Special) Exhibitors Award

Special awards from ALA were presented to three companies at the 1977 Annual Conference for 50 years of participation at Annual Conferences.

RECIPIENTS: Gaylord Bros. Inc., Walter Curley, President. Library Bureau, Robert May, President. H.W. Wilson Co., Leo Weins, President.

Grolier Foundation Award

$1,000 and a citation of achievement, established in 1953, presented annually to a librarian in a community or in a school who has made an unusual contribution to the stimulation and guidance of reading by children and young people. The award is usually given for outstanding work with children and young people through high school age, for continuing service, or in recognition of one particular contribution of lasting value. Donated by the Grolier Foundation. Administered by the ALA Awards Committee.

RECIPIENT: Elizabeth T. Fast, Groton (Massachusetts) Public Schools (posthumously).

Hammond, Inc., Library Award

$500 and a citation, established in 1962, presented annually to a librarian or library in a community or school for making an unusual contribution through continued service or a single contribution of lasting value to the effective use of or increased interest in maps, atlases, and globes by children and young people through high school age. Donated by Hammond, Inc., it is administered by the ALA Awards Committee.

RECIPIENT: Upper Hudson Library Federation, Albany, New York.

Health and Rehabilitative Library Services Division Exceptional Service Award

A citation, established in 1957, presented to a member of the HRLSD in recognition of exceptional service to HRLSD or any of its component areas of service—namely, patients; the homebound; medical, nursing, and other professional staff in hospitals; and inmates—and professional leadership, effective interpretation of program, pioneering activity, and significant research or experimental projects. Donated and administered by HRLSD.

RECIPIENT: Grace J. Lyons, Public Library of the District of Columbia.

Bailey K. Howard Award:
see **ALA Goal Award.**

(John Phillip) Immroth Memorial Award for Intellectual Freedom

An annual award, established in 1976, of $500 and a plaque presented to a fighter for intellectual freedom who has made a notable contribution to intellectual freedom and demonstrated remarkable personal courage. Donated and administered by the Intellectual Freedom Round Table.

RECIPIENT: Irene Turin, Island Trees School District, Levittown, New York.

J. Morris Jones Award:
see **ALA Goal Award.**

Kohlstedt Exhibit Award

A citation and plaque, established in 1972, given each year at the Exhibits Round Table Banquet recognizing the best single and multiple booth displays at the Annual Conference. The criteria on which judgment is made are as follows: Clear identification of exhibitor and product or service offered, availability of staff, and accessibility of product or service; effective use of design elements such as colors, shapes and textures and effectiveness of graphics in communicating about product or service; neat, uncluttered appearance and arrangement of booth(s) for convenient flow of traffic. All booths in each year's Annual Conference exhibits are eligible for the awards even though their companies or organizations are not members of ERT.

RECIPIENTS: Single booth: Bhaktive-Danta Book Trust, Los Angeles.
Multiple booths: 3M Company, Minneapolis.

Library Research Round Table Research Award

An award established in 1975 to encourage excellence in library research. No more than two awards of $500 each are presented annually to the persons submitting the best completed research reports. Research papers completed in the pursuit of an academic degree are not eligible. Donated and administered by LRRT.

RECIPIENTS: Robert W. Burns, Jr., Colorado State University.
Herbert S. White and Karen N. Hasenjager, Indiana University.

(Joseph W.) Lippincott Award

An award of $1,000, an engraved medal, and a citation of achievement, established in 1937, presented annually to a librarian for distinguished service in the profession of librarianship, such service to include outstanding participation in the activities of professional library associations, notable published professional writing, or other significant activity on behalf of the profession and its aims. Donated by Joseph W. Lippincott. Administered by the ALA Awards Committee.

RECIPIENT: Virginia Lacy Jones, Atlanta University School of Library Service.

(Margaret) Mann Citation

An annual citation, established in 1950, made to a cataloger or classifier, not necessarily an American, for outstanding professional achievement in the areas of cataloging or classification either through publication of significant professional literature, participation in professional cataloging associations, introduction of new techniques of recognized importance, or outstanding work in teaching within the past five years. Donated and administered by the Cataloging and Classification Section, Resources and Technical Services Division.

RECIPIENT: Phyllis Richmond, Case Western Reserve University School of Library Science.

(Isadore Gilbert) Mudge Citation

A citation, established in 1958, to be given at the Annual Conference of ALA to a person who has made a distinguished contribution to reference librarianship. This contribution may take the form of an imaginative and constructive program in a particular library, the writing of a significant book or articles in the reference field, creative and inspirational teaching of reference service, or other noteworthy activities that stimulate reference librarians to more distinguished performance. Donated and administered by the Reference and Adult Services Division.

RECIPIENT: Bohdan S. Wynar, President, Libraries Unlimited, Inc., Littleton, Colorado.

(John) Newbery Medal

A medal, established in 1921, presented annually to the author of the most distinguished contribution to American literature for children published in the United States in the preceding year. The recipient must be a citizen or resident of the United States. Donated by Daniel Melcher. Administered by the Association for Library Service to Children.

RECIPIENT: Mildred D. Taylor, *Roll of Thunder, Hear My Cry* (Dial).

(Eunice Rockwell) Oberly Memorial Award

A biennial award, established in 1923, given in odd-numbered years, consisting of a citation and a cash award from the income of the Oberly Memorial Fund, and presented to an American citizen who compiles the best bibliography in the field of agriculture or one of the related sciences in the two-year period preceding the year in which the award is made. Made possible by a fund established by colleagues in memory of Eunice Rockwell Oberly. Administered by the Association of College and Research Libraries, Agriculture and Biological Sciences Section.

RECIPIENT: Helen Purdy Beale, Ridgefield, Connecticut (posthumously).

Shirley Olafson Memorial Award:
see **Scholarships and Grants.**

(Esther J.) Piercy Award

An annual citation, established in 1968, presented in recognition of a contribution to librarianship in the field of technical services by younger members of the profession. The recipient is a librarian with not more than ten years of professional experience who has shown outstanding promise for continuing contributions and leadership in any of the fields comprising technical services by means of (a) leadership in professional associations at local, state, regional, or national levels; (b) contributions to the development, application, or utilization of new or improved methods, techniques, and routines; (c) a significant contribution to professional literature; (d) studies or research in technical services. The award is given each year in which the jury believes that there is a qualified recipient. Donated and administered by the Resources and Technical Services Division. (Not awarded in 1977.)

(Herbert) Putnam Honor Fund Award: see **Scholarships and Grants.**

Resources and Technical Services Division Resources Scholarship Award

An annual award, established in 1975, consisting of a citation and a $1,000 scholarship grant. The citation is presented to the author or authors of an outstanding monograph, published article, or original paper on acquisitions pertaining to college or university libraries. The scholarship grant is given to the library school of the winner's choice. Donated by Arnold Santos and National Library Service, Inc., and administered by the RTSD Resources Section.

RECIPIENT: Herbert S. White, for "Publishers, Libraries, and Costs of Journal Subscriptions in Times of Funding Retrenchment," *Library Quarterly* (October 1976).

(John R. Rowe) Memorial Award

An annual award of $500, established in 1965, made to an individual or group to aid or improve some particular aspect of librarianship or library service on the basis of need in the profession or in the operation of professional library associations. Donated and administered by the Exhibits Round Table. (Not awarded in 1977.)

(Distinguished Library Service Award for) School Administrators

An annual citation, established in 1969, presented to a person directly responsible for the administration of a school or group of schools who has made a unique and sustained contribution toward furthering the role of the library and its development in elementary and/or secondary education. Two meritorious school administrators may be cited each year. Sponsored and administered by the American Association of School Librarians.

RECIPIENT: John M. Franco, Rochester (New York) City Schools.

School Library Media Program of the Year Award

A $5,000 cash award, established in 1975, presented annually to the school system that displays outstanding achievement in providing exemplary library media programs in its elementary schools. Up to five school systems can receive national finalist awards and be awarded citations of achievement. Donated by Encyclopaedia Britannica. Administered by the American Association of School Librarians.

RECIPIENT: Los Alamitos School District (California).

(Charles) Scribner's Sons Award: see Scholarships and Grants.

(Ralph R.) Shaw Award for Library Literature

An award of $500 and a citation, established in 1959 as the Scarecrow Press Award for Library Literature and named for Ralph R. Shaw in 1976, presented to an American librarian to recognize an outstanding contribution to library literature issued during the three years preceding the presentation. The award will be given only when a title merits such recognition. Donated by the Scarecrow Press. Administered by the ALA Awards Committee.

RECIPIENT: Kathleen Molz, Columbia University School of Library Service, for *Federal Policy and Library Support* (MIT Press).

Trustee Citations

A citation, established in 1941, presented to each of two outstanding trustees in actual service during part of the calendar year preceding the presentation for distinguished service to library development on the local, state, or national level. Equal consideration is to be given to trustees of small and large public libraries. Donated by ALA. Administered by the American Library Trustee Association.

RECIPIENTS: C.E. Campbell Beall, West Virginia State Library Commission. Daniel W. Casey, Onondaga County (New York) Public Library.

(Laura Ingalls) Wilder Medal

An award, established in 1954, made to an author or illustrator whose books published in the United States have made a substantial and lasting contribution to children's literature over a period of years. Donated and administered by the Association for Library Service to Children. Presented every five years, this award will next be given in 1980.

(Halsey W.) Wilson Library Recruitment Award

An annual award consisting of $1,000 presented to any local, state, or regional library association, any library school, or any other appropriate group concerned with recruitment to the profession. Donated by the H.W. Wilson Company. Administered by the ALA Awards Committee.

(Not awarded in 1977.)

(H.W.) Wilson Library Periodical Award

An annual award, established in 1960, consisting of $250 and a certificate presented to a periodical published by a local, state, or regional library, library group, or library association in the United States or Canada that has made an outstanding contribution to librarianship. (This excludes publications of ALA, CLA, and their divisions.) The award is presented only in those years when a periodical merits such recognition. Donated by the H.W. Wilson Company. Administered by the ALA Awards Committee.

RECIPIENT: *Utah Libraries*, Blaine H. Hall, editor.

SCHOLARSHIPS

(David H.) Clift Scholarship

Approved by the ALA Council, January 1969, a scholarship in the amount of $3,000 given annually to a worthy student to begin library education at the graduate level without regard to race, creed, color, national origin, or sex. The recipient must be a U.S. or Canadian citizen and must enter a formal program of graduate study leading to a master's degree at an ALA-accredited school. Funded by an annual contribution from the Xerox Publishing Division and individual contributions, as many scholarships as possible are awarded, depending upon the total amount of contributed funds. The award may be withheld in any year. Administered by the ALA Awards Committee and the Library Education Division.

RECIPIENT: Daniel J. Lombardo, Wethersfield, Connecticut.

(Louise) Giles Minority Scholarship

Established in 1972 by the ALA Council, and renamed in memory of Louise Giles in 1977, the Minority Scholarship is a $3,000 cash award made to a worthy student who is a U.S. or Canadian citizen and is also a member of a principal minority group (American Indian or Alaskan native, Asian or Pacific Islander, Black, or Hispanic). The recipient must enter a formal program of graduate study leading to a master's degree at an ALA-accredited library school. Funded by an annual contribution from the Xerox Publishing Division and individual contributions, as many scholarships as possible are awarded, depending on the total contributed funds. Administered by the ALA Awards Committee and the Office for Library Personnel Resources Advisory Committee.

RECIPIENT: Patricia White-Williams, Silver Spring, Maryland.

GRANTS

Asia Foundation Grant

Grants, established in 1977, given annually to assist Asian students in ALA-accredited library schools in the United States to attend professional library meetings and to provide one-year memberships in ALA to select Asian librarians. Donated by the Asia Foundation, Administered by the Library Education Division.

RECIPIENTS: Mohammad Zummurad (Pakistan), Drexel Graduate School of Library Science.

Takako Akaboshi (Japan), Western Michigan School of Librarianship.

Chirawan Bkakdibutr (Thailand), Texas Woman's School of Library Science.

Nongnath Intasorn (Thailand), Texas Woman's School of Library Science.

Supanee Varatorn (Thailand), Kent State School of Library Science.

Mohammad Khan (Pakistan), State University of New York (Geneseo) School of Library and Information Science.

Ladda Yindeemak (Thailand), Indiana University Graduate Library School.

Amporn Tikhara (Thailand), Kent State School of Library Science.

Grolier National Library Week Grant

An annual $1,000 cash award, established in 1953, presented to the state library association that submits the best plan for a public relations program to be conducted in the year in which the grant is presented. Donated by Grolier Educational Corporation. Administered by the National Library Week Committee.

RECIPIENT: New Jersey Library Association.

(Frederic G.) Melcher Scholarship

An annual $4,000 scholarship established in 1956 to encourage young people to enter the field of library service to children. Donated and administered by the Association for Library Service to Children.

RECIPIENT: Lynn J. Melton, Red Wing (Minnesota) Public Library.

(Shirley) Olofson Memorial Award

An annual cash award, established in 1972, made to individuals to attend their second Annual Conference of ALA. The recipients must be members of ALA and be potential or current members of the Junior Members Round Table. Donated and administered by JMRT.

RECIPIENTS: Dallas Bagby, Winnipeg, Manitoba.

June Breland, State College, Mississippi.
Susan Broomall, Orlando.
Carolyn Clark, Ann Arbor.
Pamela Cravey, Atlanta.
Mary Johnson, Wichita, Texas.
Barbara Burkert Kiffmeyer, Bayside, Wisconsin.
Judith Ross, Middleton, Wisconsin.
Cerise Soroka, Charleston, South Carolina.

Professional Development Grant

Annual cash awards, established in 1975, are presented to librarians to attend the Annual Conference of ALA. The recipients must be members of ALA and the Junior Members Round Table. Donated by the 3M Company. Administered by JMRT.

RECIPIENTS: Robert E. Halcums, Portsmouth (Virginia) Public Library.

Paula C. Murphy, Governors State University Learning Resources Center, Park Forest South, Illinois.

Mary C. Nicolson, University of Idaho Library.

Martin F. Onieal, Framingham (Massachusetts) Library.

(Herbert) Putnam Honor Fund Award

An award, established in 1939, presented at intervals as a $500 grant-in-aid to an American librarian of outstanding ability for travel, writing, or other use that might improve his or her service to the library profession or to society. Presented when the income from the Herbert W. Putnam Honor Fund accumulates to $500. Administered by the ALA Awards Committee.

(Not awarded in 1977.)

(Charles) Scribner's Sons Award

Four annual $250 cash awards, established in 1970, presented to two school librarians and two public library children's librarians to enable them to attend ALA's Annual Conference. The recipients must also be members of the Association for Library Service to Children, have one to five years of library experience, and never have attended an ALA Annual Conference. Donated by Charles Scribner's Sons. Administered by ALSC.

RECIPIENTS:
Margaret Anne Gore, Meridian (Mississippi) Public Library.
Harriet McClaine, Blatchley Junior High, Sitka, Arkansas.
Evelyn Mott, Genessee (Michigan) Schools.
Kay Taylor, Sheppard Memorial Library, Greenvills, North Carolina.

Other Awards and Prizes

The following are selected awards given by organizations and agencies other than ALA and its units in 1977.

(Herbert Baxter) Adams Prize

$300 offered biennially since 1903 by the American Historical Association for the best book on European history by an American author who has published no more than two books.

RECIPIENT: *Recasting Bourgeois Europe* by Charles S. Maier (Princeton University Press).

(Jane) Addams Children's Book Award

A hand-illuminated certificate given annually since 1953 to a worthy author by the Women's International League for Peace and Freedom to encourage the publication of children's books of literary merit with constructive themes.

RECIPIENT: Milton Melzer for *Never to Forget: The Jews of the Holocaust* (Harper & Row).

American Academy and Institute of Arts and Letters Awards

$7,180 for the Academy in Rome Fellowship in Creative Writing.

RECIPIENT: Daniel M. Epstein, poet.

$3,000 each to writers in various categories.

RECIPIENTS:
Biographer and critic: Walter J. Bate.
Journalist: John McPhee.
Novelists: Joseph McElroy and Anne Tyler.
Novelist and Critic: Paul Theroux.
Poets: A.R. Ammons, Cynthia Macdonald, James Schuyler, Robert Watson, and Charles Wright. $1,000 for distinguished services to the arts.

RECIPIENT: James Laughlin, president of New Directions.

Gold medal for the novel, awarded every six years.

RECIPIENT: Saul Bellow.

(Hans Christian) Andersen International Children's Book Medals

Given biennially by the International Board on Books for Young People (IBBY) to a living author (since 1956) and an illustrator (since 1966) for distinguished contributions to children's literature.

(To be awarded in 1978.)

(Joseph L.) Andrews Bibliographical Award

Established in 1967, a citation presented annually by the American Association of Law Libraries for the most significant contribution to legal bibliographical literature.

RECIPIENT: *Criminology and the Administration of Criminal Justice* by Leon Radzinowicz and Roger Hood (London: Mansell).

Bancroft Prizes

Established in 1948 under the will of Frederic Bancroft and presented by Columbia University, three annual prizes of $4,000 given for distinguished works on (a) American history (including biography), (b) American diplomacy, and (c) international relations.

RECIPIENTS:
Class and Community: The Industrial Revolution in Lynn by Alan Dawley (Harvard University Press).
The Minute Men and Their World by Robert A. Gross (Hill & Wang).
Slave Population and Economy in Jamaica, 1807-1834 by Barry W. Higman (Cambridge University Press).

Besterman Medal

Given annually by the (British) Library Association since 1970 for an outstanding bibliography or guide to literature published in the United Kingdom during the preceding year.

RECIPIENT: *Guide to Official Statistics*, No. 1 (1976) by Central Statistical Office (H.M.S.O).

(Albert J.) Beveridge Award

$5,000 drawn from the Albert J. Beveridge Fund for the best book in English on the history of the United States, Canada, or

Latin America which is also the first or second work of the author. Offered biennially from 1939 to 1949 and since given annually. Administered by the American Historical Society.

RECIPIENT: *The Enlightenment in America* by Henry F. May (Oxford University Press).

BIB: see **Bratislava International Biennial of Illustrations.**

Booker Prize for Fiction

£5,000 and a trophy awarded annually since 1969 by the National Book League of England for the best novel published in English in the British Commonwealth, Ireland, or South Africa.

RECIPIENT: Paul Scott for *Staying On* (Heineman, 1976).

Boston Globe—Horn Book Awards

Three $200 prizes given annually since 1967, one for the best work of fiction for children, one for the best illustrated children's book, and one for the best nonfiction work for children.

RECIPIENTS:
Fiction: *Child of the Owl* by Laurence Yep (Harper).
Illustration: *Granfá Grig Had a Pig and Other Rhymes without Reeson from Mother Goose*, compiled and illustrated by Wallace Tripp (Little).
Nonfiction: *Chance Luck and Destiny* by Peter Dickinson (Atlantic Little).

Bratislava International Biennial (BIB) of Illustrations

Given at the biennial exhibition of Bratislava, Czechoslovakia, for children's book illustrations that have won national or international awards and for illustrations that have not received any awards. A grand prize is offered, and gold, silver, and bronze plaques are given in each competition.

(To be awarded in 1978.)

(John) Burroughs Medal

Offered annually since 1926 by the John Burroughs Memorial Association at the American Museum of Natural History for the foremost literary work in the field of nature.

(Not awarded in 1977.)

(Melville) Cane Award

Established in 1960, $500 donated by Harcourt Brace Jovanovich, Inc., given by the Poetry Society of America, one year to honor the best published work on poetry or on a poet, the next year to the best book of poems.

RECIPIENT: *Idea of the Canterbury Tales* by Donald R. Howard (University of California Press).

Carey-Thomas Award

A citation given annually since 1942 by *Publishers Weekly* for a "distinguished project of creative publishing." Candidates are nominated by the Bowker book review staff.

RECIPIENT: Edmund Engleman for *Berggasse 19* (photographs of Sigmund Freud's home and office in Vienna in 1938).

Carnegie Medal

Awarded annually since 1937 by the (British) Library Association for the most outstanding children's book published in Great Britain.

RECIPIENT: Jon Marks for *Thunder and Lightnings* (Kestrel Books, 1976).

Copernicus Award

$10,000 given annually to a poet over 45 years of age, recognizing the complete work of the poet and his or her contribution to poetry as a cultural force. Sponsored by the Copernicus Society. Administered by the Academy of American Poets.

RECIPIENT: Muriel Rukeyser.

Drexel University Graduate School of Library Science Distinguished Achievement Award

A citation awarded annually since 1959 by the Executive Board of the Library School Alumni Association to a person who has made a substantial contribution to the development of librarianship as a profession.

(Not awarded in 1977.)

(Ralph Waldo) Emerson Award

Established in 1959, $2,500 given annually by Phi Beta Kappa for an interpretive, historical, philosophical, or religious study written in the tradition of humane learning.

RECIPIENT: *Peasants into Frenchmen: The Modernization of Rural France* by Eugen Weber (Stanford University Press).

English Medal Award

Given annually since 1947 by the Canadian Library Association for the best English Canadian children's book of the year.

RECIPIENT: *Mouse Woman and the Vanished Princesses* by Christie Harris (McClellan & Stewart).

(Eleanor) Farjeon Award

Given annually since 1967 by the Children's Book Circle of England to an individual for "distinguished services to children's books."

RECIPIENT: Elaine Moss (1976).

(Christian) Gauss Award

Established in 1950 by the Phi Beta Kappa Senate, $2,500 given annually for the best book of literary scholarship or criticism published in the United States.

RECIPIENT: *Dostoevski: The Seeds of Revolt, 1821-49* by Joseph Frank (Princeton University Press).

Gavel Award

Inaugurated by the American Bar Association in 1958, a gavel presented annually to recognize an outstanding media contribution "to public understanding of American legal and judicial systems." Awards for the literary category began in 1964.

RECIPIENT: Archibald Cox for *The Role of the Supreme Court in American Government* (Oxford University Press).

Golden Kite Award

Given annually to a children's book of merit by the Society of Children's Book Writers.

RECIPIENT: *One More Flight* by Eve Bunting.

(Kate) Greenaway Medal

Given annually since 1956 by the (British) Library Association for the best illustrated book for children published in Great Britain.

RECIPIENT: Gail E. Haley for *The Post Office Cat* (Bodley Head, 1976).

Horn Book: see **Boston Globe—Horn Book Awards.**

(Amelia Frances) Howard-Gibbon Medal

Given annually by the Canadian Library Association for the best-illustrated children's book of the year.

RECIPIENT: *Down by Jim Long's Stage* (Newfoundland: Breakwater Books).

Howells Medal

Established in 1921 by the American Academy of Arts and Letters to honor William Dean Howells and given every five years to the author of the most distinguished work of American fiction published during the preceding five years.

(To be awarded in 1980.)

Hugo Award

A chrome-plated rocket ship, presented by the World Science Fiction Convention for the best science fiction novel of the year.

RECIPIENT: *Where Late the Sweet Birds Sang* by Kate Wilhelm (Harper & Row, Pocket Books).

IBBY: see **(Hans Christian) Andersen International Children's Book Medals.**

International Reading Association Children's Book Award

Established in 1974, a $1,000 prize given for a children's book by an author showing unusual promise.
RECIPIENT: *A String in the Harp* by Nancy Bond (Atheneum/Margaret McElderry).

(Association of) Jewish Libraries Award

Given annually for the most outstanding contribution in the field of Jewish literature for children.
RECIPIENT: *Never to Forget: The Jews of the Holocaust* by Milton Melzer (Harper & Row).

Kerlan Award

Given annually in recognition of the total output of a writer for children by the Kerlan Collection, a research center for children's literature at the University of Minnesota.
RECIPIENT: Wanda Gág (posthumously).

(Coretta Scott) King Award

Established in 1969, $250, a plaque, and a set of *Encyclopedia Britannica,* 15th ed., presented annually at the ALA Annual Conference for a book written in the spirit of the life and work of Martin Luther King, Jr. Donated by the John H. Johnson Publishing Company and sponsored by an independent group of American librarians.
RECIPIENT: *Story of Stevie Wonder* by James Haskins (Lothrop).

(Otto) Kinkeldey Award

Established in 1967 and presented by the American Musicological Society, $400 and a scroll given annually to a U.S. or Canadian author who has published a notable full-length study in musicology during the previous year.
RECIPIENT: H.C. Robbins Landon for *Haydn in England, 1791-1795,* vol. 3 of *Haydn Chronicle and Works* (Indiana University Press).

Lamont Award

Given annually by the Academy of American Poets for a second book of poems.
RECIPIENT: Gerald Stern for *Lucky Life* (Houghton, Mifflin).

(James Russell) Lowell Prize

Established in 1968 by the Modern Language Association of America, a $1,000 prize given annually for an outstanding literary or linguistic study, a critical edition of an important work, or a critical biography.
RECIPIENT: *Dostoevski: The Seeds of Revolt, 1821-49* by Joseph Frank (Princeton University Press).

McColvin Medal

An annual award given since 1970 by the (British) Library Association to the author or compiler of an outstanding reference book published in Great Britain.
RECIPIENT: C.G. Allen for *A Manual of European Languages for Librarians* (Bowker, 1976).

(Lenore) Marshall Poetry Prize

$5,000 given annually to the author of the outstanding book of poems published in the United States, Cosponsored by *Saturday Review* and the New Hope Foundation.
RECIPIENT: *The Names of the Lost,* by Philip Levine (Atheneum).

(Samuel Eliot) Morison Award

$5,000, established in 1977 by the American Heritage Publishing Company, given annually to an author who carries on the tradition of the late historian that "good history is literature as well as high scholarship."
RECIPIENT: Joseph P. Lash for *Roosevelt and Churchill—The Partnership That Saved the West* (Norton).

National Book Awards

Awards of $1,000 given annually to recognize the most distinguished books in several categories. Administered from 1950 to 1974 by the National Book Committee in 1975 and 1976 by the American Academy and Institute of Arts and Letters, and in 1977 by the Association of American Publishers.
RECIPIENTS:
Biography: W.A. Swanberg for *Norman Thomas: The Last Idealist* (Scribners).
Children's Literature: Katherine Patterson for *The Master Puppeteer* (Thomas Y. Crowell).
Contemporary Thought: Bruno Bettelheim for *The Uses of Enchantment: The Meaning and Importance of Fairy Tales* (Knopf).
Fiction: Wallace Stegner for *The Spectator Bird* (Doubleday).
History: Irving Howe for *World of Our Fathers* (Harcourt, Brace, Jovanovich).
Poetry: Richard Eberhart for *Collected Poems, 1930-1976* (Oxford University Press).
Translation: Li Li Ch'en for *Master Tung's Western Chamber Romance: A Chinese Chantefable* (Cambridge University Press).
Special Citation: Alex Haley for *Roots* (Doubleday).

National Book Critics Circle Award

Established in 1975, and given annually for outstanding books in a number of catagories.
RECIPIENTS:
Criticism: *The Uses of Enchantment: The Meaning and Importance of Fairy Tales* by Bruno Bettelheim (Knopf).
Fiction: *October Light* by John Gardner (Knopf).
General Nonfiction: *The Woman Warrior: Memoirs of a Girlhood among Ghosts* by Maxine Hong Kingston (Knopf).
Poetry: *Geography III* by Elizabeth Bishop (Farrar, Straus & Giroux).
These awards were given in *January, 1977.* The 1978 awards were to be given next year but have not yet been reported in the AWs received by the library.

National Medal for Literature

Established in 1964 by the National Book Committee in memory of Harold K. Guinzburg, $10,000 and a bronze medal given annually to a living author in American literature. Administered in 1975 and 1976 by the American Academy and Institute of Arts and Letters and in 1977 by the Association of American Publishers.
RECIPIENT: Robert Lowell.

NCTE Award for Excellence in Poetry for Children

Given annually by the National Council of Teachers of English to a living American poet in recognition of his or her aggregate work.
RECIPIENT: David McCord.

Nobel Prize for Literature

Established by Alfred Bernhard Nobel (1833-96), first offered in 1901, a gold medal and a sum of money ($145,000 in 1977, given annually to an author for his total literary output. Administered by the Swedish Academy in Stockholm.
RECIPIENT: Vicente Aleixandre of Spain.

(Marcia C.) Noyes Award

Established in 1948 by the Medical Library Association, an engraved silver tray presented irregularly to recognize an outstanding medical librarian.
RECIPIENT: Alfred N. Brandon, New York Academy of Medicine.

P.E.N. Translation Prize

Established in 1962 by the P.E.N. American Center, $1,000 donated annually by the Book-of-the-Month Club and awarded for the best translation of a book into English from any language.
RECIPIENT: Gregory Rabassa for *The Autumn of the Patriarch* by Gabriel Marcia Marquez (Harper & Row).
Also, $500 donated annually by Goethe House for the best booklength translation from German into English.
RECIPIENT: Douglas Parmée for *An Exemplary Life* by Siegfried Lenz (Hill & Wang).

Phi Beta Kappa Award in Science

Established in 1958, $2,500 for the best book in the physical or biological sciences or in mathematics written by a scientist.

RECIPIENT: *The High Frontier: Human Colonies in Space* by Gerard K. O'Neill (Morrow).

(Edgar Allan) Poe Award

$5,000 given by the Copernicus Society of America to honor the continuing development of a poet 45 years old or younger. Administered by the Academy of American Poets.

RECIPIENT: Stan Rice for *Whiteboy* (Mudra).

(Edgar Allan) Poe Awards

Established in 1945 by the Mystery Writers of America, ceramic statuettes, given annually for outstanding contributions to various categories of mystery, crime, and suspense writing.

RECIPIENTS:
Critical Biographical Study: *Encyclopedia of Mystery and Detection* by Chris Steinbrunner and Otto Penzler (McGraw Hill).
First Novel: *The Thomas Berryman Number* by James Patterson (Little, Brown).
Fact Crime Book: *Blood and Money* by Thomas Thompson, (Doubleday).
Juvenile Mystery: *Are You in the House Alone?* by Richard Peck (Viking).
Mystery Novel: *Promised Land* by Robert Parker (Houghton Mifflin).
Paperback Mystery: *Confess, Fletch* by Robert Parker (Houghton Mifflin).

Porgie Awards

Established in 1977 by the *West Coast Review of Books* to recognize original paperbacks.

RECIPIENTS:
Fiction Based on Fact: *Pipeline* by Milt Machlin (Pyramid).
Milestone Award: *The Godson* by Gloria Vitaza Basile (Pinnacle).
Series: *American Bicentennial Series* by John Jake (Pyramid).

Pulitzer Prizes

Instituted in 1917 under the terms of the will of Joseph Pulitzer (1847-1911), a number of prizes, currently $1,000 each, awarded annually in various categories to American authors, in most instances for work concerning American society. The following are of special interest to librarians.

RECIPIENTS:
Biography: John E. Mack for *A Prince of Our Disorder: The Life of T.E. Lawrence* (Little, Brown).
Criticism: William McPherson, editor of "Book World" of the Washington Post.
Fiction: (Not awarded in 1977.)
History: David M. Potter for *The Impending Crisis*, Harper & Row).
Nonfiction: William Warner for *Beautiful Swimmers: Watermen, Crabs, and Chesapeake Bay* (Atlantic-Little Brown).
Poetry: James Merrill for *Divine Comedies* (Atheneum).

Ranganathan Award for Classification Research

Established in 1976 by the International Federation for Documentation, a certificate of merit honoring the late S.R. Ranganathan and given annually to persons recognized for their outstanding contribution in classification research in recent years.

RECIPIENT: Derek William Austin, British Library.

Regina Medal

Given annually since 1959 by the Catholic Library Association to an author, publisher, editor, illustrator, or other person for dedication to children's literature, irrespective of religion or race.

RECIPIENT: Marcia Brown.

Shelley Memorial Award

$3,000 given annually for a poet's total volume of work by the Poetry Society of America.

RECIPIENT: Muriel Rukeyser.

(Constance Lindsay) Skinner Award

A bronze plaque given biennially since 1940 by the Women's National Book Association to a bookwoman resident in the United States for a sustained contribution to the world of books over a period of time or for a single achievement.

(To be awarded in 1978).

(W.H.) Smith & Son Literary Award

Established in 1959, a £1,000 award offered annually by the London bookseller W.H. Smith to an author of the British Commonwealth who has made a significant contribution to English literature.

RECIPIENT: Ronald Lewin for *Slim: The Standard Bearer* (Leo Cooper, 1976).

Special Libraries Association Hall of Fame

Established in 1959, an engraved medallion and a certificate given to recognize persons who over a period of years have made outstanding contributions to SLA.

RECIPIENT: Grieg G. Aspnes, Library of Cargill, Inc., Minneapolis.

Special Libraries Association Professional Award

Established in 1949, a scroll and medallion to recognize notable professional achievement in the field of special librarianship.

RECIPIENT: Audrey M. Grosch, Wilson Library, University of Minnesota.

Wheatley Medal

Awarded annually since 1962 by the (British) Library Association for an outstanding index published in the United Kingdom during the preceding three years.

RECIPIENT: Index to Vol. II of *The Works of John Wesley: The Appeals to Men of Reason and Religion and Certain Related Open Letters* by John A. Vickers (Clarendon Press).

(Walt) Whitman Award

$1,000 given annually to an unpublished poet by the Copernicus Society of America. Administered by the Academy of American Poets.

RECIPIENT: Lauren Shakeley for *Guilty Bystander* (to be published by Random House).

(Woodrow) Wilson Foundation Award

Established in 1947 and recommended by a committee of the American Political Science Association, $1,000 given annually for the "best book of the year in the field of government and democracy."

RECIPIENT: *The Changing American Voter* Norman Nye, Sidney Verba, and John Petrocik (Harvard University Press).

(Carter G.) Woodson Book Award

Established in 1973 and administered by the National Council for Social Studies, a plaque awarded annually to encourage the writing of sensitive and realistic social science books for children on topics related to ethnic minorities.

RECIPIENT: *The Trouble They Seen* by Dorothy Sterling (Doubleday).

Beta Phi Mu

Founded at the University of Illinois in 1948 to recognize high scholarship in the study of librarianship and to sponsor appropriate professional and scholarly projects, Beta Phi Mu, the library science honorary, had 40 chapters in 40 accredited library schools and 15,000 active members in 1977. Invitations to membership are based on a high scholastic achievement in the study of librarianship. Membership is open to all qualified students in accredited library schools on recommendation of their deans or directors. Students in schools without local chapters may qualify for general membership.

Beta Phi Mu annually presents an award, administered by ALA, to recognize distinguished service to library education. Russell E. Bidlack, Dean of the School of Library Science in the University of Michigan, received the award in 1977

A scholarship fund is maintained to assist students in foreign library study, continuing education, and master's-level studies. In 1977 three students received $1,000 tuition scholarships for beginning professional study. The recipients were Rebecca A. Gonzalez at the University of Texas, William Michael Serban at the University of Pittsburgh, and Valerie Jean Andersen at Emory University.

During 1977, Beta Phi Mu published *The Library at Mount Vernon,* by Frances Laverne Carroll and Mary Meacham. The 12th number in the Beta Phi Mu Chap Book Series, the book is a treatise on George Washington's private library.

Officers for 1977 were Howard W. Winger, President; Blanche Woolls, Vice-President and President-Elect; Jessie Carney Smith, Past President; Marilyn P. Whitmore, Treasurer; Frank B. Sessa, Executive Secretary; and Mary Y. Tomaino, Administrative Secretary. On the Board of Directors were Josephine McSweeney, Hester B. Slocum, Mary Alice Hunt, Herman L. Totten, Hazel Marie Johnson, and Harriet Miller. The Advisory Committee of Chapter Representatives elected George Hebben as President.   HOWARD W. WINGER

Bibliographic Processing Centers

Bibliography is usually defined as "a list of sources of information on a subject or period or a list of the literary works of an author or publisher." By popular usage within the profession, the term *processing center* has come to mean a central facility for handling processes related to librarianship, more specifically, processes of acquisitions, cataloging, and physical preparation of books for the shelves.

Centralized processing centers were one of the initial forms of administrative cooperation between libraries in the areas of acquisitions and cataloging. The various processing programs have expanded to include other library functions, and with the onset of the library technology of the last decade mechanization has begun to give way to automation of many processes.

Many librarians continue to believe that there is a substantial reduction in costs resulting from cooperative processing, but more importantly cooperative processing has created and fostered a basis for the other types of interlibrary cooperation that become more important as each day passes. The continuous evolution of library technology, library economics, and the library environment and the interaction of these components of the library universe mandate effective programs of resource sharing.

Once administrators have cracked the doors to sharing responsibilities, those doors are likely to open farther in light of new opportunities. Further administrative procedures are likely to be developed to incorporate the involvement of several libraries in common services. With the establishment of any center of activity exterior to any one library, it is probable that functions carried out by that center will grow. This tendency is a prime factor in looking at the evolution of bibliographic processing centers.

Shrinking Number. Bibliographic processing centers are not limited to the scope of technical processing of library materials. To be sure, these activities were one of the first, but other library functions have come to these centers. The dramatic growth of on-line services for libraries has revolutionized the technical services processing centers specializing in acquisitions, cataloging, and physical preparation of books. Some centers have closed because they have been unable to make the transition from mechanization to automation or could not remain competitive with the services provided by the commercial sector. In 1961 there were more than 160 technical processing centers listed in the directory compiled by the Technical Services Directors of Processing Centers Discussion Group of ALA's Resources and Technical Services Division. By 1977 this number had shrunk to about 70.

This revolution in automation has helped to carry the tenets of centralized processing into other areas of library activity. The advent of on-line services for the searching of bibliographic data bases compiled by abstracting and indexing services has suggested that handling these functions on a centralized basis might be viable and efficient. Many of the reasons for having centralized cataloging—concentration of skilled staff, sharing of tools, streamlined procedures—are logically carried over to centralized information retrieval. A skilled, trained searching staff can be used by a large number of libraries in such a center. The benefits of the on-line searching of bibliographic data bases can be made available to many libraries that otherwise could not provide this service to their users because of the high costs of a skilled staff and equipment.

The METRO Program of the Bibliographical Center for Research (BCR) in Denver has added to its growing number of libraries obtaining on-line service. Through a program called Central Access, BCR acts as a broker that contracts with the major on-line vendors for groups of libraries. By concentrating skilled staff at BCR and performing large amounts of searching from one contract with the vendors, BCR can make access to these services available to thousands of people through hundreds of libraries that are unable to operate independent services locally. South Dakota has arranged for its State Library in Pierre to operate a bibliographic data base searching service for its state government reference services through a brokerage contract with BCR. In addition, other libraries throughout the state are receiving similar services directly from BCR on Central Access. During 1977 this mix of activities brought these information-rich services to South Dakotans on an economical basis.

Multistate Services. Another early form of bibliographic processing centers to develop was the statewide or regional (multistate) union catalog centers for the centralized processing of interlibrary loan requests. The range of service runs from simple location services through actual document delivery. Examples of such programs are the Union Catalogue of Pennsylvania, the INTERLOAN Program of the Bibliographical Center for Research, and the Pacific Northwest Bibliographic Center (PNBC) in Seattle. These operations are also being affected by the changing library scene, and they continue to function with varying degrees of success. In 1977 the volume of requests processed through BCR contined to decline. There were more than 20,000 requests per year in the early 1970's; about 5,000 were projected for 1978. On the other hand, PNBC's activity continues to expand, sometimes almost uncomfortably so, to the point that 1978 promised to inundate the operation with nearly 80,000 requests.

There are numerous factors determining why there is variation in usage, growth, and decline. One of these factors is that on-line technical services systems such as OCLC and Stanford's BALLOTS continue to expand. These systems capture holdings and provide locations of materials for interlibrary loan largely as by-product operations, as opposed to the add-on operations of the regional interlibrary loan centers. This means that in OCLC and BALLOTS holdings are established in an on-line union catalog, the computer system being utilized primarily for shared cataloging by a large number of libraries. Looking at the data base's bibliographic records to locate a title is a fairly simple process. Locating a title is enhanced by the low additional cost of doing so once the use of the cataloging record is paid for and is made easier by the standardization of the records in content and format as enforced by the system itself.

In contrast, the traditional union catalog activity requires its contributors to generate additional cards. Depending on the process used for card production by the contributing library, this can be expensive. Cards must then be interfiled with the catalog, and the locations of the many libraries contributing a title must be blended onto one card in order to save space and make the catalog efficient. Retrieval must be done by hand. If the catalog has not been uniformly maintained throughout its existence and if it is in multiple sections and several sequences, the process is slow, cumbersome, and costly in comparison with electronic retrieval.

Manual Process Questioned. The viability of the manual process is increasingly being called into question, and 1977 saw the creation of more on-line data bases of bibliographic holdings to replace manual files. Florida has successfully converted the manual records of many of its resource libraries into machine-readable format retrievable electronically. Ohio—the birthplace of OCLC, perhaps the most significant automation activity in librarianship—has also converted the holdings of many of its major resource libraries into a machine-readable data base. Other states and individual libraries have moved from using bibliographic processing centers for interlibrary loan to constructing computer output microfilm (COM) data bases of bibliographic holdings. Inexpensive up to the point at which recurring cumulations become very expensive, COM union catalogs offer many librarians and libraries a solid and inexpensive bridge to on-line processes.

Another variation of the bibliographic processing center is the reference question answering service. Rapidly escalating costs for the many reference works needed to provide adequate services have promulgated the concept of housing staff and resources centrally to provide this service to a large number of libraries on a lower cost-per-question basis. Smaller libraries buying into this shared enterprise benefit since they likely would not be able even to begin to provide comprehensive service. Yet even this area is changing due to pressure from technology. More and more reference sources become on-line tools; and private entrepreneurs, who see the opportunity to offer a moneymaking service, are building an information-on-demand business.

Bibliographic processing centers cover a broad spectrum of interlibrary cooperation activity. Virtually all of the areas are under scrutiny by the profession as technology, library economics, and a changing library environment interact to bring pressure to bear on this facet of librarianship. Change is not necessarily bad unless the emphasis is on the structure of how librarians accomplish their professional roles and concerns. As bibliographic processing centers change, the emphasis must be on the continuation of effective and efficient services to users rather than on the structure of how it is done. The year 1977 has provided a mere taste of changes to come in bibliographic processing centers. (See also Networks.)   DONALD B. SIMPSON

Bibliography and Indexes

An examination of the *American Book Publishing Record* (*BRP*) shows that the number of bibliographies published during 1977 increased by about 20 per cent over 1976. Table 1 shows the overall trend for bibliographies appearing in *BPR*, divided into categories defined by Dewey subject classes. Because of the listing policy of *BPR*, the figures include only monographic items and thus underestimate the total production of bibliographies by excluding government documents and other nontrade items.

Except for the general class (000), there were increases in each class and a substantial rise in several areas, particularly in literature. Almost 40 per cent of all the items were in the social sciences, and more than half of these were published by the Council of Planning Librarians. The Council is a prolific producer of narrowly defined subject bibliographies that range in size from as few as five pages to multivolume compilations. Since 1959 more than 1,250 have been produced, and the series now includes several indexes to individual numbers.

Table 2 estimates the proportion of bibliographies to all books listed in *BPR* for six years. While the trend indicates a slight increase in the proportion, most of the increase can be accounted for by seven very active publishers. *BPR* listings indicate that there has been an increasing concentration in bibliography publishing and that more than half of the compilations are now published by just seven organizations or firms. It is not clear, however, whether this is actually the case or whether these publishers are simply more successful in getting their materials cataloged and listed in *BPR*.

1977 might best be characterized as a planning interlude before the anticipated major changes in the traditional bibliographic apparatus. Several events took place that should have considerable impact on access (intellectual and physical, subject, and other approaches) within the next few years.

At the national level, the Library of Congress has begun to distribute MARC records for the items included in the U.S. Government Printing Office's increasingly comprehensive *Monthly Catalog*. Exchange of MARC records has also begun between the United States and Great Britain, and the initiation of a computer output microfiche catalog of the Division for the Blind and Physically Handicapped was undertaken as a step toward a union list for materials in nontraditional formats. In anticipation of having all current cataloging in machine-readable form by the end of 1981 and of the "freezing" of its card catalog on January 1, 1980, the Library of Congress has begun providing its general patrons on-line access to its collections via video terminals located just off the main reading room. The Network Advisory Group of LC also published at midyear its wide-ranging report, *Toward a National Library and Information Service Network: The Library Bibliographical Component*.

As a part of its new responsibilities under the revised copyright law, the Copyright Office has made significant progress toward the on-line production of its *Catalog of Copyright Entries*, a critical tool in efforts to achieve complete national bibliographic control.

Other events of national and international significance during 1977 included the publication of the proceedings of the 1976 Chicago conference, *Prospects for Change in Bibliographic Control* (University of Chicago, 1977). New bibliographies and subject indexes, expanded from the annual UNESCO reports, are identified in the continuing surveys of previous years' achievements. The 1975 summary, compiled by Mary Jane Gibson and entitled "United States of America National Bibliographical and Abstracting Services and Related Activities in 1975," appeared in *RQ* (Winter 1976), pp. 93-119. The report covering 1976 was to be published in early 1978.

The International Congress on National Bibliographies was held in Paris in September. A working document, "The National Bibliography: Requirements and Specifications," published in the *UNESCO Bulletin for Libraries* (July-August 1977), was discussed by representatives from more than 60 countries. The discussions and recommendations on this subject and other matters of bibliographic interest will be published by UNESCO and submitted to its member nations.

Table 1. Bibliographies and Indexes in BPR: 1975-77*

Subject	Category	1975	1976	Change from 1975	1977	Change from 1976
000	General	77	54	− 23	27	− 27
100	Philosophy, Psychology	9	6	− 3	19	+ 13
200	Religion	9	12	+ 3	14	+ 2
300	Social Sciences, Education	156	230	+ 74	246	+ 16
400	Language	14	6	− 8	9	+ 3
500	Pure Science	16	14	− 2	19	+ 5
600	Applied Science	32	29	− 3	39	+ 10
700	Fine Arts	51	34	− 17	49	+ 15
800	Literature	80	66	− 14	117	+ 51
900	Travel, History, other	57	62	+ 5	81	+ 19
	Totals	501	513	+ 12	620	+ 107

* Because November and December data for 1977 were unavailable, extrapolations were made from the corresponding months of 1976.

Table 2. Comparison of Estimates of Bibliography and Book Publishing: 1972-77*

	1972	1973	1974	1975	1976	1977
Bibliographies	416	519	568	501	513	620
Total New Books	38,654	39,951	40,846	39,372	32,025	35,304
Percentage of Bibliographies to New Books	1.1	1.3	1.4	1.3	1.6	1.8

* Because November and December 1977 estimates were unavailable, the corresponding months of 1976 were substituted.

Numerous workshops and courses designed for working librarians and library school students in on-line searching and other computer-based bibliographic techniques were held throughout the year. The outlook for the future of bibliographic control is increasingly good as all of these events come together.

CHARLES WM. CONAWAY

Binding

Several developments in binding in 1977 were significant. One was the acceleration of research into the performance characteristics of various types of binding with respect to both materials and methods. The new Library Binding Institute (LBI) Book Testing Laboratory at Rochester Institute of Technology has been evaluating volumes that are oversewn, cleat laced, and adhesive fan bound and has been studying various adhesives and covering materials. The purpose is to enable librarians to know the characteristics of the products they are buying. To date, volumes adhering to Class "A" (LBI Standard) specifications outperform others in tests, but librarians are now in a position to know what the alternatives will do. Information on the test results is available from LBI.

Another development is the increased interest librarians are evidencing in learning more about the physical book. LBI together with local library associations has sponsored "Workshops on Prolonging the Useful Life of Library Materials" in California, New York, and Pennsylvania, and more are in the planning stages. They are instructional workshops dealing with specific problems. LBI's new film depicting how a volume is library bound is now available for purchase or loans. A panel of experts clinically examines and discusses the physical volume in terms of library usage.

A third development is the overall impact that the new Laboratory has begun to have on the entire book industry. The Laboratory is primarily an educational tool for graphic arts students. Book manufacturers, publishers, paper manufacturers, and others, as well as Certified Library Binders interested in book construction, have evidenced an encouraging interest in its possibilities. The Laboratory will be the focus of a future series of workshops and seminars on binding and related problems. An advisory committee is being appointed to help develop policy and direction for the Laboratory, and librarians have been invited to be members.

Further developments have taken place in the technology of library binding. A new embossing machine for printing titles and other information on the spine has been completed after several years of development. It provides unusually fine lettering with relatively high productivity. Finally, there has been increased use of LBI's Free Examination Service. Werner Rebsamen, who administers the Laboratory for the Rochester Institute of Technology, is LBI's Technology Consultant and provides the technical service in connection with such examinations.

DUDLEY A. WEISS

Biographies

BEARMAN, TONI CARBO

The Executive Director of the National Federation of Abstracting and Indexing Services since 1974, Toni Bearman previously worked at Brown University's Physical Sciences Library and Biological Sciences Library, at the University of Washington's Engineering Library as a subject specialist in technical report literature, and for *Mathematical Reviews*. She also served as Project Coordinator for a project funded by the National Science Foundation in cooperation with the Antwerp Library School in Belgium to identify and evaluate technically oriented serials published by private industry.

Bearman is Chairman of the Delaware Valley Chapter of the American Society for Information Science (ASIS) and Chairman of the ASIS Committee on Inter-Society Cooperation. She is also Chairman-Elect of the ASIS Special Interest Group on Library Automation and Networks.

She also has been active in other professional organizations. She served as Chairman of the 1978 Program Committee and Special Projects Committee of the Documentation Division of the Special Libraries Association. She is a member of the Executive Committee of the Association of Information and Dissemination Centers, of the U.S. National Committee for ICSU AB, and of the CONSER Advisory Committee and is Section T Committee Council Delegate of the American Association for the Advancement of Science. She is Chairman of Subcommittee 1 of the Z39 Committee of the American National Standards Institute.

BIDLACK, RUSSELL EUGENE

An acknowledged leader in the field of library education, Russell Bidlack received the 1977 Beta Phi Mu Award for distinguished service to education for librarianship. In 1969 he was appointed the first Dean of the University of Michigan's School of Library Science (formerly the Department of Library Science).

He was born near Manilla, Iowa, on May 25, 1920. After service in the Army Corps of Engineers from 1941 to 1946, where he advanced from private to master sergeant, he received his B.A. degree in English from Simpson College in Iowa in 1947. In 1948 he went to the University of Michigan where he earned an A.B. in L.S., an A.M. in L.S. an A.M. in history, and in 1954 a Ph.D. in L.S.

Bidlack's teaching career began in 1951 when he became a predoctoral Instructor in the Department of Library Science. He attained full professorship and was Acting Chairman of the Department when it was made a graduate school.

Combining his interests in history, education, and library science, Bidlack has written histories of the City Library of Detroit from 1817 to 1837; of Henry Colclazer, the University of Michigan's first librarian; and of the ALA Catalog. He has compiled Michigan bibliographies and written historical scripts for radio broadcasts. Since 1972 he has published an annual analysis of salaries of library school faculties in the *Journal of Education for Librarianship*.

Bidlack has been an active member of the Michigan Library Association, the Special Libraries Association, the Association of American Library Schools, and ALA. He has served in many capacities in ALA, including a term on Council from 1972 to 1976. One of his outstanding contributions has been as Chairman of the Committee on Accreditation's Subcommittee to Rewrite the Standards on Accreditation. He was a member of the Committee from 1972 to 1977 and was Chairman from 1974 to 1976.

The citation accompanying the 1977 Beta Phi Mu Award reads in part, "As chairman of the subcommittee which developed the Standards, he provided direction, energy, and dedication. As member and chairman of the Committee on Accreditation...he rendered meritorious service during the principal period of implementation of the Standards. ...Fair-minded and unselfish, warm and friendly, thoughtful and sensitive to the needs and problems of others, he gives generously of his time and attention."

BROWN, MARCIA

Winner of the Regina Medal for 1977 for her continued distinguished contribution to children's literature, Marcia Brown is well known as an author, artist, and storyteller. Born on July 13, 1918, in Rochester, New York, she grew up in a family interested in art and music in which all liked to read and enjoyed listening to stories. She attended the New York College for Teachers at Albany, receiving a B.A. degree in 1940. She spent the summer of 1938 at the Woodstock School of Painting. She later studied at the New School for Social Research, the Art Students League, and Columbia University, all in New York City.

After teaching English and drama in the Cornwall, (New York), High School from 1940 to 1943, she worked in the New York Public Library from 1943 to 1948. In 1953 she taught puppetry at the

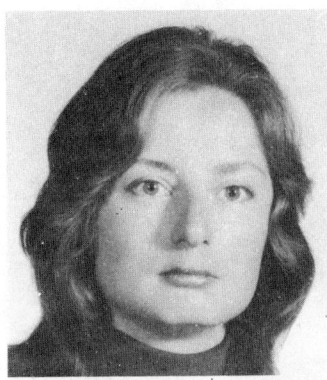

Toni Carbo Bearman

Russell Eugene Bidlack

Marcia Brown

Biographies

University College of the West Indies in Jamaica.

Books that Brown has written and illustrated include *Stone Soup, Henry-Fisherman, Skipper John's Cook, The Bun,* and *All Butterflies.* She has translated and illustrated Charles Perrault's *Puss in Boots* and *Cinderella.* She has illustrated numerous other books, including Hans Christian Andersen's *The Steadfast Tin Soldier, The Wild Swan,* and *The Snow Queen;* Theophile Gautier's *Giselle;* and Peter C. Asbjornsen's and J.E. Moe's *The Three Billy Goats Gruff.*

Awards that have honored Brown's work include Caldecott Medals in 1955 for *Cinderella* and in 1962 for *Once a Mouse.* In 1972 she received the University of Southern Mississippi Medallion "for her distinguished contribution to children's literature."

Her experience in storytelling as a librarian has influenced her decision to retell and illustrate a number of folktales, always considering the use of the books by storytellers.

BYRUM, JOHN DONALD, JR.

The ALA representative to the Joint Steering Committee for Revision of the Anglo-American Cataloging Rules, John Byrum has been appointed Chief of the Descriptive Cataloging Division of the Library of Congress. A career marked by honors has characterized his service in the profession.

Born in Wenatchee, Washington, on June 10, 1940, Byrum attended Harvard on a Harvard College Honorary Scholarship, receiving his A.B. degree magna cum laude in 1962. While pursuing graduate studies at the University of Washington in Seattle, he served as Assistant to the Serials Librarian in the University Library. In 1965 he entered the Graduate School of Library Service at Rutgers University, and after receiving his M.S. in L.S. degree he joined the Catalog Division of the Princeton University Library in 1966. He was made Head of the Division in 1968, a position he held until his recent appointment.

In the Resources and Technical Services Division (RTSD) of ALA, Byrum was the assistant to the editor of *Library Resources & Technical Services* for two years. He became the ALA representative to the committee of the International Federation of Library Associations (IFLA) working on International Standard Bibliographic Description for Serials and Chairperson of the Catalog Code Revision Committee of RTSD.

A Library Resource Fellowship from the Council on Library Resources was awarded to Byrum in 1974, enabling him to make a study to determine the uses of the *Anglo-American Cataloging Rules* by general research libraries and to gather suggestions for the improvement of the Code. In 1975, Byrum received the Esther Piercy Award, recognizing contributions in the field of technical services by younger librarians with not more than 10 years of professional experience who give outstanding promise for continuing contributions and leadership. On this occasion, William S. Dix, then Librarian of the Princeton University Libraries, characterized Byrum as "a library professional with a firm intellectual grasp of theory and insistence upon high standards, and a recognition of the opportunities offered by new attitudes and new technology."

In what some are calling the Age of Cataloging, Byrum has taken a leading role. His has been seen as having an appropriately modern style in adapting the technological approach to the intellectual problems of acquisition and organization of resources.

CABELLO-ARGANDOÑA ROBERTO

President of REFORMA 1977-1978, Cabello-Argandoña is branch librarian at the Anaheim Public Library in California. He was born in Chile in 1939. At the University of California at Los Angeles he earned the B.A. degree in 1970 in political science, the M.L.S. and the M.P.A. in 1975 and in 1977 was working toward the Ph.D. at the School of Planning and Urban Studies at the University of Southern California.

The author of several articles and papers on library services to the Spanish-speaking in the U.S., he directed the Bibliographic Research and Collection Development Unit of the Chicano Studies Research Center at UCLA from 1970 to 1977.

CLAUSMAN, GILBERT JOSEPH

Librarian of the New York University Medical Center since 1955, Gilbert Clausman was elected President of the Medical Library Association (MLA) for 1977-78. A member of many committees in MLA, he has also served as the chairman of a number of them, as the MLA representative to the Joint Committee to Study the Relation between the Libraries of the U.S. and the Federal Government in 1952-53, and as the representative to the American National Standards Association's Z39 Committee in 1958-59.

Born in Los Angeles, California, on November 8, 1921, Clausman moved to Salem, Oregon, when he was 12 years old. He attended Willamette University in Oregon, interrupting his studies to serve three years in the U.S. Navy as a pharmacist's mate, first class, and received his A.B. degree in English literature in 1947. Columbia

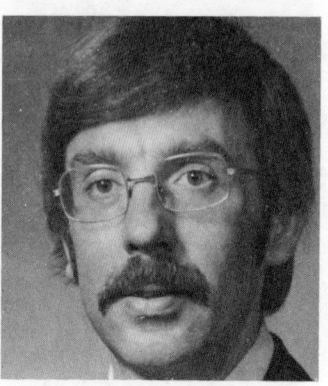

John Donald Byrum, Jr.

Roberto Cabello-Argandoña

Gilbert Joseph Clausman

University's School of Library Service conferred the B.S. in L.S. degree on Clausman in 1948 and the M.S. in L.S. degree in 1952.

Clausman began his career as a reference assistant in the Library of the New York Academy of Medicine and assumed his present position 22 years ago. From 1959 to 1963 he was a Director of the MLA and from 1960 to 1962 the Exchange Manager, reorganizing the entire structure of that operation. He served as Co-chairman of the 1971 Annual Meeting Committee and was an active and effective member of the Legislation Committee. He has been equally active in the New York Regional Group, holding various offices, including that of Chairman in 1956-57.

In addition to his MLA activities he has been Chairman of the Task Force of the Library Committee of the Associated Medical Schools of New York and New Jersey and has been a consultant to the Milton Helpern Library of Legal Medicine since 1963. A colleague has written of him, "[he] comes to us well equipped to cope with the considerable and arduous duties entailed in being President of the Medical Library Association."

COCO, ALFRED JOSEPH

Professor of Law and Library Science and Law Librarian at the University of Denver College of Law, Alfred Coco was elected President of the American Association of Law Libraries (AALL) in 1977. He has been a member of many committees of AALL and has served as Chairman of committees on Publicity, Placement, and Exhibits. In 1965 he was President of the Southwestern Chapter. Since 1974 he has been a member of the Law School Inspection Team, and he is also a member of the Inspection Team of the Section of Legal Education of the American Bar Association.

Born in Moreauville, Louisiana, on February 28, 1933, Coco was on active duty in the U.S. Air Force from 1951 to 1953 and was in the reserves until 1958. He received his A.B. degree in psychology from the University of Texas in 1957, his J.D. degree from St. Mary's University School of Law in Texas in 1960, and his Master of Law Librarianship degree from the University of Washington in 1962.

After practicing law privately for six years, Coco became Reference Law Librarian in the King County Law Library in Seattle in 1961. A year later he returned to St. Mary's University School of Law as Librarian and Assistant Professor of Law. From 1970 to 1972 he was Professor of Law and Law Librarian at the University of Houston College of Law in Texas.

Coco has written many articles, chapters of books, and television scripts. With others, he wrote *The Impact of the Environmental Sciences and the New Biology on Law Libraries* (Oceana Publications, 1973). He was given the Domanque Award of St. Mary's University School of Law for the best research paper in the field of law in 1959. Coco is licensed to practice law in Texas and Colorado.

DAINTON, SIR FREDERICK SYDNEY

A British scientist and administrator, Dr. Lee's Professor of Chemistry at Oxford University, and since 1973 Chairman of the University Grants Committee (UGC), Sir Frederick Dainton was President of the Library Association (LA) during 1977, the first nonlibrarian to hold the office since Sir Charles (now Lord) Snow in 1961. In appointing him, the LA Council could be said to have acted on the principle "if you can't beat them, have them join you," for librarians had bitterly opposed the UGC's recent expenditure cuts, especially the recommendation of its Atkinson Report in 1976 for "self-renewing libraries," with old stock regularly discarded to accommodate new. In the crisis of professional identity currently afflicting British librarians, the LA's choice of Dainton suggested that librarians saw their future as information scientists rather than as "archivists."

Born in Sheffield, Yorkshire, on November 11, 1914, Dainton was educated at Sheffield's Central Secondary School, where his interest in chemistry was stimulated by a master who encouraged inquiry and private experiment. A Scholar at St. John's College, Oxford, he moved to Sidney Sussex College, Cambridge, for postgraduate research and became a University Lecturer. Appointed as Professor of Physical Chemistry at Leeds University in 1950, he later served as Vice-Chancellor of Nottingham University from 1965 to 1970. He was a Visiting Lecturer at several North American universities and was Visiting Professor at Toronto in 1949 and at the Massachusetts Institute of Technology in 1959.

Elected a Fellow of the Royal Society in 1957 and the recipient of its Davy Medal in 1969, he was knighted in 1971. His specific contributions to chemistry lie in the identification of discrete steps in chemical reaction and their use in predicting the stability of high polymers. He published *Chain Reactions* (1956; 2nd ed., 1966) and *Photo-chemistry and Reaction Kinetics* (1968). He was chairman of the committee that produced the so-called Dainton Report in 1968 on the proportion of entrants to higher education studying science and technology. He was also Chairman of the National Libraries Committee that devised the framework on which the British Library was established in 1973.

During 1977 Dainton lectured about the LA in Germany, and presided at the Centenary Conference held in October. In his address he referred to the "burden of leisure" that might afflict society in the future and urged librarians to be ready to meet its challenges, assuring them that highly professional skills would be increasingly required.

Alfred Joseph Coco

Frederich Sydney Dainton

Biographies

Shirley Echelman

Dena Julia Epstein

Margaret T. Fischer

ECHELMAN, SHIRLEY

Assistant Vice-President and Chief Librarian of the Chemical Bank in New York City, Shirley Echelman was elected President of the Special Libraries Association (SLA) for 1977-78. A member of SLA since 1965, Echelman was Second Vice-President and the editor of the bulletin of the New York Chapter from 1968 to 1970, Chairman of the Business and Finance Division in 1971-72, Division Liaison Officer from 1972 to 1974, a member of the Conference Advisory Committee from 1972 to 1976, and Division Cabinet Chairman in 1975-76. In 1974 she received the H.W. Wilson Award for the best paper—"Libraries Are Businesses, Too"—published in *Special Libraries* during the year.

Born in Omaha, Nebraska, on October 7, 1934, Shirley Echelman was educated at the University of Wisconsin and at the University of Omaha, from which she received a B.A. degree in economics in 1956. She received her M.S. in L.S. degree from Rutgers University in 1966. From 1960 to 1965 she was the Librarian at Basic Economic Appraisals in New York City. In 1966 she assumed her present position.

An energetic practitioner of her profession, Shirley Echelman writes provocative articles for its journals and serves as a member of the Board of Trustees of the Public Affairs Information Service. An Adjunct Lecturer at Rutgers, (1970-71), she is a member of Pi Gamma Mu, the national social science honorary association, as well as of Beta Phi Mu.

EPSTEIN, DENA JULIA (POLACHECK)

Assistant Music Librarian of the Joseph Regenstein Library at the University of Chicago, Dena Epstein was elected President of the Music Library Association (MLA) for 1977-78.

Born in Milwaukee on November 30, 1916, she received a B.A. degree from the University of Chicago and B.S. and M.A. in Library Science degrees from the University of Illinois with a thesis on *Music Publishing in Chicago Prior to 1871*. After working as Art and Music Cataloger in the University of Illinois Library, she was appointed Senior Music Librarian in the Newark Public Library following her marriage to Morton B. Epstein in 1942. At the end of World War II, she went to the Library of Congress as a music cataloger and reviser in the Copyright Cataloging Division.

While her children were young, she began research into the history of Black folk music in the United States and in 1963 produced a two-part article, "Slave Music in the United States Before 1860: A Survey of Sources," published in MLA *Notes*, and a biographical sketch, "Lucy McKim Garrison, American Musician," published in the New York Public Library *Bulletin*. She resumed professional work at the University of Chicago in 1964. A revision of her master's thesis was published in 1969 by Information Coordinators of Detroit as *Music Publishing in Chicago before 1871: The Firm of Root & Cady, 1858-1871*.

A member of ALA for almost 40 years, her activities in music librarianship have included serving as a regular staff member for *Notes*, the MLA journal, from 1961 to 1966; as a member of MLA's Board of Directors from 1970 to 1973; as a member of MLA's Cataloging and Classification Committee from 1973 to 1976; and as coordinator from 1974 to 1976 of the seven libraries contributing card copy to *Music, Books on Music, and Sound Recordings*. She served as a consultant to the Phelps-Stokes Fund for the article on Negro music in *The American Negro Reference Book*, and has contributed articles to *Notable American Women: 1607-1950*, the *Dictionary of American Biography*, *Civil War History*, and the forthcoming 6th edition of *Grove's Dictionary of Music and Musicians*. In 1973 her introduction to the reprint edition of the *Complete Catalogue* (1870) of the Board of Music Trade of the United States of America was published by Da Capo Press, and in 1974 she was named a member of the Advisory Board for the *Yearbook* of the Inter-American Institute for Musical Research.

In 1970 her work on the history of Black folk music was expedited by grants from the American Council of Learned Societies, the Illinois Arts Council, and the National Endowment for the Humanities. The resulting publications were "African Music in British and French America" in *Musical Quarterly* (1973), "The Librarian as Detective: The Search for Black Music's African Roots" in the *University of Chicago Magazine* (1973), "The Folk Banjo: A Documentary History" in *Ethnomusicology* (1975), "Documenting the History of Black Folk Music in the United States: A Librarian's Odyssey" in *Fontes Artis Musicae* (1976), and a full-length book, *Sinful Tunes and Spirituals: Black Folk Music to the Civil War* (University of Illinois Press, 1977).

FISCHER, MARGARET T.

Consultant from 1975 in business management, design and implementation of new products, and new technology in information processing, Margaret Fischer was President of the American Society for Information Science, 1976-77.

She was born July 10, 1924. After graduation from Bucknell University, she joined Time, Inc., in New York in 1946 as a researcher. Later a reporter and writer, she was Head Reporter for Life (1956-58). As a member of the Time-Life New Building Committee (1958-61), she led in reorganizing the library. In 1961 she was named Manager of the Time Information Processing Department. From 1972 she was associated with the Xerox Education Group, directing its Information Services and serving as Manager, Data Services, for R. R. Bowker, a Xerox company.

Margaret Fischer contributed to many publications, including Time, Life, Sports Illustrated, and reference and professional publications in librarianship and information science. She became a trustee of Bucknell University in 1970.

GOODRUM, CHARLES A.

A librarian and author, Charles Goodrum created the new Office of Planning and Development at the Library of Congress and has published the first murder mystery with a librarian as the detective.

Charles A. Goodrum

Born in Pittsburg, Kansas, on July 21, 1923, Goodrum completed his undergraduate work in American history and political science at Princeton and Wichita State universities. He received an M.S. in L.S. degree and the Joseph Towne Wheeler Award from Columbia University in 1949.

His library career began as Circulation Librarian at Wichita State in 1947-48. He went to the Library of Congress in 1949 as a member of LC's first intern class. At LC he joined the Legislative Reference Service (LRS) as Reference Librarian in 1950 and then served as the LRS Librarian and later as Coordinator of Research. He was Assistant Director of the Service, renamed the Congressional Research Service (CRS), from 1970 to 1977. Goodrum counts among his accomplishments the major role he played in creating the CRS computerized bibliographic SDI system, its automated issue brief system, and its on-line legislative information tracking system.

In January 1977, Goodrum was asked to set up the new Library of Congress, Office of Planning and Development that would, among other responsibilities, implement the recommendations of the year-long Librarian's Task Force on Goals, Organization, and Planning.

Goodrum has been a frequent contributor to library journals and also wrote *The Library of Congress* (1974), the volume on LC for the Praeger Library of U.S. Government Departments and Agencies. He uses his typewriter for recreation as well and wrote a humorous account of coming of age on the prairie, *I'll Trade You an Elk* (1967). It was a book club selection and was made into a motion picture by Walt Disney Studios, starring Hal Holbrook, Cecil Kellaway, and Wally Cox. He has contributed humorous articles to *The New Yorker* and *Atlantic*, and in 1977 he published a murder mystery entitled *Dewey Decimated*, which was set among librarians at the mythical Mall-side Washington Werner-Bok Library.

GORMAN, MICHAEL

The joint editor, with Paul W. Winkler, of the second edition of *Anglo-American Cataloguing Rules* (AACR), Michael Gorman assumed the post of Director of Technical Services, with the rank of Professor, at the University of Illinois Library in 1977.

Gorman was born in Oxfordshire, England, on March 6, 1941. He attended the Library Association (LA) course at the Ealing School of Librarianship from 1964 to 1966, winning the Cawthorne Prize for the best results nationwide when he took the intermediate examination. In 1967 he became an Associate of LA. He worked in public libraries before attending school, and from 1966 to 1972 he served the British National Bibliography, first as a research assistant, then as Author Cataloging Reviser, and later as Head of Cataloging. He was attached to the British Library Planning Secretariat from 1972 to 1974, when he spent a year as Visiting Lecturer at the Graduate School of Library Science of the University of Illinois. His last position in England was as Head of the Bibliographic Standards Office at the British Library from 1974 to 1977, where he edited the Bibliographic Services Division *Newsletter*.

Gorman has been a member of committees of the British Library, of the British Standards Institution, and of LA. In 1974 he was appointed to the Library Association/British Library Committee on Revision of AACR. He has presented papers at library conferences in Britain, Denmark, Hungary, Switzerland, and the United States and has served on a number of international committees.

From 1969 to 1973, Gorman edited *Catalogue and Index*. In addition to chapters in books, magazine articles, and reviews, he has written *A Study of the Rules for Entry and Heading in the Anglo-American Cataloguing Rules* (1967) and *Format for Machine Readable Cataloging of Motion Pictures* (1973). The revised AACR, under his joint editorship, is expected to be published in the fall of 1978.

Michael Gorman

HAYCOCK, KENNETH R.

President of the Canadian Library Association (CLA) in 1977-78, Kenneth Haycock was born in Hamilton, Ontario, on February 15, 1948. He received a B.A. degree from the University of Western Ontario in London in 1968. He received the Diploma in Education from the Althouse College of Education of the University of Western Ontario in 1969 and the Intermediate Certificate in School Librarianship in 1970. Haycock also received the Specialist Certificate in School Librarianship from the Ontario Department of Education and the Faculty of Education of the University of Toronto in 1971, the M.Ed. degree from the University of Ottawa in 1973, and the M.A. in L.S. degree from the University of Michigan in 1974.

Haycock was a history teacher and Head Librarian at Glebe Collegiate Institute in Ottawa in 1969-70 and Head of the Learning Media Centre of Colonel By Secondary School in Ottawa from 1970 to 1972. From 1972 to 1976 he served as Educational Media Consultant for the Wellington County Board of Education in Guelph, Ontario. In September 1976 he assumed his present position as Coordinator of Library Services for the Vancouver School Board in British Columbia.

During these years associated experience has included teaching courses related to school librarianship in various institutions: from 1970 to 1972 at Queen's University in Kingston, Ontario; in 1973 at the Ontario Ministry of Education and the Waterloo County Board of Education in Kitchener, Ontario; in 1975 at the University of Toronto; and during the summers of 1976 and 1977 at the University of British Columbia in Vancouver. He served as an educational consultant for the Canadian Children's Literature Project, Methuen Publishers, in 1975-76, during which time he also was a trustee of the Guelph Public Library Board.

Haycock is a member of provincial, regional, national, and international professional associations.

Specific assignments with CLA have included the following: President, 1974-75, Canadian School Library Association (CSLA); Chairman of Committee on Committees (CSLA), 1975-76; and Chairman of Awards Jury, 1975-76. Haycock served on the editorial and Publication Policy Board (CLA),

Kenneth R. Haycock

Biographies

1974-75; and was Vice-President and Governor of Committee on Committees, 1976-77. Other activities include Editorial Board of *Index to Free Periodicals*, and National Advisory Board of Canadian Nonbook Media Selection Project, Center for Research in Librarianship, Faculty of Library Science, University of Toronto.

His publications include *A List of Subject Headings on Drugs* (1971); *The School Media Center and the Public Library: Combination or Cooperation* (1973); *Free Magazines for Teachers and Libraries*, 2nd ed. (1977); *Security-Secondary School Resource Centers* (1975); and the keynote speech in *Crucial Issues in School Library Development and Professional Education*, the proceedings of the 1976 Conference of the International Association of School Librarianship.

He lectures frequently at meetings and workshops of professional organizations, schools of library science, and faculties of education throughout Canada and the United States. Haycock's honors include Beta Phi Mu Award from the University of Michigan in 1976. In 1977 he received the Silver Jubilee Medal presented by the Governor-General of Canada for contributions to Canadian society. During 1977 he was one of 12 educators invited to a seminar discussion on the state of Canadian studies and learning resources sponsored by the Canada Council/Canadian Commission for UNESCO.

HOAGLAND, SISTER MARY ARTHUR, I.H.M.

President of the Catholic Library Association (CLA) in 1977, Sister Mary Arthur was born in New York City on May 12, 1915. She received an A.B. degree from Immaculata College in Pennsylvania and an M.S. in L.S. degree from Marywood College in Scranton, Pennsylvania. She did postgraduate study in English, education, and library science at Villanova, Temple, Fordham, and Columbia universities.

Sister Mary Arthur is the Director of Library Media Services for the Superintendent of the Office of Schools of the Archdiocese of Philadelphia. Her educational experience includes 18 years of teaching in elementary schools and 12 years as a teacher and librarian in secondary schools. She has been a Lecturer in the Department of Library Science at Villanova University in Philadelphia since 1963.

Active in local, state, and national library associations, Sister Mary Arthur is a member of the Pennsylvania State Advisory Board on Media and Certification, the Title II State Advisory Board, the Legislative Committee of the Pennsylvania Library Association, the Board of the Pennsylvania School Library Association, and the Steering Committee of the Philadelphia Children's Reading Round Table. Her professional writing includes articles in *Catholic Library World*.

HUMPHRY, JOHN AMES

Formerly State Librarian and Assistant Commissioner for Libraries in the New York State Education Department, John Humphry has been appointed Executive Director of Forest Press, publishers of *Dewey Decimal Classification*. He succeeds Richard Sealock who has retired. Humphry has been a member of the Board of Directors of Forest Press and a trustee of the Lake Placid Education Foundation since 1965.

A native of Springfield, Massachusetts, he was born on July 21, 1916. He received his A.B. degree from Harvard University in 1939 and his B.S. in L.S. degree from Columbia University in 1941. He studied further at Harvard from 1942 to 1943 while he served as an assistant in the Harvard College Library. After a term as Field Service Consultant in the Office of the Chief of Naval Operations in Washington, D.C., he was Director of Book Processing at Enoch Pratt Free Library in Baltimore from 1946 to 1948 and Library Director of the Springfield (Massachusetts) Library and Museums Association from 1948 to 1960 and Executive Director from 1960 to 1964. He resigned in 1964 to become Director of the Brooklyn Public Library and in 1967 accepted the New York State Library post, which he held until March 1977.

Humphry has always served his profession generously. He has been President of the Massachusetts Library Association and of ALA's Association of State Libraries and a member of the Board of Directors of the New England Library Association and of ALA's Resources and Technical Services Division and Association of College and Research Libraries. From 1960 to 1964 he was a member of the ALA Council. He has served on innumerable advisory committees and councils. In 1977 he was appointed to the Board of Trustees of the Metropolitan Reference and Research Library Agency. He is also a member of the board of the Council on Library Resources.

A teacher of library science at Simmons College, at the American International College in Springfield, Massachusetts, and at Pratt Institute, Humphry has also been a library surveyor. One survey resulted in the publication in 1963 of *Library Cooperation: The Brown University Study of University-School-Community Library Coordination in the State of Rhode Island*, an example of the breadth of interests and the vision of its author.

LATHEM, EDWARD CONNERY

Dean of Libraries and Librarian at Dartmouth College, Edward Lathem was President of the Association of Research Libraries in 1976-77.

Under his presidency, ARL issued two volumes with contributions by a number of librarians—*76 United Statesiana* (1976) and *Thirteen Colonial Americana* (1977).

A native of Littleton, New Hampshire, he was born on December 15, 1926. Lathem received his B.A. degree from Dartmouth College in 1951 and his M.S. in L.S. degree from the Columbia School of Library Service in 1952. The Harvard-Radcliffe Institute of Historical and Archival Management awarded him a diploma in 1954, and in 1955 he received a diploma from the American University-National Archives Institute on the Administration of Archives, Advanced. In 1961 he received his Ph.D. degree from Oxford University.

Lathem joined the staff of the Dartmouth College Library in 1952 and held the posts of Assistant to the Librarian, Director of Special Collections, Assistant Librarian, Associate Librarian, and Librarian, as well as Dean of Libraries. He assumed his present position in 1968. From 1953 to 1964 he was literary editor of the *Dartmouth Alumni Magazine*.

Deeply involved in his community, Lathem has been one of the

Sister Mary Arthur Hoagland

Edward Connery Lathem

Town of Hanover's Fence Viewer's since 1962, and copublisher of the *Coos County Democrat* since 1970. He holds directorships in the North Country Publishing Company and several other businesses in New Hampshire and Vermont.

Lathem, who has written extensively in the fields of history and literature, is a specialist on Calvin Coolidge and Robert Frost. Of his four books on Coolidge, *Your Son, Calvin Coolidge: A Selection of Letters from Calvin Coolidge to His Father* received the Award of Merit of the American Association for State and Local History in 1970. Eight of his published books have concerned Frost.

LERNER, LOUIS ABRAHAM

A member of the National Council on Libraries and Information Science (NCLIS) since its inception, Louis Lerner was appointed U.S. Ambassador to Norway by President Carter in 1977.

A member of the Chicago Public Library Board of Trustees since 1967, he was Vice-President of the Board when he resigned to assume his diplomatic post. Lerner is a native Chicagoan, born on June 12, 1935. He attended the University of Chicago from 1951 to 1954. After attending seminars in 1956 and 1957 in Copenhagen, Denmark, he returned to Chicago where he received his B.A. degree at Roosevelt University in 1960.

Lerner, a prominent newspaperman, is on leave as the Publisher of the Lerner Home Newspapers. He began as a reporter for the *North Town News* in Chicago in 1954, and was a correspondent for the Accredited Home Newspapers of America while he was in Copenhagen. He has been Director of the Myers Publishing Company and of the Lincoln-Belmont Publishing Company and President of Lerner Suburban Communication. He served on the Board of Directors of the Chicago Better Business Bureau, was a member of the Lyric Opera Guild, and served on the Northtown Chamber of Commerce, of which he was a Director from 1963 to 1965. He was a member of the Canadian-American Trade Commission. Under his direction the Lerner Newspapers have made frequent grants to the programs of the Public Broadcasting System.

In 1960, Lerner was given the Public Service Award of the Accredited Home Newspapers of America. He is a member of Sigma Delta Chi, the honorary journalism fraternity. He was Cochairman of the Chicago Public Library Centennial Celebration Committee, served on the Illinois State Advisory Board on Libraries, and was a member of the Advisory Committee on the White House Conference on Library and Information Services.

LEWIS, PETER RONALD

Chairman of the Joint Steering Committee for Revision of Anglo-American Cataloging Rules (AACR), Peter Lewis is University Librarian at the University of Sussex. He is the representative of the British Library on the Committee.

Born in Oxford, England, in 1926, Lewis was educated at the Royal Masonic School. He became a Fellow of the Library Association (LA) in 1955 and received his M.A. degree from Queen's University in Belfast, Ireland, in 1968. He served on the staffs of the Brighton Public Library, the Plymouth Public Library, and the Chester Public Library between 1948 and 1955, and from 1955 to 1965 on the Board of Trade Library in London. In 1965 he went to Queen's University as Lecturer in Library Studies. He became University Librarian at Skinner's Library at the City University in London in 1969 and in 1972 accepted the post at the University of Sussex.

Lewis wrote a widely used standard text, *The Literature of the Social Sciences* (1960), and has been a steady contributor to professional journals. He was a member of LA Council in 1971 and in 1972 became Chairman of the Editorial Board of the *Journal of Librarianship*, the quarterly publication of the Association. In 1974 he was appointed Chairman of the Media Cataloguing Rules Committee. He has been Chairman of the Joint Steering Committee for Revision of AACR since its inception in 1974. Publication of the revision is expected in the fall of 1978.

McNAMARA, BROOKS

Professor of Drama in the School of the Arts at New York University since 1968 and a contributing editor of *The Drama Review*, Brooks McNamara served as President of the Theatre Library Association from December 1976 to November 1977. He has written three books—*The American Playhouse in the Eighteenth Century* (1969), *Step Right Up* (1976), and, with Richard Schechner and Jerry Rojo, *Theatres, Spaces, Environments* (1976). He has also written articles that have been published in *The Drama Review, The Connoisseur, Educational Theatre Journal, Theatre Quarterly,* and other journals and has contributed entries to various reference works.

McNamara was born on February 1, 1937, in Peoria, Illinois. He attended Knox College, where he received a B.A. degree in 1959. He received an M.A. degree in 1961 from the University of Iowa and a Ph.D. degree in 1965 from Tulane University.

McNamara has designed stage settings for Cafe La Mama, The Performance Group, and the New York Cultural Center, as well as for many university theatre productions. He has lectured at the Museum of Modern Art, the British Architectural Association, and the University of Sussex and in cultural institutions in various countries, including a number of American universities. He has appeared on radio and television in the United States and Canada.

He served as a director of the American Society for Theatre Research in 1975 and has been a director of the Theatre Library Association since 1969. He was a member of the Delaware Arts Council in 1967-68 and has been an advisor to the Council for International Exchange of Scholars. At the end of 1977 he was working on a history of the English street entertainer and was directing a project to catalog the papers of the Shubert Corporation.

ROGERS, RUTHERFORD DAVID

Librarian of the Yale University Library, Rutherford Rogers was made an officer in the Kroonorde by King Baudoin of Belgium at the 50th anniversary meeting of the International Federation of Library Associations (IFLA) in Brussels in 1977 when he was given the IFLA Medal.

As a member of the International Relations Committee from 1959 to 1964, Rogers has long pursued an interest in overseas matters. In 1961 he was a member of the American Library Mission to Moscow and in 1964 served as a consultant to the UNESCO Conference in Manila on National Libraries in Asia and the Pacific Area.

Biographies

Louis Abraham Lerner

Peter Ronald Lewis

Brooks McNamara

Biographies

Born in Jessup, Iowa, on June 22, 1915, Rogers received an A.B. degree in English, summa cum laude, in 1936 from the University of Northern Iowa, which also honored him with its Alumni Achievement Award in 1958 and a doctor of literature (honoris causa) in 1977. In 1937 he received an M.A. degree with honors in English and in 1942 the B.S. in L.S. degree from Columbia University. In 1938 he joined the staff of the Columbia College Library, where he was Librarian when he left for military service from 1942 to 1946.

In 1948 Rogers became Director of the Grosvenor Library in Buffalo and in 1952 became Director of the Rochester Public and Monroe County (New York) Library. In 1954 he joined the staff of the New York Public Library, and in 1957 he became the Deputy Librarian of Congress. He went to Stanford University as Director of University Libraries in 1964, where extensive development of computer technology marked his five-year term. In 1969 he became the Librarian of Yale University Library.

Rogers' involvement in ALA includes service on the Intellectual Freedom Committee for 10 years—as Chairman in 1950 and 1951—on Council from 1959 to 1963, on the Executive Board from 1961 to 1966, and as Endowment Trustee in 1966-67. He was President of the Association of Research Libraries in 1967-68.

Rogers has served on various advisory committees in New York and California. He was Chairman of the Advisory Screening Committee in Library Science for the Fulbright and Smith-Mundt Grants from 1961 to 1964, the Committee on White House Libraries in 1963-64, and the Joint Libraries Committee on Copyright from 1964 to 1966. He is a member of the U.S. Advisory Council on College Library Resources, a director of the H.W. Wilson Company, and a member of the Board of Governors of the Yale University Press.

A quiet man with reserves of humor and energy, Rogers gives generously to any community of which he is a part. His principal commitment was emphasized in 1971 when, with David C. Weber, he wrote *University Library Administration*, a basic book on the subject.

SHANK, RUSSELL

University Librarian at the University of California at Los Angeles, Russell Shank was elected First Vice-President and President-elect of ALA for 1977-78. He was a member of the ALA Council from 1961 to 1965, and 1974 to 1978, member of the Executive Board, 1975-77, Chairman of the Personnel Administration Section of the Library Administration Division in 1965-66, and President of the Information Science and Automation Division in 1968-69 and of the Association of College and Research Libraries in 1972-73.

Born in Spokane, Washington, on September 2, 1925, Shank received an engineering degree from the University of Washington in 1946, and served from 1943 to 1946 in the U.S. Navy as a midshipman and ensign. In 1949 he was awarded the B.S. in L.S. degree, and the University gave him its Distinguished Alumni Award in 1968. In 1952 he received an M.B.A. from the University of Wisconsin at Madison. Columbia University granted him the Doctorate in Librarianship in 1966.

Beginning as Reference Librarian at the University of Washington in 1949, Shank later in the year went to the Engineering Library at the University of Wisconsin at Madison. In 1952 he joined the Milwaukee Public Library, and from 1953 to 1959 he was the Engineering and Physical Sciences Librarian at Columbia University. He held the post of Assistant University Librarian at the University of California at Berkeley from 1959 to 1964, when he became Senior Lecturer at the School of Library Service at Columbia University.

In 1967, Shank became Director of Libraries of the Smithsonian Institution. Among the activities of his 10-year period there was leadership in the development of the Federal Library and Information Network (FEDLINK).

Shank has taught part time and during summers at the School of Librarianship of the University of Washington, at the Graduate School of Library and Information Studies of the University of California at Berkeley, and at the School of Library Service at Columbia University. Another special activity was participation in the New York Metropolitan Library Project; he wrote the report *Regional Access to Scientific and Technical Information: A Program for Action*, which was published in 1968.

Casual and friendly, his ease in communicating with all kinds of people belies his technical background. Having been called upon for every type of service in ALA, and always having responded efficiently and with good humor, Shank's background indicates that he will be a President for all interests—approachable, informed, and diligent.

SHEEHY, EUGENE P.

Editor of the ninth edition of the American Library Association's *Guide to Reference Books*, generally referred to as "Winchell" after the editor of the seventh and eighth editions, Eugene Sheehy is recognized as a distinguished reference librarian and literary bibliographer. Born on October 10, 1922, in Elbow Lake, Minnesota, from 1942 to 1946 he served in the U.S. Marine Corps. He received a B.A. degree from St. John's University in Collegeville, Minnesota, in 1950, an M.A. degree in English from the University of Minnesota in 1951, and a B.S. in L.S. degree from the University in 1952.

He was Reference Librarian at Georgetown University Library in 1952-53 and Reference Assistant at Columbia University Libraries from 1953 to 1965. He has been Head of the Reference Department at Columbia University Libraries since May 1965.

In 1968, 1970, and 1972 he edited supplements to the eighth edition of the *Guide*, all published by the American Library Association. Compilation of the ninth edition of the *Guide*, a volume describing some 10,000 selected reference works in 829 pages of bibliographic information and including a 185-page index, was a tremendous enterprise.

Sheehy is known also as a literary bibliographer. Publications in this field include *Joseph Conrad at*

Russell Shank

Eugene P. Sheehy

Mid-Century (1957), *The Achievement of Marianne Moore* (1958), *Yvor Winters* (1959), *Frank Norris* (1959), *Sherwood Anderson*, (1960), *Index to "The Little Review"* (1961), and *Index to Little Magazines* (1953-63). He has edited a semiannual column, "Selected Reference Books," in the January and July issues of *College & Research Libraries* since 1964.

TAYLOR, MILDRED D.
Awarded the Newbery Medal in 1977 for the most distinguished contribution to American literature for children published in 1976 for *Roll of Thunder, Hear My Cry*, Mildred Taylor was praised for her moving story of a Mississippi family's struggle against the indignity of prejudice.

Taylor was born in Jackson, Mississippi, and brought up in Toledo, Ohio. She received a B.E. degree from the University of Toledo in 1965. After graduation she joined the Peace Corps and worked in Ethiopia where she taught English and history. Returning to the United States in 1967, she recruited college students in the Midwest for the Peace Corps and during the summer of 1968 prepared Peace Corps trainees for teaching in Ethiopia.

In the fall of 1968 she entered the University of Colorado where she became involved in Black studies programs. After receiving an M.A. degree from the School of Journalism in 1969, she worked as a skills coordinator in the newly created Black Education Program at the University.

By the time she entered high school she knew that she wanted to be a writer, and she wrote throughout her educational career. After two years of work in the Black Education Program at Colorado she decided to concentrate on writing. Moving to Los Angeles, she took a job during the day that left her evenings free for writing.

She entered a manuscript in the competition sponsored by the Council on Interracial Books for Children and won first prize in the African-American category in 1973 for *Song of the Trees*, a story of a Black family named Logan. Published in 1974, it was a runner-up for the Coretta Scott King Award and was a New York Times Outstanding Book of the Year.

Her second book about the Logans—*Roll of Thunder, Hear My Cry*—portrays rural Black life in the South in the 1930's. It includes teachings of her childhood and incorporates stories that she had heard about her family and others. Unforgettable scenes depict the family's grim determination to hold on to the land that is rightfully theirs, and the book shows their warmth, love, and pride as they struggle to survive. She plans other books about the Logans that will chronicle the growth of the children into adolescence and adulthood.

Taylor dedicated the award-winning book to her father and has indicated that she writes the verbal history he gave his family because it exemplifies aspects of Black pride and Black heritage that are not often recorded.

TROTTI, JOHN BOONE
President of the American Theological Library Association, 1977-78, and Vice-President, 1976-77, John Trotti became Librarian of Union Theological Seminary, Richmond, Virginia, in 1970 and Associate Professor of Bibliography there in 1972. He joined that faculty in 1968 after serving as Pastor of the Altavista Presbyterian Church in Virginia, 1964-68.

He was born in Asheville, North Carolina, December 11, 1935. After graduation from Davidson College in 1957, he studied at Union Theological Seminary (B.D., 1960) and Yale University (Ph.D. in Old Testament, 1964). He also earned the M.S. in L.S. from the University of North Carolina in 1964. He taught at Yale Divinity School (1961-62) and Randolph-Macon Woman's College, Lynchburg, Virginia, 1965-67, and 1974.

Trotti was President of the Presbyterian Library Association, 1973-74. He edited *Aids to a Theological Library*, issued in 1977

Mildred D. Taylor

and is editor of *Scholars Choice*, a periodical.

VIRGO, JULIE A.C.
Becoming the Executive Secretary of the ALA's Association of College and Research Libraries in 1977, Julie Anne Virgo had previously been the Director of Education of the Medical Library Association.

Born in Adelaide, South Australia, on June 14, 1944, she came to the United States in 1966 to attend the University of Chicago Graduate Library School which granted her an A.M. in L.S. degree in 1968 and a Doctorate in Librarianship in 1974.

Holding the Registration Certificate from the Library Association of Australia, in 1961 she became an assistant in the Children's Library of the Public Library of South Australia in Adelaide. In 1962 she became a Librarian in the State Library of South Australia and in 1963 the Librarian of the Repatriation Department, where she served until 1966.

While she studied at the University of Chicago, she was successively Research Assistant, Teaching Assistant, and Lecturer, a post she has continued to hold. From 1970 to 1972 she was a library consultant to the Department of Public Aid of Chicago. Her honors have included fellowships from the University of Chicago, the National Library of Medicine, and HEW under Title II-B; a National Library of Medicine Research Grant; a Doctoral Dissertation Award from the American Society for Information Science; and election to Beta Phi Mu. She has been a member of the Advisory Board of the Continuing Library Education Project funded by the National Commission on Libraries and Information Science (NCLIS) and of committees of the American Society for Information Science, the Council of National Library Associations, the Board of Directors of the Continuing Library Education Network, the Council on Library Technology, and the Library Education Division of ALA.

Virgo was the first person to hold the position of Director of Education of the Medical Library Association. Her staff work enabled the Association to extend and strengthen its long-established program of continuing education until it has become a model for

Biographies

John Boone Trotti

Julie A. C. Virgo

Biographies

other associations. She was deeply involved in the drafting of the new certification code, a document that sets new goals and directions for the field of library continuing education.

VOSPER, ROBERT GORDON

Professor of the School of Library and Information Science at the University of California at Los Angeles and Director of the William Andrew Clark Memorial Library, Robert Vosper was made an officer in the Kroonorde by King Baudoin of Belgium during the 50th anniversary meeting of the International Federation of Library Associations (IFLA) in Brussels in 1977.

Since 1961, when the Commission on Higher Education in the American Republics sent him on a university library survey in Central America, Vosper has been involved in international library matters. As a Guggenheim Fellow, he studied in Great Britain in 1959-60 and was a Fulbright lecturer in Italy the following spring. He was a member of the University Library Visitation Team of the Federal Republic of Germany in 1964 and in that year was made an Honorary Commissioner of the Friends of the Gennadius Library in Athens, Greece. From 1970 to 1975 he was on the advisory commission on overseas book and library programs for the U.S. Department of State and from 1968 to 1973 was a member of the U.S. Commission to UNESCO.

He served as Vice-President of IFLA from 1970 to 1977 and in 1977 was elected an honorary fellow. In 1974 he wrote "National and International Library Planning," an introductory working document for the 40th general Council meeting of IFLA in Washington, D.C. In 1973-74 he became an Honorary Research Fellow of the School of Library Studies of University College in London, and in 1974 he was made an Honorary Vice-President of the Library Association of Great Britain.

Born in Portland, Oregon, on June 21, 1913, Vosper received his B.A. and M.A. degrees in classics from the University of Oregon and the Certificate in Librarianship from the University of California at Berkeley in 1940. After a term in the Library at Berkeley he went to the libraries of Stanford University in 1942 and the University of California at Los Angeles in 1944, where he was Associate Librarian from 1949 to 1952. He then became Director of Libraries at the University of Kansas, returning to UCLA as University Librarian and Professor of Library Science in 1961. He taught library science throughout his term as University Librarian, and in 1973 resigned that post to teach full time.

Scholarly, a polished speaker, and an intellectually curious man, Vosper's services have been sought by many organizations in the United States. In 1957-58 he was Research Director for the Farmington Plan Survey of the Association of Research Libraries (ARL). He was a member of advisory committees of *Chemical Abstracts* from 1965 to 1967, the Massachusetts Institute of Technology Libraries from 1965 to 1968, and the National Science Foundation Information Council from 1965 to 1970. Since 1968 he has been a director of the Council on Library Resources. He was President of ALA's Association of College and Research Libraries in 1955-56, a member of the ALA Executive Board from 1964 to 1967, and ALA President in 1965-66. In ARL, Vosper has been a member of the Board of Directors and was Chairman in 1963.

WATANABE, SHIGEO

Japanese author, translator, reviewer, and teacher of children's literature, Shigeo Watanabe delivered the 1977 May Hill Arbuthnot Lecture on April 28 in Boise, Idaho. The lecture was sponsored by the Department of Teacher Education and Library Science at Boise State University, Idaho State Library, Boise Public Library, the State Department of Education, Boise Public Schools, and the Boise Chapter of the Children's Reading Round Table.

Born in Shizuoka, Japan, on March 20, 1928, Watanabe received a B.A. degree from the Library School of Keio University in 1953 and an M.S. in L.S. degree from Case Western Reserve University in Cleveland in 1955. He worked as a Children's Librarian in the New York Public Library from 1955 to 1957. During 1970-71 he was Visiting Scholar at the School of Librarianship at Western Michigan University in Kalamazoo. He taught for 18 years at the Library School in Keio University.

Author of a number of books for Japanese children, he received the Minister of Welfare and the Sankei Press Awards in 1969 for *Teramachi 3-chome 11-banchi* (*A Big Family in Temple Street*), a story for older children based on his happy childhood in a large family. Other books he has written include *Shobojidosha Jiputa* (*Jiputa, the Small Fire Engine*), *Futago no Densha* (*Twin Street Cars*), and *Mori no Henasuro* (*A Funny Dinosaur In the Forest*).

Watanabe has introduced a number of well-known American titles to Japanese children through translation. They include *The Moffats* by Eleanor Estes, *Secret of the Andes* by Ann Nolan Clark, *Wrinkle in Time* by Madeline L'Engle, *The Bronze Bow* by Elizabeth G. Speare, and *Make Way for Ducklings* by Robert McCloskey. For adults in Japan he translated *Unreluctant Years: A Critical Approach to Children's Literature* by Lillian H. Smith. He has also published many articles on children's literature and Japanese library service in professional journals in Japan and in the United States.

Active in international groups, he is a member of the executive committee of the International Board on Books for Young People, and an international Jury member of the Bratislava International Biennial of Illustrations.

Robert Gordon Vosper

Shigeo Watanabe

Blind and Physically Handicapped, Library Services for the

U.S. libraries serving blind and physically handicapped individuals circulated more than 14,000,000 items during FY 1977. A survey determined that, in addition to support provided by the Library of Congress ($28,000,000) in FY 1977, regional and subregional libraries received more than $12,238,000 from state, city, county, and selected federal sources. More than $415,000 was received in the form of bequests and gifts. The U.S. Postal Service contributed more than $9,000,000 in providing free mailing privileges. The total resources available to blind and physically handicapped individuals in 1977 approximated $50,000,000 or $16 per person.

RESEARCH AND DEVELOPMENT

Since the establishment of the Division for the Blind and Physically Handicapped (DBPH) in the Library of Congress 46 years ago, research and development of new materials have played an important role in improving the equipment used by handicapped readers. As early as 1934, for example, the American Foundation for the Blind, working closely with DBPH, developed long-playing records. More recently, a project supported jointly by DBPH and Recording for the Blind resulted in the development of the four-track cassette. Other improvements have reduced recording speeds so that readers need handle fewer records or cassettes.

Flexible discs, which improved and expanded the system of direct circulation of magazines, were used in 1977 to produce on a large scale and expedite to readers a recorded version of *Roots* by Alex Haley. It was available to readers shortly after the television showing. Because the flexible disc format is inexpensive, large quantities of each title can be produced, satisfying reader demand for popular titles on a timely basis. The Division is currently producing 50 titles with mass appeal on flexible disc, including the Bible and President Carter's *Why Not the Best?*

All of the titles produced on flexible discs are also being recorded on cassettes. *Roots*, produced in April 1977, was the first four-track, 15/16 ips mass-produced cassette title. The four-track system allows up to six hours of recording on each cassette. Ten cassettes would have been required to produce *Roots* in the two-track format, doubling the cost of each copy produced.

Several development projects are currently being studied by the staff of DBPH. These, or perhaps similar innovative devices, may be incorporated in the future into the national library program for blind or handicapped persons.

Portable Braille Recorder. Developed in France, this device can record and play both braille and sound on standard Philips cassettes, which can hold up to 300,000 braille characters, the equivalent of three braille volumes. Braille is put on the cassette using a seven-key electric keyboard, and reading is done on twelve-character lines that follow each other at a rate controlled by the reader. It is possible to duplicate the braille tapes by using only slightly modified tape duplication equipment.

The recorder is equipped with a microphone and loudspeaker for recording and playback, and a switch changes the machine from sound to braille automatically. The braille recorder can be connected to computers and to electronic pocket or desk calculators. The Division has acquired two machines to test the ease of their use by blind or handicapped readers. The device is available commercially, and designers are seeking ways of reducing its cost, currently about $2,400.

Ealing Reader. The device is designed especially for use by visually impaired persons or by physically handicapped individuals who lack sufficient manual dexterity to handle printed books or magazines. The reader is a metal box measuring 11″ x 11″ x 6″. A book printed in large type on a reel of paper is attached to the take-up spool and placed in the box just as film is placed in a camera. A motor advances or rewinds the paper one page at a time or at a continuous rate. Various control devices that require only slight pressure from hands, arms, or other parts of the body can be attached to the equipment for use by physically handicapped persons. DBPH has purchased several Ealing Readers and plans limited field testing with 30 users in cooperation with the Division's machine-lending agency in Cambridge, Massachusetts. The six-month test should determine the ease of operation, reliability of equipment, and user reaction.

Kurzweil Reading Machine and Telebook. Ongoing projects (see *ALA Yearbook 1977*, p. 66) include the Kurzweil Reading Machine, which "reads" a wide variety of printed matter and yields output in the form of full-word English speech, and the Telebook project. Telebook is an experimental concept in talking book service that provides blind or handicapped readers with instantaneous access to recorded material merely by dialing a central toll-free number and requesting that talking books be played over the telephone or special FM receivers.

The Library of Congress has purchased one Kurzweil Reading Machine. It will be located in the main Library of Congress building and will be modified to include a braille production capability.

The third and final phase of the Telebook

Greg Fulton, blind since birth, provides the Service for the Handicapped Department of the Mississippi Library Commission with feedback from the blind community regarding the department's services.

Blind and Physically Handicapped Library Services for the

project has begun. The first phase was completed during the fall of 1975 with a sample of 75 readers in the Washington, D.C., area. They liked the convenience of instantly listening to a book rather than waiting for it to arrive by mail. The second phase of the experiment planned the far-reaching six-month third phase that began in October 1977. The third phase, which involves 600 talking book readers in Columbus, Ohio, is intended to give the project a direct exposure to a large heterogeneous audience. A new feature to be tested is automatic indexing, which will allow the operator to mark a spot if a reader wishes to stop in the middle of a book or magazine and resume reading later.

A sample from the test group will be asked to experiment with an automated system designed so that a reader can call up a book or magazine without the help of an operator. When the third phase is complete, the reader responses will be evaluated. The findings are expected to have a significant effect on future planning.

INTERNATIONAL COOPERATION

Many countries are seeking closer contact through their public libraries and libraries for the blind with their counterparts in the United States. Until now, libraries serving blind readers have neither organized internationally nor entered into formal multinational agreements to exchange reading materials or equipment. Frank Kurt Cylke, Chief of DBPH, made the "Proposal for International Coordination of Library Service for Blind and Physically Handicapped Individuals" to the meeting of the Section on Libraries in Hospitals of the International Federation of Library Associations and Institutions (IFLA), held in September 1977 in Brussels. The proposal called for the development of common technical and service guidelines for materials in braille and recorded formats. It stated the rationale that "library service for the handicapped has the same philosophical base as that for the nonhandicapped. Many of the service and technical approaches are identical; those not identical are quite closely allied."

Recommendations. According to the proposal, five areas require immediate attention: (1) the development of an international inventory of library resources; (2) the need for identification of existing production formats; (3) the standardization of production formats; (4) the development of an effective international interlibrary loan mechanism; and (5) the need for a coordinated application of existing and future technologies to production requirements. At the September 6 meeting, D. Heleen Rosskopf, Chief Librarian for the Blind, Amsterdam Public Library, Netherlands, supported the proposed development of an IFLA-oriented coordination effort and asked that librarians "standardize original products so that exchange may be possible." Rosskopf stated that the original recording of talking books should be standardized so that copies of every sort of audio material could be made on request and that all braille books should be produced in full script so that libraries could borrow books easily from each other.

Sixteen representatives commented on the points of the proposal in a discussion moderated by Cylke. All speakers supported the establishment of an IFLA working group. George Chandler, Director General of the National Library, Canberra, Australia, asked that the concept of the "transmission of the heritage of literature" be foremost in everyone's thoughts. Cylke suggested that library service to handicapped individuals be addressed by an organization of librarians such as IFLA rather than by an organization devoted to the welfare of the blind.

Supporting statements were received from librarians representing Bermuda, Belgium, Canada, Tobago, South Africa, Germany, and the United States. D. Zarkov, Director of the Republican Central Library for the Blind of the Soviet Union, recommended that a special IFLA commission be established, citing the volume of work that would be required of an IFLA group.

Coordinating Group. In a special meeting of librarians serving the blind, plans were made to establish a coordinating group to ensure continuation of the work begun at the IFLA meeting in Brussels. By agreement, the user group to be addressed would include blind, visually handicapped, and physically handicapped persons. There was also common agreement that seven areas require immediate attention: (1) copyright, (2) bibliographic control, (3) postal regulations and custom laws, (4) format, (5) identification (directory), (6) international and national liaison, and (7) research and development.

Under Cylke's direction, responsibilities for developing position papers and circulating them at the 1978 IFLA meeting were assumed by the following IFLA representatives: (1) mission statement, Frank Kurt Cylke, U.S.; (2) copyright, Francoise Hebert, Canada; (3) postal regulations and custom laws, H. Fidder, Netherlands; (4) format, Saleh Muhanna, Saudi Arabia; (5) bibliographic control, Frank Kurt Cylke, U.S.; (6) identification, Ulla Cahling, Sweden; (7) international relationships, Anna Ubostad, Norway.

Following the discussions, the Section on Libraries in Hospitals of IFLA, under the chairmanship of Petra B. Leeuwenburgh of the Netherlands, issued a resolution calling for the creation of a working group to pursue proposed efforts related to library services for the blind and physically handicapped.

New Multistate Service Centers. Two additional multistate service centers (see *ALA Yearbook 1976*, p. 116) were created in 1977 by the Library of Congress to speed delivery of reading materials to libraries serving blind and physically handicapped persons. The addition of these two centers brings the total that are currently in operation to four. One of the two new centers is located in Philadelphia, where the Volunteer Services for the Blind will supply recorded and braille books, publications, talking book machines, and accessories to regional libraries from West Virginia to Maine. Another is located in Oglesby, Illinois, affiliated with the Starved Rock Library System. The latter will serve libraries in 11 midwestern states. Addition of these centers completes the DBPH plan for a decentralized broad structure to bolster the efforts of the library network.   FRANK KURT CYLKE

Bookselling

Meetings and Conventions. Enthusiasm, optimism, excitement, and energy among American booksellers was never greater than in San Francisco, May 28-31, 1977, during the most successful American Booksellers Association (ABA) convention in history. Lured by the combination of San Francisco and the growing international reputation of ABA convention trade exhibits, booksellers and publishers came from around the world to join their American colleagues in four days of hard work and high festivity. It appeared that the tradition they established would be enlarged upon at the ABA convention in Atlanta, May 27-30, 1978.

The convention's purpose of presenting fall titles and the best of publishers' back lists to the trade remained unaltered. The inclusion of exhibits from other countries only added to the value of the event, as did the exchange of information between booksellers from numerous nations who discovered that they share similar problems. Distribution and discount were discussed in many tongues by the nearly 16,000 in attendance.

ABA Executive Director G. Roysce Smith and President Robert D. Hale attended the London Book Fair in October, going the following week to the Frankfurt Book Fair, and held conversations in both cities with booksellers and publishers. From their discussions it became apparent that the international aspect of bookselling on the retail level will develop rapidly in the next few years.

Before the San Francisco convention, Michael Alan Fox, formerly of the University Bookstore, Seattle, became Educational Director of ABA. He was hired to expand the already extensive educational programs of the Association.

Schools and Workshops. The Traditional Bookseller Schools, cosponsored by the National Association of College Stores (NACS) and ABA, were held in Boston in February and in Colorado Springs in March, with 216 students (prospective as well as practicing booksellers) attending each of the two Schools. Under Fox's direction the Bookseller Schools will be changed from seminars on all aspects of bookselling at all levels of experience to completely separate courses designed for prospective booksellers, for booksellers needing basic training, and for experienced booksellers seeking advanced information. Each of these Schools will be limited to 80 students, with six sessions planned for the spring of 1978.

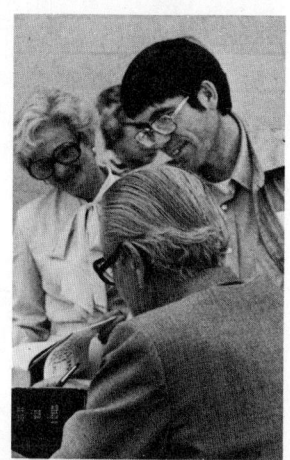

Fourteen one- or two-day workshops were conducted by Fox and ABA Associate Director Barry Hildebrandt between July and October in Tarrytown (New York), Chicago, Kansas City, Nashville, San Diego, Phoenix, Los Angeles, Seattle, Cincinnati, Anchorage, Houston, and New Orleans. Attending were 1,765 booksellers from 40 states. Eleven of the workshops covered the basics of buying and selling books. Three concentrated in depth on accounting and financial matters.

Two regional meetings sponsored by ABA in 1977 were held in Washington, D.C., in September and in Denver in October. During the Washington meeting, members of the ABA Board of Directors made the quadrennial presentation of books to the White House Library. Mrs. Carter received the delegation in the President's absence. Although not sponsoring them, the ABA was involved in panel presentations at meetings held by independent regional associations of booksellers in Fort Lauderdale; Salt Lake City; St. Louis; Eugene, Oregon; and Sturbridge, Massachusetts.

New Magazine. As part of its expanded eductional program, ABA began publication in September of *American Bookseller*, a monthly magazine created to bring specific practical information to booksellers on a regular basis and to serve as a constant conduit for dialogue between booksellers and publishers. Early

Robert Baensch of Harper & Row signing a contract with Khvdozhestvennaya Literature at the First International Moscow Book Fair held in September 1977.

The 1977 ALA convention in Detroit included many authors such as Eric Severeid who autographed his book at the Atheneum exhibitor's booth while a geisha promoted Asian titles at the Charles E. Tuttle booth.

issues of the magazine covered trends, children's books, markdowns versus returns and just plain returns, basic book lists in specialized areas, regional news, and interviews. Mary Edwards, with past experience in bookselling and in publishing, was appointed the first editor of the journal.

In the midst of planning the fall regionals, creating a new magazine, getting out the prospectus for the Atlanta convention and everything else that goes on in the Association's office, ABA moved in August from 800 Second Avenue to 122 East 42nd Street, New York 10017.

Give-A-Book. Despite everyone's best efforts, the long-anticipated Give-A-Book Certificate project did not get under way in 1977. To be operated by a new corporation owned equally by ABA and NACS, the nationwide program's legal and accounting details were greater than expected. Under the program a person will be able to buy a Give-A-Book Certificate anywhere in the nation and send it to a person in another part of the country. The recipient can take it to a local bookstore and exchange it for a book. With the forms, racks, cards, and campaign ready at the end of the year, a new starting date was set for April 15, 1978.

Survey. A statistical survey of retail bookselling was conducted during 1977 by an accounting firm hired by ABA, with the hope that the resulting information would provide guidance for booksellers on all levels to improve profit performance. Much can be learned by finding out what is wrong as well as what the most successful stores do to achieve their success. The last such survey was conducted in 1968.

Other Activities. Although no sensational censorship battles were fought during the year, the Media Coalition, of which ABA is part, continued to assist wherever trouble did occur. In a positive fashion the Coalition helped several states with prospective legislation to protect freedom of speech.

Roysce Smith and Robert Hale continued to work during 1977 with the Nigeria Task Force, comprised of booksellers, librarians, and publishers. They planned Bookweek '78 in Ife, Nigeria, a follow-up project to the very successful Bookweek '76. The 1978 event will be held in conjunction with the Ife Book Fair.

Representing retail booksellers, Hale attended and was one of the speakers at the October planning meeting for the Center for the Book at the Library of Congress. Seeking ideas for the Center, Hale urged examination of the methods of teaching reading in the United States and the adoption of programs that will get more books into the hands of children.

In what was considered a first, authors and artists, editors, publishers, librarians, and booksellers joined forces for a "Celebration" of children's books in Sturbridge, Massachusetts, in October. The one-day event was attended by approximately 1,300 persons, inspiring the planners to proceed with more cooperative efforts.

Members of the ABA staff and Board of Directors participated in various publishing procedures courses across the country in 1977: Richard and Judy Noyes in Boulder; Roysce Smith and Michael Fox at New York University; Barry Hildebrandt at Hofstra; and Robert Hale at Radcliffe.

The business of bookselling was basically up in 1977, although there were disturbing soft spots and soft seasons. Declining unit sales in many stores in both clothbound and paperback books took away some of the pleasure of increased dollars taken in. Almost without exception, booksellers were looking for ways to increase profits by cutting costs, a difficult feat made worse by continuing inflation.

While economic indicators were cautiously optimistic at best, the expansion of the book market continued to brighten, with more new people coming into bookstores each year. Many of them were not buying the standard types of books, but were seeking the endless variety of how to do everything from repair a 1957 Chevrolet to start a new religion. These new book buyers of all ages have somewhat taken up the slack of those who have been weaned away from reading by other diversions. Inasmuch as bookselling has survived since the 5th century B.C., there is no doubt that it will continue in 1978 and on into the 21st century. ROBERT D. HALE

Buildings

Public libraries continued to dominate library construction during 1977, while academic and school library building lagged behind earlier years. In part, this reflected the channeling of at least a limited amount of federal and state funds into public construction. Academic and school libraries seemed to encounter the two major barriers of declining enrollment and limited funding. Rising construction costs tended to hamper library construction projects of all types, especially where bond issues, tax overrides, and other forms of referendums were required.

TRENDS AND ACTIVITY

Additional stimulus to new library construction, additions, and remodeling was found in response to retrofitting for energy conservation and removing architectural barriers for the physically handicapped. While some observers claimed that the burgeoning use of computerized technology and microforms should substantially reduce, if not eliminate, the need for expanding library buildings, most library construction projects seemed to be in response to the seemingly inexorable growth of collections and expansion of services in libraries of all types.

National Inventory. Among the many important pieces of information released as part of the *National Inventory of Library Needs* by the National Commission on Libraries and Information Sciences (NCLIS) was a new evaluation of library space needs. According to these figures, public libraries are presently in need of 55,000,000 more square feet of floor space; academic libraries require an additional 38,000,000 square feet, while public school libraries have an even greater shortage, amounting to some 205,000,000 square feet. The total deficit is estimated at some 298,000,000 square feet. Assuming this to be net or "assignable" square footage, the challenge is staggering. During 1977 academic and public libraries added only 4,000,000 net square feet to their facilities, compared to the 93,000,000 square feet estimated as needed by the *National Inventory of Library Needs* for these two types of libraries. Unfortunately, figures are not available for making a similar comparison of school library facilities.

Additions and Remodeling. Although construction continued to account for the bulk of the dollars spent for library space in 1977, additions and remodeling appeared to be on the increase. This trend can be expected to accelerate as construction costs mount and as land acquisition becomes increasingly expensive. Among the larger additions and remodeling projects completed during the year was a 91,000-square-foot expansion of the library of the University of California at Santa Barbara. Foresight in design of the original structure had provided a capability for incremental expansion. The library now totals more than 200,000 gross square feet. Nearly half a dozen other academic libraries completed major additions and renovations of 100,000 or more square feet.

Additions to and renovations of public library buildings in 1977 consisted of smaller projects, averaging less than 10,000 square feet. Many of these additions were for branch libraries or small community libraries and resulted from the use of public works funds, Economic Development Administration grants, and revenue sharing funds. At the end of the year, the Public Library of Cincinnati and Hamilton County broke ground on the first phase of a 200,000-square-foot addition and the remodeling of the original 187,000-square-foot building that received wide attention when it was opened in 1955.

Of all the renovations in 1977, completion of the Chicago Public Library's $13,000,000 proj-

The Metropolitan Toronto Library, the largest in North America, opened in 1977. The five story building, which includes four balcony tiers, open stair cases and glass-enclosed elevators, can seat 1,300 patrons.

ect led the list. With many of the Library's functions and collections relocated elsewhere, the 80-year-old building was completely refurbished and rededicated on October 17 as the Chicago Public Library Cultural Center. While major changes were held to a minimum, every effort was made to restore the many decorative features of the building such as the two Tiffany domes and the numerous artistic embellishments of walls, arches, and other surfaces. The building was saved by the growing consciousness of individuals wanting to preserve the architectural heritage of earlier periods, something which well might not have occurred a few years ago.

New Structures. The opening of the Perry-Castenada Library at the University of Texas at Austin merited special attention as the largest library facility completed during 1977. With 500,673 gross square feet, the library can house more than 3,000,000 volumes and seat more than 3,000 users. The project cost $21,700,000. Other notable new academic library buildings included the State University of New York Library at Plattsburgh, the Idaho State University Library at Pocatello, and the South Dakota State University Library at Brookings.

Renovation of the Chicago Public Library Cultural Center which opened in 1977 included restoration of the two enormous Tiffany glass domes and installation of high intensity light sources to simulate daylight. Left, the Chicago Symphony String Quartet in the Preston Bradley Hall and (right) the Grand Army of the Republic Rotunda with even more elaborately decorated leaded glass.

Construction of two-year college learning resource center buildings kept pace in 1977 with the record for the five previous years. Among the 36 new centers finished in 1977 were several larger buildings including Shoreline Community College in Seattle (47,000 square feet), Southmost College in Brownsville, Texas (48,000 square feet), and College of Alameda in California (34,000 square feet).

Among new public library buildings, the Long Beach (California) Public Library facility was probably the largest completed in the United States in 1977. Besides boasting many innovative features, the 155,000-square-foot library facility is unique in that it is tied to the adjoining 14-story City Hall Tower at its lower level, sharing delivery access and mechanical equipment. The two-level library emerges only one story above grade, allowing space for a municipal park along its flanks and on the roof of the building. Other large new public library buildings were dedicated in Springfield, Illinois (94,500 square feet), Eau Claire, Wisconsin (63,855 square feet), Omaha (124,500 square feet), and Amarillo, Texas (60,000 square feet). The completion of many smaller libraries, including branch buildings, was evidence of the commitment of both local and federal funds in many communities.

Data on school libraries, media centers, and learning resource centers was very sparse. The trend for placing such facilities near the hub of school activity seemed to be continuing. A few news items indicated that experiments in consolidating school and public library facilities continued to be tried, but with only limited success.

Building Conversion. While more or less unusual in years past, the conversion of structures originally used for other purposes appears to be gaining popularity as an alternative to new construction. Although all types of libraries seem to be sharing in this trend, it is most frequently used for public libraries. Large open buildings such as shopping centers, markets, department stores, and warehouses are prime candidates. Former banks, fire stations, and other commercial and public buildings are also popular.

Echoing the move of such libraries as those in Spokane and in Boise, Idaho, several years ago, the Jackson Metropolitan Library System in Mississippi is renovating a Sears Roebuck store to serve as its headquarters and as the main library for Jackson. The Public Library of Columbus and Franklin County is moving its administrative and technical services operations into a 21,000-square-foot former commercial building. The Library is also converting three storefront structures into branch libraries. The Charlottesville and Albemarle County Library in Virginia is converting the old post office building in Charlottesville to house the library, ending a 35-year effort to replace the present facility.

Unfortunately, there are too many variables to make "rule-of-thumb" cost comparisons between new construction and conversions. A sample of available data indicates that conversion costs run from 60 to 85 percent of new construction. Such figures cannot, of course, consider the inherent costs or advantages and disadvantages that a particular situation may hold.

OTHER DEVELOPMENTS

Metropolitan Toronto Library. The largest new public library to open its doors in North America in 1977 was the Metropolitan Toronto Library. Representing a $30,000,000 investment, the structure contains 364,000 square feet of floor space. The building rises 5 stories and will accommodate nearly 1,250,000 volumes and seat 1,300 people. The design features an enormous atrium surrounded by four tiers of balconies tied together by open staircases and glass-enclosed elevators. Interior landscaping is extensive, combining planting and pools to control traffic and invite exploration. Considerable attention was given to energy conservation with full use of internal heat generated by people, lighting, and solar radiation. It is a building guaranteed to attract attention for years to come.

Library of Congress. Work on the James Madison Memorial Building of the Library of Congress continued in 1977. While the exterior of the structure has long since been completed, interior work continues. The 2,112,492-square-foot building contains 1,560,582 net assignable square feet. The fourth phase of the project, which includes the interior and all related work, was approximately 50 percent complete at the end of 1977. The Architect of the Capitol has granted an extension of time for completion to the end of May 1979. A contract has been awarded for the construction of motorized compact bookshelves to house the 2,500,000 volume Law Library which will occupy 76,000 square feet.

Energy Conservation. While some of the libraries opening during 1977 boasted energy conservation features, the announcements of buildings in the planning stages reflected even greater recognition of this need. Among new libraries, the Los Alamos Scientific Laboratory Library has moved into new quarters with full solar heating and cooling. Special computerized equipment monitors the system and provides a basis for accurate measurement of savings in fuel. The Troy Public Library in Miami County, Ohio, has a solar system that is designed to meet up to 77 percent of its heating requirements. Other new libraries such as the Lincoln Public Library in Springfield, Illinois, have installed heating and air-conditioning systems that can be readily converted to solar systems at a future date.

An increasingly popular method of improving energy conservation has been the use of site development. The new Scripps Institute of Oceanography Library in La Jolla, California, is an outstanding example of this technique. Built into the side of a sea cliff, much of the building is permanently insulated. Large windows overlooking the ocean are shielded from direct sunlight by being recessed into the outer walls. Ample natural light is supplied through these windows and by means of an elongated light well piercing the multifloor building. The Camden County Library in New Jersey uses earthen berms on one side and a window wall on the opposite side for much the same purpose. Smaller libraries such as the new town library in Groton, Connecticut, have followed this trend, combining earth berms, heavy insulation, and reverse-cycle cooling/heating systems to conserve energy.

Energy conservation is also showing up in remodeling and expansion projects. By replacing its old windows with tinted reflective glass, the Newberry Library in Chicago claims to have achieved a substantial reduction in winter fuel costs. Other libraries have been using remodeling and expansion projects as an opportunity to replace old light fixtures with more economical light sources. High-intensity discharge (HID) lamps appear to be growing in popularity because of their efficacy and long life. Task lighting is also being used increasingly, both in public reading areas, where it can be incorporated into carrels, and in work areas.

Instant Libraries. Experimentation continues with various concepts for creating "instant libraries." West Virginia has had considerable success with two types—an octagonal prefabricated building and a smaller rectangular structure. The Washington, D.C., Public Library has opened stations in highly

The Kenmore Branch of New York's Buffalo and Erie County Public Library solved its small site and parking problem by constructing the Tonawanda Public Library on stilts with a garage underneath the reading room.

The Illinois Regional Library for the Blind and Physically Handicapped in Chicago was completed in 1977. The barrier-free design includes windows at wheel chair eye level and an easy-to-memorize linear circulation pattern with soft corners to avoid collisions by patrons.

The Long Beach (California) Public Library shares its lower level with the City Hall (tower in background) and its second story includes a municipal park on the roof.

visible buildings designed as kiosks. The large amount of glass and the modular nature of these units make them especially adaptable to changing service patterns. The growing need for library buildings that can be constructed economically in both urban and rural settings has created a market that will undoubtedly attract other designers with innovative solutions. To date the prefabricated units share claims for durability, energy conservation, low maintenance, and simplicity of construction.

Barrier-Free Design. The impact of government regulations requiring public buildings, including libraries, to remove all barriers to access for the physically handicapped continued to grow through 1977. This requirement sometimes triggered building projects that included remodeling and, in some instances, replacement. Current regulations, however, are expected to be extensively revised as a result of a new code being prepared by the American National Standards Institute for adoption in 1978. These standards are expected to become the basis for barrier-free design for all public buildings. "Accessibility" and "nondiscriminatory" are the key concepts that Arthur F. Duncan, Assistant Director of the Codes and Regulations Center at the American Institute of Architects, believes "will cause fundamental changes in building design." Agencies receiving federal funds must make a "reasonable" attempt to remove barriers. The Department of Health, Education and Welfare allows three years for correcting architectural barriers involving structural change. It is expected that financial assistance will be forthcoming in the form of new federal grants to ease the financial burden of these improvements.

Funding Building Projects. While local funding sources continued to supply the bulk of the money for library projects, public libraries seemed to be making increasing use of federal funds, particularly those available through the revenue sharing program to local governments. Public works grants, community development funds, and similar sources have assisted some projects. States such as Mississippi, Maryland, and Georgia were fortunate to have state funds that could be used for construction. At least one state called attention to the urgent need for funding LSCA Title II to continue the program of construction that began under the law nine years ago. Ohio estimated its immediate needs for the next two years as $24,500,000 in LSCA funds for building new structures and another $18,000,000 to help eliminate architectural barriers. With the new *National Inventory of Library Needs* adding further testimony, it is expected that increasing pressure will be felt for the funding of all federal programs that can be used to finance library construction.

RAYMOND M. HOLT

The W. Dale Clark Library which opened in 1977 is situated at the head of the Central Park Mall in downtown Omaha.

Making Do in Times of Budget Stringency

Like children who outgrow their clothing with no regard to their parents' financial situation, libraries continue to require additional space irrespective of their parent agencies' ability or willingness to provide for their needs. If the *National Inventory of Library Needs* can be used as a barometer of library space needs, the situation is acute and, in many places, approaches a crisis. Perhaps more librarians than ever before are searching for a solution to their facility needs at a time when purse strings are being tightened and costs are rising dramatically.

Each librarian must obviously seek a solution for his or her library based on local factors as well as the desire to safeguard collections, promote services, and improve operational efficiency. The parameters of "making do" will certainly vary in every situation, and only general guidelines can be given.

Needs Assessment. The first step should consist of a thorough analysis of space needs. This can begin by determining the amount of space the library *should* have for the present collections and services, user accommodations, and staff. A simple inventory and a few quick calculations based on standard allocations of space will provide the needed information. For instance, libraries with active open-stack collections should allow for from 10 to 14 volumes per square foot. For reference books, bound periodicals, and oversized books a lower standard of from 8 to 12 volumes per square foot is applicable.

Seating standards are fairly well established at 25 square feet per person with slightly more for lounge furniture. Public service desks require 150 or more square feet per person, while staff work areas should range from 125 to 150 square feet per staff member. Special calculations will be needed for nonprint media collections and for meeting rooms, shipping and receiving, and other functions. Meeting rooms normally require from 8 to 10 square feet per seat plus space for a platform or stage. When these estimates of space have been assembled and totaled, the result can be compared with the space available to provide a very rough estimate of the deficit.

The second step is to project space requirements for the future. Using available forecasts of the student body or community size for the next 5, 10, 15, and 20 years, the corresponding figures for collections, personnel, and user accommodations can be estimated on the basis of accepted standards and guidelines. After completing this, the librarian will have rough figures in hand that represent the amount of space needed to house the present library adequately as well as an estimate of the space that will be required in future years.

As a third step, a comparison should be made between the assembled data and the space presently available. In general terms, the differences represent the total space deficit. Such figures should, of course, be refined as part of a total building program statement. One warning is that these guidelines give requirements for *net square feet*. Their aggregate should be compared to the actual "assignable" or net square feet available for library collections, services, and staff in the present building. Space occupied by walls, halls, staircases, rest rooms, and custodial facilities, for example, is "nonassignable" footage that, along with the assignable square footage, makes up the total or gross square footage in the building.

Alternatives. With this preliminary data in hand, it is time to look at the alternatives. The first is to consider the capacity of the existing building and how it can be improved. Libraries caught in a simultaneous budget and space squeeze oftentimes find at least temporary relief by rearranging the space in the existing structure to suit current requirements more satisfactorily. Getting the opinion of an outsider familiar with library operations and how they are performed in other situations often provides additional insight in making better use of available space. Some questions that can be asked at this point include the following:

1. What portion of the collections might be deemed "infrequently used" and how would services be affected if such materials were stored elsewhere—accessible only upon request and perhaps with a delay of several hours?

2. Given the current circulation system requirements, is the present configuration of the charging desk and the space it requires necessary?

3. Could usable space be increased significantly if certain partitions and other barriers were removed?

4. Are there office and workroom spaces that might be more effective if present partitioning were removed and large open spaces created?

5. Is there a basement or loft space that could be better utilized through installation of adequate stairs, book lifts, or elevators?

6. Could space be saved if nonprint materials were integrated with print on open shelves and if circulation of all materials were consolidated at the central circulation point?

7. Would relocation of circulation and other service desks save space?

8. Are ceiling heights sufficient to create an intermediate floor or mezzanine in part of the building?

9. How can shipping and receiving be handled to improve efficiency?

10. Are there ways of increasing the stack capacity by adding sections or by changing aisle widths?

The foregoing questions are merely samples. Many additional questions should be asked in each situation.

A valuable technique at this point is to use a scale drawing of the library building that shows only the load-bearing walls, columns, stairwells, and other structural elements. Cutouts of furniture and shelving can then be arranged and rearranged in many different configurations with minimum effort, creating

Buildings

layouts that can be tested for capacity and effect. Such layouts often call attention to possibilities that might otherwise be overlooked, and this "clean sheet" approach helps overcome barriers created by habit and familiarity. Questions such as "why?" and "what if?" are especially pertinent. During this process, it should become apparent if sufficient space can be reclaimed from within the present structure to make remodeling feasible. If more space is needed, perhaps an addition offers an effective solution. If the building is to be extended, how much space will be added and where?

When the best possible arrangement has been determined, it is time to consider remodeling requirements. What must be done to make the necessary changes? Where will partitions have to be moved? What will happen to floor coverings? Will changes be needed in the location of the plumbing? What will be the effect on heating and cooling systems? What should go into a new addition and what should be retained in the remodeled portion? This is the time to bring an architect into the process to examine the structure itself.

Condition of Physical Plant. The foregoing has assumed that the library building can be modified in whatever ways may be necessary to accommodate changes in layout. In some instances, however, this may not be the case. It may be necessary, therefore, to make a survey of the physical plant with attention focused on the structure and on electrical, mechanical (heating and air-conditioning), and plumbing systems. An architect and local building official familiar with code requirements and structural adequacy should inspect the building and provide a written report on the building's condition, citing deficiencies that need attention and changes that will be required if remodeling is done. Approximate cost estimates will prove helpful and should include any matters pertaining to requirements for the handicapped and other codes.

In some states only a very limited amount of remodeling work can be done without bringing the entire structure into conformance with current electrical, plumbing, and structural requirements. Sometimes the cost of such modifications makes it necessary to consider other solutions to the building problem. In addition, it is now the intent of the federal government that public buildings meet the requirements of access for the physically handicapped within the next three years. Many libraries must, therefore, include improvements beyond those concerned with maximizing space utilization. For instance, barrier-free access to the library may entail a new entrance, installation of an elevator or ramp, or some other structural solution. Rest rooms are also a prime target, and the solutions are demanding in terms of space and cost. These are factors, nonetheless, that must be considered in the ultimate solution.

Remodeling. If the present library building is structurally sound and has adequate land for expansion, an addition, coupled with remodeling, may provide another effective alternative. Many libraries, especially those designed in the last 25 years or so, are modular structures that can be expanded with relative ease; in fact, some have been planned for just such an eventuality. Older buildings may present special problems since many have load-bearing walls that must be retained in part or in whole. If exterior design is a problem, as it is with many older structures, an architect can be helpful in assessing the feasibility of remodeling. In considering an extension to the present structure, perhaps the primary question to be answered is "Can sufficient space be added to the building in the proper place or places at a reasonable cost and without adversely affecting other library operations?" Ideally, additional stack space should be added adjacent to existing shelving, user accommodations next to reading areas, and workroom area close to present staff spaces.

In some instances, an addition may become a major piece of construction used to overcome physical barriers for the handicapped, provide adequate rest rooms, and accommodate public services. The existing structure may then be used primarily for staff work areas, collections, and storage. This is particularly true where site conditions and orientation permit creating a sizable structure that improves accessibility. Such an arrangement often facilitates compliance with various codes.

Depending on the configuration of the original structure, the amount of space required in the addition, and the site, additions take many forms. Typical are "fill-ins," in which an irregularly shaped building becomes a rectangle; "wings," which extend one or more portions of the structure; "extensions," which elongate the building; and "wrap-arounds," which enclose part or all of the original building. The latter type of addition often creates an entirely new facade for the library, with the existing structure more or less disappearing into the total building. If large enough, such additions may absorb most, if not all, user accommodations. This solution has been effectively used for older buildings of the Carnegie period that are structurally sound and worthy of preservation.

Conversion Alternative. Libraries are increasingly looking at the conversion of existing structures as an alternative to a totally new building. Gymnasiums, multipurpose buildings, and similar types of structures offer open space opportunities for academic and school libraries. Public libraries have even greater variety, with supermarkets, department stores, banks, post offices, and fire stations among the most popular.

As in the case of remodeling the existing library, the rehabilitation of a structure originally designed for some other purpose requires careful review and planning. The amount of space available is only one of many factors. What about the location in terms of user access? Are there major problems to overcome in handling electrical requirements, heating and cooling systems, and plumbing? Is the available space adaptable to library needs or are there architectural and structural barriers that will be difficult and costly to surmount? What is the potential "useful life" of the building as a library, given projected space requirements for the next 5, 10, and 20 years? How will the cost of the converted structure compare with that of a similar number of square feet in a new library building? Again, these and many other questions must be addressed by the librarian, architect, and the building official.

The Historical Monument. In recent years, public libraries in many communities have been named as "historical monuments" by local, state, or national organizations wanting to preserve older buildings. Because such a designation limits the nature and extent of remodeling that can be done, such libraries face additional difficulties. Depending on the reasons for qualifying the building as a historical monument, both internal and external remodeling may be inhibited. In such cases, the library desperately in need of more space must seek another solution. Oftentimes this may mean relinquishing the building to use for an art gallery, museum, or community building. The library may then be free to move to other quarters sufficient for its needs.

If converting the building to another use proves impossible, library officials must determine what latitude exists for remodeling or expansion. It may be that only the front facade, for instance, must be preserved, in which case an addition might be designed for the rear of the building. Perhaps citizens want to preserve the "mood" rather than the total appearance of the building and will find it possible to accept a remodeling or expansion of the structure providing that it retains the original atmosphere. If only exterior preservation is required, the interior may be changed rather dramatically by inserting a new floor in spaces with high ceilings or by removing old partitioning to create more useful open areas. Again, however, whenever any structure is being remodeled, all concerned must be fully aware of the requirements imposed for meeting current building codes. This cost alone may require the consideration of other solutions.

Putting It All Together. Facing a space crisis in a time of budget stringency limits alternatives but does not preclude effective action. Librarians, working closely with architects, must carefully analyze present and future space needs and then look at a variety of alternatives. By employing ingenuity, solutions can be found that stretch facility dollars, provide at least temporary relief from space shortages, and improve the effective delivery of library services. Many seemingly crowded library buildings may still contain space that can be used more effectively as a result of remodeling.

Space gained through remodeling and additions will vary immensely with each project. The projected costs should be studied carefully and compared with the cost of new construction. Additions may actually prove more expensive per square foot because of special requirements such as the need to use building materials that will blend in with the original building. Remodeling costs will also increase if extensive rewiring, added heating and cooling capacity, and new plumbing are required. Replacing or supplementing staircases with other forms of vertical access for the physically handicapped will add further costs as well as occupy considerable space.

Regardless of the difficulties encountered, the lack of funds appears to be forcing an increasing number of libraries of all types to consider "make-do" solutions to their space requirements. For the librarian who can weigh alternatives, improvise, and work closely with architects and officials, making do in a time of budget stringency will be an interesting challenge—not a situation for despair.

RAYMOND M. HOLT

COMMON RE-CONFIGURATION OF STRUCTURES THROUGH ADDITIONS

1. "Wing" addition

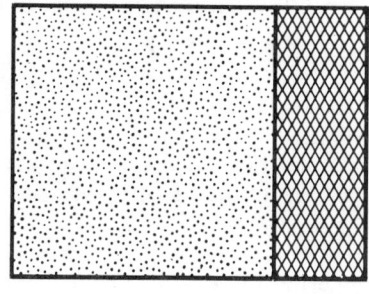

2. "Extension" addition

3. "Fill in" addition

4. "Fill in" addition

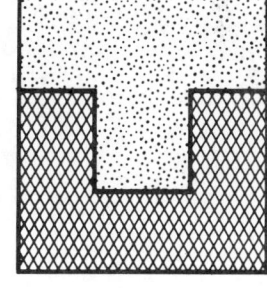

5. "Wrap-around" addition

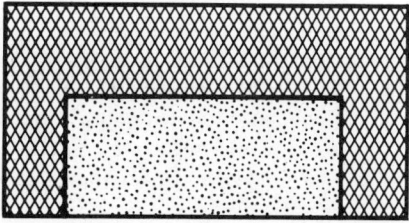

From left, Canadian National Librarian Guy Sylvestre, Secretary of State John Roberts, and President of the Canadian Jewish Congress Gunther Plaut examine the only extant copy of a Jewish prayer book printed in 1621 which was presented to the National Library in October by Jacob M. Lowy. The complete Lowy gift included some 2,000 incunabula and rare first editions in the area of Hebraic and Judaic culture.

Canadian Library Association

MAJOR CONCERNS

The Canadian Library Association (CLA) established and represented its position on six broad concerns in 1977. Toward the end of 1976, the National Library of Canada had announced the undertaking of a comprehensive review of its objectives, services, and organization and had invited CLA to submit a brief. Because of the Association's long and close involvement with the National Library, CLA welcomed the opportunity. It was appropriate that on the eve of the National Library's 25th anniversary in 1978, CLA should prepare a report assessing the institution's services and recommending priorities for the future.

Proposal and Response. The entire membership was invited to make suggestions on the brief's contents, and early drafts were circulated widely within the Association. National Library officials were freely consulted throughout the exercise, which culminated in November with the formal presentation of the brief to the National Librarian. Among its recommendations, the brief urged the establishment of a national computerized bibliographic center, which would enhance the development of a national network serving the bibliographic needs of all Canadian libraries. The brief also recommended the creation of a formalized resource network whereby the National Library would carefully delineate its own acquisitions responsibilities, and would negotiate contracts with other major libraries to make their collections generally accessible.

In response to a 1976 CLA recommendation to the federal government calling for government subsidization of the costs of interlibrary lending by major libraries, the Minister of State for Science and Technology and the Secretary of State conveyed to the Association a counterproposal in mid-1977. It suggested that the National Library and the Canada Institute for Scientific and Technical Information should strengthen their collections to serve as national lending collections of first resort. In its reply in November, CLA agreed basically with the proposal, spelling out the types of materials (periodicals, current Canadian monographs, government documents, report literature) that should be emphasized and recommending that the federal government encourage the development of provincial or regional interlibrary lending systems.

Copyright. In November, the Association completed the writing of a response to the federal government's working paper on copyright revision, issued in April. The general approach of the government study was to make creators' rights its central preoccupation. Among other things, the study touches on fair dealing, photocopying, and libraries. CLA took the lead in developing a consolidated library position by establishing a copyright liaison group comprised of representatives from all major library and library-related associations across the country who contributed valuable input. The CLA brief was written by the Association's Copyright Committee. Emphasizing the effects of copyright law on the users of libraries, the brief by and large endorses the government proposals. It does, however, recommend that the principle of fair dealing be extended to unpublished works held in libraries and archives and that, if the collective exercise of copyright is to be encouraged as a means of satisfying the needs of authors and users, these collectives should be limited in number. The brief also objects to the paucity of copyright exemptions on materials for the handicapped.

Import Issue. In a controversial pronouncement in the spring, the Association issued a policy statement supporting the freedom of libraries to buy foreign books and periodicals directly from the country of origin if they wish rather than from Canadian agencies. This statement says that the Association would oppose any move to make direct importation illegal or more costly. The CLA position is opposed by Canadian publishers, many of whom contend that they rely on agency business to support indigenous publishing.

Preparatory to the federal government's reconsideration of the subject, CLA reaffirmed its 1966 recommendation that Canada should become a party to the Florence Agreement, which eliminates customs tariffs on the importation of books, thereby permitting their unhindered flow among signatory countries. Late in the year the Association renewed its interest in the issue of public access to government information by establishing a working group to study and reply to the government's green paper, which outlines a range of legislative alternatives.

INTERACTION WITH OTHER ORGANIZATIONS

The practice of the Association is to develop and maintain firm and productive working relationships with other bodies within and outside Canada with which it shares common objectives. In view of the vast number of such organizations, it is necessary for CLA to concentrate its limited resources on those to which it can make a reasonable contribution in the pursuit of joint activities.

The Association is a member of the Book and Periodical Development Council, an organization that brings together bodies representing Canadian writing, publishing, and distribution interests in order to consolidate, wherever possible, their representation to government. CLA maintains close contacts with its French language sister association, L'Association pour l'avancement des sciences et des techniques de la documentation (ASTED). The two associations are represented on each other's governing Council and, through a liaison committee, coordinate their representation to the federal government. CLA and ASTED produce a joint workshop each year, alternating between each other's conference.

CLA enjoys productive dealings with the American Library Association. From time to time the two associations collaborate on publishing endeavors such as the second edition of the *Anglo-American Cataloguing Rules* (which also involves the Library Association). CLA is represented on ALA's Committee on Accreditation and its Joint Advisory Committee on Nonbook Materials.

CLA is also actively involved with the International Federation of Library Associations and Institutions (IFLA), taking part in the projects of many divisions, sections and committees. A CLA nominee for the IFLA Executive Board, former CLA President H.C. Campbell, Chief of the Toronto Public Library, was elected to the position for a further term of office in 1977. CLA serves as the national coordinating agent for the five other Canadian member associations of IFLA.

ASSOCIATION ACTIVITIES

Meetings and Workshops. The 1977 annual conference in Montreal, June 9-15, was entitled "Increasing Library Effectiveness" and attracted 1,450 delegates to an ambitious program of 105 events. In the spring the Association sponsored a series of meetings with Guy Sylvestre, the National Librarian, in Winnipeg, Saskatoon, Jasper, and Vancouver to discuss the role and future of the National Library. Local chapters of CLA's special libraries division continued to show the way in local programming by organizing several well-attended professional workshops in Ottawa, Toronto, Calgary, and Edmonton.

On the initiative of CLA President Ken Haycock of the Vancouver School Board, in November, the Association convened for the first time a meeting of the presidents of seven provincial and regional library associations to discuss a wide range of association management topics. CLA Council, the legislative body of the Association, met three times in 1977, while the Board of Directors, responsible for management activities, met on five occasions.

Special Projects. Under the direction of the public libraries division of CLA, work continued on the planning of "Project: Progress," a major study on the future of public libraries in Canada. Two main tasks occupied the project's steering committee: refining the research design in a way that will permit the study to be carried out in phases according to funds available, and soliciting funds from the public library community. In November, the CLA Board of Directors approved a list of corporations and other prospective funding bodies that will be invited to support the study.

In 1977 the Association produced its seventh survey of library technician programs in Canada. Conducted by Michael Angel and Gerald Brown and published in *Canadian Library Journal* (February 1977, pp. 41-55), the survey provides useful information on 17 programs across the country.

The Association participated with the British Council in arranging an exchange of visits by professional librarians between Britain and Canada. Alex Wilson, Director of Libraries and Museums for the Cheshire County Council, visited libraries in London (Ontario), Toronto, Ottawa, and Montreal.

Alex Wilson, Director of Libraries and Museums for the Cheshire County Council, England, presents former CLA President Anne Piternick a set of Library Association books published for the Centennial celebration. The presentation was made at the inaugural luncheon for incoming CLA president Ken Haycock at the CLA conference in June at Montreal.

Publications. Publications revenues account for slightly less than 50 per cent of the Association's annual income. CLA's major publishing project, the *Canadian Periodical Index,* issued monthly and with an annual cumulation, appeared in its new automated format in 1977. In January, the *Index* increased its coverage to 103 titles. *Canadian Materials,* a reviewing tool for public and school libraries, received a further operating grant of $13,700 from the Canada Council. At the end of the year, CLA's Information Services Coordinating Group completed work on a revised directory, procedures manual, and code for interlibrary lending, all of which are to be published in 1978.

CLA continued to work closely with the American Library Association and the Library Association on the joint publication of the second edition of *Anglo-American Cataloguing Rules* (AACR2) while also being represented, through the Canadian Committee on Cataloging, on the Joint Committee for Revision of AACR2. The Association continued to serve as the North American distributor for IFLA's Universal Bibliographic Control (UBC) publications. CLA publishes a monthly membership newsletter, *Feliciter,* and a bimonthly professional periodical, the *Canadian Library Journal.*

Divisional Activities. The Canadian Association of College and University Libraries (CACUL) in 1977 revised its guidelines for academic status for professional librarians in community and technical colleges. CACUL also approved a streamlining of its constitution. The Canadian Association of Public Libraries (CAPL) submitted to the National Library a brief on library srvices to the handicapped and carried out liaison with the federal government on library statistics. The Canadian Association of Special Libraries and Information Services (CASLIS) carried on an active program of local workshops, while the Canadian Library Trustees' Association (CLTA) planned a major membership drive. The Canadian School Library Association (CSLA) completed work on a set of resource service guidelines for Canadian schools, began planning the implementation of the guidelines, and continued publication of its newsletter, *Moccasin Telegraph.*

At the end of the fiscal year, June 30, 1977, CLA membership stood at 4,542, of which 3,569 were personal members and 973 institutional.

Awards and Presentations. The Association presented the following awards in 1977:

Howard V. Phalin-World Book Graduate Scholarship in Library Science: Diane Mittermeyer, Toronto, Ontario.

H.W. Wilson Education Foundation Scholarship: Heather Bishop, Truro, Nova Scotia.

Elizabeth Dafoe Scholarship: Paula Rohrlick, Montreal, Quebec.

Canadian Library Trustees' Association Merit Award: Thomas Boyd, North Battleford, Saskatchewan.

Canadian School Library Association Distinguished Service Award for School Administrators: Lloyd Rogers, Vancouver, British Columbia.

English Medal Award for the best English Canadian children's book of the year: author Christie Harris for *Mouse Woman and the Vanished Princesses* (McClelland and Stewart).

Amelia Frances Howard-Gibbon Illustrator's Award for the best-illustrated book of the year: artist Pam Hall for *Down by Jim Long's Stage* (Breakwater Books).

Elizabeth Homer Morton. The Canadian library community lost one of its pioneers and best-known practitioners when Elizabeth Homer Morton, CLA's first Executive Director, died in Ottawa on July 6. Miss Morton served the Association for 22 years before retiring in 1968.

PAUL KITCHEN

CLA Officers

PRESIDENT (June 1977-June 1978):
Ken Haycock, Vancouver School Board, British Columbia

FIRST VICE-PRESIDENT/PRESIDENT-ELECT:
Ronald Yeo, Regina, Saskatchewan

SECOND VICE-PRESIDENT:
Flora E. Patterson, National Library, Ottawa, Ontario

TREASURER:
Bruce Cossar, Trent University Library, Ottawa, Ontario

EXECUTIVE DIRECTOR:
Paul Kitchen

Headquarters: 151 Sparks Street, Ottawa, Ontario K1P 5E3

Cataloging and Classification

The concerns of the fields of cataloging and classification were again of international scope in 1977. Early in the year the Library of Congress Information Office reported to the library world that representatives of the British Library, the National Library of Australia, the National Library of Canada, and the Library of Congress had discussed "the impact that will result from the promulgation of two major compilations of cataloging standards that are now in the final stages of editing."[1] The first of these is the second edition of the *Anglo-American Cataloguing Rules* (referred to as *AACR* II); the second, the 19th edition of *Dewey Decimal Classification* (*DDC* 19). The four libraries recommended ";that machine input of new titles in conformity with *AACR* II should begin in late 1979, based on the lead time required to prepare and process entries appearing in the first 1980 issuances of printed and machine-readable cataloging records."[2] January 1, 1980, was also recommended as the date on which *DDC* 19 should be adopted.

Anglo-American Cataloguing Rules II. With the stage set for adoption, the Joint Steering Committee for Revision of the Anglo-American Cataloging Rules continued its meetings to prepare the text of *AACR* II and presented its arguments for proceeding on schedule at the Annual Conference of the American Library Association in Detroit. The Committee had earlier in the year requested review and comments on both Part I, "Rules for Description," and Part II, which deals with choice of entry and form of headings, from various groups concerned with the adoption of new cataloging standards.

Controversy erupted over a possible delay in publication to permit more time for evaluating the possible impacts on local cataloging systems. Following testimony by involved groups, a vote of the Board of Directors of the Resources and Technical Services Division (RTSD) in June 1977 gave permission for the Committee to proceed with a final draft. The Joint Steering Committee met for a final time in August. As it was reported, "It is expected that the completed text will be submitted for printing in January 1978. Publication is expected later the same year."[3] It should be noted that "the title of the second edition of *Anglo-American Cataloguing Rules* will follow British practice in the spelling of *cataloguing*."[4]

RTSD proposed a J. Morris Jones and Bailey K. Howard-World Book Encyclopedia-ALA Goals Award to develop a training program to introduce *AACR* II. The proposal was not successful.

Subject Cataloging. Criticism of certain Library of Congress subject headings continued to appear in the library press during 1977. "Policy for Subject Heading Change" was enumerated in the Library of Congress Cataloging Service *Bulletin* 123 (Fall 1977). Guidelines for the subject analysis of audiovisual materials have been composed by a subcommittee of the Subject Analysis Committee of RTSD's Cataloging and Classification Section. Specialized concerns were treated by the Subject Analysis Committee's Ad Hoc Subcommittee on Subject Analysis of African and Asian Materials.

New Bibliographic Tools. Comment on a range of new bibliographic tools proposed for publication by the Library of Congress was requested in September 1977. On the premise that the *National Union Catalog* and other bibliographies could be upgraded, the Library of Congress is hopeful of cutting the publication costs and size of these publications and of improving access to information. A series of *Master Registers* is proposed—the registers to be noncumulating, regularly produced monthly records of all data provided on LC catalog cards for a variety of media. A series of *Cumulative Brief Entry Catalogs,* or indexes, would augment the *Master Registers.*

Of considerable interest to serials catalogers using the Ohio College Library Center system was the information on terminal screens October 17, 1977, indicating that "serial card production programs are now operational."

Conferences. Catalogers and classifiers attended several meetings of national importance during 1977. Joint sponsorship by ALA's Information Science and Automation Division and RTSD provided an April institute in New York City and a May institute in Los Angeles on "The Catalog in the Age of Technological Change." Both meetings provided a forum for the examination of the most critical issues concerning the impact of technology on the traditional values and changing forms of the catalog. The papers read were made available on audio cassette.

The future role of processing centers and the Cataloging Distribution Service of the Library of Congress were topics discussed by those attending the ALA Annual Conference in Detroit. The National Commission on Libraries and Information Science and LC also sponsored a program on various aspects of the library bibliographic component of the National Library and Information Service Network. In March the Network Advisory Group issued a document in a preliminary edition with the title *The Library Bibliographic Component of the National Library and Information Service Network.*

"Closing the Catalog," a meeting sponsored by METRO, a New York City reference cooperative, focused on the closing of catalogs in their present form and the forms of catalogs available as alternatives, including on-line technology.

Grant Support. The Council on Library Resources (CLR) awarded at least two grants in 1977 of interest to catalogers. The Library of Congress received $55,000 for continuation of the COMARC (Cooperative Machine-Readable Cataloging) project, covering the salary and benefits for calendar year 1977 of three persons hired by LC for this project. The COMARC project involves receipt of bibliographic records based on LC cataloging

Cataloging and Classification

copy but converted to machine-readable form by other institutions, verification of access points, updating, and distribution without charge to COMARC participants and on separate subscription through the MARC Distribution Service.

The International Federation of Library Associations and Institutions (IFLA) received $150,000 from CLR to continue the work of IFLA's International Office for Universal Bibliographic Control (UBC). The UBC Office promotes the international standardization of bibliographic records and national plans for the improvement of national bibliographic control. It has helped especially in the development of the International Standard Bibliographic Descriptions (ISBDs) for different types of library materials.

Publications. Noteworthy among publications of 1977 was the sixth edition of *Akers' Simple Library Cataloging*, completely revised and rewritten by Arthur Curley and Jana Varlejs. Updated sections include revised rules for descriptive cataloging and the use of printed catalog cards.

Library historians interested in classification were able to read *Charles Ammi Cutter: Library Systematizer* by Francis L. Miksa. The author explains that Cutter has been given less scholarly attention than any other major American library leader even though he was chiefly responsible for the dictionary catalog common to American libraries. His work in classification laid the groundwork for the Library of Congress Classification system.

Contemporary issues in bibliographic control formed the basis for the July 1977 issue of *Library Quarterly*.

Awards. The Margaret Mann Citation in Cataloging and Classification for 1977 was awarded to Phyllis Allen Richmond "in recognition of her outstanding teaching of cataloging and classification, her scholarly publications and major contributions to the understanding and application of information science, of the theory and practice of subject analysis, and of the formulation of cataloging rules."[5] Richmond is currently professor of library science at Case Western Reserve University.

Concerns of catalogers and classifiers in 1977 seemed once again to center on the need for improved access to information and the forms in which this can be transmitted to the library user. Strenuous months lie ahead in the establishment of new standardized rules and in the transformations of catalogs as access points.

MARY POUND

REFERENCES

1. Library of Congress Information Office Press Release No. 77-3 (January 11, 1977).
2. Op. cit.
3. Library of Congress Cataloging Service *Bulletin* 123 (Fall 1977), p. 5.
4. Library of Congress Information *Bulletin* (July 29, 1977), p. 508.
5. "Margaret Mann Citation, 1977: Phyllis Allen Richmond," *Library Resources & Technical Services* (Fall 1977), p. 381.

A Comparison of AACR 1 and 2

The surface appearance of *AACR 2* will differ markedly from that of the first edition of the rules. This is seen first in the rearrangement and renumbering of the rules, with the result that none of the numbers will correspond with those of the first edition. Part I of *AACR 2* will be devoted to bibliographic description, with Part II covering choice and form of entry—the reverse of the first edition's order. The bias of the first edition towards books was manifest in the use of chapter 6 as the base chapter, with all chapters for nonbook material dependent on it. Chapter 6 will be replaced in Part I of the second edition by a general chapter on bibliographic description, followed by dependent special chapters for the various types of material (books, sound recordings, and microforms, for example). Finally, *AACR 2* will be distinguished from its predecessors by a new color, making it other than the "red," "green," or "blue" book.

Inside the covers there will be a true second edition rather than a brand new code, but with a number of major changes nonetheless. The most significant of these changes are the following.

Choice of Entry.

The concept of corporate authorship has been abandoned, although corporate main entry is still possible in a few cases. Corporate main entry is now appropriate only for certain types of works emanating from a corporate body. These types are such that the number of works allowed main entry under corporate bodies is much less than in the first edition. There is no special rule for the main entry of serials, the restriction in corporate main entry applying equally to serials and monographs.

Personal Name Headings.

Authors writing under more than one name and not predominantly identified by one of these names may be entered under multiple headings, one for each name used. When initials representing part of a name are used by authors and the full forms for which these initials stand are needed for cataloging purposes, the heading includes the initials followed by the full forms within parentheses. Catalogers' abbreviations, e.g., "Bp." or "Abp.," are not used. If a title or term of address must be used in the heading, it is given in the full form.

Corporate Name Headings.
All form subheadings ("Laws, statutes, etc.," or "Liturgy and ritual, etc.") have been abandoned. In many cases main entry may still be under the same basic corporate heading as before, but without the form subheading. All catalogers' additions to a corporate name are placed within parentheses (in contrast to the variable use in the first edition of parentheses or a comma with no parentheses). In providing for the choice between independent and subordinate entry for government bodies, *AACR 2* uses the type of name as a major criterion (function of the body being almost the single criterion used in the first edition). No catalogers' abbreviations, e.g., "Dept.," are used.

Uniform Titles.
Except for musical works and sacred scriptures, parts of works have uniform titles consisting of the title of the part shorn of the title of the whole, e.g. "Du cote de chez Swann," *not* "A la recherche du temps perdu. Du cote de chez Swann."

Bibliographic Description.
ISBD provisions for the arrangement and punctuation of data elements are applied to the description of all library materials, whereas the revised chapters of the first edition applied ISBD provisions only to printed monographs and the nonbook material covered in the revised chapter 12. Microform reproductions (e.g., of book material) are described primarily as microforms and not as the original, in contrast to the first edition where the emphasis was on the original, not on the microform reproduction.

BEN R. TUCKER

Catholic Library Association

The 56th year of the Catholic Library Association (CLA) was marked by a significant increase in the number of publications that were responses to the demands of continuing change in the Association's programs. As noted in the 1977 *ALA Yearbook*, CLA is meeting the challenge imposed by the development of Religious Education Media Centers. Of major importance was the publication of the *Guide to the Organization and Operation of Religious Education Resource Centers*, a well-received 78-page booklet that provides librarians, volunteers, and religious educators with basic information on the establishment and continued operation of a religious resource center. A specialized bibliography, *The Holocaust*, compiled by Harry James Cargas, is an annotated list of books and periodicals on a subject that has recently made newspaper headlines. The 18th cumulative volume of *The Catholic Periodical and Literature Index*, CLA's major contribution to librarianship, was published in May. The first draft of a CLA officers manual was presented to the Executive Board for study. When completed, the manual will effect closer ties between the component parts of the Association.

The growing importance of religious archives encouraged CLA to recognize an official interest section for Religious Archivists within the Association. A week-long continuing education institute on religious archives was developed and sponsored by the Association. The content of the institute will be updated during CLA's 1978 convention in St. Louis. Continuing education institutes were also offered as preconvention options in 1977. The institutes covered the subjects of the relationship of the library to instructional systems and the librarian's inter- and intra-relationships with his institution and his patrons. With the presentation of the 1978 institutes, CLA will be able to offer Continuing Education Units through an arrangement made with Marywood College in Scranton, Pennsylvania.

The CLA Executive Board in 1977 responded to the growth of continuing education programs by voting to close the collection of funds for the self-supporting Bouwhuis Scholarship Fund and to establish a Continuing Education Fund to be supported by donations from CLA members and friends. This means that additional institutes can be planned for presentation throughout the year. Target areas for these institutes will be cities in which CLA will not have an annual convention. The Executive Board also voted to increase the annual Rev. Andrew L. Bouwhuis Scholarship Award to $1,500. World Book-Childcraft International, Inc., again granted $1,000 for continuing education study by CLA members in the field of children's and school librarianship.

CLA Officers

PRESIDENT (April 1977-April 1979):
Sister Mary Arthur Hoagland, I.H.M., Philadelphia Diocesan School Libraries

VICE-PRESIDENT/PRESIDENT-ELECT:
Sister Franz Lang, O.P., Barry College, Miami, Florida

EXECUTIVE DIRECTOR:
Matthew R. Wilt

Headquarters: 461 W. Lancaster Ave., Haverford, Pennsylvania 19041

The 19th Regina Medal, CLA's highest award, was given to Marcia Brown in recognition of her continued distinguished contribution to children's literature. The Regina Medal, established in 1959 through the

Children's Book Council

generosity of an anonymous donor, has been awarded to the following: Eleanor Farjeon (1959), Anne Carroll Moore (1960), Padraic Colum (1961), Frederic G. Melcher (1962), Ann Nolan Clark (1963), May Hill Arbuthnot (1964), Ruth Sawyer Durand (1965), Leo Politi (1966), Bertha Mahony Miller (1967), Marguerite de Angeli (1968), Lois Lenski (1969), Ingri and Edgar Parin d'Aulaire (1970), Tasha Tudor (1971), Meindert De Jong (1972), Frances Clarke Sayers (1973), Robert McCloskey (1974), May McNeer and Lynd Ward (1975), Virginia Haviland (1976), Marcia Brown (1977). The 1978 recipient will be Scott O'Dell.

MATTHEW R. WILT

Children's Book Council

The membership of the Children's Book Council (CBC) stood at approximately 60 children's book publishers in 1977. The Council lost two members early in the year, one that ceased publishing children's books and another whose list became more fully integrated into the list of a publishing house that had purchased it a few years ago.

Recent new Council members—including Avon Books, Bantam Books, and Pocket Books—publish paperbacks exclusively. The trend toward more children's paperback publishing, which began modestly in the 1960's, has accelerated greatly. Possibly one-half of CBC members now have at least a token paperback publishing program that complements their hardcover publishing. Although there can be no single explanation for the emergence of so many paperback editions of children's books, one of the factors involved is the high prices of hardcover books. Because manufacturing costs continue to rise, book prices will inevitably rise with them. In addition, there is a far greater use of children's literature in classrooms as a supplement to textbooks (and in certain rare instances, as a substitute for textbooks and other more conventional teaching devices). There is also an increasing awareness that children's books must become more widely available to the general public and to children in bookstores, where many children's paperbacks have been warmly welcomed.

The Council's 1977 President was Judith Whipple, Publisher of Four Winds Press. Dorothy Briley, Vice-President and Editor in Chief, Children's Books, J.B. Lippincott Co., chaired the 1977 Book Week Committee, for which artist Anita Lobel prepared a stunning poster that illustrated Book Week's theme, "Read All about It." As usual, libraries and classrooms throughout the country conducted book-related programs and fairs and festivals, and major newspapers expanded their children's book coverage in observance of Book Week. Booksellers, too, appeared to observe Book Week more widely than they had in recent years, in part, perhaps, because the new magazine *American Bookseller,* a project of the American Booksellers Association, devoted its entire October issue to children's books and reproduced Lobel's Book Week poster on its cover.

Two other promotional programs, with materials distributed nationally, were well received. Kay Chorao prepared enticing items for "Summer Reading" programs, and Bernard Waber topped a fine group of other artists with his humorous poster prepared for "Pets," the year-round reading theme for 1977–78.

The two newest areas in which the CBC worked in 1977 were in parent education and with booksellers. In cooperation with the Princeton (New Jersey) Public Library and various Princeton-area schools, the Council sponsored a series of programs about books for parents. The programs proved to be instructive and led the Parent Activities Committee, chaired by James Giblin, Vice-President of Seabury Press and Editor in Chief of Clarion Books, to announce a plan for CBC to make a small number of $500 grants to persons or institutions for the development of book and reading programs for parents in their communities in 1978–79. For booksellers, 1977 saw the establishment of the American Booksellers Association—Children's Book Council Joint Committee, cochaired by Robert Hale of Hathaway House, Wellesley, Massachusetts, President of the American Booksellers Association, and Judith Whipple.

The 1977 Showcase, the sixth sponsored by the Council, included 42 children's books identified as creative solutions to various bookmaking and designing situations. The jury included critic Barbara Bader, designer Betty Binns, and Alvin Eisenman, School of Art, Yale University. Showcase has increasingly come to be regarded as a book award program. Because the clear intention of CBC in sponsoring Showcase has been that it be an educational program, the Showcase activity was being reexamined at the end of 1977, with a view toward developing alternate programming or materials relating to design and bookmaking in the future. The CBC's third "Prelude" program, a series of 30-minute taped sessions about aspects of children's books, appeared in 1977. The sessions covered "Books and Reading for Babies" by Nancy Larrick; "Folklore in the Culture of the Child" by Virginia Haviland; "Cognifective Domain" by Lazer Goldberg; "Trade Books as Remedies for Reluctant Readers" by William Jenkins; "Humor in Children's Books" by Caroline Bauer; and "American History Through Fiction" by Jean Fritz. The biennial revision of the

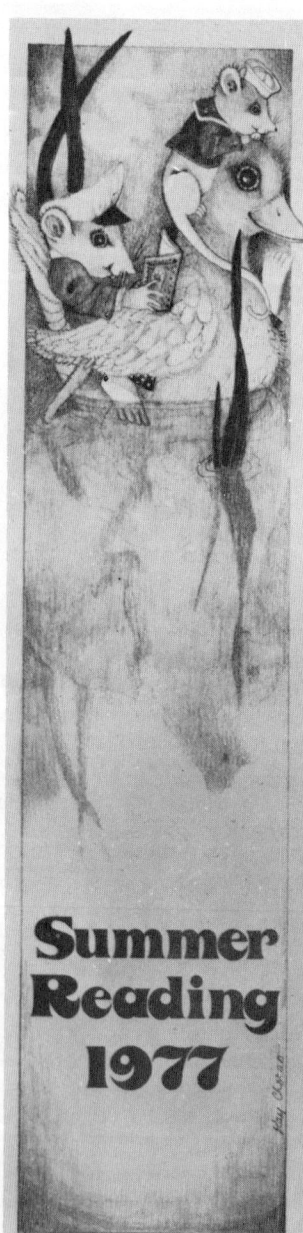

Bookmark created by Kay Chorao for the 1977 Summer Reading Program sponsored by The Children's Book Council, Inc.

Council's standard reference volume, *Children's Books: Awards and Prizes*, also appeared, with a cover by Edward Gorey.

Various other CBC joint committees with the ALA, Association for Childhood Education International, International Reading Association, National Science Teachers Association, National Council on the Social Studies, and National Council of Teachers of English had a busy year. They developed programs and conferences or, in the case of three committees, sponsored yearly bibliographic projects.

JOHN DONOVAN

Children's Library Services

1977 began with a blast of cold air that literally shut library doors. Fuel shortages and low temperatures in the eastern half of the country closed libraries, schools, and other "nonessential" services.

Conferences. In spite of a chilly start, 1977 warmed up to be the year in which the profession paid official attention to children's services in public libraries. Clara Stanton Jones, President of ALA, called a one-day preconference on June 16 in Detroit. Children's librarians and administrators were invited to attend to discuss "The Changing Role in Children's Work in Public Libraries." The proceedings of the conference are available from the Association for Library Service to Children (ALSC) headquarters.

During the ALA Annual Conference in Detroit, the Public Library Association's Service to Children Committee devoted a morning to "Children's Librarians as Administrators and Managers." Budgeting, supervision, grants, and evaluation and analysis were discussed in four sessions.

The fall 1977 Allerton Park Institute sponsored by the University of Illinois Graduate School of Library Science dealt with "Children's Services of Public Libraries." From November 13 to 16 speakers and participants identified and thrashed out concerns about the past, present, and future of work with children in public libraries. In addition to these meetings, Dorothy Broderick's *Library Work with Children* (H.W. Wilson) was published in December.

Preschool Services. If 1977 did not see the development of new trends, it did highlight the increased interest in service to children with special needs, service to very young children, and programming for parents especially in the area of early childhood education.

With the passage of The Education of All Handicapped Children Act (PL 94-142), effective in 1978, children's librarians have stepped up efforts to serve this group and other children with special needs. The Princeton (New Jersey) Public Library cooperates with the Out-Patient Department of the Princeton Medical Center by welcoming children with individualized service based on their needs and wants. In Youngstown, Ohio, "Toys of Love," a toy lending library for the mentally and physically handicapped works with social service agencies and special school classrooms.

The preschooler is no longer identified as the three- to- five-year-old, but is considered a client of the library at birth. In Prince George's County (Maryland) the new mother is sent home from the hospital with an application for a library card for her child, who obviously is not expected to wait until he or she can print a name to become a borrower.

Toy lending arrangements of various kinds are frequently a component of service to the very young child as well as to the child with special needs. Clovis-Carver Public Library in New Mexico has developed the Parent/Child Toy Lending Library that combines service to preschool children with parent education workshops.

Other programs that have been launched for the very young child include a storytime for toddlers in Greenburgh (New York) Public Library and craft classes for two- and three-

Youngster in the South Side Branch of Des Moines Public Library reads in comfort in a baseball glove manufactured by Stendig Office Furniture.

Book Week theme "Read All About It" as illustrated in this streamer by Eve Rice for The Children's Book Council, Inc.

(Above) The invincible comic book hero Spider Man awards prizes in the Chicago Public Library's Eckhart Park Branch summer reading program. (Top right) Story telling takes on a new dimension in the "magic bubble" at the Nassau County (New York) Center for the Fine Arts. (Right) Frankenstein himself showed up for the "Haunt Your Library" summer reading club sponsored by the Delaware County (Pennsylvania) Public Library.

year olds in Fairfax County (Virginia) Public Library.

Adult Services. Accompanying the growth in service to the very young child is the growth in parent support services. Reflecting this trend, the "Parent Support Program Sampler" was held in Detroit during the 1977 ALA Conference, giving librarians the opportunity to see many types of programs for parents of different kinds of children. The adult who works with children in any manner is a frequent user of such services. Parent/teacher collections in children's rooms of the library are an increasingly common sight. In addition, community resource files for parents and other adults working with children are available. The Parma (Ohio) Regional Library has developed the Information and Referral Service for parents of preschool children.

Experiences for the child from birth to three years and information for their parents is the goal of "Project: Little Kids" developed by the Greenville County (South Carolina) Library with funding from the Appalachian Regional Commission. In Westchester County, New York, the Westchester Library System and the County Youth Division cosponsored a series of workshops in three libraries for parents on child development.

The Children's Book Council (CBC) is offering seed grants to libraries and other cooperating agencies in 1978–79 for workshops for parents about children's books. A pilot program was held at the Princeton (New Jersey) Public Library in February and March 1977, funded primarily by CBC. Another program for parents on children's books and reading was held in the fall of 1977 by the East Brunswick (New Jersey) Public Library.

Storytelling and Puppetry. Traditional programs have taken on new life and sometimes a new look. Although most regularly scheduled storytelling in libraries is for preschoolers, interest in the art of storytelling is reviving. Established programs grow, and new ones are appearing around the country. Festivals in Westchester (New York), Pittsburgh, and Raleigh, are only a few examples of this widespread activity. In November 1977 the District of Columbia Public Library inaugurated the first annual Elva Young Van Winkle storytelling festival. The Danville (Illinois) Public Library held a workshop on storytelling for special groups, primarily the handicapped and the elderly.

Publications about storytelling in 1977 included Caroline Feller Bauer's *Handbook for Storytellers* (ALA), *Storytelling: Art and Technique* by Augusta Baker and Ellin Greene (Bowker), and *The World of Storytelling*, a historical study by Anne Pellowski (Bowker).

Puppetry, an ancient art and a staple of library programming for children, is also experiencing a renaissance in libraries. A donation of an old puppet theatre sparked a program of workshops and performances in the Piscataway (New Jersey) Public Libraries. Lancaster Public Library in Pennsylvania has developed a repertoire of puppet plays. A demonstration of their program inspired children's librarians in the Carnegie Library of Pittsburgh to create a puppet repertoire theatre that will circulate to branches and community groups.

Ten Mississippi libraries cooperated to present "Puppet Extravaganza '77," a three-part program that included a puppet display, a live performance, and a seminar on puppetry for adults. Sponsorship was shared by the Mississippi Library Commission, the 10 participating libraries, the Mississippi Arts Commission, and the National Endowment for the Arts.

On-line Activities. The stepped-up activity in networking and the use of on-line systems has caused librarians who work with children to becoming increasingly concerned with insuring that materials for children are included in these systems. They are also concerned that children have access to this wealth of material through interlibrary loan systems. At the 1977 Allerton Park Institute, librarians representing 26 states sent a resolution on the subject to the ALSC Board of Directors for their consideration at the 1978 ALA Midwinter Meeting.

Funding. That money is still a major problem was vividly brought home with the announcement of drastic staff and service cuts in the Buffalo and Erie County Public Library. If it is not possible to report great strides in

Children's books were included at the Memphis Public Library's Friends' fall book sale and one small patron couldn't wait to start reading!

funding for staff, materials, and services, it is heartening to be able to recognize the joint funding for special services that has been taking place. Grants, government agencies, and industry are sources that have been tapped for some of the programs.

Many questions continue from year to year with no dramatic breakthroughs. With the school population dropping in some areas, especially in suburbs, the question of school and public library cooperation is sure to come to the forefront again.

Marie Winn's thesis that television is a "plug-in drug" has renewed the debate over the role of television in library services. School and public librarians know that television can stimulate reading even as it robs children of the time to do it. How to serve the television generation is a concern all librarians who work with children must cope with.

AMY KELLMAN

Children's Literature

Two of the most dramatic events during 1977 in the children's book world were the acquisition of T.Y. Crowell by Harper & Row and the winning of the Randolph Caldecott Medal for a second consecutive year by Leo and Diane Dillon. Both sent sizable tremors coursing through the library and publishing worlds—the first because it meant a chain reaction of shifting positions for editorial, production, and promotion staffs, and the second because it had never happened before.

Publishing. The publishing of books for children and young people remained in a fairly robust state in 1977 despite the continued convalescence of the economy. The high prices of books were caused by rising production costs, and there was an attendant attrition of backlists. John Keller, children's book editor at Little, Brown, wrote in an article in *The Calendar* (September 1976-February 1977) that publishers can no longer afford to carry titles when orders are low and costs are high and that publishers are therefore obliged to make the painful decision to let good, but old, books go out of print.

Despite this situation, the figures for the total output of new trade books and paperback books held steady. The February 14, 1977, issue of *Publishers Weekly* cited more than 2,000 new juvenile titles, and the August 22 issue brought the figure up to 2,478, including 206 new editions of earlier titles. In 1977 the volume of publication was maintained, with approximately 2,400 titles (including books from alternate and irregular presses) and with more than 1,000 mass market titles in addition.

As reported in *Publishers Weekly* (April 18, 1977), sales of children's hardcover books were $109,100,000, and sales of paperbacks increased 16 per cent for a total of $17,400,000. Judith Duke, in *The Children's Literature Market* (Knowledge Industry Publications, 1977), prophesied that the children's literature market should reach $523,000,000 by 1982 (it is now $407,000,000) but that publishers will have to alter distribution and marketing practices to increase revenues.

Publishers are currently attempting to overcome buyer resistance by putting out books in

(Above) Margaret Musgrove author of "Ashanti to Zulu" (right) which won the 1977 Caldecott Medal for illustrations by Leo and Diane Dillon. (Above right) "Roll of Thunder, Hear My Cry" by Mildred Taylor won the 1977 Newbery Medal.

Katherine Paterson, author of Master Puppeteer, *won the National Book Award in 1977.*

Milton Meltzer, author of Never to Forget: The Jews of the Holocaust *won the Jane Addams Award in 1977.*

cheaper bindings, by publishing hardback and paperback editions simultaneously, and by making arrangements with publishers in other countries for cooperative publishing that can increase print runs for first editions and can also bring imported books to a new audience more quickly. Atheneum has such an arrangement with Jonathan Cape of London; and Doubleday, with Ernest Benn of London. Through book clubs publishers are also reaching for new ways to attract parents and children directly. Scholastic, long a leader among juvenile paperback book clubs, is launching its first hardcover club. The British parents organized in the "Books for Your Children" movement have joined the "Books for Children Club" in order to reach a larger number of parents. And a U.S. Justice Department consent decree has opened the Australian market to publishers in the United States.

Promotional Programs. Further impetus to increased sales may come from the "Books as Gifts" campaign. Sponsored by the Association of American Publishers, the program has been tested by advertising in nine major cities. It is tied to the purchase of books as Christmas gifts and is being checked against the holiday book purchases in cities in which there has been no advertising. Possibly a greater catalyst may be the long-planned "Give-a-Book Certificate" program, first sponsored by the Children's Book Council and later accepted by the American Booksellers Association (ABA) and the National Association of College Stores. The program is near the launching point. One day of the 1978 ABA convention will be set aside as Children's Book Day.

Another observance, International Children's Book Day, will be sponsored by the Australian International Section of the International Board on Books for Young People (IBBY). The occasion celebrates the birthday of Hans Christian Andersen on April 2, with an international sponsor chosen each year. IBBY itself has its 25th anniversary in 1978. The Friends of IBBY, a supportive organization instituted by the U.S. National Section, heard Maria Gripe speak at the ALA Midwinter Meeting. Gripe, a Swedish author, received the 1974 Hans Christian Andersen Medal.

A record number of U.S. participants attended the 1976 IBBY congress in Athens. Because of its proximity both in space and time to the Frankfurt Book Fair, the 1978 IBBY congress in Würzburg is expected to draw even more U.S. registrants. Because of the upcoming International Year of the Child in 1979, the Frankfurt Book Fair will put special emphasis on children's books. A more permanent demonstration of the increasing interest in children's literature is the establishment of the Children's Book Center in Toronto under the aegis of the Canadian Books for Children Project (a section of the Book and Periodical Development Council). It is hoped that the Center will be a resource agency as well as a catalyst for expanded publication of children's books in Canada.

NYC Auction. Rare books, original art work by many distinguished illustrators, first editions, and autographed books were contributed by publishers, authors, artists, collectors, and generous individuals for a rare event in the children's book world. The Friends of Children's Services of the New York Public Library held an auction on December 5 that, through sales and donations, netted approximately $10,000. The money will go to a special fund designed "to restore and enrich library programming for children" at a time when such programming has been severely curtailed by New York City's—and its public library system's—fiscal crisis.

The Children's Book Council (CBC), which played an active role in organizing the auction, has also supported children's literature by funding a program in which seed grants of $500 will be made available to organizers of qualifying programs directed to parents about children's books. In addition, CBC has agreed to contribute the prize money and judges' honoraria for the children's book award in the 1978 National Book Award Program. CBC has continued publishing materials for a year-round poetry program and for a series of cassette tapes on using books creatively. CBC has also made available kits of varied materials for a summer reading program and for Children's Book Week.

AWARDS

Added to the long-standing awards in children's literature was a new prize instituted by the National Council of Teachers of English. Given to a living American poet in recognition of the body of his or her work for children, the award went for the first time to David McCord. The International Reading Association's choice for a book written by an author "who shows unusual promise in the children's book field" was *A String in the Harp* by Nancy Bond (McElderry/Atheneum), and the winner of the National Book Award was *The Master Puppeteer* by Katherine Paterson (Crowell). These awards, given in 1977, were for books published in the previous year, as is the practice with all major awards in children's literature. Other finalists for the National Book Award were *Never to Forget: The Jews of the Holocaust* by Milton Meltzer (Harper & Row), *Ox under Pressure* by John Ney (Lippincott), *Roll of Thunder, Hear My Cry* by Mildred Taylor (Dial), and *Tunes for a Small Harmonica* by Barbara Wersba (Harper & Row).

Caldecott-Newbery. The Randolph Caldecott Medal and the John Newbery Medal are given by the Frederic Melcher family under the supervision of the Association for Library Service to Children (formerly the Children's Services Division) of ALA. The Caldecott Medal goes to "the illustrator of the most distinguished picture book" and the Newbery Medal to "the most distinguished contribution to literature for children" in the preceding year. In 1977 the Caldecott Medal was won by Leo and Diane Dillon for their illustrations for *Ashanti to Zulu: African Traditions* by Margaret Musgrove (Dial). The Caldecott Honor Books were *Fish for Supper*, by M.B. Goffstein (Dial); *The Contest, An Armenian Folktale*, adapted and illustrated by Nonny Hogrogian, a former Caldecott winner (Greenwillow); *The Golem: A Jewish Legend*, by Beverly Brodsky McDermott (Lippincott); *Hawk, I'm Your Brother*, illustrated by Peter Parnall and written by Byrd Baylor (Scribners); and *The Amazing Bone* by William Steig (Farrar, Straus & Giroux). Steig's *Abel's Island* (Farrar, Straus & Giroux) and Nancy Bond's *A String in the Harp* (McElderry/Atheneum) were the Newbery Honor Books. The winner of the Newbery Medal was Mildred Taylor for *Roll of Thunder, Hear My Cry* (Dial).

Batchelder and Addams. As selected by the ALA, the Mildred L. Batchelder Award for translation went to Atheneum for its publication of *The Leopard*, translated by Gunnar Poulsen from the original Danish text by Cecil Bodken, the winner of the 1974 Hans Christian Andersen Award. Given by the Women's International League for Peace and Freedom and the Jane Addams Peace Association for a book that "most effectively promotes peace, social justice, and world community," the Jane Addams Award was won by Milton Meltzer's *Never to Forget: The Jews of the Holocaust* (Harper & Row).

Canadian and British. In Canada, the 1977 award for the best children's book of the previous year went to Christie Harris for *Mouse Woman and the Vanished Princesses*, illustrated by Douglas Tait (McLelland & Stewart; published in the United States by Atheneum). The illustrator's award went to Pam Hall for her illustrations in Al Pittman's *Down by Jim Long's Stage: Rhymes for Children and Young Fish* (Breakwater Books). Both awards are given by the Canadian Library Association. The Library Association of Great Britain confers the Carnegie and Greenaway Medals, the first for literary quality and the second for illustration. The Carnegie Medal was given to Jan Mark for *Thunder and Lightning* (Kestrel). The Greenaway Medal went to Gail Haley, a former winner of the Caldecott Award, for *The Post Office Cat* (Bodley Head; published in the United States by Scribners).

Gail Haley, author and illustrator, won the Greenaway Medal for The Post Office Cat

IBBY Contenders. Leo and Diane Dillon were nominated as candidates for the 1978 Hans Christian Andersen Award to an artist, and Paula Fox was nominated as a candidate for the Award to an author. The two Hans Christian Andersen Awards, conferred biennially by a jury chosen by IBBY, are given for the body of an author's and an artist's work. The jury was to meet in Tehran in April, 1978; the awards are to be presented formally at the IBBY congress in October. The titles chosen for the U.S. honors list were Natalie Babbitt's *Tuck Everlasting* (Farrar, Straus & Giroux) and Margot Zemach's *Hush, Little Baby* (Dutton). In 1977, each country was invited to submit the name of a translator for the honors list; the U.S. choice was Sheila La Farge.

Trends. Among the new or continuing trends in books for children and young people were books about death and adjustment to bereavement; problems of aging; physically, emotionally, or mentally handicapped persons; child abuse; and members of ethnic minority groups. There were many books designed to help very young children adjust to new concepts and new experiences or to guide them to an understanding of their own emotions.

More and more books, both fiction and nonfiction, have been published for young adults that seem equally appropriate for adult readers. There were also an increased number of biographies of women and books about careers for women. For younger readers there was an increase in fiction that avoided stereotyped sex roles, although many of these unfortunately seemed to place more emphasis on their messages than on good literary qual-

Nancy Bond, author of A String in the Harp, *won the 1977 award of the International Reading Association.*

"Books That Cross Boundaries" was the topic for the Children's Literature Conference sponsored by the St. Louis Public Library in May 1977.

ity. There seemed, also, to be a discernible trend toward more and better fantasy.

In all parts of the United States, panels, seminars, workshops, speeches, and conferences on children's literature proliferated. A conference at the Boston Public Library was held in conjunction with a large exhibit of foreign children's books, reaffirming the (not new, but growing) awareness of the importance of international exchange in children's literature. The speaker for the Arbuthnot Honor Lecture, subsidized by Scott, Foresman and administered by ALA, was Shigeo Watanabe, who spoke at Boise State University. A teacher, publisher, and translator, Watanabe is on the executive committee of IBBY.

Deaths. Among the children's book authors and artists who died in 1977 were Catherine Clark, Shirley Graham DuBois, Sulamith Ish-Kishor, William Kurelek (who had just been selected as the Canadian nominee for the Hans Christian Andersen Award for an artist), Maria Leach, Jennie Lindquist, Hans Rey, and Hildegarde Swift.   ZENA SUTHERLAND

Beatrix Potter at about age 30.

Peter Rabbit

PETER RABBIT, Beatrix Potter's famous lagomorph, celebrated his 75th anniversary of publication in October 1977. The incorrigible Peter had squeezed into Mr. McGregor's garden to eat the lettuces and radishes as early as 1893 in an illustrated letter which Beatrix Potter sent to a five-year-old boy. In 1900 she decided that the story would make a book. The carefully preserved picture letter was lengthened, the illustrations redrawn, and Peter Rabbit was dispatched to a publisher—and returned! This procedure recurred at least five times before, in 1901, Beatrix Potter considered having her story privately printed. She again sent the now more professional-looking Peter Rabbit to Frederick Warne & Company, whose rejection letter had been more polite than the others, and this time they agreed to publish.

But Peter was to have adventures almost as hair-raising as those with Mr. McGregor before he was presented to the general public: he narrowly escaped being "done into rhyme" by a friend of the Potter family; his text had to be cut (some of it was used later in *The Tale of Benjamin Bunny*—Peter's cousin); and his illustrations were redrawn in color, some more than once. When finally published, he became a success overnight. He and Benjamin returned in 1904 to face more hazards in their bid to retrieve Peter's blue coat and shoes, shed in Peter's panic flight from Mr. McGregor, whose wife had put Peter's father in a pie. Although Peter later reappeared in some of Beatrix Potter's other tales, his reputation was made in his own *Tale,* which has been translated into 12 languages and Braille. Peter Rabbit has also been recorded, and has even taken to ballet.

ANNE EMERSON

Peter Rabbit

Chinese American Librarians Association

The Chinese American Librarians Association (CALA) was established in 1973 as a regional organization under the name of Mid-West Chinese American Librarians Association after a series of informal gatherings among Chinese American librarians at Rosary College in 1969, Northwestern University in 1970, and the University of Chicago in 1970. In 1976, the Association was renamed to reflect properly its nationwide membership. It affiliated with the Chinese Language Computer Society in 1976 and with ALA in 1977. The purposes of the Association are to promote better communication among Chinese American librarians in the United States, to serve as a forum for the discussion of mutual problems among Chinese American librarians, and to support development and promotion of Chinese and American librarianship.

Membership is open to all interested librarians and library science students with variations in annual dues: $10 for regular membership, $5 for nonsalaried or student membership, and $30 for organizational membership. The fee for permanent membership is $100. The membership grew 90 per cent in 1977 and now totals more than 150.

The Association has held board meetings frequently and has held a general membership meeting once a year since 1973. The first annual meeting was held at Rosary College. Five papers were presented on topics such as the Chinese language, the Chinese classification scheme, acquisition of Chinese materials, and Miss Mary Elizabeth Wood. "Library Science Education for Foreign Students and the Problem of Their Employment in the United States" was the theme for the 1974 annual meeting, also held at Rosary College. Lester Asheim was the main speaker. David Kaser addressed the meeting on "Humanism, Librarians and the Quality of Life" at the third annual meeting in 1975.

In 1976, George Bonn gave a talk on "The Librarians and the Library Community" at the annual meeting held at De Paul University. The 1977 annual meeting was held in Detroit in June. The theme was "Chinese Contributions to American Librarianship," and three papers were presented: "A Profile of Chinese American Librarians in the United States," "Chinese Cataloging in the United States," and "A Biographical Study of Alfred K'ai-ming Chiu."

The Association publishes the *Newsletter* three times a year and the *Journal of Library and Information Science*. The *Journal*, a semi-annual in Chinese and English, is published by CALA in cooperation with the Department of Social Education, National Taiwan Normal University in Taipei. A biographical directory, *Directory of Chinese American Librarians in the United States*, was published in 1977.

TZE-CHUNG LI

CALA Officers

CHAIR (1977–1978):
Robert P. Chen, Eastern Illinois University, Charleston

VICE-CHAIR
Roy Chang, Western Illinois University, Macomb
Amanda Yu, York Technical College, Rock Hill, South Carolina

PAST CHAIR
Tze-chung Li, Rosary College Graduate School of Library Science, River Forest, Illinois

TREASURER:
Theresa Hwa, De Paul University, Chicago

SECRETARY:
Alana Ho, George Mason University, Fairfax, Virginia

EXECUTIVE DIRECTOR:
Tze-chung Li

Circulation Systems

For automated library circulation systems, 1977 in many respects marked their entry into adulthood. This could be measured partly in terms of the number of vendors in the marketplace. It could also be measured by the increasing levels of sophistication used in selecting a system and by the publication of a book entirely devoted to a discussion of the subject. This maturity has been made possible by the perfection of mass-storage technology—ranging from easily updated and inexpensive computer output microform (COM) to substantial reductions in the cost of machine-addressable random access files.

Publications and Systems. *Automated Library Circulation Systems, 1977-78* by Paula Dranov[1] provides a comprehensive overview of progress up to early 1977. It not only establishes a benchmark against which the progress of 1977 as a whole can be gauged but also gives detailed descriptions of the commercial systems that were available or announced by that time.

During 1977 the position among vendors enjoyed by CLSI as having the most circulation systems in service remained unchanged. At the ALA Annual Conference, Cincinnati Electronics Corporation (CE) unveiled its system called CLASSIC (Circulation Library Automated System for Inventory Control). The system very closely follows the description CE had provided earlier.[2] CE claims to have designed flexibility into the system. It is offered as a full turn-key package, completely installed and made operational by CE, or as a package for installation on the library's (or its parent institution's) local computer. CE is offering as its basic terminal the JRL-1000, which consists of a light-pen and ticket printer. The unit can be coupled to a cathode-ray tube terminal. In addition CE is offering the CS-200 portable data terminal, which consists of a light-pen, a numeric and control-character keyboard, a cassette tape recorder, and a rechargable power supply. The CLASSIC utilizes the CODABAR™ labels on material to be identified and on borrower cards. CE offers a barcode label printer as an option.

DataPhase Systems, Incorporated, entered the scene with three installations in 1977, including what many consider the coup of the year—a contract with the Tacoma Public Library to install the system that will serve as the pilot for the Washington Library Network (WLN) Circulation Module. The DataPhase offering appears to provide a flexible and expandable system. While it can utilize a barcode label for item and borrower identification, DataPhase is placing more marketing emphasis on a formated Optical Character Recognition (OCR-A) label. In addition to providing both a human- and machine-readable label, the OCR-A label can be easily generated by a variety of techniques ranging from typewriting to commercial printing.

Statewide Efforts. In an effort to achieve an early success story for its circulation module,

Collection Development

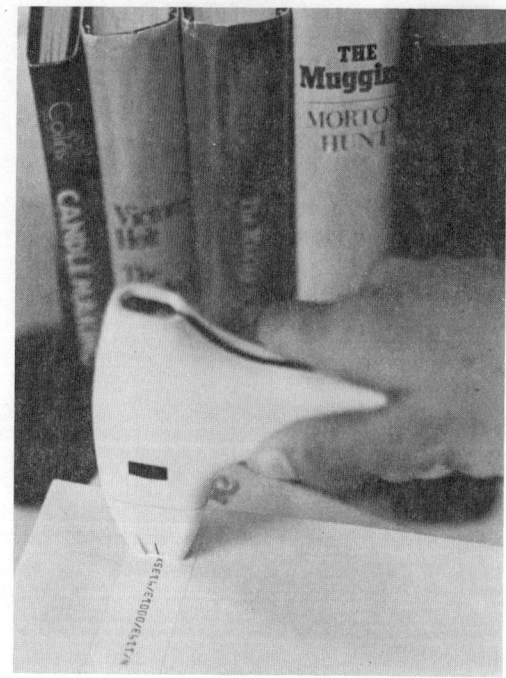

The wand attached to the OCR Circulation Station, installed by CLSI, scans labels printed in OCR-A-font in which alphabetical and numeric characters are both eye-readable and machine-readable.

WLN arranged for the Tacoma Public Library to serve as its pilot site. Tacoma sought to fulfill this role by selecting a turn-key circulation system through a tightly constructed bid process and was assisted by a consultant from Blackwell North America, Inc. Although the Tacoma Library would be the immediate purchaser, the bids were evaluated both in terms of the long-term costs of the proposed systems and of their adaptability to the expansion that WLN participation required. The bid from Data-Phase emerged as the successful contender. Although Tacoma Public cast its lot with a relatively late arrival on the scene, it is apparently well protected since the bid specifications and the resulting contract are reported to require the vendor to post performance bonds against dated benchmarks of implementation.

In April the New Mexico State Library Commission approved a grant for $10,000 "for the purpose of establishing a Task Force to study the needs for and benefits of a state-wide library system that would provide easy access to the cumulated holdings, location, and availability of materials in participating libraries...."[3] The Task Force on a State-Wide Interlibrary Cooperative System for New Mexico held to an intensive schedule of deliberations, including a circuit of meetings around the state to gain as much local input as possible.

It soon became evident that some in the state perceived the sole objective to be the creation of a state-sponsored circulation control system. The majority view, however, was that a state-wide circulation (or inventory) control system should be just one element of an expanded resource sharing system to be called the New Mexico Information System—Phase II (NEMISYS—II). The Task Force strongly suggested that any statewide circulation system take advantage of the economies of distributive processing rather than a massive central computer to service the system. A system based upon distributive processing could make inexpensive terminals available for low-volume users and could easily provide the additional locator and message transfer benefits that are necessary in a resource sharing network.

The development of automated message transfer to facilitate resource sharing, which some vendors of automated circulation systems have been claiming as a spin-off benefit of their primary product, is becoming the major objective to which automated inventory control systems may become a subservient element.

Manual Systems. More libraries retain manual systems than have adopted automated systems. For many there is no need to consider automation unless it is being organized on a network basis. One variation in 1977 merits notice. The Library of the College of the Southwest in Hobbs, New Mexico, adapted a system originally used in Colorado. This adaptation uses a four-part call slip printed on carbonless paper. The multiple parts provide a circulation file and statistical form, two recall notices, and a billing form—all filled in by the borrower at the time of the checkout of the material. While this system does not eliminate the need for human file maintenance, it is said to reduce substantially the clerical time necessary to send recall notices.

Predictions. As the state of the computing art advances, libraries are likely to see substantial reductions in the cost of automated circulation systems. This cost reduction, coupled with increased reliability of hardware and software, will begin to make automated systems attractive to smaller libraries. When the inventory control systems provide the mechanism for message switching and other resource sharing routines, they will have become attractive to a majority of libraries.

R. PATRICK MALLORY

REFERENCES

1. Paula Dranov, *Automated Library Circulation Systems, 1977-78* (White Plains, New York: Knowledge Industry Publications, Inc., 1977).
2. R. Patrick Mallory, "Circulation Systems," *The ALA Yearbook 1977* (Chicago; American Library Association, 1977), pp. 90-92.
3. *Task Force on a State-Wide Interlibrary Cooperative System for New Mexico, Final Report, December 5, 1977* (Albuquerque: General Library University of New Mexico, 1977), p. 6.

Collection Development

During 1977 collection development conferences, grants, and studies stressed analysis, planning, and measurement. Collection development is no longer an internal selection function, dependent only on local factors, but is becoming a management function affected by numerous external factors. Collection policy statements, allocation of funds, resource sharing arrangements, and centralized storage facilities are examples of a few of the elements that can affect selection. The collection development librarian is becoming a collection manager who is aware of and concerned about trends in publishing, local funding, user needs, collection strengths and weaknesses, and local, regional, and national cooperation. This trend towards more effective resource planning was clear in five areas of collection development activity during 1977: continuing education, use studies, collection development studies, resource sharing, and collection development funding.

CONTINUING EDUCATION

The Collection Development Committee of the Resources Section of ALA's Resources and Technical Services Division (RTSD) sponsored an "Institute on Collection Development" at the ALA Annual Conference in June. The preconference featured workshops on collection development policies, allocation of materials budgets, evaluation of collections, and weeding. The conference attendees were encouraged to participate in reviewing draft guidelines on these topics. Conference workshops emphasized the role of planning and analysis in the development of collections. Another significant conference on "Third World Acquisitions" was held in February at the Library of Congress. This acquisitions workshop, attended by librarians from colleges, universities, and public libraries, concentrated on the most effective means of obtaining materials from Third World countries.

Greater interest in improved acquisition techniques was also manifested in the creation of two journals in 1977: *Library Acquisitions Practice and Theory* and *LC Acquisition Trends*. Both of these publications cover acquisition activities. The latter publication replaces the National Program for Acquisitions and Cataloging (NPAC) *Bulletin* and the *Special Foreign Acquisitions Program Newsletter*. Another publication that covers acquisition questions appropriately changed its name in 1977 from *De-acquisitions Librarian* to *Collection Management*.

In October the Association of Research Libraries (ARL) devoted its semiannual membership meeting to the theme of "Collection Analysis in Research Libraries." A major topic of interest was the Collection Analysis Project (CAP) that entered the pilot study phase in 1977, first at the Massachusetts Institute of Technology Libraries, and later at the libraries of Arizona State and the University of California at Berkeley. Organized by Duane Webster and Jeffrey Gardner of the Office of Management Studies at ARL and supported by a Mellon Foundation grant, CAP intends to review, describe, assess, evaluate, and change the collection process at participating libraries.

CAP assumes that collection funds can be used effectively by focusing on institutional needs, collection strengths and weaknesses, and user needs. CAP maintains that effective collection management requires that libraries be attuned to changes in institutional programs, be aware of local political factors, measure the needs and behavior of users, promote realistic expectations from faculty and administrators, produce collection development policies, and be involved in resource sharing. One product of CAP will be a manual that can be used by libraries for self-study. During 1977 ARL has devoted many of its Systems and Procedures Exchange Center

(Above) Chicago Public Library Board President Ralph G. Newman (right) with Mr. and Mrs. Joseph Lutz who donated 4,000 volumes including rare Civil War histories to the Special Collections Department of the Chicago Public Library Cultural Center.

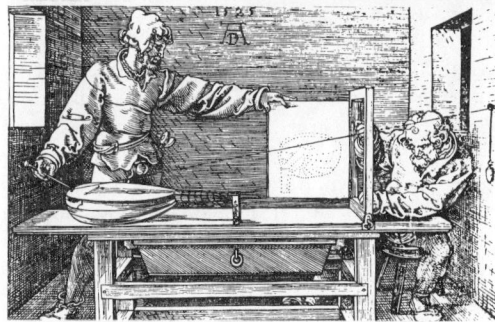

(Left) Illustration from Albrecht Durer's Underweysung der messung, mit dem zirckel und richtscheyt in Linien ebnen und gantzen corporen, *the first comprehensive book in German on practical mathematics written for builders, painters and sculptors. The volume, published in 1525, was the 1,000,000th volume acquired by the University of Houston Libraries.*

Courtroom drawings of the murder trial of Jack Ruby, accused of killing Lee Harvey Oswald, alleged assassin of President John F. Kennedy, were purchased by the Dallas Public Library in 1977.

Collection Development

(SPEC) kits to collection development topics: allocation of resources, preservation of library materials, allocation of materials funds, and collection development policies.

A major publication by the Collection Development Committee of the Resources Section of RTSD during 1977 was the *Guidelines for the Formulation of Collection Development Policies,* a step-by-step guide to producing a collection policy statement.[1] Another RTSD-Resources Section committee, the Bookdealer-Library Relations Committee, published *Guidelines for Handling Library Orders for Microforms* and the *Pre-Payment Dilemma: A Consumer's Guide.*

USE STUDIES

A significant collection study of 1977 was the Pittsburgh Study, an analysis by Allen Kent and his associates of the economics of acquiring and using materials at the University of Pittsburgh Libraries. A progress report released in April 1977 revealed that 44 per cent of all books and monographs acquired at the University of Pittsburgh in 1969 had not circulated externally in six years.[2] The study indicated that libraries need to measure the use of materials in order to evaluate more effectively resource sharing as an alternative to owning material. Maintaining rarely used titles in research collections has been determined to be a very costly investment, and the Pittsburgh Study suggests that libraries need to be more aware of user preferences and consider more precisely the trade-offs between borrowing and acquiring titles. Although the study is a milestone in user surveys, the progress report does not address the issue of research libraries as national institutions for preserving the heritage of a state, region, or nation or the issue of the significant role of special collections in a research library.

At the 1977 Rhode Island Library Association meeting, Daniel Gore reported on a use study at Macalester College in Minnesota. He concluded that the duplication of heavily used books at the expense of unique book purchases enhanced the ability of his library to serve its users, and limit the growth of Macalester's acquisitions intake.

COLLECTION DEVELOPMENT STUDIES

The CAP study was only one of the major studies in the area of collection development supported by grants in 1977. Cornell University Libraries received a grant from the Mellon Foundation for the development of a model for future allocation of financial resources and management of collection growth and costs in academic libraries. Another Mellon grant at Princeton University will assist in collection development by computer analysis of circulation data to identify heavily used material that should be duplicated and rarely used materials that should be sent to storage. The Central Administration of State University of New York completed work on a project funded by the U.S. Office of Education (USOE) to develop programs for analyzing management data on collection growth from OCLC-MARC tapes and also began work on a project funded by USOE to develop a responsive library acquisitions funding formula.

RESOURCE SHARING

In April 1977 the Task Force on a National Periodicals System of the National Commission on Libraries and Information Science (NCLIS) released its report on "Effective Access to Periodical Literature: A National Program." It recommended the establishment of a National Periodicals Center as early as 1978 or 1979. NCLIS proposed that the Library of Congress manage the Center, which would house a collection of about 50,000 titles.[3] As an alternative, the Center for Research Libraries (CRL) in Chicago proposed the establishment of a National Central Lending Library (NCLL) that would have as its first objective the acquiring of a national periodicals collection.[4] The NCLL, however, would not only acquire periodicals but also would accept deposits of less frequently used books and other library materials and serve as a complete lending library. At year's end the Council on Library Resources (CLR) announced that it had undertaken preparation, on behalf of the Library of Congress, of a detailed implementation plan for a center. The implications of the copyright law on the operations of a National Periodicals Center are not clear at this time. The NCLIS report concludes that the responsibility for adhering to the copyright guidelines rests with the borrowing libraries.

In an ALA prizewinning article in *American Libraries,* Richard DeGennaro of the University of Pennsylvania suggested that resource sharing will not result in major economies for libraries since the highest library expenditures are for personnel. He underscored the importance of resource sharing, however, for access to little-used materials. DeGennaro also maintained that concern over the new copyright law is unwarranted in view of the insignificant number of copies that may require royalty payment.[5] (See *also* Copyright.)

CRL added its 100th member in 1977 (by year's end there were more than 100 members). Stanford University and the University of California at Berkeley announced a cooperative program of exceptional scope, including a coordinated acquisitions policy. Supported by Sloan and Mellon Foundation grants, this venture will require two years to adjust and coordinate acquisitions services. A direct borrowing service between the institutions is already a feature of the program.

The Research Library Group (RLG) continued its program of resource sharing, with the result that its interlibrary loan transactions almost doubled from 1975 to 1977. Rapid interlibrary loan is an important aspect of the RLG program.

The Illinois State Library announced a proposed statewide collection development plan for Illinois. It would include a statewide directory of resources, bibliographic access to all collections by 1985, systematic collection of data base services, and a feasibility study for a statewide last-copy storage center.

During the year CLR announced a grant for an experimental project to develop a national serials location system. The pilot program will link local and regional holdings statements to the national automated data base being built through CONSER.

DEVELOPMENT FUNDING

Libraries continue to be beset by inflationary trends in materials prices. A 1977 study of academic research libraries by Miriam Drake of Purdue University showed that the average annual rate of increase in volumes held decreased in the majority of research libraries during the previous five years despite increased expenditures for materials.[6] This decrease in book buying power was evident in other types of libraries. Ohio libraries reported in 1977 that 1976 expenditures had increased 4 per cent, but 2 per cent fewer books had been purchased. Some types of libraries have shifted purchasing towards serials, and the number of books purchased has decreased. According to ARL figures in 1977, research libraries during the previous five years (1971-72 to 1975-76) subscribed to more serials, but added fewer books.

In the face of fierce inflation there was, fortunately, some encouraging news for materials funding. During 1976-77, USOE spent approximately $10,000,000 under Title II-A of the Higher Education Act to help supplement resources in the libraries of some 2,951 public and private nonprofit library agencies and institutions of higher education. Congress also approved Title II-C of the Higher Education Act and agreed to supply $5,000,000 for "strengthening research library resources" during FY1978.

Major support for collection development was made available to Florida academic libraries when the state legislature approved funds for capital expenditures in education. Florida State and the University of Florida received $7,000,000 for collection development during fiscal 1977-78 when it was decided that "library materials" qualified as a capital investment. A total of $10,000,000 was appropriated for all state-supported academic libraries in Florida.

The National Endowment for the Humanities (NEH) has provided monies for collection development and preservation. In 1977, for example, NEH made an award to Vanderbilt University to microfilm ancient manuscripts of the Ethiopian Orthodox church, available only in the hinterland of Ethiopia. Another award went to Case Western Reserve University Libraries for a program of conservation and preservation of library materials, including refurbishing storage areas for little-used materials. Many research libraries were beneficiaries of the Humanities Challenge Grants for Research Collections during 1977. (*See also* National Endowment for the Humanities.)

As Richard DeGennaro has noted, personnel costs are escalating at a rapid rate in libraries, and budgets have been consumed by a combination of rising salaries and wages and materials costs. The major proportion of a library budget (sometimes as much as 60 to 65 per cent) goes to personnel, and libraries are now beginning to utilize this personnel resource more effectively for collection development. In 1977 more effort and funds than ever before went into analysis of the collection development process.

FREDERICK C. LYNDEN

REFERENCES

1. Collection Development Committee, Resources Section, Resources and Technical Services Division, American Library Association, "Guidelines for the Formulation of Collection Development Policies," *Library Resources & Technical Services* (Winter 1977) pp. 40-47.
2. Allen Kent, et al., Progress Report on *"A Cost-Benefit Model of Some Critical Library Operations in Terms of Use of Materials"* (Pittsburgh: University of Pittsburgh, April 1, 1977, revised April 29, 1977).
3. Task Force on a National Periodicals System, National Commission on Libraries and Information Science, *Effective Access to the Periodical Literature: A National Program* (Washington, D.C.: U.S. Government Printing Office, 1977).
4. Center for Research Libraries, *A Proposal for a National Central Lending Library for the U.S.* (Chicago: Center for Research Libraries, 1977).
5. Richard DeGennaro, "Copyright, Resource Sharing, and Hard Times: A View from the Field," *American Libraries* (September 1977), pp. 430-35.
6. Miriam A. Drake, *Academic Research Libraries: A Study of Growth* (West Lafayette, Indiana: Purdue University, 1977).

Community Delivery Services

Although the search for alternative methods of delivering library services continued in 1977, variations on familiar themes appeared to be the most newsworthy. One of the unique attempts to reach library users during the year was the Detroit Public Library's "company

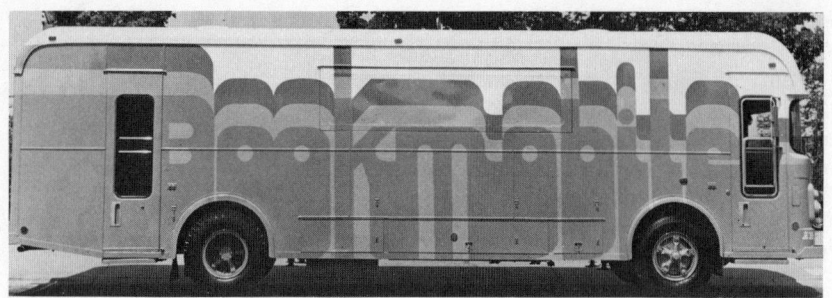

A Milwaukee Public Library bookmobile was repainted in bright colors using a graphic design supplied by a student at the Milwaukee School of Arts and painted by library staff volunteers.

card" plan. Designed to make noncirculating materials available to local organizations, the service listed "users" such as Ford, General Motors, Burroughs, and Detroit's leading banks.

Not content to bring books to people, the Mayne Williams Library in Johnson City, Tennessee, worked with local schools in a summer school bus program that delivered elementary school children to the library. Johnson City's elementary schools served as bus depots.

Bookmobiles continued to be the most traditional extension service, with more than 1,500 vehicles in operation. Modifications in conventional service, however, appeared to gain in popularity. It was even suggested that bookmobiles carry citizen band radios to improve service to CB fanatics. Perhaps a patron (CBer) could talk with the bookmobile staff to learn if materials on a particular subject were available and then meet the mobile unit at the stop closest to him to retrieve his find.

Inner-city and senior citizen bookmobiles brought materials to locales outside the central libraries' service areas. The West Florida Regional Library in Pensacola outfitted a Step Van and, cooperating with the county health department and other area social service agencies, took nurses with health information to people residing in housing projects.

Cooperating with community agencies, libraries continued to expand services to the homebound. Working with the Retired Senior Volunteer Program, the Louisville Free Public Library assembled more than 40 volunteers who took books, records, and films to citizens not able to leave their residences.

Because of increasing costs and studies indicating that many patrons disliked choosing materials from printed catalogs, mail-order programs showed no appreciable upsurge. A North Carolina survey found that rural patrons were most enthusiastic about extension services in the form of bookmobiles and least enthusiastic about books-by-mail service.

Port-a-Kiosks, port-a-structures, outpost libraries, and instant libraries emerged in 1977 as means by which to extend library services to the greatest number at affordable costs. These prefabricated designs, many of them sold as kits, provided quick branch libraries ranging from 400 to 1,600 square feet and costing from $13,000 to $50,000.

There was increased service in 1977 to the blind and physically handicapped and to imprisoned juveniles and adults. The Alabama Regional Library for the Blind and Physically Handicapped built a new facility featuring rounded wall corners and signs in Braille. In Louisville, the Sub-Regional Library for the Blind and Physically Handicapped recorded local newspapers on cassettes. And in Texas, the State Library cooperated with the Texas Library Association to develop statewide county jail standards for inmates' libraries. LSCA funds enabled the DuPage Library System in Illinois to acquire and maintain a library of vocational and self-help materials for inmates housed in facilities within the system's service area. Continued modification of delivery services will surely be influenced by the financial constraints of libraries and the energy constraints of the nation during the next decade.   RONALD S. KOZLOWSKI

REFERENCES

Arlan G. Bushman, "Prefabricated and Portable Library Units Offer Quick and Easy Extension of Service," *American Libraries* (November, 1977), pp. 546-48.

Timothy Hays, Kenneth Shearer, and Concepcion Wilson, "The Patron Is Not the Public," *Library Journal* (September 15, 1977), pp. 1813-18.

Pat Partovi, "CB Radio in the Library," *Library Journal* (October 15, 1977), pp. 2135-36.

Continuing Professional Education

For those concerned with continuing professional education for library, information, and media personnel 1977 might be summarized as a year of issue raising; experimentation with nontraditional forms of learning; self-study of missions, goals, and objectives by institutions, associations, and agencies as they serve lifelong learners; and an increase in communication about continuing education offerings across the nation.

The gradual realization of the value of continuing education in combating obsolescence in the profession and the threat of a decrease in beginning students have motivated more and more schools to increase their continuing education offerings to practitioners. It has also led to an increase in the number of post-Master's certificate programs offered—50 per cent of the ALA-accredited schools in the United States as of October 1977. None of the six Canadian schools has taken this route; but they, like the U.S. schools, are increasing their workshops, institutes, and special programs for practitioners. This has also brought about greater interaction between schools and practitioners and holds the potential of greater interaction in planning between state agencies and professional associations, and among the schools themselves.

The increase in concern for continuing education has also led many library associations and divisions of ALA, especially the Information Science and Automation Division (ISAD) and the Association of College and Research Libraries (ACRL), to sponsor more continuing education national and regional conferences and workshops. The Southwestern Library Association and the Medical Library Association have also continued their major efforts in taking learning experiences to practitioners.

This nationwide concern has been furthered and made more visible by the support of states, organizations, and agencies for the Continuing Library Education Network and Exchange (CLENE). During 1977 CLENE began working on a suggested plan to provide recognition for those who regularly participate in continuing education and for the providers who meet criteria of excellence in their programs. The proposed model includes the use of the Continuing Education Unit (CEU). CLENE also worked during 1977 for the development of more quality nontraditional forms of learning, particularly the development of home study programs, that would be available to all regardless of geographic location.

Model for Voluntary Recognition. A significant research and demonstration study in the area of continuing library, information, and media education was released at the end of 1977. The study was conducted by CLENE with Higher Education Act (HEA) Title II-B funds from the Office of Libraries and Learning Resources of the U.S. Office of Education (USOE). The development of a proposed model recognition system for presentation to the profession was the result of the 15-month project. The model includes the purposes of a voluntary recognition system for the profession, benefits to practitioners, eligibility for participation (all persons who work "in and with" libraries, information, and media resource centers), categories for which recognition is given, policies for continuing education program measurement, conversion charts for assignment of contact hours to type of activities, criteria for planned program development, and specifics on how to apply for recognition. The system provides recognition not only to the individual who participates in continuing education but also to the providers of opportunities who meet the criteria agreed upon for the programs. The system makes provision for the inclusion of academic credit hours and the use of the CEU and develops policies that permit the use of planned and guided independent study.

The development of a voluntary recognition system for library, information, and media practitioners who participate regularly in con-

Workshops in Casper, Wyoming, sponsored by the Wyoming State Library and the State Department of Education in 1977 were designed to familiarize librarians with services offered by those two agencies.

tinuing education and the development of quality nontraditional learning modes such as home study does not provide the total answer to the problem of obsolescence in the profession. This study does conclude, however, that recognition would stimulate more participation in continuing education by practitioners and that it contains enough benefits over the present status of continuing education in the profession to warrant the time, energy, and money involved in establishing such a system. Furthermore, recognition, by stimulating participation, also means that recognized (and thus quality) traditional and nontraditional continuing education programs will become increasingly better.

Nontraditional Forms. During 1977 a number of experiments demonstrated the growing conviction throughout the profession that means of delivering continuing educational offerings must not be limited by the usual time and space restrictions of the traditional system. There was also evidence that programs should be delivered at times and places convenient to the nontraditional learner and that the use of currently available delivery methods such as home study courses, independent study and tutorials, radio, television, newspapers, and satellites should be fully explored.

Prototype Home Study Course. An important part of the CLENE-USOE recognition project was the development of a prototype home study course. Its purpose was to demonstrate that geographical location need not be a barrier to learning and that home study can meet criteria of quality that warrants its inclusion in continuing education recognition systems. The title of the course developed was "Motivation: A Vital Force in the Organization." The home study course developed was to be offered by Catholic University of America starting in 1978. The guidelines for groups involved in the development of home study programs are available from CLENE.

Talkback TV. In Oklahoma the Library Technical Assistant (LTA) Training Program was offered from August to December through Oklahoma's Higher Education Instruction System. The Program was a joint venture of the Oscar Rose Junior College and the Oklahoma Department of Libraries. It pro-

99

Continuing Professional Education

vided an opportunity for academic, public, and school library clerks, aides, and other non-professional staff members—freshman and sophomore college students—to expand their library skills. The course was braodcast live and beamed via microwave satellite stations across the state. Oklahoma is the first state to incorporate this particular method of learning for library instruction.

Idaho Libraries and TV. With a $243,305 grant from the W.J. Kellogg Foundation to the University of Idaho, education resource centers with videotape equipment will be established in libraries throughout the state. The first five or six centers were to open in January 1978. Each library location will have a video playback unit—essentially a television console—and required accessories. The major group for whom the service is designed is the professional seeking certification or recertification in order to practice in such fields as education, engineering, and forestry.

Job Enrichment Experiences. The New Mexico Library Association announced an innovative program by which the Association makes grants of $200 to individuals to help defray their expenses to spend a minimum of 10 days as visiting librarian in a library that they feel will enhance their perspective on their own institution or position. A similar program was inaugurated by the Mountain Plains Library Association in which grants of $200 were made to individuals to visit an outstanding library program in another state to observe and work with the program for one week.

On-Line Systems. In November a conference on "On-Line Revolution in Libraries" at the University of Pittsburgh's Graduate School of Library and Information Sciences drew a spectacular attendance of 700 persons from across the nation. Such a record attendance dramatically demonstrates the importance of this subject for the continuing education of librarians. At the conference, it was announced that an On-Line Bibliographic and Information Systems Training Center would begin in March 1978 to provide individualized instruction for practitioners in searching on-line data bases.

OTHER DEVELOPMENTS

The twenty-five states that participated in the 1976-77 Institute for State Library Agency Personnel Involved in Continuing Education, sponsored by CLENE and USOE and funded by HEA Title II-B, examined their objectives for continuing education and their relation to their states' overall library development plans. The Institute developed a "Continuing Education Planning Inventory: A Self-Evaluation Checklist" for general distribution; it is available from CLENE. Another product of the Institute was a *Continuing Education Resource Book* that gives examples of propsed policy statements on continuing education, examples of statewide planning, and recommendations for continuing self-assessment of needs.

The College Libraries Section of ACRL formed a Continuing Education Committee in 1977 with the charge to examine the needs for continuing education for college librarians and to make such proposals as may be necessary to meet those needs. The Committee was to meet the first time during the ALA Midwinter Meeting in January 1978. The Continuing Education Committee of the Chief Officers of State Library Agencies is undertaking a project to study the continuing education needs of state library agencies.

In September 1977 the Continuing Library Education Planning Coordination Project (COLEPAC) published the 412-page *Directory of Wisconsin Continuing Library Media Education Producers and Programs* (University of Wisconsin: Madison), the first publication of its kind in Wisconsin. The Continuing Education for Library Staffs in the Southwest, a major project of the Southwestern Library Association, took an assessment in 1977 of accomplishments since its founding and is using the report by Brooke Sheldon as a tool for future planning and programming.

The Medical Library Association, a longtime leader in continuing professional education, took a major step in December 1977 with the publication of their *Examination Booklet*. In addition to graduation from an ALA-accredited library school program, qualifications for certification include a passing grade on a competency-based examination in three functional areas—public services, technical services, and administration (approximately one-third of the questions dealing with each function)—and two years of post-library-degree experience in a health sciences library at the professional level. The first competency-based examination at testing centers across the United States and Canada was scheduled for April 1978. The *Examination Booklet* specifies the competencies to be tested in each of the three functional areas. Recertification of health sciences librarians and library technicians will be required every five years in order to ensure continuing competence. Recertification will require satisfactory completion of continuing education courses and/or formal education courses, or an examination (with specifics to be announced later).

In view of this development and as more and more states are requiring professionals to continue their education, CLENE wrote to State Library Agencies to learn the status of certification requirements in their states. Replies from 60 per cent of the states indicated that, in addition to certification for school and media librarians, 14 states had requirements for certification of public librarians, 2 for junior or community college librarians, 3 for college and university librarians, and 2 for special librarians. In 9 other states certification for libraries was being discussed;. 7 states reported that it was not an issue at this time.

CLENE. Founded in the fall of 1975, CLENE continued to carry out its basic core services, engaged in research and demonstration activity, serviced state library agency personnel through an institute on statewide planning for continuing education, and initiated some new services. The *CLENExchange*, a quarterly interdisciplinary newsletter in the field of continuing education, was issued regularly. The second edition of the *Continuing Education Opportunities Directory* was published, and an analysis of the listings received showed that of the 239 programs reported the largest percentage (65 per cent) was offered by library education programs. Associations accounted for 15 per cent, and the remainder were offered by state library agencies and other miscellaneous sponsors. The largest number of offerings was in the field of management and administration (as was true in the 1976 listing). The second largest was in reference services, and the third largest was in information systems and networks. The method of instruction listed most often was the lecture method; a close second was the discussion method, followed by open questions. There was an increse over 1976 listings in the use of television or videotapes, in simulation methods including role playing, and in the use of games as a learning technique.

CLENE also issued two new Concept Papers, bringing the total number to five. The last issued was *Continuing Library Education Needs Assessment and Model Programs*. Two CLENE membership assemblies, each of which included workshop components, were held during 1977. In January the theme was "Lifelong Learning: Continuing Education and Staff Development;" in July the theme was "Continuing Education Delivery Systems." In addition to completing the USOE-funded research project for the development of a model recognition system and a prototype home study program, CLENE also provided substantive leadership through the conduct of a "Training Institute for State Library Agency Personnel Involved in Continuing Education."

As the only organization dedicated solely to continuing education in the profession, the unique strength of CLENE is the opportunity for sharing ideas across many different organizations and interests. The sharing of ideas on issues was strengthened during 1977 by the formation of six action groups (representing types of members) to make recommendations both to CLENE and to the profession at large for continuing education. Continuing Education Communicators have been identified for states, for library education programs, and for associations. Information is now being collected monthly to present quick access to continuing education opportunities in the form of the *Continuing Education Communicator*. It is distributed on the 20th of each month to the Communicators, who, in turn, are responsible for distributing information to their groups.

CLENE is a vehicle for the implementation of Objective Four of the National Program Statement of the National Commission on Libraries and Information Science (NCLIS): to "Ensure basic and continuing education of personnel essential to the implementation of the National Program." The CLENE groundwork laid for long-term improvement of continuing education for library, information, and media personnel is descirbed in the lead article, "CLENE: A Success Story" by Barbara Conroy, in the July 1977 *Library Journal*.

ELIZABETH W. STONE

CONTU

The National Commission on New Technological Uses of Copyrighted Works (CONTU) during 1977 continued "to study and compile data on the reproduction and use of copyrighted works of authorship in conjunction with automatic systems capable of storing, processing, retrieving, and transferring information . . . and the reproduction and use of such copyrighted works by various forms of machine reproduction . . ." as mandated by Public Law 93-573, which established the Commission.

Meetings. At its 11th meeting held in January, the Commission examined issues concerned with the photocopying of coyrighted works. Current photocopying practices at the National Agricultural Library and the Exxon Corporation were outlined. The National Technical Information Service (NTIS) discussed its proposed system for supplying its customers with authorized photocopies of journal articles, and the Commissioners heard an analysis of the technological capabilities of copying equipment. Representatives from the Association of American Publishers, the Information Industry Association, and the Authors' League of America also testified on photocopy issues.

The February meeting was devoted to Commission discussion of copyright protection for computer software and automated data bases and methods to check unauthorized photocopying of copyrighted materials.

At the March hearings a proposal for a copy payment center, which later evolved into the Copyright Clearance Center, was presented to the Commission. At the same session the Commissioners heard reports on the sampling, licensing, and payment systems of the American Society of Composers, Artists and Performers (ASCAP) and Broadcast Music, Inc. (BMI), and a summary of the publishing and reprint sales activities of the American Institute of Physics. A progress report was also presented on a study being conducted for the Commission by the Public Interest Economics Center analyzing computer and photocopy issues from the point of view of the general public.

Following discussions at the May meeting, reports from the Subcommittees on Computer Software and Data Bases with Additional Views were distributed to approximately 1,000 interested parties who were invited to respond either through written comments or requests for the opportunity to testify at future meetings.

Speakers and Studies. In July William Baumol presented views on economic issues relating to property rights of computer software and data bases. Fritz Machlup presented his views on the economics of photocopy clearance mechanisms. Vernon Palmour reported on a study for the Commission (*Costs of Owning, Borrowing, and Disposing of Periodical Publications*, PB 274 821), comparing the costs to a library of subscribing to a journal as opposed to requesting photocopies of individual articles through interlibrary loan. Bernard Fry, Dean of the Graduate Library School at Indiana University, summarized the results of a study on the attitudes and practices of journal publishers in supplying copies of articles or licensing authorized photocopies. The study is entitled *Survey of Publisher Practices and Present Attitudes on Authorized Journal Article Copying and Licensing. . . .* (PB 271 003). The Commission also heard testimony by the Public Interest Economics Center and the Public Interest Satellite Association on whether the interests of consumers would be advanced by increasing or decreasing the stringency of the present copyright law.

In September representatives of computer industry organizations (Association for Computing Machinery, Applied Data Research, Computer and Business Equipment Manufacturers Association, and Information Industry Association) testified on the issue of copyright for computer software in response to the Commission's Subcommittee report. The results of a study conducted by King Research, Inc., for CONTU, the National Commission on Libraries and Information Science (NCLIS), and the National Science Foundation were presented to the Commission. The study, *Library Photocopying in the United States and Its Implications for the Development of a Copyright Royalty Mechanism*, is available from NTIS. This study examined library photocopying practices and surveyed American libraries on various proposed copyright royalty payment mechanisms. A representative of University Microfilms summarized the present and future licensed photocopying activities of the firm and described a pilot project for automatically recording microform copying transactions.

Other Issues. The October meeting was devoted entirely to photocopying with testimony presented by representatives of the Council of National Library Associations, the Authors' League of America, and the Association of American Publishers. All three recommended no changes in the 1976 act. The Commission heard a description of the Original Article Tear Sheet (OATS) and authorized photocopying services of the Institute for Scientific Information. In addition the Commission received a progress report on the organization of the Copyright Clearance Center and received a document outlining further the NTIS plans to arrange for the supply of authorized, royalty-paid photocopies of journal articles by various organizations dealing with NTIS.

The technologies that affect the development, collection, retention, organization, and delivery of information were studied and discussed at the November Commission meeting. Also reported were the results of a Harbridge House study for the Commission on the methods of protecting computer software currently being used by the industry. The study, *Legal Protection of Computer Software: An Industrial Survey*, is available from NTIS.

In view of the fact that an act to extend the term of CONTU by an additional seven months was signed into law by President Carter in late October, the Commission revised its timetable and made plans for further study of the computer software, data base, and photocopy issues. The final report to the President and Congress was due not later than July 31, 1978.

ARTHUR J. LEVINE

Copyright

The year 1977 may well be called the Year of Deja Vu of the U.S. Copyright Law of 1976. The new law had been enacted by Congress in 1976 and signed by the President on October 19, 1976, with an effective date of January 1, 1978. The arena for issues relating to library photocopying moved from Capitol Hill to the National Commission on New Technological Uses of Copyrighted Materials (CONTU). The American Association of Publishers and the Authors League of America attempted—during the year—to convince CONTU that the Commission should issue guidelines and definitions beyond the three sets of Guidelines already contained in the Congressional reports prepared before enactment of the law. In brief, the thrust of the attempts by the AAP and Authors League was to increase the kinds of photocopying eligible for fee payments beyond the kinds stated in the CONTU Guidelines. The efforts and arguments put forth have been almost identical to those used during the Congressional consideration of the revision bills.

Representatives of the library community have presented testimony to CONTU to resist such efforts to issue additional guidelines. The testimony was presented by the Committee on Copyright Law Practice and Implementation[1] of the Council of National Library Associations (CNLA). The CNLA Committee emphasized that Subsection 108(i) of the law provides for a review by the Register of Copyrights five years after the effective date of the law and every five years thereafter. The addition of Subsection 108(i) had been initially recommended by the library association so that adjustments equitable to all parties can be made. Publishers and authors had agreed to the addition of Subsection 108(i). If CONTU were to issue additional guidelines, after enactment of the law, such guidelines would have dubious validity because CONTU is not a regulatory agency nor is it a legislative body.

Five conclusions were expressed by the CNLA committee in its presentation to CONTU on October 21, 1977:

(1) Libraries exist to serve their users, and libraries are the agents of the users. Librarians are concerned that the public interest be served and protected through ready access to all information. Fair use assures access to information by all Americans who are library users. Their rights should prevail. There should be no bias to any segment of American society.

(2) Creative works of authorship and publications in the arts and humanities must receive the same consideration as works in science and engineering.

(3) There are a number of areas of possible ambiguity yet to be finally resolved. At the same time it is the CNLA Committee's considered belief that after the extensive negotiations and sometimes difficult compromises that were reached during the legislative phase, the law that has emerged represents a reasonable compromise plan which needs to be tested during the next five years (as is mandated in Subsection 108(i) of the law).

(4) There is no evidence in the data of the statistical photocopying study by King Research, Inc., to suggest that there is any need for any actions before the five-year review mandated in Subsection 108(i). It is not appropriate that additional guidelines or definitions be prepared at this time. It is first necessary to collect factual operating data under the new law during the five years before the mandated review.

(5) From the experiences to be gained during the next five years with the new law, *all* parties concerned will be better able to fully assess the impact of the new law on their individual goals and on their common goals to provide all users of copyrighted works with ready and reasonable access to information.

It is necessary to record, according to the transcripts, that CONTU has spent a disproportionate amount of its time in consideration of photocopying. (The transcripts of the CONTU meetings from October 1975 through September 1977 have 1,209 pages relating to photocopying issues out of a total of 2,663 pages for the 15 meetings.) Time spent was disproportionate to the other defined purposes of CONTU as stated in P.L. 93-573 (December 31, 1974):

TITLE II—NATIONAL COMMISSION ON NEW TECHNOLOGICAL USES OF COPYRIGHTED WORKS

Establishment and Purpose of Commission

SEC. 201. (a) There is hereby created in the Library of Congress a National Commission on New Technological Uses of Copyrighted Works (hereafter called the Commission).

(b) The purpose of the Commission is to study and compile date on:

(1) the reproduction and use of copyrighted works of authorship—

(A) in conjunction with automatic systems capable of storing, processing, retrieving, and transferring information, and

(B) by various forms of machine reproduction, not including reproduction by or at the request of instructors for use in face-to-face teaching activities; and

(2) the creation of new works by the application or intervention of such automatic systems or machine reproduction.

Clause (1)(A) and Clause (2) of Subsection 201(b) above were intended for a study of the introduction of copyrighted works into computer data bases as well as consideration if computer programs or software could be copyrighted. The life of CONTU was defined to be two years from January 1, 1976 to December 31, 1977. President Ford did not appoint

Members of the Arkansas delegation to the ALA Conference in Detroit wear appropriate tee shirts for the copyright meeting. The shirt was a project of the Arkansas Library Association to alert the public to the new law.

the members of the Commission until seven months of its lifetime had passed. Therefore, in 1977, the Commission asked Congress to extend its life by seven months. The House had authorized the extension on April 11, 1977, but the Senate did not act until October 13. Recommendations from CONTU will not be known until some yet undetermined time after July 31, 1978. The Commission's final report is to be submitted to Congress within 60 days after July 31, 1978.

Photocopying Study. The long-awaited statistical study of photocopying by King Research, Inc., was completed in August 1977. The study was jointly funded by the National Commission on Libraries and Information Science, National Science Foundation and CONTU. Although draft copies of the King Report[2] have become available, final copies had not been released by the time that this annual survey was prepared.

Although the King study reports a total of 114,000,000 photocopies prepared by libraries per year, less than half this quantity (54,000,000 copies) were of copyrighted materials. Of these, about 39,000,000 were from serials—the materials of greatest expressed concern by the AAP and Authors League.

The new Copyright Law [Subsection 108(g)] addresses only the preparation of photocopies in lieu of interlibrary loan. Similarly, the so-called CONTU Guidelines refer only to photocopies in lieu of interlibrary loans. The King study shows that only 500,000 photocopies out of the 54,000,000 copies of copyrighted materials or 0.9% were apparently "eligible" for royalty payments under the CONTU Guidelines. The word "apparently" is used in the preceding sentence because photocopies made under "fair use" (Section 107) were not identified and, therefore, not excluded from the reported 500,000 copies.

The King Report presents many tabulations that require careful reading and careful study. These statistics can serve as the basis for a comparative study in the mandated five-year review.

Copyright Clearance Centers. The AAP has incorporated a Copyright Clearance Center as a centralized collection center for payments of fees. The AAP/CCC does not provide photocopies. The CCC was planned by the Technical, Scientific and Medical Division of AAP with the cooperation of the Authors League of America, the Information Industry Association and some scientific societies.

Each publisher-participant in the CCC will establish his own fee per article; apparently publishers of more than one periodical will set different fees for each title. The Center will deduct $.25 from the fee paid for each article in 1978 as the Center's handling charge. Publishers' fees announced to date range from $1 to $7 per article.

A federal agency, The National Technical Information Service (NTIS), has announced a service for users of NTIS by which photocopies will be ordered from a supplying library for delivery to the requesting library. NTIS has announced a flat fee of $.50 per article to be paid to participating publishers. It is interesting to note that some publishers who have agreed to the NTIS fee of $.50 are also participating in the AAP/CCC at higher rates.

The Institute for Scientific Information (ISI) in Philadelphia also provides copies of articles thru its OATS service for about 4,000 serial titles. ISI pay royalties directly to some of its participating publishers. Xerox University Microfilms (Ann Arbor) through its hard copy service also pays an established royalty of 10 per cent to publishers who have assigned reprint rights to University Microfilms.

It is important to note that NTIS, ISI, and University Microfilm all provide copies as well as royalty payments. The AAP/CCC does not provide copies but only collects fees. This Center offers as a supposed advantage a centralized billing service which is supposedly so simplified as to save work for librarians. It is doubtful that the simple billing procedure proposed will meet with the approval of the accounting and auditing functions of most institutions.

Publisher Attitudes. The Indiana University Graduate Library School conducted a survey of publisher practices and attitudes on copying and licensing under a contract from CONTU.[3]

The survey population was 2,552 scholarly and research journals distributed by 1,672 publishers in the U.S. The response rate for publishers was 31.8 per cent (531 out of 1,672) and the response rate for journals was 38.2 percent (974 out of 2,552). About 60 per cent of the non-responding journals were copyrighted. Of the responding journals, 89.5 per cent (or 872 titles) were copyrighted.

The research team found it somewhat difficult to draw clear conclusions. Many respondents had little if any expectations of receiving payment through any payment mechanism. In many cases, there was an unwillingness to give permission, while at the same time having no expectation of return.

When the voluminous date of the Indiana University study is carefully considered, the reader may well ask why there has been the continuing barrage of publicity from the AAP concerning the need for its Copyright Clearance Center. One apparently reasonable explanation is that the AAP represents only a fraction of U.S. publishers.

It appears that a number of major publishers, both for-profit and not-for-profit, expect increased income from the copying fees. Scholarly and research publishing is predominantly that of relatively small not-for-profit journals. Of the responding publishers, 84.6 per cent (449 out of 531) publish only one title; and 95.5 per cent (507 out of 531) publish five or fewer titles.

Recommendations for Libraries. Advisory materials have been developed by the CNLA Committee in cooperation with committees of the individual library associations:

(a) Revised Interlibrary Loan Form with added lines to show compliance with the new law by the requesting library—when the ILL Form is ued to request photocopies. The revised ILL Form is accompanied by instructions for its use.

(b) Recommendation for the *Notice* of copyright to be included on reproductions as required by Subsection 108(a) (3).

(c) Recommendation for the *Notice* to be displayed on unsupervised reproducing equipment in a library or archives as required by Subsection 108(f) (1).

(d) Recommended Record Maintenance and Retention Procedures for Interlibrary Loans (i.e. when photocopies are requested in lieu of a loan).

(e) "Copyright Clearance" Procedures for Photocopying: Information for Librarians (as required by CONTU Guideline No.4).

The above materials are being published in the journals of the library associations or are being distributed to the members of the associations. These materials have also been submitted to CONTU for information of the members of the Commission.

FRANK McKENNA

[1] Members of the CNLA committee represented American Association of Law Libraries, American Library Association, Association of Research Libraries, Medical Library Association, Music Library Association and Special Libraries Association.
[2] "Library Photocopying in the United States and Its Implications for the Development of a Copyright Royalty Payment Mechanism." King Research, Inc., Bethesda, Md. 20852 (August 31, 1977)
[3] "Scholarly and Research Journals: Survey of Publisher Practices and Attitudes in Authorized Journal Article Copying and Licensing." Bernard M. Fry, Herbert S. White and Elizabeth C. Johnson. Bloomington, Indiana (June 30, 1977)

The New U.S. Copyright Law: A Bibliography

A flood of articles and several books dealing with the text of the new copyright law (Public Law 94-553), with its legislative history, with the three sets of guidelines provided in the legislative history, and with the probable impact on individuals and institutions appeared during the interim year before the law took effect on January 1, 1978. As providers of information in a variety of forms, as administrators of institutions serving all those affected by copyright, and as producers, on occasion, of copyrighted works, librarians are being forced to look at the copyright law from many points of view.

In this list an effort has been made to provide some background material, especially bibliographies, to represent different opinions on controversial points, to cover the various aspects of the law, and to avoid a narrow concentration on the problem of library photocopying. The list focuses on publications that appeared between September 1976 and December 1977. It is limited to English-language publications.

Basic Documents

Public Law 94-553: Title 17—Copyright (October 19, 1976). The new copyright law is the first overall revision of U.S. copyright law since 1909 and replaces the previous Title 17 of the U.S. Code. The effective date of the new law was January 1, 1978.

Senate Report SR 94-473, November 20, 1975: Report of the Senate Committee on the Judiciary (to accompany S 22). The Report contains an earlier version of PL 94-553 along with the Committee's interpretation of it.

House Report HR 94-1476, September 3, 1976: Report of the House of Representatives Committee on the Judiciary (to accompany S 22) with corrections in the *Congressional Record*, September 21 and 22, 1976 (Reprinted in *Copyright Office Announcements* ML-130 and ML-132.) The Report contains the "Guidelines on Multiple Copies for Classroom or Teaching Uses" (pp. 68-70) and the "Guidelines for Educational Uses of Music" (pp. 70-71). These guidelines explicate Section 107 of the law and were agreed to by representatives of the educational community and publisher-author representatives.

Conference Report HR 94-1733, September 29, 1976: Report of Senate-House Conference Committee (to accompany S 22, which became PL 94-553). This contains the CONTU (National Commission on New Technological Uses of Copyrighted Works) Guidelines for the Proviso of Subsection 108 (g) (2). These guidelines deal with the limits on interlibrary arrangements for photocopying.

"Warning of Copyright for Use by Libraries and Archives," *Federal Register* (November 16, 1977), pp. 59264-65. This specifies the wording of warnings required by Section 108 (d) and (e).

Governmental Sources of Current Information

Federal Register. This carries notices of the adoption of regulations to implement the new law (see example above). As the Copyright Office calls for hearings on, or reactions to, its proposals for such regulations, the official notices also appear in the daily issues of the *Federal Register.*

Library of Congress Information Bulletin. This carries news of the activities of the Copyright Office in its weekly issues and also carries the "Semiannual Report on Developments at the Library of Congress," which summarizes the work of the Copyright Office.

Circulars. The Copyright Office publishes numerous free cir-

Copyright

culars on specific copyright subjects (e.g., *Copyright and the Librarian, Duration of Copyright under the New Law.*, and *Highlights of the New Copyright Law (1976)*. A useful circular, which is periodically revised, is *Selected Bibliographies.*

A list of the publications of the Copyright Office may be obtained free upon request. You may have your name added to the Copyright Office Mailing List by sending a written request. Address requests to Copyright Office, Library of Congress, Washington, D.C. 20559.

ALA Kit

American Library Association, *Librarian's Copyright Kit: What You Must Know Now* (Chicago: American Library Association, 1978). A clearly marked file folder contains the following items.

American Library Association, Reference and Adult Services Division, Interlibrary Loan Committee, "Guidelines: Records of Interlibrary Photocopying Requests," *American Libraries* (December 1977), p. 624. This is an advisory statement on what records libraries should maintain to assure compliance with PL 94-553 and to provide documentation for the five-year review of the law's effect (Section 108i).

American Library Association, Resources and Technical Services Division, Implementation of the Copyright Revision Act Committee, "Guidelines for Seeking or Making a Copy of an Entire Copyrighted Work for a Library, Archives or User." This is an advisory statement on procedures libraries should follow to obtain replacement copies of copyrighted works unavailable from normal trade sources.

"Copyright Law Prompts New ILL Form," *American Libraries* (October 1977, p. 492B-C. This shows the new ALA Interlibrary Loan Form with an explanation of all changes and directions for its use.

Council of National Library Associations, Committee on Copyright Practice and Implementation, "Proposed Copyright Clearance Procedures," *Washington Newsletter* (October 28, 1977). This explains when and how to seek permission to reproduce copyrighted material.

Lewis I. Flacks, "Living in the Gap of Ambiguity: an Attorney's Advice to Librarians on the Copyright Law," *American Libraries* (May 1977), pp. 252-57. An attorney on the staff of the U.S. Copyright Office gives his personal opinions in response to nine questions that librarians have frequently asked him about Section 108.

Edward G. Holley, "A Librarian Looks at the New Copyright Law," *American Libraries* (May 1977). The Dean of the University of North Carolina School of Library Science and a Past President of the American Library Association warns that there are no quick and easy answers to the questions posed by the new law. The text of Sections 107 and 108 is included.

Librarian's Guide to the New Copyright Law (Chicago: American Library Association, 1976). This is a reprint of the special issue of the *Washington Newsletter* (November 15, 1976) on copyright. It gives guidance in studying the law and contains excerpts from the statute, the text of the three sets of guidelines, and excerpts from the House and Senate reports.

The New Copyright Law; Questions Teachers and Librarians Ask (Washington, D.C.: National Education Association, 1977). In as clear and simple a manner as possible, answers are provided for common questions about reproducing print and nonprint materials.

William D. North, "An Interim Look at the Copyright Revision Act of 1976" (Chicago: American Library Association, 1977). Speaking as legal counsel of ALA, North analyzes Section 108 and suggests a program of action that libraries might adopt in preparing to comply with the new law.

"Warning Notices for Copies and Machines," *American Libraries* (November 1977), p. 530. Language is suggested for the warning notices required by Section 108a3 and fl.

In addition the *Kit* contains language and specifications for "Display Warning of Copyright" and for "Order Warning of Copyright" as required by Section 108d and e and issued by the U.S. Copyright Office.

Other Useful Materials about the New Law

Association for Educational Communications and Technology, *Copyright and Educational Media: A Guide to Fair Use and Permissions Procedures* (Washington D.C.: Association for Educational Communications and Technology and Association for Media Producers, 1977). This is a helpful manual for those involved with all educational media.

Association of American Publishers, *Explaining the New Copyright Law: A Guide to Legitimate Photocopying of Copyrighted Materials.* (Washington, D.C.: Association of American Publishers, 1977). This pamphlet includes the text of the three sets of guidelines related to the law as well as the publishers' interpretation of the law and the guidelines and information on obtaining permission to copy.

Luciana Chee, "How to Research Copyright Law," *Law Library Journal* (May 1977), pp. 171-83. A law librarian provides citations and descriptions of tools needed for basic current and retrospective copyright research and arranges them in order of use.

Commerce Clearing House, *Copyright Revision Act of 1976: Law, Explanation, Committee Reports* (Chicago: Commerce Clearing House, 1976). This is a comprehensive standard source providing a CCH explanation of the law.

"Copyright: A Report," in *The Bowker Annual of Library & Book Trade Information,* 22d ed. (New York: R.R. Bowker Company, 1977), pp. 116-71. Besides reprinting ALA's *Librarian's Guide to the New Copyright Law,* this section offers articles by Julius Marke and Charles H. Lieb, both lawyers. The text of the statute is reprinted in Appendix 4 of this edition of the *Bowker Annual.*

Bernard M. Fry, Herbert S. White, and Elizabeth L. Johnson, *Survey of Publisher Practices and Present Attitudes on Authorized Journal Article Copying and Licensing* (Springfield,

Virginia: National Technical Information Service, 1977). CONTU commissioned this study of publishers of scholarly and research journals carried out by the Research Center of the Indiana University Graduate Library School.

Melinda V. Golub, "'Not by Books Alone: Library Copying of Nonprint, Copyrighted Material," *Law Library Journal* (May 1977) pp. 153-70. The problems created by the widespread use of photocopying machines, microform reader-printers, and audiotape and videotape copiers are discussed in the light of such court cases as *Williams & Wilkins* and *CBS, Inc.,* v. *Vanderbilt University.*

Donald Johnston, *A Copyright Guide* (New York: R.R. Bowker Company, in preparation).

Julius J. Marke, "United States Copyright Revision and Its Legislative History," *Law Library Journal* (May 1977), pp. 121-52. This is a detailed, documented account of copyright legislation from the 18th century to the present with much information about the writing of the new law and the guidelines.

David J. Martz, Jr., "Manuscripts as Literary Property: Everybody's Problem," *Manuscripts* (Winter 1977) pp. 23-27. This provides a clear explanation of the difference between physical custody or ownership of a manuscript and ownership of literary rights to the manuscript.

Medical Library Association, *The Copyright Law and the Health Sciences Librarian* (Chicago: Medical Library Association, 1978).

Jody Newmyer, "Art, Libraries, and the Censor," *Library (Quarterly* January 1976), pp. 38-53. This deals with the relationship of the visual arts to American law and to copyright law in particular.

Melville B. Nimmer, *A Preliminary View of the Copyright Act of 1976: Analysis and Text* (New York: Matthew Bender, 1977). This is the 1976 Special Alert Supplement to Nimmer's authoritative treatise on copyright law.

Marybeth Peters, *General Guide to the Copyright Act of 1976* (Washington, D.C.: U.S. Copyright Office, 1977). This instructional material used for training the Copyright Office staff includes a chart comparing the Acts of 1909 and 1976, the three sets of guidelines, and a list on "Official Source Materials on Copyright Revision."

Leon E. Seltzer, "Exemptions and Fair Use in Copyright: The 'Exclusive Rights' Tensions in the New Copyright Act," *Bulletin of the Copyright Society of the U.S.A.* (April-June 1977), pp. 215-77, 279-337. This is a scholarly study that concludes with some suggested solutions for problems in the area of the fair use of copyrighted materials.

John C. Stedman, "The New Copyright Law: Photocopying for Educational Use," *AAUP Bulletin* (February 1977), pp. 5-16. This is a thoughtful, well-documented article by the Chairman of the Committee on Copyright Revision of the American Association of University Professors.

Patricia Whitestone, *Photocopying in Libraries, the Librarians Speak* (White Plains, New York: Knowledge Industry Publications, 1977). This reports on a survey of photocopying practices in academic, government, public, and special libraries. The survey was conducted by Knowledge Industry Publications early in 1976.

Copyright News. News and comment about the implementation of the copyright law can be found in such columns as "Copyright Today" in *Audiovisual Instruction* and "Interlibrary Loan Issues" in *RQ* as well as the frequent articles by Susan Wagner in *Publishers Weekly.* Volumes 9 (1974) and 10 (1975) of *Annual Review of Information Science and Technology* (ARIST) had chapters reviewing the literature on copyright of special interest to the information community. The *Bulletin of the Copyright Society of the U.S.A.* carries an annotated bibliography that includes government publications, law review articles, and materials in some foreign languages.

MILDRED VANNORSDALL

Council, ALA

The issue for the American Library Association and for ALA Council during 1977 was *The Speaker,* a 40-minute documentary educational film sponsored by the Intellectual Freedom Committee (IFC). The controversy and debate which the film sparked fueled the week-long Annual Conference in Detroit. For the first time in many an Association meeting, the "nuts and bolts" of ALA business were overshadowed by debate on the ethical, moral, and social responsibilities that concern the profession.

The Speaker presents the dilemma faced by a typical community when a well-known speaker who supports the view that Blacks are genetically inferior to whites is invited to speak at the local high school. The film's promotional material states that *The Speaker* "aims to challenge indifference to the First Amendment by presenting a controversy in which it is not easy to take sides.... the film strives to encourage individuals to seek a deeper understanding of the role of free expression."

ALA Debate. The film officially premiered at the first membership meeting at the Annual Conference. ALA President Clara Jones opened the floor for membership discussion. The reactions, whether pro or con, were emotional and outspoken. It was charged that the film was racist, demeaning, and stereotyped in its portrayal of Blacks and was not concerned with issues of the First Amendment and librarianship. Those arguing in favor of the film contended that the ongoing debate proved the film's value as a discussion tool and that by leaving no easy answers, the situation presented in the film challenged everyone to rethink the issue of intellectual freedom. As the first membership meeting closed, the ALA Black Caucus issued a call for a special meeting to plan a response.

At the second membersip meeting Councilor Nancy Kellum-Rose introduced a resolution demanding that ALA's imprimatur be removed from the film. An attempt was made to amend this resolution by substituting a document sponsored by the Black Caucus that specifically cited racial arguments against the film and resolved that the Association withdraw its name from the film. The debate that followed was lengthy and spirited. When the vote was called for, the amendment sponsored by the Black Caucus failed. In considering the original resolution, the membership decided by a margin of only four votes (326–322) that *The Speaker* would retain the name of the ALA. At the conclusion of the meeting it was apparent that the issues and the anger were still alive.

The debate continued at the Council meeting that afternoon. Council member E.J. Josey introduced a resolution that "out of respect for its Black members and out of real concern for the preservation of the integrity of the Association in terms of its own Library Bill of Rights, the Black Caucus requests that the ALA withdraw its name from the film." The Council voted by a large majority not to remove the ALA's name from *The Speaker*, but the dissension was obviously not satisfied. In an effort to bridge the gaps that had widened in a week of divisive debate, Ella Gaines Yates, a member of IFC and the Black Caucus, asked that the rules be suspended to introduce a resolution directing that a statement be added to the film and the accompanying study guide to "clarify the purpose of the film." This resolution provided a welcome compromise, and it was passed and sent to the Executive Board for implementation. It was clear from the discussion at the Executive Board meeting the next day, however, that the resolution would not be easy to implement and that the controversial debate on *The Speaker* would be continued at the 1978 Midwinter Meeting in Chicago.

Other Matters. At the 1977 Midwinter Meeting, Council considered matters relating to the restructuring of ALA in light of the implementation of the new dues structure. Council met as a committee of the whole at the Annual Conference to discuss the issues and ramifications of reorganization. Council took a first vote to approve the dissolution of the Library Education Division (LED). (A second vote, as directed by the ALA Constitution and Bylaws, was to be taken at the 1978 Midwinter Meeting.) A Council Committee on Library Education and a Library Education Assembly would replace LED. The merger of the Association of State Library Agencies and the Health and Rehabilitative Library Services Division was approved with little discussion; a second vote was to follow. Council also voted to approve establishment of a new ALA round table on library instruction.

Reflecting the growing autonomy and independence of the ALA divisions that have survived the change in dues structure, Council voted to approve a motion to give each division one elected Council representative. This overturned one of the recommendations of the ACONDA/ANACONDA restructuring carried out in the early 1970's whereby the divisions lost their seats on Council. An effort to control the total number of Councilors by reducing the number of Councilors at Large by the same number of division representatives was defeated. Council gave strong support to the Equal Rights Amendment (ERA) by passing a resolution from the Committee on the Status of Women in Librarianship committing ALA to meet only in those states that have ratified ERA. A similar resolution had been defeated at the 1975 Annual Conference in San Francisco. The resolution passed handily in 1977, and an effort was soundly defeated to amend the resolution by adding that it would be considered null and void if ERA were to become a constitutional amendment or fail.

Council took another turnabout at the 1977 Annual Conference in approving a resolution supporting free access to information in public and publicly supported libraries. At the Midwinter Meeting five months earlier a similar resolution had been turned down. The resolution introduced at the Annual Conference contained some rewording and came to Council with the strong endorsement of the membership. In introducing the matter, Councilor Gerald Shields stated that the resolution was "intended to guide the Association as it develops necessary policies . . . as the whole concept of the use of technology in the distribution of information becomes more and more apparent. . . ."   PAT HARRIS

Council on Library Technical Assistants

During 1977 the Council on Library Technical Assistants (COLTA) published a brochure on library paraprofessionals and held workshops, seminars, and institutes to serve the needs of library/media technical assistants (L/MTA), including students, graduates, employers, and educators. COLT also sponsored a program on L/MTA in conjunction with the Annual Conference of the American Library Association.

The COLT directory listing colleges offering L/MTA programs and courses published late in 1976 was widely distributed during 1977.

Biennial Regional meetings are to be held in 1978. The first meeting was scheduled for the

> **COLT Officers**
>
> PRESIDENT (July 1977-January 1978):
> **Margaret Barron,** Cuyahoga Community College, Cleveland, Ohio
>
> VICE-PRESIDENT/PRESIDENT-ELECT:
> **John Johnson,** Durham Technical Institute, Durham, North Carolina
>
> EXECUTIVE SECRETARY:
> **Dorothy Smith,** Community College of Philadelphia

Northeaster Region in Washington, D.C., in May. Other regions are sponsoring meetings periodically during the year. The next annual conference of COLT will be in Dallas in 1979 in conjunction with the ALA Annual Conference.

COLT was organized in 1966 as a clearinghouse for information relating to paraprofessionals. Its purpose is to advance the status of paraprofessionals as well as to promote communication between library educational programs and paraprofessionals. COLT members include students, professionals librarians, publishers, library associates, and L/MTA organizations.   MARGARET R. BARRON

Data Bases, Computer-Readable

The topic of data bases is growing in importance as computer-readable data bases are coming to be *the* way of searching the literature. The majority of the world's A&I (abstracting and indexing) sources are in machine-readable form, and more than half of the current A&I records are on-line either in America or Europe. More than two dozen data bases were brought up on-line by U.S. venders in 1977, and another dozen and a half were announced in 1977 for 1978. The volume of on-line searching exceeded the 2,000,000 mark, and batch SDI runs exceeded 1,000,000. The volume of activity has been so high that all major on-line venders upgraded their computer configurations. Marketing of data base services has been active and has reached new types of users, principally in the academic and public library areas. Meetings, conferences, workshops and publications dealing with data bases and their use in on-line systems continued to grow and prosper.

Data Bases On-Line. The number of bibliographic/natural language data bases available through on-line systems has continued to grow in number and variety. The number of on-line searches has increased significantly, and there has been no indication of a leveling off. The major on-line venders appear to be enjoying this steady, rapid, and surprising growth. The increase has been experienced in the government sector—principally the National Library of Medicine (NLM)—and in the private sector where the major bibliographic on-line venders are Lockheed Information Service (LIS), System Development Corporation (SDC), Bibliographic Retrieval Service (BRS), and the New York Times Information Bank (NYTIB).

There continues to be a competitive situation among venders in putting up large numbers of data bases, unusual data bases, more retrospective years of particular data bases, and exclusive data bases. At present LIS with its 60 data bases has the largest number up on any one system. LIS added 11 data bases to its collection in 1977. SDC added 14, which is more than in any other year since SDC initiated its publicly available search service in 1972. BRS, the newcomer to the commercial on-line field, started its service in January 1977 with the 9 most highly used data bases.

Data bases brought up on-line by the big three venders—BRS, LIS, and SDC—that cover a general mix of subject area data bases are given in the accompanying list. Some of the data bases that were mounted in 1977 by the venders listed were previously available through other venders. This list includes only those data bases put up in 1977 by the vender indicated.

Vender*	Data Base Mounted in 1977
S	Accountants' Index
L	Art Bibliographies
S	BIOCODES (a dictionary-type data base including terms, codes and synonyms)
S	BIOSIS 69-73, 74-present; put up as 2 files at SDC
L	CACon-CASIA; put up as a merged file at LIS
S	Canadian Business Periodicals Index
S	Canadian Newspaper Index
L	Child Abuse and Neglect Abstracts
L	CLAIMS Classification Index
B S	Comprehensive Dissertation Index
L	Current Research Information Systems (CRIS) of the USDA
L	Defense Market Measures (DM^2) of Frost and Sullivan

Scholarship recipients for the Library Technical Assistants Training Program are matched to their geographical locations in Oklahoma by the staff at the Oscar Rose Library, left to right are Dell Hewey, Jim Beaver, and John Hinkle.

Data Bases, Computer-Readable

L	Energyline
S	Enviroline
B	Exceptional Child Abstracts
L	Federal Index
L S	Food Science and Technology Abstracts
S	Grant Information Systems
S	Library and Information Science Abstracts
S	Management Contents
B	NIMIS
S	Oceanic Abstracts
S	Pestdoc
B	Pharmaceutical News Index
B	Pollution Abstracts
L	Public Affairs Information Service
S	Society for Automotive Engineers Data Base
L	TOSCA Candidate List

*BRS initiated its service in January 1977 with BIOSIS, CAIN, CACon, ERIC, INFORM, INSPEC, MEDLARS, NTIS, and Psychological Abstracts, all of which were previously available via LIS, SDC, or NLM. B = BRS; L = LIS; S = SDC.

On-Line Searches. All of the major commercial venders have pushed hard in the marketing area, and the payoff can be seen in the extremely encouraging growth in the number of on-line searches in 1977. Since 1974 annual statistics on the number of on-line searches for each year have been gathered by consultation with on-line venders. Only aggregate data are published, and confidentiality is maintained for all privileged data. The data refer to searches, a search being defined as one subject area query against one data base. If three data bases are used to answer one query, it is considered three searches. If a logical data base such as BIOSIS is split into two files (SDC puts up 1969-1973 and 1974 to the present as two separate files), they are treated as two physical data bases. The use of on-line services for library activities other than reference activities is not included in these figures. The numbers refer to on-line venders in the United States and Canada.

In 1974 there were 700,000 on-line searches; in 1975, 1,000,000; in 1976, 1,200,000; and in 1977, more than 2,000,000. The 2,000,000-plus figure includes the major venders of bibliographic on-line searches. It does not include legal data base services or numeric data base services (scientific, business, financial securities, econometric, and social). Figures represent publicly available systems only. The only government on-line service included is NLM; thus the majority of the activity reported here is in the for-profit sector.

The increase from 1976 to 1977 is significant. The large increase is due to a number of factors, including the introduction of BRS into the field, which made inroads into the relatively untapped academic market (63 per cent of BRS use); the doubling of the New York Times Information Bank's customer base to 600; a 45 per cent increase in the number of searches run on the NLM system, the biggest single on-line system; and substantial increases for all of the comercial venders.

Data Bases Going On-Line. Each of the major venders has, of course, plans for adding data bases in 1978, and a few have been announced. SDC will put up its chemical dictionary file called CHEMDEX. CHEMDEX will be similar to the Chemline file of NLM and the Chemname file of LIS in providing chemical names and synonyms to aid searchers in using CAS-generated data bases. CHEMDEX was derived from CASIA and includes nomenclature enhancement. It goes back to 1972 and includes names for about 2,000,000 substances.

SDC has also announced plans to put up a merged CACon-CASIA file, all three of the INSPEC data bases in one SDC file, Psychological Abstracts, the Federal Register (of Capital Services, Inc.), and TITUS (the textile information data base from France). Five of SDC's current data bases—Compendex, Energyline, ERIC, Inform (with added vocabulary), and Pollution Abstracts—will be reloaded in 1978 to conform with the new ORBIT-4 format.

LIS has announced that it will put up the Smithsonian Science Information Exchange (SSIE) data base; Geoarchives; International Pharmaceutical Abstracts; Environmental Periodicals Bibliographics; the Shirley Institute's Textile Abstracts; the PIRA data base containing paper, printing, and packaging abstracts; Excerpta Medica, and the Magazine Index. Excerpta Medica (EM) had previously been put up by Informatics but was dropped in about a year's time. Presumably LIS was able to negotiate more favorable terms with the Excerpta Medica Foundation. It will be interesting to observe in 1978 whether the wide availability of EM through LIS will have an impact on the use of MEDLINE. Hopefully, the difference in coverage and in indexing practices will make it a desirable adjunct and not a true competitor.

The new Magazine Index is being produced by Information Access Corp. It covers the contents of 350 popular magazines including the majority of the 260 entries in the *Readers' Guide to Periodical Literature*. The file will be updated monthly. Initially, LIS will put up approximately 25,000 records representing the first half of 1977. Information Access Corporation anticipates about 50,000 citations per year. LIS will charge $45 an hour. This file, like the Information Bank, should appeal to the general public and may help to increase the use of on-line services in public libraries.

BRS has announced that in 1978 it will put up the Envirnomental Protection Agency's serials file called EPAA, the National

Oceanographic Atmospheric Administration serials data base called NOAA, Management Contents, and the Department of Agriculture serials file called STAR.

Volume of Batch Searches. While *on-line* is the buzz word in data base circles, it should not be overlooked that batch searching continues. In Europe particularly there is more batch searching than on-line searching. In the United States, on-line has largely replaced batch services for retrospective searching; batch searching, however, is still dominant for SDI (current awareness) searches. Although many centers and companies have closed down their batch operations, some of the places where batch searching is still going on include the New England Research Applications Center (NERAC), IBM, Ohio State University's Mechanized Information Center (MIC), and the University of Georgia's Computing Center (UGACC).

An SDI search is defined as one query run against one data base update. UGACC runs about 10,000 SDI searches a month or 120,000 annually. The largest SDI operation in the world is run at NERAC where the IBM 145 runs 24 hours a day all year long, processing about 1,000,000 SDI searches a year. In addition, off-searches or batch searches of prior years of data bases that are not kept up on-line are run at night by NML and by BRS. Some of the on-line venders also run SDI searches in a batch mode as they process incoming update tapes. On-line is here to stay, but batch is still used too.

Marketing. The venders are marketing aggressively both in the United States and in other countries and are making their systems more accessible by increasing the number of hours that they are up and by improving the terminal/telecommnication situation. The New York Times Information Bank increased its customer base in 1977 to 600, mostly U.S. organizations. It opened a Chicago office and opened a London marketing office to access the European market. The Bank also negotiated marketing agreements with Infomart in Canada and with Teleinformatica in Mexico and in early 1978 will begin active promotion in the Far East. NYTIB will be available 22 hours a day in 1978 through both Telenet and Tymnet. The Bank now supports all Telenet and Tymnet-compatible terminals, which includes most 30 cps and 1200 baud full-duplex terminals. NYTIB also supports 1200 baud half-duplex terminals for foreign exchanges in New York, Washington, D.C., and other locations through a toll-free 800 number.

SDC now has users in Australia, Hong Kong, Manila, and Tai Pei. A node has been installed in Hong Kong and is awaiting SEC approval of tariffs. Both SDC and LIS established Midwest offices in Chicago. Lockheed established Learned Information, Ltd., as its European representative, and 1977 was the year that formal European data communications were established.

Computer Upgrading. Because of the increased demand on on-line systems in terms of data base searches, the number of data bases put up, and the ever-growing number of records in the data bases, many on-line venders have had to upgrade their computer configurations. SDC installed an AMDAHL 370/V5. SDC has been through a continuous series of computer changes, starting in 1970 with an IBM 360/67 and upgrading through a 370/155 in 1973, a 370/158 in 1975, a 370/158 mod/3 in 1976, to the AMDAHL in 1977. The AMDAHL operates several times faster and is rated at more than twice the processing power of the fastest 158. Although its internal speed (cycle time) is 3.5 times faster, the I/O slows it down. The new machine permits SDC to do timely data base updating and to increase the user load without degrading response time.

The New York Times Information Bank announced a computer upgrading for early 1978 to an IBM 370/148 and a conversion of its disc storage from 3330s to 3350s.

BRS started operation on a dual processor IBM 370/168 belonging to the Carrier Corporation Data Center in Syracuse, New York. After less than a year of providing on-line search service BRS bought its own IBM 370/155 with 2,000,000 bytes of high-speed memory and 32 mod/2 3330s, providing a total of 6,400,000,000 bytes of disc storage.

LIS replaced one of its two IBM 360/65s with a 370/165. LIS has replaced all of its data cells with discs and will increase its disc storage capacity from 17 billion bytes in 1977 to 23 billion bytes. These changes will permit LIS to accommodate easily the new data bases and records planned for the near future. By the end of 1977 LIS had 18,000,000 bibliographic records in its system and had announced eight new data bases for 1978.

Clientele. A change in the clientele using on-line services is apparent. The industrial and federal government users were the first group of clients to use on-line systems and were responsible for the majority of the growth in use of the systems for several years. The academic and public library groups were far behind. Academic groups were next to get on the bandwagon, and a considerable increase in interest is now evident on the part of public libraries. In BRS service 63 per cent of the use is by academic and educational organizations, 20 per cent by government, and only 17 per cent by industrial and private organizations. A rough indication of the developing interest by public librarians is their attendance at on-line meetings. A show of hands at a meeting at the

University of Pittsburgh indicated the following breakdown: academic, 50 per cent; industrial and government, 25 per cent; public libraries, 20 per cent; and suppliers, 5 per cent.

Meetings. Two major meetings devoted entirely to on-line use of data bases were the University of Pittsburgh's "On-Line Revolution in Libraries" in November and Learned Information's "First International On-Line Retrieval Meeting" in London in December. The University of Pittsburgh meeting was attended by 750 people, and the Learned Information meeting was attended by 450 people from more than 20 countries.

Publications. Two new journals devoted to on-line use of data bases, *On-Line* (published by Jeff Pemberton) and *On-Line Review* (published by Roger Bilboul's Learned Information, Ltd., Oxford, England), began publication in 1977. Subscriptions continue to come in, and most of the major libraries in the United States subscribe to both. The two journals have a somewhat different emphases, with *On-Line* providing more "popular" and newsy information and *On-Line Review* providing "scholarly" papers in addition to news items. On-line practitioners consider both journals essential for keeping up in the field.

Two major bibliographies covering the literature dealing with on-line systems were published in 1977. In the United States, Donald Hawkins prepared a reference bibliography, "On-Line Information Retrieval: 1965-1976," that was published as an appendix to the first issue of *On-Line Review* (March 1977). In England, Aslib published a 125-page bibliography, *On-Line Information Retrieval: 1965-1976*, prepared by J.L. Hall. These two 1977 bibliographies—together with the bibliography at the end of the chapter on "On-line Systems--Techniques and Services" by Beatrice Marron and Dennis Fife in the *Annual Review of Information Science and Technology* (1976), edited by M.E. Williams and published by the American Society for Information Science—provide excellent coverage of the on-line use of data bases.

Volume 12 of the *Annual Review of Information Science and Technology*, also edited by Williams, was published by Knowledge Industry Publications of New York City in September 1977. It included several chapters that directly or indirectly covered data bases. A chapter on numeric data bases (or data banks) entitled "Numeric Data Bases and Systems" was written by J. Luedke, Jr., G.J. Kovacs, and J.B. Fried. A chapter on "Evaluation and Design of Bibliographic Data Bases" was written by B.T. Stern, and A. Tomberg's chapter on "European Information Networks" discussed European networks for using information contained in bibliographic and numeric data bases.   MARTHA E. WILLIAMS

Disadvantaged, Library Service to

The year 1977 was not impressive as far as library service to the disadvantaged was concerned. Some strides were made, but many of them were superficial and short-lived. The public library continues to fail its disadvantaged clientele. Public libraries want the disadvantaged to change instead of preparing them to cope with changes in their own way. Consequently, in 1977 public libraries still were not serving the needs of the disadvantaged.

Basic Changes Lacking. Nationally, a number of gimmicks have been introduced to identify the disadvantaged, to predict the needs of the disadvantaged, and to serve those needs. Boards of trustees and library directors have placed top priority on the use of such gimmicks, but they have not worked. Special library activities for the disadvantaged are not necessarily well attended, and neither library facilities nor resources are well used.

Part of the failure of special programs has been attributed to the disadvantaged's inability to change to meet library standards. The blame must rest equally on the shoulders of government officials, library policymakers, funding sources, administrators, and staffs. Among funding sources and government officials, concern for the disadvantaged has declined. In the hearts of policymakers, administrators, and staffs, the concern is superficial. Substantial library services to the disadvantaged are more often discussed than actually provided.

The unrest of the 1960's should not need repeating to make the library rise to provide the kind and level of services that anchors its purpose for existence. Concern for the disadvantaged should have led the profession to accept the challenge to provide library and information services to all people. Unfortunately, public libraries still probably rely too heavily on labels to identify and serve their users. Public libraries are still not sensitive to the fact that basic human needs are very much the same for different people, despite the differences in types and levels of needs and in the ability to use services. In addition, procedures and policies are too often developed and implemented around costs rather than human needs. Not nearly enough has been done to rectify this problem.

Problems Abound. Throughout the country special programs for the disadvantaged are planned and implemented and activities are schedules. People attend such activities, and sometimes never return to the library. They often do not return because they have not discovered any tangible usefulness in the library's resources. In many cases, the regular services that the library provides are completely unrelated to the programs and activities they hold to attract the disadvantaged. Therefore, the users make no connection between the two.

In many libraries the focus on the disadvantaged is shallow. Libraries move in the direction of the grant monies and whatever is popular or is the fad at a particular time. The library's commitment to provide services to all people shifts with those fads.

The problems that confront libraries are difficult to resolve because many librarians have not learned to be flexible and to make adjustments or changes in policies and procedures that will address the real issues surrounding user needs. The problems that confront libraries are far-reaching in that libraries have the capability of serving human needs of everyone from the infant to the senior citizen. But libraries do not execute their fullest potential.

Changes taking place in today's society affect the pattern of library services to the disadvantaged. Monies are limited and population growth and the migration from rural to urban and from urban to suburban areas have left a concentration of non-library-oriented people in some locations. As public librarians learn to be empathetic with the social and economic status of the disadvantaged, they will find it easier to understand and respond to their library service and informational needs. Librarians working with disadvantaged clientele need to be conscious of the ways in which they turn people off, and they must strive to generate an atmosphere of trust and good will. Within the disadvantaged community itself the dominant means of getting information is by asking a friend, someone who is trusted. The library's charge should be to become that friend.

In spite of the many programs and activities designed with the specific intent of reaching out to and serving the disadvantaged, the trend seems to be to push a program aside when it does not work. Librarians should be asking what indicators they have to measure the effectiveness of what is being done or who in the community can assist the library in being more responsive to the needs of all people. Because the profession is lacking in accountability, perhaps the disadvantaged themselves should assume the responsibility for holding public libraries accountable for the services that they are designed to provide.

MONTERIA HIGHTOWER

Education, Library

Reduced enrollments in library schools and continuing difficulty for new graduates in locating appropriate employment were two of the obvious problems faced by library educators during 1977. Confusion over the competencies expected of the beginning professional librarian and questions about the fifth-year master's degree as the only access to "professional" assignments suggested that some employers might face discriminatory employment charges, and the issues had direct implications for library education. The rapidly diminishing support from the federal government for higher education in general and library education specifically and the few granting agencies or foundations finding library education of interest suggested that little assistance for seeking solutions will be available from these sources. The ALA Council Standing Committee on Library Education and the related Library Education Assembly proposed to replace the Library Education Division (LED) as the structure within ALA for matters pertaining to library education, raising hopes for providing a means for library practitioners and educators to work collectively toward solutions for the advancement of library service.

ORGANIZATION ACTIVITIES

The Board of Directors of LED under the leadership of President Lester Asheim succeeded in obtaining the ALA Council's initial approval for this new structure to provide leadership in library education. The plan proposed the phasing out of LED following the 1978 Midwinter Meeting and the creation of an ALA Council Standing Committee on Library Education. Each Division or unit within the Association would be encouraged to establish a committee on library education related to the Division's or unit's concerns. Representatives from these committees would provide liaison between membership and the Standing Committee by participating in a Library Education Assembly. The original request for a full-time

An Outpost Library deep in the hills was part of the West Virginia Library Commission's 1977 efforts to make service available in every location in the state. Commission Director Frederick J. Glazer was cited as HEW's 1977 Outstanding Citizen for leadership in library programs for the disadvantaged and remote areas.

Edward P. Miller, Dean of the Library School at the University of Missouri-Columbia, and three graduate students studying information science under fellowships awarded to UMC by the U.S. Office of Education.

education officer was deleted from the proposal due to financial necessity, and it was proposed that staff liaison support be provided the Standing Committee and Assembly through the Office for Library Personnel Resources. It was hoped that the new structure would provide the Association means for speaking out "at the national and international levels on matters related to the preparation of library personnel, and in a voice that reflects the needs, interests and concerns of all kinds of libraries and all levels of library staff."

Although the Association of American Library Schools (AALS) appointed a Task Force on Organizational Alignment, the opportunity for AALS to influence the development of a revised library education unit within ALA seems to have passed. AALS also approved the establishment of a Task Force on Education for Non-Clerical Support Staff in Libraries, charging the Task Force specifically with concern for the Library Technical Assistant and the Library Associate as defined in the ALA "Library Education and Personnel Utilization" statement.

The LED Librarians of Library Science Collections Discussion Group published the 1977 *Directory of Library Science Collections*, updating information provided by the earlier *Directory* and extending coverage to collections integrated into university libraries. Data are included on 46 collections related to accredited programs and to 17 other programs.

TESTING OR TRAINING

The LED program at the 1977 ALA Annual Conference revived the old debate about the adequacy of library experience validated through examinations for the assignment of personnel to professional library positions. Certain municipalities in California have given impetus to this debate by questioning the legitimacy of degrees as valid requirements for employment. California librarians, concerned over the possibility of being accused of discriminatory employment practices, are seeking justification for the master's degree as a requirement for professional library employment and are examining alternate methods for identifying qualified employees. The California State Library, with the assistance of 13 of the state's public libraries, has employed the Selection Consulting Center of the California State Personnel Board to determine procedures and policies that will protect employing libraries from discrimination lawsuits. The first phase of the Center's assignment was to identify tasks performed by beginning librarians in the cooperating libraries. Although 244 tasks were identified, only 22 were found to be common to all the cooperating libraries. The Center has identified 36 basic tasks that the entry-level librarians should be capable of performing and projects the development of an entry-level selection system, an appraisal procedure for the evaluation of performance, and development and evaluation of a promotional system.

A sensitivity to Affirmative Action and non-discriminatory employment practices is a factor in the profession's revived concern over assuring appropriate competence for professional employment. There is, however, another influential factor—the awareness of the ineffectiveness of some employees who meet current educational standards. In many cases this is a heritage from the years of the shortage of professional librarians, when anyone who could obtain the degree was practically assured a choice of jobs. Libraries, rapidly increasing in staff size, collections, and physical facilities, have been slow in delineating appropriate stratification of job assignments and in relating them to education and experience. In 1970 ALA, recognizing the resulting confused personnel situation, adopted the statement on "Library Education and Manpower" (now "Library Education and Personnel Utilization") to provide guidelines for solving the personnel dilemma. Personnel and classification restructuring, however, can be more easily recommended than implemented, and confusion persists over the responsibilities to be performed by the various levels of library personnel.

This problem, though receiving considerable publicity in California, is expressing itself on a broader geographical base and in a different fashion in the area of school library media services. School library personnel, who received minimum certification through limited undergraduate library science programs and who were assigned school library media responsibilities due to the shortage of librarians, are now protected in these assignments through longevity but are recognized in many cases as being inadequately prepared. A number of states concerned with this problem are in the process of revising their certification requirements. Increased library science course work at the undergraduate and graduate levels, a limitation on the time period for the fourth-year certification to remain in effect, and the requirement for proving competency through certification examinations are being considered as possible means of improving the effectiveness of the certification process.

California has won a reputation in recent years as a barometer in predicting trends and developments for the nation, and training for school library service traditionally has had a strong influence on education for librarianship. It seems inevitable that the profession will have to give increased attention to the training requirements for library employees at all levels if agencies outside the profession are not to determine these requirements. The proposed new structure within ALA for matters pertaining to library education could be the appropriate unit to develop solutions to these problems.

ACCREDITATION

Having completed in 1976 the first round of accreditation visits under the 1972 Standards for Accreditation, the ALA Committee on Accreditation (COA) gave attention during the year to an evaluation of the standards and the accreditation process. John Eastlick surveyed the chairpersons of visiting teams, and Russell Bidlack surveyed the 67 library schools visited. (A report of the Bidlack survey, *The ALA Accreditation Process, 1973-1976*, was published by ALA in 1977.) From the experience gained in the application of the standards and the information from the two surveys, the COA revised the self-study guide and the *Manual of Procedures for Evaluation Visits*. Major changes include means for a school seeking initial accreditation to insist on a site visit even though COA does not consider the program ready for evaluation, permission for a visiting team to vary in size from three to six members depending on the size and complexity of the program to be visited, provision for the school to approve the proposed members of a visiting team prior to their being consulted on visiting the school, and the extension of continuing accreditation visits from the previously projected four to six years to every five to eight years. The ALA Executive Board approved new "Accreditation Appeals Process Guidelines," specifying that "each party to an appeal will bear its own costs."

AALS created a Task Force on Accreditation Issues under the leadership of Sr. Lauretta McCusker to study the accreditation process for librarianship. Interviews were conducted by the Task Force with library school faculty members and administrators during the Association's annual meeting. The preliminary report from the Task Force indicated, as did the overall response to the Bidlack survey completed for COA, that library educators generally held favorable attitudes toward the accreditation process and were appreciative of the conscientious manner in which COA has attempted to apply the standards.

Advanced Programs. Sixth-year programs were introduced at Long Island, Saint John's, and Syracuse. Of the 58 U.S. schools offering accredited programs, 29 also now offer a sixth-year program; in 14 of these schools the sixth year is the terminal program. New doctoral programs were introduced at North Carolina and California at Los Angeles, and the Buffalo library school introduced a cooperative Ph.D. program with the university's Department of Education. These made a total of 25 doctoral programs which were offered at year's end by schools with accredited programs, including two of the Canadian schools.

Federal Support. The Department of Health, Education and Welfare—under the Higher Education Act (HEA) Title II-B Fellowship Program—provided more than $1,000,000 in 1977 in support of 160 fellowships that were awarded through 37 academic programs. Students enrolled in doctoral programs were designated to receive 18 of these fellowships; post-masters, 3; masters, 134; and associates in art, 5. It is anticipated that this would be the final period of funding for the fellowship program. The HEA Title II-B Training Program received less than $1,000,000 in funding for 1977. Most of this amount was expended on 23 institutes, 18 of which were sponsored by institutions of higher education, including 10 library schools offering accredited programs.

CONTINUING EDUCATION

As in the past, continuing education opportunities in 1977 were provided by a variety of agencies, organizations, networks, and schools. A few of these were funded, as in the case of the HEA Training Programs and programs supported through LSCA funds, but most were expected to be at least self-supporting if not income producing for the sponsoring unit. More than 900 registered for the 26 short courses offered prior to the Seattle meeting of the Medical Library Association, and more than 700 attended the Pittsburgh three-day conference on "The On-line Revolution in Libraries."

Unique continuing education opportunities were available also to library educators. With HEA Title II-B support, Denver sponsored a Senior Faculty Library Research Institute for 25 faculty members from library or information science programs. The Public Library of Columbus and Franklin County (Ohio) announced a faculty residency program, inviting faculty members associated with ALA- accredited programs to apply for a three- month summer appointment with the library. The program is designed to permit the resident to gain insight into current public library practices and to share academic experience with the library staff.

More than 95 groups of librarians met throughout the country at the request of the Continuing Library Education Network and Exchange (CLENE) to discuss means of structuring a recognition system for continuing education in librarianship. The summary report of these discussions indicated that there was little consensus among the approximately 800 individuals who participated in

Education, Library

the groups on the appropriate means for the development of such a recognition system.

CLENE continued to be a clearinghouse for continuing education opportunities and the *1977 Directory of Continuing Education Opportunities for Libraries, Information, and Media Personnel* included approximately 240 programs, a substantial extension of coverage over the 1976 edition. To increase awareness in CLENE's activities, regional meetings were planned during the year.

PLACEMENT, SALARIES, AND HONORS

The number of graduates of fifth-year programs continued to decline in 1977, and the initial placement of new graduates continued to be a challenge, requiring both patience and persistence on the part of the graduates.

The Learmont and Darling 1977 report on the placement of 1976 graduates of fifth-year ALA-accredited programs indicated that 5,415 persons received the degree from the 53 responding schools. The number was 595 fewer, or almost 11 per cent less, than the number reported by 51 schools for 1975. Of the 1976 graduates, 57 per cent were reported as employed in libraries or in library-related assignments, including both part-time and nonprofessional assignments. Seventeen per cent were not in library positions, and the occupations of 25 per cent were unknown. The median salary for all graduates was $10,576, a 5.8 per cent increase over the median salary reported in 1975 and equivalent to the percentage increase in the Cost of Living Index for the same period. Although some schools indicated an awareness of a greater need for librarians in certain types of libraries, the actual variation in reported placement by type of library was less than four per cent among public, school, academic, and other libraries and library agencies.

Faculties and Salaries. The Bidlack study on faculty salaries for 1976-77 reported 707 full-time library educators employed in the 64 schools with ALA-accredited programs, indicating an average faculty size of 11.05. Of these full-time educators 420 or 59.4 per cent were men, and 287 or 40.5 per cent were women; 69 per cent of the men held doctorates as did 50 per cent of the women. Average salaries for the academic year for teaching faculty ranged from $24,814 for professors to $13,174 for instructors. Of the 47 new appointments reported by 62 of the schools, 20 were men and 27 were women.

Appointments and Vacancies. New deans or directors appointed during the year included Conrad Rawski at Case Western Reserve, Timothy Sineath at Kentucky, Keith Wright at Maryland, Yves Courrier at Montreal, Richard Hyman at Queens, Antonio Rodriguez-Buckingham at Saint John's, and Brooke Sheldon at Texas Woman's. Don Swanson returned to the deanship at Chicago. John Farley resigned the Albany deanship as did Donald Foos at Louisiana State, to return to full-time teaching. Guy Marco resigned from the Kent deanship to accept the position as Chief of the General Reference and Bibliographic Division at the Library of Congress, and Doralyn Hickey resigned the directorship at Wisconsin at Milwaukee for a faculty position at North Texas.

Oregon School Closing. The Oregon Board of Higher Education approved suspension of the University of Oregon School of Librarianship at the end of the 1978 summer term. The Board stipulated that the decision would be reviewed in two years. University President William Boyd, who recommended the action to the Board, reportedly justified the closing because reduced full-time university enrollment required budget cuts, there were unemployed and underemployed librarians, and the school had failed to develop a strong curriculum and faculty.

Retirements. Library educators retiring during the year included Hallie Beacham Brooks at Atlanta, Jean Freeman and Margaret Kalp at North Carolina, and Mary McSwain at Texas.

Honors. Kathleen Molz, Columbia, was presented the Ralph R. Shaw Award for Library Literature in recognition of the outstanding contribution of her publication *Federal Policy and Library Support*. Virginia Jones, Atlanta, received the Joseph W. Lippincott Award for distinguished service to the profession. Russell Bidlack, Michigan, received the Beta Phi Mu Award for distinguished service to education for librarianship, and Herbert White and Karen Hasenjager, Indiana, received one of the two Library Research Round Table Research Awards for excellence in library research. White was also presented with the Resources Scholarship Award of the Resources and Technical Services Division for his article "Publishers, Libraries and the Costs of Journal Subscriptions in Times of Funding Retrenchment," published in *Library Quarterly* (October 1976). Phyllis Richmond, Case Western Reserve, was awarded the Margaret Mann Citation for outstanding achievement in classification and cataloging.

A. VENABLE LAWSON

REFERENCES

Russell E. Bidlack, *The ALA Accreditation Process, 1973-76* (Chicago: ALA, 1977).

Russell E. Bidlack, "Faculty Salaries of 62 Library Schools, 1976-77," *Journal of Education for Librarianship* (Spring 1977), pp. 199-213.

Carol L. Learmont and Richard L. Darling, "Placement and Salaries 1976: A Year of Adjustment," *Library Journal* (June 15, 1977), pp. 1345-51.

Ethnic Groups, Library Service to

AMERICAN INDIANS

Recent developments in library and information services for American Indian people indicate gradual changes in two major areas: (1) national recognition of Indian library and information needs and (2) the qualitative and quantitative growth of American Indian community libraries and services.

National Planning. The National Commission on Libraries and Information Science planned a White House Pre-Conference on Indian Library and Information Services On or Near Reservations in October 1978. The conference, sponsored by the Department of Interior, Office of Library and Information Services, will provide Indian people an opportunity to express their information concerns in a climate of receptivity.

The goals include the following:

1. To raise awareness among Indian people of the potential benefits of library/media/information services and their relevance to Indian concerns, issues, and interests;

2. To provide an opportunity for Indian people throughout the United States to reach consensus on a long-range plan to improve and develop library/media/information services on or near reservations;

3. To provide focused input on library/media/information needs and services as they relate to national Indian issues into the White House Conference on Library and Information Services.

The White House preconference can be viewed as an indicator of the awareness, at the national level, of the need for a national plan of information services for Indian people.

A vital consideration in the development of such a national plan would be the current Bureau of Indian Affairs (BIA) Plan for the Improvement of Library/Media/Information Programs. This document has been planned, written, and revised by Indian and non-Indian librarians and educators. Drafts have been submitted to Indian communities throughout the United States to maximize the breadth of critical input. During the preconference in 1978 additional opportunities for discussion and revision of the BIA plan will be provided.

The intent of the BIA plan is to improve library and information services to Indian people. This would be accomplished by the reassessment, development and expansion of the existing BIA plan and would enable Indian communities to develop and provide access to those library services that address their information needs in the areas of programs, resources, and facilities.

Community Library Services. Both reservation and urban Indian communities have con-

The California Library Association's conference in December included this exhibit of the state's Library Service Construction Act demonstration project at the Tule River Indian Reservation.

tinued to demonstrate their interest in developing local Indian library services. Recognition of the need for the improvement of urban Indian library services has been demonstrated in several cities, including Chicago and Grand Rapids, Michigan. Members of the Chicago Indian community, ALA, the staff of the Office for Library Service to the Disadvantaged, the Chicago Public Library, and the National Indian Education Association have met to discuss the creation of a library planning strategy. Realization of this goal would lead to the development of specific proposals for addressing the information needs of Indians in the Chicago area.

Grand Rapids Public Library received a LSCA grant from the state library to work with the Ottawas, Chippewas, and Potawatomies in creating an oral history project. One of the results of the project is a greater awareness of the Indian communities on the part of the non-Indian library staff and community. This awareness was precipitated by the library committees that were formed to locate and visit the appropriate Indian families.

The varied approaches in developing rural and reservation community libraries can be determined by scanning the country. The Kickapoo Reservation in Horton, Kansas, is developing the octagonally shaped Kickapoo Tribal Library. The library is part of the tribe's reservation development program and includes a small shopping center, a community recreation center, and the tribal administrative offices.

The Akwesasne Library and Cultural Center in Hogansburg, New York, has been serving the Mohawk community since 1971. Lack of sufficient funding, however, has hampered the library's ability to address the community's information needs. Now, because of the New York Indian Library Bill signed into law on August 1, 1977, by Governor Hugh Carey, financial support for the library will be increased. According to the governor's press release, Senate Bill 3045-A, Chapter 476, "is an act to amend the education law, in relation to Indian libraries, making an appropriation therefore." New York may be noted for recognizing through legislation that Indian libraries are a facet of the educational process.

Library services continue to be provided in the Oneida, Standing Rock, Ft. Hall, Laguna, and Zuni communities. The interest and desire for library service has resulted in an increasing number of tribal community libraries. The trend appears to be that of a growing awareness on the part of national and state library leaders of the necessity of a national plan for Indian library service to meet the information needs of the Indian people in rural, urban, and reservation communities.

CHERYL METOYER

ASIAN AMERICANS

The Asian American Librarians Association entered its third year in 1977. The purpose of this organization is to (1) provide a forum for the discussion of the problems and concerns of Asian American librarians; (2) provide a forum for the exchange of ideas by Asian American and other librarians; (3) support and encourage library service to Asian American communities; (4) recruit Asian Americans into the library and information science profession; and (5) seek funding for scholarships in library and information science schools for Asian Americans.

Under the leadership of Elsie Wong of the San Francisco Public Library the Bibliography Committee completed its first project, *Asian Americans: An Annotated Bibliography for Public Libraries*. The bibliography was published by ALA's Office for Library Service to the Disadvantaged in the summer of 1977. The 47-page publication contains annotated titles for the four major Asian American groups (Chinese, Japanese, Pilipino and Korean) as well as a listing of Asian American periodicals and a directory of bookstores and small publishers. The Bibliography Committee is continuing its review of new titles, and it plans to update the list with a supplemental bibliography.

T.C. Li of Rosary College, Chairperson of the six-member Ad Hoc Committee on Library Service to Asian Americans, issued a preliminary report based on a survey to study the public library needs and usage of Asian Americans. The survey found that library resources and services to Asian Americans are quantitatively inferior compared to what is available to other Americans. A further study is necessary to assess the needs and demands of Asian Americans before final judgment of the quality of library services and resources can be made. A proposal to seek funding for the second phase of the project, a survey of Asian Americans' use of the public library in Chicago, is being prepared.

At the 1977 ALA Annual Conference, David Kaser of Indiana University spoke on the use of libraries, professional organizations and librarians, and sources for continuing education. Mya Thanda Poe of the Library of Congress and Roy Chang of Western Illinois University served as reactors. Poe also briefly discussed the training program at the Library of Congress.

Members voted to change the name of the organization from the Asian American Librarians Caucus to the Asian American Librarians Association. The change was made in order to facilitate incorporation in Illinois as a nonprofit organization and to seek affiliation with ALA.

Officers for 1977-78 are Vivian Kobayashi, chairperson; Raymond Lum, Vice-chairperson; Tamiye Trejo, secretary; and Albert Milo, treasurer.

VIVIAN KOBAYASHI

BLACK AMERICANS

Spurred by a long and influential impact on America's cultural landscape and galvanized by increased national and local recognition of their contributions to American life, Black Americans in 1977 continued to play an important role in the shaping of America. This may be witnessed through a roll call of achievements: in library building construction; in Black academic library development; in special collections development and promotion; in professional development; in individual recognition and achievement; and last, but by no means least, in reaction to ALA's controversy of the year—*The Speaker*.

Construction. In Black library construction, perhaps the highlight of the year was in Atlanta, where the six member institutions of the Atlanta University Center announced plans for a new million-volume library scheduled to open in 1979 to mark the 50th anniversary of the Center. The largest private enterprise in Black higher education in the world, the Center includes Atlanta University, the Interdenominational Theological Center, and Clark, Morehouse, Morris Brown, and Spelman Colleges. The 400,000-square-foot building will be constructed of warm-toned concrete panels and bronze-tinted insulated glass. Its four main levels will provide space for the main collection, faculty offices, seminar rooms, study areas, a media services center, and a special collections area. A small penthouse level will also house the Center's famed art gallery. A special function of the library will be to serve as a documentation center for the Black experience in America, thereby strengthening and promoting further the historic role of the present library located on the Atlanta University campus. Priceless manuscripts, first editions, artifacts, and other items that chronicle America's Black heritage will serve the scholar's need for research materials on Black themes.

Holte Collection. The achievements of Black Americans may well be preserved through the efforts of those who in 1977 gathered additional Black collections to augment the rich and valuable resources already collected in libraries. Perhaps the single most important development in this area involved the Clarence L. Holte Collection of Africana. To the chagrin of many American libraries but to the great fortune of African libraries, it was acquired by Ahmadu Bello University in Zaria, Nigeria. The collection, appraised at $650,000, represents 30 years of tireless efforts to gather written evidence of Black American and African achievements and to provide cultural weapons in the fight to free African peoples all over the world. The collection includes numerous first editions in mint condition, which Holt preferred and which are more often than not inscribed to him by the author or otherwise signed. More than 2,000 items in the collection are inscribed or signed. The range and richness of the collection help make it particularly noteworthy. Works on the slave trade, antislavery movements, slave life and conditions, and fugitive slaves, as well as slave narratives, are particularly outstanding. The collection is a useful tool for research and study in African and Black American history and culture.

Clarence LeRoy Holte, born in Norfolk, Virginia, spent his early years in Norfolk and moved to Philadelphia with his family during the last semester of his high school year. He studied at Lincoln University in Pennsylvania and much later pursued public relations courses at the New School of Social Research. His interest and concern for Black books led him first to assemble a "reading collection" and later to expand it into a "reference collection." He thus acquired the key scholarly and relevant works on every aspect of history and contemporary life for Africans and people of African descent. His collection was publicized in *Ebony* (April 1970) and subsequently in the New York *Times*, other publications, and various radio and television programs. Such publicity spurred many people to contact him and to offer their collections to him "for the right price," and he acquired many of them.

Thus, Clarence Holte takes his place alongside Arthur Spingarn, Arthur Schomburg, and other notable collectors of works by and about Black people. Even though the collection that he once owned is now housed in Africa, his efforts have been and continue to be vital to Black scholarship. What is important is that the Black heritage is preserved in greater detail as a result of his work.

Black Press. On March 18 the Moorland-Spingarn Research Center of Howard University in Washington, D.C., and the National Newspaper Publishers Association dedicated the Black Press Archives and Gallery of Distinguished Newspaper Publishers on the occasion of the sesquicentenary of the founding of the Black press in the United States. The center has long been recognized as one of the world's largest and most comprehensive repositories for collecting and preserving materials that document the history and culture of Black people in Africa, Latin America, the Caribbean, and the United States.

The Gallery of Distinguished Newspaper Publishers had as its first honorees early notable publishers and editors. They included John Brown Russwurm (1799-1851), coeditor of the first Black newspaper in the United States and a leading Black exponent of the Back-to-Africa movement of the 1830's; Samuel E. Cornish (1795-1858), known for his impassioned style of journalism that spearheaded the antislavery crusade among Blacks in New York during the late 1820's and early 1830's and coeditor (with Russworm) of the country's first Black newspaper, *Freedom's Journal,* initially published on March 16, 1827; Philip Alexander Bell (c.1800-1889), often called the "Napoleon of the early Negro press" and one of the most analytical and productive publishers and editors of that period; Martin Robison Delany (1812-1885), one of the most talented and forthright publishers and editors of the 19th century and an outstanding physician, explorer, and soldier; and Frederick Douglass (1817-1895), the greatest advocate of the Black press during the 19th century and a renowned abolitionist.

Glenn Carrington. On June 25 the Glenn Carrington collection of Black literature was formally installed in Moorland-Spingarn. Carrington was a New York City social worker who spent more than 50 years collecting books, records, manuscripts, and other items on Black history and culture. He pledged to donate his collection to Howard, his alma mater.

The Carrington collection includes more than 2,200 books in 15 languages, 500 recordings, and 19 storage boxes of correspondence,

Members of the Hansberry family join Librarian Raymon Hightower (center) at the opening day ceremonies in August of the Lorraine Hansberry Branch of the Chicago Public Library named for Black playwright and the first library in the Chicago system named for a woman.

Ethnic Groups Library Service to

personal papers, newspaper clippings, broadsides, pamphlets, and other items. It is especially strong in books about African art and also contains a complete set of *The Crisis*, the official publication of the National Association for the Advancement of Colored People.

Toward the year's end, Moorland-Spingarn announced the acquisition of two additional outstanding collections that are sure to open new vistas of research on Black thought, religion, and education. Benjamin E. Mays, President Emeritus of Morehouse College in Atlanta and former Dean of the School of Religion at Howard University, agreed to donate his personal papers and other items to the research center. Papers of Max Yergan, a clergyman, author, and YMCA secretary, were given to Moorland-Spingarn in late 1977 and support the center's research programs as well as complement Yergan's private library at Shaw University in Raleigh, North Carolina.

Atlanta University, already steeped in the tradition of collecting, preserving, and administering Black primary resources, launched Black History Library Project which focuses on materials in Georgia. Among the Project's first acquisitions are the papers of David Scott, currently serving in the Georgia Legislature.

Archive Discoveries. Xavier University Library in New Orleans searched its Heartman Collection and "rediscovered" a work entitled "Liberty," a notebook version of a 129-year-old poem by Frederick Douglass. An earlier work—"Niagra," written in 1843 and Douglass's earliest poem—and "Liberty"—an eight-line poem dated September 13, 1847—help to mark a creative period in his life. "Liberty" was written two years after the publication of his autobiography, *Narrative of the Life of Frederick Douglass*, and after he had his first real taste of freedom in England. Copies of the poem have been sent to the Frederick Douglass Papers Project at Yale and to the Library of Congress.

As if 1977 were the "year of the rediscovery," Fisk University rediscovered a number of rare and important documents vital to its history and to Black higher education. A search through old storage areas and records produced the original deed to the site where the university stands, the articles of incorporation, financial notes, and other items dating from the University's early years in the 1860's.

During the fall of 1977 Fisk dedicated the William L. Dawson Collection in the special collections room of the library. On hand for the occasion, which also marked the inauguration of Fisk's ninth president, were relatives, colleagues, and friends of Dawson. A Fisk graduate of 1909, Dawson became one of the nation's leading and most influential Black political figures and was the first Black to head a committee in the U.S. Congress.

Other Collections. The year also might be called one of dedication—at least for Black libraries. The Carter G. Woodson Regional Library in Chicago held dedication ceremonies for the Charlemae Hill Rollins Collection of Children's Literature which helped to bring national attention to a renowned authority on Black children's books and libraries. The Rollins Collection makes an invaluable addition to the Vivian G. Harsh Collection of Afro-American History and Literature at the Library.

The Rollins Collection complements the recently named William Tucker Collection of works on Black authors and illustrators of children's materials in the School of Library Science at North Carolina Central University in Durham. Tucker is believed by scholars to be the first Black child to have been born in the English-speaking Colonies. A number of valuable and original works have been added to the Collection.

Both the Rollins and Tucker collections were complemented by the Black Films for Young Children shown in the Second Annual Film Festival January 7 in the Marie Reed Learning Center and presented by the University of the District of Columbia Black Film Institute. The Institute during the year presented a variety of Black films to the Washington community, including *Amos n' Andy*, *The Green Pastures*, *Song of Freedom*, *Leadbelly*, and *Pinky*.

While some Black libraries strengthened or dedicated special collections, others promoted the works of those who produce writings. Such was the case at Lincoln University in Pennsylvania, where on November 19 Friends of Lincoln University joined the Langston Hughes Library in presenting Charles L. Blockson, a Black bibliophile of national acclaim and author of *Black Genealogy*, a fast-selling book in 1977. Born in Norristown, Pennsylvania, Blockson attended Pennsylvania State University, played on its football team, and held records for the shot put and discus. But his interest in record making extended to Black bibliography, and he has devoted the past 30 years to collecting books, pamphlets, documents, and manuscripts on the Black experience from Colonial times to the present. For Black Americans, Blockson's new work is a how-to-do it book which helps to meet the challenge of a new surge of genealogical interest and research.

Research Projects. Faculty at the University of the District of Columbia are collaborating with colleagues at Southern Illinois University in a research project supported by the National Science Foundation. Through the research grant, the extensive former slave narratives file—collected by the Works Progress Administration (WPA) Federal Writers Project between 1936 and 1941 and housed in the Library of Congress's Archive of Folk Song—will be organized, cataloged, and annotated. While there are some 15,000 to 20,000 original manuscripts in the collection representing interviews with former slaves and children of slaves, only 2,000 narratives have been microfilmed and deposited in the Rare Book and Special Collections Division. The remainder of the materials are inaccessible to scholars primarily because they are unorganized and unprocessed.

Compounding the problem are the extensive files originating in Louisiana and located in the Louisiana State Library in Baton Rouge that are vital to the slave narratives project. Some scholars believe that narratives of former slaves and children of slaves from all of the Southern states and from border states including Missouri, Illinois, Indiana, and Ohio are included in the Louisiana files. O. Marvene Couch of the District of Columbia and Herman R. Lantz of Southern Illinois, the two collaborating project directors, expect to produce an invaluable resource to shed new light on the controversial issues surrounding the impact of slavery on the nation. They also will try to ascertain the narratives' authenticity. Once processed and perhaps published, these additional narratives will fill the voids in existing volumes of slave narratives already collected in the nation's libraries.

Grants. Developments in Black academic libraries generally have been legion. Examples of these may be seen at Johnson C. Smith University in Charlotte, North Carolina, and at Hampton Institute in Virginia. Both institutions were awarded grants in 1977 under the Council of Library Resources (CLR) library development program. Johnson C. Smith became the 24th institution to receive funding through the College Library Program, supported jointly by CLR and the National Endowment for the Humanities (NEH), each providing $25,000 matched by $51,160 from the institution toward the five-year program. As required by the grant, the University will make changes and improvements in its library program so that the library can become "fundamentally a teaching facility of the institution."

Hampton Institute became one of the 13 colleges and universities to receive awards under the CLR Library Enhancement Program. All recipients must designate project librarians who come from their senior staff and who will work with faculty, students, and administrators to design ways of integrating the library into the institution's curricular programs. Jason C. Grant, III, Hampton's chief librarian, and Elois A. Morgan, project librarian, will promote the new program at Hampton.

Four Black libraries announced the receipt of awards earmarked for developing special collections projects. Bishop College in Dallas, Texas, was awarded a $40,000 grant from NEH to direct an historical research project, concentrating on a survey of Blacks in the Southwest. Harry Robinson, Jr., project director and head of the Southwest Research Center and Museum for the Study of African-American Life and Culture, aims to identify and to acquire primary and secondary resources by and about Blacks in the Southwest, thus fulfilling one of the Center's goals.

Under a grant from the National Historical Publications and Records Commission, Atlanta University will process the papers of the Southern Regional Council, also located in Atlanta.

In historic Richmond, Virginia, Union University has begun a special and unique oral history project that focuses on the memories of Black Virginians, especially those who have a close relationship to religion. Faculty and students of the University as well as those of the School of Theology will conduct the interviews. The three-year project is supported by a grant from the Educational Ministries of the American Baptist Board of Education and Publication.

And in historic Hampton, Hampton Institute received a grant from NEH to process its rich and valuable archives, including those from its earlier history that relate to Indian students who once attended the Institute through a special training program. As these papers are processed and made available to researchers, there is no doubt that many gaps in Black and Indian higher education will close.

The roll call of Black American achievements points to professional develoment activities. A prime example is the Association of College and Research Libraries (ACRL) fourth-year internship program for administrators of predominantly Black college and university libraries. Funded by a grant from the Andrew W. Mellon Foundation, the internship is intended to accelerate management abilities of librarians in these institutions by making available to them experiences in   and p progressive   academic   library. Those selected in 1977 were Virgia Brocks-Shedd, reference-serials librarian, Tougaloo College (Mississippi); Alma Dawson, head periodicals librarian, Prairie View A & M University (Texas); Doris M. Gosier, head, public services, Fort Valley State College (Georgia); George M. Martin, librarian, Social Science Reading Room, Howard University (Washington); Millie M. Parker, head librarian, Paine College (Georgia); and Jean Frances Williams, acquisitions librarian, Virginia State College.

Awards, Publications, Controversy. Virginia Lacy Jones, Dean of the School of Library Service at Atlanta University, received the 1977 Joseph W. Lippincott Award consisting of $1,000, a medal, and a citation for distinguished service in librarianship. The

Ethnic Groups, Library Service to

Pennsylvania Library Association presented a Certificate of Merit to Emery Wimbish, Jr., librarian at Lincoln University, in recognition of his contribution to the Association and to the profession.

Honors were given to Louise Giles posthumously for her extensive and dedicated service to ALA and to academic and educational fields, including her work as chairperson of ACRL's Community and Junior College Libraries Section, as president of ACRL, and as a leader in cooperative and advisory programs. In her honor the ALA Minority Scholarship was renamed the Louise Giles Minority Scholarship. JESSIE C. SMITH

HISPANIC AMERICANS

The development of library service to Hispanic Americans gathered momentum in 1977 in a number of different areas. Several new library programs and collections were expanded, and in California a statewide project was funded to help solve some basic problems of collection and service development for minority communities.

In March the Los Angeles County Public Library initiated a successful Spanish-language radio program for children. "La Biblioteca Infantil del Aire" is broadcast Sunday mornings over KALI, one of the largest Spanish-language radio stations in southern California. The program consists of stories, riddles, and music selected and performed by librarians Hilda Prieto, Hortencia Hernandez, Burt Gallegos, and Carmen Martinez.

The Chicano Resource Center in the East Los Angeles Library received LSCA funds to continue to develop its resource and reference capabilities to serve the southern California area. The Center published a Spanish-language pamphlet on rape and is developing a number of other publications to meet specific Chicano information needs.

Collections. In Arizona a new research collection of special interest to school, children's and young adult librarians has been established. Housed at the University Library at Arizona State University, the comprehensive collection includes books in Spanish for children and young adults by Hispanic authors. Isbel Schon, Assistant Professor in the Department of Educational Technology and Library Science, was primarily responsible for its development.

The Miami-Dade Public Library System continued to expand the active cultural and educational activities at the Hispanic Branch. A new service begun in 1977 was the 658 Club, which provides large-print materials for shut-ins in the Spanish-speaking community.

The New York Public Library expanded the Hispanic Reference Collection at the Hunt's Point Regional Library. The Collection emphasizes Puerto Ricans and contains reference materials about every aspect of Hispanic culture and history. The active cultural and educational programs initiated as part of the federally funded South Bronx Project have been continued. One of the programs held in 1977 brought together well-known members of the Hispanic comunity who appear in *Las Memorias de Bernardo Vega*, a popular account of Puerto Ricans in New York from 1916 to 1946.

Guidelines and Services. At the ALA Annual Conference in Detroit, Spanish-speaking librarians discussed the first draft of "Public Library Guidelines for Serving the Spanish-Speaking." The draft, prepared by Patricia Tarin of the Los Angeles County Public Library and Yolanda J. Cuesta of the California State Library, was presented to the members of REFORMA (the National Association of Spanish-Speaking Librarians) for comments and reaction. A second draft was to be published in a 1978 issue of *Wilson Library Bulletin*. The guidelines will then be presented for possible adoption and distribution ay ALA.

The California Ethnic Services Project was initiated in 1977 to develop tools and methodologies to assist California librarians in establishing library services to minority communities. The project is under the direction of the California Ethnic Services Task Force, a 15-member group of minority librarians appointed by State Librarian Ethel Crockett. Task Force members are Robert Trujillo, Chairperson, University of California, Santa Barbara; Laura Bareño, San Diego County Library; Rafaela Castro Belcher, Contra Costa Community College; Barbara Clark, Los Angeles Public Library; Eleanor Crary, Alameda County Library; Nelly Fernández, Alameda County Library; Vivian Kobayashi, San Francisco Public Library; Cheryl Metoyer, School of Library Science at the University of California, Los Angeles; Anita Peterson, Inglewood Public Library; Hilda Prieto, Los Angeles County Public Library; Oscar Sims, University of California, Los Angeles; Rita Torres, San Jose Public Library; Anita Vejar, Tulare County Library; Gwendolyn Weaver, Bro-Dart; and Irene Yeh, Chinese Librarians Association. A cooperative on-line Spanish-language catalog is being developed as a prototype for a statewide catalog and will include Spanish-language subject access. Initially, the catalog will include the holdings of the East Bay Cooperative Library System, the Oakland Public Library, and the Los Angeles County Public Library.

In the area of library education, an important event was the funding for a second year of the Graduate Library Institute for Spanish-Speaking Americans at the University of Arizona Graduate Library School. The in-

The first Puerto Rican Book Fair in Chicago featured exhibits, book sales, and lectures on Puerto Rican literature at the Chicago Cultural Center and two branch libraries in heavily populated Puerto Rican communities.

stitute will train 14 bilingual-bicultural librarians. Participants were selected from approximately 67 applicants representing 12 states as well as Mexico, Puerto Rico, and Panama. Arnulfo D. Trejo and Luis Herrera, a graduate of the first year's institute, are coordinating the program.

Title VII. At the ALA Annual Conference in June the Minority Recruitment Subcommittee and ALA's Office of Library Personnel Resources invited library school representatives to meet with the staff of the Office of Bilingual Education to discuss development of proposals to train bilingual-bicultural librarians utilizing Bilingual Education Title VII funds. As a result of the meeting several library schools developed and submitted proposals. The contacts were initiated by Marilyn Salazar, former ALA Minority Recruitment Specialist, to encourage revision of the regulations governing Bilingual Education funds to include library schools as eligible applicants.

As the number of bilingual-bicultural librarians has slowly increased, a corresponding increase in the number of groups and organizations formed to further the development of library service to Hispanics has occurred. During 1977 Chicano librarians in El Paso, Texas, organized a chapter of REFORMA and presented a program at the joint conference of the Texas Library Association and the New Mexico Library Association in April. The chapter is sponsoring a Reading Is Fundamental Program in the "Chihuahuita" area of El Paso, a community with 97 per cent Mexican-American population.

In the San Francisco Bay Area a new group called Bibliotecas para la Gente (Libraries for the People) was organized to further the development of library service to Spanish-speaking people. The group is seeking chapter status within the California Library Association.

Another group organized in California was La Asociacion de Bibliotecas Chicanas (Association of Chicano Libraries), whose objectives are to promote better library and information services to Chicanos throughout California and to provide a communications link and base of support between people actively engaged in library service to Chicanos. The Association is participating in a project to develop a list of standardized subject headings for Chicano collections.   YOLANDA J. CUESTA

ITALIAN AMERICANS

Survey Results. The Italian Cultural Institute and the Library Association for Italian American Studies and Materials surveyed more than 900 public and 400 university libraries in the United States in the latter part of 1977. The survey led to several important conclusions.

Large research libraries generally have language specialists who buy through agents or book vendors anything that they determine necessary for their collections. The largest Italian collections in public libraries in the United States are in the New York Public Library, which houses 19,600 Italian publications; Cleveland Public Library, 9,300; Los Angeles Public Library, 8,000; Free Library in Philadelphia, 3,000; California State Library in Sacramento, 1,800; Stockton/San Joaquin County Library (California), 1,600; Milwaukee Public Library, 1,500; and Public Library of the District of Columbia, 1,000 volumes. All other public libraries surveyed have fewer than 1,000 works. Some have none or have only dictionaries and grammars. The Library of Congress ranked Italian language information bulletins as fifth in language priority should funding be available.

Circulating libraries in areas of 10,000 to 50,000 population with 400 or more first-generation Italian Americans have little or no programming, area histories, staff, or outreach services oriented towards Italian Americans. Such libraries must rely on additional funding for more significant collections. Their relationship to local Italian American organizations is functional and sometimes remunerative. In these libraries slightly more fiction than nonfiction is read, and it is read in paperback rather than in hardcover books. More classical than popular Italian records are requested. In Iowa the average starting age for first-generation Italian American library users is 19 years and older. In all other states reporting, the average Italian American library reader is 34 years and older, with the largest percentage of users being 48 years or older. Except in Rhode Island, where the average first-generation Italian American speaks English moderately well, library users speak English well. Where they speak English poorly, readers' families assist librarians in translating instructions to them. None of the libraries polled had forms or instructions in Italian. More of the libraries might avail themselves of the experimental and research opportunities under state and federal LSCA Title I funding for Italian American library services.

Universities such as Harvard, with 200,000 Italian books; University of California, 72,000; University of Pennsylvania, 25,000; and Yale and Dartmouth acquire from 300 to 1,600 Italian books annually through distributing agencies. Most public universities and colleges average from 500 to 1,000 books in their collections. Where Italian is not taught, universities often do not have any Italian books.

Of the specialized libraries, the Instituto Italiano di Cultura has 27,000 different titles and publishes a newsletter in English containing print and nonprint reviews or entire issues devoted to specific subjects. A unique collec-

Ethnic Groups Library Service to

tion on Italian American folklore is housed in the folklore archives of the University of Michigan. Otherwise, university and special libraries are generally restricted to specific disciplines as outlined through course requests or fields of specialization. *Italian-americana*, a quarterly review edited by Dr. Bruno Arcudi at the State University of New York in Buffalo, publishes material on a variety of aspects of Italian American history.

ALA Association. ALA's Library Association for Italian American Materials and Studies is updating its *Writings on Italian Americans* and expanding it to include directory information for community library use. The Association, formerly the Italian American Librarians Caucus, elected Carmine Diodati, Chair; Dina Malgieri, Vice-Chair; Joseph Stetson, Secretary; and Lorenzo Gureri, Treasurer.

At the ALA Annual Conference in Detroit, Alphonse Trezza, Executive Director of the National Commission on Libraries and Information Science, spoke on "Ethnicity and Librarianship," and Ronald De Paola, editor of *IAM Magazine*, spoke on "Ethnic Publications in the United States." The Association cosponsored the resolution on prejudice, stereotyping, and discrimination that was passed by Council at the Conference. It also cosponsored the membership resolution for ethnic representation at the White House Conference on Libraries. Diodati received the New York State Award of Merit for his services to the state.

Members of the Association advised mayoral candidates Edward Koch and Mario Cuomo in New York City. The Association is exploring the possibility of a meeting with representatives of the Superior Council of Academies and Libraries and the Division of Cultural Cooperation in Rome with the Association of Italian Editors and interested ALA membership as part of an institute on Italian American publications. The Association has initiated efforts to write an objective test for ethnic materials as a guide for librarians and readers. It will continue to support the efforts of the Intercommunity Arts Project and the National Italian American Foundation in Washington, D.C., in their various studies as well as the national study of ethnic museums, libraries, archives, and art galleries by the Center for the Study of Ethnic Publications of the School of Library Science at Kent State University under Lubomyr R. Wynar.

Modular programs and studies by David Cohen, Director of Ethnicity and Librarianship Institute at Queens College School of Library Science; national surveys by Paul Asciolla, Executive Director of the Italian American Foundation, and Virginia Cassiano of the Intercommunity Arts Project in Washington, D.C.; foreign language circuit collections in the Cleveland and New York Public Libraries; community information files in the branches of the New York Public Library; seminal research in urban librarianship by Lawrence Sherrill at Pratt Institute; and the ethnic awareness of ALA's Office for the Disadvantaged under Jean Coleman, Executive Director, will provide answers to outreach to Italian Americans through library service.

C. MICHAEL DIODATI

JEWISH AMERICANS

Computer Retrieval. A significant step towards the bibliographical control of a large body of scholarly Judaica material was undertaken in 1977. It is a project that will use a computer to make accessible a great portion of the Responsa literature, a body of rabbinic work that deals with questions of religious law and social customs. There are currently some 500,000 Responsa in existence; they span 12 centuries and are the contributions of approximately 5,000 different scholars. This literature is extremely valuable for the study of history, language, literature, religion, Jewish-Christian and Jewish-Moslem relations, jurisprudence, political science, and almost all other facets of human relationships.

Searching for an answer in the Responsa literature has been a long and arduous task, especially since most of the Responsa have not been properly indexed. The computer, a 370/168 IBM model located near Tel Aviv, Israel, that has the ability to find an answer in seconds at a cost of $50, is expected to greatly expedite matters.

The project is of particular interest to Jewish Americans since plans are being made at Yeshiva University in New York City to set up a computer terminal to obtain access to the base via satellite. According to the plan, the computer in Israel will run the searches through the Responsa and transmit the information to the Yeshiva University computer for an analysis and printout. It is intended that anybody in the Western Hemisphere who wants access to the Israeli retrieval unit will be able to make use of the Yeshiva University hookup. Long-range plans call for a direct on-line contact with the Israeli computer. To help fund this operation, the National Endowment for the Humanities has given a $175,000 grant that is being matched by private funding.

Bibliography. Many important bibliographic tools used extensively in the area of Judaica continued to be of importance in 1977. In its *Jewish Book Annual* the Jewish Book Council each year publishes bibliographies dealing with various fields of Judaica and also publishes *Jewish Bookland*, which reviews publications in these areas. Since 1953 the Hebrew Union College in Cincinnati has published the journal *Studies in Bibliography and Booklore*, a scholarly analysis of different aspects of Jewish bibliography. *Kirjat Sepher* is a quarterly published in Israel dealing primarily with Israeli materials. It has been published since 1924 under the auspices of the Jewish National and University Library.

The current efforts in the field of bibliography continue a long line of tradition in this field. The first real bibliography of Hebrew books was Giulio Bartolocci's *Bibliotheca Magna Rabbinica*. A four-volume work published between 1675 and 1693, it is arranged in alphabetical order by authors with a list of subjects in Latin as well as an abridged listing in Hebrew. An important subsequent bibliography was *Siftei Yeshenim* (1680) by Shabbetai Bass, arranged by title followed by the name of the author, the name and date of publication, and an indication of content. It contains some 2,200 listings including manuscripts. Another very early bibliographic work of note was *Shem ha-Gedolim* by J.J.D. Azulai, originally published in 1774.

The development of Jewish studies in the 19th century produced important new bibliographies. L. Zunz's *Zur Gesichte und Literatur* (1845) contains a complete section on bibliography. Moritz Steinschneider in his works *Catalogus Librorum Hebraeorum in Bibliotheca Bodleiana* and *Die Hebraischen Ueberstzunden des Mittelalters* (1893) was also extremely significant in helping to lay the basis for modern bibliography.

Abraham Yaari, Alexander Marx, Menahem Kasher, Dov Mendelbaum, S. Weiner, and S. Shunami have been important bibliographers in the modern period. Shunami's work, *Bibliography of Jewish Bibliographies* (1965, with a supplement in 1969), has been of importance in all areas of Jewish scholarship. It is comprehensive in its scope and is a constant reference tool.

Literary Awards. The Jewish Book Council each year presents awards for outstanding achievement in different areas of Judaica. Awards presented in 1977 included the following:

Jewish History Award, Irving Howe, *World of Our Fathers* (Harcourt Brace Jovanovich, 1976). This book has been universally acclaimed as a comprehensive social and cultural history of East European Jewry in its migration and settlement in America. It describes the economic and social struggle of the immigrant wage earners. Howe also received the National Book Award.

Jewish Thought, David Hartman, *Maimonides: Torah and Philosophic Quest* (Jewish Publication Society, 1977). This work tries to present the relationship between Maimonides' Halakic writings and the *Guide to the Perplexed*, his most famous philosophic work. Hartman maintains that there is a definite synthesis between Maimonides' legalistic and philosophic approach.

Jewish Fiction, Cynthia Ozick, *Bloodshed and Three Novellas* (Knopf, 1976). This book is another in a series of works by a talented author who has already become known for other works. The book covers various themes of Jewish social and cultural life.

Juvenile Literature, Chaya Burstein, *Rifka Grows Up* (Hebrew Publication Society, 1976). The scene for this work is a Russian Czarist village just prior to the Revolution. The book is based on the character of Burstein's mother who strives to get an education during this turbulent period of oppression.

Book on the Holocaust, Efraim Oshry, *Sefer Sheelot-U Teshuvot Mi-Maamakim*, Part 4 (Gross Printing, 1976). This is the last of a four-volume work that deals with the Responsa literature of the Holocaust period. It is written by a distinguished Talmudic scholar and gives insight into the manifold problems of Jews during this period.

Book on Israel, Howard M. Sachar, *A History of Israel from the Rise of Zionism to our Time* (Knopf, 1976). This work by Sachar is directed to a widely based audience. It addresses itself to many of the problems involved in the development of Zionism and Israel.

Poetry Award, Myra Sklarew, *From the Background of the Diaspora* (Pyrad Press, 1975). This is a collection of poems that show the poet's talent in the area of metaphorical imagery.

English Translation of a Jewish Classic, Zvi Lampert, *Maimonides: Introduction to the Talmud* (Judaica Press, 1975). This book by a scholarly writer is the first translation of its kind and makes accessible to the general public one of the most important of Maimonides' works.

Acquisitions. During 1977 an important collection of Rabbinic and Hasidic literature was acquired when the Polish government presented some 250 rare books and 130 manuscripts to the library and archives of the Lubavitch Hasidic movement in New York City. The works represent the writings and collections of five generations of Hasidic leaders in eastern Europe. This was a collection that was last known to be in the possession of the sixth grand rabbi of Lubavitch but that was lost in his flight from the Nazis in 1940. The acquisition promises to be an important key to aspects of Hasidic life in the 19th and early 20th centuries.

MAX CELNIK
DAVID ARONOVITCH

POLISH AMERICANS

The objectives of the Polish American Librarians Association (PALA) include exposing librarians to the history of Poles, Poland,

Ethnic Groups Library Service to

and Polish Americans so that they can serve their patrons more knowledgeably when asked about this ethnic group. In 1977 there were two unique opportunities for librarians to learn about this area. Both events were historical firsts. One was an ethnic landmarks tour of the Detroit metropolitan area on June 18. The other was a four-week librarianship and cultural seminar and travel workshop in Poland from July 17 to August 16.

Detroit Tour. The tour, sponsored by PALA and the Slavic and Eastern European Section of the Association of College and Research Libraries, was a ten-hour introduction to the history of Polonia in the Detroit area. (Polonia is the collective term used of all persons of Polish descent outside the geographical borders of Poland.) The tour included visits to two of the oldest and most beautiful Polish churches in Detroit, Sweetest Heart of Mary and St. Albertus. At both churches the group heard lectures regarding their histories. Another stop was made at the downtown branch of the Detroit Public Library, which houses the foreign language collection of the system. Polish publications comprise the bulk of this section. Another library visited was Hamtramck Public, which also has a considerable Polish language collection as well as English language resources pertaining to the ethnic group. The tour included a visit to the library at St. Mary's College northwest of Detroit and a view of the beautiful grounds and complex on Orchard Lake.

At midafternoon PALA hosted a reception at the Polish Century Club. Dinner at the Polish American Century club, with entertainment, a boutique, and a photographic exhibit of famous women of Polish descent, concluded the tour. Local PALA members had compiled a packet for each participant in which was included the itinerary with explanatory notes, bibliographies of various kinds, copies of the PALA *Newsletter,* and other informational material.

Workshop in Poland. The four-week lecture and travel workshop in Poland was also a first. Librarians working with, or interested in working with, Polish-oriented materials were eligible to attend. Of the 32 participants, 18 were either PALA members or supporters. Countries represented at the workshop were the United States, Canada, West Germany, Sweden, Italy, and Finland.

The first three weeks were spent in Warsaw, the capital of Poland. Mornings and afternoons were spent attending lectures, special receptions and events, and meetings with Polish librarians and visiting libraries, museums, and bookstores. Evenings were spent at the theatre, cinema, concerts, and special receptions and in exploring Warsaw. Weekends were devoted to sight-seeing trips of the countryside surrounding Warsaw.

The final week was a four-city tour of central Poland with stops along the way at historical sites. At Kraków, Czestochowa, Poznań, and Toruń the group was invited to see special collections and national treasures housed in university libraries. At Czestochowa's Jasna Góra monastery, Poland's national shrine, the group was permitted to enter the library, marking the first time in history that women were allowed to do so.

Colleagues in Poland had one request: preserve Polonica. Because of the stormy history of Poland, especially the events of World War II, much of Poland's archives and library collections have been destroyed or looted. Just as ethnic groups in the United States are concerned with preserving information for future generations, so too Poland is concerned about materials that can be utilized by historians, teachers, and librarians.

The Detroit tour and the workshop in Poland had one memorable aspect in common—the genuine, warm, generous hospitality extended by the hosts. The two events gave participants insights into the Polish ethnic group that could never be obtained through reading alone.

VICTORIA GALA

Exhibits Round Table

1977 was an interesting and fulfilling year for the Exhibits Round Table (ERT). In addition to the regular services provided for exhibitors and librarians, ERT staged a successful banquet at the Annual Conference, surveyed state and regional conferences, and released a revised *Exhibit Procedures Manual.*

Activities. After a hiatus in 1976 due to the ALA Centennial Celebration, ERT continued its tradition of a gala Conference banquet, held at the Detroit Plaza Hotel in June. Eric Sevareid spoke to the exhibitors, librarians, and guests on the role of television journalism in American life.

The four-week summer lecture and travel workshop in Poland in 1977 included an informal reception in Warsaw. Attending were: T. Wojnowski, W. Stankiewiez, Director of the Polish National Library, and V. Gala, President of PALA, fourth from left.

> **ERT Officers**
>
> CHAIRPERSON (July 1977-June 1978):
> **Jane Burke,** Schaumburg, Illinois
>
> CO-VICE-CHAIRPERSONS:
> **Teresa Mitchem,** Chilton Book Company
> **Ernest A. DiMattia,** Stamford, Connecticut
>
> SECRETARY:
> **Jeannette Mester,** H. W. Wilson Company
>
> TREASURER:
> **Walter W. Curley,** Gaylord Brothers
>
> Membership (August 31, 1977): 372

A committee formed in 1976 under the direction of Mary Daume to consider revision of the *Exhibit Procedures Manual* determined that the edition published in 1964 contained some valuable advice but that much of the material was outdated or unnecessary. A new edition was published in late summer, and free copies were sent to all state exhibit committees. During 1978 a committee was to be formed to formulate a plan for continuous revision of the *Manual*.

The ERT Standards Committee, chaired by Jean Mester of the H.W. Wilson Company, surveyed library and educational association conventions and rated the exhibits. The ratings—including such items as exhibit facilities, exhibitor services, amount of traffic, and hotel facilities—were passed on to the respective exhibit chairpersons who were to use the comments as guidelines in future exhibit planning.

Awards. ERT continued in 1977 to honor those exhibits judged most outstanding at the Annual Conference. The Donald W. Kohlstedt Award for the outstanding multiple booth went to the 3M Company. The winner for the best single booth was Bhaktivedanta Book Trust. Junior Members Round Table (JMRT) presented its first annual Friendly Booth Award. Organized by Beth Bingham, the JMRT liaison to ERT, the judges selected Time-Life as the friendliest booth in Detroit.

JANE BURKE

Federal Librarians Round Table

Following the strong leadership of Robert Lane, President in 1975-76, and Catherine Zealberg, President in 1976-77, the Federal Librarians Round Table (FLIRT) in 1977 decided to explore topics related to planning toward the year 2000 and to encourage projects that had the best chance of having an impact on the future of federal libraries. Accordingly, a one-day seminar, "The Federal Librarian in the Next Century," was held at the ALA Annual Conference in Detroit. This was the third seminar sponsored jointly by FLIRT and the Armed Forces Librarians Section (AFLS) of the Public Library Association (PLA). The 1977 program highlighted keynote speaker Brigitte L. Kenney from Drexel University, who spoke on "Survival in the Tricentennial." The President of FLIRT, Joan Maier, reported on the status of the satellite project that FLIRT and AFLS had agreed to sponsor when they met at the ALA Annual Conference in July 1976. Maier is chairman of the project. FLIRT and AFLS shared booths in the exhibit hall in 1977, as they had in 1976.

In cooperation with the University of Denver Graduate School of Librarianship, the Federal Library Committee and a group of federal libraries requested grant funding from various sources for the experimentation on Communications Technology Satellite for such applications as teleconferencing, training, document delivery, literature searching, and data transmission. This same consortium of federal libraries also jointly funded a six-month experiment in the use of slow-scan television and rapid telefacsimile for improving document delivery and the sharing of resources. They are seeking grant funding to continue the experiment for an additional year following Phase I from January to June 1978. Agencies represented in the consortium are the National Oceanic and Atmospheric Administration (NOAA), the National Bureau of Standards, the Army Corps of Engineers, the Environmental Protection Agency, and the Department of Energy. In addition, Portland Public Library, and the University of Maine Library, the Maine State Library have joined the project. The Federal Library Committee is also a sponsor and is monitoring the project. NOAA Libraries in Boulder, Colorado, Miami, and Rockville, Maryland, conducted a series of satellite teleconferences in the fall of 1977. Grant funding is also being sought for satellite experimentation.

> **FLIRT Officers**
>
> PRESIDENT (July 1977-June 1978):
> **Joan M. Maier,** National Oceanic and Atmospheric Library, Boulder, Colorado
>
> VICE-PRESIDENT/PRESIDENT-ELECT:
> **Samuel Waters,** National Agricultural Library, Beltsville, Maryland
>
> SECRETARY:
> **Susan Vita,** Library of Congress, Washington, D.C.
>
> Membership (August 31, 1977): 481

Another thrust into the future was the determination of FLIRT to articulate the need for issues concerning federal librarians to be included in the 1979 White House Conference on Library and Information Services. In September FLIRT's President and Vice-President met with Alphonse Trezza, Executive

Logo adopted by the Federal Librarians Round Table in 1977.

Director of the National Commission on Libraries and Information Science, about the planning for the Conference. Trezza agreed that federal librarians should have a preconference to define their own issues. FLIRT is assisting the Federal Library Committee in activities that identify these issues succinctly.

FLIRT publicized and helped plan the first Combined Book Exhibit for Federal Librarians and Program Specialists, held at the National Agricultural Library in Beltsville, Maryland, in December. The exhibit may become a yearly event in the Washington, D.C., area.

Personnel topics presented by experts drew crowds to FLIRT meetings throughout the year. At the 1977 ALA Midwinter Meeting in Washington, D.C., Eris Roth from the Social Security Administration discussed the new factor analysis system for preparing position descriptions and its potential impact on classification. In June Elizabeth Knauff of the Office of Management and Budget gave an update on classifications and Civil Service plans to revise the GS 1410, 1411, and 1412 Standards. Margaret Sellers of the Detroit Public Library spoke on "Unions for Professionals," describing this new influence on the future of federal librarianship.

During 1977, under the new editorship of Judy Schmidt of the Library of Congress, the FLIRT *Newsletter* has been an indispensable medium for FLIRT business, and, with its influence, membership grew to 479. Schmidt has also served as secretary to the meetings of the telecommunications projects in order that FLIRT members may be kept fully informed.

In October, Don Culbertson, Head of Public Services of the Argonne National Laboratories Library, agreed to fill the Board position vacated by Mareen Fiorica until June 1978. Also in October, David Hoyt, Management Assistant at the National Agricultural Library, was appointed Membership Chairman. Hoyt organized a luncheon for members in the Washington, D.C., area in December 1977.

All of these activities supported the three purposes of FLIRT: (1) promotion of library service and the library profession in the federal community; (2) promotion and appropriate utilization of federal library resources and facilities; and (3) provision for an environment for the stimulation of research and development and operation of federal libraries.   JOAN M. MAIER

Films

Films as a library medium are now firmly established in public libraries, school media centers, and many universities. Criteria for collection building and standards for cataloging continue along guidelines that evolved during the 25 years after World War II. During 1977, however, there were some major innovations and changes in the film field that are having a profound effect on library collections and services. Most of the developments come about through economic changes in the industry itself and through the burgeoning independent film movement. Paradoxically, the opportunities that the independent movement provides by making a wider variety of films and better films available to libraries have occurred at a time when many libraries have faced serious disruptions in their funding.

Year of Uncertainty. For the industry, 1977 began as a year of uncertainty for filmmaking and film distribution and especially for film libraries. Since the mid-1970's there has been a nationwide pattern of budget cuts for public libraries and school systems combined with fewer federal grants in the area of nonprint materials. Overall during this period, film budgets in public libraries seem to have suffered relatively less than in schools. Those public library film collections that were tied to federal funding have suffered the most. In some states where city library film budgets have been reduced, state library agencies have strengthened their film collections to help fill the demand at the local level. The situation varies from state to state. This is perhaps best illustrated in the policies of the neighboring states of New York and Connecticut. The New York State Library, which has had a large central film collection of long standing, almost totally disbanded it in 1977; at the same time, Connecticut expanded its statewide film services to public libraries.

But it is in schools that audiovisual budgets have been hardest hit. This has led to serious repercussions in film production and distribution and has caused reverberations throughout the film industry. The result has been that a sizable number of large and small film distributors either went bankrupt, merged with other firms, or became almost totally inactive. Even the most established film distributors have gone through various reorganizations and have had to reduce their staffs. The resulting cutbacks in services have caused librarians problems. In addition, distributors withdrew from circulation many titles considered uneconomical. Unfortunately, librarians thought many of these withdrawn items to be classics and staples of their collections. By the beginning of 1977, a significant segment of the 16mm field was in sufficient disarray that the normal flow of films from the filmmaker to the distributor to the library customer was undergoing major changes. Some of the changes were disruptive, and some of them were healthy.

Growth of Independents. One of the

strengths of a country the size of the United States is that it fosters anomalous situations. While the conventional 16mm marketing world was shrinking, independent filmmaking outside the confines of regular production and distribution was expanding at a remarkable rate. The barometer of this growth was the annual American Film Festival, the largest and most important of the 16mm film festivals, sponsored by the Educational Film Library Association in New York City. In 1976, 760 films were entered in 40 categories at the festival. In 1977 there were 911 films entered in 48 categories.

One reason for this growth, which flew in the face of economics, was the number of independent films entered. The growth of independently made films stemmed in part from the rapid development of film courses in colleges and universities in recent years. In the last decade there have also been many more production grants available for independent production, mainly from national endowments, state councils (especially the New York State Council on the Arts), and the American Film Institute, but also from a growing number of private foundations. Today young people are taking up the camera, whereas in an earlier age they turned to the pen.

At the same time, when independent filmmakers complete their works, they are turning to alternative methods of film distribution. The reasons are partly philosophical—many came out of the anti-Vietnam War movement and do not want to do business with the establishment—and partly economic. Inflation has so driven up distribution costs that a distributor will often be able to give a filmmaker only 20 per cent of gross sales. Given the modest size of the 16mm market, this is an arrangement that almost guarantees that the filmmaker will fail to get back his production costs, let alone make additional money to finance another film. Thus, many independents are taking the route of self-distribution, either singly or through co-ops. To help themselves, filmmakers have formed their own organization, (the Association of Independent Video and Filmmakers, 99 Prince Street, New York, New York 10013) to swap information and promote their work. Their *Newsletter* provides useful information on the growing movement.

As a group the independents are producing more compelling and innovative films than any other segment of the film industry. They are unlike most of the films produced for television. Barbara Kopple's *Harlan County U.S.A.* illustrates the unique strength of the independent movement. Kopple made the film in the face of great odds and often in the face of great physical danger. The production moved ahead by fits and starts as the director raised funds from a variety of sources. Because they

believed in the message of the film, the many people who worked on it took no pay against possible future royalties. The subjects of the film, the striking coal miners of Harlan County, Kentucky, cooperated with the filmmakers because they wanted to get their message across to the American people. It received many awards, including the grand prize at the American Film Festival and the festival's John Grierson Award for the most promising new documentary director. The film also opened at a first-run movie house in New York City. *Harlan County U.S.A.* stands as an exemplary independent work in that it exhibits the kind of personal commitment to a subject of social concern that seems only to come out of the independent movement.

Film List. The independents are not only producing political works such as *Harlan County U.S.A.* In addition to public issues, their involvement includes subjects such as the arts, experimental approaches to cinematic form, anthropology, and the study of interpersonal relationships. Following is a list of 10 films appropriate for library collections that are indicative of the range of the independent movement:

Hansel and Gretel: An Appalachian Version; 14 minutes, a new interpretation of an old fairy tale; available from Tom Davenport, Pearlstone, Delaplane, Virginia 22025.

Union Maids; 51 minutes; biographies of three women labor leaders; available from New Day Films, P.O. Box 315, Franklin Lakes, New Jersey 07417.

Attica; 80 minutes; the rebellion at Attica State Prison in New York; available from Tricontinental Films, 333 Sixth Avenue, New York 10014.

Betty Tells Her Story; 20 minutes; an ex-

(Top left) Scene from "Harlan County U.S.A." from Cinema 5. (Lower left) "Union Maids" from New Day Films, and (Above) "The Girl with the Feeling" from Phoenix Films, Inc.

Scene from "Hansel and Gretel: An Appalachian Version" produced by Tom Davenport.

129

perimental approach to a psychological study of personality; available from New Day Films, P.O. Box 315, Franklin Lakes, New Jersey 07417.

The Girl With the Incredible Feeling; 39 minutes; an unusual profile of singer Elizabeth Swados; available from Phoenix Films, 470 Park Avenue, South, New York, New York 10016.

Homage to Magritte; 9 minutes; an experiment in magic realism; available from Anita Thacher, 33 Second Avenue, New York, New York 10003.

Eat the Sun; 25 minutes; a satire of America's infatuation with Eastern cults and religions; available from Specialty Films, 2200 Eastlake Avenue, East, Seattle, Washington 98102.

Behind the Veil; 50 minutes; marriage customs in the Arab state of Dubai; available from Impact Films, 144 Bleeker Street, New York, New York 10012.

Potters of Hebron; 30 minutes; an anthropological examination of ancient craft techniques; available from Phoenix Films, 470 Park Avenue, South, New York, New York 10016.

The Ona People; 55 minutes; an ethnographic study of the last of a tribe in South America; available from Documentary Educational Resources, 24 Dane Street, Somerville, Massachusetts 02143.

Other Sources. Although independent production tends to be more provocative and certainly is more personal than television productions, television is, nonetheless, still an important source for library collections. The television industry has the budgets to take on big subjects and long series. An independent could hardly afford to produce an extensive investigation such as CBS News' *The CIA's Secret Army* (available from Carousel Films, 1501 Broadway, New York, New York 10036), one of the most important films to come from the networks in 1977. The wide-ranging *Six American Families,* six one-hour films that were produced by Westinghouse Broadcasting (also available from Carousel Films), is a penetrating series on family life in America presented on a scale never before recorded on film. It is interesting, however, that Westinghouse hired leading independent filmmakers to direct the six segments, which may account for their unusual effectiveness.

It is not only American television that is important to the 16mm field, for British television has entered the American market in a strong way. The British Broadcasting Corporation has been selling its films in the United States for more than a decade. Thames Television has also entered the market with valuable contributions. It is releasing its nine-part series *Destination America* (available from Heritage Visual/USCAN International, 205 West Wacker Drive, Chicago, Illinois 60606). The film examines in a particularly thoughtful way the various national and religious groups that emigrated from Europe to the United States in the 19th and early 20th centuries.

By the fall of 1977, much of the dust caused by the economic recession was beginning to settle in the 16mm world. The film distribution companies had gone through their period of retrenchment and had learned to live with a changed and shrunken market. Many audiovisual departments in public libraries, and to a lesser extent in school libraries, had reached a level of stability. Reports by the end of the year were that film sales had bottomed out and were climbing again at a healthy rate. On the whole, the 16mm field seemed to be on a new track. The influx of new independent works had invigorated film production, and because the subject interests of the independents often parallel the interests of librarians, the result was a much wider selection of titles to choose from than had existed in the past for collection building. A valuable resource book on the independent movement is *A Guide to Independent Film and Video,* edited by Hollis Melton and published in 1976 by Anthology Archives (80 Wooster Street, New York, New York 10012). The 87-page book sells for $4.00.

WILLIAM SLOAN

Films, Children's

1977 was a remarkable year for the serious attention given to children's films. A three-day conference, "Personal Cinema and the Child Viewer," coordinated by D. Marie Grieco as part of the Film and Personal Vision Seminars funded by the New York State Council on the Arts, was presented in March at the Port Washington Public Library in New York. The Children's Film Theatre (CFT) held a workshop in New York City called "A Long Overdue Workshop on the Nature of Children's Films." In April the CFT held the "First International Symposium on Child-Made Films." This three-day conference, held in upper New York State, resulted in the creation of the first major archive of child-made films. With the support of the Young Filmaker's Foundation the films

Scene from "Potters of Hebron" from Phoenix Films, Inc.

were presented to the Donnell Film Library of The New York Public Library on video cassette for viewing by the public.

Other CFT activities during 1977 were the week-long Children's Film Festival in New York City during Christmas week, and the first issue of *Young Viewers* magazine, which will be a regular quarterly feature of *Sightlines* (published by the Educational Film Library Association). In June the American Center of Films for Children, based in Los Angeles, presented its seventh annual International Children's Film Festival. The week-long program featured shorts and full-length films from around the world. For the first time the location was a commercial theater rather than the Los Angeles County Museum of Art. Thousands of children attended the program which included shows by magicians, clowns, mimes, and acrobats outside the theater and guest appearances by costumed characters from animated films made in Hollywood.

Award winners in the 1977 American Film Festival category of Children's Films were the following:

Blue Ribbon—*Maurice Sendak's Really Rosie Starring the Nutshell Kids*. Director: Maurice Sendak. Distributor: Weston Woods Studios.

Red Ribbon—*The Amazing Cosmic Adventures of Duffy Moon*. Director: Larry Elikann. Distributor: Time-Life Multimedia. Both of these films were based on popular children's books and were originally made for television.

Other significant events at the Festival were a program on "Films by Children," coordinated by Dee Dee Halleck, and "Documentaries for Children," coordinated by Maureen Gaffney.

The ALA's Association for Library Service to Children (formerly the Children's Services Division) announced its list of Notable Children's Films for 1977. The sixteen films cited were *Angel and Big Joe* (Learning Corporation), *Boy and a Boa* (Phoenix), *Bridge of Adam Rush* (Time-Life), *Butterfly* (Carousel), *Chick Chick Chick* (Churchill), *The Concert* (Pyramid), *Mr. Frog Went A-Courting* (Films, Inc.), *Nature Adventure* (Universal Education), *Red Ball Express* (Perspective), *Rookie of the Year* (Time-Life), *The Shopping Bag Lady* (Learning Corporation), *The Skating Rink* (Learning Corporation), *Snow Monkeys of Japan* (ACI), *The Soap Box Derby Scandal* (Weston Woods), *Taleb and His Lamb* (Barr), and *Tangram* (Pyramid). The list was made available for the first time as a separate brochure published by ALA. A program at the 1977 ALA Annual Conference highlighted the choices.

The American Broadcasting Company's "After School Specials," which were introduced to television five years ago on a monthly schedule, have been so successful that they have changed to a twice-monthly schedule. Many of these films, which are based on children's books, find their way to library markets, and in 1977 the series won the Television Critics Circle Award. An innovation for ABC in 1977 was the six-part first "family novel for television," based on Doris Gate's *Little Vic*.

There were two other notable examples of children's books being transformed into films for the television market in 1977. J.R.R. Tolkien's *The Hobbit* was made into an animated special by Arthur Rankin and Jules Bass. In a further example of cross-pollination of the media Abrams published a new hardcover edition of the book with artwork from the film. Late 1976 provided the first television screening of *Ballet Shoes*, a delightful live-action film from Britain based on Noel Streatfield's classic.

Feature films based on children's books and released for theatrical distribution this year included Mary Rodgers's *Freaky Friday* (Buenavista), and Johnny Gruelle's *Raggedy Ann & Andy* (20th Century Fox).

An interesting development in feature-length theatrical films was noted in 1977 by many critics in the release of several critically acclaimed films for adults that also gave serious consideration to the lives of children. The previously released *Spirit of the Beehive*, directed by Victor Erice, was followed in 1977 by Carlos Saura's *Cría* (starring the same remarkable child actress, Ana Torrent) and by François Truffaut's *Small Change* and Dyan Cannon's *Number One*.

MARILYN BERG IARUSSO

Filmstrips

The static performance of the filmstrip medium during 1977 underscores the 1976 media industry forecast. Nevertheless, sound filmstrips—three quarters of which include cassettes—have replaced 16mm film as the first-place contender for the largest share of the audiovisual educational materials market. Until 1975, a peak sales year, there was concrete hope that for the educational market AV materials sales backed by sizable federal funding would reach that of textbooks. The withdrawal and reallotment of federal funds to include other areas, however, mean that the AV-to-text ratio of 25 per cent to 75 per cent of the combined sales of $1,464,800 is approximately the same for 1976 as it was in 1970.

Nonetheless, the gains made up to 1970 have held, and for the filmstrip format have actually strengthened because of four factors. Filmstrips, whether sound or silent or combined with other media, have become increasingly sophisticated in content and production, and users have become more knowledgeable

Frame from filmstrip "The Growing Trip" from Marsh Film Enterprises, Inc.

Frame from filmstrip "American Revolution: Roots of Rebellion" from Coronet Instructional Media.

Financing Libraries: see Public Libraries, Special Libraries, School Libraries and Media Centers. See also Foundations and Funding Agencies.

about them. Like film, of which it was a spin-off, the filmstrip has become a spin-off staple in multimedia kits, which account for the largest wholesale dollar amount. The filmstrip also retains a price that is within the comfortable reach of the educational market. Finally, the marketplace now has a larger number of filmstrip projectors in the field than ever before (and most of them for automatic cassette, which helps to make the strips technically exciting).

The Canadian figures for 1976 suggest that the 16mm film dollar volume sales are still larger than filmstrip sales in that country. The National Film Board of Canada remains a powerful force without parallel in the United States. For the United States sound and silent filmstrips together with multimedia kits make up 46 per cent of the media market; 16mm films, 24 per cent; with games—in 10th place in 1970—now in 4th position.

The foreign market, including Canada, into which AV firms have been moving since 1970, still accounts for only a relatively small 5 per cent of sales. The United States accounts for the lion's share (almost 95 per cent) of the sales of AV materials. California, New York, Texas, and Pennsylvania are the top buyers by state. The only state to show an increase in dollar volume sales, however, is Texas.

As expected, language arts, social studies, and science and math hold the top places in sales for subject areas for both elementary and high school. For postsecondary schools, career training and nursing and medicine are the most popular. Sales are distributed among the levels as follows: elementary, 59 per cent; high school, 29 per cent; postsecondary, 11 per cent.

The October 1977 AV announcement issue of PREVIEWS, published by R. R. Bowker, reported the materials scheduled for release between May 1977 and April 1978. It reported a total of 1,414 series and individual titles, 541 in the filmstrip format. This number corresponds closely to the 510 titles sent to the reviewers over the previous year. The filmstrips were categorized under subject and curriculum topic, indicating that the headings representing the language arts once again claimed the most titles (151). There were 122 titles for social studies and 83 for science and math. A few other categories showed continuing or increasing strength: vocational and career training, 46; psychology, religion, and medicine, 30; and health, first aid, and safety, 18.

There are some additional trends. Drugs and alcohol and death and dying seem to have peaked, while environment and ecology and energy are maintaining their level. Small peaks seem to be developing in early childhood and special education, study and library skills, and business and economics.

To experience the stimulation of filmstrips as a learning and recreational-informational material, one need only see any of those cited in the best filmstrips feature in PREVIEWS for April 1977. Seeing some of the best filmstrips can help one understand more fully just how exciting filmstrips can be. DIANA L. SPIRT

Foundations and Funding Agencies

Grants to libraries from private foundations and from the U.S. Office of Education are reviewed in this section. The data concerning foundation grants were furnished by the Foundation Center in New York City. This summary includes only grants of $5,000 or more and only grants made to organizations or institutions. (See also Gifts, Bequests, Endowments; and National Endowment for the Humanities.)

Private Foundations. The information included in Table 2 has been updated by the Foundation Center. Foundation donors continued to give priority to library buildings in 1977 and approximately 40 per cent of all donations were in this category. As usual, about 15 per cent was designated for books and other library resources. In 1977 as in the previous two years there was evidence of increased interest in library cooperation and networks. The Council on Library Resources has provided financial support for and stimulated interest in basic work on national cooperative systems.

Several types of libraries received increased support from foundations. In 1977, 8 of the 15 members of the recently organized Independent Research Libraries Association were awarded grants totaling more than $4,700,000 from 26 foundations. These libraries have taken steps in the past few years to present their needs more effectively to foundations and other funding agencies.

Libraries serving the medical professions also benefited from special grants in 1977. The Helene Fuld Health Trust furnished aid to 30 medical institutions for acquiring library materials for schools of nursing. The largest single library grant of the year was $2,500,000, given by the Kresge Foundation to

West Virginia Governor John D. Rockefeller IV tries on the first library tie to initiate the 1977 "Tie One on for the Library" campaign to increase legislative funding for West Virginia libraries.

the Columbia Presbyterian Medical Center in New York City for its Library-Health Sciences Teaching Center.

Libraries in theological schools received more than $1,500,000 from various foundations in 1977. Women's interests were recognized by the Andrew W. Mellon Foundation grant of $240,000 to help expand Catalyst's Library and Information Center on Women and Work. Few grants for projects associated with minorities were made in 1977, and only one grant was made to a state library.

An examination of the geography of grants shows that 88 per cent of the total of all funds came from foundations in five states and the District of Columbia. In New York 41 foundations donated $10,723,000. Other totals were Michigan, $4,652,000; California, $2,507,000; Texas, $1,373,000; Washington, D.C., $1,017,000; and Minnesota, $1,012,000.

The recipients of these grants were located in 40 states and the District of Columbia. However, 75 per cent of the year's total went to five states and Washington, D.C.; New York, $8,300,000; California, $4,100,000; Washington, D.C., $2,100,000 (including $1,000,000 to the Council on Library Resources); Texas, $1,400,000; Pennsylvania, $1,150,000; and Illinois, $1,000,000. The number of grants and the total amount awarded to foreign countries declined during the year.

U.S. Office of Education. Table 3 includes appropriations but omits obligations, which were reported in the 1976 and 1977 ALA Yearbook. A significant addition to federal funding for libraries was the appropriation in 1977 of $5,000,000 for Title II-C "to aid in the strengthening of research library resources."

FOSTER E. MOHRHARDT

Table 1. Foundations Making Grants of $400,000 or More to Libraries

Foundation Name	Amount	Grants
Mellon (Andrew W.) Foundation	$5,655,500	21
Kresge Foundation	4,375,000	15
Hewlett (W.R.) Foundation	1,687,500	1
Rockefeller Brothers Fund	1,540,000	4
Houston Endowment	1,285,000	8
Council on Library Resources	837,479	19
Bush Foundation	523,866	5
Astor (Vincent) Foundation	510,000	2
Mellon (Richard King) Foundation	500,005	1
Fuld (Helene) Health Trust	481,362	31
Ahmanson Foundation	440,000	7
Other Foundations Making Five or More Grants		
Davis (Arthur Vining) Foundations		8
Ford Foundation		8
De Rance, Inc.		7
Rockefeller Foundation		5

Table 2. Grants to Libraries by Private Foundations

	Total Foundation Grants		Grants to Libraries		Proportion of Library Grants to Total Grants	
Year	Number of Grants	Total	Number of Grants	Total	Number of Grants	Total
1974	9,596	$701,000,000	212	$28,370,000	2.2%	4.0%
1975	10,678	677,000,000	265	18,460,000	2.5	2.7
1976	12,119	753,000,000	254	22,130,000	2.1	2.9
1977	14,276	769,900,000	292	24,152,000	2.0	3.1

This revised table replaces the data provided in the 1976 and 1977 ALA Yearbook articles and includes all of the data in the records of the Foundation Center as of December 1977.

Table 3. Summary of LSCA, ESEA, and HEA Appropriations

	FY 1974	FY 1975	FY 1976	TQ*	FY 1977	FY 1978
LSCA						
Title I	$44,156,000	$49,155,000	$49,155,000	$12,289,000	$56,900,000	$56,900,000
Title III	2,593,000	2,594,000	2,594,000	648,000	3,337,000	3,337,000
ESEA						
Title IV-B			147,330,000		154,330,000	167,500,000
HEA						
Title II-A	9,975,000	9,975,000	9,975,000		9,975,000	9,975,000
Title II-B (research and development)	1,425,000	1,000,000	1,000,000		1,000,000	1,000,000
Title II-B (training)	2,850,000	2,000,000	500,000		2,000,000	2,000,000
Title II-C						5,000,000
Title VI-A	11,875,000	7,500,000	7,500,000		7,500,000	7,500,000

*Transitional Quarter

A grant from the New York Council for the Humanities to the Nassau Library System, Hofstra University, and the Nassau County Office of Cultural Development funded an art and lecture program "The Politician as Seen Through the Eyes of the Artist" in Garden City, New York.

Freedom to Read Foundation

Founded in 1969, the Freedom to Read Foundtion acts as a legal defense arm for the American Library Association in bringing to the attention of the courts important cases having implications for the First Amendment rights of libraries, librarians, and library users.

Smith v. United States. During 1977, the Foundation took its first case, *Smith* v. *United States*, before the U.S. Supreme Court. The case involved petitioner Jerry Lee Smith, an Iowa publisher and bookseller, who had been convicted in Federal District Court for violating Section 18 of the U.S. Code (a Comstock law) proscribing the mailing of obscene matter. He was convicted even though the material had been mailed within the borders of Iowa itself, a state that under current statutes exempts adult reading material from proscription. In effect, the ruling of the District Court imposed a national standard for adults in Iowa, a seeming contradiction of the U.S. Supreme Court's decision in *Miller* v. *California* (1973), which established that "obscenity" was a "question of fact" to be measured by the "contemporary standards of the community." Smith's appeal was supported by the Foundation, which filed an *amicus curiae* brief in the U.S. Court of Appeals for the Eighth Circuit, but the conviction was upheld. Subsequently, the Foundation supported Smith's appeal before the U.S. Supreme Court.

On May 23, 1977, the Supreme Court in a five to four decision upheld the District Court in its conviction of Smith. The Court's majority included Chief Justice Burger and Justices White, Powell, Blackmun, and Rehnquist; the dissenting jurists were Justices Brennan, Stewart, Marshall, and Stevens. In a vigorously worded dissent, Justice Stevens commented that "in my judgment, the line between communications which 'offend' and those which do not is too blurred to identify criminal conduct. It is also too blurred to delimit the protection of the First Amendment.... In the end, I believe we must rely on the capacity of the free marketplace of ideas to distinguish that which is useful or beautiful from that which is ugly or worthless. In this case the petitioner's communications were intended to offend no one."

In its editorial comment on the outcome of the Smith case, the Washington *Star* (May 26, 1977) made this statement: "The Smith case was decided by five votes to four. Perhaps Justice Stevens will one of these days persuade a colleague of the superior wisdom—and, in our view, the superior legal responsibility—of his line of reason."

Even though the decision was expected, it was, nonetheless, a disappointment for the Foundation. General Counsel for the Foundation, William D. North, prepared a thorough analysis of the Court's decision, noting that "the significance of the Smith case to librarians is enormous in that it appears to clarify, at least until there is a change in the Supreme Court composition, the nature and scope of the risks and liabilities of disseminating works which may be deemed sexually explicit." (North's statement appears in *Freedom to Read Foundation News* for Spring-Summer 1977.) North further recommended the adoption of six policies or procedures that he believed would minimize the risk of criminal prosecution and conviction that librarians or their trustees may face in distributing works that may be deemed explicitly sexual.

Chelsea Right to Read. Other important litigation in which the Foundation became involved during 1977 included the case of *Chelsea Right to Read Committee* v. *Chelsea School Committee*. On July 28 the Chelsea (Massachusetts) School Committee voted to ban an anthology of poetry, *Male and Female Under 18*, edited by Nancy Larrick and Eve Merriam, because of its inclusion of a 17-line poem written by a 15-year-old girl. The anthology, published by Avon, has sold 40,000 copies, of which some 3,500 are in public libraries. The case involving the school librarian, Sonja Coleman, her colleagues in the school, and several students went to trial in November.

Pico v. Board of Education. Another important case in which the Foundation showed great interest was *Pico* v. *Board of Education* (the Island Trees case). The case involves a class action suit brought by students in the junior and senior high schools in the Island Trees Union Free School District, Long Island, New York. The students protested the removal of nine books from the school libraries and the prohibition of the use of these books in the curriculum. The books included such important titles as Kurt Vonnegut's *Slaughterhouse Five*, Bernard Malamud's *The Fixer*, and *Down These Mean Streets* by Piri Thomas. Following several delays, the case was filed in a federal court, and the Foundation is sponsoring the filing of a friend-of-the-court brief on behalf of the students. Whatever the outcome of these cases, the Foundation's support is essential to provide additional support for the plaintiffs in these suits and to uphold the principles of the First Amendment. R. KATHLEEN MOLZ

Friends of Libraries

Friends of Libraries are citizens who care about libraries and want the best of services. To get quality service, they are willing to band together to help library administrations and boards achieve it. Friends of Libraries assist through lobbying, public relations, and fund raising. They can be one of the most powerful public relations tools a library has. Unlike other publicity devices such as news releases, there are no easy or standard techniques for Friends groups, because their work is, above all, to serve as human publicity tools.

The American Library Association has recognized the value of citizen support groups and has established a Friends of Libraries Committee in the Public Relations Section of the Library Administration Division. The Committee has the responsibility of putting together a luncheon program at the Annual Conference. In 1977 the Committee's program featured John Toland, author of *My Search for the Real Adolf Hitler*, as the guest speaker. The Committee also presented a panel discussion entitled "Friends of Libraries: A Time for Sharing."

The Friends of Libraries Committee has two major projects under way. It is continuing work on revising the book *Friends of the Library*, edited by Sarah Leslie Wallace (ALA, 1962). In addition, the Committee is developing a directory of groups of Friends of Libraries. The directory, done on a geographical basis, will include academic, public, statewide, and other Friends groups.

Not only is there national interest in Friends, but also there are many statewide Friends associations. The California group continues to be one of the most active, with regional workshops, a regular publication, and a nationally known kit of sample materials. Some other states also have active state associations. The Ohio Friends, for example, hold workshops and publish a regular newsletter. In addition, many local libraries attempt to help other libraries learn about Friends groups. In Northern Pennsylvania, the Warren and Clarion District Libraries cosponsored a one-day workshop on Friends. More than a dozen libraries sent representatives.

Most Friends of Libraries groups are concerned with local problems, not with attempting to educate others about Friends of Libraries. It is on this local level that most activities of Friends take place. In 1977, as in previous years, local Friends groups actively supported their libraries, helped to pass needed referendums, raised public consciousness, and of course raised funds. Book sales continued to be a major money-making method. The Friends of Northland Library in suburban Pittsburgh raised more than $3,000 in four days. In November, the Friends of Orlando Public Library raised $5,300 in three days.

Other Friends of Libraries had similar success stories. Groups in Milwaukee, San Francisco, and other areas have made their annual book sales into gala events. Some Friends groups have used other methods for fund rais-

(Above) Friends of the Memphis Public Library sponsored their 14th book sale in October and in seven years have provided $45,000 for library equipment (Left) Lee Fikes of the Friends of the Dallas Public Library introducing author and astronomer Carl Sagan at the Friends annual luncheon.

ing: bridge parties, rummage sales, fashion shows, auctions, talent shows, and sales of special items. Much of the money earned is used to buy needed items that libraries could not otherwise afford. In Orlando, the earnings from the book sale went toward purchasing a film inspector and cleaner. In Northland, the Friends are using the funds to help furnish the meeting rooms of the new library building.

Friends of Libraries throughout the United States contributed much to the success of their libraries in 1977. They served as a tremendous force in the political arena as well as a bridge in reaching the community by making more people aware of and bringing them into the library.

LAURA SHELLEY

Gifts, Bequests, Endowments

Perhaps the most unusual gift in 1977 came from a successful football team. The University of Pittsburgh announced that $100,000 from its Sugar Bowl football game would be given to the University Library to use for acquisitions; $20,000 was to be earmarked for the purchase of nonprint materials.

The largest gifts of the year were separate donations of $1,000,000. Edmund and Louise Ureff Kahn made three $1,000,000 gifts—to the University of Pennsylvania Library, the Smith College Library, and the Dallas Public Library. Kahn, a graduate of the Wharton School made the gift to Pennsylvania; Mrs. Kahn, a cum laude graduate of Smith, made the gift to that institution. They jointly made the gift to the public library of Dallas, where they reside. The fourth million-dollar gift came from the Boettcher Foundation, which

Gifts, Bequests, Endowments

presented $1,000,000 to the Colorado School of Mines for acquisitions in the fields of public policy, environment, and energy, and for a special center for the Arthur Lakes Library.

Endowments. The von Klein Smid World Affairs Library at the University of Southern California received an endowment of $300,000 from a trust established by the late Rufus B. von Klein Smid. He was the former Chancellor of USC and had arranged that the income from the endowment be used for acquisitions to enrich the World Affairs Library's holdings. The Japan World Exposition Fund gave the General Libraries of the University of Texas a $10,000 grant to enable the Libraries to "continue Japanese-Language acquisitions at the past rate, despite sharp increases in the price of Japanese books."

Two libraries received special gifts when they reached the 1,000,000-volume level, while another celebrated its arrival at the 4,000,000-volume level. The rare *Prose and Poetry of the Livestock Industry of the United States* (Denver and Kansas City, 1905) was presented to the Texas A&M Libraries by Mrs. M.F. Driscoll of Midland. It was the one-millionth volume in that library's collection. The one-millionth volume in the M.D. Anderson Library of the University of Houston was Albrecht Dürer's *Underweysung der Messung* (1525). Its 999,999th volume was Gellius's *Noctes Atticae*, a great rarity printed in Venice in 1474 by Nicholas Jenson and presented by the university's President, Philip Hoffman.

The four-millionth volume to be added to the University of Texas Library at Austin was the two-volume first edition of Noah Webster's *An American Dictionary of the English Language* (1828). It was presented by Mrs. Dolph Briscoe, wife of the Governor of Texas. On yet another commemorative occasion, on their 25th anniversary, the Friends of the Columbia University Libraries purchased and presented to the Libraries the original Rockwell Kent drawings for the 1936 edition of Walt Whitman's *Leaves of Grass*.

Manuscripts. The Jean Webster McKinney family papers, which included more than 600 letters and telegrams from Mark Twain, "as well as a vast array of manuscripts, notebooks, and other documents by or relating to the noted author" were presented to Vassar College. The papers also contain a large collection of material by and about Jean Webster McKinney, Mark Twain's grandniece and a well-known author who wrote as Jean Webster. This significant gift was made by her daughter, Jean Connor, and son-in-law, Ralph Connor, of La Grangeville, New York. They also contributed $750,000 to establish an endowed chair in American literature, creative writing, or drama at Vassar.

The complete manuscript of Ernest Hemingway's *The Sun Also Rises* is now at the University of Virginia as a result of the purchase by the university of a 15-page fragment and Marguerite A. Cohn's gift (in memory of her late husband, Captain Louis Henry Cohn, Hemingway's first bibliographer) of the remainder of the manuscript. • Anais Nin's diaries, correspondence, manuscripts, and related papers have been acquired from her literary estate by the University of California at Los Angeles. The acquisition was made possible by a generous gift from UCLA alumna Joan Palevski. The papers of playwright and biographer Robert Sherwood have been presented to the Houghton Library at Harvard University by his widow, Madeline H. Sherwood. The collection is said to be extensive and to reflect nearly every aspect of his life and work.

The Seeley G. Mudd Manuscript Library at Princeton has received George Field's papers covering his service as Executive Director (1941-69) of Freedom House. The archives of the two organizations that founded Freedom House in 1941—the Committee to Defend America by Aiding the Allies and Fight for Freedom—have already been given to the Mudd Library. Mudd will also house the archives of Common Cause. Beginning with the years 1970-71, these archives contain materials concerning the founding, governing board, staff, studies and reports, press releases, and miscellaneous records of Common Cause. The papers will be generally available as soon as they are processed. The National Libertarian Party has given Alderman Library at the University of Virginia an archival collection of its papers.

Possibly the largest manuscript gift reported in 1977 was that of some 800,000 items comprising the papers of John D. Rockefeller, Sr. (1839-1937), received by the Rockefeller Archive Center of Rockefeller University. On September 27, 1976, Archbishop Fulton J. Sheen dedicated the Sheen Room at St. Bernard's Seminary, Rochester, New York, to house books and pamphlets he had written, some "1,500 tapes of sermons, retreats, lectures, and informal talks; phono recordings and TV tapes of the 'Life is Worth Living' series, 1951-57; radio and TV tapes of 'The Catholic Hour' broadcasts, 1930-52," as well as his general records and memorabilia.

George J. Barrere presented the papers of the late Philip Dunning, actor, stage manager, writer, director and producer, to the Curtis Theatre Collection of the University of Pittsburgh Libraries. Covering the period 1915-68, the papers are "essentially Dunning's personal script collection (stage, radio, TV and film)." Mrs. E.C. Parsons gave the collection of scrapbooks, correspondence, photo albums, and personal papers of her husband Admiral Parsons to the University of Texas at El Paso. Parsons was a pioneer aviator who learned to fly in 1912 and who served in Mexico and in the Lafayette Esquadrille and SPAD 4 squadrons.

Other Manuscripts. The personal and professional papers of Andrew W. Cordier, former President of Columbia University and Under Secretary of the United Nations, were bequeathed to Columbia. This collection of more than 125,000 items, including letters from Ralph Bunche, Henry Cabot Lodge, Adlai E. Stevenson, Harry S. Truman, and others, was opened to use early in the year. Bella S. Abzug has given her congressional papers, consisting of some 500,000 items, to Columbia University. The collection documents her six years in Congress (1970-76) and her concern for women's issues, housing, unemployment, urban problems, the environment, peace and amnesty, and New York City. John Warner, former Secretary of the Navy and Administrator of the American Revolution Bicentennial Administration, announced that he would present his papers, which cover 13 years of public service, to Alderman Library at the University of Virginia. The papers of Tennessee Congressman Joe L. Evans, who served 15 terms in the House of Representatives, were given to Tennessee Technological University, and U.S. Senator Harry F. Byrd, Jr., gave a collection of his senatorial papers to the University of Virginia.

Lotte Lenya, internationally known star of theatre, films, and the concert stage, donated the autograph orchestral score of *The Seven Deadly Sins* by her late husband Kurt Weill to the Music Division of the New York Public Library's Performing Arts Research Center. L.A. Whitehill of San Angelo presented the unique autograph collection of his father, Samuel Weiselberg, to the Library of Texas Technological University. Nicolaas Steelink has given the University of Arizona Library his translations into English of the publications of the important Dutch social philosopher, Edward Douwes Decker (1820-87). He wrote under the name Multoti, and few of his works have been translated into English.

Book Collections. The most significant gift ever received by the Norlin Library of the University of Colorado was the personal collection of Sam Goldman of Denver. Consisting of about 5,000 volumes on music, art, modern first editions, and "the revival of printing as an art," the Goldman gift contains every one of the 53 books published by the Kelmscott Press (including the *Chaucer*), 32 of the 40 books published by the Ashendene Press, 42 books from the Doves Press (including a magnificent copy of the five-volume Bible), plus a number of T.J. Cobden-Sanderson's inscribed presentation copies to his wife. There are also 67 books from the Golden Cockerell Press, a full set of the publications of the Nonesuch Press, books from the Greggnog, Vale, and Eragny presses, as well as books from the Heritage Press, the First Editions Club, the Folio Society, and the Imprint Society, and a complete set of the publications of the Limited Editions Club. Many items are in special bindings; there are many high spots in the collection, such as T.E. Lawrence's translation of the *Odyssey*, privately published by Bruce Rogers and Emery Walker, and Thomas Browne's *Urne Buriall*, illustrated by Paul Nash and published in London by Cassell.

Richard Morris of Indianapolis has presented to Indiana University's Lilly Library what was described as "one of the most complete collections of material relating to the United States Constitution." Beginning with the first newspaper printing of the Constitution in the *Pennsylvania Packet and Daily Advertiser* on September 19, 1787, the collection includes early works such as John Dickinson's *Letters of Fabius, a Pennsylvania Farmer* (1788), Jonathan Elliot's 1827-30 publication of the debates and proceedings on the adoption of the Constitution, and Richard Henry Lee's *Letters from the Federal Farmer to the Republican, Leading to the Fair Examination of the System of Government proposed by the Late Convention* (1788).

Herman B. Chilson of Webster, South Dakota, has presented his Western American collection of 20,000 books, documents, maps, and pamphlets in many rare, first and special editions to the I.D. Weeks Library at the University of South Dakota. Although major emphasis is on the Dakotas and Minnesota, of particular significance are the large number of works by regional authors. The collection was acclaimed as "the finest private library in the Dakotas" and is expected to provide students and scholars with an invaluable source for research.

Erskine Caldwell gave the University of Georgia Library a personal collection that contains a copy of each edition of every one of his books. Caldwell's books are said to have sales aggregating to 75,000,000 copies in 50 languages, "more than the works of any other living author." Jacob M. Lowy of Montreal presented his 1,560-title library of Hebraica, valued at $2,000,000, to the National Library of Canada. The collection consists of Hebrew and Latin incunabula, rare bibles and liturgy, Talmud editions and codes, and Hebrew books from the 16th to the 19th centuries. This major gift, the largest ever received by the Library, was considered one of the three most important Hebraic libraries in North America.

Other Book Gifts. John E. Howe has presented eight rare Siberian primers to the

Gifts, Bequests, Endowments

University of Washington Libraries. These primers constitute "some of the earliest and in certain cases the first attempts to transcribe these Siberian languages: Selkup, Karyak, Golds (Nanai), Lamut, Kamchadal (Itelmes), Udi, Gilyak (Niukhi), and Eskimo." Prepared by Soviet ethnographers in the 1930's, they illustrate early attempts to educate northern peoples who had until that time been relatively isolated from the Russian Revolution.

Trinity University Library has dedicated the Karl J. Pelzer Collection of Asian and International Studies. The collection of more than 10,000 volumes was presented by Pelzer of Yale University and contains monographs, pamphlets, serials, documents, anthologies, proceedings, and reference works. The primary emphasis is on Southeast Asia, but there is a large section covering all aspects of geography, and other areas and disciplines are also represented.

James A. Leftwich of La Jolla, a noted writer on the *Monitor* and the *Merrimack*, has given "the largest collection of Civil War naval history materials on the West Coast" to the Library of the University of California at San Diego. The collection is particularly rich in material dealing with the 1862 battle between the two ironclads. Nathan D. Grundstein presented his 2,000-volume collection of material on public and urban management, management science, sociotechnical systems, public law, and allied subjects to the John Brister Library of Memphis State University.

Collections. The Max A. Goldstein collection of some 700 volumes about education for the deaf and otology was given to the Washington University School of Medicine by the St. Louis Central Institute for the Deaf. In the collection are a 1496 Venetian work by Guarinus Veronensis, "about a dozen 16th Century works, many anatomical volumes and a fine collection on sign language." Harold Jantz has given his 9,000-volume collection of books on German literature and early German-American cultural and literary relations to Perkins Library at Duke University. This collection "reflects Professor Jantz' interests in German Baroque literature of the seventeenth and early eighteenth centuries and in literature concerning the Rosicrucians and the occult."

The distinguished musician Harold B. Lee gave his private collection of materials pertaining to the viola and viola music to Brigham Young University. The University of Pittsburgh received a gift of books and musical materials from William Steinberg, former musical director of the Pittsburgh Symphony Orchestra. It included some 1,400 books in the field of literature and about 800 titles of music, largely scores, many being presentation copies of symphonic works.

Clifton Fadiman announced that he will give his 2,000-volume collection of books for children and about children's literature to the Historical Collection of Children's Books at the University of Pittsburgh Graduate School of Library and Information Science. Helen Detwiler Robbins of Oceanside, California, has given a collection of juvenile literature concerning Pennsylvania Germans to the Myrin Library of Ursinus College. The collection is particularly strong in the works of the author-illustrator Katherine Milhous, who autographed copies of most of her books.

To foster stronger relationships between Mexican and Texan educational institutions, the Universidad National Autónoma de México gave a collection of all of the titles available that have been published by its University Press to the Yeary Library of Laredo Junior College and Texas A & I University at Laredo. Ambassador Nicolae M. Nicolae of the Socialist Republic of Romania, presented a 260-volume collection of current Romanian art, archaeology, history, poetry, and children's books to Wayne State University Libraries "to strengthen the exchange of materials between Wayne State University and the academic institutions and scholarly societies of Romania."

The Center for Applied Research in the Apostolate has presented a collection of more than 3,000 books and 200 current subscriptions concerning Africa to the University of Notre Dame. The collection was originally assembled by priests of the Society of Missionaries of Africa and covers governmental,

Sculptor Richard Hunt (at microphone) explains his work entitled "Jacob's Ladder" which was donated to the Woodson Regional Library by the Chicago Community Trust and the Board of Directors of the Chicago Public Library.

cultural, and scientific areas. The American Society of Interior Designers donated its library to the Cooper-Hewitt Museum in New York, substantially enriching its library resources. The Bibliographic Systems Center Collection of the Case Western Reserve University School of Library Science was transferred to the Library Science Library of the University of Toronto. The collection constitutes a major library of classification schemes, thesauri, and subject heading lists.

The Baltimore-D.C. Society and Institute for Psychoanalysis presented a first edition of Sigmund Freud's *Die Traumdeutung* to the Library of Congress. Two rare medical books, both printed in 1543, were given to the Thomas Jefferson University Library by Robert L. Phillips. The books are Andreas Vasalius's *De Humani Corporus Fabrica* (one of four copies in the United States), and Ambroise Paré's *Cing Livres de Cherugie*. The E.H. Little Library of Davidson College received from William P. Cumming the unusual elephant folio edition of the *Works of William Hogarth from the Original Plates* (London: n.d. but circa 1835). Arthur C. Nielson, Jr., of Northbrook, Illinois, enriched the Cordell Collection of Dictionaries in the Cunningham Memorial Library at Indiana State University with his gift of the magnificiently printed and rare Zacharias Calliergis's *Etymologicum Magnum Graecum* (Venice: N. Vlasatos, 1499).

Grants. The National Science Foundation awarded O. Marvene Couch $125,800 to organize and annotate the approximately 15,000 to 20,000 unorganized and uncatalogued original manuscripts of ex-slave narratives collected by the WPA Federal Writers Project now located in the Library of Congress Archive of Folk Song. This project will make available previously unusable primary research materials dealing with the history of slavery in the United States

The National Endowment for the Humanities gave a three-year grant of $45,296 to the University of Illinois at Urbana-Champaign to "extend intellectual control through subject and name access" to the archives of the American Library Association located at the University. The Research Libraries of the New York Public Library received a general-purpose grant from the Commonwealth Fund of $100,000. The grant is said to be one of the largest made by the Fund "not directly related to the field of medicine."   CLYDE C. WALTON

Government Documents Round Table

Robert Wedgeworth, in his "State of the Association" address at the 96th ALA Annual Conference in Detroit, gave Government Documents Round Table (GODORT) a handsome fifth birthday gift with these words: "We tend to think of ALA as a giant. It's also important for us to recognize that, while we may be big, we are also flexible, hospitable as well as helpful to small specialized interest groups. One case in point is the Government Documents Round Table, a group that has enhanced ALA and has, in turn, drawn strength from our size. The Round Table has made significant contributions in revitalizing the Advisory Committee to the Public Printer, in establishing guidelines for the use and servicing of state documents, in reviewing the function of the depository law, and has become a respected representative able to speak for the problems, needs, and goals of document librarians."

GODORT appreciated those remarks, but there is more to be said about GODORT, its six task forces and numerous work groups, as well as its individual members. Separate task forces concentrate on federal, state, local, and international documents, as well as documents in microform and education for work in documents. There is an interest group for people involved with machine-readable data files. If a member finds that an area is not being covered within the existing structure, a new task force or work group can be formed. GODORT is a viable, responsive group; evidence of this is that a four-year-old task force, Administration and Organization, voted itself out of existence at the Detroit meeting because it felt that its work was being or could be accomplished by the other task forces. At the same time, the Education Task Force, under the able leadership of Ellen Gay Detlefsen, has expanded its focus, and five work groups were organized at the Detroit meeting.

After a shaky year or two, *Documents to the People*, GODORT's newsletter, has stabilized into a regular bimonthly publication that is distributed free to members and maintains a healthy subscription list. The up-to-date, otherwise hard-to-find information that it offers makes it mandatory reading for anyone interested in government publications. Indexing is proceeding and should be available by midwinter 1977-78 for volumes 1-4.

GODORT Officers

CHAIRPERSON (July 1977-June 1978):
Nancy Cline, Pennsylvania State University

ASSISTANT CHAIRPERSON:
Francis Buckley, Detroit, Michigan

SECRETARY:
Robert Schaaf, Library of Congress

TREASURER:
Giles Robertson, University of Illinois, Chicago

Membership (August 31, 1977): 1,276

Government publications and Depository System

GODORT members are actively concerned with matters outside its organizational structure. Bernadine Hoduski is continuing to chair an ad hoc committee of GODORT members attempting to make an impact on the Anglo-American Cataloguing Rules revisions. The Ad Hoc Committee on Federal Depository Legislation was formed two years ago as a subcommittee of the ALA Legislation Committee, and all of its members are also GODORT members. GODORT continues to send a representative to the Freedom to Read Foundation because of its concern with the problems that the Foundation considers.

Three GODORT members testified at national hearings in 1977. Nancy Cline, Pennsylvania State University, and LeRoy C. Schwarzkopf, University of Maryland, both appeared before the National Study Commission on Records and Documents of Federal Officials on behalf of the ALA in Washington, D.C., on January 12, 1977. Transcripts of their testimony appear in *Documents to the People* for March 1977. Francis Buckley, Detroit Public Library, testified for the GODORT and ALA position on designating law schools as depository libraries before the Subcommittee on Libraries and Memorials of the Committee on House Administration on June 22, 1977. This statement appears in the September 1977 issue of *Documents to the People.*

In 1975 GODORT established the James Bennett Childs Award to recognize outstanding contributions to the field of documents librarianship. The first recipient in 1976 was James Bennett Childs himself, and the recipient in 1977 was Bernadine Hoduski, the first coordinator of GODORT, presently employed by the Joint Committee on Printing. A second award was established in 1976 in conjunction with the Congressional Information Service (CIS). The first recipient, announced at the ALA Annual Conference, was Joe Morehead, Associate Professor, School of Library and Information Science, State University of New York at Albany, and a prolific author of articles concerned with government publications. The ALA/GODORT/CIS award was first proposed by James Adler, president of CIS, to honor an individual or institution that has most effectively encouraged the use of federal documents in support of library service.

LOIS MILLS

Government Publications and Depository System

The best known and most used U.S. government publications are those printed by the Government Printing Office (GPO) at its own plant in Washington, D.C., or under contract to the GPO Central Office and its 14 regional procurement offices. These are called GPO publications, although the Government Printing Office acts as the printer rather than the publisher. Many U.S. government publications are also printed in-house by most federal agencies (who are the U.S. government publishers) at some 300 field printing plants authorized by the Joint Committee on Printing, or on various types of office duplicating equipment. These are called non-GPO publications.

A third type of U.S. government publication is the technical report. The National Technical Information Service operates a central clearinghouse to catalog and distribute government-prepared or government-sponsored technical reports under Section 1152, Title 15, of the U.S. Code. This article discusses the sale of selected GPO publications under Section 1708, Title 44, of the U.S. Code; distribution of most GPO publications and selected non-GPO publications to depository libraries under Chapter 19, Title 44; and cataloging and indexing of GPO and non-GPO publications under Sections 1710 and 1711, Title 44, of the U.S. Code. These three functions are assigned to the Superintendent of Documents, a GPO official designated as Assistant Public Printer. The incumbent, Carl A. LaBarre, was appointed in July 1975.

New Public Printer. John J. Boyle, Deputy Public Printer (operations) from June 1973, was nominated by President Carter as Public Printer and confirmed by the Senate on October 27, 1977. During the tenure of the previous Public Printer, Thomas F. McCormick, outstanding improvements were made in providing U.S. government publications to libraries and the public. These resulted from the move of the Superintendent of Documents and his operating units to modern leased office and warehouse space in 1975 and early 1976, with the concurrent introduction of automated equipment and systems.

By early 1976 most of the Documents Sales Service had moved into the new Union Center Plaza office building on North Capitol Street, a block north of the two main GPO buildings. The Warehouse Division, responsible for bulk storage of sales publications, had moved in 1975 to a new one-story warehouse in Laurel, Maryland, about 18 miles northeast of the Central Office. The Retail Distribution Division, responsible for mailing sales publications, had moved in early 1976 to an adjacent warehouse in Laurel. By early 1976 the Library and Statutory Distribution Service had completed its move to new warehouse and office space in Alexandria, Virginia, about 12 miles southwest of the Central Office. Its Library Division is responsible for the cataloging and depository library programs.

Sales Publications Program. The McCormick era saw a major reduction in publication order processing time from 24 workdays in

1973, using manual procedures, to less than 10 workdays by mid-1977, with estimates that the goal of 5 workdays would be met well before the target date of FY 1979. The Publications Receipt and Control System had brought on-line inventory control to warehouse and shipping functions in 1975. The Publications Fulfillment System, introduced in late 1976, had automated processing of orders for individual sales publications. The Subscription Fulfillment System went on line in late 1977 to automate order processing of periodicals and other subscription services, along with 1,200 mailing lists having more than 3,500,000 entries.

A major component of the overall GPO sales management automation plan, called Sales Order and Information System, is the Publications Reference File. This on-line system stores bibliographic and sales information on more than 25,000 GPO sales publications. About 19,000 publications are in print, 2,000 are new or on order, and 4,000 are out of stock or superseded but held in the file for 12 months before deletion. The file is arranged in three sequences: stock number; Superintendent of Documents classification number; and dictionary arrangement of authors, titles, and subjects. The file is produced weekly on 48x microfiche for in-house use. In May 1977 distribution of the microfiche file to depository libraries was begun on a monthly basis. Paid subscriptions were to be offered on a bimonthly basis starting in January 1978.

Depository Library Program. The number of depository libraries increased from 1,201 in October 1976 to 1,216 in October 1977. The number of regional depositories increased from 48 to 51, and the number of states served from 40 to 42. States not served by a regional depository are Alaska, Arkansas, Delaware, Missouri, Rhode Island, South Carolina, South Dakota, and Tennessee. Nearly 18,000,000 publications were distributed free to depository libraries in FY 1977. On July 28, 1977, Daily Depository Shipping List number 10,000 was mailed. The practice of enclosing a shipping list (invoice) with each regular depository shipment was begun on August 1, 1951.

HR 4751 introduced by Lucien Nedzi (D.-Mich.) would grant special depository designation to 164 accredited law school libraries. Hearings were held in June by the Committee on House Administration. An amended bill (HR 8358) was reported (House Report 95-650) and passed by the House of Representatives on October 25. If the bill becomes law, 34 law school libraries that are now depositories would vacate their Congressional designations, making them available to other libraries.

Other Projects. A modified GPO microform program was approved by the Joint Committee on Printing on March 25, 1977. It authorized the Superintendent of Documents to convert to microfiche for distribution to depository libraries only non-GPO publications and selected GPO publications when "savings in cost are clear and demonstrable." Filming has begun on several categories of non-GPO publications, and distribution of the first category, General Accounting Office reports, began in November.

Cataloging of entries for the *Monthly Catalog of U.S. Government Publications* was converted to MARC format and entered into the OCLC data base in early 1976. The new *Monthly Catalog* in MARC format began with the July 1976 issue. Entries for periodicals, subscription services, and serials issued more than three time a year were converted to MARC format and published in the annual *Serials Supplement* in April 1977.

Hearings were held in May 1977 by the House Committee on Public Works and Transportation on a prospectus recommending the construction of a new Government Printing Office for $164,000,000. It would consolidate scattered GPO facilities on a 33-acre site near the Rhode Island Avenue subway station, about one and a half miles north of the GPO Central Office.

LEROY C. SCHWARZKOPF

Health and Rehabilitative Library Services

In 1977 there were changes in the evolution of health and rehabilitative library services on several levels as librarians, joining forces with an increasing number of individuals and agencies, gave concerted attention to both the needs of people with special requirements and those who work with them. Long-standing concern with the individual library and information needs of users was increasingly heightened as focus was given to civil rights, assistive devices, the removal of architectural barriers, and the growing significance of library networks related to the organization and administration of library services.

LEGISLATION

It is now clear that "the educational revolution" of the 1970's will be based on educational rights and services to the handicapped. The Education of All Handicapped Children Act (PL 94-142), signed into law on July 29, 1975, moved closer to implementation. Although this legislation represents requirements established by the courts, legislatures, and other policymaking groups, it can be perceived as a continuing component in the evolving federal role in meeting the needs of the handicapped. By September 1978 it will be a violation of federal law for any public educational agency to deny a handicapped child in need of special education an appropriate program.

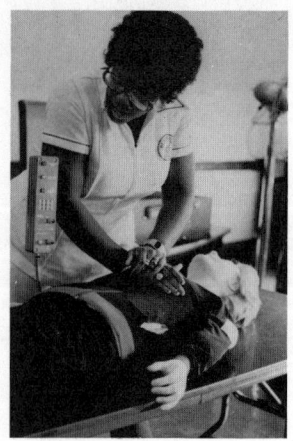

More than 1,000 library patrons attended the 1977 Health Fair at Chicago's Kelly Branch Library which featured blood pressure testing (right) and cardiac arrest first aid procedures (below) as well as hearing and sickle cell anemia tests.

This ushers into being civil rights for the handicapped, rights now guaranteed by both law and national policy.

Guaranteed Rights. Demands for these new rights provided a theme considered throughout the world of education in 1977. As the nation moved to establish appropriate practices for implementing the law, federal, state, intermediate, and local governments were immersed in rules and regulations and guidelines and bylaws in order to provide agency personnel and the general public with instruction and guidance in mounting programs. Congress discovered as part of its study leading to passage of the law that more than 1,750,000 children with handicaps were excluded from public education solely on the basis of handicaps and that more than one half of an estimated 8,000,000 handicapped children were not receiving appropriate services.

It is the primary purpose of the act to assure that all handicapped children have free appropriate public education that emphasizes special education and related services designed to meet the individual's unique needs. Handicapped children are defined by the law as those who are "mentally retarded, hard of hearing, deaf, orthopedically impaired, other health impaired, speech impaired, visually handicapped, seriously emotionally disturbed, or children with specific learning disabilities who by reason thereof require special education and related services."

Although this law concerns directly all school librarians, major legislation impacting on the publicly supported library community— Section 504 of the Vocational Rehabilitation Act of 1973 (PL 93-112)— asserts basic rights by guaranteeing that no otherwise qualified handicapped individual solely by reason of handicap can be excluded from any program or activity receiving federal financial assistance. Provision of equal rights throughout society is now a matter of statutory record; violations can result in the withholding of all federal funds.

In 1977 the library community sought tangible ways to utilize resources for effective implementation of this legislation, designing and developing public awareness campaigns, initiating staff development, conducting needs assessments, and administering plans and programs.

Of special significance for publicly supported libraries were requirements mandating user access to library settings and programs. Regulations, effective in 1977, included citizens with mobility and sensory impairments, educational and psychological illnesses, learning disabilities, mental retardation, and chemical dependency. When viewed in its entirety, each library program and activity must be readily accessible to handicapped persons and be offered in the most integrated setting possible.

National Center and Conference. This new era of civil rights requires a variety of support services; special attention should be given to the National Center for Law and the Handicapped (NCLH), located at 1235 North Eddy Street, South Bend, Indiana 46617. The center is charged with protection and extension of legal rights for handicapped persons often neglected under the law or discriminated against by public agencies. The work of NCLH is divided into two programs: legal assistance and public education. While serving as counsel in court cases, the center is primarily involved as a friend of the court. In addition, its attorney training and legal and social science intern programs focus on rights to education, treatment, work, accessibility, transportation, and housing.

1977 also brought the first White House Conference for Handicapped Individuals. Thousands of issues were debated in Washington, D.C., by 800 delegates and 2,500 observers and attendees at this landmark conference generated by Title III of the Vocation and Rehabilitation Act of 1973, as amended in 1974 (PL 93-516). The conference stressed national assessment of the problems and potentials of individuals with mental and physical handicaps, raising national awareness and formulating recommendations for the President and Congress to assure that individuals with handicaps can live independent lives founded on dignity and full participation in community life.

As librarians considered this array of legislation it was understood that general application of the label "handicapped" could not bridge the needs of individual persons and that library programs must be maximized to meet individual needs.

IMPACT ON LIBRARIES

Of special impact, handicapped individuals used their political sophistication and growing power to effect legislation and to mandate social change. In 1977, for example, the elderly, including the impaired elderly, emerged as a powerful political force. So called senior citizens comprised 10.7 per cent of the population and were expected to reach 20 per cent within 50 years. Recent legislation prohibiting mandatory retirement before age 70 for most workers is tangible evidence of effective lobbying that assures older citizens of increased independence. Momentum also accelerated changes in health care, nutrition programs, social security, and crime prevention. The elderly echoed the goal of the new civil rights: dignity and respect without stereotyping.

Innovative Changes. Within library associations 1977 brought additional innovations reflecting general changes within society. There were two areas of especial note. At the ALA Annual Conference in Detroit, ALA Council voted unanimously to approve the merger of the Health and Rehabilitative Library Services Division with the Association of State Library Agencies. A significant step toward worldwide standardization of reading materials for the handicapped was made at a meeting of the Hospital Libraries Section of the International Federation of Library Associations during its 50th conference in Brussels. Work is under way to facillitate international exchange of materials and to study copyright, postal regulations, custom laws, formal bibliographic control, and identification of individuals.

All of these activities, both legislation and library programs, reflect social attitudes about labeling. It is increasingly clear from both research and experience that labeled individuals are too often victimized by stigmas associated with labels. Assigning labels to the handicapped often suggests to those working with them that their behavior should conform to stereotyped expectations. The library community, as an integral element in services for the handicapped person, is becoming sensitive to the fact that all handicapped individuals are people first, and only secondarily people with special library and information needs.

Literature. Expansion of literature on health and rehabilitative library services was significantly represented by the first issue of *Library Trends* to focus on library services in correctional settings and final plans for the first issue on institutional libraries (published in February 1978). Eleanor Phinney's *The Librarian and the Patient; An Introduction to Library Services for Patients in Health Care Institutions* was also published by ALA.

Health and rehabilitative library services stand at the crossroads in an era of new services and service possibilities for library users with special library and information needs. Although much remains to be done, the new legislation represents a bold approach that emphasizes individually designed programs and extensions of civil rights. Librarians may anticipate important effects on the total library community. Obviously, as health and rehabilitative library services practitioners have long realized, close involvement with users with special needs, with the general society, and with peers in the library community is primary.

HARRIS C. McCLASKEY

Health and Rehabilitative Library Services Division

It would be easy to think of 1977 primarily in terms of the time and effort that went into bringing about the ALA Council approval of the merger of the Health and Rehabilitative Library Services Division (HRLSD) with the Association of State Library Agencies (ASLA). HRLSD began the year as one of the financially endangered Divisions whose very existence was threatened, and the future merger of HRLSD and ASLA will mean that the specialized library services that HRLSD champions will continue to be represented in ALA at the Divisional level. In addition, other important events occurred for HRLSD during the year.

Programs. HRLSD sponsored programs at the Annual Conference that attracted librarians from all types of libraries. The program on "The Deaf Community and Libraries: Programs For Interaction," which was cosponsored by HRLSD with the ALA Library Service to the Deaf Committee, attracted a large crowd. The three-hour program offered practical advice on how librarians can fulfill their responsibilities to the deaf and hearing impaired. It is a growing area of service about which much more will be heard in the future. A program on bibliotherapy, which was cosponsored by the HRLSD Bibliotherapy Committee and Bibliotherapy Discussion Group, used a poster format as the basis for discussing existing programs, materials, educational offerings, theoretical considerations, research needs, organizations, and controversial issues in that field.

An Awards Champagne Brunch was cosponsored by HRLSD with its Library Service to the Blind and Physically Handicapped Section. Grace J. Lyons was the recipient of the Exceptional Service Award of the HRLSD, and Adeline Franzel received the Section's Francis Joseph Campbell Citation and Medal. The Section offered a timely program on "Information Concerning the Rights and Opportunities of the Handicapped Citizen." With the emphasis on assisting the handicapped to achieve and maintain independent living, the session dealt with programs and services to foster the handicapped's "Right to Know, Right to Work, and Right to Independent Access to Information."

Publications. Despite its tight financial circumstances, HRLSD did continue to publish its *Newsletter,* although on an irregular basis, so that its membership could be kept informed of the newest developments in specialized library services and of upcoming activities of the Division and its Sections. Although the *HRLSD Journal* was issued only once in 1977, the requests for copies of past issues, especially those on the "Information Needs of Hearing Impaired People" and "Library Services for the Blind and Physically Handicapped," continued throughout the year.

> **HRLSD Officers:**
>
> PRESIDENT:
> **Susan M. Haskin,** Michigan Department of Education
>
> VICE-PRESIDENT/PRESIDENT-ELECT:
> **Phyllis I. Dalton,** Sacramento, California
>
> EXECUTIVE SECRETARY:
> **Sandra M. Cooper**
>
> Membership (August 31, 1977): 1,563
> (545 personal and 1,018 organizational)

Other Activities. HRLSD Sections were involved in many activities during the year. The Library Service to Prisoners Section prepared a progress report for ALA Council on its midwinter 1976 resolution that directed HRLSD "to assist public libraries in extending their services to local jails and detention facilities." The Section is compiling the results of its 50-state survey of library services to local institutions and is planning a program for the 1978 Annual Conference on public library services to local jails and detention centers. The HRLSD/American Correctional Association Joint Institutional Library Committee is reviewing a draft of "Library Standards for Jails and Detention Facilities," and a Section Committee has been formed to develop a manual for librarians on the issues and implications of security in correctional institutions.

The Library Service to the Blind and Physically Handicapped Section continues to find ways of furthering the improvement and extension of those services. A contract was signed with the Library of Congress, Division for the Blind and Physically Handicapped, to write standards for the services administered through the Library's national, multistate, regional, and subregional network. After this contract is fulfilled, it is hoped that standards can be written for services for the blind and physically handicapped by state, public, school, academic, and institutional libraries. A survey conducted by the Ad Hoc Special Committee to Assess the Needs for Vocational Materials found that the handicapped respondents overwhelmingly expressed a need for vocational materials and that the preferred format is cassette tape. The Committee will work to encourage the production of such materials.

During 1977, the HRLSD Board authorized the establishment of a Library Service to the Impaired Elderly Section. Officers and committees were appointed, bylaws were drafted, and a program is planned for the 1978 Annual Conference.

Staff. By year's end a new Executive Secretary, Sandra Cooper, had replaced Mary Power, who resigned in August. Cooper will be working to build a strong new division as HRLSD moves towards the merger with ASLA in January 1979.　　　SUSAN M. HASKIN

IFLA

Two events marked 1977 for the International Federation of Library Associations and Institutions (IFLA): the anniversary meeting of IFLA at Brussels and the implementation of the new statutes adopted at Lausanne in 1976. The "normal" affairs—international cooperative library projects—not only were taken care of as usual, but in many cases developed spectacularly.

Universal Bibliographic Control (UBC). The UBC Office, supported by the Council on Library Resources in Washington D.C., and by a range of national libraries, was involved in the preparations of the UNESCO/IFLA Congress on National Bibliographies, a meeting that might go down in history as having opened new and exciting ways towards the realization of UBC. More than 80 national bibliographies were represented at the meeting, held in Paris in September 1977 following the IFLA World Congress at Brussels. IFLA provided the main working document. Also during the course of the year, editions of the various International Standard Bibliographic Descriptions (ISBDs) were issued by the IFLA Office. The international exchange format, *UNIMARC,* was published in March 1977. More information about the work of the Office can be found in *IFLA Journal* and *International Cataloguing.*

International Lending. The IFLA Office for International Lending has been in existence for nearly three years and has done much towards improvement of international lending. Special attention has been given to the development of the International Loan Request Form, to the removal of barriers to interlending, and to the concept of Universal Availability of Publications (UAP). This logical component of UBC will be IFLA's main new program item in the coming years.

The continuing support of the Canadian International Development Agency enables IFLA to establish realistic regional programs, coordinated by regional bureaus in Mexico City, Kuala Lumpur, and Dakar. In June 1977 representatives of 16 nations gathered at a conference on library legislation and the legal status of librarians in Dakar. A conference on the development of public library services was held in Kuala Lumpur in March 1977.

New Statutes. Assisted by a grant of the Council on Library Resources, IFLA tackled the complicated task of making the new statutes work. In the course of 1977 more than 850 members in more than 100 countries (a 25 per cent increase in 1977) were invited to register for the 27 Sections and to nominate candidates for election in the standing committees of the Sections. The necessary national consultations on these matters led in many cases to the establishment of National IFLA Commissions. IFLA's field of activity was widened by the establishment of a Working Group of Libraries for the Blind, a Conference of National Librarians, and a Round Table for Music Librarians.

All seats on the IFLA Executive Board were open for election at Brussels, and Preben Kirkegaard (Denmark) was reelected as President. Other officers are First Vice-President, H. C. Campbell (Canada); Second Vice- President, G. Pflug (Federal Republic of Germany); and Treasurer, J-P Clavel (Switzerland). Members include L. Gvishiani (U.S.S.R.), E. Granheim (Norway), and E. R. S. Fifoot (U.K.). Fifoot was elected Chairman of the newly established Professional Board, which took over the responsibility for IFLA's professional program. Other members of the Professional Board are D. Hickey (U.S.), V. Popov (Bulgaria), P. J. Van Swigchem (Netherlands), J. S. Soosai (Malaysia), D. A. Clarke (U.K.), H. P. Geh (Federal Republic of Germany), and R. Sievanen-Allen (Finland).

Each member of the Professional Board represents one of the 8 Divisions that in the new structure coordinate the work of the 27 Sections. The Professional Board is engaged in bringing order to the jungle of plans put forward by the very active Sections. It is expected that UNESCO's new Division for the General Information Program will sponsor many IFLA programs. Other funding sources will, however, have to be opened up by the IFLA Executive Board in order to give all Sections the indispensable support they need.

IFLA's 50th Anniversary. In September, Brussels was a beehive of librarians. Nearly 2,000 participants from more than 100 countries took part in the 50th anniversary celebration, September 5–10 in Brussels. The theme of the World Congress was "Libraries for All: One World of Information, Culture and Learning." Distinguished users from various disciplines expressed their views on the importance of libraries. Daniel Boorstin of the Library of Congress; A. Nikolajev, Russian astronaut; C. N. Parkinson, British economist; Joyce Robinson, representing the Third World; A. M. M'Bow, Director-General of UNESCO; President Senghor of Senegal, "Government, Law and Politics"; Robert Triffin, "Business, Commerce and Industry"; and C. P. Snow, "The Book World," were among the many speakers.

During the conference Americans received honors for their dedication to international library cooperation. Royal Belgian Orders were given to Robert Vosper and Rutherford Rogers. The Honorary Fellowship of IFLA went to Vosper, and IFLA Medals to Rutherford Rogers and Fred Cole. Honorary Citations were awarded to Karl Baer, D. W. Bryant, Jack Dalton, and Milton Lord.

MARGREET WIJNSTROOM

Independent Research Libraries

A growing awareness of the problems of independent research libraries, those often neglected stepchildren of the library world, has been noted in recent years. In 1977 this growing awareness resulted in some positive consequences, even though the problems for the most part remain unsolved. There was scattered evidence that a growing number of private individuals were supporting independent libraries. A number of significant grants were made by private foundations, most notably the Andrew W. Mellon Foundation. The federal government, principally through the National Endowment for the Humanities (NEH), which has been a sympathetic supporter for several years, provided some basic support. The support totaled too little, but was possibly not too late. The problems are still surmountable.

Federal Aid. Under Margaret Child's supervision, the Research Division of NEH continued to develop a series of three library programs for which independent libraries are eligible. These are programs for processing collections, for developing new collections, and for focused research in collections. Several independent libraries received grants in the first category for ongoing traditional library activities that had been postponed because of severe financial constraints.

New federal support, however, came chiefly as the result of congressional appropriations in 1977, following the 1976 authorization legislation for the National Endowment for the Arts and NEH. Both announced challenge grant programs in 1977, and many independent research libraries applied under the program at the NEH.

In June NEH announced its initial round of grants totaling $30,000,000 of which some $4,000,000 went to a score of independent libraries (including historical societies). The largest library grant under this program was $850,000; the smallest, $8,000. Eight grants went to members of the Independent Research Libraries Association: American Antiquarian

(Top) Soviet astronaut A. Nikolajev and (above) U.S. Librarian of Congress Daniel Boorstin addressing the opening session of the 50th anniversary IFLA meeting in Brussels.

Independent Research Libraries Association Statistics (Fiscal Year Ending in 1976)

	Material Acquisitions	Binding and Conserv. Cost	Binding and Conserv. Salaries	Total Acquisitions	Physical Maintenance	Maintenance Salaries	Total Other Salaries
American Antiquarian Society	$ 75,809	$ 924	$ 9,900	$ 86,633	$ 36,727	$ 21,000	$ 169,699
American Philosophical Society	$ 95,111	$ 11,293	$ 23,300	$ 129,704	$ 67,883	$ 12,000	$ 115,400
John Crerar Library	$ 257,388	$ 9,979	$ 33,450	$ 300,817	$239,187		$ 812,212
Folger Shakespeare Library	$ 128,633	$ 988	$ 23,471	$ 153,092	$ 66,076	$170,131	$ 678,829
Linda Hall Library	$ 412,844	$ 24,372	$ 24,400	$ 461,616	$ 55,364	$ 51,100	$ 320,835
Historical Society of Pennsylvania	$ 18,110	$ 2,022	$ 8,300	$ 28,432	$ 48,831	$ 28,800	$ 163,228
Henry E. Huntington Library	$ 415,975			$ 415,975	$ 52,687	$ 44,826	$ 421,338
Library Company of Philadelphia	$ 37,262	NA	$ 18,381	$ 55,643	$ 58,745	$ 18,843	$ 109,072
Massachusetts Historical Society	$ 45,000	$ 4,000	$ 6,992	$ 55,992	$ 59,505	$ 19,452	$ 129,929
Pierpont Morgan Library	$ 539,392	$ 9,291	$ 40,200	$ 588,883	$ 50,784	$ 65,300	$ 628,500
Newberry Library	$ 208,775	$ 11,025	$103,565	$ 323,365	$176,040	$ 83,248	$ 591,306
New York Academy of Medicine	$ 194,555	$ 29,959		$ 224,514	$540,383	$120,768	$ 801,770
New-York Historical Society	$ 139,000	$ 8,000		$ 147,000	$241,000	$230,000	$ 370,000
New York Public Library	$2,128,000	$360,000	$140,000	$2,628,000	$348,000	$733,000	$9,359,000
Virginia Historical Society	$ 78,126	$ 4,531		$ 82,657	$ 39,258	$ 64,600	$ 181,449

	Total Fringe Benefits	Benefits % of Salaries	Other Operational Expenditures	Total Library Expenditures	Research and Education Programs	Grand Total Operations
American Antiquarian Society	$ 43,695	21.8%	$ 74,670	$ 432,424	$118,255	$ 550,679
American Philosophical Society	$ 53,297	28.2%	$ 32,153	$ 450,437	$ 21,841	$ 472,278
John Crerar Library	$ 79,811	9.4%	$ 372,597	$ 1,804,624		$ 1,804,624
Folger Shakespeare Library	$ 86,075	9 %	$ 612,662	$ 1,766,865	$174,343	$ 1,941,208
Linda Hall Library	$ 27,363	6.9%	$ 56,844	$ 973,122		$ 973,122
Historical Society of Pennsylvania	$ 31,207	16 %	$ 55,382	$ 355,880		$ 355,880
Henry E. Huntington Library	$ 77,756	16.7%	$ 192,408	$ 1,204,990	$126,309	$ 1,331,229
Library Company of Philadelphia	$ 20,520	18 %		$ 281,823		$ 281,823
Massachusetts Historical Society	$ 47,768	30 %	$ 23,083	$ 335,729		$ 335,729
Pierpont Morgan Library	$ 83,542	14.5%	$ 245,000	$ 1,672,010	$ 5,612	$ 1,677,622
Newberry Library	$ 128,181	16.5%	$ 288,182	$ 1,590,322	$839,032	$ 2,429,354
New York Academy of Medicine	$ 150,718	16.3%	$ 417,448	$ 2,255,601		$ 2,255,601
New-York Historical Society	$ 90,000	15 %	$ 135,000	$ 1,213,000	$ 97,225	$ 1,310,225
New York Public Library	$2,746,000	26.8%	$1,710,000	$17,524,000		$17,524,000
Virginia Historical Society	$ 41,064	16.7%	$ 36,166	$ 445,194	$ 24,271	$ 469,465

	Total Endowment	Gifts and Grants for Endowment	Endowment Income	Operations Income	Gifts for Current Use	Grants for Current Use
American Antiquarian Society	$ 3,666,619	$ 106,107	$ 217,055	$ 76,650	$ 40,940	$ 30,437
American Philosophical Society	$20,549,496		$1,079,007	$ 7,425	$ 8,835	$ 14,592
John Crerar Library	$ 7,975,523		$ 483,815	$ 752,054	$ 235,400	
Folger Shakespeare Library	$22,983,503		$ 983,284*	$ 475,509	$ 116,106	$219,565
Linda Hall Library	$31,905,000		$1,401,350	$ 162,550		
Historical Society of Pennsylvania	$ 3,721,702		$ 244,406	$ 117,825	$ 12,500	
Henry E. Huntington Library	$32,329,183		NA	$ 43,729	$ 22,644	$114,700
Library Company of Philadelphia	$ 4,600,000		$ 254,506	$ 28,255		$ 8,930
Massachusetts Historical Society	$ 9,119,865	$ 139,589	NA		$ 39,399	$ 30,500
Pierpont Morgan Library	$13,400,000	$ 375,000	$ 657,798	$ 48,948	$ 50,680	$ 36,500
Newberry Library	$21,227,913	$ 362,105	$1,122,775	$ 392,415	$ 201,651	$525,465
New York Academy of Medicine	$30,834,917		$1,407,717	$ 500,669		
New-York Historical Society	$13,000,000	$ 27,000	$ 650,000	$ 110,000	$ 149,775	$ 88,725
New York Public Library	$69,950,000	$1,451,000	$3,692,000	$1,280,000	$3,275,000	$701,000
Virginia Historical Society	$ 4,926,000	$ 5,000	$ 302,883	$ 81,266	$ 54,133	$ 91,962

*available for operations

	Total Operating Income	Total Volumes	Total Microform Units	Total Manuscripts	Volumes Added	Professional Staff	Non-Professional Staff
American Antiquarian Society	$ 474,887	613,984		3,500	1,484	11	17
American Philosophical Society	NA	144,034	32,644	5,000,000	899	8	6
John Crerar Library	$ 1,788,856	1,174,390	412,572	NA	19,527	25	59
Folger Shakespeare Library	$ 1,794,464	214,500	1,000	40,000	2,075	41	27
Linda Hall Library	$ 1,563,900	428,786	525,766		16,503	16.25	34
Historical Society of Pennsylvania	$ 374,731	211,000	11,820	14,000,500	1,000	10	12
Henry E. Huntington Library	NA	545,192	NA	5,000,000	11,798	19.6	40.2
Library Company of Philadelphia	$ 291,691	NA	NA	NA	unknown	6	9
Massachusetts Historical Society	$ 69,899	322,428*	52,810	4,950*	1,905	6	12
Pierpont Morgan Library	$ 793,926	68,759	2,400	unknown	1,211	31	22
Newberry Library	$ 2,242,306	1,295,753	214,603	unknown	13,547	47	70
New York Academy of Medicine	$ 2,325,834	613,710	512	2,227	6,540	20	34
New-York Historical Society	$ 997,725	606,500*	47,500	1,510,000	400	6	18
New York Public Library	$14,613,000	4,672,995	1,262,246	10,804,211	99,359	168.5	253.5
Virginia Historical Society	$ 535,234	263,000	2,250	4,081,000	1,500	9	18

*titles *running feet

Note: In the case of the New York Ac. of Med., the Am. Phil. Soc., and the Huntington, both income and costs include other than library activities.

Society ($285,000); Folger ($750,000); Huntington ($850,000); Library Company of Philadelphia ($15,000); Pierpont Morgan ($235,000); New-York Historical Society ($60,000); New York Public Library ($425,000); and Newberry Library ($797,000). In the second round of grants made in late summer, the John Crerar Library was awarded $123,000.

NEH challenge grants, which require a three-for-one match over a period of three years, may be used for any library purpose, except that the federal dollars themselves cannot be used for endowment or for new construction. This latitude constitutes a significant departure from the tradition of program grants, allowing institutions to address their fundamental problems rather than requiring them to dilute their resources in new activities. At the Folger, for example, the challenge encouraged the mounting of a major campaign for $9,700,000.

NEH Grant Questions. It remains to be seen, of course, how symbolic or how real this promising program will prove to be. First, the required three-for-one match, all from new sources of support or in excess of normal support, puts a great deal of pressure on the private sector to come up with new money in a stagnant economy. Second, libraries that had regularly been raising substantial sums every year will be hard pressed to increase that support beyond their usual pool of supporters and well-wishers. Third, it can be argued, without denying the importance of the program, that much larger grants, in some cases at least, could have provided permanent solutions to deep-rooted problems. Finally, the degree of success the institutions experience in meeting the challenges will certainly be decisive in shaping congressional support for an extension of the program beyond the present authorization and appropriation. Should that important result occur, the challenge grant program can provide major help to independent research libraries struggling to overcome historical conditions over which they have had no control.

Symbolic of these conditions in society at large were the rumors, not ill founded, of renewed tax problems perhaps more hazardous than the 1969 tax legislation under which some independents are still taxed on endowment earnings and which annually threatens the loss of their status as "not a private foundation." The current threat, which at the end of 1977 seemed merely postponed rather than eliminated, applies to changes in capital gains taxes that could reduce the deductibility of gifts (in kind or in appreciated securities) to the initial cost, plus 50 per cent of the appreciation. The direct and immediate consequences of this proposed change could be enormous, and the indirect and long-range consequences (because of the impact on giving to foundations) are equally great. The New York Times reported in December that the portents are ominous. It is ironic that at the very time that Congress is encouraging institutions to seek additional support through the NEH challenge grant program, the administration is rumored to be considering a serious reduction in that support.

Other potential federal support for independent research libraries was linked to the abortion issue in 1977, because HEW funding was held up awaiting a resolution of that question. At the end of 1977 the House and Senate had compromised, and the conference appropriation of $5,000,000 for Title II-C of the Higher Education Act, buried in the vast appropriation for HEW, was passed. As interpreted by the guidelines, the legislation seems to favor university libraries but the intent (as suggested by the language of the bill) is to include, or at least not to exclude, major independent research libraries.

Public Sector Support. Because independent research libraries have been denied basic federal support in the past, the new more favorable situation deserves extended coverage. But it is chiefly private voluntary resources, not tax money or tuitions or fees, on which these libraries continue to depend. Even in the case of federal support, especially the new challenge grants, private support continues to be fundamental. But the federal government can do much to create a favorable or unfavorable climate for private investment in independent research libraries in the future.

Emphasis on dollars and on the federal government should not obscure the fact that independent research libraries continued in 1977 to do what all good libraries do. They bought books, processed them, conserved them, and made them available to readers. The selected statistics for a group of them, members of the Independent Research Libraries Association, tabulated for the fiscal year ending in 1976, testify to research libraries' activities. It is instructive and worthwhile to compare these statistics with the figures previously reported for 1975 and 1974.

LAWRENCE W. TOWNER

Information and Referral Centers

In 1977–78 the information and referral (I and R) movement in the United States began to crystalize. The existence of the professional information and referral specialist is now generally recognized. Advertisements now appear in professional literature for I and R specialists to work in public libraries and social service I and R centers. At least one university has a graduate program to train

Indexing and Abstracting Services: see Abstracting and Indexing Services

Information and Referral Centers

Right, a full time librarian is at each of Houston's 26 branch libraries staffing a neighborhood information Center. (Right) The LIBS 100 Title query produced by CLSI displays the bibliographic holdings and location of each copy of the title available in the library.

such professionals. The Community Information Specialist Program at the University of Toledo awards the Master's Degree in Library and Information Services. Personnel working in I and R centers have an active, growing, and influential professional organization, the Alliance of Information and Referral Services (AIRS). In 1977 its membership exceeded 800. It publishes the *AIRS National Standards for Information and Referral*. A revised edition of these standards is to be published in 1978 to take into account a growing concern with definitions, confidentiality of records, advocacy, and accountability.

Need for Standards. The issue of standards as guides to quality service and as models for new centers is a current concern. The United Way of America also publishes national standards for I and R. Other major national organizations concerned with I and R such as the Easter Seal Society and the National Organization of Crisis Centers and Hotlines have expressed a need for clear standards. ALA is beginning to give formal recognition to the existence of I and R as a public library function. At the 1977 Annual Conference the first workshop on I and R sponsored by ALA was held at the Detroit Public Library. The one-day workshop was jointly sponsored by the Public Library Association, the ALA Office for Library Service to the Disadvantaged, and the Alliance of Information and Referral Services.

Numbers. There is no tally of how many I and R centers exist in the United States. In general, what is considered to be an I and R center is any organization or unit that performs I and R and has at least one full-time professional devoted to that activity. Thomas Childers of the School of Library Science at Drexel Institute of Technology, under a grant from the Library Research Division of the U.S. Office of Education, is currently conducting a survey to determine how many libraries have I and R centers. United Way of America completed a survey in 1977 of agencies it funds that are engaged in I and R as a major activity. More than 3,000 such agencies were identified. A very informal estimate of the number of social service agencies with I and R centers was made by Corazone Doyle, the Executive Director of AIRS, at the AIRS national conference in 1977. She estimated that there were between 8,000 and 10,000 such agencies in the United States.

It seems clear that I and R centers are numerous, that public libraries are increasing their services in the area, and that changes in both library and social work education will be made to meet the need for trained I and R specialists.

Funding. I and R centers today are funded from a variety of sources. Those specializing in areas such as services to the handicapped, the elderly, welfare recipients, and the mentally ill are likely to be funded by appropriate public or private sources, e.g., an office on aging, the Easter Seal Society, or a state department of public welfare. Generalized I and R's serving the entire population of a community are likely to be funded by Community Chest or United Way, tax revenues from the city or area, community development money, or federal money under Title XX of the Social Security Act of 1965.

The funding picture is very unclear, and there is undoubtedly duplication of effort among I and R's in a given community as well as competition for existing funds. The Government Accounting Office GAO has become concerned about possible duplication of effort among federally funded I and R's. In 1976–77 GAO undertook a survey of the federal agencies funding I and R's and the effectiveness with which that money was being spent. The report was expected to be released in 1978. Before the study was completed, however, the Interagency Committee on Information and Referral was formed among the major federal funding agencies. One of the major purposes of the Committee is to begin sharing information among the agencies concerning their activities in the I and R field. The Chairperson of the Committee is Eva Nash, Director of the National Clearinghouse on Information for the Aged of HEW's Office of Aging.

There appears to be a growing belief among public libraries with I and R centers that coordination or liaison with a community can best be performed by libraries. A five-day institute on cooperation among I and R centers was held at the University of Toledo in January 1978 under the sponsorship of the Library Education and Training Division of the U.S. Office of Education. Teams of I and R specialists from cities in 13 states met to form action plans for future cooperation.

MILES MARTIN

Information Industry

The information industry has achieved special prominence in today's "information age." It is a many-faceted, flexible, trend-setting area of human activity and is spearheaded by individuals whose skills, insights, and seemingly inexhaustible energy are aimed at mastering, controlling, and communicating the exponential growth in primary data, reports, and literature. Without the complex system of indexes, data bases, microforms, directories, on-line and on-demand services, information systems and concepts, and other information tools produced by this industry, our society—dependent on a managed information explosion—would be paralyzed and unable to locate the goods and services it needs. The information society is actually a society dependent on the information industry.

During 1977 several major developments were manifesting themselves within the information industry:

1. The information industry—manufacturers, distributors, and retailers—is taking on the economic structure of industries concerned with other goods and products.

2. Similarly, the emergence of the information manager responsible for the quality and flow of information through organizations provides a framework of relationships for information-related functions.

3. Vigorous growth throughout the industry is being stimulated by the emergence of on-line information services, including the initial signs of full-text retrieval services.

4. The copyright laws continue to be the primary set of rules governing relationships in the information marketplace.

5. Relationships between government and industry have been recognized as a crucial unresolved question of the information age.

These issues are being addressed by programs and activities of the Information Industry Association (IIA), which represents and serves the industry as a whole. IIA's existence has focused public attention on the contributions made by the information industry. Its membership directory, *Information Sources*, features detailed descriptions of IIA's 120 corporate members, a names and numbers section, and an index to the industry's products and services. Because IIA members form the vanguard of the rapidly changing industry, IIA itself is in the forefront of activity in these areas.

Economic Structure. The preponderance of information activities in the United States is shifting from government and government-subsidized services provided free of charge in support of specific social policies to the treatment of information as an economic entity or good to be supplied by the private sector. In an expanding universe of activity, this means increased economic activity in information, not diminished social services.

It is now commonly accepted that the industry is composed of firms that are active in one or all of the traditional economic functions—manufacturing, distribution, and retailing. This is particularly evident in the context of current on-line information developments.

Data base producers such as Congressional Information Service, Data Courier, the Information Bank, Economic Information Systems, and Environment Information Center perform the manufacturing function. They assemble, sort, organize, process, and produce information on magnetic tapes or other machine-readable media.

Information retrieval services such as Lockheed Information Systems, SDC Search Service, Interactive Data Corporation, and Control Data Technotec specialize in the distribution function. Acquiring data bases from manufacturers and making the contents available for on-line searching, these firms seek out users, install terminals, and assist in training people in the use of data bases via their on-line distribution systems.

The retail function is performed on a fee basis by full-service on-demand information companies such as FIND/SVP, Roberts Information Services, Warner-Eddison Associates, Information Unlimited, and Information for Business. In the library field this function is performed by "intermediaries" trained to perform computerized on-line searching for users. In many libraries this on-line service is beginning to carry special fees suggestive of the retail functions of the full-service information companies.

This market structure analysis applies equally to books, journals, and other information media. It also includes companies that perform more than one of the market functions.

The Information Manager. 1977 marked the emergence of the information manager as a new type of executive. Information, like finance, personnel, space, and materials, is a resource with costs and benefits. In every organization a variety of professionals are engaged in various information-related functions—librarianship, data processing, records management, word processing, research and development, information science, marketing, and promotion. Top management uses the results of these activities and has begun to recognize the need to apply sound management practices to what is clearly a significant part of the organization's efforts that involves considerable investments.

Reflecting this trend, the National Information Conference and Exposition (NICE), sponsored by IIA and chaired by James Kollegger, President of the Environment Information

Information Science: see Automation; Data Bases, Computer-Readable; Serials, Networks; Bibliographic Processing Centers; Circulation Systems. See also American Society for Information Science and National Commission on Libraries and Information Science.

Information Industry

Center in New York, was held in Washington, D.C., in April 1977. Its theme was "The Emerging Information Manager: Bridging the Gap between Information Resources and Needs." The Conference was attended by more than 1,000 professionals, featured 45 exhibitors, and generated wide interest in this new management discipline. As a result, a trade magazine and a professional journal for information managers were to be launched in 1978 by commercial publishers. Joseph Fitzsimmons, President of University Microfilms International and Chairman of NICE '78, announced that the 1978 conference would be held April 16-19 at the Sheraton Park Hotel in Washington, D.C. Its theme was to be "Attaining Organizational Goals: The Role of the Information Manager."

IIA has also created a Program for Information Managers (PRIM), an individual membership program to provide a continuing forum for this new managerial group. PRIM will offer publications, seminars, the annual NICE meeting, and other benefits to its members.

Industry Growth. Mirroring the national growth rate of the industry, IIA experienced a 20 percent net growth in its membership and a 65 percent growth in activity as measured by its annual budget in 1977. The thrust of this growth is strongly toward on-line services. IIA's 1977 Product of the Year Award went to such an information service, Control Data's Technotec, a computerized technology transfer system. Two of the Association's new members are engaged in full-text on-line access. Mead Data Central offers on-line access to full-text court decisions, and Dow Jones News Retrieval provides on-line retrieval of full-text news stories. With continuing reduction in on-line storage costs, some IIA members as a matter of company policy publish only material that is computer-composed so as to yield a machine-readable, as well as an ink-print, product.

This trend was reinforced by the creation of a trade association in Great Britain, called the Association of Data Base Producers, for creators of machine-readable data bases. At a December "on-line" conference in London, this new organization and IIA adopted a resolution creating a joint committee to study international federation. The marketing of U.S. data bases in Europe has encountered some nontariff barriers from countries seeking to give their own national capabilities time to catch up with the U.S. information industry.

The significance of the full-text trend for journal publishers and libraries is also profound. Today journal subscribers use the journal as a device for "keeping up" with developments in their profession. By contrast, on-line bibliographic data bases can be used to identify relevant articles for users who want to "catch up" with happenings in a specific subject area. The economics of journal publishing are based on the core group of users subscribing to the journal. When journals are published as Dow Jones publishes the *Wall Street Journal,* however, the articles are available for on-line searching before they are available for printing in journal format. Libraries, too, will be affected, since extensive full-text repositories will be readily available on-line to the user at his place of work.

Copyright. With the advent of the new copyright law, information professionals have had to familiarize themselves with its details. IIA and the American Association of Publishers (AAP) jointly published *The Essential Elements of a Copyright Clearinghouse,* the proceedings of a 1976 conference that outlined the premise of the Copyright Clearance Center (CCC). In addition, IIA worked diligently with the AAP committee that in September 1977 established the new nonprofit CCC. The Center was created to provide a process by which users of photocopies could (1) sort out what is "fair use" from what is "systematic" and requires permission; (2) determine whether a copy could be made upon payment of a copying charge; and (3) know how and to whom to report and pay for such copying. Until the establishment of CCC, no mechanism existed by which a publisher could expect to derive any economic return from copies made for "catch-up" purposes. Journal publishers now have the opportunity to develop experience in pricing photocopies via CCC so as to deal with future subscribers who use full-text on-line services for keeping up with new developments but who subscribe to the journal for other purposes.

Another significant effect of CCC is to formalize the structural relationship between the information retail function and the suppliers and distributors. It provides a new "after-market" for published literature. A common function of retailers is to search on-line data bases and, using CCC, provide photocopies of articles cited in the bibliographies produced by the on-line searches. Major new entrants in the retail section of the business are expected soon since data base searching, document fulfillment, custom research, and user training in "information literacy" skills are a growing part of the information industry.

As 1978 began CCC was organized, and approximately 1,000 journals were included in its coverage. The publishing, information, and user communities had contributed some $150,000 in start-up capital to support the Center's services through the end of the year.

In order to explore the copyright question further, the National Commission on New Technological Uses of Copyrighted Works (CONTU) sought comments on its committee reports on software and on data bases. IIA supported CONTU's recommendations outlining copyright protection for both but made two additional suggestions. The first was that microform compositions be specifically recognized as copyrightable subject matter. IIA also urged the creation of a copyright for data base creators beyond the traditional rights of copyright owners in ink-print products. The proposal concerned the right "to search a data base." In the absence of such a right no copyright would be involved in those cases in which an inventor searches a patent data base and finds no existing patent covering his invention. No copies would be made, but the full and intended value of the data base would have been obtained. Such searches may be provided for by contract, but a copyright system should produce national uniformity and not require the drafting of supplementary contracts for each producer and user.

During 1977, IIA registered strong opposition to the proposal of the National Technical Information Service to operate a document fulfillment service on privately published materials. At least two firms, the Institute for Scientific Information in Philadelphia and University Microfilms International in Ann Arbor, already provide licensed photocopying services. In addition, with the creation of the CCC numerous other commercial sources will become available. IIA argued that the government should not engage in information services except in the absence of competitive or adequate services in the private sector.

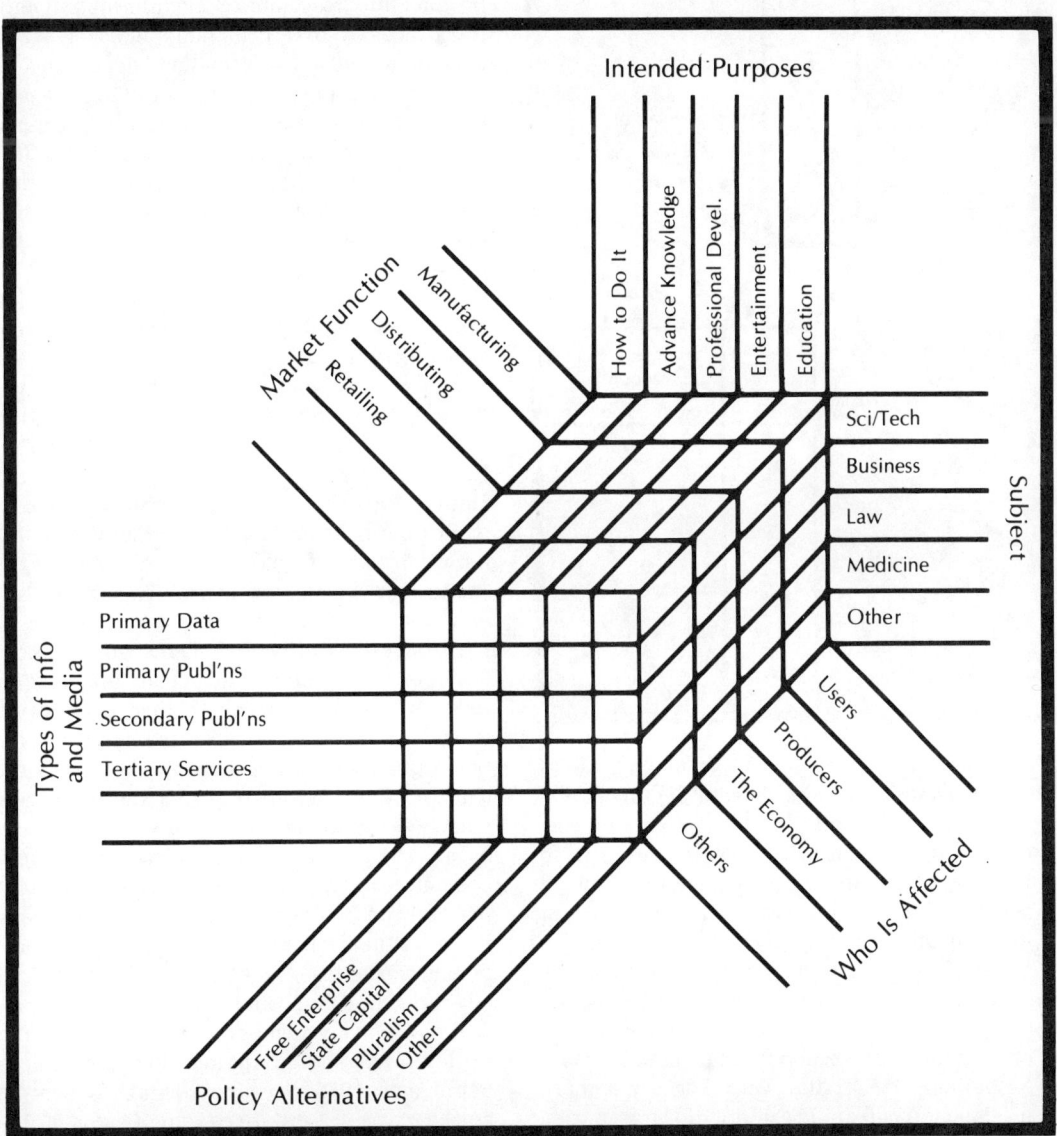

Each subset or single cube raises distinctive policy issues. To discuss information policy issues it is necessary first to agree which subset of the large cube is under consideration. For example, the policy best suited to encourage the manufacture of primary publications advancing the knowledge of business among users may very well be different from that which would promote the retailing of primary data detailing "how to do it" in the area of science and technology and affecting the economy.

Information Industry

[Diagram labels: Manufacturing, Advance Knowledge, Primary Publications, Business, Users, Policy???, Retail, How to Do It, Sci/Tech, Economy, Primary Data, Policy???]

The White Paper does not offer easy answers. One of its conclusions is that, in the information age it is necessary to re-examine the "industrial age" rules and laws to determine their current applicability in view of the greatly enhanced pluralistic information capabilities of the country. It is hoped that the White Paper will help stimulate an eventual resolution of the remaining questions regarding the relationships of government and private industry in the business of information.

As 1978 dawned the information industry was both stimulated by the great opportunities for service and somewhat awed by the responsibilities to the public interest inherent in the information business. But the developments demonstrate clearly that the industry's impact on society at large will continue to expand as the value of information in all its complexity is increaasingly recognized throughout the world.

Government and the Private Sector. A major report, *National Information Policy*, became available early in 1977. It presaged an important trend in government—a pronounced concern for policies governing the roles of government and the private sector in the business of information. At the same time, the National Science Foundation (NSF) created the Science Information Activities Task Force to analyze the NSF responsibilities in science information. One of the Task Force members was Loene Trubkin, President of Data Courier and Director of IIA.

IIA Board Chairman Herbert R. Brinberg, Vice President of the Information Technology Group of American Can Company, announced an IIA effort to draft a white paper on the subject. IIA also planned to hold a national conference in May 1978 to allow diverse sectors of the information community to critique and comment on the draft paper.

Preparation of this white paper has stimulated detailed thinking within the industry on the unique and complex characteristics of information, the relationship of America's economic system to it, and the meaning of such constitutional provisions as freedom of the press. The IIA white paper offers a conceptual framework involving two principles.

First, information is defined as "the collection, storage, processing, dissemination, and use of data, reports, and literature." Second, information is distinguished from intellectual work product. For example, the work of a design engineer results in the creation of a design blueprint. This is the engineer's work product and does not become information until it is processed to be communicated. If it is then communicated as information, depending on its applicability to the work of others, it may enter commercial information channels. Similarly, the work of the Bureau of the Census is the intellectual work product of that agency. It becomes information after it has been put in a format and protected for privacy.

The difficulty of determining an information policy is illustrated by the following Information Policy Cube.

Association Notes. In 1977 the IIA Board of Directors elected Robert F. Asleson, R.R. Bowker Company, Vice-Chairman; Robert H. Riley, Chase Manhattan Bank, Treasurer; and Haines B. Gaffner, LINK, Secretary. Herbert R. Brinberg, American Can Company, remains as Chairman of the Board; and Jerome D. Luntz, Newsweek, Inc., former Vice-Chairman, continues as a Board member.

As part of its effort to acknowledge the contributions of individuals in the information field, IIA in 1977 enrolled Eugene Garfield, President and Founder of the Institute for Scientific Information, into its Hall of Fame. Garfield has long been one of the industry's most creative and active leaders.

In 1977 IIA established two new committees—the Financial Planning Committee and the National Information Policy Task Force. Other IIA committees deal with proprietary rights, government relations, and education and marketing.

A new weekly member services bulletin, the *Friday Memo*, was inaugurated by IIA in September 1976. This publication is sent to corporate representatives and IIA committee members free of charge and provides a quick update on developments within the industry. *Information Times,* IIA's other serial, appears bimonthly, with two issues per year in tabloid form.

David Carvey, formerly Vice-President of Disclosure, Inc., and an attorney, joined the IIA staff as Special Counsel for National Information Policy. He has been and continues to serve as editor of the tabloid issues of *Information Action*. The additional IIA staff comprises Paul G. Zurkowski, President; Helena M. Strauch, Communications Director; Faye W. Henderson, Bookkeeper; Margaret S. Jennings, PRIM Coordinator; and James Sattler, Secretary. — PAUL G. ZURKOWSKI

Information Science and Automation Division

The year 1977 was one of radical change within the Information Science and Automation Division (ISAD), change that will reorganize the Division into a structure that will better meet the members' needs. Because of the rapid expansion of ISAD into areas of library technology other than the use of computers in libraries, the Division changed its name to the Library and Information Technology Association (LITA) and broadened its function statement. The changes in the statement were the inclusion of "systems analysis and design" and "communications technology" as the broadened areas of interest of the Division. These changes were approved by the ISAD membership through a special mail ballot at the end of 1977 and were to become effective after certification by the ISAD Board during its meetings at the ALA 1978 Midwinter Meeting.

New Section. In order to conform with the structure of the other divisions within ALA, the Information Science and Automation Section was formed. The Section will carry out the activities and programs that were the interest of the entire Division in the past. It became operational near the end of 1977 with the appointment of Kenneth Bierman as Interim Chairperson.

New Editor and Award. A change also took place in the editorship of the Division's journal, the *Journal of Library Automation* (JOLA). Susan Martin, the editor since the June 1972 issue, resigned in order to work on a doctorate. The ISAD Board of Directors appointed William Mathews of the National Commission on Libraries and Information Science (NCLIS) as editor beginning with the publication of the first issue of 1978.

During the year, Walter A. Winshall of C.L. Systems, Inc. (CLSI), of Newtonville, Massachusetts, approached the ISAD Board with a proposal to establish an annual award for the outstanding contribution to library technology. The award would be in cash to an individual or individuals and would be known as the CLSI/LITA Award for Achievement in Information Technology. The first presentation was planned for the 1978 ALA Annual Conference.

Other Activities. Several times during the course of the year, members of ISAD gave testimony before congressional committees and federal regulatory agencies on legislation and regulations concerning certain technical areas of interest to the Division. Brigitte Kenney of Drexel University and Larry Molumby of the District of Columbia Public Library testified at various times. Congress in 1977 began consideration of the revision of the Communications Act of 1934, and eight ISAD members and ALA staff members responded to ISAD's need for testimony. They provided a jointly written document delineating the needs of the nation's libraries now and in the future in the various facets of telecommunications being considered by Congress.

The ISAD Board established a Legislation and Regulation Committee in the Division during the course of the Annual Conference meetings. During the same Board meetings, discussion was held on the matter of establishing a full-time liaison position in the ALA Washington Office. The position would carry out the same functions as the newly established Legislation and Regulation Committee except that an individual devoting full-time to these functions could provide far better liaison and could work much closer with legislators and regulatory agencies. While this idea seemed not likely to come to fruition because of the high cost, it illustrates the importance of such liaison to the library profession. The Video and Cable Communications Section (VCCS) of ISAD has had a committee active in this area for about a year.

ISAD Officers

PRESIDENT (July 1977–July 1978):
Maurice J. Freedman, Columbia University

VICE-PRESIDENT/PRESIDENT-ELECT:
Susan K. Martin, University of California

PAST PRESIDENT:
Joseph A. Rosenthal, University of California

EXECUTIVE SECRETARY:
Donald P. Hammer

Membership (August 31, 1977): 3,456 (1,800 personal and 1,656 organizational)

As in every year, ISAD was very active in 1977 in the sponsorship of institutes in various parts of the country. They were sponsored through the Program Planning Committee, chaired by S. Michael Malinconico and, during the latter part of the year, Bonnie Juergens. The Division sponsored six institutes in 1977:

February 24-25, Chicago, "The National Bibliographic Network: Networks III"; April 22-23, New York City, "The Catalog in the Age of Technological Change"; April 25, Albany, "Conference on Education for Information Science"; May 19-20, Los Angeles, "The Catalog in the Age of Technological Change"; June 16-17, Detroit, "Media Futures—Impact and Utilization of Newer Media Technology"; December 1-2, Dallas, "Automated Circulation Systems."

Among the many activities carried out by the Division aimed at increasing membership in ISAD, the Board of Directors approved the suggestion of crediting the $15 differential institute registration fee for non-ISAD ALA members toward a one-year ISAD membership. This was to be implemented at the first institute in 1978.

The Technical Standards for Library Automation (TESLA) Committee produced two proposed standards which were forwarded to the appropriate American National Standards Institute committees. One was on sound-emission labels for equipment used in libraries, and the other was on a system for library location symbols for use in union catalogs and computer systems.

ISAD cooperated with the Resources and Technical Services Division, the Anglo-American Cataloging Rules (AACR) Revision Committee, and the Joint Steering Committee for Revision of AACR in reviewing the revised rules and forwarding its suggestions and comments. The ISAD representative to the Revision Committee was Barbara Gates.

The ISAD Board retained Oryx Press to publish the proceedings of the three ISAD institutes concerning the future of the catalog. The proceedings of the 1975 New York City institute on "The Catalog" will be combined with the papers given at the 1977 New York City and Los Angeles institutes and published in one volume. It was expected that the volume would be published in 1978.

Both the VCCS and Audio-Visual (AV) sections were active during the year. The AV Section sponsored the preconference out of which grew plans to hold an institute in October or November 1978 in Washington, D.C., on information storage media. The AV Section also held hearings during the 1977 ALA Midwinter Meeting on Project Mediabase. Sponsored by NCLIS and the Association for Educational Communications and Technology, the Project is developing a set of functional specifications for a national data base for nonprint media.

DONALD P. HAMMER

Insurance for Libraries

The Insurance for Libraries Committee of the Library Organization and Management Section of ALA's Library Administration Division has been concerned with the insurance needs of libraries for many years. In a 1968 article that appeared in the *ALA Bulletin*, a Committee report stated:

> Libraries of the United States, which represent a multibillion dollar investment, are so little insured that widespread public knowledge of this inadequacy would result in a nationwide scandal. Librarians and library administrators are so shockingly ignorant of the insurance needs of their institutions, and so derelict in educating themselves in this area, that it is hard not to think of them as verging on incompetency. If only three of over one hundred major libraries which could be named, had a serious fire in 1968, the uninsured loss would exceed fifty million dollars: what is worse is that proper solutions have been available for sometime.[1]

Apparently, this "nationwide scandal" is continuing in the 1970's. Several journal articles indicate that misconceptions about fire hazards in libraries are still prevalent and that fire prevention equipment continues to be a low priority.[2,3] Library managers appear to lack the necessary knowledge to obtain proper insurance and loss prevention coverage. Basically, it may be an attitude that, because disasters do not happen often in libraries, there is no reason to be overly concerned about them. Unfortunately, the literature belies this misconception. Library managers should know about several useful manuals and pamphlets. As an integral part of managing the business operations, managers should become more knowledgeable about current insurance practices and loss prevention systems.

Nationwide Insurance Manual. A well-written manual—*Insurance Manual for Libraries* by Gerald E. Myers—is an excellent and useful book to make library managers and library boards more aware of an insurance program and of the responsibilities essential in establishing a program. This revised manual was originally prepared in 1972 for the member libraries of the Illinois Library Systems (Bur Oak, Du Page, Northern Illinois, North Suburban, Starved Rock, and Suburban Library Systems). The manual is composed of nine chapters. Chapters three through nine analyze insurance coverage and programs. They cover (1) analysis of risks, (2) appraisals and valuation of property, (3) insurance coverages, policies, and policy forms, (4) new construction, (5) insurance rates and premiums, (6) loss prevention and safety, and (7) losses and claims. These chapters can be an aid to both the library board and the library manager as an indication of the types of insurance programs available to libraries.

Chapter one (a philosophy of insurance for libraries); chapter two (procedures for handling the insurance program); the appendixes (a sample risk management statement, an example of a valuation study, an analysis of insurable values, a special library policy, a typical analysis of *Bowker Annual Prices*, and a checklist for library insurance); and a glossary of terms complete this manual, probably one of the best published within the past 15 years. It has all of the essential components for the development of a sound insurance program.

Two Pamphlets. The National Fire Protection Association has published two pamphlets that would benefit library boards and library managers. *Recommended Practice for the Protection of Library Collections from Fire*[4] states its purpose in chapter one:

> ...to give guidance in fire safety, fire protection, and fire loss contingency planning to library trustees, chief librarians and other staff officers who are responsible for the fire safety of the library's collections and for the life safety of those persons who visit libraries or work in them. It emphasizes the responsibility at every library to analyze the fire hazards and vulnerabilities embodied in its building(s) and operations.

Other chapters discuss such subjects as library fire experience based on past fires, construction, building equipment and facilities, fire protection equipment, improving protection in existing buildings, alterations and renovations, special facilities, operation and maintenance, and organization and training.

Fire Safety Self-Inspection Form for Libraries[5] is specifically designed for staff use. It is an excellent evaluative form that can be easily implemented in any library. It will serve as an indication as to whether the library is prepared for a possible disaster and will show if corrective measures are necessary to prevent losses. With this form and periodic inspections by fire inspection personnel and other agencies, library managers can initiate a fairly complete safety and fire prevention program.

Protection by insurance coverage and loss prevention programs is a safeguard against any possible loss from the ever-present destructive nature of fires. Until library managers are more cognizant of the various safeguards for protecting library buildings, and more importantly their centers, the perpetuation of possible financial and academic losses to society will continue.

DONALD L. UNGARELLI

REFERENCES

1. American Library Association, Insurance for Libraries Committee, "Making of a National Scandal: A Report," *ALA Bulletin* (April 1968).
2. Bruce K. Harvey, "Fire Hazards in Libraries," *Library Security Newsletter* (January 1975).
3. Burns Security Institute, *National Survey on Library Security* (New York: Burns Security Institute, 1973).
4. National Fire Protection Association, *Recommended Practice for the Protection of Library Collections from Fire*, NFPA No. 910-1975 (Boston: National Fire Protection Association, 1975).
5. National Fire Protection Association, *Fire Safety Self-Inspection Forms for Libraries* (Boston: National Fire Protection Association, 1976).

Heavy smoke damage at the Central Dallas Public Library resulted from a 1977 fire. The National Fire Protection Association published two pamphlets in 1977 relating to library collection and staff protection.

Intellectual Freedom

YEAR OF CHANGE

"The times they are a-changing"—but not in the direction foreseen by Bob Dylan almost 15 years ago. In 1977, the environment in which the library profession practiced intellectual freedom underwent a noticeable and somewhat abrupt shift to the right. In addition, the issues that faced the profession were also changing. When shifting issues meet a shifting environment, the result can be explosive, and indeed 1977 was such a year for intellectual freedom.

It started rather quietly, but with a few hints of what was to come. There did seem to be a growing number of concerned citizens groups closely examining school curricular materials and additions to library collections, more fund-raising requests from a greater variety of conservative causes, and a more strident conservative press. In the bitterly cold months of January and February the pattern seemed to fit the ascending conservative curve of the past few years. It was not until the spring thaw that the impact was fully felt. The awakening jolt was a concerted nationwide attack on the film version of Shirley Jackson's short story "The Lottery." Within a few weeks, the controversy was raging in at least a dozen localities, from Vermont to Florida, from Detroit to Omaha.

The remainder of the year made it clear that the country is in the midst of a sharp turn to the right. A "born again" right wing learned from the movement of the 1960's the techniques and the values of organizing the grass roots. The result has been a ground swell of concerned people who look with dismay and bewilderment at the United States of the late 1970's. With a lack of understanding comes fear, a fear of anything that is new and different, be it life-style or books that discuss new life-styles. Simultaneously, there appeared a

Intellectual Freedom

belief that "if we go back to the principles that made America great," not only would understanding result but also the problems causing confusion would either disappear or be resolved.

Knights in shining armor appeared in 1977 in myriad forms. Among such knights were the "textbook watchers," whose bywords were "back to basics." For many of these people, back to basics means more than renewed emphasis on fundamental learning skills. The slogan means the elimination of learning materials, both in classrooms and in libraries, that challenge their basic values. It often seems to the textbook watchers that educational programs question values or discuss problems that are better dealt with by the family in the home.

Anita Bryant's antigay campaign in Dade County, Florida, constituted the most stunning example of a grass-roots response to a violation of deeply held traditional principles and values. Bryant's campaign complemented the "Stop ERA" campaign of Phyllis Schlafly. The attempt to slow down the ratification process, and eventually defeat, the Equal Rights Amendment was surprisingly, almost unbelievably, successful. Some women were convinced that, if passed, the new amendment to the U.S. Constitution would foist coed toilets, battlefield breast feeding, and compulsory female ditchdigging on helpless American womanhood.

These campaigns and many others were fought by well-meaning average American citizens in order to protect the family. The old formulas for marriage, religion, and sexual roles were long ago compromised in content. But believable alternatives to the old family forms and social values had not been devised. Conservative forces convinced a large percentage of Americans that they could accomplish a return to the past. The result was, if not a new religion, at least a new religious fervor that by the end of 1977 had spread throughout the United States. Campaigns conducted under the banner of "protection of the family" included support for the death penalty, laetrile, nuclear power, local police, the Panama Canal, saccharin, the FBI, the CIA, the defense budget, public prayer, and real estate growth, in addition to the movements against equal rights for women and homosexuals. While there were exceptions to this general rule, most people who believed in these things more likely than not fought negative campaigns against busing, welfare, public employee unions, affirmative action, amnesty, marijuana, communes, gun control, pornography, the 55-mile-per-hour speed limit, day-care centers, religious ecumenism, sex education, car pools, and the Environmental Protection Agency.[1]

EFFECT ON PROFESSION

The library profession found itself in the middle of this swing to the right. According to the Library Bill of Rights, the responsibility of librarians is to provide information and materials not on "both" sides but on all gradations between the extremes concerning each issue of import. Still unanswered at year's end was the questions of how well the libraries of the nation provided information covering the spectrum of thought on each major public question. What information was provided by the libraries in Dade County, Florida, on the issue of gay rights and how accessible to the general public was that information?

The Speaker. The principles of the Library Bill of Rights and librarians' adherence to them were tested many times during 1977. By far, the most heated controversy centered around *The Speaker . . . A Film About Freedom.* Sponsored by the Intellectual Freedom Committee (IFC) and aimed at the average American adult, the film was developed as an educational tool to engender debate and discussion on First Amendment rights. By graphically portraying the ever-present potential for bit-by-bit erosion of these basic rights, the IFC hoped to rekindle in the American public an awareness about and devotion to the most basic freedom.

The Speaker features Mildred Dunnock in the role of Victoria Dunn, a high school history teacher for 30 years, in her final year before retirement. Dunn also serves as adviser to the student-run Special Events Committee, which brings provocative speakers to campus for voluntary discussions and lectures on issues and points of view not covered in the curriculum. For the final assembly of the year, the Special Events Committee chooses to invite James Boyd, a university scientist who advocates a theory of genetic inferiority. With the issuance of the invitation to Boyd, the polarization of the community begins, a process that ultimately leads to a deep rift and a cancellation of the speaker by people in positions of authority.

The Debate. The controversy over the film within ALA began at a screening for the Executive Board during its spring meeting. Because some members raised doubts about the appropriateness of the topic and the manner in which the content was portrayed, the Executive Board suggested postponement of the film's release until it had been viewed by the Intellectual Freedom Committee, the sponsoring body, and by the full ALA membership at the 1977 Annual Conference in Detroit. Subsequently, the suggestion that the film's release be postponed was rejected as a possible breach of the contract between ALA and Vision Associates, which had joined with ALA in a joint venture to produce and distribute the film.

The Speaker's first public screening was held at the Annual Conference. The film engendered fierce discussion pro and con, with the most severe and frequent charges directed at its alleged "racism." The controversy focused on the film's choice of subject, the manner in which Blacks were portrayed, the stereotyped relationships and characters, and the manner in which the film project was developed. Other attacks focused on some of the film's technical aspects and its lack of a strong librarian character. The film also had its supporters, who called it "courageous," "a slice of life," and a "superb discussion vehicle." A motion introduced during the 1977 membership meeting to remove ALA's name from the film was narrowly defeated after extensive debate, and ALA's name remained on *The Speaker*. The Council came to the same conclusion by a greater margin.

At year's end, the controversy was still alive, although approximately 240 prints had been purchased, and preview requests numbered well over 400. Many library associations throughout the country have used the film in intellectual freedom programs with almost universally positive results. The film was accepted for screening at the San Francisco International Film Festival, and reviews in film periodicals praised the film's intellectual content and technical quality.

Resolutions. At its fall meeting, nevertheless, the ALA Executive Board adopted two resolutions recommended by members of the ALA Black Caucus. One resolution established a committee of representatives from the Executive Board, the Intellectual Freedom Committee, and the Black Caucus; in turn the committee was to appoint an interdisciplinary panel of experts "to advise the Association as to whether or not [*The Speaker*] actually addresses the First Amendment." The second resolution disclaimed any racist intent on the part of the Association in the production of the film. During the same meeting, the Executive Board decided against "unnecessary proliferation" of the film, the majority of the Board members voting to forbid video cassette reproduction of *The Speaker* by schools and other agencies.

The intense reactions to the film led to several observations by various ALA members. Many saw irony in the fact that the Association itself appeared to be acting out on a daily basis the fictionalized portrayal in the film. A second reflection concerned the effect of the medium on the content of the message. At least a few ALA members believed that the intense reaction to *The Speaker* was brought about in part by the fact that it is a film rather than a book. This viewpoint was given some credence in view of the spring controversy over the film *The Lottery*. In most instances, the film was banned while the print version was permitted to remain in library collections.

BILL OF RIGHTS

While controversy swirled around *The Speaker*, IFC was involved in a related controversy involving the Resolution on Racism and Sexism Awareness, adopted by the ALA Council in July 1976, and the Library Bill of Rights. The question of a conflict between the two documents was brought to IFC by the Board of Directors of the Children's Services Division (CSD)—now the Association for Library Services to Children—which observed that the Resolution on Racism and Sexism Awareness "seems to be in direct conflict with the Library Bill of Rights and Sexism, Racism, and Other-Isms in Library Materials—an interpretation of the Library Bill of Rights, adopted by Council in 1973." The CSD Board further informed IFC of its belief that the phrase "raising the awareness of library users" in the Resolution on Racism and Sexism Awareness "violates our professional responsibility to promote no cause and further no movement and can only result in the expurgation, labeling and removal of materials for content."

CSD Consideration. At the CSD Board's request, IFC placed the matter on its agenda for discussion during the Midwinter Meeting. Lengthy and at times acrimonious debate ensued over the several days of the meeting. In her report to Council on February 4, Florence McMullin, Chairperson, stressed IFC's belief in "the clear consensus of the American Library Association against racism and sexism and our fundamental belief in intellectual freedom as set forth in the Library Bill of Rights." She announced that IFC would begin work toward the development of a compatible set of Association policies and requested the cooperation of all concerned units of the Association in the endeavor.

At the 1977 Annual Conference, members of IFC agreed that it was their responsibility to assume the initiative in preparing a statement, or statements, to which other units of ALA could react with suggestions. Toward this end, a subcommittee was appointed, composed of Miriam Braverman, Stephen Oppenheim, Elliot Shelkrot, and Grace Slocum, Chairperson. In addition, the subcommittee agreed upon a timetable for its work. The first step was to draft a statement prior to the 1978 Midwinter Meeting for distribution to all concerned units so that subcommittee members could meet with unit representatives at the meeting. In late fall 1977, however, it became apparent that there was a division among the

Intellectual Freedom

members of the subcommittee and that a draft statement could not be prepared. The matter of a perceived conflict between the Resolution on Racism and Sexism Awareness and the Library Bill of Rights, therefore, was once again an agenda item for IFC's 1978 Midwinter Meeting.

Revision Sought. Also on IFC's 1978 Midwinter Meeting agenda was a proposal to revise the Library Bill of Rights. The issue was brought to the Committee during the 1977 Annual Conference by the ALA Committee on the Status of Women in Librarianship, which requested that sexist terminology in the document be removed immediately. Reluctant to move so quickly to change a basic document of the Association, but cognizant that the language of the Library Bill of Rights might require revision, the Committee determined to study the policy in depth prior to the Midwinter Meeting and to be prepared to suggest changes in January. Presented with a firm timetable for review and revision of the Library Bill of Rights, Council referred the resolution of the Committee on the Status of Women in Librarianship to IFC.

LEGISLATION

1977 presented intellectual freedom forces with more problems than solutions. One such problem was S. 1437, introduced in the 95th Congress shortly after it convened in January. The bill was dubbed "son of S. 1" by Nat Hentoff; and, like its predecessor from the 94th Congress, the bill was designed to "codify, revise, and reform" the U.S. Criminal Code. As the result of a compromise between Senators Edward Kennedy (D.-Mass.) and John McClellan (D.-Ark.), the language of S. 1437 modified many of the problems that had caused a halt to S. 1. In addition, many of the troublesome parts of S. 1 had been dropped, to be considered at a later date as separate pieces of legislation.

Obscenity Issue. One section of the bill of great concern to librarians was Section 1842, dealing with obscenity. The ALA presented a statement on this section in July 1977. The testimony repeated arguments frequently urged by the ALA with regard to federal laws on obscenity, namely, that the difficult question of obscenity should be removed from the criminal arena to the civil.

In a surprise move in November, the Senate Judiciary Committee approved new language for Section 1842 that would preclude the use of federal law to prosecute individuals who undertake action, for example, distribution of materials, that would be entirely legal under state law. If the new language is retained, it appears that the issue fought in the case of *Smith* v. *United States* would be won, despite the fact that the U.S. Supreme Court held otherwise. (See Freedom to Read Foundation.)

In the House, concern expressed by the Criminal Justice Subcommittee of the Judiciary Committee in regard to the wording of many chapters and sections of the bill, the major issues of energy and taxes that still face Congress, and the fact that 1978 is an election year made it unlikely that the recodification would be passed during the 95th Congress.

State-Level Action. On the state level, obscenity bills continued to be introduced at a rapid pace. At least a dozen state legislatures were faced with new or revised proposals. A new twist to such bills was the attempt to control the abuse of children through child pornography. Although repulsed by the use of children in sexually explicit materials, the Intellectual Freedom Committee of the Young Adult Services Division (YASD) asked the ALA/IFC to join in a statement cautioning against making such legislation so sweeping that it could render illegal legitimate sex education materials in libraries. A case in point was a bill that had been introduced into the New York legislature, under the provisions of which *Show Me!*, a pictorial sex education manual for adults to use with young people, would be illegal. Representatives of the YASD/IFC, the CSD/IFC, and the ALA/IFC developed a statement on legislation to control the abuse of minors, while protecting sex education materials. Council approved the statement on June 22.

Titles at Issue. The ALA statement was presented to appropriate state legislatures during the fall. In New York, the ALA resolution led to an exemption for libraries and librarians, but did not preclude the passage of an otherwise stringent measure. The exemption for libraries notwithstanding, attacks throughout the state of New York on *Show Me!* continued. Neither the exemption in the New York child pornography law nor library exemptions in other state obscenity measures precluded attacks on other sex education materials.

Our Bodies, Ourselves, prepared by the Boston Women's Health Book Collective, was

Above, actress Mildred Dunnock in a scene from the film "The Speaker". Controversy over the film included resolutions offered by the ALA Black Caucus protesting alleged racism and ALA sponsorship of the film. (Below) The Black Caucus meeting with newsmen at the Detroit Conference.

published by Simon and Schuster in 1973 and reissued in a revised edition in 1976. Acclaimed for its scope and treatment of female sexuality, it was widely purchased for young adult and adult library collections throughout the United States. In 1977, however, it became apparent that *Our Bodies, Ourselves* deals with subjects and with values and principles that a large percentage of Americans believe to be better dealt with by the family in the home. *Ms.* magazine, dealing with similar formerly taboo issues and stressing, in addition, equality for women, also became a focal point for would-be censors. While these materials and others dealing with female sexuality and equal rights were being withdrawn from library collections throughout the country, articles on the rapidly increasing rate of teenage pregnancies were making headlines in more and more cities.

OPPOSITION AND REACTION

As the year progressed, it became increasingly clear that would-be censors were better organized, better funded, more sophisticated, and more persistent than many educational and library professionals understood. Those wanting to turn back the clock enlarged their concerns to include educational methods as well as materials, series as well as books, and ideology as well as content. Erosion of trust in public service institutions, the frustration of parents in the face of seemingly ineffective education, and less availability of public service money contributed to organized conservatism.

In the face of the growing pressures being exerted on schools and libraries, representatives of eight national education organizations met in November to plan strategies for meeting the increasing challenges. In the belief that the best defense is a strong offense, the coalition, calling itself the Academic Freedom Group, determined to work together in educating their respective constituents to the breadth of the problem and to help them analyze and deal with local problems. The organizations comprising the Academic Freedom Group are the American Association of School Administrators, the American Federation of Teachers, the American Library Association, the International Reading Association, the National Council for the Social Studies, the National Council of Teachers of English, the National Education Association, and the Speech Communication Association. As a first step, a regional workshop was scheduled for the spring of 1978. The workshop was designed for representatives from the eight organizations in Illinois, Indiana, Ohio, Michigan, and Wisconsin.

Although most of the organizations represented in the Academic Freedom Group are also members of the National Coalition Against Censorship (NCAC), they believed a more detailed and specific action program was required for their constituents, all of whom are on the firing line in libraries and schools. By working together and drawing on one another's established programs and strengths, the Academic Freedom Group hopes to raise the consciousness of its constituents to the nature and extent of successful efforts at thought control and intimidation in educational settings. The group hopes to analyze and understand the approaches and strategies used by individuals and groups to restrict the availability of educational and library materials and to work together to develop preventive measures and counterstrategies that can be used in the preservation of the climate of academic freedom.

While limited in the action that it can undertake, the National Coalition Against Censorship has a similar purpose in raising awareness to the dangers of censorship. NCAC's target group, however, is the general public, and the Coalition is more broadly based, including religious and communications organizations as well as library and educational ones. Although hampered by a lack of funding, NCAC pursued its goals during 1977 by holding a one-day conference in February. Titled "Rights in Conflict," the conference focused on the question of the traditional concept of the First Amendment freedom of the press versus the First Amendment rights of special interest groups that seek to change media presentations in such areas as film and television violence and stereotyped images of ethnic groups and women. In addition, two plenary sessions were held, at the second of which *The Speaker* was screened. In October, NCAC and the New School for Social Research jointly sponsored a three-session series, "Freedom of Expression: An Inquiry," that addressed the topics of government secrecy, obscenity, and censorship of the arts.

The Coalition added several groups during 1977 increasing the total of participating organizations to 28. The director of the ALA Office for Intellectual Freedom (OIF) continued to serve as a member of the NCAC Steering Committee.

Another group with whom IFC and OIF have had a long and fruitful relationship is the Freedom to Read Committee of the Association of American Publishers. Continuing the pattern of the past several years, the two committees held joint sessions at the ALA Midwinter Meeting and Annual Conference. The 1977 sessions were particularly helpful in comparing and testing perceptions regarding the shifting issues and the shifting environment.

In the late fall, an old problem reappeared

Intellectual Freedom Round Table

in several libraries. The problem was the attempt of law enforcement officers to use library circulation records as evidence of improper conduct. Whether the attempt was to identify people who carry "improper" ideas, as evidenced by the materials they read, or to build a case of criminal conduct on the basis of reading habits, the disclosure of library circulation records is condemned by the ALA "Policy on Confidentiality of Library Records." Dissent is protected under the First Amendment, and charges of criminality should be based on actions, not thoughts.

We may in the not-too-distant future look back on 1977 as the watershed year. Having felt its strength, grass-roots America will continue to fight for a return to traditional values and principles. The full impact of the swing to the right was not felt by the library community in 1977, but the warning signals were visible. Unfortunately, as the year drew to an end, our own house was not in order; internal questions regarding ALA's position on intellectual freedom in the coming decade remained unresolved.

JUDITH F. KRUG

REFERENCE
1. Andrew Kopkind, "America Turns Right," *New Times* (September 30, 1977), p. 22.

Intellectual Freedom Round Table

The purpose of the Intellectual Freedom Round Table (IFRT) is to provide a forum on intellectual freedom as it is related to libraries and librarians and to promote growing opportunities for responsibility and involvement among members of the ALA in this concern. To further this purpose the Round Table has continued its policy of sponsoring an intellectual freedom program at the ALA Annual Conference. Charles Rembar was the featured speaker at the 1977 Conference.

At the meeting the John Phillip Immroth Memorial Award for Intellectual Freedom was given to Irene Turin, Head Librarian of the Island Trees (Long Island) School District. In its desire to contribute to the intellectual freedom involvement on the state and local level, the Round Table carried out a special "roll call of the states" during its membership meeting at the Annual Conference. Representatives of many states reported on activities and problems for the purpose of learning from one another and sharing their concerns.

The thrust of the deliberations at the membership and other meetings has been to increase local involvement of ALA membership in intellectual freedom awareness and action. As part of the effort of strengthening the effectiveness of the Round Table, it appoints annually one liaison person each to the ALA Intellectual Freedom Committee and to the Board of Directors of the Freedom to Read Foundation and the LeRoy C. Merritt Humanitarian Fund. At the 1977 Annual Conference the Round Table fulfilled its commitment to the Freedom to Read Foundation by a contribution of $500.

The membership of the Round Table represents the deep concern of the library community for the protection of intellectual freedom as the genius of the library and as the foundation of professional self-fulfillment and security. IFRT will continue to carve out its particular place and function in the organizational network of ALA.

KARL WEINER

International Board on Books for Young People

1977 marked the 24th year of the International Board on Books for Young People (IBBY). At the two regular meetings of IBBY's Executive Committee in Basel, Switzerland, in March and in Bratislava, Czechoslovakia, in September, a great deal of attention was devoted to planning IBBY's Jubilee Year in 1978. The 1978 IBBY Congress will immediately follow the Frankfurt Book Fair, whose theme for the year will be children's books to commemorate the International Year of the Child in 1979. The biennial Congress will be in Würzburg, Federal Republic of Germany, near Frankfurt.

Under IBBY's President, Hans Halbey, Director of the Gutenberg Museum, Mainz, Germany, the organization has strengthened its relations with both UNESCO and UNICEF. IBBY's representative at UNESCO is Niilo Visapaa, from Finland, IBBY's Immediate Past President. Its representative to the Non-Governmental Organizations associated with UNICEF is Augusta Baker, the well-known U.S. librarian and storyteller. A committee consisting of Baker, Anne Pellowski of the U.S. Committee for UNICEF, and Ann Beneduce, of Collins & World and a member of IBBY's Executive Committee, did the preparatory work on a comprehensive policy statement on

---

IFRT Officers

CHAIRPERSON (July 1977-June 1978):
Karl Weiner, Skokie Public Library, Skokie, Illinois

VICE-CHAIRPERSON/CHAIRPERSON-ELECT:
Lee B. Brawner, Oklahoma County Libraries, Oklahoma City

SECRETARY:
Ione Pierron

TREASURER:
Anna M. Curry

Membership (August 31, 1977): 974

Interlibrary Cooperation: see Networks

IBBY's relation to the International Year of the Child. "Priorities in Children's Books and Related Materials for Intellectual Development of Children," containing IBBY's recommendations to UNICEF, UNESCO, and governments, was adopted at the Bratislava Executive Committee meeting. IBBY has also prepared a special statement for the International Year of the Child, "Children's Books for a Better World." The complete text will appear in the *Friends of IBBY Newsletter* (Summer-Fall 1978).

IBBY's membership stands at approximately 40 National Sections. Certain of the Sections have experienced vigorous growth in the past few years, particularly those of Japan, Brazil, and, now, Canada, with the formation in 1977 of a Friends of IBBY activity. The National Sections of both Israel and Venezuela were reformed in 1977 in the expectation of becoming more active in IBBY. International Children's Book Day was sponsored in 1977 by the French National Section of IBBY, which prepared a somewhat startling poster for the occasion, and for which Jacques Charpentreau prepared a special message.

IBBY solicited nominations for the 1978 Hans Christian Andersen Medals during 1977. The medals are given to an author and an illustrator for the entire body of their work for children. The U.S. nominees, selected by a committee of the Association for Library Service to Children (ALSC), chaired by Paul Heins, are author Paula Fox and illustrators Leo and Diane Dillon. The two 1978 Honor Books from the United States are *Tuck Everlasting* by Natalie Babbitt (Farrar) for text and Margot Zemach's *Hush, Little Baby* (Dutton) for illustration. For the first time in 1978, the IBBY Honor List is to cite a translator for a body of work. The U.S. children's book translator on the Honor List will be Sheila LaFarge, with her translation of *The Glassblower's Children* by Maria Gripe (Delacorte/Seymour Lawrence) singled out as an example of her work. The 1978 Andersen Jury is chaired by Lucia Binder of Austria; Zena Sutherland from the United States is a jury member.

Members of the Executive Committee of the U.S. National Section of IBBY have been involved in various projects in support of IBBY. A committee headed by Amy Kellman selected 20 realistic children's books to represent the United States at the 1978 IBBY Congress. Virginia Haviland selected 50 titles from the ALSC list "Children's Books of International Interest" to represent the United States at the 1978 Frankfurt Book Fair. Paul Heins continued to act as U.S. Associate Editor of *Bookbird*, a publication closely identified with IBBY. Members are also participating in the editorial work for IBBY's *International Guide to Sources of Information about Children's Literature*, to be published in 1978 in a handy travel-sized format.

The U.S. National Section's Friends of IBBY numbers about 225 members. The 1977 annual meeting was in Washington, D.C., on January 30. Leena Maissen from the IBBY Secretariat in Switzerland spoke at the meeting. Judy Taylor, Director, The Bodley Head, London, also spoke about current British publishing. Virginia Haviland of the Library of Congress continues to chair Friends of IBBY; Isabella Jinnette is Treasurer. John Donovan edits the *Friends of IBBY Newsletter*, which appears twice yearly.

JOHN DONOVAN

International Federation for Documentation (FID)

In 1977, the 82nd year of the International Federation for Documentation (FID), much attention was given to developing a revised FID program as directed by the General Assembly in 1976. A draft document worked out by the two vice-presidents was distributed to national members, and a final document was expected at the time of the September 1978 General Assembly in Edinburgh.

During 1977 the organization of the 39th FID Conference and Congress in Edinburgh was also completed. The program for the Congress, with the theme "New Trends in Documentation," was to be issued in early 1978.

FID/CLA. The regional Comisión Latinoamericana (CLA) published its proposed program for 1977–78 in *Informaciones FID/CLA*, No. 27. The program includes a large number of projects and other activities in the field of information science for Latin America. FID/CLA held its 16th General Assembly in December 1977 in Venezuela in conjunction with a Latin American seminar on the utilization of data bases.

FID/CAO. The Commission for Asia and Oceania (CAO) in 1977 directed its efforts toward achieving a more active role for the developing countries in the region. Bangladesh was admitted as the 65th FID national member. The 4th Congress and 5th General Assembly of FID/CAO is to be held in India in September 1978.

Committees. FID/CCC (Central Classification Committee), the body responsible for the operation and supervision of the Universal Decimal Classification (UDC), underwent a major reorganization during 1977 to create a more viable Committee that could cope with the increasingly pressing need for an up-to-date UDC. FID/CR (Classification Research) published the fifth volume of its quarterly newsletter. The Committee has also become a cosponsor of the journal *International Classification*.

International Relations

FID/ET (Education and Training) published its third occasional paper, *Common Features of Training of Information Specialists,* and also held its annual business and technical meetings in Warsaw in May. In conjunction with FID/II and Aslib, FID/ET has organized a seminar on education and training to be held during the 1978 FID Conference.

FID/II (Information for Industry) held its annual meeting in Lisbon in October. The meeting was followed by an open forum on "Information Sources for and within Industry." Subsequent to its meeting FID/II issued a five-page recommended structure on a "Training Course for Officers of Information Service for Industry."

FID/RI (Research on the Theoretical Basis of Information) published a collection of articles, *On Effectiveness of Scientific Information Activities* (FID 527). FID/LD (Linguistics in Documentation) held a meeting in Stockholm in September.

FID/PD (Patent Information and Documentation) held two meetings, one in March in Vienna and another in December in The Hague. Through its efforts FID's observer status with the WIPO bodies has been broadened.

General Secretariat. A new edition of the *FID Yearbook* was published in 1977, and work proceeded on the compilation of an annotated bibliography of thesauri and on lists of subject headings to be published in 1978.

KENNETH R. BROWN

International Relations

The largest and grandest event in the annals of international librarianship took place in Brussels, Belgium, September 3-10, 1977, when the International Federation of Library Associations and Institutions (IFLA) celebrated its 50th anniversary. Some 1,700 librarians from around the world were present at this historic occasion, and of these more than 200 were from the United States. The congress's theme, "Libraries for All: One World of Information, Culture and Learning," was designed to appeal to a wide spectrum of the library world. Robert Vosper, IFLA Vice-President and former ALA President, was Chairman of the IFLA Program Planning Committee.

In recognition of IFLA's 50th anniversary, the ALA Council authorized a gift to the Federation of $250 to help defray the cost of membership for library associations from developing countries. IFLA chose the following associations: AIDBA Section Togolaise, Library Association of Uruguay, and Association Zairoise des Archivistes.

IFLA Delegates and Elections. The American Library Association was represented at the 43rd IFLA Council meeting by an "official" delegation including Eric Moon, President; Robert Wedgeworth, Executive Director; E.J. Josey, Chair, IRC; Rosemary Weber, ALSC; Doralyn Hickey, RTSD; Jane Flener, ACRL; Barbara Ford, SRRT; Bernadine Hoduski, GODORT; Keith Doms, PLA; Virginia Young, ALTA; Rosalind Miller, AASL; and Edward Moffat, IRRT.

During the week, the various IFLA sections and round tables held programs and business meetings. U.S. librarians elected officers of section standing committees were W.J. Welsh, Secretary, Section on National Libraries; Jane G. Flener, Secretary, Section on University Libraries and Other General Research Libraries; Linda Beeler, Secretary, Section on School Libraries; Lucia Rather, Chairman, Section on Cataloging; Doralyn J. Hickey, Secretary, Section on Cataloging; Frank L. Schick, Chairman, Section on Statistics; P.A. Molholt, Chairman/Secretary, Round Table on Astronomical and Geophysical Libraries; and Virginia Haviland, Chairman, Round Table Centers of Research and Documentation on Children's Literature.

In addition, Doralyn Hickey was elected Chairman of the Division of Bibliographic Control and was elected to the IFLA Professional Board. Earlier in the year elections were held for membership on the various section standing committees. The following librarians from the United States are serving on IFLA section standing committees: A.J. Eaton, University Libraries and Other General Research Libraries; G. Gude, Parliamentary Libraries; V.D. Hewitt, Social Science Libraries; F.E. McKenna, Social Sciences Libraries; W.W. Ristow, Geography and Map Libraries; M.N. Coughlan, Children's Libraries; W. Boyd Rayward, Bibliography; N.R. Einhorn, Exchange of Publication; J.W. Price, Serial Publications; W. Matheson, Rare and Precious Books and Documents; R. Rouse, Library Buildings and Equipment; H.D. Avram, Mechanization; J.P. Franck, Statistics; A.F. Trezza, Statistics; J.R. Fang, Library Schools and Other Training Aspects; and M.V. Rovelstad, Library Schools and Other Training Aspects.

A reception was held at the U.S. Embassy residence by Ambassador Ann Cox Chambers for the U.S. participants in the congress.

UNESCO. During the year, ALA again acted on several UNESCO matters of concern to librarians in the United States. A resolution on UNESCO funding, initiated by the International Relations Committee (IRC), was adopted by the ALA Council on February 4. It urged the U.S. Congress to authorize and appropriate funds to pay arrearages and other assessments owed by the U.S. to the organization, as well as the assessment due in fiscal years 1977 and 1978. At the ALA Annual Conference, IRC initiated a resolution urging the approval of the Florence Agreement Protocol. Adopted by Council on June 20, the Protocol represents a major step forward in the further removal or reduction of barriers to international trade for educational, scientific, and cultural materials.

At the meeting of the 19th General Conference of UNESCO in Nairobi in 1976, a resolution was passed creating the new General Information Programme of UNESCO. As a result, the new Division of the General Information Programme (PGI) has become responsible for most of the activities, including the UNISIST and NATIS programs, formerly executed by the Division of Scientific and Technological Documentation and Information (STI) and the Division of Documentation, Libraries and Archives (DBA). Also approved at the General Conference were statutes establishing an Intergovernmental Council for the PGI with 30 member states, one of which is the United States. Robert Wedgeworth, ALA Executive Director, served as the Library Advisor to the U.S. representative on the Council at its inaugural meeting in late November in Paris.

Recognizing the need within the United States for a mechanism to coordinate U.S. interests in this new unified information program, Wedgeworth called the first of several meetings held during 1977 to consider the creation of a U.S. National Committee for the UNESCO General Information Program. Wedgeworth has served as chairman pro tem of this group since its inception. A proposed charter was drafted, and it is expected that the charter will be presented for approval in 1978 to a plenary meeting of organizations representing the U.S. information community concerned with the activities of PGI.

Library Association Centenary. In 1877, one year after the founding of the ALA, a delegation of U.S. librarians was present at the Inaugural Conference of the British Library Association. Royal Festival Hall in London was the scene of the Library Association's 100th birthday celebration in October 1977. ALA President Eric Moon, Past President Clara Jones, and Executive Director Robert Wedgeworth officially represented ALA at the Centenary Conference and presented the Library Association with a special plaque to mark the occasion. President Moon was the featured speaker at the session sponsored by the Association of Assistant Librarians. He spoke on "The State of the Union, Jack."

Other ALA staff members present at the historic event were Alice Fite, Executive Secretary of the American Association of School Librarians (AASL); Babetta Jimpie, AASL Professional Assistant; and Jean Coleman, Director of the Office of Library Service to the Disadvantaged.

International Representatives. ALA is represented in the following international units: the Joint Steering Committee for Revision of the Anglo-American Cataloging Rules, John D. Byrum, Jr., and Frances Hinton, Deputy; the U.S. Mission to the United Nations, Gloria P. Brown; the United Nations Non-Governmental Organizations Section/Office of Public Information, Donald Jay; the U.S. National Commission for UNESCO, Esther J. Walls (who also serves as a member of the Executive Committee); and the International Board on Books for Young People, U.S. Section, Barbara S. Miller, Amy Kellman, and Mary Jane Anderson. JANE WILSON

Delegation of U.S. Librarians to the U.S.S.R.

U.S. librarians who visited the U.S.S.R. in November 1976 released their report on "Libraries and Information Services in the U.S.S.R." at the Midwinter Meeting in January 1977. The primary purpose of the visit was to discuss appropriate exchange relationships between Soviet and American librarians under the Helsinki Agreement and the new bilateral cultural agreement between the two countries. The trip was also designed to provide a basis for assessing the present status of library service in the U.S.S.R. in order to determine more precisely the needs and interests of Soviet and American librarians upon which exchange programs might be developed.

The delegation came away from their visit with several definite impressions about Soviet librarianship:

1. The bibliographical work performed by Soviet librarians is quite extensive in depth and staggering in quantity.
2. Soviet libraries give a high priority to library research.
3. Library staffs tend to be much larger than in comparable libraries in the United States.
4. Management information for planning and analysis is given a high priority.
5. There is a heavy dependence on exchange and on depository arrangements for building collections, especially of foreign materials.
6. There is much interest in library automation but little capability and questionable motivation.

With the agreement of their hosts at the Ministry of Culture, the U.S. delegation recommended that the American Library Association pursue the possibility of holding a joint Soviet-United States Seminar on Library and Information Services featuring invited papers from each country to address certain topics. Topics that appear to be fruitful for such a format include information needs and users, library planning and development, application of technology to library procedures, library statistics, library service to children, national subject bibliography, library education,

International Relations Round Table

and technical services. This seminar would be held in the United States in 1978 or 1979 and might be followed by a formal exchange agreement consisting of periodic seminars, exchange of individual librarians, and exchange of exhibits.

At its January 1977 meeting the ALA Executive Board authorized the Executive Director to pursue the possibility of organizing such a seminar, and it was anticipated that a three-person Soviet delegation would visit the United States in January 1978 to further discuss the planning of the first such seminar.

In March 1977, at the suggestion of the Department of State, a second proposal was prepared for a four-member delegation of librarians to visit the U.S.S.R. to be conierned solely with library service to children. It was hoped that this mission would take place in the summer of 1978.

Members of the ALA delegation to the U.S.S.R. were Nathalie P. Delougaz, Chief, Shared Cataloging Division, Library of Congress; Susan K. Martin, Head, Library Systems Office, General Library, University of California, Berkeley; and Robert Wedgeworth, ALA Executive Director. Most of the introduction to their report of their impression of Soviet libraries and librarianship appeared in LEADS, the publication of the International Relations Round Table. Another extract, which includes the itinerary with the exception of the descriptions of the Leningrad Public Library and the various youth and children's libraries visited by the delegation, appeared in the July-August 1977 issue of Special Libraries.

International Relations Round Table

The structure, sponsored events, and the newsletter Leads were the focus of Mohammed M. Aman's article on the International Relations Round Table (IRRT) in the 1977 ALA Yearbook, for it is through the Midwinter Meetings and Annual Conferences of ALA, as well as Leads, that the work of IRRT becomes visible.

Area reporters are also important to IRRT. During 1977, the reporters were as follows: Africa, Hans Panofsky; East Asia, Josephine R. Fang; International Organizations, Richard A. Steele; Latin America, Martha Tomé; Middle East and North Africa, Rosalie Cuneo Amer and Beverly Brewster; and South East Asia, Lian Tie Kho. Brief reports and helpful suggestions were given to the Executive Board, both at the Midwinter Meeting and at the Annual Conference.

At Detroit an address by Mohamed H. Zehery, Director of Kuwait's Institute for Scientific Research, and a slide presentation by Josephine Fang, Simmons College, on libraries in China that she had visited provided information for those interested in international and comparative librarianship. The formal general program sponsored by IRRT was "The American Library Association and International Library Organizations: Trends for the Next Decade and Beyond." Speakers included Robert Wedgeworth, Executive Director of ALA, speaking on ALA's commitment; Robert Vosper, UCLA, speaking as Vice-President of IFLA on its new structure and on the 1977 Brussels conference; Frank McKenna, Executive Director of the Special Libraries Association (SLA), speaking on the SLA's commitment to international relations; and Jean Lowrie, Western Michigan, speaking as President of the International Association of School Librarianship. A cassette recording of the program is available from ALA.

IRRT Officers

CHAIRPERSON (July 1977-June 1978):
David C. Donovan, Agency for International Development, Washington, D.C.

VICE-CHAIRPERSON:
Jane P. Franck, Teachers College Columbia University

SECRETARY-TREASURER:
Robert Booth, Wayne State University, Detroit, Michigan

Membership (August 31, 1977): 626

The formal social program sponsored by IRRT was the Reception for Foreign Librarians, organized by Indra David, Oakland University, and assisted financially by Blackwells of North America. At the Annual Conference note was taken of the contributions of the members at large: Abdul Huq, Saint John's University, and Jane R. Moore, City University of New York. Their replacements for 1977-78 are Alan Veaner, University of California at Santa Barbara, and Mary Maack, Minnesota.

The liaison lines to the International Relations Committee (IRC) of the ALA Council were continued by the IRRT Chairperson's representation on the IRC Board, as well as IRC's invitation to the editor of Leads to participate as an observer. Edward S. Moffat, who continues as the editor of Leads, was also appointed to represent IRRT on the ALA delegation to the IFLA Brussels conference in 1977. IRRT's interconnecting relationships of people and associations have been facilitated by the assistance of Jane Wilson, International Officer of the American Library Association.

EDWARD S. MOFFAT

Junior Members Round Table

The Junior Members Round Table (JMRT) is the group within ALA that promotes and supports the interests of new members of the profession. Membership is extended to persons under 36 years of age, or to those who have been in the profession for fewer than six years.

The national JMRT organization began in the 1930's with a handful of beginning professionals who found themselves facing common problems. Their original motive was to find a source of support in each other. The national organization still meets that need for many beginning professionals. More recently regional, state, and local affiliates have developed to meet the same need in smaller geographical areas. The goals of the organization are to learn more about the profession and ALA and to support the development of affiliate JMRT groups.

JMRT Officers

PRESIDENT (July 1977-June 1978):
Marilyn Hinshaw, Pecos Library System, El Paso, Texas

VICE-PRESIDENT/PRESIDENT-ELECT:
David Warren, Cumberland County Libraries, Fayetteville, North Carolina

SECRETARY-TREASURER:
Rose Caruso

Membership (August 31, 1977): 1,125

Much of JMRT's work during the 1976-77 year culminated in the Annual Conference in Detroit. The continuing service projects were Conference Orientation and *Cognotes,* the Conference newsletter. They were presented by JMRT teams headed by Joyce Wyngaarden and Bill Cooper (Orientation), and Lafaye Cobb (*Cognotes*). The 1977 Annual Conference "Students to ALA" Social and the accompanying student guide were produced by a JMRT committee headed by June Breland. JMRT continued the outstanding 3M/JMRT Professional Development Grant program. Four new professionals attended the Conference as grant recipients. They participated in Conference meetings and observed ALA leaders in action through a planned agenda of events that included committee meetings and the meetings of ALA's Executive Board and Council. The 1977 project was chaired by Patty Landers. The Olafson Memorial Project, chaired by Crystal Bailey, provided nine new professionals with the cost of registration for their second Annual Conference. Shirley Olafson, for whom the Project is named, died while in office as JMRT President in 1971.

The national JMRT internal structure was probed by David Warren, Vice-President/President-Elect, in a series of self-study exercises during the year. David and Bridget LaMont of the Illinois State Library prepared and presented a group interaction program for JMRT's Board and committee teams at the 1977 Midwinter Meeting. The project was directed toward the discovery of needs felt by JMRT members as represented by JMRT's national leadership. The Midwinter examination was followed by a survey of the general membership by the Committee on Governance, chaired by Doyal Nelms. The outcome of the survey confirmed JMRT's general direction. These two activities were the major tools used to plan the work of the succeeding year (1977-78).

The Affiliates Committee recommended its own termination, and the Executive Board gave the responsibility for developing new affiliates to the ever-stronger Affiliates Council. The Council includes a representative from each JMRT affiliate, and its elected officers sit on the national JMRT Board. The Council also broadened its role during 1977 by sponsoring the JMRT suite at the Annual Conference in Detroit. Different affiliates hosted the suite, which was open to JMRT members, students, and friends. Affiliates Council President Jeri Baker and Vice-President Margaret Stewart guided The Council's activities in 1976-77.

JMRT continued a liaison program that identifies other groups in the ALA organization with concerns that are of interest to JMRT. A JMRT representative is sent to observe, participate, and report to JMRT members. Those reports and all other internal communications appear in *Footnotes,* JMRT's newletter. Ann Scott served as editor for 1976-77.

A major internal structural change was voted by the membership at the Annual Conference. In preceding years, as JMRT national activity has increased, the number of committee teams organized to work on specific projects has also increased. The vote of membership at Detroit changed the vague member-at-large positions of the national Board to working directorships. Persons elected to those positions in the future will coordinate the work of several committees that are grouped together by activity. Joe Edelen headed the Constitution and Bylaws Committee, which researched and recommended the change.

In addition to JMRT's regular activities, the 1976-77 year was dubbed the "Year of Firsts." JMRT's first organizational manual was completed by a committee headed by Jacquelyn McGirt. The first midwinter issue of *Cognotes* was produced. Orientation to 1976-77 JMRT operations and activities, presented at the end of the 1976 Annual Conference, was the first of its kind for the national Board. Sale of JMRT T-shirts, a project organized by Virginia Amos, was a first in fund-raising ventures for JMRT.

Susan Broomall headed a committee that produced and staffed a new JMRT promotional booth for the 1977 Annual Conference. Another first was the All-Conference Social at Detroit. The Social was a private demonstration of success for Beverly Papai, who organized the event, and Beth Bingham, who shared a large portion of the work of selling tickets. 1976-77 was significant for JMRT's national organization and highly successful in continuing to provide support and learning opportunities to participating JMRT members.

MARILYN HINSHAW

Labor Groups, Library Service to

The most significant happening during 1977 in the area of library service to labor groups was the publishing of the results of the 1976 survey of public libraries in communities of more than 10,000 people that have a central labor council. The survey was conducted by the AFL-CIO/Reference and Adult Services Division (RASD) Joint Committee on Library Service to Labor Groups. It was the first survey of libraries concerning their service to labor groups since 1967. The number of special labor collections, the number of staff with job assignments related to labor service, and the number of libraries working with labor organizations and their membership has steadily declined since the 1967 survey. Only 18 libraries identified themselves as having a special collection of materials for use by labor unions and organizations. Fourteen libraries identified a staff member who was assigned to work with labor organizations and labor-related materials, compared with 22 in the 1967 survey.

Surprising Responses and Results. "Do we have any unions in Huron, South Dakota?" typifies some of the responses to the 1976 survey. Of the 53.2 per cent (385) that returned the questionnaires, many responses indicated that the librarians assumed that labor unions are well established and have large amounts of money to spend for special services. Other librarians were not even aware that there are unions or central labor councils in their area. The questionnaires were sent only to libraries in cities having central labor councils.

The Joint Committee has a dual responsibility to both the AFL-CIO and the ALA. With this in mind the survey included a question to determine what type of cooperation from labor organizations would be useful if a library wants to establish a special collection of services to labor unions. A total of 177 libraries said that they would like advice or cooperation of some type from unions, yet it is interesting to note that only 45 libraries had ever approached unions or the central labor council even once, and 88.4 per cent had never approached them. Libraries indicated that they want support, including financial support, advice and consultation, coordination, and improved communications from unions, yet rarely have they asked for it. Twenty-two libraries replied that they would like unions to prepare bibliographies, a task usually considered the domain of professional librarians.

Since the late 1960's there has been a shift in emphasis in many libraries from treating labor as a special group and providing them with special services to treating labor as a group of patrons with no "special" needs. The shift away from treating labor as a special group can be seen as part of the general shift in emphasis (brought on in part by LSCA Title I grant priorities) to the economically and culturally disadvantaged and to the bilingual patron. There also appears to be a general shift away from all special collections. Many librarians indicated in the survey that they had shifted the emphasis of their service to special business collections.

Mistrust of Unions. A surprising amount of mistrust and lack of understanding of anything connected with unions was shown by the librarians answering the questionnaire. Although it was echoed in many others, mistrust was illustrated by one comment in particular—"Ask members to check them [books] out, not steal them." Others indicated that it would not be worth their while to provide specialized materials since union members would not use them anyway. Another librarian stated, "... unions will ruin the United States. This library does not wish to assist in our country's downfall." Perhaps many librarians are from a socioeconomic group that makes them unfamiliar with organized labor.

Additional information on the survey and the results can be found in *Labor Collection and Service in Public Libraries throughout the United States—1977* by Kathleen Imhoff and Larry Brandwein, available from the RASD offices. The Joint Committee will use the information collected to develop materials to help libraries that would like to improve, expand, or organize a collection of materials to be used by labor groups.

A bibliography, *Labor Union in America: A Reading List*, was compiled by Jean Webber of the AFL-CIO Library for the AFL-CIO/ALA (RASD) Joint Committee. It was distributed to all of the libraries that participated in the Committee's survey and is currently available from the AFL-CIO/RASD offices.

Jack Sessions. The long-term Cochairman of the Joint Committee, Jack Sessions, died in January. Assistant Director of the Department of Education of AFL-CIO, Sessions had been instrumental in committee work for many years.

He contributed numerous articles to the labor press on library services to labor groups and was a dedicated person in promoting cooperation between unions and libraries.

KATHLEEN IMHOFF

Law and Legislation

The most vital piece of library legislation at the federal level in 1977 involved a package of bills designed to extend and amend the Library Services and Construction Act (LSCA), due to expire on September 30, 1977. House bill (H.R. 3712) was introduced by Rep. John Brademas (D-Indiana) on February 21. A Senate bill (S. 602) had been introduced on February 3 by Senator Claiborne Pell (D-Rhode Island). In addition, Senator Jacob Javits (R-New York) introduced a bill (S. 941) that was a verbatim draft of the Title V amendment as originally initiated and sponsored by the Urban Libraries Council.

Compromise Bill. Hearings were held on H.R. 3712 and S. 602 at which representatives of the ALA, the National Commission on Libraries and Information Science, the Urban Libraries Council, and other organizations testified. The House bill was passed on March 21 by a vote of 368 to 1. The Senate bill (S. 602) was passed on May 20 by unanimous consent. A House-Senate conference committee later reconciled the differences between the two bills. After a number of meetings extending over a period of almost three months, the committee reached an agreement on September 8 that was approved by both the House and Senate.

The approved bill extends LSCA for five years and authorizes a substantial increase in the appropriations for Title I. It also earmarks special financial assistance to public libraries in cities of more than 100,000 in population. This provision is designed to strengthen "major urban resource libraries," defined as "any public library located in a city having a population of 100,000 or more individuals, as determined by the Commissioner." Title I was, therefore, amended to require that a portion of the appropriations in excess of $60,000,000 be reserved for public libraries in cities of more than 100,000 in population. The reserved funds would be available to large urban libraries in the same ratio as their aggregate population compares to the total population of a given state. For example, if in a particular state 30 per cent of the population lives in cities of more than 100,000 in population, 30 per cent of the state's share of the amount appropriated in excess of $60,000,000 would be reserved for the public libraries in such cities. No more than 50 per cent of a state's share of the amount appropriated in excess of $60,000,000 can be earmarked for urban libraries.

The bill also requires that urban libraries receiving such funds must serve users throughout the regional area in which the library is located. In supporting the bill, Representative Brademas stated, "By giving additional support to libraries in metropolitan areas, the legislation will strengthen urban public libraries that are the repository of our cultural heritage and provide important resources to smaller libraries across the country."

FEDERAL ACTIVITIES

An event of great interest for the library world occurred on May 4 when President Carter signed into law H.R. 4877, which provides for an appropriation of $3,500,000 to the National Commission on Libraries and Information Science for the purpose of conducting a White House Conference. The funds are to be used in part to help defray the cost of convening state conferences.

Federal regulations were revised, effective January 17, 1977, that make public libraries meeting specified criteria eligible for construction funds under the Housing and Community Development Act of 1974. The definition of a "neighborhood facility" was broadened to permit a wider use of federal construction funds for central library purposes. Construction funds under the act are also available for removing architectural barriers that impede access for handicapped persons.

Bills were introduced in the House (H.R. 6214) and in the Senate (S. 1331) to provide for the establishment of a Center for the Book in the Library of Congress. The Center would be designed to stimulate public interest and to promote research in the role of the book in the diffusion of knowledge through such activities as a visiting scholar program, lectures, exhibits, publications, and other related activities. The President signed the law after final congressional action (P.L. 95-129).

The Wake County Public Library, which has been providing an accelerated information and referral service for the past five years, has received its first grant under Title XX of the Social Security Act. The funds, amounting to $69,137, were made available under a contract between the Library and the Wake County Department of Social Services. The grant enabled the Library to add two new information and referral specialists to its staff.

On May 13 President Carter signed into law a bill (H.R. 11) amending and extending the Public Works Employment Act. This law authorizes an additional $4,000,000,000 for local public works projects. At the White House signing of the act, Commerce Secretary Juanita Kreps declared that "... in addition to creating jobs in the private sector, the local public works legislation will give to the people

Law and Legislation

in the towns and cities throughout the nation new facilities, new public facilities, libraries, municipal buildings, water treatment plants, which they very much need."

The U.S. Department of Health, Education and Welfare in 1977 issued final regulations prohibiting discrimination against handicapped persons. The regulations apply to all recipients of federal assistance from HEW. Major provisions of the regulations affect libraries. All new facilities are to be constructed so as to be readily accessible to and usable by handicapped persons. Activities or programs in existing facilities are to be made accessible within 60 days of the effective date of the regulations. If structural changes are necessary to accomplish this, they must be made within three years.

A U.S. Circuit Court of Appeals ruled that the Medical Literature Analysis and Retrieval System (MEDLARS) tapes are not subject to the Freedom of Information Act. The System Development Corporation of Santa Monica, California, had attempted to acquire the MEDLARS data base under the Freedom of Information Act for the cost of reproduction ($500 as opposed to the $50,000 that the National Technical Information Service charges). The court ruled that there is "a qualitative difference between the type of records Congress sought to make available to the public by passing the Freedom of Information Act and the library reference system sought . . . ."

The U.S. Civil Service Commission ruled that a public library employee may not run for public office. Mark Morse, Director of the Mifflin County Library, Lewistown, Pennsylvania, was nominated to run for a seat on the Board of Directors of the Mifflin County School District. Morse was advised by the Civil Service Commission that an employee of a library receiving funds under LSCA is subject to the Hatch Act. Although the law excludes educational institutions, the Commission ruled that, for purposes of the Hatch Act, a public library is not an educational institution.

STATE ACTIVITIES

At the state level the most significant legislative action continued to be in the area of state aid for public libraries. California librarians experienced a stunning legislative victory in the passage of S.B. 792. The law is designed to encourage the sharing and coordination of library resources and services between library systems, state reference centers, and specified libraries. It provides grants and reimbursements to library systems that meet qualifying conditions and also makes provision for upgrading services to underserved residents. The act calls for the establishment of state reference centers to handle reference requests that cannot be met by systems and libraries participating in programs authorized under the act. It also provides for the creation of a computerized bibliographic data base to facilitate the location of information and library materials. The governor approved an appropriation of $5,300,000 for FY 1978-79.

On July 6, the governor of Oregon signed into law the first bill providing state aid to public libraries in the history of that state. Climaxing a six-year campaign by the Oregon Library Association, the new law empowers the State Library to administer an appropriation of $300,000 for developing and extending public library service. Grants are made available to any unit of local government, with the provision that such units may not reduce their existing support for library operating expenditures.

State appropriations were increased in a number of other jurisdictions. The Alabama legistature voted $2,000,000 for public library service, lifting state aid from $.18 to $.31 per capita. Michigan won a $2,500,000 increase in state aid, bringing the state's total to more than $7,000,000, the highest in its history. Maryland's program of per capita aid to public libraries was substantially increased. Its public library building incentive aid was also strengthened from a 1977 total of $28,139 to $94,816 for 1978.

The Massachusetts Board of Library Commissioners proposed legislation for the second time to transfer the Bureau of Library Extension from the Department of Education to the Secretary of Educational Affairs. Although the measure was previously opposed by the Massachusetts Library Association, it now has the support of the group. The purpose of the move would be to give the Board greater freedom and control in carrying out its statutory responsibilities. The Connecticut State Library is currently faced with a governmental reorganization scheme in which the State Library would be placed under the jurisdiction of the Department of Education. The State Librarian is opposing the move. At its annual meeting the National Federation for the Blind passed a resolution urging that library service programs for the blind be removed from the jurisdiction of state library agencies and be transferred to government agencies that provide total service for the blind.

Bills were introduced in the legislatures of Illinois and Ohio to afford greater security for library collections. The bills are an adaptation of already existing shoplifting statutes. The Illinois bill makes library theft a separate and distinct crime. It also permits any library agent or employee who has reasonable grounds to believe that a person has committed library theft to detain that person for purposes of investigation and, if necessary, to turn the offender over to the police. It also provides the library agent or employee with a legal defense against civil actions that may arise out of such detention. Two other states, New York and Iowa, are considering introducing similar legislation.

Librarians from the San Diego Public Library filed a complaint with the city's Equal Employment Investigative Officer. It was claimed that there exists a disparity in pay between library classifications and other professional positions requiring similar levels of education and experience. This situation, it is charged, is a subtle form of discrimination in which salaries for professional librarians are depressed because these positions have been historically held by women. A similar complaint has been filed with the Equal Employment Opportunity Commission by librarians employed at Temple University. The same argument is made that librarians are paid lower salaries because they work in a "women's profession."

A ruling of the North Carolina Supreme Court in 1977 attracted national attention of librarians, archivists, collectors, and manuscript dealers. Two Colonial bills of indictment, dated 1767 and 1768 and signed by William Hooper, who later was one of the signers of the Declaration of Independence, appeared in a catalog issued by B. C. West, Jr., a manuscript dealer. Upon learning that the documents were in the possession of West, the North Carolina Division of Archives and History filed a suit against him, requesting the court to order the return of the document to the Division. The plaintiff contended that it was the lawful custodian of public records in the State of North Carolina and that it possessed the right of ownership of all public records that had not been officially discarded.

The lower court ruled in favor of the defendant, but the North Carolina Court of Appeals reversed the decision. West appealed to the Supreme Court of North Carolina, which upheld the Appeals Court decision. The Supreme Court held that the statute of limitations does not run against the state as argued by the appellant. Furthermore, the court would not accept the argument that the documents were discarded. The court stated, "The fact that other, contemporaneous records of the Superior Court of Justice of the Salisbury District still remain in the possession of the State tends to negate the supposition of the defendant that the documents here in question were intentionally discarded." The case has caused concern that the decision may serve as a precedent for placing the burden of proof on the private owner of a public record to prove that the document in question was officially discarded.   ALEX LADENSON

Law Libraries

Statistics and a proposed reorganization of the Law Library of the Library of Congress were concerns of the law library community during 1977. Copyright revision, of course, was also of primary interest to all librarians, and law librarians collaborated on the matter with other library organizations through the Council of National Library Associations.

Law School Libraries. The American Bar Association (ABA) annually requests approved law schools to report the total number of volumes of law and related books held at the end of the fiscal year. This questionnaire has been a matter of contention between law school librarians and the ABA because it did not provide for inclusion of microform material holdings in the total count of the reporting library. The Executive Committee Regulations of the Association of American Law Schools state that "... each volume reproduced in micromaterials should count as a volume on the same basis as if reproduced in book form." Materials for which there is no readily ascertainable book equivalent are generally accounted for by law librarians on the basis of eight microfiche being equivalent to one volume and one roll of microfilm for five volumes.

In 1977 for the first time, the ABA acceded to the law librarians' demands and released a listing to law school deans of a volume count of law libraries that indicated the number of microform materials held by the libraries. The number of microform materials was added to the total count of volumes officially held by the libraries. Under the ABA standards, volume equivalents of microform materials will be based on 800 pages of original materials as equivalent to 1 volume. Original material in countable volumes will be included as volume equivalents.

As a result of this new development, law librarians are now seeking uniform standards for determining the total volume count of the holdings of law school libraries. The U.S. Office of Education, National Center for Educational Statistics, could play a significant role in this context by reaching agreement on a definition for "microforms."

Statistical Survey. The eighth annual survey of law school libraries appeared in the *Law Library Journal* (May 1977). Prior reports can be found in the May issues of the *Journal* for the appropriate years. Alfred J. Lewis, who compiled the statistics, reported that law library budgets and expenditures increased substantially over the previous year. The mean total budget of U.S. law libraries was $291,478 in 1975-76 and $337,870 in 1976-77—a 14 per cent increase. The mean total expenditures were $269,198 in 1974-75 and $304,818 in 1975-76—a 12 per cent increase.

The Salaries of head librarians were as follows:

The salaries of full-time professional law librarians (excluding heads) ranged from a high of $31,000, with fringe benefits of $2,350, to a low of $5,160, with fringe benefits of $717.

Directories. The American Association of Law Libraries (AALL) publishes a *Biographical Directory* of law librarians in odd years and a *Geographical Directory* in even years. The third edition of the *Biographical Directory* (1977) in 118 pages was available at year's end. The price was $5 for additional copies to AALL members (one copy distributed free to members) and $10 for nonmembers. The 1977 edition contains 1,220 biographies. The second edition, published in 1971, contained 733 entries.

The Directory of Law Libraries (1976) lists AALL members geographically. It also lists the librarian in charge, the names of supporting staff, the number of volumes, and the address and telephone number for each law library in the United States and in foreign countries.

Eventually both data bases will be interfaced and the information in them will be available in one volume on a more current basis. Both directories can be purchased from the AALL, 53 West Jackson Street, Chicago, Illinois 60604.

Law Library. An organizational change proposed by the Librarian of Congress, subordinating the Law Library of Congress to a newly restructured Research Services Department, has aroused the law library community to defiant opposition. In challenging the downgrading of the Law Library, law librarians throughout the nation protest that it is contrary to the intent of Congress as currently reflected in legislation in force. Law librarians have been denouncing the move not only to Daniel J. Boorstin, Librarian of Congress, but also to members of Congress. They stress that an obvious result of the reorganization would be a decline in the quality of the legal collection, loss of stature to the professional law library staff, and a downgrading of service to Congress.

The Law library community is particularly incensed by the manner in which the proposal was announced and point to its obscure origin. The report of the Law Advisory Group rejected the integration of the Law Library into the Research Services Department, and it was not recommended by the Librarian's own Task Force on Goals, Organization, and Planning or by any law library supervisor. The law library profession was given no opportunity to review the merits of the plan.

Law librarians are concerned not only that the national trend toward autonomy among law libraries in university library systems and elsewhere would be jeopardized by ending the departmental status of the Law Library but also that the move would increase the isolation of the Library of Congress within the law library community. It could even affect adversely the Librarian's purpose to provide "strong, enhanced, responsive service to the scholarly and research worlds" and a "new, expanded National Law Center and Library, called for by so many professional and advisory groups."

JULIUS J. MARKE

Libraries and Learning Resources, Office of

The Office of Libraries and Learning Resources (OLLR) continues to administer 10 library and educational technology programs. For FY 1978, Congress appropriated $277,212,000 for the operation of seven discretionary programs (HEA II-A; HEA II-B, Training; HEA II-B, Research and Demonstration; HEA II-C; HEA VI-A; Educational Broadcasting Facilities Program; and Educational Television and Radio Programming) and three state formula programs (ESEA IV-B; LSCA I; and LSCA III).

During 1977 it was announced that the regional library program officers would be reassigned to the Washington, D.C. office. A new program, Stengthening Research Libraries (HEA II-C), was added to the list of program responsibilities of OLLR.

Public Library Services. (Library Services and Construction Act, Title I; FY 1978, $56,900,000) When LSCA was enacted in 1956, 23 states had programs for statewide public library development, with expenditures amounting to $5,000,000. At the present time, 15 additional states, a total of 38, have grant-in-aid programs, with annual appropriations exceeding $100,000,000. Perhaps this is the best tribute to the role of LSCA as a federal catalyst.

In October 1977, Congress reauthorized LSCA (P.L. 95-123) with a special provision for the support of major urban libraries if the funding were to go above $60,000,000. That

Learned Society Libraries: see Independent Research Libraries

Legislative Activities, Federal: see Washington Report; Law and Legislation; Copyright

Legislative Service: see Library of Congress

Salaries of head librarians (fringe benefits are indicated in parentheses):				
Size of library involved		High	Median	Low
Small	(50,000 or less)	$23,000 (2,993)	$18,690 (1,439)	$13,394 (735)
Medium	(50,001-100,000)	$36,000 (5,417)	$22,979 (3,060)	$14,000 (1,166)
Medium-Large	(100,001-200,000)	$36,418 (6,161)	$27,500 (3,687)	$17,000 (1,956)
Large	(over 200,000)	$43,000 (7,665)	$34,000 (5,456)	$22,500 (2,150)

level was not reached with the FY 1978 congressional appropriations.

A second edition of *Library Programs Worth Knowing About,* prepared by the State and Public Library Services Branch of OLLR in September 1977, contains many fine examples of programs supported by LSCA in 34 states and territories. The publication is available from OLLR.

Interlibrary Cooperative Services. (LSCA, Title III, FY 1978, $3,337,000) Program data indicate that participation by all types of libraries in telecommunication or information processing systems has increased. Planning within states as well as multistate planning for coordination of library services has also increased to the level that approximately 7,500 libraries are involved in Title III projects.

Along with HEA II-B, Research and Demonstrations, the effectiveness of the programs is being evaluated by Applied Management Sciences under contract with the Office of Planning, Budgeting, and Evaluation of the U.S. Office of Education. The results were to be available early in 1978.

School Libraries and Learning Resources. (Elementary and Secondary Education Act, Title IV-B, FY 1978, $167,500,000) Title IV-B of ESEA continues to provide services to 12,551 local educational agencies through grants to states for school library and instructional resources, including guidance, counseling, and testing. States and local educational agencies have made a basically smooth transition from categorical legislation to the consolidated status of Title IV. Under the consolidated program substantial amounts are directed to local educational agencies that make a substantially greater tax effort for education than the state average and to those agencies that have the greatest proportion of students whose education imposes a higher average cost, e.g., low-income or rural students.

The program continues to provide funds to private as well as public schools. In 1977 more than 46,000,000 students were served by funds under the program, with approximately 10 per cent of the funds providing benefits to students in private schools.

An analysis of the impact of Title II of ESEA on the development of media standards—*Survey of School Media Standards* (Washington, D.C.: GPO, 1977)—is available from the program branch. Another publication—*Aids to Media Selection for Students and Teachers* (Washington, D.C.: GPO, 1976)—was revised to combine the 1971 edition and a supplement containing a selected list of bibliographies and journals that review books, periodicals, and audiovisual materials for elementary and secondary school instructional programs.

College Library Resources. (Higher Education Act, Title II-A, FY 1978, $9,975,000) Once again the appropriation for the HEA Title II-A program in FY 1977 provided for the minimal basic grant of $3,855. It was awarded to more than 2,500 institutions of higher education and other public and private nonprofit library institutions of higher education and other public and private nonprofit library institutions whose primary function is to provide library and information services to institutions of higher education on a formal cooperative basis. It was anticipated that the FY 1977 expenditure patterns would hold for the FY 1978 competition for the basic grant.

Library Research and Demonstrations. (HEA Title II-B, FY 1978, $1,000,000) The FY 1977 appropriation of $1,000,000 supported 19 Research and Demonstration projects that focused on the following priorities: support of studies and demonstrations of improved library service, particularly to groups and persons with special information needs; institutional cooperation; improvement in library methods and procedures; and improvement of library education. The *FY 77 Abstracts* (September 1977) describes these projects in detail and is available from OLLR.

Library Career Training. (HEA, Title II-B, FY 1978, $2,000,000) With $2,000,000 in FY 1977 funds the program supported 210 undergraduate and graduate-level fellowships and traineeships and 600 participants in institutes for skills retraining. The program has continued to contribute significantly to the training and recruitment of minorities, with 70 to 80 per cent of those involved in the programs listed as ethnic minorities.

Strenghthening Research Libraries. (HEA, Title II-C, FY 1978, $5,000,000) The competition for funds to improve and expand research collections and to encourage major research libraries to share these library resources with others was announced for the first time in October 1977.

Awards were to be made in the spring of 1978. The new law (P.L. 94-482) specifies that no more than 150 research library institutions may receive grants under this program in any given year. A reasonable effort must also be made to achieve a regional balance in the distribution of the awards to assure adequate resource sharing across the nation.

College Instructional Equipment (HEA, Title VI-A, FY 1978, $7,500,000) In FY 1977 825 grants were made to higher educational institutions for the purchase of instructional equipment. More than 200 of the grants were used for the acquisition of closed-circuit television equipment, materials, and attendant remodeling. These grants were made from state allocations determined by a formula based on higher education enrollment and per capita income. State commissions rank the applications and recommend the federal share, which cannot exceed 50 per cent of the total project cost.

Educational Broadcasting Facilities. (Communications Act of 1934, Part IV of Title III, FY 1978, $19,000,000) Since federal assistance has been made available under this program, 729 matching grants totaling $132,241,838 have been made for the acquisition and installation of noncommercial radio and television transmission and reception equipment. The program staff is currently monitoring the mandatory 10-year federal interest in 505 projects. Approximately 100 of these projects were awarded from FY 1977 funds. Eligible grantees are educational television and radio stations, higher educational institutions, a nonprofit entity operating a station, or a municipality operating a facility for noncommercial educational broadcasting. Grants made to eligible licensees are for up to 75 per cent of the cost of the equipment, with grant periods ranging from 6 to 30 months.

Educational Television and Radio Programming Support. (Special Projects Act, P.L. 93-380, Section 402, FY 1978, $5,000,000) The program provides contract or grant support for television programming, including the production, evaluation, dissemination, and utilization of programs such as "Sesame Street" and "The Electric Company." With a FY 1977 appropriation of $7,000,000, all but $2,000,000 went to Children's Television Workshop (CTW) for the support of these two children's programs.

In FY 1977 money not going to CTW went for the production of "Footsteps," the series on parent education; the production and evaluation of a series on the diversity of cultures called "The Storytellers"; work to upgrade 3 of 12 existing programs for KLRN-TV in Austin, Texas, on bringing multisensory perceptions to children 5 to 8 years old; and for the completion and dissemination of the "Music" series originally funded in FY 1975 and FY 1976.
ROBERT KLASSEN

Library Administration Division

The Library Administration Division (LAD) was organized and became an official unit of the ALA on January 1, 1957. In 1964 the ALA Council adopted a field of responsibility statement that provided an organizational framework for encouraging the study of administrative theory, for improving the practice of administration in libraries, and for identifying and fostering administrative skill. Toward these ends, the Division is responsible for all elements of general administration that are common to more than one type of library. These may include organizational structure, financial administration, personnel management and training, buildings and equipment, public relations, and relations with library governing bodies.

LAD Officers

PRESIDENT (July 1977-June 1978):
Richard L. Waters, Dallas Public Library

VICE-PRESIDENT/PRESIDENT-ELECT:
(to be elected)

EXECUTIVE SECRETARY:
Donald P. Hammer

Membership (August 31, 1977): 4,002 (2,242 personal and 1,760 organizational)

Sections and Goals. To accomplish its goals the Division is organized into five sections: Buildings and Equipment Section (BES), Circulation Services Section (CSS), Library Organization and Management Section (LOMS), Personnel Administration Section (PAS), and Public Relations Section (PRS). In addition, there is a Small Libraries Publication Committee charged with the responsibility of preparing publication materials for the guidance of personnel in small libraries.

LAD attempts to accomplish its purposes, for both the librarian and the layperson, primarily through educational services in programs, institutes, publications, committee work, and advisory services. It publishes a quarterly newsletter, the *LAD Newsletter*, that is sent to all members. It also sponsors two awards for excellence in two of its areas of concern. The annual John Cotton Dana Public Relations Award is sponsored jointly with the H.W. Wilson Company and is awarded to libraries that have developed excellence in their public relations programs. The American Institute of Architects—ALA Library Buildings Awards Program is held biennially and will be conducted in 1978.

In 1975 the ALA Council, the governing body of the Association, mandated through a new personal dues structure that all Divisions become financially self-sufficient no later than 1976-77. LAD accepted this challenge and immediately embarked on a program of self-study designed to improve the Division's program of service and governance. A Special Committee on Division Development, chaired by Don Wright, was appointed (see *ALA Yearbook 1977*, p. 189).

Recommended Action. The Special Committee's final report was accepted by the LAD Board during the 1977 Annual Conference. The report recommended several actions that are being carried out:

1. An ad hoc committee, chaired by Carolyn Snyder, is developing a formal orientation program.

2. An ad hoc committee, chaired by Joanne

Klene, is studying and making recommendations on all LAD programs and activities.

3. An ad hoc committee, chaired by Ralph Edwards, is studying the publishing needs within the Division.

4. Goals for headquarters staff development are being formulated by an ad hoc committee chaired by Frank Van Zanten.

5. A further study of the structure of LAD is being undertaken by an ad hoc committee chaired by Neal K. Kaske.

6. Communication with membership through the *Newsletter* will be strengthened by improving the delivery of the publication. The President, Editor, and Executive Secretary are at work on this matter, in cooperation with ALA Publishing Services.

In addition to these actions, all designed to be completed no later than the Midwinter Meeting in 1979, three additional planning committees have been formed in an effort to better address the needs of library administrators and managers. Nancy Wise is chairing a committee charged with the responsibility of developing plans for the establishment of a Middle Management Discussion Group. The Ad Hoc Network/Systems Administration Planning Committee, chaired by Jeanne Henning, is studying and analyzing what related activities, if any, are presently under way within the ALA. The Committee is also studying what LAD's relationship should be with current Association endeavors and what structural form LAD should develop. Plans for the establishment of a Women Administrators' Discussion Group are being developed by a planning committee cochaired by Kay Cassell and Sherrie Bergman.

The Small Libraries Publications Committee has been restructured, and a new editor of the series appointed. Under the direction of Mary E. Clark, Chairperson, and Elizabeth Ohm, Editor, the Committee anticipates the publication of two works shortly after the 1978 Midwinter Meeting in Chicago.

Future Plans. CSS, in cosponsorship with the Information Science and Automation Division, is holding a series of workshops dealing with automated circulation systems. The first program was held in Dallas in December 1977. CSS's report on fines and penalties was accepted by the Council at Detroit, and Council invited LAD to present a plan to carry out the research recommended by CSS. The plan will be presented in 1978. ALA Council also requested that the Division develop a vehicle for a model in-service training workshop on racism awareness. A PAS ad hoc committee, chaired by Mary A. Hall, is at work on the matter and expects to hold the workshop during the 1978 Annual Conference.

Recognizing the need for and importance of continuing education, the Division is planning a series of cassette tapes designed to focus on specific aspects of library administration. The tape scripts will be written by library practitioners and recorded by professional actors. In addition, LAD is studying the feasibility of developing a network of librarians who can quickly respond to brief questionnaires designed to determine the pulse of administrators on specific topics.

In 1978 LAD will again provide librarians with a meaningful range of program opportunities at the ALA Annual Conference. PRS will host a "Nuts & Bolts" preconference and will join the Chicago Public Library in cosponsoring a radio and television day of ideas. A second LAD preconference, sponsored by BES, will focus on library building and energy conservation. During Conference week, LOMS will feature "Budgetary Planning for Libraries," and PAS will study "Hidden Dollars: Your Fringe Benefits." A look at shared facilities—school, public, and community college libraries operating under one roof—will be the topic of the LAD program.

Meaningful programs, a renewed small libraries publication series, and an increase in membership—such features indicate a bright picture for the Division.

LAD joins the Association in mourning the passing of Betty Fast, who had just been elected President of the Division. Her death was a loss for all librarianship. We will miss her leadership, her vision, and her dedication. *See* Obituaries.   RICHARD L. WATERS

Library Education Division

Activities. Concern for library education reached a new dimension within ALA during 1977. After much soul-searching, heated debate, and long deliberations that included membership input, the Library Education Division (LED) Board developed a proposal for restructuring the activities and policymaking channels for those involved with and interested in library and information science education and training at all levels. LED suggested—and the ALA Executive Board and Council seemed to concur—that, if education is a priority of ALA, perhaps an alternative structure that would not compete with a single type of library or activity Division should be developed.

Using this premise, the LED developed a formal proposal that was discussed within meetings of the Divisions, published in the library press, and presented to the ALA Executive Board. The Board endorsed the concept in principle but referred it to the Committee on Program Evaluation (COPES) for consideration of the financial implications. Based on the COPES report, the Executive Board voted to recommend to Council that no action

Library Education Division

be taken on the proposal until there had been staff input to the Board and to Council. After lengthy discussion, Council passed a motion to take no action at the 1977 Midwinter Meeting.

During the spring of 1977, members of the LED Board met with the ALA Executive Director and Associate Director. Slight revisions were made on the proposal to prepare it for presentation to Council at the Annual Conference in Detroit. On June 17 Council voted to approve the proposal. This was the first step in a two-step process that requires Council to vote at two consecutive sessions in order to dissolve a Division. The second vote of Council was to be taken at the 1978 Midwinter Meeting.

Briefly stated, the proposal reflects the following premises:

1. The ALA should speak out at the national and international levels on matters related to the preparation of library personnel with a voice that reflects the needs, interests, and concerns of all kinds of libraries and all levels of library staff;

2. Library education represents an Association interest at a different level of magnitude than do the typical interests of the Divisions since there is no aspect of librarianship that is not affected by library education;

3. A library education unit should not be in competition with other units at the structural level but should be organized so as to permit all of the others to contribute to policy decisions that deal with preparation for quality library service;

4. The focue should be broad, not narrow, representing not simply a single interest within librarianship or a single group of librarians;

5. Library education involves the whole profession and not just educators for the profession. Any new structure should provide a forum and meeting place for all library personnel who are interested in or affected by the nature and quality of education or training for library service;

6. The new structure should have the capacity to coordinate and rationalize the many viewpoints and recommendations in order to avoid unnecessary duplication and to assure effective progress toward the achievement of profession-wide goals.

The plan for reorganization is as follows:

1. The Library Education Division would be phased out on January 31, 1978, and replaced by a Standing Committee on Library Education (SCOLE);

2. Membership participation in matters relating to library education and training will be made through committees on library education within Divisions or other units of the Association;

3. The liaison between membership and the Standing Committee will be provided by a Library Education Assembly made up of representatives of each of the units mentioned above; and

4. Staff liaison and support will be provided by the Office for Library Personnel Resources during the first year of planning.

LED Officers

PRESIDENT (July 1977-June 1978):
Robert D. Stueart, Simmons College, Boston

VICE-PRESIDENT/PRESIDENT-ELECT:
Annette L. Phinazee, North Carolina Central University, Durham

EXECUTIVE SECRETARY:
Margaret Myers

Membership (August 31, 1977): 1,757 (605 personal and 1,152 organizational)

Programs. Major Division programming during the 1977 Annual Conference, June 17–22, included the LED program entitled "Testing or Training." After a three-person panel discussion, current students, new graduates, professional and preprofessional staff members, library educators, library administrators, and personnel experts expressed their interest and concern over different aspects of the topic. The session was taped and is available from ALA.

Guadalupe Carrion Rodriguez from the Office of Science and Technology of the Mexican government was the Carl Milam International Lecturer sponsored by the International Library Education Committee of LED. She lectured at several library schools during October.

The Continuing Education Committee sponsored a program on "Cost Considerations in Continuing Education and Staff Development." The Training of Library Supportive Staff Committee cosponsored a program on "Training Programs and Classification Plans for Library Supportive Staff." The Committee on Education for Resources and Technical Services, a joint LED/Resources & Technical Services Division committee, sponsored a program on "Education of Librarians for Serials Management Positions."

With the Office for Library Personnel Resources and the Library Administration Division, LED co-sponsored a preconference on "Effective Personnel Utilization: LEPU Guidelines and Principles." The Interdivisional Committee on Education for Health and Rehabilitation Library Services, a joint LED/Health and Rehabilitative Library Services Division (HRLSD) committee, cosponsored a program on "Information Concerning the Rights and Opportunities of the Handicapped Citizen."

The Education for Information Science and Automation Committee, a joint Information Science and Automation Division/LED committee, sponsored a "Conference on Education for Information Science: Strategies for Change in Library School Programs" at the School of Library and Information Science, State University of New York at Albany, April 24–25. The Committee on Education for Health and Rehabilitation Library Services, a joint LED/HRLSD committee, sponsored a workshop on "Serving Special Populations—Strategies for Inclusion" at the Library of Congress on January 30.

Publications. The annual LED directory, *Financial Assistance for Library Education*, was published with the assistance of an H. W. Wilson Foundation grant. The second edition of *Directory of Library Science Librarians*, compiled by the LED librarians of the Library Science Collections Discussion Group, was also completed. The quarterly *LED Newsletter*, which gives advisory service and answers inquiries relating to library education, continued to be edited by the LED staff.

Awards. Russell E. Bidlack, Dean of the School of Library Science at the University of Michigan, was awarded the 1977 Beta Phi Mu Award which is administered by LED. The award was made for "distinguished service to the education for librarianship."

ROBERT D. STUEART

Library of Congress

At a gala event in May 1977 Librarian of Congress Daniel J. Boorstin told the black-tie audience gathered in the Library's Great Hall:

> Knowledge, which is our true commodity here, is unlike most other resources. It is nondepletable. You do not know any less because you give me what you know. The more widely knowledge is diffused, the most knowledge there is to diffuse, and the more speedily knowledge is increased. Knowledge grows as it is shared.

If there was a unifying theme for the first two years of a new administration at the Library of Congress, it was this idea—that the knowledge, the information, the talents, and the resources of the national library should be shared, that the Library should be opened up.

PLANNING FOR THE FUTURE

The beginning of 1977 saw the conclusion of a year of self-examination and analysis. On January 28 the final report of the Task Force on Goals, Organization, and Planning was transmitted to the Librarian, and a new Office of Planning and Development was established to act on the ideas stimulated by the Task Force and the eight outside advisory groups. Directed by Charles A. Goodrum, former Assistant Director of the Congressional Research Service, the Office set to work on a major reorganization of LC's administrative structure. A draft plan appeared on August 19, and it was expected to be completed early in 1978.

The Office simultaneously began analyzing the more than 100 specific suggestions that came out of the Task Force review and began organizing staff efforts to combat what Goodrum called the questions of "Why don't they ever do anything about . . . ?" High on the list is the Library's perennial problem of book delivery—the "not-on-shelf" phenomenon.

Under the guidance of Boorstin and Deputy Librarian William J. Welsh, the Library of Congress continued to expand its role as a center for scholarship and as a source of bibliographic leadership. Further emphasis was added to this purpose on September 12 when Carol Nemeyer, Senior Associate for Education and Library Services at the Association of American Publishers, joined the LC staff as Assistant Librarian for Public Education.

During 1977 the Library also engaged Erik Barnouw, the distinguished scholar of broadcasting, to assist in the design of an American Television and Radio Archive mandated by the revision of the copyright law. With Barnouw's counsel the Library was to begin collecting representative television news and feature films from copyright deposits and other sources when the new law took effect in January 1978. The intention of the Library is to create a record of this modern cultural medium that will complement other research collections and indexing projects already in existence.

Plans also progressed for a satellite reading room and reference center in the performing arts to be constructed on the top floor of the John F. Kennedy Center for the Performing Arts. Architectural specifications have been completed, construction is about to start, and purchase of resources has begun for this new facility. It will act as an introduction to and advertisement for the Library's extensive research collections in the arts.

ACQUISITIONS AND OTHER DEVELOPMENTS

The Library continued to acquire and catalog extensive research materials in all fields. The Research Department staff has nearly completed a comprehensive guide to the numerous special collections of the Library, which brought more than 112,000 visits by readers to these specialized divisions in 1977. The collections guide, which is the first comprehensive guide since 1949, is expected to be published in 1978.

In its role as a national cultural repository, LC added more than 1,000,000 pieces to its collections in 1977, including 321,879 volumes and pamphlets added to its shelves. The excep-

Library of Congress

tional items acquired, either by purchase or donation, included the following:

1. the Western Publishing Company's archival collection of Dell paperbacks;
2. an 800-volume collection on anarchy and radicalism in the United States, including many ephemera;
3. the complete microfilm of the Spanish newspaper *El Socialista*, published from 1886 until the fall of Madrid to Francisco Franco in 1939;
4. 1,500 three-dimensional maps from the Defense Mapping Agency and 18,500 Canadian fire insurance maps;
5. more than 3,000,000 manuscript pieces, including the personal files of former Vice-President Nelson Rockefeller pertaining to the Presidential Commission on CIA Activities in the United States.

Since World War II the Library of Congress has become a national center for the acquisition and cataloging of foreign materials, and today nearly a third of the Library's book collections are in languages other than English. In 1977 the Library purchased 558,771 pieces from abroad, including books, maps, newspapers, magazines, and other materials. In addition many more items were acquired through exchange agreements with foreign governments and institutions such as the Academica Sinica in Peking, with which an agreement was concluded through a personal visit to the People's Republic of China by a Library staff member.

In February LC held a "Workshop on Acquisitions from the Third World" at which specialists from libraries around the country pooled their information about publishing, distribution, and bibliographic problems in the Mideast, Africa, and Latin America. To provide better acquisitions assistance to other institutions LC also combined its foreign acquisitions reports in July into a single new publication, *LC Acquisitions Trends*, which discusses regional reports from staff, publishing trends, and Library acquisitions decisions.

Meetings and Conferences. While participating in a 1976 Bicentennial celebration in Ottawa, Librarian of Congress Daniel Boorstin suggested that annual meetings be held with the National Library of Canada to stimulate cooperation between the two national libraries. In March eight staff members from LC led by the Deputy Librarian met with their counterparts in Ottawa to discuss numerous topics of mutual interest including collection building, subject cataloging, automation, and reorganization. The Canadians were scheduled to journey to Washington, D.C., in March 1978.

The Library was also host to the fourth Assembly of State Librarians in May. At that meeting representatives of state library agencies worked with LC staff to develop better ways to share resources and talents and to establish a permanent working relationship between the national library and the state libraries.

Access and Automation. After several years of discussion the Library formally announced in November that it intends to stop filing new entries in its massive card catalogs on January 1, 1980, and thereafter to rely primarily on automated bibliographic records to provide access to its collections. Because automation of non-Roman scripts is not expected to be completed by that time, these materials will continue to be listed in a parallel manual catalog. By the end of 1977 virtually all Roman-alphabet languages had been added to the MARC data base, and the total number of verified records input since 1969 stood at 874,922. The Library's official card catalog, by contrast, included 24,820,570 cards, growing by 1,048,718 entries in 1977 alone.

Automation continued to spread through the Library's technical processing activities. The name authority list for English language and serials cataloging began to be automated in 1977, with the result that 9,500 new name authority records were made part of this emerging data base. The Library concluded an arrangement with the Government Printing Office (GPO) to work toward a common name authority file for government publications, and discussions were also held on the desirability of LC distributing GPO's *Monthly Catalog of Government Publications* on magnetic tape through the MARC Distribution Service.

Combating rumors that the Library of Congress intends to stop printing catalog cards for other libraries when it freezes its manual catalog in 1980, the Cataloging Distribution Service purchased a new Xerox 9200 nonimpact printer that will allow printing of cards within 5 days for any of the 6,300,000 non-MARC titles cataloged since LC began printing cards. In addition, the Library contracted for a major automated card printing system to produce cards from MARC tapes. These investments are evidence of the Library's intention to continue printing catalog cards so long as a need for them exists.

The Library's commitment to the development of a national bibliographic network was confirmed by the formal establishment of the Network Advisory Committee and two subcommittees that will give administrative and technical coordination to decisions of national import. The year saw the continuation of studies begun in 1976 on the organization and structure of a nationwide bibliographic network, including data base configurations (bibliographic, authority, and location files), hardware and software configurations needed at LC, pricing structures for access to LC records, and expansion of the existing computer-to-computer link with the Research Libraries Group to work in a bidirectional mode.

CATALOGING AND SERVICES

Decentralized cataloging was given a further boost in 1977 with the publication by the International Federation of Library Associations (IFLA) of the international MARC format (UNIMARC) and the launching of a pilot project to test the concept of "centers of excellence" in which libraries with specialized collections will catalog items and convert these records to machine-readable form for contribution to the national data base. Northwestern University, the first pilot participant, will convert its *Joint Acquisitions List of Africana* to machine-readable form using Library of Congress standards and files in a combination of on-lilne and off-line procedures.

The Library's serials cataloging increasingly represents the equivalent of a national bibliographic source record. In 1977 the Library cataloged a total of 11,779 serials titles, adding to an active serials file of well over 100,000 titles. The CONSER data base, the cooperative effort to build a machine-readable data base of serials cataloging, is currently maintained by the Ohio College Library Center (OCLC) and contains some 165,000 cataloging records of which 55,000 have been verified by either LC or the National Library of Canada. In August LC began putting the descriptive cataloging for serials into the CONSER data base to speed up the availability of at least a partial cataloging record.

Steady progress was also made in other areas of cataloging in 1977. The Joint Steering Committee for the Revision of the Anglo-American Cataloging Rules concluded its work in August on the second edition, leaving to the Library staff the preparation of the final manuscript for publication. The 19th edition of the *Dewey Decimal Classification* was completed with the submission of 2,700 manuscript pages to the printer. The Cataloging in Publication Office processed 26,484 titles from 1,500 publishers, which represented 64 per cent of U.S. titles published (with many of the remainder out of the scope of library collections).

The *National Union Catalog: Pre-1956 Imprints*, which has been in production since 1967, was 80 per cent complete by the end of the year. On September 30, the end of the fiscal year, editing had reached "Stapleton, England." At that point 9,277,652 cards had been processed and 525 of the projected 610 volumes (minus 4 volumes that contain entries under "Bible") had been sent to subscribers.

Preservation. The Library has for many years taken the lead in developing technology for paper and book preservation. In hopes of enlisting national support in an area of critical cultural concern, in late 1976 the Librarian established a National Preservation Program Office to coordinate the battle against paper deterioration. In June 1977 a six-person committee representing the Library and institutions with technical expertise in book preservation was appointed to assist the Office in designing a national program. Work is proceeding on the project, and an early goal of the Office will be automation of the *National Register of Microform Masters*.

In a somewhat different aspect of preservation, through the American Folklife Center the Library extended its help to several state organizations wanting assistance in preserving local folk arts. In addition to lending sophisticated recording equipment to six states, the Center assisted the Illinois Arts Council in assessing ethnic traditions in Chicago and carried out a six-week prototype inventory of folk habits in eight south Georgia counties during the summer.

Copyright. The Copyright Office, having shepherded through Congress the first revision of the copyright law since 1909 (PL 94-553, signed by President Gerald Ford on October 19, 1976), spent much of 1977 undergoing massive reorganization in preparation for substantial new duties on January 1, 1978. As an indication of public concern over the effect of the new law, the Office experienced a 25 per cent increase in telephone calls and written inquiries about copyright matters, answering 47,235 letters and 66,000 calls.

Research and Service. The Library of Congress is an enormous reference machine. In 1977 its staff responded to more than 50,000 letters and 110,000 telephone calls from private individuals and libraries seeking research and reference assistance. More than 220,000 books were loaned; most of them went to Congress, but 29,067 items went to out-of-town libraries on interlibrary loan. To improve services to the blind and physically handicapped the Library opened two new multistate service centers providing materials to library networks in the Northeast and the Midwest, thus completing nationwide coverage through regional centers.

The Congressional Research Service, which is perhaps the largest reference operation in the world, answered 295,635 inquiries from members of Congress and their staffs and undertook 1,077 major research projects with a stress on interdisciplinary approaches to public policy problems.

Despite a necessary preoccupation with the mechanics of survival, libraries are guided by a larger purpose—the transmission of human experience through the printed word. To reinforce this sense of mission, on October 20 the Librarian called together 45 leaders from the worlds of publishing, bookselling, and libraries to establish a Center for the Book in the Library of Congress. Authorized by PL 95-129 (signed by President Jimmy Carter on October 13, 1977), the Center is dedicated "to the continued study and development of written record as central to our understanding of ourselves and our world."

This article is based on draft chapters of *The Annual Report of the Librarian of Congress for the Fiscal Year Ending September 30, 1977*. All statistics are for the fiscal year October 1, 1976 to September 30, 1977.

CHRISTOPHER WRIGHT

The Center for the Book

The Center for the Book at the Library Congress was established on October 13, 1977, when President Jimmy Carter signed PL 95-129. At a planning meeting held at the Library of Congress a week later, Librarian of Congress Daniel J. Boorstin described why the Center was needed and why it should be at the Library of Congress:

"You may wonder why the Library of Congress, which, of all places on earth, is a center for the book should not become a place for the establishing of *The Center for the Book*. It is to organize, focus, and dramatize our nation's interest and attention on the book, to marshal the nation's support—spiritual, physical, and fiscal—for the book.

"The Times call for it. Why? Because this is a multimedia, electronic, media-ridden, annual-model age.

"The Place is here. This institution has a greater vested interest in the book than any other place on earth. For us, the book is not only a vested interest but a vested idea. Because we at the Library of Congress collect knowledge and entertainment resources in all media—in film and on tape, on phonograph records and on motion pictures, in manuscsript, from radio and television, on maps—as well as in books, and we have the world's great collections in these media; because we are the greatest copyright deposit in all formats; because we collect in all languages (468 at the last count!); because we have been doing this for 177 years, and will go on for more centuries. Because of all this, we know, better than anyone else, the dangers of the book being stifled, drowned, suffocated, buried, obscured, mislaid, misunderstood, ununderstood, unread—both from neglect and from the rising level of the increasing flood. Because we do serve the Congress, whose interests know no bounds, because we serve all libraries, scholars of all sorts and conditions, teachers, readers, quasi-readers, semi-readers, and even, we suspect, non-readers.

"As the national library of a great free republic, we have a special duty and a special interest to see that books *do not* go unread, that they *are* read by all ages and conditions, that books are not buried in their own excess, under their own dross, not lost from neglect nor obscured from us by specious alternatives and synthetic substitutes. As the national library of the most technologically advanced nation on earth, we have a special duty, too, to see that the book is the useful, illuminating servant of all other technologies, and that all other technologies become the effective, illuminating acolytes of the book.

"The Library of Congress is our mission headquarters, but we hope and expect to train and encourage missionaries all over our nation. Unlike some other missions, this mission is explosively ecumenical. No other mission can be more ecumenical. For the book is the most conservative and the most liberal, the most traditional and the most revolutionary of media, the most atheistical and the most reverential, the most retrospective, and the most futuristic. It is our duty to keep that mission energetically alive. The book is the reservoir of all the ideas that we have forgotten, and will be the reservoir for ideas still unborn.

"Today we are here, encouraged by our Congress and our President, hosted by the greatest library on earth, to find ways to fill the special needs of our time and our nation, to seize the opportunities I have suggested, to find new opportunities, and to keep ourselves ready for still newer opportunities. Here we shape plans for a grand national effort to make all our people eager, avid, understanding, critical readers. To make this age, this nation, and this place the staging ground for a Renaissance of the Book."

Forty-three persons from various parts of the United States attended the planning meeting. They represented many segments of the book world—authors, publishers, booksellers, librarians, scholars, and readers. Participants helped the Library define major areas of concern for the Center, which include the book in modern society, authorship, the book as a physical object, publishing and bookselling, libraries and book use, reading, and international book programs. The Center will be privately funded.

JOHN Y. COLE

Library Press

The four major general monthly periodicals in the library field reported the following average paid circulation figures for the year 1977:

- School Library Journal 40,834
- American Libraries 38,167
- Library Journal 31,518
- Wilson Library Bulletin 28,521

After three years of issuing *School Library Journal* separately from its parent publication *Library Journal*, R.R. Bowker made *SLJ*'s autonomy official with a masthead change. As of December 1977, Lillian Gerhardt was the only editor in chief listed. Previously, *SLJ* had also carried th name of *LJ*'s editor in chief, John Berry, as editor in chief of *LJ/SLJ*.

In the spring of 1977, Audrey Eaglen became the sole editor of the ALA publication *Top of the News*, the official journal of the Young Adult Services Division and the Children's Services Division (now the Association of Library Service to Children). *TON* had previously had two editors, one from each division.

New Features. Several new features were added during 1977 to the regular monthly coverage of the library field. *Library Journal* introduced a new series, "The Practicing Librarian," in October. Reporting that readers had asked for more practical advice and suggestions from the field, *LJ* explained, "The library magazines do not provide much of this kind of material, and yet it should be one of their primary functions." Opening with an article on "CB Radio in the Library," by Orange (California) Public Library Intern Pat Partovi, the series was designed for library practitioners "to share that new program, a solution to an old problem, or to tell how any old or new idea worked, or didn't work, in your library."

American Libraries launched an international news department in September with editor Art Plotnik's firsthand report on libraries in Bolivia, "Born Again in the Andes." This was followed in October by coverage of the British Library Association's Centennial celebration and in December by a review of the 50th anniversary meeting of the International Federation of Library Associations and Institutions (IFLA) held in Brussels in September.

The Year's Top Story. By all accounts, the story of the year in 1977 was the controversy surrounding the release by ALA's Intellectual Freedom Committee (IFC) of its film *The Speaker*. In March, long before the film was issued, *Wilson Library Bulletin*'s Harriet Rosenfeld reported on the film's story line as presented at the Midwinter Meeting. Previewing the plot, she asked, "And what the devil does the IFC film have to do with libraries, anyway?" Subsequent reporting on the issue would echo this question and raise others. (*See also* Intellectual Freedom.)

Another example of the library press's participation in *The Speaker* debate occurred in June, when *LJ*'s John Berry recounted his impressions of the film after a viewing at the spring ALA Executive Board meeting in Chicago. Calling the film "provocative, almost compelling," he was deeply critical of the underlying point of view and titled his editorial "A Whimper for Freedom."

Reporting on the film's premiere and the emotional response to it took precedence in the library press's coverage of ALA's Annual Conference in Detroit. *LJ* devoted a separate section of its Conference account to what it called "The Debate Nobody Won." In September *Wilson Library Bulletin* printed ALA President Clara Jones's "Reflections on The Speaker," and in October *AL* ran an article by Dorothy Broderick on the subject, along with shorter pieces by other ALA observers. Letters to the editors of all of the library magazines reflected the controversy from before the film's release through the year's end.

Library Reviewers. An interesting sidelight of library press activities in 1977 was the use of library book reviewers in publications geared for the general public. Bowker's new *Book Views* magazine draws from the 10,000 reviews printed in *Library Journal* and *Publisher's Weekly*. Intended as an alternative to bookstore-oriented, best-seller reviews in the mass media, *Book Views* will make some 3,000 reviews a year available to the general reader.

According to *Library Journal*, Bowker designed *Book Views* to be of use to libraries in several ways. "Libraries can sell it, give it away, or just make it available in quantity for browsers to borrow, and in this way bring the serious reader into the book selection process in a way convenient to him and the librarian." Library bulk orders for *Book Views* will get a discount from the jobber handling the account.

Another book review medium prepared by library professionals is ALA's "About Books" column syndicated by Newspaper Enterprise Association and distributed weekly to 575 daily papers in the United States. The majority of the papers that regularly use "About Books" have circulations of less than 50,000. The column thus provides a regular reviewing mechanism for papers that previously offered book coverage irregularly, if at all. "About Books" also serves several large urban papers—for example, Detroit, Cincinnati, and San Antonio.

Each "About Books" column covers from two to five books on a single theme. Adult fiction and nonfiction are highlighted in most of the columns, with one column a month devoted to children's books. Both libraries and book stores have reported requests for the titles reviewed in "About Books."

Prizes and Awards. The first winners of the two-year *American Libraries* $1,000 prize article competition—financed with the 1976 J. Morris Jones/Bailey K. Howard/World Book Encyclopedia/ALA Goal Award—were announced in 1977. The Round I winners of $1,000 were Lawrence and Ruth McCrank. Their article on the Portland-Multnomah County (Oregon) Library levy, "How a Levy Was Won in the West," was published in November's special "money" issue of *American Libraries*. Lawrence McCrank is Assistant Professor at the University of Maryland's College of Library and Information Services, and Ruth McCrank has had library experience in Portland and elsewhere.

The Round II winner was Richard de Gennaro, whose "Copyright, Resource Sharing, and Hard Times: A View from the Field" appeared in the September *American Libraries*. De Gennaro is Director of the University of Pennsylvania Libraries. Round III was won by Pauline Wilson, Assistant Professor at the University of Tennessee Graduate School of Library and Information Science. Her survey of the roles of librarianship and ALA in the postindustrial society is scheduled for publication in 1978.

The 1977 winner of the H.W. Wilson Library Periodical Award was *Utah Libraries*, edited by Blaine H. Hall.

ELIZABETH PRYSE MITCHELL

Library Research Round Table

The Library Research Round Table (LRRT) was established in 1968 to promote and improve research in library and information science. During 1977 the Round Table continued its established programs and embarked upon several new programs and activities.

At LRRT's Annual Conference program for ALA's general membership, Ferdinand Leimkuhler of Purdue University spoke on "Operations Research: Applications to Library Management." The program has brought to ALA outstanding researchers whose work is of special interest to library and information scientists. The 1976 speaker was Manfred Kochen of the University of Michigan; and the 1975 speaker, Lee Bolman of Harvard University.

Another established component of LRRT's Annual Conference programming is the Research Forum Series, which usually presents five forums, each consisting of several papers on related topics. Charles Curran of the University of South Carolina College of Librarianship was the coordinator of the 1977 series. Forum I, moderated by William E. McGrath, considered techniques for assessing library performance; the presenters were Chai Kim, Edward T. O'Neill, and Edward Johnson. Forum II also focused on research methodologies and featured papers by Esther Dyer on the Delphi technique and R. Kent Wood on fault tree analysis. Moderated by John F. Harvey, Forum III highlighted research activities related to index and periodical use, presented by Charles W. Conaway and W. M. Shaw, Jr. Forum IV's theme was library networks with presentations by K. Leon Montgomery, Henry C. Chang, and Bonnie Isman; the Forum was moderated by Bernard Schlessinger. Ernest R. Deprospo, Jr., moderated Forum V, which featured the work of Masae Gotanda on statewide efforts to develop effectiveness measures for public libraries.

LRRT Officers

CHAIRPERSON (July 1977-June 1978):
Jane Robbins, Louisiana State University, Baton Rouge

VICE-CHAIRPERSON/CHAIRPERSON-ELECT:
Charles H. Davis

SECRETARY-TREASURER:
James D. Sodt

Membership (August 31, 1977): 813

Continuing its policy to cooperate in research activities with other units both inside and outside of ALA, the Round Table cosponsored research programs of the American Association of School Librarians, the Children's Services Division, and the Statistics Coordinating Committee of the Library Organization and Management Section of the Library Administration Division.

In the third year of the Round Table's Annual Research Competition $400 awards were made to Robert W. Burns, Jr., Colorado State University, for his paper on "Library Performance Measures" and to Herbert S. White and Karen N. Hasenjager, Indiana University, for their study of "Some Measurements of the Impact of the Rapid Growth of Library Doctoral Programs." The 1978 Research Competition Award was increased to $500. The winners of the Research Competition will present their papers as a 6th forum in the 1978 Research Forum Series.

Beginning with the 1977 papers, the Round Table will publish an *Annual*, consisting of the papers delivered at its membership program, in the Research Forum Series, and from the Research Competition. The program, under the direction of Ellen Altman, Publications Committee Chairperson, will further LRRT's purpose of promoting and improving library and information science research. The Round Table has become a sponsor of *Information*

Science Abstracts and has embarked upon plans to begin a library and information research newsletter for its membership.

Of interest to the profession, because of the increased awareness of the need for continuing education in library and information science, are the plans of the Round Table to begin a series of regional continuing education workshops in library research. The first workshop is expected in early 1979.

JANE ROBBINS

Literacy Programs, Library

The activities of 1977 in library literacy programs indicated the persistency, pervasiveness, and complexity of the problem; the challenge to librarians to provide leadership; the need to provide training; and the development of new as well as the extension of existing programs in libraries.

Literacy and Illiteracy. The attempts to define and measure illiteracy, functional illiteracy, and degrees of literacy among children, youth, and adults of all ages continue. The numbers in the United States are estimated at between 21,000,000 and 57,000,000, depending on the population included. There are an estimated 1,000,000,000 illiterate people in the world. The figures shock and challenge everyone concerned.

Definitions of literacy and illiteracy continue to demand attention. Readability is no less easily or firmly defined. Both the content of and the methods for teaching the elements of literacy (including abilities such as speaking, listening, reading, writing, and computation) vary. Included are a range of subjects and various techniques that are more or less successful. The controversy continues about the importance of professional knowledge and skill as opposed to the human attributes of empathy, patience, respect, and understanding.

As the need expands for people to become literate and as that need is recognized, more people are being urged to help. Various programs, resources, and methods multiply. The number of persons, agencies, and organizations that are becoming involved in the effort increases. They include a large number of students, teachers, librarians, reading specialists, community and government organizations and agencies, professional and volunteer associations, and occupational groups.

Daniel Fader, author of *The New Hooked on Books*, continues to fling down the gauntlet in his unequivocal challenge to librarians to become leaders in the effort to produce a literate reading population. Librarians must interfere and intervene in homes, classrooms, and communities, Fader claims. They must help people to understand the importance of library resources. They must demonstrate how essential the knowledge of the past and the skills to acquire that knowledge are to the present and the future. In Fader's view, librarians must actively combat illiteracy among children and adults.

Nowhere has library activity and librarians concern about the literacy problem been more evident than in the 1977 programs of professional associations and in the many developing library services, materials, collections, and experimental projects. Literacy activities, sometimes as components of broader programs, have appeared under various titles: "reading development," "literacy," "adult learning," "adult basic education," "adult independent learning," "outreach," "parenting," "right-to-read," "advisory centers," and "learning centers."

Staff Training and Leadership. Training is carried out informally in association programs and library staff development programs and formally in literacy organization workshops and schools of library science.

At the 1977 ALA Annual Conference, programs and workshops related to literacy were conducted by the Young Adult Services Division, the Reference and Adult Services Division and its Services to Adults Committee, the Office for Library Service to the Disadvantaged, the Public Library Assocation, the American Library Trustee Association, and other groups. Several hundred librarians participated in these meetings. Significant aspects of involvement in literacy programs were discussed: rewards and problems in organizing literacy programs, selection and evaluation of materials, administrative ideas, visual literacy, training for volunteers, librarians as catalysts in lifelong learning, and America's millions of functional illiterates.

ALA has supported the national effort to promote literacy programs through publication of a manual for librarians and adult educators, *Literacy and the Nation's Libraries*, as well as other relevant guides. "Libraries Literacy Learning," a colorful poster proclaiming the Association's emphasis, is available to all libraries.

In November the New York Library Association provided opportunities for librarians to learn more about libraries' role in the literacy effort. The breadth of the concern and the range of library users to be served were shown in the subjects of the programs: "Where Were You When I Needed You?" and "'I Can't Read and You Didn't Understand" (Library Literacy Committee) and "The Library Media Specialists' Role in Teaching Reading" and "'Literacy and Public Libraries: A Natural Alliance" (Reference and Adult Services Literacy Committee).

Libraries also rely on other agencies for trained staff and for training. The Free Library of Philadelphia has contractual ser-

Literacy Programs, Library

Library Science: see Management, Library; Automation; Cataloging and Classification; Education, Library; Research; Reference Services; School Libraries and Media Centers; Standards; Serials; and Continuing Professional Education. Consult Index for specific topics.

Library Systems: see Networks

vices. Many libraries across the country have turned to such major literacy organizations as Laubach Literacy International, the Right-to-Read project, and Literacy Volunteers of America, Inc., for training library staffs and volunteers.

Programs and Services. These same agencies and many local groups collaborate with libraries in developing community literacy programs. For example, alliances are being formed between libraries and Literacy Volunteers of America in many communities. During 1977 approximately 20 libraries sponsored Volunteers programs and assisted nearly 800 new readers. Additional libraries have cooperated with the group's program by making available to the tutor and students a collection of low-level/high-interest materials. Some have provided space for tutoring and training workshops. Other libraries have spearheaded the establishment of Literacy Volunteers in their communities by providing a staff coordinator, telephone service, space, and public relations services. Several institutional librarians have been trained by the Literacy Volunteers staff, who have initiated tutorial programs in correctional and mental health facilities. One such program has been carried out in New Jersey's adult and youth correctional institutions under the auspices of the New Jersey State Library and the Garden State School District.

Throughout the United States the continued development of well-established programs and of creative new library programs is evident. Successful programs continue in libraries in Austin, Dallas, Denver, Forsyth County (North Carolina), Mt. View Public Library (California), New York City, New York State, Philadelphia, and Westchester County (New York). The New England states and Florida also have strong programs.

Ten such programs are described in *Library Programs Worth Knowing About*. The 10 programs are *Community Reading Development* (Library Extension Service, Arizona); *Target Children: Urban 5* (Connecticut State Library); *Literacy Volunteers of Southbridge* (Massachusetts); *Outreach to the Disadvantaged in Sunflower and Bolivar Counties* (Mississippi); *Adult Independent Learning* (Nassau Library System, New York); *Project Able: Adult Basic Library Education* (Columbus, Ohio); *News in Review*, a statewide Right-to-Read project in cooperation with the press (Oklahoma Department of Libraries); *Adult Learning Program* (Free Library of Philadelphia); *Forsyth County Public Library Children's Outreach* (Winston-Salem, North Carolina); and *English As a Second Language* (Nashville, Tennessee).

Materials. The Free Library of Philadelphia has pioneered special collections through its Reader Development and Life Coping (Survival) skills collections and its adult basic education and learning collections. The importance of a well-developed collection of materials on general and special subjects is evident. Through its newsletter *Pivot*, the program at the Free Library of Philadelphia continues to serve not only Philadelphia's adult educators and librarians but also librarians across the nation with critical evaluations of materials and news in adult basic education. The completely revised edition of *Reader Development Bibliography* was published in 1977 by New Readers Press. Supplements will be issued to review current materials.

HELEN HUGUENOR LYMAN

Management, Library

Continuing pressure from external forces appeared to grow increasingly stronger on library administrators during 1977. These external forces included increasingly aggressive library unions, local budget officials who insisted on zero-based budgeting or variations thereof, new legislation that affected public employee records and personnel transactions, and increasing pressure to investigate fee-based services.

In recent years there has been increasing emphasis on achieving greater effectiveness and efficiency within existing or declining library budgets. Although these pressures did not end in 1977, new factors became ever more important for library administrators to deal with.

Zero-based Budgeting. Zero-based budgeting, achieving new impetus because of President Carter's use of it on the federal level, placed another burden on both library administrators and staff members engaged in the budgeting process. Zero-based budgeting requires a significantly larger input of data and greater analysis of alternative decisions than does the more standard approach of budgeting by line item or program. The need for detailed data, together with the necessity of breaking library operations into so-called decision-making packages with many alternatives, requires more time by budget makers. Perhaps even more importantly, it requires a more thorough understanding of the pieces of the library operation than do other methods of budgeting.

Like other new techniques, however, many of the procedures for zero-based budgeting are similar to practices of the past but are dressed up in new terminology. The procedures do put more emphasis on specific detail than was previously required. In addition, new budgetary techniques are forcing library managers to a more thorough understanding not only of the practices and procedures of their own library but also of general accounting principles. Library managers need more specific financial and evaluation data in considering proposals for continuing or increasing service programs.

Participatory Management. Participatory management advocates proved once again in 1977 that the idea is not only not dead but that the demand for it is growing. Participatory management took many different avenues, including continuing agitation by unions. This was coupled with increasing demands by library staffs for additional in-service training and involvement, not only in the day-to-day operations of the library but also in long-range planning and in defining the goals and objectives of libraries. The Seattle Public Library, in cooperation with the University of Washington Library School, produced a significant study on staff development needs. The results of the Seattle study indicated an increasing concern by the staff for the need for better internal communication, increased supervisory skills, better understanding and involvement in the library's goals and directions, and more information on the budget philosophy of the library.

The study was perhaps only the tip of the iceberg in dealing with the general concerns of professional library staffs throughout the country. Indications are that more and more career library staff members feel they should have a greater role in the planning process and not simply in the delivery of service itself.

Increased union activity is another reflection of this trend and concern. Library unions achieved no overall significant gains in 1977, and one existing library union in Massachusetts even lost its recognition through court action. Nevertheless, union activity did increase. Much union activity was aimed not only at simply securing better salaries or working conditions but also at gaining a greater voice in the planning and development of the library service program.

Personnel Selection. Library hiring practices continued to come under attack in some quarters. There were the general problems of dealing with affirmative action quotas and goals—problems affecting all public and most private organizations. There was also increased questioning by both public officials and disgruntled employee applicants over the actual skills, education, and training needed for professional library positions. In addition to the continuing dialogue over the need for a library school degree in order to be appointed to a professional library position, the question was raised in 1977 whether any college degree should be a requirement for appointment to a professional library position. As a reflection of this concern, an intensive study was conducted in California, financed by the California State Library and a consortium of 13 public libraries, to deal with the entry-level skills required for beginning librarians. It can be anticipated that this study will be read with great concern by library administrators. But it will perhaps be studied with even more concern by library school faculties, because of the impact that the study results might have on library school education and library school students.

Fee or Free? The question of adopting fee-based services or of charging fees for existing services, at either existing or increased service levels, was again a major concern of many library administrators. Significant attention was paid to the issue at the ALA Annual Conference in June. As is often the case with such a controversial issue, there were significant arguments given by both those for and those against fee-based services, and there was no obvious resolution of the question. There is rising concern, among practicing librarians and library administrators, however, that, if fee-based services become prevalent, budgetary authorities will begin to look on the library as a self-supporting institution. If the fee-for-service process were continued to its logical conclusion, library services would be eliminated for the economically deprived members of society. This is an increasingly divisive issue among practicing librarians, and library administrators are often torn between their own professional desires and the increasing pressures from budgetary officials to generate more and more income from library services themselves. There is little doubt that increasing reliance on fees generated from library services might reach the point at which it would become more and more difficult to finance public services not supported in whole or in part from income received for those services. If that situation were to come to pass, the public library as a free institution open to all people regardless of their financial position would be threatened.

For a detailed analysis, see the feature article by Peter Watson in this volume on issues and questions concerning fee-based service.

Although not yet reaching the momentum found in some other public institutions, the trend toward contracting for management services continued in libraries. Library administrators began to view with both interest and concern the discernible tendency to contract for not only specific services (many of which, such as building maintenance or delivery service, had been contracted out in many parts of the country for many years) but also for the growing tendency in some areas to actually contract for management services.

There were specific examples in 1977 of libraries sharing chief administrators with other libraries or systems. The best-known of these shared service arrangements, however, was actually ended in 1977 when the incumbent left a position in which he was the director of a regional library system and also the director of two separate library members of that system. In that instance, the library director maintained two separate residences in order to hold his three-part administrative role. The procedure ended with the incumbent leaving for another position and both the system and the two separate libraries deciding to return to individual directorships. Nevertheless, based on some history in the Midwest, particularly where librarians have served not only as directors of a local public library but also as director of a regional system of which that library is a member, there will be increasing consideration by policymakers to explore dual administration or contract management. The practice has been done in hospitals, clinics, schools, and, to a limited extent, public libraries. As increasingly sophisticated management skills are needed for efficient library operation, this trend will perhaps develop in public libraries on a level not yet anticipated by most librarians.

Trend Pressures. There were no precedent-shattering developments in library management in 1977, but the erosion of the manager's traditional ability to control decision making continued with the increasing pressures of external legal and political forces and increasing staff involvement in management decisions. Such pressures extended even to such basic criteria as what qualifications are needed for professional staff positions. With increasing staff agitation, union development, official budgetary requirements, legislation limiting decision making and requiring more extensive public and private involvement in the decision process, library management becomes less desirable for many in the profession. Academic libraries have more and more involved university faculty members in library decision making. Increasing staff activity in management concerns is bringing this type of group decision making into play in the public library field. These events may well presage the end of the old-fashioned "director" who acts unilaterally. There may be an increasing need for managers trained not only in management skills but also in the dynamics of group participation and group action. The day of the authoritarian library manager seems ended.

ROBERT H. ROHLF

Measurement and Evaluation

In his speech to the ALA Council at the 1977 Midwinter Meeting, Executive Director Robert Wedgeworth cited major agenda items that the Association should press for immediately. The first was better statistics on library usage "... to provide accountability to the funders and users of libraries; to plan library programs; to manage libraries better and more efficiently." He went on to say that "such a statistical reporting system does not exist" and pointed out that "to date NCES [National Center for Educational Statistics] has not been able to implement a program that produces the needed data from all libraries on a regular and timely basis."

Studies and Grants. The federal government has been lackadaisical about improving its present and inadequate statistical reporting system; reports on public and school libraries since the 1970's became available only in 1977. There is great interest within the profession itself, however, in having a statistical reporting system that satisfies the three criteria Wedgeworth specified—accountability, planning, and more efficient management—a system that would measure and evaluate the quality of library services. In 1977 one new study to measure library effectiveness was begun; and another, designed to develop a broad-based statistical reporting system, was completed. A third study, completed nearly five years ago, continued to attract attention.

The Oklahoma State Library funded a study of "public library effectiveness" directed by Beverly Rawles of Battelle Memorial Institute. The focus of the research is an assessment of the financial, resource, and personnel needs of public libraries in the state. The results of this asssessment will serve as the basis for recommendations for a 10-year development plan for public libraries, including proposed changes in legislation and state aid. A large part of the study is devoted to interlibrary cooperation and includes a "satisfaction index for consolidated systems," an evaluation that the profession has badly needed for some time. The final report was to be presented at the Oklahoma Governor's Conference on Libraries in the spring of 1978.

In 1976 the U.S. Office of Education awarded a grant of $59,000 to the Western Interstate Commission on Higher Education to develop and demonstrate a statistical data base system for library and network planning and evaluation. Two documents pertaining to the study were issued in 1977—"Library Statistical Data Base Formats and Definitions" and "Commentary." The major categories of information to be collected are organizational characteristics, finance, personnel, facilities, activity measures, and user and client descriptors. The measures are basically of two types—inventories similar to the LIBGIS/HEGIS data of NCES with fine breakdowns within categories, and transaction counts like the number of volumes reshelved and the number of reference questions asked. Plans for the actual implementation of the data base system among libraries have not yet been clarified. The data base system calls for so much detailed information, however, that many libraries may be reluctant to participate.

Performance Measures. The performance measures techniques of Ernest De Prospo and Ellen Altman continue to be influential in assessing public libraries and were a major element in the recently completed Hawaii State Library study. The results were presented at the Library Research Round Table Research Forum Series at the 1977 Annual Conference by Masae Gotanda, Head, Research and Evaluation Services for the Hawaii State Library.

A 1977 publication by the Urban Institute and the International City Managers Association, *How Effective Are Your Community Services? Procedures for Monitoring the Effectiveness of Municipal Services*, draws heavily on the De Prospo and Altman techniques for the evaluation of local public libraries. Since this publication is aimed at local government officials, it will undoubtedly have an impact on their assessment of the quality of their own community libraries.

The Minnesota State Library Agency sponsored two workshops on "Performance Measures for Library Operations" in which Altman trained 100 participants in the techniques of data gathering and analysis, using the Minneapolis Public Library as a laboratory.

Performance measures are having an impact in Canada as well. During 1977 Ontario public libraries in Barrie, Richmond Hill, Markham, and Brampton conducted self-studies using the techniques. The public library and trustee divisions of the Canadian Library Association are sponsoring a performance measures program for the 1978 annual conference in Edmonton.

The most important publication of 1977 in the area of analyzing library performance was F. W. Lancaster's *The Measurement and Evaluation of Library Services*. This state-of-the-art monograph summarizes all of the major works written on measurement and evaluation for a wide variety of library services. The monograph is the first published on the topic that is suitable as a text for library school students. Perhaps its availability will spur library educators to begin offering courses in this vitally important area. Unless more people entering librarianship appreciate the importance of measurement and are trained in the techniques, real progress in developing more sensitive indicators that better evaluate service is a long way in the future.

ELLEN ALTMAN

Mediation, Arbitration, and Inquiry

In 1977 the Staff Committee on Mediation, Arbitration and Inquiry (SCMAI) received seven Requests for Action. Five of the requests related to public libraries, and two related to academic libraries. The complainants included librarians, trustees, and library patrons. The major complaints in these seven cases focused on such diverse problems as incomplete termination payments, dismissal without notice, dismissal without cause, dismissal without the authority to dismiss, and unfair library access practices.

In addition to the seven formal Requests for Action, SCMAI also received inquiries from nine other persons regarding the ALA Program of Action. These nine inquiries related to a variety of personnel problems in public, academic, and state libraries. One of the nine inquiries related to inadequacies in a contract for part-time employment.

Case Investigations. In 1977 the Committee continued work on the resolution of several cases that had been filed in 1976, as well as on cases filed in 1977. One of the more complex cases on which the Committee worked in 1977 centered on union representation of librarians. The complainant originally contended that the librarians' salaries were not being paid in accordance with the union contract. During the SCMAI investigation of this salary complaint, it became clear that there were serious problems in the case relating to both the collective bargaining structure of the institution and the representation of the librarians within the structure. (While this Request for Action investigation was ongoing, the union contracts of the institution were found to be null and void.) In the contract the status of the librarians was unclear, and the responsibility of the union to bargain for librarians was not understood in the same way by librarians, administrators, and union officials. The Committee has recommended to the concerned ALA unit that it work with all parties to recommend a future structure that will assure that librarians' rights are fully protected.

In one of the cases in which several complainants alleged unfair employment practices, the Committee was unable to resolve the problems through informal activities and recommended that a formal fact-finding inquiry be held. In this instance, all complainants decided that they preferred not to have an inquiry conducted, and SCMAI was unable to proceed further in helping to resolve the case.

Investigation into another case, in which lack of due process was alleged, determined that the employee was at fault in not confer-

Media Centers: *see* School Libraries and Media Centers. Consult Index for specific topics.

ring appropriately with the board. In this instance the Committee conferred with all concerned parties regarding termination pay and assisted the complainant in searching for a new position.

In one of the cases in which the complainant alleged that due process had not been afforded, the Committee recommended to the library board that a hearing be provided, and the legal counsels of the two principals arranged for such a hearing. The complainant has not requested further assistance.

In one of the cases an employee's contract had not been renewed. The librarian contended that he was being dismissed for unsubstantiated complaints of a former student, which the librarian believed were related to social or political activities. He also alleged that due process had not been afforded him to respond to complaints. The Committee assisted this complainant in having grievance procedures followed, and the case was resolved with his exoneration and reinstatement.

In the case alleging a lack of access to library materials there were questions of intellectual freedom, security of materials, and financial costs. In another case in which unwarranted dismissal was alleged, there were also questions of the availability of materials to the community. These cases were still in process at the end of 1977.

Formal Inquiries. A formal inquiry was held in the Request for Action by Rose Smith regarding her dismissal from Milton College. The complete report of that inquiry was published in *American Libraries* (January 1978). In brief, the conclusion of the inquiry was that the manner in which Smith was terminated was improper and unprecedented, that she was not a member of the faculty, that no adequate grounds for termination were found, and that she was denied due process. Four policies of ALA were violated: "Security of Employment in Libraries," "Standards for College Libraries" "Joint Statement on Faculty Status of College and University Librarians," and "Standards for Faculty Status for College and University Librarians."

A formal inquiry was also held in another Request for Action, but that inquiry had not yet been reported to the ALA Executive Board. That Request for Action alleged unwarranted dismissal by an agency without the authority to dismiss.

Summary. The Committee's 1977 activities again make clear the need for improvements in library personnel policies and practices, and the need for the expansion of libraries' attention to personnel administration. Detailed personnel policies and procedures are imperative for all libraries. Specific termination procedures are often lacking even though specific hiring procedures may have been developed. Adequate and reasonable notice of unsatisfactory performance is lacking in a very large portion of those personnel problems that come to SCMAI's attention.

In addition to these somewhat general problems, the Committee has noted that the increasing number of institutions with collective bargaining contracts makes it imperative that librarians determine how they (a relatively small percentage of the total employees of an institution or municipality) will be adequately represented in collective bargaining. It has also been noted that librarians do not always understand the impact of collective bargaining on their institutions and how its implementation affects their own status. Another problem that warrants increased attention is the need of some public library boards for a clearer understanding of their own responsibilities and authority and clarification of their relationships to municipal officials.

The Committee reiterates the need for libraries, library organizations, trustee organizations, and library schools to expand their attention to education and training in all areas of personnel administration and to observe the principles of intellectual freedom.

Requests for information about the ALA Program of Action should be sent to Robert Wedgeworth, Executive Director, ALA, 50 East Huron Street, Chicago, Illinois 60611.

RUTH R. FRAME

Medical Libraries

Certain years in the chronicles of Venerable Bede are labeled "annus mirabilis"—a wonderful year—a year in which many outstanding events occur. A new emperor is crowned; a comet is seen crossing the heavens; a terrible drought ruins the crops; there is peace throughout the kingdom. The year 1977 can be considered an annus mirabilis for medical librarianship because so *few* things happened. It was a year when most things were waiting resolution rather than starting or concluding—a "time between times."

The details by which the new copyright law's provisions were to be carried out remained unknown; data bases that would provide real data instead of bibliographic pointers to the data were still being promised but not produced; for the third year the President had not yet appointed a Board of Regents for the National Library of Medicine; the conceptual foundations of the widespread clinical librarian's program were still unstudied; and the Consumer Education Act, which might provide funds for medical information to laymen, had not yet had an impact. In addition, the Medical Library Assistance Act's future was still uncertain, with only a one-year extension of its authority so that the President could study the matter in depth. Altogether, an annus mirabilis indeed.

Two things did come to completion during 1977, however, and both are likely to have an impact. One was the actual start-up of the Bibliographic Retrieval Services (BRS). Founded by a group of medical librarians, the purpose of BRS is to bring down the cost of connect hours to commercially offered data bases and to have the data bases tailored to medical library needs. In addition, during 1977 an entirely new system of certification for medical librarians went into effect.

Retrieval Services. BRS had been in the planning stages for some years, but it was not until 1977 that the critical mass of subscribers was reached and that the founders were able to go directly to the producers of the data bases instead of through a commercial layer of middlemen. They were successful in purchasing the bases and offering them to subscribers at a substantial reduction in price from what the commercial companies charged. The savings did not necessarily imply that the commercial companies had been gouging their customers. BRS was able to use many volunteer workers, whereas Lockheed and System Development Corporation necessarily had to use well-paid staff members. Nevertheless, with the play of the marketplace against them, the commercial vendors had to reduce their prices in turn to be competitive with BRS, and medical libraries were the gainers in the long run. Whether BRS will be able to offer the same fringe services—such as manuals and training programs—that the commercial companies offered in the past and whether BRS will be able to continue obtaining such high-level volunteer work in the future remains to be seen.

Certification. Medical librarians have been one of the few library groups that has accepted certification voluntarily and from within—as opposed to school librarians, for example, whose certification is usually mandated by state and local hiring groups. Since the 1940's, when certification was first established by the Medical Library Association (MLA), it has been based primarily on previous schooling, with only an occasional equivalence examination for those whose education has been out of the normal stream. For some years MLA has been working toward a total revision of this scheme, with a mixture of schooling, examinations for all, and recertification through continuing education and/or examinations every five years. The difficulties in arranging a smooth transfer from the old system to the new made the planning complicated and time consuming. As a result it was not until 1977 that the old certification system came to a halt and the new one began. The first examinations, written by a committee of educators and practicing librarians, was administered in the spring of 1978. The results will be studied carefully to see whether any changes need to be made in either the basics of the plan or in the details of carrying them out.

After many advances in life, a pause for regrouping and for consolidation of gains is necessary. Such a pause can give time to understand the changes that have come about and to chart courses for the future. On the other hand, a pause after great advances may mean only that the imagination has faltered—that the concepts have come to their ultimate conclusion and that new ones need to be sought—or that the people involved are just plain tired. It would be a brash individual who could say definitively today what the annus mirabilis of 1977 means to the onward movement of medical librarianship.

ESTELLE BRODMAN

Medical Library Association

Medical librarians form one of the oldest and more innovative groups within the library profession. They can trace the specialized identity of medical libraries to a chapter contributed by John Shaw Billings to the *Centennial Report* on libraries in 1876. Medical librarians, then largely doctors of medicine, banded together to found the Medical Library Association (MLA) in 1898. The first 20 of the Association's presidents were physicians. Not until 1933 did the Association elect a layperson—Marcia C. Noyes, after whom the medical library profession's highest award is now named—as its president.

The traditional affinity of medical librarians with the health sciences communities they serve is reflected in many of the Association's activities. Inspired by models developed by the medical and health professions, MLA established a certification and accreditation program in 1948.

The Association's successful continuing education program gained strength from the priorities assigned by the medical community to the updating of professional skills. The profession's unique relationship to the National Library of Medicine in developing programs under the Medical Library Assistance Act of 1965 has led to one of the more innovative epochs of American librarianship. During the 12 years since the passage of the Act, the national Biomedical Communications Network has been established with a systematized use of interlibrary loans unmatched elsewhere. On-line searches of MEDLINE and related data bases are commonly available to medical libraries, and members of the Association have made continuing effort to update their professional skills. The medical library profession is, therefore, a partner in the national health enterprise in all its variety, a circumstance that accounts in part for the profession's vitality and at the same time for its occasional fractionation.

Membership. As of April 1977, the MLA had 4,101 members, including 2,971 individual and 1,130 institutional members. (Traditionally, institutional membership has been a requirement for access to the MLA Exchange, which has operated since 1898.) The total represents a 25 per cent increase in membership since 1976 and a 53 per cent increase since 1972. Attendance at the 1977 annual meeting in Seattle was 1,400.

The MLA's voluntary certification program continues to gain support. A total of 447 applicants qualified for certificates in 1977; 59 were rejected. A total of 3,006 medical librarians have been certified since the program started in 1948.

The Association conducts an honors and awards program featuring the honorific Janet Doe Lectureship, the Ida and George Eliot Prize for the most distinguished published paper, the Gottlieb Prize for the best essay in medical history, the Rittenhouse Award for the best paper published by a student, and the Marcia C. Noyes Award for career accomplishment. The 1977 Noyes Award was given to Alfred N. Brandon of the New York Academy of Medicine.

MLA Officers

PRESIDENT (June 1977-June 1978):
Gilbert J. Clausman, New York University Medical Center

PRESIDENT-ELECT:
Erika Love, University of New Mexico, Albuquerque

EXECUTIVE DIRECTOR:
John S. LoSasso

Headquarters: 919 N. Michigan Ave., Chicago 60611

Structure and Function. In common with other library associations, MLA undergoes periodic reexamination of its goals and of the optimal organizational arrangements for approaching them. The proliferation of unofficial local and special interest groups in the rapidly growing Association has become a matter of concern. The Ad Hoc Committee to Study MLA Group Structure, chaired by James Williams III of Wayne State University, studied the question for over two years and submitted its report at the 1977 annual meeting. The report, which proposed guidelines for the formation of geographic as well as special interest groups, was accepted after vigorous debate. A related effort to change the name of the Association and of its official publication, the *Bulletin,* to reflect more appropriately the pluralistic composition of the Association was defeated by a mail referendum during 1977.

MLA is no stranger to activist movements in the library profession. During 1977, a Medical Library Relevance Group, having proposed that MLA take a position on the layperson's right to medical information, continued to study the issue in depth. A Hospital Library Interest Group studied the medical and legal aspects of disseminating information from the hospital library.

Education. More than 900 members came early to the 1977 Seattle meeting and registered for one or more of the 29 continuing education (CE) courses offered. In addition, during the fiscal year ending June 1, 1977, 967 persons registered for 48 CE courses offered at 29 locations across the United States from Rockport, Maine, to San Diego, California. Nine new courses are under development for 1978, bringing the total available for presentation to 49.

Julie A. Virgo, who had been responsible for coordinating the CE program from the MLA headquarters in Chicago, resigned as the Association's Director of Education during 1977 to become Executive Secretary of the Association of College and Reference Libraries. She was succeeded by Robert A. Berk of the University of Oregon Library School.

Publication Program. The Association's serial publications include its professional journal, *The Bulletin of the Medical Library Association;* a news organ, *MLA News;* a register of medical journal births and deaths, *Vital Notes;* an annual *Directory;* and, in cooperation with the National Library of Medicine, *Current Catalog Proof Sheets.* The *Handbook of Medical Library Practice* is now under revision by a committee headed by Louise Darling of UCLA, and there are plans to update Estelle Brodman's classic *Development of Medical Bibliography.*

Legislation. Recent efforts to impose statutory controls over library photoduplication have been viewed with considerable apprehension in medical libraries. The Association's Legislative Committee was particularly active during 1977 with representatives of other national library associations during the passage of the new copyright act.

Now that the legislation is law, interest in the implementation of the provisions is high. At its 1977 meeting, the Association established a subcommittee to draft a set of guidelines for medical libraries to observe in their compliance with the new copyright law.

SCOTT ADAMS

Mitrographics

In the field of library micrographics, 1977 was a year of continuing growth, with the enlargement of library microform collections, the expansion of reading facilities, and the implementation of computer output microfilm

(COM) systems in conjunction with machine-readable catalogs and circulation files.

Equipment. With the exception of the IZON Corporation's demonstration of a working prototype of the "Fly's Eye" micrographic system, the new equipment of particular interest to libraries was evolutionary in nature. Of more than routine interest were a new 35mm microfilm reader aimed specifically at the library market and a pair of reader/printers.

At the joint meeting of the National Micrographics Association (NMA) and the International Micrographics Congress (IMC) held in Washington, D.C., in September, conferees were given a demonstration of the latest generation of the Fly's Eye microform reader, invented by Adnan Waly, the distinguished scientist and inventor. Five years earlier, Waly had introduced the first prototype which was about 1 inch thick with a height and width about the size of a standard 8½-x-11-inch sheet of paper. The reader was nicknamed the Fly's Eye because, instead of having a single projection lens system as do conventional readers, it utilized a system of 3,500 lenses set in a sheet of plastic and located ½ inch below the projection screen. In the original prototype, Waly had reduced each letter or character 25 times and then stored 625 characters (25 x 25) in the area originally occupied by a single character, thus enabling him to store 625 pages of information on a transparent piece of film the size of one original page. This type of filming, however, required that the original be specifically prepared for filming with characters spaced evenly both horizontally and vertically.

The current generation of Waly's reader is 2¾ inches thick and contains only 504 lenses operating in parallel. The new system can store 195 pages of information on 1 sheet of film (called an IZON film), which is 8½ inches wide and 10 inches long. It can be used for graphics as well as printed text and requires no special preparation of the source document. Movements of the film within the reader are very slight—the maximum movements on the X-Y grid are .348 inch. The grid coordinates are dialed on two thumb wheels, which makes locating a particular page simple and precise.

The new system is called the IZON Model 200 Reading and Information Display System and is being developed by the IZON Corporation of Stamford, Connecticut. Initial applications will be in commercial and industrial fields rather than in libraries. There have been large development costs involved in refining the Fly's Eye into a working system, and the high-quality optics rather than the originally planned molded plastic lenses are expensive. The hoped-for low price, once given as a prime objective by Waly, will have to wait for yet another model generation. The announced price of the current reader, when and if it actually goes into production, is $275 per unit when purchased in quantities of 500 or more. The IZON 200 is obviously a closed system with no possibility for hardware compatibility. It will be interesting to see how this ingenious system develops further.

A new 35mm library microfilm reader designed by Ferril Lossee, Professor of Electrical Engineering at Brigham Young University, was exhibited at the ALA Annual Conference in Detroit by Alpine Micrographics, a company formed specifically to manufacture the reader. A prototype of the reader had been in use for several months at Brigham Young, and it was hoped that this new reader would be in full production by the autumn of 1977. After the preproduction trial, however, certain design changes were found to be desirable, and the company decided to hold up production until these changes could be made. As exhibited, the reader had a front projection screen, a motorized film transport activated by small push buttons on the front of the machine, and a single-lens optical system. The film supply is in the upper rear portion of the machine. At first glance this would appear to be inconvenient, but the top part of the reader swings down during loading and can be loaded conveniently from the seated viewing position. There was some speculation, given the design elements of the reader and the company's manufacturing site in Utah, that this would be the reader chosen for the genealogical collections of the Mormon church.

During 1977 Minolta corporation began marketing its RP405 universal tabletop microform reader/printer in the United States. The RP405 is described as an all-purpose unit that will handle a wide spectrum of microformats including various fiche formats, 16mm and 35mm roll film, and aperture cards. The machine produces positive electrostatic copies from either negative or positive film interchangeably using the Electrofax process (paper stock coated with zinc oxide and a li-

(Left) IZON Model 200 Reading and Information Display System, a working prototype exhibited at the September meeting of the National Micrographics Association and the International Micrographics Association in Washington, D.C. (Above) Alpine Micro Viewer for 35mm library microfilm exhibited at the ALA Conference in Detroit.

quid toner). A total of 15 drop-in lens systems from 8x to 45x magnifications are available as options. In Canada, the same unit is marketed by Bell & Howell as the 16-35F, and in Great Britain it is known as the Regma LR6

During the year, Xerox Corporation announced its reentry into the microform reader/printer market with the introduction of its Xerox 740 Microfiche Reader/Printer. Somewhere in between a console and a tabletop unit, the machine is 38 inches high, 26 inches wide, and 20 inches deep and weighs 250 pounds. The rear projection type screen measures 11¼ x 9¼ inches and is recessed to shield it from ambient light. The 740 is designed to accommodate microfiches only, in sizes 4 x 6 inches or smaller, with reduction ratios ranging from 24:1 to 48:1. Positive prints (black print on a white background) can be produced from either positive or negative film. The 740 is not bimodal, however, and separate machines are required for positive and negative input. Currently, no plans for modifying the 740 to accommodate roll film have been announced.

GPO Micropublishing Program. Late in the year the first shipments of U.S. Government Printing Office (GPO) microfiches were sent to depository libraries, signaling the implementation of GPO's long-awaited micropublishing program. GPO had been authorized by the Joint Committee on Printing to convert both GPO and non-GPO documentation to microfiches as necessary and as requested by depository libraries. To this end, GPO invited bids to convert an initial 6,000 non-GPO documents to a standard fiche format (4-x-6-inch 98 frame, R24x). The average publication will contain approximately 110 pages and will require 550 distribution copies for the depository system. The 48 Regional Depository Libraries will receive two copies of each micropublication, one silver halide copy and one diazo copy. All other distribution copies will be on diazo film. Through its conversion to a microfiche format, much information not previously available through the depository system will be made accessible to the American public. According to a GPO official, the initial reaction to the micropublishing program by the depository community has been extremely favorable.

Preservation by Microfilm. Microfilming rare and deteriorating material to preserve its intellectual content for future generations is perhaps best exemplified in the United States by the Library of Congress's "Brittle Book" program, through which tens of thousands of deteriorating books have already been captured on film. The concept of preservation microfilming may have gotten an added boost in 1977 with the appointment of Norman Shaffer as Program Officer of LC's National Preservation Program. Shaffer was formerly Assistant Chief of the Library's Photoduplication Service.

The Administration of the Library's present preservation microfilming operation is located within the Preservation Office and has been in existence since 1968. Starting out as a two-person operation with an annual operating budget of less than $40,000 and an annual production of approximately 500,000 exposures, the current operation, headed by Lawrence Robinson, has a staff of 18 and an operating budget of $535,000. The current annual production is in excess of 5,000,000 exposures (10,000,000 pages). It is possible that in the future this operation will be expanded still further and may form the basis of a national preservation microfilming program.

Standards. The National Micrographics Association—through its various standards committees and through its sponsorship of the American National Standards Institute (ANSI) Committee on Photographic Reproduction of Documents, PH5—continued its fine work in the development and promulgation of industry standards. In addition, a subcommittee of the ANSI Committee on Standardization in the Field of Library Work, Documentation, and Related Publishing Practices, Z39, has been formed to formulate standards for information for microfiche headers. The subcommittee is chaired by Francis F. Spreitzer of the University of Southern California Library.

HOWARD S. WHITE

Multimedia Materials

Expenditures by libraries and educational institutions for audiovisual and multimedia materials began to increase again in 1977. In 1976 sales had dropped for the first time in a decade. Statistics compiled by the Association of Media Producers showed a decline of 7.5 per cent in sales in 1976, from $281,000,000 in 1975, to approximately $260,000,000.[1]

Expenditures in 1977. A survey of 44 companies in October 1977 showed an overall increase in sales of 13 per cent through the third quarter, broken down as follows:

	January to September 1976	January to September 1977
	(millions of dollars)	
16mm film and prerecorded videotape	40.3	45.0
Filmstrips	24.2	25.5
Records and prerecorded tapes	1.1	1.2
Multimedia kits		
Other building-level materials (slides, transparencies, 8mm films, study prints, manipulatives)	9.6	11.5
Total	94.5	106.4[2]

When the statistics are available for the entire year, estimates are that a growth of approximately 8-10 per cent will be shown. Future growth, especially in the school library area, will depend in great measure on congressional reauthorization of Title IV-B (Libraries and Learning Resources) of the Elementary and Secondary Education Act and the level at which this program is funded by the federal government.

In 1975, the National Commission on Libraries and Information Science published a study on the "National Inventory of Library Needs" that called libraries in the United States significantly underfunded. The study said that school libraries need at least $4,500,000,000 "to allow acquisition of nonprint materials, additional print materials and equipment needed for effective use of A/V materials."

Library Services and Construction Act (LSCA). The reauthorization of LSCA, which Congress extended for five years, may provide some support for the acquisition of multimedia materials. In an effort to deal with the fiscal problems faced by urban libraries, Congress provided that when LSCA Title I appropriations (library services) exceed $60,000,000, part of the excess funds will be set aside for libraries serving cities with more than 100,000 in population.

The additional funds for urban libraries will be used to support and expand the library services that, "because of the value of the collections of such libraries to individual users and to other libraries, need special assistance to furnish services at a level required to meet the demands made for such services."

Copyright. With the passage in late 1976 of new copyright legislation, copyright owners and users turned their attention to interpreting the new law, which took effect on January 1, 1978. Section 107, which defines "fair use" of copyrighted materials, will in all probability be ultimately defined through a series of court cases. Guidelines for photocopying of print materials have been developed, but a major unresolved issue is that of off-the-air recording.

Schools and libraries are making increasing use of the video recording technology, now enjoying a surging rate of development in the institutional as well as the home market. As video becomes a widely used information delivery system—be it in the form of disc or tape—immediate attention must be given to developing mechanisms through which the public's information needs are served while granting copyright proprietors a just rate of compensation and control over how the works are used.

The House Judiciary Committee has stated that "the problem of off-the-air taping for non-

David Shouldis (left) and John Calvert of the West Virginia Library Commission's new Video Services Division produce video tape cassette programs on a variety of subjects for library use.

profit classroom use of copyrighted audiovisual works incorporated in radio and television broadcasts has proved to be difficult to resolve. The Committee believes that the fair use doctrine has some limited application in this area, but it appears that the development of detailed guidelines will require a more thorough exploration than has so far been possible of the needs and problems of a number of different interests affected, and of the various legal problems presented."[3]

The Judiciary Committee urged the interested parties to work towards the resolution of this issue, and in July 1977 representatives of education, libraries, broadcasters, producers, and performers met at a conference cosponsored by the Copyright Office and the Ford Foundation. Subsequent to that conference, efforts began in two major areas: development of guidelines for the "fair use" of copyrighted works recorded off the air for nonprofit educational use; and establishment of a mechanism through which libraries and schools could obtain permission for extended or repeated use of these materials. It is hoped that resolution of these issues will be accomplished in 1978.

Two court cases filed in 1977 will undoubtedly have a bearing on this subject in varying degrees. The first case involves Universal City Studios and Walt Disney Productions against the Sony Corporation, its advertising agency, some Sony retailers, and Betamax owners. The suit contends that home videotaping of television programs for subsequent viewing violates copyright protection and provides viewers with access to film libraries of inestimable value. Litigation is bound to be long and complex and involves the attempt of manufacturers of videodisc and videotape recorders to position themselves advantageously in the marketplace.

The second suit was brought by Encyclopaedia Britannica Educational Corporation, Learning Corporation of America, and Time-Life Films against the New York Board of Cooperative Educational Services (BOCES) in the First Supervisory District in Erie County and several named individuals. The complaint alleges that the infringement of the plaintiff's copyrighted films resulted from the videotaping of those films off the air without having secured prior permission or licenses. The complaint also alleges that BOCES made additional copies of the videotapes on demand from various educational institutions and that these tapes were used in classrooms—all in violation of the copyright laws. A resolution of this case is expected in 1978.

International Standard Book Number (ISBN). The ISBN system, which was developed from the book numbering system introduced in the United Kingdom in 1967, is now being applied to 16mm films. According to a recent analysis of the *Educational Media Yearbook,* 164 (63.5 per cent) of the 248 major listed publishers and producers are numbering their 16mm films. Use of the ISBN system will help to organize film collections within libraries and media centers and will improve order processing and inventory control within companies. DAPHNE PHILOS

REFERENCES

1. *Survey and Analysis of 1976 Educational Media Sales* (Association of Media Producers, 1977).
2. *Quarterly Survey of Educational Media Sales* (Association of Media Producers, 1977).
3. U.S. House of Representatives, Report 94-1476, 1976.

Music Library Association

Activities of the Music Library Association (MLA) during 1977 maintained a vigorous pace both internally and in cooperation with other organizations. As a result of the coordination of publications functions through the recently established council on publications, editorial policies were beind codified. The production of publications, in particular of monographs and monographs in series, was increasing as it proceeded according to the planned schedule. Design was to receive increased attention, and new means of distribution were being explored. While increased costs required certain reductions in expenditures for various Association activities, efforts to organize business procedures more efficiently were under way. To assist in securing financial support for professional programs undertaken in the future, an endowment campaign will begin early in 1979. The campaign will be coordinated with MLA's 50th anniversary, to be celebrated in 1981.

The new copyright law received widespread scrutiny in 1977, especially in view of its apparent restriction on library photocopying of music. The topic appeared on the programs of both national and chapter meetings, at which attorneys were among the speakers. Other legislation of interest to members was the proposed Arts and Education Bill, for which the Association has indicated its support.

In 1977 MLA established three annual prizes. One is for the author or compiler of the best book-length bibliography. The second is for the author or compiler not beyond the age of 40 of the best article length bibliography or the best article on music librarianship. The third prize is for the author of the best review in *Notes,* the quarterly journal of the Association. The first awards will be made early in 1979. Nominations may be made internationally, and recipients will receive honoraria.

In response to numerous requests, the subject of music library consultants was reviewed by the Board of Directors. Although the recommendation of individuals is not a practice in which the Association participates, guidelines for selecting consultants and for acting in the capacity of a consultant were published in *Notes* (March 1977).

MLA Officers

PRESIDENT (February 1977-February 1979): **Dena J. Epstein,** University of Chicago

RECORDING SECRETARY: **George Hill,** Baruch College, New York

TREASURER: **Shirley P. Emanuel,** Library of Congress, Washington, D.C.

Headquarters: 343 S. Main St., Ann Arbor, Michigan 48104

Among members who are catalogers of scores and sound recordings, close attention was being given to developments nationally and internationally. As MLA's OCLC Task Force for Music submitted its final report, the Music OCLC Users Group, a new organization independent from MLA, was formed. The proceedings of the Joint Steering Committee for Revision of the Anglo-American Cataloging Rules, attended by an invited representative of MLA, were given special attention during the year. It was with satisfaction that MLA members learned of the modification of certain of the proposed rules whose original form they had found especially controversial.

Walter Horban is one of the Chicago Symphony Orchestra's four librarians responsible for the symphony's library of over 6,000 orchestral works with separate scores for up to 135 musicians each.

As an ISBD for nonbook materials is being formulated by IFLA, similar problems in the proposed rules for sound recordings are being dealt with both through direct communication with IFLA and in cooperation with the International Association of Music Libraries. Participation in other IFLA activities has increased as MLA has developed relationships with other U.S. members and, for the first time, has had the benefit of several of its own members' attendance at an international congress.

In 1977 members of the Association voted to have one national meeting a year instead of two. Consolidating past special committees on professional education, continuing education, and institutes as well as the work of a special officer for exchange of librarians, a new standing committee on education was established. After a systematic review of policies and procedures, the need for a constitutional revision committee was also recognized. Its work will include consideration of recommendations made by a committee on goals and objectives, whose final report had been submitted previously. Upon formal request, a Public Librarians Interest Group was initiated, and organization of a new, Rocky Mountain, chapter was begun. Work continued on a project for a bibliography of American sheet music since 1826, for which a planning conference supported by a grant from the National Endowment for the Humanities was held in the spring.

The establishment of new lines of communication with ALA was promising. MLA is participating in the reexamination being given by ALA to the role of affiliates. MLA's contacts with the ALA's Publishing Committee and with the Audiovisual Committees of the Association of College and Research Libraries, the Public Libraries Association, and the Resources and Technical Services Division were also productive. Participation in the Joint Committee on the Union List of Serials continued in 1977. In cooperation with the Répertoire Internationale des Sources Musicales (RISM), MLA is assisting in the revision of Part 1 ("Canada and the United States") of the *Directory of Music Research Libraries* (Iowa City: University of Iowa, 1967), in which there will be greatly expanded coverage of music collections in American libraries. MLA holds membership in the Council of National Library Associations and is represented on its joint committees on library education and American National Standards Institute Z39. The Association maintains joint committees with the U.S. Branch of the International Association of Music Libraries, the American Musicological Society, and the Music Publishers Association.

The Music Library Association is an organization of approximately 1,750 individuals and institutions. In addition to its journal, the Association publishes an *Index and Bibliography Series*, a series of *Technical Reports*, the *Music Cataloging Bulletin*, a newsletter, and occasional monographs. MLA has a placement service to assist in placing candidates trained in the field of music librarianship and to aid libraries in locating qualified personnel. There are 12 local and regional chapters, membership in which is not contingent on membership in the national organization. GERALDINE OSTROVE

National Agricultural Library

During October 1977 the one-millionth citation was recorded in the AGRICOLA (Agricultural On-Line Access) family of data bases. AGRICOLA consists of CAIN (Cataloging and Indexing), the major National Agricultural Library (NAL) data base; AGECON (Agricultural Economics), a data base on agricultural marketing policies, program policies, program products, demand, supplies, and prices; and the FNIC (Food and Nutrition Information and Educational Materials Center) data base that includes citations on journal articles, monographs, and audiovisual materials in applied human nutrition, food service, food sanitation and safety, volume food storage and preparation, and administrative management. The CAIN data base includes all materials cataloged as well as selected agricultural articles indexed by NAL. Canadian publications on cooperatives are now being processed for inclusion in AGECON by Agriculture Canada. When available, other data bases dealing with specialized aspects of agriculture will be added to AGRICOLA.

NAL Officers

DIRECTOR:
Richard A. Farley

ASSOCIATE DIRECTOR:
Samuel T. Waters

DEPUTY DIRECTOR FOR RESOURCE DEVELOPMENT:
Jeanne M. Holmes

DEPUTY DIRECTOR FOR LIBRARY SERVICE:
Wallace C. Olsen

EXECUTIVE OFFICER:
Gerald J. Sophar

Headquarters: National Agricultural Library
10301 Baltimore Blvd., Beltsville, Maryland 20705

Cooperative Projects. Microfilming land-grant college agricultural research documents under cooperative agreements has been continued and expanded. Filming of documents from 17 states was completed in 1977, and new agreements were negotiated with a group of 5 states in the Southwest. The cooperative project to provide current awareness and free document delivery services to sorghum researchers on four land-grant campuses was completed and evaluated.

In 25 states document delivery services to U.S. Department of Agriculture personnel are provided near their work location through state land-grant college libraries. This service is providing fast response to 72 per cent of the requests received.

National Programs. The agreement between NAL and Cornell University Libraries to add bibliographic records of agricultural serials and journals to the CONSER (Conversion of Serials) data base continues. More than 2,600 titles held by both NAL and Cornell had been processed by the end of 1977 and entered into OCLC records. NAL has also entered 4,700 local data serial check-in records for 3,400 titles into OCLC.

As the amount of information included and the number of libraries on the system increase, the OCLC data base becomes more and more useful as a processing and location tool. During 1977 there was significant growth in the use of OCLC to locate libraries holding publications and to locate in NAL's own collection recently received publications that had not yet been fully processed and entered into the NAL catalogs.

The National Agricultural Library has taken an active role in training new users of on-line systems to access AGRICOLA data bases. Approximately 60 people have attended one-week instruction courses in the theory, practice, and economical use of the AGRICOLA on-line searching.

International. During 1977 the AGRIS Documentation Center and NAL cooperated in efforts to convert CAIN records to the AGRIS format. The first automatically converted entries appeared in the September issue of *AGRINDEX*. The process will increase the number of records of U.S. publications in agriculture appearing in this international index.

Publications. The results of on-line searches of subjects that are of interest to a number of users are now issued as *Quick Bibliographies*. The citations are checked and nonrelevant material removed. A limited number of copies are prepared, and the titles are announced in *Agricultural Libraries Information Notes*. Approximately 30 of these bibliographies were issued in 1977, and 750 copies were distributed.

Symposia. Two important symposia were sponsored in 1977 by the Associates of National Agricultural Library, Inc., at NAL. "The One-Millionth Citation Symposium" was a review of the development, present status, and impact of on-line retrieval services and of the possibilities for future information organization and control. The second symposium was entitled "International Agricultural Librarianship: Continuity and Change." Appropriate to the subject matter of this symposium was a special tribute to Foster Mohrhardt, a former director of NAL and a Past-President of the American Library Association.

RICHARD A. FARLEY

National Commission on Libraries and Information Science

1977 was a year in which a number of projects of the National Commission on Libraries and Information Science (NCLIS) produced final reports. These reports have provided a wealth of information, which will be invaluable to the Commission and the library/information community in their efforts to implement the NCLIS National Program. Described in the document *Toward a National Program for Library and Information Services: Goals for Action*, the plan was almost immediately endorsed in principle and concept by all of the major library and information professional associations when it was published in 1975. Since that time, the Commission and the library/information community have been working toward implementing its eight objectives, concentrating in the early stages on collecting the information needed to make intelligent decisions, developing consensus on strategy and tactics, and improving the utilization of existing resources.

Public Library Funding. The report *Evaluation of the Effectiveness of Federal Funding of Public Libraries* was published in 1977. The report demonstrated that, while categorical aid programs such as the Library Services and Construction Act (LSCA) are not only useful but absolutely necessary to healthy survival of public libraries, they can be described as only moderately effective. On the other hand, block grant programs such as general revenue sharing have been virtually useless in providing support to libraries. The report recommends revised and expanded federal legislation for categorical aid to libraries, with administrative as well as dollar volume improvements.

In 1977 NCLIS published a study undertaken for the Urban Library Council. The study, *Improving State Aid to Public Libraries*, focuses on the disproportionate share of library support that falls on the local community, in contrast to the balanced funding of similar activities such as education. Increased state participation in public library funding is recommended, and suggestions for promoting such participation are offered.

Inventory of Library Needs. Because there

had not been a comprehensive comparison since 1965 of the library resources available with the needs for these resources, NCLIS commissioned a new examination. The final report of this study, *National Inventory of Library Needs—1975*, compares available resources with sets of need indicators derived from existing service standards by a widely representative advisory committee. This comparison shows that, although there has been improvement in the provision of library service over the past 20 years, there are still some 5-10,000,000 people with no library service at all and many millions more with inadequate or substandard library service. The report recommends strenuous efforts to correct the deficiencies with more funding at the state and federal levels and more effective use of existing funding.

Periodical Access. A major problem for librarians has always been locating sources for and obtaining copies of articles from scholarly journals not in the local collection. With tens of thousands of periodical titles extant, no library can possibly afford to subscribe to all of them, much less obtain or maintain back files. Libraries have traditionally acquired articles from infrequently used titles from other libraries on a quid pro quo basis. The system as it currently exists does provide some access to other than local collection materials, but it is inefficient and inequitable, overburdening some libraries and underutilizing others. NCLIS attacked this problem by funding a research study to define the parameters of the problem, sponsoring a conference to set priorities and overall strategy, and supporting a task force to develop a specific program.

The program, published as *Effective Access to the Periodical Literature: A National Program*, describes a three-level, hierarchical system, in which it is estimated that 80 percent of requests would be filled at state or regional levels. About 5 percent of the requests—those for the least-used titles—would be filled from a combination of existing resources (e.g., the large research libraries). The remainder would be filled by a new collection of approximately 50,000 periodical titles. This National Periodicals Center is to be established as a separate operation under the direction of the Library of Congress. As the year ended, the Council of Library Resources (CLR) had agreed to undertake for the Library of Congress the design phase for the establishment of the Center.

Standards. The principal instrument for standardization in the library/information field for many years has been the American National Standards Institute's Committee Z39 on Standardization in the Field of Library Work, Documentation, and Related Publishing Practices. When Jerrold Orne, the long-time chairman of Committee Z39, announced his retirement effective in mid-1978, it became necessary to find a new chairman and a site for the administrative office for the Committee. At the same time, NCLIS and the agencies that have been providing the bulk of the funding for Committee Z39, the National Science Foundation (NSF) and CLR, believed that it would be appropriate to reexamine Z39 with an eye to possible future directions.

This proposed reexamination would provide a response to some proposals for expansion of the scope of the Committee and to some criticisms that had been voiced. Accordingly, NCLIS with the cooperation of NSF and CLR selected a task force to represent the broad community of interests and commissioned them to develop criteria for and recommend a Secretariat. The task force was also to examine present and future modes of operation and make recommendations with respect to these. After four meetings the task force submitted a report that recommended retention of the present Secretariat, the Council of National Library Associations. The Task Force also recommended extensive reorganization, including modification of both the title of the Committee and its scope, changes in organization and operations, and a search for additional sources of funding. The report, *American National Standards Committee Z39: Recommended Future Directions*, will be given wide circulation in the community for reaction and response.

The Commission continued its support with NSF and CLR of the Committee for the Coordination of National Bibliographic Control, which in an active year examined such varied subjects as bar codes, formats for journal article citations, and name authority files. The most basic standardization effort, however, was the sponsorship with the National Bureau of Standards (NBS) of a task force charged with developing the computer-to-computer protocols necessary to permit disparate systems and hardware to intercommunicate. The report of this Task Force, *Computer Network Protocol*, not only describes the protocol but also points out that building such a protocol is only one part of the task of providing for intersystem communication. The report points out that maintaining a protocol is a never-ending task. At the very least, there must be a continuously maintained registry of codes as they are assigned, plus modifications and error-recovery requirements that will surface as operational implementation is achieved.

Library of Congress. There can be no question that the Library of Congress must play a crucial role in any national network undertaking. Defining that role for the near term was the purpose of a study that was to be pub-

National Commission on Libraries and Information Science

lished early in 1978. It defines a number of specific tasks for LC to undertake, ranging from expanding and expediting its cataloging activities, through increasing on-line access to its files, to continuing the creation and maintenance of the Union Catalog. Still another study that is being performed by LC is of the role and structure of authority files in the national network. Because of the extraordinary complexity of this topic, the study will be performed in phases over several years. A preliminary study, which was performed in 1977, was designed to develop the strategy and methodology to be used for this significant investigation.

Library Photocopying. Possibly the most significant report of those produced in 1977 was *Library Photocopying in the United States*, which presents the results of a year-long, nationwide study of photocopying in all types of libraries, except school library/media centers. This study reports that libraries made photocopies of some 114,000,000 items in 1976, totaling almost 1,000,000,000 pages. Less than half of that material, however, was copyrighted, and nearly three-quarters of the copyrighted items were articles from serials such as scholarly journals. The overwhelming majority of these copies were either for local users or for other branches within the same library system, with only about 11 per cent, or 4,300,000 copies being made for interlibrary loans.

When the guidelines developed under the aegis of the National Commission on New Technological Uses of Copyrighted Works (CONTU) are applied to the interlibrary loan photocopies, the number of copies drops. The number of copies of domestic serials articles under six years old, not for replacement or classroom use, and including more than five articles from a given serial title (not issue) obtained by a given library, drops from 2,400,000 to about 500,000. There is also high concentration of photocopying within each class, about one-fifth of the libraries doing about three-quarters of the photocopying, and about two-thirds of the local-use photocopies and 86 per cent of the interlibrary loan photocopies being made from only 20 percent of the serials. Having been performed just prior to the effective date of the new copyright law, this study can serve as a benchmark against which changes in photocopy patterns as a result of the new law can be measured.

Other Activities. Early in 1977, NCLIS published *National Information Policy*, a report of the Domestic Council Committee on the Right of Privacy, which recommends the establishment of a structure in the Executive Office of the President to deal with questions of information policy. A second management institute for chiefs of state library agencies was held in the spring, with the emphasis on the future and the development of multitype library networks within each state. The Task Force on the Role of the School Library/Media Center in the National Network was formed and began its deliberations. An examination continued on the state of bibliographic control of nonprint media, being performed jointly with the Association for Educational Media and Technology. Preliminary reports show that the only element common to all bibliographic record types now in use is the title, indicating an urgent need for standardization in this area.

White House Conference. The official call in 1976 for the White House Conference on Library and Information Services was followed by the appointment of the Presidential contingent of the Advisory Committee and the inclusion of the Conference budget in the first supplemental appropriations bill for fiscal 1977. This $3,500,000 budget was appropriated in late spring; but the Commission, concerned with the tight schedule requirements, had already used its own funds to bring together the Advisory Committee to make the necessary early decisions. A program coordinator was selected in midsummer and the professional staff began reporting shortly thereafter. Before the end of the fiscal year, initial grant payments had been made to more than 40 states and territories for their pre-White House Conferences, and by year-end virtually all states and territories were committed to holding preconferences. Two states, Georgia and Pennsylvania, have already held their conferences. One of the decisions made at the preliminary Advisory Committee meeting had been to provide for a preconference for Native Americans on reservations if there were no legal or other barriers to prevent it. This has been cleared and confirmed by the Advisory Committee, and the Commission and the Bureau of Indian Affairs of the Department of the Interior will act as administrators.

The momentum toward implementation of the NCLIS National Program, which began to develop in 1976, was maintained and accelerated during 1977. Continued progress was expected in 1978 as the White House Conference process continues. Already the heightened awareness of library/information resources engendered by the publicity about the preconferences can be seen. This will intensify as the time for the White House Conference itself—scheduled for late fall 1979—approaches. If this heightened awareness can be maintained after the Conference—and the Commission intends to see that it is—progress toward implementation should be able to move with fewer hesitations and stumbling blocks.

FREDERICK BURKHARDT

National Endowment for the Humanities

The National Endowment for the Humanities (NEH) is an independent federal agency created by Congress in 1965 to support projects of research, education, and public activity in the humanities. The Endowment's operations are conducted through four major divisions: Fellowships, Education Programs, Research Grants, and Public Programs. Other projects are eligible for support through the Office of Planning and Policy Assessment and through Special Programs in the Chairman's Office of the Endowment. In addition, the Office of State Programs makes grants to citizens' committees in each state to provide support for local humanities projects. All of the Endowment's divisions support library projects.

Fellowships Division. Through its programs of Fellowships Support to Centers for Advanced Study, the Fellowships Division provides funds to independent research libraries for stipends to resident scholars. In 1977, such grants were made to the Folger Shakespeare Library and the Huntington Library.

Education Programs Division. The College Library Program, cosponsored by the Council on Library Resources and NEH, focuses on increasing the involvement of college and university libraries in academic teaching. Its purpose is to enhance these libraries' resources and activities in order to allow them to play a more meaningful role in the teaching and learning process. Grants were given under this program in 1977 to DePauw University, Ball State University, the University of Toledo, the University of Wisconsin-Parkside, Northwestern University, the University of Evansville, and Saint Olaf College.

The Division's Cultural Institutions Program assists libraries and museums in providing formal and systematic educational programs designed both for students and for the general public. In 1977 a grant was made under this program to the Tucson Public Libraries, whose National Learning Library Program will focus on the theme "Sonoran Heritage."

Support for libraries is available in a number of other programs of the Division of Education Programs. In 1977, for example, through the Higher Education Projects Program the John F. Kennedy Library in Waltham, Massachusetts, received a grant to initiate a collaborative program with community colleges.

Research Grants. The Research Collections Program focuses on making the raw materials of research more accessible to scholars. It increases access to materials through projects that address national problems in the archival and library field, through projects that serve as models in systems development and library automation, and through processing grants that are used to catalog, inventory, or otherwise gain bibliographic control of significant research collections.

The Collections Program also helps to develop collections, either by microfilming materials in foreign repositories so that they will be available in the United States or by collecting data through oral history techniques. The third objective of the program, encouragement of the use of important research collections, is achieved by projects for long-term collaborative research that focuses on making use of unique collections of research resources. Approximately 60 grants were made through the Research Collections Program in 1977.

Public Programs. The Program Development area of this Division makes a limited number of grants to test new ways of making the humanities increasingly available to the adult public. Current priorities include the support of projects that enable public libraries to increase the public's use of humanities holdings and services—especially those projects that involve unique and previously untested ideas. In 1977, grants were made to the New Jersey State Library, the Newberry Library, the State Library of Ohio, the Office of Public Libraries and Interlibrary Cooperation in St. Paul, the Houston Public Library, the Southwestern Library Association, the University of North Carolina School of Library Sciences, the Dallas Public Library, the Alabama Public Library, the Denver Public Library, the Oklahoma Library Association, the Tri-County Regional Library, and the Chattahoochee Valley Regional Library.

Office of Planning and Policy Assessment. This office of the Endowment made one new library-related grant in 1977. The American Association of Community and Junior Colleges and the ALA received a grant for a joint survey of community college and public library cooperation in humanities education.

Challenge Grants. Libraries are also eligible

The Houston Public Library received a $135,000 grant from the National Endowment for the Humanities for a nine-month project titled "City!—Our Urban Past, Present and Future". Urban-oriented books purchased under the grant were available at the Central library and four branches.

National Librarians Association

for support under the Endowment's new program of Challenge Grants. The grants are designed to stimulate increased support for humanities institutions from private citizens, business and labor organizations, state and local governments, and civic and other groups by offering one federal dollar for every three raised in the private sector. Unlike most other Endowment grants, Challenge Grants may be used for basic operating support. Libraries that were recipients of Challenge Grants in 1977 included the Eleutherian Mills-Hagley Foundation, the Folger Shakespeare Library, the John Crerar Library, the Library Company of Philadelphia, the New York Public Library, the Newberry Library, the Pierpont Morgan Library, the Research Libraries Group, and the libraries of Case Western Reserve University, Princeton University, Radcliffe College, the University of Florida, the University of Notre Dame, the University of Oklahoma, the University of Rochester, and the University of Tulsa.

GLORIA R. WEISSMAN

National Librarians Association

The National Librarians Association (NLA) was founded in 1975 in order to meet the need for a national association dedicated specifically to the protection and advancement of the concerns of professional librarians. Membership is restricted to librarians who have earned the M.L.S. Through its committees and chapters, the NLA focuses national attention on such crucial issues as certification, identification of the core content for graduate study, upgrading library school admissions standards, and providing swift and substantial aid to librarians who have been victims of unprofessional treatment by their employers.

NLA Officers

PRESIDENT (through June 1979):
Peter Dollard, Alma College, Alma, Michigan

SECRETARY (through June 1978):
Ronald W. Johnson, Washington, D.C.

TREASURER (through June 1979):
June Stratton, South Bend Public Library, South Bend, Indiana

---

Activities. During 1977, NLA focused its attention on expanding its membership. These efforts were successful, and there was a 500% increase in membership, which stood at nearly 250 by the end of the year. The first NLA chapter, the Librarians Association of Hawaii, was accepted into NLA, and NLA organizational efforts were under way in Iowa, California, Montana, Michigan, the District of Columbia, and Texas, as well as in a half dozen other areas.

Three major NLA committees became active late in 1977: Professional Welfare, chaired by Julio Martinez, San Diego State University Library; Professional Education, chaired by Shirley Gaventa of the National Agricultural Library; and Certification Standards, chaired by T.R. Lynch, St. Tammany Parish (Louisiana) Public Library.

Reva Brick, who is a librarian at Chicago's Joint Reference Library, was named NLA Membership Director in October. The NLA's first Nominating Committee was also appointed in October, since NLA's initial Executive Board is constitutionally empowered to serve only through June 1978. The Committee, chaired by Ellis Hodgin of the College of Charleston (South Carolina), will designate a slate of candidates to fill the positions of vice-president/president-elect, secretary, and one at-large position.

Programs and Publications. NLA sponsored its first program at the ALA Annual Conference in Detroit. A panel of four distinguished librarians addressed the question "What Should Librarians Expect from Their Professional Association?" The panelists were Richard Dougherty, University of California at Berkeley; Jerry Shields, State University of New York at Buffalo; Gail Schlachter, University of California at Davis; and Martin Erlich, Orange (California) Public Library.

The Association will sponsor a program at the 1978 Annual Conference concentrating on the ways in which unprofessional trends are eroding the job environments of many librarians. The NLA has issued a nationwide call for papers on the subject, the best of which will be presented at the Conference.

The major communications organ for members of NLA is the *NLA Newsletter: The National Librarian.* This newsletter is published quarterly, is free to members, and was being received on a subscription basis by an additional 130 libraries at the end of 1977. The newsletter has grown regularly in order to keep up with NLA's growth and now includes articles and book reviews as well as news updates.

Plans are being made for the creation of an NLA series of Occasional Papers, the first of which will be the text of the NLA's 1977 program. The second in the series will be the best papers received for the 1978 program. Other suitable papers will be published in the series.

PETER DOLLARD

National Library of Medicine

Especially noteworthy in 1977 was the beginning of construction work for the new Lister Hill Center building. A $13,600,000 contract to erect the Center was awarded on June 17. The facility, being built on the south side of the present National Library of Medicine (NLM)

NATIS: see UNESCO

building, is expected to be completed by the spring of 1980. The new building will house the communications technology and network engineering programs of NLM's Lister Hill Center and the closely related functions of the National Medical Audiovisual Center, now in Atlanta. The Library's Extramural Programs, the Office of Computer and Communications Systems, and the Toxicology Information Program will also move to the new building.

The authority of the Medical Library Assistance Act was extended for one year in 1977. Under the act, NLM's Extramural Programs administer grants for improving health sciences library resources, for research and training in information sciences related to health, and for support of biomedical scientific publications.

In 1977 there were continued increases in requests for library and information services. MEDLINE (MEDLARS On-Line), the Library's on-line bibliographic data base of journal article references, was widely used by researchers, educators, and practitioners throughout the United States. In FY 1977, almost 900,000 on-line and off-line searches were done at the 800 institutions in the United States that belong to the NLM network. This represented an increase of about 50 per cent over 1976. Impressive gains in productivity were also achieved in the area of reference inquiries, which were up 33 per cent in FY 1977.

Another area of success was the automation of technical services. New computerized procedures have eliminated backlogs in acquisition processing, speeded up binding, and improved the ability to identify and quickly fill gaps in the serials collection.

A new satellite terminal facility at the National Library of Medicine made its debut in 1977. Using the Communications Technology Satellite (CTS) in geostationary orbit some 22,500 miles away, crisp color pictures and clear voice signals are now regularly exchanged within an experimental network that includes terminals in Seattle, Fairbanks, Bozeman (Montana), Lexington, and Denver. NLM's facility is operated by the Lister Hill Center and serves as the coordinating center of the network. The network is being used by several Public Health Service agencies to conduct experiments in continuing health education and for conferences over interactive satellite television.

CHEMLINE, the Library's on-line chemical dictionary, has been enlarged to include information on 243,373 unique chemical substances. This is a major expansion (CHEMLINE previously contained records on 98,860 substances) that will extend its usefulness in supporting other data bases dealing with chemical substances. Prominent among the added records is the Environmental Protection Agency's Toxic Substances Control Act (TSCA) Inventory Candidate List, numbering some 33,000 items.

Another accomplishment in 1977 involving an on-line data base was the successful reorganization and implementation of an up-to-date on-line file of nonprint materials called AVLINE (Audiovisuals On-Line). It provides educators in many fields of health science with a unique data base of peer-reviewed audiovisual material that has been critically assessed for quality of content and educational objectives. AVLINE contains sufficient descriptive material to enable the educator to make an intelligent selection for his teaching needs.

Architectural drawing of the library and 10-story Lister Hill National Center for Biomedical Communication in Bethesda, Maryland, which was under construction in 1977 and scheduled for completion in 1980.

Two new catalogs of audiovisual materials used in health science education were published in 1977. The *National Medical Audiovisual Center Catalog*, computer generated for the first time, lists all motion pictures and video cassettes available on short-term loan from the Center. In addition, a listing of all audiovisuals in AVLINE was published as the *NLM AVLINE Catalog*. Both catalogs are available from the Government Printing Office.

MELVIN S. DAY

National Micrographics Association

From its beginnings in 1943, the National Micrographics Association (NMA) has grown into a highly professional organization serving more than 8,000 individuals and 250 trade member companies. With its headquarters in Silver Spring, Maryland, adjacent to Washington, D.C., NMA has the facilities and resources available to carry out its varied programs of education and information services.

Publications produced during 1977 included the *1977 Buyer's Guide to Micrographic Equipment: Products and Services*; a supplement to the *Guide to Micrographic Equipment*; and a completely new edition of the *Micrographics Index*. Three NMA Resource Reports were revised: *Bibliography of Micrographics*; *Micrographic Audiovisuals* (an annotated listing); and the *Micrographic Standards* directory. In addition, several new publications were introduced: *All About Microfilm*

NMA Officers
PRESIDENT (1977-78):
Richard J. Conners

VICE-PRESIDENT:
Warren Cole

TREASURER:
Louis J. Zeh, Jr.

EXECUTIVE DIRECTOR:
O. Gordon Banks

TECHNICAL DIRECTOR:
Don M. Avedon

Headquarters: 8728 Colesville Road, Silver Spring, Maryland 20910

Cameras, a consumer series booklet; Resource Reports covering a list of *Micrographic Industry Surveys and Market Studies* and *Automated Micrographic Retrieval Systems,* which lists and describes systems currently available; and the second in a series of Personal Learning Packages, *COM: Systems and Applications.*

NMA's Resource Center's collection of micrographic information has grown by more than 54 per cent in the past 12 months. Since April 1976, 782 new books, articles, manuscripts, and microforms have been added to NMA's already comprehensive library of micrographic data. The total number of items in the collection is now 2,500. The number of technical inquiries to the Resource Center has also grown substantially.

NMA in 1977 revised and published American National Standards (ANS) covering *Reader Screen Luminance* and *16mm Cartridges.* A new NMA industry standard, *Standard Test Chart for Rotary Microfilm Cameras,* was issued. A new book, *Basic Microfilm Standards,* was also published in 1977. The book contains the five ANS specified in the Internal Revenue Service Procedure 76-43, which covers microfilming general books of account in addition to several other related documents.

Four new NMA standards committees were established: Procurement Guidelines, Engineering Drawings, Color Microforms, and Ecology. These committees will be responsible for developing industry standards and recommended practices or issuing informative white papers.

The 16th meeting of the International Organization for Standardization (ISO) Technical Subcommittee TC46/SC1 on Documentary Reproduction was held in Washington, D.C., in May. The meeting marked the first time the committee had convened in the United States. NMA cosponsored the meeting with the ANS Institute. Thirty delegates representing eight countries participated. Much of the work of the past several years is now beginning to result in either final International Standards or in draft documents ready for ballot.

NMA's Speakers Bureau continued to be an active program, providing speakers for the National Computer Conference and the American Society for Information Science annual meeting, among other functions. In its continuing commitment to education, NMA held tutorial seminars the day before its two major meetings on such topics as "Fundamentals of Micrographics," "Retrieval and Systems Design," "Inspection and Quality Control," and "Computer Output Microfilm."

NMA's vital and active chapter program grew, with chapters being formed in Missouri, North Carolina, Florida, and Illinois, resulting in a total of 37 chapters.

A first for NMA in 1977 was the Service Company President's Forum held in June. The objectives of the meeting were to draw the decision makers of service companies into an atmosphere of fellowship, to provide a framework for the presentation of solutions to specific business problems, and to explore the values of improved communication within the service company community.

NMA conducted a technological assessment of the micrographics industry during the year. On several occasions experts representing all areas of the industry were questioned about the future of micrographics, particularly in relation to other information processing technologies. The results of the assessment were submitted to NMA's Long Range Planning Task Force, which is developing a five-year plan for the Association.

The NMA's 26th annual conference and exposition was held in Dallas in May with 7,300 in attendance. There was record-breaking attendance at educational sessions. Exhibits of the latest in micrographics equipment covered 42,800 square feet. A special midyear meeting with an international flair was held in Washington, D.C., in September. This meeting was held in conjunction with the International Micrographics Congress and featured speakers from all parts of the world.

O. GORDON BANKS

National Technical Information Service

Today's information revolution challenges the world's ability to organize information and to retrieve and manipulate it to solve problems. As the quantity of information—in the form of books, reports, journal articles, papers, manuals, guides, statistical data, and magnetic tapes—grows at a staggering rate, the world tries to keep pace by using an array of sophisticated equipment.

The National Technical Information Service (NTIS) is in the forefront of those leading this revolution. As an agency of the Department of Commerce, it is the most important single source for public access to research, development, planning, and analytical studies. NTIS uses computers, electronic copiers, telex, other long-distance communications devices, and even automated camera equipment for volume reproduction. In turn, these devices have provided flexibility and growth in the number of information products available from NTIS.

1977 Growth. NTIS growth continued in all phases of operations for 1977. Input of new reports progressed from 65,000 reports in 1976 to more than 75,000 in 1977. Subscriptions in 1977 totaled 39,000, compared with 30,000 in 1976. Distribution of NTISearches increased from 30,000 in 1976 to more than 32,000 for 1977.

To keep pace with this input and announcement growth, several innovative products were developed in 1977. The government has long been interested in promoting better use of its patents and of ideas uncovered as part of government research. The NTIS conducts a promotion and licensing program that encourages the adoption of government patents in commercial ventures. The program has created a comprehensive *U.S. Government Patent Portfolio* that lists 16,000 patents issued from 1966 through 1974. This publication is updated each year by the *Government Inventions for Licensing Annual Index,* which contains 3,500 inventions from 12 different government agencies.

Innovative Services. A related innovation is the NTIS *Tech Notes* series, which promotes the results of government research. It packages the latest high-technology applications in 11 diciplines from agencies such as the National Aeronautics and Space Administration, the National Institutes of Health, the Air Force, the Navy, the Army, the Bureau of Mines, and the Forest Service. This special nonbook format, which includes drawings, functional charts, and formulas, was designed to present the most important and promising new applications to the actual users of this sophisticated information.

An entirely new approach, an information referral service, was also introduced in 1977. The purpose of the program is to make federal laboratory experience available to private industry by providing direct contact between people in small- and medium-sized firms and government specialists. Industry requirements are channeled to NTIS through university extension centers. Solutions can then be reached through the combined efforts of the technical information services of NTIS and the technical aid of more than 60 federal research and development laboratories.

Customer Service. The NTIS customer base also continued to grow in 1977. It includes more than 150,000 names, 13,000 of whom have NTIS deposit accounts that they actively draw on to order products and services. To aid these customers, NTIS offers a broad array of ordering mechanisms: telex, telecopier, telephone, in-person, mail, and on-line computer ordering. A broad range of payment methods is also available: credit card, cash, ship and bill, NTIS deposit account, purchase orders, and a special charge account for state and local government units.

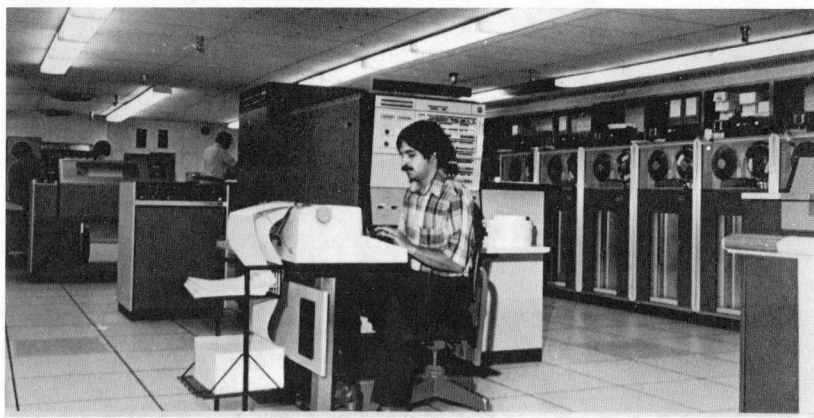

In 1977 NTIS emphasized flexibility and convenience in remodeling the delivery services from which a customer can select. Rush Handling guarantees that an order will be shipped the day of its receipt if it is in stock or the following day if it requires special printing. Premium Service is a toll-free telephone order service, with delivery within 5 to 12 days. Regular Service includes the option to request air mail or first-class delivery if desired. The rationale of this flexibility in ordering and payment is that, although information, service, and products cost money, customers should have a choice in the cost that they pay.

This rationale will continue to prosper in 1978. The thrust of developmental programs will be in technical information services for state and local governments and expanded foreign marketing. New products and services will include a Journal Article Copy Service and a Keyword-Out-Of-Context (KWOC) Title Index for all reports in the NTIS collection.

TED RYERSON

National Technical Information Service

Above and left, the National Technical Information Service processes nearly 7,000 requests for demand and standing order items daily through its computer center supplying scientific, technical and business information. The center also produces tapes for periodical publications by electronic photo composition techniques.

Networks

The "library bibliographic component" of the Nationwide Library and Information Service Network was the scene of a considerable number of important activities during 1977. The library bibliographic component is made up of those organizations involved in the creation, processing, dissemination, and use of bibliographic information for a wide variety of purposes. Together with other components concentrating on such areas as resource allocation, information delivery, reference services, and continuing education, the library bibliographic component is an important part of the "full-service" network.

LC AND NCLIS ACTIVITIES

LC Network Development Office. On the national level, many activities pivoted around the Library of Congress and especially the LC Network Development Office (NDO). An examination of the role of the Library of Congress in the emerging nationwide network was completed by Inforonics, Inc. This study, funded by the National Commission on Libraries and Information Science (NCLIS), surveyed the plans and activities of multistate, state, and local library networks and concluded that the Library of Congress should assume a strong leadership role in the development of the nationwide bibliographic network.

Network Advisory Committee. Elaborating on that theme, the LC Network Advisory Group (NAG), composed of top administrators from many organizations involved in computerized bibiographic networking, completed a draft document entitled "Toward a National Library and Information Service Network: The Library Bibliographic Component." This document outlines broad steps that must be taken to insure the rational development of this component. The draft was presented and widely discussed at the 1977 ALA Annual Conference. Reactions have been invited from the library community, and a final version of the document is expected to be ready early in 1978. Among other things, the document calls for further efforts aimed at a definition of technical issues relevant to the network, an exploration of network governance options, and an examination of the relationship of authority files to the network. During the year the NAG membership was expanded slightly, its charge was refined, and it was renamed the Network Advisory Committee (NAC).

Network Technical Architecture Group. To begin attacking technical issues relevant to the nationwide network, the LC NDO established the Network Technical Architecture Group (NTAG). This group consists of technicians knowledgeable in computer systems, telecommunications, data bases, and library automation generally. The first two meetings of this group were sponsored by the Research Libraries Group (RLG) who were particularly interested in sharing details of their experience with a communications link to LC. As its first task, NTAG began to define a phased approach toward implementation of a computerized bibliographic network that would join together several networking organizations. The first phase called for interconnection by methods similar to those used by RLG. Subsequent phases were postulated that would widen participation and improve the modes of communication providing for bilateral and eventual multilateral sharing of information by all organizations involved. Subsequently, NTAG has engaged in specifying the technical issues that must eventually be resolved before an effective electronic network can be put into place. These include such topics as network topology, reliability, and performance characteristics. At the same time, NTAG has been building a schedule for the completion of technical tasks, clarifying interrelationships between tasks, and suggesting how each task might be accomplished.

Other LC Activities. Also in line with recommendations of NAC, a subcommittee of that body was formed to look into legal and governance issues. This subcommittee is formulating a work description for an investigation that will explore options and alternatives for the fiscal, legal, and organizational structure of the eventual network. It will take into consideration the role of various federal, multistate, state, and local entities in that network.

NDO has also begun an in-depth study of the role of authority information in a nationwide network. There is a recognition that use of authority information in a network is likely to differ substantially from use of this information within a single institution. The methodology for conducting this investigation had already been formulated as the result of earlier work. This new study should result in a general, high-level design for a comprehensive authority system to support the needs of a nationwide bibliographic network. Among the topics to be looked at in detail are the following: (1) a requirements definition for authority control in all segments of the American library community; (2) the relationship between these requirements for the various types of institutions involved; (3) the interrelationship between different and possibly incompatible authority systems, and (4) differences between requirements of LC and those of the network.

Yet another aspect of the complex picture presented by networking is embodied in a pilot project between LC and Northwestern University, which is testing the concept of using "centers of excellence" as the source of authoritative bibliographic records. In this pilot project Northwestern will catalog its Africana materials, using procedures that conform to LC cataloging practice. Northwestern will supply records in MARC communications format for subsequent distribution by LC. This project should pinpoint some of the problems and difficulties surrounding the construction of an authoritative bibliographic data base from multiple sources.

Task Force on Protocol. A group working outside the Library of Congress on issues related to nationwide networking was the NCLIS/NBS (National Bureau of Standards) Task Force on Computer Network Protocol. This group of telecommunications experts was chaired by NCLIS with a secretariat and staff support from NBS. The Task Force addressed itself to devising standards for facilitating computer-to-computer interchange of bibliographic information using telecommunications. After a 15-month effort, the Task Force produced a final report that contains a draft protocol and a series of recommendations. The protocol enables one computer to transfer bibliographic information to another computer in spite of different system architectures. This work represents the clearing away of a major, time-consuming technical roadblock to the eventual construction of a coherent computerized network. Among several recommendations made by the Task Force was that a means be pursued for making this draft protocol into an officially recognized national and international standard. The Task Force also cautioned that many issues regarding the precise operation of the protocol would only be understood as the protocol is actually implemented.

Protocol Planning Study. Acting on one of the recommendations of the NCLIS/NBS Task Force, the LC's NDO began still another related effort called the Protocol Implementation Planning Study (PIPS). Under contract with the New York Public Library, a subset of the original Task Force has begun to describe the steps required to conduct an adequate implementation of the NCLIS/NBS protocol in a realistic operating environment.

OTHER ORGANIZATIONS

At the same time that activities were being orchestrated at the national level, significant developments were taking place at a number of bibliographic utilities and other related organizations.

Ohio College Library Center. The Ohio College Library Center (OCLC) has by far the largest clientele for automated library information processing, with more than 1,800 terminals connected on-line to its computers from more than 1,000 libraries in 46 states. Two events must be mentioned with respect to the Center.

Of special significance was the completion during the year of a study of new governance alternatives for OCLC. Funding for this study was provided by the Council on Library Resources (CLR), and the study itself was carried out by the management consulting firm of Arthur D. Little, Inc. Based on this study, specific recommendations for a change in governance structure were presented to the OCLC membership for their vote in December 1977. Although OCLC has served libraries in almost every state of the union, only Ohio libraries have had membership status in the organization.

The study details several alternatives to the present organization and analyzes the problems and difficulties posed by each alternative. Most of the alternatives aim at providing wider and more representative membership and governing structures. At its annual meeting in December 1977, the OCLC membership voted to amend the OCLC articles of incorporation, adopting the new name "OCLC, Inc." Members voted to extend membership to libraries participating in the system regardless of their geographical location. They created a User's Council and adopted changes in the composition of the Board of Trustees and their manner of election. They also voted to form a separate, autonomous network for Ohio participants to be known as OHIONET.

Also of some note was the formulation of a long-range development plan. This plan, which covers a six-year period, signals the beginning of an era of planned and controlled growth for OCLC. It was the previous policy of OCLC to bring new terminals, institutions, and applications onto the system on a first-come-first-served basis. In 1977 it became imperative to allocate the number of terminals added to the system, and in future years it seems likely that there will be close scrutiny of use patterns and demands made on the system to insure a more equitable distribution of this computerized resource. This situation confronts libraries with the reality of a second-order scarcity—that is, a scarcity even in those mechanisms that libraries have been turning to as a way of improving the use of other scarce resources.

Research Libraries Group. A link from RLG to the Library of Congress became operational during 1977. This link consists of a computer-to-computer connection from the New York Public Library (NYPL) to the Library of Congress for deriving pertinent records from the LC MARC file to supplement a file maintained at NYPL. Catalogers at Columbia and NYPL first search their own data base for a record, and, if it is not found, may then search the LC data base. The link is unidirectional with respect to bibliographic data flow. Records are derived from LC, but not returned or updated to LC from RLG. Further observation and measurement of the effectiveness of this technique is in progress.

Concurrently, RLG has formulated its needs more specifically in terms of the computerized system it believes is most appropriate for large research libraries. This statement of needs was then turned into a request for proposals from suppliers who could support those needs. Responses to this request were received from BALLOTS, NYPL, the University of Chicago, and OCLC among others. Site visits and evaluation of these proposals took place in the last quarter of 1977, with a decision expected by March of 1978.

Ballots. The BALLOTS system of Stanford University experienced a year of remarkable growth subsequent to its initiation of on-line shared cataloging in November 1976. There are now more than 120 libraries regularly using BALLOTS. About 40 of these libraries are creating records for cataloging purposes. Since the system provides subject searching and several other modes of access, another 80 libraries are using BALLOTS for reference services. During 1977 BALLOTS established new goals and priorities and underwent a change in management. Placing overall emphasis on a "quality data base," BALLOTS sees its services as especially suiting the needs of large academic and research libraries. This by no means excludes smaller libraries from benefiting, and BALLOTS intends to focus its marketing efforts on all types of libraries in California and the Western states. BALLOTS now reports directly to the provost of Stanford University instead of to the Stanford Center for Information Processing. The new management has announced its firm intention to make BALLOTS a nationwide service and to formulate a sound business plan that will make BALLOTS self-sustaining.

Washington Library Network. 1977 was a banner year for the Washington Library Network (WLN). In July, after a brief pilot operation, WLN began full production using its on-line bibliographic subsystem which provides cataloging support services. In this subsystem, WLN places particular emphasis on network-wide authority control. While bringing its technical network on-line in July, the WLN network also became a legal entity and implemented a governance structure that includes a Representative Assembly and an Executive Council. Within the state, WLN sees itself as a proving ground for the concept of a full-service network, complementing its automated services with resource sharing, collection building, interlibrary loan, and continuing education networks.

An expansion in service is also under way with a test implementation of an acquisitions subsystem at the Washington State Library and subsequent extension of this service scheduled for the library at Washington State University. A circulation control system at the Tacoma Public Library, based on a stand-alone minicomputer, will also be interfaced with network functions as it is developed. This interconnection should become a prototype for other circulation systems in that state.

Rapidly extending from a base of 40 on-line terminals, WLN has accepted its first member from Alaska. This move toward multistate service has already brought about a review of the WLN governance, as the network management stresses its commitment to keep the network's administrative form in step with its new constituencies.

R.R. Bowker Company. In the commercial sector, the R.R. Bowker Company conducted a marketing and application study for a Library/Bookstore Acquisitions System. Such a system would build on the massive bibliographic files Bowker already maintains for production of *Books in Print*. It would serve not only libraries but also booksellers, jobbers, and publishers alike, creating a method for ready interchange of data between publishers and their marketplace. Bowker is continuing to examine the results of this study and is in the planning stages of possible system development.

C L Systems, Inc. Another interesting innovation in the commercial sector is an experimental connection between the CLSI Libs 100 circulation systems of CL Systems, Inc., and the on-line bibliographic inquiry system offered by Bro-dart. This interconnection allows a user at a CLSI terminal to log-on to the Bro-dart system to derive more complete bibliographic information, which can then be automatically incorporated into the circulation file data base. The Libs 100 user can at the same time order preprocessed books, cards, and spine labels through Bro-dart. In this way the two systems complement each other in a primitive symbiosis. The Marin County Public Library has demonstrated an interest in the installation using this kind of connection. CLSI is negotiating to make a similar connection between its systems and BALLOTS. These offerings may then become options that can be provided to any CLSI user.

SOME OBSERVATIONS

Several concepts surfaced during 1977 which will continue to influence the development of the library bibliographic component. First, it is almost superfluous to point to the common thread of governance concerns. Clearly, this indicates a new appreciation for the importance of building bibliographic service organizations on a firm footing and a realization of the difficulties inherent in continually reworking governance once an organization is on its way.

Second, in spite of the seeming omnipresence of computerized bibliographic services, it is well to recognize that only a small portion of the library community is being reached. Mostly restricted to academic libraries, these services have hardly made a dent in public and special libraries. Moreover, the products offered are surprisingly unrefined and, for the most part, oriented narrowly toward cataloging support and reference services.

From this perspective, it is clear that the library bibliographic component is still in its infancy. Optimal patterns for information delivery have not yet emerged. Much work remains before this component is integrated with other elements of a full-service network—a network not restricted to bibliographic information or computerized data, but encompassing all methods and techniques that can improve access to information for all the nation's citizens.

Third, although it is often claimed that economic considerations have impelled the development of network services, no convenient economic model exists for gauging the impact of new network products. This leaves network planners without a succinct basis for judging that a network approach is reasonable in one case but not in another. Nor does there seem to be any general agreement on principles of cost recovery, cross-subsidization, importance of market stability, appropriate stimuli for market growth, or acceptable bases for tariff construction. A model that provides a common conceptual framework and helps us to cope with the large-scale economic forces is sorely needed.

Fourth, standards for computerized network services are, for the most part, lacking or embryonic. Almost no standards exist for log-on procedures, command languages, query syntax, bibliographic responses, error messages, library and patron identifiers, and so forth. Very little of this crazy quilt of practices enhances the competitive advantage of the products concerned. It immerses the user in a quandary of expectations; normal behavior on one system is exceptional on another. There should be a thorough examination of pertinent areas for standardization, together with careful scrutiny of processes for creating and modifying those standards.

Finally, computerized networks are riding a tide of technological innovation. It has recently become clear that rapid advances in technology have outpaced our collective ability to make cogent policy decisions regarding the best use of that technology. New attempts to deal with this situation, now evident at the highest levels in the government, will surely affect the delivery of library services.

In the past few years, Congress has been bombarded by information-related bills of every description. Copyright, freedom of information, privacy, electronic funds transfer, and communications reform are just a few of these. In the communications area, the House Subcommittee on Communications is reviewing technological advances such as fiber optics and satellites as well as sociological outgrowths of technology such as the phenomenal boom in video games and CB radios. It seems probable that one result will be a substantial revision of the Communications Act of 1934 to establish a new framework for national communications policy that will influence us well into the next century.

The Office of Technology Assessment (OTA), an agency of Congress, has been asked to study this area of communications together with technological innovations in computers, digital storage, and consumer electronics to assist in the formulation of guidelines for information policy generally. It seems likely from this and other initiatives that a comprehensive national information policy will evolve during the next decade and profoundly affect many aspects of electronic networking.

AL TREZZA

Notable Books

The American Library Association's 1977 *Notable Books* list was released during Midwinter Meeting in Chicago in January 1978. Compiled for use by the general reader and by librarians who work with adult readers, the list includes titles selected for their significant contribution to the widening of knowledge or for the pleasure they can provide to adult readers. The criteria for selection also included wide general appeal and literary merit. (See the 1976 *ALA Yearbook* for a list of *Notable Books* from 1944 to 1975.)

The Notable Books Council of 1977 included Jerome K. Corrigan, Prince George's County Memorial Library (Oxon Hill, Maryland); Kay Ann Cassell, Bethlehem Public Library (Delmar, New York); Robert Donahugh, The Public Library of Youngstown and Mahoning County (Ohio); Elizabeth Egan, Helen M. Plum Memorial Library (Lombard, Illinois); Jeanne Gelinas, Hennepin County Library (Edina, Minnesota); Lyn Hart, George Peabody Library (Baltimore); Jane K. Hirsch, Montgomery County Public Library (Rockville, Maryland); Joan Hoagland, Cleveland Public Library; Martha Reynolds, Frederick County Public Library (Maryland); Ross Stephen, University of Wisconsin (Oshkosh); Susan Sutton, Bloomfield Township Public Library (Bloomfield Hills, Michigan); Wendell Wray, University of Pittsburgh; and Dorothy Snowden, a consultant for *Booklist*.

Notable Books

John Ashbery
: *Houseboat Days* (Viking)

Mikhail Baryshnikov with photos by Martha Swope
: *Baryshnikov at Work* (Knopf)

W. Jackson Bate
: *Samuel Johnson* (Harcourt Brace Jovanovich)

Anthony Berlant and Mary Hunt Kahlenberg
: *Walk in Beauty: The Navaho and Their Blankets* (Little Brown)

John Berryman
: *Henry's Fate & Other Poems, 1967-1972* (Farrar, Straus & Giroux)

Elizabeth Bishop
: *Geography III* (Farrar, Straus & Giroux)

Robert Brain
: *Kolonialagent* (Harper & Row)

Philip Caputo
: *A Rumor of War* (Holt, Rinehart & Winston)

Patricia Cooper and Norma Bradley Buferd
: *The Quilters: Women and Domestic Art* (Doubleday)

Milovan Djilas
: *Wartime* (Harcourt Brace Jovanovich)

Elizabeth Drew
: *American Journal: The Events of 1976* (Random House)

Gloria Emerson
: *Winners and Losers: Battles, Retreats, Gains, Losses and Ruins from a Long War* (Random House)

Willard R. Espy
: *Oysterville: Roads to Grandpa's Village* (Clarkson N. Potter)

Marilyn French
: *The Women's Room* (Summit Books)

John Gardner
: *The Life and Times of Chaucer* (Knopf)

Thomas Gavin
: *Kingkill* (Random House)

Boyd Gibbons
: *Wye Island: Outsiders, Insiders and Resistance to Change* (Johns Hopkins University Press)

James Hanley
: *A Dream Journey* (Horizon)

Marvin Harris
: *Cannibals and Kings: The Origins of Cultures* (Random House)

Margaret Hennig and Anne Jardim
: *The Managerial Woman* (Doubleday)

Michael Herr
: *Dispatches* (Knopf)

Claire Joyes
: *Monet at Giverny* (Two Continents)

Richard E. Leakey and Roger Lewin
: *Origins* (Dutton)

Robert Lowell
: *Day by Day* (Farrar, Straus & Giroux)

David McCullough
: *The Path between the Seas: the Creation of the Panama Canal, 1870-1914* (Simon and Schuster)

John McPhee
: *Coming into the Country* (Farrar, Straus & Giroux)

Jessica Mitford
: *A Fine Old Conflict* (Knopf)

Elsa Morante
: *History: A Novel* (Knopf)

Toni Morrison
: *Song of Solomon* (Knopf)

V.S. Naipaul
: *India: A Wounded Civilization* (Knopf)

Vance Packard
: *The People Shapers* (Little, Brown)

Walker Percy
: *Lancelot* (Farrar, Straus & Giroux)

Carl Sagan
: *The Dragons of Eden: Speculations on the Evolution of Human Intelligence* (Random House)

Anthony Sampson
: *The Arms Bazaar: From Lebanon to Lockheed* (Viking)

Thomas Savage
: *I Heard My Sister Speak My Name* (Little, Brown)

Paul Scott
: *Staying On* (William Morrow)

Richard Selzer
: *Mortal Lessons: Notes on the Art of Surgery* (Simon and Schuster)

Susan Richards Shreve
: *A Woman like That* (Atheneum)

Peter Taylor
: *In the Miro District and Other Stories* (Knopf)

Paul Theroux
: *The Consul's File* (Houghton Mifflin)

Gore Vidal
: *Matters of Fact and Fiction; Essays 1973-1976* (Random House)

E.B. White
: *The Essays of E.B. White* (Harper and Row)

Marie Winn
: *The Plug-In Drug* (Grossman/Viking)

Richard Wright
: *American Hunger* (Harper & Row)

Obituaries

BATCHELOR, LILLIAN L.

(1907-1977), died in Moorestown, New Jersey, on June 28. Born in Camden, New Jersey, on November 17, 1907, she received a B.S. degree from the University of Pennsylvania in 1930, a B.S. in L.S. degree from Drexel Institute, an M.A. degree from Columbia University in 1946, and an Ed.D. degree from Columbia in 1952.

She was Librarian of Ogontz Junior College in Pennsylvania from 1930 to 1932 and a teacher and Librarian in the Junior-Senior High School in Prospect Park, Pennsylvania, from 1932 to 1937. In 1937 Batchelor became a teacher and Librarian in the Vaux Junior High School in the Philadelphia School District. The rest of her career was spent in Philadelphia, as Librarian and Head of the English Department of Bok Technical High School (1938-48), Supervisor of School Libraries for the Board of Education (1948-66), and Assistant Director in Charge of Libraries (1966-74).

From 1958 until her retirement she served as Adjutant to the faculty of the Graduate School of Library Science at Drexel University and was frequently a consultant to workshops throughout the United States on various aspects of school library service.

Active in local, state, and national professional organizations, she served as President of the American Association of School Librarians and served on the ALA Council.

In 1966 she received the Alumna of Distinction Award from the University of Pennsylvania and in 1967 the Drexel Alumni Award. The Pennsylvania Library Association presented her with an award of merit in 1971.

CHILDS, JAMES BENNETT

(1896-1977), member of the Library of Congress staff from 1925, is credited with making the library one of the world's greatest repositories of official publications. His appreciation of the value of government documents, including legislative proceedings, agency reports, executive documents, and treaties and statutes led him to compile bibliographies of domestic and foreign agencies, to write the first guides to the use of such publications, and to develop improved methods for maintaining collections.

Born in Van Buren, Missouri, on March 2, 1896, Childs attended the University of Illinois, with time out for service in World War I. He received his B.A. degree and his B.S. in L.S. degree in 1921. He worked in the Cataloging Division of the John Crerar Library in Chicago from 1921 to 1925. When he went to the Library of Congress in 1925, his first post was in the Catalog Division of which he became Head in 1930. In 1934 he became Chief of the Division of Documents, moving to Acquisitions in 1943 and to Processing in 1948, where he was the Chief Documents Officer. In 1954 he became the Specialist in Government Documents Bibliography in the Reference Department, a position he held until his retirement in 1965. The Library appointed him Honorary Consultant in Government Bibliography. In 1976 he was appointed to a fourth three-year term.

A long career of international activity began in 1929 when Childs was a delegate to the World Library and Bibliographic Congress in Rome, the first of many international congresses he attended. His publications were concerned not only with U.S. documents but also with those of Central America and other American republics, the German Federal Republic, the German Democratic Republic, and the Spanish government. The catalog of the Library of Congress listed 55 publications, the earliest dated 1921, at the time of his retirement in 1965.

In 1971 Childs was awarded the ALA Gilbert Mudge Citation. In 1976 he received the first James Bennett Childs Award, established by the ALA Government Documents Round Table, for distinguished contributions to document librarianship. The Award was presented in a ceremony at the Library of Congress, at which Childs's family was present.

Many workers in the field of documents librarianship, looking always to Childs for leadership, feel that his formal honors were too few and too late. They value not only his dedication, his scholarship, and his published works, but also his willingness to share his intellectual wealth. Letters from younger librarians seeking assistance were answered promptly at length, and with gentle encouragement and general humor. He was delighted with the recognition by his colleagues in establishing the Childs Award in his name in 1976, less than a year before his death in Washington, D.C., on May 14, 1977.

FAST, ELIZABETH

(1931-1977), ALA Executive Board member (1975-77), school librarian and winner of the 1977 Grolier Award, died on June 16. Three days later ALA Membership passed a resolution mourning "the loss of an outstanding leader and articulate advocate for libraries and librarianship."

Born in Brooklyn on February 8, 1931, she received an A.B. degree from Radcliffe College in 1952, an L.S. degree from Southern Connecticut College in 1966, an M.L.S. degree from the University of Rhode Island in 1968, and the Sixth Year Professional Certificate in Education from the University of Connecticut in 1972. She was a candidate for a Ph.D. at Connecticut at the time of her death.

James Bennett Childs   *Elizabeth Fast*

OCLC: see Cataloging and Classification; Networks; Automation. *See* also various State Reports.

Obituaries

After work as a volunteer she became an elementary school librarian in the Groton Public Schools in Connecticut in 1962, Director of Library Services for the system in 1965, and Director of Education Media in 1968, continuing in that position until her death.

Her numerous professional activities included chairing the Groton School Library Advisory Committee from 1960 to 1964 and serving as Instructor in the Continuing Education Program at the University of Connecticut since 1968 and as Instructor at Columbia University in 1967.

Activities within ALA included membership on Council from 1969 to 1972 and from 1975 to 1977 and membership on COPES (Program Evaluation and Support from 1971 to 1977 and on ANACONDA in 1970-71. She held many committee assignments in the American Association of School Librarians. She was a member of the Newbery and Caldecott Awards Committee of the Children's Services Division in 1973-74 and a member of the Budgeting, Accounting, and Costs Committee of the Library Organization and Management Section of the Library Administration Division from 1971 to 1974.

She was an alternate to the White House Fellows Program in 1965 and received a Council on Library Resources Fellowship in 1972. She wrote many articles on media and related fields and edited the bulletins of the Connecticut Audiovisual Education Association and the Connecticut Educational Media Association. She contributed the article on "School Libraries and Media Centers" to the second volume of this series of *Yearbooks* (1977).

For more than 15 years Elizabeth Fast stood at the vanguard of school librarianship and gave strong leadership to the development of school media programs. The Grolier Award citation commended her for "sharing with her colleagues new ideas for better library service" through ALA committee and Council service and "continued involvement in all areas of library work."

GROSS, MASON WELCH

(1911-1977), President of Rutgers University from 1959 to 1971, Mason Gross was Chairman of the National Book Committee from 1968 to 1971. He had been Vice-President of the Committee from 1964 to 1968. He was a principal speaker at the 1963 ALA Annual Conference, opening the Conference within a Conference on "An Inquiry into the Needs of Libraries, Students, and the Educational Process."

Born in Hartford, Connecticut, on June 3, 1911, he went abroad after completing his secondary education in Connecticut. After two years at the University of Aberdeen in Scotland, he went to Cambridge University where he earned A.B. and M.A. degrees in classics. He received his Ph.D. degree from Harvard University in 1938. From 1942 to 1945 he served in the U.S. Air Force and was awarded the Bronze Star.

After holding teaching posts at Harvard and Columbia Universities, Gross went to Rutgers as Assistant Professor of philosophy in 1946. He held the positions of Vice-President and Provost and attained the rank of Professor before his appointment as President in 1959. He retired in 1971.

Under his tenure, the enrollment doubled and the University grew phenomenally in physical facilities and in educational scope and prestige. Gross was known principally, however, for his encouragement of innovation, his role in urging the legislature to increase higher education and cultural opportunities in New Jersey, his tenacious defense of civil liberties, and his expert and humane handling of student protests in the 1960's. He and the Board of Governors were given the Ninth Annual Meiklejon Award in 1966 for refusing to dismiss a competent professor who had been criticized for political views.

Gross edited *Alfred North Whitehead: An Anthology* (1953). He received nine honorary degrees and served on numerous boards of academic, cultural, and business institutions. In 1972 he became President of the H.F. Guggenheim Foundation.

At Gross's death October 11 in Red Bank, New Jersey, the newest division of Rutgers, the School of Creative and Performing Arts, was named the Mason Welch Gross School.

KAMINSTEIN, ABRAHAM LOUIS

(1912-1977), formerly Register of Copyrights at the Library of Congress, had held that post from 1960 until 1971 when he retired because of ill health. He had been deeply involved in the development of the copyright law enacted in 1976, presiding over the meetings of panels of consultants and testifying before Congress. Upon his retirement he was made Honorary Consultant in Domestic and International Copyright Affairs at the Library of Congress.

Born in New York City on May 3, 1912, Kaminstein received a B.A. degree from City College of New York in 1933. He received B.A. and M.A. degrees from Harvard Law School and was a Research Fellow at Harvard in 1936-37. He was a member of the New York Bar and was admitted to practice before the U.S. Supreme Court. He joined the Library of Congress in 1947, after serving as an attorney for several government agencies. He became Chief of the Copyright Examining Division and later Deputy Register of Copyrights.

A frequent contributor of journal articles on copyright law, Kaminstein was active in international as well as national copyright affairs. He served as the U.S. representative at various sessions of the Intergovernmental Copyright Committee established under the Universal Copyright Conven-

Mason Welch Gross

Abraham Louis Kaminstein

tion and was Chairman of the U.S. delegation to the International Convention for the Protection of Performers, Producers of Phonograms, and Broadcasting Organizations held in Rome in 1961. In the controversies between developing and developed countries over international copyright, his clarity and accuracy of expression and his gentlemanly tact were highly valued.

The German Society for Performing and Mechanical Rights in Music conferred the Richard Strauss Medal on Kaminstein in 1971. In 1972 he received the Jefferson Medal of the New Jersey Patent Law Association. He was given the 1977 Award of the Copyright Society of the U.S.A. before his death on September 10 in Washington, D.C.

KURTH, WILLIAM H.

(1917-1977), the first librarian to propose a methodology for measuring the changes in the prices of library materials, died on February 27.

Born July 4, 1917, in Union Hill, New Jersey, he received a B.A. degree from the University of Virginia in 1942 and an M.S. in L.S. from Catholic University of America in 1958. He worked at the Library of Congress as Filer-Searcher for the National Union Catalog (1943-44); as Head of the Order Section of the Order Division (1944-48); and as Assistant Chief of the Order Division (1948-59). From 1959 to 1962 he was Chief of the Circulation Division of the National Library of Medicine.

After serving as the Latin American Bibliographer at the University of California at Los Angeles in 1963, he moved to Washington University Library in St. Louis, where he advanced from Acquisition Chief to University Librarian.

While Assistant Chief of the Library of Congress Order Division he wrote "A Proposed Cost of Books Index and Cost of Periodicals Index" that appeared in *College & Research Libraries* (October 1955). His master's thesis, *Cost of Books Index Applied to Mexican Book Production—1947-1957*, completed at Catholic University in 1958, was a practical demonstration of his theory. As Chairman of the Cost of Library Materials Index Committee of the Resources Section of ALA's Resources and Technical Services Division, he issued the first price index of U.S. books in 1960. An expanded price index, coauthored with Frank Schick in 1961 and entitled *The Cost of Library Materials: Price Trends of Publications*, laid the foundation for all subsequent American price indexes.

From 1969 to 1971 he compiled a table of Mexican book prices for the Library Materials Price Index Committee. In 1972 he addressed the International Federation of Library Associations (IFLA) Committee on Statistics and Standards in Budapest on the need for international price indexes.

Kurth served as Chairman of the American National Standards Institute Z-39 Sub-Committee, which drafted the *American National Standard Criteria for Price Indexes for Library Materials*. Published in 1974, this standard has been officially adopted by the Library Materials Price Index Committee and was recommended as an international model to the IFLA Committee on Statistics and Standards.

His work on price indexes was only one facet of William Kurth's many contributions to librarianship. The library world is indebted to his vision and work in developing indispensable tools of library management.

LEVY, EVELYN

(1909-1977), a pioneer in library service to the disadvantaged, had a distinguished career in public libraries. Starting as a children's librarian in the Boston Public Library, she became a branch librarian and in 1956 went to the Enoch Pratt Free Library in Baltimore. She served as Assistant Coordinator of Adult Services and Head of the Book Selection Room until 1965 when she became the Library Supervisor in the city's Community Action Program. At the time of her retirement in 1974, she was a regional librarian.

Born in Boston on September 15, 1909, she was educated at Radcliffe College, where she received a B.A. degree in English literature in 1930. In 1947 she received a B.S. in L.S. degree from the Simmons College School of Library Science and in 1968 an M.A. from Johns Hopkins University. Always interested in library education, she served on the Advisory Board for Research Projects of the University of Maryland College of Library and Information Services, taught at the School of Library Science of Florida State University, and led seminars on library service to the disadvantaged at the University of Wisconsin Library School at Madison.

Through her professional associations, Evelyn Levy pursued her concerns for the social responsibilities of libraries and for the freedom to read. In 1965-66 she was President of the Maryland Library Association. For ALA she served on the Intellectual Freedom and Program Policy Committees of the Adult Services Division (now the Reference and Adult Services Division) and on the Board of the Freedom to Read Foundation. She was a charter member of the Social Responsibilities Round Table and served on the ALA Executive Board from 1970 to 1974. She played a key role in the work leading to the merger of the ALA Editorial Committee and the Publishing Board as the new ALA Publishing Committee (1975).

Always a well-prepared and thoughtful professional and participant, Evelyn Levy was also a person of great compassion, a delightful companion, and a warm friend. All of her qualities were called upon when she organized library service in the Community Action Program in southeast Baltimore, a poverty area and Black ghetto. With few precedents for guidance, she started by getting to know the people on the streets. In training Youth Corps and other lay assistants, collecting materials, and making them available, she used tradition when it served and created new approaches when they were needed. She died in Baltimore on February 17.

LINDQUIST, JENNIE D.

(1899-1977), librarian, author, and second editor of *The Horn Book Magazine*, died on February 8 in Manchester, New Hampshire, where she had been born on March 9, 1899. She attended the University of New Hampshire and the Simmons College School of Library Science, the latter as the first recipient of the Caroline M. Hewins Scholarship. After doing public library practice work in New York City she returned to work in the Carpenter Memorial Library in Manchester. She then went to the University of New Hampshire Library in Durham as

Obituaries

Consultant in work with children and young people for two years, leaving to become Director of work with children at the public library in Albany, New York.

In 1941 she became the first editor of "Hunter's Fare," the book inquiry column of *The Horn Book Magazine*. In 1948, she was named managing editor of the *Horn Book*, becoming editor in 1951 upon the retirement of the founder and first editor.

Lindquist's Caroline M. Hewins Lecture, entitled "Caroline M. Hewins and Books for Children," was published in *Horn Book* in 1951. She wrote three books for children: *The Golden Name Day*, a Newbery Medal Honor Book; *The Little Silver House*; and *The Crystal Tree*. These stories were based on reminiscences of a full year's seasons and of Swedish holidays during her own childhood.

In 1958 she retired from *Horn Book* to work with a friend in the John Mistletoe Bookshop in Albany, New York, where she spent the mornings writing and the afternoons selling children's books. She frequently taught summer courses in children's literature at the University of New Hampshire.

MORTON, ELIZABETH HOMER (1903-1977), distinguished Canadian librarian and educator, died July 6 in Ottawa. She retired in 1968 from the position as Executive Director and Editor in Chief of the Canadian Library Association—Association Canadienne des Bibliothèques.

Born in Tunapuna, Trinidad, on February 3, 1903, in 1926 she received a B.A. degree from Dalhousie University in Halifax, Nova Scotia, and certificates from the Nova Scotia Normal School and the Ontario Library School. In 1947 she studied at the University of Chicago, specializing in library science and adult education.

She began her career as a teacher in Nova Scotia and New Brunswick and was Executive Secretary of the New Brunswick Library Commission in 1930-31. From 1931 to 1944 she was a reference librarian in the Toronto Public Library, and she was Executive Secretary and editor for the Canadian Library Council in Ottawa from 1944 to 1946. An organizer of the Canadian Library Association (CLA), in 1946 she became its first Executive Director, administering its projects to expand library facilities throughout the country. Following retirement in 1968 Morton continued contributing to her profession as a free-lance library consultant, editor, and compiler.

During her career she worked in many national groups including the Canadian Association for Adult Education, Canadian Education Association, Canadian Federation of University Women, and National Council of Women. She was a member of the National Library Advisory Council, Canadian Citizenship Council, and Canadian Centenary Council. Her many honors included the Merit Award of the Canadian Library Trustees Association, the Centenary Medal of 1963, the Order of Canada in 1969, and an honorary LL.D. from the University of Alberta in 1969.

She was an important writer on librarianship, with significant contributions to professional journals, including her work as editor of *Canadian Library* for 24 years and of *Feliciter* for 12 years.

Elizabeth Morton was also an active member of the American Library Association, supporting joint action and cooperative programs such as the joint CLA-ALA Conference in Montreal in 1960. A longtime friend and colleague describing her years of service wrote that she served "with gaiety, imagination, wisdom, and boundless patience."

NESBITT, ELIZABETH (1897-1977), a library science teacher and specialist in library work with children in Pittsburgh, died August 17 in Atlantic City, New Jersey. Born in Northumberland, Pennsylvania, on April 15, 1897, she received a B.A.

Elizabeth Nesbitt

degree from Goucher College in 1918, a B.S. in L.S. from Carnegie Library School in 1931, and an M.A. from the University of Pittsburgh in 1935.

She began her career as a children's librarian in the Pittsburgh Public Library in 1922, becoming Supervisor of Storytelling in 1924. From 1926 to 1929 she was Librarian of the Pennsylvania State Teachers College in Clarion. Returning to Pittsburgh, she became Associate Professor at Carnegie Library School in 1929, and was Associate Dean and Professor from 1948 to 1962. From 1962 until her retirement in 1965 she was a member of the faculty of the University of Pittsburgh School of Library and Information Sciences.

Throughout her career, Nesbitt was honored many times for her achievements in library work with children. She was the coauthor of *A Critical History of Children's Literature*, first published in 1953. In 1958 she was named a Distinguished Daughter of Pennsylvania. In 1968 she spoke for the United States on training for children's services in libraries at an international conference on that subject sponsored by the Children's Section of the International Federation of Library Associations (IFLA).

The Elizabeth Nesbitt Room, which houses an important historical collection of children's books, was dedicated at the University of Pittsburgh Graduate School of Library and Information Sciences in 1976, honoring her for her devotion to librarianship and to education.

RICKING, MYRL, (1918-1977) Director of the Office of Recruitment of the American Library Association when it was established in 1962, died in Washington, D.C., on May 5, 1977.

Born in Ohio on August 2, 1918, she received a B.A. degree from the University of Cincinnati in 1940. She worked at the Board of Education Office in Cincinnati as an administrative secretary from 1940 to 1943 and then went to New York City where, from 1944 to 1946, she worked with the American National Red Cross. In 1946 she accepted a position in the Personnel Office at Yale University, and she became Executive Secretary of the Yale Library in 1947.

From 1951 to 1953 she was an editor at Field Enterprises Educational Corporation in Chicago. She went to Milwaukee as Chief of In-Service Training and Personnel Control of the Milwaukee Public Library in 1953. During the years in the Milwaukee position she was active in ALA and had chaired the Recruiting Committee of the Library Administration Division since 1957, when she was appointed Director for the new Office of Recruitment in 1962.

She effectively and successfully launched and developed ALA's recruitment program in a highly professional and imaginative manner. In 1967 she left the position to accept appointment as the Chief of the Manpower Utilization Office of the Library of Congress. After three years in that position she resigned to set up Manpower Resources, a consulting service for libraries that provided services of practical assistance to libraries in developing staff and revitalizing organizational structures.

SHIPMAN, JOSEPH COLLINS
(1908-1977), Librarian of the Linda Hall Library in Kansas City, Missouri, made that institution one of the outstanding science libraries in the country. When he was appointed Director in 1945, nothing existed but the bequest that was to make the Library possible. Shipman developed the collection and services from scratch, saw them appropriately housed, and attracted to the Library serious students and scientists from all over the world.

Born in Winnipeg, Manitoba, Canada, on January 20, 1908, he received his B.A. degree in chemistry and biology in 1929, and his B.S. in L.S. in 1932 from Western Reserve University in Cleveland. After working as an assistant in the Technical Division at the Cleveland Public Library for four years, he went to Union College in New York as a library counselor for 1937 to 1939. He was the Technical Librarian at the Toledo Public Library from 1939 to 1942, and the Head of the Science and Technology Division of the Enoch Pratt Free Library in Baltimore from 1942 to 1943 when he became Assistant Director of the Library. He was at Linda Hall from 1945 to his retirement in 1974.

Always active in professional associations. Shipman served as President of the Maryland Library Association in 1944-45 and of the Missouri Library Association in 1947-48 and as Treasurer of the ALA Association of College and Research Libraries from 1952 to 1955. He wrote two books, *Milestones in the History of Science* (1956) and *William Dampier, Seaman-Scientist* (1962). With Louis Nourse he made a survey of the Wichita Public Library in 1948. In 1963-64 he served on the Missouri Governor's Science Advisory Committee, and he was a Trustee of the Midwest Research Institute in Kansas City after 1966. He received honorary degrees from Park College in Missouri and the University of Missouri at Kansas City.

When Shipman died in Kansas City on June 13, Charles O'Halloran wrote a tribute in *Show-Me Libraries*, the publication of the Missouri State Library: "(He had) an ability to see the future and an ability to adhere steadfastly to the vision (that) manifests character, strength, and a certainty of purpose . . . a deep conviction."

SPIVACKE, HAROLD
(1904-1977), music librarian and musicologist, was an Honorary Consultant in Musicology to the Library of Congress. He had come to the Library in 1934 as Assistant Chief of the Music Division. In 1937 he was made Chief of the Division, a post he held until his retirement in 1972.

Born in New York City on July 18, 1904, Spivacke received his B.A. and M.A. degrees from New York University in 1923 and 1924. He received his Ph.D., magna cum laude, from the University of Berlin. From 1933 to 1934 he was a research assistant to Olin Downes, music critic of the New York *Times*.

A man of eclectic musical interests, Spivacke almost tripled the holdings of the Music Division, covering every type of music from jazz to neoclassic, and every form from manuscripts to scores to recordings. He supervised the establishment in 1940 of the Music Division's Recording Laboratory, and in 1959 instigated the first research study on the preservation and storage of sound recordings.

The Library of Congress concerts that Spivacke planned made Washington, D.C., according to one music critic, the "Chamber Music Capitol of the World." From the foundation funds available to the Library he commissioned works by such composers as Aaron Copland, George Crumb, Paul Hindemith, and Gian Carlo Menotti, works that had their premier performances at the Library.

Spivacke's advice was sought by the U.S. government in World War II when he became a member of the Joint Army and Navy Committee's subcommittee on music. From 1949 to 1955 he was a member of the Fulbright Advisory Selection Committee on Music, and he was Chairman of the U.S. Joint Commit-

Myrl Ricking

Joseph Collins Shipman

Harold Spivacke

Obituaries

tee on the International Inventory of Musical Sources for more than 10 years.

Frequently honored, Spivacke was awarded honorary degrees from Baldwin-Wallace College in Ohio in 1947, the University of Rochester in 1955, and the Cleveland Institute of Music in 1967. The Organization of American States (OAS) gave him citations in 1965 and 1971. He received the Library of Congress Distinguished Service Award in 1965 and the National Music Council Citation in 1972. One of the citations from OAS mentions his contributions to the "advancement of mutual understanding, solidarity, and cooperation among the peoples of the Western Hemisphere." Spivacke died in Washington, D.C., on May 9.

WIESE, BERNICE (MARION) (1905-1977), Retired Director of Library Services for the Baltimore public school system and a library consultant, died December 12 in Baltimore.

Born in San Francisco on April 18, 1905, she earned a B.A. degree at Goucher College in 1926, an M.A. degree at Duke University in 1929, and a B.S. in L.S. degree at Columbia University in 1948. After teaching in Baltimore in 1926, she moved to Augusta, Georgia, in 1929 where she taught in a high school for five years. She returned to Baltimore as a junior high school librarian in 1935. In 1946 she was given a year to organize a city elementary school library system and was then named Director of Library Services, the position she held at her retirement in 1968.

During a sabbatical in 1964-65 she served as a school library consultant to the Malaysian Ministry of Education under a Fulbright-Hays Grant. After retirement she returned to Southeast Asia, again on a Fulbright Grant, to lecture on library science at the Teachers Training College in Singapore. In addition to teaching abroad she taught summer courses in library science at John Hopkins University, the University of Delaware, the State University of New York at Geneseo, and Drexel Institute.

Wiese was active in professional organizations. She was a member of ALA Council; Secretary of the Buildings and Equipment Section of the Library Administration Division from 1956 to 1960; Second Vice-President of the American Association of School Librarians in 1962-63; and Chairman of the Committee on Planning School Library Quarters from 1955 to 1959. She was active also in the Association for Supervision and Curriculum Development, the National Association of Secondary School Principals, and the National School Public Relations Association—all departments of the National Education Association. She held offices in the Maryland Library Association and also in the Maryland Association of School Librarians, serving as President from 1944 to 1946.

She was a frequent contributor to professional journals and was editor of the *International Association of School Librarianship Newsletter* from 1971 until her death.

WOFFORD, AZILE M. (1896-1977), faculty member of the University of Kentucky Department of Library Science (now the College of Library Science) from 1938 to 1961, died in Asheville, North Carolina, on April 21. Born in Laurens, South Carolina, on February 1, 1896, she received a B.A. degree from Winthrop College in South Carolina in 1915, a B.S. degree from George Peabody College in Tennessee in 1935, and an M.S. degree from Columbia University in 1938.

From 1915 to 1918 she was a principal in rural schools in South Carolina. She worked in the U.S. Navy Bureau, Supplies and Accounts, in Washington, D.C., in 1918-19. From 1927 to 1934 Wofford was Librarian at the high school in Laurens, South Carolina, and she was an assistant reference librarian in Greenville, South Carolina, from 1935 to 1937. In 1938 she went to the University of Kentucky Department of Library Science as Assistant Professor. She became Associate Professor and during two interim periods was Acting Head of the Department.

Always active in professional associations, she was President of the Kentucky Library Association in 1947-48. She served as Chairman of the Section on Work with Children and Young People of the Southeastern Library Association and upon her retirement in 1961 was given the Association's Certificate of Honor. She worked closely with school library supervisors in other Southern states as well as Kentucky and made significant contributions to the committees of the Southern Association that worked on preparing standards for elementary and secondary schools.

Azile Wofford's writing, as well as her teaching, reflected her deep interest in training students to handle the practical aspects of running a library. *Know the South* (1943), a bibliography on the South for use in high schools; *The School Library at Work* (1959); and *Book Selection for School Libraries* (1962), widely used for years, were highly valued by school librarians.

Oral History Association

The Oral History Association (OHA), founded in 1965, is an international society of organizations and individuals interested in advancing the practice and use of oral history. The Association also promulgates standards and is concerned with professional ethics.

OHA Officers

PRESIDENT:
William Wyatt, Western Health System, Rapid City, South Dakota

PRESIDENT-ELECT:
Waddy Moore, University of Central Arkansas, Conway

EXECUTIVE SECRETARY:
Ronald E. Marcello, North Texas State University, Denton

Membership (August 31, 1977):

Activities. OHA holds an annual workshop and colloquium each fall. The workshop is designed to meet the needs of novices, with concentration on establishing a program, funding, interviewing techniques, and transcribing. The colloquium covers a variety of topics in the field of oral history and usually features several keynote speakers of national reputation. An annual business meeting is also held in conjunction with the colloquium.

OHA cooperates fully with the activities undertaken by state and regional oral history organizations. OHA provides publications at discount rates to these groups, supplies keynote speakers for their annual meetings, and encourages joint membership arrangements. OHA has recently established an evaluation service for ongoing programs in order to develop standards. OHA will provide regional evaluators for any program desiring this service.

Publications. OHA publishes an annual *Oral History Review* and a quarterly *Newsletter*. Both publications are part of the yearly membership package. Single issues of the *Review* and *Newsletter* may also be purchased by writing the executive secretary. All out-of-print publications are reproduced for sale in microform by the Microfilming Corporation of America. Occasional publications include the *Bibliography on Oral History* and *Oral History in the United States: A Directory*.

Annual Meetings. The 12th annual meeting was held October 20-23 at Coronado, California, and was attended by 330. The 1978 annual meeting is scheduled for October 19-22 at Savannah, Georgia.

Membership. The membership categories and dues are $10 for individual members, $25 for institutional members, $250 for life members, $10 for library members (nonvoting), and $7.50 for student members (nonvoting).

RONALD E. MARCELLO

Organization of American States

As a priority activity of the Library and Archives Development Program of the Organization of American States (OAS), progress was made in 1977 in the development of the necessary infrastructure for an inter-American network for transmitting bibliographic information, both that of a cataloging nature and that available through automated data bases. Decentralized activities have been carried out in the field, primarily through national and multinational projects requested by member states. The activities have included advisory services, training programs, library materials and equipment for the project centers, and technical meetings and reports, with planning, coordination, and technical supervision provided by the OAS General Secretariat.

The standardization of cataloging practices and procedures in Latin America and the Caribbean that are essential for their eventual automation and participation in Universal Bibliographic Control received special attention in 1977. The AMIGOS Bibliographic Council was contracted to provide technical assistance to the University of Costa Rica to develop a centralized cataloging service for Central America and to the Colombian Institute for the Promotion of Higher Education (ICFES) for a cooperative cataloging project. They are to serve as pilot projects for comparison of two approaches to national and regional cataloging problems.

The development of an adequate authority control system for both subject headings and name headings gained momentum through technical assistance to ICFES in 1977. A technical meeting was held in Colombia with outside experts, and there was a study tour of U.S. and Canadian automated cataloging projects by those responsible in Colombia for the cooperative cataloging project and the expansion of the Rovira list of subject headings in Spanish. Brazilian librarians were urged to plan for the development of a similar authority control system in Portuguese, to be coordinated with the system for Spanish. Plans were made and funds approved for technical assistance in 1978 to create Inter-American Centers at the University of Costa Rica for library standardization and at the Mexican Consejo Nacional de Ciencia y Tecnología (CONACYT) for library automation. Both would serve as training centers and research and demonstration projects and for the production of work and training manuals. The first definitive edition of *MARCAL: Manual de*

Older Adults, Library Services to: *see* Adults, Library Services to

Organizations and Associations

la Automatización de las Reglas Catalográficas para América Latina was submitted for printing, and authorization was granted for the translation into Spanish of the Library of Congress format for authority records. The first automation project of CONACYT will be the production of the Mexican national bibliography as a by-product of cataloging at the National Library.

National library and information systems continued to be of prime concern during 1977, with assistance given to Bolivia, Costa Rica, and Nicaragua for national school library system. Assistance was given to Peru for a regional educational documentation network, to Colombia for public school libraries, and to El Salvador for planning to strengthen national libraries in order to centralize the development of school and public libraries. A few "centers of excellence" received OAS assistance for purposes such as creating a learning resources center at a teacher training school in El Salvador.

Information services to industry from a university library were initiated in 1977 with OAS assistance in a pilot project at the University of Trujillo in Peru. The project will organize the university's library system, build a new building, and expand reference services, with a view to creating a national university library network.

Training programs continued to receive OAS support in 1977 in the form of professors, fellowships, and travel grants for regional and national schools for librarians in Colombia and Bolivia and for archivists in Argentina, the Dominican Republic, and Spain. The regular OAS fellowship program gives first priority to library school teachers for advanced study in the United States and Puerto Rico. Attention was given to planning for graduate level professional training in Brazil and Mexico, with funds anticipated for a school in Guanajuato, Mexico, in 1979. Plans for a library research program were developed at the Inter-American Library School in Medellín, Colombia. A modest grant requested by Jamaica made possible a one-day course in restoration and conservation of paper in the tropics at a joint meeting of Caribbean library and archives associations in Curaçao.

Some 16 projects of an inter-American and national nature were carried out in 1977 in Argentina, Barbados, Bolivia, Chile, Colombia, Costa Rica, the Dominican Republic, Ecuador, El Salvador, Jamaica, Nicaragua, Paraguay, Peru, and Uruguay, with expenditures from $10,000 to $84,000.

For the 1978-79 biennium 42 new project proposals were received from member states, evaluated by the four library and archives specialists, and reviewed by a series of five inter-American committees and councils. The OAS General Assembly in December approved funds for 9 new and 15 continuing projects in 1978. Of the $500,000 contributed for the first time by the U.S. government to the cultural program, some $45,000 was approved for library projects. The production of books for children in Venezuela adds a new dimension to the concerns of countries for libraries and information services.

In response to the May 1977 mandate of the Inter-American Council for Education, Science, and Culture (CIECC) for the coordination of all library and information activities of the OAS by the Library and Archives Development Program, a draft plan was prepared for an integrated project in library and information services and systems. The design of the library-bibliographic component of the proposed inter-American system would include not only perfection of the infrastructure on which the OAS has already embarked but also the creation of a library network among the member states for transmitting bibliographic data, accessing data banks, and creating data banks in the various countries. The system would also establish a central data bank of publications from or about Latin America as well as a documents delivery system coordinated by the Columbus Memorial Library of the OAS in Washington, D.C.

Advisory services were continued in 1977 to member states for the Spanish translation of *Dewey Decimal System* and to the Books for the People Fund and Project LEER.

MARIETTA DANIELS SHEPARD

Organizations and Associations

The American Library Association has a special relationship with the organizations and associations cited here. All data given are as of the end of 1977 unless otherwise indicated. (The asterisk denotes ALA membership in the organization.)

Adult Education Association of the United States of America*
(founded 1951)

PURPOSE: To further the concept of education as a continuing process throughout life. The Association makes available knowledge about adult continuing education, alerts key leadership and the general public to the need for lifelong learning, and provides an organizational framework for persons who make adult education their professional commitment. The Association works with program development and legislation at the federal and state levels and seeks to stimulate local, state, and regional adult education activities. Special interest sections and commissions are created to advance theory and research and to translate educational or social concerns of the adult learner into practice.

MEMBERS/SUBSCRIBERS: 5,600.

PRESIDENT: Huey B. Long (November 1977-October 1978).

PRESIDENT-ELECT: Donnie Dutton (November 1977- October 1978).
EXECUTIVE DIRECTOR: Linda S. Hartsock.
PUBLICATIONS: *Lifelong Learning: The Adult Years* (10 issues a year); *Adult Education* (quarterly).
HEADQUARTERS: 810 18th Street, N.W., Washington, D.C. 20006.

Alliance for Information and Referral Services

PURPOSE: To serve as a clearinghouse for exchange of technical, operational, and research ideas and information.
Annual Expenditure: $10,000.
PRESIDENT: Rosendo Gutierrez.
VICE-PRESIDENT/PRESIDENT-ELECT: Risha Levinson.
SECRETARY: Jean Coleman.
EXECUTIVE DIRECTOR: Corazon Esteva Doyle.
PUBLICATIONS: *National Directory of Information and Referral Services in the United States and Canada* (biannually); *Proceedings of the AIRS Roundtable* (on conference years); *National Standards for Information and Referral* (biannually).
HEADQUARTERS: P.O. Box 10705, Phoenix, Arizona 85064.
ALA REPRESENTATIVE: Jean Coleman.

Alliance of Associations for the Advancement of Education*
(founded 1970)

PURPOSE: To improve the quality of education in America through promoting cooperation among member associations in the exchange of information, in the conduct of research, in the issuance of substantive statements on crucial issues in education, in the development of projects which are of concern to member organizations and in the provision of special services to association operations.
MEMBERSHIP: 8; *Annual Expenditure:* $6,000.
PRESIDENT: Alberta L. Meyer (July 1, 1977-June 30, 1978).
VICE-PRESIDENT/PRESIDENT-ELECT: E. Glenadine Gibb.
EXECUTIVE SECRETARY/TREASURER: Elvie Lou Luetge.
EVENTS: Quarterly Round Table Meetings.
HEADQUARTERS: 3615 Wisconsin Avenue, N.W., Washington, D.C. 20016.

American Association for Gifted Children
(founded 1945)

PURPOSE: To recognize and stimulate creative work among gifted children, to foster appreciation of their capabilities, to promote plans to further their interests, to encourage public sentiment in support of early recognition of gifted children and their welfare, to arouse community agencies such as ALA as to the needs of the gifted, and to publish supporting materials.
MEMBERSHIP: 200; *Annual Expenditure:* modest.
PRESIDENT: Anne Impellizzeri (1976-77).
VICE-PRESIDENT AND EXECUTIVE DIRECTOR: Marjorie L. Craig.
PUBLICATIONS: *Guideposts; The Gifted Child* (as needed), cooperative publication with ALA entitled "The Library Is My Best Friend."
HEADQUARTERS: 15 Gramercy Park, New York, New York 10003.
ALA REPRESENTATIVE: Naomi Noyes, Association for Library Service to Children (1976-77).

American Association for the Advancement of Science
(founded 1848)

PURPOSE: To further the work of scientists, to facilitate cooperation among them, to foster scientific freedom and responsibility, to improve the effectiveness of science in the promotion of human welfare, and to increase public understanding and appreciation of the importance and promise of the methods of science in human progress.
MEMBERSHIP: 128,560; *Annual Expenditure:* $8,522,207 (1976).
PRESIDENT: Emilio Q. Daddario (1977).
VICE-PRESIDENT/PRESIDENT-ELECT: Edward E. David, Jr.
EXECUTIVE SECRETARY: William D. Carey.
PUBLICATIONS: *Science* (weekly); *Science Books & Films* (quarterly).
HEADQUARTERS: 1515 Massachusetts Avenue, N.W., Washington, D.C. 20005.
ALA REPRESENTATIVE: Russell Shank, Association of College and Research Libraries (1977-80).

American Association of Community and Junior Colleges.
(founded 1920 as American Association of Junior Colleges)

PURPOSE: To provide national direction and leadership and promote the development of community and junior colleges in America and internationally.
MEMBERSHIP: 900; *Annual* Expenditure: $2,500,000.
CHAIRPERSON: Richard H. Hagemeyer (July 1976-July 1977).
VICE-CHAIRPERSON: Lee G. Henderson.
PRESIDENT (executive officer); Edmund J. Gleazer, Jr.
PUBLICATIONS: *Community and Junior College Journal* (8 issues a year); *Community, Junior and Technical College Directory* (annually).
HEADQUARTERS: National Center for Higher Education, One Dupont Circle, N.W., Washington, D.C. 20036.
ALA AFFILIATION: Joint Committee on Learning Resources Programs. Association for College and Research Libraries; chairperson, William J. Hoffman (1975-76).

American Association of University Professors (AAUP)
(founded 1915)

PURPOSE: Organization of college and university teachers, research scholars, and academic librarians for the promotion of professional and educational interests.
MEMBERSHIP: 83,500; *Annual* Expenditure: $2,000,000.
PRESIDENT: Peter O. Steiner (through June 1978).
VICE-PRESIDENT: Martha Friedman.
GENERAL SECRETARY: Morton S. Baratz.
PUBLICATIONS: *Academe* (quarterly); *AAUP Bulletin* (quarterly).
HEADQUARTERS: One Dupont Circle, Washington, D.C. 20036.

American Booksellers Association (ABA)
(founded 1900)

PURPOSE: To create and maintain favorable trade conditions and foster good bookseller-publisher relations. To increase the sale of books of all types by assisting members in dealing with operational and public relations problems.
MEMBERSHIP: 5,045; *Annual Expenditure:* $1,100,000.
PRESIDENT: Robert D. Hale.
VICE-PRESIDENT: Robert Dike Blair.
EXECUTIVE DIRECTOR: G. Roysce Smith.
PUBLICATIONS: *Newswire, Basic Book List, Book Buyer's Handbook, Sidelines Directory* and *American Bookseller.*
HEADQUARTERS: 122 East 42nd Street, New York, New York 10017.
See also article in text: *Bookselling.*

American Civil Liberties Union*
(founded 1920)

PURPOSE: Defense of civil liberties; freedom of inquiry

Organizations and Associations

and expression; due process of law; equal protection of the laws, and privacy.
MEMBERSHIP: 200,000; *Annual Expenditure;* $8,000,000.
CHAIRPERSON: Norman Dorsen (1977-78).
EXECUTIVE DIRECTOR: Aryeh Neier.
PUBLICATIONS: *Civil Liberties* (quarterly); *Privacy Report* (monthly); *First Principles* (monthly).
HEADQUARTERS: 22 East 40th Street, New York, New York 10016.

American Correctional Association
(founded 1870 as National Prison Association)
PURPOSE: To strengthen and increase recognition of corrections as a profession and contribute to the professionalization of correctional personnel.
MEMBERSHIP: 10,000; *Annual Expenditure:* $1,500,000 (December 31, 1977).
PRESIDENT: William D. Leeke (August 1976-July 1978).
VICE-PRESIDENT: Katherine Gable.
EXECUTIVE DIRECTOR: Anthony P. Travisono.
PUBLICATION: *American Journal of Correction* (bimonthly).
HEADQUARTERS: 4321 Hartwick Road, Suite L-208, College Park, Maryland 20740.
ALA AFFILIATION: Joint Committee on Institutional Libraries, Health and Rehabilitative Library Services; chairperson, Barratt Wilkins (1976-78).

American Council on Education
(founded 1918)
PURPOSE: Composed of institutions of postsecondary education and national and regional educational associations to provide through voluntary and cooperative action "comprehensive leadership for improving educational standards, policies, and procedures."
MEMBERSHIP: 1,500; *Annual Expenditure;* $9,000,000.
PRESIDENT: Jack W. Peltason.
CHAIRPERSON, BOARD OF DIRECTORS: Robben W. Flemming.
EXECUTIVE SECRETARY: Richard A. Humphrey.
PUBLICATIONS: *Educational Record* (quarterly); *Higher Education and National Affairs* (weekly).
HEADQUARTERS: One Dupont Circle, Washington, D.C. 20036.

American Federation of Labor/ Congress of Industrial Organizations—ALA, Library Service to Labor Groups
(founded 1945)
PURPOSE: To promote library service to labor groups through the ALA and the AFL-CIO.
MEMBERSHIP: 15; *Annual Expenditure:* $200.
ALA COCHAIRPERSON: Kathleen Imhoff.
HEADQUARTERS: c/o Reference and Adult Services Division, ALA, 50 East Huron Street, Chicago, Illinois 60611.
ALA AFFILIATION: Joint Committee on Library Service to Labor Groups, Reference and Adult Services Division.

American National Standards Committee X3—Computers and Information Processing
(founded 1960)
PURPOSE: To identify and develop data processing standards necessary to achieve: efficient and economic interchange of data and computer programs within and between present and projected information processing systems; and to enhance the national and international marketability, utilization, and life expectancy of data processing equipment and systems.
MEMBERSHIP: 51.
CHAIRPERSON: John F. Auwaerter (October 1976-October 1979).
VICE-CHAIRPERSON: Robert M. Brown.
EXECUTIVE SECRETARY: William F. Hanrahan.
SECRETARIAT: Computer and Business Equipment Manufacturers Association (CBEMA), 1828 L Street, N.W., Washington, D.C. 20036.
ALA REPRESENTATIVE: James A. Rizzolo, Information Science and Automation Division (1976-77).

American National Standards Institute: American National Standards Committee on Instructional Audio-Visual Systems Standards (PH7)
(founded 1968)
PURPOSE: To develop "standards, recommended practices, performance specifications, nomenclature, and test methods for instructional audiovisual systems."
MEMBERSHIP: 17.
CHAIRPERSON: Marvin I. Mindell.
VICE-CHAIRPERSON: Richard G. Nibeck.
SECRETARY: Richard Hittner.
PUBLICATION: *Standards and Recommended Practices* (variable).
HEADQUARTERS: 1430 Broadway, New York, New York 10018.
ALA REPRESENTATIVE: Howard S. White, *Library Technology Reports* (1975-76).

American National Standards Institute: Sectional Committee on Library Work, Documentation and Related Publishing Practices (Z39)
(founded 1940)
PURPOSE: To establish standards for concepts, definitions, terminology, letters and signs, practices, and methods in the field of library work, in the preparation and utilization of documents, and in those aspects of publishing that affect library methods and use.
MEMBERSHIP: 55; *Annual Expenditure:* $30,000 (1977-78).
CHAIRPERSON: Jerrold Orne (June 1975-June 1978).
VICE-CHAIRPERSON: Toni C. Bearman.
PUBLICATION: *News about Z39* (quarterly).
HEADQUARTERS: School of Library Science, University of North Carolina, Chapel Hill, North Carolina 27514.
ALA REPRESENTATIVE: Susan Vita, Resources and Technical Services Division.

American National Standards Institute: Sectional Committee on Micrographic Reproduction (PH5)
(founded 1953)
PURPOSE: Standardization of terminology, definitions, sizes, format, quality, apparatus, and procedures for the production and use of microform reproduction.
MEMBERSHIP: 41; *Annual Expenditure:* $62,500.
CHAIRPERSON: Henry C. Frey (January 1977- December 1979).
VICE-CHAIRPERSON: Lester O. Kruger.
SECRETARY: Don M. Avedon.
HEADQUARTERS: Secretariat, National Micrographics Association, 8728 Colesville Road, Silver Spring, Maryland 20910.

American Vocational Association
(founded 1925)
PURPOSE: To develop and promote comprehensive programs of vocational education through which individuals are brought to a level of occupational performance commensurate with their innate potential and the needs of society.

MEMBERSHIP: 55,000; *Annual Expenditure:* $1,700,000.
PRESIDENT: Gordon I. Swanson (July 1, 1977-June 30, 1978).
EXECUTIVE DIRECTOR: James E. (Gene) Bottoms.
PUBLICATIONS: *American Vocational Journal* (monthly except June, July, and August); *Yearbook of the American Vocational Association* (annual).
HEADQUARTERS: 1510 H. Street, N.W. Washington, D.C. 20005.
ALA AFFILIATION: Joint Committee, American Association of School Librarians; chairperson, Joseph Blake.

Associated Organizations for Teacher Education

PURPOSE: To develop a network of organizations dealing with the certification and accreditation of teacher education programs and to respond to the effect of these programs upon the educational profession.
MEMBERS: 23 organizations; *Annual Expenditure:* None.
PRESIDENT: Charles Byrd, Director of Instructional Technology and Media, West Virginia State College.
VICE-PRESIDENT/PRESIDENT-ELECT: Mearl Guthrie, Bowling Green State University, Bowling Green, Ohio.
EXECUTIVE DIRECTOR: Joel Burdin.
HEADQUARTERS: One DuPont Circle, Washington, D.C. 20036.
ALA REPRESENTATIVE: Anna Mary Lowrey.

Association for Asian Studies
(founded 1941)

PURPOSE: To further interest in and scholarly study of Asia by publishing scholarly research and other materials designed to promote Asian studies; sponsoring research through conferences, fellowships, and programs; and carrying on related activities "to encourage cooperation and exchange of information within the field of Asian studies in the United States and Canada and among scholars and scholarly organizations in these and other countries of the world.
MEMBERSHIP: 5,500 (October 1977); *Annual Expenditure:* $284,495 (1977).
PRESIDENT: John M. Echols (April 1977-March 1978).
VICE-PRESIDENT: Richard L. Park.
SECRETARY-TREASURER: Rhoads Murphey.
PUBLICATIONS: *Journal of Asian Studies* (quarterly); *Bibliography of Asian Studies* (annually); *Asian Studies Newsletter* (5 issues a year); *Committee on East Asian Libraries Newsletter* (3 issues a year).
HEADQUARTERS: 1 Lane Hall, University of Michigan, Ann Arbor, Michigan 48109.
ALA AFFILIATION: Committee on East Asian Libraries, Eugene W. Wu, Harvard-Yenching Library, Harvard University.

Association for Childhood Education International
(founded 1892)

PURPOSE: To work for the education and well-being of all children; to promote desirable conditions, programs and practices for children from infancy through early adolescence; to raise the standard of preparation and to encourage continued professional growth of teachers and others concerned with the care and development of children; to bring into active cooperation all groups concerned with children in the school, the home and the community; to inform the public of the needs of children and the ways in which school program must be adjusted to fit those needs.
MEMBERSHIP: 25,000; *Annual Expenditure:* $500,000 (estimated 1977-78).
PRESIDENT: Ruth L. Roche (April 1977-April 1979).
EXECUTIVE SECRETARY: Alberta L. Meyer.
PUBLICATION: *Childhood Education* (6 issues a year).
HEADQUARTERS: 3615 Wisconsin Avenue, N.W., Washington, D.C. 20016.
ALA AFFILIATION: Joint Committee, American Association of School Librarians; chairperson, Dorothy S. Heald (1975-77).

Association for Educational Communications and Technology*
(founded 1923)

PURPOSE: To facilitate humane learning through the systematic development, utilization and management of learning resources, which include people, processes and media in educational settings.
MEMBERSHIP: 8,423 (November 18, 1977; *Annual Expenditure:* $1,016,200 (1977-78).
PRESIDENT: William Grady (April 1977-April 1978).
VICE-PRESIDENT/PRESIDENT-ELECT: Marie McMahan.
EXECUTIVE DIRECTOR: Howard B. Hitchens.
PUBLICATIONS: *AVI (Audiovisual Instruction)* (9 issues a year); *AVCR (AV Communication Review)* (quarterly).
HEADQUARTERS: 1126 16th Street N.W., Washington, D.C. 20036.
ALA AFFILIATION: Joint Advisory Committee on Nonbook Materials, William Quinly; Resources and Technical Services Division, Committee on Catalog Code Revision, William Quinly.

Association of American Colleges
(founded 1915)

PURPOSE: To enhance and promote humane and liberating learning. To strengthen institutions of higher education as settings for humane and liberating learning.
MEMBERSHIP: 618; *Annual Budget:* $1,400,000.
CHAIRPERSON: Paul F. Sharp (February 1977- February 1978).
VICE-CHAIRPERSON: Sister Joel Read.
PRESIDENT: (executive officer); Frederic W. Ness.
PUBLICATION: *Liberal Education* (quarterly).
HEADQUARTERS: 1818 R Street, N.W., Washington, D.C. 20009.
ALA AFFILIATION: Joint Committee on College Problems, Association of College and Research Libraries; ALA staff liaison officer, Beverly P. Lynch (1975-76).

Association of American Library Schools
(founded 1915)

PURPOSE: To promote excellence in education for library and information science as a means of increasing the effectiveness of library and information services. Affiliated with ALA, Council of National Library Associations, International Federation of Library Associations, and Council of Communication Societies.
MEMBERSHIP: 710 personal, 99 institutional; *Annual Expenditure:* $40,000.
PRESIDENT: Margaret K. Goggin.
VICE-PRESIDENT/PRESIDENT-ELECT: Gary R. Purcell.
EXECUTIVE SECRETARY: Janet C. Phillips.
PUBLICATION: *Journal of Education for Librarianship* (quarterly)
HEADQUARTERS: 471 Park Lane, State College, Pennsylvania 16801.
ALA AFFILIATION: Library Education Division, Robert Stueart.

Association of American Publishers
(formed in 1970 by merger of American Book Publishers Council and American Educational Publishers Institute)

PURPOSE: To improve the status of intellectual prod-

Organizations and Associations

Organizations and Associations

ucts in the United States and to nurture and strengthen the public understanding that books and allied media play a central role in society. Provides members with information on the conditions of the book trade, government policies, and pending legislation on matters such as copyright and censorship. Also provides a framework within which groups comprising the combined general trade and educational publishing industry and interested professional associations can exchange ideas and work together.

MEMBERSHIP: 325; *Annual Expenditure:* $1,000,000.
CHAIRMAN: Harold T. Miller (July 1, 1977-June 30, 1978).
VICE-CHAIRMAN: Winthrop Knowlton.
PRESIDENT: Townsend Hoopes.
PUBLICATIONS: *AAP Newsletter* (monthly); divisional newsletters.
HEADQUARTERS: One Park Avenue, New York, New York 10016.
ALA AFFILIATION: Joint Committee, Resources and Technical Services Division; chairman, Connie R. Dunlap; ALA staff liaison officer, Carol R. Kelm (1975-76).

Association of Research Libraries (ARL)
See article in alphabetical order in text.

Atlantic Provinces Library Association*
(founded 1950)
PURPOSE: To promote library service throughout the Atlantic Provinces; to cooperate with other associations on matters of mutual concern; and to serve the professional interests of librarians in the region.
MEMBERSHIP: 230; *Annual Expenditure:* $6,000 (1975-76).
PRESIDENT: Alan MacDonald.
VICE-PRESIDENT/PRESIDENT-ELECT: Terence K. Amis.
PUBLICATION: *A.P.L.A. Bulletin* (4 issues a year).
HEADQUARTERS: c/o School of Library Service, Dalhousie University, Halifax, Nova Scotia, Canada.

Big Brothers/Big Sisters of America
(Big Brothers of America merged with Big Sisters International in June 1977; the movement dates from 1903)
PURPOSE: To promote friendships between mature adult volunteers (Big Brothers and Big Sisters) and children from single-parent homes under the guidance and supervision of professional social workers, a one-to-one concept aimed at filling the child's need for someone to listen, to respond, and to care on a regular and reliable basis.
MEMBERSHIP: 360 agencies; *Annual Expenditure:* $857,000 (1977).
PRESIDENT: Don A. Wolf (June 1977-June 1978).
VICE-PRESIDENT/ADMINISTRATION: William J. Mashaw.
VICE-PRESIDENT/RESOURCES: John J. Frank.
EXECUTIVE VICE-PRESIDENT: Lewis P. Reade.
PUBLICATIONS: *Correspondent* (10 issues a year).
HEADQUARTERS: 220 Suburban Station Building, Philadelphia, Pennsylvania 19103.

Boys' Clubs of America
(founded 1906)
PURPOSE: To promote the health, social, educational, vocational and character development of all boys throughout the country, irrespective of race, color, creed or national origin.
MEMBERSHIP: 1,086,000; *Annual Expenditure:* $3,430,266 (September 30, 1976).
PRESIDENT: John L. Burns.
EXECUTIVE DIRECTOR: William R. Bricker.

PUBLICATION: *Keynote Magazine* (quarterly).
HEADQUARTERS: 771 First Avenue, New York, New York 10017.
ALA REPRESENTATIVE: Elga M. Cace, Association for Library Service to Children.

Chief Officers of State Library Agencies (COSLA)
(founded 1973)
PURPOSE: To provide a means for cooperative action among its state and territorial members to strengthen library services to the American people through the work of the respective state and territorial agencies. Its purpose is to provide a continuing mechanism for dealing with the problems faced by the heads of these agencies which are responsible for state and territorial library development.
MEMBERSHIP: 50 states, 1 territory.
CHAIRPERSON: Joseph F. Shubert, State Librarian, New York State Education Department, (November 1976-1978).
VICE-CHAIRPERSON: William G. Asp, Director, Minnesota Office of Public Libraries and Interlibrary Cooperation, Department of Education.
SECRETARY-TREASURER: Carlton J. Thaxton, Director, Division of Public Library Services, State Department of Education, 156 Trinity Avenue, S.W., Atlanta, Georgia 30303.
ALA AFFILIATION: Executive Secretary: Sandra Cooper of ALA; President: Donald Simpson of the Association of State Library Agencies.

Child Development Associates Consortium
PURPOSE: To establish competencies for early childhood personnel and the assessment of the competency of such persons who apply for the CDA credential.
MEMBERSHIP: 39 organizations; *Annual Expenditure:* $1,468,263.
PRESIDENT: Richard Orton.
VICE-PRESIDENT/PRESIDENT-ELECT: Maureen McKinley.
SECRETARY: Mary Jane Anderson.
EXECUTIVE DIRECTOR: Robert J. Harper, II.
HEADQUARTERS: 805 15th Street, N.W., Suite 500, Washington, D.C. 20005.
ALA REPRESENTATIVE: Mary Jane Anderson.

Coalition for Children and Youth
(formerly National Council of Organizations for Children and Youth)
(founded 1973)
PURPOSE: "To serve as an umbrella agency for local, state, and national organizations working for and with children and youth; to collect and disseminate information pertinent to public policies, legislation, and program implementation as they relate to children and youth, specifically in our five cluster areas; day care, foster care and adoption, health, juvenile justice, and families and parenting. Primary function is to represent and document the needs of children and youth so that, as a coalition, we can more effectively advocate on their behalf."
MEMBERSHIP: 100 full, voting, national organizational members, 1,300 associate member organizations and individuals; *Annual Expenditure:* $300,000.
PRESIDENT: Chauncey Alexander, National Association of Social Workers (September, 1977-September 1979).
FIRST VICE-PRESIDENT: Marilyn Smith, National Association for the Education of Young Children.
EXECUTIVE DIRECTOR: Margaret J. Jones.
PUBLICATIONS: *FOCUS on Children and Youth* (monthly); *America's Children '76; Directory for*

Child Advocates (1977-78); *How to Raise Money for Kids.*
HEADQUARTERS: 815 15th Street, N.W., Washington, D.C. 20005.
ALA REPRESENTATIVES: Alice E. Fite, American Association of School Librarians; Lyle Eberhardt, Association of State Librarian Agencies; Mary Jane Anderson, Association for Library Service to Children; Dorothy M. Sinclair, Public Library Association.

Coalition of Adult Education Organizations

PURPOSE: To operate on a nonprofit basis for the promotion of social welfare by developing, maintaining, and improving a balanced system of adult and continuing education.
MEMBERSHIP: 20 organizations; *Annual Expenditure:* $2,000.
PRESIDENT: Robert A. Allen, Jr.
PRESIDENT-ELECT: John R. Mackenzie.
SECRETARY: Suzanne M. Fletcher.
HEADQUARTERS: 810 18th Street, N.W., Washington, D.C.
ALA REPRESENTATIVE: Andrew M. Hansen.

Continuing Library Education Network and Exchange (CLENE)
(founded 1975)

PURPOSE: To provide equal access to continuing education opportunities and to ensure library and information science personnel and organizations the competency to deliver quality library and information services to all. Also, to create an awareness and a sense of need for continuing education of library personnel on the part of employers and individuals as a means of responding to societal and technological change.
MEMBERSHIP: 550 (December 1, 1976) *Annual Expenditure:* $53,000.
PRESIDENT: Travis Tyer (1977-78).
PRESIDENT-ELECT: Peggy O'Donnell.
EXECUTIVE DIRECTOR: Elizabeth W. Stone.
PUBLICATIONS: *CLENExchange* (quarterly); *Directory of Continuing Education Courses and Programs for Library Personnel, Information and Media Specialists* (annually); *CLENE MEMBERSHIP Directory; Concept Papers; An Annotated Bibliography of Recent Continuing Education Literature; CLENE Proceedings—First Assembly—January 1976; CLENE Proceedings—Second Assembly—July 1976; CLENE Proceedings—Third Assembly—February 1977; Continuing Education Communicator* (monthly).
HEADQUARTERS: 620 Michigan Avenue, N.E., Washington, D.C. 20064.
ALA AFFILIATION: ALA staff liaison officer, Margaret Myers (1975-76).
See also article in text: *Continuing Professional Education.*

Council of National Library Associations*
(founded 1942)

PURPOSE: To promote closer relationship among the national library associations of the United States and Canada.
MEMBERSHIP: 14 national associations; *Annual Expenditure:* $3,000.
CHAIRPERSON: John T. Corrigan (1977-78).
VICE-CHAIRPERSON: Theodore Weiner.
SECRETARY-TREASURER: Susan T. Sommer.
HEADQUARTERS: Catholic Library Association, 461 W. Lancaster Avenue, Haverford, Pennsylvania 19041.

Council of Specialized Accrediting Agencies
(founded 1971)

PURPOSE: To strengthen the effectiveness and quality of postsecondary, professional, and specialized education through accreditation and related activities.
MEMBERSHIP: 47; *Annual Expenditure:* $4,000.
CHAIRMAN: David R. Reyes-Guerra (February 1977-February 1978).
VICE-CHAIRPERSON: Dorothy Ozimek.
SECRETARY-TREASURER: Ruth M. Greenspan.
HEADQUARTERS: c/o Council on Postsecondary Accreditation, One Dupont Circle, Suite 760, Washington, D.C. 20036.

Council on Postsecondary Accreditation*
(founded 1975)

PURPOSE: To improve Postsecondary Education through the accreditation process.
MEMBERSHIP: 4,000 accredited institutions and an estimated 8,000 programs through 55 recognized accrediting bodies; *Annual Expenditure:* $275,000 (estimate).
CHAIRPERSON OF THE BOARD: Dana B. Hamel (July 1, 1976-June 30, 1979).
VICE-CHAIRPERSON: Glenn S. Dumke.
PRESIDENT(executive officer): Kenneth E. Young.
PUBLICATIONS: *Accreditation* (quarterly); occasional papers on various topics.
HEADQUARTERS: One Dupont Circle, Suite 760, Washington, D.C. 20036.

Educational Film Library Association*
(founded 1943)

PURPOSE: To stimulate the production, distribution, and utilization of films and other audio-visual materials in libraries, schools, and universities. Also to serve as a clearinghouse of information about nontheatrical film.
MEMBERSHIP: 1,900; *Annual Expenditure:* $237,000 (1976-1977).
PRESIDENT: Edward A. Mason (July 1977-June 1978).
VICE-PRESIDENT/PRESIDENT-ELECT: Laura Murray.
EXECUTIVE DIRECTOR: Nadine Covert.
PUBLICATIONS: *Sightlines* (quarterly); *EFLA Evaluations* (10 issues a year).
HEADQUARTERS: 43 West 61st Street, New York, New York 10023.

Educational Media Council

PURPOSE: To keep members of the Association informed of one anothers' activities.
MEMBERSHIP: 14 national associations; *Annual Expenditure:* None.
PRESIDENT: Howard Hitchens.
EXECUTIVE DIRECTOR: Harriet Lundgaard.
PUBLICATIONS: *Standards and the Education Consumer; Media Milestones in Teacher Training,* and *New Relationship in ITV.*
HEADQUARTERS: 1346 Connecticut Avenue, Washington, D.C. 20036.
ALA REPRESENTATIVE: Alice Fite.

Education USA Advisory Board

PURPOSE: To provide a communications network for public school information officers and to communicate with educational professionals about current issues and trends at the state and national level.
EXECUTIVE DIRECTOR: John Wherry
PUBLICATIONS: *Education, U.S.A.* (weekly).
HEADQUARTERS: 1801 N. Moore Street, Arlington, Virginia, 22209.
ALA REPRESENTATIVE: Alice Fite.

Girls Clubs of America
(founded 1945)

PURPOSE: To guide girls for miltiple roles in home work

Organizations and Associations

Organizations and Associations

and civic affairs, to help girls find their own identity, develop potential talents and skills and achieve a sense of responsibility.
MEMBERSHIP: 215,000; *Annual Expenditure:* $932,954 (December 31, 1976).
PRESIDENT: Mrs. J. Michael Prejean.
VICE-PRESIDENT: Mrs. Harry C. Pratt.
EXECUTIVE DIRECTOR: Edith B. Phelps.
PUBLICATION: *Girls Club News* (quarterly).
HEADQUARTERS: 133 East 62nd Street, New York, New York 10021.

Illinois Regional Library Council*
(founded 1971)
PURPOSE: To serve as a coordinating agency for all types of libraries, information centers, and library agencies in the Chicago metropolitan area with improvement of access to information by all metropolitan area residents being its primary objective.
MEMBERSHIP: 202 paid members; *Annual Expenditure:* $101,951.40 (June 30, 1977).
PRESIDENT: Robert R. McClarren.
VICE-PRESIDENT: Howard Dillon.
EXECUTIVE DIRECTOR: Beth A. Hamilton.
PUBLICATIONS: *Multitype Library Cooperative News* (monthly); *Libraries and Information Centers in the Chicago Metropolitan Area* (triennially); *Union List of Serial Holdings in Illinois Special Libraries* (1977); occasional papers (irregularly).
HEADQUARTERS: 425 North Michigan Avenue, Chicago, Illinois 60611.

Illuminating Engineers Society of North America
(founded 1906)
PURPOSE: To establish scientific lighting standards and recommendations and to develop and communicate this information to all interested parties. Comprised of professionals who are actively engaged in the practice of teaching of illumination.
MEMBERSHIP: 10,000; *Annual Expenditure:* $850,000.
PRESIDENT: David Patterson (July 1, 1977-June 30, 1978).
PRESIDENT-ELECT: W.S. Fisher.
EXECUTIVE VICE-PRESIDENT: Frank M. Coda.
PUBLICATIONS: *Lighting Design and Application* (monthly); *Journal of the Illuminating Engineering Society* (quarterly).
HEADQUARTERS: 345 East 47th Street, New York, New York 10017.
ALA REPRESENTATIVE: Sub-Committee on Library Lighting. Howard S. White, *Library Technology Reports* (1975-76).

Interagency Council on Library Resources for Nursing
PURPOSE: To promote the use of libraries by nurses, to give support to libraries serving nurses, and to promote the exchange of information about libraries serving nursing.
MEMBERSHIP: 20.
PRESIDENT: Emi Akiyama.
ALA REPRESENTATIVES: Fred Pattison and Mary Shopa.

International Association of Law Libraries
PURPOSE: To encourage and facilitate the work of librarians and others concerned with the acquisition, bibliographic processing, and administration of legal materials.
MEMBERSHIP: 480.
PRESIDENT: Igor I. Kavass.
VICE-PRESIDENT/PRESIDENT-ELECT: Willi A.F.P. Steiner.
PUBLICATIONS: *International Journal of Law Libraries; IALL Newsletter.*
HEADQUARTERS: Vanderbilt University Law Library, Nashville, Tennessee 37203.

International Association of School Librarianship*
(founded 1970)
PURPOSE: To encourage development of school libraries and library programs throughout all countries, to promote the professional preparation of school librarians, to bring about closer collaboration between school librarians in all countries (including loan and exchange), to encourage the development of materials, and to initiate and coordinate activities, conferences, and other projects.
MEMBERSHIP: 450; *Annual Expenditure:* $3,634 (1976-77).
PRESIDENT: Jean E. Lowrie (August 1975-July 1977).
VICE-PRESIDENT: Axel Petersen.
PUBLICATIONS: *IASL Newsletter* (quarterly); *Annual Proceedings.*
HEADQUARTERS: Western Michigan University, Kalamazoo, Michigan 49008.

International Board on Books for Young People (IBBY)
See article in alphabetical order in text.

International Federation for Documentation (FID)
See article in alphabetical order in text.

International Federation of Library Associations (IFLA)
See article in alphabetical order in text.

International Reading Association
PURPOSE: Improvement of quality of reading instruction, promotion of the lifetime reading habit, and development of every reader's proficiency to the highest possible level.
MEMBERSHIP: 70,000; *Annual Budget:* $2,412,962.
PRESIDENT: William Eller.
VICE-PRESIDENT/PRESIDENT-ELECT: Ralph C. Staiger.
PUBLICATIONS: *The Reading Teacher* (9 issues a year); *Journal of Reading* (8 issues a year).
HEADQUARTERS: 800 Barksdale Road, Newark City, Delaware 19711.

Joint Council on Educational Telecommunications*
(founded 1950)
PURPOSE: To advise the educational community regarding educational and social applications of communications technology and implications of telecommunications policy; to assist in experimentation and projects to meet those ends.
MEMBERSHIP: 23; *Annual Budget:* $150,000.
VICE-PRESIDENT: Harold Wigren.
EXECUTIVE DIRECTOR: Frank W. Norwood.
PUBLICATION: *JCET Monitor* (monthly).
HEADQUARTERS: 1126 16th Street, N.W., Washington, D.C. 20036.
ALA REPRESENTATIVE: Lawrence E. Malumby, Assistant Director, District of Columbia Public Library.

National Affiliation for Literacy Advance
PURPOSE: To eradicate illiteracy among adults using materials published by New Readers Press; to work with native speakers of English and of other languages who want to learn to read and write English.
MEMBERSHIP: 20,000; *Annual Expenditure:* $92,488.
PRESIDENT: Mary F. Kumley.
VICE-PRESIDENT: Marylyn M. Hanson.
SECRETARY: Barbara C. Roper.
EXECUTIVE SECRETARY: Adelaide L. Silvia.

PUBLICATIONS: *Literacy Advance* (quarterly); highlights of NALA activities.
HEADQUARTERS: 1320 Jamesville, P.O. Box 131, Syracuse, New York 13210.

National Association for Bilingual Education

PURPOSE: To promote bilingual education as a logical process to enhance educational success of the student with limited English proficiency; to encourage implementation of quality programs; to promote recognition of the total community; to promote bilingual instruction within the context of awareness and appreciation of cultural linguistic differences.
MEMBERSHIP: 3,000; *Annual Expenditure*: $100,000.
PRESIDENT: Maria Madina Swanson.
VICE-PRESIDENT/PRESIDENT-ELECT: Juan D. Solis.
SECRETARY: Henry Oyama.
PUBLICATIONS: *NABE Journal* (3 times a year), *NABE Newsletter* (periodically).
HEADQUARTERS: 500 South Dwyer, Arlington Heights, Illinois 60005.

National Association for the Education of Young People

PURPOSE: To serve and act on behalf of the needs and rights of young children (from birth to eight years) with primary focus on the provision of educational services and resources.
MEMBERSHIP: 28,000.
PRESIDENT: Bernard Spodek.
EXECUTIVE DIRECTOR: Marilyn Smith.
PUBLICATIONS: *Young Children* (bimonthly); books and pamphlets on related topics.
HEADQUARTERS: 1834 Connecticut Avenue, N.W., Washington, D.C. 20009.
ALA REPRESENTATIVE: Faith Hektoen.

National Association of Elementary School Principals*
(founded 1921)

PURPOSE: To facilitate positive educational leadership; to serve as an agency for the collection and dissemination of information pertinent to elementary school principalship; to provide services such as publications, conferences, and research; to promote the principle of equal rights; and to enhance harmonious relationships between elementary school principals and teachers.
MEMBERSHIP: 25,000; *Annual Expenditure*: $1,093,286 (August 31, 1977).
PRESIDENT: Bill M. Hambrick (September 1, 1977-August 31, 1978).
PRESIDENT-ELECT: Nellie B. Quander.
EXECUTIVE DIRECTOR: William L. Pharis.
NATIONAL CONVENTION: April 18-22, 1977, Las Vegas, Nevada.
PUBLICATIONS: *National Elementary Principal* (quarterly); *Communicator Newsletter* (biweekly).
HEADQUARTERS: P.O. Box 9114, 1801 North Moore Street, Arlington, Virginia 22209.

National Association of Exposition Managers*
(founded 1928)

PURPOSE: To advance the arts and sciences pertaining to education through the use of exhibits, exhibitions and expositions for the dissemination of knowledge and information.
MEMBERSHIP: 1,000; *Annual Expenditure*; $200,000.
PRESIDENT: Ruldolph Lang (December 1977- November 1978).
EXECUTIVE DIRECTOR: Thomas J. Sullivan, Jr.
PUBLICATION: *Exposition Managers' News* (bimonthly).
HEADQUARTERS: 108 Wilmot Road, Suite 105, Deerfield, Illinois 60015.
ALA REPRESENTATIVE: Christopher Hoy.

National Coalition Against Censorship

PURPOSE: Education through national organizations and the general public on freedom of thought, inquiry, and expression.
MEMBERSHIP: 27 organizations; *Annual Expenditure*: $30,000.
COORDINATOR: Leanne Katz.
PUBLICATIONS: *Censorship News* (3 issues a year).
HEADQUARTERS: 22 East 40th Street, New York, New York 10016.
ALA REPRESENTATIVE: Judith Krug.

National Conference on Social Welfare

PURPOSE: Education and information through annual forums on a broad spectrum of human services.
MEMBERSHIP: 4,000 independent, 1,000 agencies.
PRESIDENT: John B. Turner.
VICE-PRESIDENT/PRESIDENT-ELECT: Mitchell I. Ginsberg.
SECRETARY: Dorothy Hollingsworth.
EXECUTIVE DIRECTOR: Margaret E. Berry.
PUBLICATIONS: *Social Welfare Forum* (the annual proceedings); *Forum Council Bulletin* (4 issues a year).
HEADQUARTERS: 22 West Gay Street, Columbus, Ohio 43215.

National Council of Teachers of English
(founded 1911)

PURPOSE: To improve the quality of instruction in English at all educational levels; to encourage research, experimentation, and investigation in the teaching of English; to facilitate professional cooperation of the members; to hold public discussions and programs; to sponsor the publication of desirable articles and reports; and to integrate the efforts of all those who are concerned with the improvement of instruction in English.
MEMBERSHIP: 45,000; *Annual Expenditure*: $2,000,000.
PRESIDENT: Marjorie Farmer.
EXECUTIVE DIRECTOR: Robert F. Hogan.
PUBLICATIONS: *Language Arts* (8 issues a year); *English Journal* (9 issues a year); *College English* (8 issues a year); *College Composition and Communication* (quarterly); *English Education* (quarterly); *Abstracts of English Studies* (9 issues a year); *Research in the Teaching of English* (4 issues a year); *CSSEDC Newsletter* (quarterly); *Council-Grams* (5 issues a year).
HEADQUARTERS: 1111 Kenyon Road, Urbana, Illinois 61801.
ALA AFFILIATIONS: Joint Committee, American Association of School Librarians; cochairpersons, Douglas Brown (NCTE) and Thomas Downen (AASL) (1977-78).

National Council of Teachers of Mathematics
(founded 1920)

PURPOSE: To assist in promoting the interests of mathematics in America . . . and to revitalize and coordinate the work of local organizations of teachers of mathematics.
MEMBERSHIP: 48,000; *Annual Expenditure*: $1,960,000.
PRESIDENT: John C. Egsgard (April 1976-April 1978).
PRESIDENT-ELECT: Shirley A. Hill.
EXECUTIVE DIRECTOR: James D. Gates.
PUBLICATIONS: *Mathematics Teacher* (9 issues a year); *Arithmetic Teacher* (8 issues a year).
HEADQUARTERS: 1906 Association Drive, Reston, Virginia 22091.
ALA AFFILIATION: Joint Committee, American Association of School Librarians; cochairperson, Eloise Brown, Public Schools Libraries, Washington, D.C.

National Micrographics Association (NMA)
See article in alphabetical order in text.

Organizations and Associations

National Story League
(founded 1903)
PURPOSE: To encourage the creation and appreciation of the good and beautiful in life and literature through the art of storytelling.
MEMBERSHIP: 1,300; *Annual Expenditure:* $5,815 (1976-1978).
PRESIDENT: Mrs. James Lea (July 1976-July 1978).
VICE-PRESIDENT: Mrs. J.A. Reynolds.
EDITOR: Marylouise Reighart.
PUBLICATION: *Story Art Magazine* (bimonthly).
HEADQUARTERS: 555 Tod Avenue, N.W. Warren, Ohio 44485.
ALA REPRESENTATIVE: Linda Oscarson, Association for Library Service to Children.

National University Extension Association
(founded 1915)
PURPOSE: An association of institutions of higher education which have a commitment to continuing education and extension.
MEMBERSHIP: 261 institutional, 1,058 professional, *Annual Expenditure:* $295,000.
PRESIDENT: Phillip E. Frandson (March 1977-April 1978).
PRESIDENT-ELECT: William L. Turner.
PUBLICATIONS: *Newsletter* (biweekly); *Continuum* (quarterly); *Guide to Independent Study* (biannually); *On-Campus/Off-Campus Degree Programs for Part-time Students.*
HEADQUARTERS: One Dupont Circle, Suite 360, Washington, D.C. 20036.
ALA AFFILIATION: Joint Committee on university library extension services, Association of College and Research Libraries; Barry E. Booth; ALA staff liaison officer, Frank MacDougall (1976-1977).

New England Library Information Network (NELINET)
(founded 1966)
PURPOSE: A multistate network of academic, research, public, and other libraries with a mission "to facilitate the sharing of library and information resources and services for the people of New England."
MEMBERSHIP: 50; *Annual Expenditure:* $1,558,616 (July 1976-June 1977).
CHAIRPERSON: Charles Churchwell (July 1, 1977-June 30, 1978).
VICE-CHAIRPERSON: Margaret Otto.
EXECUTIVE DIRECTOR: A. John Linford.
PUBLICATIONS: *Channel* (newsletter, 5 issues a year); *NELINET Technical Memoranda* and *NELINET Administrative Memoranda* (variable).
HEADQUARTERS: 40 Grove Street, Wellesley, Massachusetts 02181.

Parents Without Partners, Inc.
(founded 1957)
PURPOSE: An international, non-profit, non-sectarian educational organization devoted to the welfare and interests of single parents and their children.
MEMBERSHIP: 160,000; *Annual Expenditure:* $1,000,000.
PRESIDENT: Freda Mark (July 1977-July 1978).
FIRST VICE-PRESIDENT: Belle Golden.
EXECUTIVE DIRECTOR: Virginia Martin.
PUBLICATION: *The Single Parent* (10 issues a year).
HEADQUARTERS: 7910 Woodmont Avenue, Washington, D.C. 20014.
ALA REPRESENTATIVE: Mary B. Bauer, Association for Library Service to Children (1975-76).

Public Service Satellite Consortium
PURPOSE: To help nonprofit organizations achieve low-cost telecommunications services through efficient use of satellite systems.
MEMBERSHIP: 90 nonprofit organizations.
PRESIDENT: John P. Witherspoon.
VICE-PRESIDENT: Robert A. Matt.
SECRETARY: Frank Norwood.
PUBLICATIONS: *PSSC Newsletter* (monthly); proceedings of annual conference.
HEADQUARTERS: 4040 Sorrento Valley Boulevard, San Diego, California 92121.

Puppeteers of America
(founded 1937)
PURPOSE: To raise the standards of the art of puppetry through an educational program of annual conferences, institutes, workshops, lecture programs, exhibitions, publications, and advisory services.
MEMBERSHIP: 2,500; *Annual Expenditure:* $25,000.
PRESIDENT: Nancy Staub (July 1976-June 1977).
VICE-PRESIDENT: John Miller.
EXECUTIVE SECRETARY: Olga Stevens.
PUBLICATION: *The Puppetry Journal* (bimonthly).
HEADQUARTERS: P.O. Box 1061, Ojai, California 93023.
ALA REPRESENTATIVE: Donald Reynolds, Association for Library Service to Children (1975-76).

Round Table of National Organizations for Better Education*
(founded 1953 as Round Table for the Support of Public Schools)
PURPOSE: To meet annually and exchange information on major issues in education, to learn what organizations are doing for and in education and to obtain expert information on trends. Round Table is a clearinghouse, not a decision-making body.
MEMBERSHIP: 45; *Annual Expenditure:* $1,785.
CHAIRPERSON OF THE PLANNING COMMITTEE: Jerry Cordrey (January 1977-December 1977).
SECRETARY-TREASURER: Harold V. Webb.
HEADQUARTERS: 225 Touhy Avenue, Park Ridge, Illinois 60068.

Salvation Army, The
(founded 1865)
PURPOSE: Expressed by a spiritual ministry to preach the Gospel, disseminate Christian truths, provide personal counseling, and undertake the spiritual, moral and physical rehabilitation of all persons in need who come within its sphere of influence regardless of race or creed.
MEMBERSHIP: 380,618 (1976).
NATIONAL COMMANDER: Commissioner Paul S. Kaiser.
NATIONAL CHIEF SECRETARY: Colonel Orval A. Taylor.
PUBLICATIONS: *War Cry* (weekly); *Young Soldier* (monthly); *SAY* (monthly).
HEADQUARTERS: 120-130 West 14th Street, New York, New York 10011.
ALA REPRESENTATIVE: Marya Hunsicker, Association for Library Service to Children.

Society of American Archivists
(founded 1936)
PURPOSE: To provide a means of contact, communication, and cooperation among archivists and archival institutions through its publication program, annual meetings, symposia, and committee activity. Also advances professional education and training, offers job placement services, supports research, and represents archivists in areas involving related professions.
MEMBERSHIP: 3,100.
PRESIDENT: Walter Rundell, Jr. (October 1977-October 1978).
VICE-PRESIDENT/PRESIDENT-ELECT: Hugh A. Taylor.
EXECUTIVE SECRETARY: Ann Morgan Campbell.

Outreach: see Disadvantaged, Library Service to

PUBLICATIONS: *American Archivist* (quarterly); *SAA Newsletter* (bimonthly).
HEADQUARTERS: P.O. Box 8198, Library, University of Illinois, Chicago, Illinois 60680.
ALA AFFILIATION: Joint Committee on Library Archives; ALA staff liaison officer, Robert Wedgeworth.

Universal Serials and Book Exchange (USBE)
See article in alphabetical order in text.

Women's Joint Congressional Committee*
(formed 1920)
PURPOSE: A coalition-type clearinghouse for the legislative work of national organizations engaged in promoting federal measures pertaining to the general welfare.
MEMBERSHIP: 25.
CHAIRPERSON: Betty B. Blouin (October 1977-September 1978).
VICE-CHAIRPERSON/CHAIRPERSON-ELECT: Diane Fassett.
ALA REPRESENTATIVES: Eileen D. Cooke, Jane B. Nida (1977-78).

Personnel and Employment: Affirmative Action

In 1977 librarians were torn by conflicts between the values of intellectual freedom and the dangers of racial stereotyping facing the need to recruit and promote minorities and women in a time of little staff turnover, complicated by the possible elimination of mandatory retirement rules. New federal regulations on removing barriers to the handicapped as well as the increasing militancy of disabled applicants and other citizen groups caught some libraries by surprise. Many librarians' concern for outreach to those with limited access to library service perhaps masked a lack of awareness of the needs of their own handicapped employees, if, indeed, there were any. It was a good year for consciousness raising, a time of sudden realization that most libraries still were inaccessible to all but the mobile and that libraries had not developed or implemented Affirmative Action plans as required by local, state, and federal law and by American Library Association policy.

HANDICAPPED

When the ALA Equal Employment Opportunity Policy was first passed in 1974, it did not include the handicapped as a protected class. The policy was amended in 1976 to include the group, long neglected by library employers.

In 1,399 replies to a 1975 survey of 5,000 public and academic libraries, the U.S. President's Committee on Employment of the Handicapped found that 627 libraries employed 1,265 handicapped workers in full- and part-time capacities. Unfortunately, 771 libraries responded that they did not employ the handicapped; of the 199 who answered the question as to why none were employed, a number gave negative reasons. W.A. Zerface's article, "Hire the Handicapped Librarian!" in *Wilson Library Bulletin* (April 1977), confirmed that, while library managers have become aware of the need to remove architectural barriers for patrons, they have not been much concerned with such barriers limiting handicapped employees. Basing his conclusions on the experiences of some applicants for library positions, Zerface suggested that certain libraries have taken a position that actually is weighted against the disabled applicant. He scored the 1967 ALA policy statement on hiring the handicapped in libraries as innocuous and far from positive in its inclusion of physical requirements such as visual ability and acuity of hearing as major considerations in library employment. Also called into question was the long-held assumption that emotional equilibrium is essential to professional achievement, as espoused by Neal Harlow in "Admission to the Profession: Counseling the Handicapped" in *Wilson Library Bulletin* (December 1968).

Given this demonstrated need for educating librarians to the job potential of handicapped employees, the publication in 1976 and 1977 of federal regulations implementing Sections 503 and 504 of the Rehabilitation Act of 1973 (PL 93-112) probably threatens the majority of libraries that are not now in compliance—and which receive more than $2,500 in federal assistance—with the loss of federal funds.

Rehabilitation Act. The Rehabilitation Act of 1973 defines a handicapped person as anyone who has a physical or mental impairment that substantially limits one or more major life activity, or who has a record of or is regarded as having such an impairment. Included are those who have been in mental hospitals or who have a history of heart condition or cancer, as well as the blind, deaf, retarded, paraplegic, and others. A July 1977 news release from the Labor Department's Equal Employment Opportunity (EEO) Program reminded federal contractors that alcoholics and drug abusers are also covered under this legislation, although there is some confusion in this area. Key requirements of Section 503 mandate that employers make "reasonable" efforts to accommodate the physical and mental limitations of both employees and applicants, undertake recruitment activities at social service and educational agencies, and review mental and physical job qualifications for all positions to ensure that no qualified handicapped persons are screened out. Institutions with contracts of $50,000 and 50 or more employees must have a written Affirmative Action plan that is reviewed and updated annually.

Architectural Barriers. Regulations on architectural barriers became effective June 3, 1977, shortly after the White House Con-

Personnel and Employment: Affirmative Action

People: see Biographies; Obituaries; State Reports. Consult Index.

Personnel and Employment

Major Fair Employment Laws

According to the March 1977 issue of *The EEO Report*—a monthly publication of The Institute for Management, Old Saybrook, Connecticut—among the most significant laws defining fair employment are the following: Titles VI and VII of the Civil Rights Act, the Equal Pay Act, the Age Discrimination in Employment Act, Executive Order 11246, the Rehabilitation Act of 1973, the Vietnam-Era Veterans Readjustment Act of 1974, the Revenue Sharing Act of 1972, and Title IX of the Education Amendments of 1972. The impact of each of these laws is outlined below:

Title VII of the Civil Rights Act:

This Act is the most all-encompassing of the fair employment laws. It prohibits discrimination on the basis of race, color, sex, religion, or national origin, and applies to private and public employers, labor unions, employment agencies, and apprenticeship committees. To be subject to the law, an employer has to meet two criteria: 1) there must be at least 15 employees during 20 or more calendar weeks during the present or immediately preceding year; and 2) the employer's operations must be a part of, or affect, interstate commerce. Because interstate commerce has been interpreted in an extremely broad fashion, businesses should assume that they are involved in interstate commerce unless otherwise advised by counsel.

Title VII is enforced by the Equal Employment Opportunity Commission (EEOC), which despite its many well-publicized problems, still has many powerful weapons in its arsenal. Back pay, reinstatement, affirmative action, and attorneys' fees and costs are the most common remedies and, especially in class actions, they can be staggering.

The Equal Pay Act:

This Act applies only to sex discrimination in pay or benefits, but while its scope may be less than Title VII, it applies to any employer who has two or more employees engaged in interstate commerce, so almost all employers are covered. It is enforced by the Wage and Hour Division of the U.S. Department of Labor's Employment Standards Administration. Under the Act, employees may bring their own suits or the Labor Department may sue on their behalf. Back pay and attorneys' fees are the most common remedies.

Age Discrimination in Employment Act:

There are actually two Age Discrimination acts. The 1967 Act applies to all public and private employers who have 20 or more workers on their payrolls during 20 weeks of the year; however, it protects only workers who are between the ages of 40 and 65. As in the Equal Pay Act, either the aggrieved employee or the Labor Department may sue for back pay, attorneys' fees, or other appropriate relief.

The 1975 Act is broader in some respects, but narrower in others. It prohibits all discrimination based on age, regardless of the employee's age (contrast the 1967 Act, which applies only to workers between 40 and 65); however, it applies only to employers who receive federal financial assistance, and remedies are much more limited than in the 1967 Act. There is no provision for private suits by aggrieved employees, and the relief is limited to a cutoff of federal funds.

Rehabilitation Act of 1973:

This Act applies to private employers who are performing work on federal contracts or subcontracts which exceed $2,500 in value. It prohibits discrimination on the basis of handicap, except when the handicapped employee cannot do the job required, and it also requires that covered employers take affirmative action to hire and advance handicapped employees. Enforcement is by the Office of Federal Contract Compliance, which can cancel present contracts or debar the contractor from future contracts.

Vietnam-Era Veterans Readjustment Act of 1974:

Under this Act, federal contractors and subcontractors are required to take affirmative action to employ Vietnam-era veterans. The Assistant Director for Employment Standards in the Department of Labor is in charge of enforcement. Remedies are usually limited to cancellation and debarment.

Executive Order 11246:

Under EO 11246, federal contractors and subcontractors are prohibited from discriminating in employment because of race, color, religion, sex, or national origin. It also requires most employers who have 50 or more employees and contracts worth more than $50,000 to develop written affirmative action plans.

Enforcement is by the Office of Federal Contract Compliance, which in turn delegates responsibilities to contracting and administering agencies. Until late 1976, remedies were limited to cancellation and debarment, but a U.S. district court has now given its stamp of approval to an award of back pay.

Revenue Sharing Act of 1972:

State and local governments which receive federal revenue sharing funds are prohibited from discriminating against employees or applicants on the basis of race, color, national origin, age, handicapped status, religion, and sex. The Secretary of the Treasury is in charge of enforcement. Unlike Executive Order 11246, private individuals may bring suit under this Act.

Title IX of the Education Amendments of 1972:

Title IX is concerned only with sex discrimination in educational institutions receiving federal financial aid. Its main concern is in the area of equal opportunity in curricula but it also prohibits employment discrimination because of sex. The U.S. Office of Education is in charge of Title IX enforcement. Its principal remedy is a cutoff of funds.

Personnel and Employment: Affirmative Action

ference on Handicapped Individuals. Among the main provisions of Section 504 published in the *Federal Register* (May 4, 1977, pp. 22676-702) is the requirement that all new facilities be constructed to be readily accessible and usable by both disabled patrons and employees. The regulations also require that architectural or other barriers limiting access to activities in existing facilities be removed by July 20, 1977, with the completion of necessary structural changes by 1980. At hearings in September 1977 before a House subcommittee, the American Library Association testified that more than 8,000 public library buildings are inaccessible. It was calculated that $260,600,000 would be required to make them barrier-free, at an average cost of $30,700 per building. ALA urged the funding of Title II of the Library Services and Construction Act, which provides for public library construction and remodeling, as recently amended to include the costs of the removal of barriers as an eligible category.

Funding was also recommended for Title VII of the Higher Education Act (HEA) as revised by the Education Amendments of 1976 (PL 94-482) to include renovations making academic facilities accessible. An amendment to the proposed Rehabilitation Cost Assistance Act (S. 2302) was introduced in November 1977, authorizing $6,000,000 in grants to educational institutions to pay a share of compliance costs. Meanwhile, the Public Library of Rudd, Iowa (with an annual operating budget of $3,591 and one part-time librarian) won a reprieve in November from the U.S. Office of Civil Rights from a requirement that it build a ramp to make the meeting room in the basement of the building accessible to wheelchairs if it were not to lose city revenue sharing funds as well as access to a regional library funded by federal money. None of the 429 residents of Rudd uses a wheelchair.

STATUS OF WOMEN

Carol L. Learmont and Richard L. Darling's annual survey, "Placements and Salaries 1976: A Year of Adjustment" in *Library Journal* (June 15, 1977), noted that the average women's salary for 1976 graduates was $275 less than the men's average. While men continued to fare better overall, some small improvement was noted in the mean high salary for women—$16,832, which is generally for those with previous library experience—$879 higher than that for men, continuing a reversal of a pattern first noted in 1974.

In an unpublished memo updating library school deans on his survey of 1975-76 faculty salaries at 62 library schools in the *Journal of Education for Librarianship* (Spring 1976), Russell Bidlack revealed a continued five per cent pay differential in favor of male faculty on fiscal year appointments. A previous 14 per cent discrepancy had decreased to 10 per cent, however, for women faculty appointed on an academic year basis.

As reported in *Library Journal* (January 15, 1977), in December 1976 a group organized as the San Diego Public Library Concerned Librarians filed a formal complaint of sex bias against the city, charging disparities between library classifications and other professional positions requiring similar education and experience. In the spring of 1977, a similar suit, filed in December 1976 by a group of Denver nurses, won its first round in court according to *The Spokeswoman* (May 15, 1977). By fall 1977 another class action complaint had been filed with the EEO Commission by Temple University librarians, charging that librarians get lower salaries because they work in a "woman's profession." Similar actions can be expected by library women's groups in the future. (*See also* Women in Librarianship, Status of.)

MINORITY STATUS

Although librarianship has a better record in the area of minority recruitment than other professions such as medicine or law, racial parity is a goal not yet achieved. The annual "Degrees and Certificates Awarded by U.S. Library Education Education Programs, 1975-76," (to be published in 1978) reflected that again less than 10 per cent of graduating library students were minorities, about comparable to the number now in the profession. The only change from the year before was a decrease in Blacks and Asian Americans and an increase in Hispanics. Much of the impetus sustaining recruitment efforts in 1977 was due to the availability, under HEA Title II-B, of $2,000,000 in fellowships and institutes during the 1977-78 fiscal year. This amount was up from only half a million dollars the previous year. The HEA Title II-B program gives very high priority to minority and bilingual persons for graduate library education at the profes-

Nick, Canadian Review

"Our token Black—is that how you think of yourself, Ms. Corwin? You're much more than that, I assure you. You're also our token woman." (Handelsman (C) Punch)

sional entry level. Funding was available for 134 minority fellowships at the master's level and 18 doctoral-level fellowships; 80 per cent were awarded to minority persons. An additional 35 students (including a few bilingual Anglos) were in graduate institutes at the University of Arizona, Atlanta University, and California State at Fullerton.

Major credit for a slow but steady increase of minorities in the field must be given to the strong leadership efforts of minorities already in the profession. During five years as ALA's first Minority Recruitment Specialist, Marilyn Salazar has effectively directed two major projects and developed many useful contacts with outside agencies, especially minority educational organizations, as well as encouraging library school deans to increase minority programs. E. J. Josey and Kenneth E. Peeples, Jr., edited *Opportunities for Minorities in Librarianship* (Scarecrow Press, 1977), a book of articles by minority librarians writing about their own career experiences in the hope that they would provide role models for young people considering a career in the field. Writing in a special report on education for *American Libraries* (March 1977), "Modifying Library Education for Ethnic Imperatives," Arnulfo D. Trejo stated that, because the profession has had little appeal to Chicanos, positive images must replace the negative ones that have characterized librarians and that librarianship as a career must be introduced early in the student's life.

Although a decision was not expected until sometime in 1978 in one of the most important civil rights cases before the U.S. Supreme Court in a generation, *Regents of the University of California* v. *Allan Bakke*, a qualified victory for the Los Angeles County Public Library's Affirmative Action program was achieved in a settlement of agreement, with final approval by the State Appellate Court expected in December. Terms included a total of $42,500 in compensation for the seven librarians who had brought the suit in 1972 on a charge of "reverse discrimination" in the promotion of two minority librarians. The two will retain their positions as principal librarians.

GAY RIGHTS

Many library employers may not be aware that the ALA Equal Employment Opportunity Policy provides protection on the basis of "individual life-style," which includes sexual preference. Of course, local ordinances or state legislation under which some libraries operate may guarantee full rights for homosexuals, which also goes beyond federal EEO requirements. A common shortcoming of the 25 library Affirmative Action plans critiqued by the ALA Equal Employment Opportunity Subcommittee of the Office for Library Personnel Resources Advisory Committee during the past two years has been the omission of this category from policy statements. The setting of hiring or promotional goals for gays probably would violate privacy rights and is therefore not feasible. A positive step was taken by the ALA Council in June 1977 in its reaffirmation of support for equal rights for gay library workers. The resolution also recommended that libraries "reaffirm their obligations under the Library Bill of Rights to disseminate information representing all points of view on this controversial topic."

AGE DISCRIMINATION

Age Discrimination. Contrary to popular misconceptions, the federal Age Discrimination in Employment Act of 1967 does not forbid all discrimination based on age, but only forbids discrimination against workers between the ages of 40 and 65. The 1975 Act, however, which applies only to employers who receive federal assistance, would include most libraries, and it does prohibit all age discrimination. Similarly, many state statutes also outlaw discrimination based on age, making it as illegal to discriminate against an 18-year-old as it is under federal law to discriminate against a 55-year-old. Libraries developing Affirmative Action plans will need to be in compliance with legislation at all levels of government, as well as with the ALA policy.

The U.S. Department of Labor's Bureau of Labor Statistics 1975 report on *Library Manpower: A Study of Demand and Supply* (Bulletin 1852, Government Printing Office) forecast that about three-fourths of the 11,000 job openings annually would be to replace librarians who retire, die, or leave for various reasons. Pending federal legislation that would modify or eliminate mandatory retirement could limit seriously the already short supply of jobs for new graduate librarians, as well as promotional opportunities for both minorities and women who are currently underutilized at higher administrative levels. In September, California went a step further than the federal government and banned mandatory retirement at any age.

ACTIVITIES WITHIN THE PROFESSION

Affirmative Action requires employers to determine to what extent affected groups are underutilized in their work forces by comparing their work forces with the labor market. Libraries developing Affirmative Action programs have had little or no data, particularly on current availability of qualified minority personnel in the national labor pool. In an attempt to supply this information, the ALA Office for Library Personnel Resources sought and received a $13,856 grant from the Council on Library Resources to conduct a comprehensive survey of employers of librarians in order to determine the percentages of minorities and women with the requisite skills. The survey instrument will be designed to obtain a work force profile using variables such as race, sex, type of library, type of job, education, and geographic location. A sample of 1,300 libraries will be drawn from all public, academic, and school libraries identified by the National Center for Education Statistics. The results should be available by late 1978.

In 1977 ALA took action on a number of issues relating to equal rights and Affirmative Action. A "Resolution on Prejudice, Stereotyping, and Discrimination" was a follow-up to the 1976 "Resolution on Sexism and Racism Awareness." It committed most major ALA DIvisions to develop programs to raise the awareness of library users in these areas and instructed the Personnel Administration Section of the Library Administration Division to develop a model in-service training program on discrimination awareness for library employees.

One resolution committed future ALA Conferences only to states that have ratified the Equal Rights Amendment. Another resolution urged state library agencies and ALA Chapters to seek involvement of racial, ethnic, handicapped, and other minorities in regional and state conferences leading to the 1979 White House Conference on Libraries.

The most comprehensive summary to date of the many issues involved is contained in "Affirmative Action and American Librarianship," published in *Advances in Librarianship* (Spring 1978), by Elizabeth Dickinson and Margaret Myers.

Libraries interested in developing Affirmative Action plans are encouraged to write to the ALA Office for Library Personnel Resources for an *Affirmative Action Packet*, available for $1. Also helpful is the July-August 1976 issue of *American Libraries*, which includes the ALA policy mandating the review of library Affirmative Action plans by the Association, as well as a checklist used by the EEO Subcommittee in its review process. Drafts or completed plans should be sent directly to Association headquarters and will be reviewed on a confidential basis.

AGNES M. GRIFFEN

Personnel and Employment: Job Market

Library budget cuts that resulted in elimination of staff positions continued to be reported throughout 1977. A few libraries reported restored funding or the ability to hire new employees through Comprehensive Education and Training Act (CETA) funds. During the summer of 1977, Brooklyn Public Library reopened many of its branches with a group of 44 CETA employees. During the previous two years, Queens Public Library had lost 286 staff members in addition to all part-time employees, but in 1977 was able to restore branch services because of 151 CETA positions. The New York Public Library branch system had been forced to lay off 439 staffers since 1975, but hoped to restore some branches through increased contributions.

Hit by the economic crunch, some libraries have depended more on volunteers for both ongoing and extra services, although a few employers have emphasized that no volunteers will be used to replace full-time staff members whose jobs have been vacant because of the budget situation. Some employers have also questioned the value of CETA personnel on grounds that they are unable to replace trained professionals and take valuable time to break in. No reports have appeared to show whether or not employers are continuing to pay the salaries of these persons from regular funds once the temporary CETA money ends.

In the fall of 1977, Detroit Public Library received a $3,100,000 increase in state and city funds, enabling the library to call back personnel laid off in 1976 and allowing it to enlarge the staff for the first time in three years.

Survey and Outlook. Shortages in staff (as well as materials, other resources, space, and operating expenditures) were identified in the *National Inventory of Library Needs—1975*, a study submitted to the National Commission on Libraries and Information Science in March 1977. Existing information on library staff employed in 1975 is compared with "indicators of need," showing what would be necessary to provide "adequate" library services to the U. S. public. According to the study, another 8,500 public librarians, 100,000 school librarians, and 9,750 academic librarians are needed, nearly doubling the 121,700 professionals reported in service in 1975. Similar gaps in support staff are also reported. It must be pointed out, however, that these positions are not funded, but refer to the numbers needed if the goals for full service as described in the study were to be met. A similar inventory in 1965 produced the often-quoted projection of a shortage of 100,000 librarians in the field.

Because trends point to continued tight or reduced budgets, combined with increasing pressure for higher wages and salaries, many questions relating to the job market arise. To what degree will labor costs be reduced through automation and increased cooperation? What will be the effect of increased unionization on salaries and hiring? What will

The placement service at the ALA Conference in Detroit drew some 1,400 participants for approximately 400 available positions.

be the effects of proposed legislation removing mandatory retirement regulations? The Bureau of Labor Statistics (BLS) report in 1975 on library supply and demand predicted that 75 per cent of all job openings until 1985 will result from replacement needs caused by retirement, death, and other exits from the profession rather than from new openings. Will the older professionals keep working longer than originally anticipated?

According to Money magazine (November 1977), librarians faced the second poorest career opportunities as newcomers between now and 1985. Money used BLS statistics projections and devised a rating system to sort out which professions have the best and least possibilities for recent graduates. Doctors, veterinarians and systems analysts got top ratings, while school teachers, librarians, and protestant clergymen received the worst.

As reported in the annual Library Journal (June 15, 1977) survey of recent graduate placements and salaries, it is clear that the job market continues to be very tight for new graduates, and they are finding that the job search takes longer. The job market picture improved for the 1977 class of college graduates over the previous year, and employers felt that this upward trend would continue into 1978. The 1977 College Placement Council survey of 701 employers in industry, government, and nonprofit organizations showed that 1977 graduates at all degree levels and in all disciplines received approximately 18 per cent more job offers than the class of 1976. It must be recognized, however, that engineering, accounting, and business majors were in the greatest demand and that there was little improvement for graduates in nontechnical fields. Perhaps the general upswing in private company hiring is, however, also reflected in the slightly more than two per cent increase in special library placements of new graduates in 1976. This category of library employment is the only one showing a steady annual increase for new professionals. In 1976 public library placements dropped three per cent, and school and academic placements remained constant.

Reflecting the longer time period needed for job searches by recent graduates are estimates of unemployment for three, four, and six months after qualifying for a degree. The median for those unplaced dropped from 35 per cent at 3 months to 15 per cent after 4 months and 13 per cent at 6 months.

Of the total known library placements of recent graduates in 1976, 6 per cent were reported to be in nonprofessional positions, compared to 11 per cent in 1975. There was no explanation for this change. At the same time, 17 per cent were reported in nonlibrary positions, compared to 12 per cent in 1975. Whether these persons returned to former fields or sought a new area because of the difficulty in finding library employment is not known. Another unknown each year is the whereabouts of some 26 to 30 per cent of the graduates. Have they left the field altogether or are they operating in some area of "alternative" librarianship?

Letters to the editors of Australian and British library periodicals from new professionals in those countries reflect the same frustrations held by graduates in the United States and Canada. There is a feeling that individuals without library experience are confronted by employers who demand experience but are reluctant to supply the means of acquiring it.

There is some evidence that turnover rates are decreasing, thus making it more difficult for new entrants to be hired. Figures compiled by the Library of Congress Personnel Office from July 1976 to June 1977 showed 25,797 applications received while only 6.8 per cent of those employed left the Library. In two years, the applications had approximately doubled while the percentage of separations fell by half.

Little new data exists since the BLS report of 1975 regarding the job market for persons other than new professionals. At the ALA 1977 Annual Conference placement center,

1,515 registered applicants pursued 455 job vacancies. A perusal of job vacancy ads continues to show a preponderance of openings requiring considerable experience. The possibility of inflated qualification requirements may come under closer scrutiny as employers become more aware of the need to assure that personnel selection procedures are related to the jobs.

In addition to needing an update of the 1975 BLS report, the profession needs more information on the supply and demand for information professionals outside of traditional library jobs. The University of Pittsburgh Manpower Consortium for the Information Profession has begun exploring this market. Articles and workshops on alternative librarianship are becoming more evident.

Professionalism Issues. Debates on "professionalism" continue in the literature and at conferences. A Library Education Division (LED) program on "Testing vs. Training" drew a large audience at the 1977 ALA Annual Conference. A bibliography on the subject is available from LED. The ALA Office for Library Personnel Resources (OLPR) Advisory Committee sponsored a 1977 preconference on personnel utilization to revitalize the use of the 1970 ALA "Library Education and Personnel Utilization" policy. It also adopted a statement on "Comparable Rewards: The Case for Equal Compensation for Non-Administrative Expertise." OLPR is establishing a task force to recommend ALA action relating to whether the master of library science degree can be used as a valid selection requirement.

The Medical Library Association completed test development for its new certification code, to take effect in 1978. The Selection Consulting Center of Sacramento completed the first phase of the California Library Selection Project, identifying those "tasks" that are "properly validated" minimum requirements for entry-level positions. —MARGARET MYERS

Personnel and Employment: Performance Appraisal

Library personnel remained the most valuable and costly library resource in 1977. Little attention has been given to the appraisal of this resource, however, if one judges by the lack of attention given performance appraisal systems in the literature of librarianship. Most attention seems to have been given to the care and feeding of library collections. This situation may be the result of the problems of preserving, storing, and protecting collections, or it may be the result of librarians not wanting to change from the old "check list of characteristics" such as punctuality, creativity, and neatness that have served as performance appraisals.

Some librarians say that the new systems take too much time and are too hard to use. Librarians using the check list might ask themselves if their systems of personnel appraisal assist in the improvement of individual and organizational performance. If their appraisal system does not, they should adopt a better system. In changing systems, librarians must remember that a good performance appraisal system provides employees with (1) information on what is expected of them, (2) information on what standards are being used to judge performance, and (3) regular feedback as to progress or lack of progress toward the goals of the library.

1977 Activities. During 1977 a number of activities occurred that will have a direct effect on personnel performance appraisal systems. These activities have been in the areas of professionalism and certification, library effectiveness studies, continuing education for librarians, and current trends in the personnel management field.

For a good explanation of the question of professionalism and certification in librarianship a symposium in *Library Journal* (September 1, 1977, pp. 1715–31) is valuable. The symposium raises many questions that relate directly to personnel performance appraisal systems. Should there be certification of librarians? If so, who should do it? How long should the certification last before it needs to be renewed? How should competence be tested? Are librarians professional in attitudes and actions?

All of these questions deal with the evaluation of personnel within libraries. If certification and maintenance of certification become a requirement of employment, the effect on performance appraisal systems for librarians will be significant. Two library groups working for the certification of librarians are the National Librarians Association (Certification Standards Committee) and Concerned Librarians Opposing Unprofessional Trends (CLOUT), a chapter of the California Library Association. The progress of these groups should be noted by everyone.

Studies and Publications. The area of library effectiveness studies needs to be analyzed for data on how the effectiveness of librarians is evaluated. During the 1977 ALA Annual Conference, Masae Gotanda, Head, Research and Evaluation Services, Office of Library Services, Department of Education, State of Hawaii, presented a paper on "Performance Measures for Public Libraries: The Hawaii State Library System" at one of the Library Research Round Table sessions. Parts of the study relate directly to the performance evaluation of library staff members and their work. F.W. Lancaster's book *The Measurement and Evaluation of Library Services* was published in 1977 by Information Resources Press. The work brings together much of the information on evaluation of library service. Some of the information relates directly to the appraisal of librarians. In *LJ/SLJ Hotline* (June 27, 1977, pp. 2–3), it was reported that Battelle Laboratories of Columbus, Ohio, will conduct a "statewide study of the effectiveness of libraries in Oklahoma in meeting user needs...."

The work of the Continuing Library Education Network and Exchange (CLENE) is helping librarians keep up to date through programs and publications. CLENE provides home study courses for librarians, and its publication *Continuing Education Communicator* lists learning opportunities for librarians throughout the country. Librarians are taking advantage of these programs, and what they learn from these programs cannot help but influence their performance appraisals.

Trends. The literature of personnel management points to a number of trends regarding performance appraisals, of which librarians should be aware. Recent literature indicates that performance appraisals are becoming more quantitative in the public sector. This fact is pointed out by Gary Craver in his article "Survey of Job Evaluation Practices in State and County Governments" in *Public Personnel Management* (March–April 1977, pp. 121–31). The article "Performance Appraisal—A Survey of Current Practices" in *Personnel Journal* (May 1977, pp. 245–47, 254) by Alan H. Locher and Kenneth S. Teel reports what techniques are being used to appraise, who is doing the appraising, and how often the appraising is being done. The authors point out that "recent Equal Employment Commission (EEO) actions and court decisions have underscored the necessity of organizations having accurate, objective records of employee performance to defend themselves against possible charges of discrimination in discharges, promotions and/or salary increases." "The Annual Performance Review Discussion—Making It Constructive" in *Personnel Journal* (October 1977, pp. 508–11) by Herbert H. Meyer provides an excellent format for the appraisal discussion. Those librarians using appraisal discussion between the employee and supervisor will find Meyer's ideas useful.

A call for more frequent (bimonthly) appraisals is by far the most striking trend in the literature of personnel management. The advantages of more frequent administration of performance appraisals are discussed by Robert C. Ford and Kenneth M. Jennings in "How to Make Performance Appraisals More Effective" in *Personnel* (March–April 1977, pp. 51–56). Some of the advantages claimed are more feedback for the employee, better accuracy in the evaluation, a lowering of the "recency effect" and the "central tendency error," and better data for EEO.

If libraries follow, as they have in the past, the management trends of business and government, some real changes in performance appraisal systems will be seen. These changes will be toward a more quantitative appraisal and the possible use of performance standards. These changes will add to the professionalism of librarians and help in the definition of the role of libraries and librarians in society. — NEAL K. KASKE

Personnel and Employment: Staff Development

The challenges facing library managers increased in 1977 as budgets stabilized and as library users made greater and more sophisticated demands on the library system. Although available technology holds the promise of revolutionizing the way libraries function, there remain the expense and difficulty of implementation. Thus, library managers were expected to do more with less in virtually every area of library operations in 1977.

The critical element in implementing change, coping with new demands, and improving library performance is a competent, active, and growing library staff. The library's personnel resources have long been recognized as a strength, but with increasingly rapid changes and mounting pressures for better performance, libraries are examining their views of personnel utilization and development. Part of this review is based on the recognition that people-related problems in library organizations are keeping libraries from meeting their full potential in serving users. Thus, many library organizations are addressing these personnel issues in a concerted fashion.

Supervisory Training and Development. Managerial responsibility centers on building on the natural motivation that most people have by creating an atmosphere that will encourage talented people to do a good job. To do this, library managers are responding to the needs of their library staffs by developing a sense of worthwhileness that allows the staff to be active contributors to library work, get feedback on those contributions, and be part of successful library programs.

In response to the circumstances faced by library administrators, programs for supervisory training have been undertaken. One of the more intensive projects to help librarians understand their role as supervisors is the CLENE (Continuing Library Education Network Exchange) home-study course on motivation. Through a grant from the U.S. Office of

Education, CLENE has successfully tested five modules that employ case studies and readings on employee and self-motivation.

Other ways of developing supervisors have included workshops and institutes. The Office of University Library Management Studies (OMS) of the Association of Research Libraries conducted two Library Management Skills Institutes during 1977—one in Kansas City, Missouri, and the other in Columbia, Maryland. These four-day institutes were aimed at developing middle managers' interpersonal and organizational skills.

Another example of a supervisory development program is the Special Focus Workshop designed by OMS. The first of these was tested at the State University of New York at Binghamton, where a two-day workshop on supervisory skills was held for unit and department heads. The Management Training Film Program offered by OMS serves a similar function. Management films are selected for their applicability to library organizations, and the specially designed training materials accompanying the films have made them heavily used sources for in-house training programs.

The U.S. Office of Education has funded at least two programs for supervisory development among media specialists. The Oklahoma State Department of Education and the South Dakota Department of Education and Cultural Affairs received grants for designing leadership training programs.

Ongoing programs for administrative development continued during 1977. The University of Maryland and Washington University continued to offer such programs. There were some efforts, too, on the part of librarians to take advantage of nonlibrary courses in order to develop their potential. A number of librarians, for example, are pursuing second master's degrees in business administration. There is increasing interest among librarians in continuing education opportunities provided by the American Management Association, the National Training Laboratory, and University Associates. The ALA also offers a variety of professional development opportunities at each Annual Conference.

Individual Development. In an effort to be responsive to the needs of individual staff members, libraries have adopted a number of professional development programs. Sabbatical and research leaves have been incorporated into many academic library policies. In a few instances, a portion of the regular workweek is set aside for individual research in publications for librarians. A few libraries have experimented with job rotation or exchange, either within the library or with other institutions. Virginia Conrad of the University of Massachusetts Library conducted a survey of libraries and discovered that nine have at least a limited exchange or rotation plan for individual staff members.

The most notable source of outside funding for professional development continues to be the Council on Library Resources (CLR). In 1977 CLR made 25 awards to libraries as part of their Professional Development Program. A total of 5 awards were made in the Management Intern Program, 4 in the Advanced Study Program, and 16 in the Fellowship Program. In each of these programs, the individuals who receive grants are able to further their professional interests. Although not formally a part of the Professional Development Program, the CLR Library Services Enhancement Grants have led to release time for 13 librarians who have worked with faculty and administrators on their campuses to make library services more responsive to their needs. The Association of College and Research Libraries also offers internships for minority librarians; five such awards were made in 1977. The key issues in such programs are organizational support for personal development that includes a good climate and encouragement for growth and that allows individual responsibility to exercise, initiate, and actively pursue a plan for development.

Organizational Development. A great deal of pressure is exerted on libraries by their boards, university administrators, and users. One of the results of this emphasis on accountability is that individual staff development efforts are becoming more difficult to justify. It is difficult to demonstrate that staff development activities lead to increased effectiveness. Tied to this difficulty are the research findings indicating that training is most effective when it is directly related to the day-to-day work of those in the training programs.

Library administrators are interested in organizational efforts that have a staff development component but that are primarily directed at improving the effectiveness of their organizations. An example of such an effort is the Management Review and Analysis Project (MRAP) developed by OMS under a grant from CLR. An extensive organizational effort like MRAP uses a number of task forces and a study team, both of which allow for professional development of the members. But the primary tasks of MRAP are identifying problems and generating recommendations for their solutions.

The Academic Library Development Program (ALDP), a CLR-sponsored project similar to MRAP but designed for small and medium-sized academic libraries, serves similar functions. ALDP was being tested in three libraries during 1977.

Many libraries have not been willing to invest time in projects such as MRAP or ALDP and have looked to alternative methods for organizational improvement. The Princeton University Library staff, for example, in 1977 held a "Problem-Identification, Problem-Solving Retreat" for unit heads using an outside facilitator to help focus on priority issues. Other examples are the University of Michigan Libraries' planning project, which is now in the implementation phase, and the Duke Libraries' planning program now in the process of operating a number of task forces. A benefit of such sessions is that staff members learn much about conducting successful meetings, but a more important result is that organizational goals tend to be more widely shared by all of the staff when there are open discussions of the problems and challenges.

Conclusion. Libraries in 1977 faced many financial and technological challenges, and the effects on staff development were noticeable. The accountability required of libraries has led to some innovation in staff development. Greater utilization of existing training expertise in the governing structure is taking place. Cooperative training programs are also being offered to groups of libraries.

Staff development and personnel officers of different types of libraries are meeting regularly at professional conferences in order to share ideas and methodologies. The *Staff Development Newsletter* and the *CLENE Communicator* are noteworthy attempts to keep librarians up to date regarding staff development opportunities. These examples serve to illustrate that librarians are looking more to one another for help in staff development.

Outside sources of funding are scarce, but the demands of the staff do not diminish. In-house or on-campus training have become crucial components of staff development programs. Perhaps the key to staff development programs in the future will be the initiation of programs at the regional level. The Northeast Academic Science Information Center and the Southeastern Library Association have been leaders in this regard. Travel funds for staff development tend to be scarce, and resource sharing of personnel becomes as important as the sharing of collections. — DUANE WEBSTER
DEANNA MARCUM

Preservation of Library Materials

Interest in preservation activities continued to burgeon in 1977 as evidenced by the large number of seminars and workshops. There were several developments of major importance. A patent was granted to researchers at the Library of Congress (LC) Preservation Office for a method of deacidifying paper in solutions. A new ALA Preservation Discussion Group was formed, many grants were awarded for conservation programs, the New England Document Conservation Center (NEDCC) moved to larger quarters and expanded, the Barrow Laboratory closed, and progress was made on the National Preservation Program.

National Preservation Program. Norman J. Shaffer was appointed National Preservation Program Officer in the Office of the Assistant Director for Preservation at LC. The Ad Hoc Advisory Committee, supported by the Council on Library Resources (CLR) and set up to pursue the development of programs discussed at the 1976 National Preservation Program Planning Conference, met twice during 1977. An account of the conference—"Preservation: a National Plan at Last?" by Pamela W. Darling—appeared in *Library Journal* (February 15, 1977). Information on the program and subsequent meetings appeared in the *LC Information Bulletin* (December 1977). The members of the Ad Hoc Advisory Committee are Frazer G. Poole, Assistant Director for Preservation at LC; Paul N. Banks, Conservator at the Newberry Library; Pamela W. Darling, Head of the Preservation Department at Columbia University Library; Robert L. Feller, Director of the Center on the Materials of the Artist and Conservator at the Carnegie-Mellon Institute of Research; Carl M. Spalding, Program Officer for the Council on Library Resources; David H. Stam, Librarian of the Milton S. Eisenhower Library at Johns Hopkins University and Chairman of the Preservation of Library Materials Committee of the Association of Research Libraries; and Allen B. Veaner, Director, University of California at Santa Barbara Library. The group is presently exploring the development of an automated on-line data base of microform masters to assure greater bibliographic control and to aid coordination in this area.

Other Activities. A patent was granted to John C. Williams and George B. Kelly of the LC Preservation Office on the deacidification of paper. Dated September 27, 1977, U.S. Patent 4,051,276 describes a method of deacidifying paper by passing it through a solution of organometallic compound and a liquid solvent that will not dissolve ink or cause discoloration. After the paper is permeated, the organometallic compound is hydrolyzed to an alkaline material. The method requires dipping or spraying the paper, and it permits the use of compounds such as diethyl zinc that are highly volatile in vapor form but safe in solution. Since all reactions must take place in an inert gas atmosphere, its greatest application is in mass deacidification.

The Barrow Laboratory of Richmond, Virginia, closed in 1977 after the death of its director and the completion of the major projects under study. The laboratory was originally headed by William J. Barrow and later, after his death in 1967, by Bernard Walker. Walker's death in 1977 was greatly mourned; his dedication to the lab and its work was intense and entire. The laboratory produced excellent in-depth work on the causes of deterioration in book papers and on the development of permanent and durable paper. After 20 years of support by CLR and supplementary funding in the latter phases from the National Endowment for the Humanities (NEH), the laboratory was closed and dismantled. Much of the equipment is on indefinite loan to the Carnegie-Mellon Institute of Research for use by Robert Feller on experiments on paper. Walker's report on "Morpholine Deacidification of Whole Books" appeared in *Advances in Chemistry* (Series No. 164) and was submitted to NEH. Research Corporation, Inc., will be handling the patent and its promotion when it is released.

A new Preservation Discussion Group has been formed to provide an informal forum for the exchange of expertise and information in the Resources and Technical Services Division (RTSD) of ALA. The Group will meet at both the Midwinter Meetings and Annual Conferences and will be chaired by Pamela W. Darling, a Past Chairperson of the RTSD Committee on the Preservation of Library Materials. Gay Walker, Head of the Preservation and Preparations Department at Yale University Library, is the chairperson of the Committee. The Committee's program at the ALA Conference,—"Preservation: What You Always Wanted To Know But Didn't Know Who To Ask"—was coordinated by Darling and created much interest and audience participation. An RTSD booth, a popular location in the exhibit hall, focused on preservation problems with expert on-the-spot advice.

More reports on fires, floods, and other disasters were made in 1977. The University of Pittsburgh's Langley Library experienced an explosion in January that took two lives, destroyed furnishings, and damaged many books. About 3,000 soaked books were frozen, and their drying and cleaning were carried out with help from faculty and student volunteers. A multi-million-dollar fire at the University of Toronto destroyed the Sandford Fleming Laboratory along with about 8,000 engineering books. Easily replaceable volumes were discarded, but about 500 rare books were freeze-dried. A leaky toilet at Case Western Reserve caused water damage in the Music Library, and a formulated disaster plan did not prevent severe damage of some rare music materials.

The Milton S. Eisenhower Library at Johns Hopkins University has established the "Bindery Traineeship Program," a five-year apprenticeship program under the direction of John F. Dean, designed to produce bookbinders and restorers with a certificate of proficiency. Ellen Fink, Head of the Academy Book Bindery in Ann Arbor, has developed "Apprenticeship Program for the Craft of Hand Bookbinding," a four-year program documented with standards, contracts, an evaluation schedule, and schedules for work experience and related instruction. Fink also edits *The Abbey Newsletter*, a quarterly publication on binding, conservation, and related techniques.

The Research Library Group (RLG) has given each of its four members (Harvard, Yale, Columbia, and the New York Public Library) $15,000 to microfilm selected serials and other multivolume sets that have deteriorated. The University of California's system-wide Task Group on the Preservation of Library Materials completed a survey of conditions and preservation needs. The National Conservation Advisory Council, established in 1973 to study the needs for preserving the nation's cultural and historical patrimony, is in the process of being reorganized to allow a more uniform representation of sectors involved with conservation. Paul Banks, Chairman of the Library and Archives Committee within the Advisory Council, wrote an interim statement on "Control of Environmental Conditions in Museums, Libraries and Archives in Situations of Energy Shortage" that appeared in *Special Libraries*, (November 1977) and includes specific guidelines for conditions.

Workshops and Seminars. A two-day course entitled "Preservation of Library Resources," conducted by Donald Etherington and Peter Waters of the LC Preservation Office, was followed by a three-day special advanced course on the "Conservation of Library and Archival Materials" as a part of the seventh Annual Library Institute held on the Santa Cruz Campus of the University of California during the summer. The seminar focused on practical applications of conservation methods developed by the LC Preservation Office. At the ALA Conference in Detroit, Frazer Poole of LC spoke on "The Marking of Rare Books and Manuscripts: Safeguard or Defacement?" at the meeting of the Rare Books and Manuscripts Section of the Association of College and Research Libraries. An archivally safe manuscript marking ink has been developed by the LC Restoration Office and the Government Printing Office. Poole also spoke on the "Preservation of Music Materials" at the Music Library Association's annual meeting in Santa Barbara.

The Library Binding Institute (LBI), together with local library associations, sponsored several "Workshops in Prolonging the Useful Life of Library Materials." Three workshops were held in cooperation with the Mid-Eastern Regional Medical Library Service; another was cosponsored with the Law Library

Preservation of Library Materials

Association of Greater New York. These instructional workshops were aimed at specific binding problems and made use of the expertise of Werner Rebsamen, who directs the LBI Book Testing Laboratory at the Rochester Institute of Technology, School of Printing. The workshops also featured LBI's new film, "Binding the Past for the Future." A 16mm color film, about 20 minutes long, it shows how a volume is library bound and is available for loan or purchase from LBI.

A two-day "Seminar on the Conservation of Long Island's Historical Collections" was held at the C.W. Post Center of Long Island University. The workshop was funded by a grant from the New York State Council on the Arts; the participants included Laura Young, Noel Kunz, Nancy Donaldson, Gerard Reese, and C.R. Jones. The demonstration workshops covered mylar encapsulation (mylar is an inert polyester film), storage of flat paper items, mounting of prints and maps, treatment of bindings and minor repairs, and the care of photographs. New York's Clinton-Essex-Franklin Library System held a series of workshops on "Historic and Library Materials Conservation." Carolyn Horton, Edward Weldon, Noel Kunz, and Nancy Donaldson were the speakers. The Society of American Archivists (SAA) sponsored two workshops on the "Care of Historical Records," the first on the campus of the University of Notre Dame and the second in conjunction with the October SAA annual meeting in Salt Lake City. A special course on "The Binding, Maintenance, and Restoration of Books" was sponsored during the summer by the Arts Education division of the Civic Arts Program in Walnut Creek, California.

The NEDCC conducted a five-day seminar in conservation administration for the Archdiocese of New Orleans at Saint Mary's Dominican College. The NEDCC and the Resources and Technical Services Section of the New York Library Association cosponsored a seminar on the "Conservation of Materials" in Syracuse. The NEDCC also presented a workshop in conservation in October for the New England Archivists. Pamela W. Darling spoke on "What Technical Services Librarians Should Know About Preservation" at the April meeting of the New England Technical Services Librarians, a sign of the growing awareness of the need for all librarians to become more knowledgeable about the subject.

The year was the first for the federal support of an accredited program in preservation education. The "Institute on the Development and Administration of Programs for the Preservation of Library Materials" will be offered by the Columbia University School of Library Service in July and August of 1978. The institute will prepare 12 experienced librarians as administrators to plan, organize, and administer comprehensive preservation programs. The director of the project is Susan O. Thompson, Assistant Professor in the School of Library Service. Paul Banks, Conservator at the Newberry Library since 1964, again taught a four-week summer course on "The Conservation of Research Library Materials." Offered in alternate years since 1971, the course is designed for those responsible for the physical care of rare and research books and manuscripts.

Grants. NEH announced its Humanities Challenge Grant Program, in which awards will go to more than 120 institutions. Each NEH dollar must be matched by at least three from the private sector. Many awards have already been announced, and at least three have been given for conservation purposes. Case Western Reserve University Libraries received a $390,000 NEH grant that will be used to establish a broad-gauged conservation program. Planned measures include low-use storage, provision of appropriate facilities to insure the preservation of special collections, treatment of library windows with ultraviolet filtering material, and binding, boxing, and repairing of heavily used out-of-print materials. Case Western Reserve also received a $10,782 LSCA grant to do a survey of library conservation programs in Ohio and to determine the feasibility of setting up a regional center for the conservation of library materials.

A grant of $73,745 from the National Historical Publications and Records Commission was received by NEDCC through the New England Library Board to establish a microfilm reproduction capability of archival quality and an archival microfilming consulting service. To relieve crowded conditions and provide room for the new facilities, the NEDCC moved to Abbott Hall on the Phillips Academy Campus in Andover, Massachusetts. The Center now includes a microfilm preparation and filming room, processing, testing, and inspection laboratories, three paper restoration workshops, an auditorium and gallery, and a materials control center.

Several conservation surveys of library collections and buildings were made by the NEDCC during 1977 and included recommendations for changes and cost estimates. Assistance was given in more than 30 emergencies throughout the year. The National Historical Publications and Records Commission awarded two grants to the NEDCC to support special programs. A grant for $5,800 will partially fund four one-week conservation seminars in six New England states, and the other grant of $11,850 will aid in the first year's training of a technician and an apprentice.

Publications. Papers presented at a symposium sponsored by the Division of Cellulose, Paper, and Textile Chemistry at the 172nd meeting of the American Chemical Society in 1976 were published in the *Advances in Chemistry* series (No. 164). Published by the American Chemical Society and edited by John C. Williams of the LC Preservation Office, *Preservation of Paper and Textiles of Historical and Artistic Value* contains 25 papers, 11 of which apply to books and manuscripts. Several deal with mass drying and deacidification techniques. Two are of special interest: Bernard Middletown's "Book Preservation for the Librarian" and the late Bernard Walker's report on "Morpholine Deacidification of Whole Books."

Several papers of interest were presented at the American Institute for the Conservation of Historic and Artistic Works (AIC) summer conference in Boston. They covered such topics as heat-set tissue, the health hazards of solvents used in conservation, the conservation of archives materials, and rebinding practices at the Newberry Library. Reprints are available from the Executive Secretary of the AIC National Office (1522 K Street, N.W., Suite 804, Washington, D.C. 20005).

An updated list of academic preservation education courses was produced by the Preservation of Library Materials Committee of the Resources & Technical Services Division and is available from ALA. The Guild of Bookworkers, an affiliate of the American Institute of Graphic Arts, updated the booklet *Opportunities for Study in Hand Bookbinding and Calligraphy.*

Robert A. Weinstein and Larry Booth coauthored *Collection, Use, and Care of Historical Photographs*, published by the American Association for State and Local History. The book covers both the technical and philosophical aspects of photographs and their care. Two new titles appeared in the leaflet series on preservation available from the LC Preservation Office: *Marking Manuscripts* (No. 4) and *Preserving Newspapers and Newspaper-type Materials* (No. 5). *The Journal of Academic Librarianship* (March 1977) contained an article by E.G. Kesler on "A Campaign Against Mutilation" that described a unique campaign to educate staff and patrons. The final report of the salvage and restoration methods used on the Corning Museum Collection damaged in the 1972 flood, *The Corning Flood: Museum Under Water*, edited by John H. Martin, became available from the Museum. It includes chapters on the restoration of the glass collection, the library, and the photo and tape collection as well as the useful section "Planning to Protect an Institution and Its Collections."

Library Scene, a periodical published by the LBI in Boston, continued to offer interesting and helpful articles on binding and preservation, the library/binder relationship, and quality standards. The Office of Management Studies of the Association of Research Libraries (ARL) produced a Systems and Procedures Exchange Center flyer and kit (No. 35) on the "Preservation of Library Materials" in August. The kit contains reprints of 14 documents on preservation and binding provided by ARL libraries. The new Reprint Clearing House (M.G. Carlson, P.O. Box 2658, Detroit, Michigan 48231) has announced the planned publication of a seven-volume set of *Reprints Published to 1977*, a "Monthly Data Service" to update prices and availability status of reprints, and *New Reprints*, a monthly listing of LC proofsheets for reprints with current prices.

A survey taken at the Harvard University Libraries helped set guidelines and goals for a broad-gauged attack on the problems of the conservation of library materials. The informative report appeared in *HUL Notes* (April 7, 1977). — GAY WALKER

Public Libraries

It will be remembered as the Winter of '77, whose severe cold, ice, snow, and fuel shortages caused cutbacks, layoffs, closings, damaged facilities, inoperative equipment, and untold hardships on personnel. Yet public libraries, in those hours that they were open, were jammed with kids, teachers, and other adults—and circulation zoomed.

Spurred by a Governor's Conference in one or two states and planning activities in many others as a preliminary to the White House Conference on Libraries and Information Services, grass-roots participation in library planning and operations was on the upswing. Here and there, declining incomes and skyrocketing costs prompted library administrations to ask the people what they wanted. In Columbus, two years of testing and $248,927 of LSCA funds disclosed that the people wanted—at least in the inner city—all- around media centers with a staff that was in tune with the community and had a feel for the specific information needs of the residents.

At year's end, the new copyright law that had been hovering like a threatening cloud was destined to usher in the new year—some thought with hail and lightning, while others foresaw it as a windstorm that would blow through without damage.

Public Library Universe. The "universe" of public libraries in the United States numbers more than 10,000. If very small public libraries are excluded (those with less than $2,000 in annual income), the number is reduced to 8,500.

If only those serving a population greater than 100,000 are considered, the universe

Private Libraries: see Independent Research Libraries

Processing Centers: see Bibliographic Processing Centers

Public Libraries

numbers about 250. If only those serving a wholly urban population in cities of more than 100,000 population, they number about 150, with 11 states excluded since they have no cities over 100,000.

The universe of information from which news about public libraries is drawn is limited, since only those libraries and librarians whose activities or conditions are reported in the national mass media, trade magazines, association-controlled media, or government publications can be examined for trends, issues, and major developments.

Buildings. A record high was reached in the year ending June 30, 1977, when more than $130,000,000 was spent in construction and reconstruction of public library buildings. Local funding accounted for about 72 per cent, federal 17 per cent, gifts 6 per cent, and state funding 5 per cent.

In Alaska, Anchorage voters rejected an $11,500,000 bond issue for a new building, but in Nome they approved bonding for a $364,000 addition. In Texas, Fort Worth voters failed to pass a referendum for library building, while in Austin they approved a $1,900,000 expansion of the central library.

Three members of the Suburban (Illinois) Library System were among the first of many to tap Public Works Employment Act funds for construction. Others included Framingham (Massachusetts), $4,500,000 for a new 53,000-square-foot main building; Henrietta (New York), $1,450,000 toward a new 20,000-square-foot building; Stark County (Ohio) District Library, $4,600,000; Portland (Maine), $3,300,000 to be supplemented by local funds for a $5,400,000 building; and Woodburn (Oregon), $1,100,000 for renovation and an addition.

A remodeled supermarket building became the new library at Salamanca (New York) with all kinds of gimmicks to finance it: "selling" materials to be used in the remodeling, a one-night "night club" operation in the partially remodeled building, an auction of donated goods and services, and volunteer labor.

At Birmingham, voters approved an $11,000,000 bond issue for a new main and branch library. Seattle received a grant of $2,700,000 for remodeling. Vigo County (Indiana) broke ground for its new $3,000,000 main library during National Library Week, while Springfield (Ilinois) celebrated the week with a formal dedication of its new $7,800,000 main building.

The Hendrik Hudson Free Library (Montrose, New York) remodeled an old fire station on a $125,000 budget as its new headquarters. A branch of the Josephine County (Oregon) Public Library moved into a relocatable building on a school ground and is sharing space with the school library. Voters at St. Cloud (Minnesota) approved a $2,200,000 bond issue for a 59,000-square-foot structure, of which some 15,000 square feet will be rented to the Great River Regional Library for its headquarters.

An old main post office building at Charlottesville (Virginia) will become the new library after a $1,500,000 remodeling; the original cost of the post office was $250,000. In Paterson (New Jersey) a branch library will serve as the major core function when it shares a new building with a multipurpose community room, police community relations office, and a fire department ambulance. The architectural firm sees this as a trend "as the costs of separate but related community facilities begin to price out any new construction for each individual facility."

Smatterings of solar energy construction appeared. The new Springfield (Illinois) library is said to be "one of the first libraries in the U.S. to have a cooling/heating system planned for easy adaptation to solar energy when it becomes economically feasible." At New Rochelle a grant of $274,855 from the Federal Energy Research and Development Agency is to provide for installation of a solar energy system in the new 60,000-square-foot main library already under construction. A solar-heated building is in the planning for Lake Villa (Illinois) following approval of a referendum by voters for a building to be insulated from the outside rather than the inside.

The long-debated fate of the Los Angeles central library was decided when the Community Development Agency approved a $30,900,000 project to renovate and expand the old building. A $44,000,000 combination of federal funds, gifts, and bond issues will construct a new main library for Dallas. In Chicago, the 1897 Chicago Public Library (CPL) building was reopened October 17 as the CPL Cultural Center with a new civic reception hall. The building still houses the circulating library, the children's collection, and materials on the arts.

The District of Columbia Library opened its second and third kiosk libraries, each housing some 1,000 books in a 100-square-foot structure. The indomitable Frederic Glazer, Director of the West Virginia Library Commission, went beyond his "instant libraries" to "outpost libraries," "port-a-kiosks," and "port-a-structures," all designed to extend library services to the greatest number at an affordable cost. (See "Prefabricated and Portable Library Units Offer Quick and Easy Extension of Service," *American Libraries* (November 1977) pp. 546-48.)

Cooperation. Cooperative systems and networks—multistate and/or multitype—were much in the news during 1977, kicked off by a legislation hearing at the ALA Midwinter

Public Broadcasting: see Telecommunications and Public Broadcasting

Publishing, Newspaper: see Publishing Serials

Meeting sponsored by the Association of State Library Agencies. Although cooperative efforts across the country are uneven and varied, most of those in attendance seemed to support the national network envisioned by Al Trezza of the National Commission for Libraries and Information Science (NCLIS) and published by NCLIS as *Toward a National Program for Library and Information Services.*

Nearly 30 states have enabling legislation for multitype library cooperative systems, but only about one-third have allocated funding. Most systems were started with and are being maintained by LSCA funds, although fiscal stability likely will not be achieved without a mix of federal, state, and local funds. In Indiana, LSCA Title III is used for several multitype projects: an Interlibrary Communication Project utilizing teletype machines; the Indiana Cooperative Library Services Authority, a statewide bibliographic network tied into OCLC; and Area Library Services Authorities, voluntary municipal corporations of member libraries, which are now established in 12 of the state's 14 regions. An 18-month study on "Development of a Plan for the Integration of Indiana Libraries into the National Plan for Library and Information Services" is scheduled for completion in early 1978.

FINANCES

In a year in which the public economy was in trouble, libraries at large fared better than many had expected. Typically, library budgets increased slightly in 1977—Seattle 2 per cent, Baltimore County 7 per cent, for example—but inflation and rapidly rising costs wiped out the gains and libraries were less well off than in 1976. Especially hard hit were materials purchases: the 9.2 per cent increase in the average price of a periodical and the 7.4 per cent increase in the average price of a book meant that fewer were purchased.

There is evidence of priorities being reexamined, or being established, with hard choices made among the many alternatives. Techniques of zero-based budgeting were used in some places for projected levels of funding, with operational goals spelled out for increased funding, status quo funding, or reduced funding.

At the top of the bad news was the wave of budget cutbacks in the large metropolitan systems in New York. Salary increases were banned in Monroe County, and cuts up to 10 per cent were ordered on salaries over $12,000. The budget was reduced 8 per cent at Queens Borough, bringing the total cutback to about $3,500,000 since 1974. A 50 per cent decrease in the staff was a result of a 25 per cent cut in the budget at Buffalo and Erie County.

Brooklyn and Queens Borough, among several libraries whose crippling losses included all part-time staff, made heroic efforts to keep the system going. Queens Borough used hundreds of Comprehensive Employment and Training Act (CETA) employees. Brooklyn formed a "Book Brigade" of volunteers, each to work at least three hours per week, with recruitment and coordination chores performed by community organizations that agreed to "adopt" their neighborhood branch library.

The Illinois Library Association obtained federal funds for a project aimed at better funding of public libraries by providing library boards with information on funding sources, holding workshops, and providing technical assistance. The objective was to encourage the boards to go after additional dollars.

State Aid. Some gains were made in state aid to public libraries. A 300 per cent increase in Alabama brought the per capita aid to $.18. In Maryland, the Governor's Committee on Funding of the State Library Resource Center (the Enoch Pratt Free Library) recommended 100 per cent funding of interlibrary lending and reference service, acquisition of specialized informational, reference, and research materials, and the services of the audiovisual department. Florida boosted state aid from $1,400,000 to $3,218,603. First aid came to Oregon's public libraries on July 6 when Governor Robert Stráub signed a bill providing $300,000 for local library services.

In Ohio, the $1,700,000 appropriation for state aid in 1977-79 was a 32 per cent increase over 1975-77. Federal revenue sharing funds were used for Colorado's appropriation of $1,421,091, up slightly over the previous year. In Maryland, per capita state aid was increased from $3 to $4 on a 60 per cent local and 40 per cent state basis. California, which had been providing $.05 per capita, enacted a new Library Services Act with wide-ranging provisions and an appropriation of $5,300,000, a whopping increase of 500 per cent.

Public Libraries

Margaret Mitchell was one of seven outstanding readers who finished 190 books while participating in the 1977 Summer Reading Club at the Cleveland Public Library.

The Brooklyn Public Library's "Get Ready to Read" program was advertised on the Spectacolor signboard at Times Square during a two week period in March as a public service announcement.

Houston Public Library's fund raising fashion show featured models from Neiman-Marcus department store on a runway built on top of the information desk in the library's lobby.

Acceptance by the state for the responsibility of maintaining public library resources for the citizens was given a boost in 1976 when Michigan designated the Detroit Public Library as a state resource center and assumed responsibility for funding the main library. In 1977 Michigan increased its appropriation for Detroit's main library by $1,000,000 to $6,500,000. In addition, state aid to all Michigan libraries was increased to $7,100,000.

City aid in a new form came to the Palm Springs Public Library when it latched onto a share f the "bed tax" that is added to motel and hotel bills of out-of-state tourists.

NCLIS Support. Added support for increased state aid was given by NCLIS with the release of its study *Improving State Aid to Public Libraries*. The study stresses the educational role of libraries and places the responsibility for their development with the state as part of the state's mandate to provide public education. Sources of funding shown in the study's 1975 statistics were 82 per cent local, 13 per cent state, and 5 per cent federal, with the libraries receiving less than 2 per cent of local government expenditures. Noting that public schools get 44 per cent of their funds from the state, and that state aid per capita is $146 for schools compared to $.68 for libraries, the study urged a closer alignment for schools and libraries: "librarians, local and state library boards, commissions, and advisory boards should deliberately seek to establish closer planning, operating relationships, and joint service agreements with public education groups, officials, and institutions."

Federal Assistance. The Library Services and Construction Act Amendments of 1977 were signed by President Carter on October 7, without the Title V provision for direct aid to urban libraries that had been sought by the Urban Libraries Council (an ALA affiliate of member libraries serving cities of more than 100,000 in population). Title I now provides, however, for a percentage of any funds over $60,000,000 to be earmarked for large urban libraries, the only problem being that an appropriation in excess of $60,000,000 is unlikely.

The *National Inventory of Library Needs, 1975* was published by NCLIS in March. Comparison of the 1975 statistics with a similar inventory in 1965 showed an 81 per cent increase in professional staff from 19,900 to 36,000; a 65 per cent increase in bookstock from 241,000,000 to 397,000,000 volumes; and a 290 per cent increase in operating expenditures from $261,000,000 to $1,018,000,000. In this ten-year period the population grew only 10 per cent.

Nevertheless, the "indicated needs" are horrendous. According to the *National Inventory*, "Libraries in the United States in 1975 were grossly underfunded—hence, lacked sufficient staff, collection materials, and space to give adequate library service, including sufficient hours of service." Based on the indicated needs, the nation's public libraries were short 240,000,000 volumes, 8,450 professional and nearly 48,000 support personnel, and 55,000,000 square feet of building space. In operating expenditures alone, meeting the minimum indicated levels of $9 to $12 per capita would have required an additional $1,000,000,000, or twice the actual annual expenditure.

Fees. Probably the liveliest topic of debate involving public librarians was the charging of fees for specialized services, such as the online data base. While certain charges, relatively small, had become commonplace over the years—photocopy fees, for example—the idea of charging by the minute to search a data base via computer terminal or by the hour for specialized research was abhorrent to many.

The Virginia Beach Public Library was selling city histories that cost $1.40 each at $3.50, a profit of 150 per cent. And the annual used book sales of some libraries have developed into year-round discard bookstores in the public libraries at Columbus and Hennepin County (Minnesota), with the latter realizing $20,000 annually. Apparently, it is all right for public libraries to be out for the buck as long as the charge is not by the minute or by the hour.

The matter came to the floor of the ALA Council in a resolution that "ALA reaffirm the concept of access to information without charge to individuals in public libraries and tax-supported libraries... and go on public record against the charging of fees by tax-supported libraries for providing information and reference services which have traditionally been free." Council rejected the resolution by a three to one majority, but was amenable to looking into the kinds of fees being charged. Council apparently could not both reaffirm the concept of free access and condemn those who are violating it. As Eric Moon aptly put it from the chair, "Let's establish the principle, and then we can deal with the practice."

News of fee chargers came to light now and then. The Public Library of Cincinnati and Hamilton County charged $3 for a filled interlibrary loan request, reduced to $2.50 for an unfilled request. When the Onondaga County Public Library (New York) was to be assessed $2 for each interloan "imbalance" with the Mid-York Library System, it promptly became neither a borrower nor a lender.

At the 96th ALA Annual Conference in Detroit, the membership and the Council overwhelmingly reaffirmed its advocacy of free access to all information in public and publicly supported libraries. President Moon argued for a national information policy whose principle is "that free access to information for all is the very foundation, not only of our profession and our services, but of individual liberty."

The Chicago Public Library in cooperation with the Illinois Regional Library Council announced the availability of the New York Times Information Bank at $10 for a search of up to three minutes and $2.50 for each additional minute. As CPL pointed out, the same information was free—if the patron did a manual search. Cuyahoga County (Ohio) was offering the same service with the first 15 minutes free, and $1.50 for each additional minute. Columbus installed a telecopier on a facsimile transmission network to share the Times Information Bank with other libraries, with the first 10 minutes free and $1.50 per minute beyond that.

Information Alternative, Woodstock, New York, published *The Directory of Fee-Based Information Services 1977*, listing individuals and organizations in the United States and Canada in business to provide answers for a price. The cost of the *Directory* is $3.

Fines. A national policy on fines for late or nonreturn of borrowed materials did not materialize from the work of the Circulation Services Section Ad Hoc Committee on Fines and Penalties of the ALA Library Administration Division. Following two years of meetings, discussions, and public hearings, the committee submitted a final report to ALA Council with the conclusion that "the issue of fines and/or penalties still remains a matter of local consideration requiring a local solution." Council accepted the report with appreciation.

The Buffalo and Erie County Public Library contemplated an increase in fines until a committee reported that not only would the action fail to increase revenue and get more books returned on time but also would result in a net financial loss. The Board of the Chicago Public Library recommended severe penalties of up to $1,000 for overdue and damaged books, and punishment under statutes governing property damage so that harsher fines could be imposed for damaged materials. The King County Public Library in Seattle contracted with a local collection agency to recover fines for overdue books and payment for lost books.

On the other hand, the Oklahoma County Libraries System converted five trailer bookmobiles and a small branch from hardback to paperbound book collections, eliminated all overdue fines, and sent overdue notices only to those borrowers who had an "excessive" record of unreturned books. "Experienced, interested personnel and overdue book notices are the primary means to maintaining a low book loss" was the conclusion of the two-year study.

Funds and Things. The National Endowment for the Humanities (NEH) designated its third and fourth Learning Library. A $330,000 grant to the New Orleans Public Library will support a three-year educational program called "Jambalaya" with courses in the library on just about everything that makes up New Orleans. "The Sonoran Heritage" is the subject of a similar multiyear project at the Tucson Public Library, which will focus on those things that are unique to the Southwest. The first to be designated as a Learning Library was Boston, the second was Chicago.

Houston was awarded $135,000 by NEH for a nine-month program entitled "City—Our Urban Past, Present, and Future." A $36,100 planning grant to the Indiana Library Association and the Indiana Library Trustees Association for the investigation of ways that academic humanists can assist public libraries in staff education, program planning, and collection development produced an action plan presented in a one-day conference of the two associations. The plan was subsequently submitted to NEH as a proposal for a three-year project.

For the past several years, funds for adult community programs related to public policy issues have been available to public libraries through the NEH state-based programs operated by citizen committees. With its National Learning Library program, direct grants to public libraries, and its Challenge Grant experience with New York, NEH seems headed for a major push of the humanities through the nation's public libraries. (*See also* Gifts, Bequests, Endowments; National Endowment for the Humanities.)

OTHER DEVELOPMENTS

Health and Medical. Medical and health information, which over the past years was dispensed sparingly and uneasily by public librarians, is now being provided to the public by means of prerecorded audiotapes accessed by telephone. Prince George's County (Maryland) developed its health information service using TEL-MED tapes, revised and updated by local doctors and dentists, with start-up costs estimated at $30,000 and annual operating costs at $8,000. Columbus used an LSCA grant to initiate a health information and referral service called MED-LINE with a core of some 300 tapes prepared by the San Bernardino Medical Society; tapes run from three to five minutes, and the system will also make referrals.

Funding from LSCA and a National Library of Medicine grant is supporting a Community Health Information Network in the Boston area, with five public libraries serving as outlets for medical information from the Mount Auburn Hospital. The libraries are cooperating in collection development, training of reference personnel, and interlibrary loans, and local residents are participating through a community advisory committee.

Audio-Video. While audio systems are on a slight upswing, video systems are dragging, according to a study released by Knowledge Industry Publications called "Video in Libraries, A Status Report, 1977-78." "Lack of local support has forced curtailment—and in some cases abandonment—of promising experiments launched with federal funds," says the report, which found not more than 5 per cent of public libraries "seriously committed to video."

Among those libraries committed to video is the Cambridge (Massachusetts) Public Library, which puts on a city-funded weekly 30-minute television series on city issues.

Although video systems may be sparse, the conversion of libraries from print to multimedia continues, sometimes in dramatic fashion. San Francisco transformed a branch library into an LSCA-funded "communications center and media literacy demonstration project," adding audio cassettes, videotapes, films, projectors, wireless headsets, and other AV hardware and software. San Francisco previously had provided little in the way of AV services.

Other Demands. Libraries with genealogy collections have been inundated with requests for information and assistance in the wake of the wide public exposure to the book *Roots* by Alex Haley. The search for roots, the celebration of the Bicentennial, the energy shortage, reduced buying power for conventional materials, and numerous other factors are causing a resurgence of interest in local history, creating what many feel is a healthy atmosphere of localism and regionalism. One such project is under way at a branch library in Cleveland where young adults are researching the history of rock and roll music in the Cleveland area through taped interviews and photographs, with a slide/tape show planned to be shown in libraries and schools.

Technology. Prevalent among the new technology reports during the year were installations of automated circulation control systems on line to a minicomputer with light-pen scanning of bar-code labels. Two prepackaged systems dominated the market in 1977—LIBS 100 from CL Systems, Inc., and Gaylord's Computerized Circulation System. (*See also* Networks.)

Also frequently in the news were reports of COM (computer output microfilm) catalogs, with many switching from the book catalogs that had replaced the card catalogs not too many years ago. Some chose microfiche instead of microfilm, and some chose both. And some, having chosen neither the book catalog nor the COM catalog on microfilm or microfiche, were waiting for affordable technology to put the whole thing on line, a move that hopefully might last at least until one's career ends.

EDWARD N. HOWARD

Public Library Association

1977 began with the Public Library Association (PLA) searching for solutions to the plight of the nation's public libraries and working to strenghthen the Association itself. The Goals, Guidelines, and Standards for Public Libraries Committee, long working toward a new set of public library standards, promised substantial progress toward the resolution of this major problem. The membership of the Association continued to support a viable Secretariat at ALA headquarters. Innovative programs were planned for the ALA Annual Conference. The *PLA Newsletter* continued to provide a dynamic forum for public library and Association ideas. Furthermore, the stirrings of the Alternative Education Programs Section offered additional evidence of the viability of PLA.

New directions for PLA were planned. The New Directions Committee met in the spring and submitted its report to the PLA Board of Directors at the Annual Conference. Major revisions were made in the Association's statement of missions and goals, and the organization was restructured. Priorities were established for the allocation of Association resources, and appropriate activities were recommended.

Missions Outlined. As adopted by the Executive Board, the missions of PLA are (1) to advance the development and effectiveness of

Public Library Association

public library service to the American people; (2) to speak for the library profession at the national level on matters pertaining to public libraries; and (3) to enrich the professional competence and opportunities of public librarians.

In order to accomplish its missions, the Association goals will include: (1) conducting and sponsoring research about how the public library can respond to changing social needs and technological developments; (2) developing and disseminating materials useful to public libraries in interpreting public library services and needs; (3) conducting continuing education for public librarians by programming at national and regional conferences, by publications such as the newsletter, and by other delivery methods; (4) establishing, evaluating, and promoting guidelines and standards for public libraries; (5) maintaining liaison with other relevant national agencies and organizations engaged in public administration and human services; (6) maintaining liaison with other divisions and units of ALA and with other library organizations such as the Association of American Library Schools and the Urban Libraries Council; (7) defining the role of the public library's service to a wide range of user and potential user groups; (8) promoting and interpreting on a national level the public library to a changing society, including legislation and other programs.

To accomplish these goals, several new sections were proposed for the Association. The Alternative Education Programs Section was created with responsibility for defining the role of the public library in literacy and providing liaison with educational agencies working in that area. The responsibilities of the Metropolitan Libraries Section will include funding resources for urban libraries, the relationship between urban and suburban libraries, issues related to equity, service to the disadvantaged and minorities, and other similar areas. The Public Library Management Section will be responsible for the areas of public relations, personnel, budget, evaluation, and related subjects of special concern for public libraries.

The Small and Medium-sized Libraries Section was created with responsibility in the areas of funding resources, service to the disadvantaged and minorities, and other problems of small and medium-sized libraries. Retained were two existing sections. The Armed Forces Librarians Section will continue to be responsible for relations with other federal libraries and for liaison with military and public libraries. The Public Library Systems Section will continue to be responsible for the relationship of public library systems to multi-type networks.

Priorities Set. Six priorities for the Association were adopted. They relate to the roles of the public library as a nontraditional educational agency, as a cultural agency, as a rehabilitation agency, as a partner and coodinator of all public and private library and information resources, as an information and referral agency, and as a public institution.

The effort to create new output and user-oriented standards for public libraries based on research continued throughout the year. A subcommittee of the Goals, Guidelines, and Standards Committee was also developing a mission statement for public libraries.

The mission statement adopted by the Executive Board directed attention to the current plight of the public library as an institution. The mission statement attempted to show that the needs of present and future society require that the public library change as an institution and assume a strong leadership role. The document pointed out that the pace of social change, the exponential increase in the volume and complexity of the record of human experience, the movement toward egalitarianism, and the depletion of natural resources have so changed the environment of the public library that a new focus is required for the mission of the institution. Furthermore, corresponding changes are required in its governance and administration, its delivery systems, its materials (in both content and form), its personnel and their competencies, its services, and its relationships to other libraries and other types of agencies and institutions. An updated library vocabulary and responses to the new environment were proposed.

PLA Officers

PRESIDENT (July 1977-July 1978):
Genevieve M. Casey, Wayne State University, Detroit

VICE-PRESIDENT/PRESIDENT-ELECT:
Ronald A. Dubberly, Seattle Public Library

EXECUTIVE SECRETARY:
Andrew M. Hansen

ASSOCIATE EXECUTIVE SECRETARY:
Mary Jo Lynch

Membership (August 31, 1977): 4,177 (2,631 personal and 1,546 organizational)

Research Grant. A grant was received from the U.S. Office of Education for $140,000 to support research on the process of standards development for community library service. The 21-month project was approved for the development and testing of a process by which public libraries could plan and evaluate services within the context of community goals and objectives. Manuals were to be developed to assist in the assessment of community information needs, to identify current library and

Public Relations

information services within the community, to establish priorities, and to develop service programs.

The year closed with the national economy and public libraries in a mixed but improving situation. Furthermore, the year had produced significant movement toward an Association more responsive to the needs of public libraries and librarians across the nation. It also had produced a professional statement of direction for public libraries and substantial effort toward initial tools for measuring progress toward their goals.

RONALD DUBBERLY

Public Relations

In 1977 most libraries sought increased support both in use and in funds. There were also signs of advances in the management function of public relations. This indicates that public relations is being accepted more and more in libraries as an essential of good management.

Merchandising Skills. For more than 75 years, aggressive public library administrators have been gaining support by offering and promoting new services. In 1977 libraries that were in tune with their communities included the Public Library of Columbus and Franklin County (Ohio), which offered on-line automated information on health; the Watertown (Massachusetts) Public Library, which sponsored programs for women on finding jobs, legal rights, and assertiveness; and the Watertown (Minnesota) County Library, which loaned repair manuals for tractors to farmers throughout the region. To reach out to new users the Los Angeles County Public Library System launched a Spanish-language radio program for children and the Bossier City (Louisiana) Parish Library added sign language interpretations for deaf children during story hours.

In a major expansion of services that should enlarge its body of supporters, the Chicago Public Library opened its new Cultural Center with a profusion of free programs of dance, theater, music, and art that were offered almost daily to adults and children. Following the pattern utilized by the country's leading museums, the Library gained financial backing for its ambitious cultural program from corporations, as well as from foundations and private benefactors.

Although a study by the editor at the State Library of Ohio revealed that most of that state's public libraries issue no annual report for community distribution, many of the country's libraries reported the year's events with wit and vigor. The Cheshire (Connecticut) Public Library announced to its citizens: "Last year we saved you $1,790,291.83." The sum was the total cost if all items borrowed had instead been bought by library users. The Public Library of Cincinnati and Hamilton County told its story succinctly in a report entitled "We're Number 2!" The New Orleans Public Library used the format of a menu in an elegant restaurant for its imaginative year-end report.

Administrators of small public libraries, whose budgets only rarely can support even part-time public relations help, continued to assess community interests and then develop and publicize services to meet these needs. James Swan, Director of the Pickens County (South Carolina) Library, provided valuable guidance for staffs of small libraries in his article "New Visibility for the Small PL" in *Wilson Library Bulletin* (January 1977), pp. 424-27.

School Media Centers. Public relations is one of the many management tasks assumed by every administrator of a school media center. With school budgets threatened in most communities in 1977, media centers faced the dual challenge of serving students effectively and presenting the need for more resources. The Rocky River (Ohio) High School Library utilized a slide/tape presentation to present its resources as an essential part of a lifelong process of learning. In Youngstown, New York, Lewiston Porter Central School Library successfully promoted to the community its concept of what a good school library media program can be. Both centers won John Cotton Dana Public Relations Awards for their programs.

Betty Fast, the former Director of Media Services for the Groton (Connecticut) Public Schools died during the year; but she left a legacy to the profession through her contributions to standards for public information in media centers. The standards to which she contributed are found in *Media Programs: District and School,* published by ALA and the Association for Educational Communications and Technology.

Systems, State and National Libraries. Leading public library systems, like the one in Nassau County (Long Island), continued to offer member libraries a wide range of materials, training workshops, and consultation services. Among the newer multitype library systems the New York Metropolitan Reference and Research Library Agency (METRO) broke new ground by winning a John Cotton Dana Public Relations Award for its "result-oriented techniques" of communication.

The major national event in state libraries was the ending of financial support for Wisconsin's Coordinated Library Information Program, Inc. (CLIP). Through the newsletter (*Tips from CLIP*), posters, pamphlets, and radio and television spot announcements, Marian S. Edsall had supplied libraries throughout the country with sound public rela-

Tennis pro Arthur Ashe endorses libraries over sports for the Michigan Library Association.

tions counsel and imaginative materials. Although created for Wisconsin libraries of all types, the program grew through demand into a supplement to ALA's public information program. A new publication, Library PR News, was announced for a January 1978 premiere, but only demand by enlightened librarians can assure that CLIP's other programs will have a rebirth under new sponsors.

The West Virginia Library Commission continued to demonstrate skill in lobbying for funds. The Commission's graphics program called "Exposure" remained the only statewide supplier of library posters and pamphlets—a wide array of sometimes irreverent but always compelling publications.

In Illinois, the ILLINET Public Information Project, which had aroused national interest and envy when its $400,000 LSCA grant was announced several years earlier, still was not operational in 1977. An Illinois official announced that the project's future was uncertain. Librarians around the country who bought and benefited from the Houston Public Library's television spot announcements made by Ketchum, MacLeod & Grove, Inc. (including the so-called Watergate spot) welcomed the news of a new Texas Library Association (TLA) project. LSCA and TLA funds totaling $40,000 will finance television and radio spots, some of the latter in Spanish as well as English, made by the same advertising and public relations firm. The spots, which will be available for sale nationally, have as their goal the improvement of the image of the librarian.

In 1977 the Division for the Blind and Physically Handicapped in the Library of Congress developed plans for a massive radio and television campaign to inform the 3,000,000 eligible persons who are not borrowers about the free reading program. The program, which will be tested early in 1978 in seven regional areas, will be supported by public education programs conducted by local libraries and will offer a toll-free telephone number. In previous promotions the Division relied on printed publications and exhibits, with most messages directed toward librarians and sighted persons from whom referrals were sought.

The Library of Congress set a good example in communications in other ways. The 1,600-person Processing Department commissioned an analysis of its internal communications and a plan for an internal communications program. Under the direction of the Assistant Librarian of Congress (Public Education)—a new top-level position held by James Parton until midyear when he was succeeded by Carol Nemeyer—the Library expanded its exhibition program and installed handsome new directional signs in the Main Reading Room, where the staff offered orientation and assistance to users.

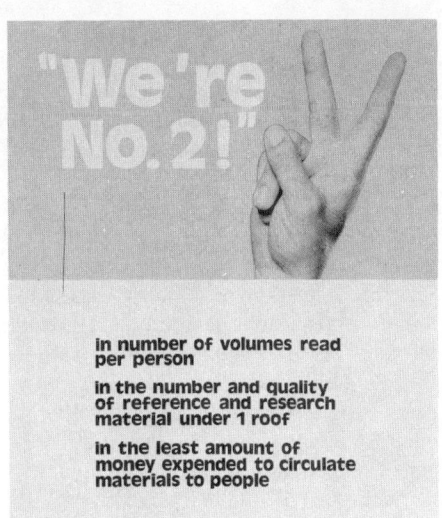

The Public Library of Cincinnati and Hamilton County cited three areas in which they were second in the nation and the statistics were published in their 1977 annual report.

Academic Libraries. Academic libraries, even those with large staffs, have been slow to centralize their public relations functions. Only three libraries—the University of Texas at Austin, the University of Utah, and Case Western Reserve University—are known to have full-time public relations positions on their staffs. Financial pressures in 1977 increased the need for better communication with students and faculty to gain support and save staff time. When the new open stack Perry-Castaneda Library opened at the University of Texas in Austin, fans read about it in the football program. Earlier the Library had announced receipt of its 4,000,000th volume by turning on orange lights in the tower building, an honor previously reserved for sports victories.

Public Relations Staffing. No one has yet made a census of library public relations staff members or analyzed their qualifications. The total is probably fewer than 200 full-time positions for the United States; an incomplete list at ALA has 53 names. Probably about half of the state libraries have public relations specialists who coordinate the state library's public relations program and, in some cases, offer leadership and assistance to libraries in the state. The Washington State Library was among those who added this new position in 1977. Announcements of job openings in the library press indicated that the total grew slightly in 1977, mostly in public library systems and state libraries, and that more libraries were seeking persons with public relations training and experience than were requiring professional library degrees.

A former press secretary (not a librarian) for an Ohio governor joined the staff of the Public Library of Columbus and Franklin County and helped turn the Library's new services into media events that rated prime television news coverage. Wisconsin's excellent standards for public relations in systems of libraries, large, medium, and small, continued

Public Relations

Above and below, ALA graphics for 1977 National Library Week.

to provide an example that other states, and the profession as a whole, would be wise to follow. In many libraries salaries for a public relations specialist without a graduate library degree still lag behind those of librarians.

Bleak news came from the Los Angeles Public Library, which eliminated three public information positions including that of the director, in order to add staff to branch libraries. The Denver Public Library lost one public information position and reduced its printing budget substantially. Connecticut libraries followed three staffing paths that some other libraries throughout the country were following. The Hartford Public Library used Comprehensive Employment and Training Act (CETA) funds for one-year appointments of a public relations coordinator, a writer, an artist, and six community contact staff members. The Southwestern Connecticut Library System, with a staff of 1½ persons, hired a local advertising and public relations firm to develop a short-term countywide promotion program. In Windsor, Connecticut, the public library called on corporate public relations expertise to help sponsor promotional and staff training programs in cooperation with a local McDonald's restaurant.

ALA Activities. ALA continued to function as the country's major communicatiol for libraries, a huge task for the small headquarters Public Information Office directed by Peggy Barber and the volunteer members of the Public Relations Section of the Library Administration Division, the National Library Week (NLW) Committee, and other ALA units. One of the goals of ALA is the "promotion of libraries and librarianship to assure the delivery of user-oriented library and information service to all." Among the many activities carried out in 1977 by ALA's Public Information Office staff with the guidance of the Public Relations Board, Inc., ALA's public relations counseling firm, on behalf of all libraries were the following:

—stimulating the national media to report library news and to develop library features for audiences throughout the country.

—supplying a syndicated book column, "About Books," through Newspaper Enterprise Association for use by about 375 newspapers. This successful, self-supporting activity expanded to include "Book Hot Lines," a 60-second public service spot announcement series broadcast on the CBS radio network.

—serving as a center of information on innovative library services and programs and offering guidance to librarians in the field of public relations.

—directing and coordinating the National Library Week program, the only national program that promotes all types of libraries. NLW focuses on one week each April but produces materials that libraries can use year-round. With the advice and assistance of ALA's National Library Week Committee (Alice Norton, Chairperson for 1976-77, and Lawrence Molumby, Chairperson for 1977-78), the ALA staff arranged for the production of posters, banners, bookmarks, and sample news releases and radio spots which 6,000 libraries bought for state and local observances.

The 1977 NLW theme of "Use Your Library" had subthemes such as "Get Carried Away" and "Get Your Fatcs Straight." The graphics, produced by one of the country's leading design firms, drew praise and also brickbats from some librarians who asked for more realistic art. The Florida Library Association used the "Fatcs" theme and NLW graphics for a statewide, yearlong campaign to publicize library information services, with many locally produced materials. Distribution of NLW materials, including brisk sales in Australia, continued to bring financial benefits to ALA. In 1977 profits paid for 60 percent of the operation of the association's Public Information Office.

The staff of ALA and the Public Relations Board supplied library stories to national magazines, radio and television networks, and national wire services, They resulted in thousands of newspaper articles, public service advertisements, and features in major magazines and on national radio and television programs. In April hundreds of librarians and citizens converged on Congress and on state and city legislatures during NLW's Legislative Day, with national efforts guided by ALA's Washington Office.

The NLW Committee awarded the third annual Grolier Award to the New Jersey Library Association (NJLA) for the funding of its program "Influencing City Hall: Good Libraries Are Good Business and Deserve Good Budgets." NJLA produced materials that local public libraries used for communication with governing officials and also sponsored training workshops at which librarians and trustees learned political skills. In addition to buying NLW materials from ALA and some state associations the country's librarians bought everything from posters to T-shirts from Upstart, a Maryland producer of imaginative, nontraditional library promotion materials.

The NLW Committee, expanded by its request to 10 persons with the purpose of including representatives from all types of libraries, reported to ALA's Executive Committee and Council during the ALA Annual Conference. The Committee also produced the first three in a series of fact sheets for ALA members that can be ordered from ALA's Public Information Office. The Committee also made initial plans to conduct a series of campaigns directed toward specific library public relations needs. At the Annual Conference, ALA demonstrated its support for the NLW program by awarding the J. Morris Jones/Bailey K. Howard/World Book Encyclopedia/ALA Goal Award to the NLW Committee and ALA's Public Information Office. The generous grant funded the creation of a television spot for promotion of libraries nationwide. In addition, ALA's Executive Director named the NLW program as one of the Association's major accomplishments.

Public Relations Section. Among the Section's major activities of 1977 were.

—sponsoring the one-day "Swap and Shop" session at the ALA Annual Conference, during which hundreds of librarians and trustees visited exhibits, gathered sample library promotional materials, watched library audiovisual presentations used by local libraries, and sought advice from public relations specialists.

—producing five pamphlets offering advice and reading suggestions to beginners in the field on such topics as "Public Relations: What It Is/Who Does It" and "Get It in Print: The Library News Release."

—cosponsoring with the H. W. Wilson Company the 32nd annual John Cotton Dana Library Public Relations Award. The winners, who received certificates during the ALA Annual Conference, were Greenville (South Carolina) County Library, West Virginia Library Commission, New York Metropolitan Reference and Research Library Agency (METRO), University of Utah Library, Rocky River (Ohio) High School Library, and Clark Air Force Base Library, Philippines. Seventeen other libraries received honorable mention and special awards. Through interlibrary loan the ALA Headquarters Library lends scrapbooks and audiovisual materials submitted as entries by the winners.

—sponsoring through the Friends Committee a luncheon at the ALA Annual Conference, offering guidance to Friends groups throughout the country, and continuing work on a master directory of Friends groups.

Children's Book Week. The Children's Book Council continued its long and valuable tradition by creating promotional materials designed by leading illustrators for Children's Book Week in November. CBC also continued its recent program of producing funny and useful materials for a year-round reading program. The State Library of North Carolina launched a statewide campaign during the 1977 Children's Book Week with the aim of registering every child in the state for a public library card. (See also Children's Book Council.)

Other Associations. The Library Public Relations Council in 1977 offered members its annual packet of the best library promotional materials and sponsored the annual competition for excellence in library promotion. Among the state and regional library associations that sponsored public relations workshops during their conferences was the New York Library Association. During a daylong session on "How Is Your Library Image?" participants explored the library's image among the staff, with the community, and with legislators.

The Association of American Library Schools (AALS) sponsored a public relations audit and preparation of a public relations program by a consultant in 1977. Within a month after receiving the report AALS had begun to implement the recommendations, which included a more vigorous communications program under the direction of a new committee chaired by the past president.

Education in Public Relations. Interest increased in 1977 in seminars and short courses on public relations sponsored by library schools. Catholic University of America, the University of Denver, Simmons College, Case Western Reserve University, and Western Michigan University were the graduate library schools that sponsored such courses directed by Alice Norton. The University of Missouri offered a new semester-long public relations course developed by Edward P. Miller, Dean of the School of Library and Informational Science, and Sue Fontaine, a library public relations specialist. Long Island University continued to offer its course in public relations under Betty Rice, Associate Professor.

Search for Dollars. Accompanying the more aggressive push for tax dollars among publicly supported libraries was a growing trend among privately supported libraries for donations. Harvard's Houghton Library for rare books used gifts from two donors to transform one area into an 18th-century enclave for the display of books and artifacts. The New York Public Library's privately supported Research Libraries also received munificent gifts, including a $5,000,000 challenge grant from the Vincent Astor Foundation. In 1977 the Library's aggressive fund-raising campaign, which now attracts donations from 34,000 persons a year, offered gala functions and previews of exhibitions to the thousands of members of Friends of the Library. One of the most imaginative of the Library's campaigns was a one-month "Gifts of Gold" event during which donors gave tax-deductible gold items they no longer wanted. Wedding bands, gold teeth, jewelry, and other items brought in $19,800. The National Endowment for the Humanities pledged a challenge grant to the Library for its $52,000,000 development campaign.

ALICE NORTON

West Virginia Library Commission's EXPOSURE staff produced materials aimed at increased recognition and state funding in it's 1977 "Tie One On For The Library" campaign.

The ALA publishing committee's 1977 spring meeting chaired by Peggy Sullivan (right background). Counter clockwise from the chair are Don Stewart, Director of Publishing, George Bobinski, Guy Marsh, Ed Howard, Helen Cline, Lillian Gerhardt, Herbert Bloom, and Doris Saunders.

The February cover of Booklist was a valentine to libraries. The design was also available as a four-color poster.

Publishing, ALA

ALA Publishing Services issued 34 new titles in 1977. Among them were *Handbook for Storytellers* by Caroline Feller Bauer, *Literacy and the Nation's Libraries* by Helen Huguenor Lyman, and the fourth edition of *Guides to Educational Media*, a compilation of published catalogs of nonprint educational media by Margaret I. Rufsvold. The largest volume published in 1977 was *Subject Index to Poetry for Children and Young People, 1957-75*; it covers 2,000 subjects in 1,050 pages. Among the shortest ALA publications in 1977 was the six-page *Libros a tu Gusto*, prepared by the Commmittee on Library Services to the Spanish-Speaking (RASD).

On administration, ALA published *Public Library Finance* by Ann Prentice, *The Personnel Manual: An Outline for Libraries* (Personnel Administration Section, LAD), and *Insurance Manual for Libraries*, with a glossary, by Gerald E. Myers.

Other Books and Pamphlets. Of general interest are *Langston Hughes: The Poet and His Critics*, the fourth volume in the series and the first full-length critical treatment of the poet. *The Library Connection* comprises personal essays written by public figues on the significance of the public library; among the contributors are Norman Cousins and George Plimpton. *Libraries and the Life of the Mind in America* is a volume of six ALA Centennial Lectures; it was designed in a handsome format worthy of the content by Vladimir Reichl, who retired in 1977 as ALA Production Manager for Books and Pamphlets. *Oral History: From Tape to Tape* is a practical manual on a growing activity.

Of special interest to librarians who serve younger patrons are *Paperback Books for Young People: An Annotated Guide to Publishers and Distributors*, second edition; *Media and the Young Adult: A Selected Bibliography, 1950-1972*, a 400-title bibliography on needs and access prepared by the Research Committee of YASD; *More Films Kids Like*; *Children's Books of International Interest*, second edition; and *Notable Children's Books, 1940-70*. *Literature and Young Children*, published by the National Council of Teachers of English, was distributed by ALA.

Among *Guidelines* published were those on book catalogs and on professional contracts, professional placement in libraries, and job decisions.

The second volume of *The ALA Yearbook*, edited by Robert Wedgeworth, appeared in June 1977. At year's end, an ALA selection of useful documents and reprints on copyright matters appeared as the *Librarian's Copyright Kit*. (See further the list of basic copyright documents accompanying the article "Copyright" in this volume.)

Sales revenues for the fiscal year ending August 31, 1977, totaled $1,384,900, and expenditures were $1,233,700, providing a margin of $151,200.

American Libraries. A survey of ALA members conducted in the fall of 1977 by Market Data Retrieval of Chicago indicated that 59 per cent of *American Libraries* readers (327 respondents) viewed it as "the publication with the most reliable information about professional associations and activities"; other library publications were cited by 32 per cent (176 respondents). The "publication most frequently read from cover to cover" was also *American Libraries*, according to 51 per cent (284) participating in the survey. *American Libraries* during the year covered CONSER (the cooperative conversion of serials project); presented Eugene P. Sheehy, the "modest but heroic editor" of the ninth edition of the *Guide to Reference Books*, in a portrait of the reference librarian at work by Editor Art Plotnik; published the $1,000 winner in Round II of its prize article competition ("Copyright, Resource Sharing, and Hard Times..." by Richard De Gennaro); and brought to attention the forgotten K. August Linderfelt, President of ALA in 1891-92, in articles on "The Wayward Bookman" by Wayne A. Wiegand. A special issue explored the many facets of "money." At year's end, in addition to its general circulation to ALA members (see Table 3), *American Libraries* went to more than 1,800 institutional subscribers.

LTR. During its 13th year of publication, *Library Technology Reports* continued in 1977 to inform the profession on products and services used in libraries. Among topics were test reports on microfiche duplicators, 35mm microfilm readers, 16mm sound motion picture projectors, and electric typewriters; a survey of word processing equipment; an industry

ALA Periodicals (1977)

Periodical	Editor(s)	Publication Frequency	Subscription*	Circulation
American Indian Libraries Newsletter (OLSD Committee on Library Service for American Indian People)	Cheryl Metoyer, Editor Graduate School of Library and Information Science, University of California, Berkeley	Quarterly	Free	2,500
American Libraries	Arthur Plotnik, Editor ALA, Chicago	11 issues a year; July/August combined	Free to ALA members; available to institutions at $20 per year.	37,831
Booklist	Paul Brawley, Editor ALA, Chicago	23 issues a year	$28 per year.	38,640
CHOICE (ACRL)	Louis Sasso, Editor Middletown, Connecticut	11 issues a year; July/August combined	$40 per year.	6,000
College & Research Libraries (ACRL)	Richard D. Johnson, Journal Editor State University of New York, College at Oneonta John V. Crowley News Editor State University of New York College at Oneonta	17 times a year (6 bimonthly journal and 11 monthly news issues; July/August combined)	Free to Division members; subscription $25 per year; single journal issues $3; news issues $2.	12,000
Documents to the People (GODORT)	Patricia Reeling, Editor Rutgers University, New Brunswick, New Jersey	Bimonthly	Free to Round Table members; otherwise by a contribution of $10 per year.	1,800
Exhibit Newsletter (ERT)	Jane Burke, Editor CLSI, Schaumburg, Illinois	Quarterly	Free to Exhibits Round Table members.*	350
Financial Assistance for Library Education, Academic Year 1978-79	Margaret Myers, Editor ALA, Chicago	Annually	50¢ a copy.*	8,000
FLIRT Newsletter (FLIRT)	Judith G. Burke, Editor 1408 D St., S.E. Washington, D.C.	Quarterly	Free to Federal Librarians Round Table Members.*	500
Footnotes (JMRT)	Ann Scott, Editor Virginia Beach, Virginia	Quarterly	Free to Junior Members Round Table members.*	1,000
HRLSD Journal (HRLSD)	Robert F. Ensley, Editor State Library, Springfield, Illinois	2 issues a year	Free to Division members.*	1,700
HRLSD Newsletter (HRLSD)	Mary Power ALA, Chicago	Irregular	Free to Division members.*	1,700
IFRT Report (IFRT)	Ione Pierron, Editor Eugene, Oregon	Irregular	Free to Intellectual Freedom Round Table members.*	900
Journal of Library Automation (ISAD)	Susan K. Martin, Editor University of California, Berkeley	Quarterly	Free to Division members; subscription $15 per year; single issues $4.	5,500
LAD Newsletter (LAD)	John F. Harvey St. Johnsbury, Vermont	Quarterly	Free to Division members.*	5,000
Leads (IRRT)	Edward Moffat, Editor Palmer Graduate Library School, C. W. Post Center, Long Island University, Greenvale, New York	Quarterly	Free to International Relations Round Table members; subscription $10 per volume.	650

Publishing, ALA

Title	Editor	Frequency	Availability	Circulation
LED Newsletter (LED)	Margaret Myers, Editor ALA, Chicago	Quarterly	Free to Division members.*	1,800
Library Resources & Technical Services (RTSD)	Wesley Simonton, Editor University of Minnesota, Minneapolis	Quarterly	Free to Division members; subscription $15 per year; single issues $4.	9,500
Library Technology Reports	Howard S. White, Editor ALA, Chicago	6 issues a year	$125 per year.	1,500
Newsletter on Intellectual Freedom (IFC)	Coeditors: Judith F. Krug, Roger L. Funk ALA, Chicago	6 issues a year	$8 per year.	3,100
PLA Newsletter (PLA)	Nancy Doyle, Editor Winston-Salem, North Carolina	4 times a year	Free to Division members.*	5,000
ASLA President's Newsletter (ASLA)	Irma R. Bostian, Editor State Library, Springfield, Illinois	4 times a year	Free to Division members.*	1,400
Public Library Trustee (ALTA)	Robert L. Faherty, Editor Alexandria, Virginia	Periodically	Free to Division members.*	2,400
RQ (RASD)	Geraldine King, Editor Ramsey County Public Library, St. Paul, Minnesota	Quarterly	Free to Division members; subscription $15 per year; single issues $4.	7,000
RTSD Newsletter (RTSD)	Mary Pound, Editor University of Texas, Austin	Quarterly	Free to Division members and *Library Resources & Technical Services* subscribers.	9,000
School Media Quarterly (AASL)	Glenn Estes, Editor Graduate School of Library and Information Science, University of Tennessee, Knoxville	Quarterly	Free to Division members; subscription $15 per year; single issues $4.	7,500
SORT Bulletin (SORT)	Marywave Godfrey, Editor Pierce County Library, Tacoma, Washington	Semiannually	Free to Staff Organizations Round Table members.*	300
SRRT Newsletter (SRRT)	Rick Speer, Editor Community Library of Allegheney Valley, Tarentum, Pennsylvania	3 issues a year	Free to Social Responsibilities Round Table members; $3 to individuals; $20 to institutions.	1,500
Top of the News (ALSC/YASD)	Audrey Eaglen, Editor Cuyahoga County Public Library, Cleveland, Ohio	Quarterly	Free to Division members; subscription $15 per year.	11,000
Washington Newsletter	Eileen Cooke, Editor Director of ALA Washington Office	Irregular (minimum of 12 issues)	$8 per year.	2,200

*Asterisk indicates not available by subscription (December 1977).

Booklist (1977)

Books reviewed	**4,756**
Adult	3,256
Young Adult	337
Children's	1,163
Nonprint materials reviewed	**1,756**
16mm films	294
Filmstrips	813
Recordings	419
Slides	29
Videocassettes	102
Multimedia kits	99
Books and galleys received	**17,400**
Adult	15,031
Children's & Young Adult	2,369

Reference and Subscription Books Reviews (1977)

Books and sets received	1,162
Rejected	333
Reviews published	99
General encyclopedias	2
Other forms	97
Notes published	343
Special lists and articles	26

report on 16mm educational films; a special report on the strength design of library tables and chairs; and an evaluation of automated circulation control systems. Revenues for fiscal year 1976-77 totaled $204,660, and expenditures were $184,150 for a margin of $20,510.

Booklist. The "Annual Index" of *Booklist* in August brought the total number of pages for volume 73 (September 1, 1976, through August 31, 1977) to 1,862—an increase of 154 over volume 72. Revenues for the same period fell short of expenditures by $12,622, which were covered by earnings of a dedicated endowment fund that supports such publishing activities. Revenues totaled $1,213,305, and expenditures were $1,225,927, including $224,000 paid in overhead charges in support of general fund activities and $101,600 for costs of the "Reference and Subscription Book" reviews. In most years *Booklist* returns a substantial margin to the Association.

Under editor Paul Brawley, *Booklist* continued to offer innovations in 1977. The success of an "Easy Reading" column in the "Children's Books" section led to the publication of a "High-Low Reading" column for Young Adults, introduced in the October 1977 issue by Barbara Duree, editor of that section. A "Love Your Library" poster, adapted from a *Booklist* cover (February 1), was offered for sale and bought by almost 1,900 libraries. An additional 1,500 libraries received the poster as part of the National Library Week Kit. About 900 librarians and others attended *Booklist*'s "Open Forum on Children's Books" at ALA's Annual Conference in Detroit. Cataloging and classification data for all nonprint materials was begun in the issue of January 1, 1977. Specialists on and outside the staff contributed new special columns and lists on "Canadian Books," "Popular Reading for Children," "Sports Books for Children," "Alternative Press Scene," "Small Press Poetry," and "Women's Presses." In 1977 many non-English-language bibliographies appeared in addition to 13 continuing columns, which included "Films," "Filmstrips," "Video," "Multimedia Kits," and "Recordings."

During the year *Booklist* editors reviewed criticisms concerning its treatment of Children's and Young Adult books containing elements of vulgarisms, violence, and sexual expression. In *Letters* and through editorials editors explained their approach in listing and evaluating such books. (For statistics *see* Table 1.)

Choice. The February 1977 issue of *Choice*, a program of ACRL, completed volume 14. The total number of reviews was 6,690, compared with about 6,500 in volume 13. The staff reported a decline of about 20 per cent in

Publications and materials produced by ALA.

university press books received, a loss offset by increases in two other publishing activities— increases in books published by English and Canadian publishers and distributed in the United States and increases in the output of the private and small presses. *Choice* often provides the only recognition a small press book receives. Louis Sasso became editor of *Choice* on January 3, 1978, succeeding Richard Gardner, who had resigned as of June 1, 1977. Sasso was formerly Assistant to the Director of the Boston Public Library.   DONALD E. STEWART

Publishing, Book

Book publishing, which topped the $4,000,000,000 sales level for the first time in 1976 and remained above that level in 1977, is expected to reach $4,700,000,000 in 1978, according to the *U.S. Industrial Outlook* of the Department of Commerce. As in the recent past, the anticipated increase of some $350,000,000, or 8 per cent, is expected to represent about 25 per cent real growth and about 75 per cent expansion due to price increases.

The long-term outlook for the industry is also for growth and for an increase in book title output, which turned slightly downward between 1972 and 1976. The Book Industry Study Group, Inc., an independent research organization, issued the first of a planned annual series on industry trends and predicted dollar sales of $5,700,000,000 for 1981. Unit sales also were expected to rise by 4.1 per cent between 1976 and 1981 to a total of 1,400,000,000. Among the wealth of figures in the 399-page study is the prediction that by 1981 annual dollar acquisitions of books by libraries, schools, and institutions, which increased 17.6 per cent between 1972 and 1976, are expected to rise another 21.1 per cent above 1976 levels. Unit acquisitions by these same institutions, which declined 16.6 per cent from 1972 to 1976, are expected to continue the downturn by another 17.8 per cent by 1981.

Inflation vs. Growth. Again, as in recent years, there was little doubt that the dollar growth of book publishing in 1977 reflected inflation rather than a substantial increase in unit sales. "Publishing is a mature industry, no longer growing in real terms," according to Winthrop Knowlton, President and Chief Executive Officer of Harper & Row. He added, "Our visible prosperity is highly dependent on raising of prices."

During 1977, however, some new benchmarks for measuring the industry's growth were registered. John Dessauer, the statistician of the Association of American Publishers (AAP), developed a new figure—the number of book units sold in a given year, estimated for 1976 at 1,361,000,000. There was a new approach, also, to reporting "book title output," the number of new books and new editions issued by the industry each year in various categories. Deciding first that numerous new factors have combined in recent years to increase delays in listing new books, the R. R. Bowker Company decided to issue 18-month title counts in the future (*Publishers Weekly*, August 22, 1977). For 1976, the 12-month count was 35,141 (26,983 new books and 8,158 new editions) while the 18-month count through June 1977 came to 41,698 (32,352 new books and 9,346 new editions). The average price per hardcover volume issued, by 12-month counts, rose from $14.09 in 1974 to $16.32 in 1976.

Paperback Boom. Of the industry's major segments, paperback—both mass market and trade—and mail-order and book club sales were especially brisk. There were some 125,000 paperback titles in print, and the public was reportedly buying 400,000,000 copies a year. The hardcover novel also appeared to be flourishing. The New York *Times* reported during 1977 that all of the top-selling novels of 1976 sold more than 100,000 copies.

The year was not without the usual phenomenal deals. Avon bought reprint rights to *The Thorn Birds*, a second novel by the Australian writer Colleen McCullough, from Harper & Row for a record $1,900,000. This occurred within weeks of another major Avon/Harper & Row deal—a $1,500,000 package for Erich Segal's *Oliver's Story* and *Love Story*. The sale of the paperback rights from Simon & Schuster to its Pocket Books Division of ex-policewoman Dorothy Uhnak's *The Investigation* brought $1,600,000, and former White House aide William Safire's *Full Disclosure* brought $1,300,000 to Doubleday from Ballantine. The death in August of Elvis Presley caused a single retail chain (Kresge) to place a record order for 2,250,000 copies of *Elvis: What Happened?*—an original paperback published by Ballantine.

There were several other noteworthy publishing developments during the year. Simon & Schuster announced plans to publish a specially written biography of Soviet President Leonid Brezhnev, with a foreword by Brezhnev himself addressed "to the American Reader." Random House mounted a major public relations effort for a one-volume encyclopedia, developed jointly with Mitchell Beazley in England at a joint cost, excluding production, of some $7,000,000. The encyclopedia was the culmination of a 10-year international joint publishing venture that will also see 14 publishing houses in Europe, Africa, Asia, and the Middle East producing editions of their own by 1980. Houghton Mifflin reported unprecedented domestic demand for and intense international interest in *The Silmarillion*, a posthumously issued work by J. R. R. Tolkien, author of *The Hobbit* and the *Lord of the Rings* series. The work was described as an account of the founding of Middle-earth and the creation of the world.

Random House sprang a major surprise on the publishing world by developing and publishing in great secrecy and without government clearance "Decent Interval," a critical appraisal of the CIA's role in South Vietnam by Frank Shepp, a former CIA senior analyst.

Mergers and Acquisitions. The year's major recombinations of publishing houses included the agreement of Time, Inc., and the 51-year-old Book-of-the-Month Club to merge. Harper & Row acquired Thomas Y. Crowell, a diversified house that had been a subsidiary of Dun & Bradstreet, and, late in the year, Harper & Row was chosen from among several "suitors" by the J.B. Lippincott Co., Philadelphia, as the firm to which that family-owned house preferred to sell 100 per cent of its stock, in a deal said to exceed $15,000,000. A 51 per cent interest in Bantam Books was purchased by the Bertelsmann Group, Germany's largest publishing house, which acquired the interest from IFI International, an Italian conglomerate that retained a 49 per cent interest. IFI, which has ties to the Italian Fiat automobile manufacturing concern, had paid $70,000,000 for Bantam in 1974 and received "more than $36,000,000" for its 51 per cent interest. In still another acquisition, Holt, Rinehart & Winston acquired Praeger Publishers from Encyclopaedia Britannica in late 1976 and announced that Praeger would function as a separate department within Holt's college operation. A cliff-hanger that never went over the edge was the attempt of the Times-Mirror Company of Los Angeles to acquire Random House from RCA; the deal fell through for numerous reasons.

Such ferment of ownership changes did not pass without critical comment. Rep. Morris Udall (D-Arizona), who for some time had cosponsored with Rep. Robert Kastenmeier (D-Wisconsin) a bill to study economic concentration in various industries, announced to the 1977 AAP annual meeting in Bermuda that he would add book publishing to the list of industries to be studied in order "to begin a dialogue, to establish that there may be a problem." Udall's concern was welcomed by the Authors Guild, a 5,000-member organization of writers, which issued a tough statement a month after Udall's comment, charging that book publishing mergers and takeovers had "passed far beyond the warning line" drawn by the antitrust laws threatened competition in the literary marketplace, imperiled the individual author's bargaining power and "endangered the uninhibited 'marketplace of ideas' guaranteed by the First Amendment." Commenting on these claims in an address to the annual Radcliffe College summer publishing procedures course, AAP President Townsend Hoopes said that "in the judgment of most experienced observers, including lawyers, the Guild does not have much of a case."

"The trend toward merger is discernible and continuing," Hoopes added, "but there are still nearly 1,200 book publishers in the United States, which makes it difficult for authors to claim that rejection of their manuscript by two or three houses is a serious bar to their being published." Senior publisher Knowlton of Harper & Row said on another occasion, "I am very impressed with the fact that 173 new book publishing houses have been founded since 1971 and that those houses last year published over 4,000 titles—or 10 per cent of the industry total." It was reported, nevertheless, that both the Justice Department and the Federal Trade Commission were scrutinizing some of the major recent mergers for possible anticompetitive implications.

Clearinghouses. With the new copyright law enacted in 1976, attention turned to its implementation in advance of the January 1, 1978, effective date. Specifically, two clearinghouse mechanisms were created to facilitate authorization and payment for photocopies of journal articles beyond those permitted under the new law.

Publishers, through the Technical, Scientific and Medical Division of AAP, initiated and financed the creation of the Copyright Clearance Center (CCC) to allow each copyright holder to establish individual royalties for copying of articles. The CCC, now independently organized and financed, will collect fees and distribute them to copyright holders. Libraries will be able to tell which publications are participating in the CCC by appropriate designations included in the journals. An eight-person board representing authors, publishers and libraries will oversee policy, and operations are directed by David Waite, an experienced data management executive, with Michael Harris of John Wiley & Sons as first Board Chairman.

The National Technical Information Service (NTIS) of the Department of Commerce created Journal Article Copying Service (JACS). JACS pays a flat royalty and acts as an intermediary between the private sector fulfillment source and the deposit account customer. NTIS will also use the CCC.

Librarians and others may receive a copy of the CCC Users Manual by writing directly to David Waite, President, CCC, 310 Madison Avenue, New York, New York 10017. For further information on JACS, write to NTIS, 5285 Port Royal Road, Springfield, Virginia 22161.

International. The international market for books continued to grow. The U.S. Commerce Department's 1978 *Industrial Outlook* estimated combined U.S. book exports and imports at $500,000,000 in 1977, up from $212,000,000 in 1967. Exports alone were pegged at $325,000,000 in 1977, up 9 per cent over the preceding year's $299,000,000, with Canada accounting for nearly half of the U.S. export total. Imports were estimated at $175,000,000 in 1977, higher by 11 per cent than the 1976 volume.

AAP's International Division, created in 1976 with Robert Baensch (Harper & Row) as its first Chairman, became one of the Association's busiest sectors, and it was a dispute over international trade and ideology that produced one of the year's liveliest debates within the industry. The Soviet Union staged the first Moscow Book Fair in September, and whether U.S. publishers should exhibit or not became a major issue dividing the publishing community. The New York *Times* set off the public debate with an editorial entitled "Selling Out at Moscow's Book Fair." The editorial claimed that the 40 or so U.S. publishers planning to exhibit there would be "selling not just their books but their prestige to the tormentors of Solzhenitzyn, Sakharov and so many others" since such dissident Soviet authors would, of course, go unrepresented at Moscow. There followed a lively exchange of letters to the editor in which exhibitors and nonexhibitors defended their respective positions, each professing that his represented the way for free-world ideas to be asserted but each proclaiming his respect for the integrity of the other faction.

The Fair was widely acclaimed as a successful event in which Soviet censorship of exhibited works was held to a minimum. Knowlton of Harper & Row, one of those who had defended Moscow exhibitors, attended the Fair in his triple role of a leading U.S. publisher and as chairman of the Committee on Freedom to Publish of both AAP and the International Publishing Association. Knowlton startled the Soviet publishing establishment and his U.S. critics by entertaining some 40 dissident and independent Soviet writers at a dinner in a Moscow public restaurant. He also shipped copies of Solzhenitzyn's *Gulag Archipelago* to the Fair, but predictably, they never reached the exhibit stands. He expressed the view that both publishers who went to Moscow and those who stayed away helped to further the cause of international freedom of expression.

In November, AAP received a 14-member delegation of Soviet publishing figures at a seminar in New York and Washington, conducted as an exchange for a 1976 visit of U.S. publishers to Moscow.

Activities of the AAP International Division included promoting attendance and active participation at international book fairs; proposing the reinstatement of a currency convertiblity program; seeking reforms in application of international copyright; pursuing more equitable freight rates for book shipments, and strengthening publisher relations with the Third World.

Book Distribution. Recognizing that the profitability of the industry depends significantly on its efficiency—and that both could stand improvement—AAP created a Book Distribution Task Force to analyze the book distribution and fulfillment process and to determine how it might be improved by wider application of computer and other modern data processing techniques.

The Task Force has determined that much work is now in process by organizations within and beyond the industry to achieve the end goal of improved distribution systems throughout the industry. To keep the industry involved and aware of these developments, the Task Force periodically issues Bulletins describing one area of concern. The 1977 Bulletins were concerned with: proper use of ISBNs; the advantages of Cataloging in Publication (CIP) in getting title information to customers prior to publication; the potential advantages and difference between computer and library networks; the status of the ANSI Standard Account Number; and a summary of those areas of concern to the Task Force in the 1977-1978 year.

In addition, the Task Force is attempting to develop specifications for any generalized title data base and for the most appropriate media and format for up-dating title information in the College Bookstore and Mass Market Paperback areas. The group also plans to assess computerized data-based systems available now or under development, to determine the most appropriate area(s) for publisher interface.

Awards and Other Activities. The AAP was pleased with the apparent success of a "Books as Gifts" television commercial blitz in two selected market areas at Christmastime in 1976. With outside support from other sectors of the publishing community, the AAP General Publishing Division conducted a vastly enlarged effort in nine markets during the 1977 holiday season. The campaign slogan was "A Book is a Loving Gift" and encouraged gift purchases of books.

The National Book Awards changed hands during the year. Following what were described as "friendly discussions" with the American Academy and Institute of Arts and Letters, which had functioned as the sponsor of the awards for two years, AAP assumed responsibility for conducting the annual program. AAP's sponsorship was facilitated by the promise of substantial financial support from the Franklin Library, an AAP member and a division of the Franklin Mint Corporation. Franklin planned publication of a compendium of the winners.

Another book award almost made its debut. Books eligible for the Readers Book Awards were to have been nominated by their publishers in several categories, after which readers visiting local bookstores were to ballot during January 1978 for "the book I liked most" among nominated works in 23 categories. Some 4,000 to 5,000 bookstores were to have participated, but scheduling and other difficulties forced the suspension of the program in December, and publishers' "seed money" was returned.

William Kaufman of the Los Altos, California, house bearing his name, received AAP's second annual Curtis G. Benjamin Award for creative publishing. AAP's TSM Division established several awards for excellence in technical, scientific and medical publishing.

Following two years of study and the completion of a wide-ranging survey of the status of education of people "in, for, and about" book publishing, a special AAP committee issued a major report. "The Accidental Profession: Education, Training and the People of Publishing" derived its title from the conclusion that book publishing is a vocation "in which most people find themselves by accident." The report urged the Association to assume the lead in an extensive educational and training effort. Before committing itself to implementing the costly long-range effort called for in the report, the AAP retained the veteran and respected industry leader Curtis G. Benjamin as a short-term consultant to examine the feasibility of carrying out the Committee's recommendations.

New Periodicals and Best-sellers. Two new industry-related national magazines appeared on the book scene. *Bookviews,* a monthly compendium of reviews and features about new books, was issued by Bowker in September. In the same month, the American Booksellers Association (ABA) began publication of *American Bookseller,* another slick-paper monthly, intended primarily for ABA's far-flung membership. McGraw-Hill inaugurated the monthly *Legal Briefs,* containing a wealth of courtroom and legislative reporting directed at editors, publishers, writers, and "everyone who creates, uses or disseminates information." Another new publication, one with regional orientation, was *Bookletter/ Southeast.* Published in Morgantown, West Virginia, it reported on the activities of some 60 publishers located in the 10-state Southeast region and on the activities of many authors with ties to that portion of the country.

White House Conference. With the White House Conference on Libraries and Information Services scheduled for October 1979 and state conferences due to precede it, AAP formed a special committee to formulate issues of concern to publishers and methods for getting them discussed at the various conferences. The committee was headed by Shirley Sarris (Bowker). Sarris also chaired the Libraries Committee of AAP's General Publishing Division.

Censorship Watch. Domestically, AAP's Freedom to Read Committee continued to monitor and intervene selectively in areas of actual or potential censorship of reading materials. Of three lawsuits in which AAP intervened as a friend of the court, it was on the prevailing side in two—both libel actions that resulted in ringing court defenses of the right to publish controversial opinions. AAP was on the losing side in an obscenity case that challenged the federal right to impose standards for sexually explicit materials stricter than those already supported by a state legislature (Iowa).

Nearly 20,000 copies of the Freedom to Read Committee pamphlet, *Books and the Young Reader,* were disseminated to schools and libraries in various states as well as in several foreign countries and Canadian provinces. The publication supports a broad and varied reading experience for young people and deplores the condemnation or boycotting of a publisher's total output on the basis of a single book. But pending federal legislation may, if approved, reverse the effect of that ruling.

New LC "Accession." In what amounted to a major coup for the Library of Congress but a major loss for the AAP, Carol Nemeyer, the senior staff member in the AAP New York office in charge of liaison with the library community, left in September to become an Assistant Librarian of Congress. Nemeyer will direct several major national programs, including the Library's publishing ventures, public relations efforts, and special events.

RICHARD P. KLEEMAN

Publishing, Serials

PERIODICALS CENTER

The proposal for the National Periodicals Center, with service to begin in late 1978 or early 1979, proved to be the major event of 1977. Closely linked to the proposal were continued escalating journal costs, tighter acquisitions budgets, and what promises to be an interminable discussion over the copyright law revision.

The Plan. The National Periodicals Center, as envisioned by the National Commission on Libraries and Information Science, would be developed by the Library of Congress, have a core collection of 50,000 titles, and cost $3,500,000 to start and operate, at least for the first year. The model is the highly successful British Library Lending Division, which expedites interlibrary loan and photocopying and takes the economic pressure off the few large libraries that generally provide most of the interlibrary loans of periodical materials. The purpose of the U.S. Center is much the same—to serve as a link in the national information network slowly being forged. But in less ambiguous terms, librarians see the Center as a way of meeting the rising costs of journals. Less frequently used titles will be readily available, and given this backup, librarians will have to buy only the more frequently used, less esoteric journals.

Richard DeGennaro, an articulate critic and director of the University of Pennsylvania Libraries, pointed out in his $1,000 Prize Competition Article in *American Libraries* (September 1977, p. 433) that the Center is not likely to solve the budget crunch. He also noted the fears that publishers have about the proposed Center:

> Publishers still have the idea that if they can discourage interlibrary loan and photocopying, libraries will be forced to spend more money to buy books and journals. This is bunk. Libraries can't spend money they don't have. The fact is that with or without effective sharing mechanisms [e.g., the National Periodicals Center, for one], with rising prices and declining support, libraries simply do not have the funds to maintain their previous acquisitions levels.

Publisher Reservation. Journal publishers were less than enthusiastic about the proposed Center and less than convinced their fears were "bunk." They proceeded to set up mechanisms for collecting fees that they believed would pour in when the new copyright law revision became effective in 1978. Called the Copyright Clearance Center, it was to collect fees from libraries and others when more than five articles a year were copied from the previous five years of any one journal. Not all publishers think such a procedure necessary. In addition, neither librarians, publishers, nor lawyers are sure that the new copyright law can be interpreted on the five-copy/five-year rule. They also do not know how librarians will enforce the law, or even if they should try. As one wag put it, the primary benefit of the copyright provision for book publishers is selling new books, articles, and seminars on what the law means.

The interpretation of the copyright law and the fate of the National Periodicals Center remained uncertain in 1977, but not so the familiar continued rise in periodical prices. According to the annual survey in *Library Journal* (July 1977, p. 1462, and October 1, 1977, p. 2011), the average cost of a U.S. title in 1977 was $24.95, almost a 13 per cent jump over 1976. Annual price hikes total nearly a 100 per cent increase since 1970. More significant is what inflation has meant to general acquisitions. According to one study in *American Libraries* (February 1977, p. 70), research libraries increased their periodical budgets on an average of 36 per cent between 1970 and 1975, but cut back on the gross number of book titles ordered by 14 per cent.

Cost Problems. How are librarians to solve the financial crunch? In 1977 there were almost as many proposed solutions as librarians. If there was consensus about networks and local cooperation one month, the next month there was equal agreement that a major cure was going to require selective surgery on periodical standing orders. New subscriptions were being watched. At the same time libraries were bringing pressure on scholarly publishers to check the price increase of the 1960's or risk the loss of library support. Some of the talk found its way into actual guidelines, e.g., "Guidelines for the Formulation of Collection Development Policies" in *Library Resources & Technical Services* (Winter 1977, pp. 40–45).

A possible solution to rising journal costs was suggested by John Senders ["An On-line Scientific Journal," *The Information Scientist* (March 1977), pp. 3–9], who believes that in 15 or 20 years the majority of scientific journals will be "published" only as data bases, accessible via the on-line computer terminal. Original publication on microform has been used in an extremely limited way for the past 15 years. Furthermore, an in-depth study of the economics of serial publishing and libraries reveals that at least 50 per cent of librarians are skeptical about cutting costs through automation. In fact, half of them think that money can be saved by eliminating automation.

The same study showed considerable pessimism about any resolution of the syndrome of rising costs and lower library budgets. As the researchers put it, "The economic model is not viable." They foresee either subject areas in which journal publication will disappear entirely for lack of financial support or a federal subsidy to keep the journals in business. [See Herbert S. White and Bernard M. Fry, "Economic Interaction Between Special Libraries and Publishers," *Special Libraries* (March 1977), pp. 109–14.]

Of the 100,000 or so journals now being published, however, only about 200 are a continuing concern to either the average library user or the scholar. The layperson is more concerned with *Reader's Digest* and *Time* than the more than 98,000 titles that represent the bulk of journal literature in large research libraries. But even in such libraries, as numerous surveys have discovered, half of the total reading is done by scholars and scientists in fewer than 300 of the journals. Another sobering experience for the librarian is the ongoing citation study in *Science Citation Index*. The annual survey reveals that only a handful of the 2,000 or so titles cited are of any concern to the majority of readers.

THE COMMERCIAL FIELD

In the commercial marketplace in 1977 most of the action took place with popular periodicals. By far the most dramatic story was the takeover of Clay Felker's *New York Magazine*, *New West*, and *Village Voice* by newspaper magnate Rupert Murdoch. (The sure way of measuring news importance was met in this case. Both *Time* and *Newsweek* featured the takeover story on the covers of their magazines.)

Censorship and Gossip. Almost as much publicity was generated by the *Hustler* censorship trial in Cincinnati. Larry Flynt, the brash publisher of the hard-core men's sex magazine, was found guilty of "pandering obscenity." Many librarians, who normally might be somewhat less than interested in the outcome, joined forces with the American Civil Liberties Union to help Flynt appeal the case, possibly to the U.S. Supreme Court. The reason was that the case was a major test of the validity of a Supreme Court judgment of more than four years ago. In that case the justices found national standards no longer an acceptable way of judging sexual printed materials and ruled that local juries have to decide for their own communities. The problem is that, in so doing and in harassing publishers, some communities virtually clamp national censorship on titles otherwise acceptable in other communities. This is the argument that is the heart of the Flynt appeal. The irony, always expected in such cases, was that the newsstand sales of *Hustler* jumped after the decision, keeping the magazine in third place (behind *Playboy* and *Penthouse*) among men's titles.

The Felker-Flynt stories caused publishers and critics to take another long look at the magazine press. Almost surprised, a writer for *U.S. News and World Report* (August 15, 1977, p. 32) discovered that "trivia, gossip, sex and leisure currently make up the hot subjects for today's magazines—and many are including material that would have shocked the sensibilities of average readers a few years ago." Few would argue with such an observation, and such titles as *People* and *Us* supported the judgment. Strong on photographs, short on copy, long on gossip, the new versions of the *Life* confessional gained immediate popularity. Why is this so? An educated guess is that the majority of readers are young, devoted to television, and more interested in short picture presentations than in editorial copy.

Specialized Journals. Not all of the approximately 300 new American magazines in 1977 were built around trivia or gossip. Most were more concerned, as in years past, with meeting the highly specialized reading requirements of select audiences. In 1977, for example, self-explanatory titles such as *Skateboard* and *Moped Biking* were born. *Nuestro* was introduced to serve the special needs of Latinos in the United States. Most of the new magazines cost about $1 an issue, but there were some exceptions. *Human Nature*, a takeoff on *Psychology Today*, sold on the newsstands for $1.75 a copy; *Quest*, a lively general magazine of features and photographs for the family, sold at $2 a copy; and the familiar hardback *Horizon* changed its format to a soft cover with a $2.50 selling price. These prices, however, hardly compare with those of many scholarly journals, which average $25 to $35 a year for only four issues. The quarterly *Probe Telecommunication* costs $340 a year, and the first issue in 1977 was only 46 pages long with one article. There were numerous subscribers, however, including a few large libraries, because the article was by experts about a potentially money-making communication system using fiber optics and light waves.

Sales and Circulation. Publishers continue to show increased interest in newsstand sales and subscriptions. Circulation profits were hardly important in the 1960's. The Magazine Publishers Association noted that in 1966 only 30 per cent of magazine revenue came from sales. Today the figure is close to 50 per cent and increasing. Publishers see this as a healthy development because revenues from readers make the publisher more independent of the whims of advertisers, who heretofore completely determined magazine failure or success. The attention to spot sales—particularly in the supermarket—is evident to almost any American. Currently about 50 per cent of the total sales of consumer magazines in the United States are made in food stores and related outlets.

Under continued pressure from increased postal rates and production costs, publishers are looking for ways besides boosting cover prices to survive economically. Among those ways favored in 1977, and sure to increase in importance, were switching to lighter paper and reducing the page size. The result is a production savings as well as a chance to cut costs for storage and transportation. Another way of trimming postal charges, sure to be explored further, was to drop postal services. Threats of rising postal rates have caused numerous magazine publishers to test alternatives for delivery. Among consumer magazines now experimenting with such techniques as delivery of the magazine by the newspaper boy or by independent trucking outfits are *Time*, *Newsweek*, and *Reader's Digest*. Since August 1974, the latter has delivered 3,000,000 copies outside the U.S. postal system through a special home delivery system. Predictions vary, but publishers now believe that by 1980 some 25 to 50 per cent of their subscriptions may be delivered by alternate means.

Only large-circulation magazines can presently hope to profit by avoiding the postal service, and there is always the threat that a conglomerate will get the corner on a new, inexpensive method of delivery. Thanks to diversity in the U.S. magazine publishing world, most experts consider the threat of magazine conglomerates as not serious. There was, however, a flurry of mergers and buying and selling of magazines in 1977. CBS, which owns more than 60 special-interest magazines, paid $50,000,000 for Fawcett Publications (*Woman's Day* is the best known of their titles). On a less grand scale, Time purchased the Book-of-the-Month Club, and for the third time in six years Norman Cousins sold *Saturday Review/World*.

A small but increasingly enthusiastic audience helped to boost the number of little magazines in the United States in 1977. The number of "littles" is variously estimated at between 1,500 and 3,000. The variance is due to the fact that almost as fast as one is published another one dies. Who reads these titles devoted to poetry and avant-garde thinking? In numbers, their circulation is not impressive. Most have fewer than 500 readers, and only about 10 per cent can claim more than 2,500 subscribers. The readers, according to a Council of Literary Magazines survey, are teachers, writers, publishers, or students. Why do they

Realia

read little magazines. "One reads a little to keep from becoming a statistic," was one reply. A boost to little magazines has been the annual *Pushcart Prize,* an anthology of the best of the littles, published by Bill Henderson and his Pushcart Press.

Serials Librarian. Serials librarians welcomed two in-house titles in 1977. *The Serials Librarian,* with Peter Gellately as editor, is the first quarterly journal devoted exclusively to the subject, and the Haworth Press publication received enthusiastic support from librarians. The second edition of that key to the mystery, *Periodical Title Abbreviations,* appeared from Gale Research Company with 20,000 entries.

Space hardly permits discussion of fascinating bibliographical developments in 1977. The dedicated reader should check *The Serials Librarian* for a running account of such matters as Conversion of Serials (CONSER) or Catalog Code Revision Committee (CCRC), as well as the able summary of serial activities in the summer issue of *Library Resources & Technical Services.*

The "jargon discovery" of the year—the editor of *IEEE Transactions on Education* (May 1977, pp. 84–85) wrote an entire editorial around the term *niche,* which is "commonly used in this context in biology and describes the species' complex interaction with its surroundings and the unique place it has found for itself—its niche.... It would seem that such a niche description could be applied to archival journals as well." Dean Swift put it somewhat more felicitously in 1729: "If I can but fill my Nitch, I attempt no higher Pitch" (*OED,* Vol. 7, p. 128). No wonder so few scientific journals are read.   BILL KATZ

Realia

The use of realia, chiefly in public libraries, continued to develop slowly during 1977 around the perimeter of traditional library services and is not yet in the mainstream. News items reflected two main kinds of realia use. Objects are used by library patrons to reinforce or expand the usefulness of print media in doing or learning (Jane Doe borrows a timing light and dwell-tachometer in order to learn how to use the instructions and specifications in the manual for her car as she does a tune-up). On the other hand, patrons borrow equipment in order to make use of nonprint media (John Doe continues his search of old newspapers on microfilm at home with the use of a circulating portable reader).

During the year there was recognition of realia by the Toys, Games, and Realia Committee of the Children's Services Division in an article (*Booklist* January 1, 1977, pp. 671–74) giving a rationale, criteria for selection, and a classified list of recommended realia complete with annotations, prices, and sources.

A good example of imaginative use of realia in the interest of the entire community is the Chester County Library of West Chester, Pennsylvania, which in cooperation with the Chester Board of Realtors loans an engraving tool. Suggested uses are the engraving of one's driver's license or other identifying marks on personal possessions subject to loss or theft. The practice helps in the return of lost goods, and law enforcement officials endorse the practice as a crime deterrent.

The Santa Fe (New Mexico) Public Library reported the loan of audiovisual equipment in a *Wilson Library Bulletin* article (January 1977, pp. 397–98) that features a sample of their contract for AV loans that was developed in consultation with an attorney. The article also demonstrates how a library can begin this service on a shoestring, using underused equipment that it already owns. Circulation techniques, maintenance problems, and costs are covered in this remarkable success story.

In its small but diversified program of realia use, the Canal Fulton (Ohio) Public Library has made available to the general public a complete black and white darkroom and provides training in its use to photographic neophytes. The library also features a sphygmomanometer for in-house use by those wanting to monitor their blood pressure, a practice advocated by many physicians.

A Client Library serving the developmentally disabled in the Monroe Development Center at Rochester, New York, was reported by Cindy O'Mara, Client Librarian. The library serves adults and children and provides diversified services to fit individual needs. Among realia used are toys, games, goldfish, and filmstrips, as well as printed materials.

The Salt Lake County (Utah) Library System has a fully equipped AV production center in which patrons have free use of a spirit duplicator, dry-mount press, 8mm splicer-editor, close-up photography setup, lighted tracing table, drafting table, music typewriter,

(Below left) Panels for displaying the circulating framed print collection in the Skyline branch of the Dallas Public Library were purchased by the Friends of the library, and, (right) circulating sewing patterns were introduced in 1977 in the library.

transparency maker, collator, and sound filmstrip synchronizer.

Although similar reports of success and innovation continue to surface concerning the use of realia, abiding needs for the practitioner and potential practitioner remain: an idea-sharing forum where good and bad experiences can be recycled, and a better term than the educator's "realia" or everyman's "stuff." TOM BROWNFIELD

Recordings, Sound

One year after the founding of the ALA in 1876, Thomas A. Edison invented a small mechanical device that captured, stored, and reproduced the sounds of the human voice. Although sound had been recorded as early as 1857, it remained for Edison to reproduce it successfully. The centennial of this event was celebrated throughout the Western world in 1977. One of the most spectacular of these celebrations took place at the Royal Scottish Museum in Edinburgh, where an American librarian and Edison scholar, Raymond R. Wile of Queens College Library, read the opening paper at an Edison symposium and exhibit. The proceedings of the symposium and a catalog of the exhibit have been published by the Museum.

In the United States major exhibits were held at the Library of Congress and at the Rodgers and Hammerstein Archives of Recorded Sound. In November the Syracuse University Libraries presented a symposium that brought together archivists, scholars, technicians, and major figures from the recording industry to explore the past and the future of recorded sound and its technology. Since Syracuse University is the home of the Audio Archives and the Thomas Alva Edison Foundation Re-Recording Laboratory, it was an appropriate site for this important symposium. At Brooklyn College, the Institute for Studies in American Music sponsored a centennial conference devoted to the cultural and social (rather than technical) impact of sound recordings. Earlier in the year, the Association of Recorded Sound Collections (ARSC) devoted the bulk of its 11th annual meeting to the centennial. Whether it was because of the Edison centennial is hard to say, but 1977 was a notable year for sound recordings, as it was for archivists and librarians concerned with their preservation and diffusion.

Acquisitions. The archives of the National Broadcasting Company's radio broadcast materials, which include around 150,000 transcription discs covering the years from 1932 to 1960, have been entrusted to the recently founded Museum of Broadcasting in New York City. The radio archival material from the American Broadcasting Company has been donated to the National Archives. Another unique event in 1977 was the donation by the British rock group Foghat of a collection of recordings documenting the history of the blues to the Rodgers and Hammerstein Archives. The group also presented a benefit concert to raise money to expand the Archive's blues collection.

The Audio Center and Popular Library of the Center for the Study of Popular Culture at Bowling Green State University in Ohio has developed into what seems to be the fastest-growing archival collection of popular recordings. It has rich holdings in rock and roll and all other forms of current and older popular music, genres that have not usually been collected extensively by general archives or those devoted to jazz. In 1977 the Bowling Green collection amounted to around 150,000 items. The documentation of a rather different aspect of American culture is taking place at the American Music Center in New York City, which, in addition to its many other activities, is now the archives for musical works produced under grants from the National Endowment for the Arts. It will include recordings of Endowment-funded musical compositions.

ARSC. In 1977 ARSC began to issue the quarterly *ARSC Newsletter*, a small quarterly publication that includes short notices, news of interest to collectors, and inquiries concerning various aspects of sound recordings and discography. The early issues (somewhat tentative and still trying to define a purpose, format, and style) have laid the foundation for a tool that will be useful to both collectors and librarians. It is already functioning as a source for answers to difficult reference questions by drawing on the considerable pool of expertise of the ARSC membership. The Executive Secretary of ARSC is now compiling a directory that will be classified according to the specialties of the ARSC members. Several "invisible colleges" will thus become somewhat less invisible, and librarians will have access to these information sources in serving their users.

ARSC's growth continues at the rate of around 50 new members a year and is well over 500. Having arrived at an unusual state of financial solvency, ARSC is now ready to move ahead with its publication program. In keeping with its commitment to all types of sound recordings collections—public and private, music and nonmusic—ARSC is planning a joint meeting with the Library of Congress and the National Archives. Most of what happens at the ARSC annual meetings is never issued in published form. It was appropriate that the proceedings of the 11th annual meeting in 1977 have been made available commercially on audio tapes by Merritt Sound Recordings, 223 Grimsby Road, Buffalo, New York 14223.

AAA. The Associated Audio Archives (AAA) has been established as a means of dealing with certain policies and problems faced by the six large general sound archives in North America—the Library of Congress, the Rodgers and Hammerstein Archives, and university archives at Yale, Stanford, Syracuse, and Toronto. The major problem is getting archival material cataloged. Working with ARSC, the AAA has acquired funds to prepare a union catalog of their holdings of commercially issued pre-LP classical music and spoken word recordings. Work will begin with a pilot project in 1978 to test the plan before the full project gets under way. In time, it is expected that jazz and other popular forms will be included. When finished, the work may be considered a union catalog of recorded incunabula. Although there is not a general consensus as to a definition of recorded incunabula, many discographers would place all pre-LP material in this category.

Cataloging. The manual being developed for the AAA union catalog project will be congruent with the *Anglo-American Cataloguing Rules* in so far as this is possible without compromising the unique requirements of descriptive cataloging necessary for sound recordings. At the meeting of the International Association of Music Libraries, in Mainz, Germany, it appeared that the major international thrust for standards for cataloging and discography will come from the Association's Sound Recordings Commission rather than from the International Association of Sound Archives. Agreement was reached at Mainz and standards were endorsed for discographic references. In the United States, Sub-Committee Four of the Z39 Committee of the American National Standards Institute endorsed standards for bibliographic citations that include the citation of sound recordings.

Publications. If discographic control is the key to organizing and providing public access to sound recordings, the bibliographic control of published discographies is an important step toward an efficient system of access. The publication of the first volume of Michael Gray and Gerald Gibson's *Bibliography of Discographies* (Bowker, 1977), covering classical music discographies between 1925 and 1975, is now available. Subsequent volumes will deal with discographies of jazz, popular music, and other genres of recorded sound. The long-awaited cumulation of Kurtz Myers's *Index to Record Reviews* is now in press and will be published in 1978 by G.K. Hall & Company.

Archives and Collections. 1977 saw the retirement of two archivists who have made major contributions to the preservation and scholarly use of sound recordings. Edward E. Colby retired as Director of the Archive of Recorded Sound at Stanford University. George List retired as Director of the Archives of Traditional Music at Indiana University.

David Hall, Director of the Rodgers and Hammerstein Archives, succinctly evaluated the present state and future possibilities of sound archives and with singular clarity defined the functions and activities of archives and other types of collections in "Storing Solid Gold for the Future," which appeared in *Billboard* (May 21, 1977). If public and private collections and archives are included, according to Hall, there may be as many as 15,000 historical collections in the Western Hemisphere. Among the major archives, that of the Library of Congress is unique, with special responsibilities not found in other archives. The Library of Congress currently is establishing a Broadcast Archives, a new organizational structure that will include its massive collection of sound recordings and other broadcast materials.

Few librarians have contributed to research in sound recordings or their use. Uses and attitudes are particularly important in determining public library policy. To the small number of Ph.D. dissertations in library science devoted to sound recordings, Frank W. Hoffman's "Methodological Study of Librarian and Community Attitudes toward Phonorecord Collections in Public Libraries" (University of Pittsburgh, 1977) can now be added.

GORDON STEVENSON

Reference and Adult Services Division

Creative work in the areas of professional help, programs, and publications characterized the activities of the Reference and Adult Services Division (RASD) of the American Library Association in 1977. These activities ranged from a preconference on library service for the aging, to a listing of Spanish books for young adults called *Libros a tu Gusto*, to information for librarians on the new copyright law. In addition, a new section emerged, awards were given, notable books and outstanding reference books were selected, and divisional planning was emphasized.

Copyright. Public information and professional help for complying with the Copyright Law (Public Law 94-553, Title 17, U.S. Code) were forthcoming from a subcommittee of the RASD Interlibrary Loan Committee. The Interlibrary Loan Request Form was revised to accommodate representation of copyright. Wording for the notice of copyright, which must be included on the reproduction of a work, was suggested. Wording for the notice of copyright was also outlined for unsupervised reproducing equipment located in a library or archive. A record retention plan was devised to help organize records of reproductions of library materials. Information was given through the library press, through contributions to numerous workshops throughout the country, and by discussions and lectures at library meetings and conventions.

Conference Programs. Reflecting the myriad interests of the members of the Division, the Annual Conference programs covered a wide range of topics. The program on the economics of providing information and service included such areas as economic interdependencies between libraries and publishers, adjusting services to needs and resources, and technology and organization. A preconference institute on "Library Services in Support of Independent Living for the Elderly" was offered by the Library Service to Aging Population Committee. Other program topics included a new look at adult services, charging fees for computer-based reference service, changes in technical processing that affect reference work, copyright law, public service and the on-line catalog, the role of interlibrary loans in networks, business data bases, and reference policies. The History Section's program was on pictorial source material. The AFL/CIO—ALA (RASD) Library Service to Labor Groups Joint Committee toured the Archives of Labor History and Urban Affairs at Wayne State University in Detroit.

Publications. Publications for 1977 reflected the many interests of the division. *Interlibrary Loan Basics: A Workshop Package,* compiled by Virginia Boucher, was designed for trainers of interlibrary loan service practitioners. The materials had been tested at a preconference at Rosary College in 1976.

Labor Collections and Services in Public Libraries throughout the United States, by Kathleen Imhoff and Larry Brandwein, appeared both as a separate publication and in *RQ* (Winter 1977, pp. 149-58). *Labor Unions in America—A Reading List,* by Jean Webber, was also published.

Libros a tu Gusto, a listing of Spanish-language books for young adults, was first published in *Booklist* (May 1, 1977, pp. 1341-42) with annotations in English. It was later published as a separate pamphlet with annotations in Spanish.

On-Line Bibliographic Services: Where We Are, Where We're Going, edited by Peter G. Watson, is the proceedings of an all-day meeting organized by the RASD Information Retrieval Committee at the 1976 ALA Centennial Conference. The *Directory of State and Local History Periodicals,* compiled by Milton Crouch and Hans Raum, was published by ALA Publishing Services. *RASD,* a new membership brochure, was published.

Notable Books 1976, compiled by the Notable Books Council, was published by ALA Publishing Services for use by the general reader or for the librarians who work with adult readers. *Outstanding Reference Books of 1976* was compiled and appeared in the April 15 issue of *Library Journal.* A collection of these books was made available for loan to library associations and other interested groups.

Under the editorship of Geraldine B. King, *RQ,* the official quarterly of the Division, continued to provide pertinent materials to reference librarians, bibliographers, and others interested in user-oriented library services. Two new columns made their appearance in *RQ*: "Backtalk," containing adult services news relating to innovative programming ideas and materials; and "Interlibrary Loan Issues," containing information on new developments in the field, particularly information on the new copyright law.

Dartmouth Medal. In 1977 the Dartmouth Medal was awarded for the *Atlas of Early American History: The Revolutionary Era, 1760-1790.* This work was published for the Newberry Library and the Institute of Early American History and Culture by Princeton University Press in 1976. Lester J. Cappon served as editor in chief.

Mudge Citation. The Isador Gilbert Mudge Citation for distinguished contributions to reference librarianship was awarded in 1977 to Bohdan S. Wynar in recognition of "outstanding work as a publisher of reference books, as an author of numerous books and articles covering the whole range of librarianship in several languages, and as an editor who encourages excellence in writing by other librarians."

History. Among other activities of the History Section, the Local History Committee conducted a survey of local history collections and services. The information from this survey is to be used in developing guidelines.

MARSS. At the Annual Conference the RASD board approved establishment of a new section, the Machine-Assisted Reference Service Section (MARSS). This Section represents the interests of those planning, managing, teaching, or conducting computer-based reference service in libraries. The Section seeks to be a means of sharing experiences and information among interested librarians and to be a forum for discussion between librarians and the suppliers of computerized search services. Sarah Knapp, Chairperson of the former Machine-Assisted Reference Services Discussion Group, is chairing the Organizing Committee for 1977-78. *Messages from MARSS,* an occasional newsletter edited by Martha Packer, is published by this Section.

In addition to MARSS, two new discussion

groups were approved: Interlibrary Loan and Women's Materials and Women Library Users.

Membership Survey. With the objective of gathering opinions and information that would help the RASD Board respond to the needs of the membership and explore possibilities for increased participation by members, a membership survey was mailed to a random sample of 640 RASD members in August 1977. Questionnaire items were grouped into five categories: (1) extent of participation in RASD, (2) preference for Annual Conference formats and topics and other Division activities, (3) continuing education, (4) characteristics of respondents, and (5) general comments. Although the complete results are too detailed to list here, it is interesting to note that respondents preferred present Conference programming, rated RQ very highly as contributing significantly to professional development, and recommended an expanded continuing education program, preferably in the form of workshops.

RASD Officers

PRESIDENT (July 1977-June 1978):
Virginia Boucher, University of Colorado, Boulder

VICE-PRESIDENT/PRESIDENT-ELECT:
Larry Earl Bone, Mercy College, Dobbs Ferry, New York

SECRETARY:
Barbara J. Brown

EXECUTIVE SECRETARY:
Andrew M. Hansen

ASSOCIATE EXECUTIVE SECRETARY:
Mary Jo Lynch

Membership (August 31, 1977): 5,502 (3,396 personal and 2,106 organizational)

Planning. Where the Division has been, where it is now, and what direction the Division should take in the future concerned the RASD planning group that met for two days in Des Plaines, Illinois, in October. The membership survey results and comments from the RASD Board, the RASD Secretariat, and committee chairpersons, along with discussion by those present, all helped in planning for the future. Representatives from two new ad hoc committees, Continuing Education and RASD Goals, contributed to the proceedings. The most important decisions included reaffirmation of continuing education as an overall activity of the Division, commitment to all forms of service to the library user, and the need for reference and adult service management training that includes emphasis on an assertive role for the librarian. The results of the meeting will concern the Division as new programs are designed and old ones are strengthened. — VIRGINIA BOUCHER

Reference Services

Anyone who attempts to review reference service for 1977, or for any year, must be puzzled by what he finds. What passes for research in most journals directed at reference librarians is at best disappointing. The journals themselves are devoted less to analyses of reference service than to lists of key works in various fields and reviews of new tools. Many developments that will have an impact on reference work originate with other specialties or outside the profession altogether. Reporting on reference service becomes in part, therefore, explaining what the catalogers or the historians or the literary types or the scientists are up to.

Part of the explanation for this lies in the kind of work reference librarians do. It is not so much a science as a craft, and like other crafts it is supported by a theoretical framework that may be charitably described as modest but that must carry a considerable weight of practical details. Catalogers, by contrast, work within an apparatus of classification theory, descriptive cataloging rules, subject authority lists, and the like that are being constantly refined but that do provide some procedural security. Reference librarians stand between the variety of readers that frequent any library and the writers, scholars, bibliographers, publishers, catalogers, and others who contribute to or attempt to organize the published record.

The record is so large, its sources so various, and its users so diverse that efforts to understand how these elements interact have discouraged all but the most heroic researchers. At its best, as for example in the work of Thelma Freides, the research undertaken by reference librarians is directed toward understanding the literature of various disciplines and the specialists working in them rather than toward the delivery of reference service itself. One might say that the proper study of reference librarians is the structure of information transfer in publishing, in libraries, and in the learned disciplines. There seems to be little to discover about methods for the delivery of reference service, which has become a matter for administration rather than research. As Gil McNamee pointed out in "References Services" in the 1977 ALA Yearbook, the way reference librarians perform and interact with the public has changed little in the 100 years since Samuel Green stalked the catalogs of the Worcester Public Library.

Kinds of Services. Reference librarians have not always been sure where the boundaries of reference service lie, and they have seemed to engage in many kinds of activities that have had an uncertain bearing on their regularly assigned duties. In a working paper presented at the annual meeting of the Reference Services in Large Research Libraries Discussion Group of the Reference and Adult Services Division (RASD) at the 1977 ALA Annual Conference, Paula Watson and Martha Landis reported that the range of responsibilities assigned to reference departments varies greatly. Some do one-on-one reference work and little else. Others take care of documents, periodicals, interlibrary lending and borrowing, microforms, newspapers, bibliographic instruction, maps, exhibits, book selection, computer-aided information retrieval, and so forth.

Staff size varies with the range of assignments. Responsibility for documents and bibliographic instruction adds staff more heavily than anything else, but there is no relation between the size of the staff and the size of the collections or the student body. About half of the libraries surveyed had added or augmented their programs of computer-aided information retrieval or bibliographic instruction over the previous five years. Although reference work loads have in general increased, this has not been reflected in staffing levels. Some libraries have lost staff, but others have added. The study showed little pattern in the administration of reference departments, in the size of reference collections, or in the amount of time spent on desk assignment. It would appear that reference work consists of whatever it is that reference departments do.

The Bible: Revised Standard Version. However they spend their time, reference librarians in North America were delighted to have the ninth edition of the *Guide to Reference Books*, published by ALA and edited by Eugene Sheehy, Reference Librarian at Columbia University, with assistance from the Columbia reference staff. The new edition is about the size of the Manhattan telephone book and lists some 10,000 titles. Although quarrels might be made with the inclusion or omission of individual titles, the ninth *Guide* shows admirable balance and objectivity in selection, is helpfully annotated and usefully organized, and maintains high standards of accuracy and reliability. In Sheehy, the editorial mantle has descended on an able successor to Isadore Mudge and Constance Winchell.

It is gratifying to know that plans for a tenth edition are already being laid. At a breakfast meeting during the ALA Annual Conference in Detroit, Donald Stewart of ALA's Publishing Services announced that Sheehy has agreed to continue as general editor for a new edition of the *Guide* and that editorial assistance would be sought for the social sciences and natural sciences sections. New editions may be published in more than one volume, but the general arrangement in five sections is expected to continue.

To Fee or Not to Fee. Computer-assisted searching is becoming common in libraries of all kinds in the United States and Canada; but the costs of acquiring equipment, bringing the staff to an appropriate level of training, and paying connect charges for searching various sources have become so high that libraries have found it necessary to pass part of the cost of providing this service back to the user. Charging for services was the hottest topic of the year at the Annual Conference before such varied groups as the Machine-Assisted Reference Service Discussion Group, the Social Responsibilities Round Table and the RASD membership meeting. The topic has also found its way into print, particularly in the October 1 issue of *Library Journal*, where articles by Fay Blake and Edith Perlmutter and by John Linford aired aspects of the question.

Briefly, the argument advanced by librarians such as Blake, Haynes McMullen, Zoia Horn, and Richard Hill is that services to readers have been provided free of charge in publicly supported institutions for a very long time as one manifestation of the national belief that every citizen should have equal opportunity and, consequently, equal access to information. When libraries began to offer access to computer-based sources, they quickly found that the cost of providing the service could become so large that it might threaten libraries' ability to maintain other services or to build collections. Consequently, user fees have been assessed as the most convenient means of regaining part of the cost of computer searching.

There are, according to these librarians, several difficulties with the practice, however. Some searching is done free of charge (on OCLC terminals, for example). Well-heeled users can more easily afford to pay fees than can less affluent users, who may need information more urgently. The service may be paid for once out of public funds and may also be supported by government grants; user fees may thus be the third payment, something that Blake calls the "triple dip." Users who can pay may get a disproportionate share of the reference librarian's time, and there are other problems. In short, the ability of libraries to provide equal access to information for all users may be weakening.

The other side of the argument, advanced by Linford, Ann Lipow, Allen Veaner, Richard De Gennaro, and others, recognizes that charging for services may not be ideologically palatable, but these librarians point out that it is done out of necessity. Libraries, they argue, have charged for some services all along

Reference Services

(photocopying, interlibrary lending, and genealogical searching, for example). Such fees are usually assessed when the service provided is specific to an individual user and is not transferrable to other readers. In any case, libraries must charge for expensive services, or not offer them, or curtail services elsewhere.

Libraries need to give this issue careful thought. Some libraries are not supported by public funds and can charge for services without challenging cherished notions of free service, but many libraries cannot. Some computer-based sources that libraries have been quick to make available to users are poorly compiled and edited and show little promise of being useful. In many cases, librarians have not been careful enough in searching printed sources before calling on computerized substitutes. Libraries offering computer searching should seek alternate means of funding. Reference staffs should be thoroughly schooled in both printed and computer-based data sources and should refrain from recommending computer searches unless no other approach is satisfactory. And libraries should offer computer searching only after carefully examining the sources available and the potential local market to determine whether the sources will meet a local need and whether the use made of them will justify the expense in relation to other resources in which the library might invest.

Countdown. Not all reference librarians have understood why, but interest in the application of statistical analysis to reference work has continued. Sometimes this has been a modest undertaking, such as Dee Birch Cameron's analysis of 50 reference questions at the libraries of El Paso and the University of Texas at El Paso. Marcella Cuicki, writing in *RQ*, compiled samples of forms used in recording reference transactions from academic, public, special, and school libraries around the country. But it is Katherine Emerson who has become a "Mother of Us All" in statistical matters. Her *RQ* paper on national reporting of reference transactions summarized the reporting of information contacts that libraries will be asked to submit as part of the Library General Information Survey covering the years 1976-78. She also described the work of ALA's Committee on Statistics for Reference Services. Awareness that statistics on reference service can have managerial usefulness, and that reference librarians need to become more statistically knowledgeable, seems to be growing. A preconference at the Annual Conference on "Statistical Methods for Reference Services" was fully subscribed, and librarians who attended learned how to code for keypunching, were introduced to sampling techniques, and had brushes with such concepts as chi square, the uncertainty coefficient, and Yule's Q.

Instruction. Bibliographic instruction continues to be discussed in regular columns in the *Journal of Academic Librarianship* and in articles in a variety of other library journals. John Mark Tucker described a program at Wabash College funded by the Council on Library Resources that featured freshman tutorials and student assistants trained by the library staff. Hannelore Rader found nearly 70 articles on library instruction published during 1976. Bibliographic instruction has come of age, the chief rite of passage being the organization meeting at the Annual Conference of the Bibliographic Instruction Section of the Association of College and Research Libraries, chaired by Tom Kirk, who presided over the formation of no fewer than nine subcommittees. Bibliographic instruction seems to have become an established feature of academic reference work, both in universities and colleges, and it should no longer be necessary to prove that it is something worth doing.

AACR 2. The Catalog Code Revision Committee met at the Annual Conference, seemingly without a break, and delivered a text of the revised version of the *Anglo-American Cataloguing Rules* (AACR 2) to the Resources and Technical Services Division Board with a recommendation that it be published, a recommendation that the Board approved. This seemingly innocent event will shake the profession. Although details of the changes that AACR 2 will bring have been guarded carefully, news is beginning to leak out. The ISBD format for descriptive cataloging is affirmed, and title entry will be far more common. Corporate bodies (being called "corporate emanations")

The ninth edition of the Guide to Reference Books published by ALA in 1977 was edited by Eugene Sheehy (right) and assistant editors Rita G. Keckeissen (left) and Eileen McIlvaine.

will enter under their names rather than under place (ending forever the delightful conceit of entering UCLA as "California. University. University at Los Angeles"). A separate section will specify rules for cataloging microforms. The Library of Congress has already announced that it will finally carry out its standing threat to close its catalogs, in part as a result of the AACR 2 changes. The closing date is set for January 1, 1980.

Reference librarians, who must interpret card catalogs to users and who now face yet another cataloging upheaval, may be tempted to throw the whole thing over. In many libraries, committees to consider closing local catalogs are hard at work, with the likely result that libraries will have multiple searching files. In an effort to prepare for the impending changes, METRO sponsored a meeting in New York City on November 4 on "Closing the Catalog." Joseph Rosenthal pointed out that closing card catalogs is only one step libraries will take in reforming attitudes toward bibliographic records and that our sights must be raised beyond card files to the possibilities presented by machine manipulation of records. John Knapp listed some of the plans libraries must lay if automated catalogs are ever to materialize: authority files must be linked to bibliographic records, costs must be distributed among libraries, decisions must be taken as to whether to close old catalogs or convert them to some other form, links between catalogs must be provided, and a suitable alternative to the catalog (probably COM) must be provided. Carol Weiss described the University of Toronto's experiences in closing catalogs and converting to COM. The future of card catalogs, at least in large libraries, is at best uncertain. Reference librarians will become, by force of circumstance, used to consulting multiple files, and they will become more conversant with cataloging principles than they have been in the past. (See also Cataloging and Classification.)

Questions. A number of issues continued to vex the profession. How should nonprofessionals be used in reference service, and if they are used, how much training is it necessary to give them? Policy statements and department manuals exist in some institutions but not others. How necessary are they? Many departments have endured staff cuts in the past year or so. What effect will this have on services, and what services should reference departments properly offer? All these chickens came home to roost in Vern Pings's article on accountability and measurement in *RQ*, where it was argued that reference librarians, immune to charges of malpractice, will be held increasingly accountable for the quality of service they offer and that they must develop criteria against which performance can be measured and objective means of applying the criteria. Although some have said that computerization of catalogs will provide the opportunity for libraries to place more emphasis on public service, it seems more likely that financial pressure will fall as heavily on public services as on other parts of libraries and that reference librarians will have to become more sophisticated in justifying their function and in using staff skillfully.

ROBERT BALAY

REFERENCES

Fay M. Blake and Edith L. Perlmutter, "The Rush to User Fees: Alternative Proposals," *Library Journal* (October 1, 1977), pp. 2005-8.

Katherine Emerson, "National Reporting on Reference Transactions, 1976-78," *RQ* (Spring 1977), pp. 119-207.

John Linford, "To Charge or Not to Charge: A Rationale," *Library Journal* (October 1, 1977), pp. 2009-10.

Vern M. Pings, "Reference Services Accountability and Measurement," *RQ* (Winter 1976), pp. 120-23.

Hannelore B. Rader, "Library Orientation and Instruction—1976: An Annotated Review of the Literature," *Reference Services Review* (January/March 1977), pp. 41-44.

John Mark Tucker, "An Experiment in Bibliographic Instruction at Wabash College," *College & Research Libraries* (May 1977), pp. 203-9.

Paula D. Watson and Martha Landis, "Working Paper on Staffing, Services and Organization of Reference Departments in Large Academic Libraries," prepared for the Discussion Group on Reference Services in Large Research Libraries, Reference and Adult Services Division, American Library Association (Urbana: University of Illinois Library, June 1977).

REFORMA

REFORMA, the National Association of Spanish Speaking Librarians in the United States, is committed to uniting and supporting all librarians who feel strongly about providing better service for the millions of Americans of Spanish heritage. REFORMA experienced a good year in 1977, began to make its name and its purpose more widely known, and made strides in gaining recognition and respect for its accomplishments. For the first time REFORMA's participation in state and national conferences was given prominent coverage in the professional literature. In the near future *Wilson Library Bulletin* will devote an issue to services to Americans of Hispanic heritage. The editors will be Roberto P. Haro and Elizabeth Martinez Smith.

The largest concentration of REFORMA members is found in California, where efforts to improve library service to the Hispanic population have been steady and have won a measure of success. REFORMA has established legislative, legal, and service standards committees through which it is attempting to correct disparities in the Los Angeles Public Library's Branch Services. It is working to increase the number of Spanish-speaking librarians in systems serving the Hispanic community through lobbying, recruitment, and newspaper advertisements. It has succeeded in having a Spanish Speaking Consultant established at the California State Library and is working at having a Spanish Speaking Minority Services Coordinator established at the Los Angeles County Library.

REFORMA Officers

PRESIDENT (July 1977-June 1978):
Roberto Cabello-Argando$a, University of California, Los Angeles

VICE-PRESIDENT/PRESIDENT-ELECT:
Daniel Durham, Anaheim, California

SECRETARY:
Iliana Sonntag, University of Arizona, Tucson

Headquarters: 2093 N. Medina Ave., Simi Valley, California 93063

REFORMA successfully sponsored a resolution at the Midwinter Meeting. Submitted by REFORMA founder Arnulfo Trejo, the resolution proposed that ALA encourage graduate library schools to expand their curricula with courses taught by bilingual and bicultural faculty, specifically reflecting the cultural heritage and needs of the Spanish-speaking people of the United States.

In order to give more strength and purpose to REFORMA librarians around the country, regional chapters are being promoted. Successful ones are the Pacific Coast Chapter, with headquarters in Los Angeles (Humberto Gallego, President), and the El Paso Chapter in Texas. These chapters function with a great deal of autonomy, choose their own officers, and split their dues equally with the national association. Both chapters have set up special programs for Spanish-speaking users in conjunction with their state associations.

The El Paso Chapter presented a program on "Library Services to the Spanish Speaking" at the conference held jointly by the Texas and New Mexico Library Associations in April. The Chapter has been promoting radio and television exposure of library-related activities and has sponsored a public service announcement in Spanish on a local television station to promote reading and use of libraries. It is also sponsoring a "Reading is Fundamental" program in the Spanish-speaking Chihuahuita area of El Paso. Officers of the El Paso Chapter are Cesar Caballero, President; Trini Delgado, Secretary; and Susana Luevano, Treasurer.

Cooperation also exists between REFORMA and other organized groups such as the Committee on Recruitment of Mexican American Librarians, the Chicano Librarians Caucus, the Asociación de Bibliotecarios Chicanos, the ALA Social Responsibilities Round Table's Chicano Task Force, and the Graduate Library Institute for Spanish Speaking Librarians at the University of Arizona. Other chapters are being organized in Phoenix, under the leadership of Josefa García; Chicago; Wrentham, Massachusetts; Miami; Austin; and Provo. Some of these expect to be functional in time to participate in their states' Pre-White House Conferences.

At the California Library Association's annual conference in San Francisco, REFORMA and the Pacific Coast Chapter will cosponsor a one-day preconference, "The Spanish Speaking and California Libraries: Planning for Multicultural Consciousness," under a grant from the California Council for the Humanities and Public Policy. Public policymaking administrators, planners, librarians, and scholars will deal with planning library services for the Hispanic community, preservation of critical materials and resources created by this community, and their organization and dissemination.

ILIANA L. SONNTAG

Regional Library Associations

MOUNTAIN PLAINS LIBRARY ASSOCIATION

The Mountain Plains Library Association (MPLA) strives to promote library service in the states of Colorado, Kansas, Nebraska, Nevada, North Dakota, South Dakota, Utah, and Wyoming. In 1973 a Master Plan Task Force outlined three goals that the Association now works toward: (1) to establish a viable organization and structure; (2) to initiate and develop viable programs for continuing education and resource coordination; and (3) to strengthen communications between MPLA and the various state library organizations.

In addition to the elected officers MPLA State Representatives work closely with the Association in state activities. This has resulted in the annual conferences being held jointly with a state association each year. Because the Association represents a wide variety of individuals, the members may choose to belong to one of several sections: Children's and School, College and University, Public, State, Technical Services, and Trustees. In addition, there is a Junior Members Round Table. Committees are appointed to aid in MPLA operations and include Awards, Continuing Education, Constitution and Bylaws, Finance, Nominating, Public Relations, and Scholarship.

Continuing education was the MPLA emphasis for 1977. The annual conference was held in Rapid City, jointly with the South Dakota Library Association. Two important preconference seminars were held: "The Basics of Managing People" and "The New Copyright Law and You." More than 450 attended and participated in meetings covering copyright, censorship, organization of media, documents, performance measures, community analysis, acquisitions based on circulation, signs, library instruction, and the Library of Congress. Six special MPLA awards were given at the awards luncheon: Legislative Support Award—Michael O'Callaghan, Governor of Nevada; News Media Support Award—*The Laramie Boomerang,* Laramie, Wyoming; Intellectual Freedom Awards—Richard H. Noyes, owner of the Chinook Book Shop in Colorado Springs, and James Crawford, *Rocky Mountain News,* Denver; Literary Contribution Award—Robert G. Athearn, Professor, Western History at the University of Colorado, Boulder; Beginning Professional Award—Hal Brown, Kansas Public Library, Wichita; and Outstanding Service Award—Lucile Hatch, University of Denver, Graduate School of Librarianship.

MPLA Officers

PRESIDENT (November 1977-October 1978):
Robert Malinowsky, University of Kansas Library, Lawrence

VICE-PRESIDENT/PRESIDENT-ELECT:
James Dertien, Bellevue Public Library, Bellevue, Nebraska

SECRETARY:
Shirley Flack, Scottsbluff Public Library, Nebraska

EXECUTIVE SECRETARY:
Joseph R. Edelen, University of South Dakota Library, Vermillion

The Association is working towards more involvement with continuing education and is now developing a one-on-one program in which individuals may apply for grants to work in other libraries in the region to gain new experience. Continuing education units and continuing education scholarships are among the priorities of members. A committee has been formed to work on the White House Conference at the regional level with programs being planned for the Lake Tahoe, Nevada, meeting in 1978.

H. ROBERT MALINOWSKY

PACIFIC NORTHWEST LIBRARY ASSOCIATION
The Pacific Northwest Library Association (PNLA) is dedicated to the promotion and improvement of library service in the Pacific Northwest. Its first constitution was adopted June 10, 1909. The states and Canadian provinces represented by the association are Alaska, Idaho, Montana, Oregon, Washington, British Columbia, and, joining in 1977, Alberta. PNLA is thus the only regional library association with international membership. The membership includes 832 individuals and 146 institutions.

PNLA Officers

PRESIDENT (October 1977-October 1978):
Mary Bates, Blue Mountain Community College, Pendleton, Oregon

VICE-PRESIDENT/PRESIDENT-ELECT:
Gary Strong, Washington State Library, Olympia

SECRETARY:
Milo Nelson, University of Idaho Library, Moscow

Special interests of the membership are reflected by eight divisions: Children and Young People, Circulation, Academic Libraries, Library Education, Public Libraries, Reference, Technical Services, and Trustees. Activities of the divisions include the sponsorship of workshops at the annual conferences and the undertaking of special projects. Two current projects of the Reference Division, for example, are compilation of a list to specify all libraries in the region that collect comprehensively in a specialized area and identification of all newspapers and special materials being indexed within the PNLA region. Projects under discussion include the publication of a manual on library policies by the Public Libraries Division and the creation of a bibliography of regional continuing education materials available for interlibrary loan by the Library Education Division. The Children and Young People's (CYP) Division sponsors the Young Reader's Choice Award, given annually since 1940. The 1977 winner was the book *Blubber* by Judy Blume, who was the featured speaker at the CYP Award Breakfast.

Two major projects aimed at meeting the needs of libraries and librarians of the region are currently under investigation: the updating of Charles W. Smith's regional bibliography, *Pacific Northwest Americana,* which presently covers imprints only to 1948, and the creation of a PNLA job line. The latter would be a regional job listing service available by telephone to people seeking employment in the Northwest. Although specific details are still to be decided, PNLA has appropriated funds to underwrite development costs.

PNLA's commitment to the concept of continuing education has resulted in the decision to institute workshops as the major feature of every annual conference. The 1977 conference

Regional Library Associations

in Spokane, Washington, presented six five-hour workshops: "Maximum Use of Networks," "Library Orientation/Instruction," "Working with the Different Patron," "Human Rights," "Automated Circulation Systems," and "Public Relations." Also featured at the conference were a progress report by Margaret Warden, State Senator from Montana, and Marian Gallagher, Professor and Librarian, University of Washington Law School, on the White House Conference on Library and Information Services and an address by Raymond G. Holt, a library consultant, on the future of libraries.

The *PNLA Quarterly,* the official journal of the association, has been published since 1936 and was an ALA—H.W. Wilson Library Periodical Award Winner in 1964 and 1974. Circulation currently is more than 1,300. Special features include the annual publication since 1957 of the "PNLA Checklist of Books and Pamphlets Relating to the Pacific Northwest," compiled by the PNLA Bibliography Committee with the assistance of librarians in each state and province, and the quarterly "Continuing Education Calendar," which lists continuing education activities open to librarians throughout the Northwest. Book reviews focus on books pertaining to the region, while articles range from subjects of general interest to those specifically concerned with Northwest library problems. The membership is kept informed through quarterly news columns and announcements and the annual publication of the conference proceedings, reports, and membership list. Special issues in the past have been edited by students from the region's graduate library schools. The summer issue in 1977 was prepared by students from the University of Oregon School of Librarianship.

PNLA will hold its 1978 conference, August 17–19, in Anchorage, Alaska.

MARY P. NELSON

SOUTHEASTERN LIBRARY ASSOCIATION

For an "off year," as the year between the biennial conferences is frequently described, much was accomplished in the Southeastern Library Association (SELA) during 1977.

Executive Board. Early in 1977 the Executive Board initiated the detailed planning required of the Association in following the implementation of the first recommendation set forth in *Libraries and Library Services in the Southeast: A Report of the Southeastern States Cooperative Survey, 1972–74,* compiled by Mary Edna Anders and published by the University of Alabama Press in 1976. The recommendation stated that "if it expects to provide effective leadership and support for the growth of libraries and the expansion of library service, the SELA needs to establish and staff the office of a full-time executive director."

SELA Officers

PRESIDENT (November 1977-October 1978):
J. B. Howell, Mississippi College Library, Clinton

VICE-PRESIDENT/PRESIDENT-ELECT:
Helen D. Lockhart, Memphis/Shelby County Public Library, Memphis

SECRETARY:
Larry T. Nix, Greenville County Library, Greenville, South Carolina

EXECUTIVE DIRECTOR:
Johnnie Givens, Tucker, Georgia

Accordingly, Johnnie Givens, formerly Director of the Austin Peay State University Library, joined the staff on January 3 as the Association's first full-time Executive Director. In addition to Ann W. Morton, who continues to serve on a part-time basis as Assistant Director, a secretary has been employed, and the headquarters offices have been expanded.

The Executive Board is assisting G. Sheppeard Hicks, Chairman, and the members of the Program Committee in planning for a joint conference with the Southwestern Library Association in New Orleans, October 6–8, 1978.

Sections. Two of the Association's eight sections sponsored workshops during 1977. A seminar on the recently enacted copyright law was conducted by the Special Libraries Section, chaired by Thomas T. Rogero of the University of Miami Library, in Chattanooga in October. Under the auspices of the University and College Section, with Leland M. Park of Davidson College as Chairman, a SELA/Southern Association of Colleges conference on the "Accreditation of Academic Libraries in the Southeast" was held in Atlanta in November.

Committees. Interim reports indicated significant progress on the activities and projects of several committees during 1977. Immediately following the Georgia Governor's Conference on Libraries (the nation's first Pre-White House Conference) in September, the Governmental Relations Committee of SELA sponsored a seminar to assist local steering committees in planning Pre-White House Conferences in the other nine states of the Southeast.

As announced in the fall of 1976, a regional Library Orientation-Instruction Exchange (LOEX) has been organized at David Lipscomb College in Nashville by James E. Ward, Chairman, and the members of the Library Orientation and Bibliographic Instruction Committee. The first *Southeastern Bibliographic Instruction Directory: Academic Libraries* has been compiled by the Committee and will be available for distribution early in 1978. The Special Collections Committee has completed its survey, and a descriptive list of the special collections in the libraries of the Southeast is scheduled for publication in 1978.

In addition to the 25 standing and special committees that were appointed at the beginning of the biennium, four additional ad hoc committees are working directly with the Executive Director. The committees are working on several projects: (1) compiling job descriptions for headquarters personnel; (2) reviewing grant proposals; (3) converting the Association's membership records into machine-readable form; and (4) establishing guidelines for SELA-sponsored workshops and preconferences.

Special Project. In collaboration with the Tennessee State Library and Archives, SELA has received a grant from Union Carbide's Oak Ridge National Laboratory to assist in the acquiring of special resources in the area of solar technology and making them available to potential users through the public libraries of Tennessee. Eileen Janas, a recent graduate of Emory University's Division of Librarianship, joined the staff as Assistant to the Executive Director for this pilot project in Tennessee. She will continue to work with the project in the states selected for development during 1978.
J.B. HOWELL

SOUTHWESTERN LIBRARY ASSOCIATION

The Southwestern Library Association (SWLA), an organization embracing six southwestern states, continued in 1977 to stress a strong commitment to continuing education and humanities programming. It was midyear between a highly successsful joint conference with the Mountain Plains Library Association in Albuquerque in November 1976 and the projected joint conference with the Southeastern Library Association in New Orleans in October 1978. To facilitate involvement and to further the development of continuing education, a short conference was held in November in Dallas.

SWLA's major work projects are administered by its Southwestern Library Interstate Cooperative Endeavor (SLICE) Office. Continuing Education for Library Staffs in the Southwest (CELS) is a project of SLICE. Peggy O'Donnell serves as Director of the SLICE Office and as CELS Coordinator. In 1976 funding of SLICE projects was provided by SWLA, the six state library agencies in the SWLA region, and the National Endowment for the Humanities.

SWLA Officers

PRESIDENT (November 1976-October 1978):
John F. Anderson, Tucson Public Library

VICE-PRESIDENT/PRESIDENT-ELECT:
Sam A. Dyson, Prescott Memorial Library, Louisiana Technical University, Ruston

EXECUTIVE SECRETARY:
Marion Mitchell, Dallas

CELS Project. CELS project activities dominated the work of the Association in 1977 as workshops were developed, planning extended, publications produced, and evaluation undertaken. One of the most successful workshops was on copyright. CELS continued to sponsor previously developed workshops on grants, training the trainers, and computer applications.

Planning activities in addition to frequent visits to the states by the Coordinator included a planning meeting in Santa Fe in July for the continuing education coordinators of the state agencies. The CELS Coordinator acted as a consultant to Louisiana and Arkansas in developing statewide continuing education plans.

The *CELS Needs Assessment* report was published and the "Current Awareness" audio cassette series entered its second year. This unique bimonthly service digests professional literature from 29 publications. A *Learner's Advisory Service Training Workshops* series of six manuals was developed by Tulsa City-County Library and edited and published by CELS. *CELS Update* continued as a valuable coordinating publication for continuing education opportunities.

A conference on continuing education in Dallas involved 200 librarians in five workshops: "Copyright," "Networking," "Communications in Libraries: Insight and Strategy," "Professional Effectiveness," and a "System

Two-day workshop on the Copyright Revision Act sponsored by the Arkansas Library Association, the Arkansas Library Commission, and CELS. From left, speakers William Nasri, Ron Naylor, and Robert Stevens, with Chairman Richard Madaus at lectern.

Approach to Media." Appended to these workshops were meetings of the AMIGOS Bibliographic Council and interest groups and boards of SWLA.

Of special significance was an evaluation study by Brooke E. Sheldon, *The CELS Project—1974-1977: A Progress Report with Recommendations for the Future.* The study provided the foundation for serious discussions on the future of the project as well as the very structure and financing of the SWLA organization. The CELS project was judged a success and of significant impact on continuing education in the region as well as the nation.

Humanities Project. A National Endowment for the Humanities grant for production of three program packets, begun in 1976, was completed in 1977. "The Southwestern Mosaic: Living in a Land of Extremes" included three packets: "Our National Environment: Perspectives and Challenge"; "Melting Pot or Mosaic"; and "Political Institutions: The Challenge to Public Choice in Southwestern Politics." These packets were distributed to 960 public libraries in the region. The $120,000 project was extended for a year with a $40,000 grant to publicize and evaluate the project. An eight-minute slide and tape program was produced and an independent evaluator retained. Other materials emerging from the project included a program planning manual and the commercial publication of *Guide to Humanities Resources in the Southwest.*

Other Activities. Emphasis was placed on development of a cooperative program with Mexico after a group of SWLA members visited Mexico City libraries following the 1976 biennial conference. A survey of border library services was undertaken, and programs were in the formulation stage for exchange of library school students, faculty, and librarians.

Bibliographic networking activities shifted gears as the Association helped support research by John Corbin on "A Study of Cooperative, Networking, and Computer Activities in Southwestern Libraries." This provided the basis for planning by the newly constituted Bibliographic Networking Interest Group.

The year saw the publication of *A Selected Buying Guide to In-Print Children's Books about the Southwest,* edited by Will Howard and sponsored by the Youth Services Interest Group. The *SWLA Newsletter* continued its bimonthly publication under the editorship of Patricia Smith. SWLA once again moved its offices, to share quarters in a new building with the AMIGOS Bibliographic Council. As the year ended, SWLA and SLICE were pondering the future in financing and structure and at the same time planning new services such as a job hot line for the region.

JOHN F. ANDERSON

Research

Research in library and information science continued to advance in 1977. Several federal agencies awarded grants for library research projects. A number of significant research studies were completed, and the reports of two ongoing surveys were published. As they had done in previous years, programs on research and research-related topics drew large audiences at the 1977 ALA Annual Conference in Detroit.

RESEARCH GRANTS

During FY 1977 the U.S. Office of Education funded 18 library research projects with money appropriated under the Higher Education Act, Title II-B, Library Research and Demonstration. The total funds awarded, $994,493, were almost exactly the same as the amount awarded in FY 1976 ($999,918) and FY 1975 ($999,338). The funded projects are listed in Table 1.

Under the authorization of the Medical Library Assistance Act (1965) and its extensions, the National Library of Medicine (NLM) administers a program of grants to assist medical libraries in the development of better health information services, especially those that relate to the development of biomedical information networks. In 1977, NLM awarded funds for the 11 library-related research projects that are shown in Table 2.

In 1977 the National Science Foundation (NSF) awarded funds for library and information science research projects in five areas: access improvement, economics of information, information science, national/international, and user requirements. As in previous years, NSF had a far larger amount of money for funding library and information science research projects ($4,623,440) than either the Office of Education ($994,493) or NLM ($805,199). The funded research projects in the five areas are listed in Table 3.

RESEARCH STUDIES

Several noteworthy research studies were completed during 1977. Among the most important studies completed were the library photocopy study conducted by King Research, Inc., for the National Commission on Libraries and Information Science (NCLIS) and others. The National Commission on Higher Education Management Systems (NCHEMS) statistical data base system and the *National Inventory of Library Needs—1975* were among other important research projects completed. The Book Industry Study Group's *Trends—1977* and the National Research and Management Project, of the Council for the Advancement of

Small Colleges National Research Project, *Library Cost and Service Module*, also were completed during the year.

Funded jointly by NCLIS, the Division of Science Information of NSF, and the National Commission on New Technological Uses of Copyrighted Works (CONTU), the study of library photocopying was undertaken to collect data about the amount of photocopying of library materials that is being done by library staffs for users, intrasystem loans, and interlibrary loans. The results were analyzed to determine the implications they might have for alternative royalty payment mechanisms that may be established under the new copyright law and CONTU guidelines.

The study found that while there is in fact a substantial amount of photocopying of library materials being done by library staffs, a large proportion of the copied material is not eligible for royalty payment. Of all the libraries in the United States, less than one-quarter (23 per cent or about 5,000 libraries) are estimated to have more than 1,000 eligible photocopies per

TABLE 1: Projects Funded under the Higher Education Act, Title II-B, Library Research and Demonstration, FY 1977

Organization	Principal Investigator	Project Title	Funding
American Library Association	Mary Jo Lynch	The Process of Standards Development for Community Library Services: A Proposed Research Study	$140,000
University of California, Los Angeles	Robert M. Hayes	The Use of an On-Line Microfiche Catalog for Technical Service and Retrieval of Bibliographic Data	76,361
City University of New York, Herbert H. Lehman College	Paul E. Vesenyi	Development of a Model System for Bilingual Subject Approach in a Minority Oriented Information Center	35,590
Drexel University	Thomas Childers	Survey of Public Library Information and Referral	45,000
Elgin Community College	Jack Weiss	Research and Demonstration for a Comprehensive Package of Computer Programs to Serve Community College Learning Resource Centers	70,500
MITRE Corporation	Sidney Polk	The Role of Microcomputers in Library Automation	64,000
New England Board of Higher Education	John Linford	Implementation of a Computerized Interlibrary System to Provide Market Value Information for Resource Sharing to a Multi-type Regional Library Network	94,460
University of North Carolina at Greensboro	Theodore C. Hines	Children's Media Data Bank and Information Center: A Library Research and Demonstration Project	69,100
Oakland University	Eileen Hitchingham	A Study of the Relationship Between the Intermediary Searcher and the System User, and the Assessment of Search Results as Judged by the User	23,600
Oklahoma State Department of Education	Leroy Ireton	Library Media Specialists: Leadership Training	54,500
University of Pittsburgh	Sara Fine	Resistance to Technological Change in Libraries	98,700
University of South Carolina	Daniel Barron, Charles Curran	Information Needs Assessment of Rural Groups for Library Program Development	17,398
South Dakota State Department of Education and Cultural Affairs	Ardis Ruark	Training Program for Library Media Specialists to Serve the Handicapped Student	28,100
State University of New York at Albany	Glyn T. Evans	Development of a Responsive Library Acquisitions Formula	90,000
State University of New York at Buffalo	Gerald Shields	The Design and Testing of Values to be Derived in the Training of Librarians through a Systematic Data Gathering Project on Graduates of a Program in Education for Librarianship	15,150
Virgin Islands, Department of Conservation and Cultural Affairs	Henry C. Chang	Virgin Islands Demonstration Library Network Study	31,100
Washington State Library	Mary Jane P. Reed, Hugh T. Vrooman	A Network Management Tool: Computer Simulation	20,934
Western Michigan University	Marguerite Baechtold	Early Childhood Library Programming: Identification and Demonstration of Competencies Needed	20,000
		Total	$994,493

Research Libraries: see under type of library—Academic, Public, School, Special; see also Independent Research Libraries, Association of Research Libraries; Association of College and Research Libraries.

Research

year. The extensive and detailed findings of the study are expected to be very useful in the planning and establishment of royalty payment mechanisms in accordance with the new copyright law that became effective January 1, 1978.

NCHEMS developed and demonstrated a statistical data base system for library decision makers in academic and public libraries. The four objectives of the project were to design and develop cooperatively a statistical data base system, to demonstrate its use, to evaluate the system, and to disseminate the components of the new system. The project was funded by the U.S. Office of Education with matching funds from the Western Council of State Libraries.

In meeting its objectives, the project produced a number of important documents. The *Commentary to Library Statistical Data Base* provides an overview of the framework and the conceptual approach used in the project. The *Library Statistical Data Base Formats and Definitions* presents a detailed set of data structures for categorizing information, terminology, and definitions used in the project. The *Summary of the Pilot Test and Demonstration of the Library Statistical Data Base* is an evaluative summary of the results of the application of the data base in the demonstration. In addition, a bibliography of library management information needs and statistical data was prepared, and the final report of the project documents the process used to develop and demonstrate the statistical data base.

NCHEMS has been awarded a contract to continue work on the data base project by applying it to school and special libraries and at the same time by continuing to refine the academic and public library components of the data base. The objective of this contract is to produce a handbook of library management information and a guide to standard terminology.

The *National Inventory of Library Needs—1975* sponsored by NCLIS is a source book showing resource data and relationships among resources of different kinds. In the report, two sets of data are juxtaposed: indicators of need for resources of measurable kinds for public, public school, and academic libraries; and reports from these three types of libraries about their resources. The kinds of resources analyzed are ones that are measurable and recognized as significant. The resources considered are ones for which nationally representative data have been collected, thus limiting resources to the data elements included in the Libraries General Information Surveys (LIBGIS) of the National Center for Education Statistics. The main thrust of the report is the presentation of particular quantitative measures from multiple points of view.

An earlier study, the *National Inventory of Library Needs—1965*, examined the books, professional staff, and the operating expenditures available to academic, school, and public libraries in the United States and identified what libraries needed in those areas to attain professionally accepted standards of resource availability. The 1975 *Inventory* follows its predecessor in that it attempts to develop empirical evidence concerning the resources of staff, materials, space, and operating expenditures available to academic,

TABLE 2: Research Grants Awarded by the National Library of Medicine under the Medical Library Assistance Act (1965), FY 1977

Organization	Principal Investigator	Project Title	Funding
Beth Isral Hospital, Boston	Warner V. Slack	Counseling in Nutrition by Computer	$100,901
Case Western Reserve University	William Goffman	Problem Oriented Bibliometry	47,438
University of Cincinnati Medical Center	Leonard T. Sigell	A New Model for Medical Information Communication System	87,888
University of Connecticut Health Center	Gertrude Lamb	A Shared Patient Care Information System	73,719
Georgia Institute of Technology	Vladimir Slamecka	Extended Utilization of Biomedical Information	95,672
Lehigh University	John J. O'Connor	Retrieval of Answer-Passages from Biomedical Papers	79,419
University of Marlyand School of Medicine	Murray M. Kappelman	Information Needs of Practicing Physicians	52,529
New York University	Naomi Sager	Computer Structuring of Medical Narrative	17,757
University of Southern California School of Medicine	Phil R. Manning	Individualized Library Services for Office Practice	102,429
Syracuse University School of Information Studies	Marta L. Dosa	Development/Evaluation of Health Information Sharing	104,915
Tufts University School of Medicine	Norman S. Stearns	Documented Reading for Improved Patient Care and CME Credit	42,532
		Total	$805,199

school, and public libraries in 1975 in comparison with indicators of need as developed through professional judgments and expressed in standards.

Book Industry Trends—1977, by John P. Dessauer, Paul D. Doebler, and E. Wayne Nordberg, is the Book Industry Study Group's Research Report No. 4. The first in a contemplated annual series, the publication presents data and analyses needed by book industry managers and planners. Doebler's article is entitled "Recent and Anticipated Events, Developments, and Perceptions in the Book Industry"; Nordberg's article, "Economic Trends and the Book Industry: 1976 and Beyond"; and Dessauer's article, "Book Industry Markets 1972-1981." The volume concludes with an essay by Barbara O. Slanker, "The Need for Further Research."

Sponsored by the Council for the Advancement of Small Colleges (CASC), the Library Cost and Service Analysis Module is one part of the National Research and Management Project that investigated a number of different aspects of small colleges. The objective of the library module was to design and test a data system for the libraries of private liberal arts colleges. The purposes of the data system are to provide usable management data for librarians and to develop a set of descriptive data about college libraries that is useful for planning public policy. Based on the HEGIS (LIBGIS) data system for academic libraries, the data system was adapted for use by small college libraries.

SURVEYS

Two surveys completed in 1977 are especially important because they have been done for several years, making the accumulated data particularly valuable for comparative analyses and for the identification of trends. The *Annual Salary Survey—1976-1977* by the Association of Research Libraries (ARL) and *Degrees and Certificates Awarded by U.S. Library Education Programs—1973-1976* by the ALA Office for Library Personnel Resources report the results of continuing surveys.

The ARL *Annual Salary Survey—1976-1977*, compiled by Suzanne Frankie, was expanded in 1977 to include a group of supplementary tables that report average salaries for the filled positions in ARL's academic libraries. For the first time, the report also includes information about ARL salaries by position, sex, minority group membership, and the geographical location, size, and type of institution. The report has the traditional tabulation of median and beginning professional salaries for budgeted positions in all ARL libraries.

In the introduction to the *Survey*, Frankie notes that the data in the supplementary tables make possible many kinds of analyses, and several are given. For example, one table shows that, of the professional librarians employed in the 83 U.S. academic libraries reporting, 9 per cent were members of minority groups. Of the minority persons employed, men had higher average salaries than women, and the minority librarians holding top administrative positions were paid less than the nonminority librarians in the same catagories. Another table shows that, with the exception of the top administrative positions, librarians working in public institutions had higher average salaries than those working in private institutions. Generally, librarians in the Pacific region were paid the highest salaries, while librarians in the East South Central region had the lowest salaries.

Analysis of data for the past eight years (1969-77) shows that median salaries have increased about the same amount as the consumer price index, but beginning professional salaries began to drop below the consumer price index in 1972, and they have fallen farther behind each year. (*See further* Association of Research Libraries.)

Annually since 1973-74 the ALA Office for Library Personnel Resources has surveyed U.S. library education programs to get information about the number and types of degrees and certificates they awarded and the ethnicity and sex of the recipients of the degrees. The purpose of the annual survey is to collect and publish information for librarians to use in the development and implementation of their libraries' affirmative action plans. Librarians can also use the data to measure the effectiveness of their efforts to recruit members of minority groups to the profession of librarianship.

In the report of the 1975-76 survey, data from the first two surveys are included, and data from all three surveys are considered together. The number of degrees awarded by U.S. library education programs has dropped about 5 per cent each year since 1973-74. Although U.S. library education programs award five different degrees, four-fifths of the degrees awarded are master's degrees. Substantially more degrees are awarded to women than to men for four of the five types of degrees; more doctoral degrees are awarded to men than to women. White persons receive about nine-tenths of the degrees awarded, and of the minority groups, Blacks receive the greatest number of degrees.

For the last two surveys, data about the geographic distribution of the degrees awarded were collected. The 10 regions defined by the U.S. Department of Health, Education and Welfare were used to identify the regions of the United States. In both years library education programs in Region V (Illinois, Indiana, Michigan, Minnesota, Ohio, and Wisconsin) awarded the greatest number of degrees.

Research

TABLE 3: Research Library Projects Funded by the Division of Science Information, National Science Foundation, FY 1977

Organization	Principal Investigator	Project Title	Funding
Access Improvement Projects			
American Chemical Society	F. Tate	Contract for Development of Computer-Managed Data Bases for the Fields of Chemistry and Chemical Engineering	$119,290
American Geological Institute	J. Mulvihill	Designing an Experimental Information and Data Network for Geologists	74,400
Capital Systems Group, Inc.	J. Strawhorn	A Planning Guide on Innovations in the Dissemination of Scientific Information	312,086
Council on Library Resources	L. Livingston	National Bibliographic Control Activities	25,000
University of Dayton	J. Martino	A Computer Conference on Futures Research Methodology	62,500
George Washington University	S. Umpleby	Electronic Information Exchange Among General Systems Theorists to Integrate Scientific Disciplines	73,600
Innovative Systems Research, Inc.	J. McCarroll	An Assessment of the Utilization of Electronic Information Exchange by an Interdisciplinary Research and Development Community in the Area of Devices for the Disabled	51,143
Lehigh University	L. Freeman	Electronic Information Exchange by a Social Networks Research Community	71,900
NCLIS	—	Task Force on the Activities and Future Direction of the American National Standards Institute (ANSI) Committee Z39	12,300
NFAIS	T. Bearman	Meeting Between NFAIS/ASIDIC and European Information Services	5,100
New Jersey Institute of Technology	M. Turoff	Electronic Information Exchange Test Facility	474,657
Stanford Research Institute	O. Whitby	Editorial Processing Center—Prototype Operational Experiment: Conclusion and Evaluation	88,400
U.S. Department of the Air Force	D. Stone	Workshop Utility Service IV	45,674
U.S. Department of the Army	S. Taylor	Workshop Utility Service IV	29,326
		Total	$1,445,376
Economics of Information			
Case Western Reserve University	P. Kantor	Levels of Output as Related to Cost of Operation in Scientific and Technical Libraries	$ 93,800
Charles River Associates, Inc.	D. Evans	Development of a Discrete Model for the Demand of Scientific and Technical Information	101,764
Indiana University	B. Fry	Impact of Economic Pressures on American Libraries and Their Decisions Concerning Scholarly and Research Journal Acquisition and Retention	51,500
Kent State University	C. Casper	Estimation of the Demand for Library Services	31,500
King Research, Inc.	D. King	Data Gathering for Statistical Indicators of Scientific and Technical Communication from Primary Sources	149,800
King Research, Inc.	D. McDonald	An In-Depth Study of the Interaction Between Scientists and the Publishing of Scientific Journals	49,800
Metrics, Inc.	R. Mason	A Study of the Economic Costs and Benefits of Federally-Sponsored Information Analysis Centers (IAC's)	83,800
New York University	F. Machlup	The Production and Distribution of Scientific and Technological Information	35,000
Purdue University	J. Talavage	The Economic Characteristics of Information Analysis Centers	57,700
		Total	$654,664

Information Science

George Washington University	I. Cisin	Study of Methods Used in Reviewing and Synthesizing Research in the Behavioral Sciences	$ 34,700
Georgia Institute of Technology	P. Zunde	Study of the Empirical Foundations of Information Science	58,800
IIT Research Institute	D. Becker	Investigations into the Logical Foundations of Information Retrieval	143,800
Lehigh University	D. Hillman	Research into the Architecture of Large-Scale Science Information Systems	166,200
University of Maryland	J. Kidd	Cognitive Process Models as Theoretical Foundations for the Design of Information Retrieval Systems	133,700
Massachusetts Institute of Technology	J. F. Reintjes	Networking of Interactive Information Retrieval Systems	169,500
		Total	$878,600

National/International Projects

Denver Research Institute	T. Schlie	Strengthening Scientific and Technical Information Service Support of Technology Transfer to Latin America	$ 7,500
Franklin Institute Research Laboratory	Alex Peters	Support for Coordination of Scientific and Technical Information Activities	182,266
George Washington University	M. Head	Exploring Critical Issues Facing S&T Information Activities in the U.S.	22,208
National Academy of Sciences	J. J. Lloyd	Committee on International Scientific and Technical Information Programs (CISTIP)	190,390
National Academy of Sciences	W. Spindel	U.S. Support of the International Committee on Data for Science and Technology (CODATA)	10,250
		Total	$412,614

User Requirements Projects

American Institute of Physics	R. Lerner	Assessment of Data Base Searching and Document Delivery via Communications Satellite	$141,200
Capital Systems Group, Inc.	J. Spargur	Research Relating to the Use of STI and the Effectiveness of Scientists and Engineers	86,369
Florida State University	G. Jahoda	Effect of On-Line Search Services on Chemists' Information Style	77,000
Industrial Research Institute Research Corporation	A. Gerstenfeld	An Experimental Trial of Improving the Transfer of Interdisciplinary Information Among Scientists and Engineers	140,200
Institute of Electrical and Electronics Engineers, Inc.	J. Lufkin	Publication of Proceedings for the Third (1977) IEEE Conference on Scientific Journals	12,000
University of Kansas	D. Rummer	Improving the Use of Computer-Based Information Resources Within the Engineering Classroom	14,600
University of Michigan	D. Lingwood	A Study of Science Information Instruction by College Science and Engineering Educators	59,000
University of Michigan	R. Havelock	Development of a Theory to Improve the Understanding of Interdisciplinary Information Transfer	63,100
NTIS	W. Knox	Comprehensive Information Services to Include Document Processing, Announcement and Distribution Services in Paper Copy and Microfiche, Magnetic Tape Services and Bibliographic Data Search Services	17,000
Northwestern University	A. Rubenstein	Field Experiments on Key Communicators and the Dissemination and Utilization of Scientific and Technical Information	141,500
Participation Systems, Inc.	C. Stevens	Assessment of a Legislative Resource Network	108,100
University of Pennsylvania	P. Davis	SCATT: The Third Phase Extension, Dissemination and Implementation of the SCATT Idea	102,000

Research

Polytechnic Institute of New York	H. Kaufman	Factors Related to Use of Scientific and Technical Information and Effectiveness of Engineers: A Longitudinal Study	80,000
Stanford Research Institute	E. Michael	Innovations in Engineering Publications	149,000
Temple University	J. Grashof	Measurement and Evaluation of an Operational Experiment for the Marketing of Scientific and Technical Information	16,600
United Engineering Trustees, Inc.	J. Price	Engineering Foundation Conference—Innovative Management of Technical Information Functions in Industry	14,500
Westat, Inc.	E. Olson	Relationship of Organization Climate to the Transfer of Scientific and Technical Information in Industrial Settings	10,017
		Total	$1,232,186
		Grand Total	$4,623,440

ANNUAL CONFERENCE PROGRAMS

Programs on library research and research-related topics attracted large audiences at the 1977 ALA Annual Conference in Detroit. Among the units sponsoring programs on research were the Library Research Round Table (LRRT), the ALA Office for Research, the Research Committee of the American Association of School Librarians (AASL), the Research and Development Committee of the Children's Services Division (CSD), and the Library Organization and Management Section, Statistics Coordinating Committee, of the Library Administration Division (LAD).

LRRT Programs. Of all the ALA units, the LRRT sponsored the greatest number of programs on library research—five programs in the Research Forum Series, another major program, and the Information Exchange Suite where library researchers gave informal reports of their work in progress.

As it has done since 1975, LRRT presented its Research Forum Series which covered a variety of research topics. Cosponsored by the ALA Office for Research, the series was directed by Charles C. Curran.

Forum I, "Measurement," was moderated by William E. McGrath, and included three papers: "Cost per Capita as an Indicator of Library Performance and Service," by Chai Kim; "Measures of Library Performance: Traditional and New; Quantitative and Qualitative," by Edward T. O'Neill; and "Assessing the Impact of MRAP on Several Research Libraries," by Edward Johnson.

Moderated by Robert W. Burns, Jr., the topic of Forum II was "Techniques for Finding Out." It included two papers: "The Delphi Technique: History, Development, and Use with Specific Reference to Library Applications," by Esther Dyer; and "Fault Tree Analysis (Employing Delphi Input): The Systems Tool Used to Analyze Possible Modes of Failure in a System," by R. Kent Wood.

Forum III, "Indexes and Periodical Use," was moderated by John F. Harvey, and the following papers were presented: "The Coefficient of Index Usability of 'Off the Shelf' Indexes," by Charles W. Conaway; and "Techniques for Monitoring Use of Periodical Collections and for Rating Relative Liability of Unused Titles," by W. M. Shaw, Jr.

"Networks," Forum IV, was moderated by Bernard Schlessinger and included two presentations: "WEBNET: An Experimental Network Consisting of Six Libraries Who Share Resources and Acquisitions, Cataloging, and Circulation Data," by K. Leon Montgomery; and "The Virgin Islands Demonstration Library Network Study: The Feasibility of Library Networks in Remote and Disadvantaged Areas," by Henry C. Chang and Bonnie Isman.

Forum V, "Effectiveness Measures for Public Libraries," was moderated by Ernest R. DeProspo, Jr. Masae Gotanda presented the paper, "State-wide Efforts to Develop Effectiveness Measures in Public Libraries."

LRRT and the ALA Office for Research also sponsored a program by Ferdinand F. Leimkuhler, Professor of Industrial Engineering at Purdue University. He spoke on the topic "Operations Research: Applications to Library Management."

The winners of the 1977 LRRT Research Competition were announced, and checks for $400 were presented by Gary R. Purcell, the Chairperson of LRRT, to Robert W. Burns, Jr., Colorado State University Libraries, for his paper, "Library Performance Measures As Seen in the Descriptive Statistics Generated by a Computer Managed Circulation System"; and Herbert S. White and Karen Hasenjager of the Graduate Library School at Indiana University for their paper, "Some Measurements of the Impact of the Rapid Growth of Library Doctoral Programs." The papers were presented in the LRRT Information Exchange Suite. (See also Library Research Round Table.)

Division Programs. The "Forum for Research" presented by the Research Committee of AASL and cosponsored by the ALA Office for Research drew a large audience of conferees. David V. Loertscher, Committee Chairperson, presided over the program that reported on current research projects affecting school media programs. The following speakers presented the results of their research: R. Kent Wood, "Teacher Use of Library Media Centers in the Future: The NATUL Project"; Janet G. Stroud, "Evaluation of Media Center Services by Media Staff, Teachers and Students in Indiana Middle and Junior High Schools"; Esther R. Dyer, "Cooperation in Library Services to Children: A Fifteen Year Forecast of Alternatives Using the Delphi Technique"; Therese Bard, "The Effects of Developmental Level, Adult Intervention, Sex, and Reading Ability on Response to Four Filmed Versions of Explanatory Folk Tales"; and Joanne Troutner, "Usage of Professional Time in the Media Center."

The Research and Development Committee of CSD sponsored a Research Forum presenting the results of research concerned with library service to children. Mary Kingsbury, Committee Chairperson, presided and introduced the following speakers: Christine E. Thorndill, "The Renovation of Nancy Drew and the Hardy Boys: A Critical Evaluation"; Peggy Whalen, "A Study of Children's Strategies for Making Meaning of Visual Narrative in Peter Wezel's *The Good Bird*"; and Joseph Turow, "Client Relationship and Juvenile Publishing: A Case Study of Mass Market Production and Distribution of Children's Books."

The Statistics Coordinating Committee of the Library Organization and Management Section of LAD and the ALA Office for Research presented the program "Using Statistics as an Internal Management Tool." Speakers who addressed the topic, "Different Needs and Uses of Statistical Data," were Janis C. Keene, public libraries; Roderick E. Banks, academic libraries; and John A. McCrossan, state library agencies.

BARBARA O. SLANKER

Resources and Technical Services Division

The Resources and Technical Services Division (RTSD)—with 6,164 members (as of August 31, 1977), 4 divisions, 21 divisional and interdivisional committees, 14 discussion groups, and 25 regional groups—is one of the largest and most diversified Divisions in ALA, and 1977 saw all of these units at work on a wide variety of tasks.

International Cooperation. Involvement in international cooperation occurred on a number of fronts in 1977. The Special Committee on International Cataloging Consultation met to discuss options for future catalog code revision and ways in which ALA might participate most effectively in all international library deliberations. The RTSD Board named a number of RTSD members to represent ALA as official voting delegates to the various sections at the International Federation of Library Associations (IFLA) World Congress of Librarians in Brussels in September. These delegates included Doralyn Hickey (Cataloging), Nathan Einhorn (Exchange of Publications), Mary Sauer (Serial Publications), and Frances Hinton (Conservation). In addition, Doralyn Hickey, who also went to the Congress as the RTSD official representative to the IFLA Council, was elected Chairman of the Division of Bibliographic Control and was elected to the IFLA Professional Board, the only U.S. librarian to have gained such a position in IFLA.

The Catalog Code Revision Committee (CCRC) continued its work on the preparation of its input to the second edition of *Anglo-American Cataloguing Rules* (AACR). A six-month review of the draft of the second edition was undertaken early in the year by the national committees and their constituents that make up the Joint Steering Committee. CCRC administered this draft review program within the American library community, inviting all the groups that had been involved with the code revision effort, including several RTSD units, to participate. More than 700 pages of comments were received as a result of this review, and these were collated and examined by the Committee during its meetings in June at the ALA Annual Conference, with a number of changes in the draft resulting. CCRC then recommended to the RTSD Board of Directors that it endorse publication of the second edition of AACR. After hearing comments from a number of interested groups, the Board gave its endorsement.

RTSD Officers

PRESIDENT (July 1977-June 1978):
Norman Dudley, University of California, Los Angeles

VICE-PRESIDENT/PRESIDENT-ELECT:
Pauline Atherton, Syracuse University

EXECUTIVE SECRETARY:
To be appointed

Membership (August 31, 1977): 6,029 (3,850 personal and 2,179 organizational)

The New Copyright Law. ALA has been concerned about providing assistance to librarians in the implementation of the new copyright law. In the spring of 1977 the RTSD President was asked to appoint a committee to prepare guidelines for a library or archive that wishes, under the new law, to make a single copy of a published copyrighted work for a user or to replace a copy in its collection that is damaged, deteriorating, lost, or stolen. The committee completed its work in October, and its statement, with some minor revisions, is being included in the ALA Librarians Copyright Kit, which will be made available to members early in 1978.

Collection Development Preconference. The Annual Conference in Detroit featured a successful two-and-a-half-day collection development preconference sponsored by RTSD and its Resources Section. More than 260 attendees heard talks on the formulation of collection development policy statements, the selection process, evaluating selection tools, allocating book funds, selecting materials for storage, and the evaluation of library collections, interspersed with small workshops on these subjects. Papers and guidelines prepared for the preconference will be published by ALA.

Awards. RTSD has three awards that it presents annually for outstanding achievements in technical services. The 1977 recipient of the Margaret Mann Citation, given for outstanding professional achievement in the areas of cataloging and classification, was Phyllis Richmond of Case Western Reserve University. The Resources Scholarship Award, given to honor the author of an outstanding monograph or article on acquisitions or collection development in academic libraries, went to Herbert S. White for his article "Publishers, Libraries, and Costs of Journal Subscriptions in Time of Funding Retrenchment," published in *The Library Quarterly* (October 1976). The Esther J. Piercy Award, established to recognize outstanding achievement and promise in a librarian with less than 10 years of professional experience, was not given in 1977.

Discussion Groups. ALA members are finding it increasingly useful and interesting to get together at Annual Conferences and Midwinter Meetings with others and to discuss mutual problems. The result has been a great proliferation of discussion groups throughout the Association within recent years, and RTSD has contributed its share. For several years RTSD has had groups for chief collection development officers of research libraries of different sizes, technical services directors of various sizes and types of libraries and processing centers, serials librarians, and those who are interested in the reproduction of library materials. Recently RTSD has added groups on acquisitions, preorder and precataloging searching, the preservation of library materials, and the role of the professional in academic research technical service departments. These groups provide a forum that is not available anywhere else in ALA, and their almost phenomenal growth, in numbers and size, is testimony to their effectiveness.

In December 1977 Carol Kelm, RTSD Executive Secretary, resigned. She provided RTSD with outstanding support for nine years.

Running full tilt to stay in the same place is a commonplace in the wonderland of librarianship. In 1977 RTSD ran a little faster than that in a number of areas, and may even have advanced a square or two.

NORMAN DUDLEY

School Libraries and Media Centers

In 1977, dissatisfactions that had earlier manifested themselves as expressions of vague remonstrances against the permissiveness of open education became fullblown movements. These fears were fueled by apprehensions about the negative impact of the addictive viewing of television by youth. It was argued that television, because it does not further the ability of learners to read, write, or express themselves clearly and because it encourages passive intake only, is a clear danger to the American educational system.

Also evident in 1977 was a more generalized reaction against all of the media as purveyors of attitudes and as methods of teaching and learning that are at best suspect and at worst ineffectual. These attitudes emerge cyclically, and in 1977 their time had come again. Rooted mainly in a fear of the unknown and of too rapid change, they reflected the unfortunate tendency of intimidation, and many school library media programs were put in defensive postures. The profession primarily reacted to its critics, seeking to justify its worth by asserting its contribution to the basic education of learners and by proving that library media programs are true instructional programs with clear learning goals and objectives.

PROBLEMS

If 1977 was a tallying time, school library media programs themselves had much to do with the fact that they were judged with increasing harshness by critics who, quite unjustly, laid all of the faults of "open education" at the door of the library media center. The response of library media professionals and their programs to these criticisms, and their determination to persevere in spite of them, strengthened their ability to survive and even move ahead into new program areas. Professionals who had shown the wisdom not to promise all things to all people and the integrity to keep the promises that were made, and their library media programs did survive in a time of restricted program growth. 1977 will be marked as much for its promising new starts and its bold assertions of the relevance of library media programs to the teaching and learning process as for its negative events.

At the building and the district level, however, reduced financial support for school library media programs remained a harsh reality. Because many school library media program budgets are based on per capita enrollment figures, budget decreases were directly related to the precipitous nationwide decline in elementary school enrollments. Some school districts simply refused to pledge any more tax money to support school programs, and schools in Ohio and Oregon closed their doors when funds to operate them ran out. These budget restrictions were aggravated further by the uncertainties that prevailed during the first full year of funding for library media programs under Title IV-B of the Elementary and Secondary Education Act.

Yet the austerities of reduced budget support sometimes forced positive results. Although "increased productivity" and "more efficient delivery of services" are sometimes code words used to justify cuts in professional and support staff and materials and equipment budgets, many school library media programs have been forced, because of budget restrictions, to rethink their purpose and their accountability to the school's instructional program. This demanding process has led to a greater clarification of the purpose of the library media program within the entire instructional program with better focus on instructionally related services.

Teaching Goal. In the past decade, the school library media specialist has increasingly assumed a teaching role. The transition from traditional librarian to special teacher is related directly to the publication of three major documents: *Standards for School Media Centers* (1969); *Media Programs: District and School* (1975); and the *Certification Model for School Media Specialists* (1976). Each of these publications supports the notion that "the media program exists to support and further the purposes formulated by the school or district *of which it is an integral part*, and its quality is judged by its effectiveness in achieving program purposes."

Today the school library media specialist is expected to teach specific learning activities to students. Helping learners achieve adequate skill levels in retrieving and using media effectively has become a major focus for library media programs. Contemporary teaching and learning require, more than ever before, that the learner be able to find, retrieve, and use a wide variety of media to learn effectively. This kind of teaching reflects the thoughtful integration of media skills teaching into subject area and classroom ac-

Above and below, fifth graders at Margaret M. Seylar School in Perkasie, Pennsylvania, work on their own in the library using books, records, and slides.

tivities, a highly sophisticated process.

In 1977 reading was rediscovered. The national preoccupation was sometimes carried to extremes, manifesting some peculiar attitudes. Reading became an absolute virtue, and doubters were punished with excommunication. In this attitude lies perhaps the greatest danger to the openness traditionally associated with the school library media program. The proper reaction to any real or imagined failings of the open education era is not regimentation and barracks-style discipline in which rote learning from reading primers becomes the order of the day. The baby-bathwater syndrome is in effect, and in 1977 sensitive school library media specialists became articulate proponents of maintaining an openness of attitude and style about teaching young learners by demonstrating that their programs provide the structure within which sound basic learning can proceed.

The accelerative thrust of the future described by Alvin Toffler in *Future Shock* has not slackened its pace. Our ability to manage or cope with the future and not be demolished in the process relates directly to our ability to manage the media. The teaching of "basics" must reflect this compelling reality, for future survival and well-being will be dependent on much more than a simple ability to read at an eighth grade level, do fifth grade computational math, and articulate at the "you know" level. To the extent that school library media programs were able to accommodate themselves to these changing expectations and still provide innovative leadership, they found new purpose in 1977.

During the last decade teachers and students have become far more sophisticated media users and producers, and this too has had a positive impact on the development of school library media programs. In effect, teams composed of teachers, library media specialists, and students are often involved in the diagnosis of learning needs and the prescription of the proper media use to satisfy these needs. Just as important, each team member assumes an accountability for his or her role in the teaching-learning process. This process supports the concept that the library media program involves within it the widest number of teachers, students, administrators, support staff, and parents, as opposed to the more limited concept of a library media center to which learners are sent to have some sort of service or activity performed upon or for them. This thrust of the library media program into the educational mainstream of the building and even into the community must be identified as one of the most important trends of the decade.

These developments placed still more demands on the professionals who manage the building, district, and state library media programs. Increasingly, the focus is being placed on the ability of the professional to manage a program that manifests itself in a number of instructional formats, uses a variety of media, and involves many different people in several locations. Improving professional capabilities to meet these new challenges through staff development has become a major need for school library media specialists. Staff development programs to help library media professionals upgrade their ability to manage library media programs, evaluate the success (or failures) of these programs, and plan for new strategies for media program development and implementation grew in importance in 1977.

Program Changes. Equally significant was the growing involvement of library media professionals in teaching other professionals new skills or in shaping new attitudes. These activities carried with them the expectation that improved teaching abilities and attitudes related directly to better use of library media programs. The role of the library media specialist as a teacher and staff developer gave credibility to the teaching role of the library media specialist.

These program changes eventually will have an impact on the kind of facilities that are designed and built to house the library media center. There were discernible signs in 1977 that some careful reconsideration about some cherished notions concerning the form and function of school library media centers was taking place. At the American Association of School Librarians meeting in Detroit, for example, Jane Hannigan of the Columbia University School of Library Science stated that the profession should divest itself once and for all of the notion that without an elegant library media center there can be no library media program. Although no one is opposed to attractive surroundings that invite students into them to use their materials, the facility is not the ultimate purpose of the library media program.

Reflecting another reality of contemporary American life, in 1977 school library media programs were also forced to confront some important decisions imposed by government fiat. Bilingual programs and the laws governing the education of handicapped children (PL 94-142) provide two examples. The growth of bilingual programs requires that library media specialists become more knowledgeable about and sensitive to the selection and use of media for those of different cultural and linguistic heritages. It is too early yet to measure the full impact that the mandates imposed by PL 94-142 will have on school library media programs. Whether one considers barrier-free facilities or the prescription of a media-based individualized educational program for the handicapped learner, it is hardly visionary to predict that, within a few years, such effects will be profound.

Copyright. School library media programs also began to pay careful attention in 1977 to the fact that on January 1, 1978, a new copyright law would take effect. Although the tendency of many has been to ignore the new law in the vain hope that it would go away, others have looked carefully at the effect that it will have on their programs. The question of the legitimacy of the use of off-the-air taping is a matter of extraordinary concern. Increasingly sophisticated equipment fosters widespread videotaping, but the new law is frustratingly vague about what is "fair use" in this area. A conference held at Airley House in Warrenton, Virginia, discussed the issue thoroughly but failed to reach a consensus, and the issue remains to be settled, perhaps by litigation. The use of laminating machines for the multiple reuse of workbook pages, of copy machines to make thermal masters of book pages, and of audio and video tape recorders to tape broadcasts off the air will receive careful scrutiny in light of the regulations of the new copyright law. The law will have a direct impact on the delivery of library media program services, on which many teachers and students have become dependent.

Funding. 1977 represented the first year of full funding for ESEA Title IV-B and Title IV-C. The law consolidated programs administered by the Office of Education concerning school libraries and learning materials (IV-B) and educational innovation and support (IV-C). Certainly the most controversial part of Title IV-B is the section that unites counseling and testing services with school library media programs. As with many shotgun marriages, the union has not always been a happy one. Mary Barry, Assistant Secretary for Education, testified to the Subcommittee on Education of the Senate Human Resources Committee that Title IV "has resulted in the improvement of school libraries and media centers, and it has led to improvements in teaching techniques and effective forms of participation by nearly all eligible public and private school children and teachers." Also testifying before the Subcommittee, David Bender of the Maryland State Department of Education, Office of Media Services, addressed himself to the provision of the law that allows the funding of guidance and counseling salaries from Title IV-B funds. He stated that this provision places people and materials in competition and should be removed when the law is amended.

Barry alluded to a potential value of Title IV programs—the growing involvement of parents and community-based organizations in the operation of public schools. Volunteers have traditionally been a major resource component for many school library media programs, but their roles have been essentially passive and submissive. This is no longer true. Parents now assert an articulate and demanding role about the quality of the education that the school delivers to their child. School library media programs have shown themselves more comfortable with this phenomenon than have other parts of the educational community. Perhaps their attitude reflects their long and relatively harmonious association with volunteer workers or the openness of attitude that excellent library media programs have always displayed.

Community outreach, a concept more familiar to the public library world, became more important to many school library media programs in 1977. Federal legislation ranging from funding for magnet schools to the Community Employment Training Act required that local education agencies work with other community-based organizations in planning the delivery of their programs and services. Such laws affected and changed the focus of school library media programs.

Parental Involvement. Parental involvement in the operation of school programs manifested itself in other, less pleasing, ways. In such divergent locations as West Virginia, North Dakota, Maryland, and California, the issue of censorship by the public of school library materials was raised. In North Dakota the Drake Public School District actually removed and burned such books as Kurt Vonnegut's *Cats Cradle*. In Montgomery County, Maryland, through legal actions parents challenged the right of the school library media centers to own such titles as *The Learning Tree, A Choice of Weapons, Naomi in the Middle,* and *I Never Loved Your Mind*.

Defending the selection and acquistion of materials solely on the basis of intellectual freedom or professional expertise became an increasingly difficult posture to maintain. Even the American Civil Liberties Union, whose credentials in the defense of individual liberty are impeccable, went on record as supporting the right of parents and students to some measure of protection from compulsory use of instructional materials that they believe infringe on genuine religious and moral beliefs. Some school systems have already adopted this approach. In Littleton, Colorado, citizens serve on textbook review committees whose function it is to examine textbooks prior to their adoption for classroom use. This may presage a new era of citizen involvement in school library media programs. Although the professional's integrity to select and acquire materials that support the needs of a diffuse and sometimes controversial learning program must remain inviolate, it is not unhealthy to have parents involved in a supportive way in knowing why materials are selected and how they are used. Professionals have asserted for years that students and teachers should have a role in selection procedures. Accordingly, parental involvement need not be a threat. It can be an opportunity to involve parents in ways that can lead to increased support for library media programs.

STATE AND REGIONAL

At best during 1977, most state education agencies maintained their efforts to provide leadership for effective library media programs. The states of Maryland, Indiana, Colorado, North Carolina, and Florida—through

School Libraries and Media Centers

their publications, staff development activities, and assertive program leadership—provided examples of excellent state agency programs. Other states, however, lacked even any state agency personnel to work with school and district library media programs. The Title IV-B legislation will hopefully eventually be amended to mandate the use of administrative funds to develop effective state education department leadership personnel for library media programs. There is little cause for optimism that the states, acting on their own, will do this, and a national legislative mandate may be the only realistic method to achieve this critically needed dimension for school library media program development.

District-level supervision for school library media programs experienced similar problems. As many supervisors retired, they were not replaced, or additional and often unrelated duties were assigned to the remaining library media supervisors. There was a diminution of district program support, and abolishment of these key leadership positions became a reality for some.

AASL. Meeting in Detroit in June 1977, the membership of the American Association of School Librarians (AASL) confronted the frustrating reality of how to help professionals who, because of budget restrictions, were losing their jobs. At this meeting AASL's Board of Directors went on record again as supporting the vital need to maintain school library media programs and professional staffing for them. These actions reflect a deep concern with a major problem of the times. But reality dictates that, although effective national association leadership can make more visible and substantive the role of the excellent school library media program, it cannot in the end save these programs from prevailing local conditions.

Alice Fite, the Executive Secretary of AASL, provided a statement of support for maintaining staffing for the elementary school library media program in Philadelphia. The statement affirmed AASL's position that quality library media programs make a difference in the level of excellence achieved by a school district.

The *Survey of School Media Standards*, edited by Milbrey L. Jones, was released by the Office of Libraries and Learning Resources of the Department of Health, Education and Welfare. This document surveys such categories as programs of service, personnel, facilities and equipment, materials, expenditures, and organizations. Although diminished local and state support for school library media programs generally translates to mean little or no adherence to whatever standards have been developed for these programs, their

A statistical survey of U.S. public school libraries and media centers released in 1977 by National Center for Education Statistics, Department of Health, Education, and Welfare, indicated that during the fall 1974:

There were 507,000,000 library books and 68,000,000 titles of audiovisual materials available to students attending the 74,625 public schools that had libraries.

Public schools employed 78,219 certificated library staff members.

Of the 12,840 public schools without libraries, 12,163 were elementary or combined schools.

Mean salaries of public school library staff, by state

State	Mean salary	State	Mean salary
Aggregate United States	$11,219		
Alabama	$ 9,000	Montana	$10,019
Alaska	16,209	Nebraska	8,581
Arizona	11,999	Nevada	13,994
Arkansas	(*)	New Hampshire	10,200
California	16,221	New Jersey	12,000
Colorado	11,544	New Mexico	10,702
Connecticut	12,874	New York	15,428
Delaware	12,123	North Carolina	10,816
District of Columbia	15,344	North Dakota	9,674
Florida	10,290	Ohio	10,654
Georgia	10,599	Oklahoma	9,218
Hawaii	14,769	Oregon	11,812
Idaho	9,844	Pennsylvania	11,853
Illinois	13,061	Rhode Island	11,814
Indiana	12,205	South Carolina	10,050
Iowa	11,227	South Dakota	8,690
Kansas	9,001	Tennessee	9,028
Kentucky	9,930	Texas	9,881
Louisiana	9,165	Utah	11,199
Maine	9,636	Vermont	8,219
Maryland	12,350	Virginia	9,919
Massachusetts	(*)	Washington	(*)
Michigan	14,587	West Virginia	9,371
Minnesota	12,854	Wisconsin	12,655
Mississippi	8,196	Wyoming	10,317
Missouri	9,388		

*Data not available

Source: Nicholas Osso, National Center for Education Statistics, "Statistics of Public School Libraries/Media Centers/Fall 1974," p.2.

existence is nonetheless important. Standards continue to provide the measure whereby library media programs can be evaluated in relationship to the quest for quality education.

Networking. Another significant occurrence that provided some national focus on the needs of school library media programs was the formation of a task force to study the role of the school library media program in networking. The task force, formed by the National Commission on Libraries and Information Science (NCLIS), set a goal of establishing procedures and plans whereby school library media programs would participate in a national networking of all libraries to provide the greatest possible access to information and services for all citizens. A network that would provide access to media and information resources and service, help with selection of material, provide technical services and broadly based support for financing would, of course, be of great benefit to many school library media programs.

To participate in networking, the basic resources of the individual building library media program must be rich enough to be shared with others, but such is not always the case. Boyd Ladd, in a study done for NCLIS, stated that "the acquisitions behavior (of school library media programs) suggests replacement of print materials, accepting some obsolescence, and for nonprint a very modest rate of building in addition to normal replacement." If networking comes to be accepted as a method for doing away with the building-level library media program, irreparable damage might result.

The White House Conference on Libraries and Information Services, whose existence is closely interwoven with NCLIS, is scheduled for October 1979. Essentially a citizens' effort aimed at the widest possible participation by citizens in deciding the future course for all American libraries, the state-level pre-White House Conferences offer school library media programs opportunities to place their needs and expectations before state lay and professional leadership.

At the national level in 1977, an encouraging sign of interdivisional cooperation within ALA and among commercial interests and school library media specialists was the *Survey of the Marketing, Selection and Acquisition of Materials for School Library Media Programs.* The survey, which sampled publishers, producers, wholesalers, distributors, and school library media programs, yielded significant information about the review and evaluation of print and nonprint materials, the resources used in selection of materials, and a host of other timely information.

The average number of direct library material loans was 28 per pupil during the school year.

More than 26 per cent of the public schools spent less than $2 per pupil for books.

The full-time-equivalent certificated library staff comprised more than seven times as many women as men.

Thirty-eight per cent of the schools reported fewer than 1,200 square feet of space assigned for library purposes.

Eighty-three per cent of the school libraries were open 30 or more hours per week.

Certificated library staff, by sex and employment status and by school level and membership

School level and membership	Number of schools with libraries	Certificated staff			
		Men		Women	
		Full-time	Part-time	Full-time	Part-time
All schools	74,625	6,040	3,574	46,218	22,387
Secondary schools	22,315	4,027	1,550	20,687	4,914
2,000 or more	1,409	637	120	2,870	120
1,000 – 1,999	5,297	1,561	531	7,225	670
700 – 999	4,089	852	210	3,944	373
500 – 699	3,169	431	210	2,800	349
300 – 499	3,413	323	78	2,486	652
Under 300	4,938	223	401	1,362	2,750
Elementary and combined schools	52,310	2,013	2,024	25,531	17,473
2,000 or more	44	8	–	94	–
1,000 – 1,999	2,322	340	81	2,327	315
700 – 999	6,770	342	264	5,174	1,047
500 – 699	12,567	789	190	8,123	2,695
300 – 499	16,861	359	776	7,400	5,922
Under 300	13,746	175	713	2,413	7,494

Source: Nicholas Osso, National Center for Education Statistics, "Statistics of Public School Libraries/Media Centers/Fall 1974," p.6.

Volumes of books added and held at end of year, and audiovisual materials held at end of year, by school membership

School membership	Volumes of books		Audiovisual materials held at end of year
	Added during year	Held at end of year	
All schools	37,500,000	506,900,000	68,000,000
2,000 – above	2,600,000	31,400,000	3,600,000
1,000 – 1,999	8,202,000	95,000,000	11,200,000
700 – 999	6,400,000	91,500,000	13,200,000
500 – 699	7,400,000	108,600,000	15,000,000
300 – 499	8,000,000	114,600,000	16,500,000
Under 300	4,900,000	66,800,000	8,500,000

Source: Nicholas Osso, National Center for Education Statistics, "Statistics of Public School Libraries/Media Centers/Fall 1974," p.5.

The Outlook. While anxiety, pessimism, and a concern with what the short- and long-term future may portend for school library media programs are attitudes that prevail in many places, these feelings cannot stand as the dominant mood of 1977. The plenteous days of the 1960's, fueled by generous infusions of federal funds and aggressive plans to create new frontiers for school library media programs, are gone. Yet such expectations as program accountability, productivity, measurable results from program involvement, and program performance budgeting have not destroyed the school library media program, which has continued to function as an integral part of the school's instructional program. In fact, teachers, administrators, and taxpayers can and will fight hard to support and save these programs when they have experienced the true measure of their value to the students' learning opportunities.

The shaking-out process of the mid-1970's has bruised and damaged some library media programs while challenging many firmly held, if casually founded, beliefs about them. The essential core of belief that school library media programs are, more than ever, critical to the learning needs of all students must continue to be a vision. In the end, this vision, more than any fears about what the future may bring, will provide the drive to serve traditional clients—the students, teachers, and the community. This sense of optimism and a willingness to meet new challenges and differing expectations will, after all else passes, remain as the preeminent mood of the school library media profession in 1977.

D. PHILIP BAKER

REFERENCES

American Association of School Librarians, Networking Committee, *The Role of the School Media Program in Networks and Interlibrary Cooperation*, Exhibit #16, ALA 1977 Annual Conference.

American Association of School Librarians, Resources and Technical Services Division, American Library Association, and Association of American Publishers, *Survey of the Marketing, Selection and Acquisition of Materials for School Library Media Programs* (Chicago: ALA, 1977).

American Library Association and Association for Educational Communications and Technology, *Media Programs: District and School* (Chicago: ALA, 1975).

Milbrey Jones, *Survey of School Media Standards* (Washington, D.C.: Government Printing Office, 1977).

Boyd Ladd, *National Inventory of Library Needs, 1977: Resources Needed for Public and Academic Libraries and Public School Library Media Centers* (Washington, D.C.: National Commission on Libraries and Information Science, 1977).

Thomas Walker and Paula Montgomery, *Media Skills: An Instructional Program for Elementary and Middle School Students* (Littleton, Colorado: Libraries Unlimited, 1977).

Marie Win, *The Plug-in Drug: Television, Children, and the Family* (New York: Viking Press, 1977).

Science Information, Division of

The Division of Science Information (DSI), formerly the Office of Science Information Service (OSIS), National Science Foundation (NSF), supports basic and applied information science research. Both types of research are expected to contribute to strengthening information science as a scientific discipline and to providing knowledge for improving communication services.

Programs. During 1977 DSI operated through four main programs. Information science research included fundamental research on information science problems, the development of theoretical bases for new communication systems, the development of performance measures for information systems, and applications of advanced communication technologies for improvement of communication services.

User requirements research included applied research on conditions affecting the use of scientific and engineering information, the impact of organizational policies and practices on the use of scientific information, information requirements of various user groups, the development of curricula and training materials on the use of scientific and technical information resources, and the development of user-responsive and cost-effective information services for scientists and engineers.

Access improvement research included researching ways of getting newly discovered information into the public record; providing access to the public record of science and technology; and identifying, locating, obtaining, and using information.

Management studies and coordination included research on the economic and structural characteristics of the U.S. scientific and technical communication enterprise, national issues affecting scientific and technical communication, and the economics of information transfer; analyses of public issues related to scientific and technical information services; and support for exchange of scientific information with other countries and for U.S. participation in international scientific and technical information organizations.

Projects. During FY 1977, DSI received 150 proposals, of which 62 (41 per cent) were funded. The award decisions rested heavily on assessments provided by hundreds of persons who served as proposal reviewers. The actual amounts awarded totaled approximately $4,900,000 (DSI's budget allocation). This represented nearly 31 per cent of the total amount requested. The average amount of an award was just over $79,000.

Virtually all DSI-sponsored projects are relevant to current library operations or point to future modes of operation. Among those started in FY 1977 and related directly to library activities were the following: Bernard M. Fry and Herbert S. White, Graduate Library School, Indiana University, "Impact of Economic Pressures on American Libraries and Their Decisions Concerning Scholarly and Research Journal Acquisition and Retention"; Jerold Orne, University of North Carolina, "ANSI Committee Z-39: Libraries and Documentation"; Rita G. Lerner, American Institute of Physics, "Assessment of Data Base Searching and Document Delivery via Communications Satellite"; Cheryl A. Casper, Kent State University, "Estimation of Demand for Library Services"; Lawrence G. Livingston and Paul B. Lagueux, Council on Library Resources, "National Bibliographic Control Activities"; Paul B. Kantor, School of Library Science, Case Western Reserve University, "Quantitative Output Measures and Cost of Knowledge"; Douglas S. Price, National Commission on Libraries and Information Science, "Task Force on ANSI Committee Z-39 Activities and Future Directions"; and Donald W. King, King Research, Inc., "Library Photo-Copying Study" (funded through the National Commission on Libraries and Information Science (NCLIS), with support shared by NSF, NCLIS, and the National Commission on New Technological Uses of Copyrighted Works).

(In October 1977, DSI assumed new directions. Emphasis was placed on basic and applied information science research; other changes included establishment of the User Requirements Program and reduction of national and international coordination activities. A new program announcement, *Information Science Research*, (WSF FF-77), was issued in December 1977).

Additional information about the DSI program is available in (1) program announcements for submission of proposals; (2) *Summary of Awards—FY 1976*; (3) *Summary of Awards—FY 1977*; and (4) *Bibliography of Reports from DSI Projects*. For copies, write to the Division of Science Information, National Science Foundation, 1800 G Street, N.W., Washington, D.C. 20550.

LEE G. BURCHINAL

Security Systems

"A Tenant Checks Out, Leaving 7,000 Library Books" read a caption in the New York *Times* for August 29, 1977. According to the article, a building superintendent in Queens found more than 7,000 technical books from public libraries as far away as Chicago in an apartment he managed. The tenant had left several months before, leaving the books scattered around the apartment in piles and in shopping bags. Stories such as this emphasize the need for improved library security.

Checkpoint Technology. The major manufacturers of library security systems reported gains in sales, improvements in technology, and, for Checkpoint Systems, Inc., favorable government action during 1977. The Federal Communications Commission (FCC) adopted an amendment to Part 15 of the FCC rules to allow the operation of wide-band swept radio frequency equipment used by the Checkpoint Mark II system; the amendment took effect on September 12. Checkpoint had been operating under a temporary waiver of FCC regulations since December 13, 1974. Since that time the FCC had given considerable study to comments received from other antipilferage manufacturing firms and to the fact that it had received no complaints of interference by the Checkpoint Mark II system. Under the new amendment the FCC had ruled that existing Checkpoint Mark II equipment and expansion of that equipment are acceptable on the condition that any interference complained of must be eliminated immediately. New installations of Checkpoint Mark II equipment must be modified to operate on a center frequency of 4.5 MHz (existing systems operate at 5.0 MHz).

New technology introduced by Checkpoint during 1977 included a refined circuit design to simplify installation and improve operating reliability; a hand-held device to insert Checklabels in pockets in six seconds; an improved entrance/exit gate; color-coordinated sensing screen bases to match existing library decor; and a method to protect headsets, phonodiscs, and other audiovisual equipment. Checkpoint Systems has been spun off from its parent, Logistics Industries Corporation, and is now an independent, publicly owned company.

Other Manufacturers. Gaylord Company, responsible for the Gaylord/Magnavox System,

SCMAI: see Mediation, Arbitration, and Inquiry

Security Systems

the newest book security system, reports that it now has 52 installations throughout the country. During 1977 the detector tag was improved with the addition of a tab pull to release the backing paper. Detector strips are now available to protect noncirculating magazines and reference books or for use in the bypass system. Gaylord also lowered the price of the system.

The Knogo Corporation has initiated an aggressive advertising campaign for its book detection system. The company developed a four-inch detection strip for use both in the spines and gutters of books and for bookplates and pockets. Semicircular targets for use directly on records and tape cassettes have been patented and are available.

The major news from General Nucleonics, Inc., manufacturer of the Sentronic ScanScope security system, was the issuance of a pamphlet entitled *The Comparator: The Inside Story on Theft Detection Systems*. According to the preface it is "a comprehensive and factual guide in the selection of a theft detection system for those concerned with the protection of library resources as well as for the safety and welfare of the public and the employee." The pamphlet begins with a warning to prospective customers of the dangers of low levels of electromagnetic radiation (EMR). It cites various studies and points out the strictness of some European countries in their low level of tolerance of EMR. The pamphlet points out that Sentronic and its licensee, Book Mark, sold by Library Bureau, operate on a magnetic principle and are the only systems free from EMR. The pamphlet is available from General Nucleonics, Inc., P.O. Box 116, Brunswick, Ohio 44212.

The 3M Company, manufacturer of the Tattle-Tape and Spartan systems, reported that 1977 was a year of growth. The company has more than 1,500 systems installed worldwide. Improvements in library security systems as well as a continuing and widespread acceptance of the systems as a deterrent to costly theft of library property were apparent during 1977. — NANCY H. KNIGHT

Disasters

A variety of disasters resulting from both natural and unnatural causes were reported during 1977.

Fire, Bombs, and Water Damage. A multi-million-dollar fire at the University of Toronto Sanford Fleming Laboratory destroyed about 10 per cent of the 80,000-volume collection. Easily replaceable books were discarded, and approximately 500 rare and valuable books were freeze-dried in an attempt to restore them eventually.

The Rhodes Memorial Library in Gideon, Missouri, was completely destroyed by a fire caused by a faulty dryer in an adjacent coin-operated laundromat. It was estimated that water destroyed approximately 50 per cent of the 30,000-volume collection.

An explosion at the University of Pittsburgh's Langley Library resulted in two deaths, damage to library furnishings and bookstacks, and water damage to many books. About 3,000 water-soaked books were put in a nearby freezer and procedures were established for drying and cleaning them.

A pipe bomb exploded in the fountain in front of the New York Public Library on 42nd Street. Damage was limited to the fountain statue and some of the marble facing on the building. Several hundred staff members, however, were evacuated while a search for other bombs was conducted. At Case Western Reserve's Music Library water from a leaking toilet caused damage to some rare music materials.

The Cambria County Library in Johnstown, Pennsylvania, suffered a double disaster during the summer of 1977. After it was severely damaged by flood waters, HUD's Federal Disaster Assistance Administration ruled that the library was not eligible for federal disaster relief because it was not an educational facility as defined by the Code of Federal Regulations.

Vermin. Thirty-seven recently imported books in the Beinecke Rare Book and Manuscript Library at Yale University were discovered to be infested with a borer bug previously undetected in America. A Yale entomologist recommended a deep-freeze technique whereby the books are wrapped in plastic and held at −20° F for three days. The cold kills insects, eggs, and larvae without injury to the books.

Collapsed Shelves. The shelves collapsed in the basement of the Penrose Public Library in Colorado Springs, Colorado, causing 20,000 volumes to crash to the floor. The library director determined that the one-eighth-inch screws and plastic anchors were inadequate to secure the shelf braces to the concrete wall. The resulting cleanup took four months.

Theft. A total of 5,880 missing books were discovered in a Flushing, New York, apartment. The earliest date stamped on the books was 1952, and the latest was in the mid-1960's. Books came from the libraries of New York, Queens, Brooklyn, Cooper Union, Greenwich, Connecticut, and from other libraries as far away as Florida State University.

The San Francisco Public Library has suffered more than 50 burglaries, most conducted with keys. Items missing included money from coin-operated copying machines, fine boxes, and other sources of ready case.

More than 500 volumes from 15 multivolume sets of reference works on the 18th-century romance have disappeared from Harvard University Libraries.

At least $10,000 worth of historic manuscripts have been stolen from the New York Public

Library. David Zuckerman, who apparently convinced library officials that he was a philatelist, is accused of the theft. He had secured a six-month pass to the documents room, which he visited regularly and where he allegedly tore and cut items out of volumes.

The Carnegie Library of Pittsburgh reported the theft of 11 music scores, 10 of which are rare and valuable. The loss is estimated at approximately $3,000. Three paintings valued at $15,000 were stolen from the Harwood Foundation Library in Taos, New Mexico. Winslow Homer prints were cut from 19th-century journals in a number of Northeast academic libraries. Cornell lost 156 prints and Harvard lost 45.

The Charlestown Library Society, a private subscription library in South Carolina, reported that Audubon prints valued at over $350,000 were missing. The theft was discovered only after a closed, normally locked case was found unlocked.

The Royal Library in Copenhagen reported 21 missing books including a 16th-century volume illustrated by Albrecht Durer. Interpol agents were called in, but Danish officials suspect that the thief may be one of the library's 400 staff members.

As a result of such disasters and thefts a number of libraries have established emergency procedures to deal with unexpected crises. A study prepared by the Research Group of Predicasts, Inc., in Cleveland, predicts that spending for protective services, deterrent and monitoring equipment, and fire control devices will triple between 1975 and 1990 and approach the $13,000,000 mark. The research organization predicts that protective services will be the largest product group with revenues approaching $6,000,000, deterrent equipment will show above average growth, and monitoring and detection equipment sales will grow the fastest of all categories.

The Society of American Archivists has introduced an archival security consultant service to help repositories plan and carry out security measures. Consultants with knowledge of both archival administration and security will help in areas such as establishing staff security procedures, designing reading rooms, and convincing the public of the seriousness of the problem. This consultant service is supported by a National Endowment for the Humanities grant and is to be operated on a cost-sharing basis.

OCLC. The Ohio College Library Center (OCLC) has taken precautions against major disasters. At least three times a week the Center makes tape and disc copies of the entire union catalog. Five copies of the catalog exist; one copy is stored in a fireproof vault, and others are in a fireproof warehouse and an underground storage site outside Ohio. In addition, an electronic security system allows only those persons with appropriate security clearance into the headquarters. The equipment is protected by an automatic fire control system that includes smoke detectors, sprinkler systems, and fire walls.

OCLC plans to develop an independent electric power supply in the event of a power blackout. The need for an independent power source was emphasized in 1977 when a lightning bolt brought the on-line system to a halt for several hours. Operations were also stopped when a leak in the roof required the machines to be shut down and covered with plastic sheets to prevent them from being damaged.

Death. Security programs can have their hazards, however. An elderly woman trapped in a remote corridor died in the Boston Public Library as a result of security deficiencies. She had wandered into an emergency exit corridor and had been unable to open an emergency door. Investigators suggested that the alarm signal indicating that someone was in the corridor had worked but that no one had heard it. To save money, the central alarm system had been turned off four years previously.

NANCY H. KNIGHT

Serials

Resource sharing, networking, and copyright concerns joined the increasing costs of serial subscriptions and the expanded thinking regarding a National Periodicals Center to constitute some of the 1977 highlights in serials.

The transitional and fluctuating state of many activities typified 1977. The new copyright law, which so intimately involves the acquisition and lending of serials, did not officially take effect until 1978. A great many preliminary steps were taken in 1977, however, to make the transition as gentle as possible. Although there is some documentation as to what form the proposed National Periodicals Center might take, the matter still retains a good many amorphous qualities. The state of networking and computerized control of serial sharing and bibliographical matters is some distance from being indelibly outlined. Jockeying for position in various areas was much in evidence during 1977, particularly among the large research libraries. CONSER (CONversion of SERials) moved forward in an interesting and useful manner. Now under the management of the Library of Congress, CONSER received assurances of continued and expanded support from the Ohio College Library Center (OCLC).

COST OF SERIALS

Serial budgets in 1977 again were subjected to close scrutiny as prices continued to rise, although at a rate somewhat lower than in 1976. The annual cost index compiled by Norman B. Brown indicated a 9.2 per cent increase for 1977 as compared with the 12.9 per cent increase in 1976. For 1977, Brown examined 3,218 titles and published the results in his article "Price Indexes for 1977: U.S. Periodical and Serial Services" in *Library Journal* (July 1977). The periodical that cost $22.52 in 1976 cost $24.59 in 1977. Serial services, on the other hand, increased a fraction more than did serials in 1977. An examination of 1,432 U.S. serial services showed a 9.9 per cent increase over the 1976 prices. Thus, the serial service purchased in 1976 for $129.47 cost $142.27 in 1977.

An article by Richard De Gennaro, "Escalating Journal Prices: Time to Fight Back" in *American Libraries* (February 1977) pointed out sharply the horrendous budget problems created by the proliferation of scholarly journals. Coupled with differential and inflated pricing by some publishers, the situation serves to keep libraries financially backed to the wall.

A comparative study of periodical prices was done again in 1977 by F.F. Clasquin in his article "Periodical Prices: 1975-77 Update," published in the October 1, 1977, issue of *Library Journal*. Among other things, the study indicated that multiple-year rates from some publishers still provide the opportunity to save in serial costs but that these opportunities are becoming more rare. The development of "average" prices is a tricky matter, and work continues to establish an authority, possibly through CONSER activities, that will, as Clasquin puts it in his article, "select and maintain groups of titles in each subject class as the data base to be used in the annual price study."

In the July 29 issue of *Science*, Clasquin and Jackson B. Cohen provided a profile of the problems faced by academic libraries in using their limited funds to supply the science technology community with the serials it requires. They indicated that special financial support for the exorbitantly expensive journals in this area is needed through federal grants in the same manner that expensive scientific equipment is funded.

Serial Use. A study of the use and costs of monographs and serials conducted by a team of investigators at the University of Pittsburgh is nearing completion and has produced information on the use of serials in a large research-centered operation. The Pittsburgh study, begun in 1975 and slated to be completed in December 1977, was made possible through grants from the National Science Foundation. It provides some insight into the patterns of use and nonuse of serials, particularly in the area of science and technology (physics, engineering, and life sciences, including psychology). The study basically shows that many journals subscribed to are used infrequently and some not at all, especially as the up-to-dateness of the journal issue fades. In this respect, the study provides confirmation of some basic principles already known about journal use and nonuse. Thomas G. Galvin's and Allen Kent's article on "Uses of a University Library Collection: A Progress Report on a Pittsburgh Study" in the November 15 issue of the *Library Journal* presents an important summary of the study.

Another look at the expenditures of funds for collection development is being set up at Cornell University. The problems involved with the acquisition of serial and other library material will be surveyed through a study being conducted by Cornell University Libraries and supported by a $240,000 grant from the Andrew Mellon Foundation. The intent of the grant to Cornell is "to develop a long-term plan for the future allocation of resources at the libraries and for the management of collection growth and costs." The project will probably require about two and a half years.

NATIONAL PERIODICALS SYSTEM

As the CONSER project continues to evolve and grow, additional nuances accompany the action. Joseph W. Price, Chief of the Library of Congress MARC Development Office, referred to CONSER as being "capable of providing the glue in a national program of serial access," according to the *LC Information Bulletin* for April 1.

In accordance with the goal set by the National Commission on Libraries and Information Science (NCLIS), the National Periodicals System, a segment of the total program, is governed by the general guidelines adopted for the overall operation. These were stated in the NCLIS publication *Toward a National Program for Library and Information Services: Goals for Action* (Washington, D.C.: 1975):

> "To eventually provide every individual in the United States with equal opportunity of access to that part of the total information resource which will satisfy the individual's educational, working, cultural and leisure-time needs and interests regardless of the individual's location, social or physical condition or level of intellectual achievement."

Average Cost of Periodicals and Serial Services							
	1970-71	1971-72	1972-73	1973-74	1974-75	1975-76	1976-77
U.S. Periodicals	$ 11.66	$ 13.23	$ 16.20	$ 17.71	$ 19.94	$ 22.52	$ 24.59
U.S. Serials Services	90.95	95.38	103.45	109.31	118.03	129.47	142.27

Source: *Library Journal*, July issue of each year except for 1976 (August).

In an effort to examine the specifics of this charge, the NCLIS Task Force on a National Periodicals System prepared the report *Effective Access to the Periodical Literature: A National Program*, published by the Superintendent of Documents in April 1977. The views and recommendations were those of the Task Force and did not necessarily reflect an official policy or position of NCLIS.

Plans for the National Periodicals Center focus on a three-level program, with the Library of Congress to be responsible for developing and managing the Center. According to the Task Force, the levels would be structured as follows:

Level 1—Local, state and regional library systems responsible for meeting a substantial portion of routine needs for periodicals.

Level 2—A comprehensive periodicals collection dedicated for lending and photocopy service to meet the majority of unfulfilled requests derived from Level 1. Initially, a single National Periodicals Center would be developed, but experience and demand may warrant more than one.

Level 3—Existing national libraries and other unique collections to back up the first two levels.

It is planned that the Center will be operational in late 1978 or early 1979 and will have approximately 50,000 current subscriptions. Projections as to the number of requests that will be filled by the National Periodicals Center are as follows: 1978—300,000; 1979—375,000; 1980—469,000; 1981—586,000; 1982—732,000. The initial collection will be dependent on the resources of the Center for Research Libraries (CRL); Chemical Abstracts Services (CAS); and the Universal Serials and Book Exchange (USBE), with assistance from academic and research libraries. It is estimated that the operating budget for the first year will be about $3,500,000.

A National Periodicals System Advisory Committee, comprised of nine people selected from recommendations made by such organizations as the American Library Association, Association of Research Libraries, and the Special Libraries Association, will serve to coordinate the various elements involved in setting up the Center. Thus, the Library of Congress and its Advisory Committee will work together in developing and designing the facilities.

A detailed plan for the Center is in preparation, with CLR in the role of overseer. The plan will include recommendations for equipment, site, staffing, and prices. C. Lee Jones of the Health Science Library at Columbia University is to be the project director, and Warren Haas will oversee the work for CLR as well as several other foundations that are assisting with financial support in preparing the plan. An issue yet unresolved is the impact that the new copyright law may have on the National Periodicals Center. It will be imperative for NCLIS to work closely with the Commission on Technological Uses of Copyrighted Works (CONTU) if the Center is to set a solid example of a streamlined national network for sharing serial resources on a grand scale.

CONSER/OCLC

CONSER, which began in 1974 with a goal of developing a data base of 200,000 to 300,000 records, continued to grow in 1977. There are now 15 institutions participating: Library of Congress; National Library of Canada; National Library of Medicine; National Agricultural Library; Boston Theological Institute; University of California, Systemwide Administration; Cornell University; University of Florida; Harvard University; U.S. Department of the Interior; University of Minnesota; New York State University; Ohio College Library Center; State University of New York; and Yale University.

The CONSER data base has more than

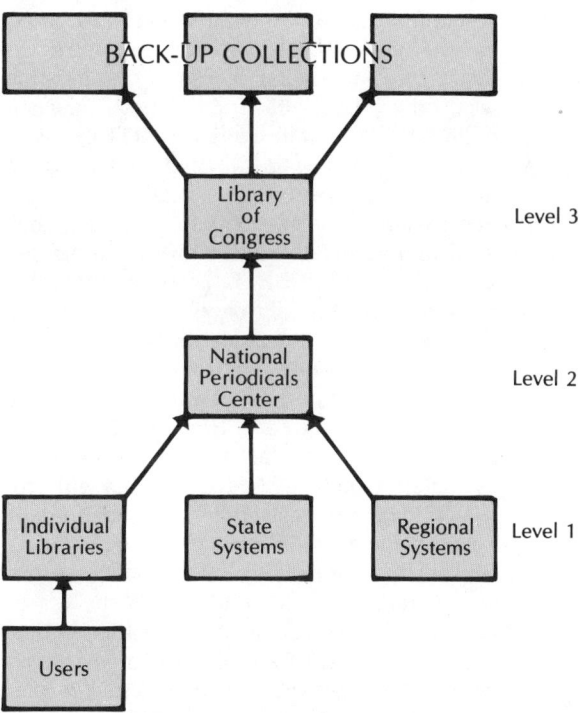

Flow of requests in proposed national periodicals system

(Taken from Effective Access to the Periodical Literature: A National Program, page 43 Prepared by Task Force on a National Periodicals System National Commission on Libraries and Information Science, April 1977)

165,000 records, of which about 40,000 have been distributed on tape through the MARC Distribution Service-Serials after having been authenticated by the CONSER centers. In conjunction with keeping procedures up to date, a revision of the *CONSER Manual* funded by CLR is being done by an outside serials consultant. A revision of the *MARC Serials Editing Guide: CONSER Edition* is also under way. This revision will incorporate modifications to the MARC serials format and additional interpretations needed for the on-line CONSER conventions.

Under the management of the Library of Congress, CONSER I is using the on-line facilities provided by OCLC with emphasis on buildilng up the present operation and striving for greater efficiency. It is planned that the next phase, CONSER II, will provide for the incorporation of more detailed and expanded information on locations and holdings on serial records. Present estimates are that it will be a number of years before the CONSER files will contain holding records detailed enough to handle interlibrary loans at a peak operational level.

The development of a low-cost, efficient method of linking local and regional holdings statements to CONSER was begun this year in a continuing effort to expand this automated national serials base. The prototype of a national location system received its impetus when the Minnesota Interlibrary Telecommunications Exchange (MINITEX) was granted $25,000 by CLR to plan a pilot project for the development of a national serials location system. It is planned to bring together local and regional serial holdings statements and link these to CONSER, the national data base. Because the Library of Congress is taking over the management of CONSER from CLR, it will be involved in the project.

An on-line holdings file will be created by using the location data from the *Minnesota Union List of Serials* (MULS), one of the bases used in developing CONSER. This file will provide a means to test on-line maintenance of serial holdings and compare it with batch mode or manual holdings operations. Location information from the *Indiana Union List of Serials*, a five-volume nonstandard list with a single supplement, will be put in standard form and merged with MULS to create a common on-line data base. This data, in turn, can be linked to the National Serials Data Program (NSDP) machine-readable records, to CONSER, or to the National Union Catalog by such access points as the International Standard Serial Number (ISSN) or the LC card number, or to the OCLC base by the OCLC control number. This file of location information will be maintained by a minicomputer with an online update capability. *Linkage* is the all-important word in this effort to bring together the scattered location and holdings information that abounds in the numerous independent networks and thousands of local, state, and regional union lists of serials.

During the year OCLC increased its support of the CONSER project by installing additional equipment to improve the response time and the overall capability of the CONSER operation. This renewed effort on the part of OCLC was cited in the *OCLC Newsletter*, No. 111. The support will be continued until CLR, the Council's CONSER Advisory Group, and the Library of Congress indicate that the body of machine-readable serials records produced is essentially complete. In addition, OCLC has announced that charges for computer file memory space occupied by CONSER records, along with charges for CONSER utilization of OCLC staff and central installations, was to be discontinued as of December 1977. It is intended that the same relationships that CONSER participants and OCLC have had over the past two years will continue between OCLC and the project's Library of Congress management. OCLC will make exceptions to general policies in order to facilitate CONSER activities. As of October there reportedly were more than 200,000 serial records in the OCLC system, but not all of these had been authenticated as a part of the CONSER project.

OCLC's progress in the serials check-in module deserves particular mention. According to its 1976-77 annual report, one of the objectives of OCLC is to make available the serials control function to participating libraries within the next three years. A growing number of libraries are using OCLC's serials check-in module, which provides the capabilities of checking in, recording holdings, claiming, binding, and predicting the appearance of the next issue based on the serial's frequency. As of January 1977 approximately 150 institutions were using the OCLC subsystem, and plans for expanding the number were under way. Two videotapes on OCLC's serials control subsystem, "The Check-In Record" and "Automated Check-In," have been produced by and are available from Kent State University Libraries. The serials control subsystem, hardly removed from its infancy, already provides some idea as to the problems networking must face to prepare for the "sophistication" yet to come.

Serials and Networking. As mentioned above, several steps toward sharing have been taken. These include the activities of OCLC and CONSER; the designation of the Library of Congress by NCLIS to develop and operate the National Periodicals Center; and a variety of related and fundamental activities such as the development of NSDP and ISSN.

The need to share resources and the heavy

financial problems that have assailed libraries in recent years was brought home quite soundly in Richard De Gennaro's award-winning paper, "Copyright, Resource Sharing, and Hard Times," in *American Libraries* (September 1977).

The emphasis on networking and its importance to the bibliographical control of serials is growing rapidly, and as it does, the number of articles, talks, and general communiques on the subject also grows. The June issue of the *Journal of Library Automation* (*JOLA*) emphasized the plethora of semantic problems involved by presenting a wide variety of viewpoints ranging from the idea of a monolithic solidarity to the concern over separate operations that lend themselves to a state of general confusion.

The papers in this issue represented the proceedings of the February 1977 Information Science and Automation Division institute on the subject of a national bibliographic network. Although the papers did not center on serials as a particular concern, they did bring out much that applies to this form of publication in relation to networking. Among the presentations in the *JOLA* issue were "Network Brew: Hints from a Misty Crystal Ball," by Joseph A. Rosenthal; "The Role of the Library of Congress in the National Bibliographic Network," by Henriette D. Avram; "The National Bibliographic Network: The View from the Research Library," by John G. Lorenz; "Getting It All Together: International Cataloging Cooperation and Networks," by Lucia J. Rather and Peter J. De La Garza; and "The NCLIS View—A Full-Service Network," by Alphonse F. Trezza, Executive Director of NCLIS.

The preliminary edition of *Toward a National Library and Information Service Network: The Library Bibliographic Component*, edited by Henriette D. Avram and Lenore S. Maruyama, was issued in 1977 and is available from the Subscriber Accounts Unit of LC's Cataloging Distribution Service.

Serials Cataloging. According to Joseph Howard, Director of the Processing Department, among the primary goals of the Library of Congress in serials cataloging during the next several years will be the creation of an on-line catalog in conjunction with the closing of the card catalog in 1980. The *Library of Congress Information Bulletin* (November 4, 1977), however, states that among the points LC had identified for consideration, "the problems of serials and the freezing of the catalogs have yet to be fully addressed at the Library."

During 1977 the LC serials cataloging policy was revised to provide, if possible, the complete publishing history of a serial title rather than a record of the Library's holdings of a title. LC's Serial Division is continuing its project of cataloging the newspaper holdings of the Library of Congress. As of June more than 200 titles had been added to the CONSER data base and 600 more had manuscript copy completed.

In its October *Newsletter*, OCLC announced plans to produce "...catalog cards for serials cataloged on-line by participating libraries. The exact day when serials card production will begin will be announced via log-in message, and after that date, PRODUCE command on a record will result in printed catalog cards. OCLC intends to print retrospective catalog cards for serial records PRODUCED before implementation of serial catalog card production, but will first contact libraries that used the PRODUCE function for serials to confirm that cards are still desired."

In an effort to provide assistance in using OCLC cataloging information, *A Serials Workbook: A Problem-Solving Manual for OCLC Serial Catalogers* written by E. Sue Weber is available from the Libraries of the State University of New York at Stony Brook. The 83-page book provides answers to the practical problems encountered in on-line serials cataloging.

Miscellany. During 1977 R.R. Bowker Company published *Sources of Serials*, an international directory of corporate authors and publishers. This sizable volume containing 1,547 pages brings together all serial publishers and corporate authors listed in *Ulrich's International Periodicals Directory, Irregular Serials and Annuals*, and *Ulrich's Quarterly*. The total assemblage includes 63,000 publishers and corporate authors organized under 181 countries and encompasses a listing of 90,000 current serial titles issued by them. It is the most in-depth and comprehensive listing of serials and their sources that has been developed in recent times. This machine-readable file, which will be updated, provides access to serials information through a number of approaches and will be of significant help in various areas of serials work including cataloging, claiming, collection development, ordering, and selection. According to Emery Koltay, Director of the Bowker Serials Bibliography, "The use of *Sources of Serials* is limited solely by the imagination of the user."

The master pages for the 680-page catalog of ISSN (International Standard Serials Numbers) and corresponding Key Titles were run off at the Library of Congress by the Cataloging Distribution Service's automated Data Processing Office. This *ISSN Key Title Register* is a Government Printing Office publication and will contain a "Register Section" of 8,396 entries arranged by ISSN as well as an index by Key Titles, variant titles, and authors.

In September two meetings of the IFLA Section on Serial Publications were held with Marie Louise Bossuat, Conservateur en Chef of the Centre Bibliographique Nationale in Paris, presiding. Of major importance was the attention brought to the first standard edition of the *International Standard Bibliographic Description for Serials* (ISBDS) and the application of it by cataloging units. This first standard edition incorporates numerous modifications to the edition published in 1974. Several papers were presented, among them "The ISDS International Register of Serial Publications" by Marie Rosenbaum, Director of the International Centre of the International Serials Data Systems.

During 1977, as in the past, some serial services revised their approach to bibliographical control. An announcement was made in July that the Public Affairs Information Service data bases were to become available for on-line searching on the Lockheed Dialog system. *Chemical Abstracts* advised they would be charging $4,200 for their service and that they expected to keep this price for 1979. H.W. Wilson reworked its coverage for the *Reader's Guide to Periodical Literature*. These are but a few examples of the types of revamping that occur each year.

The newest journal in the field, *The Serials Librarian* under the editorship of Peter Gellatly, continued to grow and gain stature as the best specific source for information on serialism.

The increasing importance of the deacquisition of serials escalated as budgets stabilized and serial prices continued to rise. Not only were titles cancelled, but the use of serials in microform grew more attractive in terms of subscription costs, space utilization, usage of retrospective volumes, and binding costs. Members of the Committee on Micrographics of the Depository Library Council to the Public Printer were presented with a lengthy report in October. This document carried information that as many as 6,000 non-GPO documents could be converted to microfiche, which would encompass many serial publications. It was pointed out, moreover, that significant cost reductions were possible if microfiche were used for certain categories of documents including annual reports, Census Bureau documents, Senate and House appropriations hearings, and all bills. Although these matters are in an exploratory stage, there is a significant trend toward using microforms where only hard copy would have been considered a few years ago. Commercially, microforms of serials are gaining recognition, and one publisher has reached the stage where a catalog of secondhand microfilms is being made available. The micrographics industry is growing in the private and public sectors. Interest in this form is on the upswing, particularly where serials are concerned.

WILLIAM H. HUFF

Social Responsibilities

The social responsibility role of librarians, information specialists, and libraries has grown enormously in recent years, and social responsibility involvement is found in almost every sphere of human endeavor. If one attempts to develop a balance sheet for the library world in 1977, some would say that there were more positive events to place on the credit side and others would argue that the debit side of the ledger is filled with significant setbacks. In spite of one or two setbacks in the library and information science world, significant social responsibility responses occurred in 1977 and are cited here. It is not possible to report all of them here.

PUBLIC LIBRARIES

Public libraries continue to lead in social responsibility as reported in the literature and reflected in professional conference programming. One could argue that this is true because of the diverse clientele they serve; that is not the whole story, however, for other types of libraries are also following a social responsibility course of action.

Because of fiscal problems, large numbers of libraries have lost staff by attrition. Rather than close branches in many public library systems, staff members have agreed to "pairing plans" under which they work at more than one branch. This happened in the Brooklyn Public Library, Queens Borough Public Library, and the New York Public Library systems. The District of Columbia Public Library reported that despite a severe loss of staff, the library staff generously agreed to a program that would "keep all branches open on Saturday without closing *all* branch libraries on a weekday." The regionalization has improved efficiency and increased quality of service.

The Chicago Public Library inaugurated new services to meet the special needs of several of its constituencies. Emphasis was on the cultural and educational enrichment of life in the downtown Chicago Loop area as well as in several neighborhoods in the city. Alice Scott indicated that "The former Central Library building was renovated and opened as a new Cultural Center with refurbished marble, coffered ceilings and Tiffany designed domes and decorative mosaics. In addition to being the setting for cultural events the Center also houses the Fine Arts Collection of art and music and a Popular Library. At the dedication ceremonies Commissioner Reich emphasized that it is a people place, pointing out that the guiding philosophy behind the

Cultural Center is to create exhibits and programs for people to see, touch and hear as well as books to read. CPL's social responsibility for an informed citizenry was expanded through the addition of the Information Bank to the Central Library Information Center. The Information Bank makes available for a fee computerized searches of data from the New York Times and other current events publications. Community life at the local level was enriched by the opening of the Lorraine Hansberry Branch as a part of the new Martin Luther King Community Center. Local residents can conveniently make use of both social welfare and library services within the same building. Another noteworthy new service was the development of a Black genealogy collection at the Vivian G. Harsh Collection of Afro-American History and Literature at the Carter G. Woodson Regional Library. The collection brings together materials for use of those of Afro-American background interested in tracing their family history."

Job Information Centers that have been established in many public libraries in New York State continue to offer invaluable service to unemployed citizens. The Rochester (New York) Public Library Job Information Center began its third year in September. During the year it moved from service to individuals to group service through two programs: (1) a series of video-taped showings on job seeking and a series on jobs and careers via talks and discussions led by personnel from community agencies; (2) the JIC expanded via satellites in other libraries in Newark, Canadaigua, Geneseo, and Warsaw in the Pioneer Library System.

Several library systems are working with the Internal Revenue Service in providing a unique service to their users. An example of such cooperation is at the Rochester Public Library. In cooperation with IRS it offers the facilities and services of four inner-city branches for specific periods of Income Tax Counseling for residents.

The Port Washington (New York) Public Library continued its many social action projects that are blue ribbon examples of what libraries can do in the area of social responsibilities. For four consecutive weeks, on Tuesday afternoons, the library sponsored Teen Baby Sitting Workshops; topics discussed included Basic Child Care, First Aid and Handling Health Emergencies, Handling Emergencies, and Ideas on Entertaining Children. Other forums and seminars offered were "A Musical Salute to the United Nations, A Career Planning Forum, Discussions on Single Parent Families and The Step Parent Family, Children and Television, Consciousness Raising for Women, and the Opportunities and Challenges of Single Life in Port Washington.

The Singles Night Forum has led to the formation of a Singles Club that meets once a month in the library.

Service to Institutions. Service to persons who are in correctional facilities is continuing as well as being initiated in many public libraries across the country. While service is growing in a number of libraries in the country, this is still a tremendous underdeveloped area and may be considered on the debit side of the 1977 ledger. On the credit side, however, the Detroit Public Library, the District of Columbia Public Library, the Los Angeles County Public Library, and the Chautauqua-Cattaraugus Library System (New York) institutional programs are persevering and flourishing.

One of the most heartwarming reports in 1977 came from Lillian Lopez, Coordinator of Special Services, New York Public Library. NYPL works with 10 institutions in Manhattan, the Bronx, Staten Island, and Rickers Island. Lopez reported:

> This is the first year we have been permitted to use funds to support the salary of a full time librarian to work on the project which has certainly increased our sensitivity to inmate readers, and hopefully greatly improve the quality of services.

"Before ordering materials we arranged meetings with inmates to ask what they wanted from the library...their requests were not unusual. Tastes range from cowboy and detective stories to philosophy and religious history. Among adult men current events topics are popular, while young people prefer music and sports. In short, tastes of those inside and outside prison do not differ dramatically. Of course, library users are a small minority of the prison population. In general, inmates were not part of the libaray's clientele on the outside. Little is done in prison libraries to change their attitude. Part of our job is to help spread the word about the benefits of library use. We have tried to serve special interest groups also. We brought a Chinese librarian from Chatham Square branch to Rikers Island to speak to Chinese inmates and find out what Chinese material they would like. . . .

Social Responsibilities

Children from a day care center make a weekly visit to the Topeka Public Library for a story hour in the children's department.

Social Responsibilities

"Among these teenage male inmates sports and action films are naturally most popular. On several occasions we tried slipping in films about drugs; social problems in the United States and the world; and films about different cultures. The most successful program by far has been the continuing showing of the 12 part film *Roots*, borrowed from the Central Harlem Project...."

Bilingual Programs. Public libraries have become increasingly responsive to the needs of their bilingual residents. The Chicago Public Library Informacion Center operates El Centro de Information (Spanish Information Center). This service is staffed by Spanish-speaking personnel and was initiated for those who can converse only in Spanish. Most of the inquiries concern information that will aid in adjustment to urban life, such as citizenship procedures and locations of English-as-a-second language classes. The Rochester Public Library's Biblioteca Manuel Alonso (Spanish Language Library) reached its fifth birthday in 1977, and LSCA funding received during the course of the year would support the opening of a satellite operation on the west side of Rochester to serve the Spanish speaking population in that area of the city. There are many outstanding bilingual programs in public libraries. One excellent program that must be mentioned is at the East Los Angeles County Library. One of the most notable Hispanic reference colections is located at the Hunt's Point Regional Library of the New York Public Library.

The South Bronx Project funded for the last decade from LSCA funds began in 1967. Materials have been acquired in Spanish and English relevant to the Hispanic community. The special value of this collection is that it is a strong bilingual reference collection designed to serve the entire South Bronx area through nine neighborhood libraries. While it is a great repository to serve the large Puerto Rican community, students of Spanish and Latin American Literature and History use this extensive reference and research resource extensively.

Community Information and Referral Services. Access to all kinds of information and resources has become the hallmark of American public librarianship. Libraries that pioneered in this service, such as the Detroit Public Library, continue in a leadership role among public libraries. They have been joined by many other libraries in the country. Several libraries are publishing what they call *A People to People Index*; the Schenectady County Public Library (New York) published its *Index* in 1977. Wonja Brucker of SCPL reported that "the index covers more than 100 subjects and offers the volunteer services of about 80 persons who are experts in fields ranging from beer and wine-making to bird watching." SCPL worked cooperatively with the Schenectady County Chamber of Commerce in developing the *Index*. It was described as "an educational network established to facilitate exchange of knowledge." The Chautauqua-Cattaraugus Library System published its second edition of a *Directory of Human Resources* in 1977, and Murray L. Bob, the Director, in his comment on the importance of this tool to support community information and referral service, declared, "this represents an interesting experimental effort to extract reference information from people as well as books." The District of Columbia Public Library launched a new community information service in a cooperative effort with the libraries of the public junior and senior high schools and the libraries of the University of the District of Columbia in October 1977.

OTHER LIBRARIES

College and University Libraries. The social responsibility role of college and university libraries is most visible through their participation in library networks and consortia and in the lending of materials and resources beyond their campuses to users of all types of libraries. Many have provided their users access to data-base services for a fee. One of the most dramatic reports issued during 1977 came from R. Dean Galloway, Library Director, California State College, Stanislaus. The library began automated data-base searching during the fall term. Galloway stated that "we shall *not* charge fees to students. The reference librarian will determine whether or not such a search would be helpful in solving the student's problem. If the decision is affirmative the library will absorb the cost...." For interlibrary loan, the library also absorbs the costs that are sometimes charged by libraries of major universities.

Community college libraries have joined forces with public libraries to respond to the information needs of citizens. In the assembling of resources in nonprint formats, it appears that community college libraries throughout the country are miles ahead of most of the traditional liberal arts colleges and the universities. Regarding the massive revolution in the various technologies of communication, Irwin S. Stein, Director of the Corning Community College, Arthur A. Houghton, Jr. Library, mused that "libraries must recognize this facet of their social responsibility if they are to preserve their viability as institutions freely serving society; libraries must consider home-based video recording, communication satellites, videodiscs, capable of storing and instantly retrieving 30 times as much information as today's magnetic discs...." To provide resources to meet the needs of bilingual education, college and university libraries from the East coast to the West coast are acquiring books and materials. During 1977 Herbert H. Lehman College, City University of New York, received a $35,590 grant under Title II-B (Research and Demonstration) of the Higher Education Act to develop a bilingual subject approach to its card catalog. Lehman College, in the Bronx, has a large Hispanic student body, and this new tool will be of invaluable assistance in guaranteeing access to the library's resources for Spanish-speaking students.

School Libraries. 1977 was not a good year for school librarians and libraries. Fiscal problems resulted in some school librarians being returned to classroom teaching assignments, and school library budgets were still woefully inadequate. In some areas, taxpayers denied budgets to school libraries, and there was no funding for the purchase of library materials. The American Association of School Librarians and the various school library state associations, nevertheless, are alive and well and are working in a vigorously and socially responsible way to strengthen the position of school library media centers. Because of the strong school library leadership in New York State, a creative and dynamic school librarian, Lucille C. Thomas, captured the presidency of the New York Library Association and became the first Afro-American elected to the presidency of that body. In another strategic spot in the NYLA leadership in 1977 was Patricia Mautino, serving as Chairperson of the powerful legislative committee. Many Southern states are strengthening school library media programs in elementary schools for the purpose of
Hallie Jordan, State School Library Media supervisor of Alabama, reported, "the commitment of local school systems to the establishment of school library media programs is evident in the increase of 135 new library media personnel from the 1974-75 to the 1975-76 school year. Most of the growth occurred at the elementary level in order to achieve accreditation by the Southern Association of Colleges and schools." Continuing, she observed, "we have grown from 600 school library media personnel five years ago to more than 1,100 today." Most of the improvement in the quality of school library media programs in the country is the result of the dedication and hard work of one of the most dynamic groups in the information profession, school library media specialists. The strength and influence of school library media personnel will grow in the years ahead, for at the AECT convention in April, the board of directors, after hearing concern from Peggy L. Pfeiffer, AASL's 1976-77 President, passed a resolution that declared, "We the AECT board extend an invitation to explore areas of cooperation betwen AASL and AECT for the benefit of membership of both associations ... of the profession."

Publications. Alternative publications continue to make their way into libraries. Libraries are actively promoting small presses. COSMEP (Committee of Small Magazine Editors and Publishers) created a regional structure—COSMEP East, COSMEP South, and COSMEP West. At the urging of Noel Peattie, Editor of *SIPAPU*, a twice yearly newsletter for librarians and others interested in Third World Studies, the counter culture, and the free press, COSMEP found grant money from the Coordinating Council of Literary Magazines to distribute free poetry and broadsides, accompanied by promotional materials, to all libraries requesting the materials. Announcements in several of the nation's leading library periodicals indicated that the materials were available. About 500 libraries requested the free packages of materials.

On the eve of the Fourth Annual New York Book Fair, LACUNY (The Library Association of the City University of New York) in October, sponsored a seminar, "Small Talk: Librarians and the Alternative Press." Lee Johnson, Editor of RAIN, called attention to a significant publication venture, *Rainbook: Resources for Appropriate Technology* (Schocken Books). This publication "best exemplifies the integration of our life and work in a socially responsible way. The magnum opus besides answering the oft-asked 'what is appropriate technology,' and doing so in many areas of life, including communications, libraries, and networking...has been most useful to librarians as a guide to the best resources for their libraries." Of special interest to the library and information science specialist is its section on Information Centers, which includes "Community Information Project in Libraries" and Homegrown Libraries.

Urban Information Interpreters, Inc., College Park, Maryland, updated its *Prison Directory*. Two additional titles from UII are *Guide to the Literature of Social Change*, a landmark bibliography, and *Alternatives to Traditional Library Services: A Case Book*, "prepared for the use of people in and out of the library profession who are interested in the utilization of information for social improvement and toward the related goal of citizen participation in government...." The Council on Interracial Books for Children in the fall issue of the *Bulletin* devoted its entire issue to the theme "Intellectual Freedom and Racism"; of special note is its coverage of the ALA's controversial film, "The Speaker," and the inclusion of a discussion guide on "The Speaker" as a vehicle of propaganda. Among nonprint resources,

Social Responsibilities

films for inter-cultural study were released by Pyramid Films, Santa Monica, California. Of special interest is the 15-minute color production on "Scott Joplin" and a 12-minute production, "The Gift of the Black Folk."

Library Education. Library schools are educating future librarians and information specialists, and social responsibility from this quarter is encouraging. A number of library schools through their curricula are sensitizing their students and professionals in the field of the sociocultural impact of media. A perusal of catalogs reveals a number of seminars and courses on the importance and function of media in libraries and information centers. The growing number of video workshops in continuing education programs is also a trend in this direction. A few social responsibility activities of the programs that might be classified as prototype are the following:

At North Carolina Central University, Dean Annette L. Phinazee indicates that Professor Benjamin Speller "has initiated voluntary service of our students in two correctional institutions and in a mental institution. Projects have included a practicum, preparation of a bibliography, selection of materials, and development of service in a reading room. One of our graduates was appointed Institutional Consultant for the N.C. State Library this year after serving as librarian in a correctional institution for two years."

Dean Thomas J. Galvin at the University of Pittsburgh reported, "A member of our faculty is in the process of developing a new course in the area of bibliography of minority cultures which we hope to soon be in a position to add to our existing offerings. A Committee on Minority Student Concerns, with representatives from among students, faculty and alumni has been formed to advise us in all areas relating to minority students and their educational and career goals. In the area of research, Dr. Patrick R. Penland, with support from the United States Office of Education, has completed a national study titled 'Individual Self-Planned Learning in America.' This study addresses the learning patterns of adults and focuses on the actual and potential roles of the public library in facilitating the dissemination of information throughout the total community." At Columbia University a new course was designed by Miriam Braverman and a New York State Senator, Major Owens, who is a professional librarian, on "Information and Referral Services," aimed at providing new tools for the age of information.

Support for Libraries in a Period of Austerity. Friends of Libraries groups, citizens groups, and interested citizens continued their efforts to gain more fiscal support for their libraries in 1977. *The New York Times* of April 12, 1977, reported in a column with bold headlines "BEAME HOPES TO END PUBLIC LIBRARY CUTS." The Mayor's office announced that it intended to use Federal public service job funds...being considered as part of President Carter's economic stimulus program to restore personnel in the city's library systems to their 1975 levels. Of special interest is the assertion that "Of these 14,000 new employees, Mayor Beame was said to have made a preliminary decision to use 500 for the libraries because of the 'enormous pressure' he has felt from community groups opposing the curtailment of hours in the city's three library systems. One city official said that there has been no subject of greater concern to letter writers to the Mayor's office than the library cutbacks."

Martin Lewin, Deputy Director, Buffalo & Erie County Public Library System, described in the March issue of *American Libraries* not the disastrous 1977 winter in the city of Buffalo but the financial woes of the Buffalo & Erie County Public Library. The Committee to Save the Libraries organized in the fall of 1976 along with "library trustees, friends and citizens groups are forging long-range efforts to enlist broad community support for library funding."

In addition to the citizens groups that are guarding their libraries, one of the most provocative essays in a nonlibrary periodical on the fiscal difficulties of the nation's libraries was Pete Hamill's "Libraries' Decay Speaks Volumes," which appeared in the May 4th issue of *The New York Daily News*. While the article was about the Park Slope Branch of the Brooklyn Public Library, it bespeaks well of the importance of the free public library in a democracy and, more importantly, Pete Hamill's essay had a profound effect on the political leaders of one of the greatest cities in the world.

American Library Association. ALA continues to focus on social responsibility issues. While there is a growing trend toward conservatism among some who seem tired of these concerns, it appears that a large majority of the membership is still committed. The most auspicious act of the Association in support of social responsibility was at the June 1977 ALA Conference when the Public Library Association's Board adopted a draft "Mission Statement for Public Libraries." The statement asserts a political and social leadership role for public libraries. Noteworthy actions of the Council, the legislative body of the association, included (1) a resolution which mandated that beginning in 1982, ALA would hold conferences only in States ratifying ERA; (2) the membership and council reaffirmed a policy of free access to information; (3) democratized the council by adding divisional representation; (4) passed a Gay-Rights Resolution; and (5) passed a resolution on the Florence Agreement Protocol. On the debit side of the ledger was the membership and Council's disregard of the opinion and feelings of the overwhelming majority of Black members of the Association regarding the film "The Speaker," produced by the Intellectual Freedom Committee. In spite of the fact that the ALA Black Caucus argued that the film is racist and does not do justice to the First Amendment or Intellectual Freedom, the Black Caucus Resolution was defeated; critics held that it was a sad day for the Association, for the film made the 1977 Annual Conference the most divisive Conference in the history of the Association. President Clara S. Jones, in a moving statement, said, "it has caused a separation along racial lines...racial trust has been lost here." One of the hopeful and reassuring signs of the ALA Conference was Eric Moon's inaugural address, in which he called for the development of a national policy on freedom of access to information to be developed by the American Library Association. Of great significance to those who advocate social responsibility is President Moon's admonition that "we need to take a hard look at the rights of the young to access to information. It is an issue we have avoided for far too long. And what seems to have become our traditional stance—that it is up to parents to control the reading and viewing of their offspring— may be politically expedient but it isn't particularly principled."

Finally, another ray of hope is the growing participation of librarians in political action. The election of Mrs. Isablla Cannon, a 73-year-old retired library staff member, as the Mayor of Raleigh, North Carolina, astonished the political observers. Active in the peace movement and the civil rights movements for 25 years, Mayor Cannon had a long and distinguished history of fighting for social justice. The election of someone from the library community to the mayoralty may be a portent of things to come.

E.J. JOSEY

Social Responsibilities Round Table

The Social Responsibilities Round Table (SRRT), in keeping with the commitment implied by its name, was in the forefront of the effort at the 1977 Annual Conference to remove ALA endorsement from the film *The Speaker*. SRRT continues to support the ALA resolution to boycott states that have not supported the Equal Rights Amendment and also is committed to the implementation of the Resolution on Racism and Sexism Awareness as passed by the membership and Council of ALA in June 1976.

SRRT itself sponsored a major session at the Annual Conference in Detroit on the "Prostitution of Information." The meeting featured M.

Blake, Rick Hill, Bernadine Hoduski, and Ann Lipow. The annual ALA membership meeting responded by passing a resolution supporting free access to information. The ALA Council also endorsed this resolution.

Gail Sheehy, author of Passages, *was the speaker at the Social Responsibilities Round Table's Task Force on Women program at the annual Conference.*

SRRT Officers

COORDINATORS:
Mary Biblo, Chicago
Elizabeth Morrissett, Denver

TREASURER:
Nancy D'Amico, Providence, Rhode Island

Membership (August 31, 1977): 993

SRRT task forces continued to be active on all fronts. At the Annual Conference the Ethnic Materials Information Exchange (EMIE) Task Force cosponsored with the Office for Library Service to the Disadvantaged a program on "Ethnic Pluralism: The Merging American Identity, from Fragmentation to New Pluralism."

The Task Force on Women also had a well-attended program. Gail Sheehy, author of *Passages*, spoke to an overflow crowd about her research, past and future. The Task Force on Women elected a nine-member steering committee at its business meeting.

The Task Force on Gay Liberation announced that *Familiar Faces, Hidden Lives: The Story of Homosexual Men in America Today* by Howard Brown was the winner of the 1977 Gay Book Award. At the same meeting the Task Force's invited speaker was Professor Sol Gordon of Syracuse University, whose speech was entitled "It's Not Okay to Be Anti-Gay."

Task force publishing activities continued in 1977. The 1977-78 edition of *Alternatives in Print* became available; Bowker International will distribute the edition internationally. The Gay Task Force continued working on a sixth edition of the widely used *Gay Bibliography*. The EMIE Task Force was about ready to go to press with the first issue of its newsletter, the *EMIE News Quarterly*. A revision of the EMIE Task Force's *Directory of Ethnic Publishers and Other Resource Organizations* was in preparation; the current edition is still available from ALA. The SRRT Clearinghouse continued to publish the *SRRT Newsletter*.

MARY BIBLO

Special Collections

ESTC

Many of the events and undertakings of 1976 continued to bear fruit in 1977. Most notable of these was the continuing torrent of activity that, it was hoped, would lead eventually to an 18th-century short title catalog (ESTC) of books printed in the English language and of all books in any language printed in the British Isles and in North America during that period. The earlier investigations conducted by individuals and the various institutional ventures such as the London-Oxford-Cambridge Project, the Hand-Printed Book Project, FAUL (New York), and the Western Kentucky Project had served both as catalysts and learning devices. All were useful as preliminary background for the intensive undertaking now in progress.

Joint Project. This latest and largest drive for an ESTC got under way in June 1976 with a conference of English and American experts in London. The conference was initiated by the American Society for Eighteenth Century Studies and supported by a grant from the National Endowment for the Humanities (NEH). Chaired jointly by Douglas Bryant of Harvard University and Sir Frank Francis, former Director of the British Museum, the conference considered problems of scope and methodology and raised questions of inclusion and definition, of data collection and editing, and of staffing and financing. A smaller Organizing Committee was formed to explore the intellectual and practical problems raised by the conference and to resolve the questions identified by it. Although the unprecedented complexity and magnitude of such a bibliographic enterprise was sobering, the conference was in essential and optimistic agreement about the feasibility of the project through the use of advanced computer technology under scholarly direction.

Through the Drafting Committee which it set up as a working subcommittee, the Organizing Committee came to the conclusion that the scope was larger than anticipated (at least 800,000 items). The Committee also concluded that a smaller percentage of these than was first thought to be the case (only 40 percent) would be held by the British Library. After conducting an initial feasibility study, the British Library committed itself to recataloging its 18th-century holdings and appropriated £250,000 to its project headed by Robin Alston. It was the first sizable financial commitment to the idea of ESTC, and a significant psychological one.

Future Plans. Further development of the ESTC Project depends on finding the necessary funding, and the Drafting Committee has prepared and submitted grant proposals to support the detailed plans drawn up for American participation. If supported by NEH, the plans call for a project divided into several stages over six or seven years. There would be a six-month Operational Test Project at the New York Public Library sometime in 1978, followed by an 18-month American Imprints Publication Project from late 1978 to 1980 and a United States—United Kingdom Enrichment and Publication Project from 1980 to 1984. The last phase would convert to machine-readable form, merge the two national files, and enlarge them with the holdings of other libraries. Publication in a computer output microform (COM) catalog would complete Phase I of ESTC and would produce the results now being sought.

Phase II, if it were to be initiated at some later date, would seek further enrichment of the file from some 400 libraries around the world and produce final publication of the file in printed volumes. It is possible that during the latter stages of Phase I interim publications or listings might make available to libraries and scholars partial files based on initial institutional holdings.

Caxton Commemorative. Other events of 1976 also left their mark on 1977. The furor over the United States Bicentennial finally subsided after a year marked in the rare book world by some notable exhibitions and handsome catalogs that served to document the event in terms of the significant historical holdings of a number of the nation's most distinguished libraries and institutions. The rare book world had its own quincentenary to celebrate in 1976, the 500th anniversary of William Caxton, the first English printer. The International Caxton Congress was held in London in the fall of 1976, with a week-long series of commemorative events honoring Caxton and his translation and printing of the *History of Troy*, the first book printed in English. In the spring of 1977 a one-day Caxton Celebration in New York City honored the man who in 1477 published his *Dictes or Sayengis of the Philosophers*, the first book printed in England. There were numerous Caxton exhibits, more than 50 in England alone, and many publications. Foremost among the publications was George Painter's *William Caxton: A Biography.*

RARE BOOKS

19th-Century Interest. The 19th century also claimed its share of attention in 1977, with Toronto the scene of much of the activity. The annual Toronto Conference on Editorial Problems looked at the editing of 19th-century fiction. The Rare Books and Manuscripts Preconference sponsored by the Association of College and Research Libraries (ACRL) also met in Toronto to consider the topic "Book Selling and Book Buying: Aspects of the Nineteenth Century British and North American Book Trades." It was the first time the annual meeting had been held outside the United States, and interest was high among American librarians and dealers in the Canadian and Toronto book scene, including the Thomas Fisher Rare Book Library of the University of Toronto. The papers of the 1975 preconference on "Eighteenth Century English Books" appeared at the beginning of 1977 in an ACRL monograph, and the Toronto papers will be edited by Richard Landon. Papers of the 1976 meeting held in Ann Arbor on "Maps and Atlases: A New World in Rare Book and Manuscript Collections" were published in the *AB Yearbook* for 1976.

Special collections librarians and curators in 1977 were still caught up in the same cat-and-mouse game with the budget which has bedeviled them in recent years. They were again forced to look carefully at new titles (and old ones as well) while desiderata lists grew longer in a number of institutions. Once more the financial "moment of truth" hit newer collections with more crippling force than the established or more prestigious ones. Creative projects for collections development and promotional display and use of the collections were sought, and grant proposals assumed new importance as a facet of institutional life.

LC Activities. The Library of Congress in 1977 initiated the free series of Engelhard Lectures on the History of the Book. Congress itself passed enabling legislation establishing a Center for the Book at the Library of Congress "to stimulate public interest and research in the role of the book in the diffusion of knowledge." Funding is to come, hopefully, from donations and bequests from nongovernmental sources, according to the law establishing the Center. A series of conferences will discuss the proposed role of the Center and seek to outline specialist programs and objectives. The Center will, according to the Librarian of Congress, "draw together all the Library's resources and help awaken our nation to the world of books."

Publications. Public interest in rare books and collecting in general continued its upward spiral in 1977. Some of it was tied primarily to the investment aspects of the book as a market commodity, but much of the interest was based on a genuine appreciation of the intellectual and aesthetic lure of the printed word. Publishers responded to this interest with a plethora of new books on various aspects of the book and the collecting game, paying considerable attention to pricing and value and making occasional extensions into such specifics as bookbinding, conservation, and the book as history or artifact. Many of the books offered to the public were of dubious value and filled at times with inaccuracies or misinformation.

On the other hand, a few of the books were first-rate, written by experts in their field and filled with useful information. Foremost among these were Gordon N. Ray's *The Illustrator and the Book in England, 1790-1914,* and Joseph Blumenthal's *The Printed Book in America.* The former is an informal but solid survey of English book illustration, centering on various artists and processes and done with the usual meticulous scholarship associated with Ray. The latter promises to become a classic reference along with Blumenthal's *Art of the Printed Book* published four years earlier.

The *Atlas of American History,* which appeared in the Bicentennial year, assembled a wealth of information on early American printing, publishing, newspapers, engravers, and paper mills and made maps and text available for the researcher in publishing and printing history. It is a most welcome piece of scholarly lagniappe indicative of the thoroughgoing nature of the whole project. A definitive study of very early book production was reported in *The Making of the Nuremberg Chronicle* by Adrian Wilson, the distinguished West Coast printer who studied the design and production background of the *Chronicle* and analyzed the "Exemplars" or manuscript-design models on which it was based. Although the influence of this new work on the market for copies of the *Chronicle* itself is as yet unknown, a disbound copy of the Latin edition sold in 1977 for $10,000, setting a new record. Other useful reference titles were Roderick Cave's *Rare Book Librarianship* and Bowker's *Book Collecting: A Modern Guide,* with chapters by established experts.

New Periodicals. New periodicals have been cropping up with some regularity for the past few years, often in the form of bibliographic newsletters or more substantial publications put out by institutions or individual scholars. The audience they have sought has ranged from the general to the specialist, and the subjects covered have varied from publishing and printing history to the miniature book and the market for collec-

Special Collections

tors. The quality overall has been high, and in some cases there has been a substantial contribution to scholarship in the material carried. At a time when libraries have faced stringent serial cutbacks and even established journals were encountering difficult times, these new titles have made a contribution worthy of support.

Among the latest journals to appear were *Publishing History,* edited by Michael Turner of the Bodleian Library; Northern Illinois University's *Analytical and Enumerative Bibliography;* and the polysyllabic *Microbibliophile,* for the specialist in miniature books. A useful article on the proliferation of newsletters appeared during 1977 in the *Antiquarian Book Monthly Review.*

Conservation. In addition to building collections in 1977, curators were constantly seeking ways to conserve them. Budgets often did not support the professional conservation work needed, but librarians were increasingly sophisticated about the possible dangers of in-house operations by untrained personnel. This was fortunate since simplified but questionable techniques were still being advanced with disarming regularity and imprimatur. Regrettably, formal training programs for book conservators were as yet unrealized. Knowledge and skills were still being transmitted on the job in apprentice-type situations for those lucky enough to find work with one of the experts. The move to establish regional conservation centers seemed in decline, and some announced cooperative ventures for conservation work never advanced beyond the planning stage.

The Library of Congress continued its major contributions to research and the planning of scientifically based work in conservation. At the 1976 ALA Annual Conference, Frazer G. Poole, the Assistant Director for Preservation at LC, spoke on "A National Preservation Program and the Library of Congress." Among the five points he outlined as part of a possible program were an academically affiliated training program for conservators at LC, establishment of regional conservation centers, a center to house master negatives, further research on paper, and a national preservation collection stored under ideal environmental conditions, perhaps underground. In 1977, the Library named Norman J. Shaffer as National Preservation Program Officer, responsible for planning, organizing, and managing a broad-based national program; an ad hoc advisory committee was also established.

Security. Security of collections remained a matter of much concern in 1977. Attempts were made to counteract the sometimes alarming loss by theft encountered by a growing number of libraries, and some progress was being made. In the middle of the year, a column for announcing the theft of specific rare books was inaugurated in *AB Bookman's Weekly.* The same support was expected from dealers which had already been given the register of lost or stolen archival materials begun by the Society of American Archivists in 1976. Court actions that resulted in legal judgments, with fines or jail sentences invoked, were looked on as possible deterrents to thefts.

Continuing apprehension of individuals involved in large-scale thefts from various institutions served as a constant reminder of the scope of the problem, as did the end-of-the-year reports from London of the intensification of thefts from well-known book dealers and auction houses. The subject and format of material stolen varied considerably. Their size did not prevent the theft from Audubon House in Key West, Florida, of the four elephant folio volumes of Audubon's *Birds of America,* later recovered with the volumes geographically separated but intact. Size notwithstanding, Audubons may have been especially vulnerable in a year that saw the folio reach the staggering price of $352,000 in a sale at Christie's, well over the estimate. Other Audubon titles and multiple copies of the octavo edition of the *Birds* moved in a steady stream through the New York auction houses.

Cost Escalation. Books and manuscripts continued to increase in price, less perhaps from an increase in intrinsic worth than from the inflationary influences at home and the resulting debasement of the dollar abroad. New collecting fields continued to be sought or devised, but past experience showed that once established these too soon joined the price march upward. Some of the endowed libraries held more or less firm, but most felt the larger public changes. A few, like the Morgan, were conspicuously successful in finding outside funds; and NEH continued support for a few selected libraries, principally the New York Public. At the same time, the Independent Research Libraries Association continued its successful cooperative approach to lobbying to explain and support the needs of its members.

Yale Center. In contrast to the static or reduced circumstances that have pertained generally in the past few years, the Yale Center for British Art was opened with much-deserved fanfare in the spring. Originally known as the Mellon Center for British Art and British Studies, the Center brings together the magnificent private collections of books, paintings, drawings, and prints belonging to Paul Mellon. Housed in a striking modern building designed by the late Louis Kahn, the collections include about 16,000 rare books, among them the famous Major Abbey Collection of color plate books. The 1978 ACRL Rare

Books and Manuscripts Preconference will be held at the Center, which lends itself well to its role as a modern research center in the American mode with programs of conferences, seminars, exhibits, and fellowships. This same type of model has also emerged outside the United States, where the great library at Wolfenbüttel in Germany has developed similar programs.

IFLA. American rare book librarians, never insular in their approach to the book, continued to watch and participate in developments abroad. The International Federation of Library Associations (IFLA) reorganized in 1976 with a section on rare and precious books and documents having American representation and able to monitor such things as the earlier IFLA work on an ISBD for older books. Cooperative work on the revision of the *Anglo-American Cataloguing Code* was also watched with interest, sparked by attempts to adapt AACR-2 and OCLC to the cataloging of older books.

AUCTION-SALE ACTIVITY

Christie's. A major event in the auction world was the entry of Christie's into New York sales with the opening of a permanent salesroom at Christie's Park Avenue. This move by the venerable firm brought a healthy edge of rivalry and new activity to the season. It also introduced to the United States for the first time the commission structure established in England in 1975 and now used by most of the leading English firms. The structure imposes a percentage fee on the buyer with a reduced fee on the seller. Christie's 10 percent buyer's fee on the Audubon elephant folio helped in part to account for the record price. It also accounted for Christie's claiming a record over Sotheby Parke Bernet when both houses sold copies of Edward S. Curtis's *The North American Indian*; the buyer's fee put Christie's price just $500 above the $60,000 realized earlier at Parke Bernet.

Christie's opening sale also had a number of works by John Gould, Audubon's contemporary and rival, several of which reached new highs. All of this was in keeping with the fact that color plate and natural history books continue to be among the stars of the salesrooms. The prices realized help flush out other copies and titles, as indicated by a second Audubon folio in a late-year sale at Christie's.

Manuscripts. Manuscripts, both illuminated and modern literary and historical ones, were strong contenders at auction. Following hard on the 1975 sale of a set of the *Signers of the Declaration of Independence* for $120,000, the Historical Society of Pennsylvania divested itself of the Sprague set, one of three it owned, for $180,000 in a reassessment of its holdings. The archive of William Beckford's literary manuscripts and correspondence sold in London for £120,000. The sale of the first third of Jonathan Goodwin's outstanding collection of modern literature in prime condition contained a group of Hemingway's letters to his parents which brought $65,000 and a typescript of the first two unpublished chapters of *The Sun Also Rises,* which sold for $22,000 to the University of Virginia. The two parts of the manuscript were reunited when Mrs. Louis Henry Cohn of the House of Books generously donated to the University the remaining part of the manuscript in honor of her late husband. He had bought the manuscript intact as a dealer and had subsequently returned the unpublished chapters to Hemingway.

Other Sales. The Goodwin sale at Parke Bernet set world records for modern first editions, exceeding the prices set in the same gallery the previous year. Several other name sales placed their own special cache of material on the market. The library of Niels Hansen Christensen, a clergyman-scholar turned book dealer in retirement, brought forward 80 incunabula (only one of which was listed in Goff); they brought prices ranging from $300 to $3,750. The Francisco J. Duarte Library of the History of Mathematics included the most extensive collection of Euclid ever to appear at auction.

Scrope Davies Find. Not all material of note surfaced in the auction rooms. At the beginning of 1977 the Scrope Davies Papers were placed on display immediately after their arrival at the British Library. The papers had been found only a short time earlier in a locked trunk in the vaults at Barclay's Bank where they had lain since their deposit there in 1820. Scrope Davies was Byron's greatest friend, and the chest contained a series of treasures, one of the most exciting literary finds of recent years. Most important were two notebooks used by Byron and one used by Shelley. One of the notebooks was in Byron's hand and contained the third canto of "Childe Harold"; the other held his "Prisoner of Chillon." The Shelley notebook contained "Mont Blanc" in his own hand, plus copies of the "Hymn to Intellectual Beauty" and two unknown sonnets. Also included in addition to personal and business papers of Scrope Davies were 16 letters of Byron to Davies. A publication is planned that will include a biography of Davies, a catalog of the trunk's contents, and an anthology of the more interesting items.

Less rarefied publications issued in reprint editions continued to serve the interests of rare book librarians and their patrons. Useful titles were issued in reprint programs covering special areas such as the series by Garland Press on "The English Book Trade, 1660-1853." Other publishers served similar specialist needs, although some of the smaller

Special Collections

and less stable firms that proliferated during the peak of the reprint boom have disappeared.

Book Fairs. The constantly expanding number of antiquarian book fairs and the increase in their size and geographic dispersal brought curators, collectors, and dealers new opportunities along with attendant problems. Librarians ran far behind dealers and collectors as purchasers at such fairs, but librarians used them with good advantage to expand their knowledge and their contacts. Although the idea of a fair for new books stretches back to the 15th century, the first attempt at an antiquarian book fair was in London only 20 years ago. They now seem almost endemic, and recent meetings of both the Antiquarian Booksellers Association of America and the International League of Antiquarian Booksellers have wrestled with the demands imposed by the complexities of organization and public relations required by larger and more successful fairs. Opinion among dealers was divided as to whether their professional organizations should maintain control or should allow private entrepreneurs to take over their management. Whatever the sponsorship, their future seems assured for the moment, as more dealers seek to take part and many issue special catalogs to mark their participation.

Deaths. The year 1977 took its untimely toll of the rare book world with the passing of a distressing number of prominent men and women. By the end of 1976 death had claimed Graham Pollard, an unassuming scholar, onetime bookseller, and associate of John Carter in the exposure of the T.J. Wise forgeries;

Lew D. Feldman, a flamboyant dealer in spectacular literary manuscripts and association copies, whose long association with the University of Texas helped build the collections there; and

John S. Van Eisen Kohn, a partner in the Seven Gables Bookshop, compiler of a series of landmark catalogs devoted to authors' first books, and friendly mentor to many a collector and curator of American literature.

The losses in 1977 included Leslie Bliss, former librarian of the Huntington, who directed its development from a private library to a major research institution;

J. Terry Bender, a gentleman and host par excellence, and most recently an appraiser of books and manuscripts after service as university librarian or curator of rare books at Stanford, Syracuse, and Hofstra; and

David Magee, a veteran rare book dealer, former president of the ABAA, and bibliographer of the Grabhorn Press.

Two celebrities who were partisans and friends of books and bookmen also died: Ben Grauer, radio announcer and broadcast journalist and dedicated bibliophile and devotee of the hand press; and

Anais Nin, author, critic, essayist, and sometime publisher and printer under her Gemor Press imprint. She was one of the distinguished proteges of Frances Steloff, founder of the Gotham Book Mart, who once loaned Nin funds to buy a small press.

Frances Steloff, only partially retired and still a doyen of American bookselling, helped bring the year to a joyous close by celebrating her 90th birthday on December 31.

ROBERT J. ADELSPERGER

Special Libraries

Special librarians must be managers. Shirley Echelman, in her inaugural address in June as President of the Special Libraries Association (SLA), spoke of librarians as dealing with a commodity—information—and dealing with it in competition with systems analysts, computer managers and programmers, and marketing people. "Librarians are now locked in competition for their livelihoods in what was once their nearly exclusive domain. In order to maintain a similar connection with information in the future as the one which we have traditionally enjoyed, we need to sharpen and extend all of our traditional skills and to master a number of new ones. We need to learn how to apply our considerable knowledge about information itself to augment our competitive position as organizers and managers of the information resource—to enhance both our intellectual and economic standing," she said. It is not enough, however, to be able to manage information, although that is the real skill of special librarians. They must also manage staff, produce accurate and valid budgets, statistics, and cost-benefit analyses, and be able to justify their work to the senior management of the institutions of which they are a part.

Special Libraries Association. Most special librarians would agree that the cornerstone of their profession is SLA. The Association achieved a milestone in 1977 in that for the first time the membership exceeded 10,000.

	1971	1977
Membership	6,600	10,214
Chapters	37	47
Divisions	23	29
Student Groups	0	32
Conference attendance	1,647	4,154
Exhibitor booths	76	182

Because the Association has changed significantly in other ways recently, many older members miss the intimacy and the cheerful "do-it-yourself" devotion of earlier years. As organizations grow, more and more work must of necessity be left to paid experts, and SLA's professional staff has grown to match its membership growth. In 1977 emphasis was placed on the education of members, and the new position of Professional Development Coordinator was instituted. The Coordinator will work to provide more and better opportunities for continuing education for members and will work closely with SLA's Education Committee, which has been one of SLA's most active and adventurous. During 1977, its chief accomplishment was four regional seminars in Kansas City, Seattle, Atlanta, and Toronto, carried out with the help of the local chapters. This project is to be continued in other regions and is one type of activity that the Professional Development Coordinator will foster.

"Worldwide Information Sources" was the theme of the 1977 SLA conference held in New York City. More than 4,000 people were in attendance, an increase of 1,400 over 1976's previous high of 2,694. As the host, the New York Chapter, led by Ron Coplen of Harcourt, Brace, Jovanovich, prepared a program that revolved around the "worldwide" theme. Vivian Hewitt, Librarian at the Carnegie Endowment for International Peace and President-Elect of SLA, arranged for distinguished speakers, including Preben Kirkegaard of Denmark, President of the International Federation of Library Associations and Institutions (IFLA), John Woolston of Canada, and Andrew Aines of the National Science Foundation. Two absorbing speakers at another general session were Pat Carbine of *Ms.* ("But Can He Type?") and James Adler of the Congressional Information Service ("Entrepreneurs of Information: How Publishers Think"). A panel of speakers on copyright spoke to a standing-room-only crowd and gave advice to librarians, publishers, and the general public on various aspects of the new law and its implications for libraries.

Awards and Honors. SLA's 1977 Professional Award was given to Audrey N. Grosch, who designed and developed the Minnesota Union List of Serials (MULS), an enriched data base of the Marc II format that is proving to be a prototype for other such data bases. SLA's Special Citation for 1977 was awarded to its own Executive Director, Frank D. McKenna, in recognition of his service to librarians in connection with revision of the copyright law. SLA in 1977 added the names of three special librarians to its Hall of Fame: Grieg Aspnes of the Minnesota Chapter, Sam Sass of the Boston Chapter, and the late Rocco Crachi of the Southern California Chapter. All three have, in different ways, contributed immeasurably to the Association. Two distinguished women were elected Honorary Members of SLA: Barbara Ringer, United States Register of Copyrights, and Margreet Wijnstroom, Secretary General of IFLA.

(Above) General Session III on Copyright Law: Practice and Implementation at the Special Libraries Association conference in New York. (Left) SLA 1977-78 President Shirley Echelman and outgoing President Mark Baer at conference.

Committee Work. The Government Information Services Committee of SLA, which had conducted a user survey to pinpoint and document some of the problems in dealing with the Government Printing Office, prepared a report, a summary of which was published in *Special Libraries* (February 1977). The final report is being distributed to the members and staff of selected House and Senate committees. The SLA Committee has cooperated with other associations to put pressure on the Government Printing Office, and noticeable improvement in service can be attributed to their work.

The Networking Committee made considerable progress in 1977. A brochure entitled *Networks and Special Libraries: Why and How* was mailed to all members in January, and *Getting into Networking: Guidelines for Special Libraries* was published in April. An excellent program was produced at the conference in New York City to an overflow audience. Beth Hamilton of the Illinois Regional Library Council emphasized the importance of special libraries getting into state and regional networks.

The Positive Action Committee in 1977 developed several interesting projects. Among them is a stipend program approved by the Board in June. Money has been set aside to assist minority students interested in a career in a special library. Articles highlighting minority special librarians have appeared in *Special Libraries*, and programs involving other SLA Committees have been instituted.

Student groups now exist in library schools in the United States and Canada. This program has proved a highly successful recruiting technique and has attracted students because of its potential for interesting and practical programs and contact with practicing librarians.

After the copyright law was passed in 1976, SLA continued to be active in drawing up regulations for implementing it. Frank McKenna is SLA's representative on the Ad Hoc Committee on Copyright of the Council of National Library Associations and has continued work on this complicated topic.

IFLA's 50th Anniversary. IFLA in 1977 celebrated its 50th anniversary in Brussels. IFLA's structure was changed in 1976, and the new structure was tested in 1977. The newly formed Special Libraries Division, chaired by Frank McKenna, held several meetings, and various organizing sessions were held by subgroups that proposed to form Sections. In former years, librarians had organized several narrow Sections: Geography and Map Libraries, Astronomy and Geophysical Libraries, Administrative (i.e., governmental) Libraries, and Social Science Libraries. These will now be grouped under the Special Libraries Division. Several other provisional Sections have been formed: Art, Music, Science and Technology, and Biological and Medical Science. The names and goals will need clarification, but a start has been made toward a more logical organization of the Division. Derek A. Clark of the British Library of Political and Economic Science in London is the new Chairman of the Division.

A special 50th anniversary program was prepared under the title "Libraries for All: One World of Information, Culture and Learning." Emphasis was on information, the key commodity of the special library. Chairmen, organizers, and speakers came from the special library field, a field that becomes more and more involved in IFLA and its work. Several of the themes were closely related to special librarianship. MIRIAM H. TEES

Staff Organizations Round Table

At the ALA Midwinter Meeting in January the Steering Committee of the Staff Organizations Round Table (SORT) established the following working objectives: (1) to provide library staffs that are considering the formation of a staff association or organization with information needed for making that decision, and (2) to develop effective ways of publicizing the activities of the Round Table.

The Steering Committee also set the following tasks for itself for 1977: (1) to survey organizational members of the Round Table to determine what types of staff organizations exist and what needs they might have for SORT's assistance, and (2) to survey nonmember public and academic libraries to obtain similar information. At the year's end, both surveys were in process, with compilation of data awaiting completion.

Another Steering Committee project was the preparation of a revised membership brochure. Ruth Leek was responsible for developing the new brochure, which was ready for distribution at the Annual Conference in Detroit.

SORT's program at the Annual Conference was a discussion on the topic "'Library Staff Organizations and Their Relationships with Library Trustees." Speakers were Albert Herling, President of Friends of the Greenbelt Library in Prince George's County, Maryland, and President of the International Labor Press Association; Richard Nagler, Chairperson of the Negotiating Team of the Professional Organization of Librarians at Detroit Public Library; and George Reed, Executive Vice-President of the Staff Association of Denver Public Library.

Members of the Round Table elected Lee Ash, Fran Jones, and Tom Muth to the Steering Committee for three-year terms. The Steering Committee named Fran Jones and Margaret Jones to the offices of Chairperson and Secretary-Treasurer respectively.

Membership voted to revise the bylaws on two major points: (1) the addition of the office of vice-chairperson/chairperson-elect to Steering Committee offices, and (2) revision of the dues structure for organization members, making it more favorable to smaller libraries.

FRANCES JONES

Standards

Standards in library work, information science, and documentation and publishing are voluntary and are developed and agreed to by members of the user community. The American National Standards Institute (ANSI) is the official agency for promulgating and publishing nongovernmental standards in all areas in the United States. The International Organization for Standardization (ISO) is its international counterpart. Other agencies and associations, both national and international, are also involved in the development and application of standards and normative (standards-like) documents for their respective fields of interest.

Legislation and ANSI. The principle of voluntary standards developed by the user community upon which ANSI is based received a setback when the bill Voluntary Standards and Accreditation Act of 1977 (S. 825) was introduced in the U.S. Senate. The bill would give the authority to promulgate and develop standards to an agency of the federal government. Proponents of the bill say that the current standards-developing agencies favor big business and the status quo. According to ANSI President John W. Landis, the enactment of S. 825 would result in the destruction of the voluntary standards system. He contends that S. 825 would replace the present free and diverse system, which gives the nation the most technologically advanced standards in the world, with a monolithic one involving excessive control. Landis also believes that the bill would impair the effective presentation of U.S. positions in voluntary, nongovernmental international standards activities and that it would sound the death knell for certification and testing in the private sector.[1]

The work being done by the ANSI sectional committees and other agencies continued undaunted, however, by the possibility of governmental intervention. The ANSI Sectional Committee Z39 on Library Work, Documentation and Related Publishing Practices had a productive year in 1977. Three standards were published, two of which are important to the library community: *Format for Scientific and Technical Translations* (Z39.31–1976), *Bibliographic References* (Z39.29–1977), and *Development of Identification Codes for Use by the Bibliographic Community* (Z39.33–1977). *Bibliographic References*, which has long been in the making, sets guidelines for writing bibliographic references. The examples given in Appendix A, "Applications of the Standard," are a noteworthy accomplishment by themselves, listing all manner of bibliographic references including, but not limited to, books, journals, journal articles, titles in series, all types of audiovisual media, and computer data bases. An abridged version of the standard appeared in the *Journal of the American Society for Information Science* (January 1977).

Other Z39 standards approved by ANSI in 1977 but not yet published include the revision of *Periodicals: Format and Arrangement* (Z39.1–1967) and a new standard, *Synoptics* (Z39.34). *Synoptics* is a relatively new term in American journal publishing that refers to a concise (usually two-page) publication by the author in a primary journal of those key ideas and results from a full paper or completed work that he believes to be most important and useful to others. A synoptic is longer and more informative than an abstract and, in fact, includes an abstract. The standard lists requirements for a synoptic's length, style, use of figures and tables, and manner of publication and for the availability of the full paper.

A number of previously published Z39 standards were circulated in 1977 for reaffirmation in compliance with ANSI's five-year review of published standards. Two were reaffirmed without change: *Directories of Libraries and Information Centers* (Z39.10–1971) and *Trade Catalogs* (Z39.6–1965). The following received comments and negative votes, indicating that revisions were necessary: *Identification Number of Serial Publications* (Z39.9–1971), *Advertising of Books* (Z39.13–1971), *Writing Abstracts* (Z39.14–1971), *Title Leaves of a Book* (Z39.15–1971), and *Preparation of Scientific Papers for Written or Oral Presentation* (Z39.16–1972).

Z39 technical subcommittees during 1977 were writing new standards or revising old ones in the following areas: machine-input records, transliteration of Yiddish, library statistics, standard account numbers, standard order forms, journal article codes, microform publishing statistics, serial holdings statements, serial claim forms, book spine layout, newspaper and journal publishing statistics, indexes, library identification codes, and dissertations. Draft standards for a number of these areas were circulated for comment during the spring and summer. A draft of the proposed standard for microform publishing statistics appeared in *Microform Review* (July 1977).

Three sets of Romanization tables were circulated for a vote to the Z39 Committee: Lao, Khmer, and Pali; Burmese and Thai; and Armenian. These tables were developed by the Library of Congress in conjunction with others and were forwarded to Z39 by the Descriptive Cataloging Committee of the Cataloging and Classification Section of the Resources and Technical Services Division of ALA.[2]

Also in 1977, the Z39 Office published a revised and updated edition of the *Compilation of Terms and Definitions Appearing in Z39 Standards*, a glossary of terms found in published Z39 standards. The office began an expansion of its activities and has been working to collect information and act as a clearinghouse for the standards development activities of other national and international organizations. These include not only standards organizations but also international agencies with a special subject interest who nevertheless have an interest in standardization.

Other ANSI committees that develop standards of interest to librarians are X3—Com-

State Library Agencies: see Association of State Library Agencies

Standards

puters and Information Processing, especially subcommittee X3L8—Data Elements and Coded Representations, and Committee PH5–Microcopying. An important development in 1977 was the revision of *Code for Information Interchange* (ANSI X3.4–1968) to bring it into greater conformity with *Bibliographic Information Interchange on Magnetic Tape* (Z39.2–1971). The standard provides a coded character set for the general interchange of information between information processing systems and associated equipment. A related standard is *Message Heading Formats for Information Interchange Using the American National Standard Code for Information Interchange for Data Communication System Control* (X3.57–1977), a new standard published in July 1977. Another new standard is *Representations of Local Time of the Day for Information Interchange* (X3.43–1977), published by ANSI in October.

ANSI Committee PH5, of which the National Micrographics Association (NMA) holds the Secretariat, has been working on revising standards and developing new ones. They have submitted for ANSI's approval a revision of *Specifications for 16mm and 35mm Microfilms in Roll Form* (PH5.3–1967), revised in 1973, which covers general specifications for 16mm and 35mm microfilms for roll applications and references standards that address the type of microfilm and its dimensions. A new proposed standard is *Microfilming Newspapers* (BSR/NMA MS-11), which would establish uniform formats and minimum quality criteria for microfilming newspapers on 35mm black-and-white silver halide roll film used for archival storage or permanent use collections.

ALA Activities. The ALA's Standards Committee was active with internal work but did not issue any new documents during the year. It should be noted, however, that their standards manual was approved and published in 1976, after many years of hard work.

The ALA was awarded a contract by the Library of Congress to formulate standards for library service to the blind and physically handicapped. It will be the responsibility of the Health and Rehabilitative Library Services Division of ALA to develop standards that will cover administration, staffing, resource development, services and activities, public relations, and physical facilities. The ALA will also work on standards for organizations and agencies that are developing and maintaining print collections about visual and physical handicaps.[3]

During 1977, the Technical Standards for Library Automation Section of ALA's Information Science and Automation Division forwarded several proposals to ANSI/Z39 for consideration and processing as national standards. Two of these, a first draft of the "Identifier for a Library" and a second draft of the "Identifier for an Item in a Library Collection," were forwarded for consideration by the appropriate Z39 subcommittees.

The Resources and Technical Services Division of ALA issued two new guidelines. Of particular interest to college and public libraries will be the "Guidelines for Selecting a Commercial Processing Service."[4] This was in first draft form and is being developed by the committee. Also of interest in the Acquisitions Guidelines series is *Guidelines for Handling Library Orders for Microforms* (No. 3), published in 1977.

The Association of College and Research Libraries issued additional guidelines during the year. The *Statement on the Reproduction of Manuscripts and Archives for Commercial Purposes* was approved by the Board in May. This is a sequel to the *Statement on Reproduction of Manuscripts and Archives for Non-Commercial Purposes* approved in 1976. These statements and others issued by the Rare Book and Manuscripts Section, Committee on Manuscripts Collections, were published as a single document, *Guidelines on Manuscripts and Archives*. In April, the *Guidelines for Bibliographic Instruction in Academic Libraries* was approved. Other committees are currently working on developing standards for university libraries, quantitative standards to accompany the *Guidelines for Two-Year College Learning Resources Programs*, and draft guidelines and procedures for the screening and appointment of academic librarians.[5]

Other Activities. Along the same lines as the guidelines for screening and appointment of academic librarians, the Board of the Art Libraries Society/North America approved the first document of their standards committee, *Standards for Staffing Art Libraries*. This is intended to serve both museum libraries and academic branch art libraries of all sizes.[6]

The National Commission on Libraries and Information Science (NCLIS) in 1977 became involved in standards as a reviewer and a developer. At the request of the National Science Foundation, NCLIS established a Task Force on Standards Committee Z39 to study the organization and activities of Z39, how its operations might be improved, and the possibilities of additional funding from other sources. Their report and recommendations were completed in the fall.

With the assistance of the National Bureau of Standards, Institute for Computer Science and Technology, NCLIS has established a Task Force on Computer Network Protocol. It is the intent of the Task Force to identify specific areas requiring standardization to assure effective and efficient information interchange, to identify and select appropriate existing standards for adoption by the library and information science communities, and to develop essential standards, including a high level data interchange protocol. Their final report was scheduled for the end of 1977.[7]

What was happening on the international level was also important. The International Organization for Standardization, Technical Committee 46 on Documentation (ISO/TC 46), held a constituent meeting of its Steering Committee in January in Geneva. The United States and five other countries make up the membership of the Steering Committee, which was organized to assist the Secretariat in planning for TC 46. Rules of procedure dealing with membership, meetings, and working and voting procedures were drafted, and the question of priorities and target dates for the work of TC 46 was discussed.

In May, NMA and ANSI cosponsored a meeting of TC 46/SC 1—Documentary Reproduction. The aim of this meeting was to bring the work of previous years to a conclusion as international standards or as final balloting drafts. The subcommittee also considered the desirability of becoming a separate technical committee. Also involved in this change is a redefinition or refinement of the scope of SC1. Potential overlap with the work of ISO/TC 42—Photography was carefully considered. This question was before the membership of TC 46 at the plenary session in November.[8]

In June there was a meeting in London of TC 46/Working Group 6—Bibliographic and Similar Tasks, the Task Group on the revision of *Bibliographic References—Essential and Supplementary Elements* (ISO 690-1975). The Task Group also began work on the revision of *Bibliographic References—Abbreviation of Typical Words* (ISO 832-1975). The ISO/TC 46 plenary meeting was held in Paris, November 14-23.

New Standards. In 1977, ISO/TC 46 published the following new standards: *Patents—Bibliographical References—Essential and Complementary Elements* (ISO 3388) and *Documentation—Presentation of Translations* (ISO 2384). Member countries of TC 46 are currently voting on a revision of *Codes for the Representation of Names of Countries* (ISO 3166, corresponding to Z39.27-1976, *Structure for the Representation of Names of Countries of the World for Information Interchange*). TC 46 recently published an Amendment I to ISO 3166, listing changes made in the country codes since the publication of ISO 3166. The revision includes the changes made in Amendment I and other more recent changes and additions.

The following draft international standards (DIS) have obtained the necessary majority of votes and will be published as ISO standards: *Presentation of Periodicals* (DIS 8), *International System for the Transliteration of Greek Characters into Latin Characters* (DIS 843), *Vocabulary of Information and Documentation (VID)—Chapter 1* (DIS 5127/1), and *Abstracts Sheets in Serial Publications* (DIS 5122).

TC 46 subcommittees and working groups are active in several areas, many of them similar to ANSI/Z39, preparing new standards and revising old ones: abbreviations of typical words; transliteration of Slavic-Cyrillic characters and non-Slavic languages using Cyrillic characters, Arabic characters, Hebrew characters, and Japanese; bibliographic strip; abstracts; microcopying, both microfilm and microfiche; and bibliographic information interchange formats.

Also on the international scene, the World Science Information System (UNISIST) within UNESCO has been working on the development of an international standards information network (ISONET) in cooperation with ISO. As a first step, the organizations have published two standards handbooks. *International Standards in Documentation and Terminology* (Bibliography 7, November 1976) contains details of ISO standards, draft standards, and draft proposals dealing with documentation and terminology, as well as standards and other normative documents in the same fields issued by other international organizations. *The ISO Standards Handbook I* has photographic reproductions of 56 international standards relating to bibliographic references and descriptions, abstracting and indexing, transliteration, document copying, microforms, bibliographic control, library and information systems, mechanization and automation in documentation, and principles of terminology. UNISIST also sponsored a Symposium on International Standards Information Networks in Paris in October to expand international understanding of the need for information on standards and their uses, including the important aspect of technical transfer.

It is obvious from the steadily increasing volume of standards being produced and agencies now vying for dominance in the standards field that the information transfer community is more aware and concerned than was the case a few years ago. Current developments in network development and application of computer technology speak for even more rapid development in the years ahead.

DEBORAH BODNER
KATHARINE SILVASI

REFERENCES

1. "Landis Stresses Value of Voluntary Actions," *ANSI Reporter* (July 1, 1977), pp. 1-2.
2. American National Standards Committee Z39 on Library Work, Documentation and Related Publishing Practices, *Status Report—1977* (Chapel Hill: University of North Carolina, 1977).

3. "ALA to Formulate Standards for Blind, Physically Handicapped Services," *LC Information Bulletin* (October 21, 1977), pp. 716–17.
4. Commercial Processing Services Committee, "Guidelines for Selecting a Commercial Processing Service," *LRTS* (Spring 1977), pp. 170–73.
5. Connie R. Dunlap, "Association of College and Research Libraries: Annual Report of the President, 1976–77," *College & Research Libraries News* (July–August 1977), pp. 191–93, 195.
6. "Standards for Staffing Art Libraries," *ARLIS/NA Newsletter Supplement* (April 1977).
7. NCLIS/NBS Task Force on Computer Network Protocol (CNP), "Memorandum of Understanding Between the National Commission on Libraries and Information Science and the National Bureau of Standards (CNP-3)" (June 1977).
8. Don Avedon, "Standards: 1977 ISO Report," *Journal of Micrographics* (July-August, 1977), pp. 343–46.

Telecommunications and Public Broadcasting

While the field of telecommunications—and that small part of it which is public broadcasting—is often said to be in flux, the more apt term for its state in 1977 might have been *transition*. A new administration in the White House, changed committee assignments on Capitol Hill, and a resolve to reexamine roles and goals in public broadcasting all contributed to "something in the wind" that suggested that actions initiated in 1977 might have consequences that would be fully revealed only in future years.

CPB Activities. In mid-December, Henry Loomis, President of the Corporation for Public Broadcasting (CPB), announced his intention to resign by the time of CPB's 1978 annual meeting in September or earlier if the CPB board named a successor before that time. While Loomis's resignation was not thought to be the result of outside pressures, there were political overtones.

Early in the years of the administration of former President Richard Nixon, CPB's first president, John W. Macy, resigned in protest against White House attempts to stifle public affairs programming. The present board feels it important that Loomis's leaving not be perceived to be a direct consequence of the coming of the Carter administration. The authors of the Public Broadcasting Act of 1967, which created CPB as a nongovernmental agency to distribute federal funds, strived to avoid politics. With its Nixon-appointed majority, the board thus hopes to fill the vacancy before the appointment of six new board members shifts the balance to Carter nominees.

Public broadcasting's five-year funding authorization will run out in 1978, and the White House proposed a new financing act. For FY 1980, the act would authorize $180,000,000, with $200,000,000 for each of the following four years. To the objection that the authorizations would hit a ceiling too low and too soon, the White House responded that higher subsequent authorizations might be considered, depending on the outcome of several other provisions of the bill.

The role of CPB would, for example, be substantially changed from that of an active participant in programming to one more nearly like that of a foundation, providing unencumbered block grants to selected production agencies. CPB would also be charged with responsibility for long-range analysis and planning. If CPB's planning function documented the need for more money for the system, the $200,000,000 limit might be raised. In keeping with CPB's new duties, four members would be added to the present board, two appointed by the Public Broadcasting Service and two by National Public Radio. The number of board members would later be reduced by attrition from 19 back to 15.

Other highly controversial aspects of the proposal included requiring CPB to set aside at least 25 percent of each year's appropriation for national programming and the move of the Educational Broadcasting Facilities Program from the Office of Education of HEW to CPB. Since 1963, the Facilities Program has provided matching grants for the construction, improvement, and expansion of noncommercial radio and television stations. In recent years, the Program has had little high-level support within HEW, and appropriations have been made on the floor of the House. If the program is shifted to CPB, the White House Office of Management and Budget has promised to support an increase to $30,000,000, twice what Congress provided in 1977.

For the first time, the Program would provide grants for nonbroadcast facilities such as low-power translators, interface with cable systems, and ITFS (Instructional Television Fixed Service), all of which would extend public broadcasting coverage. For the first time, matching grants for such gear could be made to educational entities that are not public broadcast stations.

Remaining at HEW would be the Telecommunications Demonstrations Program, which would get an additional year of funding at the $1,000,000 level. Designed to encourage innovative applications of communications technology, the Program had not made its first grant by the end of 1977. The delays, it was said, were due to bureaucratic wrangles within HEW.

Other developments in public broadcasting included the reorganization of National Public Radio, which combined with the Association of Public Radio Stations and hired Frank Mankiewicz, an associate of Senator Robert Kennedy, as its new president. The Carnegie

Corporation of New York (whose earlier study, *Public Television: A Program for Action,* led to the 1967 Public Broadcasting Act that established a pattern of federal funding and the Corporation for Public Broadcasting) was persuaded to give the matter a fresh look. It established the Carnegie Commission on the Future of Public Broadcasting (Carnegie II). William J. McGill, President of Columbia University, chairs the new commission, and the staff is headed by Sheila Mahony, formerly Executive Director of the Cable Television Information Center. Carnegie II expects to complete its work during 1978 and to issue its findings early in 1979.

New Policies Planned. Within the executive branch, the fate of the Office of Telecommunications Policy (OTP) was decided but not carried out. The OTP, an executive branch agency to deal with long-term issues in communications, was urged by former President Lyndon Johnson's Task Force on Communications Policy but put into place under the Nixon administration. The Carter executive branch reorganization plan decided to abolish the agency and distribute its responsibilities. Some policy questions will go to the White House staff (for example, the Public Broadcasting Financing Act). Other areas, including debates about frequency assignments, will become the responsibility of the Office of Management and Budget; and much of what the OTP concerned itself with will be assigned to a new subsection within the Department of Commerce. Commerce's Office of Telecommunications has long provided technical support to OTP. With its staff and responsibilities greatly increased, it will have a new name (probably the National Telecommunications and Information Administration) and a new head with the title of Assistant Secretary of Commerce. Henry Geller, former FCC general counsel, who more recently has been with the RAND Corporation and the Aspen Program on Communications and Society, was expected to assume the post early in 1978. Geller will be President Carter's principal adviser and spokesman on telecommunications matters. His special assistant will be Forrest Chisman, with experience in the Aspen Program and the Markel Foundation.

In the White House, the Domestic Policy staff concerned with communications, included Si Lazarus, an associate director who once served as a legal assistant to former Federal Communications Commissioner Nicholas Johnson; Richard Neustadt, an assistant director who had a large hand in the public broadcasting bill; and Steve Simmons, another assistant director who was on the law faculty of the University of California at Irvine.

1934 Act Revision. The House Subcommittee on Communications, chaired by Lionel Van Deerlin (D.-Calif.), held a full schedule of hearings and round table discussions on commercial and public broadcasting, cable television, women and minorities in broadcasting, and broadcast ratings and advertising. The data developed are to serve for what Rep. Van Deerlin hopes will be a "basement-to-attic" rewriting of the Communications Act of 1934. An advisory committee of 15 commercial broadcasters, asked to help establish priorities for such a revision, surprised the subcommittee by recording their opposition to the idea of rewriting the 1934 act. Rep. Van Deerlin remained determined, but said that the revision will probably be a "longer range problem than I first thought."

Carter appointed Charles D. Ferris, former general counsel to House Speaker Thomas (Tip) O'Neil (D.-Mass.) to the FCC and named him as chairman. Also appointed was Tyrone Brown, a Black attorney from the Post-Newsweek stations. Ferris's early appointments included Frank Lloyd, principal author of the Public Broadcasting Financing bill, as administrative assistant to the chairman and Robert Bruce, formerly director of planning for PBS, as FCC general counsel.

Cable TV. For two young segments of the telecommunications industry, 1977 was a bullish year. "Pay cable"—the distribution of recent films, sporting events, and original "spectaculars" on a cable channel for which subscribers pay an additional fee—established its economic viability. The principal pay cable operator, Home Box Office (a Time-Life subsidiary), moved into black ink after five years of operation. Pay programming gives increasing evidence of being that long-sought-for plus that makes cable television attractive

Patron at the Museum of Broadcasting in New York which has a five-year goal of collecting 20,000 commercials. Agreements have already been signed with CBS and NBC and negotiations were initiated in 1977 with ABC, PBS, and the National Public Radio for access to program archives.

The Clark County (Nevada) Library district programming staff filming scenes in a Clark County courtroom for a documentary on medical malpractice in Nevada. The program was aired by the local PBS station as well as being used for public discussion at the library.

to subscribers in large metropolitan areas where over-the-air signals are already plentiful. In the suburbs of New York City and Los Angeles, householders are signing up for cable at $6 a month in order to be able to spend another $8 for the pay channel.

Home Box Office distributes its programming to subscribing cable systems via two channels that it leases on RCA's Satcom satellite. About 150 system-owned satellite earth stations were in operation as 1977 ended, and it is anticipated that double that number will be in place by the end of 1978. Home Box Office will soon have a major competitor when Viacom International begins satellite distribution of its "Showtime" service. Broadcast pay television, in which a scrambled signal is sent over the air and subscribers rent decoders, began in 1977 in New York City and Los Angeles, but it was too early to predict success or failure.

Puppets used in Mississippi's Educational TV programs toured 10 libraries in the state in 1977 under a grant from the National endowment for the Arts, the Mississippi Library Commission, and the Mississippi Arts Commission.

Video Cassettes. The other big winner of 1977 was home video cassettes, which wound up under more Christmas trees than any but its most devoted enthusiasts would have predicted. There are, at present, four incompatible formats for ½-inch cassettes, but it appears that the market will eventually shake down to two—Sony's Betamax and Matsushita's VHS. Almost all of the major manufacturers have lined up behind one or the other, and it appears that both options will survive.

Recording programs off the air, a task to which the home video cassette machines are ideally suited, raises legal questions that are not yet answered. The 1976 suit by Universal City Studios and Walt Disney Productions to challenge off-the-air recording at home was yet to be tried. A new action regarding off-the-air copying by schools was filed in the U.S. District Court against the Erie County (New York) Board of Cooperative Educational Services by three major educational film companies.

Both producers and institutional users such as teachers and librarians recognize that the new copyright legislation leaves unanswered questions of "fair use" and further access to broadcast materials. As the year ended, the Association of Media Producers and the Joint Council on Educational Telecommunications announced plans for a joint effort to explore and, it is hoped, to resolve such issues.

FRANK W. NORWOOD

Theatre Library Association

The Theatre Library Association (TLA) is a nonprofit organization made up of librarians and other individuals interested in collecting and preserving material related to the theatre and in stimulating general interest in the building and use of theatre collections. The Association was founded in 1937 by Harry M. Lyndenberg, who was then the Director of the New York Public Library, and George Freedley, Curator of the Library's Theatre Collection. The membership is now international and includes librarians, private collectors, historians, professors, and lay people interested in theatre study and memorabilia.

Events of 1977. The Association's annual book award presentations were made at a reception May 9. The George Freedley Memorial Award for a distinguished book on live theatre was presented by producer Morton Gottlieb to Gerald Kaban for *Jacques Callot: Artist of the Theatre* (University of Georgia Press). Honorable mention went to Charles Shattuck for *Shakespeare on the American Stage* (Folger). The Theatre Library Association Award honoring a book in the field of recorded performance was presented by

Robert Saudek to Fred W. Friendly for *The Good Guys, The Bad Guys and the First Amendment: Free Speech and Fairness in Broadcasting* (Random House). There was no honorable mention. About 85 people attended the ceremony, which was broadcast over WNYC radio. The reception also included an open house at the Songwriters' Hall of Fame.

TLA Officers

PRESIDENT (December 1977-November 1978):
Brooks McNamara, School of the Arts, New York University

VICE-PRESIDENT:
Louis A. Rachow, The Walter Hampden-Edwin Booth Theatre Collection and Library, The Players, New York

SECRETARY-TREASURER
Richard M. Buck, The New York Public Library at Lincoln Center, New York (serves as executive secretary)

RECORDING SECRETARY:
Paul R. Palmer, New York

Headquarters: 111 Amsterdam Ave., New York 10023

The annual TLA program meeting was held in Detroit June 19 during the American Library Association Annual Conference week. The featured speaker was Schuyler G. Chapin, formerly the General Manager of the Metropolitan Opera, and now the Dean of the School of the Arts at Columbia University, and the author of the memoir *Musical Chairs* (Putnam). Chapin spoke on "The Arts: World's Best Hope for Morality." He was preceded by two panels of theatre librarians and curators discussing the contribution of the specialized theatre, film, and communications librarian to the work of the circulation and reference librarian. Ten panelists covered the activities of various theatre collections from coast to coast and several film, videotape, and communications collections that offer specialized services for research in the field.

The annual business meeting of TLA was held on November 17 in the Vincent Astor Gallery of the New York Public Library at Lincoln Center. At that time four new members were elected to the Executive Board. The full board for 1977-78 includes:

Mary Ashe, Art and Music Department, San Francisco Public Library.
Tino Balio, Wisconsin Center for Film and Theater Research, University of Wisconsin.
Mrs. Robin Craven, private collector, New York City.
Ford E. Curtis, Curtis Theatre Collection, University of Pittsburgh.
Alfred S. Golding, Ohio State Univesity Theatre Research Institute.
William Green, Department of English, Queens College.
Frank C.P. McGlinn, private collector, Philadelphia.
Paul Myers, Curator, Theatre Collection, New York Public Library at Lincoln Center.
Jeanne T. Newlin, Curator, Harvard Theatre Collection, Harvard College Library.
Sally Thomas Pavetti, Eugene O'Neill Memorial Theatre Center, Inc., Waterford, Connecticut.
Elizabeth D. Walsh, Research Center for the Federal Theatre Project, George Mason University, Fairfax, Virginia.
Mrs. John F. Wharton, Theatre Collection, New York Public Library at Lincoln Center.

A panel discussion on appraisals was presented at the meeting, covering such aspects for theatre collections as the insurance and tax situation, the evaluation of stage and scene designs, and the appraisal of theatrical museum artifacts.

Publications. The Theatre Library Association is responsible for the publication of a quarterly newsletter, *Broadside*, edited by Louis A. Rachow of the Walter Hampden- Edwin Booth Theatre Collection and Library at the Players, 16 Gramercy Park, New York City 10003, and *Performing Arts Resources*, edited by Mary C. Henderson, c/o R.M. Henderson, of the General Library and Museum of the Performing Arts, 111 Amsterdam, New York City 10023.

Organization Information. Any person or institution interested in the aims and activities of TLA may become a member. Dues are $15 annually for personal members and $20 for institutional members, based on the calendar year. As of November 17, 1977, TLA had 248 personal and 217 institutional members. Expenditures of TLA from November 1976 to November 1977 were $4,619.

RICHARD M. BUCK

Toys and Games

Early in December 1977, Alice Honig of Syracuse University, the author of *Parent Involvement in Early Childhood* published by the National Association for the Education of Young Children in 1975, evaluated the first year of the Greenville County (South Carolina) Public Library's "Project: Little Kids." Funded with a grant from LSCA, it is the first major library project for infants to age three and includes their parents and child care personnel. Mary Aiken, Head of Children's Services, reported a hectically busy year with heavy use of the toys and games, attendance by many

Schuyler Chapin, author of Musical Chairs: A Life in the Arts, *was the featured speaker at the Theater Library Association's 1977 meeting in Detroit.*

Fred Friendly, winner of the Theater Library Association book award for 1977 for The Good Guys, The Bad Guys and the First Amendment.

Theological Libraries: see American Theological Library Association

Trustees

Pre-schoolers using toys and games purchased by the Friends of the Memphis Public Library.

parents, and involvement of 35 parents in a training program.

Nancy De Salvo, Coordinator of Children's Services in the Village Library at Farmington, Connecticut, inaugurated a series of programs in 1977 called "The Terrific Two's," with registration limited to eight two-year-olds and their mothers. While the children play with toys and realia and listen to stories and records, their mothers learn about the uses and meaning of toys, games, and realia. The emphasis is on visual discrimination. The program is in great demand and a special series was given in the fall in a Farmington nursery school. The project is organized along the same lines as the Connecticut State Library's LSCA-supported seminar series on "Reading as a Process," held in the late spring and summer of 1977. A revised grant application to support more intensive training was being designed.

At the ALA Annual Conference in Detroit, the major program of the Children's Services Division, now the Association for Library Service to Children (ALSC), was a daylong hands-on presentation called "Parent Support Program Sampler." Four of the presenters showed uses being made across the country in public libraries of toys, games, and realia. In library schools, students are increasingly choosing projects on the use of toys and games as library materials and on their relationships to communities.

Several recent important publications delineate research on the importance of toys, games, and realia on the development of the very young child and clearly demonstrate the value of play with objects. Play by Catherine Garvey (in The Developing Child series published in 1977 by the Harvard University Press) shows how through discovery and exploration children use objects in creative problem solving, social contacts, dramatic play, and language skills in a regular important progression. The other books in the series—Play and the World of Objects and Tools, Play and the Social World, and Play and the World of Symbols—collect exceedingly important research studies from around the world that offer valuable insights for librarians using toys and games and planning training programs for parents. Jerome Bruner, Alison Jolly, and Kathy Sylva edited Play, published in 1976 by Basic Press. A 1977 publication of the National Association for the Education of Young Children, Current Issues in Child Development edited by Myrtle Scott, includes a paper by Ira Gordon on "Parent Education and Infant Research." The pamphlet Encouraging Language Development by the Toy Library Association of England details specific activities for parents.

The 23rd Allerton Park Institute of the University of Illinois held a program on "Issues in Children's Services," November 13–16. There were references to the library use of toys and games in five speeches: "Adult Perceptions of the Children's Librarian" by Faith Hektoen, Connecticut State Library; "Services in the Large Public Library" by Barbara Rollock, New York Public Library; "Special Services to Children" by Amy Kellman, Carnegia Library of Pittsburgh; "Services for the Exceptional Child" by Bridget Lamont, Illinois State Library; and "Materials" by Mary Margaret Kimmel, University of Pittsburgh, and Dudley Carlson, Princeton (New Jersey) Public Library.

The ALSC Toys and Games and Realia Committee has ready for publication a second list of recommended materials, carefully selected for children from ages 8 to 12. Sara Long, Head, Children's Division, Columbus Public Library and Franklin County (Ohio) Library System is readying a $100,000 LSCA grant application for toys and games in public library community services. Three trained volunteers will provide the necessary support.

FAITH H. HEKTOEN

Trustees

The dominant concern of trustees of public libraries in 1977 continued to be problems of financing, both finding adequate funds and making wise use of the monies available. The effort to obtain support for their libraries pushed trustees to a heightened level of political activity and toward increased participation in library associations.

Securing Funds and Lobbying. In the search for public funds, trustees became a more visible force at federal, state, and local levels. As laypersons in the library community with no personal monetary interest in a piece of legislation, trustees are powerful spokesmen for library needs. During the ALA Midwinter Meeting in Washington, D.C., trustees were in the forefront, contacting legislators and seeking support for federal library programs.

Similar scenes occurred in state capitals

and in city and county buildings throughout the nation. Appearing before the New York State Board of Regents in September, for example, Marguerite B. Yates, president of the New York State Association of Library Boards, declared that "a crisis exists" in the public library systems throughout the state, particularly in the major urban areas. Calling the existing state formula for aid to libraries "woefully inadequate," she urged "increased dollar amounts for the support of these public libraries."

The terms *lobbyist* and *lobbying* as applied to trustees gained acceptance in 1977, and trustee organizations were urging trustees to become active lobbyists. A handbook for trustees published in 1977 by the Minnesota Library Trustees Association (MLTA) defines lobbying as "the process of expressing opinions to the decision makers and pushing in support of one's opinions." After listing several guidelines for "effective lobbying," the handbook concludes, "If you, as a trustee, see lobbying as a continuous information process for aiding elected officials, as well as a right of every citizen to be heard and express an opinion, you will be comfortable with the political process and develop skill in lobbying that will benefit all libraries and the public they serve."

The American Library Trustee Association (ALTA) mounted an effort to establish a legislative network of trustees across the country. The goal of the network was to have a well-informed person in each legislative district. This person would be responsible for staying in contact with the district legislator and giving the legislator and his staff information about library-related aspects of specific pieces of legislation, particularly information about how the legislation would affect his own district. The contact person would also be responsible for feeding information about legislative matters in that district into the network.

Trustees also increased their efforts to obtain private funds. In Troy, Michigan, for example, a campaign was launched to inform taxpayers of an amendment to the state income tax law that provided a credit against personal income tax for charitable contributions to public libraries. ALTA inaugurated an award to honor benefactors of public libraries. The first awards were given to donors in Duncan, Oklahoma; Greenville, South Carolina; Muscatine, Iowa; Seward, Alaska; North Syracuse, New York; Clinton, Louisiana; and King George, Virginia.

Participation in Associations. Although the majority of the nation's 60,000 library trustees were still not actively involved in any library association in 1977, the number who were involved was growing as librarians urged their trustees to participate and as trustees realized their need to learn, to share experiences, and to gain strength in numbers. Among new trustee organizations was the California Association for Library Trustees and Commissioners, which was formed in late 1976 and had its first meetings in 1977.

Most of the associations, as well as many library systems, offered workshops for trustees. The subjects for such workshops included the whole range of trustee concerns: budgeting, public relations, library law, personnel relations, censorship, collective bargaining, legal responsibilities of trustees, and other matters. In order to meet the increased requests for such workshops, the ALTA Speakers' Bureau expanded both the number of speakers available and the topics treated.

Some associations have publications specifically for trustees; most states have a manual for trustees. During 1977, for example, handbooks were prepared for trustees in Min-

Trustee Louis A. Lerner (right) is congratulated on his appointment as U.S. Ambassador to Norway by Chicago Mayor Michael Bilandic (left) and Library Commissioner David Reich at a party hosted by the Library Board for Lerner and his wife (right).

Bessie Moore, vice-chairman of the National Commission on Libraries and Information Science, addressing the trustees division of the Arkansas Library Association at the state 1977 annual conference.

(Above) A one day "Trustee Institute '77" was sponsored by the Nassau (New York) Library System. From left, speakers Dorothy C. Smith, Daniel McDonnell, Minnie-Lou Lynch, and Charles E. Reid. (Right) Commissioner of the West Virginia Library Commission C. E. Campbell won the 1977 ALA Trustee Citation Award for Distinguished Service to Library Development.

nesota and Pennsylvania. The Trustee Relationships Committee of the New Jersey Library Association began publishing an occasional publication called *Trustee Alert*, and *Illinois Libraries* devoted its March issue to trustees.

Personnel Policies. An ongoing concern of trustees in 1977 was the need for personnel policies, particularly with respect to evaluating the performance of the chief librarian. The need for such evaluation guidelines has been demonstrated by SCAMI (Staff Committee on Arbitration, Mediation, and Inquiry) investigations, 90 per cent of which have involved the dismissal, without due process, of the library director. Attention was thus focused on a pilot project in New Jersey sponsored by the state library and the New Jersey Library Trustee Association (NJLTA).

In January the members of the NJLTA Executive Board and their directors (about 30 persons in all) participated in a three-hour workshop on "Evaluating the Library Director," conducted by a member of the Professional Institutes of the American Management Association. Six teams of librarians and trustees attended a six-hour follow-up session in June. The purpose of the project was to establish the concept that the evaluation of the library director cannot be an isolated procedure but must be an integral part of the library planning process. The library board and the director as a team must establish goals for the library. These goals then form the basis for setting performance standards, against which the work of the director can be measured.

Similarly, Ann Prentice of the State University of New York at Albany was developing a program on "Trustee-Librarian Relationships" that would outline the duties and responsibilities of both trustees and library directors and their proper relationships. The program was intended to be presented in each of the 10 ALTA regions with adaptations appropriate to each region.

Other Issues. The issue of whether or not to charge fees for library services attracted the attention of trustees in 1977. Fees have crept into libraries—especially for the use of special collections, expanded reference services, computer access services, and the like. Some people see such fees as a necessary source of revenue if the library is to offer certain new services. Others see these fees as a breach of one of the basic traditions of democracy—a free people dependent on free access to information. It is a difficult question that trustees increasingly will have to face as they find themselves caught in the dilemma of how to maintain services despite rising costs.

A growing number of trustees worked to exploit the potential of the public library in the war against functional illiteracy. After conducting a successful pilot project in Lockport, New York, an ALTA task force on illiteracy sought funds to create an educational program for trustees that would make them aware of the problem and would suggest ways of using the library to combat it.

White House Conference. Trustees were deeply involved in planning the Pre-White House State Conferences. Several trustees were members of the National Commission on Libraries and Information Science and the Advisory Committee on the White House Conference, and trustees were serving in various capacities on the states' planning committees. If 1977 was a year of continued struggle for trustees to obtain adequate support for the nation's public libraries, it was also a year of anticipation that the White House Conference and the State Conferences would create an atmosphere in which the library needs of the nation could be evaluated and the means to meet those needs could be determined.

ROBERT L. FAHERTY

Trustees and Personnel Policy

"Most of the cases which have come to SCMAI have reemphasized the necessity for libraries to have clearly established and well-delineated personnel policies and procedures.

"Some libraries have personnel policies and practices which appear to be reasonably well defined but which are not applicable to the chief librarian.

"The Committee suggests that PLA and ALTA may want to jointly develop a guide for public libraries recommending some specific personnel policies and practices regarding the employment of the chief librarian and his or her relation to the library board. This should include guidelines for performance evaluations, warnings of unsatisfactory performance, notice periods for resignations and dismissals, terminal payments, and grievance procedures."

The above words were addressed by the ALA Staff Committee on Mediation, Arbitration and Inquiry (SCMAI) to the American Library Trustee Association (ALTA) and the Public Library Association (PLA) (1975).

The ALTA Board in 1976 empowered its President to set up a task force to deal with the problems outlined. The PLA Board decided not to set up a special committee or task force. PLA felt that the matter was basically a trustee concern and that the trustees should draft a document covering the solutions needed, at which time PLA would act as a reviewer of the draft, as would, of course, the ALTA Board. Both divisions voiced the opinion that the Library Administration Division (LAD) also had a stake in the matter and should be asked to contribute its ideas on a draft.

When the ALTA task force met, it became apparent that paragraphs stating that the Director should be evaluated at regular intervals and should have certain channels to follow in order to appeal or modify results forthcoming from the evaluation would not solve, or even ameliorate, the problems SCMAI was addressing. Granted, it was the performance of the Director that the library Board should look at. But the performance as compared with what? The library when he or she came? The library as it was at the last evaluation? The library as related to the community? Other libraries? If other libraries, what size? What location?

If performance is to be stacked up against the job description, what was the job description when the Director arrived? Was it up-to-date when he or she was hired? Has it been looked at critically since the Director was hired? If the Board and the Director each wrote a current job description, would one recognize the other?

Regarding the immediate and long-range future, what is the Director to do? Why is the Director to do it? How is the Director to do it? How is the Director to know if it is going well? How is the Director to proceed if it is not going well?

In short, if the Board does not know its library intimately from many viewpoints, it has an insurmountable task even to attempt to evaluate its Director, let alone plan for the future operations it wants the Director to administer.

Many trustees would agree with the current enthusiasm for setting up a management by objectives (MBO) program in a library. A useful book on the subject is *MBO for Nonprofit Organizations* by Dale D. McConkey (1975). Limitations of space preclude a discussion here of the way MBO operates. But a study of the subject is considered by many to be necessary for trustees, directors, and staff, all of whom are involved. A primary conclusion, however, is that all trustees should be included in the process.

The rational, economic, and logical way to achieve this necessary education is at the national level. ALTA, PLA, and LAD should devise a workable modus operandi. ALTA has a potential membership of many thousands of trustees, but its potential has never begun to be tapped. Many trustees are interested only in the local aspects of their libraries. Some are interested in state organizations, but relatively few are interested in state and national concerns as well. Many trustees are not even aware of a national organization. There may be some excellent leadership among these trustees.

ALTA has attempted to do most of its recruiting directly with trustees. It is an impossible task—the shot is far too scattered, the cost too high, and the results have been proved to be negligible. More trustees must be led to join the channels of the national and state organizations. The membership must be increased in order that there can be cadres to go back to the local level to instruct the individual boards on what is transpiring for the well-being of the public library. Each Director of a public library should, and must, make an ongoing effort to interest the Board in the vital necessity of a strong national organization for the strengthening of all types of libraries.

When library directors do their work well, there will be excellent geographical coverage, which is as important as numbers. ALA and ALTA will then be in a far stronger position to promulgate education for the library service all members talk about achieving for their local libraries, as well as for the libraries with which they are in active cooperation. As the service grows better, so will the public response to it. The library will gain stature and the ability to command more funds with which to carry on and further enhance service. Better statistics and public support pay off.

SCMAI's reasonable and basic request is that every public library have a policy regarding hiring, evaluating, and terminating personnel up to and including the Director; that such a policy be written to contain safeguards for all parties concerned; and that such a policy be reviewed at reasonable intervals.

This request for the enhancement of the library world, particularly the public library world, must be complied with, but it can be done only by educated, dedicated trustees, directors, and library personnel. The word *cooperation* is used constantly in talk concerning library matters. Only if there is active cooperation, can the requested results be accomplished.

JEAN M. COLEMAN

UNESCO

"The book is a passport to the world... a faithful companion, a spinner of dreams, or a source of wisdom, at the choice of its user." These opening words in the introduction of "Books for All," the long-term program of action initiated by UNESCO to continue the impetus begun by the International Book Year of 1972, express the completeness and universality of books. But while in some parts of the world more and more books are being produced, in many others "the book hunger" increases year by year as the growing numbers of literate adults and young people cry out for reading materials that their own national book production industry, if it exists at all, cannot always provide.

To help remedy this situation is one of the goals of the new UNESCO Division of Book Promotion and International Cultural Exchanges, established in 1977 within the Sector of Culture and Communication. The Division will carry out the "Books for All" program, which relies largely on the cooperation and support of professional organizations of authors, publishers, translators, booksellers, librarians, readers, and specialists in children's books. These organizations coordinate their activities through the International Book Committee, which they set up to support UNESCO's program.

At its fifth plenary session in Stockholm in May 1977, under the chairmanship of its President, Sigfred Taubert, the Committee approved activities to promote books for young people that could be undertaken by the world community during the International Year of the Child in 1979. These activities include promotion of national book development councils, national book committees, or similar institutions; wide diffusion of the Charter of the Book in as many languages as possible; issuance of a special stamp showing young people reading; an international bibliography on "the reading chilld"; an international information guide providing basic facts about the situation of children's books in different countries; support for the quarterly *Bookbird* the only international periodical on literature for children and young people, published by the International Board on Books for Young People; a report on children's books during the International Year of the Child; and possible publication of a series of case studies.

The international book prize, which the Committee awards each year for eminent services rendered to the cause of books by a person or an institution, was given in 1977 to Julian Behrstock. A former UNESCO official, for 12 years Behrstock was in charge of the program for book development in developing countries and for encouraging international cooperation in the book world.

Multilingual Publishing. Books written by authors in the national language and produced by a national book industry can contribute considerably to the assertion of cultural identity, one objective of UNESCO's medium-term plan (1977-82). Many countries, however, are multilingual, which causes difficulties for their book industries.

In 1976, UNESCO organized a Symposium on Book Publishing in Multilingual Countries in Moscow to study some of these difficulties. The proceedings of the Symposium have been edited and analyzed in a publication entitled *The Book in Multilingual Countries* that appeared in the series *Reports and Papers on Mass Communication*. Another publication in this series is *The Economics of Book Publishing in Developing Countries* by Datus G. Smith, Jr., former President of the Franklin Book Program. The publication is based on the findings of a survey of publishers in Africa, Asia, Latin America, and the Middle East and gives a general picture of each of the regions surveyed and an indication of the issues meriting further attention.

To assist developing countries in establishing their own book industries and distribution networks, UNESCO has set up regional book development centers at Yaoundé, Cameroon, for Africa; at Bogotá, Colombia, for Latin America and the Caribbean; at Cairo, Egypt, for the Arab states; and at Karachi, Pakistan, for Asia. The Karachi center has recently widened its scope to cover cultural activities as well as book development. Each center works actively in the countries of its region, holding seminars on various aspects of book production and distribution and organizing practical training courses for writers and editors, particularly of children's books. They also issue regular liaison bulletins, bibliographies, and other information materials.

Assistance is also given to the Tokyo Book Development Center, in particular for the Asian Program for Copublication of Children's Books and for the development of new printing characters for Asian languages that do not use the Latin alphabet. The Asian Copublication Program plans to issue 48 stories from 18 countries in Asia in its *Folktales from Asia* series, of which some titles have already been published in 15 Asian languages. Other projects under way include publication of *Let's Play Asian Children's Games*, introducing 50 games with photographs and instructions for the use of teachers and recreation leaders of youth groups, publication of a bibliography of children's picture books in Asia, and production of audiovisual materials.

Cross-cultural Publishing. Simultaneously with its program for national book production as a means of asserting cultural identity, the

Division has undertaken a program to promote wider participation in cultural life through knowledge of the literatures of other countries. The objective is to make known at the international level works written in languages not widely known, works that remain inaccessible to the vast cultivated public of the world if they are not translated into widely used languages such as English or French. Since the launching of this program, 500 literary works have been translated and published. Texts of 60 literatures representing nearly 40 Asian languages and about 20 European languages, to which should be added non-Slavic languages of the U.S.S.R. and African languages, have been translated and published.

Similarly, the program also encourages the translation and publication of Western literary works in the languages of Africa and Asia. In all, the works of about 30 major European writers have been translated into Arabic, Burmese, Persian, Thai, Vietnamese, and various Indian languages. A new edition of the catalog of all the titles translated has recently been issued. These translations are also listed in *Index Translationum*, the international bibliography issued by the International Institute of Intellectual Cooperation from 1932 to 1940 and continued by UNESCO since 1950 as a means of making the literature of the world accessible to all. Volumes 27 and 28 are scheduled for publication early in 1978.

To increase public awareness of culture and of its impact on modern living and to promote understanding and appreciation of all cultures is the aim of *Cultures*, a quarterly that acts as a forum for discussion. Two recent issues dealt with fundamental aspects of Islamic civilization and with cultural trends in contemporary society. The latter issue was devoted to books and reading as well as sociocultural aspects of sports, and includes a selected bibliography on sports and politics.

Other 1977 activities of the new Division of interest to librarians included the publication of two important reference books: *Catalogue of Reproduction of Paintings Prior to 1860*, which has been revised and brought up to date, and *Study Abroad*, Vol. 21, listing international scholarships and courses for 1977-78 and 1978-79.

I. BETTEMBOURG

The Standardization of International Library Statistics: 1853-1977

The city of Brussels, Belgium, the birthplace of international library statistics in 1853, became in 1977 the location of their latest revision during the 50th anniversary of the International Federation of Library Associations (IFLA). When the first International Statistics Congress met in Brussels 125 years ago, library data were discussed because they were considered among the national assets that could provide an indication of educational developments and cultural resources for various countries.

1853-1964. During the 80 years following 1853 no notable progress was made, but discussions at other statistical congresses kept library statistics in a semicomatose condition. There were no associations organized to collect data based on international terminology that would also be responsible for their tabulation and publication. Five years after its founding, in 1932, IFLA established a statistics subcommittee. This small group, which met irregularly, saw to it that the hope to develop international library statistics was kept alive.

Due to IFLA's concern and the interest of member states, the League of Nations collected and published the first international library data. UNESCO, the U.N.'s eductional, scientific, and cultural organization, the successor to the League of Nations, organized its first statistical services in 1950 and published its first library statistics in 1952. Since that time, IFLA has acted as the statistical spokesman for the international library community, and UNESCO has been the collector and publisher of library statistics based on the data supplied by member states. Since 1964 the International Organization for Standardization's Technical Committee 46 (ISO/TC46) has joined in these efforts, representing the international library and reformation activities concern for standardization.

1964-1970. During the 1960's the IFLA and ISO/TC46 statistics committees held a number of joint meetings with UNESCO representatives to develop principles and appropriate terms to update the UNESCO statistical surveys dealing with libraries. This difficult task was partly based on the ALA *Library Statistics Handbook* of 1966. The joint IFLA/ISO-TC46 statistics committee meetings were usually held in conjunction with ISO or IFLA conferences. Partial but essential financial assistance was provided by the Council on Library Resources.

The efforts of the various drafts worked out in these meetings culminated in 1970 when UNESCO held a library statistics conference in Paris, to which 47 countries and 7 international organizations sent more than 80 delegates and observers to draft the text of the UNESCO "Recommendation" on library statistics. The delegates unanimously completed a draft that was ratified by UNESCO's governing body.

Two years later, ISO/TC46 adopted the "Recommendation" as an international standard without changes in the text but with a separate introduction. The United States, like most UNESCO member states, recognized the "Recommendation" by having it signed by the Secretary of State. (Recommendations are international documents of a lower type than treaties, which require ratification by the Senate.) When recognitions were given to the UNESCO "Recommendation" by the Department of State and ISO/TC46, this writer was gratified that the work he had participated in as Chairman of the combined IFLA-ISO/TC46 meetings and the UNESCO statistics conference had been nearly completed.

When the 1970 "Recommendation" was adopted, most participants realized that a number of areas had to be omitted because the international library community's experience was insufficient to provide adequate technology and quantifications. For this reason a proviso was inserted in the final report of the drafting committee indicating that, as soon as possible, steps should be taken by UNESCO to fill the missing gaps regarding these matters: (a) library buildings (physical facilities) statistics; (b) manuscripts (or library holdings) statistics; (c) audiovisual materials and microfilm statistics; (d) interlibrary loan statistics (nationally and internationally); (e) user statistics; and (f) library automation activity statistics.

It was felt that a few years' experience with international library statistics by UNESCO and the member states' statistics offices would help to provide the means to complete the work.

1970-1977. The collection of national library statistics was greatly influenced by the UNESCO "Recommendation" and the ISO/TC46 standards. UNESCO cannot collect original data from millions of libraries around the world but has to rely on the statistical offices of member states to provide the data in national aggregations to comply with their triennial request. The national offices have to supply the requested statistics in a format compatible with the "Recommendation." Obviously, if the UNESCO requests are not adaptable to national data collections, no information is forthcoming.

To complete the work on the "Recommendation" in the six areas, a number of steps were taken between 1970 and 1977 to fill the gaps.

1. The UNESCO statistics staff inserted a series of questions in their 1972 survey dealing with the physical space occupied by libraries.

2. Between 1971 and 1975 the combined IFLA/ISO-TC46 committees completed guidelines regarding manuscripts and interlibrary loan statistics.

3. In January 1976, Joanna Eggert, Executive Secretary of ISO/TC46, organized a conference in Strasbourg, France, that dealt primarily with the question of how to fill the existing gaps in the "Recommendation" and the ISO/TC46 standards.

4. As a result of the efforts of Margreet Wijnstroom, Secretary-General of IFLA, UNESCO awarded IFLA a contract late in 1976 to complete the work of the "Recommendation." This contract enabled the IFLA statistics section to employ a project consultant to arrange for a two-day preconference meeting in Brussels with ISO/TC46 representatives. A draft was reviewed in the fall by the combined IFLA/ISO members and submitted by the end of the year to the IFLA Secretariat for submission to UNESCO.

The final document included the following suggestions for revision:

1. While keeping the data collections based on public, academic, special, and national libraries, it (a) defines more fully major nonspecialized libraries and (b) refers specifically to library automation activities, indicating areas subject to statistical assessment.

2. It leaves the previous recommendations intact on how to count books, periodicals, and other items already in the collection as well as annual additions to the collection but adds how to count manuscripts, microfilms, and audiovisual docouments.

3. It supplies definitions for new and revised terms that relate primarily to audiovisual materials and microfilms.

4. It expands the concepts that were used to tabulate library loan transactions on the national and international level.

5. It recommends the elimination of questions regarding the production of photo and other types of copies of library materials.

6. It reviews the UNESCO library statistics surveys conducted in 1972 and 1975 and makes suggestions on how to improve the percentage of returns from UNESCO member states for the next scheduled survey.

UNESCO will, it is hoped, incorporate the recommendations into a new survey instrument that is to deal with the 1978 survey year.—FRANK L. SCHICK

Universal Bibliographic Control

The program of the International Federation of Library Associations and Institutions (IFLA) for Universal Bibliographic Control (UBC) is a long-term program that aims to ensure the preparation at the national level of bibliographic records of the national imprint in accordance with internationally accepted standards and the universal availability of these records in both printed and machine-readable form. The program is the particular responsibility of the IFLA International Office for UBC, which cooperates with a number of IFLA Sections and Divisions and national and international organizations (such as ISO/TC46 and UNESCO) in promoting projects related to UBC.[1]

During 1977 progress was made on many projects with particular emphasis on the International Standard Bibliographic Description (ISBD) program. During the year ISBDs for *Serials* (1st standard edition), *Cartographic Materials,* and *Non-Book Materials,* as well as the general framework for the description of all library materials on which the specialized ISBDs are based, the ISBD(G), were published.[2] Work also continued on the ISBDs for *Printed Music* and *Older Books,* and a revision process has been initiated for ISBD(M), which will be amended and updated to conform with the provisions of ISBD(G) and the specialized ISBDs. The texts of the ISBDs will then remain constant for a period of five years, although their use and application will be kept under review.[3]

One of the major highlights of the UBC year was the International Congress on National Bibliographies, which was jointly organized by IFLA and UNESCO and held in Paris, September 12–15. Participants from countries producing or intending to produce national bibliographies met to discuss the Congress's working document, *The National Bibliography: Present Role and Future Developments,* prepared by the UBC Office. Recommendations were made on minimum standards for the content, coverage, presentation, arrangement, and availability of national bibliographic records and the requirements for their international exchange.[4]

Other projects completed during 1977 and published by the UBC Office were *UNIMARC,* an international exchange format for machine-readable bibliographic records; *International Target Audience Code,* a proposal for a code to be included in bibliographic records; and *Names of Persons,* details of national name usage in 60 countries, together with recommended forms of entry for library catalogues. Projects undertaken by working groups or by the UBC Office included a list of uniform titles for anonymous classics of European literatures, the establishment of international principles for the form and structure of corporate headings, a limited survey of the provisions and processing of non-Roman script material in some public libraries, and a new project to prepare international principles and procedures for establishing authority control systems.

The UBC Office also participated with a number of national libraries in preparing a series of studies related to the establishment of an international Machine Readable Cataloging (MARC) network for the exchange of bibliographic records under the auspices of the International MARC Network Study Steering Committee.[5]

The IFLA UBC Office will be actively involved in 1978, together with UNESCO's General Information Program, in the implementation of the recommendations of the Paris Congress. Regular reports on the publications and projects of the UBC Office appear in *International Cataloguing* and *IFLA Journal.*

DOROTHY ANDERSON
ROSAMOND KERR

REFERENCES

1. *See* "Universal Bibliographic Control" in *ALA Yearbook 1976* for the objectives and functions of the IFLA International Office for UBC.
2. Published texts of the following ISBDs are available for North American readers from the Canadian Library Association, 151 Sparks Street, Ottawa, Ontario K1P 5E3:
    ISBN 0-903043-02-5 ISBD(M), 1974 (1st standard edition)
    ISBN 0-903043-13-0 ISBD(S), 1977 (1st standard edition)
    ISBN 0-903043-12-2 ISBD(NBM), 1977
    ISBN 0-903043-16-5 ISBD(CM), 1977
    ISBN 0-903043-18-1 ISBD(G), 1977
3. These were decisions reached by the Standing Committee of the IFLA Section on Cataloguing at its meeting during the IFLA Congress in Brussels in September 1977.
4. The final report of the Congress with its recommendations is available from UNESCO.
5. Two studies, the *Senior Consultant's Report* and the *Bibliographic Study,* have been published by the IFLA UBC Office as Occasional Papers No. 3 and 4.

Universal Serials and Book Exchange

Recycling of library materials through the refining processes of Universal Serials and Book Exchange (USBE) reached one milestone in late 1977 and looked forward to another in early 1978. In November USBE's distribution to libraries reached 13,000,000 publications, sent in response to library requests during nearly 30 years of operation. On February 26, 1978, USBE would celebrate its 30th anniversary in the service of resource sharing among libraries.

(Above) Universal Serials and Book Exchange staff. (Below) Gordon D. Cooke, assistant director for serials, examining incoming periodicals at the Exchange.

The member libraries that form the cooperative network of USBE are multitype and multidisciplinary. They number 1,625 institutions, of which half are academic and half special, plus 60 public libraries, the group showing the greatest increase in 1977. The special libraries include those of government, commercial, and nonprofit agencies. Libraries ranging in size from specialized collections housed in a single room to the Library of Congress are both the contributors of the stock and the beneficiaries of the distribution.

The members placed 146,400 requests with USBE in 1977 and received in response 318,057 periodicals and 19,930 books and documents. They paid an average fee of $2.14 each for the periodicals and $5.87 each for the books and documents. A new feature of the distribution in 1977 was the accelerated backorder system initiated in January, whereby incoming periodical issues that answer a request on file at USBE are sent out immediately on receipt.

Consideration of USBE's role in the plans for the National Periodicals Center continued to be a special concern of the USBE staff and Board of Directors under President Joseph H. Treyz, Director of Libraries at the University of Wisconsin in Madison. In anticipation of requirements of the proposed Center, the USBE development of procedural changes was accelerated in areas in which the results could both improve the efficiency of the manual operation and provide a surer base for the possible handling of automated programs. Treyz appointed a committee of experts in library automation to review USBE procedures and plans and to make recommendations for additional steps to be taken.

A second committee was appointed to advise USBE in another major area of interest, the expansion of services to libraries outside the United States and Canada. USBE has a tradition of international activity that dates from its earliest operations, which were supported by a Rockefeller Foundation grant partly aimed at aiding libraries abroad. Expansion of distribution to institutions outside the United States and Canada is of value to all concerned. It serves to put to use publications needed in one part of the world more than in another and introduces new publications of the developing nations to libraries in the rest of the world. USBE foreign membership increased in 1977 to 280 libraries in 53 countries, which are cooperating with the 1,345 institutions in North America. The advisory committee is seeking channels whereby the increase in members abroad can be accelerated by bringing information to the attention of key personnel in the institutions that can benefit from USBE's cooperative services and substantial resources.

Of significance for USBE's areas of special interest was the fact that the number of visitors to USBE in 1977 doubled over 1976. The visits featured tours by groups of librarians, starting with those who attended the ALA Midwinter Meeting in Washington, D.C., in January. Other visitors included groups from individual libraries, groups with special program interests, and groups from countries abroad. Visitors came from 14 countries outside the United States as well as from 16 states and the District of Columbia.

ALICE D. BALL

Urban Libraries Council

In the late 1960's, the board members and administrators of urban libraries became acutely aware of the problems of their institutions.

City budgets, which began to reflect declining income and rising costs, placed severe financial pressures on many urban institutions. Many of the trustees of the affected libraries became concerned because they perceived a danger to the nation as well as to their own local institutions. If library services were to become weaker at a time when there was an increasing demand for informational and educational materials and services, the nation might inadvertently deprive itself of an irreplaceable asset. It became evident to these trustees that adverse developments in any one city had a profound relationship to the totality of library service and to the political response to library needs.

After a series of informal meetings beginning in 1970, trustees from several urban libraries, with the help of key administrative personnel from their own and other institutions, urged the creation of a new national organization to be known as the Urban Library Trustees Council. The Council was incorporated under an Illinois charter in 1971. Since that time the Council has met regularly, and its Executive Board has gradually and patiently sought a common base of interest upon which state and national programs might be built. Among its efforts, the Council subsidized the research that led to the report on the urban library condition entitled *Better Libraries Make Better Cities*. The findings of the report confirmed the pessimistic forebodings: library budgets were declining, and the usefulness of city libraries was being jeopardized.

ULC Officers

PRESIDENT:
Ralph Newman, Chicago Public Library

PRESIDENT-ELECT:
Randolph A. Brown, Louisville, Kentucky

EXECUTIVE DIRECTOR:
Paxton Price, St. Louis, Missouri

Headquarters: Chicago Public Library, 425 North Michigan, 60611

The Council gradually developed the view that federal intervention was necessary not only to save libraries but also to make them more effective than ever before. In this opinion the Council finds itself in complete harmony with the National Commission on Libraries and Information Sciences (NCLIS), whose studies and reports reinforce the Council's judgment.

After three years of activity, the Council determined that it needed to include more than trustees in its deliberations. Professional librarians, whose collective experience and knowledge keep our libraries operating, were invited to hold membership on the Executive Board. Because it was thought that the organization should focus public attention on the institutions represented, it was decided to drop the word *trustee* from the name of the Council. In July 1974, the group therefore renamed itself the Urban Libraries Council.

As a national consensus emerged in favor of direct federal funding of urban public libraries, the Council sought the introduction of legislation providing that assistance. Consequently, when in 1977 Congress considered the five-year renewal of the Library Services and Construction Act, an amendment was made to Title I mandating the direct distribution of federal funds to libraries in large cities in each state.

The evidence is now overwhelmingly persuasive that if libraries are to survive their funding must be more widely shared by states and the federal government. The Council's effectiveness will be directly related to the base of its membership and, incidentally, to its ability to command sufficient resources to influence legislative judgments.

In pursuit of its objective to improve legislative and financial support at the state and federal levels for urban library programs, the Council commissioned a significant study entitled *Improving State Aid to Public Libraries*. The study was conducted by Government Studies and Systems and was published in 1977 under the auspices of NCLIS by the Government Printing Office. The study is a follow-up to the earlier NCLIS report of 1974 entitled *Alternatives for Financing the Public Library*. As a service to its membership the Council will publish biennially, beginning in 1978, selected information and statistical data about its member libraries.

In 1977, the Council pledged its support to the National Citizens Emergency Committee to Save Our Libraries founded in New York City. The purpose and aims of the Committee parallel, in the main, those of the Council.

The membership of the Urban Library Council now numbers more than 80 libraries. The current officers are president, Ralph G. Newman, Chicago; vice-president, Randolph A. Brown, Louisville; secretary, Harold F. Herring, Huntsville; treasurer, Paulette Holahan, New Orleans. The members of the Executive Board are Arthur C. Banks, Jr., Hartford; Lucille Clifton, Baltimore; David M. Hennington, Houston; James R. Hunt, Cincinnati; Wyman Jones, Los Angeles; Edward Miller, Denver; Rt. Rev. Edward G. Murray, Boston; Whitney North Seymour, Jr., New York; Bruce D. Smith, Minneapolis; A.C. Strip, Columbus; and Sidney C. Volinn, Seattle. The executive director is Paxton Price, St. Louis; the editor of *The Lamp*, the Council newsletter, is Eva R. Brown, Chicago; and the legal consultant is Alex Ladenson.

Membership is institutional, with all members having an equal vote. The Urban Libraries Council is an affiliate of the American Library Association.

RALPH G. NEWMAN

Washington Report

Mixed reviews followed the close of the first session of the 95th Congress. Depending on which side of the aisle one was inclined to believe, it was the most productive session ever—House Speaker Thomas (Tip) O'Neill (D.-Mass.)—or it left a sorry record of accomplishments—Senate Minority Leader Howard Baker (R.-Tenn.). Putting partisan posturing aside, it was generally agreed that legislative achievements were about par for the course, with some 200 new public laws enacted during 1977. Expectations were considerably higher when the year began in view of the fact that the administration and the majority in Congress were of the same party and could, therefore, be counted on to work as a united team. This view was quickly put in perspective, however, by those who recalled that Jimmy Carter campaigned against entrenched Washington ways while the congressional majority, used to bucking the White House for the previous eight years, ran free of any White House political coattails.

Library Bills. On Capitol Hill, a number of library-related bills were approved by Congress and sent to President Carter for his signature. Other issues with library implications, some tied to Presidential reorganization plans still winding their way through legislative and executive channels, remained to be dealt with in the second session of the 95th Congress during 1978.

Foremost among the library issues was a five-year extension of the Library Services and Construction Act (LSCA). The new law (PL 95-123) includes an urban library amendment providing that when appropriations for LSCA Title I exceed $60,000,000, each state's portion of the excess will be reserved for libraries in cities of more than 100,000. For example, in a state with 20 per cent of its population in three cities of more than 100,000, 20 per cent of the state's share of the allocation over $60,000,000 would go to libraries in those three cities. (The remaining 80 per cent of the new money would be used for other Title I activities.) A state cannot earmark more than 50 per cent of the additional funds for urban libraries, and if there are no cities over 100,000, there is no formula earmarking funds for urban libraries. Although Title I has been funded for nearly two decades, this is the first time that Congress has specified funds for urban libraries. The next battle will be to get the funding level for Title I (now $56,900,000) increased enough to make the new urban library provision work.

Supplemental appropriations were provided for the White House Conference on Library and Information Services ($3,500,000), college library resources ($9,975,000), library training ($2,000,000), and research and demonstration ($1,000,000) under Title II of the Higher Education Act (HEA). Extensions of the Comprehensive Employment and Training Act (PL 95-44) and the Public Works Employment Act (PL 95-28) promised additional sources of funding for library positions being cut back by local budget stringencies.

Early in the year President Carter submitted his revision of the FY 1978 budget to Congress, proposing an increase for library programs of nearly $10,000,000 over the budget proposed by former President Ford. In April Carter issued a heartening National Library Week statement concluding with these words:

"This Library Week can serve as a rallying point for all concerned citizens to express their support for the nations's library system and to acknowledge the fact that libraries are a critical national resource we cannot afford to neglect."

FY 1978 Appropriations. Both House and Senate appropriations committees moved ahead in timely fashion to consider library and education funds in HR 7555, the FY 1978 money bill for the Department of Labor and the Department of Health, Education and Welfare (L-HEW), only to find themselves at a complete standstill by the end of July after resolving their dollar differences. The impasse was over federal funding of abortions, and it was not finally reconciled until the week before Congress adjourned in December, after 16 different votes over the intervening months. Due to the fact that thousands of federal workers were likely to go payless, House and Senate conferees then took an unusual shortcut procedure and passed House Joint Resolution 662, a stopgap money bill to cover the entire fiscal year. This bill took the place of the regular L-HEW bill as PL 95-205 and provided, among other items, a total of $245,712,000 for the three major library programs—LSCA, $60,237,000; HEA Title II, $17,975,000; and the consolidated Elementary and Secondary Education Act (ESEA Title IV-B) for school library materials, equipment, and guidance, counseling, and testing, $167,500,000.

ESEA Title IV-B. During the second half of the year, House and Senate education subcommittees reviewed how the ESEA Title IV-B consolidation was working as part of their deliberations over legislation to extend the program for another five years (HR 15 and S 1753). School librarians testified before both bodies, on July 27 in the House and on October 13 in the Senate, and urged continuation of the program but removal of the unduly competitive guidance and counseling salaries from what is basically needed to undergird all educational activities—school library resources and equipment. Final action is not expected until mid-1978 at the earliest.

Minimum Wage and Social Security. On November 1 President Carter signed into law the Fair Labor Standards Amendment (PL 95-151), increasing the minimum wage to $2.65 in 1978, $2.90 in 1979, $3.10 in 1980, and $3.35 in 1981. On December 15, the day of adjournment, Congress approved and sent to the White House the Social Security Financing Amendments of 1977. Signed into law on December 20 (PL 95-216), this comprehensive measure is designed to bolster the national Social Security system which was in peril of going broke within a couple of years. It will, among other things, increase employer and employee payroll taxes by $227 billion over 10 years, starting in 1979.

Once Congress adjourned, the focus of Washington's attention shifted back to the President, with speculations and rumors running rampant over what would be on his agenda in 1978 and in his first budget due to be submitted to Congress on January 23. (The past year—FY 1978—was a combination of Ford with some Carter revisions.) Major issues with implications for libraries and librarians will be Carter's urban policy, resolution of the conflicts in the energy legislation, and revision of the tax laws.   EILEEN D. COOKE

Women in Librarianship, Status of

As in previous years, the 1977 report on the status of women in librarianship must give a fragmentary and incomplete picture. This is due to the lack of data for the profession as a whole and the fact that information on sex is still not included as a variable in all studies of the various segments of the profession. When it is included, information on sex is frequently not correlated with other variables such as education, length of career, experience, or personal characteristics.

The data available, however, clearly show that women are underrepresented in management roles in proportion to their number in the profession and that the larger or more prestigious the library or library-related institution, the more likely that the administration will be male. Where men and women hold equal positions, the data also show that men tend to earn higher salaries than women. Other segments of the profession in addition to management tend to be segregated by sex. School librarianship, for example, has roughly 25 per cent more women practitioners than does academic librarianship, and men predominate in library education. Studies reported in 1977 corroborate this picture.

Social Responsibilities Round Table's Task Force on Women formed a steering committee at this meeting at the ALA Conference in Detroit.

Degree Distribution. The sexual distribution of degrees awarded in 1974-75 by U.S. library education programs, including those not accredited by the American Library Association, remained essentially the same as previously reported. (See *Degrees and Certificates Awarded by U.S. Library Education Programs, 1974-75,* ALA Office for Library Personnel Resources.) Women received 91.7 per cent of the associate of arts degrees and 90.3 per cent of the baccalaurate degrees awarded. More women (78.9 per cent) than men (21.1 per cent) received the master's degree in librarianship, but the percentage of women receiving unaccredited degrees was higher (87 per cent) than of those receiving degrees from ALA-accredited programs (78.9 per cent). Sixty-two per cent of the sixth-year certificates awarded went to women, but only 37.2 per cent of the doctorates were awarded to women. While the number of women enrolling in doctoral programs is increasing, the increase has not yet had an impact on the number of degrees awarded. Women receiving degrees in librarianship still follow the general pattern of women in higher education: the higher, the fewer.

Salaries. Salary and placement data are available only for graduates of U.S. and Canadian ALA-accredited library education programs. The results of the 1976 annual placement survey show that male graduates of the 53 ALA-accredited schools responding continued to be offered slightly higher salaries than women (See C.L. Learmont and R.L. Darling, "Placements and Salaries 1976: A Year of Adjustment," in the June 15, 1977 issue of *Library Journal.*) The 1976 median salary for all graduates was $10,576: $10,500 for women and $10,900 for men. The salary differential (3.7 per cent) was similar to that reported for 1975.

If the gap between the entry-level salaries of

321

male and female librarians is to be narrowed, women's salaries must increase at a pace faster than men's. This is not happening, however, despite the fact that the mean (average) beginning salary for women ($11,019) increased by 5.4 per cent over 1975 while that for men ($11,264) increased by only 3.2 per cent. Women's higher rate of advance can probably be accounted for by beginning salaries in the high range rather than an overall improvement in salaries for women.

For the third consecutive year women's median high salaries were higher than men's, and the difference—$16,750 for women, $14,300 for men—was greater than in the previous year. The median low salary reported for women ($7,590) also continued to fall below that for men, in 1976 by $1,200; and there were more women in the lower salary range than in the higher. In the five years that the placement survey data have been analyzed by sex, women's median salaries have increased at approximately the same rate as men's—$1,744 for women, $1,737 for men, a difference of only $7 in favor of women.

Sex segregation within the profession is also highlighted by the 1976 placement report. Eighty-five per cent of the placements in school libraries were women; 64 per cent, in college and university libraries; 76 per cent, in public libraries; and 76 per cent in other libraries and library agencies.

Type of library sex distribution affects salaries. School library positions, where placement of women is highest, accounted for 44 per cent of the 1976 high salaries, reflecting prior experience in a school system, and only 13 per cent of the low salaries. Public libraries accounted for only 16 per cent of the high salaries but for 41 per cent of the low salaries. The most frequently reported reason for accepting a low salary was geographic location.

The status of women whose career is in library education changed little from the previous year according to the 1976-77 survey of faculty salaries among schools accredited by ALA. (See R.E. Bidlack, "Faculty Salaries of 62 Library Schools, 1976-77," in the Spring 1977 issue of *Journal of Education for Librarianship*.) Women continued to account for 41 per cent of the faculty and 20 per cent of the heads of programs, the same percentages as in the previous year despite four schools having been added to the survey and four having been dropped due to accrediting and reporting changes. The median salary for women faculty ($32,415) remained less than that of male faculty ($33,494), but the salary differential was down from 5 per cent to 3.2 per cent.

Whether women had an earned doctorate or not, their salaries were lower than men's for both fiscal and academic year appointments with two exceptions, both without doctorates—full professors having a fiscal year appointment, and associate professors having an academic year appointment. As in the previous year women outnumbered men in the lower ranks of instructor and lecturer but were not represented in any rank in proportion to their number in the profession at large. Of the full professors only 28.8 per cent were women.

Medical Libraries. In a 1976 Medical Library Association (MLA) survey of U.S. and Canadian medical school libraries, men (one-third of the respondents) were found to be more heavily concentrated in better paying positions and at higher levels of responsibility than were women. (See P. Strange and W.N. Hoke, *A Survey of Salaries of Medical School Librarians in the United States and Canada, 1976-77*, Medical Library Association Surveys and Statistics Committee, May 1977.) The higher the administrative responsibility of medical school librarians, the lower the proportion of women—from 4.6 women to each man for librarians to .6 women to each man for directors.

Mean salaries for women were consistently lower for all subsets examined: librarians, department heads, assistant librarians, and directors. The differences between men's and women's salaries increased with administrative responsibility, a pattern reported for academic librarians as a whole for 1975-76. (See *Salary Structures of Librarians in Higher Education for the Academic Year 1975-76*, ALA, August 1976.) Administrative assignments were found to determine the level of compensation more powerfully than any other variable examined, including experience and education. Thus male predominance in the higher levels accounted for some, but not all of the large difference (27 per cent) between male and female levels of compensation in medical school libraries. Administrative assignment itself was not found to correlate strongly with variables analyzed but with characteristics reported to be intangible.

Rachel K. Goldstein reported in "Women and Health Science Librarianship: An Overview" in the *Bulletin of the Medical Library Association* (July 1977) that almost 30 per cent of the medical school libraries listed in the most recent directories of MLA and the Association of American Medical Colleges and in *MLA News* announcements have either been founded since 1972 or have had a new director. Nevertheless, the ratio of men to women administrators reported in the 1972 study by R.K. Goldstein and D.R. Hill in "The Status of Women in the Administration of Health Science Libraries" in the *Bulletin of the Medical Library Association* (October 1975) has remained virtually unchanged. Men have continued to assume more than 60 per cent of the new or vacated medical school library administrative positions during the past few years. The membership of MLA, by contrast, is approximately 85 per cent female.

Status Action Issues. Women have attempted to remedy their underrepresentation in the more powerful and lucrative segments of the profession and to remedy the inequality of salaries where equality of position exists by organizing in their professional associations and on the job.

Librarians at Temple University in Philadelphia and at San Diego County Library have filed sex discrimination complaints charging that both male and female librarians receive lower salaries because they work in a "women's profession." Individuals have also continued to file complaints such as one that resulted in the recommendation that the Justice Department bring suit against the Milwaukee Public Library for sex discrimination.

The ALA's Standing Committee on the Status of Women in Librarianship sponsored the major political action in a professional association in 1977—a resolution passed by Council "committing future ALA conference meetings to states that have ratified the Equal Rights Amendment." In 1975 a similar resolution had been defeated. ALA thus joined other professional associations such as the National Education Association in a boycott that the Chicago Convention Bureau indicated might cost its city alone some $15,000,000 in convention revenue. The ERA resolution has been sent to appropriate governors, state legislators, and convention bureaus and has already aroused vocal opposition from the heads of state library agencies in Louisiana and Alabama.

ALA's membership organization for those concerned with the status of women in librarianship, the Task Force on Women of the Social Responsibilities Round Table, completed restructuring begun in 1976. Goals were redefined, and a coordinating council was established. The Task Force's discussion group for women administrators continued to meet and faced the unresolved issue of whether to be a broad-based group or to limit itself to women actually in administrative positions. Members of the Task Force also actively lobbied for passage of the ERA resolution.

Within ALA's Reference and Adult Services Division a discussion group on service to women and on women's materials was formed. Official approval was obtained, and the initial meeting was held at the Annual Conference.

ALA's Association for Library Service to Children sponsored a day-long discussion at the Annual Conference on sexism in children's materials through its Discussion Group on Sexism in Library Materials for Children. The Young Adult Services Division's Sexism in Adolescent Literature Committee also met.

In compliance with the resolution on sexism and racism passed by ALA membership and Council in 1976, the various divisions and offices of ALA have been developing plans to combat sexism and racism in library education, staff development, cataloging procedures, and among library users. The section of the resolution committing ALA to increase library users' awareness of sexism and racism has been criticized as being in opposition to the concept of intellectual freedom, and the controversy is expected to continue. Full reports from the divisions and offices will be made at the 1978 Annual Conference.

Women were also active in related associations. The Interest Group on Women in Librarianship was officially recognized by the Association of American Library Schools. The Affirmative Action Committee of the Association for Educational Communications and Technology (AECT) sought to move the Association's 1978 and 1979 convention sites to cities in states that have ratified ERA, but the resolution was not considered because of a procedural matter. AECT's Women in Technology group, however, continued its strong conference programs and cassette tape exchange. While the women's caucus in the American Society of Information Scientists did not meet in 1977, the informal group was expected to continue.

Canadian Report. Canadian women librarians continued the level of activity reported in the 1977 *ALA Yearbook* (see Sherrill Cheda, "Women in Canadian Librarianship"). The Status of Women Committee of the Canadian Library Association (CLA) sponsored assertiveness training for its program at the CLA annual conference and requested Provincial Library Association liaison to provide contact with librarians throughout Canada. At Dalhousie University's School of Library Service Canada's first course on library service to women, Women's Studies Collections, was offered during the 1977 summer session. *Emergency Librarian,* the independent feminist library journal in its fourth year, was to devote its March 1978 issue to the first report from the "National Study of Career Paths of Librarians." The Study was undertaken in 1976 to examine career variables such as motivation, mobility, and career interruption as well as education and experience for men and women. The first report was to be on salary.

WLW Growth. For Women Library Workers (WLW) 1977 was a period of consolidation and steady growth. Individual membership increased by 24 per cent from 650 to 850 Canadian and U.S. professional, technical, clerical, and administrative library staff members.

Women's National Book Association

Twenty-four local chapters were registered with the national organization. Sixteen of these were actively working on projects that included planning the 1978 national WLW conference, a pay-parity survey, and workshops on career management and job skills. National bylaws were ratified by the membership, and the organization received not-for-profit tax-exempt status. Chapters appointed a coordinating council, a coodinator and recorder were elected, and a new staff person was hired.

Despite these efforts the status of women in librarianship remains one of economic and power disadvantagement in a profession they dominate in number. The causes of this disadvantagement are still being researched and debated, but women's status itself has been overwhelmingly documented in the past few years.

KATHLEEN WEIBEL

Women's National Book Association

On October 29, 1917, 15 women met at Sherwood's Book Store at No. 19 John Street in New York City to discuss ways and means of organizing a club "among all the women in the book trade." In 1977 the Women's National Book Association (WNBA) celebrated its 60th anniversary with a variety of programs across the country. Its 1,100 members—women and men—belong to 11 chapters and are supported by 35 sustaining members—publishers, wholesalers, and other commercial firms. The chapters and the years of their founding are: New York, 1917; Cleveland, 1952; Boston, 1954; Nashville, 1955; Binghamton, 1962; Detroit, 1966; Little Rock, 1967; San Francisco, 1968; Grand Rapids, 1968; Pittsburgh, 1976; and Southern California, 1976. A chapter in the Baltimore-Washington area is being organized.

The WNBA is the only organization in the book world open to women and men in all occupations allied to the publishing industry—publishers, authors, librarians, literary agents, editors, illustrators, educators, booksellers, and others. Each chapter elects its own officers and conducts its own educational programs. In 1977 these programs dealt with a wide variety of topics—writing, publishing, book production, women at work, women in sales, and the history and purpose of the WNBA. A major focus was a seminar, "Publishers on Publishing: A Dialogue with Teachers of English," sponsored by the WNBA and the Women's Committee of the National Council of Teachers of English (NCTE) on November 22 in New York City. Among the 20 speakers were Marilyn Abel of Penguin Books; Jane Howard, the author of *A Different Woman* and (forthcoming) *Families*; Dan Lacy, Senior Vice President of McGraw-Hill; Donald S. Lamm, President of W. W. Norton & Company; Kay Lee, Director of Design, General Books, Harcourt Brace Jovanovich; and Samuel Vaughan, Publisher and President of Doubleday Publishing Company. Several chapters held prior meetings with their local NCTE affiliates, and others asked NCTE members to attend and report.

Since 1940, the WNBA has presented the Constance Lindsay Skinner Award to a living American bookwoman whose contribution to books and to society through books—over and above her daily work—has been exceptional. In 1976 the award was presented to Frances Cheney of Nashville, Helen Meyer of New York City, and Barbara Ringer of Washington, D.C. It was decided in 1976 to make the award thereafter only in even-numbered years. The jurors for the 1978 award were Arthur Brody of Brodart, Charlotte Gallant of the Cuyahoga County (Ohio) Library, and Connie R. Dunlap of

Chapter Presidents, 1977–78

BINGHAMTON
  Miss Kay Brando
  Kay's Book Studio
  86 Front Street
  Binghamton, New York 13905

BOSTON
  Adeline Oakley
  24 Reynolds Avenue
  Randolph, Massachusetts 02368

CLEVELAND
  Winifred Dean
  4015 West 213 Street
  Fairview Park, Ohio 44125

DETROIT
  Edith Phillips
  23260 Russell Street
  Southfield, Michigan 48075

GRAND RAPIDS
  Margaret Bird
  60 Wallinwood Avenue, N.E.
  Grand Rapids, Michigan 49503

LITTLE ROCK
  Jane Cazort
  1 Sunset Circle
  Little Rock, Arkansas 72207

NASHVILLE
  Gladys Beasley
  5909 Hillsboro Road
  Nashville, Tennessee 37215

NEW YORK
  Sandra Paul
  Random House, Inc.
  201 East 50th Street
  New York, New York 10022

PITTSBURGH
  Amy Kellman
  Carnegie Library of Pittsburgh
  4400 Forbes Avenue
  Pittsburgh, Pennsylvania 15213

SAN FRANCISCO
  Peggy Sarasohn
  173 Buena Vista Avenue East
  San Francisco, California 94117

SOUTHERN CALIFORNIA
  Sylvia Cross
  19824 Septo Street
  Chatsworth, California 91311

the Duke University Libraries. The three nominees are Mary Stahlman Douglas of Nashville, Charlotte Huck of Columbus, and Anne Pellowski of New York City. The award will be presented at a time and place of the winner's choice in the spring of 1978, to coincide with the annual meeting of the Board of Managers of the WNBA.

National Officers and Committee Chairs, 1976-78

PRESIDENT: Ann Heidbreder Eastman
  716 Burruss Drive, N.W., Blacksburg,
  Virginia 24060; (703) 951-4770

SPECIAL ASSISTANT TO THE PRESIDENT: Mary Glenn Hearne
  3838 Granny White Pike, Nashville,
  Tennessee 37204

SECRETARY: Adeline Oakly
  24 Reynolds Avenue, Randolph,
  Massachusetts 02368

TREASURER: Anne J. Richter
  55 North Mountain Avenue, Apartment A2, Montclair,
  New Jersey 07042

ASSISTANT TREASURER: Sister Patricia A. Hodge, RSM
  Librarian, Trinity College, Colchester Avenue, Burlington,
  Vermont 05401

PAST PRESIDENT AND MEMBERSHIP: Mary V. Gaver
  300 Virginia Avenue, Danville,
  Virginia 24541

CORRESPONDING MEMBERSHIP: Marian Young
  1057 Yorkshire Avenue, Grosse Pointe Park,
  Michigan 48230

EDITOR, *The Bookwoman:* Diana L. Spirt
  17 Wayaawi Avenue, Bayville,
  New York 11709

CONSTANCE LINDSAY SKINNER AWARD (1978):
  Gaylyn Fullington
  1036 Berwick Trail, Madison
  Tennessee 37115

UN/NGO REPRESENTATIVE: Claire Friedland
  36 East 36th Street, New York
  New York 10016

Other major activities of the WNBA are numerous. *The Bookwoman* is published three times a year. As a Non-Governmental Organization of the United Nations, WNBA is heavily involved in planning for the International Year of the Child in 1979. Preparations are under way for publication of a chapbook containing a letter from Constance Lindsay Skinner to a young man about her interest in poetry. The chapbook will contain essays about Skinner—one by Helen Hoke Watts, who knew her in the last years of her life—and a complete bibliography. The WNBA has published two other books—*Women in the World of Words* (1967) and *Americana: As Taught to the Tune of a Hickory Stick* (1954)— both of which are available from the chapter presidents.   ANN HEIDBREDER EASTMAN

Young Adult Library Services

PROGRAMS

1977 will be remembered in young adult (YA) library services as the year of the skateboard, thanks to redesigned and more flexible boards that produced overwhelming YA interest (and accidents), and the release by Pyramid Films of *Magic Rolling Board*, a super program-starter. Prince George's County (Maryland) Library System (the only public library system in the country with a full-time YA programming specialist in addition to a YA coordinator) did an entire countywide "sidewalk surfing" series stressing skateboard safety. Orlando (Florida) Public Library audiences averaged from 150 to 200 for a series of skateboard symposiums. The Port Richmond Branch of the New York Public Library sponsored a skateboard contest, while kids in Ossining and Rye (New York), carried boards to repeated and begged-for showings of the Pyramid film.

Chess and science fiction competed for second place in YA programming interest, with tournaments, tutorials, and clinics in chess everywhere from White Plains, New York, to Bowie, Maryland, to Contra Costa County, California, to Osterhout, Pennsylvania. The Queensborough (New York) Public Library held a YA science fiction program featuring authors Isaac Asimov and Frederick Pohl for a packed house; the Contra Costa County and the Westchester (New York) Library Systems each offered countywide science fiction feature film festivals. The release of *Star Wars* fanned the flames as a new post-"Star Trek" cult emerged among the already rabid YA science fiction fans.

Encouraging creativity was the goal of many YA programs. Poetry workshops in six New York Public branches and a citywide YA poetry contest sponsored by the Los Angeles Public Library resulted in YA publications. Pleasant Hill (California) Library sponsored its sixth annual teenage art show; White Plains had a Halloween YA "paint-in" contest. Tulsa City-County Library sponsored a young filmmakers' festival, and Boston Public Library had a summer YA workshop in creative writing. Orlando did a mime workshop, and Grand Rapids (Michigan) Public Library held a film and video festival. Branches of the Cuyahoga County (Ohio) Public Library had teens paint a mural for the meeting room, displayed YA art with a reception for parents and community, held a mime workshop and a YA poetry and story collection, and planned a slide and tape history of rock and roll in Cleveland. Branches in the Prince George's County Library System featured concerts by local YA bands. The New York Public Library sponsored 25 library-based events and cosponsored 7 other presentations of the Youth Theatre Festival, including 50 Chinese teenagers from the Young People's Chinese Cultural Center performing traditional dancing and singing. New York Public also held four YA videotape workshops.

Although many programs resulted in publications or productions of original work by YA's, many libraries continued well-established review and creative writing publications such as "Thoughtwaves" in Prince George's County or "Teen Talk" from the Young People's Service of the National Library of Singapore. Several libraries produced new publications such as "ACTA BRAP" by the teen advisory board to the Arlington County (Virginia) Public Library or special issues such as one on YA reactions to *Roots* in "Your Choice" from the Central North Carolina Regional Library-Project ACEE.

YA interest in comics was seen in Los Angeles Public's mammoth regional comics and cartooning program that drew about 1,000 teenagers. There was a program on how to write and publish comics at the Walnut Creek Branch of the Contra Costa County Library System, and the Ossining Public Library established the Comic Freaks Club. Many libraries have also added comics to their YA collections.

Crisis problems of young adults were considered in programs on adolescent suicide in Prince George's County and Orlando, on delinquency diversion in Mount Pleasant, on rape prevention in Greenburgh and Yonkers (New York), and on jobs and college placement almost everywhere.

The Hawaii State Library System's Young Adult Services Unit produced a succinct information and referral brochure for young adults called appropriately, "The Yellow Page"; a booklist called "Dear Blabby," presenting teen problem novels in the form of letters to a mythical advice columnist; and several attractive bookmark booklists of topical interest.

As part of an ongoing, cooperative effort with the local Council on Adolescents, the Montgomery County (Md.) Department of Public Libraries initiated a project called READ WHILE YOU WAIT, to provide portable displays of lists and easy reading material for adolescents who "wait," often involuntarily, outside Juvenile Courts, counselor and parole offices, and in receiving homes and detention centers.

The National Runaway Hotline number (800-621-4000) was distributed nationwide through state library agencies, thanks to the vision of Pauline Winnick of HEW's Library Services Section.

In addition to those programs, many film, book discussion, and crafts programs continued to attract YA's to public libraries. New York Public probably set a record for longevity as its "Teen Age Book Talk" radio program (an "unrehearsed discussion of books and reading with authors and others from the publishing field") continued successfully into its 31st year on the air. Several libraries opted for single, general, large-appeal YA programs such as "Teen Nite II" at the Leon County (Florida) Public Library and the National Library Week discotheque at the Forsythe County (North Carolina) Library. "Levels," the only library-sponsored YA cultural center in the country, completed its third successful year of operation at the Great Neck (New York) Public Library.

CONTINUING EDUCATION

In cooperation with local YA librarians at the Denver Public Library and the Southeastern Metropolitan Board of Cooperative Educational Services, the University of Denver Graduate School of Librarianship sponsored an April institute on adolescent literature featuring YA authors S.E. Hinton and Richard Peck. The University of Alabama School of Library Service and the Alabama Library Association cosponsored a YA workshop, also featuring author Peck. The School of Library Science of the University of North Carolina, and the North Carolina Library Association cosponsored "Hot Stuff," a preconference workshop on catching kids. The program included Mary K. Chelton, Past President of ALA's Young Adult Services Division (YASD), and Joan Lipsitz, author of *Growing up Forgotten*, as speakers with an afternoon idea exchange program. The Palmer Graduate Library School of Long Island University (C.W. Post Center) sponsored a YA literature day in cooperation with Harper & Row in December, and the Children's and Young Adult Services Section (CYASS) of the New York Library Association (NYLA) featured YA author Robin Brancato and a panel of paperback publishers at the NYLA annual conference. NYLA's CYASS also formed a committee on current professional issues to keep its Board better informed on state and national problems related to library services to youth. The New York Chapter of the Women's National Book Association held a January program on YA publishing, and the Colorado Library Association's keynote speaker, Dorothy M. Broderick, addressed library responsibilities and the First Amendment rights of youth.

Wisconsin's Division for Library Services sponsored an April conference on "What Concerns Young Adults Most?" with guest author John R. Powers. The Maryland Library Association's Adult and Young Adult Services Division sponsored two regional meetings on

YA services. The Ohio Library Association featured author Robert Cormier at its YA program on "Access to Diversity" and honored YA Task Force Coordinator, Barbara Newmark of the Cuyahoga County Public Library, with its Diana Vescelius Memorial Award. Carol Starr, editor of the *Young Adult Alternative Newsletter*, now in its sixth year, appeared at programs in Arizona and Nebraska, and the Minnesota Library Association held a spring meeting on literature and services for young adults. In a unique move toward closer cooperation, the Bay Area Young Adult Librarians met with the YA library class at the University of California at Berkeley to give students and teacher a closer look at actual YA selection practices.

PUBLICATIONS AND PROJECTS

Most public libraries continued to produce book and materials lists for their YA publics. Boston Public was possibly the most prolific with a series on all U.S. ethnic groups and their heritages. The publications included "Bee Pel's Choice," a YA list for people who hate books; and "Black on Black," a list of books on the Black experience by Black authors. Others done in cooperation with the Eastern Massachusetts Regional Library System included "Versus," "Paperback Power II," "Books Build Background," a series called "Easy Reads," and "And Ain't I a Woman?"

Prince George's County continued a bookmark-booklist series of "If You Liked _____, Try ..." and integrated topical reading lists on YA programming fliers. New York Public, despite budget problems, continued to produce its invaluable "Books for the Teenage" annual list.

A recurring trend in YA reading lists is to allow YA readers to do the selections and annotations on the lists. Examples are the "Science Fiction Booklist" from Novato, California, a mystery list, "You Said It," from Chappaqua, New York, and "The Cat: A Teen Catalog" from Rockville Centre, New York. One of the best topical YA booklists in 1977 was "Runaways: Unhappy Teenagers" from the Fresno County (California) Public Library.

While most YA librarians shy away from the summer reading clubs common in children's services, the Charlotte and Mecklenburg County (North Carolina) Public Library sponsored "16 Ways to Read Your Summer" for students in grades 7 to 12. Done in conjunction with a local radio station, the project documented 2,600 YA readers getting library cards and 747 completing the reading requirements for free records. Ironically, this immensely successful program led to demands from children for a reading club of their own.

To reinforce the YA services commitment to booktalking, the four Bay Area YA coordinators (Carol Starr, Virginia Carpio, Susan Henderson, and Jeannie Goodhope) produced a training videotape on booktalking through their local cable video project for use by practitioners and library educators.

The Young Adult Task Force of the Ohio Library Association produced the "Whole YA Catalog," and the Central North Carolina Regional Library Project ACEE put together "Young Adult Program Ideas That Worked." "Y-A Hotline" is being compiled by the Dalhousie University School of Library Service YA classes under the direction of Professor Loren Amey.

YARNS (YA Roundtable News), the Alabama Association's YA services newsletter, spawned by the 1976 Institute on YA Services at the library school of the University of Alabama, went into its second year of publication.

"In the YA Corner" continued as a feature in *School Library Journal*, and *Booklist* introduced YA reviewing of high-interest/low-literacy-level titles. Unfortunately, the demise of *Booklegger* lost for YA librarians Patty Campbell's wonderful column "Se Habla YA Aqui?"

Two surveys of YA services were completed or launched in 1977. The Bay Area YA Librarians polled local school and public YA librarians on job-related concerns, the results of which were turned over to the YASD and Library Education Division Joint Committee on Library Education for Service to Young Adults at the Pre-Service Level. YASD Board member Lelia-Jane Roberts initiated a national survey through *School Library Journal* to find out who was really serving adolescents in public libraries.

Trends. Although "it is a fact that YA librarians seem to be an endangered species," as Valerie Brooker, the lone YA librarian in New Mexico, said in an article in *Notes from the Examination Center for Children's Books*, it was heartening to learn that Chicago Public was actively searching for a YA services specialist and that San Diego Public Library "elevated" the YA coordinator to special groups coordinator. The Tampa-Hillsborough (Florida) Library also created a new YA coordinator position.

Christy Tyson, an LSCA-funded YA librarian in the Mesa Public Library, Arizona, managed to form an exemplary, ongoing young adult advisory committee, consisting of eight volunteers from ten of the city's secondary schools and one person not in school, to help plan program and review materials. She regards the YA committee as "the most effective check we have against any tendency toward insularity and misapplication of other people's programs and principles."

The Texas State Library is using a $240,000

LSCA grant to test video program collections in 29 libraries; based on the participants' preferences, children and young adults came second after general entertainment. Guitar Workshop of Roslyn received funds from the New York State Council on the Arts to offer 75 folk music performances, an obvious YA interest area, in public libraries in the state.

While the funding and administrative support varied widely for services, it must be said that YA services managed to hold their own in 1977 with enthusiasm and creativity at the national, state, and local levels.

MARY K. CHELTON

Young Adult Literature

If any general statement can be made regarding young adult literature in 1977, it is this the best way to insure that teenagers would read any given book was to make a film or television program out of it or to base advertising of the book on the movie or television program made from it. A media tie-in gives a book an automatic, instant national exposure. The most prominent example of the media tie-in's success in promoting a book for teen readership in 1977 was *Star Wars*—a movie probably seen by as many teens as listened to the Beatles 10 years earlier. George Lucas's book was available before the movie was distributed but went largely unnoticed. It was later revised slightly to fit the movie's image and became an instant hit among teen readers. (And just as 1977 was drawing to a close, Steven Spielberg's film *Close Encounters of a third Kind* gave birth to a paperback novelization that promises to be as popular as *Star Wars* has been among young adult readers.)

Media Tie-ins. Variations of the media tie-in were used to promote scores of books read by teens in 1977. This is not a new phenomenon; what is new is that it no longer is a once- or twice-a-year happening. The media tie-in can now be counted on to sell books to teens in and of itself—almost regardless of what the subject is.

Not only does the success of *Star Wars* as a book point up the influence of the media tie-in, but it also establishes a focal point for science fiction—and although still in space, it is miles away from *2001* (a media success of the late 1960's). Perhaps it is coincidental, but teens in 1977 did not find as many serious science fiction novels to read as they had in previous years. Space opera—which is what *Star Wars* is—seems to have monopolized young adult interests in the science fiction field.

To emphasize this even more, teenage readers found great interest in Gary Garano's and Paul Schulman's *Fantastic Television*, a documentary paean to the previous 30 years that included scripts of "Star Trek," "Superman," and "Batman."

Although serious science fiction seems to have been deemphasized in 1977, young adults continued to read well-written fantasy. *Tsuga's Children* by Thomas Williams is a rich, imaginative tale of a family and their adventures in an isolated past or future world that forces them to spend their days just trying to survive their harsh winter environment—a human *Watership Down*. Also published in 1977 was *The Sword of Shannara* by Terry Brooks, an epic fantasy of good and evil in conflict. Although often compared to Tolkien's novels—primarily because of the imaginary world set up in the story—the book is more of a "fantasy opera" than an allegory. This quality, of course, makes it a good story and has given it appeal among teen readers. And Anne McCaffrey has added another episode to her Dragonsong series, a novel entitled *Dragonsinger*. Her heroine is depicted trying to make a place for herself on her remote planet in a vocation in which women were formerly excluded.

Sexual Themes. If it is still possible, three books published in 1977 broke new ground in writing about sex for teenagers. Peter Mayle's *"Will I Like It?"* attempts to prepare teens to enjoy their first sexual experience. Although it is an interesting attempt to provide an extended, liberal answer to an "Ask Beth" question, it does not work because of the irrelevant and confusing photographs of nudity arbitrarily placed throughout the text and because it asks the question without providing a thorough discussion of sexuality and adolescent emotions and feelings. In short, it puts the cart before the horse.

Homosexuality is the theme of two books. Morton Hunt's *Gay: A Young Person's Guide to Homosexuality* sympathetically tries to delineate the various modes of homosexual life, but the book is badly flawed by the author's bias against gay life-styles different from the homosexual couple living together like a middle-class hetereosexual couple. Hopefully, this first book on a formerly taboo subject will inspire others to write on gay men and women with more understanding and

Cover photo from The Sidewalk Racer and Other Poems *by Lillian Morrison.*

knowledge. Of more interest to teens in 1977 was pro football player David Kopay's autobiography, *The David Kopay Story*, in which he candidly talks about his homosexuality and describes his inner conflicts in deciding finally to make public his sexual preferences.

Don Bredes' novel *Hard Feelings* also charts new paths in writing about sexuality for teens. The story is a humorous and realistic account of male teenagers growing up in the 1960's on Long Island. It emphasizes their preoccupation with sex in language, thought, and activity. Some have objected to the frequent use of four-letter words (and combinations therof), and many have been critical of the macho attitudes expressed by the young men in the story, but the novel accurately reflects the milieu of the 1960's and is one of the best contemporary novels portraying the rites of change in male adolescents.

Music, Sports, and War. Music is still the focus of many teenagers' reading interests. In 1977, a somewhat unusual expression of this interest was seen in the popularity of a large-size paperback called *An Album of Albums*, edited by Storm Thorgerson and Roger Dean. The book contains colorful reproductions of record album covers—most of them from the world of rock music. Published originally as a serious art and music book with detailed information on making album covers, the book has fascinated young adults.

The most widely read sports books in 1977 were about the decathlon and soccer. Bruce Jenner's *Decathlon Challenge*, though often reading like an old "This Is Your Life" television program, successfully communicates to readers the great willpower of Jenner in training for the 1972 and 1976 Olympics and relates his amazing athletic feats in the 1976 Olympic Games. His wife Chrystie also wrote a book entitled *I Am Chrystie* about her life during this period of time, and it was just as popular among many young adult readers. Pelé, the world's most famous soccer player, retired in 1977, but his autobiography, *My Life and the Beautiful Game: The Autobiography of Pelée*, has made all the cheap profiles written about him almost worthless.

Although quality books on the Vietnam War were published in 1977, teenage readers largely ignored them and instead turned their reading interests to World War II. Among the many books young adults read on the subject in 1977, the best were Fred Uhlman's *Reunion*, about the friendship between a Jew and a non-Jew in Nazi Germany, and Ilse Koehn's *Mischling Second Degree*, a memoir of a Hitler youth participant who looks back on her experiences after realizing that she is partly Jewish.

Other themes. Consciousness raising among women has filtered down to young adult females in books on many topics. One of the

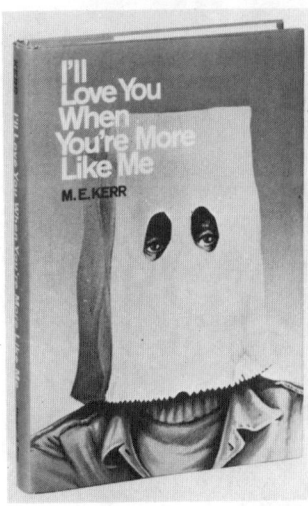

(Top) Robert Lipsyte, author of One Fat Summer.
(Middle) M. E. Kerr, author of I'll Love You When You're More Like Me.
(Bottom) Nicholasa Mohr, author of In Nueva York.

Young Adult Literature

(Top) Robert Cormier, author of I Am the Cheese.
(Right) Harry and Norma Fox Mazer, authors of The Solid Gold Kid.

most unusual books related to this phenomenon in 1977 was a book for girls and women entitled *Self-Defense And Assault Prevention For Girls and Women* by Bruce Tegner and Alice McGrath. The authors have perhaps minimized the danger of violent assault by strangers in their emphasis on preventing seduction and rape by people known to their victims. But their emphasis on building self-worth and self-reliance along with developing techniques of self-defense is welcome and helpful advice.

Two excellent books on American Indians attracted interest among older teen readers. *Anpao: An American Indian Odyssey* by Jamake Highwater is a skillfully woven tale—beautifully illustrated by Indian artist Fritz Scholder—combining many Indian myths, showing the deep feelings and strong beliefs many Native American tribes had about the close relationship between human beings and nature. James Houston's novel *Ghost Fox* is a long and involving story of the kidnapping of a New Hampshire 17-year-old girl by the Abnaki Indians, her captivity and assimilation into the tribe, and the adoption of the Indian way of life.

Older young adult readers also were attracted to two books describing personal tragedies of American families, both having significant implications for legal system reform. Joan Barthel's *A Death In Canaan* uncovers the story of an 18-year-old Connecticut boy wrongly accused and almost convicted of killing his mother. And Karen Ann Quinlan's parents movingly tell her tragic story and their own reactions to what happened to her (*Karen Ann: The Quinlans Tell Their Story*).

Animal lovers were fascinated by two heart-warming books about people dealing with animals on a daily basis. David Taylor's *Zoo Vet* details his experiences as a vetinarian treating sick and injured animals around the world. And for older readers, James Herriot's best selling *All Things Wise And Wonderful* tells about the author's well-known veterinary experiences.

Other 1977 adult best sellers which were favorites among teen readers are: Robin Cook's *Coma*, a fast moving suspense story

(Above) Anita Heyman, author of Exit From Home.

(Right) Lois Ruby, author of Arriving at a Place You've Never Left.

(Left) Alice McGrath, co-author with Bruce Tegner of Self-Defense & Assault Prevention for Girls & Women.

mixing strong feminism with strange medical ethics in an urban hospital setting; *The Book of Lists* by David Wallechinsky; TV newsman Dan Rather's memoir *The Camera Never Blinks*; Jay Akson's *The Amityville Horror*, an account of his family's 28-day encounter with a haunted house; and Wil Huygen's *Gnomes*, an imaginative recreation of imaginary creatures.

What of Fiction? In the past two years, novelists such as Ursula LeGuin and Norma Fox Mazer have successfully revived the short story form for teens. Two 1977 anthologies deserve special mention—Lois Ruby's *Arriving at a Place You've Never Left* and Nicholosa Mohr's *In Nueva York*. Ruby's anthology is composed of short, simply told stories of young people, their friends, and their parents experiencing fear, love, sickness, and hope—all in very different settings. Mohr's stories are set on the Lower East Side of New York City and are interconnected slice-of-life portraits showing the grief and humor of Puerto Rican street life.

Many authors quite familiar to young adult readers came out with new books in 1977. M.E. Kerr, a perennial favorite among younger teenagers, added to her famous characterizations of teenagers in a novel called *I'll Love You When You're More like Me*, about teenagers who disagree with their parents' plans regarding their futures. Paul Zindel, whose novels have always included a mixture of humor, humanism, and cynicism along with zany characters, has continued true to form in his short novel *Confessions of a Teenage Baboon*. The book concerns a teenager and his itinerant nurse-mother and their relationship with a self-pitying and strange 30-year-old man whose contact with humanity is limited to befriending confused adolescents.

Riding the wave of explicit sex in teen novels (such as Judy Blume's trend-setting *Forever*), Norma Klein has written a novel called *It's OK If You Don't Love Me* that inverts the usual stereotypes—here the female is relatively sexually experienced and the male is not. Two favorite authors of books for younger teenage readers, Harry Mazer and Norma Fox Mazer, have for the first time collaborated on a novel,

Young Adult Literature

The Solid Gold Kid, a suspense adventure about the kidnapping of a teenager from a rich family, his new friends, and their escape from their captors.

The most talked about novel of the year was Robert Cormier's second novel for teenagers, *I Am the Cheese*. It is a fragmented and often confusing narrative about a teenager whose parents' identities, his own past, and his present sanity are question marks until the end— and even then there are questions left unanswered. However, the studied craftsmanship and the careful interweaving of episodes mixed with the author's creative handling of the theme of government power and the dehumanization of the individual, make for exciting and provocative reading.

Female teenage readers in 1977 were treated to a follow-up novel to Blossom Elfman's very successful *The Girls of Huntington House*. The story, *A House for Jonnie O.*, is about unmarried pregnant teenagers trying to forge meaningful lives for themselves as parents-to-be. Although the characters are stereotyped, the story is involving, and the theme of independence hits home with young adults.

One first novel deserves special mention, Anita Heyman's *Exit from Home*. It is set in Czarist Russia in the Jewish ghetto. Evoking a combination of *Fiddler on the Roof* and Chaim Potok's *The Chosen*, the novel tells of a bright Yeshivah student who outgrows his parochial education and his overly strict father, becomes involved in anti-Czarist politics, and finally decides to leave Russia to go to the United States.

Two anthologies of poetry stood out as being especially attractive to young adult readers. Lillian Morrison's collection *The Sidewalk Racer And Other Poems of Sport And Motion* contains poems largely for younger teenagers, combining short verse with pictures illustrating the activity portrayed in the poems. Nancy Larrick's anthology *Crazy To Be Alive In Such A Strange World* (Evans, 1977) is an extremely rich and varied collection of poems for teenagers by well-known poets showing different life situations, often with an ironic twist.

Reading Problems. Discussion of young adult literature in 1977 would not be complete without mention of a recently discovered fact of social reality—fewer and fewer teenagers graduate from school knowing how to read. In schools across the country, remedial reading, once set aside for special classes, is now being incorporated into regular high school English classes. The publishing industry has only recently begun reacting to this phenomenon. "High-interest—low-reading-level" series have been started and are beginning to be pushed on schools and libraries. Many of them are clearly inferior and exploitative. The Scholastic Action series of graded original novels in paperback format with black and white photos illustrating scenes from the narratives, however, have been widely used and accepted by teenage readers. The novels cover adolescent interests—cars, parental troubles, sports, trouble with the law, male-female relationships, and other subjects. The characters are easily identifiable, and the stories, while not didactic, express positive and believable attitudes.

In addition, some publishers in the past two years have brought out easy-to-read novels as part of their regular trade line of books. Because of their clearly drawn characters, subject matter, and easy-to-read writing, books such as Kin Platt's *Headman* and Judy Blume's *Forever* have appealed to and have been read by many young adults who are poor readers. In 1977, *One Fat Summer* by Robert Lipsyte fell into this category. The book is not about drugs or sex, but tells the story of a very overweight teenager growing up in the 1950's, coping with his adolescence and his fatness. The book is easy to read and very humorous, and contains a main character with whom younger teenagers will easily identify.

The need for such books is rapidly increasing. To help librarians identify titles with high interest, low reading level use with young adults, *Booklist* has recently begun to review and grade books falling into this category. High school librarians and public librarians working with teenagers should expect an increasing number of easy reading, high interest books in coming years.

JACK FORMAN

Bibliographical Information on Title Cited
Young Adult Literature, 1977

Star Wars by George Lucas (Ballantine, 1976, 1977)
2001: A Space Odyssey by Arthur Clarke (Norton, 1968)
Fantastic Television by Gary Garano and Paul Schulman (Harmony Books, 1977)
Tsuga's Children by Thomas Williams (Random House, 1977)
Watership Down by Richard Adams (Macmillan, 1975; Avon, 1976)
Sword of Shannara by Terry Brooks (Random House, 1977; Ballantine, 1977)
Gay: A Young Person's Guide to Homosexuality by Morton Hunt (Farrar, 1977)
The David Kopay Story by David Kopay (Arbor House, 1977)
Hard Feelings by Don Bredes (Atheneum, 1977)

An Album of Albums edited by Storm Thorgerson and Roger Dean (A&W Publications, 1977)
Reunion by Fred Uhlman (Farrar, 1977)
Mischling Second Degree by Ilse Koehn (Greenwillow, 1977)
Self Defense and Assault Prevention for Girls and Women by Bruce Tegner and Alice McGrath (Thor, 1977)
Arriving at a Place You've Never Left by Lois Ruby (Dial, 1977)
In Nueva York by Nicholosa Mohr (Dial, 1977)
I'll Love You When You're More like Me by M.E. Kerr (Harper, 1977)
Headman by Kin Platt (Greenwillow, 1975; Dell, 1977)
One Fat Summer by Robert Lipsyte (Harper, 1977)
Scholastic Action Series (Scholastic Press)
Decathlon Challenge by Bruce Jenner (Prentice Hall, 1977)
I Am Chrystie by Chrystie Jenner (Celestial Arts, 1977)
My Life and the Beautiful Game: The Autobiography of Pelé by Edson A. Nascimento (Pelé) and Robert Fish (Doubleday, 1977)
Zoo Vet by David Taylor (Lippincott, 1977)
Coma by Robin Cook (Little Brown, 1977)
The Book of Lists by David Wallechinsky (Morrow, 1977)
Confessions of a Teenage Baboon by Paul Zindel (Harper, 1977)
Forever by Judy Blume (Pocket Books, 1976)
It's OK If You Don't Love Me by Norma Klein (Dial, 1977)
The Solid Gold Kid by Harry Mazer and Norma Fox Mazer (Delacorte, 1977)
I am the Cheese by Robert Cormier (Pantheon, 1977)
The Girls of Huntington House by Blossom Elfman (Houghton, 1972)
A House for Jonnie O. by Blossom Elfman (Houghton, 1977)
Exit from Home by Anita Heyman (Crown, 1977)
The Chosen by Chaim Potok (Simon and Schuster, 1967)
The Sidewalk Racer and Other Poems by Lillian Morrison (Lothrop, 1977)
Crazy To Be Alive In Such A Strange World by Nancy Larrick (Ed.) (Evans, 1977)
Dragonsinger by Anne McCaffrey (Atheneum, 1977)
Ghost Fox by James Houston (Harcourt, 1977)
Close Encounters Of A Third Kind by Steven Spielberg (Dell, 1977)
The Amityville Horror by Jan Anson (Prentice-Hall, 1977)
All Things Wise And Wonderful by James Herriot (St. Martins Press, 1977)
Gnomes by Wil Huygen (Abrams, 1977)

Young Adult Services Division

Membership continued to be a problem in 1977, although interest in the Young Adult Services Division (YASD) most certainly was not. After an increase in organizational dues received by the Division became a fact, the Executive Secretary was able to go to full-time status as of November 1. The contacts made and the effectiveness of the Division's office staff enabled YASD to be heard at ALA headquarters and among the entire ALA membership. Inquiries about young adult services and the work of the Division were handled efficiently by the staff, and interest in YASD grew. Participation on the Divisional Interests Special Committee helped YASD understand and cope with the problems arising from the new independence of divisions.

Programs. The YASD meeting at the ALA Annual Conference in Detroit had its largest attendance ever. "The Librarian as Youth Counselor," a two-part program, drew more than 400 people for the lecture on human sexuality by Sol Gordon of Syracuse University. Professor Gordon discussed a basic theme—too many people are hung up on their own sexuality, whereas loving, caring, and consideration for the partner is the important thing. If this feeling exists, a good sexual relationship will follow, he said. The second half of the program was limited by registration to 200 participants. A dinner in designated groups was followed by workshop sessions in active listening. These involved role playing and listening and interview techniques that would be helpful for drawing young adult patrons out of themselves to find their real information needs. The sessions were directed by Sara Fine.

A second program was produced by the Publishers' Liaison Committee. "Paperback Power" was discussed by a panel composed of Richard Peck, YA author; Audrey Eaglen, Cuyahoga County (Ohio) Public Library System; Marilyn Abel, Viking-Penguin Publishers; Marvin Scilkin, Director of Orange (New Jersey) Public Library and editor of the U*N*A*B*A*S*H*E*D Librarian; and Dan Fader, author and advocate of reading for all ages. The discussion covered phases of the purchase and use of paperbacks—techniques of writing for and effective purchase of paperbacks, publishers' and distributors' views of the library market, emphasis on the fact that libraries do not return books as retailers do, and location of materials by title. There was a final plea from Fader that unless everyone works together reading will become a thing of the past since most people get their information from radio and television. Sol Gordon's speech was taped and is available from the YASD office. Hints and highlights from

Flyer from the Fresno (California) County Public Library advertises the "toll free, hassle free" telephone number for runaway teens.

Young Adult Services Division

"Paperback Power" will be available in a reprint from *Top of the News*. A sampling of films from the annually produced list, "Selected Films for Young Adults—1977," was also shown during the Annual Conference week.

Projects. Among the ongoing projects continued in 1977 by YASD committees were preparation of bibliographies for *Teachers' Guide to Television* and other related publications; preparation of a services guide, *Directions for Library Services to Young Adults*, to be published in 1978; a draft of a position paper on "Library Education for Librarians Working with Young Adults in Public Libraries"; continued work on an award list of the "Top Ten Pops List" to be chosen by young adults themselves; selection of "Best Books for Young Adults—1976" and "Selected Films for Young Adults—1977"; the implementation of a procedure for public discussion by the Best Books for Young Adults Committee that would be an efficient working model for book discussion committees to follow; and circulation by the Activities Committee of a questionnaire to locate audiovisual programs in in-service training and promotion of YA services. Circulation and rejuvenation of "Living Library Patterns" and the "Survival Kit" continued; both of these packages on programming and management have been so popular that the Executive Secretary has reservations through 1978 for these tools in work with young adults. Also circulating is a packet on services to the blind, physically handicapped, and shut-in, prepared by the Library Service to Young Adults in Institutions Committee. A still-popular aid for promoting young adult services is the brochure *If You Work with Young Adults . . .*, distributed from the YASD office. Another promotional project is the "Youth People's Person-YASD" T-shirt sale. The shirts are still available for $4.50 prepaid to YASD T-shirts, Mayfield Regional Library, 6080 Wilson Mills Road, Cleveland, Ohio 44143. Specify S/M/L. Colors: red, yellow, gold, blue, orange.

Skateboard safety was stressed in many libraries in 1977 and included a symposiusm at the Orlando (Florida) Public Library (above) and a clinic at the Bowie branch of the Prince George's County memorial Library System.

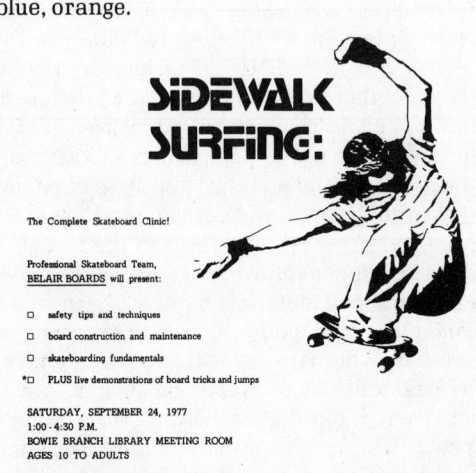

New Committees. During the year the YASD Board authorized several new committees. Those just becoming active included the YASD Intellectual Freedom Committee, which alerted Council to pass a resolution on Legislation to Control Sexual Abuse of Minors and was very vocal in discussion of *The Speaker*. The Sexism in Adolescent Literature Committee had a new project under way. The High-Interest/Low-Literacy-Level Materials Evaluation Committee was in the process of planning a joint preconference with the Association for Library Service to Children (ALSC) for the 1978 Annual Conference; and a revision committee was at work on *Selected Materials for Children and Young Adults* (ALA, 1967). New committees for 1978 resulted from a split of the Media Selection and Usage Committee into two committees. The Library Services to Young Adults in Institutions Committee continued the outstanding work done by the Task Force, and the Legislative Committee served as a watchdog on legislation that might affect young adults. The ALSC/YASD *Top of the News* Editorial Joint Committee worked with the new editor, Audrey Eaglen. The YASD Advisory Committee to the Collection Development Section of the Library of Congress continued to recommend young adult titles for Talking Books. New liaisons were established with the Library Instruction Round Table, the Girl Scouts of America, and the Planned Parenthood Federation of America.

YASD Officers

PRESIDENT (July 1977-June 1978):
Rosemary Young, Denver Public Library

VICE-PRESIDENT/PRESIDENT-ELECT:
Bruce E. Daniels, Free Library, Philadelphia

EXECUTIVE SECRETARY:
Evelyn Shaevel

Membership (August 31, 1977): 4,022 (1,847 personal and 2,175 organizational)

Publications. Lists that continue to be popular are the five "Outstanding" lists revised in 1976, and "Still Alive: The Best of the Best, 1960-1974," "Best Books for Young Adults," and "Selected Films for Young Adults." A new publication now available is *Media and the Young Adult: A Selected Bibliography—1950-1977*. It is available for $5 from ALA Order Services, 50 East Huron Street, Chicago, Illinois 60611. The "YASD Survival Kit" is available for $2.25 prepaid from the YASD office at the ALA address. The Division also has made available "Booktalking: You Can Do It" by Mary K. Chelton, reprinted from *School Library Journal*. *Top of the News* continues as the quarterly journal of both ALSC and YASD. — ROSEMARY YOUNG

Canadian Correspondent's Report

During 1977, Canadian libraries faced a repeat of the economic situation of the previous year, described in the 1976 report as "characterized by inflation, slow growth and federal government price and wage controls." Once again library budgets were severely strained, making it difficult or impossible to develop new services or to expand existing ones.

Some of the highlights of 1977 included publication by the federal government of position papers on copyright and freedom of information and of a study on library use by Canadians; acquisition of the Lowy Collection by the National Library; publication of the report of the Canadian Union Catalog Task Group; publication of a report on library-publisher relations; a workshop on Canadian abstracting and indexing services; and the offering of M.L.S degree courses in Ottawa.

Abstracting and Indexing Services

A workshop on Canadian abstracting and indexing services was convened by the Committee on Bibliographical Services for Canada (CBSC) at the National Library of Canada, March 7-8. Participants included members of CBSC, representatives from 18 Canadian abstracting and indexing services, and resource persons from the National Library and the Ottawa Public Library. Position papers were delivered on the coverage of Canadian materials by Canadian abstracting and indexing services, on the financing of such services, on their editorial production, and on their technical production. Following the workshop, CBSC formulated a series of recommendations that were transmitted to the National Library Advisory Board and other appropriate bodies for consideration.

CBSC recognized that it is a Canadian responsibility, as a national contribution to universal bibliographical control, to ensure the coverage of Canadian materials by abstracting and indexing services. CBSC stated that effective coordination of Canadian services could only evolve through a proper assessment of the existing coverage of Canadian materials. As an initial step, CBSC recommended that an inventory of all Canadian materials already abstracted or indexed by Canadian services be compiled, indicating the extent and level of coverage for each individual item.

The Committee also recommended that a standard set of criteria be applied in the assessment of proposals soliciting financial support for abstracting and indexing services, such criteria to include coverage, market, quality of output, cost-effectiveness, national interest, and alternative sources of income. In order to provide a basis for the exchange of information between services with similar subject interests, the Committee recommended that each abstracting and indexing service be asked to prepare a statement of possible areas of cooperation. As a result of its deliberations, the Committee recognized the need in Canada for better information about existing Canadian services and expertise in the field of abstracting and indexing and the need to facilitate better communication between the creators and producers of data bases. In order to review the implementation of its recommendations, CBSC recommended that a similar meeting be convened in 1978.

Academic Status for University Librarians

Final approval was given to one remaining clause of the *Guidelines on Academic Status for University Librarians*, the report of the joint task force of the Canadian Association of University Teachers (CAUT) and the Canadian Association of College and University Libraries (CACUL). With the exception of one clause dealing with salaries, the report had received approval by CACUL at its 1976 annual meeting, and approval of the remaining clause was given at the 1977 meeting on June 12.

One of the clauses in the *Guidelines* that has created some controversy is article I.G.1. which recommends a pattern of ranks for librarians corresponding with that of faculty. Academic rank for Canadian academic librarians has been the exception rather than the rule, and there has been some apprehension about whether the new guideline is workable. To the library administrator, the prospect of a staff of librarians performing normal library functions at the pay of a full professor is dismaying. On the other hand, while rank and file librarians welcome improved status and salary, they have shown concern about the implications of the normal criteria for faculty promotion, which require possession of a Ph.D. degree and a satisfactory record of research and publication.

In most Canadian academic libraries, the norm is the traditional hierarchical administrative structure in which librarian positions are defined and classified. From the viewpoint of the administrator, the advantages of this system are clarity of function, authority, and responsibility and the fact that payment is based on the worth to the institution of the work being performed. From the viewpoint of the librarian, the advantages are that a person is paid for the level of work performed, no matter what the extent of experience. The great disadvantage of the system both to the administrator and to the librarian is that the only avenue for advancement is the administrative route. This can result in a multiplicity of middle management positions to satisfy the career needs of librarians and can also result in inappropriate placement in these positions of librarians who seek and accept management positions in order to "get ahead." It can also result in limited career prospects for librarians who have little interest in or talent for administration, with a consequent lowering of morale.

The *Guidelines on Academic Status* recommend that librarians take their place in the academic community alongside the teaching staff and accept their role as an integral part of the education process by providing well-organized access to information and research skills. Despite apprehension about the ranking of librarian positions, there seems to be a strong feeling among academic librarians that such ranking and the move towards a collegiate structure will hasten fulfillment of their newly redefined role.

Acquisitions

In June the National Library of Canada announced its acquisition of the Lowy Collection, gathered over a 45-year period by Jacob M. Lowy of Montreal. The collection, consisting of 2,000 Hebraic and Judaic rare books with an estimated market value of $2,000,000, was described by Guy Sylvestre, National Librarian, as "the most valuable single bequest that the National Library has received since it was created in 1953." Scores of the individual books in the Lowy Collection are described as invaluable, and several are unique. One of the outstanding features of the collection is a group of 27 early editions of the work of the renowned Jewish historian, Flavius Josephus, who lived during the first century of the Christian era. The collection also includes more than 40 incunabula in Greek and Latin and several very rare Bibles and editions of the Talmud and its Codices, many of which are unique. The collection will be housed in the Jacob M. Lowy Room on the second floor of the National Library.

Appointments

Major appointments during 1977 included:

PATRICIA ANGLIN as Librarian for the Western (Newfoundland) Regional Library, Corner Brook;

GRACE A. ARMSTRONG as Head Librarian of the Learning Resources Centre, Southern Alberta Institute of Technology, Calgary;

R.H. ARNER as Chairman of the Ontario Provincial Library Council, Toronto;

GORDON C. BARHYDT as Chief Librarian of the North York (Ontario) Public Library;

ROBERT C. BRANDEIS as Chief Librarian of Victoria University, Toronto;

MOIRA C. CARTWRIGHT as Chief Librarian of the Kingston (Ontario) Public Library;

HOPE E. A. CLEMENT as Associate National Librarian, National Library, Ottawa;

YVES COURRIER as Directeur of L'Ecole de Bibliothéconomie de l'Université de Montreal;

DORIS DAEHN as Chief Librarian, Yellowhead Regional Library, Spruce Grove, Alberta;

RUTH DALLAS as Librarian of the Ameliasburg (Ontario) Public Library;

THOMAS R. DRYNAN as Chief Librarian of Mohawk College of Applied Arts and Technology, Hamilton, Ontario;

JOHN DUTTON as Chief Librarian of the Winnipeg Public Library;

SHIRLEY EDGAR as Coordinator of the Library Technician Program at Fanshawe College, London, Ontario;

LARRY ESHELMAN as Director of the Eastern Ontario Library System, Ottawa;

A. RAZZAH FATTAH as Librarian of the Manitoba Museum of Man and Nature, Winnipeg;

HOWARD FORD as Director of the South Central Regional Library System, Windsor, Ontario;

DEAN HALLIWELL, Chief Librarian of the University of Victoria (British Columbia) as part-time Special Assistant to the President for a three-year period;

FRANCESS G. HALPENNY, Dean, Faculty of Library Science, University of Toronto, as a member of the National Library Advisory Board;

BRIAN HEENEY as Director of Trent University Library, Peterborough, Ontario;

GARTH HOMER as Head, Learning Resources Centre, Grant MacEwan Community College, Edmonton;

SHEILA KIERAN as Executive Director of the Book and Periodical Development Council, Toronto;

JOHN LOVE as Chief Librarian, Gananoque (Ontario) Public Library;

MARGOT B. McBURNEY as Chief Librarian of Queen's University at Kingston, Ontario;

CATHERINE O'NEIL as Chief Librarian of the Lakeland Library Region, North Battleford, Saskatchewan;

LAURA POGUE as Librarian for the Saskatchewan Department of Municipal Affairs, Regina;

VINCENT RICHARDS as Director of the Edmonton Public Library;

PAUL SHEPPARD as Chief Librarian of the Cranbrook (British Columbia) Public Library;

DEBORAH SPENCER as Chief Librarian of the Yorkton (Saskatchewan) Public Library;

GENE WILBURN as Head Librarian of the Royal Ontario Museum Library, Toronto;

PHYLLIS YAFFE as Director of the Children's Book Centre, Toronto.

Awards and Prizes

HENRY C. CAMPBELL, Chief Librarian, Toronto Public Library, was elected First Vice-President of the International Federation of Library Associations (IFLA) for a four-year term.

FRANCESS G. HALPENNY, Dean, Faculty of Library Service, University of Toronto, was elected a Fellow of the Royal Society of Canada.

NORMAN HORROCKS, Director, School of Library Service, Dalhousie University, was elected to serve on the Executive Board of the American Library Association for the period 1977-81.

WILLIAM F.E. MORLEY, Special Collections Librarian, Queen's University at Kingston, Ontario, was awarded the Tremaine Medal by the Bibliographical Society of Canada.

Several Canadian librarians were among those who received the Queen's Silver Jubilee Medal 1977. These included Robert H. Blackburn, Chief Librarian, University of Toronto; Henry C. Campbell, Chief Librarian, Toronto Public Library; Barbara Clubb, Consultant, Public Library Service, Department of Tourism, Recreation and Cultural Affairs, Winnipeg; Bruce Cossar, former Chief Librarian, Trent University, Peterborough, Ontario; Rev. Edmond E. Desrochers, Directeur, Bibliothèque, Maison Bellarmin, Montreal; Agnes Florence, Chief Librarian, Teachers' Library and Resource Centre, Winnipeg School Division; Gertrude Gunn, University Librarian, University of New Brunswick, Fredericton; Ken Haycock, Head, Library Services, Vancouver School Board; Esther Jacobsen, Secretary-Treasurer, Bibliographical Society of Canada, Toronto; Brian Land, Professor of Library Science, University of Toronto; Douglas Lochhead, Professor of English, Mount Allison University, Sackville, New Brunswick; Diane MacQuarrie, Chief Librarian, Halifax City Regional Library; Frances Morrison, Chief Librarian, Saskatoon Public Library; Sylvia Morrison, Editor, *Canadian Periodical Index*, Ottawa; Anne Piternick, Associate Professor of Librarianship, University of British Columbia, Vancouver; Jean Weihs, Director, Library Technician Program, Seneca College of Applied Arts and Technology, Toronto; and Ronald Yeo, Chief Librarian, Regina Public Library.

Four retired and two active members of the Faculty of Library Science of the University of Toronto received Sesquicentennial Long Service Honor Awards from the University on the occasion of its 150th anniversary. Those honored were Winifred G. Barnstead, Director Emeritus; Bertha Bassam, Professor Emeritus and Director Emeritus; Mary E. Silverthorn, Professor Emeritus; Katharine L. Ball, Professor Emeritus; Francess G. Halpenny, Professor and Dean; and Margaret E. Cockshutt, Associate Professor.

Buildings

On March 17 Winnipeg opened its $10,000,000 Centennial Library, the new central building for its public library system. The three-story, 130,000-square-foot library was designed by the architectural firm of McDonald, Cockburn, McLeod and McFeetors and occupies one city block in the heart of downtown Winnipeg. The main floor of the building houses the reference and nonfiction collection and current periodicals. The second floor houses the fiction and paperback collections, children's books, microforms, audiovisual materials, and an art print collection. The third floor is reserved for staff and administrative functions. The new building has a 100-seat auditorium and a storage capacity for 600,000 volumes.

The new Metropolitan Toronto Library was officially opened November 2 by the Lieutenant Governor of Ontario, Pauline McGibbon. The new reference library, which is located on Yonge Street near Bloor Street in the heart of downtown Toronto, was designed by architect Raymond Moriyama and was built at a cost of $23,000,000 plus an additional cost of $7,000,000 for the site. The new building is five double stories in height, and is highlighted by a large atrium from the ground level to the glassed roof. It has seating accommodations for 1,305 and a capacity for nearly 1,250,000 volumes and provides 364,000 square feet of floor space.

The new St. Catharines (Ontario) Centennial Public Library was officially opened June 22 by the Ontario Minister for Culture and Recreation, Robert Welch. The new library contains 63,000 square feet on four levels and cost $3,600,000 to build. The library has space for 30,000 volumes and seating accommodations for 314 patrons.

Canadian Union Catalog Task Group

The Canadian Union Catalog Task Group, established by the National Library in 1972 "to study and make recommendations on the nature, scope, maintenance and use of the Canadian Union Catalog, which would form the bibliographic base of the national library network, with international interfaces," presented its final report in 1976. Recommendations from the Task Group, which was chaired by Basil Stuart-Stubbs, Chief Librarian of the University of British Columbia, were published in *National Library News* (March-April 1977), pp. 7-16.

In its report the Task Group advocated the development, with the guidance and support of the National Library, of a Canadian library network whose objectives would be to equalize opportunity for access to information and to make more cost-effective the use of total Canadian library resources. The network would be made up of three interrelated components—a bibliographic network, a resource network, and a communications network. The bibliographic network would be based on a

Canadian national bibliographic data base compiled at the National Library. This data base would be used to support the production and maintenance of union catalogues, union lists, and cataloguing support services at both the National Library and provincial and regional bibliographic centers.

The resource network would be made up of the holdings of the National Library and other federal government libraries, designated resource libraries across the nation, and unique items held in other libraries. Support for this resource network would be provided by the federal government for library collections both at the National Library and other libraries. A periodicals resource center and a storage center to be operated by the National Library and by the Canada Institute for Scientific and Technical Information were also proposed.

The communications network would consist of a delivery system for the actual transfer of items by such means as the postal service and interorganizational delivery and information transmission systems. Costs of transmitting materials among libraries and of communications among libraries should be absorbed, alleviated, or, at the least, regionally equalized by the federal government.

The National Library is studying the report of the Canadian Union Catalog Task Group in order to assist it in evolving a policy, program, and schedule for the development of the national component of a Canadian library network and related services.

Cataloguing

Beginning with the January 1978 issue of *Canadiana*, the national bibliography compiled and issued by the National Library, a new service, called *Canadiana: Microfiche* is to be offered. The new microfiche publication will be a COM (Computer Output Microform) version of the monthly computer-produced *Canadiana* proof list. The text of *Canadiana: Microfiche* will contain entries for each current monthly issue of *Canadiana*, and the monthly indexes will be cumulated with each issue to cover all previous issues for the current calendar year. This new microfiche service is intended as an interim measure to improve the currency of service to *Canadiana* users until the implementation of the revision of *Canadiana* services planned for 1980. Publication of regular issues of *Canadiana* in hard copy will continue.

The National Library's MARC Records Distribution Service, which began in 1976, continues to grow at a steady rate, both in terms of the number of libraries subscribing to the service and in the resources that the service makes available to subscribers. Various options are available to small libraries with manual cataloguing systems and to large automated libraries that are able to obtain cataloguing data either in machine-readable form on tape or in the form of printed unit cards. For libraries compiling their own source files, the regular weekly tape services provide both *Canadiana* cataloguing data and records from foreign cataloging agencies converted to the Canadian MARC communications format. For those libraries wanting selected records only, another option provides an inexpensive means of acquiring cataloguing data for their own holdings either on tape or on printed cards. As of July 1, 1977, the MARC Records Distribution Service data base contained more than 815,000 records. Present coverage includes Library of Congress records created since January 1, 1968, *Canadiana* records created since January 1, 1973, and U.K. MARC records created since January 1, 1975.

In April 1977 the full subscription service to CAN/MARC: Authorities became available from the National Library. CAN/MARC: Authorities is an authority listing on microfiche produced by COM techniques from the Library's automated authority system. The microfiches contain a unified list of all name headings in the authority data base, including both English and French forms, complete with associated references and history notes. At present this data base consists largely of Canadian federal and provincial government headings and some personal names, but it is rapidly being expanded to include all types of name headings. The base file is published in microfiche on a quarterly basis with cumulating supplements issued biweekly.

Mowat (McClelland and Stewart); and *Sally Go Round the Sun*, by Edith Fowke (McClelland and Stewart).

Classification

In 1977 the classification schedule for Canadian law, *Class K, Subclass KE: Law of Canada*, became available from the Library of Congress. The appearance of Subclass KE is the result of a cooperative effort between the National Library of Canada and the Library of Congress. Anne Rae of the National Library developed the schedule around the LC collection of Canadian legal materials and the printed shelflist of the holdings of the Osgoode Hall Law School Library of York University. The section on Quebec law was developed by Guy Tanguay, Law Librarian at l'Université de Sherbrooke. As the schedule was being developed, it was reviewed periodically by a committee of Canadian law librarians and appropriate staff members of the Library of Congress. The National Library has been assigning classification numbers from this schedule to the entries in the 1977 *Canadiana*.

Community College Libraries

During the year, the Community and Technical College Libraries Section of the Canadian Association of College and University Libraries approved revised *Guidelines for Academic Status for Professional Librarians in Community and Technical Colleges*. The *Guidelines* indicate areas in which librarians in postsecondary, non- degree-granting institutions require academic status and academic freedoms generally granted to teaching faculty, and they define and describe those conditions of employment generally termed "academic status." The *Guidelines* relate to conditions of employment, rather than to personal qualifications of individual librarians, and apply to positions that are usually held by professional librarians. Topics covered are appointment, salaries, promotion, termination of appointment, grievance, research and travel funds, and leave.

Copyright

The long-awaited working paper on copyright, *Copyright in Canada: Proposals for a Revision of the Law*, by A.A. Keyes and C. Brunet, was published March 29 by the federal Department of Consumer and Corporate Affairs. The 245-page study cites a number of reasons for revision of the Copyright Act of 1924. The present law is antiquated and difficult to interpret and to enforce and does not cover recent technological developments such as sound recordings, films, videotapes, television, photocopiers, computer programs, or information storage and retrieval systems. The proposed revisions are based on certain basic principles: that copyright be vested in property law; that the law should

Children's Literature

A nationwide poll of public librarians conducted by *The World of Children's Books*, a semiannual review published in Edmonton, produced a list of the 20 best Canadian children's books in English. Public librarians in 170 English-speaking communities were asked to select the top five Canadian children's books on the basis of literary merit. The first-place winner in the poll was *Alligator Pie*, by Dennis Lee and Frank Newfeld (Macmillan). Second place went to *Anne of Green Gables* by Lucy Maud Montgomery (McGraw-Hill Ryerson). The third most popular children's book was *Mary of Mile 18*, by Anne Blades (Tundra Books).

The remainder of the top ten children's books included *Jacob Two-Two Meets the Hooded Fang*, by Mordecai Richler (McClelland and Stewart); *The Incredible Journey*, by Sheila Burnford (Paper Jacks); *A Walk out of the World*, by Ruth Nichols (Longman); *The Marrow of the World*, by Ruth Nichols (Macmillan); *How Summer Came to Canada*, by William Toye and Elizabeth Cleaver (Oxford University Press); *Owls in the Family*, by Farley protect the pecuniary as well as the moral rights of creators; that copyright should operate as an incentive to publish; and that conveyance of information should be a chief objective of copyright law.

General recommendations advocated by the working paper include the following major points:

Given Canada's status as a net importer of copyright materials, participation in international conventions should not be extended beyond the present levels (the 1928 Rome text of the Berne Convention and the 1952 text of the Universal Copyright Convention). Any increase in copyright protection at the international level would only result in increased royalties flowing out of Canada.

Canada should maintain the present level of domestic protection over traditional categories of works (literary, dramatic, musical, and artistic), but that protection should be broadened to cover new technological developments such as sound recordings and cable television.

The revisions should provide greater access to copyright materials, yet increase the share of creators and authors in copyright returns.

Collectives, along the lines of existing performing rights societies, should be established to facilitate public access to copyright materials and to remove the exercise of individual rights from state control.

A Copyright Tribunal, to replace the Copyright Appeal Board, should be the regulatory agency for the operation of collectives, the appeal of disputes, and for subsequent revisions of the Copyright Act.

The study recommends that, for published work, the general term of copyright protection remain the life of the author plus 50 years. For literary, dramatic, and musical works unpublished at the author's death, the paper proposes that the term of protection be until publication or public performance and for 50 years thereafter (but that the total term not exceed 75 years after the author's death or 100 years after the author's death if the work has been deposited in an archives).

The paper proposes substantial revisions for materials not covered in international conventions such as sound recordings, broadcasts, computer programs, published editions of works in the public domain, and performance of works. It recommends that a public lending right not be provided in a new Copyright Act and that the present law of "fair dealing" be left unchanged.

Concerning photocopying, the working paper recommends that photocopying not be the subject of any specific provisions and that no statutory exceptions be provided to libraries and archives other than to permit them to make a copy for the sole purpose of preserving material that is deteriorating or damaged. The paper also rejects the proposal that there be a copyright exemption for special media materials produced on a nonprofit basis for the use of the visually and physically handicapped.

Under the present Copyright Act, the rights of authors are divided into pecuniary rights and moral rights. The working paper proposes that the exclusive rights of authors be formulated as the right to have their work reproduced, performed in public, published, adapted, or broadcast, and that they have the power to authorize the exercise of any of these rights by others.

Clarification is also provided for the moral rights of the author. These are defined as the author's right to enjoy respect for his authorship, to restrain any distortion, mutilation, or modification of his work, and to stop a publication or to withdraw a work from circulation provided that the publisher receives compensation. The term of protection, the ownership of moral rights, and the remedies for infringement would be the same as those accorded in the case of pecuniary rights.

The likelihood is that it will be months or perhaps years before the proposals or amended proposals are enacted into law. In the meantime, authors, publishers, and librarians will be engaged in study of the working paper and in the preparation of responses to its philosophy and its recommendations. It was expected that a national conference on copyright revision would be held in Ottawa in the spring of 1978.

Financial Support for Libraries

Canadian libraries suffered a double blow to their purchasing power during 1977. First, there was the inevitable increase in book and periodical prices that made it difficult, if not impossible, for most libraries to maintain their buying power given modest budget increases of 10 per cent or less. Second, the devaluation of the Canadian dollar on foreign exchange markets contributed to a further decrease in purchasing power of approximately 10 per cent, thereby offsetting budget increases.

In general, library budgets across Canada showed little cause for satisfaction, with the notable exception of public libraries in Alberta and Quebec. In Alberta, provincial grants to regional libraries doubled to $1.50 per capita, provided the grant is matched by local government. Grants for establishment of regional systems jumped from $1 per capita to $6. In Quebec, the Ministry of Cultural Affairs decided to improve subsidies to libraries as part of the Parti Québecois government's emphasis on cultural development. As a result, provincial library grants rose by $2,000,000 or 55 per cent, bringing the total to approximately $6,500,000.

Freedom of Information

A federal government "green paper" (proposals for public discussion) suggesting alternatives for possible future legislation on public access to government publications was tabled in the House of Commons on June 29 by the Secretary of State. The green paper, entitled *Legislation on Public Access to Government Documents*, suggests that, although greater public access to documents is desirable, full and systematic access could have serious implications for cabinet ministers' responsibility to Parliament and for the neutrality and anonymity of the public service.

The green paper also suggests that a parliamentary review procedure for decisions made by ministers on whether or not material was exempt would not affect ministerial responsibility and would not be too costly, even though it could be slow and time consuming. The paper discusses the possibility of appointing an information auditor who would receive complaints from disappointed applicants, examine the documents in question, and make a regular report to Parliament. Other options include the appointment of an information commissioner who might either have advisory powers not binding on the government or have the power to order the release of documents. Judicial review, the paper states, could threaten the independence of the court. The paper argues that under the Canadian system of government, which combines the executive and legislative branches through the system of cabinet ministers responsible to Parliament and, through Parliament, to the electorate, judges could not be asked to rule on a minister's decision.

The paper suggests the possibility of phasing in the implementation of legislation on public access in order to reduce initial expenses and to obtain an accurate estimate of costs. It estimates that implementing freedom of information legislation at the federal level would cost $10,500,000. In October, the federal government announced its intention of bringing in freedom of information legislation. So far, only one province has a freedom of information act; Nova Scotia enacted and proclaimed such legislation during 1977.

Joint School-Public Libraries

Developments in joint school-public libraries during 1977 included a decision by the Newfoundland Public Library Board not to set up any future joint libraries. The decision came about as the result of a survey which indicated that, although teachers and students saw the joint library situation as successful, there was reluctance on the part of the adult public to use a library located in a school. The decision halted three other joint library projects in the planning stages. Meanwhile, in Coquitlam, the largest joint school-public library in British Columbia signed a contract to operate for another year. A public library board, established in 1976, had not yet been able to find accommodation or funds for a separate library in Coquitlam.

A country-wide study, known as the Canadian School-Housed Public Library Project, was announced by Lorne J. Amey of the Dalhousie University School of Library Service in Halifax. The purpose of the project is to produce a Canada-wide review of school-housed public library activities. The survey will provide up-to-date information on school-public libraries in each province. The study will also include a literature search and report on local journal and newspaper articles commenting on joint library experiments, as well as a list of names of such libraries and their founding dates.

Library Associations

The Library Association of Alberta presented a brief to the provincial government requesting an increase in grants to $2,500,000; a $650,000 grant to establish a provincial library system; establishment of 150,000 as the minimum population base for regional libraries; funds to make available the computerized circulation systems of Calgary and Edmonton to the medium-sized public libraries of the province; and funds to continue school library development, the multilingual biblioservice, service to the handicapped, and the northern and southern Alberta library projects that provide service to outlying areas.

The Atlantic Provinces Library Association passed a resolution urging Information Access, publisher of the new *Canadian Newspaper Index*, to expand its coverage to include a major newspaper from the Atlantic region.

The Manitoba Library Association received a $1,250 support grant and the Manitoba Library Trustees Association a $140 grant from the Manitoba government. These two organizations, along with the Manitoba School Library Audio-Visual Association and the Manitoba Association of Library Technicians, helped to sponsor Manitoba Library Week, October 1-8.

The Ontario Library Association arranged for placing a plaque at the Niagara-on-the-Lake Public Library, the oldest public library in the province, in conjunction with the Association's 75th conference in Niagara Falls.

The Saskatchewan Library Association (SLA) presented a brief to the provincial government urging the amendment of the Public Libraries Act of 1969 to ensure universal participation in regional library systems. SLA also asked for funds for the development of the Provincial Library's special collections and for the establishment of effective school library service at all levels and urged the development of more efficient means for cataloging and distribution of provincial government publications.

The Council of Administrators of Large Urban Public Libraries was formed in October to supersede the ad hoc group of Administrators of Large Public Libraries which has been in existence for many years. The purpose of the Council is to identify the issues and choices available in devloping urban library service and to influence legislation and financing for these libraries. A new organization, the Polish Canadian Librarians' Association, was formed in order to ensure proper representation of Polish materials in Canadian libraries and to provide a forum for dissemination of this information.

Library Education

In the autumn of 1977, the School of Library and Information Science of the University of Western Ontario began offering courses in Ottawa for credit for the M.L.S. degree. In the autumn of 1977, the Faculty of Library Science of the University of Toronto conducted a continuing education workshop in Ottawa on Canadian children's literature and announced that it would begin offering M.LS. credit courses in Ottawa early in 1978. The course offerings in Ottawa have been provided in response to a request from the Ottawa-Hull Committee on Continuing Education and to an earlier recommendation made by the Advisory Committee on Academic Planning of the Ontario Council on Graduate Studies.

During the academic year 1975-76, six Canadian library schools awarded a total of 495 degrees as follows: Alberta, 45; British Columbia, 60; Dalhousie, 33; McGill, 61; Montreal, 69; Toronto, 127; and Western Ontario, 100. The total full-time and part-time enrollment during the autumn of 1976 was as follows: Alberta, 29; British Columbia, 132; Dalhousie, 66; McGill, 139; Montreal, 150; Toronto, 295; and Western Ontario, 142.

Those graduating during 1975-76 found an increasingly tight employment market. Provided that graduates were willing to relocate where the jobs were, however, most were able to find employment within months of graduation. The largest single number of graduates (30.3 per cent) found employment with public libraries, closely followed by special libraries (29.9 per cent) and academic libraries (26.3 per cent). School libraries employed 13.5 per cent of the new graduates during 1975-76.

Library-Publisher Relations

The report of the Library Information Project, sponsored by the Canadian Book Information Center and published in 1977, reinforced some old prejudices and raised some new points about library-publisher relations. The project used questionnaires and interviews with 48 Canadian publishing houses and 32 public libraries across the country.

The report found that 96 per cent of the publishers surveyed received orders from Canadian library wholesalers, and 60 per cent received orders from Baker & Taylor. One-quarter of the publishers complained about library orders with incorrect author or title information or orders for books that the firm did not publish. Half of the publishers stated that they reported on orders to library customers by invoice only, meaning that libraries were not informed about books out of print or otherwise unavailable. Most publishers offered some discount to libraries, ranging from 10 to 40 per cent, but nearly one-third offered no discount. Nearly two-thirds of the publishers made no sales visits to libraries.

All libraries found publishers' catalogues effective tools for book selection and 88 per cent also listed advance notices as helpful for selecting Canadiana. The most common flaw in catalogues was the omission of publication dates for both new and backlisted titles. Only 27 per cent of the libraries indicated that they were satisfied with the service they received from Canadian publishers, and although all libraries expressed interest in receiving publishers' newsletters, less than half of the libraries surveyed actually did.

Library Service to the Blind and Print-Handicapped

During 1977, the Oakville (Ontario) Public Library was granted a licence by the Canadian Radio-television and Telecommunications Commission to begin a radio service for the blind and other print-handicapped persons. The library plans to use a subsidiary channel of a nearby Burlington FM radio station to broadcast its programs. The broadcast signal will cover a 50-mile radius, which includes a potential audience of 20,000 blind and print-handicapped persons, and the programs will be picked up only by those with a special receiver. Oakville and the other 29 member libraries of the South Central Regional Library System will supply receivers free to those who qualify. For copyright reasons, only persons unable to use normal print materials will be eligible for receivers.

Plans call for an almost complete reliance on volunteer labor, but even with this help it will cost an estimated $100,000 to get the programs on the air and a further $40,000 a year to maintain the service. Studios and technical equipment are to be installed in the Woodside Branch of the Oakville Public Library. It is expected that there will be about 19 hours of programs a day, some of which will be rebroadcasts. Much of the programming will be provided by excerpts from current newspapers and magazines read over the air and community-oriented announcements. The tentative date for the opening of the service is mid-1978.

Library Technicians

Guidelines for the Training of Library Technicians, developed in 1976 by a committee of the Canadian Library Association, are being used in Canada by many local advisory committees for evaluating their respective programs. The *Guidelines* deal with the role of the library technician, admission requirements, the program of instruction, academic studies (50 per cent), library technical studies (25-30 per cent), related technical studies (20-25 per cent), field practice, the program director and instructional staff, library services, supporting facilities, administration and budget, location of programs, local advisory committees, provincial advisory committees, extension programs and the implementation of the *Guidelines*.

In recent years, there has been a trend in Canada toward two-year library technician programs with their own instructional staff rather than adjunct staff from the college library. An increasing number of extension programs offered in the evenings, on Saturdays, and off campus have appeared. In addition, specialist programs such as the Health Sciences option at Sheridan College in Oakville, Ontario, are being introduced.

A recent survey of library technician programs (excluding French-language programs) indicated that in 1975 there were 286 graduates; in 1976, an estimated 338 graduates; and in 1977, an estimated 266 graduates.

Library Use Study

According to a survey on "Selected Leisure Activities" conducted by Statistics Canada, the federal government statistical agancy, approximately 4,400,000 adult Canadians, or one in four, visited a library in their leisure time during the 12-month period preceding October 1975. Approximately 29 per cent of the total population (14 years of age and older) who responded to the survey, which covered a variety of activities from attending ballet performances to watching television, reported that they had visited libraries. The survey analysis was based on 32,000 individual responses.

The proportion of library users varied considerably between provinces. The highest proportion was found in British Columbia where 40 per cent of the responding population used a library, and the lowest population (18 per cent) was in Quebec. The percentage of adults who were users of the library averaged 28.9 per cent for Canada as a whole, but the regional variations were quite distinct (see Table 1).

Table 1. Responding Adult Population, Users, and Percentage Distribution of Users, 1974-75

Region	Responding Adult Population* (000)	Adult Users (000)	Percentage of Adult Users
Atlantic	1,368.0	300.7	22.0
Quebec	4,350.2	788.6	18.1
Ontario	5,628.2	1,965.5	34.9
Prairie	2,311.1	715.9	31.0
British Columbia	1,671.2	668.2	40.0
Canada	15,328.8	4,439.2	28.9

*Nonrespondents totalled about 1,800,000 or 15 per cent.

Table 2. Estimated Circulation and Book Holdings per Adult Population and per User, 1974-75

Region	Adult Population Book Holdings	Adult Population Circulation	Adult User Book Holdings	Adult User Circulation
Atlantic	1.5	4.5	7.5	23.0
Quebec	1.0	2.3	6.3	14.0
Ontario	2.6	8.0	8.3	25.3
Prairie	2.0	6.3	7.4	23.3
British Columbia	2.1	8.7	5.8	24.3
Canada	1.9	5.9	7.4	22.7

Table 3. Estimated Total Operating Expenditure per Adult Population, Adult User, and Adult Visit to the Library, 1974-75

Region	Adult Population	Adult User	Adult Visit
Atlantic	$3.90	$20.20	$1.70
Quebec	2.20	13.20	1.20
Ontario	9.90	31.40	2.50
Prairie	5.90	21.90	1.90
British Columbia	7.10	20.00	1.50
Canada	6.30	24.10	1.90

The survey also examined book holdings available to library users and found that there were almost two books available for borrowing by every adult Canadian. Ontario had the greatest number of holdings available for each adult while British Columbia had the highest circulation figures for each adult. The circulation rate in British Columbia of 8.7 items for every adult was twice the circulation figure for the Atlantic Provinces and three times the ratio for Quebec. Book holdings and circulation ratios for the user population indicated that almost seven books were held for each user and that the average number of borrowings per book was 23 per year (see Table 2).

According to the survey, the total operating expenditures per adult was $6.30. The regional variations in operating expenditures were quite distinct, ranging from a low of $2.20 in Quebec to a high of $9.90 in Ontario. For each adult user, the estimated operating expenditure for 1974-75 was $24.10 for Canada as a whole. Ontario's expenditure was $7 above the national average, making it the highest operating expenditure per adult user of all the provinces. Except for Quebec, all other regions had expenditure-to-user ratios close to the overall national average. The Atlantic Provinces had a low expenditure-to-total-adult-population ratio, but the expenditure-to-user ratio was not substantially below the national average because of the lower proportion of library visitors in this region (see Table 3).

The general results of the survey of leisure time activities carried out with the assistance of Statistics Canada are contained in *A Leisure Study—Canada, 1975*, published by the Department of the Secretary of State, Ottawa. Statistics Canada plans to publish its own report, *Library Visitors and Library Resources*, which will furnish more detailed information about the use of libraries in Canada.

National Library

The National Library of Canada carried on with the major review begun in 1976 of its role, objectives and services. The senior staff of the Library prepared the following draft statement of the National Library's overall mission:

"The mission of Canadian libraries and other documentation centers is to provide access to information for all Canadians. The mission of the National Library is to facilitate the fulfillment of the mission of Canadian libraries and documentation centres by:

"1. Providing library and information services relating to Canadian materials and studies by organizing comprehensive and in-depth programs for (a) acquisition; (b) conservation; (c) bibliographic control; (d) promotion of use and assistance to research.

"2. Ensuring access to library resources in Canada by (a) provision of bibliographic information; (b) provision of documents (e.g., through interlibrary loan).

"3. Encouraging the development of Canadian libraries and information systems by (a) leading and coordinating the various components of the national information system; (b) developing standards and promoting compatibility; (c) providing advisory, liaison, and referral services; (d) supporting research, development, and implementation; (e) working the interface between the Canadian information systems (regional and national) and the international systems."

The first phase of the review involved input from the National Library's own staff, from other libraries, and from library associations and other organizations. The second phase involves the development of broad recommendations to the National Librarian for consideration. The final phase, which is planned for completion by 1978 on the National Library's 25th anniversary, is to involve formulation of specific recommendations for implementation by the Library.

Obituaries

Elizabeth Homer Morton (1903-1977), retired Executive Director of the Canadian Library Association, died in Ottawa, on July 6. Born in Trinidad, she graduated from Dalhousie University and, after a period of teaching in Nova Scotia, received her library training at the Ontario Library School in Toronto. From 1930 to 1931 she was Executive Secretary of the New Brunswick Library Commission. From 1931 to 1944 she was a reference librarian at the Toronto Public Library, and she also served from 1936 to 1943 as Secretary-Treasurer of the Ontario Library Association. In 1944 she went to Ottawa as Executive Secretary to the newly established Canadian Library Council. When this organization was succeeded in 1946 by the Canadian Library Association, she became its first Executive Director and Editor in Chief, a position she held until her retirement in 1967. She was responsible for the establishment of publishing, microfilming, and other programs for CLA and was instrumental in organizing library developments across Canada, including representations to the federal government that resulted in the creation of the National Library of Canada in 1951.

Angus Mowat (1893-1977), retired Director of Public Libraries for the Province of Ontario, died in Kingston, Ontario, on September 21. Born in Trenton, Ontario, Mowat graduated from Queen's University and served as librarian of the Trenton, Belleville, and Windsor, Ontario, and Saskatoon, Saskatchewan, public libraries. He became Inspector and later Director of Public Libraries in Ontario in 1937, a post he held until his retirement in 1960. Among his achievements were the development of county and regionsl library cooperatives and the enactment of certification regulations for Ontario public librarians.

Vernon Ross (1901-1977), Professor Emeritus and retired Director of the McGill University Graduate School of Library Science, died in Montreal on February 28. Professor Ross was a native of Montreal and received her B.A. and M.A. degrees in history and a Library School Certificate from McGill. In 1926 she joined the staff of McGill's Redpath Library, where she served for 10 years as a cataloguer and reference librarian. In 1936-37, she attended the School of Library Service at Columbia University where she earned her B.S. in L.S. degree. On her return to Montreal, she joined the teaching staff of the McGill Library School on a full-time basis, and in 1949 she was appointed Director, a post she held until 1966. In 1964, during her tenure as Director, McGill abolished its one-year B.L.S. program and replaced it with the two-year M.L.S. program, the first Canadian library school to do so. Professor Ross continued to teach until 1969 when she retired with the rank of Professor Emeritus. She served as President of the Quebec Library Association, the Bibliographical Society of Canada, and the History Association of Montreal and was also a Director of the Association of American Library Schools and a Councillor of both the Canadian Library Association and the American Library Association.

Other members of the Canadian Library community who died during 1977 included Jean-Charles Bonefant, retired Chief Librarian of the Legislative Library of Quebec; M.I. Belle Grant, retired Head of the Arts Reference Department, University of Waterloo; Mabel Florence (James) Blyth, retired Chief Librarian, Department of Finance and Treasury Board, Ottawa; and Mary Whittendale, Accounting Supervisor, Canadian Library Association, Ottawa.

Public Libraries—Statistics

Statistics Canada, the federal government's statistical agency, reported that, during 1975, 739 public libraries had total holdings of 35,490,537 books and other materials catalogued as books. Total operating expenditures were $132,172,397 and the full-time professional staff totalled 1,577. Other details are included in the following table:

Summary Statistics of Public Libraries in Canada, 1975

Total population	22,799,000
Libraries reporting	739
Books and other materials catalogued as books	35,490,537
Newspaper and periodical titles	117,519
Nonprint materials	2,186,514
Circulation	108,044,499
Full-time professional librarians	1,577
Total operating income	$147,948,801.
Total operating expenditures	$132,172,397.

Research

The Centre for Research in Librarianship of the Faculty of Library Science of the University of Toronto reported involvement with several funded research projects. They included a user study of children for the Regina Public Library; an annotated list of Canadian books and periodicals for public libraries, a project commissioned by the Metropolitan Toronto Library Board; a study of children's library services for the South Central Regional Library System, Hamilton; a research design for a full-scale study of the University of Toronto's card and COM catalog; and compilation of a Canadian nonprint materials catalog.

Retirements

The following librarians retired during 1977: Gladys Mitchell, Head of the Family Reading Centre and Assistant Librarian, Main Library, Windsor (Ontario) Public Library, after more than 50 years of service to the same library system in a succession of positions; and Ted Wiltshire, Director of Library Services, Province of Alberta, after 18 years of service.

School Libraries

The Vancouver School Board introduced changes during 1977 in its method of purchasing for its libraries. For a two-year period the Board is to buy fully catalogued and processed library books from one supplier, the Co-operative Book Centre of Toronto. The decision to use one supplier means that Vancouver schools no longer have to determine the origin of a title or choose which edition to buy since the agreement with the supplier requires the Canadian edition if there is a choice. The Vancouver School Board has also set up a small demonstration collection of recommended books for elementary and junior grades that is maintained by the Library Services Department. The ordering procedure for school libraries has also been changed from bulk purchasing to school-based selection although a certain number of titles, such as award winners, are still purchased in bulk. The 1977 figure for purchase of school library materials was more than $10 per student, nearly twice the 1976 figure.

In Toronto, the Board of Education added a special one-time grant of $1 per student to the 1977 materials budget for the purchase of Canadian books. The extra funds meant that the money spent per student in Toronto school libraries for 1977 rose to $4.94 for primary grades, $6.22 for grades seven and eight, and $9.33 for secondary schools. The decision to increase the amount provided for Canadian materials was the result of recommendations made in the report *Canadian Books in Canadian Schools*, which was published in 1977.

School Libraries—Statistics

According to Statistics Canada, 63.1 per cent of all public schools in Canada (excluding Quebec, which did not participate in the survey) reported having centralized school libraries which served 81.6 per cent of the total student enrollment during 1974-75. A centralized school library is defined as an area specifically designated for study and reading and for the custody, circulation, and administration of a collection of books, periodicals, and graphic or audiovisual materials for the use of the student body and staff of the school. Classroom collections and centralized book collections in the corridor or auditorium do not qualify as school libraries under this definition.

Ontario had the highest proportion of schools with centralized libraries (72.2 per cent), while Newfoundland had the lowest proportion (24.9 per cent). British Columbia had the highest proportion of students enrolled in schools with centralized libraries (90.2 per cent), while Newfoundland had the lowest proportion (39.8 per cent).

Book holdings in centralized school libraries grew by 21.2 per cent over the figure reported for the 1972-73 survey, while expenditures for print materials increased by 16.5 per cent. Newfoundland had the largest percentage increase in book holdings (52.2 per cent) in the two-year period since the previous survey. The highest rates of growth in expenditures for print materials were reported by Prince Edward Island and Nova Scotia with increases of 182 per cent and 107 per cent respectively over 1972-73. By contrast, expenditures for print materials in Ontario schools were only 5 per cent higher than those for the 1972-73 period.

Serials

In January 1974 ISDS was established within the National Library of Canada as the Canadian national center for the International Serials Data System. In this way Canada is contributing to a worldwide undertaking to improve identification and bibliographic control of international serials publication. During its first three years of operation ISDS Canada registered approximately 13,000 Canadian serials, both current and discontinued. Since January 1975, *Canadiana*, the national bibliography, has included ISSN (Interna-

Summary Statistics of Centralized School Libraries in Canada (Excluding Quebec), 1974-75

	Elementary	Elementary and Secondary	Secondary	Total
Number of schools reporting centralized libraries	5,228	1,021	1,413	7,662
Percentage of schools reporting centralized libraries	62.6	52.8	76.6	63.1
Enrollment in schools reporting centralized libraries	1,757,518	367,277	1,119,577	3,244,372
Percentage of students attending schools with centralized libraries	80.2	69.2	89.4	81.6
Book holdings	25,014,395	4,892,478	12,464,440	42,371,313
Book holdings per student	14.2	13.3	11.1	13.1
Expenditures				
Print	8,747,459	1,815,325	6,624,636	17,187,420
Nonprint	2,083,014	372,817	1,096,484	3,552,315
Total	10,830,473	2,188,142	7,721,120	20,739,735
Expenditure for student				
Print	$4.98	$4.94	$5.92	$5.27
Nonprint	1.19	1.02	.98	1.09
Total	6.16	5.96	6.90	6.39
Full-time library staff				
Professional librarians	99	31	336	466
Trained school librarians	1,843	176	737	2,756
Total	1,942	207	1,073	3,222
Students per full-time library staff	905	1,744	1,043	1,007

Special Libraries in Canada by Subject and Type of Sponsor, 1976

	Company	Government	Other	Total	Per Cent
Arts and Humanities				54	4.9
Fine Arts		13	10	23	2.1
Humanities		7	4	11	1.0
Religion, Theology			20	20	1.8
Social Sciences				498	45.4
Business, Economics, etc.	71	46	14	131	11.9
Education		28	15	43	3.9
Environment		10	3	13	1.2
Geography, History, etc.	1	11	11	23	2.1
Law	22	31	22	75	6.8
Military Science		8	1	9	0.8
Publishing, Current Events	31			31	2.8
Social Welfare, Recreation, Tourism		39	6	45	4.1
Sociology, Politics		61	9	70	6.4
Urban and Regional Planning, Transportation	6	42	10	58	5.3
Science and Technology				546	49.7
Agriculture, Forestry, etc.	11	40	3	54	4.9
Biological Sciences		24	6	30	2.7
Earth Sciences	32	13	2	47	4.3
Engineering, Technology	98	41	3	142	12.9
Health Sciences—General		7	39	46	4.2
Health Sciences—Hospital-Administered on Clinical Medicine			125	125	11.4
Marine Science and Fisheries	1	16	1	18	1.6
Physical Sciences	46	17	2	65	5.9
Science and Technology—General	1	15	3	19	1.7
Total	320	469	309	1,098	100.0

tional Standard Serial Number) in its serials entries. In January 1976 this coverage was extended to selected federal and provincial government serials. CAN/MARC tapes contain both ISSN and key titles for these *Canadiana* records. In addition, the CONSER (CONversion of SERials) data base is building a machine-readable file of authenticated ISSN and key titles for serials held by North American libraries.

Special Libraries—Statistics

According to an analysis based on data extracted from the special libraries section of part 2 of the *Canadian Library Directory*, there were 1,098 special libraries in Canada in 1976. Beryl Anderson, Chief, Library Documentation Centre, National Library of Congress, prepared the analysis. A special library is defined as one that is, "for its primary clientele, a tool for the furtherance of the objectives of the library's sponsoring organization." Subject departments of public and university libraries are excluded. Of the total number of libraries, 54 (or 4.9 per cent) were in the arts and humanities, 498 (or 45.4 per cent) were in the social sciences, and 546 (or 49.7 per cent) were in the sciences and technology.

BRIAN LAND

London Correspondent's Report

Academic Libraries

In academic libraries the main theme during 1977 was "Coping with the Cuts", the title of a London conference in July organized by the Books and Students Committee of the National Book League and attended by representatives of LA, the publishing and book trades, and many university associations. Statistics showed that in library expenditure, which in any case had not kept up with inflation, more was proportionately spent on salary increases (up from 50.59 per cent to 54.68 per cent in 1974-75) than on serials (up from 16.01 per cent to 16.8 per cent) and books (down from 23.82 per cent to 19.71 per cent). In practice, expensive items were not acquired, and the decline of the pound had especially affected the purchase of foreign books and serials. The opinion, expressed in speeches, annual library reports, and letters to academic journals, was that irreparable harm had already been done to university libraries and that none but the longest established would retain sufficiently good research facilities to attract academic staff of high quality.

Lord Donaldson, minister for the arts, revealed that the Department of Education and Science had in effect adopted the policy of "self-renewal" for academic libraries as outlined in the 1976 Atkinson Report of the University Grants Committee (UGC). He thought Britain could not afford to store materials indiscriminately and emphasized the need to establish criteria for the elimination of older library stock. The Atkinson policy continued to attract a torrent of criticism, made in formal protests by bodies such as LA, SCONUL (Standing Conference of National and University Libraries), and CVCP (Committee of Vice-Chancellors and Principals) and individually by innumerable writers and speakers.

In Bristol University Library's annual report it was argued that compact storage was probably cheaper than extensive borrowing through networks. Aberdeen University's chief librarian, John Smethurst, accepted the practicality of self-renewal for undergraduate texts only. He considered that some broad distinction should be made between arts and sciences stock; investigation at Aberdeen had shown that scientific texts and serials more than 25 years old could realistically be discarded, whereas arts subjects textbooks retained their usefulness for more than 50 years. Ray Moss, chief librarian of Teesside Polytechnic, in an article in the *Library Association Record* uncompromisingly supported the self-renewal concept, adversely criticizing most university libraries as unduly arts-orientated and arguing that they, as much as industrial and technological libraries, should expect to rely on network systems.

Acquisitions and Collections

Sussex University Library was to receive custody of the Kipling papers bequeathed to the National Trust by Rudyard Kipling's daughter, who died in 1976. Lamentably, she had destroyed a quantity of material. The BL received an important bequest of early printed books in fine bindings from the late Henry Davis, a Northern Ireland businessman. The remainder of his valuable collection, including more than 60 incunabula and examples from the Gregynog, Kelmscott, and Ashendene presses, went to the New University of Ulster at Coleraine. The Ronalds Library, a collection of around 8,000 books on magnetism and the development of early telegraphic systems, was accepted by the Institute of Electrical Engineers.

The BL gave £2,000 toward repair of books in the Hurd Library at Hartlebury Castle, Worcestershire, a large number of books given by King George III to Bishop Richard Hurd. The U.S. Bicentennial Partnership Commission gave £18,000 to the Bodleian Library, Oxford, to form a collection of diaries and journals compiled by travelers in the United States and Britain.

British authorities continued to be concerned at the breakup of collections and libraries, often resulting in many items being sold abroad. The Friends of the National Libraries sought an enquiry into the dispersal of ecclesiastical libraries following the sale, for £155,000, of manuscripts and nonliturgical books, including important incunabula, from the library of Sion

Viewing the Henry Davis Collection during a royal visit in August to the New University of Ulster's library are from left; Her Majesty Queen Elizabeth II, Librarian F.J.E. Hurst, Secretary of State for Northern Ireland Roy Mason, Deputy Librarian Eileen M. Tyrrell and Prince Philip.

Library and Information Science Abstracts (LISA) on-line with the System Development Corporation Systen (SDC) were made available to the public in 1977 by SDC and Lockheed. From left: Roger Bilboul, Norman Jackson, Dale Kratsch, and LISA editor Jeremy Digger.

College, London. There was also distress at the Evelyn family's decision to sell in separate lots the library of John Evelyn, the 17th-century diarist. Valued at between £500,000 and £1,000,000, it had been on loan to Christ Church College, Oxford, since 1950. If the British wish to retain their treasures, however, the government must exempt such collections from estate duty, accept them in lieu of it, or provide institutions such as the BL with the funds to acquire them.

Automation

The British Library Automated Information Service (BLAISE) was extended in 1977 to cover the U.K. and LC MARC files, other BL databases, and MEDLARS. By agreement with the U.S. National Library of Medicine, MEDLINE, TOXLINE, SDILINE, and CHEMLINE files would also be available on-line.

Derbyshire County Library was in process of installing an ambitious integrated automation system. Selection of books would remain decentralized; but the orders, made through the County Council's IBM 370 computer, would become catalog entries when the books' arrivals were registered. The catalog was on COM cassetted roll film supplied to all branch libraries, where it could be read on Scottish Instruments' "Planet" viewers. The County Library also acquired its own Prime 300 minicomputer, to be used at first mainly for circulation control but designed ultimately to deal with everything except catalog updating. There were to be ALS label-reading terminals for issues and returns and an automatic fines indicator. Each branch library would eventually have an "Informa" VDU on-line for the organization of network loans.

Cambridge University's Computer Library received a grant of £38,750 over three years for research on indexing and searching. LA held a course on "Library Use of Computer Networks," and an Association of Database Producers was formed. The advance of automation was not without problems, however. Research by the LA's Industrial Group revealed heavy reader resistance to microform. Library automation also became involved in the general debate about threats to individual privacy posed by data banks. LA, in evidence to an official committee, submitted that personal information programmed into library computers for statistical purposes could become available to unauthorized searchers, who might also trace membership of special libraries and discover what books a student consulted.

Buildings

In 1977 the Royal Institute of British Architects gave awards to three new library buildings. They were the public library, built in brick with high windows, at Pershore in the County of Hereford and Worcester; the library at Worthing, West Sussex; and the Hugh Owen Building of the University College of Wales, Aberystwyth. The latter houses the arts teaching center as well as a library containing 500,000 volumes and seating 526 readers.

Other new academic libraries included that of St. Andrews University and Manchester Polytechnic's Central Library. In the new town district of Bretton, Cambridgeshire, a new 6,700-square-foot library forms part of a planned leisure complex and shares its book stock of 20,000 volumes with a nearby secondary school. An interesting building carefully designed to blend with the surrounding countryside and houses is the new library at Mottram-in-Longdendale in Greater Manchester's Tameside area. Built of stone with a slate roof, it holds 9,000 books in just over 1,000 square feet of space. Equally appropriate to its situation is the new library at Mansfield in Nottinghamshire, situated at one of the main entrances of a large, newly developed commercial shopping center. Serving a population of 60,000, it has 42,000 square feet of space and six floors. The first (British "ground") floor is surrounded by a circular glass drum set back from the pillars that support the rectangular walls above. The roof-lit open stairway breaks the line of the otherwise tunnellike main library on the second floor, which is also offset by a large mural.

In Nottingham a new Central Library that opened in January had been created in 13 months by the conversion of a former furniture store. The original shop windows remain an attractive feature, and the library's six floors provide 54,000 square feet of space. A problem is the weight of stock on the non-purpose-built floor; but the main reserve stack is in the basement, and the staff will not relocate shelves without consulting the architects.

Cataloging and Classification

The *British National Bibliography* (BNB) in 1977 added "Cataloguing in Publication" (CIP), covering publications scheduled for up to two months ahead, to its weekly lists. CIP was also added to the U.K. MARC tape services. CIP material was to exist in cumulative form until incorporated into the BNB itself. Similar advance information was to be provided after January 1978 in a new monthly microfiche issue of *British Books in Print*.

Members of the Music Bibliography Group, whose MARC format for music was to be issued by BL's Bibliographic Services Division, were taking part in the current revision of AACR and the proposed new standard bibliographic description (ISBD) and were advising those working out the new British music catalog to be based on PRECIS.

Bath University received a BL grant of more than £88,000 over three years for research into mechanized cataloguing and its value in academic libraries. At the LA's Medical Section's conference held at Bath, Philip Bryant, director of the Bath research program, suggested that such institutions possessing their own computers were well advised to avoid shared catalog facilities. But Stan Jenkins of the Barnes Medical Library in Birmingham University, drawing on the two-year experience of the Birmingham Libraries' Co-operative Mechanization Project (BLCMP; see 1976 *ALA Yearbook*), declared that the advantages of shared services outweighed the disadvantages. The disadvantages, including delays in cataloging and in receiving MARC tapes, were gradually being eliminated.

Education, Library

In March 1977 LA published *Training in Libraries*, the report of its working party on professional qualifications. It was proposed that all library students from 1981 onward would attain graduate status. After a three-year degree course (or one year of postgraduate study for nonlibrary graduates) and one year of satisfactory library service, an entrant would become a licentiate of LA. Three years later, on submitting an adequate work report, the person would qualify for associateship (ALA).

A second series of proposals were designed to increase the routes by which an ALA could attain fellowship (FLA), a status currently restricted to those who had submitted a thesis. The number of FLAs has seriously declined, from 32 per cent of total LA membership in 1960 to 12.5 per cent in 1975. It was suggested that after five years as an ALA a candidate could present either a thesis or an account of his or her "contribution to librarianship". Published work or a doctorate in librarianship or information science would also be accepted.

The report also considered the status and education of nonprofessional library assistants, proposing to grant certificates in library work based on a LA-controlled syllabus for which candidates could study at local authority colleges. Suitable certified assistants would have the chance to move on to library schools.

It was argued that the core of the proposals, the decision to phase out the two-year nongraduate entry to the profession, was not revolutionary because statistics clearly showed that the proportion of graduates in the profession was already steadily increasing. The only effect on presently chartered librarians (ALAs) was that their chances of becoming FLA would be increased.

Nevertheless, the proposals were much criticized. There were variously voiced doubts about whether local authorities would give adequate financial recognition to the new professional grades. Concerted opposition came from the National and Local Government Officers' Association (NALGO), to which many public librarians belong, the LA's chartered status preventing it from acting as a trade union (*see also* "Personnel and Employment"). Without giving advance warning to LA, NALGO distributed broadsheets to those attending the LA's annual general meeting (AGM). It attacked the composition of the working party as insufficiently representative of public librarians and made 10 distinct criticisms of the proposals. These were subsequently refuted point by point in a formal letter. It is difficult to find that NALGO was motivated by anything but the frequent British trade union spirit of resentment at the attainments of others.

Apart from the NALGO broadsheet, opposition was voiced at the AGM, critics affecting to disbelieve the statistics of the trend toward a graduate profession and disregarding the need to achieve professional reciprocity with other EEC countries. Although the critics were defeated in a straight vote, a sufficient proportion demanded a postal ballot; further developments thus wait upon the corporate decision of all LA members.

The roots of the criticism are difficult to identify but undoubtedly lie with the insecurity currently felt by chartered (nongraduate) librarians and seem connected with resentment that their qualified status depends on continued membership of and subscription to LA. A motion that status be maintained by payment of a minimum £3 registration-only fee was introduced at the AGM, but the issue was postponed pending a report to be made by LA Council at the 1978 meeting.

Law and Legislation

The most significant debate in 1977 concerned the possible alteration of the copyright law. It was triggered by the report, *Copyright and Design Law*, of the Whitford Committee set up in 1974. The report dealt basically with two areas of copyright law, international and internal, and attempted to state general principles that would remain valid for any currently undeveloped media of communication.

The international situation as such was comparatively straightforward. The Committee recommended that Britain ratify the Paris text of the 1886 Berne Convention, an action that would involve little change in existing British law. The report seemed, however, not to deal adequately with the increasing conflicts between British law and the terms of the EEC's Treaty of Rome, which enshrined the principle of the free flow of goods throughout the Community. A relevant case in 1977 came about when the European Commission complained that the publishers Jonathan Cape and Penguin Books had made a contract illegal under Community law by restricting the import of a continental paperback edition of Ernest Hemingway's *The Old Man and the Sea* into the U.K. and Ireland, where they were selling an exclusive edition. It seemed that the Treaty of Rome principles were at odds not only with U.K. law but also with the Berne Convention and that the issue needed resolution on an international level.

For the U.K. itself, the report attempted to sort out the enormous problems posed by "reprography," a term it adopted to cover all forms of reproduction including photocopying, holography, and microform and laser techniques. Current practice, stemming mainly from the 1956 Copyright Act, allows librarians to supply for "private study" single copies of extracts of not more than 4,000 words—or a series, none more than 3,000 words, totalling not more than 8,000 words—not exceeding 10 per cent of the "work." This is regarded by the report as unsatisfactory on many grounds. The charges only cover costs and provide no surplus toward any royalty scheme. Multiple "single" copies can, in fact, be obtained (e.g., by a class of students all applying individually), and there is no penalty if a copy

The new six-story Central Library of Nottinghamshire, converted from a furniture store, opened in January.

declaredly made for "private study" is actually intended for industrial or other use.

The Committee was unable to assess the extent of library copying, let alone the vast and totally unrecorded copying that goes on in schools and offices. It seemed to the Committee that, short of accepting the principle that no effective control could ever be established, the only solution would be the introduction of a so-called "blanket" scheme, Copy issuers would be licensed and owners of copyright, foregoing individual collecting rights, would receive royalties through appropriate central collecting bodies (one for each medium, such as books). The royalties would be allocated on estimated and not recorded reproduction of individual items.

Other Whitford recommendations were that, in general, copyright should remain with authors, speakers, and producers of computer programs and software. Exceptions should include commissioned works and those carried out by an employee. Recording agents would also be assigned copyright, provided they had the speaker's or artist's permission. It was suggested that all existing crown copyright and the general concept of perpetual copyright now enjoyed by some "nonpublished" material be extinguished.

Comment was generally favorable except with regard to the "blanket licence" proposal, and even to this reaction was mixed. Teachers favored it as allowing multiple copying, and authors and composers seemed also to approve. BL and LA, however, regarded the suggestion with suspicion, both perhaps particularly considering the effect on scholarly serials, which might be driven out of existence if readers acquired copies rather than printed issues. This would be particularly inappropriate because it seemed clear that those writing in such journals sought dissemination of their views rather than economic reward. The fears may have been groundless; an ASLIB study of the decline in subscriptions to serials attributed it to current shortages of funds rather than the increase in copying, and BLLD confirmed that 46 per cent of copy requests from special libraries was for back numbers of serials to which the libraries still subscribed. LA, which was presenting its considered criticisms to the secretary for trade, felt that the blanket licence would, by raising fees to users, prove counterproductive in information dissemination and also might be used as a precedent in any public lending right scheme for making the borrower pay toward the royalty.

Meanwhile, one public lending right bill having been "talked out" in the 1975-76 session of Parliament, another was introduced and passed in the House of Lords, but it seemed unlikely to receive Commons's time. There was discussion of a possible system of bypassing legislation, by which the government could authorize payments to authors through the Arts Council. This, however, would give the authors only ad hoc and not statutory rights.

In the first prosecution for blasphemous libel brought in 56 years, the magazine *Gay News* was fined £1,000 and its editor given a nine-month suspended sentence for publishing a poem describing a Roman centurion's homosexual love for Christ.

Networks

There was considerable debate in 1977 over whether regional networks should be further developed or abandoned in favor of universal reliance on the BL's Lending Division (BLLD) at Boston Spa in Lincolnshire. BLLD itself, at first supporting regional networks and financing various pilot schemes for them, appeared to change its policy, seeking to become the major source of interlibrary loans. Although the London and South Eastern Region's pilot scheme that used fleets of lorries for book transfers was highly successful, halving the cost of sending books by post, it was discovered in a Midlands Region experiment that it was quicker to order books from BLLD than through the regional network.

Lincolnshire's county librarian, Edward Roberts, pointed out that, because BLLD often added a handling charge of £3, the cost of borrowing a particular book several times would amount to more than its purchase price. He appeared, however, to be ignoring possible local storage problems.

In attempting to identify material most in demand, BLLD sent a questionnaire to nearly 1,000 client libraries. The 816 replies showed that most of the books borrowed were on pure and applied science published in the previous two years and costing aroung £8.80. Most requests were from public and industrial (not academic) libraries, and 85 per cent of the borrowing was for users. A surprise factor was the length of waiting time—up to six months—that was apparently acceptable.

Personnel and Employment: Supply, Salaries, and Collective Bargaining

In the field of employment the main problems in 1977 were in commanding appropriate salary scales and, for those newly qualified, in finding library work at all.

By local government reorganization in the early 1970's public libraries were administratively grouped with "leisure facilities," and the controlling recreation or amenity officer became senior to the chief librarian, thus depressing the latter's salary and those of subordinate librarians. An example of this process occurred at East Kilbride near Glasgow, where an assistant director of leisure services, a former sports manager, became the chief librarian's superior officer. In a similar case at Lambeth, LA discovered that the appointment was pending, protested to the appropriate authority, and picketed their meeting. Although the successful candidate was not currently practising as a librarian, he was qualified and had served as a librarian; it was stipulated that he renew his LA membership. LA was trying to watch for all advertisements for senior leisure appointments and also for posts in nonuniversity academic libraries, where it sought to promote the appointment of chartered librarians.

Another grievance was the widespread failure of local authorities to implement for librarians the 1975 award, based on a job evaluation study, made by ACAS (Advisory Conciliation and Arbitration Services).

A major contributory factor in librarians' salary problems appeared to stem from the fact that they work in a variety of sectors, in most of which they comprise only a minority of the total work force and therefore carry little weight in whatever trade union is operative. In the public library sector the librarians, many of whom are not and do not wish to be union members, have for years been inadequately supported by NALGO, which in its turn validly claimed that librarians have taken insufficient part in its activities. At the 1977 NALGO conference an emergency measure was introduced opposing the LA's plans for future professional training. (*See also* Education, Library.) This showed that NALGO librarians perhaps see themselves more as "workers" than as professionals, thus perpetuating outworn attitudes. The motion was, presumably, responsible for NALGO's detailed criticism of the LA proposals. As a result, although in 1977 a record number of four librarians were elected to NALGO's executive council, top-level relations between the two bodies were seriously strained.

Similarly, the National Association of Teachers in Further and Higher Education, to which many tutor-librarians in nonuniversity colleges belong, notably failed to promote their interests. It was, however, possible that LA could pressurize this union by threatening that its members would switch to the more helpful Association of Polytechnic Teachers.

Meanwhile, employment prospects, especially for the newly qualified, became increasingly bleak. An annual Department of Education and Science survey showed that of the 70 to 80 per cent of new librarians who replied to the questionnaire only 69 per cent had obtained professional employment two months after qualifying, against 90 per cent two years earlier. Of those who had failed to find library work, nearly 20 per cent said they were giving up the attempt. The situation was exacerbated by the refusal (in one sense commendable) of library authorities to appoint qualified staff to lower grade positions; one correspondent of the *Library Association Record* complained that as a result of this policy he was working in a hotel. Obviously much of this problem resulted from deliberate understaffing because of economic recession. Unless there was a notable improvement, however, existing statistics suggested that the library schools would be overproducing by about 40 per cent during the next four to five years.

Public Libraries

Faced with the continual need to economize, many local authorities had squeezed their libraries, a practice that might become self-defeating. Lord Donaldson, minister for the arts, hinted that those depriving their library services might face reduced rate support grants (government contributions to local authority funds); and Shirley Williams, secretary of state for education and science, suggested that part of the grants could be "earmarked" for library use. The Council of Local Education Authorities admitted that in 1976 excessive savings in their sector throughout the U.K. had amounted to around £88,000,000. Examples of estimated reductions for 1977-78 were Essex County Library's £500,000, and East Sussex's £69,000, of which £31,000 was to be taken from the book fund. Total estimated book fund increases for 1977-78 were 7.13 per cent; but as this figure was less than the estimated inflation of book prices, it represented a decline in real terms.

After some years of inadequate book buying many authorities tried hard to switch savings to other sectors. Some libraries were closed down (e.g., Camden's High Holborn branch, used mainly by London commuters), or hours were drastically reduced. Saturday afternoon closing was introduced in Dorset, Cheshire, and North Yorkshire; and many other libraries closed on one weekday. East Sussex invited the public to subscribe for newspapers and magazines. Somerset appealed for gifts of books, and Kensington and Chelsea introduced charges for borrowing records. Buckinghamshire, which had bought no children's books since April 1975, was considering abandoning its school library service. Kingston-upon-Thames proposed to charge schools £10 for each "box" of books borrowed.

An increasing number of authorities adopted the practice of selling surplus books. Surrey, Staffordshire, Nottinghamshire, and Lancashire had continuous sales; Buckinghamshire had monthly ones, while some libraries held "once off" events. Redbridge and Oxfordshire sold postcards made from prints and photographs in their local history collections; Norwich Central Library sold T-shirts bearing its name.

Despite retrenchment, there were isolated pockets of advance and evidence of much lively activity. Some relaxation of austerity occurred. Croydon filled two recently "frozen" posts. Greenock's Central Library actually introduced Saturday afternoon opening, and Leicestershire increased by £50,000 its original allocation for school and college libraries. New libraries were opened at Hoddesdon in Hertfordshire, at Berkeley and Charlton Kings in Gloucestershire, and at Woking and Egham in Surrey. In the London borough of Bromley the new Churchill Library, after 13 years of gestation, finally opened in April in an enormous building shared with a theater. Built and equipped at the fabulous cost of £2,250,000, it seemed that there remained insufficient funds for adequate staffing and other facilities. In Cheshire and Suffolk mobile library services were extended.

Although opening hours were reduced, the use of libraries increased. Issues were up by as much as 49 per cent at Barnsley's Central Library (new in 1976), by 42 per cent at Solihull, and 15 per cent in Cornwall. Lincolnshire loaned nearly 200,000 more books than in 1976; and Kent, 780,000 more. At Redbridge the proportion of population registered as readers went up from 33.7 per cent to 45.8 per cent; Surrey claimed that nearly 50 per cent of its population were readers.

There was no lack of invention and enterprise, and a number of children's events were staged. Nottinghamshire and the London boroughs of Islington and Lewisham ran various competitions during the summer holidays. Greater Manchester had a Jubilee children's book fair in November, while during National Children's Book Week in October Weybridge in Surrey laid on authors and illustrators and a chess champion to challenge six young players concurrently. Writers-in-residence were appointed at Sutton and Lambeth. Lambeth's awareness was shown by its production, hard upon the news of his death, of a booklet about Elvis Presley that listed all available tapes and discs of his music and indicated those that the library possessed. Wandsworth organized a Silver Jubilee literary competition throughout London. Middlesborough's Market Place branch, in a very run-down area, became an important community center, providing interest for children, pensioners, and the unemployed.

Libraries increased and diversified their services, and provisions for immigrants improved. Wolverhampton publicized its large stock of books in Punjabi, Hindi, and Urdu. Tooting provided a librarian specifically for foreign-language books; and Cleveland, Hertfordshire, and Slough also gave special attention to immigrants' needs. In a situation of general unemployment, libraries contributed to the job-creation scheme, notably at Gateshead, Rotherham, and Liverpool, where school-leavers were used mainly on local history projects.

Publishing, Book

Declining home sales and growing competition overseas forced British book publishers to push their product more aggressively in 1977. Total titles published in 1976 were 34,434, only 3.3 per cent down from 1975's record output. The January-September 1977 total of 25,601 was 4.1 per cent higher than than for January-September 1976. Cutbacks were clearly not yet biting. To boost home sales, promotional campaigns were intensified; abroad, expansion into new areas and improvement of performance in existing markets became urgent priorities.

At home, the year began with a paperback recession. Orders were cancelled, and returns percentages rose. Penguin, with January-June profits down from £807,000 to £449,000, predicted that a three-year annual 30 per cent sales rise would fall in 1977 to one of 10 per cent to 15 per cent. By September, helped by stay-at-home summer weather, increased advertising, and cutbacks, the slide seemed to have been stopped. There were fears, however, of market saturation as publishers planning for expansion continued to regard a paperback subsidiary to be essential. A main cause of the recession had been a virtual end of the impulse buying on which paperback publishers' profits largely depend. Significantly, such high-priced quality nonfiction imprints as Pan's Picador and the many popular large-format illustrated series had withstood the downward trend. Such publications were guides to a growth area successfully cultivated by two of the year's international bestsellers: Mitchell Beazley's The Joy of Knowledge Library, a "look and learn" encyclopedia; and Marshall Cavendish Editions, from a publisher described in The Guinness Book of Records, as the most efficient company operating in Britain.

Produced and printed in Britain at an investment cost of £3,500,000 for the international edition, The Joy of Knowledge Library had earned some £3,000,000 from sales of 14 foreign-language editions before its publication in the U.K. in 10 separately available volumes to be sold through bookshops in 1977-78. An initial 125,000-copy print order went to the United States, where Random House—publishing it in one alarmingly bulky volume—had acquired trade rights and Encyclopaedia Britannica Educational Corporation had acquired school and college rights. Thematically organized, it treats each topic in a double-page spread consisting of 10, mainly four-colour illustrations, with captions to supplement 850 words of text. It is aimed at a televisually conditioned home and high school readership. Man and Machines, one of the first volumes published in Britain, won the Times Educational Supplement's Senior Information Book Award.

Marshall Cavendish Editions, a glossy full-colour, high-priced nonfiction series—with books on houseplants, the small garden, and embroidery published in 1977 and four titles commissioned for 1978—combines instruction for beginners with in-depth information for specialists. A 1977-78 investment topping £350,000 was justified by substantial sales to the United States, Australia, New Zealand, France, West Germany, the Netherlands, Denmark, Sweden, and Finland. There was a 200,000-copy first print order for the home market.

Predictably, paperback ventures were in established growth areas in 1977, Robin Clark, a new paperback publisher, catered to the family, with first titles ranging from Fun on Wheels—games, puzzles, and brainteasers to amuse travelling children—to Bar Guide, instructions for mixing exotic drinks. Corgi, Transworld's popular fiction firm, launched the "Barbara Cartland Library of Love," reprinting best-sellers by such pioneer heart-throb novelists as Elinor Glyn, E.M. Hull, and Ethel M. Dell. The continued appeal of historical romance ensured success for Mills and Boon's new Masquerade imprint, with six-figure print runs of first titles fully subscribed. Futura followed its diversification from science fiction into romance with Pocket Guides, a new imprint for the absorbent "teach yourself, do-it-yourself" market. Short print runs ensured frequent updating, and pithy presentation kept prices competitive. Fontana started a science fiction series and replaced its religious books series, selling more than a million copies a year, with a new imprint, Fount Paperbacks. It also launched an international prestige project, Fontana Open Books, original titles by experts on "the developing child." The titles were simultaneously published in hardcover by Open Books in the U.K. and by the Harvard

Books en route from London's Gatwick Airport to Australia are part of Air Book Australia, a door-to-door service jointly sponsored by the Publishers Association and the Australian Booksellers to cut delivery time from three months to 14 days.

University Press in the United States and Canada, with translation rights sold to 10 continental European countries.

Although exports had risen to 43.15 per cent of turnover in 1976 and publishers with overseas companies reported higher profits from their activities than from home sales, Britain's preeminence in English-language world markets was increasingly challenged by U.S. expansion and by the growth of indigenous publishing industries. India had become the world's third largest exporter of English-language books. Australia, where Britain's share of an expanding market had dropped from 80 per cent in 1965 to 48 per cent by 1976, was developing book exports to India, Southeast Asia, China, and Japan. Australia was also buying rights to U.S. books, printed at home or in Southeast Asia, direct from U.S. publishers. In Canada, competing against U.S. domination of the growing market and expanding Canadian book production, British publishers were losing heavily. Complaints of the high price of imported British books, delivery delays, and poor market servicing were general.

To meet the challenge, publishers acted individually and corporately. Allen and Unwin, the Bodley Head-Cape-Chatto group, Dent, and the Souvenir Press started Australian companies. The Publishers Association (PA) began a weekly Air Book Australia service, cutting delivery time from three months to 14 days, with a 30 per cent cash saving on Accelerated Surface Post. PA also invited representatives of the Canadian book trade to Britain to discuss problems and prospects. As a result, publishers reduced Canadian book prices, introduced a corporate airfreight service that speeded deliveries to 15 days from 4 to 6 weeks and increased coproductions with Canadian publishers.

Thomson Publications reorganized for expansion and created a new company, Thomson Books, to rationalize worldwide distribution and develop markets in North America, Latin America, South Africa, and the Far East. By acquision of Noble and Noble of New York and Bowmar of Los Angeles (merged as Bowmar-Noble), it gained a footing in the U.S. elementary and high school textbook market, and its later takeover of Wadsworth carried it into college and academic textbook publishing. William Clowes and Rex Collings also formed new companies to handle continental European, North American, Middle Eastern, and African sales and to develop intercontinental marketing. Heinemann Educational established U. S. and Caribbean companies; Allen and Unwin set up a subsidiary to market academic titles in the United States; and Macdonald Educational joined Raintree of Milwaukee in launching Macdonald-Raintree, which acquired the assets of Purnell Educational, BPC's U.S. subsidiary. W.H. Smith Distributors formed a U.S. company to distribute British books.

The Oxford University Press (O.U.P.) and George Philip pooled resources to develop the West African and Southeast Asian cartographic markets, planning joint imprint publications. O.U.P. also opened a Cairo office.

In continental Europe, Austria has become a growth area, with the value of British book imports up 308 per cent since 1974, and the Austrian book trade offered financial backing for author visits and other promotional aids. The West German market potential was reassessed, and foreign currency book pricing and invoicing were investigated. Mills and Boon was expanding into France. As part of its planned development of EEC markets, Faber organized a successful exhibition at Lille, a city with a large university English faculty, where Faber's paperback range of poetry, drama, and literary criticism was displayed. Faber also worked through an important Conservatoire (showing its scores and music books) and France's biggest bookshop, at which its general, art, and children's books were on view. Phaidon's "into Europe" export drive also used exhibitions in Copenhagen, Amsterdam, West Berlin, Florence, Vienna, Zurich, and Oslo, where Norway's largest booksellers sold more than one-third of the titles on show within two days, with orders rolling in. David and Charles carried its "Britain's Countryside" campaign into bookshops in France, Belgium, the Netherlands, Sweden, and Denmark, with the slogan "Visit Britain with David and Charles."

Publishing, Magazines

Although costs continued to rise and library spending to fall, 1977 was a growth year for U.K. magazine publishing.

There was a £20,500,000 takeover in November of Morgan-Grampian, an up-and-coming magazine publishing chain, by trafalgar House, the engineering, property, and shipping group that in June had bought Beaverbrook Newspapers Ltd. The Takeover created a powerful, forward-looking new publishing empire, potentially capable of challenging Reed International's monolithic International Publishing Corporation (IPC). Morgan-Grampian was already expanding from technical and professional journals into the consumer market. It had launched several pop music and hi-fi magazines and had acquired the women's monthly *Over 21*. Trafalgar House planned its expansion into sport and women's interests and was on the lookout for further acquisitions.

The year's launches outnumbered its closures, and several showed the continuing appeal of the topical or special-interest magazine, with assured initial readership

Christopher Tolkien was the editor of J.R.R. Tolkien's The Silmarillion, which was published in 1977 from his father's manuscripts.

Window display of Phaidon Press books at Sandsbergs Bokhandel, Stockholm, which formed part of Phaidon's 1977 "into Europe" export drive.

and advertising revenues. Morgan-Grampian's *Weight Watchers* had a ready-made readership in the members of the 800 classes run by its parent organization, the U.K. branch of Weight Watchers, Inc., and overtook its nearest rival, IPC's *Successful Slimming*, new in 1976. *Home Grown*, Britain's first drug magazine, could count on revenues from suppliers of legal drug-growing and drug-taking equipment. *Vole*, a conservationist monthly started by Richard Boston, campaigner for real ale and columnist of the *Guardian* newspaper, gained support from advocates of alternative life-styles. *Nationwide Skateboarding*, launched by IPC on the crest of a new craze, provided a shop window for manufacturers and retailers. Closure within a year of *Prima*, a women's monthly lacking an individual approach, pointed the moral.

Deluxe, a fashion and features quarterly with West German financial backing, was founded to fill the gap between IPC's teenage fashion monthlies, *Honey* and *19*, and the up-market *Vogue*. It hoped to become a women's magazine enjoyed by men. Another gap was closed by *Good Reading*, a monthly review of paperbacks.

Private Eye, the satirical weekly threatened by a complex of legal cases brought against it by Sir James Goldsmith, millionaire financier and aspiring newspaper owner, was saved. Claiming that it had maintained a campaign of vilification against him, Sir James had tried to suppress it by private prosecution of its editor for criminal libel, a legal rarity carrying the penalty of imprisonment, and by civil libel actions against its distributors, publishers, and printers. In May, however, the criminal libel charge was dropped, and the civil actions were settled by a full-page apology in the London *Evening Standard* (owned by Beaverbrook Newspapers in which Sir James held shares) and payment of £30,000 towards his costs. Actions threatened against distributors had lost *Private Eye* 12,000 of its 100,000 circulation.

Special Users, Services to

The Newington Branch Library in Edinburgh, opened in 1975, won a prize for its excellent facilities for the disabled. It provides special parking space, ramps for wheelchairs, and catalogs and audiovisual material placed at the correct height for wheelchair occupants. There is also a braille version of the record catalog.

Some advances were made in help for the blind. Gateshead Public Libraries utilized the government's job creation scheme to effect the production of more talking books for the blind and partially sighted; and Kensington and Chelsea exempted the blind from charges for borrowing records. Greater awareness of the needs of the blind was shown when *Brio*, the journal of the British branch of the International Association of Music Librarians, printed an article by Daphne Kennard, music project officer of the Disabled Living Foundation, in which she stressed the need for braille overprinting of music catalogs. LA received £11,000 from the British National Bibliography research fund to finance an 18-month study of large-print users and their special needs. To be run by Lorna Bell, a chartered librarian working in Birmingham, the study would concentrate on identifying the users, assessing their knowledge of what resources were available to them, and also working out what type of print as well as size was most generally suitable. An attempt was to be made to discover whether there existed a section of the community in need of the large-print service, but unaware of its availability.

For late or slow readers the BBC started a television and radio series entitled "On the Move," and a number of libraries were backing up the programs by providing video recordings. The series seemed assured of success, since in the year from February 1976 to February 1977 the number of adults being helped to read had nearly doubled, reaching about 100,000. For deaf children the National College of Teachers of the Deaf issued some simplified texts in the well-known "Ladybird" children's series. A problem was that publishers were unwilling to produce simplified text versions of their books since the short runs required were unprofitable.

STEPHANIE MULLINS
DOROTHY M. PARTINGTON

State Reports

State correspondents report here on events of general interest during 1977. They provide systematic coverage on state library associations and state agencies. Data are given as of the end of 1977 unless otherwise indicated. ALA membership is given for state associations reporting it.

ALABAMA

Alabama Library Association (founded 1904)

Membership: 1,292; *Annual Expenditure:* $12,000.
President: Mozelle B. Cummings, Alabama Public Library Service (April 1977-March 1978).
Vice-President/President-elect: Betty Beal, Jefferson County Schools, Birmingham.
Second Vice-President: Mary Ella Terrill, Tuscaloosa County Schools.
Secretary: Bonnie Ledbetter, University of Alabama in Birmingham.
Treasurer: Jerry Stephens, University of Alabama in Birmingham.
Executive Secretary: Ruth Waldrop, P.O. Box BY, University, Alabama 35486.
Annual Meeting: April 6-8, 1977, Montgomery.
Publication: The Alabama Librarian (bimonthly).

Alabama Public Library Service

Anthony Miele, Director
6030 Monticello Drive
Montgomery 36130

School Library Media Supervisor

Ray Jones
Department of Education
Montgomery 36104

College and University Libraries. The year 1977 was outstanding for cooperative activities among all types of libraries, particularly in the formal study of the state's libraries and in the expanded use of SOLINET and the Union Catalog.

In October the Architecture and Fine Arts Library of Auburn University moved into new quarters in the fine arts complex, more than doubling its space. The building is an architectural and aesthetic asset to the campus. In ceremonies attended by library leaders from throughout the state, the University of Alabama in Tuscaloosa named the Special Collections Room of the Amelia Gayle Gorgas Library after W. Stanley Hoole, Dean Emeritus of the University Libraries, in recognition of his contributions to research and writing in the profession and in the field of history.

The Lister Hill Library of the Health Sciences at the University of Alabama at Birmingham is implementing all functions of the UCLA On-Line Serials Control System. This project, funded through a National Library of Medicine Resource Program Grant, will not include cataloging functions. The objective of the project is to prove that the UCLA system can be successfully implemented at a medium-sized medical library with computer facilities and programming services that are independent of the UCLA system.

School Libraries. Affiliation with the American Association of School Librarians (AASL) has come to Alabama. A letter from Alice Fite, Executive Secretary of AASL, read in part, "I have made positive recommendations to ASSL Regional Directors that the application from the Children and School Librarians Division of Alabama Library Association has met the criteria for affiliation with ASSL." Fite was to address the business session of the School Librarians Division at the state convention in April 1978.

Guidelines for School Media Programs by Raymond Jones, Ruth Johnson, and Hallie Jordan was published in 1977. Progress is being made toward accreditation to meet the State Department of Education's mandate for statewide accreditation by 1980. Montgomery County achieved accreditation within its system, employing certified librarians for 35 elementary schools. More than half of the counties in Alabama have achieved the goal. Sixteen school media supervisors now serve Alabama schools.

Public Libraries. Public libraries responded to increased support at the state level (from 18 to 31 cents per capita in 1977) by improving service and engaging in cooperative activities among themselves and with other types of libraries. Public Administration Service of Chicago is conducting a study to determine the current effectiveness of Alabama's libraries in meeting the needs of users and to propose changes to raise the level of service within the state.

The Alabama library community has recognized that the vast needs and limited resources of the state mandate a cooperative approach. All parts of the profession are represented on the System Development Committee, and there has been enthusiastic participation in area meetings addressing the needs of patrons of all types of libraries. These activities have intensified the search for a workable blueprint for methods of providing every citizen with the highest possible level of library service. John O. Hall is the director of the study; Lester L. Stoffel, Peggy Sullivan, Edward Holley, and Robert Rolfe are special consultants.

Birmingham will choose the architect for a new main library made possible by a successful bond issue, and Sylacauga received a grant from the Public Works Administration for the construction of a new building.

Statewide Activities. Robert B. (Bob) Ingram, Jr., has been chosen as the State

Library Service, the Alabama State Department of Education, the Alabama Instructional Media Association, and Auburn University at Montgomery, the conference featured Susan Bistline and Marybeth Peters of the Copyright Office, May Jo Lynch of ALA, and Ivan Bender of the Encyclopaedia Britannica Educational Corporation.

People. Upon the retirement of Richardana Ramsay at the end of 1976, George Stewart was appointed Director of Birmingham-Jefferson County Public Library. Ann Terrell Hester, Janet Norflette Day, and Jack F. Bulow were designated as Associate Directors.

O. Dallas Baillio, Jr., is the new Director of the Mobile Public Library. Other changes include Shirley Laseter, Autauga-Prattville; Lester McKiernan, Cahaba; and Miriam Martin, Macon County-Tuskegee. Alice Doughtie retired as Administrator of Choctawhatchee Regional Library, and Lydia Parker succeeded to the position.

Changes and additions to the staff of the Alabama Public Library Service (APLS) included Sue Smith, with responsibilities in planning, evaluation, and statistics; Martha Jule Blackshear, formerly APLS State Aid Coordinator, named to the newly created post of Children and Young Adult Coordinator; Bill Crowley, formerly Public Information and Continuing Education Coordinator, the new full-time Continuing Education Coordinator; Miriam M. Pace, formerly Federal Program Coordinator, the new Administrator of the new Alabama Regional Library for the Blind and Physically Handicapped; Ernie Laseter, formerly Director of Ector County Library (Texas), the new Federal Programs Coordinator; Cathy Smith, formerly Extension Specialist with the Coastal Plains Library (Georgia), the new Serials Librarian; Bob Schremser, formerly Head Librarian at Alexander City Junior College, the new Consultant for Multitype Systems and Institutional Libraries; Regina T. Finney, formerly Head of the College Library Branch of the Atlanta Public Library, the new Administrative Assistant to the Director; Ken Zaleski, formerly Head of Technical Services at Belleville Public Library (New Jersey), the new Reference Librarian.

Alabama Library Association. Ruth Waldrop of the Graduate School of Library Service at the University of Alabama became Executive Secretary of the Alabama Library Association on December 1. Her varied experience as a school librarian, library and media supervisor, state school library consultant, and professor of library science makes her uniquely qualified to serve in the post.

The highlight of the state convention held Chairman for the Governor's Committee on Libraries for the Alabama Governor's Conference on Library and Information Services. Ingram has been an active participant in Alabama affairs as a newspaperman, as Director of the State Finance Department (1968-71), and as the owner and editor of *Alabama*, a newsmagazine. Regional conferences will be held in the fall of 1978 in preparation for the state conference in January 1979. The official recommendations will be presented to the incoming governor, who will be inaugurated in January 1979.

Alabama has received a $200,000 grant from the National Endowment for the Humanities for *Perspectives: The Alabama Heritage*, a project designed to encourage out-of-school adults to use humanities resources in libraries. Rosemary Canfield of the English Department of Troy State University is the project director. Alabama Public Library Service and Troy are co-sponsors of the project, matching the grant funds with $200,000 on a cost-sharing basis. The program is to focus on books written by Alabama writers and will feature study guides available at all public libraries, model club program outlines, exhibits at district and state club meetings, local radio and television talk shows, newspaper columns, and a series of six one-hour documentary television programs to be presented on the Alabama educational television network.

Library Education. In 1977 library continuing education in Alabama acquired both a structure and a purpose. On December 4, 1976, the Executive Council of the Alabama Library Association (AlaLA) unanimously adopted a resolution "to develop a plan for the ongoing facilitation of library continuing education." Composed of representatives of all types of libraries and other institutions concerned with continuing education, the *Steering Committee on Library Continuing Education* first met in May 1977. Nancy Bush, Head of Auburn University's Department of Educational Media, was elected chairman. Outstanding conferences and workshops during the year included a statewide trustee conference on October 14-15 at Auburn University with the title "Who Runs Your Library?" Featured speakers were Nancy Stiegemeyer and E. Culpepper Clark. The conference was sponsored by divisions of AlaLA, the Alabama Public Library Service, and the Department of Educational Media and Continuing Education Office of Auburn University.

The last statewide conference of the year, "Implementing the Copyright Law in Alabama," took place on December 9-10 at Auburn University at Montgomery. Cosponsored by the Alabama Public in Montgomery in April was the Legislative Day Dinner attended by more than 100 members of the state legislature. Librarians, trustees, and library patrons were stimulated by the address of Bessie Boehm Moore, Acting Chairperson of the National Commission on Libraries and Information Science. Other programs featured Letitia Baldridge, Agnes Furruso, Alice Ihrig, Allen Kent, James Livsey, Arthur Plotnik, and Judith Krug. AlaLA Author Awards were given to William Bradford Huie for *In the Hours of the Night* and to F. Wilburn Helmbold for *Tracing Your Ancestry*. The Public Service Award went to Carl Elliott. Others recognized for outstanding service were Mary Edna Anders, Maj. Harwell G. Davis, William Cody, Bethel Fite, Joe Namath, Strode Publishers, and the Alabama Wildlife Federation Endowment.

MOZELLE B. CUMMINGS

ALASKA

Alaska Library Association
(founded 1960)

Membership: 259; *Annual Expenditure:* $7,500.

President: Peggy Cummings, Alaska State University, Juneau (March 1977-March 1978).

Vice-President/President-elect: Betts Johnson, Kodiak Island School District.

Secretary: Emma McCune, Homer High School, Minilchik.

Annual Convention: March 19, 1977, Fairbanks.

Publication: Sourdough (bimonthly).

Division of State Libraries
Richard B. Engen, Director
Pouch G. Capitol
Juneau 99801

State School Library Media Supervisor
Molly Bynum
Mountain View Elementary School
Anchorage 99504

The annual AkLA conference held in Fairbanks in March focused on networking. Featured speakers were Rod Swartz, Washington State Librarian, and Heather Nicoll, Washington Library Network trainer. The conference endorsed the "Statement on Faculty Status of College and University Librarians" sponsored by ALA's Association of College and Research Libraries, the Association of American Colleges, and the American Association of University Professors. AkLA accepted a seventh local chapter into the Association (Matanuska-Susitna) and awarded an honorary membership to Jeane Moore, retired U.S. Air Force Alaska Air Command Librarian.

Priorities of the Association for 1977 were the development of school library standards and of a continuing education plan. Additional AkLA-supported activities included the Northern Chapter's Book Tips project (30- and 60-second radio "teaser" spots), completion of the editing of the Alaska Native Oral Literature tapes and plans for a cumulative index to the stories, and publication of a handbook of procedures and policies for the Association.

Continuing Education. Continuing education planning and activities continued to be a priority of both AkLA and the Alaska State Library. The continuing education scholarship was offered by AkLA for the third consecutive year. Two federally funded training proposals were approved. The project for Village Library Workshops, funded under Title I-A of the Higher Education Act (HEA), is bringing village librarians from 10 communities on the Seward Peninsula into Nome for two sessions. At the session held in October, participants made radio spots and publicity posters and planned a project for their community library. The second meeting was to be in March 1978. A workshop on "School Library Management and Networking in Alaska," also funded under HEA, Title II-B, was to take place in 1978, bringing together 30 participants from rural schools and school and community libraries.

Tanana Valley Community College began offering a two-year Library Technical Assistant program. Classes in Introduction to Libraries and Small Library Administration and in Technical Processes I—Cataloging were offered in the fall. Course offerings were to expand in the spring of 1978. Fifty-three students were enrolled in 1977, and there is much interest around the state in having the program offered at other University of Alaska units.

The Continuing Education Committee of AkLA sent out 1,200 surveys in late 1976, seeking information on the needs of library personnel statewide. Twenty-four per cent of the surveys were returned, and results were summarized. The Committee outlined a tentative plan for the state, identifying definite course titles that were wanted immediately and specifying the continuing education responsibilities of AkLA, the State Library, and the universities in the state.

School Library Standards. An AkLA Task Force for School Library Standards began work in late 1976, drafting a plan of action to insure adequate school library resources and appropriate management of those resources. The special needs of both the rural and urban schools in Alaska, creation of library collections for the newly formed rural districts and their regional resource centers, and alternative methods of delivery were some of the areas considered. Standards have been drafted and are to be presented to the Association at the 1978 annual meeting. The Task Force also coordinated AkLA's recommendation to establish a school library consultant position in the Department of Education's Division of State Libraries and Museums.

Networking. In early fall 1977, Alaska became the first out-of-state unit to join the Washington Library Network (WLN). Initially, two computer terminals were installed, at the State Library in Juneau and at Rasmuson Library at the University of Alaska in Fairbanks. Usage is now limited to output; the input mode will follow in another step, as will expansion of the number of terminals.

A number of developments utilizing the technology of computers for networking occurred in 1977 that allow Alaskan libraries to plug into outside data bases. At least three major libraries have terminals and are using Systems Development Corporation and Lockheed Bibliographic Data Base systems. The U.S. Bureau of Mines Library in Juneau is on-line to the Minerals Availability System in Denver.

Work continued on pursuing satellite time for information transfer and on expanding the University of Alaska computer system. Immediate implications of the system include interlibrary loan, input capability to the statewide union serials list, and film booking. The statewide union list of serials is in the last stages of its pilot project. Microfiche copies of the pilot were distributed at the 1977 AkLA conference.

Construction. The Fairbanks North Star Borough Library and Resource Center was completed in the summer and dedicated on October 29. Construction of the facility, which serves the Northern Region of Alaska as well as the Fairbanks Borough, was made possible partly through the 1974 state general obligation bond. The new building covers 42,000 square feet. Special features include a small auditorium, an Alaskana room with a pegged oak floor, a room for the genealogical collection, a skylight in the foyer and five 20-foot trees, a fireplace in the informal reading area, and art work throughout by prominent Alaskan artists. There is a computerized circulation system, a microfilm card catalog, and space for 150,000 volumes (with the collection now totaling 80,000).

On the staff of the Library is the regional services librarian funded by the State Library. This position oversees the Library's part in providing the services of a regional resource center, including the mail-a-book program, lending of circulating collections to small libraries, and interlibrary loan. The Fairbanks North Star Borough Library and Resource Center will also serve as the last-copy depository for Alaskan public libraries. The opening of this major regional resource center is a significant step in the development of the Alaska library network.

A number of other new and supplemental construction grants have been approved for Alaskan community libraries, including Anderson, Dillingham, Eagle, Galena, Wasilla, and Kodiak.

Appointment. Keith Revelle, formerly the Assistant Librarian for the Municipality of Anchorage, was appointed Municipal Librarian in the summer of 1977.

Publications. *Stories of Native Alaskans*, published by the University of Alaska Press, is the result of the Alaska Native Oral Literature taping project conducted by AkLA since 1972. The book contains 14 stories from the tapes and their English translations, published as 28 broadsides. Matching graphics draw the native language and English broadsides together for the same story. At least one story is included in each of the native languages of Koyukon Athabaskan, Kutchin, Athabaskan, Inupiaq, Yupik, and Siberian Yupik.

The second edition of *High School Library Book Materials for First Year Purchase*, published by the Alaska State Library, was developed to meet the needs of small high schools beginning or updating a library collection. An accompanying list for elementary school libraries was also published in 1977. The State Library also published *State and Local Publications Received: A Ten-Year Cumulation, 1964-1974*.

NANCY LESH

ARIZONA

Activities in Arizona libraries in 1977 focused on two major concerns: an increase in activity and interest in automation, and an increase in Southwest ethnic materials and library services to minority groups.

Automation. OCLC is now used in several libraries in the state. The University of Arizona Library reported that its Catalog Department expected to process about 40 per cent more titles in 1977—an additional 15,000 or more—with the use of OCLC. Without OCLC this increased rate of acquisition would mean that these 15,000 or more titles would join the backlog.

Tucson Public Library added more new

volumes than any other public library in the state in 1977 and started two new branch libraries. The Library handled an increase of 4,000 volumes a month with no additional staff through the use of OCLC. An OCLC terminal was made operational in 1977 at the Yuma City-County Library, the headquarters library for Region IV in the state.

Both Phoenix and Tucson Public Libraries purchased new circulation and acquisition systems. Phoenix Public Library purchased the ULISYS Circulation Control System from Universal Library System of Toronto, and Tucson Public Library installed a bar-code, a commercially available turn-key system distributed by C.L. Systems, Inc. Both libraries have implemented the Baker and Taylor Automated Buying System (BATAB).

Arizona Library Association (founded 1926)

Membership: 1,035; *Annual Expenditure:* $17,260.
President: Sharon Womack, Arizona Department of Library Archives, Phoenix (October 1977-September 1978).
Vice-President/President-elect: David Laird, University of Arizona Library, Tucson.
Secretary: Linda Head, Marana Public Schools, Tucson.
Annual Conference: September 15-17, 1977, Yuma.
Publication: Newsletter (monthly).

State Library, Archives, and Public Records Division

Marguerite B. Cooley, Assistant Director,
State Capitol
Phoenix 85007

School Library Media Supervisor

Mary Choncoff
State Department of Public Instruction
Phoenix 85007

Ethnic Materials and Services. Arizona librarians demonstrated increased sensitivity to and interest in the cultural and educational needs of the Spanish-speaking and Chicano population in the state during 1977. The Ad Hoc Committee on Ethnic Materials and Services, established by Arizona State Library Association (ASLA) President Coralie Wolf, met monthly, and regular reports appeared in the Association's *Newsletter.* A highlight of the year was a State Library Extension Service videotape entitled *Minority Librarians . . . A Better Way?* Members of the Committee provided consultant services to libraries throughout the state.

The Library at Arizona State University worked to develop a comprehensive collection of books in Spanish for children and young adults by Hispanic authors. Isabel Schon, Assistant Professor in the Department of Educational Technology and Library Science, reported that it is the only collection of books for children and adolescents by Hispanic authors in the United States.

Both the Arizona and Arizona State library programs offer courses on ethnic materials for the Spanish-speaking population. For a second year in 1977 the Graduate Library School of the University of Arizona was awarded a grant to train bilingual Spanish-speaking librarians. This highly successful project, the GLISA Program, is under the direction of Arnulfo Trejo.

Grants. A number of people and institutions in the state received significant funding through national grant awards in 1977. The National Endowment for the Humanities awarded Tucson Public Library a grant for a project called "Sonoran Heritage." This three-year program will attempt to discuss the history and culture of the Sonoran region through the context of man in an arid ecosystem. Kathleen Dannreuther will direct the study.

The University of Arizona Library received a grant from the Bicentennial Commission for preserving on microfilm historic Arizona newspapers. Papers selected for the filming were the St. John's *Herald,* 1885-1912; Arizona *Journal Miner* (Prescott), 1901-05; Prescott *Courier,* 1897-1905; and the Arizona *Bulletin* (Safford), 1889-1918.

Two research grants were awarded to individuals in Arizona in 1977 from the Division of Library Programs of the U.S. Office of Education. Norman Higgins, Chairperson of the Department of Educational Technology and Library Science at Arizona State received a grant for a study entitled "Improving Library Education for Selected Minorities." Helen M. Gothberg, Assistant Professor in the Graduate Library School at Arizona, received a grant for a project called "Training Library Communication Skills: The Development of Three Video Tape Workshops." This product will be made available nationally from the National Audiovisual Library in Washington, D.C.

Workshops and Speakers. A "Southwest in the Arts" program was held in Phoenix in April and featured Ann Nolan Clark, Newbery Medal Award author, and Larry Golsh, one of the Southwest's foremost Indian artists. The program was sponsored by the Arizona Commission on the Arts and Humanities, the School Library Division of ASLA, Arizona State University, and the Arizona State Department of Education.

Wallace Stegner, noted Western author, was the featured speaker at the formal dedication ceremony of the new University of Arizona Library. John Dreyfus, a typographical advisor to Cambridge University Press and to the British Monotype Corporation, gave two talks on campus that were sponsored by the Graduate Library School, the Arizona Historical Society, and Zeitlin and VerBrugge Booksellers.

Featured speakers at the ASLA annual conference were John Holt, author and critic of American education, and Sid Fleischman, children's author. Librarians from around the state heard news of the White House Conference on Library and Information Services from Alice Irig on the national level and from Betty Ruffner on the state and local level; about intellectual freedom from ALA's Judith Krug; and on matters of service to ethnic groups from ALA's Jean Coleman. Conference Chairperson David Snider is Director of the Casa Grande Public Library.

A New Program. In July the new Space Imagery Center opened as an integral part of the University of Arizona's Lunar Planetary Laboratory. The new library contains nearly 500,000 images of planets and their satellites taken from earth and in space and a collection of topographic and geologic maps.

Publishing. The ASLA Executive Board in 1977 approved loans for publishing the index to the newspaper the Arizona *Daily Star* and for publishing an Arizona directory of libraries. In addition, the Association is currently involved with an author-title-subject index to *Arizona Highways* to cover the years 1967 through 1976.

Awards and Scholarships. Judy Blume was the recipient of the first Arizona Young Reader's Award, donated by ASLA. Twenty thousand children in kindergarten through grade eight voted Blume's *Tales of a Fourth Grade Nothing* as their favorite book.

The Association awarded the Alice B. Good Scholarship to Karen Biglin, a beginning student at the University of Arizona's Graduate Library School. The Outstanding Librarian of the Year Award was given to Donna Stephenson of the Guadalupe Town Library.

People. Jerrye Champion, former Assistant Director of the Scottsdale Public Library, was promoted to Library Director. Myriette Ekechukwu was appointed Director of the Columbus Branch Library in Tucson. She was previously in children's services at the Woods Branch Library.

Norman Higgins, Professor of Education, is the new Department Chairman of the Department of Educational Technology and Library Science at Arizona State University. Maggie Nation has been named Director of the Flagstaff City-Coconino County Public Library. She replaced Hazel Robinson, who was appointed School Library Supervisor in Flagstaff. David Snider, formerly Head of Public Services at Mesa Public Library, is the new Director of Casa Grande Public Library.

In Memoriam. Barbara Barth was killed in an automobile accident on June 10, 1977, in New Mexico. She had been the focal point for the formation of the regional board that led to the development of the Southeast Arizona Regional Library and had served as President of the Special Libraries Division of ASLA.

HELEN M. GOTHBERG

ARKANSAS

Arkansas Library Association (founded 1911)

Membership: 1,148; *Annual Expenditure:* $20,248.
President: Richard Reid, Fayetville, (January 1977-December 1977).
Vice-President/President-elect: Mrs. Bill Brothers, Helena School Libraries.
Secretary: Jean Lewidge, Tri-Lakes Regional Library, Hot Springs.
Annual Convention: October 2-4, 1977, Little Rock.
Publication: Arkansas Libraries (quarterly).

Arkansas Library Commission

Frances Neal, Librarian
506½ Center Street
Little Rock 72201

State School Library Media Supervisor

Betty Jean Morgan
State Department of Education
Little Rock 72201

Activities and Issues. The Arkansas Library Association's activities for 1977 were marked by both the hazards and the excitement of a walk on a tightrope. A precarious financial situation was balanced by productive activity and increased participation in Association affairs. Supported by a revised constitution adopted late in 1976, President Richard Reid led the Executive Board into actions that helped tighten procedures, improve understanding, and strengthen cohesiveness among the organization's divisions and its 1,148 members.

During the year 175 librarians joined as new members or renewed membership after a lapse of several years. A petition for the incorporation of a junior members group as a division of the Association was pending during a study of the organizational structure.

A two-day workshop in May on problems connected with the new copyright law was sponsored by the College and University Libraries Division (Richard Madaus of Henderson State University, Chairman) and the Reference Services Division (Kathy Essary, University of Arkansas at Little Rock, Chairperson). The workshop was coordinated by Peggy O'Donnell, Southwestern Library Association's Director of Continuing Education for Library Staffs, and was held at De Gray State Park Lodge near Arkadelphia. Robert Stevens, Head of Cataloging in the Copyright Office; Ron Naylor, Assistant Director of the University of Houston Libraries; William Nasri, Graduate School of Library and Information Sciences at the University of Pittsburgh; and H.W. McMillan, a lawyer from Arkadelphia, were resource people and speakers for the workshop which drew 66 active participants.

At the request of the College and University Division, the Executive Board endorsed and referred to membership for approval the Association of College and Research Libraries statement supporting faculty status for librarians. Membership gave its unanimous approval. Following the appearance of an official of the Arkansas Department of Higher Education at the Division program during the annual meeting, the Chairman solicited suggestions from librarians in all institutions of higher education in the state. A 20-page "Report on Post Secondary Education Library Planning and Resource Needs" to be used in the statewide master planning project was prepared and submitted to the Director of the Department of Higher Education.

Division Activities. The Public Libraries Division led by Kathryn Wright of Fordyce cooperated during the summer with Arkansas Library Commission personnel in producing a workshop on services to children. Mary Medearis, author of *Big Doc's Girl* and an Arkansan, spoke at a dinner meeting. Library Commission trustees voted to give profits from the workshop to the Arkansas Library Association's Scholarship Fund as a memorial to Mrs. W.H. McCain, a former Commission trustee who was vitally interested in improvement of standards for librarians and attraction of capable young people to the profession.

The School Libraries Division was granted affiliation with the American Association of School Libraries at the ALA Midwinter Meeting. The Division is working toward clarification of its relationship with school librarians from the Arkansas Education Association and members of the Arkansas Audio Visual Association. Chairman Kevin Blanton and Vice-Chairperson Ann Doss have worked closely to accomplish this goal.

Publications. One of the most visible improvements in the Association in 1977 was the revamping of *Arkansas Libraries*, the quarterly journal. Guided by an active Publications Committee under Don Deweese and edited by Joan Roberts of Fayetteville, the journal has assumed a new modernized format and editorial policies. Personal items and news of local rather than general professional interest are now incorporated in a quarterly *Newsletter* edited in the Association offices.

A trustee's handbook was published in the fall. A committee from the Association's Trustee Division under the direction of Mrs. Harve Taylor, Jr., Steve Bradley, and Vera Jacobs worked with the staff of the Arkansas River Valley Regional Library of which Katharine Keathley is Director.

The third edition of *Arkansas Union List of Periodicals* was produced by Arkansas State University Head Librarian Jerry Taylor. Sponsored by the College and University Libraries Division and funded through a federal program, it was released early in 1977.

The seventh Charlie May Simon Award was won by Sid Fleischman for *Ghost on Saturday Night*. The Award is made on the basis of a vote by Arkansas school children in grades four through six for titles copyrighted two years previously. Bettye Greene's *Phillip Hall Likes Me, I Reckon Maybe* was the runner-up. Bettye Greene was originally from Arkansas. Charlie May Simon (Mrs. John Gould Fletcher), in whose honor the Award was established, died during the year.

Legislation. Obscenity legislation was a matter of concern for librarians during the legislative session. Fred Darragh, Jr., a trustee of Little Rock Public Library and of the Arkansas Library Commission and Chairman of the Association's Legislative Committee, appeared with Alice Coleman of the Intellectual Freedom Committee and the Association's Executive Secretary at a legislative committee hearing in January. They expressed concern over provisions in a proposed obscenity law that had been reviewed by ALA's Intellectual Freedom Committee and by the state's attorney general. They and other interested parties were instrumental in having the bill amended to include protective clauses to prevent removal of library materials without prior determination of obscenity and to protect trustees from legal action.

Early in the year, the Legislative Committee announced priorities for activities during 1977: to monitor completion of the new Arkansas Library Commission quarters; to seek increased funding for the Commission; to seek an updating of Arkansas library laws; to support strongly a new constitutional convention; to lend more support to college, university, and school libraries; and to study a certification system for librarians.

Continuing Education. Gladys Davis of the Arkansas Library Commission staff has been named Continuing Education Coordinator for the state, and part of her professional time has been designated for such activities. The Advisory Committee—constituted by the Association's Subcommittee on Continuing Education, by persons who attended HEW institutes at Louisiana State University during the past two years, and by others invited to participate—has been organized. A quarterly continuing education calendar of events for the state and a clearinghouse for news are conducted through Davis's office.

Conferences. A happy feature of the fall conference held in October was a reception in historic Trapnall Hall that was sponsored by the Association to honor Mrs. Karl Neal, Director; Miss Freddy Schader, Consultant; and Mrs. Marie Pinckney, Administrative Assistant of the Arkansas Library Commission. These three, who have worked for a combined total of more than 100 years for Arkansas libraries, were to retire early in 1978.

Cassie Brothers, Vice-President of the Association and Program Chairman for the annual conference held in Little Rock, organized a program on "Excellence Through Continuing Education." A morning general session followed a breakfast at the conference hotel. The chief accomplishment of the membership meeting was the passage without dissent of a much-needed dues schedule change. The new schedule is based on salaries, and except for trustees all categories were raised. The life membership was abolished, and a "contributing members" category, which has received good support, was added.

KATHERINE STANICK

CALIFORNIA

California Library Association
(founded 1890)

Membership: 3,500; *Annual Expenditure:* $225,000.
President: June D. Fleming, Palo Alto Public Library (1977).
Vice-President/President-elect: Ursula Meyer, Stockton-San Joaquin County Public Library.
Executive Director: Stefan B. Moses, Suite 300, 717 K Street, Sacramento, California 95814.
Annual Meeting: December 11-15, 1977, San Francisco.
Publications: California Librarian (quarterly); *CLA Newsletter* (monthly).

California State Library
Ethel S. Crockett, State Librarian
P.O. Box 2037
Sacramento 95809

School Library Media Supervisor
Gerald W. Hamrin
State Department of Education
Sacramento 95814

Annus Mirabilis! The year 1977 saw several culminations of careful, arduous planning in previous years. It had long been recognized that there was a need for new state library legislation. Funding under the Public Library Services Act of 1963 had always been inadequate—only once exceeding $1,000,000. These parsimonious funds were distributed on a per capita basis to the various public library systems formed under the Act. The Department of Finance for some time had been seeking a different funding formula, and at the same time the State Library recognized the need for support for more types of libraries. During 1976 under the able leadership of Wallace W. Hall, an educator long concerned with library problems, the expanded California Library Association Government Relations Committee held a series of nine meetings around the state to get input and reaction for state library legislation. This careful groundwork paid off.

On April 1 Senator John F. Dunlap (D.-Napa), Chairman of the Senate Education Committee, introduced Senate Bill 792, the California Library Services Act. He was joined in sponsorship by 30 other state legislators in both houses. During the next few months the bill successfully passed various committees in both houses and was sent to the governor's desk in early September with a $6,600,000 appropriation authorization. Governor Jerry Brown signed the bill on October 1 after deleting $1,300,000.

State Librarian Ethel S. Crockett reported that special library projects for the underserved were not funded under the bill and that the State Library would provide for such projects with LSCA funds. The bill did include funding for the following program areas: universal borrowing, system reference, equal access, interlibrary loan, statewide administration, and a statewide data base. The bill goes into effect on July 1, 1978.

CLASS. Just as 1977 saw the successful passage of the new California Library Services Act, so too did it see growth of the California Library Authority for Systems and Services with its CLASSy acronym. As of December 1977, CLASS has 145 members consisting of the State Library, 14 of the 19 California State University and College libraries, all of the 9 University of California libraries (plus the Law Library at Davis), 28 community college libraries, 21 private academic libraries (including Stanford, the University of Southern California, and the Claremont Colleges), 47 public libraries (including 1 public school system resource center), and 24 special libraries (including private school libraries).

For 1976-77 its income from membership was $5,375. It had a state grant of LSCA funds in the amount of $468,750. The State Library has authorized CLASS to carry over the balance of more than $400,000 to the 1977-78 fiscal year. CLASS is governed by a Board of Directors whose membership is spelled out in the Joint Exercises of Powers Agreement. Much of its planning and progress, however, will be determined by an Authority Advisory Council made up of members appointed by the Congress of Members in the various segments of types of libraries (community colleges, public libraries, etc.).

Under its Executive Director Ron Miller, CLASS is currently working in nine program areas: (1) the California library and information service network; (2) the California data base (monographs); (3) the California data base (serials); (4) on-line reference citation support service; (5) improvement of access to and delivery of library materials; (6) storage of library materials; (7) the California conservation and preservation program; (8) continuing education; and (9) consulting.

CLA. Amidst the restrained euphoria caused by the passing and signing of the California Library Services Act, the California Library Association (CLA) met for its 79th annual conference in San Francisco in December. For the first time as far as is known, the Association was addressed by the governor. Brown spoke without notes, giving a speech in general terms that related to aspects of the library field. The governor then offered to answer questions from the audience. Ann Mitchell of the Law Library at UCLA asked what could be done so that all persons who needed it could afford to have access to expensive data base information. This question was obviously new to the governor, who asked for a more detailed explanation of the problem and more specific information. He said that it is elitist and undemocratic to have information resources that are not freely available to all who need them.

Brown's remarks agreed with those of Russell Shank, Vice-President and President-elect of ALA and University Librarian at UCLA. Shank spoke at the CLA Intellectual Freedom Committee meeting about the seemingly deliberate effort of the federal government to promote the philosophy of the marketplace, whereby the services of tax-supported entities must be paid for by users. He contrasted this policy with the generally accepted former philosophy that many services and products of tax-supported entities considered as worthwhile in themselves should be freely available to citizens for the social good.

Controversial Study. The Selection Consulting Center of Sacramento did a study to determine what qualifications should be brought by a beginning librarian to the first professional position. The Center analyzed the variety of tasks for beginning positions as reported by 14 public libraries, including the State Library. Of the 244 tasks listed by the reporting libraries, the Center could find only 22 common to all libraries.

One of the aims of the study was to demonstrate the validity of the requirement of an M.L.S. degree from an ALA-accredited school. It is doubtful that the results of this study could be used to make such a justification. Indeed, it is possible that the results might be used to justify alternative career ladders for entry and advancement into the professional ranks. The study, its methodology, and its results will certainly generate controversy within the state and within the national library community.

California is never a state to turn away from controversy. At its annual conference, CLA passed a resolution that again asked ALA to disassociate its name from the film *The Speaker*. However, the main library news in California during 1977 must be the passage of the Library Services Act. The state now has the opportunity to be in the national forefront of efforts to make all library services freely available to everyone. With its fees for membership under question, even CLASS has the opportunity to make its products and services, heavily supported by tax-generated income, available at so small a cost that all libraries will be able to offer them to everyone.

WILLIAM L. EMERSON

COLORADO

Statewide Library Program. Regional Library Service Systems completed the first year of operation with expanded membership that included all types of publicly supported libraries. Membership in the seven systems expanded from 279 to 325 members. A statewide seminar in Colorado Springs in April facilitated the development of new system programs. System publications during 1977 included *Regional Library Service Systems Needs Assessments Reports*, Volumes 1-8; *Regional Library Service Systems Management Seminar, Proceedings;* and *Accounting Manual and Uniform Classification of Accounts for Colorado Regional Library Service Systems.* Robert Audretsch was appointed the new Director of the Three Rivers Library System.

The Colorado Library Network Plan was approved by the State Board of Education and distributed to all libraries in the state. The Colorado General Assembly approved a permanent Network Coordinator for the State Library staff, and Nicholas Law was appointed to this position. The Network Coordinator will direct the Payment for Lending program, which reimburses libraries for interlibrary loan, and will coordinate implementation of the Network Plan.

Colorado Library Association (founded 1892)

Membership: 840; *Annual Expenditure:* $35,000.
President: Ron Stump, High Plains Regional Library System, Greeley (October 1977-October 1978).
Vice-President/President-elect: Claude Johns, Director, Michener Library, University of Northern Colorado.
Executive Secretary: Denise Hall, 1380 South Columbine Street, Denver, Colorado 80210.
Annual Conference: October 16-19, 1977, Denver.
Publication: Colorado Libraries (quarterly).

Colorado State Library

Anne Marie Falsone, Assistant Commissioner, Office of Library Services
1362 Lincoln Street
Denver 80203

School Library Media Supervisor

Richard DeFore
State Department of Education
Denver 80203

The Colorado Public Library Guidelines Committee met monthly throughout 1977 to draft guidelines for Colorado's public libraries. Hearings will be held throughout the state for input from Colorado's library community before the guidelines are published in the fall of 1978. *A History of Colorado Public Libraries, 1876-1976* was published by the Colorado State Library with funds from LSCA Title I. The School Media Guidelines Committee has begun meeting to revise the guidelines adopted in 1974.

The Information and Communication Network, administered by the Colorado State Library and the Bibliographical Center for Research, was funded for a second year with $79,468 of LSCA Title I monies. Additional terminals were added at Denver Public Library and at the University of Colorado at Boulder to facilitate interlibrary loan and to expand the availability of computerized information retrieval. WATS telephone lines added in each system have improved communication among members.

The Colorado State Library for the Blind and Physically Handicapped moved to a more convenient location at 1313 Sherman Street in Denver and is now accessible to the handicapped. Colorado was selected by the Division for the Blind and Physically Handicapped of the Library of Congress as one of several areas to be included in a national public education program pilot study. The study will involve the use of professionally produced radio and television spots to inform the public of library services available to persons physically unable to read conventional print.

The position of Consultant to serve institutionalized youth was added to the State Library staff by the Colorado General Assembly. Susan Loss was appointed to this position.

Several library directors were appointed for Colorado's academic libraries. They included Hartley K. Phinney, Jr., at the Colorado School of Mines in Golden and Clyde Walton at the University of Colorado in Boulder.

Awards. Elizabeth Bowers, Director of the Weld County Public Library, was named Colorado Librarian of the Year by the Colorado Library Association. Project COIN received the Library Project of the Year Award for the *Indexed Checklist to Colorado State Publications*.

The Mountain Plains Library Association awarded its Outstanding Service Award to Lucile Hatch, Professor at the University of Denver Graduate School of Librarianship.

Buildings. Summit County enlarged and remodeled its public library. A new public library was established in Lyons with community support. The Lyons train depot, built in 1887, was remodeled and renovated to provide suitable space for the library collection and programs.

ANNE MARIE FALSONE

CONNECTICUT

State Library Budget. The State Library ended the year facing a severe budget crisis. For the past several years the agency's budget proposals have been slashed, first upon incorporation into the governor's recommended budget and later by the General Assembly. In November the

Legislation Committee of the Connecticut Library Association (CLA) and the State Librarian made a strong appeal for public support of the Library's 1978-79 request for a 57.4 per cent increase over the 1977-78 appropriation. The proposed budget, if granted, would regain only part of the ground lost in recent years.

The crisis severely affected the Library's operations. Authorized full-time positions remained vacant. All monograph purchases for the Division of Reader Services were eliminated, and 10 per cent of serials subscriptions were cancelled. The purchase of materials for the service centers was cut by 50 per cent, and orders for 150 films for the statewide film service were cancelled. Continuing education and workshop activities were greatly curtailed. In December, further cost-saving actions were being considered, including the possibility of closing on Saturday or Monday.

Connecticut Library Association
(founded 1890)

Membership: 950; *Annual Expenditure:* $30,000.
President: Virginia Dowell, New Britain Public Library (July 1977-June 1978).
Vice-President/President-elect: Peggy Abrams, Fairfield Public Library.
Secretary: Patti Bandolin, Colebrook Stage, Winstead.
Annual Convention: April 20-22, 1977, Norwich.
Publication: Connecticut Libraries, (quarterly); *Clamemo* (10 issues a year).

Connecticut State Library
Charles Funk, Jr., State Librarian
231 Capitol Avenue
Hartford 06115

Legislation. Collection and control of state publications has long been frustrating to Connecticut documents librarians. Through their efforts, strongly supported by the library community, Public Act 77-561 was passed to authorize the State Library to establish and administer a Connecticut documents collection and depository library system. The legislation also carried an appropriation of $25,000 for 1977-78. Essential to the success of the system is the section of the law that requires each state agency to deposit copies of each new publication with the Library.

One provision in another piece of legislation was less warmly received by librarians. Reorganization of the Executive Branch of State Government (Public Act 77-614) places the State Library Board, heretofore independent, within the Department of Education "for administrative purposes only." Although the relationship of the Board to the Department is carefully defined in the law, there is concern that some future redefinition could lead to the loss of the identity and effectiveness of the State Library.

CLSU Program. In late 1976 the state's Cooperating Library Service Unit (CLSU) Review Board was granted $300,000 in LSCA funds to encourage the formation of cooperating units under criteria established by the Board. A fund of $50,000 was reserved for distribution on a project grant basis to each of six designated service regions in the state. As of the fall of 1977, units have been formed in each region, with members drawn from public, academic, special, and school libraries.

In creating the Review Board and accepting the concept of cooperating units in 1975, the legislature made no provisions for any state funding of the program, and a bill to assure such funding failed to pass in the 1977 General Assembly session. The intent of the LSCA grant was one-time incentive aid. The units recognize that, although some financial support must come from their member libraries, some level of ongoing state funding is essential. The State Library's proposed budget for 1978-79, which was to be considered by the legislature early in 1978, included $350,000 for support of the program.

Grants. The National Archives and Record Service awarded $5,000 to the State Library for the examination of its collection of 4,000,000 early Connecticut court records spanning more than 200 years. The study will result in recommendations as to which records should be disposed of after selective microfilming and which should be preserved.

Two proposals received funding from the National Historical Publications and Records Commission. The Stowe-Day Memorial Library in Hartford received $26,109 to publish in microfilm the letters of suffragette Isabella Beecher Stowe. Bridgeport Public Library was given $23,431 to survey and assess business and labor records in the Bridgeport area and to arrange for their deposit in or donation to the Library.

The public libraries of Cheshire, Hamden, and North Haven took a LEAP toward cooperative resource sharing. A grant of $21,869 in LSCA funds, augmented by local appropriations, began financing the initial phases of a networking project called "Library Exchange Aids Patrons" (LEAP). Joint purchase of an automated circulation system and consequent development of a common data base will provide instant access to the shared collections of the three towns. West Haven and Wallingford expect to join the project in a later phase.

Buildings. Library construction continued at a good pace in 1977, spurred in part by the infusion of federal public works money and in part by the availability of a limited amount of state funding. The State Library's Division of Library Development anticipated that from 30 to 50 communities would be engaged in major projects during the next three to five years.

Nine public libraries shared $500,000 in construction funds granted to the State Library by the State Bonding Commission. Plans approved included additions in Fairfield, New Canaan, Newtown, Norwalk, Rocky Hill, Stamford, and Watertown, a new central library in New Haven, and remodeling of a vacant school for a new central library in Hamden.

Hamden, Norwalk, Granby, South Winsdor, and Wallingford also received funding under the federal Public Works Employment Act for new buildings. New Milford, Putnam, and Stratford received funds for additions. Several other towns had projects planned or under way that were being financed entirely by local funds. These included new buildings in Essex and Westbrook, an addition in Clinton, a remodeling in Willington, and the renovation of a branch library in Bridgeport.

Finished during the year were a new building in Groton, an addition in Guilford, and a branch library in West Haven. Interior design work was completed at Mystic Seaport's G.W. Blunt Library to prepare it to serve students enrolled in the Williams College-Mystic Seaport undergraduate program in American Maritime Studies, which began in September. The 387,000-square-foot library at the University of Connecticut in Storrs, begun in 1975, was near completion at year's end. Occupancy was scheduled for June 1978.

People. With the death of Elizabeth T. Fast in June, Connecticut and the nation lost an outstanding and committed librarian. Recipient of the 1977 Grolier Foundation Award, she was a member of the ALA Executive Board and was active in CLA. At the time of her death, she was Director of Media Services for the public schools in Groton.

In September, Elinor Hashim, Chairman of the State Library Board and Director of the Welles-Turner Memorial Library in Glastonbury, became President of the New England Library Association (NELA). Brenda Claflin, Librarian of the Faxon Branch of the West Hartford Public Library, was appointed editor of NELA's newsletter.

Richard Akeroyd, Director of Planning and Research at the State Library, resigned in September to join the NCLIS Program Planning Team for the White House

Conference on Library and Information Services. Leslie M. Berman, coordinator of the LSCA grant program at the State Library, succeeded him.

Frances Davenport, Director of Special Services at the State Library, retired on July 1 after more than 44 years with the Library. John Crawford retired in January from his position as School Library Consultant with the State Board of Education. A librarian for 22 years, he served on the CLA Executive Board in various capacities for 18 years.

Daniel J. Lombardo of Wethersfield was awarded ALA's David H. Clift Scholarship. He is a candidate for a master's degree in library science at Southern Connecticut State College. Shirley Bysiewicz, Law Librarian at the University of Connecticut School of Law, was the recipient of the first Distinguished Alumnus Award of the Alumni-Student Association of Southern Connecticut's Division of Library Science and Instructional Technology.

Connecticut's Library School. The Division of Library Science and Instructional Technology of Southern Connecticut State College initiated extension work in library science at the Hartford Graduate Center in September. The program will offer four courses each semester with both core requirements and electives available on a rotating schedule. The Division now offers four joint master's degree programs: Library Science and Instructional Technology; Library Science and Chemistry; Instructional Technology and Chemistry; and, in association with the University of Connecticut School of Law, Library Science and Law.

CLA Notes. Approval of a new Public Relations Section brought the number of CLA divisions to 10. The bylaws were amended to establish a category of voting membership for sales representatives serving libraries and to make the Director of the library school at Southern Connecticut an ex officio member of the Executive Board. The Board instituted what is to be an annual practice, a review of the State Library's budget proposal with the State Librarian and the staff. The State Library closed a long-standing inactive account and donated the $3,000 balance to the CLA's Program for Educational Grants.

Publications. Two publications compiled in 1977 by cooperative library groups appeared to be vying for a longest-title-of-the-year award. Winner by a scant margin was *A Catalog of Micrographic Hardware, Microfiche Collections, and Computerized Data Bases in Libraries within the Capitol Region*, issued by the Capitol Region Library Council. Contributors included 16 special libraries, 16 academic libraries, and 3 of the larger public libraries in the area.

The Southwestern Connecticut Library System produced *A Directory of Selected Reference Materials in Libraries and Historical Societies in Fairfield County, Connecticut*. The *Directory* locates major general reference tools, special collections of print and nonprint materials, and copying and reading equipment in 35 special libraries, 25 public libraries, 16 historical societies, 10 hospital libraries, and 8 secondary schools.

Women's Studies: A Guide to Reference Sources by Kathleen Burke McKee is the sixth title in the University of Connecticut Library's Bibliography Series. Primarily an annotated bibliography, the publication also includes a special supplement listing and describing feminist serials.

BARBARA BRYAN

DELAWARE

Delaware Library Association (founded 1934)

Membership: 198; *Annual Expenditure,* $2,350.
President: Daniel E. Coons, Delaware State College, Dover (May 1977-June 1978).
Vice-President/President-elect: Florence Brown, Concord Pike Library, Wilmington.
Secretary: Barbara Weeks, Wilmington Institute.
Annual Convention: April 1977, Dover.
Publication: Delaware Library Association Bulletin (quarterly).

Division of Libraries
Sylvia I. Short, Head
630 State College Road
Dover 19901

State School Library Media Supervisor
Richard L. Krueger
State Department of Public Instruction
Dover 19901

Programs. "Librarians and Politicians" was the theme of programs and workshops at a Delaware Library Association (DLA) meeting in Dover, October 7-9. Speakers and panelists included Senator Major R. Owens, Brooklyn, New York; Joseph T. Conaway, Sussex County Administrator; Mary D. Jornlin, New Castle County Executive; Barbara Reisenfield, League of Women Voters of Delaware; and James H. Gilliam, Jr., Secretary of Community Affairs and Economic Development. Group discussions on organizing, lobbying, public relations, budgeting, and cost-effectiveness were led by Ann Jarrett and Vicky Kleinman of the League of Women Voters; Grace Parkinson, Philadelphia Free Library Public Relations Office; and Charles Robinson, Director of Baltimore County Libraries. Workshops on problems and prospects in resource sharing and on communication and staff development preceded the conference. The workshops were led by Briggitte L. Kenny, Drexel University; J.S. Kidd, Acting Director of the University of Maryland College of Library and Information Services; and Marilyn White and Michael Reynolds, Maryland library school staff members.

In March the Library Development Committee of DLA and the Delaware Learning Resources Association (DLRA) conducted a one-day workshop on resource sharing in Dover. The workshop was patterned on a conference held in Pittsburgh in 1976. The session was moderated by Lois L. Pyle, Coordinator of School Libraries in New Castle-Gunning Bedford School District. Marcy Murphy, Coordinator of Western Pennsylvania Buhl Network, wrote and delivered the position paper. Other panelists were Katherine C. Hurrey, Director of the Southern Maryland Regional Library Association, and Robert Uffelman, University of Delaware Education Resource Center. Clara S. Jones, President of ALA, was the guest speaker at the luncheon.

The Sussex County Department of Libraries conducted a series of workshops on policies and procedures, selection of materials, and cataloging and classification. The objectives were to learn how to be practical, to recognize staff needs of public libraries, and to offer an opportunity to exchange ideas and discuss problems.

Effort was made in 1977 to strengthen DLA by activating divisions in the Association. The constitution provides that a division may be formed by "at least fifteen members interested in promoting library service and librarianship within and for a particular type of library activity." The College and Research Libraries Division and the Public Library Division are currently active. Officers of DLRA rejected a proposal to become a division of DLA. The recently reactivated Library Trustees Association has been encouraged to become a division.

DLRA proposed forming joint committees in areas of mutual concern as an alternative to a merger with DLA. The Committee on Legislation was appointed and has pledged support for legislation to increase the state's grants-in-aid to public libraries from 5 cents to 10 cents per capita. An appropriation of $66,768 will double the amount of state aid the public libraries are now receiving.

Services. William Pahlmann, known as the originator of the "eclectic" look in interior design, has given his records dating from 1930 to 1977 to the Winterthur Museum Library. These include photograph albums, publicity scrapbooks, full-color renderings and sketches of interiors, and fabric, ceramic, and porcelain samples as well as other materials. The Library is a resource center for the Henry Francis du Pont Winterthur Museum, a research institution of more than 100 rooms showing American interior architecture, furniture, and decorative objects in vogue from 1684 to the 1800's. The Library's chief purpose is to document the Museum's collection, but it has extended coverage of American decorative arts into the 20th century. The Prahlmann gift is the first collection of contemporary interior design to be acquired.

Summer reading programs have gained in popularity throughout the state. The Storybook Players of the Dover Public Library, assisted with new puppets and props, presented their skits in all playgrounds and camps in Kent County and in other state recreational and health facilities. The Kirkwood Highway Library's summer readers and nonreaders illustrated segments of stories on paper plates that became segments of two bookworms snaking their way around the walls. Drive In and Read, the Newark Free Library's reading club, enrolled 434 children who completed a large mural representing a pond scene with butterflies, fish, and lily pads that were earned with each book read. A game called "Secret Squares" encouraged children to join the summer reading program in the New Castle County Library. Clues to solve mysteries were given children who read or joined storytelling groups. The Milford Public Library sponsored the Book-Worm Club for children in grades three, four, and five.

In anticipation of the court-ordered reorganization of public education in New Castle County to desegregate the Wilmington schools, the New Castle Regional Planning Board for Libraries made an in-depth study of school library services in the county and completed a report and curriculum plan to present to the New Castle County Planning Board of Education. Ruth Heisler, Librarian in the Alfred I. du Pont District, directed the study.

In 1976 the recently established Delaware Law School moved to the campus of Brandywine College in Wilmington. To accommodate the libraries of both institutions, Vincent G. Kling & Partners of Philadelphia were employed to design a building to house both collections. The new building and conversion, estimated to cost $1,900,000, makes provision for the Brandywine College Library on the first floor and the Law Library on the second and third floors. Classrooms, a moot court, and administrative offices are in the same structure.

To curtail its use as a "walk-in" library, the State Division of Libraries has proposed establishing demonstration projects in three Kent County towns where residents do not have easy access to library service. The Division will seek a federal grant to install, stock, and staff modular libraries in communities that show support for the program and are willing to continue the operation at the end of two years. Opposition to the new policy is strong among those who prefer using the State Library and from town officials faced eventually with providing support for the library units.

The Dover Public Library houses an unusual item in its collection—the skull of Patty Cannon. She lived in southern Delaware near the Maryland border in the early part of the 19th century. Cannon was accused of kidnaping slaves and poisoning travelers and was indicted for murder, but she committed suicide in jail before she could be tried. *The Entailed Hat* by George Alfred Townsend recounts her exploits.

Curtailed Services. As of July 1 the *News Journal*, publisher of the morning and evening daily papers, closed its library to the public in order to serve its news department. The library continues to provide information in answer to telephoned or written requests. It also provides publication dates of news articles and photocopies of papers no longer available.

The Eleutherian Mills Historical Library, a collection of early business records of the 19th century, planned to reduce its staff of 90 by about 10 per cent as of January 1978. The Library is supported with the income from an endowment funded initially by Pierre S. du Pont. Supplementary donations raise an annual budget of $2,000,000, but the amount is insufficient to offset expenses.

The Department of Public Instruction reported further reduction in 1977 in library staffing. Seven professional positions were eliminated in New Castle County. A number of library aides throughout the state were not reemployed.

People. Sylvia I. Short was appointed to head the State Division of Libraries in July. Delaware had been without a State Librarian since 1974 when the professional staff of the Division was reduced by 83 per cent and the supportive staff by 47 per cent. Short has been a consultant in the Division of Libraries and has been Librarian for the State Legislative Council. She is a native of Delaware and a graduate of Duke University and of the Graduate School of Library Science at Drexel University. She has had experience in school and special libraries in addition to work at the state level.

Ruth Ann Melson, former Acquisitions Head at the Dover Public Library, was appointed to fill the vacancy at the Legislative Council Library. David Burdash, Acting Director of the Wilmington Institute Library since June 1975, was appointed Director of the Library in July. Diane Francis is the new Director of the New Castle County Libraries, having served for a time as Acting Head of the system. Alyce Bower, Director of Services at the Milford Public Library, retired in October and moved to Sun City, Arizona. Phyllis Rust was appointed to fill the position of Director. Caleb Boggs, twice Governor of Delaware and a former U.S. Senator, is Honorary Chairman of the Governor's Conference to be held in 1978 prior to the White House Conference on Library and Information Services.

Martha Morris, who had retired in 1971 after serving seven years as chief hospital librarian at the Veterans Administration Hospital in Elsmere, died in a retirement home in Pennsylvania in 1977. From 1946 to 1954 she was Chief Technical Librarian to the U.S. Naval Academy at Annapolis, and from 1941 to 1946 she was Chief Hospital Librarian at the Bainbridge Naval Training Station in Port Deposit, Maryland.

HELEN H. BENNETT

DISTRICT OF COLUMBIA

District of Columbia Library Association (founded 1894)

Membership: 900; *Annual Expenditure:* $14,650.
President: Catherine A. Jones, George Washington University (June 1977-May 1978).
Vice-President/President-elect: Lillimaud Hammond, Georgetown University.
Secretary: George Arnold, American University.
Annual Meeting (banquet): May 1977, Fort Myer, Virginia.
Publication: Intercom (monthly).

School Library Media Supervisor
Olive DeBruler
District of Columbia Public Schools
Washington, D.C. 20024

Metropolitan Washington Library Council. The Metropolitan Washington Library Council, newly organized from the former Librarians' Technical Committee of the Metropolitan Washington Council of Governments, held its first meeting in January 1977. The Council is a library organization open to all library groups organized to provide library service in the Washington, D.C., metropolitan area. Almost 150 associations joined during the first formal year of membership—9 public library systems, 20 college and university libraries, 2 public school systems, more than 100 special and federal libraries, and 11 libraries which joined as affiliated members.

During the year the Council conducted a survey of automation, published under the title *Survey of Library Automation in the Metropolitan Washington Area, 1977*. Supported by the Federal Library Committee, the Council instigated a new "on-call" delivery service among Council libraries. It also offered continuing education workshops on zero-based budgeting, management skills for paraprofessionals, space planning and practical design, performance evaluation and interviewing techniques, management by objectives, graphic arts, assertiveness training, leadership skills, staffing formulas, and the use of volunteers. The Job Line continued to list positions. The reciprocal borrowing program and film cooperative called MAILS (Metropolitan Area Interlibrary Loan Service), for which LSCA Title II funds expired in September, was turned over to a commercial service for continuation. In midyear Marilyn Gell resigned her post as Chief of Library Programs to pursue graduate work. Barbara Robinson was named to replace her.

District of Columbia Library System. Patrons learned to love the bar code as public libraries in the District of Columbia adopted the CLSI LIBS 100 automated circulation system. Three new kiosks were established, two in southeast and one in northeast Washington. Prefabricated units, each kiosk displays 2,500 paperbacks or several hundred hardcover books, requires only one librarian, and comes complete with all facilities, including heating and air conditioning.

A refurbished branch in Takoma Park opened in late 1977 after extensive renovation. The newest branch of the system opened in October on the second floor of the Garnet C. Wilkinson Elementary School in Anacostia to serve all residents of the area as well as the children of the school. It is the first library of its kind in Washington, D.C., a full-fledged public library located in a public elementary school.

Hardy R. Franklin, Director, is coordinating plans for the District of Columbia for the Pre-White House Conference on Library and Information Services. A Planning Committee appointed by Mayor Walter E. Washington met in November to begin preparations for the Conference.

FEDLINK. The Federal Library and Information Network increased from 60 libraries in October 1976 to 110 by December 1977. It now includes agencies in Washington, D.C., and 25 of the 50 states. Lillian Washington, Network Coordinator for FEDLINK, resigned her post in February, and Milton Megee became Acting Coordinator.

District of Columbia Library Association. The District of Columbia Library Association (DCLA) had a full year under Presidents Marilyn Gell and Cathy Jones, beginning with a meeting on the use of international documents in January at the Pan American Union. In February, Barbara Ringer of the Copyright Office spoke on the new copyright law, and in March a meeting was held on copyright and government publications. April included a tour of the Government Printing Office and a report by John Y. Cole on the LC Task Force on Goals, Organization and Planning.

The Children's and Young Adults' Group met monthly to explore areas of interest. The Joint Spring Workshop, Microforum '77, was sponsored jointly by DCLA, the Special Libraries Association, the American Society for Information Science, and the Society of Library and Information Technicians. The workshop was a full-day program on all forms of micrographics, with a comprehensive exhibition of readers and printers. A new interest group, College and University Librarians, held a workshop on grant proposal writing for librarians in May. The climax of the year was the annual banquet, with Larry McMurtry speaking on his experiences as a novelist and film writer.

Zero-based budgeting was discussed in September, in addition to on-line retrieval of government documents in a hands-on demonstration. Eve Johannson of the British National Library was a speaker in October. The Reference Group began a series of informal luncheon discussions in September. A reception for new members at the Visitor's Center of Union Station and a program on integrating on-line reference service with traditional or manual reference service were held in November.

Special Libraries Association. The Washington, D.C., Chapter of SLA under President Sarah Thomas Kadec began the year with a meeting on freedom of information and copyright. In February there were meetings on contracting for library services and on the "State-of-the-Child" report. The chairmanship of the Joint Spring Workshop, Microforum '77, fell to SLA. Elizabeth Yeates headed this all-day exploration of micrographics in library applications. In April, Henriette Avram addressed the Chapter on the Library of Congress and the National Library Network. President Jack Speer took office in June, but in September he left Washington, D.C., for a position in Florida. Patricia Berger became President of the Chapter, and Elizabeth Knauff became Vice-President/President-Elect. In November a one-day workshop on financial management for libraries was held at the National Bureau of Standards under Chapter sponsorship.

Catholic University of America. The Department of Library and Information Science made changes in its name and transferred its activities to a consolidated location in Marist Hall on the Catholic University campus. The new quarters include the entire second floor of the building, and the Library Science Library and student lounge have quarters on the first floor.

Fred Peterson, Assistant Director of the Department, moved to Mullen Library as Acting Director of the University Libraries on the retirement of Lloyd Wagner. Kieth Wright resigned his post as Assistant Professor to become Dean of the College of Library and Information Services at the University of Maryland in College Park.

CAPCON. The Capital Consortium Network (CAPCON) increased its membership from 10 to 19 during 1977. New participants were Dominican, Columbia Union, Hood, Mount Saint Mary's, Inter-American Development Bank, Georgetown University Law Center, Washington Hospital Center, the Loyola/Notre Dame Library, and the College of Library and Information Services at the University of Maryland. The Enoch Pratt Free Library, George Washington University Medical Center, and Morgan State University were scheduled to join early in 1978.

Academic Libraries. After a long and difficult planning period, American University began construction of a new library, to be occupied in 1979. The library became the first academic library in the Washington metropolitan area to install the CLSI LIBS 100 circulation system. Gallaudet's Model Secondary School for the Deaf moved into new facilities. George Washington University received a large grant from the Scaife Foundation for the establishment of a regional center for the Vanderbilt television news archives and for related audiovisual equipment.

Lloyd F. Wagner, Director of Libraries at Catholic University of America for 10 years, resigned effective July 1. Fred M. Peterson was appointed Acting Director of Libraries. Judith Sessions was appointed Director of the Learning Resources Center at Mount Vernon College.

People. Russell Shank retired from his post as Director of the Smithsonian Libraries in July to become University Librarian at UCLA. He was subsequently elected Vice-President/President-Elect of ALA, to take office in June 1978. Gilbert Gude of Maryland, having resigned his congressional post, was appointed by the Librarian of Congress as Director of the Congressional Research Service at the Library of Congress.

Robert J. Coxe, formerly with OCLC, was appointed Assistant Coordinator of Library Programs for the Consortium of Universities effective September 1. He is primarily responsible for coordinating services for CAPCON, an OCLC-affiliate network administered by the Consortium.

James Bennett Childs, Honorary Consultant at the Library of Congress and a former specialist in government documents bibliography, died in May 1977. In 1976 the Government Documents Round Table of ALA had established the James Bennett Childs Award for distinguished work in government documents. Childs was the first recipient.

Harold Spivacke, Chief of the Music Division of the Library of Congress for 34 years, also died in May 1977.

MARY K. FELDMAN

FLORIDA

Florida Library Association
(founded 1920)

Membership: 1,337; *Annual Expenditure:* $41,855.
President: Glenn Miller, Orlando Public Library (May 1977-April 1978).
Vice-President/President-elect: John DePew, Florida State University, Tallahassee.
Secretary: Eileen Cobb, Broward County Library, Fort Lauderdale.
Annual Conference: May 11-14, 1977, St. Petersburg.
Publication: Florida Libraries (bimonthly).

State Library of Florida
Barratt Wilkins, Director
R.A. Gray Building
Tallahassee 32304

State School Library Media Supervisor
Eloise T. Groover
State Department of Education
Tallahassee 32304

State Library. The State Library of Florida started 1977 just having moved into the R.A. Gray Archives, Library, and Museum Building in Tallahassee. The State Library occupies 70,000 square feet in this new building, which has space for 500,000 volumes and meeting rooms and auditorium facilities. Designed by the Tampa architectural firm of Fletcher and Valenti that designed the University of Tampa's Merl Kelce Library, the building has a wide veranda on three sides and an adjacent parking garage for both employees and library users. It also houses the State Archives and the Museum of Florida History.

On March 25 the State Library celebrated its 50th anniversary. Established in 1925 by the state legislature, it began operations in 1927. The State Library had occupied quarters in both the Capitol and the Supreme Court Building before moving into the new facility. At the 50th anniversary ceremony, three former State Librarians—Dorothy Dodd, F. William Summers, and Cecil P. Beach—were honored. The keynote address was delivered by former Governor LeRoy Collins. The room housing the Florida History Collection was named in honor of Dorothy Dodd.

A statewide film service was started in 1977 when the state legislature permitted LSCA funds to be used to establish a film collection. With an initial budget of $150,000 for films and $16,000 for equipment and with a staff of four, the Audio-Visual Section of the State Library was just getting organized by the end of the year. It was expected that a catalog would be produced and that the lending of films would be started by March 1978.

The State Library closed its Book Processing Center during the year. A year's notice of the closing had been given to some 30 participating libraries. Originally started in the 1950's and operated by the Orlando Public Library, the Book Processing Center had been run by the State Library since 1968. A declining volume of work was the chief reason for the decision. Set up to be self-sustaining from the fees charged, the Center in recent years had required increasing amounts of LSCA funds to subsidize its operation. Member systems had dropped out due to technology (one established a book catalog and no longer needed catalog cards) or the availability of cheaper processing elsewhere. However, no employee lost a job. The State Legislature created a Bureau of Library Support Services, which will continue technical services for the State Library as well as centralize the computer systems that the Library is involved with. In addition, certain other administrative functions were transferred to the Bureau.

Adult Services. With continued emphasis on offering more than reference service to adults and with the added stimulation of LSCA funding for services to older adults, new adult readers, and handicapped adults, many existing programs expanded their service, and new programs were being implemented in 1977.

The Jacksonville Library Operated Outreach Program (LOOP), originally directed to disadvantaged children, expanded its operations to include mobile library service to adult basic education centers, senior citizens' meal sites and nursing homes, halfway houses, detoxification centers, and sheltered care centers for the mentally ill.

The Collier County Public Library System operated an extensive Mobile Migrant Program in 1977, including a mobile library with as large an audiovisual as book load. It served a rural and agricultural area in southern Florida with a large disadvantaged and migrant population spread over 1,560 square miles.

With the assistance of LSCA funding, 16 separate library systems inaugurated or expanded their services to economically disadvantaged and isolated rural people. Services include literacy tutoring and materials supplementation, film programming, and bilingual information and materials. The programs use mobile libraries, library vans, one-to-one outreach service, and books by mail.

The State Library conducted two workshops during 1977 in continuing education in adult services. A statewide two-day workshop on "Innovations in Education: Implications for Public Library Service" dealt with various new approaches to adult continuing education, with special emphasis on community education. The second workshop was developed as a series of four regional one-day meetings on "Library Service to the Mentally Retarded Adult." The objectives of the series was to assist Florida librarians in meeting the library service needs of the mentally retarded adult who is leaving an institution and returning to the community.

The Cocoa Public Library of the Brevard County Library System conducted a reference services outreach program, using a "community walk" to inform local businessmen of business resources and services.

The diversity of adult programming throughout the state continued, with many libraries providing in-depth programs such as classes on advanced principles of investing, lectures on nutrition, seminars on "Women in Society," programs on planning for retirement, a course in "Year-end Tax Strategies for the Stock Market Investor," and hobby and craft demonstrations.

Additional programming help will be available to small and medium-sized libraries with the opening of the new Film Center at the State Library. This Center will provide the planning assistance that will enable Florida's smaller libraries to provide year-round adult programs, adding another dimension to the total adult services in all Florida libraries.

Children's and Young Adult Service. Book selection and programming were featured in a two-day workshop sponsored by the State Library and the Clearwater Public Library under an LSCA grant. Representatives of six major book review journals were on an all-star panel that elicited interaction among librarians, guest authors, and reviewers. Young adult librarians demonstrated successful program ideas and warned against pitfalls in a multimedia sharing session.

The 1977 statewide Summer Reading Program with "Dig In at Your Public Library" as the theme again offered regional planning workshops organized and presented by practicing librarians. Printed publicity materials including posters and bookmarks featured a lively digging animal. Also provided were a Summer Reading radio jingle and a TV slide/script commercial, all done through the cooperation of the Orlando Public Library and its graphics department and community relations and business office, which administered the LSCA funding for the program. An advisory committee to the State Library Youth Services Consultant assisted in the initial planning of the annual Summer Reading Program and in ongoing services to children and young adults.

Two film evaluation committees, one for children's films and another for young adult films, were initiated to produce an annotated list of recommended films. The list was to be distributed in the state to aid in building the new film collection at the State Library. BARRATT WILKINS

GEORGIA

Georgia Library Association (founded 1898)

Membership: 1,284; *Annual Expenditure:* $15,016.
President: Barbara C. Cade, Atlanta Public Schools (October 1977-September 1979).
Vice-President/President-elect: Carlton J. Thaxton, Georgia Department of Education, Jekyll Island.
Annual Convention: October 19-22, 1977, Atlanta.
Publication: Georgia Librarian (semiannually).

Division of Public Libraries

Carlton J. Thaxton, Director
156 Trinity Avenue, S.W.
Atlanta 30303

State School Library Media Supervisor

Nancy Hove
State Department of Education
Atlanta 30329

Governor's Conference. Highlights of Georgia librarianship during 1977 were the Governor's Conference and the biennial conference of the Georgia Library Association (GLA).

The Governor's Conference on Georgia Library and Information Services, the first of the state Pre-White House Conferences, was held in Atlanta, September 15-16. The Conference attracted some 1,200 participants. Mrs. Lillian Carter, the President's mother, was Honorary Chairman and actively participated in the discussions. Hugh Carter, Jr., Special Assistant to President Carter for Administration, addressed the delegates at an evening dinner meeting. New York State Senator Major R. Owens gave the keynote address, "The Future Impact of Libraries on Social Change." Governor George Busbee assured participants of his continued support of libraries in his address.

In general sessions panelists reviewed the status of federal and state funding and the current status of libraries in Georgia. These reviews were based on the Georgia Library Survey completed in 1975 by a study team from the Battelle Laboratories in Columbus, Ohio, and the needs and recommendations that grew out of the Survey. Another group of panelists responded to questions formulated by participants working in small discussion groups. These questions focused on how problems associated with achieving the Survey recommendations could be effectively met. The participants also formulated recommendations for revised state and federal legislation in the 1980's and for the White House Conference.

Other notable features of the Conference included addresses by Gerald Shields on the librarian as a professional and by Elmo Ellis, a major radio figure and editorialist of the Southeast, on how a communicator looks at libraries. The Conference was sponsored by GLA and planned by a steering committee chaired by Elizabeth Cole, Consultant in the Division of Public Library Services.

GLA. The theme of the biennial conference of GLA, held in Jekyll Island, October 19-22, was cooperative service among libraries. Preconference workshops on service to the blind and physically handicapped and reference interviewing were conducted the first day. Featured speakers of the conference included Connie R. Dunlap, Librarian of Duke University and President of the Association of College and Research Libraries; Frederick G. Kilgour, Executive Director of OCLC; Shirley Echelman, Vice-President and Librarian of the Chemical Bank Research Library in New York City and President of the Special Libraries Association; Frank Blair, former NBC television newscaster; Robert Wedgeworth, Executive Director of ALA; and Richard W. Armour, author and humorist, who spoke at a dinner.

Other sessions gave concerned attention to a range of professional interests and concerns, including employee evaluation, the quality of workmanship in popular books, audiovisual programming, staff development, printing and the small press, public and school library cooperation, and revision of Georgia certification requirements for school library media center personnel.

David E. Estes, Assistant University Librarian for Special Collections at Emory University and a former President of the Association, received the Nix-Jones Award for distinguished service to Georgia librarianship. Former presidents of GLA were recognized, and several recent retirees were awarded honorary memberships in recognition of major contributions.

Well-attended workshops sponsored by various units of GLA during the year included workshops on improving management skills, intellectual freedom and privacy, reference use of census information, and political action for lay library leaders.

People. Retirees during the year included Hallie B. Brooks, Professor at Atlanta University's School of Library Service; Ursuline B. Ingersoll, Supervisor of School Libraries in Savannah; Barbara Bronson, Consultant at the Division of Public Library Service; Thera Hambrick, Director of the Library at Valdosta State College; and Ruth Walling, Associate University Librarian at Emory University.

Major appointments included Paul Cousins, Acting Director of Libraries at Emory University; Nancy P. Hove, Head of Media Field Services in the State Department of Education; David L. Ince, Director of the Library at Valdosta State College; Lila Rice, Director of the Brunswick Public Library; and Joe Zavodny, Assistant Director of Atlanta Public Library.

JOHN E. CLEMONS

HAWAII

Makiki Library. Hawaii's one public library not part of the State Library System continued in operation throughout 1977. Makiki Library opened in September 1976, staffed with volunteers and stocked with donated materials, in a building supplied by the county and city of Honolulu. This action came after criticism of the state's delay in plans to acquire land for a proposed library in the community.

The state Department of Education, which has jurisdiction over public libraries, recommended that priority for new libraries be given to other communities with less access to existing facilities. The Board of Education, however, supported the Library for Makiki. The Board asked the governor to accept for transfer to the state the land, buildings, and parking facilities that the county and city had supplied for the Library. It directed the Department to present fiscal requirements for renovating and running the Library. The Mayor advised that there were no legal impingements in such a transfer, but as the year ended the Makiki Library was still under county-city jurisdiction and staffed with some CETA-funded positions. The county and city reported that an unofficial offer must be accepted by the governor before an ordinance transferring the facilities can be issued. The state Department of Education reported that the governor had not received an official offer from the city and that consequently no action had been taken on the transfer.

Hawaii Library Association
(founded 1922)

Membership: 551; *Annual Expenditure:* $10,003.
President: Harry Y. Uyehara, University of Hawaii (March 1977-February 1978).
Vice-President/President-elect: Yvonne Bartko, Hawaii State Library, Honolulu.
Secretary: Beth Madinger, Honolulu Schools.
Annual Convention: April 1-2, 1977, Honolulu.
Publication: HLA Journal (bimonthly).

Office of Library Services, Department of Education

Mae Chun, State Librarian
P.O. Box 2360
Honolulu 96804

State School Library Media Supervisor

Patsy Izumo
Department of Education
4211 Waiala Avenue
Honolulu 96816

Reorganization Issue. The organization of the State Library System continued as the most newsworthy library activity during the year. The Commission on Organization of Government published a final report in February containing recommendations for reorganization of the System.

Proposed was a director for the State Library System who would report to an executive director in a Department of Life-Long Learning. The State Library System would operate all public libraries as well as community-school libraries. School libraries would remain under the jurisdiction of the Department of Education.

The Commission had originally proposed that school libraries be staffed by public librarians, with present school librarians being given the option of returning to classroom teaching or becoming public librarians. The school library community, supported by teachers and the library community, vigorously opposed the proposal, and it was not included in the final report. Under the original proposal, school libraries would also have become part of a lifelong learning group.

The legislative auditor of Hawaii began a study of the Department of Education's organization for the delivery of library services in 1972. The study was suspended in 1973, resumed again in 1975, and finally published in February 1977. It was highly critical of the Department.

When Hawaii became a state, county libraries were transferred to the Department of Education to facilitate coordination and cooperation between school and public libraries. The State Librarian became an assistant superintendent in the Department of Education with responsibility for all public libraries and consultative and support services for school libraries. School libraries, however, remained under the direct control of school principals. The intent of all policy since statehood has repeatedly been aimed at creating an integrated, cohesive system of libraries throughout the state. In the opinion of the state auditor, the Department of Education has failed to carry out this task.

The auditor found that the Department has failed to initiate the action required to implement a system. Hawaii has no real library system, but rather school libraries almost totally isolated, public libraries operating on their own, regional libraries operating haphazardly, and a lack of the solid backup that should be forthcoming from a state resource center.

The 59-page report offered a detailed analysis of the problems that were discovered and recommended a number of solutions. Important among these was a proposal to remove school libraries from the authority of school principals, placing them under the Department of Education's Office of Library Services. School libraries would be administered by public librarians and, where useful, be made available for use by the public. A second important proposal would convert the Hawaii State Library in downtown Honolulu into a Hawaii library resource center. It would function as an in-depth reference service center for all libraries in the state and would maintain the central resource collection.

The first proposal has not been incorporated into a reorganization plan currently being tried by the Department of Education. The school library support services have been transferred to the Office of Instructional Support Services, and school libraries remain under the control of school principals. The second proposal seems likely to be implemented in the reorganization, since an attempt is being made to free the Hawaii State Library from those functions that conflict with its primary purpose as a resource center.

Other Developments. The conversion of the Hawaii State Library union catalog to automated form has been under way for several years and was completed in 1977. Public libraries and high school libraries received their first microfilm catalogs in December as a result of the automation project.

Hawaii looks forward to the Governor's Conference on Library and Information Services scheduled for June 11-13, 1978. Rev. David Kaupu, chaplain at the Kamehameha Schools, was appointed by the governor as the planning committee's chairperson.

The Hawaii Library Association published a new edition of *A Directory of Libraries and Information Sources in Hawaii and the Pacific Islands.* The directory may be ordered from the Association.

People. Two key library positions were vacated in 1977. Stanley West, University Librarian at the University of Hawaii, retired in June, and Mae Chun, State Librarian, retired in October. During his nine years at the University, West was responsible for the planning of Phase II of Hamilton Library, which when completed in 1977 more than doubled the square footage of the Library. All special collections formerly housed in Sinclair are now in the new addition in Hamilton. The Graduate School of Library Studies also moved from Sinclair to expanded quarters in Hamilton.

Don Bosseau succeeded West as University Librarian in September. Bosseau served as Director of Libraries at Emory University in Atlanta before coming to Hawaii. Ruth Itamura, formerly Head of State Library Branches, was temporarily acting as State Librarian, with a permanent appointment expected in January 1978.
ROSE MYERS

IDAHO

In 1977 Idaho libraries experienced continued steady progress towards the extension and expansion of library services, opened several new buildings, hosted a nationally recognized lecture on children's literature, and were generally able to avoid budget cuts and other sorts of unpleasantness.

Construction. Many buildings were completed during 1977, with the new library at Idaho State University in Pocatello heading the list both in terms of size and of cost.

The $6,000,000 building contains 180,000 square feet on four floors and occupies a full city block. It is the largest structure ever erected in Idaho for educational purposes and is also noteworthy for its innovative heating and cooling system based on geothermal technology.

The new Idaho Falls Public Library opened its 62,000-square-foot buillding in August. The $2,700,000 buillding project is unusual for being funded entirely by a bond issue passed by Idaho Falls citizens in October 1974. The new building is fully accessible to the physically handicapped and contains a unique interior garden atrium—a welcome relief to patrons used to the long, gray winters of southeastern Idaho.

Ketchum, the home of Sun Valley, opened its new Community Library in the spring of 1977. The Library was built, and is operated, totally through community contributions, fund-raising events, and the proceeds of a flourishing thrift shop called The Gold Mine. The building is a striking complement to the natural setting and encourages patrons to enjoy the library and the mountains at the same time.

Salmon also celebrated with a new library, built through a combination of local contributions and a grant from the Idaho State Library. Located prominently on the town's main street, the library is accessible to the handicapped and offers 5,000 square feet to its users, as well as a community meeting room.

The Caldwell Public Library, which had opened its new building in 1976, received an award from the American Institute of Architects for its building's "straightforward and non-complicated appearance. It expressed its brick construction form ably and well."

Idaho Library Association
(founded 1915)

Membership: 400; *Annual Expenditure:* $15,077 (June 1, 1977).
President: Milo Nelson, University of Idaho Library, Moscow (June 1977-June 1978).
Vice-President/President-elect: Bill Wilson, Couer d'Alene Public Library.
Secretary: Patricia Hart, P.O. Box 8367, Moscow, Idaho 83843.
Annual Meeting: April 28-30, 1977, Boise.
Publication: The Idaho Librarian (quarterly).

Idaho State Library

Helen M. Miller, State Librarian
325 West State Street
Boise 83702

School Library Media Supervisor

Ruth Seydel
Department of Education
Boise 83701

State Library. Construction of a 12,640-square-foot addition to the State Library and Archives building began in late 1977. The addition will provide a 50 per cent increase in space, which will be used for more stack area for materials for the Idaho Historical Society and for additional stack and service areas for the program for the blind and physically handicapped.

In February, the State Library's radio station for the blind began broadcasting. The station was funded through $10,000 allocated by the state legislature. The station broadcasts four hours a day, using volunteer readers.

The State Library began zero-based budgeting in 1977. Funding for grants for the regional systems was approved by the legislature at the 1976 level, and only small cost-of-living and wage scale increases were allowed in the State Library's operating budget.

ILA Conference. The annual conference of the Idaho Library Association was held in Boise, April 28-30. Boise was selected to host the May Hill Arbuthnot Lecture in 1977, and the conference was organized around this distinguished event. In addition to Shigeo Watanabe, Arbuthnot Lecturer, Idaho librarians had the opportunity to hear and talk with people in the field such as Mary Jane Anderson, Children's Services Division, ALA; John Donovan, Executive Director of the Children's Book Council; Ethel Heins, editor of *Horn Book*; and Zena Bailey Sutherland, editor, reviewer, and writer of children's books.

Cooperation. Quorum, the organization that represents the state's regional library systems' administrators, elected Arlan Call, Director of the Twin Falls Public Library, as the 1977 chairman. Quorum went on record as supporting the State Library's efforts to set aside money to foster the investigation of automated data bases and bibliographic networks. ICASOL elected Eli Oboler, University Librarian at Idaho State University, as its new chairman and agreed to open its membership to representatives of all academic institutions in the state.

A Kellogg Foundation grant of $243,305 was awarded to the University of Idaho to establish educational resource centers throughout the state and to equip them with videotape equipment. These centers will bring videotape continuing education courses to communities without colleges or universities. Courses on forestry, agriculture, mining, education, engineering, and computers are planned.

Advances and Setbacks. In April the Lewiston-Nez Perce County System was dissolved after a six-year contractual agreement between the city and the county. City residents felt that they were short-changed in the arrangement, while county residents rejected the notion that their board should assume an advisory capacity to the city board. The difficult task of dividing the collection fell to the library staff and State Library consultants. Two separate libraries now operate within several blocks of each other in this city of 30,000.

In November, a bond election to build a new library for the Moscow-Latah County Library System failed. Two elections were required because of the city-county nature of the system. In Idaho, a two-thirds vote is required to pass a bond election. The measure passed in the city election by 75 per cent but failed in the county, receiving only a 54 per cent affirmative vote. Attempts to form library districts in the county areas surrounding Twin Falls and Nampa also failed.

The Pocatello Public Library began direct cable telecasting of locally produced programs in 1977. Library staff, community individuals, and groups present programs that include musical concerts, public meetings, hearings, dance festivals, children's story hours, health education, political candidate forums, school events, publicity for local clubs, and telecasts of visiting speakers and artists. Pocatello also managed to obtain a $45,000 budget increase.

People. Helen Miller, State Librarian, was elected to the governing board of the Chief Officers of State Library Agencies.

Timothy Brown, formerly Assistant Director for Administrative Services at the Iowa State University Library in Ames, was selected to replace retiring Ruth McBirney as Director of the Boise State University Library.

Mary Nicholson, catalog librarian at the University of Idaho Library, received a JMRT-3M Company Professional Development Grant, which paid for her attendance at the ALA Annual Conference.

Life membership in the Idaho Library Association was presented to Helen Smith of Pocatello for her many years of volunteer service to the libraries of Idaho as a member of the Idaho State Library Board and for her many activities in ILA.

The Trustee of the Year Award was given by ILA to Frank Payne of Caldwell Public Library, a longtime member of the board who gave many hours to the construction project for that library.

The Librarian of the Year was Geraldine Jacobs of the Madison County Library for her many years of service to that library, to the Eastern Idaho Regional Library System, and to ILA.

JEANNE GOODRICH

ILLINOIS

Illinois Library Association
(founded 1896)

Membership: 4,001 (1,100 ALA members); *Annual Expenditure:* $140,000.
President: Frank J. Dempsey, Arlington Heights Memorial Library (October 1977-October 1978).
Vice-President/President-elect: Dawn Heller, Riverside-Brookfield High School.
Executive Secretary: John R. Coyne, 425 N. Michigan Avenue, 13th Floor, Chicago 60611.
Annual Conference: October 26-29, 1977.
Publications: ILA Reporter (quarterly); section and round table newsletters.

Illinois State Library

Kathryn Gesterfield, Director
Centennial Building
Springfield, Illinois 62756

School Library Media Supervisor

Marie Sivak
Illinois Office of Education
Springfield 62702

New State Librarian. Alan J. Dixon was inaugurated as the 34th Secretary of State and State Librarian on January 10, 1977. Dixon stated that under his administration the post of State Librarian would be a primary function of the Office of the Secretary of State.

"The State Library," according to Dixon, "is the logical agency to coordinate statewide library development." Among his goals are to increase and improve the state's services to the blind and physically handicapped; to support full library services to correctional centers; to support continuing education and manpower activities of the State Library; and to promote a statewide public information program, scholarship and workshop programs, and participation of Illinois libraries in the bibliographic data base service.

Equalization Grants. Fifty-seven public libraries in 11 Illinois systems received Equalization Aid Grants in 1977 totaling $155,574. The program is funded under an annual appropriation approved by the Illinois legislature and is designed to equalize the incomes of libraries with low tax bases. Funds from the grants must be used for library service, including personnel, books, and other library materials and operation expenses.

System Changes. In 1977 two Illinois library systems moved into different quarters. The Illinois Valley Library System moved from the Peoria Public Library to offices located on the campus of Bradley University. The Northern Illinois Library System moved into new headquarters in Rockford.

Two of the systems appointed new directors. Starved Rock Library System's new director is Richard Willson, formerly from Ohio. Elaine Albright, former professor of library science at the University of Illinois, is the new director of the Lincoln Trail Library System.

LSCA Grants. According to Kathryn J. Gesterfield, Director, the Illinois State Library authorized $2,044,944.11 in federal Library Services and Construction Act (LSCA) grants for 1977.

The funds were allocated for a variety of projects: six shared staffing projects; nine scholarships; four PLUS projects (a program designed to extend library services to an unserved area or to help a local library to extend services to the unserved surrounding areas); one Project Pride (a program to help establish a coordinated library service program for a county library and its branches); and 10 interlibrary cooperation consultants.

The Northwest Municipal Conference was awarded a LSCA grant to organize the Intermunicipal Reference Library. The Library will provide reference support and coordination of materials to local, state, and governmental service agencies with the Northwest Municipal Conference, 15 municipalities and 4 townships of suburban Chicago. The Conference serves more than 500,000 people. The long-range goal of the Library is to coordinate governmental reference material in order to serve as a regional clearinghouse for municipal and government data.

ALSCA grant has been awarded to the University of Illinois Library Research Center to do an analysis of children's services in Illinois public libraries. The purpose of the project is to assess library goals, services, personnel, materials, and facilities in order to provide a basis for the development of standards for children's services in public libraries.

An LSCA grant was also awarded to the DuPage Library System to supply and operate the Kane County Adult Correctional Library. The Library is a cooperative effort of the Library System and several local libraries in Kane County. The project calls for the hiring of a librarian to head the Library and for providing service in cooperation with the local libraries. Additional funding was supplied by the Illinois Library Association.

Funds have also been allocated to begin a statewide audiovisual project. The project is designed to strengthen existing audiovisual libraries on all levels and to design an efficient and effective resource sharing system. A planning committee has been appointed.

Chicago Public Library. For the Chicago Public Library and for many Chicagoans, the highlight of the year was the long-awaited opening of the Chicago Public Library Cultural Center. Before extensive renovation, the building housed the Central Library. Designated a Chicago landmark in November 1976, the building houses the Library's Fine Arts Division, a popular library, an audiovisual center, and a children's library as well as refurbished areas for professional exhibits and programs. This concept of a cultural center is unique among U.S. libraries in that a large amount of space and a separate staff are assigned solely for the production of such programs and exhibits.

Other significant events in the Library's year included the Board of Directors' approval of a statement of philosophy and function. The statement described the role of a future central library and the Board's resolution to the City Council expressing the need for a new building. An extensive renovation program for all Library-owned branch buildings, sponsored by the Community Development Fund, was begun. The city approved a subsidy through its Public Building Commission for the construction of the Frederick H. Hild Regional Library (the Library's second regional) and the complete refurbishing of the Legler Branch Library. Two branches were relocated to more spacious, modern quarters. The Library's 79th branch, named in honor of the Chicago playwright Lorraine Hansberry, opened in one of the city's community service centers; and a site was selected for the 80th branch. Construction was completed on architect Stanley Tigerman's innovative building for the Illinois Regional Library for the Blind and Physically Handicapped, planned for opening in January 1978.

Special Collections received an outstanding gift of early Chicago materials from Joseph Francus containing legal documents and prefire theatre memorabilia that had been a part of the Lawrence Dicke Collection. Joseph and Jennifer Lutz donated an important collection of 6,000 volumes on the Civil War and American history.

Special Libraries. Special libraries and librarians in Illinois have moved into the mainstream of statewide library development in recent years. During 1977 they continued to have significant representation as members and participants in both the Illinois Regional Library Council and ILLINET. Early in the year the *Union List of Serial Holdings in Illinois Special Libraries* was published by the Council. The list contains an estimated 29,000 entries, reflecting the serial holdings of 142 special libraries in Illinois, and is meant to be used as a resource by all libraries throughout the state. *Getting Into Networking: Guidelines for Special Libraries* was published by the Special Libraries Association (SLA). It was completed by a small group of Illinois special librarians who worked together as a subcommittee of SLA's Networking Committee. The Illinois Chapter of SLA, which provides the focus for most of the special library activity in the state, grew to more than 600 members during the year.

Public Library Survey. The results of the Illinois Public Library Usage Survey were published in 1977. The Survey, conducted in March and April of 1976, was commissioned to determine the level of library usage, to determine the level of understanding of library services, and to define why people do or do not use the library. The Survey consisted of 899 randomly selected telephone interviews and 152 personnel interviews at local public libraries.

A summary of the Survey results indicated that 54 per cent of Illinois adult nonstudents owned or had access to a library card. Sixty-five per cent of the library card owners lived in households with children under 18, and only 41 per cent of the people with no children under 18 had library cards. Library users generally had some college education (53 per cent), were between 35 and 49 years of age (66 per cent), were employed in professional positions (72 per cent), and had incomes over $15,000 (65 per cent).

Of the people surveyed, 46 per cent did not own or have access to a library card. Of this percentage 45 per cent had never owned a card, 53 per cent had owned one in the past, and 2 per cent could not remember ever owning a card.

Forty-three per cent of the surveyed could be classified as public library users, meaning that they had used the library within the previous two years. Forty per cent of these used the library at least once a month.

Fifty-four per cent of the library users surveyed primarily used the reference and information services in the library, with 41 per cent using the library to borrow books. Among library nonusers 57 per cent had not been to a library in more than five years.

The overwhelming majority of public library users in Illinois gave "the library" an extremely high rating. The users were satisfied with library services, found their library easy to use, and rated the personnel as helpful. Sixty-nine per cent of the users saw no need for improvement.

CCD Report. The Cooperative Collection Development (CCD) Subcommittee of the Research and Reference Center Directors Committee has published a working paper called "Toward Cooperative Collection in the Illinois Library and Information Network." The report was the first step in a long-range program to increase cooperative collection development through the Illinois Library and Information Network (ILLINET), recommended several steps:

1. All libraries participating in ILLINET should adopt and foster the "User Oriented Acquisitions" report as their collection development philosophy.

2. The participants in ILLINET should work toward access for library users to materials in all participating library collections.

3. The State Library should sponsor a statewide in-depth survey to determine unmet needs and to examine subject strengths and specific system subject collection responsibilities as identified.

Illinois Library Legislation. The ILA program of the legislative year was productive. The following library bills became Illinois law: SB-210: Restores the $389,000 from bond revenues for the state's share in constructing a regional library in Chicago for the blind & physically handicapped; SB-338: Appropriates $1,319,700 to the State Historical Library for fiscal year 1978; SB-751: Appropriates $50,000 for fiscal year 1978 for the General Assembly Library Study Commission; SB-900: Recreates the General Assembly Library Study Commission, composed of the four legislative leaders and four public members appointed by the leaders; HB-284: Allows directors of library systems, upon serving six years on a system board, to serve again after an interim of at least two years off the board; HB-602: Allows all public libraries to levy an additional tax of .02% for the purchase of sites and buildings; for the rental of a building required for library purposes; and for the maintenance, repair, and alteration of library buildings and general equipment, subject to provisions of the "back-door" referendum; HB-603: Increases the working cash levy for all public libraries by an additional .02% (.05% now instead of .03%); HB-604: Increases the mortgage limitations on existing library buildings and sites from 50% to 75%; HB-750: Appropriates $25,000 in state funds and $25,000 in federal funds for the Illinois Pre-White House Conference on Libraries and Informational Services; HB-873: Provides that a new public library district may be established by referendum with a tax limit of .40% instead of .15% if the higher rate is specified on the referendum ballot and in the petition calling for the referendum; and HB-874: Provides that a new local library may be established by referendum with a tax limit of .40% instead of .15% if the higher rate is specified on the referendum ballot and in the petition calling for the referendum.

State Library. Gesterfield appointed the Illinois State Library Task Force on Copyright Guidelines for the Illinois Library and Information Network as a follow-up to copyright meetings held throughout Illinois in May 1977. The Task Force developed guidelines to be used by Illinois libraries in complying with the Copyright Revision Act of 1976. It had representatives from the components of the network: local libraries (academic, public, school, and special); systems; reference and research centers; special resource libraries; and the Illinois Library Association.

"A Fair Shake: Copying Rights for ILLINET Participants under the Copyright Revision Act of 1976" is based on the philosophy of what librarians *can do* in continuing to serve their clientele. It attempts to convey the specifics of the law as it affects the flow of information under ILLINET's statutory obligations to serve the research and reference needs of the people of Illinois. Copies were distributed to ILLINET participants through the Illinois State Library and the Illinois library systems.
JOHN R. COYNE

INDIANA

New Life for ILA. A phenomenal increase of 30 per cent in the number of personal memberships in the Indiana Library Association (ILA) followed the establishment of a joint Executive Office by ILA and the Indiana Library Trustees Association (ILTA) in April 1976. As of October 31, 1977, ILA had 1,137 personal members (up from 873 at the end of 1976) and 221 institutional members.

ILA Business. The annual conference was held jointly with ILTA in Indianapolis November 3-5, with an attendance of more than 800. The main item of business was a change in the constitution and bylaws to rename all interest groups in the association as "divisions," to provide divisional representation on the Executive Board, and to shift the status of the ALA Councilor on the Executive Board from voting to non-voting ex officio status (to conform with the ex officio status of the ILA Executive Director and the State Library Director). Under the amended constitution, divisions with fewer than fifty members are to be discontinued after a specified time.

Honorary memberships and Citations of Appreciation were approved for presentation to Congressman John Brademas (D.-Ind.) "for his continuing support of library and education programs in the United States Congress" and to Marcelle Foote "for her many contributions to library service in the State of Indiana."

Indiana Library Association
(founded 1891)

Membership: 1,137; *Annual Expenditure:* $32,609.
President: Mary McMillan, Plainfield Public Library (November 1977-November 1978).
Vice-President/President-elect: Robert Trinkle, Monroe County Public Library, Bloomington.
Executive Director: Susan Cady, 1100 West 42nd Street, Indianapolis, Indiana 46208.
Annual Meeting: November 3-5, 1977, Indianapolis.
Publication: Focus on Indiana Libraries (bimonthly).

Indiana State Library

Marcelle K. Foote, Director (retired August 31)
Jean Jose, Acting Director (September 1)
140 North Senate Avenue
Indianapolis 46204

School Library Media Supervisor

Phyllis Land
State Department of Public Instruction
Indianapolis 46204

ILTA Business. Officers elected for the 1977-78 year were William Laramore, president (Plymouth); Carol Winslow, vice-president/president-elect (Evansville); Carolyn Henson, secretary (Vigo County); and Ralph Burress, treasurer (Madison). Directors elected were Kathryn Swartz (Crown Point), Winifred Pettee (Indianapolis), and Evangeline Herr (Newburg).

A 14-member Trustee Council was formed with two members from each of the state's seven ILTA districts. The role of the newly organized Council is to serve as an advisory group on the trustee viewpoint, making recommendations to the ILA and ILTA Executive Boards. It will meet twice each year.

Legislation. ILA and ILTA initiated five bills that were introduced into the Indiana General Assembly. Three of the five passed and were signed into law by Governor Otis R. Bowen.

One bill amended the Library Services Authority Act that governs the operation of ALSAs, INCOLSA, the Indiana Library Film Circuit, and the Library Flicks Film Circuit. The amendments simplify operations through mail votes, reduce filing requirements, and change the powers of delegation.

Another bill amended the Public Library Law of 1947 to permit public libraries to appropriate funds for institutional membership in organizations of a civic, professional, or governmental nature.

The third bill amended the law governing the State Library and Historical Board by providing a formula for the distribution of state funds to public libraries: "multiplying (1) the amount appropriated by the general assembly for the purposes of this section by (2) a fraction, the numerator of which is the amount of the eligible public library district's current certified operating fund budget, and the denominator of which is the total amount of the current certified operating fund budgets of all eligible public library districts in the state." $832,000 was included in the state budget for each of the fiscal years 1977-78 and 1978-79, an increase of 4 per cent over the 1976-77 funding.

Public Library Finance. All tax-supported entities in the state—public libraries, schools, cities, towns, etc.—have been operating at a frozen tax rate since 1973. A special session of the Indiana General Assembly in 1977 amended the law to permit a 5 per cent increase in 1978 of the amount of money raised in 1977, with the tax rate for 1978 adjusted accordingly. The amended law also provides for another increase in income for the 1979 operating budget of 8 per cent over 1978 income.

Humanities Grant Planning. A $36,100 planning grant was made to ILA-ILTA by the National Endowment for the Humanities (NEH) for the investigation of ways in which humanists can assist in the improvement of public library services. An action plan was presented in a one-day preconference in November. The plan is being submitted to NEH as a proposal for a second grant.

ISLA. The Indiana School Librarians Association (ISLA) held its annual meeting April 28-30 in Clarksville. President for 1977-78 is Mary Collins of the Indianapolis Public Schools; the president-elect is Jean Christian of Huntington School Corporation. The current membership is 849.

The main project sponsored by ISLA is the Young Hoosier Book Award. Begun in 1974-75 as a response to the Right-to-Read movement, the program has been increasing in interest and participation each year. In 1977, more than 13,000 students helped select Thomas Rockwell's *How to Eat Fried Worms* as the winner.

ISLA also established the Esther Burrin Memorial Award to be given to a librarian/media specialist for promotion of a notable school media program. Esther Burrin, who died in 1975, was one of the founders of ISLA, a past president of ISLA and of the American Association of School Librarians, and the first director of school libraries in the Indiana Department of Public Instruction.

IAECT. The Indiana Association for Educational Communications and Technology (IAECT) has a membership of nearly 500 media specialists, librarians, teachers, and others in all types of schools and industries. Formed in 1947 as the Audio-Visual Instruction Directors of Indiana, IAECT is now considering a consolidation with ISLA. The executive boards of IAECT and ISLA met on November 19 and voted to dissolve the two associations and to form a new organization called Hoosier Media Association. The action was to be voted on by members when the two associations met jointly in March 1978. President of IAECT is Margarete Butz of Harshman Junior High School in Indianapolis.

Special Libraries. The Indiana Chapter of the Special Libraries Association was established in 1941. The Chapter has had a significant growth in membership with 160 members as of June 30, 1977, an increase of 17 per cent over the previous year. President for 1977-78 is Miriam A. Drake of Purdue University; president-elect is Mary Ann Roman, librarian of Barnes, Hickam, Pantzer & Boyd in Indianapolis.

Governor's Conference. The Governor's Conference on Library and Information Services is planned for August 11-13, 1978, in Indianapolis. Governor Bowen will give the keynote speech. Nominations for delegates were to be held early in 1978. A screening committee was to review the nominations, selecting 250 delegates and 100 alternates. Chairperson of the planning committee for the Governor's Conference is Alice L. Wert of Vigo County Public Library.

ASLAs. With the formation of 2 more ALSAs during 1977, 12 of the state's 14 regions now have an Area Library Services Authority. The 11 operational ALSAs (the Southeastern Indiana ALSA serves two regions) encompass 80 of Indiana's 92 counties. Each ASLA is a voluntary municipal corporation of member libraries of all types within the prescribed geographic area. Membership in the 11 ALSAs includes 143 public libraries, 93 school corporations, 8 private schools, 37 college and university libraries, and 45 special libraries.

INCOLSA. The 123 members of the Indiana Cooperative Library Services Authority include 62 public, 31 academic, 17 school, and 13 special libraries. During 1977, INCOLSA expanded its network of OCLC terminals. By the end of the year 66 terminals were in operation, and the State Library installed a terminal for interlibrary loan and reference use. INCOLSA itself manages the Indiana

Cooperative Processing Center, cataloging more than 40,000 titles for some 50 small libraries in 1977. A centralized cataloging service for small libraries was initiated (the present customers are largely school and special libraries). With the cooperation of the Indiana University School of Medicine Library, a pilot centralized cataloging service for health science libraries was also begun.

TWX. The Indiana library teletype network, officially the Interlibrary Communication Project (TWX), includes 14 public libraries, 4 state university libraries, the State Library, and the Indiana University School of Medicine Library. Other public libraries in the state are assigned as "satellites" to the 14 public libraries, which serve as TWX centers for the geographic regions in the state.

Formerly leased, the teletype machines were purchased with LSCA funds, and under the agreement in effect in 1977 each participating TWX library paid only the Western Union equipment charges, service charges, and out-of-state message costs. Each satellite library is provided a credit card for phone calls to its TWX center library. In-state toll and credit card charges amounted to $29,476 in fiscal 1976-77 and were paid from LSCA funds. During the fiscal year ending June 30, 1977, Indiana libraries originated 50,950 requests on the TWX network.

Buildings. Indiana State Library held an open house on August 9 to celebrate the completion of an addition and remodeling that added 87,053 square feet to the 120,000 in the original building. A 200-seat auditorium and two smaller conference rooms provide meeting space for library and historical groups, the legislature, and other state agencies. In addition to the State Library, the building houses the Indiana Academy of Science, the Historical Society, and the Historical Bureau.

On September 23 the Indiana Central University Library in Indianapolis was dedicated. The 93,100-square-foot structure houses the library, the instructional media center, and the University administrative offices.

The Christian Theological Seminary Library dedication took place on October 5 in Indianapolis. October 9 marked the dedication of the first remodeling of the Indianapolis-Marion County Public Library's central library since its opening in 1917. Previous office and storage space was converted into 12,000 square feet of public service space in addition to other facilities.

The Michigan City Public Library dedicated its $2,700,000 ultramodern facility on October 30. The 35,000-square-foot structure won a Distinguished Building Award from the Chicago Chapter of the American Institute of Architects.

People. Nellie Coats, 88, former head of the Catalog Division of the Indiana State Library for 35 years, died January 11. She served as president of ILA in 1925-26, and in 1962 was named Woman of the Year by the Hoosier Chapter of American Women in Radio and TV.

Marcelle Foote, director of the Indiana State Library, retired August 31. She first joined the State Library in 1956 as a field consultant after serving as a librarian in the public libraries of Albion and Connersville. In 1966 she was chosen Librarian of the Year by ILTA and in 1975 was awarded an honorary doctorate by Indiana State University.

Roger B. Francis, director of the South Bend Public Library for 25 years, retired October 1. Francis was on the staff of the New York Public Library from 1940 to 1952. He is a past president of ILA and a former ALA Councilor from the Indiana Chapter.   EDWARD N. HOWARD

IOWA

Iowa Library Association
(founded 1896)

Membership: 1,620; *Annual Expenditure:* $21,000.
President: Douglas M. Hieber, Circulation Department, University of Northern Iowa Library (October 1976-December 1978).
Vice-President/President-elect: Elaine G. Estes, Public Library of Des Moines.
Secretary-Treasurer: Gayle Burdick, 401 Securities Building, Des Moines, Iowa 50309.
Annual Conference: October 19-21, 1977, Cedar Rapids.
Publication: Catalyst (bimonthly).

State Library Commission of Iowa

Barry L. Porter, Director
Historical Building
Des Moines 50319

School Library Media Supervisor

Betty Jo Buckingham
Department of Public Instruction
Des Moines 50319

ILA Activities. ILA held its annual district meetings in the spring of 1977. Vice-President Elaine Estes chose the theme "Is It Legal?" and arranged for speakers who are experts in law related to libraries.

Patent attorneys addressed the seven meetings on the topic "The Copyright Law As It Affects Libraries," pointing out what the law will mean for libraries that provide photocopy service for their users. Ray Sullins, Head of the Criminal Appeals Division of the Iowa Attorney General's office, reported on the implications of the *Jerry Lee Smith* v. *U.S.* case. The U.S. Supreme Court convicted Smith for mailing obscene materials through the mails despite an Iowa law that allows people over 18 to read whatever materials they desire. He stated that, while interlibrary loan may very well provide a library with a situation that is technically comparable to *Smith*, obscenity laws exist not to harass libraries but to prosecute distributors of pornography.

Thomas Mann, Director of the Iowa Civil Rights Commission, discussed hiring practices in light of the laws preventing discrimination in hiring. Representatives of the Iowa League of Municipalities explained how Iowa's recently enacted Home Rule Law affects libraries' finances. Maurice Baringer, Treasurer of the State of Iowa, discussed unemployment tax liability, the Iowa Public Employees Retirement System, and the minimum wage law as they affect libraries.

Legislation Committee. The ILA Legislation Committee put much of its effort during the 1977 session of the Iowa legislature into gaining a budget and pay increase for Iowa's regional libraries. Working with other interested librarians and trustees, Committee members also attempted to have a bill passed that would establish a long-needed state documents depository system.

In order to obtain any state documents, a librarian currently must somehow become aware of the documents' existence, request the items, and sometimes pay for the documents. In preparing for the 1978 session, Committee members have coordinated contact people to persuade legislators to pass the bill. The Committee also planned to work in conjunction with the Iowa Civil Liberties Union and the Iowa Freedom of Information Council to support the bill.

Another concern of the Legislation Committee became evident when a library user requested the reading record of another user and was refused. The user had assumed that library circulation records were public information. The Iowa Code does not currently exempt these records from public scrutiny, although most public library boards of trustees have established policies to protect circulation records. The Legislation Committee has begun to work with a legislator to amend the Iowa Code to protect the privacy of library users.

Annual Conference. ILA President Douglas Hieber presided over a "Potpourri" of informative speakers and a business meeting at the ILA annual conference in Cedar Rapids. Sanford Berman,

Head of Cataloging for the Hennepin County Library in Minnesota, addressed a general session and participated in a panel discussion "In Defense of Catalogers."

The State Library Commission arranged for Lewis Flacks, Special Counsel to the Library of Congress's Office of Copyright, to clarify how librarians should handle problems that may arise under the new copyright law. Clark Mollenhoff, a veteran reporter and native Iowan, told how libraries played an important role in his career choice.

Members voted to increase ILA dues by 15 per cent and also amended the ILA Constitution and Bylaws to change the term of offices to the calendar year instead of the conference year.

The most heated debate arose from a proposal to endorse the *Minimum Guidelines for Iowa Public Libraries.* Copies of the document had been mailed to all public libraries in the state. Public hearings then provided the opportunity for people to express their feelings about the *Guidelines.* ILA members finally voted to endorse them, provided ILA establish a committee that represents public libraries of all sizes in the state to further administer the development of the *Guidelines.*

ILA presents a plaque every three years in memory of former State Librarian Johnson Brigham to an Iowa author for an outstanding contribution to literature. James Schell Hearst received the Johnson Brigham Plaque in 1977 for his works *Dry Leaves: New Poems* and *Shaken by Leaf-Fall.*

MFLA Membership. The Executive Board of ILA voted to drop MFLA membership in 1978 because the Midwest Federation of Library Associations changed its bylaws, requiring state associations not to hold a state conference with commercial exhibits during MFLA conference years. Many ILA members had registered complaints after the last MFLA conference.

Iowa OCLC Memberships. In 1977, 28 libraries in Iowa became OCLC members. They included 2 state universities accessing OCLC through MIDLNET, a private university, a library school, 2 special libraries, and 22 private, four-year liberal arts colleges accessing OCLC through the Bibliographical Center for Research (BCR) in Denver. Most of the private colleges received $8,000 Kellogg Foundation grants for start-up funds. The State Library joined BCR, providing a statewide comprehensive BCR membership for Iowa. The membership will allow access to BCR's many services other than OCLC.

Library Outreach Cooperative. Representatives of the State Library Commission and ILA attended a meeting with representatives from Missouri and Kansas to establish the Library Outreach Cooperative (LOC). A coordinator from each participating state has established a file of successful outreach library programs and unsuccessful attempts and lists of people in the state who would be willing to act as outreach consultants, advisors, and workshop speakers. Library publications in Missouri, Kansas, and Iowa are notifying their readers of the availability of the information. The representatives will meet to assess the success of the LOC program and to solicit participation by other states in the area.

National Publicity. Two Iowa libraries received national publicity in 1977. The Musser family in Muscatine received the new ALTA Honor Award for 1977. Members of the family have contributed major gifts to the Musser Public Library during the past 75 years. Barbara Prentice, ALTA Vice-President/President-Elect, presented plaques to the Musser Public Library and the Musser family in November at an awards ceremony.

The Rudd Public Library became known nationally when the city faced threats of the loss of federal revenue sharing funds. HEW directives implied that a city might lose federal funds if any public building did not allow access by physically handicapped people. The national news media pointed out that the library could not afford to build a ramp and that no one in the small town used a wheelchair. The library, however, had already planned to build a ramp. With the help of Easter Seal funds from Mason City and materials donated by a local lumber yard, the Rudd Public Library is well on its way to completing a ramp and will not close its doors to users.

GAYLE BURDICK

KANSAS

Governor's Task Force. Governor Robert F. Bennett in 1977 established the Governor's Task Force on Library Resources. Chaired by LeRoy Fox of Johnson County Public Library, the Task Force is to make recommendations to the governor regarding several questions: (1) What should be the mission of libraries within various types of institutions, i.e., what is the character of the collection each type of library should hold? (2) How should the interlibrary loan program be utilized to provide for an interconnected system of libraries that more effectively utilizes library resources? (3) What steps should be taken to avoid the unnecessary duplication of library resources in Kansas? (4) What should be the role of the state and local governments—including the State Librarian, the Board of Regents, the State Department of Education, community junior colleges, school boards, and county and city officials—in providing for library resources?

Kansas Library Association (founded 1900)

Membership: approx. 600; *Annual Expenditure:* approx. $12,000.
President: Charles Bolles, Kansas State Library, Topeka (July 1977-June 1978).
Vice-President/President-elect: Mike Tacha, Neosho County Community Junior College, Chanute.
Secretary: Helen Suellentrop, Central Kansas Library System, Great Bend.
Annual Conference: May 11-13, 1977, Topeka.
Publication: KLA Newsletter (2 or 3 times a year).

Kansas State Library

Ernestine Gilliland, State Librarian
3rd Floor, Statehouse
Topeka 66612

School Library Media Supervisor

Mona Alexander
State Department of Public Instruction
Topeka 66612

Eight subcommittees chaired by the Task Force members have been established to present respective needs, concerns, and problems to the Task Force: Private Academic Libraries, Sister Kathleen Egan, Benedictine College; Community Junior Colleges, Mike Tacha, Neosho County Community Junior College; Regional Library Systems, Duane Johnson, South Central Kansas Library System; Public Libraries, Duane Johnson; School Media Centers, Louise Dial, Derby; Special Libraries, Ernestine Gilliland, Kansas State Library; Library Education, Sarah Reed, Emporia State University; Regents' Institutions, James Ranz, University of Kansas. Once the subcommittees have reported to the Task Force, a response to the governor's questions will be formulated and reported.

Other members of the Task Force include Jasper Schad, Wichita State University, and citizens Jane Byrd, Ottawa; Gail Merrill, Marion; Mrs. Jerry Pettle, Manhattan; Carl H. Sperry, St. Francis; Fred Young, Dodge City; Judy Raile, St. Francis; and Margaret Moore, Hill City.

It is expected that the Task Force will have completed its activities by the fall of 1978 and that its findings will be incorporated into the Kansas Conference on Library and Information Services, preceding the White House Conference.

Networking. The overall goal of the Kansas Library Services Network, coordinated by the State Library, is to provide citizens of Kansas access to all levels of information at local or primary library sites. The network is made up of several components including the Kansas Information Circuit, computer-based reference and information services, automated technical services, and the Kansas Union Catalog.

The Kansas Information Circuit is a multitype interlibrary loan network of the Kansas regional library systems, their member libraries, and affiliated academic libraries. During 1977 communication within the network was upgraded by the installation of either Hazeltine 2000 or Texas Instruments 733 and 745 terminals. The installation of these terminals has allowed modifications in routing and savings in time and costs that have significantly improved service to the citizens of Kansas.

The same terminals used in the Kansas Information Circuit may also be used to provide access to a variety of on-line computerized data bases to provide literature searching capabilities and to supplement traditional reference. Such services must be initiated by the patron and may involve costs to the patron.

OCLC installations provide automated technical services information of a bibliographic and cataloging nature. Four regional library systems have central processing centers that provide OCLC access for approximately 150 public libraries. In addition, 25 academic institutions currently have access to OCLC information.

The current cataloging done through OCLC is being captured for use in developing the Kansas Union Catalog, a COM single-entry listing of materials owned by selected Kansas libraries. In addition to the current OCLC cataloging information, retrospective collections are being input as libraries go to automated circulation systems or internal COM catalogs. This activity will help provide access to information, promote interlibrary cooperation, and, most importantly, help improve resource sharing in a simple and positive way.

Information Sciences. The Kansas Association for Educational Technology, the Kansas Association of School Librarians, and the Kansas Library Association have worked together to establish the Kansas Council for Information Sciences (KCIS). The purpose of KCIS will be to promote the public welfare through access to information, communications, and education by the study of common interests and problems, by the application of educational technology to information sciences and librarianship, and by the cooperative action of the three affiliate organizations. It is hoped that KCIS will provide libraries and media specialists in the state greater visibility and impact in support of information-related programs through cooperative legislative efforts, public relations, research, and similar activities. Chairperson Rubye Downs of Salina has coordinated the organizational phase of KCIS; substantive programs are to be developed in the future.

People. New library directors in Kansas in 1977 included Father Gerald Mesmer, Benedictine College, Atchison; James Swan, Central Kansas Library System and Great Bend Public Library; Jane Hatch, Dodge City Public Library; Dean Willard, Fort Hays State University, Hays; Hans Bynagle, Friends University, Wichita; Robert Gorman, Kansas Newman College, Wichita; and Edgar Nickel, Northwest Kansas Library System, Hoxie.

CHARLES BOLLES

KENTUCKY

Kentucky Library Association
(founded 1907)

Membership: 1,114; *Annual Expenditure:* $25,000.
President: Edwin Strohecker, Murray State University, Murray (October 1977-October 1978).
Vice-President/President-elect: Barbara Miller, Louisville Free Public Library.
Secretary: Betty Hatfield, Eastern Kentucky State University, Richmond.
Annual Convention: October 6-8, 1977, Paducah.
Publication: KLA Bulletin (quarterly).

Department of Library and Archives
Barbara M. Williams, State Librarian
Box 537
Frankfort 40601

State School Library Media Supervisor
Lucy Bonner
State Department of Education
Frankfort 40601

Kentucky Library Association. During 1977, Kentucky's participation in state, regional, and national library activities was at a new high. The Kentucky Library Association (KLA) celebrated its 70th birthday at the annual conference held at Fort Mitchell, October 6-8, by honoring the Association's past presidents. Gifts were presented to Rebecca Bingham, Jacqueline Bull, Madge Davis, Elizabeth Gilbert, Vera Grinstead Guthrie, Omer Hamlin, Jimadean Ireland, Sherwood Kirk, Tom Sutherland, Joy Terhune, Clarissa Williams, and Margaret Willis.

KLA has assumed a leadership role in planning for the Governor's Pre-White House Conference on Library and Information Services to be held in Lexington in March 1979. Serving on the Steering Committee for the Conference are Vivian Hall, Barbara Miller, Edwin Strohecker, and Paul Willis.

Seven round tables were formed in KLA in 1977. They are: (1) Children and Young People's Literature; (2) Community and Junior Colleges; (3) Government Documents; (4) Health Science Librarians; (5) Independent College Librarians; (6) Junior Members; and (7) Nonprint Media. Each group cuts across sectional lines and draws together librarians with common interests.

The Professional Development Committee of KLA sponsored a one-day workshop in October on "Bibliographic Instruction and Library Orientation Update" that attracted 65 librarians representing public, school, academic, and special libraries.

Louisville Library. Effective July 11, 1977, Ronald S. Kozlowski became Director of the Louisville Free Public Library upon the retirement of C.R. Graham who had served as Director for 35 years.

From September 19 through October 31 the Library mounted two displays of books, "From Kentucky Private Presses," as its part of the Festival of Fine Print that took place in Louisville, Bardstown, and Lexington. In October the Library instituted paperback browsing collections at the main library, all 23 branches, and 3 bookmobiles. The service was enthusiastically received by the public.

The Children's Department sponsored a three-session program called "Start Early for an Early Start." It was designed for parents who wished to extend their knowledge of the nature of the young child, available media, and choice of books for preschoolers. Registration of 81 adults exceeded expectations, and plans were under way to repeat the program in branches as well as at the main library.

Library Developments. In January a new State Librarian, Barbara M. Williams, and Deputy State Librarian, Isaac Daniel Kreutzer, took office. Williams was the former Deputy Librarian, and Kreutzer had been a speech writer for Governor Julian Carroll.

A reception held during KLA's Public Library Section meeting provided an opportunity for the new State Librarian to become acquainted with librarians within the state. In July at ALA, a reception hosted by C.V. Cooper, Jr., Chairman of the Kentucky Governor's Advisory Council on Libraries, honored Williams and other state librarians.

A Steering Committee was appointed and began work to develop plans for Kentucky's Pre-White House Conference. Tentative plans include seven congressional hearings, task forces on several relevant issues, and five symposia on information-related topics, all to take place prior to the state Conference in March 1979.

The Technical Services Division processed and catalogued approximately 178,229 books and materials during FY 1976. Film circulation also increased over the previous year's record high.

Kentucky's Oral History Project continued in 1977 with additional funding ($50,000) coming from the Governor's Contingency Fund. To date the Level II project, coordinated through public libraries, has yielded approximately 250 tapes.

Two public libraries in eastern Kentucky were destroyed as flood waters swept through the towns of Pineville and Pikeville. The State Library staff worked with disaster officials to clear the aftermath and develop future plans for restoration of services.

The following public library construction projects were completed during 1977: Christian County, Hopkinsville; Simpson County, Franklin; Henry County, Eminence; Lee County, Beattyville; Estill County, Irvine; Bullitt County (North Bullitt Branch), Maryville; Casey County, Liberty; Allen County, Scottsville.

Continuing Education. Joy Terhune, Associate Professor at the University of Kentucky's College of Library Science, has been appointed Acting Director of the Office of Continuing Education. During 1977-78, the Office will undergo a review to determine its future role in continuing education in the state and nation. Ongoing activities that the Office has instituted for the College include spring and fall symposiums on topics of current interest. The Faculty Forum Series (Friday afternoon seminars for practicing professionals) was begun in the fall of 1977. Programs for the community on preschoolers, parents, and books have become a regular activity. The annual workshop for school and young adult librarians continues to be a highlight in the spring.

Morehead State University. On November 22, 1976, two Lexington firms were awarded a joint contract totaling $2,195,000 for construction of the Julian M. Carroll Library Tower, a five-story addition to the Johnson Camden Library at Morehead State University. When this new facility is completed in 1978, it will increase the Library's book capacity by nearly 1,000,000 volumes. The new addition will house a multimedia center, a dial access center, the University Archives, the Kentucky Collection, a microfilm library, a government documents library, and general reference areas and stacks.

School Libraries. Mildred Gill, Librarian at Franklin County High School in Frankfort, was named Outstanding School Librarian for the year. The award was presented at the luncheon of the Kentucky School Media Association held during the KLA annual conference.

ALA witnesses testified in support of a five-year extension of school and library media aid under the Elementary and Secondary Education Act, Title IV-B, on July 27. One of those speaking on behalf of the American Association of School Librarians was Louise Bedford, an instructional media coordinator in the Montgomery County Schools in Mt. Sterling.

People. Timothy W. Sineath, formerly Coordinator of the Doctoral Program and Associate Professor in the School of Library Science at Simmons College in Boston, was named Dean of the College of Library Science at the University of Kentucky. Thomas W. Waldhart served as Acting Dean during the 1976-77 academic year. James Nelson, Director of the Office for Continuing Education, resigned to accept a position at the University of Wisconsin as Assistant Professor of Library Science Communication Programs.

Jo Ann Rogers received the Center for Developmental Change Faculty Research Planning Fellowship for the fall 1977 semester. In cooperation with the Appalachian Education Satellite Project, Rogers explored the possibility of preparing a series of workshops on bibliographic networking to be delivered to librarians through the 45 satellite sites in Appalachia.

Ron Steensland, the newly appointed Director of the Lexington Public Library, came to Kentucky from Mesa Public Library in Los Alamos, New Mexico, where he was Director of Public Libraries. John Sheridan, the new Director of Translyvania University Libraries, came from Knox College in Galesburg, Illinois, where he was Head of Technical Services.

One of the original workers and developers of Kentucky's public library program retired July 1. Hallie Day Blackburn, Senior Extension Librarian for the northeastern area of Kentucky, worked untiringly for 25 years to establish services and support throughout the state.

BARBARA S. MILLER

LOUISIANA

Public Library Finances. The outstanding development in Louisiana public library history in 1977 was the passage of legislation designating the State Library as the state agency to receive and administer funds for state aid to public libraries. Although no state aid dollars are yet in the coffers of public libraries, the passage of the enabling legislation and the prospect of an appropriation is a tremendous victory. Much credit is due to the Louisiana Library Association Legislative Network, which in less than a year's time developed a legislative package, planned a campaign, and united to push for passage of the legislation. As 1977 drew to a close, plans were being developed to work for the passage of a $1,500,000 appropriation in 1978.

There were other outstanding successes in improved support for parish libraries in Louisiana during the year. In two parishes, the voters approved $2,200,000 bond issues for library construction. In four parishes the tax for operation and maintenance was increased, and in four others the tax was renewed at the same level. In four parishes, however, voters failed to approve public library tax increases. These failures were partially due to confusion on the part of voters caused by changes in the tax procedure mandated by the 1974 state constitution.

Louisiana Library Association (founded 1926)

Membership: 1,326; *Annual Expenditure:* $26,000.
President: Agnes Harris, Union Parish Library, Farmerville (July 1977-June 1978).
Vice-President/President-elect: Lynda Netherland, Bossier Parish Library, Benton.
Secretary: Diane F. Gustafson, New Orleans Public Library.
Annual Convention: March 31-April 2, 1977, New Orleans.
Publication: LLA Bulletin (quarterly).

Louisiana State Library

Thomas F. Jacques, State Librarian
P.O. Box 131
Baton Rouge 70821

State School Library Media Supervisor

James S. Cookston
State Department of Education
Baton Rouge 70804

Public Library Programs. The New Orleans Public Library was awarded a $330,000 grant from the National Endowment for the Humanities (NEH) to offer "Jambalaya," a three-year educational program designed to stimulate creative thought about New Orleans and to take an in-depth look at the social, cultural, and economic climate of the area. The Library is the third in the nation designated as a NEH Learning Library, joining the libraries of Boston and Chicago.

The first course, "Behind the Mask of Mardi Gras," was offered in the spring and gave many native New Orleanians new insights into the Mardi Gras celebration. In the fall a course on "New Orleans: Buildings, Streets, People" taught by local architects took an intensive look at the interrelationships between people and their old and new environment. In the "Writer's Forum," authors who have written about New Orleans shared their thoughts about the influence of New Orleans on their works—their use of the city as inspiration, setting, or symbol. In "New Orleans in Film," a film critic explored the city's prevailing image of eccentricity and allure in a series of old movies. In "The Economy of New Orleans," a university professor of economics probed the economy of the area, its trends, and its problems.

Academic Libraries. The Louisiana State Supreme Court has designated the University of New Orleans Library as the official permanent repository for its archives, which include docket books, minute books, and case files dating to 1813 when the Court was created. As part of the agreement, the Supreme Court will retain ownership. The Library will put the records in proper order and preserve and microfilm them, depositing a copy with the Supreme Court.

Institutional Libraries. Since 1968 the State Library has established pilot libraries in 12 state-supported health and correctional institutions, with the State Library organizing and supporting the libraries for two years and the institutions assuming responsibility for maintaining the projects after the pilot period. During 1977 a new approach to library service was selected to reach juvenile delinquents in a correctional institution with a traditional school library supporting the academic program.

LLA Awards. Hester B. Slocum, Assistant City Librarian at New Orleans Public Library, received the Essae M. Culver Distinguished Service Award presented annually to a professional member of the Louisiana Library Association (LLA) whose service and achievements have been of particular value to Louisiana librarianship. Slocum was cited for her professional endeavors on the local, state, and regional levels.

The LLA Modisette Awards were presented to Jacob S. Landry as the outstanding public library trustee, to the St. Mary's Dominican High School in New Orleans, and to the DeQuincy Elementary School. Landry, a New Iberia attorney, was honored for his 30 years of service on the Iberia Parish Library Board, 10 years of which he served as president.

The St. Mary's Dominican High School, headed by Margaret A. Waltzer, was cited for its outstanding collection of periodicals dating from 1950; its policy of overnight lending of reference books and newspapers; and its collection of curriculum-related government documents, a unique service for a high school library. Yvonne K. Theriot, Librarian, accepted the award for the DeQuincy Elementary School Library, which was recognized for its multimedia programs and for a program of multiple library activities.

The Louisiana Literary Award was presented to Mary Alice Fontenot and Rev. Paul B. Freeland, D.D. (posthumously), for their book "Acadia Parish Louisiana: A History to 1900." The winning book is a comprehensive, detailed, and well-documented publication.

New Buildings. Four new public library branches and one main library addition were dedicated during the year. The St. Charles Parish Library Regional Branch at Luling was formally dedicated on May 6. The total cost of the 17,000-square-foot facility was $1,000,000. A unique feature of the Luling building is a planetarium that gives visitors an opportunity to do some stargazing.

The Ouachita Valley Branch of the Ouachita Parish Library in West Monroe was dedicated on June 5. The new building contains 14,000 square feet, a 120-seat reading room, a 100-capacity meeting room, and a capacity for 60,000 books. The total cost of the building was $770,600, with $75,000 in federal revenue sharing funds and the remainder from a bond issue. With the remainder of the $1,600,000 bond issue, the main library is being remodeled and enlarged.

Dedication ceremonies for the Rayne Branch of the Acadia Parish Library were held on June 12. The 6,950-square-foot library was built at a cost of $216,038. Construction funds were derived from a local bond issue of $1,300,000, which also financed branches in Iota and Church Point and the new main library in Crowley under construction. The North Regional Branch of the Terrebonne Parish Library was dedicated on October 29. This 14,000-square-foot building was financed by the library maintenance and construction tax.

The dedication of the Sarah Jones Room of the Audubon Regional Library in Clinton was held on December 11. The 900-square-foot addition was made possible by a bequest from the late Sarah Jones, who at the time of her retirement was a public library consultant on the staff of the State Library. A native of Clinton, she dedicated 40 years of her life to the development of public libraries in Louisiana. The $25,000 bequest from Miss Jones was supplemented by $5,000 in federal revenue sharing funds. For her generosity, Miss Jones was named the posthumous recipient of a 1977 American Library Trustee Association Honor Award that recognizes major benefactors of libraries.

Continuing Education. The State Library Task Force on Continuing Education, commissioned in the fall of 1976, submitted its final report, "A Coordinated Plan for Continuing Education in Louisiana," to State Librarian Thomas Jaques in 1977. The major recommendation of the report was that the State Library, because of its resources and its focal position in the Louisiana library community, assume principal responsibility for the administration of continuing library education in the state. Other recommendations called for the appointment of a continuing education coordinator at the State Library and the establishment of a broadly based council to advise the State Library on the implementation of the plan.

In 1977 a total of 141 librarians from all types of libraries attended the personnel management workshops sponsored by the State Library and conducted by the Governmental Services Institute of Louisiana State University. A total of 108 librarians attended the Copyright Workshop sponsored by the State Library and conducted by the Southwestern Library Association/Continuing Education for Library Staffs on October 18-19.

Two workshops were conducted by the State Library to introduce library staff members to the services of various agencies serving the blind and physically handicapped. Jackie Wintle of the Division for the Blind and Physically Handicapped of the Library of Congress was the main speaker on the program. It also included representatives of agencies serving the blind and physically handicapped and individuals benefiting from the services.

Awards. Della K. Thielen, a member of the Calcasieu Parish Public Library System Board, received the Greater Lake Charles Chamber of Commerce Civic Service Award. Rosa F. Keller, a member of the New Orleans Public Library Board, was among four New Orleanians honored for their contributions to the city in the first annual Black Recognition Day. The White Contributor's Award went to Keller for her "active role in maintenance of the New Orleans public schools during the integration crisis."

Rosalynn Carter has chosen *The Cajuns of George Rodrigue* as an official State Department gift to visiting foreign heads of state. The book consists of 98 color reproductions of Rodrigue's works depicting the life-style and folklore of the Acadians of southwest Louisiana. It was also named to the Outstanding Southern Book List of 1976 by the Southeastern Library Association.

Appointments. Michael R. McKann was

appointed Associate State Librarian for Readers' and Technical Services effective January 9, 1978. He was formerly Chairman of the Acquisitions Department at the University of Florida Libraries at Gainesville. Jane Robbins was appointed Associate Professor at the Louisiana State University Graduate School of Library Science effective with the 1977-78 academic year.

Elizabeth C. Rountree assumed the responsibility of Assistant City Librarian in New Orleans on November 1. Rountree comes to New Orleans from Georgia where she was Director of the Brunswick-Glynn Regional Library and the Northeast Georgia Regional Library at Clarksville.

Larry D. Larason was appointed in August as Director of the Northeast Louisiana University Library, where he had served as Acting Director since November 1976. Ada J. Jarred was appointed in January as Director of the LSU-Alexandria Library, where she has been on the staff since 1973. Joanne R. Euster became Director of the Loyola University Library on July 1. Euster was formerly Director of the Library-Media Center at Edmonds Community College in Washington. James G. Volny became Director of the Centenary College Library in Shreveport on August 18. He was formerly Librarian of Loyola University in New Orleans.

Glenna Clark became Librarian of the LaSalle Parish Library in Jena effective January 1, 1978. Jeffrey L. Salter became Librarian of the Catahoula Parish Library effective January 1, 1978.

Retirements. Ruth M. Baldwin was appointed Professor Emeritus upon her retirement in May from the faculty of the LSU Graduate School of Library Science. Since that time she has joined the faculty of the Department of English at the University of Florida in Gainesville, where she will also be the librarian in charge of the development of a historical collection of children's literature including her personal collection of more than 35,000 children's books written in English before 1900.

Eunice H. Cotton, Librarian of the Franklin Parish Library in Winnsboro since it was established in 1950, retired on April 30. Marjorie Morgan retired on June 30 as Assistant Coordinator of Technical Services at the State Library.

Murrell C. Wellman, Associate State Librarian for Readers' and Technical Services, retired on July 31 after 19 years of service. Hazel Jones, Director of the Grambling State University Library, retired on June 12. She had been on the staff since 1949 and Director since 1974.

Thesta Ann Hogan, Coordinator of Technical Services at Louisiana Tech University Library in Ruston, retired on June 30 after more than 31 years of service to the University. Ellis A. Stringer, Librarian of the Catahoula Parish Library in Harrisonburg, retired on September 30 after 18 years of service.

Hester B. Slocum, Assistant City Librarian in New Orleans since 1967, retired on October 31. Since her retirement she has been appointed to a five-year term on the Library's Board of Commissioners. Cecil Gaddis, Librarian of the LaSalle Parish Library in Jena, retired on December 31 after 21 years of service.

Obituaries. Lois Shortess, a pioneer in the development of school libraries in Louisiana, died March 24. She was an innovator during a career that spanned 45 years in school, public, and academic libraries and in bookselling. She was the first state supervisor of school libraries in both Michigan and Louisiana and was Librarian at the University of Southwestern Louisiana. She helped develop undergraduate library science programs at several of the state's colleges and universities and operated her own book shop from 1941 to 1950, when she joined the staff of the State Library. In 1967 she organized the State Library's centralized processing center and directed the operation until her retirement in 1969. She was presented the Essae M. Culver Award for distinguished service to Louisiana libraries in 1968.

Roby Spaar, who served on the Jefferson Parish Library staff since 1958 and retired as an assistant administrator in November 1976, died on March 30.

Josephine T. Murry died on March 9. She had retired in 1974 from Southern Universsity where she had been on the library staff since 1962. From 1947 to 1960 she was on the staff of the State Library.

Consuela P. Winder died on March 13. She was the retired Librarian of the Capitol Junior High School and until June 1976 served as Research Librarian in the State Department of Education. From 1944 to 1948 she was on the staff of the State Library. — VIVIAN CAZAYOUX

MAINE

State Aid. 1977 began with an intensive effort by Maine libraries to win legislative support for a financial package that would (1) increase state aid for community library services from 10 cents to 25 cents per capita, (2) increase state support for interlibrary loan and reference services provided by the three regional resource centers, and (3) increase state aid for library development and for audiovisual services. In view of the spirit of austerity that reached from the governor's office to the halls of the legislature, it was a major triumph to have the lawmakers increase the funding to $100,000 in support of interlibrary loan and reference service.

Regional Systems. It was a triumph to secure new state aid in 1977, but the year also marked the second time that the statewide plan to widen and improve library services had won legislative endorsement. The plan, only four years in operation, joins the state's public, school, and college libraries in three regional systems.

Under the leadership of the State Library, resource sharing through the regional systems has been remarkably effective. The network of TWX and WATS lines carries thousands of reference and interlibrary loan requests from nearly 300 public and school libraries to the regional reference and resource centers. 1977 saw more than 40,000 books and other items mailed on interlibrary loan from the area resource centers.

The Health Sciences Library Information Cooperative, a separate but integrated network of libraries, has also operated for several years in Maine with great success. It gained a new director in 1977 when Margery Read assumed responsibility for the network of hospital, health agency, and academic libraries.

Maine Library Association
(founded 1893)

Membership: 854; *Annual Expenditure:* $6,558.
President: Richard Gross, Director, Lewiston Public Library (May 1976-May 1978).
Vice-President: Benita Davis, Bangor Public Library.
Secretary: Richard Sibley, Director, Waterville Public Library.
Annual Meeting: April 28-30, 1977, Rockport.
Publication: Downeast Libraries (five issues per year).

Maine State Library
J. Gary Nichols, State Librarian
Maine State Library
Augusta, Maine 04330

School Library Media Supervisor
Walter Taranko
Maine State Library
Augusta 04333

State Library. The State Library, a bureau in the state Department of Education, discovered that a special legislative committee was at work early in 1977 to establish a new state department of cultural resources. The committee report that appeared in October included a proposal to include the State Library in the new department. The Maine Library Commission and the Executive Board of the Maine Library Association (MLA) quickly went on record in opposition to the proposal. The legislature was to act on the issue early in 1978.

Maine Library Association. The annual conference of MLA was held on April 28-30 at Rockport with more than 370 members attending. The conference program centered on the theme of cooperation among school and college libraries and included workshops on audiovisual services, serials, materials selection for school libraries, standards, and state library services. Following a recent custom, the conference served as the joint annual meeting of MLA and the Maine Educational Media Association.

The fall meeting of MLA was held October 14 at Portland. The conference theme was "Energy," and those attending were involved in a series of programs centering on energy conservation and the efficient uses of energy.

Continuing Education. The Continuing Education Committee of MLA saw its goals met in 1977. With assistance from the State Library staff and a corps of qualified instructors, a series of courses on reference services and cataloging were offered at various locations around the state. Nearly 200 people from school and public library staffs participated in the program. The Continuing Education Committee plans to expand this popular and much-needed program.

Bibliographic Access. Two important bibliographic efforts were completed in 1977. The *Maine Union List of Serials*, edited by Charles Campo of the University of Maine library staff, was funded by the Larger Libraries of Maine and the Maine State Library. It is the first time Maine has had a union list of serials, and the benefit for interlibrary loan services and acquisition work was felt immediately.

Maine: A Bibliography of Its History was prepared by the Committee for a New England Bibliography. A companion to the Massachusetts volume that appeared in 1975, it organizes the sources for Maine history for the first time in many years.

Buildings. While no major building program was completed in 1977, Portland, Maine's largest city, secured funding for a new public library building. The present library, nearly a century old and seriously inadequate, will be replaced by a 76,000-square-foot building that will cost more than $5,000,000. Edward Chenevert, Director of the Portland Public Library, reported that the building program will be financed by $2,000,000 in city funds and more than $3,000,000 in federal money. Work on the new building began in the fall of 1977.

Appointments. W. Stuart Debebham was named Librarian at Colby College. The new head of the Auburn Public Library is Robert Dysinger. Patricia Weeks was named head of the public library in Gorham. The new head of the library at the University of Maine-Machias is Bert Phillips. The new head of the public library in Cape Elizabeth is Mary Stanewick.

BENITA DAVIS

MARYLAND

Master Plan. Most 1977 library activity was aimed at attaining one or more of the recommendations outlined in the state's Master Plan for library service. Within public libraries, planning efforts in the form of needs assessment studies were undertaken at local, regional, and state levels. Wherever such studies had been completed, action was being taken to acquire the necessary resources to provide the needed services. User and nonuser needs studies were initiated in the State Library for the Blind and Physically Handicapped, as well as in patient, school, and staff libraries in the Department of Health and Mental Hygiene.

State Library Resource Center. The recommendations advanced in November 1976 by the Governor's Committee to Study Funding of the State Library Resource Center (Enoch Pratt's Central Library) served as an impetus for much activity in 1977. The Committee worked to arrive at an equitable formula by which Baltimore and Maryland could share funding respon-

Maryland Library Association Inc. (founded 1923)

Membership: 1,015 (320 ALA members); *Annual Expenditure:* $34,475.
President: Ruth E. Almeida, Annapolis and Anne Arundel County Library (May 1977-May 1978).
Vice-President/President-elect: Charmaine S. Yochim, Prince George's Community College.
Executive Secretary: Jeannette Dutcher, 115 West Franklin Street, Baltimore, Maryland 21201.
Annual Meeting: April 27-29, 1977, Hunt Valley.
Publication: The Crab (bimonthly).

Maryland State Department of Education
Nettie B. Taylor, Assistant State Superintendent for Libraries and Director
Baltimore-Washington International Airport
Baltimore, Maryland 21240

School Library Media Supervisor
David R. Bender
State Department of Education
Linthicum 21240

sibilities for the Center. After delineating city and state services, percentages of monetary support were assigned.

Further recommendations addressed state and city responsibilities for planning, budget, and policy control. Spatial considerations brought a recommendation for a study to determine alternate ways to utilize present space and, if necessary, to decide appropriate means to expand the existing plant. Work began on a long-range plan for the State Library Resource Center.

Networking. The Division of Library Development and Services moved toward the realization of a definitive long-range plan for the Maryland State Library Network at a two-day workshop in May. Administrators from all types of libraries in Maryland met to study and plan for several areas of network development: communications and delivery; automation; structure, organization, and finance; policies, services, and standards; regional and local interlibrary cooperation; and national network relationships. Task forces addressed each area, and task force recommendations were referred to the Network Planning Committee. The group is charged with preparing a planning document for interlibrary networking for the five-year period from 1978 to 1982.

A committee of ten representatives from community colleges, state colleges and universities, public libraries, the State Board of Education, the State Department of Budget and Fiscal Planning, and the Maryland State Department of Education has been charged with working toward a plan for financing and studying overall library needs. Chaired by H. Joanne Harrar of the University of Maryland the committee began its tasks in 1977.

Support. A wide variety of library resources, services, and personnel existed in 1977. Per capita support for public libraries ranged from $10.98 to $3.03. As of June 30, 1976, per capita support averaged $8.41.

Support for schools also showed a wide range in per capita support for textbooks, varyng from a high of $14.12 to a low of $6.33. In the purchase of nontextbook library resources, the range was even broader, from $17.44 to $2.37 in local jurisdictions.

Pursuant to another Master Plan recommendation, legislation was passed raising state public library per capita support from $3 to $4. The new law combined operating and public library building sections from the old law. An advantage of the new bill is that a county library system may set aside up to 20 per cent of its state allocation toward capital improvements or—if new or expanded facilities are not required—may opt for using the entire amount for operating expenses.

MLA Activities. The annual conference of the Maryland Library Association (MLA) was held at Hunt Valley in April and attracted a record 558 participants. Promoting the theme of "Strategies: Present and Future," the multifaceted program featured such diverse personalities as Alphonse Trezza, Executive Director of the National Commission on Libraries and Information Science; Lucille Clifton, poet, author, and "learning mother"; Edward P. Kelly, Jr., of Academic Collective Bargaining Service; Charles H. Wheatly, Executive Secretary of the Maryland State Teachers Association; John Dessauer of *Publishers Weekly*; Alvin Schwartz, author of books for children; and a wealth of "local talent" including more than two dozen Maryland authors and educators.

MLA Awards. The Association's Distinguished Service Citation was awarded C. Keating Bowie, Chairman of the Board of Trustees of Enoch Pratt Free Library in Baltimore. Charles W. Robinson, Director of the Baltimore County Public Library, was presented the Maryland Library Association Award.

Buildings. Despite rumblings about "tight money," 1977 proved a good year for the dedication of new facilities, building additions, and ground-breaking ceremonies for getting projects under way.

The Long Branch Library of the Montgomery County Department of Public Libraries, the Woodlawn Branch of the Baltimore County Public Library, the Talbot County Free Library headquarters in Easton, and the Accident Library of the Ruth Enlow Library of Garrett County opened in 1977.

Frederick County Libraries opened its Middletown Branch in a rented storefront, and the Washington Village Library Center of Enoch Pratt Free Library opened in a renovated firehouse. The Hurlock Branch of the Dorchester County Public Library and the Frederick-Carroll Audiovisual Cooperative expanded their quarters.

Work continued on the Southern Maryland Regional Resource Center in Charlotte Hall, the Kent County Public Library headquarters in Chestertown, and the Edgewood Branch of the Harford County Library.

Construction contracts were signed in December for a 28,000-square-foot addition to the Wicomico County Free Library headquarters in Salisbury which houses the Eastern Shore Regional Resource Center and the Maryland Materials (Processing) Center. Bids were received on the construction of a 22,000-square-foot headquarters facility for the Carroll County Library in Westminster.

Potpourri. The National Endowment for the Humanities formally awarded the Regional Planning Council in Baltimore a grant of $19,841 for libraries and museums to plan for a major implementation project application.

More than 200 media professionals and administrators attended the Maryland Educational Media Organization spring conference in Hagerstown, March 27-29. Programs addressing "Sex in Young Adult Literature," "The Role of ITV in the Classroom," and "Film Study in the Curriculum" drew unusually large crowds. A second meeting in October in conjunction with the Maryland State Teachers Association was equally successful.

An overflow crowd heard William W. Warner, Pulitzer prizewinning author of *Beautiful Swimmers*, deliver the ninth annual Annis J. Duff Lecture on December 4 in the Wheeler Auditorium at Enoch Pratt Free Library.

Maryland's catalog on microfilm (Microcat) contained 800,000 titles in 1977. A third edition, including a portion of the holdings of the Johns Hopkins University, was in production.

James T. Farrell, internationally known author, helped more than 400 admirers celebrate the "Sage of Baltimore's" birthday on September 24 at Pratt Central. Farrell's topic was "The Legacy of H.L. Mencken."

Marcia Sanders, Regional Adult Field Worker at Enoch Pratt Free Library, received the 1977 William G. Baker Award for distinguished service.

People. At Enoch Pratt Free Library of Baltimore retirements included Sara L. "Bunny" Siebert, Coordinator of Young Adult Services; John F. Peacock, Superintendent of Buildings; Frances W. Covington, Adult Field Worker; Eleanor Vernon-Williams, Librarian, Gardenville; and Thelma T. Bell, Children's Field Worker. Joseph M.A. Cavanagh was appointed Systems Planner.

At Baltimore County Public Library, Donald J. Napoli, Librarian at North Point, resigned to accept the directorship of the South Bend (Indiana) Public Library. Mary Landry Eidleman, Specialist in Library Information and Referral Services, resigned from the Division of Library Development and Services to become Coordinator of Library Services at Dundalk Community College. Jean-Anne Marie South, Library Planner at the Regional Planning Council in Baltimore, left to become Program and Planning Consultant for the White House Conference on Library and Information Services.

Ending a career with the Maryland State (Law) Library that began in 1932, Nelson J. Molter retired after 45 years of state service. Michael S. Miller is the new director.

William R. Gordon was named Director of Prince George's County Memorial Library. Kieth C. Wright was appointed Dean of the College of Library and Information Services at the University of Maryland. William J. Demo was appointed Coordinator of Library Services and Douglas O. Michael has become Director of Learning Resources at Allegany Community College in Cumberland.

Deaths. Maryland's library community was saddened by the death of Evelyn Levy on February 17. Known for her special leadership qualities, she had served on ALA Council and as President of the Maryland Library Association. Her pioneering efforts were responsible for the realization of Community Action service programs set up by the Enoch Pratt Free Library to serve Baltimore's inner-city residents.

M. Bernice Wiese, retired director of library services for the Baltimore public school system, died December 12. A library consultant of international reputation, she had served as a member and officer of both the ALA and Maryland Library Association. She was a former president of the Maryland Association of School Librarians.

M. Lucia James, Professor of Curriculum and Director of the Curriculum Laboratory at the College of Education of the University of Maryland at College Park since 1965, died October 18. She had been active in many library associations including both ALA and MLA. She cochaired the ALA/AASL Committee on Treatment of Minorities in Library Materials from 1967 to 1972 and was active as a consultant and program participant.

LANCE C. FINNEY

MASSACHUSETTS

State Library Agency. 1977 was a most trying and distressing time for Massachusetts libraries and librarians as several smouldering issues developed into conflagrations. They included the resignation of the controversial Director of the Bureau of Library Extension; the reorganization of the State Agency, also a subject of some controversy; and a classic confrontation between a school librarian and a school board that reached the federal district court.

The resignation of Charles Joyce as Director of the Bureau of Library Extension marked the culmination of a long-standing disagreement between the Director and many segments of the library community. There was disagreement concerning the role and style of the Bureau and its Director, the administration of the regional library systems, and the use of federal Library Services and Construction Act

(LSCA) funds. The disagreement was first made public in February 1976 with an article written by Joyce, "LSCA: Does It Do More for Massachusetts?" The article asserted that the regional libraries in Boston, Worcester, and Springfield were unfairly obtaining too large a portion of LSCA funds.

Shortly before the article appeared the Bureau and the library community had been at loggerheads concerning representation on a committee to plan an intertype library conference. Also during 1976 and 1977 the LSCA Advisory Council had a series of confrontations with the Director and the Bureau Staff concerning the Council's right to organize itself and the failure of the Bureau to refer all proposals for LSCA funding to the Council. As 1977 began the State Agency was also faced with increasing alienation from the library community, and the unexpected resignations of two members of the Board of Library Commissioners were generally believed to be due to the growing conflict.

At the annual spring meeting of the Massachusetts Library Association (MLA) an ad hoc committee issued a report that charged the Bureau with putting too much LSCA money into the administration and strengthening of the Bureau at the expense of the regional systems and other grant programs. The report also accused the Director of bypassing the LSCA Advisory Council to get the Bureau's proposals for use of LSCA funds routinely approved by the Board of Library Commissioners.

In August upon the recommendation of the Bureau staff, the Board of Library Commissioners voted to inform the Fitchburg Public Library, one of the smaller contracting regional libraries, of the Board's intention to terminate its contract with the Library because of a two-year difference of opinion between the Bureau and the Central Regional Advisory Council concerning the regional budget. Other budget and plan-of-service problems with the Eastern Regional Library System were settled, at least temporarily, in a somewhat less dramatic manner.

With all of these issues swirling about, it was somewhat surprising that the controversy concerning the Director of the Bureau of Library Extension should culminate with a "Watergate-style" ending. A memorandum from the Director's public relations assistant belittling the efforts of an ad hoc committee appointed by the Board to deal with the regional systems was leaked to the members of the Board, to the regional administrators, and to others. The memo included disparaging remarks about the Board of Library Commissioners, several individual members of the Board, the two Bureau staff members on the ad hoc committee, and other library personnel. The resentment expressed by those mentioned in the memo and others in the library community was intense, and several weeks later the resignation of the Director of the Bureau was announced.

Despite the resignation of the Director, at the close of the year, many of the issues that had created the controversy in Massachusetts remained unresolved. The issues included the extent to which library policy in Massachusetts is to be determined in an open manner, involving the participation of all segments of the library community; the extent to which LSCA funds should be used to bolster the Bureau; and the extent to which the regional advisory councils should determine the budget and plan of service for the three regional library systems in Massachusetts.

Massachusetts Library Association (founded 1890)

Membership: 1,100 (200 ALA members); *Annual Expenditure:* $26,000.
President: Margaret Brown, Charlestown Branch, Boston Public Library (July 1977-June 1979).
Vice-President: Barbara Weaver, Worcester Public Library.
Executive Secretary: Patricia A. Demit, P.O. Box 7, Nahant, Massachusetts 01908.
Annual Conference: May 19-20, 1977, Chicopee.
Publication: Bay State Librarian (5 issues a year); *The B.S. Letter* (periodically).

Board of Library Commissioners

Alice Cahill, Acting Director
648 Beacon Street
Boston 02215

State Agency Reorganization. Despite active opposition from MLA in 1976 and less than unanimous support from the library community in 1977, legislation was enacted during the year to reorganize the State Agency. The Board of Library Commissioners and the Bureau of Library Extension were separated from the Department of Education, and the State Agency was placed under the Secretary of Educational Affairs.

The Agency, which will now be called only the Board of Library Commissioners, will continue to set standards for the certification of librarians. It will also have responsibility for the two programs of state aid to public libraries (direct grants and regional public library systems), as well as for the federally funded programs under Titles I and III of LSCA. Its former responsibility for providing school library services—including the acquisition and loan of library materials, consultative services and supporting personnel—was transferred directly to the Department of Education. In addition, the new law increased the number of commissioners from five to nine.

Chelsea School Censorship Case. In July the Chelsea School Committee removed the book *Male and Female under 18*, edited by Nancy Larrick and Eve Merriam (Avon, 1973), from the high school library because it contained an allegedly obscene poem, "The City to a Young Girl." When Sonja Coleman, the librarian, and two English teachers objected to this action, they were threatened with dismissal. Subsequently, the three faculty members, MLA, and a group of concerned Chelsea residents—claiming that both the teachers' and students' First Amendment rights had been violated—sued in federal court to have the book restored to the library.

At a pretrial hearing the federal judge ordered the book returned to the library to be loaned with parents' permission and prohibited the School Committee from seeking any reprisals against the librarian and the two teachers involved in the court case. In supporting Sonja Coleman and the two teachers, MLA stated that the Chelsea School Committee acted in violation of the First Amendment to the Constitution and the Library Bill of Rights in denying library users access to library materials. MLA noted that the librarian selected the book in accordance with policies endorsed by the profession in the School Library Bill of Rights of the American Association of School Librarians and the Students Right to Read Statement of the National Council of Teachers of English.

The trial lasted six days in November with testimony from the librarian and other witnesses, including representatives of MLA and the Simmons College Graduate School of Library Science. Many students attended the trial, which was extensively covered in the Boston newspapers and on television. The Freedom to Read Foundation has taken an interest in the case and, along with MLA, is providing financial support to the defense fund. The decision by the federal judge, which was not to be rendered until April 1978, will undoubtedly have national implications.

Financial Support. Once again legislation to increase the state aid funding for public libraries failed, primarily because of a serious fiscal crisis that has plagued Massachusetts for the past three years. In December MLA reintroduced its bill to double the per capita grants to public libraries and the three regional public library systems. Funding for these programs has not been increased since 1970. The legislature did vote approximately $125,000 in increased funding for the

Bureau of Library Extension to satisfy the federal requirement that the state match the LSCA expenditures for the administration of the Bureau.

MLA. Programming at the 1977 conferences was a mixture of theory, nitty-gritty how-to, and Association introspection. The midwinter meeting at Sturbridge centered around the keynote address on ethics delivered by Richard Hauptman. Breakout meetings dealt with the ethics of furnishing reference information that could be used in a manner to threaten society, the confidentiality of library records, open access to library shelves, and the relationships between trustees, directors, and library staffs.

The annual conference held at Chicopee in May included an all-day time management seminar. Its success was overwhelming, and similar intensive programming to parallel the standard program is planned for future meetings. The Association took an inward look in a program entitled "MLA 1890-1977, and Then What?" Feedback from participants was collected, summarized at the end of the meeting, and typed and distributed at the second day of the conference to become the basis for the adoption of new goals for MLA.

Appointments. Y.T. Feng was appointed Director of Wellesley College Libraries, succeeding Helen Brown who retired. Fay Zipkowitz was appointed Director of the Worcester Area Cooperating Libraries to succeed Ray DeBuse, now Associate Director for Networking at the Washington State Library. A. John Linford became the new Director of the New England Library Information Network (NELINET), replacing Ronald Miller, now Director of California Library Authority for Systems and Services (CLASS). C. Robin LeSueur was appointed Librarian of the Francis A. Countway Library of Medicine at Harvard University.

Barbara Pettus was elected the new editor of the *Bay State Librarian*, succeeding Karen Day, who moved to Denver. Rev. John R. Aherne, O.S.A., and Veniette O'Connor were appointed to the Board of Library Commissioners, replacing Garth Hite and Jacqueline Van Voris who resigned. ARTHUR J. KISSNER

MICHIGAN

PLA 89. August 2, 1977, was a big day for public libraries in Michigan. On that date Governor William G. Millikin signed into law Public Library Act 89. After five years of long and hard work by librarians, trustees, and friends, the new legislation became a reality and opened up a new and exciting challenge for library service in Michigan.

Taking effect immediately, the Act was funded for the first year at $7,100,000. The Act provides for the establishment of cooperative libraries, requires new levels of state funding for both public libraries and new cooperative area libraries, and provides additional funds to enable public libraries to purchase cooperative area library services.

It is now the job of the governing boards and librarians of public libraries in Michigan to write plans of service for the new cooperative service areas and to implement the law with innovative library service that will better serve the people of Michigan.

Michigan Library Association
(founded 1891)

Membership: 2,189; *Annual Expenditure:* $70,000.
President: Joann L. Wilcox, Brandon Township Library, Ortonville (November 1977-October 1978).
Vice-President/President-Elect: Robert Raz, Willard Library, Battle Creek.
Secretary: Frances H. Pletz, Lansing.
Annual Convention: September 30-October 2, 1977, Ann Arbor.
Publication: Michigan Librarian (quarterly).

Michigan Department of Education

Frances X. Scannell, State Librarian
735 E. Michigan Avenue
Lansing 48913

State School Library Media Supervisor

Mary Ann Hanna
Department of Education
Lansing 48933

Joint Annual Conference. For the first time the Michigan Library Association (MLA) and the Michigan Association for Media in Education (MAME) held a joint annual conference. Held in Dearborn, September 30-October 2, with a total registration of 1,761, the conference used the theme "Daring to Share." The banquet was held at the Ford World Headquarters with Charles Kuralt of CBS as speaker. The Great Lakes Film Conference was held at the same time as the MLA and MAME conference and had continuous film showings. Other speakers included Daniel Fader and Joyce Carol Oates.

State Senator William Faust was presented the Walter H. Kaiser Memorial Award for his outstanding work in library legislation, especially his help in the passage of Public Library Act 89. Jill Locke of the Farmington Community Library was presented the Loleta D. Fyan Award as the notable junior librarian.

The Trustee Citation of Merit went to Gretta Birchfield, trustee of the Charles A. Ransom Public Library in Plainwell. Mrs. Birchfield has served on the board for 38 years, with 20 of those years as president. Leo Dinnan, Director of the Wayne-Oakland Federated Library System, was named Michigan Librarian of the Year in 1977.

Grants. The W.K. Kellogg Foundation of Battle Creek provided $1,500,000 for the development of a statewide computer-based informational library network. The statewide Michigan program involved 24 regional library systems and 448 public and academic libraries. Grants from the Foundation ranged from $700 to $8,000, depending on the size and type of service provided. Focusing on improving services to library patrons, libraries will use the grant funds for program coordination, membership in appropriate information retrieval systems, acquisition, installation of necessary computer equipment, and in-service staff training workshops and conferences. Grants were also provided to the Michigan State Library and the Michigan Library Consortium for their program services.

The Michigan State Library distributed a grant of $400,000 under the Library Services and Construction Act (LSCA) to the four library systems that serve the state as regional film centers. The centers, each of which had previously received $150,000 in grants through LSCA, Title I, will use the current grant to increase their collections of 16mm films. Through these centers, each serving five to seven other library systems, all residents of the state have access to 16mm films. Procedures for circulating the films are determined by the systems within each region and are adapted to local conditions.

Public works grants for new buildings were received by the Cass County Library ($872,000), Sterling Heights Library ($1,600,000), and the Coldwater/Branch County Library ($721,000). Other new buildings occupied were the Portage Public Library (32,000 square feet), the Wyoming Public Library (17,500 square feet) and the Washtenaw Community College Learning Resource Center. Evart remodeled and added an addition to its building.

The branch libraries of the Kalamazoo Public Library received a federal grant for publicizing and promoting the use of the neighborhood branches and for increasing adult library usage. With the theme of "Information Places," door-to-door canvassing, a special promotional mail-a-book service, newspaper ads, radio and television spots, billboards, bus signs, and posters were the means used to reach potential patrons. In all, 50 diverse types of promotional aids were developed or purchased that centered on informing the adult nonuser of the location of the library, services, collections, and the availability of a free library card.

The Michigan Council for the Arts approved a grant to the Kent County Library for an artist-in-residence. Cynthia Nibbelink, poet and author, was selected for the position and presented programs at the 19 member libraries that emphasized Michigan folklore. The residency was for two weeks and was entitled "Festival of Michigan Folklore."

The "Read with the Radio" program is a project of the Oakland County Subregional Library for the Blind and Physically Handicapped located in Farmington and is designed for disabled persons within a 50-mile radius of radio station WDET in Detroit. A grant of $20,000 was received from the Holden Foundation for special receivers to be placed in the listeners' homes. Receivers will be used in place of radios since the broadcast will be a closed-circuit program to avoid copyright problems.

Activities. The 22 Regional Education Media Centers in Michigan have undertaken several projects that also provide benefits for the public libraries in their service areas. Repair of audiovisual equipment at low cost and with fast turnaround has recently been instituted in 17 of the Centers. Cooperative purchasing of audiovisual materials and group purchasing of films are other projects available to public libraries.

The statement "For every hour you spend on the athletic field, spend two in your library," made by the tennis star Arthur Ashe, is being used to promote libraries in Michigan. The MLA Public Relations Committee received permission from Ashe to use his statement as the focal point for publicity materials to promote libraries. Posters, bookmarks, bus signs, and radio spots were produced using Ashe's picture and statement.

The media staff of the Battle Creek Central High School ran a series of "how-to" media workshops for high school teachers. Each session had an explanation and demonstration period, followed by a supervised hands-on work time.

Two new publications became available from MLA. The Continuing Education Committee completed a publication entitled *Workshop Manual*, a step-by-step guide to planning and carrying out a successful workshop. The Academic Division of MLA published the *Directory of Michigan Academic Libraries*. The *Directory* lists employees by institution, function, and/or specialty.

People. Mary Mace Spradling, Head of the Young Adult Department of the Kalamazoo Public Library since its creation in 1957 and long active in the Young Adult Division of ALA, retired in December 1976.

Homer Chance retired as Director of the Ann Arbor Public Library in August 1977. Gene Wilson has been appointed as the new Director. Juanita Oas, Director of the Sturgis Public Library, retired in August. Fran Taube is the new Director. Beatrice Adamski retired as Director of the Hamtramck Public Library.

Arthur Curley has been appointed Associate Director for Public Services with the Detroit Public Library. Edward M. Szynaka, formerly of Massena, New York, is the new Director of the Grace A. Dow Memorial Library in Midland, replacing Karl O. Burg who retired.

Elaine Didier is the new Executive Secretary for MAME. She was formerly Materials Utilization Specialist with the Wayne County Intermediate School System.   JULE FOSBENDER

MINNESOTA

Minnesota Library Association (founded 1896)

Membership: 1,022; *Annual Expenditure:* $21,073.
President: Mary Heiges, Hopkins Public Library (September 1977-May 1978).
Vice-President/President-elect: Nancy Olson, Mankato State University.
Secretary: Darlene Weston-Elberling, Minneapolis Public Library.
Treasurer: Gary Shirk, University of Minnesota.
Annual Meeting: September 21-23, 1977, Duluth.
Publication: MLA Newsletter (9 issues a year).

Department of Education, Office of Public Libraries and Interlibrary Cooperation

William G. Asp, Director
301 Hanover Building
480 Cedar Street
St. Paul 55101

State School Library Media Supervisor

Robert H. Miller
State Department of Education
St. Paul 55101

The introduction to the Minnesota Long Range Plan for Library Service, which was revised in 1977, affirms that "facts, information, ideas and inspiration, as found in recorded communications, are absolutely necessary in the most basic sense to the growth and development of individuals and groups in contemporary society." The library in society, the responsibility of libraries as agents for the collection, retrieval, and dissemination of information to society—these ever-present issues for all librarians were particularly alive for Minnesota librarians in 1977.

Governor's Conference. The Governor's Conference on Library and Information Services, to be held in September 1978, will be Minnesota's preparation for the 1979 White House Conference. The Coordinator of the Conference is Grieg Aspnes, who for 21 years was a research librarian at Cargill, Inc. Aspnes has been deeply involved in professional activities for many years. He taught a course in special libraries for eight years at the University of Minnesota Library School. A past president of the Special Library Association (SLA), he was elected to the organization's Hall of Fame in 1977.

Access to Information. In a state whose libraries have demonstrated a commitment to shared resources and the citizen's right of access to information, the means of providing access continued to be developed and refined in 1977. Much attention was paid to bibliographic access, for physical access to documents depends on it.

The Bush Foundation of Minnesota granted the Minnesota Higher Education Coordinating Board (HECB) $134,980 to allow MINITEX (Minnesota Interlibrary Telecommunications Exchange) to install 15 additional OCLC on-line cataloging terminals in Minnesota and South Dakota. This grant and 1976 grants of $216,066 from the Bush Foundation and $88,000 from the Kellogg Foundation for a total of $439,046, provided significant support for more than 45 libraries in Minnesota, North Dakota, and South Dakota to move into on-line cataloging. The first MINITEX record was input in OCLC in December 1976, and at the end of 1977 there were more than 400,000 MINITEX records in the data base.

The Bush grant will also be used to update the South Dakota Union List of Serials and to integrate it with the existing Minnesota-North Dakota-Wisconsin serials data base. That data base, the *Minnesota Union List of Serials* (MULS), was published in its second edition late in 1977. Contained in seven volumes are more than 82,000 bibliographic entries, plus cross-references and added entries, representing the serial holdings of 220 participating libraries. On behalf of MINITEX, HECB also received a Council on Library Resources (CLR) grant of $25,000 for the planning phase of a project designed to link standard serial holdings statements to bibliographic records (CONSER).

Cooperating Libraries in Consortium (CLIC), a Twin Cities college library cooperative, received $53,422 from the

Bush Foundation for equipment to display its new COM union catalog. With special grants, MELSA (Metropolitan Library Service Agency) has been actively encouraging all libraries in its seven-county federation of public libraries to convert current acquisitions to machine-readable form. In 1977 the systems in Dakota County and Carver County began conversion of both current and retrospective records to conform to MELSA-MARC standards. MELSA funds also supported a project, currently in the systems analysis and design stage, in which the Minneapolis and St. Paul Public Libraries will convert bibliographic records to machine-readable form. The Arrowhead Library System of northeastern Minnesota began a project to convert the holdings of its member libraries to a COM union catalog housed in ROM readers. The first catalog contains 80 per cent of the holdings of the Duluth Public Library.

Bibliographic access means that physical access is possible. Statewide network services facilitate the sharing of resources among Minnesota libraries. Resource sharing in Minnesota reached an annual volume of 750,000 documented interlibrary transactions, a figure that does not represent reciprocal borrowing or measure direct use of nonlocal collections made possible by bibliographic data bases. The 150 MINITEX participants have agreed to share resources with one another through the MINITEX system. Most of the public library systems have reciprocal arrangements whereby a patron's library card is honored by neighboring systems.

Seven Minnesota counties with a total population of 141,514 began participation in regional systems to improve the quality of library service their residents receive. The number of Minnesota citizens with access to library services through regional library systems is 3,557,323, or 93.5 per cent of the state's population. A new regional library, Western Plains Library System, came into existence in 1977, as well as a new state agency library, that of the Minnesota Zoological Garden. Under the College Library Resources Program (Title II-A of the Higher Education Act), academic libraries received 52 grants totaling $197,605 for acquisition of library materials in 1977-78. Because of resource sharing, new libraries and new holdings benefit everyone in the state.

Teaching the skills patrons need to gain access to library holdings is another aspect of physical access. St. Olaf College was the recipient of a matching grant from CLR and the National Endowment for the Humanities (NEH) under their joint College Library Program. St. Olaf's Course-Related Library Instruction Program will be supported with the CLR-NEH award of $38,793 and $39,683 in institutional funds.

Legislative Activity. The 1977 Minnesota legislature voted a moderate increase in grants for public library service to $4,300,000 for the biennium 1978-79, with an additional $400,000 for 1979 contingent upon a new distribution formula. Much of this increase, however, will be directed to library regions newly eligible for services. The Office of Public Libraries and Interlibrary Cooperation (OPLIC) will have $357,000 for operating expenses in each of the two years. The Environmental Conservation Library received healthy suport, as its grant was increased from $80,000 for 1976-77 to $202,000 for the 1978-79 biennium. MINITEX Library Program funding was increased to $400,000 for 1978 and $425,000 for 1979. The University of Minnesota Libraries, whose collections are a major state resource, received a special supplementary budget for collection development.

Librarianship. The program of the Minnesota Library Association (MLA) midwinter conference offered librarians an opportunity to consider the new copyright law. At one of the most heavily attended MLA conferences ever, Barbara Ringer, U.S. Register of Copyright; Arthur Levine, CONTU Executive Director; Robert Wedgeworth, ALA Executive Director and CONTU Commissioner; Sara Case, ALA Washington Office; and Jeff Squires, CONTU Counsel, discussed the intricacies and impact of the new law. They helped Minnesota librarians develop a perspective from which to examine and implement the law.

A boon for libraries and librarians seeking continuing education information was the creation of the position of Continuing Education and Library Research Specialist by the Office of Public Libraries and Interlibrary Cooperation (OPLIC). Suzanne H. Mahmoodi, who was appointed to the new position, will help librarians and library educators by advising them on both existing opportunities and the development of new programs.

During the spring the University of Minnesota Library School organized an impressive colloquia series while Jesse Shera was on the faculty as Visiting Professor. "The Library in the Social Process" was debated by Shera and Edward Holley. Shera and William Budington discussed "Research Libraries and Society." Library service to children was considered by Shera and Peggy Sullivan. Additional guest speakers on the colloquia series were Michael Gorman, "The British Library: A Personal View" and "AACR 2," and Eileen Cooke, who spoke on the activities of the ALA Washington Office. Shera also addressed the Minnesota Special Libraries Association (SLA) and American Society for Information Science (ASIS) meeting on the "Foundations of Information Science."

Associations. An important development in 1977 was the formation of the Minnesota Statewide Library Services Forum. The Forum consists of two representatives of each of Minnesota's six library associations, with a total membership of approximately 3,000. MLA, the Minnesota Chapters of SLA and ASIS, the Minnesota Educational Media Organization, the Minnesota Health Science Library Association, and the Minnesota Association of Law Libraries have associated for the purposes of communication and cooperation in programs and services on a statewide level.

A significant event for MLA was the creation of the position of Executive Director. On January 1, Patricia Kovel-Jarboe was named to that position.

Buildings. Three new public library buildings were completed in 1977: the Minnesota Valley Regional Library headquarters in Mankato, the North St. Paul Branch of the Ramsey County Library, and the Warren Branch of the Northwest Regional Library. Construction began on the new $6,000,000 Duluth Public Library building.

Awards. Sanford Berman, Hennepin County Library Head Cataloger and editor of the *HCL Cataloging Bulletin*, was named MLA Librarian of the Year. MLA Trusteee of the Year was Dorothy Caron, a trustee of the Virginia Public Library. Audrey Grosch, of the University of Minnesota Libraries and President of ASIS, received the SLA 1977 Professional Award. The Hennepin County Library received two 1977 New County, USA Achievement Awards from the National Association of Counties for "outstanding programs that can be adapted for use by other counties in the country." The winning programs were the used bookstore and services to Vietnamese.

ALICE WILCOX
ANDREA HONEBRINK

MISSISSIPPI

Multitype Library Network. A multitype library network working paper has been prepared by Gerald Buchanan, Assistant Director for Library Operations of the Mississippi Library Commission (MLC). It has been prepared for discussion and action by the MLC Director, staff, and Board of Commissioners; the Mississippi Library Association (MLA) Long-Range Planning Committee; the LSCA Advisory Council; and the CLAM Task Force. The CLAM Task Force and MLA Long-Range

Planning Committee have officially endorsed the concepts and have adopted the working paper as a basis for further discussion and action.

The recommendations of the paper are based on the following underlying assumptions: (1) the library user's needs are paramount; (2) cooperation among libraries is essential; (3) unnecessary duplication of materials and services is wasteful and expensive; (4) local resources should be used first; (5) specialized resources should be centralized; (6) MLC should be the administrative agency; (7) authority should be delegated as needed; (8) building on existing strengths is essential; and (9) the Planning and Development Districts (PDD) should be the basic unit for public library systems.

The goal of the proposed network is to increase the availability, quantity, and quality of library resources and services and to promote their use. The two major elements of the network design are district resource libraries and state resource centers. Network support funds—including grants for personnel, building, and materials—would be channeled to and through these libraries and centers.

Other elements of the network design include (1) centralized automated cataloging through SOLINET-OCLC; (2) telecommunications of interlibrary loan requests; (3) production of a statewide union microfiche catalog based on SOLINET-OCLC archival tapes; (4) a statewide interlibrary loan code and library card; and (5) a coordinated plan of acquisitions.

Mississippi Library Association (founded 1909)

Membership: 1,235; *Annual Expenditure:* $32,225 (1977).
President: Jim Anderson, First Regional Library, Hernando (January-December 1977).
Vice-President/President-elect: Jim Parks, Millsaps College Library, Jackson.
Secretary: Barbara Carroon, Hinds County Schools, Jackson.
Treasurer: Caroline Killens, Department of Archives and History, Jackson.
Annual Conference: October 26-28, 1977, Jackson.
Publication: Mississippi Library News (quarterly).

Mississippi Library Commission

Jack Mulkey, Director
P.O. Box 3260
Jackson 39207

State School Library Media Supervisor

Yvonne C. Dyson
State Department of Education
Jackson 39206

Publications. The Mississippi State University Libraries received a grant from the Mississippi Library Commission to prepare the second edition of the two-volume *Mississippiana: Union Catalog and Union List of Newspapers.* The first edition was published in 1971. George Lewis, Director of Libraries, directed the project, while Thomas W. Henderson and Susan M. Fitzgerald compiled and edited the records reported by the participating libraries. Forty-four of the 56 libraries that participated in the first edition submitted their holdings for the second edition.

The *Mississippiana: Union Catalog*, the first of the two-volume work, contains approximately 17,600 items listed by main entry, title, and subject. The entries, which are mainly monographs, contain complete information in the author and title sections, including holding library numbers.

The second volume is a 90-page, two-column union list of Mississippi newspapers held by participating libraries in the state. Included in the publication are the beginning and ending (where appropriate) publishing dates of the newspapers plus a brief history including editors and publishers, title changes, and the frequency of publication. The *Union List of Newspapers* was set in type and published in microfiche. The *Union Catalog* was produced by computer output microfiche.

The Mississippi Research and Development Center received a grant of $8,300 from the Mississippi Library Commission to compile and publish the second edition of the *Mississippi Union List of Periodicals* in microfiche.

MLA Annual Conference. "Library Users Profit from Automation" was the topic of CLAM '77, the MLA preconference meeting. Librarians interested in automation, networking, and resource sharing came from six states to hear Allen Kent of the University of Pittsburgh and Rod Swartz, Washington State Librarian, discuss the issues related to the conference theme.

CLAM officers for 1978 are Carol West, Mississippi College Law Library, President; Jeannetta Roach, Tougaloo College, Vice-President; and Missy Lee, Mississippi Research and Development Center, Secretary-Treasurer.

The theme of the annual conference was "Can You Hear Us Now?"—an effort centered on communications between the Association and the membership. With programs on children's, reference, and technical services, bibliographic instruction to the patron, copyright law, government documents, education for librarianship, and censorship, the conference had something of interest for everyone. Guest speakers included Art Plotnick, editor of *American Libraries*; Edward Holley, Dean of the School of Library Science at the University of North Carolina; Lee Brawner, Executive Director of the Oklahoma County Libraries System; Patsy Perritte, School of Library Science at Louisiana State University; Henry Stewart, Old Dominion University; Norm Barbee, Government Printing Office; and Anthony Miele, Alabama Public Library Service. MLA planned to hold a joint conference with the Alabama Library Association in Birmingham in April, 1978.

News. Three counties joined regional libraries during 1977: Holmes County joined the Mid-Mississippi Regional Library in Kosciusko; Chicksaw County joined the Dixie Regional Library in Pontotoc; and Walthall County joined the Pike-Amite Regional Library in McComb.

Construction was completed and dedications held for 14 new or renovated public library buildings. Financing was made through state revenue sharing funds combined with matching local funds.

J.B. Howell, editor, and Evelyn Tackett, business manager of the *Mississippi Library News*, resigned their positions. Kay Miller assumed the responsibilities of business manager. New joint editors are Jim Parks, Elizabeth Long, and J.B. Howell. Carolyn Newton will continue as managing editor.

Mississippi libraries joined SOLINET during the year included the University of Mississippi, the University of Southern Mississippi, Millsaps College, the Mississippi College Law Library, and the Jackson Metropolitan Library System. Mississippi State University was a charter member of SOLINET.

The following libraries formed a consortium to acquire computer assisted information retrieval services from Bibliographic Retrieval Services (BRS): the University of Mississippi Medical Center Library, the University of Mississippi, the University of Southern Mississippi, and Mississippi University for Women.

People. Bette M. Rice was promoted from Head of Humanities Reference to Assistant Director for Public Services at the Mississippi State University Libraries. Louise Hurdle, Reference Librarian in Social Sciences at Mississippi State University, retired after eight years of service on the staff. Ed Walters, Head of Special Collections at the University of Mississippi Library, became Director of East Tennessee State University Library in Johnson City. Dennis Reed, Head of Information Services at the Mississippi Library Commission, resigned to join a private firm in California as a consultant. Linda Allman, Head of Technical Processing at the Mississippi Library Commission, resigned to return to South Carolina. Ted Campbell, Head of Services for the Handicapped at the Mississippi Library Commission, resigned to become Director of the Odessa Public Library in Texas.

Hazle Carter became Head Librarian of Northeast Mississippi Junior College in Booneville. Helen Mullen became Head Librarian of Copiah-Lincoln Junior College in Wesson. She succeeded Frances Frazier who retired. Margaret A. Guthrie retired as Librarian of Harriette Person Memorial Library in Port Gibson.

Meg Murphy joined the staff of the Mississippi Library Commission. She had previously been Parish Librarian at Jefferson Davis Library in Jennings, Louisiana. Dave Woodburn assumed the position of Director of the Washington County Library System in Greenville. Jess Nettles, Jr., became Director of the Oktibbeha County Library in Starkville.

Jane Smith assumed the position of Director of the Yazoo-Sharkey-Issaquena Library System, coming to the state from Concordia Parish Library in Ferriday, Louisiana. Lai-Ying Hsiung was named Veterinary Medicine Librarian at Mississippi State University.

Virginia F. Toliver, formerly Acting Library Director at Alcorn State University, became Reference Librarian at the University of Southern Mississippi Library. Kay Miller, Head of Reference Services at the Mississippi Research and Development Center, became Assistant Director for Public Services at the University of Southern Mississippi Library.

Joseph Rosenblum joined the University of Mississippi Library staff as Senior Reference Librarian. John Nunelee, Assistant Director and Head of Public Services at the Mississippi State University Libraries, accepted the position as Library Director at Sam Houston State University at Huntsville, Texas. J.B. Howell, Librarian at Mississippi College, was elected President of the Southeastern Library Association.

George Lewis, Director of Libraries at Mississippi State University, participated in the Science and Land Grant Libraries Conference held at Colorado State University. Lewis's presentation, "Introducing and Administering On-Line Information Retrieval Services," included comments on the Mississippi State University Library's newly established Computer Assisted Information Retrieval Service.

GEORGE LEWIS

MISSOURI

MLA. A significant step was made for library cooperation in Missouri when the MLA membership unanimously adopted a networking document at the 77th annual Conference. In preparation for nearly a year, the document proposes goals and a model for statewide library networking.

The annual conference theme was resource sharing—its problems and benefits. Allen Kent of the University of Pittsburgh and Ernest E. Doerschuk, Pennsylvania State Librarian, were the principal speakers. MLA divisions sponsored lectures by Arnold Lobel, children's author; M.E. Kerr, author of *Dinby Hocker Shoots Smack* and other popular young adult novels; and John Hinkle of the Oklahoma State Library.

Missouri Library Association
(founded 1900)

Membership: 1,256; *Annual Expenditure:* $57,500.
President: Harold R. Jenkins, Kansas City Public Library (September 1977-September 1978).
Vice-President/President-Elect: Judith Armstrong, Drury College, Springfield.
Secretary: Sue Ann Schlosser, Ferguson Municipal Public Library.
Annual Conference: September 28-30, 1977, Columbia.
Publication: MLA Newsletter (bimonthly).

Missouri State Library
Charles O'Halloran, State Librarian
308 E. High Street
Jefferson City 65101

State School Library Media Supervisor
Carl Sitze
State Department of Education
Jefferson City 65101

The Ghost on Saturday Night by Sidney Fleischman won the 1977 Mark Twain Award. Almost 45,000 children from 230 schools and libraries voted for their favorite book in the seventh annual program. The Award is sponsored by MLA and the Missouri Association of School Librarians (MASL).

Three hundred school librarians and media specialists attended the MASL spring conference held at Kansas City's Crown Center. Lillian Friedman, vice-president of Brentano's bookstores, spoke on her 40 years in the book business. S.E. Hinton, author of *The Outsider* and *Rumblefish*, talked about adolescent traumas and her successful books; and Leo and Dianne Dillon described the joint creative efforts that brought them the Caldecott Medal two years in a row. Other conference sessions included workshops on time management and assertiveness training.

The Outreach Round Table (ORRT) assumed a leadership role in forming a regional outreach group called the Library Outreach Cooperative (LOC) that will collect and disseminate information on outreach activities on interstate and intrastate levels. Representatives from a number of Midwestern states met twice in 1977 to discuss objectives and projects and to appoint area representatives.

ORRT and the Children's Services Division sponsored a workshop on library services to the mentally retarded. Exceptional children, state services, library modifications for the handicapped, evaluation of programs, and work with community groups were some of the subjects covered.

The Reference Committee offered a workshop on legal materials and services. Several questions were dealt with: When does reference guidance become legal counseling? What constitutes unauthorized practice of law? How does a librarian get patrons who need legal assistance to the right person or place?

State Library. On July 1 the State Library assumed direct management and control of the Wolfner Memorial Library for the Blind and Physically Handicapped in St. Louis. Before the change, St. Louis Public Library had administered the Library. As one of 56 regional libraries for the blind and physically handicapped in the United States, Wolfner offers statewide library service to 5,000 active readers.

Implementation of the new state documents depository law signed in 1976 was well under way in 1977. Two types of depositories, full and partial, have been established. Ten full depositories and 17 partial depositories receive publications from agencies of the state government. The State Library is the distribution center for the system.

Topics for the annual summer institutes were supervision in libraries and the health sciences. Cosponsored by the State Library and the University of Missouri's School of Library and Informational Science, the institutes drew participants and trustees from all types of libraries.

The State Library held a series of workshops for state agency personnel on commercial data bases, census materials, and services offered by the Library. Speakers included a representative from the U.S. Bureau of the Census, a consultant from SDC, and area librarians.

The third oral tradition workshop was devoted to drama and attracted children's and young adult librarians and educators and students from Missouri and a number of other states. Sponsored by the State Library and the Southwest Missouri State University's Department of Speech and Theatre, the workshop featured Tomie de Paola, children's author and illustrator;

author Bernice Carlson; Carolyn Fellman, children's theatre specialist; and Leslie Irene Coger, a noted drama teacher and author.

Meryl Atterberry, Coordinator of the Government Documents Division of the State Library for six years, resigned and was succeeded by Maggie Johnson, the Library's Federal Documents Librarian. Atterberry developed the state documents collection and was instrumental in the passage of House Bill 1021, which authorized a state documents depository system.

Programs, Services, Networks. Changes in service hours in six branches of the St. Louis Public Library went into effect April 4. Fewer morning hours are being retained, and two branches will be open only three days a week. The shorter hours will reduce operating cost for the facilities at an estimated savings of $160,000 during the next three years. The change is part of a general economy plan that will include reductions in staff, cost-cutting operational procedures, and purchase of fewer reading materials.

The Kansas City Libraries Metropolitan Information Network (MINET), a cooperative of all types of libraries, began operation in 1977. MINET provides on-line searching services to patrons in a two-state, multicity area. Selected staff members from participating libraries were trained as searchers on various commercial data bases. Patrons and libraries in the metropolitan area have access to the data bases of the National Library of Medicine, Lockheed, SDC, BRS, OCLC, and the Information Bank. T. Philip Tompkins of the University of Missouri-Kansas City Libraries serves as the project director.

St. Louis County Library patrons now scan microfilm readers instead of card catalogs to search for materials. The Library is the first in Missouri to convert to a microfilm catalog. Studies conducted by the Library revealed that $70,000 in costs could be saved by eliminating the card catalog. The new catalog is updated every three months. St. Louis County presently circulates more than six million books a year to a population of 770,000.

Conferences on the new copyright law were held in Kansas City and St. Louis. Sponsored by area library and education consortia, the conferences dealt with the effect of the law on schools and libraries. Speakers included representatives from the Copyright Office, Encyclopaedia Britannica, ALA, and the American Association of University Professors. Area lawyers and librarians attempted to answer questions and discuss adoption of policies and procedures for handling requests through interlibrary loan and network operations.

The question of censorship was the subject of an informative conference sponsored by Central Missouri State University. Primarily directed at school boards and libraries, the conference covered topics such as parental pressure on school librarians to remove "offensive" books from the library, selection policies, students' rights, and the purpose of school libraries. Also featured was a presentation by a school board member who was involved in a censorship case over the book *Go Ask Alice*.

People. John Bruce Robertson was appointed Commissioner of Higher Education for Missouri. Before coming to Missouri, Robertson was Assistant Chancellor for Research and Development in the New Jersey Department of Higher Education.

Harold E. Holland, Assistant Professor in the School of Library and Informational Science at the University of Missouri-Columbia, accepted a one-year appointment in the Department of Library Science at Pahlavi University in Shiraz, Iran.

Paxton P. Price resigned as Director of the St. Louis Public Library in November. He had been Director since 1969. Price served as Missouri State Librarian from 1949 to 1964 and held positions with the U.S. Office of Education and UNESCO. Harry C. Bock, Business Manager of the Library, is Acting Director during the search for Price's successor.

Martha Carroll was named MIDLNET (Midwest Regional Library Network, Inc.) and OCLC Coordinator for Missouri and Iowa. Bruce Russell was appointed Director of the newly established Camden County Library District.

Gertrude Zimmer, Director of the Ozark Regional Library since 1966, retired and was succeeded by John Mertens. Before accepting the job at Ozark Regional Mertens was a learning resources specialist at Three Rivers Community College in Poplar Bluff.

Isabel Evans retired after 13 years as Director of the St. Joseph Public Library. She was succeeded by Frederick von Lang who came to Missouri from Maine where he directed the Auburn Public Library.

Beth Arnett became Director of the Boonslick Regional Library after Richard Parker resigned to join the Tulsa City-County Library as Assistant Director.

Joyce Balogh succeeded Daniel Bradbury as Director of the Rolling Hills Consolidated Libraries. She had worked as an extension and branch supervisor for the Library.

Virginia Walton, Adult Services Librarian at the Mid-Continent Public Library since 1966, retired in January. Well known for her work with the handicapped and with community groups, Walton developed two resource centers for the handicapped at branches of the Mid-Continent library.

The governing board of The Poetry Society of America appointed Charles Guenther as its Regional Vice-President. Guenther was Chief of the Technical Library at the Defense Mapping Agency's Aerospace Center in St. Louis. Wendy Hartwig is the new director of the Thompson Library at Tarkio College.

Deaths. Joseph C. Shipman, Director of the Linda Hall Library of Science and Technology from its beginning in 1945 until his retirement in 1974, died June 12. Under his direction, the Kansas City institution became the second largest privately endowed library in the United States.

William Kurth, University Librarian for Washington University's Libraries since 1969, died February 27. Kurth's book, *Moving a Library*, was published in 1966 and became a standard guide for moving a library collection.

Lucy Lomax, former Director of Scenic Regional Library and one of Missouri's leading proponents of library cooperation, died October 29. She had worked with citizens' groups in three counties to establish the regional system.

Philip Brooks, the first Director of the Harry S. Truman Library, died June 24. He had spent 36 years in government service, most of which were with the National Archives and Records Service.

Sharon O. Willis, Assistant Professor in the University of Missouri-Columbia School of Library and Informational Science, died August 3. Active in both state and national library associations, Willis had served as President of the Missouri Library Association and had received many awards for her distinguished service to the profession.

Awards. The Washington University East Asian Library in St. Louis was the recipient of a matching grant of $10,000 from the Commemorative Association for the Japan World Exposition of 1970.

Charles O'Halloran, Missouri State Librarian, received the Outstanding Service Award for his work as Interim Commissioner of Higher Education.

At the annual MLA conference Jack Conroy, author of *The Disinherited*, received the MLA award for literary excellence. Virginia Walton, retired Adult Services Librarian of Mid-Continent Public Library, was honored for meritorious achievement. Dianne Myers, a former planner for the Kansas City Public Library, and Jane Weitkemper, the founder of Daniel Boone Regional Library's Outreach Department, were recognized for their leadership in establishing the MLA Outreach Round Table.

MASL honored Helen Smith as Librarian of the Year during its spring conference. Smith is Librarian at the Horton Watkins

Senior High School in Ladue.

State Librarian Charles O'Halloran is the new Chairman of the Missouri Committee for the Humanities, Inc. He was elected for a two-year term. The Committee is the state-based arm of the National Endowment for the Humanities.

MADELINE MATSON

MONTANA

Montana Library Association
(founded 1906)

Membership: 559; *Annual Expenditure:* $8,746.97.
President: Alene Cooper, Montana State Library, Helena (June 1977-May 1978).
Secretary: Darlene Preble, Montana State Library, Helena.
Vice-President/President-elect: Lucille Thompson, Montana State University, Bozeman.
Annual Meeting: May 5-7, 1977, Billings.
Publication: President's Newsletter (4 issues a year).

Montana State Library

Alma S. Jacobs, State Librarian
930 East Lyndale Avenue
Helena 59601

School Library Media Supervisor

Monica Kittock Sargent
Office of the Superintendent of Public Instruction
Helena 59601

Legislation. A far-reaching bill revising local government laws—which would have made library boards optional, limited their authority, and altered the present stipulated tax levies—was deferred for further study in 1977. This will give library friends more opportunity to seek revision or elimination of those parts of the bill seen as not in the best interests of library development in the state.

The legislature did pass a bill to provide for a historical records network involving units of the Montana University System and the Montana Historical Society; but no funds were provided in 1977, and full implementation of the network will be delayed. In the meantime, a steering committee began moving ahead with plans and with such implementation as is feasible by participants from their own budgets.

Montana Library Association. The Montana Library Association (MLA) conference in Billings on May 5-7 had as its theme "Today and Tomorrow." The conference centered around a series of continuing education workshops and a series of library-media forums emphasizing the "Library-Media Impact, Today and Tomorrow." Principal speakers were David Smith, Dean of the School of Education of the University of Montana, and Bernard Franckowiak of the University of Washington's School of Librarianship. The conference was sparked by a "Library Fair" night that featured ideas, programs, and facilities presented by libraries and librarians from throughout the state in a county fair atmosphere.

The Association's award for School Library Administrator of the Year was presented to Peggy Gadbow of Missoula, and the Trustee of the Year Award was presented to John Trangmoe of Glendive. Life Memberships were presented to Lura Currier, retiring Director of the Pacific Northwest Bibliographic Center, and to Doris Mart, Librarian of the Garfield County Free Library. Special honor was paid to Doris Wilson, a life member of the Association who is leaving the state.

State Library Activities. Although the demonstration program instituted by the State Library Commission in 1976 failed to assure adoption of the statewide levy for state funding of libraries, the effort did result in more counties joining the library federation system. In 1977, 42 of the 56 counties in the state participated in federations.

The State Library and MLA began working together in planning for the state's Pre-White House Conference on Library and Information Services in October 1978. The MLA Library Development Committee's study of multitype library cooperation and networking has contributed to preparing the background for the Conference and has pointed up the hope of achieving state funding for libraries through this approach.

The State Library is developing the capacity for automated data base search services as part of its program to serve state agencies and as a backup for federations. The State Library also is participating in planning an integrated energy information system in cooperation with the Montana Energy Office and the University of Montana Library.

Grants of $1,000 each were made to 60 Montana public libraries during 1977 as a stimulus to library development. The grants were made on the basis of criteria established by the State Library Commission.

School, Academic, and Public Libraries. Through the Office of the Superintendent of Public Instruction, school libraries in the state have undergone an extensive survey study resulting in recommended standards for school libraries and media centers. Hearings and debates over adoption of the standards will be held.

The Inter-unit Librarians Committee of the Montana University System is studying ways of establishing an automated circulation system linking the six units. At the same time the Committee is working on plans for participation in a library network, with the chief consideration being the new Washington Library Network. Both of these efforts will serve as pilots for similar developments on a state level involving all types of libraries.

The Billings Public Library is in the process of implementing an automated circulation system, which will make it the second public library in the state to do so. (Lewis and Clark Library in Helena is the other.) The Billings library also continues to expand its microfiche catalog of holdings.

Buildings. New public library buildings were completed in Malta and Sunburst during the year. The Flathead County Library was nearing completion of a major addition to facilitate its services to the city of Kalispell and to Flathead County, as well as to Flathead Valley Community College by contract. Work was to begin in December 1977 on completion of the University of Montana Library building, which was opened in 1974 with two of its five floors incomplete.

Networks. The *Union List of Montana Serials*, sponsored by MLA and funded by a grant from the State Library Commission's LSCA funds, was distributed to participating libraries in the state. As its value to the Montana Information Network Exchange was demonstrated, plans were being made for a further edition.

EARLE C. THOMPSON

NEBRASKA

1977 Priorities. At the end of 1976 Charles Gardner, President of the Nebraska Library Association (NLA), set four priorities for 1977: intellectual freedom, legislative action, library cooperation, and continuing education. At the end of 1977, a summary of the year's activities gave evidence of programs and progress in all four areas.

Intellectual Freedom. By making the Intellectual Freedom Committee (IFC) a standing committee instead of a special committee appointed at the discretion of the President, NLA emphasized its commitment to intellectual freedom. Its Executive Board also approved IFC's statement of "Procedures of the Intellectual Freedom Committee of the Nebraska Library Association," published in the Summer 1977 *NLA Quarterly*.

Judith Krug from the ALA Office for Intellectual Freedom was the keynote speaker at the annual conference of NLA, which had "Freedom of Access/Freedom of Choice: Removing Barriers to Information" as its theme. The film *The Speaker* was shown at two special sessions, each followed by a discussion period. The School, Children's, and Young People's Section of NLA had a program with Carol Starr speaking on the subject "Adolescent Materials—Access and Censorship." The conference ended with a symposium featuring the key convention speakers on "Freedom of Access/Freedom of Choice: Problems and Prospects."

Nebraska Library Association
(founded 1895)

Membership: 980; *Annual Expenditure:* $11,375.
President: Margery Curtiss, Educational Service Unit 14, Sidney (October 1977-October 1978).
Vice-President/President-elect: Ann Reinert, Nebraska State Historical Society Library.
Executive Secretary: Louise Boyd Shelledy, 3420 South 27th Street, Lincoln, Nebraska 68506.
Annual Conference: October 20-21, 1977, Omaha.
Publication: NLA Quarterly.

Nebraska Library Commission

John L. Kopischke, Director
1420 P Street
Lincoln 68508

School Library Media Supervisor

John Courtney
Department of Education
Lincoln 68509

Legislative Action. Special funding for the Legislative Committee provided financial support for the chairman's attendance at the Washington legislative workshop; the preparation of a slide/tape program which was shown at spring meetings in all of the state network regions; a special interest group program, "Opening Doors to Total Access," at the annual conference; and the development of a new legislative action plan ultimately aimed at establishing a network system to keep members informed of legislative matters.

Library Cooperation. Major efforts in library cooperation were led by the Nebraska Library Commission (NLC) and by the directors of postsecondary educational libraries. The State Library Commissioners created a study committee to review the structure and purpose of its advisory council. As a result, the Nebraska Advisory Council on Libraries was formally structured to provide advice and counsel to the Commission from all types of libraries and interests in the library community.

Major NLC projects funded and initiated or continued under LSCA monies included the following: a computer output microform union catalog of the holdings of the state's community and technical colleges to supplement the Nebraska Union Catalog begun in 1937, which has never included any such library collections; statewide extension of regional mail-a-book service for rural residents; audiovisual service with equipment and materials for a six-county region provided by libraries and bookmobiles from Thomas and Hooker Counties in the Sandoz Network; a rotating collection of large-print materials to serve all network libraries; continuation and updating of filmstrip and cassette collections to serve all networks; purchase and circulation of alcoholism resources for use throughout the Panhandle Network; development and utilization of a centralized processing center using the OCLC system in the Northern Network in conjunction with Wayne State College; cooperation in the Sandoz Network with a migrant summer school for Mexican Americans to provide story hours and activity classes for children; extension of a joint project with the Sioux City (Iowa) Public Library to provide library service to Native Americans in the Winnebago Reservation area; and updating the union list of serials developed in 1972 in the Panhandle Network.

Postsecondary Educational Library Directors of Nebraska broadened its scope to promote participation by all public and private institutions engaged in adult education. Its new name is Postsecondary Educational Libraries and Resource Centers of Nebraska (PELARCON).

Continuing Education. Through projects supported by LSCA funds, NLC directed the following activities: hired an advisor in the Sandoz Network to assess needs and demands and subsequently to assist library staff members with weeding, cataloging, and classification; employed a part-time librarian in the Metro Network to provide training as needed and to conduct one- and two-credit courses offered through the University of Nebraska at Omaha; arranged workshops for librarians, trustees, and volunteers on topics of concern in the various networks; developed a slide and tape presentation in the Northern Network to educate the public on available services and materials; prepared a bibliography of current professional library materials for continuing education; and established and set aside space for a center for readers at the Omaha Public Library for adults in beginning reading and learning English as a second language.

Outreach. Among the extension projects of Nebraska libraries in 1977 were providing film projectors for use in senior citizens homes, low-income housing units, and programs for trainable retarded adults; securing funds for purchase of library materials for jail inmates and visually impaired and physically handicapped citizens; establishing storefront collections and reading centers in communities with no public libraries; and equipping a retired bookmobile as a traveling cataloging office to serve small public libraries in the Sandoz and Central Districts.

People. NLA presented its 1977 Trustee Citation to Mrs. Glen Houston of Imperial and the Meritorious Service Award posthumously to Laura E. Berge of Lisco. Berge had been Librarian at Oshkosh Public School and at Hiram Scott College and Coordinator of the Panhandle Network.

Other librarians who died in 1977 were Ethel Jane Maurer, retired from library positions at Lincoln City Libraries and the 1975 winner of the Meritorious Service Award, and Catherine N. Beal, Librarian at Omaha Public Library since 1923 and the 1970 winner of the Meritorious Service Award.

Major new appointments in Nebraska libraries were Raymond Means, Director of Alumni Memorial Library of Creighton University, who left a position as Acting Director at the University of Nebraska at Omaha, and Robert M. Braude, Director of the Library at the University of Nebraska Medical Center, who came from the University of Colorado Medical Center. David Bishop, the previous Director of the University of Nebraska Medical Center, assumed a similar position at the University of California Medical Center in San Francisco.

Carol Dick Buell from De Vry Institute of Technology in Chicago became Coordinator of Instructional Resources for the Metropolitan Technical Community College.

Significant by virtue of their unique positions in Nebraska were Jean Hofacket, the Outreach Librarian for the Mari Sandoz Network, and Linda Bramer, the Itinerant Librarian for the Metropolitan Network.

Buildings. Two large new buildings were occupied in 1977 in Omaha—the $4,100,000 Creighton University Health Sciences Library/Learning Resource Center and Biomedical Communications Center and the $7,000,000 W. Dale Clark Library, which replaced the 1894 Omaha Public Library building. The latter is located at the head of a new Central Park Mall being developed in downtown Omaha.

It is also noteworthy that Lincoln City Libraries, which had the first Nebraska Carnegie building in 1901, celebrated its centennial in 1977 with the final phase of its three-phase construction of the Bennett Martin Library begun in 1962.

New library buildings in Blair, Elgin, and Norfolk were completed in 1977. The commitment and dedication of other small Nebraska communities to library service at a time when building costs are prohibitive was indicated by the remodeling of several different kinds of buildings for public library use. These included a former power and light building in Columbus, a converted store building in Polk, and a jail in Strang. Waterloo shares a new building with a water pumping station, and Papillion has the top floor of the three-level City Hall. Albion constructed a two-level addition to an old Carnegie building.

Publications. Several new and revised editions of publications were produced in 1977: *Nebraska Library Trustee Manual*; the revised *Nebraska Library Association Handbook*; *Manual: Procedures of the Intellectual Freedom Committee of the Nebraska Library Association*; the revised *Handbook on Intellectual Freedom*; *A Postsecondary Educational Library Inventory Information System*; *A Nebraska Regional Automated Bibliographic Information System: A Proposal to Replicate an Existing Library Bibliographic System in Nebraska*; *Guidelines for School Library Use of Public Libraries: A Cooperative Effort of the Nebraska Department of Education and the Nebraska Library Commission*; and a list of recommended qualifications for trustee appointments to a library board to be sent through the League of Municipalities to all city councils and mayors as a guide for appointments.

VIVIAN A. PETERSON

NEVADA

Library development in Nevada continues to be characterized by interlibrary cooperation. The most significant events of 1977 demonstrated this spirit of community among Nevada librarians.

Automation. The computer continues to make rapid advances in Nevada, and interlibrary cooperation plays an important role. At the end of 1977 the Clark County (Las Vegas) Library District was in the process of making arrangements with two other users of the LIBS 100 Circulation Control System in California to query one another's data bases for more efficient interlibrary borrowing.

Serial locations in Arizona libraries were added to the Serials in Nevada data base, which then became the fourth edition of the *Intermountain Union List of Serials*. The Nevada State Library has distributed the first issue of its computerized *Title Locator Index*, an alphabetical listing with locations of more than 15,000 titles held in libraries throughout Nevada. The State Library is now producing its monthly list, *Nevada Official Publications*, by computer, and by the end of 1977 the retrospective catalog of Nevada documents was in its last stages of completion.

The University of Nevada (Reno) Library joined BALLOTS in 1977. Other Nevada libraries were on the brink of doing the same or of producing microfilm catalogs or converting to computerized circulation systems. All were working cooperatively toward systems that are compatible with those already in operation.

A major figure in the development of computerized data bases in Nevada has been Robert G. Anderl of the University of Nevada (Las Vegas) Library. In recognition of his efforts, the Nevada Library Association (NLA) awarded him its Special Citation for 1977.

**Nevada Library Association
(founded 1946)**

Membership: 178; *Annual Expenditure:* $11,373.
President: Robert G. Anderl, University of Nevada, Las Vegas (January 1978-December 1978).
Vice-President/President-elect: Ann Thompson, Clark County Library, Las Vegas.
Secretary: Allen Schwartz, Boulder City Library.
Annual Convention: September 29-October 1, 1977, Ely.
Publication: Highroller (9 issues a year).

Nevada State Library

Joseph J. Anderson, State Librarian
Carson City 89701

School Library Media Supervisor

William F. Arensdorf
Nevada State Department of Education
Carson City 89710

Construction. For a state the size of Nevada, library construction has continued at a remarkable rate. A new 3,200-square-foot building was constructed for the Lyon County (Yerington) Library in 1976, and by the end of 1977 construction had started on another new building for the Mineral County (Hawthorne) Public Library. In Las Vegas the Clark County Library was expanding in all directions at once. The new Sunrise Branch Library opened in a storefront location in January 1977, and the Las Vegas Library moved into larger and more accessible quarters in a shopping center. Construction also began on a $1,800,000 facility for the Charleston Heights Library and Performing Arts Center. In Incline Village near Lake Tahoe, a new facility was under construction in 1977 for a branch of the Washoe County Library. Plans were finalized for a new branch library building for the Douglas County Public Library. An addition to its Minden headquarters was almost completed by the end of the year.

Nevada's academic libraries are growing just as rapidly. In the early part of the year the North Campus of the Western Nevada Community College moved into a new facility, as did its Learning Resources Center. In August the University of Nevada (Reno) Library opened its $3,200,000 addition, which increased stack space by 58 per cent and added 500 additional seating spaces. By the end of the year the University of Nevada (Las Vegas) Library was planning a new addition.

Intellectual Freedom. Nevada's biennial legislature took a major step forward in 1977 by unanimously enacting a bill that directs a legislative commission "to study the provisions of Nevada law which relate to obscenity, review relevant court decisions which deal with obscenity, and examine workable obscenity laws of other states" and to report findings and recommendations to the legislature in 1979. Most significantly, the resolution mandates participation in the study by representatives of NLA, which has successfully opposed anti-obscenity bills in past sessions.

The legislature also approved funding for professional librarians in two of Nevada's three correctional institutions. All three have in the past participated in LSCA demonstration projects involving professional staffing, and one institution continued to be staffed by a librarian through LSCA funding.

Continuing Education. A workshop on proposal writing was sponsored by the Nevada State Library, the first of several successful continuing education activities held for Nevada library staff members. The Clark County Library received a grant to hold a unique training activity for library aides from the remote communities of central Nevada. Members of the Clark County Library staff spent four days in Tonopah instructing the aides in a wide variety of library processes and programs, including cataloging, book selection, and children's services.

A series of workshops funded by LSCA on literature for children and young adults was held in Reno, Elko, and Las Vegas and featured Mae Durham Roger of the School of Library and Information Studies at the University of California at Berkeley. The State Library cooperated with the Extended Programs and Continuing Education Department of the University of Nevada (Reno) to make available an extension course on storytelling. The course was designed around a 13-part television series, "Once upon a Storyteller," produced by the University of California at Davis and broadcast as a public service by KTVN-TV in Reno.

NLA Annual Meeting. NLA held its annual meeting in Ely, and Nevada librarians turned out in large numbers. Both local experts and visiting dignitaries participated in a variety of stimulating programs. Professor Paul Page from the University of Nevada (Reno) outlined the elements of nonverbal communication and described a fascinating experiment in proximity carried out on the escalators of Harrah's Club. Other programs covered topics such as the reference interview, automation for libraries, storytelling, young adult programming, and publicity.

Convinced after reading the new copyright law and related reports and opinions that they knew almost as much about the law as did experts, several Nevada librarians gave a short program on the new law in a postconvention workshop. But the highlight of the convention was Nevada Assemblywoman Sue Wagner's banquet speech outlining advice for expanding the role of librarians in the legislative process. Revised bylaws included the incorporation of a new dues schedule and the revision of NLA's constituent group structure and Board of Trustees.

New Programs. With a grant from the Nevada Humanities Committee, the Clark County Library programming staff researched, produced, filmed, edited, and programmed two documentary films of local issues. *Don't Forget* investigated nursing homes in Nevada, and *Vicious Cycle* looked at medical malpractice.

Clark County Library also provided office space and support services to Nevada's first full-service public radio station during its pre-on-the-air planning stage. The Library will be participating actively in the future development of the station. Local artists traveled with the Clark County Library regional bookmobile to give demonstrations and lectures in the rural areas of southern Nevada.

The University of Nevada (Las Vegas) sponsored a course for high school students in the use of the University Library. Graduates of the three-week course received one university credit and borrowing privileges.

A "book amnesty" campaign (a fine-free week) was arranged by the Washoe County (Reno) Library. It was advertised on television over much of northern Nevada, and borrowers were advised that books could be returned to their nearest branch of the First National Bank of Nevada.

The University of Nevada (Reno) Library was the recipient in 1977 of approximately 3,600 books dealing with the trans-Mississippi West and 180 artifacts, mostly of the Plains Indians. The collection was the gift of Robert and Grace Griffen.

Nevada State Library. Nevada's Governor Mike O'Callaghan has requested the director of the Nevada State Museum to study the feasibility of creating a Department of Cultural Affairs from at least 11 miscellaneous agencies including the Nevada State Library. State Librarian Joseph J. Anderson, while welcoming such a study, has indicated that he would prefer an alternative somewhere between the present situation and full consolidation of a wide variety of disparate agencies.

LSCA and State Library development funds continued to support the rural Nevada bookmobile programs and the programs of the regional resource centers at Clark County Library, Elko County Library, and Washoe County Library. A number of new programs were also initiated through grant funds. The White Pine County (Ely) Library started a books-by-mail service to reach shut-in and rural residents of the county. The Nevada Historical Society was able to catalog historical Nevada documents in its collection. Through the State Library, Nevada continues to work for multistate library development through the Western Council of State Libraries, Inc.

State Conference. Planning for Nevada's State Conference in preparation for its participation in the White House Conference on Library and Information Services went into high gear in 1977. The Citizen's Advisory Committee of 25 members, two-thirds of whom are citizens not employed in libraries, received invitations from Governor O'Callaghan to participate in planning the Conference. The Committee is chaired by former Governor Grant Sawyer. Nevada's Conference will focus on the needs of Nevadans and on how libraries might help meet those needs.

ROBIN BARKER

NEW HAMPSHIRE

Libraries in New Hampshire during 1977 struggled with the same problems that plagued libraries throughout the country—tight budgets, competition for state and federal allocations, attacks on intellectual freedom posed by obscenity statutes, and a growing demand for wider and more varied services.

One major attempt is under way to evaluate the state's library services and needs. The core committee for the New Hampshire Conference on Libraries, chaired by Emerson Greenaway, engaged Lowell Martin to update the 1961 Ford-Holden study of the state's library services. During 1977 Martin held meetings and interviews throughout the state. A final report is expected by the fall of 1978, setting forth directions for the future. The report will be made available through the office of State Librarian Avis Duckworth and is being funded by a Title I LSCA grant.

A lack of funding caused several curtailments in services during the year by the State Library. The position of Assistant State Librarian went unfilled because of a budget shortage. Early in the year bookmobile service was curtailed for the remainder of fiscal 1977 in compliance with an executive order citing a deficit in state funds available for library and other services. The state's law library cancelled a number of subscriptions and services because of a cutoff in funds.

New Hampshire Library Association (founded 1889)

Membership: 298; *Annual Expenditure:* $5,725.
President: Jean Michie, Richards Library, Newport (June 1977-May 1978).
Vice-President/President-elect: Diane Tebbetts, University of New Hampshire Library, Durham.
Secretary: Phyllis Warnock, Somersworth Public Library.
Annual Conference: May 1977, North Conway.
Publication: NHLA Newsletter (bimonthly).

New Hampshire State Library

Avis M. Duckworth, State Librarian
20 Park Street
Concord 03301

State School Library Media Supervisor

Reginald Comeau
Department of Education
Concord 03301

Meetings. The eighth annual New Hampshire Library Council conference was held May 16-17 at North Conway. Speakers included Catherine Armstrong of the Library of Congress, who discussed the new copyright law; Art Plotnik, editor of *American Libraries*; Noel Perrin of Dartmouth College; and anthropologist Harry Shapiro. William Loeb, publisher of the Manchester *Union-Leader*, addressed the Council and predicted that support for libraries would decrease in the future as the public turns to television as a main source for information.

The New Hampshire Library Trustees Association (NHLTA) presented awards for distinguished library service during the annual Council conference. The awards went to Charlotte Hutton as Librarian of the Year; Ralph W. Balch as Trustee of the Year; Beatrice Jordan for services to librarianship; and Elizabeth Yates McGreal, retiring State Library Commission member, for outstanding service. The featured speaker at the meeting was T. Holmes Moore, the Headmaster of New Hampton School.

Two NHLTA scholarships were established during the year. They were the Natalie B. Shores Scholarship in honor of the Franconia trustee who died in 1976 and the William P. Doherty Scholarship in memory of the Sunapee trustee who died in 1977.

Helen Ogden of Manchester presided at the annual meeting of the New Hampshire Friends of the Library in Manchester in September. The Richards Free Library Friends presented the Sarah Josepha Hale Award to Roger Tory Peterson for his contribution to libraries.

State Activities. The State Library Commission approved an allocation of $6,000 under Title III LSCA funds for the continuation of the state's teletype network in 1977. The New England Serials Service continued to be funded by carry-over Title I LSCA funds.

Institutional library services were in a state of flux during the year. In August the State Library Commission voted to authorize funding for the state's institutional libraries program, but budget delays were caused when the governor and the executive council held up authorization of the funds. Carol Brown, consultant for institutional services, spent her first year coping with budget problems and seeking federal monies.

Library services to the handicapped faced similar problems. The staff continued to work under adverse conditions in a former state liquor warehouse with inadequate work space and few trained personnel. Director Eileen Keim, however, reported that statistics indicated that the regional library served 11 per cent of all eligible borrowers in the state, ranking New Hampshire seventh in the nation in that category. The Advisory Council on Libraries and the State Library Commission awarded $17,356 under LSCA grant funds to establish a high-speed, high-quality duplicating center for tapes recorded by volunteers.

Although building programs were curtailed, a few projects were under way in 1977. Projects funded by the Public Works Employment Act were started in Salem, where the Kelley Library was given $534,800 for a building project, and in Wolfeboro, where a $580,000 project was under way for the Wolfeboro-Brewster Memorial Library.

Intellectual Freedom. Two actions during the year involved the issue of intellectual freedom. The city of Claremont proposed an ordinance that would make it unlawful to furnish pornography to a minor; pornography in the statute was defined as visual material containing "photographs, pictures, sketches, or verbal descriptions of sexual acts or excretion..." and writing that "uses slang language, commonly referred to as 'four letter' words, to express thoughts about sexual acts or excretion." The staff and trustees of the Fiske Free Library in Claremont protested the proposed city ordinance and circulated a document to enlist opposition to the act.

Also during the year Governor Meldrim Thomson Jr., vetoed a bill that would have exempted librarians from prosecution on obscenity charges.

People. Library appointments during the year included Joan Donovan Blanchard as Director of the State Library's Division of Extension and Library Development, Anita Bologna as public library consultant to the New Hampshire State Library staff, Kay Herrick as institutional library consultant, Judith Kimball as district consultant for the central district, and Tom Reynolds as Legislative Reference Librarian.

Resignations included Anne Krause, Director of Extension and Library Development with the State Library, to take a position with Project Information in Ohio, and, Carol Brown, institutional library consultant, to take a position with the Concord Public Library.

The governor appointed Esther J.B. Cash, Hampton, and Shirley Walkins, Hookset, to the State Library Commission.

KATHLEEN TAYLOR

NEW JERSEY

New Jersey Library Association
(founded 1890)

Membership: 1,828; *Annual Expenditure:* $60,000.
President: John H. Livingstone, Jr., Monmouth County Library, Freehold (May 1977-May 1978).
Vice-President/President-elect: Mary Joyce Doyle, Bergenfield Public Library.
Recording Secretary: Lola Reed, West Orange Public Library.
Corresponding Secretary: Patricia Anderson, Englewood Public Library.
Annual Conference: April 20-23, 1977, Atlantic City.

Division of State Library, Archives and History, State Department of Education

David C. Palmer, State Librarian
185 West State Street
Trenton 08625

State School Library Media Supervisor

Anne Voss
State Department of Education
Trenton 08625

Spring Conference. Nearly 1,300 librarians attended the 1977 spring conference of the New Jersey Library Association in Atlantic City, April 20-23. Some 250 conference members heard Doris Beck speak at an Administration Section luncheon on "The Library's Role in the Political Area or Don't Let the *** Get You Down." Beck, a former mayor and a library trustee, urged her listeners to become active in political circles to restore library allocations through lobbying in the state legislature. She said that the battle begins at the local level and suggested that city governments should be monitored constantly for their attitudes toward libraries.

Peter Muniz, a management consultant and library trustee, headed a workshop on "The Importance of Staff Evaluations." He responded to criticisms of evaluations as too subjective, purposeless, inadequately explained, and unrelated to job performance, with little benefit to employee or employer. Speakers at the workshop included Carolyn Markuson and Marlene Rosenberg.

The advantages of evaluations were outlined as focusing communication between workers and supervisors, making possible development and promotion, and providing a way in which the employee knows where he stands with the employer. Negatives included supervisors not trained to supervise or rate, guidelines that are confusing, reluctance of employees to hear about negative aspects of their performance, and reluctance of supervisors to be objective in evaluations.

Public Libraries. Westwood Public Library became a member of the MidBergen Federation of Public Libraries on January 1. Affiliation with the regional library service extends the research and borrowing privileges of Westwood residents to the eight other member libraries in the Federation. It increased the number of books, records, films, and other materials from the 43,670 in the Westwood collection to the 588,283 in the member libraries.

The Mount Laurel Free Public Library, only one year old, inaugurated several programs to stimulate local interest and participation. Included were one-day bus trips to places of historic and scenic interest, lectures on antiques, and summer art classes.

Libraries in Essex County now form a cooperative interlibrary loan network, and the Essex County Library Directors are planning to request funds from the State Library to form an automated systems network coordinated by the area libraries in Bloomfield and East Orange and supported by a regional reference center at Newark. The network could become a statewide service.

Jan Stepan, a foreign and international law librarian at Harvard Law School, in 1977 judged the 10,000-volume collection of Soviet legal materials at the Rutgers

School of Law among the top three if not the best of such collections in the United States.

Three New Jersey public libraries benefited from the Public Works Act in 1977. Hillside received $225,000 for a 4,500-square-foot addition. Manville was granted $906,000 for a 14,000-square-foot addition, and Wharton received $467,670 for a new building with 7,400 square feet of space.

The Library Development Bureau announced three Title I LSCA outreach grants totaling $113,539 for New Jersey libraries in 1977. They were approved for programs at Gloucester City, Asbury Park, and Neptune for services to shut-in children and bookmobile services to the elderly and disadvantaged.

Five New Jersey public library projects funded under the Library Services and Construction Act have been selected for inclusion in a U.S. Office of Education publication entitled *Library Programs Worth Knowing About*. The programs are conducted by libraries in Gloucester City, Berkeley Heights, Franklin Lakes, Montclair, and Cumberland County, meeting needs for physically and emotionally handicapped children, Spanish-speaking users, retarded adults, and preschool children.

The trustees of South Brunswick Public Library announced the beginning of bookmobile services in March. Donald Taylor, president of the trustees, reported that the service was being financed without local tax aid through money saved for future services from past state aid. He said plans were under way to expand the present building through the same fund source.

State Library. The New Jersey State Library in cooperation with the New Jersey Trustee Association has begun a series of workshops throughout the state to promote the development of evaluation of library directors. A two-session pilot project workshop was attended by librarians and trustees from Bergenfield, East Brunswick, Monmouth County, Pemberton, Phillipsburg, and Ringwood.

David C. Palmer, Acting Director of the State Library, reported that a grant from the National Endowment for the Humanities was awarded to the state in support of planning prepackaged programs in the humanities for New Jersey libraries. Program ideas to be explored in the plan include Black history, Indian archaeology, New Jersey writers and artists, censorship, ethnic languages, and problems of urban areas.

Also announced during the year by Palmer was the largest bequest in recent history to the State Library from the will of Florence Taylor Tischler of Jamesburg. Under the terms of the bequest a trust fund of more than $25,000 is to be spent annually for the purchase of library materials for smaller communities throughout the state. Mrs. Tischler established the Tischler Memorial Fund in her will and did not restrict the use of the money to books alone but included magazines, recordings, and other nonprint materials.

White House Conference. New Jersey will hold a State Conference in the spring of 1979 in preparation for the White House Conference on Library and Information Services to be held in September 1979. Selma P. Kessler, State Library liaison for a planning committee, said that the committee will include some 30 members representing civic, community, industrial, historical, cultural, and ethnic interests throughout the state. The committee will select delegates to the State Conference and the White House Conference. A Conference coordinator will be hired to implement the committee's decisions.

People. New library directors in the state include Robert E. Coumbe, formerly Director of North Tonawanda, New York, now at Gloucester County; Jeanne Leubs, Cedar Grove Public Library, replacing Emily Curry who retired in 1977; Robert J. Hunter, former staff member at the Dumont Library, Director of Haddon Heights Library; Nancy J. Forester, promoted to Director from Children's Librarian at Milville Public Library; Leila Cayci, appointed Director at New Brunswick Public Library; and Margaret M. Magill, appointed Director at Woodbury Public Library.

Genevieve T. Nomer, a member of the Atlantic City Public Library for seven years, was appointed Director by the board of trustees. She had been Adult Services Librarian. Kathryn M. Evans, Assistant Director of the Camden Free Public Library and a staff member for the past 36 years, was named Director in 1977.

Karen R. Avenick, former Interlibrary Loan Librarian at La Salle College, has been appointed supervisor of reference services for the Camden County Library.

Marie Cranmer, branch coordinator at the Ocean County Library, Toms River, has been appointed Acting Director of the Library Commission.

Learned Bulman, supervisor of technical services for Morris County College, formerly Director of the East Orange Public Library, has been notified that his biography will appear in the 1977-78 edition of *Who's Who in the East*.

More than 150 officials, townspeople, and State Library dignitaries attended a reception September 25 for Elizabeth Budell, retiring as Director of the Madison Public Library.

Julius Ostromecki, Director of the Hackensack Johnson Public Library, retired in 1977. John Shine was appointed Acting Director.

Three New Jersey librarians have been informed that they will appear in the 1977-78 edition of *Who's Who of American Women*. They are Betty J. Turock, Director of the Montclair Public Library; Patricia Ann Hannon, Director of the Wood-Ridge Memorial Library; and Grace Husselman, Director of the Lee Memorial Library, Allendale.

Obituary. Genevieve Cobb, Librarian of the biology and geology departments of Princeton University for more than 30 years, died in Princeton. At her death at age 76 she was serving without pay as Librarian of the Historical Society of Princeton at Bainbridge House.

JOHN H. LIVINGSTONE, JR.

NEW MEXICO

New Mexico Library Association (founded 1924)

Membership: 436; *Annual Expenditure:* $19,000.

President: Vida Hollis, New Mexico State Library, Bookmobile Center, Cimarron (April 1977-April 1978).

Vice-President/President-elect: Lois E. Godfrey, Los Alamos Scientific Laboratories Library.

Secretary: Karen James, New Mexico Department of Education, Santa Fe.

Treasurer: Sandra Coleman, Zimmerman Library, University of New Mexico, Albuquerque.

Annual Conference: April 13-16, 1977, El Paso, Texas (joint meeting with the Texas Library Association).

Publication: New Mexico Library Association Newsletter (5 or 6 issues a year).

New Mexico State Library

C. Edwin Dowlin, State Librarian (resigned July 1977)
Paul A. Agriesti, Acting State Librarian (July 1977)
P.O. Box 1629
Santa Fe 87503

School Library Media Supervisor

Delores Dietz
State Department of Education
Santa Fe 87501

State Librarian. July 15 was Edwin Dowlin's last day as New Mexico State Librarian, a position he had held since May 1970 when he succeeded Dorothy J. Watkins. When Dowlin came to New Mexico, the A.D. Little survey of the state's libraries and library resources had just been completed. From that survey, the State Library, the New Mexico Library Association (NMLA) leaders, and the librarians of the state developed the Coordinated Library Systems of New Mexico—a plan for library development in the state.

Under Dowlin's direction, the State Library geared itself to develop the Coordinated Library Systems through "librarian power." This included the establishment of a locator unit at the State Library for bibliographic control and a communications network among the state's libraries. During this time, the state's librarians accomplished other things as well: a 400 per cent increase in funding for the state aid program for public libraries; passage of a $10,000,000 bond issue for academic library acquisitions; and appointment of a task force to study the need for and benefits of a statewide circulation system. The capstone of Dowlin's New Mexico achievements was his being named Outstanding Librarian of the Year by NMLA at its annual conference in April 1977.

Joint Conference. Some 1,400 Texas and 300 New Mexico librarians attended the four-day New Mexico Library Association/Texas Library Association joint conference April 13-16 in El Paso, Texas. In keeping with the conference theme, "In Search of Learning," 10 seminars were held at which papers on Affirmative Action, communications, career satisfaction, staff welfare, decision making, professional ethics, and other subjects were read. Each had reactor panels, and discussion time was available. To celebrate the Texas Library Association's 75th anniversary, NMLA hosted a birthday celebration that included a five-foot birthday cake. Out of it popped Doris Cox, Carlsbad High School's Librarian, who led a group singing session that included "Happy Birthday" and "Deep in the Heart of Texas." Mrs. Steve Burkstaller and Mrs. Paul Kelly—trustees of the Roswell Public Library—were honored as Outstanding Trustees of the Year for their work in the successful passage of a bond issue to erect a new library at Roswell.

Interlibrary Cooperative System. At its April 15 meeting, the New Mexico State Library Commission approved a $10,000 grant for the purpose of establishing a task force to "study the need for and benefits of a statewide library system that would provide easy access to the cumulated holdings, location, and availability of materials in participating libraries." The grant was made on the recommendation of the New Mexico Advisory Council on Libraries.

The task force members were selected to be representative of the various library and information communities and of the various constituencies that would participate in and benefit from an eventual statewide system. The task force had its organizational meeting on May 4, and subsequent meetings were held, with few exceptions, on a weekly basis. In order to assess the current patterns and extent of interlibrary loan and materials control, a questionnaire was mailed in late May to all types of libraries in the state. The responses received represented a cross section of libraries and aided the task force in the identification of needs and requirements. An additional grant of $6,000 was made available from the State Library for a series of regional meetings throughout the state, and the task force travelled to seven cities during the last week of September to explain the concepts contained in the preliminary report and to obtain input to refine the recommendations.

The task force's final report, completed in early December, recommended a system to facilitate resource sharing among the state's libraries. The recommendations were based on the current interlibrary loan operations in the state (NEMISYS). There were basically three recommendations: 1) a system of local circulation systems in the state's participating libraries; 2) an interlibrary loan system with equipment to tap information contained in the local circulation systems; and 3) the creation of a computerized master list of holdings in the state based on the NEMISYS data base containing 295,000 items. The cost of the system was set at $1,500,000.

New Buildings. The Los Alamos Scientific Laboratories Library moved into a new $4,600,000 building in March. The building contains 50,000 square feet and has solar heating and cooling systems that are expected to provide 96 per cent of the library's heat and 76 per cent of its air conditioning.

The University of New Mexico's 63,000-square-foot Medical Center Library was opened in October. Dedication activities included a reception, seminars, tours, and an exhibit of paintings by New Mexico artists. The Library serves the faculty and students at the University's School of Medicine as well as the colleges of Nursing and Pharmacy.

A $1,100,000 contract was awarded in August for the construction of a new library at Jal. The new structure will have 15,000 square feet. The present city library and the high school library will be merged to form the Woolworth Public Library, named for May and Elizabeth Woolworth of Lea County, who provided the funds in a bequest. The bequest included an endowment for the library as well as funds for the new building.

During 1977 the small New Mexico communities of Bernalillo, Estancia, and Tularoso each received grants from Title I of the Public Works Employment Act. Each of the communities are building city complexes that include new libraries.

The Las Cruces City Commission has purchased six acres as a site for a new city library. The winning design provides for a 34,000-square-foot building, sixty per cent of which will be recessed into the ground. The $1,600,000 structure will be solar heated.

People. AnnaBelle Wignall, Librarian at the Tucumcari Public Library, retired on February 25 after 18 years as Director. Helen Melton retired on March 31 after 23 years as Librarian at Carlsbad. Bert Ellen Camp retired May 15 after 15 years as Head Librarian at the New Mexico Military Institute in Roswell.

Roscoe E. Dooley died March 29 in Portales. After retiring from a 30-year career as Comptroller for the American Library Association, Dooley moved to New Mexico. He served as an architectural consultant for several building projects, including the 12-year-old State Library building.

PAUL A. AGRIESTI

NEW YORK

New York Library Association (founded 1890)

Membership: 4,500 (approx. 1,200 ALA members); *Annual Expenditure:* $193,000.

President: Mary B. Cassata, State University of New York at Buffalo, (October 1976-November 1977).

Vice-President/President-elect: Lucille C. Thomas, New York City Board of Education, Brooklyn.

Executive Director: Dadie Perlov, 60 East 42 Street, Suite 1242, New York, New York 10017.

Annual Conference: November 17-20, 1977, Niagara Falls.

Publication: NYLA Bulletin (10 issues a year).

New York State Education Department

John A. Humphry, State Librarian (resigned March 1977)
Joseph F. Shubert (October 1977)
State Education Building
Albany 12224

School Library Media Supervisor

Lore Scurrah
State Education Department
Albany 12224

CYASS. At a time when the very existence of the age specialist was being challenged, the Children's and Young Adult Services Section (CYASS) Executive Board in 1977 directed its energies toward promoting the value of library service for children and young adults to both the library community and to the public at large. With the approval of the Board the President established an Issues Committee, whose charge it was to investigate broad issues of concern to youth services librarians and to prepare background reports for the CYASS membership and Board for information and action. Mary K. Chelton was appointed to chair the Issues Committee for 1977-78.

Another major concern of the Board has been the development of a revised goals and objectives statement for the Section, as well as the realignment of the duties of Executive Board members for greatest efficiency. An Ad Hoc Committee was created to study these matters under chairperson Ristiina Wigg.

The *Newsletter* was the chief membership activity in 1977—the Spring installment having been sent to nonrenewals along with New York Library Association (NYLA) membership applications. Many CYASS publications went into second and third printings in 1977. They included three 1976 booklists—"Fantasy and Science Fiction for Children," "Science Fiction for Young Adults," and "You Be You and I'll Be Me: Liberating Children from Sex Roles." Completed in time for sale at the NYLA conference was the 1977 revision of "Films for Children," under chairperson Julie Cummins.

College and University Libraries. In April the College and University Libraries Section (CULS) sponsored a workshop at Rensselaer Polytechnic Institute on "The Librarian as Teacher: Practical Strategies for Teaching Library Courses." It also sponsored a variety of program meetings at the annual conference at Niagara Falls. Among these was a symposium on "Author to Editor to Book: The Life and Times of Book Editors, Planning the Unpredictable," which included as speakers senior editors from Doubleday, Lippincott, and Scribner's. Bibliographic instruction remains a major subject of interest to academic librarians, and with the New York Library Instruction Clearinghouse CULS cosponsored a program on "Concepts and Issues in Bibliographic Instruction." Because of concern about the new copyright legislation that was to take effect in January 1978, CULS cosponsored with the 3R's System a panel discussion on "Copyright Update" for librarians at the conference.

Public Libraries. The Executive Board of the Public Libraries Section (PLS) joined with PULISDO (the Public Library Systems Directors' Organization) in formulating statements for hearings regarding the Governor's Commission on Libraries in November 1977. These two bodies also wrote joint letters to state legislators regarding pending legislation for the State Library and regionalization. Members of PLS attended legislative hearings in New York City and other locations throughout the state and wrote as many letters to representatives in Albany.

The Buildings Committee provided suggested norms for building size based on the number of people served and the functions provided by the library. The Committee worked to document library space needs in New York State for use by the Legislative Committee and the Governor's Conference Committee and to provide a list of programs and functions of public and association libraries.

Resources and Technical Services Section. Among the highlights of activities by resources and technical services section was the successful seminar held in September on the Conservation of Library Materials. Topics discussed were paper restoration, different types of binding, conservation of photographs as well as an overview of conservation and preservation of materials. In addition to its diverse programs and on-line demonstrations at the Niagara Conference, RTSS also shared a membership booth with the RTSD of ALA. Finally, a survey by Bill Myrick on the selection and ordering practices of New York State libraries was the lead article in the October NYLA *Bulletin.*

Reference and Adult Services. The name of the section was changed from Adult Services to Reference and Adult Services. *Do It! A Manual on Information and Referral Services for Libraries,* published in 1976, was reprinted in 1977.

Committees active during the year included the Literacy Committee, which worked in conjunction with the New York State Association of Library Boards. The Adult Independent Learner Committee worked with the literacy program at the conference. The Prisons Committee performed a survey of library services available to prisoners from within and without these institutions. The Reference Committee prepared a pamphlet entitled *The Activist Librarian Quiz.* The Continuing Education Committee revised the guidelines for the awarding of the Section's Margaret E. Martignoni Study Grant. A grant of $50 to $200 is available to Section members "for the purpose of improving these individuals' potential to provide library services for adults." The Aging Committee continued to work to identify those with whom it will work and to ascertain their library needs.

School Library Media. The School Library Media Section (SLMS) of NYLA continued to gain members and to work for the improvement of both school librarians and libraries. The new and attractive *SLMS Newsletter* was launched in the fall. School Library Media Day has now become an annual event. Mass mailings in 1977 included the governor's proclamation, a booklet of ideas, and other suggestions. Evelyn Rice, a past president of SLMS, sorted out the historical files and compiled a manual of standards and operating procedures for the Association.

The SLMS annual spring conference, held in Plainview, Long Island, in May, was cosponsored by the Nassau-Suffolk School Library Association and the Suffolk School Library Media Association and was chaired by Elliot Rabner. A unique feature was the optional continuing education course, "A Literary Historical Tour of Long Island." Participants had the opportunity to hear several Long Island authors speak and to tour local literary landmarks such as Walt Whitman's birthplace.

Governor's Conference. In preparation for the New York State Governor's Conference on Library and Information Services, to be held in 1978 in preparation for the White House Conference in 1979, the Governor's Commission on Libraries held a special day of hearings for the library profession at the Niagara Falls conference in November. The NYLA Committee assisted the Commission in conducting sessions in two formats. Five morning sessions included testimony and discussion based on papers submitted to the Commission in advance on the topics of technology, access, interrelationships and resource sharing, functions and services, and finance and governance. The afternoon session was scheduled for general testimony.

Legislation. The NYLA legislative program continued to focus on proposals to benefit both specific types of libraries and library service in general. Three ongoing task forces were meeting in an attempt to resolve some identified critical areas. One issue was the study of the bill on the State Library, a major piece of legislation that would vitally affect all types of libraries in the state. The second task force continued to study new approaches to school library funding, and a third addressed the fiscal problems of public libraries. There was special emphasis on the needs for an adjusted formula base and relief for urban libraries. In addition, there were other proposals affecting special and academic libraries, correctional institutions, and the blind and physically handicapped.

Other significant activities included organization and implementation of Library Legislative Day in Albany in March; passage of a bill establishing public library service on three Indian reservations; full funding at the $300,000 level for the Schomburg Center for Research in Black

Culture; a $300,000 allocation through the supplemental budget for the two regional libraries for the blind and physically handicapped; a $76,000 allocation through the supplemental budget for the State Library to assist with the move of the collection to the Cultural Education Center; testimony at the ESEA Title IV-B hearings before the House Education and Labor Committee in Washington in July; testimony at the Regents Legislative Conference in September in Albany; and testimony before the Assembly Subcommittee on Libraries in November in Syracuse.

Intellectual Freedom. The Intellectual Freedom and Due Process Committee continued its involvement with the Island Trees case. There was a special meeting in New York City in May with representatives of ALA and the New York Civil Liberties Union (NYCLU) to discuss strategies in the case being filed by students against the School Board for removal of several titles from the school library. At the suggestion of the Committee, the NYLA Council donated $350 to NYCLU in support of the action and agreed to support an amicus curiae brief at the proper time.

The Committee also mediated a charge of professional harassment filed by a library employee against the employer and concluded plans for a series of 1978 workshops on the use of sexist, racist, and ethnically biased materials in children's and young adult collections in libraries. The Committee endorsed the resolution on intellectual freedom of the National Commission on Libraries and Information Science with recommendations to the NYLA Council for endorsement. In addition, the Committee completed plans for the presentation of two intellectual freedom policy statements on the rights of youth to access to information and protection for librarians in the dissemination of such information.

Considerable time and effort were unsuccessfully expended by the Committee to seek modification of legislation on the sexual abuse of minors that specifically denied a "test of obscenity" for published materials. The Committee planned to seek legislation in 1978 restoring the test of obscenity in prosecution for the use of children in publications. The modification would protect library acquisitions and remove the chilling effect of "prior restraint" in existing legislation.

Niagara International Conference. More than 3,200 librarians attended the NYLA international conference at Niagara November 17-20. The joint gathering titled "Between Friends" drew 2,150 American conferees and 1,100 from across the Canadian border. Trustees, exhibitors, students, and friends of libraries from both sides of the border swelled total attendance to over 4,000. The unique conference marked the third time the NYLA had met in Niagara. In 1912, 332 librarians attended and in 1937, 660 were present. The 1977 conference features a private international shuttle bus from Canada, outstanding speakers from both countries, and forums, panels, and workshops of interest to librarians from both countries. The Conference was cosponsored by the Ontario Library Association.

New Developments. The NYLA Conference in 1977 saw the development, with the approval of Council, of a new Film/Video Round Table. Its purpose is to provide a forum for the exchange of information and a base for cooperative effort for those NYLA members working with, or interested in, film and video service in libraries.

The Legislative Committee produced a revised edition of *The Library Lobbyist: A Guide to Action in the State Capitol*. The Reference Committee of the Reference and Adult Services Section developed *The Activist Librarian Quiz*. The Committee on the Concerns of Women provided *A Checklist of Materials on Selected Topics for Women*; and the Children's and Young Adult Services Section produced a revised edition of *Recordings for Children*.

The Libraries at St. Mary's School for the Deaf in Buffalo moved to spacious new quarters in 1977. The new facilities will allow new and innovative programs for deaf students, increase the study and graduate training programs cosponsored with Canisius College, and house the professional materials on the social, educational, and medical aspects of deafness and other areas of special education.

The NYLA annual conference was the occasion for presenting special awards. The L. Marion Moshier Award for outstanding service by a librarian operating a library serving a population of 7,500 or less went to Alice J. Rosenfeld, Director of Mattituck Free Library. The School Library Media Section's John T. Short Award for School Library Media Day was awarded to Irene Johnson, Library Media Specialist at Circleville Middle School. A special Award of Council went to retired State Librarian John A. Humphry for his outstanding contributions to libraries and library service. The Velma K. Moore Award of the New York State Association of Library Boards, given to an outstanding trustee, was awarded to Whitney North Seymour, Jr., trustee of The New York Public Library.

State Library Post. Joseph F. Shubert was named State Librarian and Assistant Commissioner for Libraries on October 3, succeeding Humphry who resigned in March. A native of New York, Shubert had been State Librarian of Ohio since 1966 and was previously State Librarian of Nevada. Humphry joined Forest Press, publisher of *Dewey Decimal Classification*, as Executive Director.

NYPL. The financially pressed New York Public Library in 1977 turned to a fund raiser and to a foundation executive to spur its lagging $52,000,000 capital fund drive. Richard Salomon and William M. Dietel, President of the Rockefeller Foundation, were named to help the library raise funds. The NYPL, a private corporation that receives some support from the city government, has had an annual deficit of from $1,500,000 to $3,500,000 for the past several years. Only $12,000,000 of the fund goal had been raised by the end of 1977.

MICHAEL G. DERUVO

NORTH CAROLINA

North Carolina Library Association (founded 1904)

Membership: 2,500; *Annual Expenditure:* $47,365.
President: Leonard L. Johnson, Greensboro Public Schools (October 1977-September 1979).
Vice-President/President-elect: H. William O'Shea, Wake County Public Libraries, Raleigh.
Secretary: Artemis Kares, Greenville.
Biennial Conference: October 5-8, 1977, Winston-Salem.
Publication: North Carolina Libraries (quarterly).

Division of State Library

David N. McKay, Director and State Librarian
109 East Jones Street
Raleigh 27611

State School Library Media Supervisor

Elsie L. Brumback
Department of Public Instruction
Raleigh 27602

Legislation. North Carolina's librarians went to the legislature in 1977 with a program for libraries that gained some success but also saw major disappointments, particularly with appropriations. A 1969 recommendation from a legislative library study commission that "the state gradually assume equal responsibility with local governments for operating and improving local public libraries" did not mean the same thing to librarians and legislators. A supplementary public library aid bill calling for $2,400,000 for 1977-78 and $5,800,000 for 1978-79 was reduced to $50,000 for each of the two fiscal years.

State law was amended to permit regional public librarians to participate in the North Carolina Local Governmental Employees Retirement System. The law had previously excluded the librarians who served nearly half of the state's counties.

School library funds of $500,000 were appropriated for fiscal 1977-78 to provide library/media personnel for public schools on the basis of average daily membership. The new law, however, repealed the 1976 requirement of city and county school administrative units to employ at least one half-time librarian.

The State Library gained support for SOLINET (Southeastern Library Network) in the amount of $64,000 for both years of the biennium, aid for the IN-WATS reference network, and $100,000 per year to rent more suitable space to house the library for the blind and physically handicapped. Cuts in other programs, however, resulted in the loss of three positions.

NCLA Activities. The North Carolina Library Association (NCLA) held its biennial meeting October 5-8 at Winston-Salem. A preconference workshop on children's and young adult services entitled "Catchin' Kids" drew 350 participants to hear Mary Kay Chelton, Barbara Elleman, and Joan Lipsitz. Many who attended called it the best preconference ever organized by NCLA.

The conference itself was also well attended with overflow crowds at the programs of Reference and Adult Services (to hear Mary Jo Lynch), College and University (for Ann Stone), Library Education, and other sections. The theme of the conference—planning library service for the future—held great interest for the more than 1,200 librarians, students, and exhibitors who gathered at Winston-Salem. The highlight of the week was author Virginia Hamilton's talk at the banquet. A major dues increase was passed by the membership. Increased financial support for NCLA was one of several proposals brought to the Board by the Development Committee chaired by Ken Shearer.

State Library. *Tar Heel Libraries*, a bimonthly newsletter from the State Library, appeared in September. It replaced *The Library Reporter*, which was last published in the winter of 1976. Alberta Smith of the State Library is the editor.

The second annual "Story Telling in the Park," sponsored by the State Library and directed by Diana Young, Children's Services Consultant, brought 6,000 visitors to the Capitol lawn to hear, see, and tell stories during the week-long event.

The state's first subregional library for the blind and physically handicapped opened November 1 in Charlotte. The Metrolina Library provides talking books, cassettes, and large-print materials to users in Alexander, Cabarrus, Catawba, Cleveland, Gaston, Iredell, Lincoln, Mecklenburg, Rowan, and Stanly and Union Counties.

Building Programs. The University of North Carolina at Chapel Hill completed a $3,750,000 100,000-square-foot addition to Wilson Library. Designed to house 1,000,000 volumes and provide 400 study carrels, the 10 levels of stacks were 70 per cent filled when they opened to the public in October. This is the second addition to the Library constructed in 1929 and named for Louis Round Wilson, longtime University Librarian and a leader in American librarianship. Plans were being prepared for a new $22,000,000 central research library.

Forsyth County Public Library received a $567,000 grant from the Economic Development Administration of the U.S. Department of Commerce to help pay for a 42,000-square-foot three-story addition to the main library.

Coastal Carolina Community College dedicated its new $1,400,000 Learning Resources and Student Activity Center. The Center has a capacity of 50,000 volumes in an area of 23,000 square feet. Durham County Public Library broke ground at the end of October for a new main library. Completion is expected by early 1979. Ashe County Public Library dedicated its new building on October 23.

Professional Interests. The School of Library Science at the University of North Carolina at Chapel Hill began its new Ph.D. program in August with five students. Proposed off and on for more than 25 years, the idea finally came to fruition under the guidance of Dean Edward G. Holley when three years earlier the University's Board of Governors had authorized the School to begin planning the program.

Awards. Joyce Beaman, a librarian at Saratoga Central High School in Wilson, won the 1977 Terry Sanford Award for innovation and creativity in teaching.

The Catawba County Library received a National Association of Counties Award for Rural Library Service. The Library was recognized for expansion of its service in the Sherrills Ford and Terrell communities.

Kay Taylor of the Durham County Public Library received a Charles Scribner's Sons Award. The $250 cash award enabled Taylor to attend her first ALA Annual Conference.

Lyda Moore Merrick, a member of the Durham County Library Board for more than 50 years, was awarded Honorary Membership in NCLA during the biennial conference. Among her many activities on behalf of the Library and its clients, nothing stands out more than *Negro Braille Magazine*, which she founded and continues to edit and nurture.

Appointments. Philip Barton became Director of the Rowan Public Library in Salisbury. Malcom Blowers became Director of the D. Hiden Ramsey Library at the University of North Carolina at Asheville. Nancy Brenner was named Director of the Randolph Public Library in Asheboro. Robert Burgin was named Director of the Wayne County Public Library in Goldsboro. George Craddock became Director of the Gardner-Webb College Library. Jay Chung became Director of the Thomas H. Braswell Library in Rocky Mount, replacing Walter Gray who left to become Director of the Polk County Public Library.

Mary Arden Harris was named Media Center Specialist for the Charlotte/Mecklenburg School System. Mary Holloway was appointed Supervisor of Library Services for the Wake County School System. Eugene W. Huguelet became Director of the Library at the University of North Carolina at Wilmington. Myron L. Kirkes began his duties as Director of the Haywood County Public Library. Jonathan A. Lindsey was named Director of the Meredith College Library. Jimmy McKee became Director of the Bladen County Public Library.

Lucy McGrath was promoted to Director of the Learning Resource Center at Carteret Technical Institute. Marion McGuinn became Director of the Rutherford County Library. John Pritchard was named Director of the Catawba County Public Library. Arrabelle Schokley was appointed Media Director for the Winston-Salem/Forsyth School System. Judith Sutton left the State Library to become Associate Director of the Public Library of Charlotte and Mecklenburg. Jerry Thrasher was named Assistant Director of the Forsyth County Public Library. Barbara Walker was promoted to Director of the Beaufort, Hyde, Martin Regional Library.

Retirements. Margaret Chapman, Librarian at Queens College in Charlotte retired in 1977. She received the coveted Algernon Sydney Sullivan Award for service from the College.

Charlesanna Fox retired in March after serving 28 years as Director of the Randolph Public Library in Asheboro. She had developed the Library from one room to a modern system encompassing five communities. Active in state and national associations, she had served as NCLA President and on ALA Council.

Ainsley Whitman retired in September as Director of the D. Hiden Ramsey Library at the University of North Carolina at Asheville. He was a former President of the Oregon Library Association and Vice-President of the Arkansas Library Association.

Mary Wilson, Director of the Beaufort, Hyde, Martin Regional Library since 1962, retired in March. She had inaugurated many new services in the region and had recently completed a new library in Ocracoke. DAVID P. JENSEN

NORTH DAKOTA

North Dakota Library Association (founded 1906)

Membership: 338; *Annual Expenditure:* $5,000.
President: Dina Butcher, Minot Public Library (October 1977-September 1979).
Vice-President/President-elect: Ora Stewart, Carnegie Bookmobile Library, Grafton.
Secretary: Marilyn Guttromson, North Dakota Legislative Council Library, Bismarck.
Treasurer: Cheryl Bailey, Mary College, Bismarck.
Annual Conference: September 29-October 1, 1977, Fargo.
Publication: Good Stuff (quarterly).

North Dakota State Library Commission

Richard J. Wolfert, State Librarian
Highway 83 North
Bismarck 58505

School Library Media Supervisor

Patricia Herbel
Department of Public Instruction
Bismarck 58501

State Library Commission. The 1977-78 state legislature approved a resolution recommending the relocation of the State Library to the Liberty Memorial Building on the State Capitol grounds. As a result of this move, expected to take place in 1981, the Commission will be returned to a location providing both high visibility and easy access for legislators and other citizens. The additional space available will make possible many new services such as an examination center, an exhibit collection of children's books and media materials, an expanded governmental affairs library, and a library for the visually handicapped.

Recommendations made in 1976 in the Fridley Report were implemented during 1977: the traveling library program was discontinued, MINITEX service was expanded, and a position was established to coordinate statewide library planning and development. Another study, the Palmour Report, praised the high level of networking activities in the state as exemplified by the number and speed of interlibrary loans through the teletype and telephone communication system, the union catalog, and MINITEX service. The Palmour Report cited the need for the development of a planning structure to assure that the present level of service will continue under changing demands and the tight budgets imposed by the state.

A review by national and regional officials of HEW of the administration of LSCA funds in North Dakota commended the State Library Commission for sound financial management procedures, the high quality of its publications program, its foresighted and highly effective use of modern technology, and its ongoing research into the information needs of its many clientele groups. Cited as an extremely critical weakness was the total lack of professional support staff. As a result of the study's major recommendation, two new professional positions were authorized by the legislature.

In a continuation of its long-standing philosophy of cooperation the Library Commission signed a two-year agreement with the Minnesota Higher Education Coordinating Board to provide North Dakota residents improved library and information services. The agreement is for MINITEX to provide access to Minnesota library resources through the North Dakota State Library Commission. This includes loan of books and documents as well as a variety of reference and information services. The agreement also provides for MINITEX to produce a new edition of the *North Dakota Union List of Serials.* Fifty libraries are participating in the new list.

Four cities held elections to raise existing mill levies. Bismarck and Lisbon were successful; Mandan and Wahpeton were not. Effective in January 1977, the State Penitentiary Library was being operated as a branch of the State Library. A State Library staff member is administering the service on a daily basis, and the purchase of new material is being made through the State Library.

North Dakota Library Association. The North Dakota Library Association (NDLA) completed its 71st year with a total membership of 338. More than 300 registrants attended the 1977 annual convention held in Fargo, September 29-October 1. A variety of workshops drew enthusiastic support, and several speakers developed the convention theme, "1984," by exploring the near future and librarians' unique opportunities in shaping it. Margaret Warden, a Montana State Senator and member of the National Advisory Committee on the White House Conference on Library and Information Services, examined the opportunities available to the profession through participation in both the national and local conferences. Dina Butcher, incoming NDLA President, was appointed State Coordinator for the White House Conference. Plans were under way for a preliminary State Conference in Bismarck in the fall of 1978.

Joel Barker, Director of the Future Studies Department at the Science Museum of Minnesota, outlined the vital role librarians can play in shaping the world of 2001. Among other speakers who contributed to the program were Luther Bjerke, North Dakota humorist from Grand Forks; and Nellie Yost, historian and author, who reported on the progress of her NDLA-commissioned biography of "Doc" Hubbard, a North Dakota naturalist and storyteller.

The membership approved the establishment of two new groups in NDLA—the Health Science Information Section and the Children's Round Table. They also voted to support the proposed legislative activity of the Public Library Section's Crisis Committee. Bismarck was selected for the 1978 convention with the hope that a tie-in with the proposed pre-White House State Conference might be arranged.

Public Library Section. Convention activities focused on the members' concern regarding the many long-standing and progressively worsening problems faced on the local and state levels by North Dakota public libraries. As a means of addressing these problems, the Section members voted to establish a new group called Crisis. By evaluating the needs for statewide library service and by working for grass-roots support of that service, the committee hopes to achieve its goal of significant financial support for public libraries from the state legislature at its next session.

Workshops for trustees and librarians continued as a favored program around the state, and children's activities, particularly story hours, flourished. Branches were established by the Ward County Library and the Carnegie Bookmobile Library, while the merger of the Cooperstown Public Library and the Prairie Bookmobile Library into the Griggs County Library was completed after two years of planning. An innovative program was initiated by the Grafton Carnegie Library and the Grand Forks Public Library through a cooperative paperback mail-order service to their five-county population area of 103,000.

Grants to public libraries also loomed large on the scene. Planning grants were awarded to the Devils Lake, Williston, and Bismarck Public Libraries by the State

Library. The North Dakota Council of Arts and Humanities awarded $500 to Ward County Library for the purchase of art prints. Later in the year the Ward County Library successfully wrote another proposal to the Council and was funded more than $900 for audiovisual materials.

Health Science Information. In March 1977 health science librarians gathered in Grand Forks, Minot, Fargo, and Bismarck for the spring business meeting via ETN (Educational Telephone Network). They received an invitation from NDLA President Dennis Page to affiliate with NDLA and to become a separate section of the Association. Members voted to accept the invitation and forwarded to the NDLA Executive Board a request for section status. At the same time they voted to be known as the North Dakota Health Science Information Section (NDHSIS) of NDLA. The first meeting as a section of NDLA took place at the fall convention in Fargo. A one-day workshop on a policy and procedure manual was presented; and a new President, Laurie Reule, Jamestown Hospital Librarian, was elected. Special interests were identified for future continuing education programs, and another ETN meeting was suggested for the spring of 1978.

Academic Section. Academic attention was focused on a study with great possible implications for libraries in the state. The North Dakota Post-secondary Education Commission initiated a study of academic libraries and obtained the services of an outside consultant to conduct the investigation. The report, "Planning for the Future of Academic Libraries in North Dakota," was submitted by consultant Vernon E. Palmour in August. Specific problems identified in the report were space, cooperative activities, joint storage, a planning framework, a staff to develop planning networks, and state-level policies.

Members of the Document Committee saw the successful culmination of much hard work with the passage by the 1977 state legislature of a new state documents law. In the law these materials are defined, official depositories are designated, and the responsibilities of issuing agencies in implementing the provisions of the law are specified.

The computer-based Tri-College University Union Catalog became a reality in 1977. Copies were installed in the three libraries in December of 1976. Displayed on ROM 3 readers, it contains 80,000 titles, approximately 70 per cent to 80 per cent of books added to the University Libraries since 1968. Plans are for the catalog to be updated quarterly, with each update to include a number of retrospective titles as well.

Building. The 1977-78 state legislature appropriated $2,500,000 for expansion of the North Dakota State University Library. At year's end preliminary decisions regarding location and space needs had been made. The first floor plans were being worked on, with construction scheduled to begin in the late spring of 1978.

People. Jeanne Cobb retired after 15 years as Jamestown Public Library Director. Genevieve Buresh retired from her position as Director of School Library Services at the State Department of Public Instruction. Pat Herbal was appointed to replace Buresh.

Five new directors were appointed in 1977: Amy Waite, Jamestown; Jerry Kaup, Minot; Don Kopper, Devils Lake; Janet Walsh Crawford, Mandan; and Valerie Licha, Valley City. At the Chester Fritz Library at the University of North Dakota, Sherman Hayes was named Assistant to the Director. The two newly authorized positions at the State Library were filled. Jeff Fox, Planning Director, will work with both academic and public libraries; and Ruth Mahan, Field Librarian, will work with public and institutional libraries.

PATRICIA SCHOMMER

OHIO

Ohio Library Association
(founded 1895)

Membership: 2,282; *Annual Expenditure:* $85,572.
President: Charlotte Leonard, Dayton and Montgomery County Public Library (October 1977-October 1978).
Vice-President/President-elect: Hannah McCauley, Lancaster Campus, Ohio University.
Executive Director: A. Chapman Parsons, 40 South Third Street, Suite 409, Columbus, Ohio 43215.
Annual Conference: October 27-29, 1977, Dayton
Publication: OLA Bulletin (quarterly); Ohio Libraries Newsletter (8 issues a year).

State Library of Ohio

Joseph F. Shubert, State Librarian
(resigned September 1977)

Ira Phillips, Acting State Librarian
(October 1977)
65 South Front Street
Columbus 43215

School Library Media Supervisor

Anne Hyland
State Department of Education
Columbus 43215

Library services to Ohio's citizens was improved during 1977 by many breakthroughs in interlibrary cooperation. The State Library Board made state grants amounting to $301,000 and grants amounting to $1,222,000 from federal funds in assisting the 13 regional cooperative systems.

The trend in Ohio, as well as across the nation, is towards cooperation among all types of libraries. In Ohio interlibrary loan and reference services are a basic part of the service provided through the cooperative systems to public libraries in 82 counties and to 37 academic, 16 school media center, 8 special, and 5 institution libraries. Cooperative system staffs increased 25 per cent during 1977, including many specialists in children's, adult, and audiovisual services.

Statistics. Survey forms distributed by the State Library of Ohio were integrated with Library General Information Survey (LIBGIS) forms to produce three major Ohio library statistical documents: *Ohio Directory of Libraries*, *Rankings of Ohio Public and Academic Library Statistics*, and *Academic Library Statistics*.

Ohio libraries increased expenditures for library materials 4 per cent in 1976, but added 2 per cent fewer books. Operating expenditures for 3,081 public, school, academic, institutional, and special libraries were $155,000,000, an increase from $150,000,000 in 1975.

Expenditures for the 122 academic libraries reporting amounted to $45,600,000. Personnel costs accounted for 53.6 per cent, and printed materials accounted for 25 per cent of the total expenditures. Almost 900,000 volumes were added to collections during 1976, bringing the total collections to 19,200,000 volumes. The professional staff accounted for 38.4 per cent of the total staff of 2,033.

Public library circulation totaling 62,300,000 in 1976 continued a seven-year upward trend. Books loaned to adults increased almost 1 per cent. The total number of volumes in public libraries increased 2 per cent to 28,100,000. The number of professional staff in Ohio's public libraries continued to increase. Of the 5,129 staff members in 1976, 21 per cent were professional staff, an increase of 54 persons over 1975. Income to public libraries from the legislatively earmarked classified intangible property tax (local situs) amounted to $74,600,000 in 1976, 6 per cent above the 1975 collection. More than 20 of the 249 libraries increased their income by $10,000,000 through voted tax levies, adding to the $68,400,000 allocated by county budget commissions. Total public library income for 1976 was $84,700,000, a 12.9 per cent increase over 1975. Voted library issues received an 80 per cent approval from 1974 to 1977.

The 1977 *Ohio Directory of Libraries* reported 2,523 school library media centers and 1,955 certificated school media specialists in publicly supported schools. The master's degree in library science in educational media was held by 915 persons. Ohio school library media centers held 25,500,000 volumes and added 4,500,000 volumes in 1976; total operating expenses amounted to $25,600,000. Book expenditures decreased 7 per cent, but audio visual expenditures increased by 4 per cent.

Library resources for the 24,902 people in Ohio's 42 state-supported institutions are growing. The total number of volumes available to these residents increased 8.4 per cent during 1976. Total circulation increased 22.5 per cent, while operating expenditures were increased only 3.5 per cent. In 1977 it was reported that 67 per cent of the institutionalized population of the state have direct access to an institutional library. The rate of growth (volumes added) in Rehabilitation and Corrections institutions and in Ohio Youth Commission institutions more than doubled during 1976.

The 144 Ohio special libraries reporting to the State Library indicated holdings of 3,600,000 books, 18,868 manuscripts, 1,400,000 technical reports, and 50,000 translations. Eighty-two libraries reported expenditures of $7,600,000.

State Library. Interlibrary cooperation was greatly facilitated during 1977 by the State Library Board and staff. Jane Sterzer of Dayton was elected President in June, succeeding Max Drake of Tiffin, who retired from the Board in October. H. Baird Tenney of Cleveland Heights was elected Vice-President.

Joseph F. Shubert, State Librarian, announced his resignation in September after 11 years of service. During his tenure services to state government were expanded, cooperative systems and institutional library services were developed, and automation was introduced. Ira Phillips, Assistant State Librarian for Library Development, was named Acting State Librarian on October 1.

The 112th Ohio General Assembly voted a 14 per cent increase in the State Library budget for the 1977–79 biennium. An aggressive effort with a conference committee of both houses resulted in an additional $100,000 being added to the state aid program. The $11,800,000 budget approved for the next two years includes $4,200,000 for State Library operations, $5,300,000 in federal funds, and $1,700,000 for state aid. In June 1977 the total number of authorized positions in the State Library was 137, compared to 151 in 1976 and 169 in June 1972.

Publications issued in 1977 included: *County by County in Ohio Genealogy; Libraries for College Students with Handicaps: A Directory of Academic Library Resources and Services in Ohio; Libraries for People with Handicaps; Ohio Documents Cumulated List 1971–1975;* and *Books-by-Mail in Ohio.*

The Ohio White House Conference on Library and Information Services will be held September 20-22, 1978, in Columbus. Raymond R. Brown is Chairman of the Conference.

Ohio Library Association. A major achievement of the Ohio Library Association (OLA) in 1977 was the approval by the Board of Directors of the Library Development Committee Report calling for a new Ohio Library Development Plan to supplement the plan enacted into legislation in 1969. The Report called for strengthening existing libraries and cooperative systems, expanding the cooperative systems, establishing a statewide reference and information network, establishing an Ohio Reference and Information Council, and conducting a major statewide needs assessment study. At year's end the Report was transmitted to the Ohio Multitype Interlibrary Cooperation Committee and distributed to members.

The major event of 1977 was the concurrent conference OLA held with the Ohio Educational Library Media Association (OELMA) on October 27-29 in Dayton on the theme "Getting to Know." More than 2,300 persons attended the conference, which was preceded by a workshop on "Performance Appraisal" and a postconference on "Any Number Can Play: The School-Public Cooperation Game." The concurrent conference was the first for the two associations, which were also joined by the Academic Library Association of Ohio, Ohio Friends of the Library, and the Ohio Library Trustees Association.

Correspondent Daniel Schorr spoke during the banquet to an audience of 1,100 on the subject "The Public's Right to Know." Major program participants included Eileen Cooke of ALA; Alice Ihrig, Past President of the American Library Trustee Association; Molefi Asante, Department of Communications, Buffalo, New York; Charlotte Zolotow; Franklin Walter, Superintendent of Public Instruction in Ohio; and author Robert Quackenbush.

Library Trustee Association. The 1,650-member Ohio Library Trustees Association (OLTA) sponsored 12 regional meetings and an annual conference program during 1977; more than 600 members participated in these programs. The State Library of Ohio and OLTA are participating in the writing of a new public library trustee manual. A. Robert Rogers, Acting Dean of the School of Library Science at Kent State University, is project director; and Mrs. Weldon Lynch of Oakdale, Louisiana, is project consultant. Sixty library trustees will be participating in the project.

Ohio Library Foundation. The Ohio Library Foundation began an active campaign in 1977 to secure contributions for assisting libraries throughout the state. This "Program for the Future," adopted by the Foundation's Board of Directors in December 1976, marks a new level of service. An Office of Development was opened on February 15. Walter Brahm, Director of Development, sent letters to members of OLA, OELMA, OLTA, and the Academic Library Association of Ohio, urging participation in the Foundation's efforts. Letters were also sent to some 260 retired Ohio librarians, urging them to remember the Foundation in their current programs of giving or in their wills. The Foundation received operating grants from OLA and OLTA totaling $953.75 and gifts of more than $2,000.

OCLC. The Ohio College Library Center continued its rapid growth in performance during 1977. OCLC produced 61,000,000 catalog cards, and libraries found existing records in the system for 92.4 per cent of titles cataloged. On July 1 the OCLC staff numbered 208, and the assets totaled $13,633,000. A budget of $18,428,000 was adopted for 1977–78. During the Year OCLC received grants from the Council on Library Resources, the State Library of Ohio, the U.S. Office of Education, and the W.K. Kellogg Foundation. In December OHIONET was organized to provide increased representation and improved services for Ohio members of OCLC.

OELMA's First Year. OELMA, the group formed from the merger of the Ohio Association of School Librarians and the Educational Media Council of Ohio, observed its first birthday during 1977. OELMA had Copresidents during 1977: Isabelle Pratt of Findlay Public Schools and Maxie Lambright of Defiance College. John Kerstetter of Audio Visual Services at Kent State University is the President for 1978.

Deaths. Ohio lost distinguished librarians during 1977. John T. Thackery, Jr., died August 25. He was Assistant Director at Dayton and Montgomery County Public Library, an OLA Past President, and Chairperson of the OELMA/OLA Concurrent Conference Local Committee.

A.T. Dickinson, Director of Mansfield Public Library, died in Arkansas on September 4. He had been an OLA Division Coordinator and a Director of OLA.

Mildred Krohn of Akron and Summit County Public Library died during the year in an apartment fire.

Awards. The following persons received Ohio Library Association awards during the conference in October: Hall of Fame,

Dorothy I. Strouse, retired Librarian at Maumee; and Arthur W. Marr, Trustee of Guernsey County District Public Library in Cambridge; Trustee of the Year, Florence M. Gault, Euclid Public Library; Librarian of the Year, Doris Wood, Clermont County Public Library in Batavia; Supportive Staff Member of the Year, Elsetta R. Ervin, Ohio State University; Citizens Award, Robert C. Nichols, Cuyahoga Falls; Diana Vescelius Memorial Award, Barbara Newmark, Cuyahoga County Public Library; and *OLA Bulletin* Best Article, Philip L. Koons, State Library of Ohio.

The Ohio Library Trustees Association presented its Award of Achievement to the Board of Trustees of the Public Library of Columbus and Franklin County.

The Ohio Educational Library Media Association gave its Award of Merit to Hannah McCauley of the Lancaster Branch of Ohio University and its Edgar Dale Award to Sid Eboch (deceased) of Ohio State University.

A. CHAPMAN PARSONS

OKLAHOMA

Oklahoma Library Association (founded 1907)

Membership: 931; *Annual Expenditure:* $28,777.

President: Anne Rounds, Norman Public Schools (April 1977-April 1978).

Vice-President/President-elect: Mrs. Pat Woodrum, Tulsa City-County Library.

Secretary: Kenneth Tracy, Oklahoma State University Library, Stillwater.

Annual Conference: April 21-22, 1977, Stillwater.

Publication: Oklahoma Librarian (quarterly).

Department of Libraries

Robert L. Clark, Director
200 North East 18th
Oklahoma City 73105

State School Library Media Supervisor

Clarice Roads
State Department of Education
Oklahoma City 73105

Legislation. Elementary library legislation that made provision for the funding for library media specialists in all elementary schools was drafted for introduction in the January 1977 session of the Oklahoma legislature. The legislation was deleted before passage, but Oklahoma librarians and media specialists promised that legislation would be reintroduced in the 1978 session. This important legislation is being supported by the Oklahoma Association of School Library Media Specialists, the Oklahoma Library Association (OLA), and the State Department of Education.

The Library Development Committee of OLA continued working for approval of $600,000 in state funds for assistance to public libraries. The Committee hoped to convince the governor of the importance of state aid, in order that it could be included in the governor's budget recommendations to the legislatulre.

The Oklahoma Open Meeting Act became effective on October 1, 1977. It is of interest to librarians since it describes the rules and regulations governing state public meetings. The Act pertains to all libraries in the state receiving public funds and requires advance notice of the date, place, time, and agenda of all public meetings.

Buildings and Gifts. Ground-breaking ceremonies were held for two library buildings funded through Public Works Employment Act funds. The Purcell Human Resources Center will have 12,000 square feet of its space to be used by the Purcell Public Library, a part of the Pioneer Multi-County Library. The Human Resources Center in Purcell is a joint project involving the public schools, the city of Purcell, the county's health department, and the Pioneer Multi-County Library.

The Tahlequah Public Library, part of the Eastern Oklahoma District Library System, will have a new facility adjacent to the present Carnegie Library Building. The present building will be used as a meeting area.

Oklahoma Library Association. Four persons were elected to serve as directors on the Executive Board of OLA. The directors represent various types of libraries and will give the total membership of OLA wider representation on the Executive Board. Elected were James Alsip, University of Oklahoma Libraries; Robert Clark, Oklahoma Department of Libraries; Lee Brawner, Metropolitan Library System; and Jean Harrington, Enid Public Library.

Jean Merrill's *The Toothpaste Millionaire* was the winner of the 19th annual Sequoyah Children's Book Award. More than 20,000 Oklahoma children in grades three through six participated in the selection of the book. Merrill was present at the annual meeting of OLA to accept the award.

"Kaleidoscope '77" was the theme of the annual meeting of OLA held in Stillwater, April 21-22; the meeting had a rich variety of speakers and topics. Speakers included Thomas Galvin, Van Allen Bradley, Carol Vantine, Gerald Shields, Alphonse Trezza, Donald Ely, Richard Armour, and Larry Kusche. The grand finale to the meeting was a Hawaiian luau, complete with an erupting volcano and hula dancers.

Outreach Programs. The Social Responsibilities Round Table of OLA presented its third Citation of Merit to the Stilwell Public Library for an outstanding program called Cherokee Outreach. The program included a series of instruction sessions in the Cherokee language and the addition to the Library of history books on the Cherokees, language tapes, and other pertinent materials.

Academic librarians attended an OLA-sponsored workshop at Oklahoma Baptist University in November. The topic for the workshop was "Securing Financial Support for Academic Libraries"; John Dow Gray was the principal speaker.

The Oklahoma City University Library and Education Department jointly received a federal grant to train paraprofessional aides to work in Indian information centers. The project ran from July 1976 to March 1977, and the participants were nine students from various Indian tribes in Oklahoma.

State Library. Professor Lowell Martin came to Oklahoma to give a series of lectures at the Oklahoma Department of Libraries, the Tulsa City-County Libraries, and the School of Library Science at the University of Oklahoma.

Several trustee workshops were held in various locations in the state in June. Alice Ihrig, Past President of the American Library Trustee Association, was the moderator for the workshops. Topics discussed were budgets, buildings, standards, objectives, and legislation.

Beverly Rawles was Project Manager and Dorothy Sinclair was a consultant for a statewide comprehensive survey and needs assessment study of Oklahoma libraries. The study was to determine the effectiveness of libraries in Oklahoma in meeting user needs and to develop guidelines for library development in Oklahoma for the ten-year period from 1978 to 1987. The survey was to provide a focus for the Governor's Conference on Library and Information Services to be held in the spring of 1978.

Wayne Morgan, George Lynn Cross Professor of History at the University of Oklahoma, was appointed Chairman of the Governor's Conference Steering Committee. Marilyn Vesely of the Oklahoma Department of Libraries was appointed Coordinator.

"Oklahoma Images: Multi-cultural Influence" has been funded by the National Endowment for the Humanities as a pilot project. Sponsoring organizations are the Department of Libraries, the School of Library Science at the University of Oklahoma, the Oklahoma Arts and Humanities Council, and OLA. Anne Morgan, Humanities Project Coordinator, is directing the project.

Publications. A new edition of the *Oklahoma Union List of Serials* is available for sale in printout or microfiche format. Additional information may be obtained from Norman Nelson at Oklahoma State University Library in Stillwater.

People. Guy Logsdon, Director of Libraries at the University of Tulsa, received the Stanley Draper Distinguished Service Award from the Oklahoma Heritage Association. The Award recognized his years of research and many contributions in the field of Oklahoma music.

The Oklahoma State University Library building has been named the Edmon Low Library in honor of the Oklahoman who planned and designed the building and who for many years was the Director of the Library. Low, although retired, is presently Librarian at New College in Sarasota, Florida.

Frances Kennedy, Director Emeritus of the Oklahoma City University Library, was presented a special award at the OLA meeting in April on the occasion of her retirement as Executive Secretary of the Association. Kennedy was honored for her outstanding contributions to libraries and librarianship and particularly for her untiring and valuable efforts on behalf of OLA. Aarone Corwin was appointed as Executive Secretary of OLA.

Nancy Amis retired as Secretary of the Library Development Committee of OLA. Her accomplishments were recognized at the annual meeting.

Elsie Bell, Chief of the Oklahoma County Libraries Main Library, was awarded a fellowship from the Council on Library Resources to study the relationship between main and branch libraries in several cities in the United States.

Richard Parker was appointed as Assistant Director of Public Services at the Tulsa City-County Library. The position had been held by Pat Woodrum, now the Director of the Tulsa System.

Marilyn Vesely of the Oklahoma Department of Libraries was appointed Conference Coordinator for the 1978 Governor's Conference on Library and Information Services. Barbara Spriestersbach and Clarice Roads were appointed as Library Media Coordinators in the State Department of Education.

Vickie Guagliardo became Children's Librarian at the Carnegie Library in Shawnee. Guagliardo had been Children's Librarian at the downtown branch of the Tulsa City-County Library.

Mae Jennings was appointed Director of the Choctaw Nation Multi-County Library System, following the resignation of Bill Strain, who had served as Director for five years.

James K. Zink, Director of the University Libraries at the University of Oklahoma, accepted a position as Divinity Librarian at Vanderbilt Divinity School in Tennessee. James Alsip was appointed Interim Director of the University Libraries.

Deaths. Frances Duvall died March 31 in Alva. She was retired from her position as Librarian of Northwestern Oklahoma State University. She had been instrumental in establishing the Sequoyah Children's Book Award in 1957 and in developing an undergraduate department of library science at Northwestern Oklahoma State University.

Ralph H. Funk, Director of the Oklahoma Department of Libraries from 1968 to 1976, died March 14 in Norman. Among his many accomplishments as Director were the establishment of OTIS, a statewide teletype interlibrary loan network, and the planning and construction of the Allen Wright Memorial Library Building for the Department of Libraries.

IRMA TOMBERLIN

OREGON

Oregon Library Association
(founded 1941)

Membership: 569; *Annual Expenditure:* $14,500.
President: Richard E. Moore, Director, Southern Oregon State College Library, Ashland.
Vice-President/President-elect: Edwin S. Budge, Director, Josephine County Library, Grants Pass.
Secretary: Ralph Delamarter, Oregon State Library, Salem.
Annual Conference: April 21-23, 1977.
Publication: Oregon Library News (6 issues per year).

Oregon State Library
Marcia Lowell, State Librarian
Oregon State Library
Salem, 97310

State School Library Media Supervisor
Lyle Wirtanen
State Board of Education
Salem 97310

Enactment of state aid for public libraries, establishment of a statewide resource sharing network, development of new county and regional library systems, and pending closure of the School of Librarianship at the University of Oregon highlighted the library activities in Oregon during 1977.

State Aid. Intensive lobbying during the previous three sessions of the Oregon legislature culminated in the passage of Oregon's first state aid for public libraries in 1977. The law provides that the state will make $300,000 available over the next two years on a request basis to public libraries. The Oregon Library Association (OLA) has spearheaded the effort for state funds, and while the legislation falls short of per capita assistance for all public libraries as requested, OLA and the library community are pleased that the legislature has recognized that the public library in Oregon is a function of education by the state for all ages on a self-instructional basis. Administration will be through the State Library Board of Trustees, aided by an advisory council of public librarians. Awarding of the first grants was scheduled for late 1977. For the first biennium of state aid, major emphasis will be on assistance to small libraries.

Library Planning. Several objectives for the development of Oregon libraries conceptualized at a meeting of a cross section of librarians in October 1976 were implemented in 1977. These included the establishment of a state interlibrary loan network, state funding for membership in the Pacific Northwest Bibliographic Center (PNBC) to enable all libraries to participate, provision of microfiche readers to all public libraries receiving the Oregon State Library Catalog (now published on microfiche), reinstatement of the Oregon Regional Union List of Serials with expanded library participant, and initiation of a centralized cataloging project for Oregon documents.

State Resource Network. For the first time in Oregon, funding has been provided to some of the major libraries in the state to act as resource centers. The University of Oregon, Oregon State University, Portland State University, the Health Sciences Center, and the Library Association of Portland (Multnomah County Library) will fill interlibrary loan requests from any library in the state for materials not available in the Oregon State Library (OSL). OSL acts as a central node or clearinghouse for this operation and forwards appropriate requests to the resource libraries. The microfiche catalog of the holdings of the Oregon State System of Higher Education (OSSHE) libraries provides rapid location information.

The resource libraries have used the funds to cover increased interlibrary loan costs and to provide additional interlibrary loan personnel to expedite requests. Multnomah County library has also purchased a TWX to improve communication with OSL. In addition, the Health Sciences Center will answer subject requests for health and medical information not readily located in public libraries. The program started in April and will be evaluated at the end of the first full year of operations.

Academic Libraries. The OSSHE libraries reported resource items totaling more than 6,860,000 in their report to the State Board of Higher Education in June

1977. In dealing with cooperative collection development, local holdings are being deemphasized in favor of a consortium of Oregon academic libraries to provide for, and to promote access and service from, a broader base. The OSSHE library collections are being developed and maintained in close relation to the overall academic plan, and duplication of materials has been limited to basic resources. Improved interlibrary loan service was recorded in 1977 between the state institutions through teletype and shuttle bus. In the Willamette Valley, the shuttle can provide delivery in 24 to 48 hours. Most of the larger academic libraries now have terminals linked to national commercial data bases.

There is also available a microfiche union catalog of state system library holdings, available in the State Library, which makes information available to the citizens of Oregon through their local public libraries. It is now economically feasible to produce on-demand copies of catalogs for other libraries since the catalogs are in microfiche format. The 1977 edition of the *Oregon Union List of Serials* is available in either hardcover or microfiche and includes all Oregon independent college and university libraries, the 13 Oregon community college libraries, OSL, the Multnomah County Library, the Oregon Regional Primate Research Center Library, and all OSSHE libraries.

School Libraries. The Oregon Educational Media Association (OEMA) is the focal organization for resource center librarians. A major emphasis is on development of in-service education sponsored by OEMA, particularly in the area of continuing education for school librarians. Controversy is currently raging around the state over the Portland School Board's decision not to require certification for school librarians in elementary schools. Both OEMA and OLA are discussing this issue. OEMA featured a number of local and regional media specialists at its fall 1977 conference. Around the state, there are still cases of school library censorship necessitating the need for intellectual freedom activity.

Library Development. New library programs were initiated in three areas of the state through voter action. The first regional system in Oregon has been organized in the three counties of Marion, Polk, and Yamhill, which includes Salem. Rural library service was started in Lane County, the state's second most populous area, and provision was made through the serial levy for a Council of Librarians from the cities in the county. Washington County also started a cooperative library program that includes school, public, academic, and special libraries. Interlibrary loan workshops are being sponsored by the Oregon Library Association to assist in the sharing of resources. A new public library was started in Tualitin.

Finances. When city and county budgets were defeated in 1977, local officials in several areas put the library budgets on separate ballots. Public libraries were highly successful in receiving voter approval for higher budgets, even when the remainder of local government budgets were defeated. In addition, several library budgets in major cities were increased, allowing for additional hours and personnel. For the first time, the Oregon legislature requested zero-based budgets from three state agencies, including the State Library. The staff studied the process and made an effective presentation of three levels of budgets to the Ways and Means Committee. Various librarians around the state assisted in the program assessment for the budgets. The results were very positive in terms of State Library funding and in recognition of the fiscal responsibility of the agency.

School of Librarianship. Librarians, students, and educators from across the state rallied in defense of the University of Oregon's School of Librarianship following an announcement in April by President William Boyd that the School would be closed in August 1978. Necessary budget cuts, too many unemployed librarians, and an underdeveloped faculty and curriculum at the School were cited as reasons for the decision. Testimony before the special faculty committee studying the closure and before the State Board of Higher Education pointed out that the School of Librarianship has been self-supporting, that jobs are available to those willing to leave Oregon, that 80 per cent of those employed in Oregon libraries lack professional degrees, and that the school can and should be strengthened. In spite of strong support, the Board of Higher Education suspended the School of Librarianship effective at the end of 1978 summer term. There will be a review of the decision within two years and a report to the 1979 legislature documenting the need to seek restoration funds during the 1979–81 biennium.

White House Conference. OLA is cosponsoring the Governor's Conference on Library and Information Services with the Oregon State Library. The Steering Committee has met, and plans are under way to hire a coordinator. Several regional meetings were to be held early in the state in 1978, culminating in the Governor's Conference late in the spring. Funding for the Conference was in doubt when the Emergency Board of the legislature refused to allocate the additional funds to the budget of the State Library. Support from OLA and others led to the reversal of the decision in November.

KATHERINE G. EATON

PENNSYLVANIA

Pennsylvania Library Association (founded 1901)

Membership: 2,600; *Annual Expenditure:* $90,670.
President: Richard Fitzsimmons, Pennsylvania State University, Dunmore (October 1977-October 1978).
Vice-President/President-elect: Kenneth G. Sivulich, Erie City-County Library.
Treasurer: Dorothy Cieslicki, Dickson College Library, Carlisle.
Annual Conference: September 25-28, 1977, Tamiment.
Publication: PLA Bulletin (bimonthly).

State Library of Pennsylvania
Ernest E. Doerschuk, Jr., State Librarian
Box 1601
Harrisburg 17126

State School Library Media Supervisor
Joan Diana
State Department of Education
Harrisburg 17126

Continuing Education. Continuing education was in the forefront of library activities throughout the state in 1977. Named as priorities by the Pennsylvania Library Association (PLA) President Donald Potter, workshops and seminars expanded the perimeters of librarianship in many ways. "Building the Bridges of Communication" was the theme of the PLA annual conference held at Tamiment-in-the- Poconos, September 25-28. Richard Armour addressed the conference on the "Sixth Sense and Communication," and Judge Lisa Richette questioned, "Have We Come a Long Way, Baby?"

The State Library of Pennsylvania cosponsored sessions on grants, interlibrary loan, librarianship for correctional institutions, services to special patrons, and problems and procedures for talking book lending agencies. Drexel University concentrated on media in several of its continuing education workshops. Cable television and the on-line revolution were studied at the University of Pittsburgh. International in scope, "The On-Line Revolution in Libraries" held in November attracted more than 700 participants for a three-day session. The new copyright law was studied in workshops jointly sponsored by several library organizations in the state.

The Library Media Advisory Council appointed a study committee to prepare competencies to broaden higher education programs for prospective librarians and media specialists. Cross-training will be stressed, and the Council will address itself to these recommendations and to media program guidelines.

The state correctional institutions have their required legal collections in place, and a training program to instruct librarians and resident assistants in their use was held October 26-27 at Camp Hill. The conference was sponsored by Margaret Cheeseman, the Coordinator of Institutional Library Services of the Bureau of Library Development, and directed by Elizabeth Poe, State Law Librarian, with the assistance of the Law Library staff and librarians from the field. Participants rated the training conference as highly successful. The University of Pittsburgh's Graduate School of Library and Information Sciences planned an intensive three-week institute to train professional librarians to develop an up-to-date low-cost resource center for adult citizens in public libraries.

Budgets and Buildings. Pennsylvania's state budget crisis seemed to last the entire year, with "payless paydays" in the late summer and no funding for library-related colleges by year's end. The State Library itself received a $132,000 increase in operating expenses and a $40,000 increase for library service to the blind, but no increase in appropriations for state aid to libraries.

Much thought was being given to the *Plan for Library Cooperation in Pennsylvania*, known locally as "The Drexel Report." The Plan was commissioned by the State Library with LSCA Title III funds and was prepared by a team from Drexel University's Graduate School of Library Science led by Charles T. Meadow.

Among the Plan's high-priority recommendations was the creation of a Pennsylvania Union Catalog, including the resources of a far greater number of libraries than are represented in the microfilmed Union Library Catalog of Philadelphia. Acting in response to this recommendation, the State Library agreed to fund a study, jointly proposed by the Pittsburgh Regional Library Center and PALINET, to define the needs and determine the costs of improving bibliographic access to the materials in Pennsylvania libraries. That study was scheduled for completion in 1978.

Two library buildings were dedicated in March, the Benson Memorial Library in Titusville and the Montgomery County Library. The latter is a completely new structure totally funded by the county government, while the former is a renovated building with additions for which an LSCA Title II grant had been provided through the State Library.

New Castle Public Library received $700,000 matched by a gift of $500,000 from the May Emma Hoyt Fund for a new public library and district library center. The ground breaking took place in December. The Jeannette Public Library received $500,000 for construction of a new building. Both the Oil City Public Library and the Franklin Public Library were extensively renovating and expanding existing public library buldings with funds raised through public subscription.

The Altoona Public Library began its 1977–78 year with a deficit of $105,000. The library, however received a challenge grant of $60,000 from the National Endowment for the Humanities, to be matched by $180,000 in local money.

The Hazleton Area Library was threatened by the cutoff of school district funds for 1977–78 and consequent closing of the main library and its branches. The State Library sent a letter to the Library and school board reminding them that more than $500,000 dollars was granted in 1967 to construct an addition to the Hazleton Area Library Building on the condition that the school district maintain support of the Library at a level sufficient to receive state aid and that the school board had agreed to the condition by a formal resolution. The Library remained open on borrowed money until the crisis could be resolved, presumably by passage of a school subsidy bill.

The Chartiers Township supervisors cut the local library out of its 1977 budget completely. Constructed with LSCA funds, the library receives its primary support from the school district. The library announced plans to close during the months of August and December. The Dauphin County Library undertook a drastic six-month austerity program, including the furloughing of some 30 employees, in order to eliminate a deficit.

The J. Lewis Crozer Library in Chester (Delaware County) reported that the school district withdrew $40,000 in support for 1977–78, and the library expected to run out of money in December. The Library has a new branch building constructed with LSCA Title II funds.

Governor's Conference. Pennsylvania's Pre-White House Conference on Library and Information Services took place October 31-November 1. The planning period had begun in January 1976 when the State Library solicited organizations and libraries throughout the state for names, addresses, and affiliations of potential lay and library-related delegates to the Conference and for suggested names of persons to serve on a Conference planning committee. A meeting of the heads of library and information-oriented organizations took place in the spring of 1976, and from that meeting came additional suggestions for a planning committee.

Early in the planning it was decided to commission a series of six "issue papers" for distribution to delegates prior to the Conference: *Who Makes Library Policy?* by Ernest E. Doerschuk, Jr., State Librarian; *Pennsylvania Library Futures* by Keith Doms; *Breaking Down Barriers* by Thomas J. Galvin; *How Much Can We Pay for Knowledge?* by Rodney P. Lane; *Networks for Sharing* by Jacqueline C. Mancall; and *Technology's Use Today* by Charles P. Meadow.

The 26 district library centers of Pennsylvania were encouraged to hold "Speakouts" within their districts during the summer and early fall of 1977 to give librarians and lay persons a chance to speak about library issues in their respective areas. Another means of educating delegates prior to the Conference was pre-Conference caucuses of delegates within districts. The purpose was to discuss the issues that would come before the Conference, to become acquainted with each other, and to discuss any concerns delegates wished to bring to the Conference.

Through the process, three federal goals and six state goals were placed before the delegates at the final session. The governor, who had stated the challenge to the Conference on the opening day, returned during the debate on the state goals and said that he would accept all six—"Don't bother to count the votes; I'll accept them all."

The outcome and a list of White House delegates elected was sent to each delegate immediately following the Conference. A formal presentation to the governor at one of his scheduled sessions for signing bills and performing ceremonial functions was being planned.

International Activity. The Children's, Young People's and School Librarians Division of PLA was involved during 1977 in negotiations with the City Council of London, England, to arrange for the erection of a bronze plaque to honor John Newbery, the 18th-century publisher and champion of children's literature. The memorial will be located on the site of the building where Newbery lived and worked at Number 65, St. Paul's Churchyard—actually not a churchyard but a business area across from the cathedral. When it is dedicated in 1978, PLA will sponsor a group tour for the occasion.

Structure Study. The Executive Academy of the Pennsylvania Department of Education directed a leadership workshop at which the incoming and outgoing members of PLA's Board of Directors assessed the future needs of libraries and the profession and endeavoured to design a plan for action. The group tried to predict what 1982 would require in library services insofar as skills, management, policy, and delivery systems were concerned and how best PLA could serve those needs. The five most pressing needs that emerged were (1) to develop grass-roots political action and techniques to affect legislation; (2) to develop professional standards and have an active hand in enforcing them; (3) to mandate county libraries; (4) to develop evaluative tools for libraries; and (5) to join with other groups.

People. Richard R. Chamberlin in August 1977 became the Director of Readers' Services at the University of Guyana at Georgetown in South America. After a year of service he will return to his duties at Indiana University of Pennsylvania.

Vera Hospodka is the new Head Librarian at Pennsylvania State University's King of Prussia Graduate Center. Patricia Brown Pond was appointed Associate Dean and Chairperson of the Department of Library Science and Professor at the University of Pittsburgh.

William E. Lafranchi, Director of Libraries at Indiana University of Pennsylvania, was elected President of the Pittsburgh Regional Library Center. Nicholas G. Stevens, Professor and Director of Library Science at Kutztown State College, retired effective September 1, 1977.

Louise H. Stuart was named Director of Citizens Library in Washington. Jean Wilt was appointed Librarian at the Eva K. Bowlby Library in Waynesburg. Michael J. Durkan is the new Librarian of Swarthmore College. He had formerly served the U.S. Information Centre Library in Dublin, Ireland, and most recently was Assistant Librarian at Wesleyan University in Middletown, Connecticut.

Elizabeth Rupert, Dean of the School of Library Media and Information Science at Clarion State College, was appointed Acting President of the College effective January 1, 1977, Elizabeth Harvey was appointed Director of the Schlow Memorial Library at State College.

Ann F. Painter, who had been on a leave of absence from the Graduate School of Library Science at Drexel University to teach at the University of Adelaide, resigned her position at Drexel to remain in Australia. Michael S. Miller, Librarian at Allegheny County Law Library in Pittsburgh, became the Director of the Maryland State Library in Annapolis in February. William L. Beck was appointed Director of Library Services at California State College in Pennsylvania.

Scott Bruntjen of the Library at Shippensburg State College received the Exceptional Academic Service Award from the Pennsylvania Department of Education. He was cited for his work in cataloging American publications of the 1830's. Bruntjen was to be Librarian in Residence at Dalhousie University's School of Library Service from January to June 1978.

Obituaries. Sister Joseph Catherine Roddy, C.S.J., Chairman of the Elementary Section of the Western Pennsylvania Unit, died on May 18, 1977.

Lillian M. Batchelor, formerly Assistant Director of School Libraries for the Philadelphia Board of Education, died on June 28. She had served as President of the American Association of School Librarians and was active in ALA. She had also received citations of merit from the Pennsylvania School Library Association and PLA.

Rosemary Isensee, former Head of the Central Lending Department of the Carnegie Library of Pittsburgh, died in August.

Elizabeth Nesbitt, a well-known library science educator and specialist in children's literature, died in Atlantic City, New Jersey, on August 17. Nesbitt had been honored in October 1976 by the University of Pittsburgh's Graduate School of Library and Information Sciences by the naming of the room housing a children's literature collection for her. A graduate of Carnegie Library School, she served as its Associate Dean from 1948 to 1965. Among her awards and honors was being named a Distinguished Daughter of Pennsylvania in 1958.

Joseph Blake of Millersville State College died October 25. He had been active in library and education circles within the state and nation and was widely known through his publications. He was Chairman of the Library Education Department and Director of Library Education at Millersville.

Honors and Awards. Nicholas G. Stevens, the recently retired Director of the Division of Library Science at Kutztown State College, was given the Distinguished Service Award for 1977, PLA's highest honor, for his outstanding contributions to the field of libraries and librarianship.

Six PLA Certificates of Merit were presented at the annual conference. They went to Joan Diana, Head of the state's department of school libraries; Daniel J. Flood, a Pennsylvania congressman, Phyllis A. Larson, a member of the Board of Delaware County Library; Bertha N. Miller, Dauphin County Library; Anthony A. Martin, Director of the Carnegie Library; and Emery Wimbish, Jr., of the Lincoln University Library.

PAT REDMOND
NANCY L. BLUNDON

RHODE ISLAND

Rhode Island Library Association (founded 1903)

Membership: 580; *Annual Expenditure:* $11,750.
President: Ardis S. Holliday, Westerly Public Library (November 1977-October 1978).
Vice-President/President-elect: Kathleen Gunning, Brown University Library, Providence.
Secretary: Constance E. Lachowicz, South Kingston Public Library, Peacedale.
Annual Conference: November 7-8, 1977, Newport.
Publication: Bulletin of the Rhode Island Association (10 issues a year).

Rhode Island Department of State Library Services

Jewel Drickamer, Director
95 Davis Street
Providence 02908

Incentive Grants. Limitations on funding in 1977 resulted in the small sum of $11,500 in state money being allotted for Incentive Grants by the Rhode Island Department of State Library Services. In addition, $3,300 in federal funds from Titles I and III of LSCA was used for Incentive Grants.

The list of accepted proposals and the amounts of the awards were as follows: Barrington Public Library, $1,100; Coventry Public Library, $1,700; Greenville Public Library, $2,000; Newport Public Library, $1,500; North Kingstown Free Library, $1,000; Pawtucket Public Library, $2,000; Portsmouth Free Public Library, $1,500; Woonsocket Harris Public Library, $2,000; and University of Rhode Island Library, $2,000.

Legislation. Two significant pieces of library legislation were passed by the General Assembly in 1977. House Bill 5709 provides that each regional library system be eligible for an annual grant-in-aid of $30,000 plus 25 cents per capita for the population of the cities and towns served by it. The legislation was also amended to provide an additional $5,000 to the Rhode Island Library Film Cooperative and an additional $50,000 to Providence Public Library in its role as the principal public library of the state. Also passed was an act classifying the libraries at Providence College and Bryant College as special research centers and providing appropriations therefor.

Conferences, Programs, and Workshops. In 1977 the Rhode Island Library Association (RILA) omitted its spring conference and held three spring workshops. The first workshop explored "Commercial Processing and Its Alternatives." A second workshop was held in May by the Intellectual Freedom Subcommittee. Entitled "The

Rights and Responsibilities of Librarians," it examined the personal, professional, and institutional responsibilities of librarians. A third meeting "Workshop on Statewide Borrower's Card," placed emphasis on free access systems in Connecticut and New York's Nassau County.

RILA's fall conference was held on November 14-15. It had as a general theme "Publishers: Public Pressures and Priorities." The first meeting, "Update: University of Rhode Island Graduate Library School," was addressed by Bernard Schlessinger, the Library School's new Dean.

Daniel Gore of Macalester College presented two papers. In one session he dealt with "Mischief in Measurement: A Caveat on the Hazards of Using Faulty Instruments in Measuring Library Performance." Specifically, Gore warned against using a method advocated by Ernest DeProspo in *Performance Measures for Public Libraries*. Other speakers during the conference included Rhode Island Senator Lila Sapinsley; John Berry, editor of *Library Journal*; and Celeste West of Bootlegger Press.

On August 26 Governor J. Joseph Garrahy announced a Governor's Conference on Library and Information Services for March 31 and April 1, 1979.

Publications. During 1977, RILA issued a number of noteworthy publications under the guidance of Leo Flanagan, editor of the *Rhode Island Library Association Bulletin*. The May issue of the *Bulletin* included a listing of the RILA membership. The June issue was dedicated to several bibliographic listings, including an extensive bibliography of "Rhode Island in Fiction" by Robert S. Burford, Director of the Marion Mohr Memorial Library in Johnston. The October issue of the *Bulletin* gave a history of RILA from 1903 to 1977 by Leo N. Flanagan.

Public Libraries. In Rhode Island librarians are a tremendously diverse group of people as proved by a survey of outside interests conducted by the Department of State Library Services early in 1977. The survey included the staffs of the Department of State Library Services and of the five public libraries that comprise the chief libraries of the five Interrelated Library Systems. It showed that these people were engaged in work with some 47 library-connected agencies or organizations and with some 158 other types of organizations.

School Libraries and Media Centers. On June 1, the Rhode Island Educational Media Association (RIEMA) was created from the Rhode Island School Media Association (RISMA) and the former union of the Rhode Island Audio-Visual Education Association (RIAVEA) and the Rhode Island School Library Association (RISLA).

The last meeting of RISMA was held on May 17 to discuss plans for the future and to present gifts of appreciation for service to Hope Carey (RISLA), Marian Bean (RIAVEA), and Gene Paquin (first Joint Conference Committee).

Academic and Special Libraries. The Consortium of Rhode Island Academic and Research Libraries (CRIARL), which came into existence in 1970, held further committee work during 1977 aimed toward the development of a union serials list. CRIARL also investigated the feasibility of forming a cooperative patterned after the Worcester (Massachusetts) Area Cooperating Libraries system.

On November 17, the Rhode Island Chapter of the Special Libraries Association (SLA) was installed as the 48th Chapter of the national organization. The Rhode Island Chapter had been granted full status as a chapter of SLA in January at the SLA meeting in Seattle.

Building Programs. The year 1977 in Rhode island saw the completion and beginning of a number of building programs. The Warwick Public Library completed a $750,000 renovation project. The Narragansett Pier Free Library completed construction of an addition to the building, enlarging the area from 1,500 square feet to a little less than 6,000 square feet. The library addition was built with $275,000 in Federal Community Development Funds.

During 1977, the Tiverton Library Services reopened the North Tiverton Reading Center in the new Community Center. The Reading Center replaces a center destroyed by fire several years ago.

The Pawtucket Public Library was awarded $40,000 under the city's FY 1978 Community Development Block Grant Program. The funds were to be spent to initiate an architectural and engineering design study for the rehabilitation and improvement of the library complex.

As a result of funding through the Public Works Act, the Coventry Public Library planned to build a new main library, and the Middletown Free Library planned to renovate an abandoned day-care center into a new library building. The Central Falls Free Public Library planned to add a $225,000 addition onto the present building, using money from private trusts, foundation grants, and state and federal aid. Due to lack of funds the Barrington Public Library and the Lincoln Public Library remained stalled in their plans to build new main libraries.

Networks and Interlibrary Cooperation. A conference at Rhode Island College on "A National Information Policy: Its Implication for Education and Human Development" was held November 4. James Riley, Executive Director of the Federal Library Committee, and Alphonse Trezza, Executive Director of the National Commission on Libraries and Information Science, were the principal speakers.

Both the Pawtucket Public Library and the University of Rhode Island Library announced plans to follow the lead of Providence Public Library in converting their circulation systems to the CLSI LIBS 100 computerized system.

Collective Bargaining. On January 27 400 clerical and technical workers struck the University of Rhode Island. Of the 400, 50 were library technicians and clerical workers employed at the three libraries which make up the University system. The major issue of the strike was reclassification. The union maintained that its employees were not properly paid for the work they performed. Examples of large numbers of workers classified as Senior Clerk Typists, but in reality performing the work of paraprofessionals, were cited to point out the widespread practice in the University of not matching the job title and pay classification to the job actually performed. Morale problems caused by poor lines of communication and a deterioration of services due to understaffing were also cited by the union.

The strike was settled quickly. The union members, recognizing that implementation of reclassification of library personnel and of clerical positions elsewhere on campus would take time and also be costly, settled for a collective bargaining agreement with the University administration.

Awards. At the fall business meeting of RILA on November 15, Nancy Potter was awarded the 1977 Citation for Outstanding Service in Librarianship. She had served as Acting Dean of the University of Rhode Island's Graduate Library School during a difficult year of transition.

Appointments and Resignation. After a seven-month search, the Board of Trustees of the Pawtucket Public Library appointed Lawrence Eaton as Library Director. He had been the Director of the Northwestern Kansas Regional Center before assuming the Pawtucket position.

In March Connie Lachowicz was appointed as Director of South Kingstown Public Library System. She had been Acting Director since January and Head of the Kingston Free Library since 1972.

In May the University of Rhode Island appointed Bernard Schlessinger of the University of North Carolina as Dean of the Graduate Library School. He replaced Nancy Potter, who had served as Acting Dean while a search was conducted for a permanent replacement for Edward J. Humeston, Jr., who retired in June 1976.

During May, Myron and Stephanie Kirkes, Northern Regional Coordinator and Cranston Public Library Branch Librarian respectively, resigned their positions.

Charles Taylor, Director of the Providence Public Library since 1968, announced his resignation effective July 1, 1978. Annalee M. Bundy, Director of the Somerville (Massachusetts) Public Library was appointed as his replacement.

Richard Waters, Deputy Director of the Department of State Library Services, resigned effective December 2. Anne Shaw, Government Documents Librarian at the University of Rhode Island Library (Kingston), was appointed as his replacement.

Deaths. On May 21, 1977, Marie Andrea Mulligan, former Librarian at Brown University, died after a long illness.

Later in the year Donald Medley died. He was Chairperson of the Board of Trustees of the George Hail Library in Warren. — EMIL A. CIALLELLA

SOUTH CAROLINA

South Carolina Library Association (founded 1915)

Membership: 900; *Annual Expenditure:* $9,028.
President: Margaret W. Ehrhardt, State Department of Education, Columbia (January 1977-December 1978).
Vice-President/President-elect: Lennart Pearson, Presbyterian College Library, Clinton.
Secretary: Margaret F. Huff, Calhoun Technical College, Orangeburg.
Annual Conference: October 13-15, 1977, Myrtle Beach.
Publication: South Carolina Librarian (biannually).

South Carolina State Library

Estellene P. Walker, State Librarian
P.O. Box 11469
Columbia 29211

State School Library Media Supervisor

Margaret W. Ehrhardt
Department of Education
Columbia 29201

Governor's Conference. Governor James B. Edwards has agreed that South Crolina's Pre-White House Conference on Library and Information Services shall be convened as a Governor's Conference on March 15-17, 1979. State Senator Arnold S. Goodstein of Charleston is serving as Honorary Chairman of the Advisory Committee planning the Conference. Betty E. Callaham, Deputy State Librarian, is Conference Coordinator.

Workshops and Conferences. The South Carolina State Library and the South Carolina State Personnel Division cosponsored a workshop on interpersonal communication and personnel management for the state's public library directors. Lynn Phelps, Director of Interpersonal Communication at Miami University (Ohio), and Robert Hall, Classification and Compensation Supervisor of the State Personnel Division, led the program.

In August the South Carolina State Library sponsored a two-day "Outreach Workshop" led by Wyllie F. Dennis, Chief of Children's Services and Supervisor of LOOP (Library Oriented Outreach Program) in Jacksonville, Florida.

The College of Librarianship at the University of South Carolina held several one-day workshops on the Columbia campus. Topics of the workshops were "Media Production," "Library Automation," "Workshop on Workshops," and "Cataloging: AACR Chapter 6."

The College of Librarianship held a colloquium on "Library Service Performance Measures: Where Are We? Where Are We Going?" Ernest R. DeProspo, Professor at the Graduate School of Library Service at Rutgers University, was the speaker.

The South Carolina State Library and the College of Librarianship cosponsored a copyright workshop in November. Edmon Low, Director of Libraries at the University of South Florida; Cora Paul Bomar, Assistant Professor at the University of North Carolina, Greensboro; Susan Bistline of the Copyright Office of the Library of Congress; Larry Besant, Assistant Director of Ohio State University Libraries; and Robin Mills, Law Librarian at the University of South Carolina, participated in the conference.

S.C.L.A. Members of the South Carolina Library Association approved basic changes to the Constitution and Bylaws of that organization in order to make it more responsive to its members. The changes included the employment of an Executive Secretary, creation of four new activity sections and added a 2nd Vice-President.

Public Libraries. Since 1943 the South Carolina State Library has worked for the establishment of library systems for every county of the state. In February 1977 this goal was realized when funds were appropriated to fund the Clarendon County Library. State Senator John Land, State representatives Charles Harbin, and Charles Griffin, the Manning Civic League, and the Clarendon County Library Commission were instrumental in achieving this milestone.

The South Carolina State Library and the South Carolina Wildlife Federation cosponsored the film *The Russell Dam—A Question of Values.* The film explores the pros and cons of the controversial Russell Dam Project. The dam is to be constructed on the Savannah River, which runs between South Carolina and Georgia. Research for the film was provided by the South Carolina State Library, and it was directed by Jacquelin E. Jacobs, Executive Secretary of the Wildlife Federation. The South Carolina Humanities Committee funded the project.

The South Carolina State Library made a $25,000 grant to establish an Area Resource Reference Center (ARRC) in Florence, to be administered from the Florence County Library. The initial grant will provide a salary as well as administrative expense for one year. The goal of the ARRC concept is to place a major reference and information center no more than a half-day's drive from any citizen in the state.

The Richland County Public Library added the New York Times Information Bank to its reference services in 1977, becoming the first library in South Carolina to acquire this type of information retrieval. This computer-based service provides access to the data files of the New York Times as well as 60 other publications. Through the terminal at the Richland County Public Library, it is possible to locate particular projects, research, and facts in a matter of seconds or minutes.

Institutions. A new trailer library was opened at the Manning Correctional Institute. The three-room 12-foot-by-60-foot trailer was surplus U.S. government property purchased for $100. Shelves were taken from what was the old library at Manning, and the circulation desk was formerly a department store display case. The outside of the structure will be veneered brick to create an attractive appearance.

The South Carolina Department of Corrections Library Division also opened a library at the new Kirkland Correctional Institution and included the new Aiken youth facility in its bookmobile schedule. Both additions were made late in the year and were not provided for by any special budget increments.

With the South Carolina State Library's assistance, the South Carolina Division of Youth Services is providing quality library service for institutionalized young people. The libraries at the Willow Lane School and Birchwood Campus School in Columbia function as learning centers as well as sources for recreational and leisure reading materials.

Various bibliotherapy projects were carried out in institutions associated with the South Carolina Department of Mental Health. The Crafts-Farrow State Hospital at Columbia added a one-to-one bibliotherapy project in which aides assist by reading regularly to their patients from a shelf of materials selected by the librarian. The Horger Library at the State Hospital continued a media therapy program with films chosen from the South Carolina State Library collection by the patients who were participating in the program. Book cart service, mostly paperbacks and periodicals, is the specialty of the library at State Park Health Center.

Blind and Physically Handicapped. The South Carolina State Library for the Blind and Physically Handicapped has as a major goal the recording of South Caroliniana for its patrons. To accomplish this, the Library and the Department of Theatre and Speech and the Department of Media Arts of the University of South Carolina have an agreement whereby students make talking books on a volunteer basis.

The Telephone Pioneers of America were given a special award by the State Library Board in recognition for their assistance to the Talking Book Program of the State Library for the Blind and Physically Handicapped.

Academic Libraries. A study of the library resources of postsecondary institutions in South Carolina, commissioned by the South Carolina Higher Education Commission, has been published. *Resources of South Carolina Libraries* was prepared by Edward G. Holley, Dean of the School of Library Science at the University of North Carolina; Johnnie E. Givens, Executive Director of the Southeastern Library Association; Fred Roper, Assistant Dean of the School of Library Science at the University of North Carolina; and W. Christian Sizemore, Dean of South Georgia College. The library study forms part of the Higher Education Commission's long-range planning effort "to assess needs of the higher educational institutions and make recommendations for a cohesive system of postsecondary education."

Awards and Appointments. Arthur Magilll, who served as the first President of the Friends of the Greenville Library, was presented with the 1977 Friends of the Library Award by the South Carolina Library Association (SCLA). The Award, sponsored by the Association, recognizes a nonlibrarian who has made a significant contribution to library development in the state.

The 1977 South Carolina Children's Book Award was presented to Judy Blume, author of *Tales of a Fourth Grade Nothing*, at a workshop sponsored by the University of South Carolina's College of Librarianship, the South Carolina Association of School Librarians, and the South Carolina Department of Education.

Two South Carolina public libraries received the John Cotton Dana Public Relations Award during the year. Pickens County Library won an award for its slide-sound presentation developed to support the Library's budget request. Greenville County Library won its fifth consecutive Award for a scrapbook illustrating activities connected with the celebration of the Bicentennial year.

Edward A. Scott, Director of the Instructional Materials Center and Assistant Professor of Library Science at Winthrop College, was named the 1976 Media Person of the Year by the Association for Educational Communications and Technology of South Carolina.

Jim Johnson, Librarian at South Carolina State Library for the Blind and Physically Handicapped, was appointed to represent the South on a four-member advisory committee to the Library of Congress.

Library Education. The Ad Hoc Committee on Scholarship of SCLA drew up a number of recommendations in an effort to stimulate professional improvement. Committee members were Betty Callaham, South Carolina State Library; Carolyn Tyler, Librarian of the Education Library at the University of South Carolina; and Margaret Ehrhardt, Library Consultant for the South Carolina Department of Education. The Committee is concerned with the employment prospects of beginning librarians and the need for continuing education programs for practicing librarians.

A scholarship fund of $500 a year will be set aside for SCLA members holding a baccalaureate degree who are currently employed in South Carolina.

In March the South Carolina Board of Education gave its approval to the graduate program in school librarianship offered by the University of South Carolina College of Librarianship.   CARL STONE

SOUTH DAKOTA

In South Dakota 1977 was a year of steady growth of public library service as many smaller public libraries moved to new or enlarged facilities. It was also a time of continued discussion about the place of computerized data bases in the development of the state network of libraries. No major library legislation was passed in 1977, but early in 1978 state legislators were to consider a proposal to eliminate special mill levies for municipalities under which public libraries can levy a special tax of up to three mills.

Joint Conference. Most of the year's activity centered on preparations for the joint conference with Mountain Plains Library Association (MPLA). Programs were planned with the help of MPLA under the leadership of Robert Malinowski and the South Dakota Library Association (SDLA) under the leadership of Jan Olson. The theme chosen was "Forward to Fundamentals," and a Western motif was used. Pre- and postconference workshops were scheduled.

Under the direction of Phil McCauley, Local Arrangements Chairperson, the joint meeting was held in the Rapid City Convention Center, November 2-5. About 500 persons registered for more than 60 conference activities and viewed displays by 48 exhibitors. Those attending participated in programs on performance measurement, community analysis, library instruction, the basics of managing people, copyright, library signage, film utilization, and other subjects.

South Dakota Library Association (founded 1907)

Membership: 600 (85 ALA members); Annual Expenditure: $3,200.
President: Dorothy Liegl, State Library, Pierre (October 1977-September 1978).
Vice-President/President-elect: Caroline Green, Waubay High School.
Secretary: Hugh Franklin, Devereaux Library, South Dakota School of Mines and Technology, Rapid City.
Treasurer: Cynthia Winn, Sioux Falls Public Library.
Annual Conference: November 2-5, 1977, Rapid City.
Publication: Book Marks (bimonthly).

South Dakota State Library

Herschel V. Anderson, State Librarian
State Library Building
Pierre 57501

State School Library Media Supervisor

Ardis Ruark
Department of Educational and Cultural Affairs
Pierre 57501

State Library. Librarians from across the state attended the formal dedication of the new State Library building on January 25. With its 50,000 square feet the structure houses all present services and collections with adequate space for 10 years of expansion.

The State Library budget was $911,544 with $480,432 from state funds, $395,112 from federal funds, and $36,000 from the contract with North Dakota for services to the visually and physically handicapped. These funds provided support for all State Library functions except that of providing curriculum materials for the elementary and secondary schools of the state. An attempt by the State Library to curtail direct film services for classroom use was

403

countermanded by the state legislature, and the State Library continues to serve the schools on a limited budget.

In midyear, the State Library Information Services Program financed the installation of a computer terminal that provided direct access to research data bases. Formerly, access had been through the Bibliographic Center for Research in Denver.

Due to lack of funds and the structured guidelines for a state-level White House Conference on Library and Information Services, the State Library decided not to make application for funds. SDLA also declined to participate in the program.

Public Libraries. 1977 saw a number of changes in public library facilities throughout the state. The following communities have remodeled or moved their libraries: Lemmon, Sully County (Onida), Oldham, Lennox, Edgemont, and Whitewood. In addition, Murdo, Wall, Wasta, Menno, and Gary are organizing new libraries.

Lawrence and Grant Counties are working on combining efforts to build strength. The Grant County Library was established by a popular vote and combines the Milbank Public Library and Grant County Bookmobile. This was the first such vote in the state. In Lawrence County the county commission and four public libraries joined forces. Under the Joint Exercise of Governmental Powers Law, the Lawrence County Commission and the city commissions of Lead, Deadwood, Spearfish, and Whitewood provide service throughout the county.

Mitchell Public Library has found a way to serve its community through a cooperative contract. The Mitchell Area Vocational School, which has no library, will buy materials for its students, and the public library will house them.

School Libraries. Joint school and public library projects continue to grow. The Meade School District and the West River Independent School District contract for services from the Sturgis Public Library. Willow Lake School District has contracted with the Hamlin-Codington County Library for bookmobile service. Wessington School Board and the Wessington Public Library provide a joint community library for the town. In order to better serve the citizens of Selby, the school library opened one day a week during summer vacation.

Academic Libraries. Now in its new facility, the H.M. Briggs Library of South Dakota State University has under its roof several collections that had been scattered throughout the campus. Included are the 230,000 volumes of the original library, 20,000 from the Chemistry and Pharmacy Branch, and 40,000 that had been in storage.

Sinte Gleska College on the Rosebud Indian Reservation received a $100,000 grant from the Bush Foundation of St. Paul, Minnesota, to finish and furnish its library media center.

Several campus libraries have had a boost to their local history collections. Herman Chilson of Webster donated his entire 20,000-item collection of Western Americana to the I.D. Weeks Library at the University of South Dakota. It included purchased collections of other collectors and authors, items relating to religious activity in the Midwest, and a strong section of materials dealing with the Indians of the Dakota area. The Leland D. Case Library of Western History at Black Hills State College received the collection of Rev. Eugene Szalay.

Building Programs. Dedication of the H.M. Briggs Library on the campus of South Dakota State University in Brookings was held December 17. This 121,000-square-foot building now provides space for 500,000 books, 400,000 documents, 300 study carrels, and several study lounges.

Through the Public Works Employment Act, several cities will have new or improved buildings for their public libraries. Vermillion will construct an 11,000-square-foot facility, and Grant County (Milbank) plans a building of 8,000 square feet. Sturgis Public Library will use the funds to remodel an addition to its facility.

In the northwestern part of the state, Belle Fourche citizens passed a $250,000 bond issue for a new building. Construction was expected to be completed in early 1978.

Northern State College in Aberdeen is in the process of remodeling its library. The $564,000 project will add stack and study space to all three levels of the library, modify the building for access by the handicapped, and provide housing for the college's Educational Media Center.

Networks. The teletype network in the state continued with grants from the State Library to 3 public libraries and 10 academic libraries. Under this system participating libraries use in-state locations for materials before contacting out-of-state libraries. The South Dakota Union List of Serials was scheduled for input into the Minnesota Union List of Serials data base in early 1978.

Three new libraries were to join the OCLC network. The University of South Dakota, South Dakota School of Mines and Technology, and the State Library were designated for grants from the Bush Foundation of St. Paul, Minnesota. Grant money is to be used for terminal installations, bringing the total number of OCLC terminals in the state to seven.

Awards. The following awards were given by the South Dakota Library Association: Librarian of the Year—Hershel V. Anderson, State Librarian; Trustee of the Year—Mrs. Winifred Lorentson, Trustee, Hand County Library, Miller; Friend of the Library—Herman Chilson, Webster.

People. Cleo Catchpole of Lemmon and Merle Heidenreich of Watertown were appointed to the State Library Commission. Leon Raney, Dean of Libraries at South Dakota State University, was appointed to the Board of Trustees of the Bibliographic Center for Research.

Elaine Anderson became Catalog Librarian of the Sioux Falls Public Library; and Irene Aga became Children's Librarian at Rapid City Public Library. Rebecca Bell was appointed Technical Services Librarian at the State Library; and Jerry Bowman was appointed Reference Librarian at Watertown Regional Library.

Three appointments were made at the Lommen Health Sciences Library of the University of South Dakota School of Medicine: Dave Boilard, Program Development Officer; Linda Precoda, Medical Cataloger; and Thomas Bremer, Acquisitions Librarian.

Several other appointments were made during the year: Ellen Hall, Director of Presentation College Library; Sandra Norlin, Adult Services Librarian at Brookings Public Library; John Olgaard, Documents Librarian and Archivist at I.D. Weeks Library at the University of South Dakota; Linda Watson, Director of the National College of Business Library; and Stanley Planton, Director of Learning Resources at Dakota Wesleyan University.

Carolyn Mountain, Assistant Director of Mitchell Public Library; Irma Falck, Documents Librarian of the I.D. Weeks Library at the University of South Dakota; Evelyn Dickson, Media Librarian at Northern State College Library; and Helen Herrett, Director of the Belle Fourche Public Library, retired during 1977.

EMILY K. GUHIN

TENNESSEE

Grants. The School of Library Science of George Peabody College for Teachers in Nashville received an award of $31,000 from the U.S. Office of Education. The award has been designated for five fellowships to train graduate library science students to work with the economically disadvantaged and with ethnic minorities. The College also received a grant from the Tennessee Committee for the Humanities to study the feasibility of establishing a resource center at Peabody for the Committee.

Memphis/Shelby County Public Library and Information Center received a

Rockefeller Grant from the Memphis Board of Education to teach parents how to help their children become better readers. Qualified personnel from the city schools conducted the classes to train parents in the basic principles of reading education. The Library also received a $10,000 grant from the Memphis Delta Area Agency on Aging.

Jessie Carney Smith, University Librarian at Fisk University in Nashville, received a grant from the Council on Library Resources for a study entitled "Black Academic Libraries and Research Collections: An Historical Survey."

Tennessee Library Association (founded 1902)

Membership: 1,403; *Annual Expenditure:* $42,445.
President: Gary R. Purcell, University of Tennessee, Knoxville (May 1977-April 1978).
Vice-President/President-elect: Mary Little, Caney Fork Regional Library, Sparta.
Treasurer: Willodene Scott, Nashville Public Schools.
Annual Conference: April 14-16, 1977, Memphis.
Publication: Tennessee Librarian (quarterly).

Tennessee State Library and Archive

Katheryn C. Culbertson, State Librarian and Archivist
403 Seventh Avenue North
Nashville 37219

State School Library Media Supervisor

Christine Brown
State Department of Education
Nashville 37219

Buildings. The Chattanooga-Hamilton County Bicentennial Library officially opened its new Northgate Branch with a ribbon-cutting ceremony on April 18. The Northgate Branch is a 7,800-square-foot circular building.

The Clarksville-Montgomery County Public Library broke ground on April 19 for an addition to and a renovation of the present building. A Public Works Grant in the amount of $350,000 will provide assistance.

Friends of the Library. Friends of the Mayne Williams Public Library made city commissioners aware of the funding needs of the Library by presenting each commissioner with a blackberry cobbler pie and a booklet entitled "Original Recipe for Enough Library Pie for 40,000 Johnson Citians ... and Other Palatable Goodies." Citizens were urged through the Friends of the Library newsletter to contact their commissioners. The Library's budget was increased 10 per cent.

The budget outlook for the Memphis/ Shelby County Public Library and Information Center looked bleak in the spring of 1977, with a reduction of 20 per cent facing the Library Board. A staff committee and the Friends organization stepped in with letters, phone calls, and petitions with well over 10,000 signatures. After a two-month battle, the Friends carried the day with a solid 5 per cent increase over the year before, a total gain of 25 per cent above the first proposal made by city hall. The second annual Book and Author Dinner, sponsored by the Friends of Memphis/ Shelby County, was held October 25.

The Friends of the Memphis Public Library conducted their 14th successful semiannual book sale in October, netting more than $5,000.

Friends of the Joint University Libraries held their fourth annual dinner meeting in November. The first meeting of the Friends of the Memphis State University Libraries was held on March 11.

During 1977 the Knoxville-Knox County Public Library faced the possibility of a crippling cut in its budget for the year. Library supporters rallied to the cause of obtaining the original request. Eventually, 80 per cent of the budget request cut was restored.

Programs. A two-year staff development program for 13 libraries was concluded in August by the Upper Cumberland Regional System and the Tennessee Technological University.

The Memphis/Shelby County Public Library and Information Center cooperated with the Memphis Area Chamber of Commerce and the Memphis in May Committee in the city's "Salute to Japan." "Shatter Silence," an all-day workshop, was held as part of the Deaf Awareness Week observance. During the observance of Older Americans Month in May, senior citizens were invited to visit the Memphis Room at the Main Library and to participate in the contest to see who could identify the majority of pictures of old Memphis. The Main Library and two branches, Hollywood and Parkway Village, were invaded by more than 650 children to be entertained by two Barnum and Bailey circus clowns and their talking dog. The Library, the Memphis Area Chamber of Commerce, Memphis State University, and Action for Independent Maturity sponsored a workshop on retirement planning. Peter Rabbit's 75th birthday was observed system-wide in 21 libraries during September by 1,826 Memphis and Shelby County children (see "Peter Rabbit," p. 92).

LINC (the Memphis/Shelby County Public Library and Information Center's Information and Referral service) moved through its second year with extensive "community walks" by all branches in the system. In September crowds came to the first "Christmas" workshop at the Library.

The Mayne Williams Public Library and the Johnson City School System operated a library program for elementary school children during the summer months. Bus transportation from each elementary school to the public library was provided. Bus schedules and information on the program were sent home with final report cards to all elementary school students in the city. The Dial-a-Story program, sponsored by the Junior Service League of Johnson City in conjunction with the Friends of the Mayne Williams Public Library, averaged nearly 5,000 calls a month during the year.

Video. The Knoxville-Knox County Public Library took the first steps in exploring the role of its Library in cable community television. The program used equipment from the community video center one-half block from the Main Library. The staff, headed by a former television newswriter and producer, videotaped several library programs for showing on the community cable television channel.

Tennessee Library Association. The Tennessee Library Association (TLA), the Southeastern Library Association, and the Special Libraries Association cosponsored a copyright workshop in Chattanooga. A legislative workshop was held on December 6 at the University of Tennessee in Nashville. A TLA-sponsored luncheon was held February 23-24 for state legislators.

William C. Robinson, Associate Professor at the Graduate School of Library and Information Science of the University of Tennessee in Knoxville, was selected as the new editor of the *Tennessee Librarian*.

The College and University Section held midwinter conferences in January and November. The School Libraries Section planned to present the Louise Meredith School Library Media Service Award at the next TLA convention. The citation will be given annually to the school library media specialist whose school library media program is deemed outstanding. The Public Libraries Section established five new committees on program, bylaws, audiovisual, children's services, and midwinter plans.

Appointments, Retirements. Edward M. Walters was appointed Director of Libraries at East Tennessee State University in Johnson City, July 1.

Keith Cottam was appointed Assistant Director for Public Services and Employee Relations at Joint University Libraries in Nashville. Margaret Link was appointed Director of the Management Library, and James Zink was appointed Director of the Divinity Library at Joint University Libraries.

Elsie Draper Barrette, Director of Library Service at East Tennessee State University in Johnson City, retired after 29 years of service. Dorrice Bratcher, Head of the Reference Department of the John W. Brister Library at Memphis State University, retired after 28 years of service.

Evelyn P. Fancher was appointed Director of the Tennessee State University Library. Robert H. Simmons was named Director of the Library at Austin Peay State University.

Deaths. Walter Turner Clark, Assistant Director and Business Manager of the Memphis/Shelby County Public Library and Information Center, died July 26. He had joined the Memphis Public Library in 1946 as Director of the Shelby County School Libraries operation. Active in TLA, he served as President in 1963-64.

John Morrow Bobb, Jr., former Assistant Chief Librarian at the Oak Ridge National Laboratory for 17 years, died January 12. An active member of professional associations, he had served as President of TLA.

ROBERT F. PLOTZKE

TEXAS

Texas Library Association (founded 1902)

Membership: 3,367; *Annual Expenditure:* $100,000.
President: Shelah A. Bell, Irving Public Library (April 1977-March 1978).
Vice-President/President-elect: Alvin C. Cage, Stephen F. Austin State University, Nacogdoches.
Executive Secretary: Jerre Hetherington, Houston.
Annual Conference: April 13-16, 1977, El Paso.
Publications: Texas Library Journal (quarterly); *Added Entries* (3 issues a year).

Texas State Library

Dorman H. Winfrey, Director and Librarian
Box 12927, Capitol Station
Austin 78711

State School Library Media Supervisor

Mary Boyvey
Texas Education Agency
Austin 78711

Although the Texas State Library's budget for the biennium that began in September 1977 did not rise appreciably, the beginning of a second funding cycle with significant state funding for statewide responsibilities has made a perceptible change in service. For more than a decade LSCA has enabled the Texas State Library to upgrade service to public libraries. With significant funding for the Library Systems Act for fiscal 1976 and 1977, the state also became involved. During the last biennium the state expanded service to the blind and physically handicapped, continued to develop a system for inactive records of local governments in a network of regional depositories in academic and public libraries, and expanded its program to distribute publications of state agencies to depository libraries.

The percentage of Texans served by libraries that are members of regional public library systems organized under the provisions of the Texas Library Systems Act rose from 86 per cent in fiscal 1977 to 88.5 per cent in fiscal 1978. Twenty-one libraries serve the 286,449 persons represented by this 2.5 per cent increase. Since most of the larger libraries are now members of the regional systems, the major thrust has become work with smaller libraries to upgrade local support so that they can meet criteria for system membership. Approximately half of the 12 per cent of all Texans who are not served by system members have no library service. Most of these unserved persons live in areas where cities and towns support library service but where the county does not. The organization of county libraries or systems in these counties, therefore, has become a major priority. To assist in its development, grants are being given to counties to organize systems.

Since passage of the Regional Historical Resources Depository system in 1971, the Texas State Library has been increasingly involved in management of inactive records of counties, cities, and other local governmental units. In 1977 the State Library was directed to produce a manual to assist county officials in determining what records should be kept and for how long.

Activities. In a speech prepared for a Texas Library Association (TLA) district meeting in October, Governor Dolph Briscoe announced that the Texas Pre-White House Conference on Library and Information Services will take place in Austin in the fall of 1978. More than 250 Texans will assemble for the Conference.

A program to identify and preserve Texas newspapers was proposed at a February 1977 meeting of librarians, historians, and journalists. Discussed were points to be considered in identifying files, microfilming the papers, preparing guides, and cataloging. The Texas Library and Historical Commission agreed that the State Library should serve as an umbrella agency for the project.

Lubbock City-County Library was one of the first public libraries to subscribe to the AMIGOS Bibliographic Council's computer-based reference services that will provide bibliographic citations and abstracts using the Lockheed DIALOG and Systems Development Corporation data bases.

In August, Fondren Library at Rice University was designated a Patent Depository Library by the Patent and Trademark Office of the U.S. Dept. of Commerce. This is the only patent depository in Texas.

A special CETA grant was secured by the Amarillo Public Library to prepare a brochure on its Bush/FitzSimon Collections on the Southwest. The John L. McCarty papers, a collection of 4,000 items on the Texas Panhandle, were processed. Friends of the Amarillo Library have helped employ indexers for Amarillo papers and underwrote continuing education expenses for the staff.

School Libraries. School librarians remained concerned that legislation be enacted and funded so that each Texas public school building have the services of at least one full-time learning resources specialist or librarian. The greatest need is at the elementary level. The progress of Texas school libraries was well recorded in the Winter 1977 issue of *Texas Library Journal*. The subjects covered ranged from an explanation of the Learning Resources Specialist Certificate, to explanations of Dallas area and Alief media center projects, to "How to Talk to an Architect" when planning a library.

The first Siddie Joe Johnson Award honoring achievement in library service to children was awarded to Ella Mae Platz of Lubbock. The Texas Association of School Librarians presented its annual award for Distinguished School Library Service to John F. Townley, Superintendent of the Irving Independent School District.

Acquisitions. The Dallas Public Library purchased a collection of 130 drawings by John Groth from the 1964 murder trial of Jack Ruby. Groth's drawings are the only visual record of the trial. The beginnings of a valuable collection of memorabilia from Dallas film history including movie posters, photos, and 16mm preview advertisements of films came from a garbage can. An alert janitor spotted them, called the Library, and arranged delivery by a city garbage truck to the Library archivist.

In January 1977 the University of Houston libraries was presented its millionth volume for the central campus—Albrecht Dürer's *Underweysung der messung* . . . (1525). In February the University of Texas at Austin added its four millionth volume—Noah Webster's *An American Dictionary of the English Language* (two volumes, 1828). The Texana collection of Max H. Bickler, master emeritus of protocol for Texas inaugurations, was presented in August to the

Austin-Travis County Collection of the Austin Public Library.

Grants. Bishop College in Dallas received National Endowment for the Humanities (NEH) funds for assistance in launching a bibliographic survey of historical research materials documenting the history and current status of Blacks in the Southwest. In the first phase, the survey staff will identify, locate, and describe collections in four specific locations.

A nine-month project for the Houston Public Library, with the assistance of NEH funds, will examine the city. Called "City! Our Urban Past, Present, and Future," the project involves exhibits and programs at the Central Library and three branches.

In November, the Library Board, Friends of the Library, and Neiman-Marcus staged a major fund raiser, an historical style show and dinner dance, for the Houston Public Library. The event netted some $20,000 to develop an endowment for the Library's Humanities Department.

A special one-time appropriation of $134,000 was given to Midwestern University by the Texas legislature for library development. Funds are to be matched by monies raised from private sources in a school-sponsored "Advance Midwestern" drive.

Publications. *A Comprehensive Program of User Education for the General Libraries: The University of Texas at Austin* describes a multiphase program of library instruction. With the Winter 1977 issue the *Journal of Library History* moved its editorship to the Graduate School of Library Science at the University of Texas at Austin, with publication by the University of Texas Press. "Texas Reference Sources, 1976–77," published in the Fall 1977 *Texas Library Journal*, updates a guide published in 1975 as a TLA Reference Round Table project. *Photographs from the Border: The Otis A. Aultman Collection* was published late in 1977 in a limited edition by the El Paso Library Association.

Buildings. On January 28 the University of Houston dedicated a five-story addition to the M.D. Anderson Memorial Library and dedicated the John H. Freeman wing. Additional library areas were renovated. In July the Texas A & M University Board of Regents awarded the contract for construction of an addition to the central library building. Ground breaking for Trinity University's $4,300,000 library took place July 5; it was the culmination of four years of fund raising.

The huge Perry-Castañeda Library, the new main library for the University of Texas at Austin, was opened August 29. A six-level structure of 500,673 square feet, the $21,700,000 facility offers expanded public services and includes the administrative offices, the Bibliographical Control Division and the bibliography department for the General Libraries. Basically a humanities-social sciences collection, materials in the Library represent holdings formerly shelved in the Tower and in the Business Administration-Economics and Education-Psychology Libraries. Filling the shelves meant the move of approximately 1,500,000 volumes from their former locations during the summer months of 1977.

New public library facilities opened in Amarillo, Dallas, Orange, and San Antonio. Design plans and working drawings for the first phase of construction for the new Dallas central library were completed, and the first phase of construction began. The staff at the Fort Worth Public Library spent the year getting ready for a move to their new central library to open in late spring 1978. One such project was the conversion of the card catalog to microfiche. A new central library building of 125,000 square feet was under construction in Austin. Two-year colleges located in Brownsville, Paris, and San Antonio added new learning resource centers.

Texas Library Association. Support for the Texas State Library's budget request, with particular emphasis on the budget request for the program called "Statewide Library Development," continued as a goal of TLA. The statewide development program provides for the following: regional public library systems authorized by the Texas Library Systems Act, interlibrary loan services through the Texas State Library Communications Network, and continuing education and consulting services for Texas library staffs. A coordinated TLA legislative effort was begun to assure substantial increases in the next state biennium. Another priority of TLA work in 1977 was planning and putting into action a statewide public information program with publicity prepared by a public relations agency.

Members celebrated the TLA's 75th year by meeting in El Paso in April with members of the New Mexico Library Association. Microfiches of the proceedings were prepared. Named as Librarian of the Year was Alice Green, Librarian at Amarillo Public Library; and as Trustee of the Year, Robert E. Davis, a three-term member of the Waco-McLennan County Library Board and Chairman of the Texas Library and Historical Commission. TLA members passed a resolution to seek incorporation of TLA under the Texas Non-Profit Corporation Act, endorsed the 1940 AAUP Academic Freedom and Tenure Statement of Principles and Interpretive Comments, and heard plans for the new Audio Visual Interest Group to solicit members in 1978.

TLA's annual assembly, a midyear working session for committee members and officers, was held in July. TLA now has official headquarters space in Houston. National Library Week materials were again prepared for sale; the 1977 version featured "A Curious Bird and the Written Word." Building on its strength of 75 years, TLA in 1977 saw the involvement of a great many members through committee work. Library trustees and Friends were especially encouraged to participate.

Retirements. Ella Mae Platz, Director of Children's Services at Lubbock City-County Library, retired January 31. Wanda K. Sivells, Director of Hodges Learning Center at Wharton County Junior College, retired in 1977.

Deaths. Isabel Bazan, Head of the Main Library of the San Antonio Public Library, died in February.

Siddie Joe Johnson, formerly Children's Librarian at Dallas Public Library and Children's Book Editor of the Dallas *Morning News*, died July 27.   MARY POUND

UTAH

Utah Library Association (founded 1912)

Membership: 600; *Annual Expenditure:* $12,000.
President: E. Dale Cluff, University of Utah, (March 1977–March 1978).
Vice-President/President-elect: Amy Owen, Utah State Library Commission, Salt Lake City.
Executive Secretary: Gerald A. Buttars, Utah State Library Commission, Salt Lake City.
Annual Conference: April 6-8, 1977, Salt Lake City.
Publication: Utah Libraries (semiannual).

Utah State Library Commission

Russell L. Davis, Director
2150 South 300 West
Salt Lake City 84115

State School Library Media Supervisor

Leroy L. Lindeman
State Board of Education
Salt Lake City 84111

The year 1977 could be characterized as a year of consolidation for Utah libraries. A few library systems enjoyed building expansion or celebrated ground breakings or opened new branches, but 1977 was a year for developing human and physical resources already extant. "Horizons Unlimited," the theme of the 1977 Utah Library Association (ULA) conference, referred to better utilization of existing resources and wiser selection of goals than in previous periods of expansionist growth.

College and University Libraries. Typical of the emphasis on making better use of existing resources was the major reorganization of materials and personnel undertaken during the summer months by the Marriott Library at the University of Utah. Built in the 1960's with a "subject divisional" approach to organizing the collection, the Marriott Library now has a consolidated collection and unified reference service, maintaining separate subject facilities only for science and engineering in the main building. Serials, formerly allocated by subject to various locations, have been integrated along with the staff and files into a single area that now includes the microforms collection. More than 742 bookshelves were freed by the reorganization. An all-day open house was held on September 23 to introduce returning faculty members and students to the changes.

1977 was also an outstanding year for the development of human resources training at the University of Utah Libraries. The Staff Development Committee scheduled a full series of programs on communication skills, designed particularly for new supervisors but open to all staff members.

For professional librarians at the University of Utah, 1977 will be remembered as the year they lost faculty status. On May 2, the Academic Senate of the University of Utah voted to approve an academic committee's recommendation changing the status of the university librarians from faculty rank to a newly created "librarian" rank. Arguments justifying this change stressed that benefits and privileges previously enjoyed by librarians will continue to be available. Only the rank titles will be altered to Librarian, Associate Librarian, Assistant Librarian, and Affiliate Librarian. Criterion for promotion in the sequence will be based on standards set by the library staff.

Physical conservation of the materials in the University Libraries collection began as a major program at the University of Utah Libraries with the appointment in May of a professional Books and Manuscripts Conservator, Paul A. Foulger, formerly Conservator in charge of the Conservation Room in the Historical Department of the Church of Jesus Christ of Latter-day Saints.

The major acquisition at the University of Utah Libraries during 1977 was the purchase in March of a rare 1845 edition of George Catlin's *North American Indian Portfolio*. This represents the crowning work of a gifted American artist who spent the years from 1829 to 1838 traveling in what was then known as the Far West. He painted more than 600 portraits of distinguished Indian men and women. The 31 magnificent plates in the copy given to the Marriott Library by the Friends of the Libraries are among his best work.

Brigham Young University celebrated a major growth in physical facilities. With the completion of the 225,000-square-foot addition to the Harold B. Lee Library dedicated on March 15, it became one of the largest university libraries in the United States. The new addition brings the space available to a total of 430,000 square feet. The new facilities will be able to accommodate 4,800 students, 2,000,000 volumes, and 133 faculty researchers, along with additional administrative space for the library staff.

In November, a Lee Library profile was completed and sent to the BALLOTS Center, preparatory to the Library's participation in the Center's computer-based cataloging service. Installation of terminals and personnel training were scheduled by year's end.

Public Libraries. The major addition to a public library in Utah was signaled by the formal opening of the Whitmore Library addition in July 1977. The flagship of the Salt Lake County Library System, the headquarters building grew by 16,000 square feet on two floors, with extensive remodeling undertaken along with the expansion. Among new facilities provided were the Rainbow Room in the children's area, which provides young patrons with a world of unusual experiences; the Concentrated Study area for quiet reading; a new glass-enclosed booth for the United Press International teletype; the Heritage Room for display of historic materials by the Daughters of Utah Pioneers; and a special room for computerized information retrieval.

On November 12, a 4,000-square-foot branch building in the Salt Lake County System was opened, replacing a station converted from an old bookmobile. The new shopping center branch was linked to the system-wide CLSI computerized circulation control system. Two ground breakings were celebrated in the summer of 1977 for new branches to be completed during the last half of 1978. When they are completed, the Salt Lake County Library System will consist of 12 branches plus the headquarters building.

In January, the Salt Lake City Library was selected as a participant in the national Consortium for Public Library Innovation. Consisting of nine urban libraries throughout the United States, the Consortium seeks the improvement of library service through systematic research and experimentation. It is an outgrowth of the Adult Independent Study Project, a four-year experiment in continuing education through libraries that was initiated in 1972.

Serving a metropolitan area of 2,000,000, the Salt Lake City Library has recently been directing much energy towards staff committees that are developing studies on long-range goals, staff development, policies and procedures, personnel, and branches. These internal review and evaluation activities are seen as essential in planning for the management of future library programs.

In the smaller community of Ogden, the Weber County Library witnessed a year-long picketing effort aimed at a local adult bookstore by the Citizens for True Freedom. Their efforts resulted in numerous court actions and a new city ordinance requiring business licensing of bookstores. The threatening atmosphere led to the challenge of one school biology textbook, numerous visits to school libraries by parents, and the reemergence of the Friends of the Weber County Library. Municipal elections late in the fall permitted voters to rebuff hard-line censors, and the year's end saw an uneasy quiet on the issue.

In February, the Board of Trustees of the Provo City Public Library settled on a site for a new building for the Library. Last remodeled in 1939, the present facility was designed to serve a town of 18,000, but Provo currently has a population of 60,000. The collection is badly cramped with fewer than 52 seats in the building, and the expansion in the new location is seen by Director Larry Hortin as essential.

St. George saw the launching of a public relations effort sponsored by the city's Rotarians under the slogan "1977, The Year For Our Library!" Directed toward the building of a larger and more adequate facility, the effort was spearheaded by 50 Rotary members who pledged their personal time.

A publicity effort in the remote desert town of Thompson, with a population of about 35, resulted in the opening of a 2,500 book library in February. The books were collected in book drives sponsored by Girl Scouts in nearby communities, and surplus Air Force furniture and shelves were provided by the State Library Commission to start the library. Public support was demonstrated by a successful potluck supper in the local school, and the library has the services of one volunteer librarian.

Special Libraries. The Library of the Genealogical Society of Utah, Church of Jesus Christ of Latter-day Saints, named a new Director, Ted F. Powell, in November. The Library has increased the number of its branches to 275, including branches in England and Germany. Oral history projects are currently being undertaken in three countries, and microfilming, which added 45,000 volumes in 1977, takes place in 35 countries throughout the world.

Serving a special clientele, the Intermountain Inter-tribal School Library at Brigham City has completed a Native American Room as part of a $27,000 grant project to update and improve the existing facilities. Serving 800 students representing more than 90 tribes, the school recently underwent a period of transition from a single-tribe school to a multitribal high school. The project, funded under Title IV of ESEA, is scheduled for completion in 1978.

Awards. Utah librarianship was recognized for its excellence on three different counts during the 1977 ALA Annual Conference. Competing against 150 print and nonprint entries, two libraries won John Cotton Dana Public Relations Awards on the basis of their outstanding audiovisual productions. The University of Utah Libraries placed first in the College and University Libraries category with a videotape presentation humorously designed to interest students in the Library's orientation program. The Salt Lake City Public Library won a Special Award among public libraries for a promotional video project featuring an excellent supportive sound track. The H.W. Wilson Company's 1977 Periodical Award for "sustained excellence in both content and format with consideration to size of budget and staff" was presented to *Utah Libraries*, the official publication of the Utah Library Association.

The 1977 Distinguished Service Award for Librarianship in Higher Education, sponsored by the College and University Section of ULA, was presented to Maurice "Mike" Marchant, Director of the Brigham Young University Graduate School of Library and Information Sciences. The 1977 ULA Scholarship winner was Ron Gabriel, Fine Arts Librarian at the Salt Lake City Library.

Utah Library Association. During the fall of 1977, four sections of ULA sponsored workshops to meet their separate needs. A regional workshop for small public libraries was held in Cedar City during October by the Public Library Section. In October the School Section hosted a panel discussion during the fall meeting of the Utah Educational Association. In November, the College and University Section sponsored a program entitled "The Creative Librarian" in Provo on the Brigham Young University campus. Throughout the year, the Special Library Section conducted tours of the Genealogical Library and the Dugway Proving Grounds, providing focus for a yearlong project to identify outstanding collections of technical reports or microform.

The University of Utah Libraries was named as the depository of ULA records at an Executive Board meeting in the summer.

Obituary. Just before the beginning of the year, the Utah library community was saddened by the death of August Hanniball III, Extension Librarian at the University of Utah Libraries and former President of the Mountain Plains Library Association. He had been the recipient of the Distinguished Service Award at the ULA convention in the spring of 1976 and had received the same award at the fall meeting of the Mountain Plains Library Association. A memorial service was held on January 7 in the auditorium of the Marriott Library at the University of Utah.

K. ELIZABETH RUNYON-LANCASTER

VERMONT

**Vermont Library Association
(founded 1892)**

Membership: 450; *Annual Expenditure:* $4,973.
President: Joseph Popecki, St. Michael's College, Winooski (January-December 1977).
Vice-President/President-elect: Merris Eggert, Brattleboro (January-December 1977).
Publication: Vermont Libraries (irregular).

Vermont Department of Libraries

John McCrossan (resigned 1977)
Patricia Klinck, State Librarian (June 1977)
Montpelier 05602

School Library Media Consultant

Jean D. Battey
State Department of Education
Montpelier 05602

Intellectual Freedom. In the year of Vermont's bicentennial, some important events and changes occurred in the state's library world. Extremely small but historically spirited, the rural libraries of the state take pride in their independence and Yankee individuality. Demonstrated by the library field before the state legislature in the spring of 1977, the strength and depth of that independence won a major victory over a restrictive censorship bill. The bill was the result of the arrival of two new "adult" bookstores in the state. A furor arose over the supposed moral danger to the general citizenry by the very presence of such establishments.

A very small group rose to the defense, but Vermont's librarians held their ground for the overriding principles of the freedom of speech and the right to read. They stood against tremendous odds found in the large numbers of zealots who wanted to control the minds and morals of their neighbors. As this battle stretched through many weeks and difficult hours of Senate and House committee hearings, public librarians, school librarians, college librarians, and library trustees worked together closely to express their deep concern over the threat of censorship.

Midway through the legislative session, an enormous public hearing in the chambers of the House of Representatives packed more than 300 witnesses to present formally or simply to encourage their point of view before the House Judiciary Committee. The library community seemed hopelessly outnumbered; but its voice was united and coolly rational, while the opposition's was emotionally charged and incendiary. In a crescendo of feeling, the opposition built to a climax of vituperation against the librarians themselves who refused to retort in kind. Although the opposition appeared to have carried the evening, the points made by the librarians were not lost on the Committee. In the closing hours of the 1977 legislative session some weeks later a cliff-hanger final debate and vote on the floor of the House defeated the bill by only a six-vote margin.

Department of Libraries. Under the capable direction of a new State Librarian, the Vermont Department of Libraries began to reorganize and to forge ahead with noteworthy projects. Patricia Klinck, a veteran member of the Department staff, was appointed State Librarian in June to replace John McCrossan who left to teach in the Graduate Department of Library, Media, and Information Studies at the University of South Florida in Tampa. Klinck appointed Kent Gray, Midstate Regional Librarian, to be Assistant State Librarian and Director of Extension Services.

Governor Richard Snelling announced plans to call a formal conference in preparation for the White House Conference on Library and Information Services. It will be called the Second Governor's Conference for Better Libraries.

In the area of children's services, the Department's film "Stories in Motion" was reviewed in *Booklist* and has been sold all over the world. The booklet on summer programming prepared in 1976 has sold more than 3,000 copies throughout the United States. Both projects were directed by Caroline Heilmann, Children's Services Consultant, who has begun a new project on "Poetry in the Public Library" in cooperation with the Vermont Council on the Arts. These summer sessions are planned for 5- to 12-year-olds who showed an enthusiastic response in 1977.

Annual Conference. The fourth annual combined conference sponsored by the

Vermont Library Association (VLA), the Vermont Library Trustees Association (VLTA), and the Vermont Educational Media Association (VEMA) met at Green Mountain College in Poultney. Conference highlights were a speech on library management by Robert D. Stueart, Director of Simmons College's School of Library Science; a puppetry festival sponsored by the Children and Young Adult Librarians Section of VLA; a VEMA- sponsored "bull session" for secondary school media people; and Peter Jacobs of Bro-Dart, who spoke on the services and modern problems of book jobbers.

VLA District Meetings. Noteworthy for their crowd-gathering content, the five fall VLA district meetings drew record numbers to hear presentations on copyright by Milton Crouch of the University of Vermont and on "saving time" by Sally Roberts of the Department of Libraries. Adult book review sessions rounded out the schedule of the meetings, which were said to be among the best ever in Vermont.

VEMA Fall Conference. Held at Essex Junction Education Center Library on October 21, the VEMA conference was sponsored jointly by VEMA and the Association for Early Childhood Education. An outstanding and heartwarming presentation was made by Jon Stone, the producer of "Sesame Street," now in its ninth year on television. A moving speaker with a fine sense of humor and a spirit of generous sharing with his audience, Stone captivated his listeners.

Awards and Grants. The 1977 Elva Sophronia Smith Grant Awards for the improvement of library service to children were presented to the Calef Memorial Library in Washington under the direction of Elizabeth Hunt; the Joslin Memorial Library in Waitsfield, Frances Merchant, Librarian; and the Proctor Free Library under Barbara Burns.

The Aldrich Public Library in Barre received a $50,000 grant from the federal government to establish an Ethnic Heritage Study and Program Center. Because of the granite industry in Barre, the city has a rich background of many nationalities, particularly the artists, sculptors, and craftsmen from Europe who work in monumental design. The Project Director and Research Assistant have begun their work to assess and coordinate community resources.

JOSETTE ANNE BOISSE

VIRGINIA

Virginia Meetings, Workshops. A one-day seminar on community involvement in corrections was held in June in Richmond to bring together employers, prospective employers, offenders, ex-offenders, and other interested persons to provide insight into the work-study release program, the employment of ex-offenders, and other types of community involvement. The program was sponsored by the Pre-Release Activities Center in conjunction with the Division of Probation and Parole Services of the Commonwealth of Virginia.

In Richmond in September the Virginia State Library sponsored an institute on "Community Analysis for Responsive Library Service." It was conducted by Roger Greer and his staff from the University of Denver School of Librarianship.

**Virginia Library Association
(founded 1905)**

Membership: 954; *Annual Expenditure:* $15,547.
President: Janet E. Minnerath, Virginia Medical Information Service, Virginia Commonwealth University, Richmond (December 1976-November 1977).
Vice-President/President-elect: Nolan Yelich, Virginia State Library.
Secretary: Marcy J. Sims, Department of Public Libraries, Municipal Center, Virginia Beach 23456.
Executive Director: Eugene Fischer, Campbell County Public Library, P.O. Box 317, Lynchburg 24505.
Annual Conference: November 17-19, 1977, Hot Springs.
Publication: Virginia Librarian Newsletter (6 issues a year).

Virginia State Library
Donald R. Haynes, State Librarian
Richmond 23219

School Library Media Supervisor
Mary Stuart Mason
State Department of Education
Richmond 23216

The Virginia Library Association (VLA) preconference program on budgeting was sponsored by the LSCA Title III Continuing Education Advisory Committee under the auspices of the Office of Library Cooperation at the Virginia State Library. The seminar was a follow-up on the 1976 budgeting institute in Roanoke and concentrated on direct applicability of program budgeting techniques to libraries.

Another program sponsored by the LSCA Committee was a one-day workshop in Richmond in May on "Library Automation in Virginia." Leaders in the workshop included Leonre Maruyama, Senior Information Systems Specialist in the Network Development Office of the Library of Congress; Kenneth Thomas, Training Coordinator of SOLINET; Richard S. Moschler, Jr., Director of the Virginia Department of Management Analysis and Systems Development; Charles D. Miller, the state's Management Information Systems Director for Education; Betty Dillehay of the A.H. Robins Company in Richmond; Charles H. Stevens; Wilhelm Moll of the University of Virginia's Health Services Library; Robert Seal of the University of Virginia; and Kay Durkin of BRS.

"Decisions in Automation," moderated by William R. Chamberlain of the State Library, featured Gerard B. McCabe of Virginia Commonwealth University; Lelia B. Saunders, Arlington County Department of Libraries; and Joseph F. Viar, Jr., a systems analyst for Viar and Company of Alexandria. A panel discussion on automation in various Virginia libraries included Moderator Howard Ogden, Director of the Charles H. Taylor Memorial Library in Hampton; J. Marshal Hughes of NASA/LRC Technical Library; A.R. Pierce of Carol M. Newman Library at Virginia Polytechnic Institute and State University; and William L. Whitesides of Fairfax County Public Library.

Library instruction was the theme of the College and University Section meeting held in May at the Donaldson Brown Center for Continuing Education in Blacksburg. Fred Heath, Section Chairperson, served as the planner and coordinator of the one-day meeting that featured Patricia Breivik, Dean of Library Services at Sangamon State University in Springfield, Illinois. A panel on philosophies of library instruction included papers by Gloria Terwilliger on the library-college concept and Charles Brownson on Library Orientation-Instruction Exchange. Dennis Robison served as a respondent and called for a Virginia "summit conference" on library instruction.

The VLA Library Instruction Forum was one of the afternoon sessions with Tim Williams of Radford College as convenor and Bill Prince of Virginia Polytechnic as convenor-elect. Concurrently, interlibrary loan librarians from more than 25 libraries gathered to exchange ideas and information regarding procedures and common problems.

Notable Gifts. John W. Warner, former Secretary of the Navy and former Administrator of the American Revolution Bicentennial Administration, presented his personal papers covering eight years of public service to the Alderman Library of the University of Virginia in a ceremony at the Rotunda. His wife, Elizabeth Taylor, accompanied him. Warner also deposited at Alderman Library the papers of his tenure as Under Secretary and Secretary of the Navy from 1965 to 1974.

Virginia Library Association. Programs presented to the membership of the Junior

Members Round Table during the year included a spring meeting in May at Virginia Beach entitled "Positive Assertion for the Librarian" with Diane Gramstead of Virginia Commonwealth University. A fall meeting in September in Richmond was entitled "Get to Know Your State Agencies" with representation from Virginia Polytechnic Extension Services, the Division for the Blind and Physically Handicapped, the Department of Education, the United Way Information Center, and the Virginia Travel Service. "Orientation to the VLA Conference" was held at The Homestead with presentations by VLA, VEMA, exhibitors, and The Homestead Convention Arrangements Staff as participants. Arthur Plotnik, editor of *American Libraries*, was an all-conference speaker during The Homestead conference.

The Virginia Foundation for the Humanities and Public Policy provided a $4,935 grant for the project "Education, Mass Media, and Public Libraries." The grant was awarded to the Public Library Section in October. Matching in-kind funds will raise $6,164 for the project.

Much of the work of the Children's and Young Adult Services Forum was done through regional workshops held in the spring and fall. Programs included preschool show and tell services, the use of toys in the library, techniques for buying books on an incredibly tight budget, idea swaps, and a job swap—to see what it is like to try on someone else's shoes.

Highlighting the activities was the annual conference program sponsored jointly with the School Library Section. Katherine Paterson, winner of the 1976 National Book Award for *The Master Puppeteer*, and Mary Louise Clifford, known for her *Land and People Series* books and *Bisha of Burundi*, spoke on "Presenting Other Cultures to Today's Young People." During the business meeting 1977 Notable Films were shown.

The Trustee Section of VLA conducted a campaign to promote full state funding for public libraries in the 1978-80 biennial budget. The effort was aimed at persuading the governor and legislators to appropriate fully the legally authorized amounts of state aid. Both the Virginia Municipal League and the Virginia Association of Counties agreed to support full funding.

Pat Pfeiffer and Rev. William McDermott received Trustee of the Year Awards for 1976 and 1977 respectively. Carroll Kem Shackelford received Life Membership in VLA. The Trustee section also acclaimed Leo Mason for his wisdom and organizational talent.

The Executive Board of VLA began exploring ways to initiate long-range planning. Treasurer Theda Gibson was analyzing income and expenditures for the previous three years. Each section, forum, and regional chairperson began program planning for 1978 to allow the development of a VLA annual calendar of events. Budgets were presented at The Homestead conference.

VLA and VEMA officers worked together to produce a program for the conference with distinguished speakers such as Alphonse Trezza, Louis Manarin, Eric Moon, Frank Norwood, Arthur Plotnik, and Johnnie Givens. Several VLA and VEMA representatives were present in Governor Godwin's office when he signed a proclamation for National Library Week.

Gene Fischer, VLA's new Executive Director, was employed as of September on a part-time basis. He is Director of the Campbell County Library in Rustburg. Roberta Miller resigned as Executive Director to accept a new job with the State Library.

Virginia has a new set of standards for public library service drawn up by VLA's Library Development Committee. The standards provisionally passed the VLA Executive Board and went to the State Library Board in the fall along with a new set of requirements authored by the Library Development Committee. In approving the standards, the VLA Executive Board asked the Library Development Committee to test the figures proposed. Fifteen public libraries of all sizes and types were chosen to test the new standards. They were favorably received by all who tested them in planning and by some who tested them in budgeting for 1977. A detailed survey report was made to the Library Development Committee.

The main activity of the *Intellectual Freedom Committee* was an all-day workshop to Library Trustees held in February at Chesterfield County Public Library for all Trustees from the Richmond area. The program included an area lawyer speaking on the legal implications for librarians concerning intellectual freedom.

One of the most successful projects of the *VLA Legislative Committee* was the drafting of a statement of legislative issues of concern to librarians and library users in Virginia which was sent to every announced candidate in the June 14 Virginia primary election. Individual Committee members also spoke with candidates and arranged public meetings where the issues were discussed.

People. Several notable librarians retired or resigned from Virginia libraries in 1977: Florence B. Yoder, Head of the Library Development Branch of Virginia State Library since 1956; Antje L. Smith, Assistant City Librarian at Richmond Public Library for 14 years; Josephine Bennington Wingfield, Head Librarian at Jones Memorial Library in Lynchburg; Anne Woodward, City Librarian at Staunton Public Library for 22 years; Anne Blair, Children's Services Coordinator at Fairfax County Public Library for 20 years; Mercedes Shepanek, Head Librarian of the Dolley Madison Library Branch of Fairfax County Public Library for 15 years; Milton Russell, Head of Public Services for Virginia State Library; Gertrude C. Davis, Director of the Martha S. Grafton Library at Mary Baldwin College for 20 years; June Smith, Children's Librarian at Prince William Public Library in Manassas for 18 years; Anna Margaret Dession, Head Librarian at the Charlotte County Free Library; and Phyllis Clark Moore, Director of Mary Riley Styles Public Library.

In addition to Shackelford, Davis, Smith and Yoder mentioned above, the following were voted Honorary Life Memberships in the Virginia Library Association: Frances Johnson, Professor at Radford; Roy Land, Director of Circulation at University of Virginia; Jeanne Rose, Head of Reference Section at Arlington Public Library, and Helen Keeble Scribner, Head of Cataloging Section at State Library.

As a result of retirements, promotions, and transfers, there were many changes in the Fairfax County Public Library System. New appointees included Nancy Schifrin, Coordinator of Young People's Services; Esther Beaumont, Director of Technical Operations; Mary Williams, Personnel Officer; Barbara Waserman, Head Librarian, George Mason Regional Library; Marylou Hobbs, Head Librarian, Dolley Madison Library; Joe Coleman, Head Librarian, Kings Park Library; Marie Ringle, Head Librarian, Centreville Library; and Mary Trefry, Head Librarian, Woodrow Wilson Library.

Other new appointments to Virginia Libraries included Laurie Surface, Librarian, Tazewell County Public Library; Polly W. Boaz, Head Librarian, Charlotte County Free Library; Ann Fisher, Director, Radford Public Library; Connie House, Library Director, Staunton Correctional Center; Tim Williams, Librarian, Virginia State Penitentiary, Richmond; John M. Cotham, Librarian, Mountain Empire Community College; Bobbie White, Librarian, New River Community College; Diana D. Osborne, Head Librarian, Lewis E. Smoot Memorial Library (King George); Diane Richmond Jennings, Director, Franklin County Public Library; Lottie Driver, Director, Newport News Public Library; and Deane Dierksen, Director, Mary Riley Styles Public Library (formerly Falls Church Public Library). Judith Segel, Direc-

411

tor, Loudoun County Library; William C. Pollard, Director, Martha S. Grafton Library.

Agatha Hurlbert was appointed Assistant City Librarian at Richmond Public Library. Other Richmond Public changes were Carol Wells, Branch Librarian, Broad Rock; and Ellen Agnew, Branch Librarian, Ginter Park.

State Library appointments were Roberta L. Miller, Director of the Library Division, composed of the General Library Branch and the Library Development Branch; Sarah Crews, Head of Technical Services; Toni H. Waller, Head of the Prints and Pictures Collection; and Kitty Smith, Head of Public Services.

New Libraries. The William E. Richardson, Jr., Memorial Library opened in Emporia in June. The Chesapeake Public Library opened the Judge M.M. Hillard Branch in June. The Chesterfield County Library System opened a new Central Library in October.

Added Services. The Bristol Public Library in April presented the first of its weekly story programs for preschool children over KBT, the local cable television channel. The City of Bristol and Washington County established a reciprocal borrowers' agreement between the two libraries. The Richmond City Council approved a resolution proposing library system cooperation for one year among three Richmond metropolitan area libraries—Henrico County, Chesterfield County, and the City of Richmond.

All talking book readers in Fairfax County, Arlington County, and the city of Alexandria received copies of a consumer booklet entitled *Use Your Phone for All It's Worth*, produced by the C&P Telephone Company in recorded format for the blind and physically handicapped. The latest publication from the Creative Writing Workshop at the Virginia State Penitentiary was *In Celebration*, a collection of poetry.

The first comprehensive and documented history of Virginia Beach was written by Kathleen M. Eighmey while she worked as a library assistant. *The Beach: A History of Virginia Beach, Virginia* was published by the Virginia Beach Department of Public Libraries.

Friends of the Central Library made it possible for the Fairfax County Library to become the first library to provide patrons with computerized legislative information with access to the State Legislature computer in Richmond.

Grants. The State Library Board made allocations to 21 regional, 25 county, 22 city, and 4 town libraries that met the requirements for receiving state and federal grants-in-aid in fiscal 1978.

Williamsburg signed a contract with James City County in May, thus becoming eligible for a grant based on the two political subdivisions for the first time. Fluvanna and King George Counties also received grants for the first time. Of the 72 libraries qualifying for aid, 12 did not have certified librarians. Grants for those 12 were reduced by 25 per cent.

WILLIAM L. WHITESIDES

WASHINGTON

Washington Library Network. The Washington Library Network (WLN), established in 1976 by the legislature, contains four components: interlibrary system, reference/referral, telecommunications, and computer systems. Implementation of the governance structure for the Network began after the October 1976 State Library Commission meeting when the rules and regulations in support of the establishing law were formally adopted. Seven Library Service Areas, geographic subdivisions of the state, were established by the Commission to promote multitype library cooperation as well as to elect at-large representation to the Representative Assembly, a statewide body that assists in planning Network programs, activities, and services. In March 1977 the Assembly elected a 13-member Executive Council comprised of representatives of all types of libraries to set directions for the Network. Allene Schnaitter, Director of Libraries at Washington State University, is chairperson of the Council.

By the end of 1977, 202 libraries had signed the Basic Membership agreement—70 public, 46 academic, 56 school, and 30 special libraries. Of these 28 had also signed letters of intent to become Principal Members.

Through the use of computer and telecommunications systems, WLN is based on the sharing of resources; member libraries agree to share resources of all types. During 1977 five Library Service Areas received LSCA grants to develop, document, and evaluate multitype library cooperative projects. Washington and Oregon began testing the feasibility of a regional information specialist to tap the collections of major libraries. In another project multitype libraries are providing library services to rural residents through existing school facilities. One project is evaluating the cost-effectiveness of a commercial courier serving academic and public libraries; another is linking existing library system deliveries with those of multicounty educational districts.

The WLN Computer System achieved full production status at midyear, and a

Washington Library Association (founded 1905)

Membership: 1,118; *Annual Expenditure:* $20,163.
President: Betty W. Bender, Spokane Public Library (August 1977-July 1979).
Vice-President/President-elect: Verda Hansberry, Seattle Public Library.
Secretary: Jan Ames, Washington Regional Library for the Blind and Physically Handicapped, Seattle.
Annual Meeting: April 28-30, 1977, Vancouver.
Publication: CAYAS Newsletter (quarterly).

Washington State Library

Roderick G. Swartz, State Librarian and Executive Director of the Washington Library Network
Olympia 98504

State School Library Media Supervisor

Jean Wieman
State Department of Public Instruction
Olympia 98501

total of 19 participating libraries were online by the end of 1977. Two of these were out-of-state. The bibliographic data base held more than 1,000,000 titles. It included books, serials, and projected media. The Acquisitions subsystem was to be implemented later on a pilot basis in the State Library. The Circulation subsystem was under development by an outside contractor, to be implemented on a minicomputer in 1978. Serials control was in the design phase. The computer-produced statewide *Resource Directory* of holdings of Network participants was to be joined by individual library catalogs, also in microform, during 1978.

The Reference/Referral component of the Network was in planning. A research project to study existing and possible interlibrary loan patterns was under way, to be completed by September 1978. Entitled "A Network Management Tool: Computer Simulation," the project was funded by the U.S. Office of Education to develop computer models that simulate a state-level network for interlibrary lending as well as for internal library operations dealing with interlibrary lending. Codirectors of the project are Mary Jane Reed of the Washington State Library and High T. Vrooman of the Illinois State Library.

Certification. In conjunction with the Executive Board of the Washington Library Association (WLA) and its Certification Committee, the State Board for Certification of Librarians named Dean Margaret Goggin of the Graduate School of

Librarianship at the University of Denver as a consultant. The Certification Board is having increasing difficulty working with the 1935 law and its rules and regulations. Goggin was to examine the 40-year-old certification law and make recommendations for revisions based on the current library environment.

Buildings. Several library construction projects were being assisted by the Economic Development Administration. A $550,000 project was financed through the joint effort of the Federal Economic Development Administration, $385,000; the Port of Chelan County, $100,000; and the library district, $65,000. The new 15,000-square-foot facility is owned by the Port, and the Regional Library will have exclusive use of the building for 25 years. Rental to pay back the Port's investment is not to exceed $10,000 in any one year. Construction of the center was completed in the summer of 1977.

In December 1976, two local public works grants were awarded that affected the Timberland Regional Library. The city of Centralia, which contracts with the Regional Library, was awarded $1,208,344, and the Regional Library itself was awarded $870,015 for a new service center. Centralia will remodel, furnish, and landscape an existing 1912 Carnegie building, increasing its size from 6,000 to 13,000 square feet. Construction began in March 1977, and the opening was expected in March 1978.

The space of the Timberland Regional Library Service Center increased from 3,700 square feet of rented space to 15,496 square feet when it occupied its new facility in December 1977. Total construction costs were estimated to be $997,014, of which the Regional Library contribution was $151,775.

A public works grant of $344,365 was awarded to the city of Cle Elum in December 1976 for construction of a 2,200-square-foot library. Under construction in Bremerton during 1977 was the new Kitsap Regional Library Information and Service Center. This 36,000-square-foot building has been designed with earth beams against external walls to conserve heat and a heating system that can be converted to a solar source in the future. A bond issue of $1,900,000 passed in 1976 was financing the construction.

In the city of Olympia a 21,000-square-foot building was financed by a bond issue of $1,500,000 passed by the voters in 1976. The building was scheduled for completion in 1978 to replace a 12,000-square-foot 1914 Carnegie building.

School Libraries. School library and audiovisual specialists serving kindergarten through college students voted to consolidate their organizations by July 1, 1978. The new organization, as yet unnamed, will combine the Washington State Association of School Librarians and the Washington Association for Educational Communications and Technology.

Preparation for the consolidation began in 1974 with the establishment of the Washington Educational Media Coordinating Council. The Council was charged with sponsoring joint conferences, establishing joint committees on issues of common concern, and investigating the possibility of a joint publication. The publication, *The Medium,* was first issued in 1976 and has served as the communications vehicle for keeping members of both organizations informed on planning.

People. Merle N. Boylan, formerly Director of General Libraries at the University of Texas in Austin, became Director of Libraries at the University of Washington in July 1977. He succeeded Marion Milczewski, who retired in February.

William T. (Bill) DeJohn was named Director of the Pacific Northwest Bibliographic Center effective September 1977. DeJohn was formerly Senior Consultant for Library Cooperation of the Illinois State Library Development Group. He succeeded Lura G. Currier, who retired in September.   DOROTHY R. CUTLER

WEST VIRGINIA

West Virginia libraries entered 1977 with high hopes for more money and great strides forward. A dinner honoring state legislators was held in early March. With the theme "Tie One On for the Library," the dinner was sponsored by the West Virginia Library Association (WVLA). The dinner got the ball rolling with the sale of ties and scarves featuring a logo designed by Carol Bryan of the Exposure staff of the West Virginia Library Commission. Within a day of the dinner, state funding hopes were crushed by a bill proposing the consolidation of a number of departments under one master department, to be called the Department of History and Culture. The proposal, a part of the new governor's plan, would have placed the Library Commission in jeopardy of losing its identity.

West Virginia Library Association (founded 1914)
- *Membership:* 971; *Annual Expenditure:* $10,000.
  President: Ruth Ann Powell, Technical Services Librarian, Fairmont State College (December 1977-November 1978).
  Vice-President/President-elect: Luella Dye, Director, Craft Memorial Library, Mercer County Service Center, Bluefield.
  Secretary: Karen Goff, Reference Librarian, West Virginia Library Commission, Science and Cultural Center, Charleston 25305.
  Annual Conference: November 10-12, 1977, White Sulphur Springs.
  Publication: West Virginia Libraries (quarterly).

West Virginia Library Commission
Frederic J. Glazer, Executive Secretary
Science and Cultural Center
Charleston 25305

School Library Media Supervisor
Carolyn Skidmore
State Department of Education
Charleston 25305

A campaign to stop the consolidation was mounted by WVLA under the leadership of President Barbara Bonfili. The citizens of the state responded with a massive letter-writing and telephone campaign to their individual senators and delegates. Librarians pleaded their case personally with the legislators. Newspapers took up the cause, and the final result, after many anxious weeks, was that the Library Commission was removed from the bill. The identity and integrity of the Library Commission as an independent commission remained, and libraries throughout the state could continue to serve their public without fear of political interference.

Construction. Once again under the able guidance of Frederic J. Glazer, Executive Secretary of the West Virginia Library Commission, another innovative library construction project was started. The "Outpost" library has now become a part of the scenery in rural West Virginia communities. The 12-foot-by-40-foot mobile module unit—complete with wooden bookshelves, books, tables, chairs, circulation desk, restroom, projector, screen, carpeting, air conditioning, heating and storage area, and concrete block foundation—is a welcome library facility in communities not large enough to support a larger library.

The Outpost, an idea of Glazer, was designed by Charles Hively of Wilson and Golf Associated Architects of Saint Albans, West Virginia. These modular buildings are designed with energy conservation as a primary concern. They make use of the heat pump, the most efficient heating system available. They are well insulated, with six inches of insulation in the walls and floor and nine inches in the ceiling. The power cost has been estimated to be between $35 and $50 per month. The unit provides reader seating for 12 people, film seating for more than 24, and an estimated 4,500 volumes.

Eleven Outpost libraries had been approved by the end of 1977. Nine were on their sites. Although the expenses vary from community to community, the cost averages $16,600 each, including the foundation and all utility hookups. Because many communities in West Virginia are isolated due to the terrain, some residents are unable to avail themselves of library services. These mobile modular units, trucked in and set up in a few hours, are putting library services within easy access to many more people. In a program report to HEW, the Library Commission asked that consideration be given for 12 more units to be built between January and June of 1978.

The Instant Carousel Library established in 1976 has also been a huge success. Eight were completed during 1977, three more had been approved and were under construction, and one was waiting site preparation. Larger libraries have not been forgotten. Libraries at Weirton and South Charleston began expansion programs, and a library at Moorefield was remodeling. Bids were opened for a multi-million-dollar library in downtown Huntington, and the lower bid came in at $250,000 under the budget. The Huntington Library may prove to be a unique building, for it is being designed to make use of solar energy for heating and cooling.

Section Reports. College and University librarians sponsored two conferences in 1977. The first conference in February on management techniques was attended by 77 librarians. Presenting papers were librarians from five college and university libraries. The second conference was held in April on the subject of bibliographic instruction, and 79 people attended. As a move toward better educational opportunities for education, the College and University Section worked out agreements with colleges for educational exchange programs. The Academic Common Market now makes it possible for residents of West Virginia to attend out-of-state schools on an in-state tuition basis for master's level work in librarianship. Universities participating are the University of South Carolina, Louisiana State University, the University of Kentucky, the University of Tennessee, and the University of Alabama. Participating in a doctoral-level program is Florida State University.

The Special Library Section held a workshop in May sponsored by the Medical Library Association to discuss the subject of "Human Factors in Library Administration." Fourteen persons attended. A membership directory was published by the Section. The Public Library Section became involved in the campaign to stop the political move designed to lump the Library Commission and funding procedures with other state commissions.

Many librarians again attended the Commission-sponsored Library Skills Institute at Marshall University in May. In its fourth year, the Institute attracted 100 librarians from seven states in 1977. Courses in cataloging, reference, and educational media were offered.

Annual Conference. The 1977 annual library conference was held at White Sulphur Springs in November. Approximately 325 librarians, trustees, and friends attended. Workshops featured continuing education ideas for patrons of public libraries, creative dramatics in the library, and a user needs workshop for the Special Library Section. Alice Ihrig, Chairman of the ALA White House Conference Planning Committee, spoke on the subject of the Pre-White House Conference.

Awards. West Virginia Librarians continued to reap awards for their outstanding work. Library Commission Director Glazer was cited as HEW's 1977 Outstanding Citizen. His leadership in library programs for the disadvantaged and remote areas was recognized. C.E. Campbell Beall, a West Virginia Library Commissioner, was the recipient of the 1977 ALA Trustee Citation Award for Distinguished Service to Library Development. For the third consecutive year the Exposure Division of WVLC received a John Cotton Dana Public Relations Award for outstanding public relations materials. E. Frances Jones, Field Consultant for WVLC, was named the Dora Ruth Parks Award winner for her outstanding work in libraries since 1963. Jones was presented her award at the WVLA annual conference.

LUELLA DYE

WISCONSIN

Wisconsin Library Association (founded 1891)

Membership: 1,900 (766 ALA Members); *Annual Expenditure:* $32,178 (1976).
President: Marianna Markowetz, University of Wisconsin-Milwaukee Library (January-December 1977).
Vice-President/President-elect: William D. Grindeland, Racine Unified School District.
Administrative Secretary: Bonnie Lynne Robinson, 201 West Mifflin Street, Madison, Wisconsin 53703.
Annual Conference: October 19-21, 1977, Eau Claire.
Publication: WLA Newsletter (bimonthly).

Wisconsin Department of Public Instruction, Division for Library Services
W. Lyle Eberhart, Administrator
126 Langdon Street
Madison 53702

School Library Media Supervisor
Dianne McAfee Williams
Department of Public Instruction
Madison 53702

Cooperative Activities. The 86th annual conference of the Wisconsin Library Association (WLA) had as its theme "Wisconsin Libraries: A Potpourri of Services." The conference was an occasion for looking back over a year of accomplishments and forward to building on these accomplishments to improve library services. This was particularly true of activities that cut across types of libraries.

The planning for Wisconsin's Pre-White House Conference got a boost when it was announced at the WLA meeting that Governor Martin J. Schreiber would sponsor the meeting as a Governor's Conference on Library and Information Services in September 1978. An ad hoc coordinating committee representing library continuing education producers in Wisconsin met for the first time at the WLA conference. This committee grew out of a statewide conference of continuing education producers, held in September as the culmination of the Continuing Library Education Planning and Coordinating (COLEPAC) project.

The COLEPAC project, under the direction of Kathleen Weibel, also produced the *Directory of Wisconsin Continuing Library Media Education Producers and Programs.* The annual revision of the Division for Library Service's *Comprehensive Long-Range Program for Library Services* was reported in *Wisconsin Library Bulletin* (September-October 1977). It contained a draft outline of an action-oriented five-year plan for continuing library education in Wisconsin, which would build on the work of the COLEPAC project.

The Wisconsin library community continued throughout 1977 to work toward implementation of the recommendations of the Task Force on Interlibrary Cooperation and Resource Sharing. The 1977-79 biennial budget request of the Department of Public Instruction included funds for the proposal Council on Library Development and Networking. While the state budget that was ultimately adopted did not contain such funds, it did allow the transfer of an existing library consultant for interlibrary cooperation from federal to state funding.

The budget bill also directed the Legislative Council (the research arm of the state legislature) to conduct a study of several vital library issues, a study which librarians hope will result in legislation implementing some of the Task Force recommendations. These included recommendations for a broadly based group to plan and govern state-level multitype cooperative activities. As an interim or transitional step toward the establishment and funding of such a group, the Council of Wisconsin Librarians, which operates several cooperative projects and which had previously been composed of academic librarians, broadened its membership and governing structure to include representatives of all types of libraries.

Public Libraries. In 1977 12 state-aided public library systems covered 47 of Wisconsin's 72 counties and served 68 per cent of the state's population. In 1978 there were to be 13 systems, including 58 counties and providing services for 76.5 per cent of the population. Barbara Thompson, State Superintendent of Public Instruction, requested full statutory formula funding for these systems in her 1977–79 budget request to the governor. The governor's budget proposal, however, contained funding for only 80 per cent of the formula. This proposal would also have reduced drastically the funding for the Bureau of Reference and Loan (the interloan and switching backup to the public libraries in the state) and would have removed control over the expenditure of LSCA funds from the Division for Library Services.

WLA and other interested parties engaged in intensive legislative activities as the state budget moved through the legislative process. The budget bill that was signed by the governor in June did fund public library systems at only 80 per cent of the statutory formula. It did not, however, reduce the funding of the Reference and Loan Bureau as drastically as the governor had proposed, and it contained other features for which the library community had worked. The State Council on Public Library Certificates and Standards continued its work toward new certification standards for public library personnel.

Academic Libraries. Late in 1977 the libraries of the campuses in the University of Wisconsin System began an experiment in resource sharing and library service development. Esther Stineman was appointed System Librarian-at-Large in Women's Studies. Created at the recommendation of the Women's Studies Task Force, this position is intended to develop services that will bring the library and information resources of the entire University System to bear on the women's studies programs of the individual campuses. It is hoped that the communication and other activities initiated by Stineman will result in coordinated collection development, increased bibliographic access, and more effective use of materials in teaching and research.

Wisconsin's second-largest academic library, that of the University of Wisconsin-Milwaukee, celebrated the addition of its millionth volume on January 30. The Wisconsin Association of Academic Librarians, a division of WLA, continued its active programming on behalf of its members during 1977. Among the interests that were pursued in committee work and program meetings were copyright, continuing education, the faculty status of librarians, and legislative concerns.

School Library Media Centers. A task force that had been established to revise the state's standards for school library media programs finished its work, and in the fall of 1977 the publication, *Standards for Instructional Media Programs, 1977–82*, was distributed. In November another task force that studied the certification requirements for school library media personnel submitted the final draft of its proposal for new certification requirements to the State Superintendent's Advisory Committee for Teacher Education and Certification. After asking questions of task force members and after discussing the draft, the Advisory Committee tabled the draft for study.

The state Bureau of School Library Media Programs prepared and distributed guidelines entitled "Suggestions for Dealing with Censorship of Media Center Materials: A Wisconsin Plan." A key resource for librarians in resisting censorship pressures is the review and other information that is available from the Cooperative Children's Book Center. This study and research agency for current and retrospective children's material is jointly funded by the School of Library Science and the School of Education of the University of Wisconsin-Madison and the state's Division for Library Services. School librarians joined with public library children's librarians and others in a strong legislative action program to gain additional state funding for the Center in the 1977–79 budget. Their effort was successful, and the Center expected to strengthen its services as an educational and information resource for children's materials.

Special Libraries and Services. A new association was formed during 1977. The Wisconsin Health Science Library Association (WHSLA), which is open to anyone employed by a health science library, held its initial meeting in La Crosse in September. Wisconsin chapters of the American Society for Information Science and the Special Libraries Association continued their activities on behalf of special librarians and information personnel during the year. These two chapters and the new WHSLA jointly selected a representative of special libraries to the governing board of the restructured Council of Wisconsin Librarians.

People. Barbara Thompson, State Superintendent of Public Instruction, in whose department the Division for Library Services is placed, was re-elected in June. During and after her campaign she stressed the importance of cooperation among libraries of all types. Dianne McAfee Williams was appointed Director of the Division's Bureau of School Library Media Programs.

Muriel L. Fuller, WLA President in 1968–69, retired from her important responsibilities for continuing library education on the University of Wisconsin faculty. She was succeeded by James A. Nelson, who came from a similar position in Kentucky. Elizabeth S. Bohmrich retired as Administrative Secretary of WLA and was succeeded by Bonnie Lynne Robinson. Doralyn J. Hickey resigned as Dean of the School of Library Science at the University of Wisconsin-Milwaukee to take a faculty position in Texas.

The library community was saddened by the deaths of Forrest Mills, WLA President in 1958–59, who had been the Director of the Racine Public Library, and of Dalton Johnson, Chairman of the Council on Library Development and an energetic library enthusiast.

At the WLA annual conference, the Librarian of the Year Award was presented to Nancy Elsmo of the Racine Public Library. The Library Trustee of the Year Award was given to Mrs. B.R. (Kay) Swan of Berlin. The T.B. Scott Free Library of Merrill won the Clarence B. Lester Award as the Library of the Year. The Banta Literary Award, which is administered by WLA, was given to Richard N. Current for *The Civil War Era— 1848–1873*, the second volume in his *History of Wisconsin*.

CHARLES A. BUNGE

WYOMING

Wyoming Library Association
(founded 1914)

Membership: 420 (70 ALA Members); Annual Expenditure: $7,550.
President: Wayne H. Johnson, Wyoming State Library, Cheyenne.
Executive Secretary: Irene Nakaku, Rock Springs Public Library.
Annual Meeting: May 5–7, 1977, Jackson.
Publication: Wyoming Library Roundup (quarterly).

Wyoming State Library

State Librarian, Vacant
Wyoming State Library
Cheyenne 82002

State School Library Media Supervisor

Dale Hughes
State Department of Education
Cheyenne 82001

The ongoing development of the state's energy resources, primarily coal, continued to make Wyoming one of the fastest-growing regions of the country during 1977. Some of the negative aspects of this growth were given national television exposure in the fall. While public library budgets in the state were growing, the growth was slower, in many cases much slower, than the increasing demands for service generated by the rapid population growth. With the sponsorship of the Wyoming Library Association (WLA), legislation authorizing direct state financial aid to county library systems was introduced again in 1977. Despite receiving committee endorsement, the bill died on the floor of the Wyoming House of Representatives, largely because of the opposition of the majority leader. This was the third time that such a bill had failed in the Wyoming legislature in this decade. State support of public library service is evidently an idea whose time has not yet come in Wyoming.

Notwithstanding the influx of new residents, the one new public library opened in Wyoming during 1977 was established primarily to serve the descendants of the state's first settlers. The Crowheart Branch of the Fremont County Library, dedicated April 2, is located on the Wind River Indian Reservation, and its clientele is primarily composed of members of the Shoshone and Arapaho Tribes. The library is housed in the new community center serving the western section of the Reservation.

Wyoming Library Association. Despite the traditional snowstorm, the annual conference at Jackson on May 5-7 drew a good attendance and was rated a success by those who were there. In the fall, two WLA sections began experimenting with regional meetings intended to supplement the spring convention. The Public Library Section had a one-day gathering at the Johnson County Library at Buffalo in September. In October the Academic and Special Library Section members met at Eastern Wyoming College in Torrington. The initial response from both sections was so favorable that both scheduled additional meetings, and it seemed likely that regional meetings would become an ongoing program of both sections.

Wyoming State Library. There were two changes in top leadership at the State Library in 1977. In May, William Nightingale of Lander resigned as Chairman of the State Library, Archives and Historical Board. He was succeeded by Board member Mary Emerson of Evanston, who has been active in both the library and historical fields. Near the end of the year Deputy State Librarian John M. Carter resigned. A successor had not been named at year's end.

In November the State Library issued an updated version of the catalog of its extensive collection of large-print books. In April the State Library joined the University of Wyoming Library and the Natrona County Public Library in Casper in sponsoring a workshop on government documents in Casper. During the fall the State Library and the State Department of Education jointly presented a series of workshops for public and school librarians on "How to Use Your State Library and the State Department of Education." The 1977 meeting of the State Library Advisory Council was held in Cheyenne June 3.

Around the State. Libraries and the news media share common interests, but not all of them support one other as well as the Albany County Library and the Laramie *Daily Boomerang*. With funding from a CETA grant, in October the Library began the project of preparing a complete index of the *Boomerang* and its predecessors, the first attempt to index any Wyoming daily. In November the *Boomerang* received the Mountain Plains Library Association's first News Media Support Award for its ongoing campaign to secure better funding and a new main building for the Library.

Campbell County's George Amos Memorial Library in Gillette waged a successful campaign for a major upgrading of staff salaries. The Library pointed out, among other things, that its salaries were the lowest of any county department and that it was also the only department employing a preponderance of women.

In November the University of Wyoming Science Library and the University's College of Engineering began an experimental program funded by a Department of Energy grant to deliver up-to-date energy information throughout the state.

Buildings. The University of Wyoming Library broke ground in April for a much-needed $4,000,000 addition to the William Robertson Coe Library, the main campus library. When completed in 1979, the new wing will approximately double both shelving capacity and reader accommodations. During the fall the staff of the first unit of the University's new College of Human Medicine, the Family Practice Center at Casper, gradually moved into their new building as the construction workers moved out. The facility includes a medical library and an outstanding audiovisual section. The Laramie County Library started construction in late fall of a new building to house its branch in Pine Bluffs. The branch has been renamed the Eastern Laramie County Library.

Intellectual Freedom. Like most other states, Wyoming had action on the legislative front in 1977. A stringent anti-obscenity measure received preliminary approval in the House of Representatives with a bare quorum of members present, but it was killed on the final reading with all members voting. Apparently backed by conservative religious groups, the bill seemed likely to surface again. No significant censorship attempts involving libraries occurred during the year.

Awards. At its annual convention in May, WLA presented the following major awards: Librarian of the Year, Lisa Lang, Director of Albany County Library, Laramie; Outstanding Trustee, Charlotte Vivion, Carbon County Library, Rawlins; Legislator of the Year, State Representative Bob O'Neill, Sublette County; Milstead Award (for outstanding library service to children or youth), Margaret Hall, Moorcroft School Library; and Special Project Award, Laramie County Library (Al Whitelock, Director) for its Bicentennial programs.

PAUL B. CORS

INDEX

A & I services: *See* Abstracting and Indexing Services
AACR 1, AACR 2: *See* Anglo-American Cataloguing Rules
Abbreviations and acronyms, x
"About Books", 179, 244
Abrams, Peggy, 357
Abstracting and Indexing Services, 2-3 *(See* Indexing and Abstracting Services 77, 76 eds.)
Canadian report, 335
Academic Freedom Group, 159
Academic Libraries, 4-14 *(also 77, 76 eds.)*
ACRL activities, 36-38
armed forces libraries, 31
automation, 45, 46
Black libraries, 121
buildings, 72
Canadian report, 335, 337
collection development, 97
genealogical collections, xxx
Italian collections, 123
London report, 343, 344
management issues, 184
NEH programs, 197
OLLR programs, 171
public relations activities, 243
social responsibilities, 292, 293
staff development, 231
standards, 304
women librarians, 322
Academic Library Development Program (ALDP), 4, 231
Accreditation, 14-17 *(also 77,76 eds.)*
evaluation of process, 115
ACRL: *See* Association of College and Research Libraries
Acquisitions: *See* Collection Development
Addams Children's Book Award, 51, 91
Administration: *See* Management, Library

Adults, Library Services to, 18-20 *(also 77, 76 eds.)*
Canadian library usage, 340; table, 340
CBC programs, 86
literacy programs, 181
parent support services, 88
See also 77, 76 eds.: Older Adults, Library Services to
Adult Education Association of the United States of America, 214
AFL-CIO, 166
"After School Specials," 131
Age Discrimination in Employment Act, 224
AGRICOLA (Agricultural On-Line Access), 193
AGRIS Documentation Center, 194
Ahmadu Bello University, 119
Ahmanson Foundation, 133
Aiken, Mary, 309
Air Force libraries, 31
Akaboshi, Takako, 50
Akers' Simple Library Cataloging, 84
Akron-Summit County Library, 19 (photo)
Alabama report, 350, 351
aid to libraries, 237
library legislation, 168
Alaska report, 351, 352
Alberta, Can., 338, 339
Aleixandre, Vicente, 53
Alexander, Mona, 369
Alliance for Information and Referral Services (AIRS), 148, 215
Alliance of Association for the Advancement of Education, 215
Allen, C. G., 53
Allerton Park Institute, 87
Almeida, Ruth, E., 374
Alpine Micrographics, 189
Altman, Ellen, 180, 185
Aluri, Rao, 9
American Academy and Institute of Arts and Letters Award, 51
American Association for Gifted Children, 215
American Association for the Advancement of Science, 215
American Association of Community and Junior Colleges, 215
American Association of Publishers (AAP), 102, 103, 104, 150
American Association of Law Libraries (AALL), 20, 21, 170 *(also 77, 76 eds.)*
American Association of School Librarians (AASL), 21-23, 380, 281 *(also 77, 76 eds.)*
awards, 47
research programs, 275
American Association of University Professors (AAUP), 215
American Bar Association (ABA), 169
American Book Publishing Record (BPR), 57
American Bookseller, 71, 86
American Booksellers Association (ABA), 71, 215
American Broadcasting Company, 257
American Center of Films for Children, 131
American Civil Liberties Union, 215, 216
American Correctional Association, 216
American Council on Education, 216
American Film Festival, 129
American Folklife Center, 177
American Indians and libraries, 117, 118
See also 76 ed.
American Institute of Architects/ALA/Library Administration Division Award, 47

American Institute of Architects—ALA Library Buildings Awards Program, 172
American Institute for Conservation (AIC), xxxvii
American Libraries, 179
American Library Association
ACRL joint activities, 36
affirmative action stand, 223
Archives, 30, 31, 139
awards and prizes, 47-51
CLA joint activities, 81
Conference, 228 (photo)
convention—1977, 71 (photo)
copyright kit, 106
intellectual freedom debate, 156
international library relations, 162-164
MLA contracts, 193
Notable Books, 205
preservation courses, xli
public relations activities, 244
Publishing, ALA, 246, 249, 262 (photos)
social responsibilities, 294, 295
standards, 304
See also Council, ALA, Divisions, Offices, and Round Tables by name
American Library History, 23 *(also 77, 76 eds.)*
ALA Archives uses, 30
American Library History Round Table (ALHRT), 23, 24 *(also 77, 76 eds.)*
American Library History Round Table Award, 24
American Library History Round Table Essay Award, 47
American Library Society, 24, 25 *(also 77, 76 eds.)*
American Library Trustee Association (ALTA), 25, 26, 313 *(also 77, 76 eds.)*
trustees, 311

417

American Library Trustee Association Honor Award, 47
American Music Center, 257
American National Standards (ANS), 200
American National Standards Institute (ANSI), 195, 216, 302-304
American Society for Information Science, 26, 27 (*also 77, 76 eds.*)
American Television and Radio Archive, 175
American Theological Library Association, 27, 28, 133 (*also 77, 76 eds.*)
American Vocational Association, 216
Ames, Jan, 412
AMIGOS Bibliographic Control, 213
Ammons, A. R., 51
Amos, Virginia, 165
Anderl, Robert G., 385
Anders, Mary Edna, 266
Andersen International Children's Book Medals, 51, 91, 161
Andersen, Jean, 55
Anderson, Herschel V., 403
Anderson, Jim, 380
Anderson, Joseph J., 385
Anderson, Patricia, 387
Andrews Bibliographical Award, 51
Anglo-American Cataloguing Rules, 83-85
  art cataloging, 33
  CLA work, 82
  revision completion, 177
  revision impact, 262, 263
ANSI: *See* American National Standards Institute
Arbitration: *See* Mediation, Arbitration, and Inquiry
Arbuthnot Honor Lecture, 35, 92
Architecture: *See* Buildings
Archives, 28-31 (*also 77, 76 eds.*)
  ALA Archives, 15, 139
  American Television and Radio Archive, 175
  Black collection discoveries, 120
  CLA activities, 85
  document ownership case, 169
  security consultant service, 285
  security system, 6
  sound recordings, 257, 258
Arensdorf, William F., 385
Argentina, 214
Arizona report, 352-354
Arkansas report, 354, 355
  copyright law, 103, 267 (photos)
Armed Forces Librarians Achievement Citation, 47
Armed Forces Librarians Section, 127
Armed Forces Libraries, 31, 32 (*also 77, 76 eds.*)
Armstrong, Judith, 381
Army libraries, 31
Arnold, George, 359
Art Libraries, 32-34
  standards, 304
  Yale Center for British Art, 298
Art Libraries Society of North America (ARLIS/NA), 32-34, 304
Art Publishing Awards, 33
Ash, Lee, 302

Ashe, Arthur, 242 (photo)
Asheim, Lester E., 113 (*See also Biographies 77 ed.*)
Asia Foundation Grant, 50
Asian American Librarians Association, 118
Asian Americans and libraries, 118 (*also 77, 76 eds.*)
Asleson, Robert F., 152
Asp, William G., 378
Aspnes, Grieg G., 54, 301
Assembly of State Librarians, 176
Associated Colleges of the Midwest (ACM), 7
Associated Organizations for Teacher Education, 217
Association for Asian Studies, 217
Association for Childhood Education International, 217
Association for Educational Communications and Technology, 217, 323
Association for Library Service to Children, 34-36
  intellectual freedom debate, 157
  Notable Children's Films, 131
  research forum, 275
  sexism conference, 323
  toys and games, 310
  See also Children's Services Division in 77, 76 eds.
Association of American Colleges, 217
Association of American Library Schools (AALS), 114, 115, 217
  public relations activities, 245
Association of American publishers (AAP), 217, 218, 250
  Books as Gifts program, 90
  Freedom to Read Committee, 159
Association of Assistant Librarians (AAL), xlv
Association of Audio Archives (AAA), 258
Association of College and Research Libraries, 36-38 (*also 77, 76 eds.*)
  Art Section, 32
  Black librarians internships, 121
  continuing education programs, 99
  standards, 304
Association of Data Base Producers, 150
Association of Recorded Sound Collections (ARSC), 257
Association of Research Libraries, 38-41 (*also 77, 76 eds.*)
  academic libraries, 4
  ACRL joint activities, 37
  collection development, 95
  continuing education, 100
  OMS, 231
  salary survey, 271
Association of State Library Agencies, 42, 43 (*also 77, 76 eds.*)
  merger proposal, 108, 143
Association pour l'avancement des sciences et des techniques de la documentation, L' (ASTED), 81
Astor Foundation, 133
Atkinson Report, 343
Atlanta University, 118, 120

Atlantic Provinces, Can., 339
Atlantic Provinces Library Association, 218
Auctions, 299-300
  New York Public Library, 90
Audiovisual material
  AVLINE, 199
Audiovisual materials
  cataloging and classification, 83
  holdings by schools table, 282
  realia, 256
  sound recordings, 257, 258
Austin, Derek William, 54
Automation, 43-47 (*also 77, 76 eds.*)
  academic libraries, 5
  bibliographic processing centers, 55
  bibliographic records, 263
  circulation systems, 9, 93
  CONSER project, 288
  copyright issues, 102
  fees for services, xv
  GPO sales system, 141
  Library of Congress, 176
  London report, 344
  National Library of Medicine, 199
  See also Data Bases, Computer-Readable
Authors Guild, 251
Authors League of America, 102-104
Awards and Prizes, 47-54 (*also 77, 76 eds.*)
  academic librarians, 12, 23
  ALSC policy changes, 34
  art libraries, 33
  Beta Phi Mu Award, 55, 175
  Black librarians, 121
  book publishing, 252
  buildings, 344
  Canadian report, 336
  cataloging and classification, 84
  children's literature, 90, 161
  CLA awards, 82
  documents librarianship, 140
  exhibits, 127
  films for children, 131
  information industry, 150
  information science, 27
  intellectual freedom, 160
  international cooperation, 145
  Jewish Book Council awards, 125
  LAD awards, 172
  library educators, 116
  library historianship, 24
  library press, 180
  LRRT awards, 180
  medical librarianship, 188
  MPLA awards, 265
  music librarianship, 192
  public relations, 244
  reference librarianship, 259
  research awards, 274
  service to blind and handicapped, 143
  special librarianship, 301
  SRRT awards, 295
  technical services, 276
  Theatre Library Association honors, 308
  trustees, 25, 26
  Women's National Book Association, 324
  See also individual awards, e.g. Caldecott, Newbery and recipients by name
Babbitt, Natalie, 161
Baensch, Robert, 71 (photo)
Baer, Karl, 145

Bagby, Dallas, 51
Bailey, Crystal, 165
Bailey, Stephen K., 37
Baker, Augusta, 160
Baker, Jer., 165
BALLOTS, 44, 56, 204
Bancroft Prizes, 51
Bandolin, Patti, 357
Banks, Paul, 233
Barnouw, Erik, 175
Barron, Margaret, 109
Bartko, Yvonne, 363
Basile, Vitaza, 54
Batchelder Award, 35, 48, 91
Batchelor, Lillian L., 207
Bate, Walter J., 51
Battey, Jean D., 409
Beal, Betty, 350
Beale, Helen Purdy, 49
Beall, C. E. Campbell, 26, 50
Bearman, Toni Carbo, 59 (photo)
Beatty, Samuel B., 27
Beaver, Jim, 109 (photo)
Behrstock, Julian, 314
Bell, Shelah A., 406
Bellow, Saul, 51
Bender, Betty W., 412
Bender, David, 279, 374
Bender, J. Terry, 300
Beneduce, Ann, 160
Bergman, Sherrie, 173
Berk, Robert A., 188
Berry, John, 179
Best sellers, 250
Besterman Medal, 51
Beta Phi Mu, 55 (*also 77, 76 eds.*)
  Award, 48, 116, 175
Bettelheim, Bruno, 53
Beveridge Award, 51
Bibliographic aids and services
  abstracting and indexing services, 2
  cataloging and classification, 83
  instruction by reference librarians, 262
Bibliographic Center for Research (BCR), 56
Bibliographic control
  academic libraries, 11
  automation, 45
  discographies, 258
Bibliographic Processing Centers, 55-57
  See also 77, 76 eds.: Processing Centers
Bibliographic Retrieval Services (BRS), 46, 109-111, 187
Bibliography
  Bibliographic Retrieval Services, 187
  fees for searches, xv
  Library of Congress, 176
  OAS programs, 213
  serials, 289
  Universal Bibliographic Control, 317
Bibliography and Indexes, 57, 58 (*also 77, 76 eds.*)
Bibliography and Indexing standards for references, 303
Bibliography of Discographies, 258
Bibliotherapy, 43
Bidlack, Russell E., xxiii-xxx, 14, 15, 48, 55, 59 (photo), 116, 175
Bierman, Kenneth, 153
Big Brothers/Big Sisters of America, 218
Bilandic, Michael, 311 (photo)
Bilingual programs, 292, 293
  school libraries, 278

418

Spanish-language programs, 123
Binder, Lucia, 161
Binding, 50 (also 77 ed.)
  preservation issues, xxxvi-xxxviii, xxxix
  preservation projects, 233
Biographies, 59-68 (also 77, 76 eds.)
Biomedical Communications Network, 187
Bishop, Elizabeth, 53
Bkakdibutr, Chirawan, 50
Blacks and libraries, 118-122 (also 77, 76 eds.)
  ACRL internships, 37
  Black Caucus, ALA, 108, 157, 158 (photo), 295
Black Press Archives, 119
Blake, Fay, 261
Blind and Physically Handicapped, Library Services for the, 69-71 (also 77, 76 eds.)
  academic libraries, 9
  adult services, 18
  building design, 75 (photo), 76, 78
  Canadian report, 339
  children's library services, 87
  delivery services, 98
  health and rehabilitative library services, 141
  HRLSD activities, 143
  LC services, 177
  legislation summary, 167, 168
  London report, 349
  school libraries, 278
  standards, 304
Bliss, Leslie, 300
Blockson, Charles L., 120
Blyth, Mabel Florence (James), 341
Bobinski, George, 23
Bolles, Charles, 42, 369
Bombs, losses due to, 284
Bond, Nancy, 53, 90, 91 (photo)
Bonner, Lucy, 370
Book clubs, 90, 250
Book Distribution Task Force, 252
"Book Hot Lines," 244
Book Industry Study Group, Inc., 249, 270 (also 77 ed.)
Book Industry Trends—1977, 271
Book Views, 179
Book Week
  CBC activities, 86
Booker Prize for Fiction, 52
Booklist, 249
Bookmobile: See Community Delivery Service; See also 77, 76 eds.
"Books as Gifts" program, 90, 252
"Books for All," 314
Bookselling, 71, 72 (also 77 ed.)
  media tie-ins, 328
Boorstin, Daniel J., 145 (photo), 175-178
Booth, Larry, 235
Booth, Robert, 164
Boston Globe—Horn Book Awards, 52
Boston Public Library, 327
Bouwhuis Scholarship Award, 85
Boys' Clubs of America, 218
Boyvey, Mary, 406
Braille recorder, 69
Brandon, Alfred N., 53, 188
Bratislava International Biennial (BIB) of Illustrations, 52

Brawner, Lee B., 160
Breland, June, 51, 165
Brick, Reva, 198
Briley, Dorothy, 86
British Broadcasting Corporation, 130
British Library, 343, 344
British Library Automated Information Service (BLAISE), 344
British National Bibliography (BNB), 344
Broadcast Archives, 258
Brocks-Shedd, Virgia, 37
Brodart, 46, 204
Broomall, Susan, 51, 166
Brothers, Mrs. Bill, 354
Brown, Christine, 405
Brown, Florence, 358
Brown, Marcia, 54, 59 (photo), 85
Brown, Margaret, 376
Brown, Norman B., 285, 286
Brown, Tyrone, 307
Bruce, Robert, 307
Brumback, Elsie L., 391
Brunet, C., 337
Bryant, Douglas, 145, 296
Bryant, Philip, 344
Buchinski, Edwin, 44
Buckingham, Betty Jo, 368
Buckley, Francis, 139, 140
Budge, Edwin S., 397
Buffalo and Erie Country Public Library, 75 (photo)
Buildings, 72-76 (also 77, 76 eds.)
  academic libraries, 11, 12
  Black Americans, 118
  budget vs. space, 77, 78, 79
  Canadian report, 336
  federal appropriations, 167
  handicapped persons' access, 223, 224
  Lister Hill Center, 198, 199 (photo)
  London report, 344
  prefabricated libraries, 98
  public libraries, 236
Budgeting, Accounting, and Cost Control: See Management, Library
Bunting, Eve, 52
Bureau of Indian Affairs (BIA), 117
Burdick, Gayle, 368
Burgan, John S., xxv
Burke, Jane, 127
Burns, Robert W., Jr., 49, 180, 274
Burroughs Medal, 52
Burstein, Chaya, 125
Bush Foundation, 133
Butcher, Dina, 393
Buttars, Gerald A., 407
Bynum, Molly, 351
Byrum, John Donald, Jr., 60 (photo)
Cabello-Argandoña, Roberto, 60 (photo)
Cable TV, 307, 308
Cade, Barbara C., 362
Cady, Susan, 367
Cage, Alvin, 406
Cahill, Alice, 376
Caldecott Medal, 48, 91
  1977 recipient, 89 (photo)
  policy changes, 34
California report, 355, 356
  aid to libraries, 237
  library legislation, 168
California State Library, 114
Campbell, C. E., 312 (photo)
Campbell Citation and Medal, 48, 143
CAN/MARC: Authorities, 337
Canada

  children's literature, 90, 91
  filmstrip sales, 132
Canadian Association of College and University Libraries (CACUL), 82, 335
Canadian Association of Public Libraries (CAPL), 82
Canadian Association of Special Libraries and Information Services (CASLIS), 82
Canadian Association of University Teachers (CAUT), 335
Canadian Correspondent's Report, 335-343 (also 77, 76 eds.)
Canadian Library Association, 80-82 (also 77, 76 eds.)
  Centenary celebration, 81 (photo)
  children's literature awards, 91
  women librarians, 323
Canadian Library Trustees' Association (CLTA), 82
Canadian Materials, 82
Canadian Periodical Index, 82
Canadian School Library Association (CSLA), 82
Canadian Union Catalog Task Group, 336, 337
Cane Award, 52
Cannon, Isabella, 295
Cappon, Lester Jesse, 48
CAPTAIN, 44
Card catalogs, 11
  LC closing, 289
  LC policy, 176
  OCLC serials policy, 289
  reference issues, 263
Carey-Thomas Award, 52
Carnegie Corporation, 306, 307
Carnegie Medal, 52, 91
Carrington Collection, 119
Carroon, Barbara, 380
Carter, Jimmy, 26, 178, 320
Carter G. Woodson Regional Library, 120
Caruso, Rose, 165
Casey, Daniel W., 26, 50
Cassata, Mary B., 389
Cassell, Kay, 173
Cataloging and Classification, 82-85 (also 77, 76 eds.)
  AACR 2, 262, 263
  academic libraries, 11
  art librarianship issues, 33
  automation, 44, 45
  Canadian report, 337
  Library of Congress, 176
  London report, 344
  serials cataloging, 289
  sound recordings, 258
  standardization in Latin America, 213
  UBC projects, 317
  See also Anglo-American Cataloguing Rules
Cataloging and Indexing (CAIN), 193
Catholic Library Association, 85-86 (also 77, 76 eds.)
Censorship: See Intellectual Freedom
Center for Chinese Research Materials, 41
Center for Research Libraries, 7, 96, 287
Center for the Book, 167, 178
Certification
  archivists, 29
  continuing education, 100
  medical librarians, 187
  performance appraisal issues, 229
  school librarians, 114

Chadwell, Patricia, xxix
Challenge Grant Program, 10, 197
Chang, Roy, 93, 118
Chapin, Schuyler, 309 (photo)
Checkpoint Systems, Inc., 283
Chelsea Right to Read Committee v. Chelsea School Committee (case), 134
Chemical Abstracts Services (CAS), 287
Ch'en, Li Li, 53
Chen, Robert P., 93
Cheney, Frances, 254
Chicago Public Library, 117, 119 (photo), 290, 291
  Cultural Center completion, 73, 74 (photo)
Chief Officers of State Library Agencies (COSLA), 218
Child Development Associates Consortium, 218
Childers, Thomas, 148
Children's Book Center (Toronto, Can.), 90
Children's Book Council, 86, 87 (also 77, 76 eds.)
  children's literature, 90
  parents workshop funding, 88
Children's Book Week
  public relations activities, 245
Children's Film Theatre (CFT), 131
Children's Library Services, 87-89 (also 77, 76 eds.)
  ALSC activities, 34
  handicapped childrens' rights, 141
  London report, 347
  realia, 256
  Spanish-language programs, 122
  toys and games, 309, 310
Children's Literature, 89-92 (also 77, 76 eds.)
  ALSC award policy changes, 34
  Canadian report, 337, 338
  CBC activities, 86
  IBBY projects, 160
  See also Young Adult Literature
Children's Services Division: See Association for Library Service to Children
Childs, James Bennett, 207 (photo)
Childs Award, 48, 140
Chinese American Librarians Association, 92, 93
Chinese Americans, library service to, 291
Chisman, Forrest, 307
Choice, 36
Choncoff, Mary, 352
Christie's, 299
Christofferson, Rea, 5
Chun, Mae, 363
Church of Jesus Christ of Latter-Day Saints (Mormons)
  genealogy library, xxvi
Cincinnati Electronics Corporation, 46, 93
Cincinnati Public Library, 19 (photo)
Circulation Library Automated System for Inventory Control (CLASSIC), 93
Circulation Systems, 93, 94 (also 77, 76 eds.)
  academic libraries, 9
  automated systems, 45
  confidentiality of records,

419

160
  LAD workshop, 173
  public libraries, 240
Civil Rights Act, 224
CL Systems, Inc., 45, 46, 204
Clark, Carolyn, 51
Clark, Mary E., 173
Clark, Robert L., 396
Clarke, D. Sherman, 34
Clasquin, F. F., 286
Clausman, Gilbert J., 60 (photo), 188
CLENE (Continuing Library Education Network and Exchange), 219, 230, 231
  continuing education, 99-101, 115
Cleveland Public Library, 19 (photo)
Clewer, Lisa Ray, xxv
Clift Scholarship, 50
Cline, Nancy, 139, 140
CLSI/LITA Award, 153
Cluff, E. Dale, 407
Coalition of Adult Education Organizations, 219
Coalition for Children and Youth, 218
Cobb, Eileen, 361
Cobb, Lafaye, 165
Coco, Alfred J., 21, 61 (photo)
Cohen, Jackson B., 286
Colby, Edward E., 258
Cole, Fred, 145 (See also Biographies 77 ed.)
Collection Development, 94-97 (also 77, 76 eds.)
  academic libraries, 10, 11
  art libraries, 34
  automated systems, 46
  genealogical specialization, xxviii
  Library of Congress, 175
  London report, 343-345
  NEH programs, 197
  projected increase, 249
  replacement of materials, xxxix
  serials study, 286
  See also Acquisitions in 77, 76 eds.
Collections Analysis Project (CAP), 41, 95
Collective bargaining: See Labor unions, library
College Library Program, 8
Colorado report, 356
  aid to libraries, 237
COLT: See Council on Library Technical Assistants
Colton, Flora D., 24
COM: See Computer Output Microform
COMARC, 43, 83
Combined Book Exhibit for Federal Librarians and Program Specialists, 128
Comeau, Reginald, 386
Commission on Federal Paperwork, 29
Committee of Small Magazine Editors and Publishers (COSMEP), 293
Committee on Accreditation (COA), 14-16, 115
Committee on Bibliographical Services for Canada (CBSC), 335
Committee on Program Evaluation (COPES), 173
Committee on the Status of Women in Librarianship, 158
Communications Act of 1934, 172
Communications Technology Satellite (CTS), 127, 199

Community Delivery Services, 97, 98 (also 77 ed.)
Community Delivery Services
  bookmobile, 98 (photo)
  public libraries, 236
  school libraries' roles, 279
Comprehensive Education and Training Act (CETA), 227
Computer Output Microform (COM), 337
  catalogs, 45, 240
  microfiche catalogs, 11
Concerned Librarians Opposing Unprofessional Trends (CLOUT), 229
Congressional Research Service, 177
Connecticut report, 356-358
  library legislation, 168
CONSER, 177, 285-288
  agricultural serials, 194
  ATLA participation, 28
  automation, 45
Construction: See Buildings
Continuing Education
  CLA programs, 85
  collection development, 95
  LAD cassette tapes, 173
  LED programs, 174
  library education, 115
  medical librarians, 188
Continuing Education for Library Staffs in the Southwest (CELS), 267, 268
Continuing Education Unit (CEU), 99
Continuing library education performance appraisal issues, 230
Continuing Library Education Network and Exchange: See CLENE
Continuing Library Education Planning Coordination Project (COLEPAC), 100
Continuing Professional Education, 98-101 (also 77, 76 eds.)
Continuing professional education
  ACRL program, 38
  ASLC activities, 35
  young adult librarians, 326
  See also CLENE; Education, Library
CONTU, 101, 102 (also 77, 76 eds.)
  automation issues, 44
  copyright questions, 102, 150
  photocopy issue, 4
Cooke, Gordon D., 318 (photo)
Cookston, James, S., 371
Cooley, Marguerite B., 352
Coons, Daniel E., 358
Cooper, Alene, 383
Cooper, Bill, 165
Cooper, Sandra, 43, 144
Cooperative Machine-Readable Cataloging: See COMARC
Cooperative Microfilm Project of Religion and Theology (COMPORT), 28
Coordinated Library Information Program, Inc. (CLIP), 242
Copernicus Award, 52
Copyright, 102-103 (also 77, 76 eds.)
  academic library issues, 6
  ARL guidelines, 38
  automation issues, 44
  Canada, 80
  Canadian report, 337
  clearinghouses, 251
  CONTU, 101, 102
  information industry issues,

150
  Library of Congress, 177
  National Periodical Center impact, 96
  off-the-air recording issue, 191
  serials issues, 285
  serials publishing, 254
  video recording, 191
Copyright Clearance Centers (CCC), 104, 150, 251, 254
Copyright kit, librarian's, 106
Copyright Law, 301 (photo)
Copyrighted Works, National Commission on New Technological Uses of: See CONTU
Corbin, John, 268
Cornell University Libraries, 96, 194
Corporation for Public Broadcasting (CPB), 306
Correctional facilities, service to, 98, 291
  HRLSD activities, 144
  literacy programs, 182
Cossar, Bruce, 82
Couch, O. Marvene, 121, 139
Council, ALA, 107, 108 (also 77, 76 eds.)
  International Relations Committee, 164
  position on fees, 238
Council of National Library Associations (CNLA), 103, 219
Council of Planning Librarians, 57
Council of Specialized Accrediting Agencies, 219
Council on Library Resources (CLR), 133
  academic library grants, 4, 8, 12
  Black library grants, 121
  cataloging grants, 83
  CONSER, 45
  preservation activities, xli
  Professional Development Program, 231
Council on Library Technical Assistants, 108, 109 (also 77, 76 eds.)
Council on Postsecondary Accreditation (COPA), 16, 219
Courtney, John, 384
Coyne, John R., 365
Crachi, Rocco, 301
Craver, Gary, 230
Cravey, Pamela, 51
Creps, John E., 27
Cretsos, James M., 27
Crockett, Ethyl S., 355
Crowley, John, 38
Cuicki, Marcella, 262
Culbertson, Don, 128
Culbertson, Katheryn C., 405
Cummings, Mozelle B., 350
Cummings, Peggy, 351
Curley, Walter W., 127
Curran, Charles C., 180, 274
Curtiss, Margery, 384
Curry, Anna R., 160
Cylke, Frank Kurt, 70
Dainton, Sir Frederick, xlv, 61 (photo)
Dallas Central Library, 19 (photo)
Dalton, Jack, 145
Dalton, Phyllis I., 144
Dana Public Relations Awards, 48, 172
Darling, Pamela W., xxxi-xliv, 233
Darling, Richard L., 4, 5, 23
Dartmouth Medal, 48, 259

Data Bases, Computer-Readable, 109-112 (also 77, 76 eds.)
  abstracting and indexing services, 2
  ALA Archives, 30
  bibliographic data, 55
  children's materials, 88
  CONSER, 288
  information industry, 149
  medical libraries, 187
  National Library of Medicine, 199
  photos, 45, 94, 201
  Responsa literature, 124
  UBC project, 317
Davis, Benita, 373
Davis, Charles H., 180
Davis, Russell L., 407
Davis Awards, 27
Dawley, Alan, 51
Dawson, Alma, 37
Dawson Collection, 120
DBPH (Division for the Blind and Physically Handicapped), 69
Deacidification of paper, xxxviii, xxxv (photo), 232
Dean, Frances C., 23
Dean, John F., 233
DeBruler, Olive, 359
DeFore, Richard, 356
DeGennaro, Richard, 7, 10, 96, 97, 180, 253, 261, 286 (See also Biographies 76 ed.)
Degrees, library education: See Education, Library
DeJohn, William, 42
Delamarter, Ralph, 397
Delaware report, 358, 359
Delougaz, Nathalie P., 164
Demit, Patricia A., 376
Dempsey, Frank J., 365
DePaola, Ronald, 124
DePew, John, 361
Depository Library System: See Government Publications and Depository System
Dervin, Brenda, 18
De Salvo, Nancy, 310
Dessauer, John, 250, 271
Detlefsen, Ellen Gay, 139
Dewey Decimal Classification, 177
Dewey Medal, 48
Diana, Joan, 398
Dickinson, Peter, 52
Dictionary of American Library Biography, 23
Dietz, Dolores, 388
Dillon, Leo and Diane, 48, 91, 161 (See also Biographies 77 ed.)
DiMattia, Ernest A., 127
Disadvantaged, Library Service to, 112, 113 (also 77 ed.)
Disadvantaged, Office for Library Service to the: See 76 ed.
Disasters, xxxiv, 284, 285
Discography, 257
Discrimination
  legal prohibitions, 167, 168
  sex discrimination in salaries, 5
  women librarians, 323
Distinguished Library Service Award for School Administrators, 23
District of Columbia Library, 236
District of Columbia report, 359, 360, 361
Division for the Blind and Physically Handicapped (DBPH), 69

Division of Eligibility and Agency Evaluation (DEAE), 15
Documents, government archives, 28
  GODORT activities, 139
  replevin case, 10, 169
Documents to the People Award, 48
Doebler, Paul D., 271
Doerschuk, Ernest E., Jr., 398
Dollard, Peter, 198
Donaldson, Lord, 343, 346
Donovan, David C., 164
Donovan, John, 161
Dowell, Virginia, 357
Dowlin, C. Edwin, 388
Doyle, Corazone, 148
Doyle, Mary Joyce, 387
Drake, Miriam, 4
Drescher, Robert, 42
Drexel University Graduate School of Library Science Distinguished Achievement Award, 52
Drickamer, Jewel, 400
Duckworth, Avis, 386
Dugan, Patricia, 6
Duke, Judith, 89
Duncan, Arthur F., 76
Dunlap, Connie R., 38
Dutcher, Jeannette, 374
Dye, Luella, 413
Dyson, Yvonne, 380
Eaglen, Audrey, 179, 334
Ealing Reader, 69
Earnshaw, Donald C., 25, 26
Eastlick, John, 15
Eastman, Ann Heidbreder, 325
Eberhart, Richard, 53
Eberhart, W. Lyle, 414
Echelman, Shirley, 62 (photo), 300
Ecuador, 214
Edelen, Joe, 165
Education, Library, 113-116 (*also 77, 76 eds.*)
  accreditation, 14
  LED activities, 173
  Library Association issues, xliv
  literacy program training, 181
  London report, 344, 345
  minority recruitment, 226
  OAS programs, 214
  OLLR programs, 171
  Passing Through the Turnstile: A View of Library School Admissions, xlvii-li
  preservation training, xli, 235
  public relations courses, 245
  research survey, 271
  social responsibilities, 294
  Spanish-speaking librarians, 122
  women's status, 322
  See also Accreditation; Continuing Professional Education; Standards
Education Amendments of 1972, 224
Education of All Handicapped Children Act, 87, 141
Education USA Advisory Board, 219
Educational Broadcasting Facilities Program, 306
Educational Film Library Association, 219
Educational Media Control, 219
Edwards, Mary, 72
Edwards, Ralph, 173
Eggert, Joanna, 316

Eggert, Merris, 409
Ehrhardt, Margaret W., 402
Einhorn, Nathan, 275
El Salvador, 214
Elementary and Secondary Education Act (ESEA), 191, 320
  appropriations, 133
  school library funding, 279
Elias, Arthur, 27
Elizabeth II, Queen, 353 (photo)
Emerson, Katherine, 262
Emerson Award, 52
Employment: See Personnel and Employment
Encyclopaedia Britannica Educational Corporation, 191
Energy conservation, 75
Engen, Richard B., 351
Engleman, Edmund, 52
English Medal Award, 52
Epstein, Daniel M., 51
Epstein, Dena Julia (Polacheck), 62 (photo)
Estes, Elaine G., 368
Estes, Glenn, 22
Ethics, 24 (*also 77, 76 eds.*)
Ethnic Groups, Library Service to, 117-126 (*also 77 ed.*)
  affirmative action projects, 117, 119, 122, 126 (photos)
  London report, 347
  social responsibilities, 291
  See also ethnic groups by name
Exceptional Service Award, 143
Executive Order 11246, 224
Exhibitors Award, 48
Exhibits, Commercial, See 76 ed.
Exhibits Round Table, 126, 127 (*also 77, 76 eds.*)
Explosions, losses due to, 233, 284
Equal Employment Opportunity (EEO), 223
Equal Pay Act, 224
Equal Rights Amendment, 156, 323
  ALA Council support, 108
  SRRT position, 295
Fader, Daniel, 181, 333
Fair employment laws, 224
Falsone, Anne Marie, 356
Farber, Evan Ira, 38
Farjeon Award, 52
Farkas, Conn, Irene, 27
Farley, Richard A., 193
Fast, Elizabeth T., 48, 173, 207 (photo), 242
Federal Communications Commission, 283 (*also 77 ed.*)
Federal funding for libraries
  appropriations, 133
  building projects, 76
  collection development, 97
  continuing education, 99
  handicapped persons' services, 142
  independent research libraries, 145
  information and referral centers, 148
  legislation summary, 167
  library schools aid, 115
  multimedia materials funds, 191
  NCLIS recommendations, 194
  NEH operations, 197
  preservation courses, 234
  preservation program, xli
  public libraries, 238
  school libraries, 279

  Urban Libraries Council programs, 319
Federal Librarians Round Table, 127, 128 (*also 77, 76 eds.*)
Federal Libraries: See Armed Forces Libraries; also 76 ed.
Fees
  automated searches, 46
  bibliographic searches, 8
  dilemma of fees for service, xv-xxii
  interlibrary loans, 38
  public libraries, 238
  reference services, 261, 262
Feldman, Lew D., 300
Ferris, Charles D., 307
FID: See International Federation for Documentation
Fikes, Lee, 135 (photo)
Films, 128-130 (*also 77, 76 eds.*)
  Black films, 120
  intellectual freedom issues, 156
  ISBN's for films, 192
  young adult services, 325
Films, Children's, 130, 131 (*also 77, 76 eds.*)
Filmstrips, 131, 132 (*also 77, 76 eds.*)
Financial support for libraries: See Federal funding for libraries; Foundations and Funding Agencies
Fink, Ellen, 233
Fires, losses due to, xxxiv, 154, 233, 284
First Amendment freedoms, xvii (*also 77 ed.*)
Fischer, Margaret T., 27, 62 (photo)
Fisk University, 120
Fite, Alice E., 22, 23, 280
Fitzsimmons, Richard, 398
Fleming, June D., 355
FLIRT: See Federal Librarians Round Table
Floods, losses due to, xxxii, 284
Florida report, 361, 362
Flynt, Larry, 254, 255
Ford, Robert C., 230
Foundations and Funding Agencies, 132, 133 (*also 77, 76 eds.*)
  See also Federal funding for libraries; funding agencies by name
Fox, Michael Alan, 71
Fox, Paula, 161
Francis, Sir Frank, 296
Franck, Jane P., 164
Franco, John M., 23, 50
Frank, Joseph, 52, 53
Frankie, Suzanne, 271
Franklin, Hardy, xxv
Franklin, Hugh, 403
Franz, Ray, Jr., 41
Franzel, Adeline, 48, 143
Free Library of Philadelphia, 182
Freedley Memorial Award, 308
Freedman, Maurice J., 153
Freedom of Information: See Intellectual Freedom
Freedom to Read Committee, 159, 253
Freedom to Read Foundation, 134 (*also 77, 76 eds.*)
Freides, Thelma, 260
Friendly, Fred, 309 (photo)
Friendly Booth Award, 127
Friends of IBBY, 161
Friends of Libraries, 134, 135 (*also 77, 76 eds.*)

Friends of the National Libraries, 343
Fry, Bernard, 102
Fuld Health Trust, 132, 133
Fulton, Greg, 69 (photo)
Funding for Libraries: See Federal funding for libraries; Foundations and Funding Agencies
Funk, Charles, Jr., 357
Furniture and Equipment
  baseball glove chair, 87 (photo)
  micrographics equipment, 189
  See also 77, 76 eds.
Gaffner, Haines B., 152
Gág, Wanda, 53
Gala, V., 126 (photo)
Gallego, Humberto, 264
Gallery of Distinguished Newspaper Publishers, 119
Gambee, Budd L., 24
Games: See Toys and Games
Gardner, Jeffrey, 95
Gardner, John, 53
Gardner, Richard, 36
Garfield, Eugene, 152
Garvey, Catherine, 310
Gates, Barbara, 154
Gauss Award, 52
Gaventa, Shirley, 198
Gavel Award, 52
Gay Book Award, 295
Gay rights, 226
Gaylord Company, 46, 283, 284
Geller, Henry, 307
Genealogy
  archives usage, 30
  Genealogy As It Relates to Library Service, xxiii-xxx
  public libraries, 240
General Nucleonics, Inc., 284
George Washington University Library, 29 (photo)
Georgia report, 362
Gerhardt, Lillian, 179
Gesterfield, Kathryn, 365
Giblin, James, 86
Gifts, Bequests, Endowments, 135-139 (*also 77, 76 eds.*)
  academic libraries, 10
  Black collections, 119
  Canadian report, 335
  Chicago Public Library, 138
  Chicago Public Library Cultural Center, 95 (photo)
  London report, 343
  Lowy gift, 80 (photo)
  sound recordings, 257
Giles, Louise Jones, 36, 122 (See also Obituaries 77 ed.)
Giles Minority Scholarship, 50, 122
Gilliland, Ernestine, 369
Girls Clubs of America, 219, 220
"Give-A-Book Certificate," 72, 90
Givens, Johnnie, 266
Glazer, Frederic, 236, 113 (photo), 413
Goal Awards, 47, 180
Godfrey, Lois E., 388
Godine, David R., 33
GODORT: See Government Documents Round Table
Goff, Karen, 413
Golden Kite Award, 52
Goldstein, Rachel K., 322
Gonzalez, Rebecca A., 55
Goodrum, Charles A., 62 (photo), 175
Gordon, Sol, 333
Gore, Daniel, 96

421

Gore, Margaret Anne, 51
Gorman, Michael, 63 (photo)
Gosier, Doris M., 37
Gotanda, Masae, 229
Government Documents Round Table, 139, 140, (*also 77, 76 eds.*)
Government Printing Office (GPO), 140, 301
  LC joint arrangements, 176
  micropublishing, 190
Government Publications and Depository System 140, 141 (*also 77, 76 eds.*)
  micropublishing, 190
  micrographic serials, 290
Grant, Jason C., III, 121
Grant, M.I. Belle, 341
Grants: *See* Federal funding for libraries; Foundations and Funding Agencies; funding agencies by name
Grauer, Ben, 300
Great Britain
  children's literature, 90, 91
  information industry, 150
  London report, 343
Green, Caroline, 403
Greenaway Medal, 52, 91 (photo)
Grindeland, William D., 413
Grolier Foundation Award, 48
Grolier National Library Week Award, 51, 244
Groover, Eloise, 361
Grosch, Audrey N., 27, 54, 301
Gross, Mason Welch, 208, (photo)
Gross, Richard, 373
Gross, Robert A., 51
Guide to Reference Books, 261
Guidelines on Academic Status for University Librarians, 335
Gunning, Kathleen, 400
Gustafson, Diane F., 371
Guttromson, Marilyn, 393
Haas, Warren, 287
Halbey, Hans, 160
Halcums, Robert E., 51
Hale, Robert D., 71, 72, 86
Haley, Alex, xxiii, 53
Haley, Gail E., 52, 91 (photo)
Hall, Blaine H., 180
Hall, David, 258
Hall, Denise, 356
Halldorsson, Egill A., 9
Hamilton, Beth, 42
Hammer, Donald P., 153, 172
Hammond, Inc., Library Award, 48
Hammond, Lillimund, 359
Hampton Institute, 121
Hamrin, Gerald W., 355
Hanna, Mary Ann, 377
Hansberry, Lorraine, 119
Hansberry, Verda, 412
Hansen, Andrew M., 26
Harlan, Donna B., 25
Harlan, John B., 25
Haro, Roberto P., 263
Harpole, Patricia, xxviii
Harris, Agnes, 371
Harris, Christie, 52
Harris, Michael H., 24
Hart, Patricia, 364
Hartman, David, 125
Harvey, John F., 24
Harvey, Karen, 34
Hasenjager, Karen, 49, 116, 180, 274
Haskin, Susan M., 144
Haskins, James, 53
Hatfield, Betty, 370
Haviland, Virginia, 161
Hawaii report, 363

Haycock, Kenneth R., 63 (photo)
Haynes, Donald R., 410
HEA Education Act: *See* Higher Education Act
Head, Linda, 352
Health and Rehabilitative Library Services, 141-143 (*also 77, 76 eds.*)
  activities, 143
  delivery services, 98
  public libraries, 240
  See also Blind and Physically Handicapped, Library Services for the
Health and Rehabilitative Library Services Division, 143, 144 (*also 77, 76 eds.*)
  ASLA merger, 42, 108
  Health and Rehabilitative Library Services Division Exceptional Service Award, 49
  standards, 304
HEGIS-LIBGIS, 4
Heiges, Mary, 378
Heins, Paul, 161
Hektoen, Faith H., 36
Heller, Dawn, 365
Henning, Jeanne, 173
Herbel, Patricia, 393
Herrera, Luis, 123
Hersey, John, 44
Hess, James, 25
Hetherington, Jeree, 406
Hewey, Dell, 109 (photo)
Hewitt, Vivian, 301
Hewlett Foundation, 133
Hickey, Doralyn, 162, 275
Hicks, G. Sheppeard, 266
Hieber, Douglas M., 368
Higher Education Act (HEA), 97, 224, 320
  academic library aid, 7
  appropriations, 133
  library education funding, 115
  OLLR appropriations, 170
  research library funds, 38
Higher Education General Information Survey, 4
Higman, Barry W., 51
Hill, D.R., 322
Hill, Richard, 261
Hinkle, John, 109 (photo)
Hinshaw, Marilyn, 165
Hispanic Americans, library service to, 122, 292
  REFORMA activities, 262
Ho, Alana, 93
Hoaglund, Sister Mary Arthur, I.H.M., 64 (photo), 85
Hobbit, The, 131
Hoduski, Bernadine A., 48, 140
Hodgin, Ellis, 198
Hoffberg, Judith A., 32-34
Hoffman, Frank W., 258
Holley, Edward G., 24, 106
Holliday, Ardis S., 400
Hollis, Vida, 388
Holmes, Jeanne M., 193
Holt, Raymond, 42
Holte Collection, 119
Honig, Alice, 309
Hood, Roger, 51
Hoopes, Townsend, 251
Horban, Walter, 192 (photo)
Horn, Zoia, 261
Horn Book Award: *See* Boston Globe—Horn Book Award
Houston Central Library, 19 (photo)
Houston Endowment, 133
Hove, Nancy, 362
How to Find Your Own Roots (Clewer), xxv
Howard, Donald R., 52

Howard, Joseph, 289
Howard-Gibbon Medal, 52
Howe, Irving, 53, 125
Howell, J.B., 266
Howells Medal, 52
Hoyle, Karen, 35
Hoyt, David, 128
Huff, Margaret F., 402
Hughes, Dale, 415
Hugo Award, 52
Humanities Challenge Grants, 97, 234
Humphry, John Ames, 64
Hunt, Richard, 138 (photo)
Huq, Abdul, 164
Hwa, Theresa, 93
Hyland, Anne, 394
I and R Centers: *See* Information and Referral Centers
IBBY: *See* International Board on Books for Young People
Idaho report, 363, 364
Idaho State University Library, 6 (photo)
IFLA, 144-145 (*also 77, 76 eds.*)
  art libraries, 32
  CLA joint activities, 81
  50th anniversary meeting, 145 (photo)
  handicapped persons' programs, 70, 143
  international relations, 162
  Music Library Association activities, 193
  library statistics, 315
  rare books, 299
  RTSD delegates, 275
  Special Libraries Division, 302
  Universal Bibliographic Control, 84, 317
  UNIMARC, 177
ILLINET Public Information Project, 243
Illinois report, 365, 366
  library legislation, 168
  public relations activities, 243
Illinois Arts Council, 177
Illinois Regional Library Council, 220
Illinois Regional Library for the Blind and Physically Handicapped, 75 (photo)
Illinois State Library, 97
Illuminating Engineers Society of North America, 220
Immroth Memorial Award for Intellectual Freedom, 49, 160
Independent Research Libraries, 145-147 (*also 77 ed.*). (*See Independent Libraries. 76 ed.*)
Independent Research Libraries Association (IRLA), 132
Index to Religious Periodical Literature, 28
Indexing and Abstracting Services: *See* Abstracting and Indexing Services
Indiana report, 367, 368
Indiana Union List of Serials, 288
Indians, American: *See* American Indians and libraries
Information Access Corp., 110
Information and Referral Centers, 147, 148 (*also 77 ed.*)
Information Industry, 149-153 (*also 77 ed.*)
  micrographics expansion, 290

Information Industry Association (IIA), 104, 149
Information Science and Automation Division, 153, 154 (*also 77, 76 eds.*)
  cataloging conferences, 83
  cataloging institute, 11
  circulation systems workshop, 173
  continuing education programs, 99
Insects, losses due to, xxxiii, xxxiv
Institute for Scientific Information (ISI), 104
Institute for State Library Agency Personnel Involved in Continuing Education, 100
Insurance for Libraries, 154, 155 (*also 77, 76 eds.*)
Intasorn, Nongnath, 50
Intellectual Freedom, 155-160 (*also 77, 76 eds.*)
  book publishing, 251
  Canadian report, 338
  Freedom of Information Act, 168
  freedom of access to information, xvii, 158 (photo)
  Freedom to Read Foundation, 134
  school library issues, 279
  serials publishing issues, 254, 255
Intellectual Freedom Committee, 156 (*See also 77, 76 eds.*)
Intellectual Freedom Round Table, 160 (*also 77, 76 eds.*)
Interagency Council on Library Resources for Nursing, 220
Interest Group on Women in Librarianship, 323
Interlibrary Cooperation (*also 77, 76 eds.*)
  collection development, 96
  fees for services issue, xv
  See also Networks
Interlibrary loan
  academic libraries, 6, 9
  ARL fees, 38
  children's materials, 88
  genealogical record policies, xxx
International Association of Law Libraries, 220
International Association of Music Libraries, 258
International Association of School Librarianship, 220
International Board on Books for Young People (IBBY), 90, 160, 161 (*also 77, 76 eds.*)
International Caxton Congress, 296
International Children's Book Day, 90, 161
International Congress on National Bibliographies, 57, 317
International Federation for Documentation (FID), 161, 162 (*also 77, 76 eds.*)
International Federation of Library Associations and Institutions: *See* IFLA
International library activities
  art libraries, 32
  bibliographic projects, 57
  blind persons' programs, 70
  FID activities
  handicapped persons' services programs, 143

IFLA, 144
  RTSD activities, 275, 276
  standards, 305
International Micrographics
  Congress (IMC), 189
International Organization for
  Standardization (ISO), 302
  library statistics, 315
  Technical Committee 46,
    315, 316
International Reading
  Association, 220
  children's literature award,
    90
  1977 recipient, 91 (photo)
International Reading
  Association Children's
  Book Award, 53
International Relations,
  162-164 (*also 77, 76 eds.*)
**International Relations Round
  Table,** 164 (*also 77, 76
  eds.*)
International School
  Librarianship: *See* 77 ed.
International Standard
  Bibliographic Description
  (ISBD), 317
*International Standard
  Bibliographic Description
  for Serials* (ISBDS), 290
International Year of the Child,
  161, 314, 325
Iowa report, 368, 369
  library legislation, 169
Italian Americans and
  libraries, 123, 124 (*See
  also 77, 76 eds.*)
IZON Corporation, 189
Izumo, Patsy, 363
Jacobs, Alma S., 383
Jacobstein, J. Myron, 21
Jacques, Thomas F., 371
Jake, John, 54
James, Karen, 388
Jane Addams Award
  1977 recipient, 90 (photo)
Jewish Americans, library
  service to, 124, 125
Jewish Book Council, 124, 125
Jewish Caucus, ALA: *See* 76 ed.
Jewish Libraries Award, 53
Jenkins, Harold R., xxviii, 381
Jenkins, Stan, 344
Jennings, Kenneth M., 230
Jimpie, Babetta, 23
Jinnette, Isabella, 161
John, Nancy R., 34
John F. Kennedy Center for the
  Performing Arts
  library facility proposal, 175
Johns, Claude, 356
Johnson, Betts, 351
Johnson, John, 109
Johnson, Leonard, 391
Johnson, Mary, 51
Johnson, Richard David, 38 (*See
  also Biographies 76 ed.*)
Johnson, Ronald W., 198
Johnson, Wayne, 415
Johnson C. Smith University,
  121
Joint Council on Educational
  Telecommunications, 220
  (*also 76 ed.*)
Jones, Fran, 302
Jones, C. Lee, 287
Jones, Catherine A., 359
Jones, Clara Stanton, xlv, 35,
  87 (*See also
  Biographies 76 ed.*)
Jones, Margaret, 302
Jones, Ray, 350
Jones, Sarah Irwin, 47
Jones, Virginia Lacy, 49, 116,
  121 (*see also Biographies
  77 ed.*)

Jose, Jean, 367
Josey, E.J., 108,226
Journal Article Copying Service
  (JACS), 251
Journal of Library History, 23
Journals: *See* Publishing,
  Serials; Serials
Juergens, Bonnie, 153
Junior Members Round Table,
  165, 166 (*also 77, 76 eds.*)
Kaban, Gerald, 308
Kaminstein, Abraham Louis,
  208 (photo)
Kansas report, 19, 291 (photos);
  369, 370
Kares, Artemis, 391
Kaser, David, 118
Kaske, Neal K., 173
Keller, John, 89
Kellman, Amy, 161
Kellum-Rose, Nancy, 108
Kelly, George B., 232
Kelm, Carol, 276
Kenney, Brigitte L., 127, 153
Kent, Allen, 27
Kentucky report, 370, 371
Kerlan Award, 53
Kerr, Rosamond
  1977: The Library
  Association Centenary,
  xliii-xlvi
Kesler, E.G., 235
Keyes, A.A., 337
Khan, Mohammad, 51
Kiffmeyer, Barbara Burkert,
  51
King, Kenneth, xxix
King Award, 53
King Research, Inc., 102, 268
  photocopying study, 7, 104
Kingston, Maxine Hong, 53
Kinkeldey Award, 53
Kissinger, Henry, 29
Kitchen, Paul Howard, 82. *See
  also Biographies 76 ed.*
Klene, Joanne, 172
Knapp, John, 263
Knauff, Elizabeth, 128
Knogo Corporation, 284
Knowlton, Winthrop, 250
Kobayashi, Vivian, 118
Kohlstedt Exhibit Award, 49,
  127
Kollegger, James, 149
Kopischke, John L., 384
Kopple, Barbara, 129
Kreps, Juanita, 167
Kresge Foundation, 132, 133
Krueger, Richard, 358
Kurth, William H., 209
Kurzweil Reading Machine, 69
**Labor Groups, Library Service
  to,** 166, 167 (*also 77, 76
  eds.*)
Labor unions, library, 183, 185,
  186
Lachowicz, Constance E., 400
Ladd, Boyd, 281
LaFarge, Sheila, 161
Laird, David, 352
LaMont, David and Bridget,
  165
Lamont Award, 53
Lampert, Zvi, 125
Lancaster, F.W., 185, 229
Landers, Patty, 165
Land, Phyllis, 367
Landis, John W., 303
Landis, Martha, 261
Landon, H.C. Robbins, 53
Lang, Sister Franz, O.P., 85
Lantz, Herman R., 121
Lash, Joseph P., 53
Lathem, Edward C., 41, 64
  (photo)
Laughlin, James, 51
Law and Legislation, 167-169

(*also 77, 76 eds.*)
ACRL activities, 37
affirmative action, 223
Freedom to Read Foundation
  cases, 134
depository designation, 141
handicapped persons' rights,
  141
intellectual freedom issues,
  158
London report, 345, 346
off-the-air recording cases,
  191
public document issues, 28
replevin of documents, 11
Urban Libraries Council
  programs, 319
Washington report, 320, 321
See also specific laws and
  cases by name
Law Libraries, 169, 170 (*also
  77, 76 eds.*)
Law Library Journal, 20
LEADS, 164
Learmont, Carol L., 4, 5
Learning Library, 239
Lee, Joel, 24
Leek, Ruth, 302
Leimkuhler, Ferdinand, 180
Leonard, Charlotte, 394
LeRoy C. Merritt Humanitarian
  Fund. *See* 76 ed.
Lerner, Louis Abraham, 65
  (photo), 311 (photo)
Levine, Philip, 53
Levy, Evelyn, 209
Lewidge, Jean, 354
Lewin, Ronald, 54
Lewis, Alfred J., 169
Lewis, Peter Ronald, 65 (photo)
Li, Tze-chung, 93, 118
**Libraries and Learning
  Resources, Office of,**
  170-172 (*also 77, 76 eds.*)
**Library Administration
  Division,** 172, 173 (*also 77,
  76 eds.*)
  Friends of Libraries
    Committee, 135
Library and Information
  Technology Association
  (LITA), 153 (*See
  Information and
  Automation Division*)
Library Association
  Centenary celebration, 163
  Centenary Conference
    ALHRT representation, 24
  1977: The Library
    Association Centenary,
    xliii-xlvi
Library Association for Italian
  American Materials and
  Studies, 124
Library Binding Institute (LBI),
  xxxvi, 58, 233
Library Cost and Service
  Analysis Module, 271
Library Education Division,
  173-175 (*also 77, 76 eds.*)
  dissolution, 108
  professionalism issue, 229
  reorganization plan, 113
Library Enhancement
  Program, 8
Library General Information
  Survey, 4
Library Journal, 179
Library of Congress, 175-178
  (*also 77, 76 eds.*)
  art cataloging, 33
  automation, 43, 44
  cataloging and classification,
    83
  children's literature awards,
    91
  collection development, 95

CONSER, 288
Copyright Office, 106
DBPH activities, 69
James Madison Memorial
  Building, 75
Law Library, 170
MARC project, 57
National Periodicals Center,
  287
networks, 195, 202, 203
preservation activities, xli
preservation project, 190
public relations activities,
  243
rare books, 297
sound archives, 258
Library Press, 179, 180 (*also
  77, 76 eds.*)
Library Public Relations
  Council, 245
**Library Research Round
  Table,** 180, 181 (*also 77, 76
  eds.*)
  research programs, 274
Library Research Round Table
  Research Award, 49, 116
Library Services and
  Construction Act (LSCA),
  167, 237, 319, 320
  appropriations, 133
  multimedia materials funds,
    191
Library Technology Reports,
  246
Liegl, Dorothy, 403
Light, losses due to, xxxiii
Lindeman, Leroy L., 407
Lindquist, Jennie D., 209
Linford, John, 261
Lipow, Anne, 11, 261
Lippincott Award, 49, 116, 121
List, George, 258
Lister Hill National Center for
  Biomedical Communication,
  198, 199 (photo)
Literacy Programs, Library,
  181, 182 (*also 77, 76 eds.*)
  adult services, 18
  London report, 349
Literacy Volunteers of
  America, 182
Little, Mary, 405
Livingstone, John H., Jr., 387
Lloyd, Frank, 307
Lockhart, Helen D., 266
Lockheed Information Service
  (LIS), 109-111
Locher, Alan H., 230
Lombardo, Daniel J., 50
**London Correspondent's
  Report,** 343-349 (*also 77,
  76 eds.*)
Long, Sara, 310
Long Beach Public Library, 76
  (photo)
Loomis, Henry, 306
Lord, Milton, 145
Lorenz, John G., 41
Los Alamos Scientific
  Laboratory Library, 75
Los Angeles County Public
  Library, 122, 226
Los Angeles Public Library,
  264
LoSasso, John S., 188
Lossee, Ferril, 189
Louisiana report, 371-373
Louisiana State Library, 121
Love, Erika, 188
Lowell, Marcia, 397
Lowell, Robert, 53
Lowell Prize, 53
Lowrey, Anna Mary, 23
Lowrie, Jean, 164
Lowy, Jacob M., 80 (photo)
Lubetsky, Seymour, 48
Luntz, Jerome D., 152

423

Lutz, Mr. and Mrs. Joseph, 95 (photo)
Lynch, Beverly, 36
Lynch, T.R., 198
Lynne, Bonnie, 414
Lyons, Grace J., 49, 143
Maack, Mary, 164
MacArthur, William J., Jr., xxviii
McCasland, T.H., 47
McCauley, Hannah, 394
McCay, David N., 391
McClaine, Harriet, 51
McClarren, Robert R., 43
McColvin Medal, 53
McCord, 53, 90
McCrank, Lawrence and Ruth, 180
McCrossan, John, 409
McCune, Emma, 351
McCusker, St. Lauretta, 115
Macdonald, Cynthia, 51
McElroy, Joseph, 51
McGill, William J., 307
McGirt, Jacquelyn, 165
McGrath, William E., 180
McKenna, Frank, 164, 301
McMillan, Mary, 367
McMullen, Haynes, 261
McMullin, Florence, 157
McNamara, Brooks, 65, (photo)
McNamee, Gil, 260
McPhee, John, 51
McPherson, William, 54
Machine-Assisted Reference Service Section (MARS), 259
Machine-Readable Cataloging: See MARC
Machine-Readable Data Bases: See Data Bases, Computer-Readable
Machlin, Milt, 54
Machlup, Fritz, 102
Mack, John E., 54
Macy, John W., 306
Madinger, Beth, 363
Magazines: See Publishing, Serials; Serials
Magazine Index, 110
Magee, David, 300
Mahony, Sheila, 307
Maier, Charles, S., 51
Maier, Joan M., 127
Maine report, 373, 374
Maissen, Leena, 161
Malinconico, S. Michael, 153
Management, Library, 182-184 (*also 77, 76 eds.*)
 academic libraries, 4
 collection development, 95
 LAD activities, 172
 public libraries, 237
 school libraries problems, 276, 277
 staff cuts, 227
 staff development, 230
 women's role, 321
Management Review and Analysis Program (MRAP), 4, 41, 231
Managing the Library Fire Risk (Morris), xxxiv
Manitoba, Can., 339
Mankiewicz, Frank, 306
Mann Citation, 49, 84, 116, 276
Manuscripts
 auctions, 299
 gifts to libraries, 136, 137
 North Carolina decision, 11
MARC, 43, 57
 Canadian report, 337
 CONSER, 288
 Library of Congress, 176
 Monthly Catalog conversion, 141

UBC project, 317
MARCAL, 213
Marcello, Ronald E., 213
Mark, Jan, 91
Markowetz, Marianna, 414
Marks, Jon, 52
Marshall Poetry Prize, 53
Martin, George M., 37
Martin, John H., 235
Martin, Susan K., 154, 164
Martinez, Julio, 198
Martinez Smith, Elizabeth, 263
Maryland report, 3, 374, 375
 aid to libraries, 237
 library legislation, 168
 losses due to water, xxxviii
Mason, Mary Stewart, 410
Massachusetts report, 375-377
 library legislation, 168
Master Registers, 83
Mathews, William, 153
Mautino, Patricia, 293
May, Henry F., 52
Mays, Benjamin E., 120
Measurement and Evaluation, 184, 185 (*also 77, 76 eds.*)
 adult services, 20
 Canadian library usage, 340
 library use study, 10, 96
Media: See Multimedia Materials; School Libraries and Media Centers; Telecommunications and Public Broadcasting
Media Coalition, 72
Mediation, Arbitration, and Inquiry, 185, 186 (*also 77, 76 eds.*)
Medical Libraries, 186, 187, 189 (photo). *See also 77, 76 eds.*
 grants, 132
 National Library of Medicine, 199
 women librarians' status 322
Medical Library Assistance Act, 199
Medical Library Association, 187, 188 (*also 77, 76 eds.*)
 certification, 187, 229
 continuing education programs, 99, 100
 women librarian study, 322
MEDLARS (Medical Literature Analysis and Retrieval System), 168
MEDLINE, 187, 199
Melcher Scholarship, 51
Mellon Foundation, 96, 133
 academic library grants, 8, 10, 11
 ACRL internship grant, 37
Melton, Lynn J., 51
Melzer, Milton, 51, 53, 90 (photo), 91
Memorial Award, 50
Memphis Public Library, Friends of, 135, 310 (photos)
Merrill, James, 54
Mester, Jeannette, 127
METRO Program, 56
Metropolitan Toronto Library, 73 (photo), 75, 336
Mexico, 213
Meyer, Helen, 324
Meyer, Herbert H., 230
Meyer, Mary K., xxvi, xxviii
Meyer, Ursula, 355
Michie, Jean, 386
Michigan report, 377, 378
 aid to libraries, 238
 library legislation, 168
Microfiche, microfilm, microforms: See

Micrographics
Micrographics, 188-190 (*also 77 ed.*)
 Canadiana: Microfiche, 337
 cataloging, 263
 COM catalogs, 45
 conference exhibits, 189 (photo)
 copyright issues, 150
 GPO programs, 141
 law libraries' holdings, 169
 NMA activities, 199
 reproduction of materials, xxxix
 RLG preservation project, 233
 serials, 290
 standards, 303
 See also "Micrographics— An Eventful Forty Years— What Next?" 45-56, 76 ed.
Miele, Anthony, 350
Milam International Lecturer, 174
Miller, Barbara, 34, 370
Miller, Edward P., 113 (photo)
Miller, Glenn, 361
Miller, Helen, 364
Miller, Robert H., 378
Mills, Shirley C., 42
Milo, Albert, 118
Minimum wage, 321
Minnerath, Janet E., 410
Minnesota report, 378, 379
Minnesota Interlibrary Telecommunications Exchange (MINITEX), 288
Minnesota Union List of Serials (MULS), 288
Minolta Corporation, 189
Minorities, library service to: *See* Ethnic Groups, Library Service to
Minority Scholarship, 122
Mississippi report, 379, 380, 381
 educational TV, 308 (photo)
Missouri report, 381, 382
 UMC fellowship, 113 (photo)
Mitchell, Bonnie Beth, 42
Mitchell, Gladys, 341
Mitchem, Teresa, 127
Moffat, Edward S., 164
Mohrhardt, Foster, 194
Molumby, Larry, 153
Molz, Kathleen, 50, 116
Montana report, 383
Monthly Catalog of U.S. Government Publications, 141
Moon, Eric, xliii (photo), 162, 163, 239, 295
Moore, Bessie, 311 (photo)
Moore, Jane R., 164
Moore, Richard E., 397
Moore, Waddy, 213
Moorland-Spingarn Research Center, 119
Morehead, Joe, 140
Morgan, Betty Jean, 354
Morgan, Elois A., 121
Morison Award, 53
Morse, Mark, 168
Morton, Elizabeth Homer, 82, 210, 341
Moscow Book Fair, 71 (photo), 251
Moses, Stefan B., 355
Moss, Elaine, 52
Moss, Ray, 343
Mott, Evelyn, 51
Mountain Plains Library Association (MPLA), 264, 265
 continuing education program, 100

Mowat, Angus, 341
Mudd Manuscript Library, 136
Mudge Citation, 49, 259
Mulkey, Jack, 380
Multimedia Materials, 190-192 (*also 77, 76 eds.*)
 filmstrips, 132
 public libraries, 240
 realia, 256
 See also Films; Films, Children's; Filmstrips; Realia; Recordings, Sound; School Libraries and Media Centers; Telecommunications and Public Broadcasting
Multistate service centers, 70
Murfin, Marjorie E., 9
Murphy, Paula C., 51
Museum of Broadcasting, 257
Musgrove, Margaret, 89 (photo)
Music Libraries, 192 (photo), 257
Music Library Association, 192, 193 (*also 77, 76 eds.*)
Music OCLC Users Group, 192
Musser, P.M., 47
Muth, Tom, 302
Myers, Gerald, 154
Myers, Margaret, 174
Nakako, Irene, 415
Nassau Library System, 19 (photo)
National Affiliation for Literary Advance, 220
National Agricultural Library, 193, 194 (*also 77, 76 eds.*)
National and Local Government Officers' Association (NALGO), 345
National Archives, 28, 29, 257
National Association for Bilingual Education, 221
National Association for the Education of Young People, 221
National Association of Elementary School Principals, 221
National Association of Exposition Managers, 221
National Association of Spanish Speaking Librarians: *See* REFORMA
National Book Awards, 53, 90, 252
 1977 recipient, 90 (photo)
National Book Critics Circle Award, 53
National Broadcasting Company, 257
National Bureau of Standards, 203
National Catalog of Sources for the History of Librarianship, 30
National Center for Education Statistics, 4
National Center for Law and the Handicapped (NCLH), 142
National Central Lending Library (NCLL), 96
National Citizens Committee to Save Our Libraries, 319
National Coalition Against Censorship (NCAC), 159, 221
National Commission on Higher Education Management Systems (NCHEMS), 268
National Commission on Libraries and Information Science (NCLIS), 194-196 (*also 77, 76 eds.*)

federal funding, 167
Indian library conference, 117
National Periodicals System, 286, 287
networks, 22, 202, 203
public library study, 238
research studies, 268-270
school library study, 281
standards, 304
Urban Libraries Council, 319
National Commission on New Technological Uses of Copyrighted Works: See CONTU
National Conference on Social Welfare, 221
National Conservation Advisory Council, 233
National Council of Teachers of English, 221
poetry for children award, 53, 90
National Council of Teachers of Mathematics, 221
National Endowment for the Arts
adults' services grants, 18
research library grants, 145
National Endowment for the Humanities, 197, 198 (*also 77, 76 eds.*)
academic library grants, 8, 10
adults' services grants, 18
ALA Archives grant, 30
Black library funding, 121
collection development grants, 97, 197 (photo)
historical records conference, 29
preservation funding, 235
public library funding, 239
research library grants, 145
Responsa automation funding, 124
National Federation for the Blind, 168
National Federation of Abstracting and Indexing Services (NFAIS) 2, 3 (table)
National Historical Publications and Records Commission, 234
National Information Conference and Exposition (NICE), 149
National Information Policy, 152
National Inventory of Library Needs, 73, 77, 195, 227, 238, 270
National Librarians Association, 198
certification issue, 229
National Libraries: *See 77 ed.: Principal Libraries of the World. See 76 ed.*
National Library of Canada, 34, 80, 335, 340
National Library of Medicine, 198, 199 (*also 77, 76 eds.*)
research grants, 268, 270
National Library Week (NLW)
public relations activities, 244
See also 76 ed.
National Medal for Literature, 53
National Micrographics Association, 189, 190, 199, 200 (*also 77, 76 eds.*)
National Periodicals Center, 96, 253, 285-287, 318
National Periodicals System, 287 (diagram)
National Preservation Program, 190, 232
National Public Radio, 306
National Science Foundation (NSF), 139
Division of Science Information, 282, 283
research grants, 268, 272-274
science information study, 152
National Serials Data Program (NSDP), 288
National Story League, 222
National Study Commission on the Records and Documents of Federal Officials, 28
National Technical Information Service (NTIS), 200, 201 (*also 77, 76 eds.*)
Journal Article Copying Service, 251
photocopy service, 104
publications, 140
National Union Catalog, 83, 177, 288 (*also 76 ed.*)
National University Extension Association, 222
Navy libraries, 31
NCLIS: *See* National Commission on Libraries and Information Science
Neal, Frances, 354
Nebraska report, 383-385
Needham, William, 9
Nelms, Doyal, 165
Nelson, Milo, 364
Nemeyer, Carol (Anmuth) 175, 253 (*See also Biographies 76 ed.*)
Nesbitt, Elizabeth, 210 (photo)
Netherland, Linda, 371
Network Advisory Committee, 176
Network Advisory Council (NAC), 44
Network Advisory Group, 57, 83, 202
Network Development Office (NDO), 44, 202
Network Technical Architecture Group (NTAG), 44, 202
Networks, 202-205 (*also 77, 76 eds.*)
AASL-NCLIS study, 22
academic libraries, 7, 8
automated networks, 44
bibliographic processing centers, 55
Biomedical Communications Network, 187
Canadian report, 336, 337
children's materials, 88
genealogical loan policies, xxx
international lending, 144
Latin America, 214
London report, 346
NCLIS activities, 195
preservation efforts, xl
public libraries, 236
school libraries, 281
serials, 288, 289
UBC project, 317
Universal Serials and Book Exchange, 318
See also specific networks by name; *also 77, 76 eds.*: Interlibrary cooperation
Nevada report, 308 (photo), 385, 386
New England Document Conservation Center (NEDCC), xli 234
New England Library Information Network (NELINET), 9, 22
New England Research Applications Center (NERAC), 111
New Hampshire report, 386, 387
New Jersey report, 387, 388
New Mexico report, 388, 389
New Mexico Information System—Phase II (NEMISYS—II), 94
New York report, 133, 237 (photos), 389-391
library legislation, 169
New York Board of Cooperative Educational Services (BOCES), 191
New York Public Library, 203, 291
children's services auction, 90
public relations activities, 245
young adult services, 325, 326
New York Times Information Bank (NYTIB), 109, 111
Newberry Library, 75
Newbery Medal, 49, 91
policy change, 34
1977 recipient, 89 (photo)
Newman, Ralph G., 95 (photo), 319
Newman, Simon, 27
Newspapers: *See* Publishing, Serials; Serials
Neustadt, Richard, 307
Nicaragua, 214
Nichols, J. Gary, 373
Nicolson, Mary C., 51
Nigeria Task Force, 72
Nikolajev, A., 145 (photo)
Nin, Anais, 300
Nix, Larry T., 266
Nixon, Richard, 28
Nobel Prize for Literature, 53
Non-English-Speaking, Library Service to the: *See* Ethnic Groups, Library Service to
Nonprint materials: *See* Films; Films, Children's; Filmstrips; Multimedia Materials; Realia; Recordings, Sound; Telecommunications and Public Broadcasting
Nordberg, E. Wayne, 95
North, William D., 106, 134
North Carolina report, 391-393
manuscript decision, 11
replevin case, 29, 169
North Dakota report, 393, 394
North Suburban Illinois Library System, 7
Northern Illinois University Library, 9 (photo)
Northwestern University, 177, 202
Notable Books, 205, 206 (*also 77, 76 eds.*)
Notable Children's Films, 131
Noyes Award, 53, 188
NTIS: *See* National Technical Information Service
Nye, Norman, 54
O'Brien, Elmer, 28
O'Halloran, Charles, 381
O'Neill, Gerard K., 54
O'Shea, H. William, 391
Oakville (Ontario) Public Library, 339, 340
Oberly Memorial Award, 49
Obituaries, 207-212 (*also 77, 76 eds.*)
Obscenity and pornography, 134, 158
Office for Library Personnel Resources, 226, 229
library education survey, 271
Office for Research, ALA research programs, 274, 275
Office of Education U.S., 15, 230
continuing education funding, 99
grants, 133
library study grant, 184, 241
preservation program, xli
research grants, 268
Office of Telecommunications Policy (OTP), 307
Office of University Library Management Studies (OMS), 41, 231
Ohio report, 394, 395, 396
aid to libraries, 237
library legislation, 168
photos, 19, 237, 243
Ohio College Library Center (OCLC), 7, 56, 203
automation, 44
CONSER data maintenance, 177, 287
disaster precautions, 285
NAL project, 194
serials cataloging, 83
Ohm, Elizabeth, 173
Oklahoma report, 396, 397
Oklahoma State Library, 184
Older Adults, Library Services to: *See* Adults, Library Services to (*also 77, 76 eds.*)
Olofson Memorial Award, 51
Olsen, Robert A., Jr., 28
Olsen, Wallace C., 193
Olson, Nancy, 378
Onieal, Martin F., 51
Optical Character Recognition (OCR-A) label, 93
Oral History Association, 213
Oregon report, 397, 398
aid to libraries, 237
library legislation, 168
Organizations and Associations, 214-223 (*also 77, 76 eds.*)
Organization of American States, 213 (*also 77, 76 eds.*)
Orne, Jerrold, 195
Oshry, Efraim, 125
Our Bodies, Ourselves, 158
Owen, Amy, 407
Ozick, Cynthia, 125
Pacific Northwest Library Association (PNLA), 265, 266
Palmer, David C., 387
Palmour, Vernon, 102
Papai, Beverly, 166
Paperback books, 250
British book publishing, 347
children's literature, 86, 89
YASD program, 333
Park, Leland M., 266
Parker, Millie M., 37
Parker, Robert, 54
Parks, Jim, 380
Parmée, Douglas, 53
Parsons, A. Chapman, 394
Parsons, Gerald J., xxx
Participatory management in libraries, 183
Partovi, Pat, 179
Paterson, Katherine, 53, 90 (photo)
Patterson, Flora E., 82
Patterson, James, 54
Pearson, Lennart, 402

425

Peck, Richard, 54
Peeples, Kenneth E., Jr., 226
Pellowski, Anne, 160
P.E.N. Translation Prize, 53
Pennsylvania Area Library Network (PALINET), 44
Pennsylvania report, 399, 400, 277 (photo)
Penzler, Otto, 54
Periodicals: See Publishing, Serials; Serials
Perlov, Dadie, 389
Perry-Castañeda Library, 5 (photo), 73
Personnel and Employment: Affirmative Action, 223-227 (also 77, 76 eds.)
Personnel and Employment: Job Market, 227-229 (also 77 ed.)
  academic libraries, 5
  library students' considerations, 1
  London report, 346
  new graduates' placement, 116
Personnel and Employment: Performance Appraisal, 229-230 (also 77, 76 eds.)
  chief librarians, 312, 313
Personnel and Employment: Salaries
  academic libraries, 4, 5
  academic library staff salaries tables, 13, 14
  affirmative action, 225
  ARL librarians, 39, 40
  ARL survey, 271
  Canadian report, 335
  discrimination charges, 169
  law librarians, 170
  library educators, 116
  London report, 346, 347
  mediation and inquiry, 185
  public libraries, 237
  school library staff table, 280
  women librarians, 321, 322
  See also 76 ed.
Personnel and Employment: Staff Development, 230-232 (also 77, 76 eds.)
  job assignment, 114
  management issues, 183
  school libraries, 278
Petrocik, John, 54
Pfeiffer, Peggy L. 22, 294
Phi Beta Kappa Award in Science, 54
Phillips, Ira, 394
Phinazee, Annette, 174
Photocopying
  copyright issues, 101, 102, 338
  King Research study, 268
  NCLIS study, 196
Physically handicapped persons: See Blind and Physically Handicapped, Library Services for the
Pico v. Board of Education (case), 134
Piercy Award, 49, 276
Pierron, Ione, 160
Pings, Vern, 263
Piternick, Anne, 81 (photo)
Plaut, Gunther, 80 (photo)
Pletz, Frances H., 377
Ploshnick, Mary, 35
Plotnik, Art, 179
Poe, Mya Thanda, 118
Poe Awards, 54
Polish Americans Librarians Association (PALA), 125
Pollard, Graham, 300
Pollution, losses due to, xxxiii
Poole, Frazer G., 233, 298
Popecki, Joseph, 409

Porgie Awards, 54
Port Washington Public Library, 291
Porter, Barry, 368
Potter, Beatrix, 92 (photo)
Potter, David M., 54
Poulsen, Gunnar, 91
Powell, Ruth Ann, 413
Power, Mary R., 43
Preble, Darlene, 383
Prentice, Ann, 312
Prentice, Barbara S., 25, 26
Preservation of Library Materials, 232-235 (also 77, 76 eds.)
  academic libraries, 11
  LC activities, 177
  microfilming projects, 190
  problems and solutions, xxxi-xliv
  special collections, 298
Presidential Recordings and Materials Preservation Act, 28
President's Award, 23
Price, Joseph W., 286
Prince Philip of England, 353 (photo)
Principal Libraries of the World: See 77, 76 eds.
Prints and Posters: See 76 ed.
Privacy, right of
  confidentiality of circulation records, 160
Privacy Protection Study Commission, 29
Prizes: See Awards and Prizes
Processing Centers: See Bibliographic Processing Centers; also 77, 76 eds.
Product of the Year Award, 150
Professional Development Grant, 51, 165
Professional Development Program, 231
Program for Information Managers (PRIM), 150
"Project: Little Kids," 88, 309
Public broadcasting: See Telecommunications and Public Broadcasting; See also 76 ed.
Public documents and records: See Documents, government
Public Law 94-553: See Copyright Law, U.S.
Public Libraries, 235-240 (also 77, 76 eds.)
  adult services, 18
  American Indian services, 117
  automation, 46
  blind and handicapped persons' services, 70
  buildings, 72
  Canada, 81
  Canadian report, 338, 339, 341
  children's library services, 87
  disadvantaged persons' services, 112
  federal assistance, 167
  film budgets, 128
  Friends of Libraries, 135
  genealogical collection policy, xxiv
  health and rehabilitative services, 142
  information and referral centers, 147
  Italian collections, 123
  labor groups' services, 166
  London report, 346, 347
  NCLIS funding study, 194
  OLLR programs, 170

projects and programs, 19, 237, 238, 242, 243, 256, 291, 310 (photos)
public relations activities, 242
realia, 256
social responsibilities, 290-292
toys and games use, 309, 310
trustees, 310-313
women librarians, 322
Public Library Association, 240-242 (also 77, 76 eds.)
  adult services, 20
  Armed Forces Librarians Section, 32
  ASLC joint program, 36
  trustees, 313
Public Relations, 242-246 (also 77, 76 eds.)
Publications Reference File, 141
Publishing, ALA, 246-249 (also 77, 76 eds.)
Publishing, Book, 249-253 (also 77, 76 eds.)
  ALA publishing, 246
  Canadian library relations, 339
  Children's Book Council, 86
  children's literature, 89
  London report, 347, 348
  multilingual publishing, 314
Publishing, periodicals
  library journals, 179
Publishing, Serials, 253-256
  British magazine publishing, 348, 349
  copyright issues, 104
  new periodicals, 253
  on-line journals, 150
  small presses, 293
  See also 77, 76 eds.: Publishing, Magazine; Publishing, Newspaper
Pulitzer Prizes, 54
Puppeteers of America, 222
Purcell, Gary R., 274, 405
Putnam Honor Fund Award, 51
Rabassa, Gregory, 53
Racism
  intellectual freedom debate, 157
Rader, Hannelore, 262
Radio
  American Television and Radio Archive, 175
  broadcast archives, 257
  Canadian service to blind, 339
  off-the-air recording, 191
  OLLR funding, 172
  public relations uses, 242
  Spanish language programs, 122
  young adult progamming, 326
Radzinowicz, Leon, 51
Rae, Anne, 337
Ranganathan Award for Classification Research, 54
Rare books and manuscripts, xxxi (photo), 297-299
  ACRL activities, 37
  Black collections, 119
  genealogical works, xxx
  Hasidic literature collection, 125
Rawles, Beverly, 184
Raz, Robert, 377
Readers Book Awards, 252
Reading programs
  CBC activities, 86
Realia, 256-257 (also 77, 76 eds.)
  toys and games, 309, 310
Rebsamen, Werner, 234

Rebinding
  preservation issues, xxxvi, xxxvii, xxxviii, xxix
Recordings, Sound, 257-258 (also 77, 76 eds.)
  blind persons services, 69
Reference and Adult Services Division, 258-260 (also 77, 76 eds.)
  labor groups services study, 166
  women's service group, 323
Reference Services, 260-263 (also 77, 76 eds.)
  academic libraries, 9
  adult services, 18
  automation, 46
  bibliographic processing centers, 56
  fees for services, xv
  genealogical research aids sources, xxvii
  Library of Congress, 177
Referral centers: See Information and Referral Centers
REFORMA, 263-264 (also 77, 76 eds.)
  El Paso chapter founding, 123
Regina Medal, 54, 85
Regional Library Associations, 264-268 (also 77 ed.)
Rehabilitation Act of 1973, 223, 224
Reich, David, 311 (photo)
Reinert, Ann, 384
Religion Index One: Periodical (RIOP), 28
Religion Index Two: Multi-Author Works (RITMAW), 28
Repair and restoration: See Preservation of Library Materials
Replevin of documents, 11, 29, 169
  ACLR position, 37
Research, 268-275 (also 77, 76 eds.)
  accreditation studies, 14, 15
  ALA Archives, 30
  binding studies, 58
  Canadian report, 341
  library statistics standardization, 315, 316
  reference services, 260, 261
  academic libraries, 4
  ACRL activities, 36-38
  genealogical collections, xxviii
  independent research libraries, 145
  Italian collections, 123
  OLLR funding, 171
Research Libraries Group (RLG), 8, 97, 202, 203
  art libraries, 33
  automation, 44, 45
  preservation activities, xl, 233
Resolution on Prejudice, Stereotyping, and Discrimination, 227
Resolution on Racism and Sexism Awareness, 157
  AASL reaction, 22
  SRRT position, 295
Resource sharing: See Interlibrary cooperation
Resources and Technical Services Division, 275-276 (also 77, 76 eds.)
  cataloging and classification, 83
  cataloging institute, 11
  collection development, 95, 96

Preservation Discussion Group, 233
standards, 304
Resources and Technical Services Division Resources Scholarship Award, 49, 276
Responsa, 124
Revenue Sharing Act of 1972, 224
Rhode Island report, 400-402
Richardson, Eleanor M., xxviii
Rice, Stan, 54
Richmond, Phyllis, 49, 84, 116, 276
Ricking, Myrl, 210 (photo)
Riley, Robert H., 152
Ringer, Barbara Alice, 301, 324 (See also Biographies 76 ed.)
Roads, Clarice, 396
Robbins, Jane, 180
Roberts, Edward, 346
Roberts, John, 80 (photo)
Robertson, Giles, 139
Robinson, Lawrence, 190
Rochester Public Library, 291
Rockefeller, John D., iv, 133 (photo)
Rockefeller Brothers Fund, 133
Rodgers and Hammerstein Archives of Recorded Sound, 257
Rogero, Thomas T., 266
Rogers, Rutherford David, 65, 145
Rollins Collection, 120
Rosenfeld, Harriet, 179
Rosenthal, Joseph A., 153, 263
Ross, Judith, 51
Ross, Vernon, 341
Rosskopf, Heleen, 70
Roth, Eris, 128
Round Table of National Organizations for Better Education, 222
Rounds, Anne, 396
Royal Library of Belgium, xxxi (photo)
Ruark, Ardis, 403
Rukeyser, Muriel, 52, 59
Ruscha, Edward, 33
Russo, Antonette, 21
Sachar, Howard M., 125
Sagan, Carl, 135 (photo)
Salaries: See Personnel and Employment: Salaries
Salazar, Marilyn, 123, 226
Salmon, Stephen R., 6
Salvation Army, 222
San Diego County Library, 323
San Diego Public Library Concerned Librarians, 225
Sargent, Monica Kittock, 383
Sarris, Shirley, 253
Saskatchewan, Can., 339
Sass, Sam, 301
Satellite communications
Communications Technology Satellite, 199
continuing education broadcasts, 100
telecommunications, 308
Sauer, Mary, 275
Scannell, Frances X., 377
Schaaf, Robert, 139
Schaeffer, Lorraine, 42
Schlosser, Sue Ann, 381
Schmidt, Judy, 128
School Libraries and Media Centers, 276-282 (also 77, 76 eds.)
AASL activities, 22
buildings, 72
Canadian report, 338, 339, 341, 342 (table)
certification of librarians, 114

film budgets, 128
intellectual freedom issues, 155
multimedia materials, 191
OLLR programs, 171
public relations activities, 242
social responsibilities, 293
women librarians, 322
School Library Journal, 179
School Library Media Program of the Year Award, 50
Schuyler, James, 51
Schwartz, Allen, 385
Schwarzkopf, LeRoy C., 140
Science fiction, 325, 328
Science Information, Division of, 282-283 (also 77, 76 eds.)
Scott, Ann, 165
Scott, Paul, 52
Scoville, Maxine, 25
Scribner's Sons Award, 51
Scripps Institute of Oceanography Library, 75
Scurrah, Lore, 389
Seattle Public Library, 183
Security Systems, 283-285 (also 77, 76 eds.)
academic libraries, 6
archives, 29
library legislation, 168
special collections, 298
theft prevention, 285
Sellers, Margaret, 128
Senders, John, 254
Serban, William Michael, 55
Serials, 285-290 (also 77, 76 eds.)
academic libraries, 7
Canadian report, 342
cataloging and classification, 83
LC cataloging, 177
NCLIS access study, 195
publishing, serials, 253
rising costs, 10
USBE activities, 317, 318 (photo)
Serials Librarian, The, 290
Sessions, Jack, 166
Seydel, Ruth, 364
Shaffer, Norman, 190, 232, 298
Shakeley, Lauren, 54
Shank, Russell, 66 (photo)
Shattuck, Charles, 308
Shaw Award for Library Literature, 50, 116
Shearer, Kenneth, 20
Sheehy, Eugene P., 66 (photo), 261
Sheehy, Gail, 295
Sheldon, Brooke E., 268
Shelledy, Louise Boyd, 384
Shelley Memorial Award, 54
Shera, Jesse Hauk, 23, (See also Biographies 77 ed.)
Shields, Gerald, 108, 198
Shipman, Joseph Collins, 211 (photo)
Shubert, Joseph F., xxv, 389, 394
Sibley, Richard, 373
Simmons, Steve, 307
Simpson, Donald B., 43
Sims, Marcy J., 410
Sitze, Carl, 381
Sivak, Marie, 365
Sivulich, Kenneth G., 398
Skidmore, Carolyn, 413
Skinner Award, 54, 324
Sklarew, Myra, 125
Slanker, Barbara O., 271
Slave narratives, 120
Smethurst, John, 343
Smith, Dorothy, 109
Smith, Eldred R., 38
Smith, G. Roysce, 71, 72

Smith, Patricia, 42
Smith, Rose, 186
Smith & Son Literary Award, 54
Smith v. United States (case), 134
Smoot, Ann, 47
Snyder, Carolyn, 172
Social Responsibilities, 290-295 (also 77, 76 eds.)
access to information issue, xvii
health and rehabilitative services, 143
Library Association issues, xlv
literacy programs, 181
services to disadvantaged, 112
SRRT activities, 295, 296
Social Responsibilities Round Table, 295-296 (also 77, 76 eds.)
Task Force on Women, 295, 321 (photos), 323
Social Security Act, 167
Society of American Archivists (SAA), 29, 222, 285
preservation workshops, 234
security system, 6
Sodt, James D., 180
Solar energy in libraries, 236
Sony Corporation, 191
Sophar, Gerald J., 193
Soroka, Cerise, 51
SORT: See Staff Organizations Round Table
Sources of Serials, 289
South Carolina report, 402, 403
South Dakota report, 403, 404
Southeastern Library Association (SELA), 8, 266, 267
Southeastern Library Network (SOLINET), 44
Southern Illinois University, 120
Southwestern Library Association (SWLA), 267, 268
continuing education, 99, 100
Spanish-speaking Americans: See Hispanic Americans, library service to
Speaker, The, 107, 108, 156, 158 (photo), 179, 295
Special Collections, 296-300 (also 76 ed.)
Black collections, 119
Italian literature, 123
labor collections, 166
machine-readable cataloging project, 177
sound recordings, 257
Spanish-language collections, 122
Special Libraries, 300-302 (also 77, 76 eds.)
adult services, 18
armed forces libraries, 31
art libraries, 32-34
Canadian report, 343, 342 (table)
genealogical collections, xxvii, xxviii
Special Libraries Association (SLA), 300-302
Special Libraries Association Hall of Fame, 54
Special Libraries Association Professional Award, 54
Special Projects Act, 172
Spivacke, Harold, 211 (photo)
Spreitzer, Francis F., 190
SRRT: See Social Responsibilities Round Table

Staff Committee on Mediation, Arbitration and Inquiry (SCMAI), 185
Staff Committee on Mediation, Arbitration, and Inquiry trustees, 313
Staff Organizations Round Table, 302 (also 77, 76 eds.)
Standing Committee on the Status of Women in Librarianship, 323
Standards, 302-306 (also 77, 76 eds.)
abstracting and indexing, 2
ACRL activities, 37
art libraries, 34
discography, 258
handicapped persons' services, 144
information and referral centers, 148
international library statistics, 315, 316
micrographics, 190, 200
NCLIS activities, 195
UBC project, 317
Stanford University, 96
State libraries
genealogical collections, xxix
public relations activities, 242
State Library Agencies: See Association of State Library Agencies; also 77, 76 eds.
State University of New York, 96
Statistical analysis, 262
Stegner, Wallace, 53
Steinbrunner, Chris, 54
Steloff, Frances, 300
Sterling, Dorothy, 54
Stern, Gerald, 53
Stewart, Donald, 246 (photo), 261
Stewart, Margaret, 165
Stewart, Ora, 393
Storytelling, 87, 88
Stratton, June, 198
Strohecker, Edwin, 370
Stueart, Robert D., 174
Stump, Ron, 356
Suellentrop, Helen, 369
Sullivan, Peggy, 34; 35, 246 (photos)
Survey of School Media Standards, 280
Sutherland, Zena, 161
Sylvestre, Guy, 80 (photo), 81
Swartz, Roderick G., 412
Swenberg, W. A., 53
Swetmann, Viola T., 47
Syracuse University Library, 257
Systems Control, Inc., 46
System Development Corporation (SDC), 109-111, 168
Systems and Procedures Exchange Center (SPEC), 4, 41, 95
Tacha, Mike, 369
Tally, Roy D., 27
Taranko, Walter, 373
Taubert, Sigfred, 314
Tawanda Public Library (N.Y.), 75 (photo)
Taylor, Judy, 161
Taylor, Kay, 51
Taylor, Mildred D., 49, 67 (photo), 89, 91
Taylor, Nettie B., 374
Tebbets, Diane, 386
Teel, Kenneth S., 230
Telecommunication and Public Broadcasting,

427

306-308; (*also 77 ed.*)
applications of, 29, 307, 344 (photos)
OLLR funding, 172
public relations uses, 242
See also 76 ed.: Public Broadcasting and Satellite Communications; Television in Libraries
Telecommunications Demonstrations Program, 306
Telenet, 111
Television
American Television and Radio Archive, 175
children's films, 131
continuing education broadcasts, 99
effect on youth, 276
film productions, 130
library usage debate, 89
news archives, 29 (photo)
off-the-air recording issues, 191
OLLR funding, 172
public relations uses, 242
Television Critics Circle Award, 131
Television in Libraries: *See* Telecommunications and Public Broadcasting; *also* 76 ed.
Temple University, 5, 169, 225, 323
Tennessee report, 404-406
Texas report, 406, 407
photos, 19, 95, 135, 238, 256
Texas Library Association (TLA), 243
Thames Television, 130
Thaxton, Carlton, 362
Theatre Library Association, 308-309 (*also 77, 76 eds.*)
Theatre Library Association Award
1977 book, 309 (photo)
Theft, 168, 283-285
Theroux, Paul, 51
Thirteen Colonial Americana, 39
Thomas, Lucille C., 293, 383, 389
Thompson, Ann, 385
Thompson, Susan O., 234
Thompson, Thomas, 54
3M Company, 284
Tikhara, Amporn, 51
Time-Life Films, 191
Tolkien, Christopher, 348 (photo)
Top of the News, 179
Toronto, Can., 341
Children's Book Center, 90
Metropolitan Library, 73 (photo), 75
Toronto Conference on Editorial Problems, 297
Toys and Games, 309-310 (*also 77, 76 eds.*)
children's library services, 87
Tracing and Researching to Cultivate Esteem (TRACE), xxiii
Tracy, Kenneth, 396
Translations,
UNESCO activities, 315
Trejo, Arnulfo D., 123, 226, 264
Trejo, Tamiye, 118
Trezza, Alphonse Fiore, 124, 127, 128. *See also* Biographies 76 ed.
Trinkle, Robert, 367
Tripp, Wallace, 52
Trotti, John Boone, 28, 67 (photo)
Trustee Citations, 25, 26, 50

Trustees, 310-313 (*also 77, 76 eds.*)
activities, 311, 312 (photos)
ALTA activities, 25, 26
Tucker, John Mark, 262
Tucker Collection, 120
Turin, Irene, 49, 160
Tyler, Anne, 51
Tymnet, 111
Udall, Morris, 251
UNESCO, 314-316 (*also 77, 76 eds.*)
bibliographic projects, 57
General Information Program, 317
IBBY projects, 160
international library relations, 162
statistical services, 315
UNICEF
IBBY projects, 160
UNIMARC, 177
UBC projects, 317
Union University, 121
UNISIST (World Science Information System), 305
United Way of America, 148
Universal Availability of Publications (UAP), 144
Universal Bibliographic Control, 317 (*also 77, 76 eds.*)
Canadian report, 335
CLR grant, 84
IFLA activities, 144
Universal Serials and Book Exchange (USBE), 287, 317-318 (*also 77, 76 eds.*)
University Microfilms, 104
University of Arizona ry, Library, 7 (photo)
University of California, Berkeley, 96
University of Chicago, 5
University of Georgia's Computing Center (UGACC), 111
University of Illinois
ALA Archives agreement, 30
University of Oregon School of Librarianship, 116
University of Pittsburgh, 10, 96
University of Toronto Library Automation System (UTLAS), 45
Urban Libraries Council, 318-320
Urban Professionals, Library Service to: *See* 76 ed.
U.S.S.R.
librarianship in, 163
Moscow Book Fair, 251
U.S. librarians delegation, 163, 164
Utah report, 407-409
Uyehara, Harry Y., 363
Van Deerlin, Lionel, 307
Van Eisen Kohn, John S., 300
Van Zanten, Frank, 173
Vancouver, Can., 341
Varatorn, Supanee, 50
Veaner, Allen, 164, 261
Verba, Sidney, 54
Vermin, losses due to, xxxiii, xxxiv, 284
Vermont report, 409, 410
Vocational Rehabilitation Act, 142
Voluntary Standards and Accreditation Act of 1977, 303
Volunteers, library use of, 227, 279, 292
literacy programs, 182
Vickers, John A., 54
video cassettes, 308
Vietnam-Era Veterans

Readjustment Act of 1974, 224
Virginia report, 410-412
Virgo, Julie A. Carroll, 36, 38, 67 (photo), 188
Visapaa, Niilo, 160
Vita, Susan, 127
Vosper, Robert Gordon, 68 (photo), 145, 164
Voss, Anne, 387
W. Dale Clark Library, 76 (photo)
Waite, David, 251
Waldrop, Ruth, 350
Walker, Bernard, 233
Walker, Gay, 233
Walker, Estelle, 402
Walker, William, 32
Walt Disney Productions, 191
Waly, Adnan, 189
Ward, James E., 266
Warner, William, 54
Warnock, Phyllis, 386
Warren, David, 165
Wartluft, David J., 28
Washington, D.C., Public Library, 75
Washington Library Network (WLN), 44, 204, 93
Washington Report, 320-321 (*also 77, 76 eds.*)
Washington State Cooperative Storage Center, 7
Washington state report, 412, 413
Watanabe, Shigeo, 35, 68 (photo), 92
Water, losses due to, xxxii, xxxviii (photos), 233, 284
Waters, Richard L., 172
Waters, Samuel, 127, 193
Watson, Peter, xv-xxii
Watson, Robert, 51
Weaver, Barbara, 376
Webber, Jean, 166
Weber, Eugen, 52
Webster, Duane, 95
Wedgeworth, Robert, 31, 139, 162, 163, 164
Weeks, Barbara, 358
Weiner, Karl, 160
Weinstein, Robert A., 235
Weiss, Carol, 263
Welsh, William J., 175
West, B. C., Jr., 169
West Virginia report, 413, 414
public relations activities, 243
video services, 191
Western Council of State Libraries, 44
Western Interstate Commission for Higher Education (WICHE), 44
study grant, 184
Western Interstate Library Consortium (WILCO), 44
Weston-Elberling, Darlene, 378
Whalen, Lucille, 15
Wheatley Medal, 54
Whipple, Judith, 86
White, Herbert S., 49, 50, 116, 180, 274, 276
White House Conference for Handicapped Individuals, 142
White House Conference on Library and Information Services, 196, 281, 313 (*also 77, 76 eds.*)
White-Williams, Patricia, 50
Whitelock, Margaret, 28
Whitman, Kathryn A., 25
Whitman Award, 54
Whittendale, Mary, 341
Wiegand, Wayne A., 24
Wieman, Jean, 412
Wiese, Bernice (Marion), 212

Wijnstroom, Margreet, 301, 316 (*See also Biographies 77 ed.*)
Wilcox, Joann L., 377
Wilder Medal, 50
policy change, 34
Wile, Raymond R., 257
Wilhelm, Kate, 52
Wilkins, Barratt, 361
Williams, Barbara M., 370
Williams, Diane McAfee, 414
Williams, James, III, 188
Williams, Jean Frances, 37
Williams, John C., 232
Williams, Shirley, 346
Wilson, Alex, 81 (photo)
Wilson, Bill, 364
Wilson, Jane, 164
Wilson, Pauline, 180
Wilson Foundation Award, 54
Wilson Library Bulletin, 179
Wilson Library Periodical Award, 50
Wilson Library Recruitment Award, 50
Wilt, Matthew R., 85
Wiltshire, Ted, 341
Wimbish, Emery, Jr., 122
Winfrey, Dorman H., 406
Winger, Howard W., 55
Winnipeg Centennial Library, 336
Wirtanen, Lyle, 397
Wisconsin report, 414, 415
Wise, Nancy, 173
Wittenborn Award, 33
Wofford, Azile M., 212
Wolfert, Richard J., 393
Womack, Sharon, 352
Women in Librarianship, Status of, 321-324 (*also 77, 76 eds.*)
affirmative action, 225
salary discrimination, 5, 169
Women Library Workers (WLW), 323, 324
Women's Joint Congressional Committee, 223
Women's National Book Association, 324-325
Wong, Elsie, 118
Woodrum, Mrs. Pat, 396
Woodson Book Award, 54
Wright, Charles, 51
Wright, Don, 172
Wyatt, William, 213
Wynar, Bohdan, 23, 49
Wyngaard, Susan, 34
Wyngaarden, Joyce, 165
Wyoming report, 99 (photo), 415, 416
Xerox Corporation, 190
Yale Center for British Art, 298
Yanchisin, Daniel A., xxix
Yates, Marguerite B., 311
Yelich, Nolan, 410
Yeo, Ronald, 82
Yep, Laurence, 52
Yeshiva University, 124
Yochim, Charmaine S., 374
Young Adult Library Services, 325-328 (*also 77, 76 eds.*)
Young Adult Literature, 328-333 (*also 77, 76 eds.*)
young adult library services, 326
Young Adult Services Division, 333-334 (*also 77, 76 eds.*)
Young Viewers, 131
Yu, Amanda, 93
Zehery, Mohamed H., 164
Zemach, Margot, 161
Zerface, W.A., 223
Zero-based budgeting, 182
Zummurad, Mohammad, 50
Zweizig, Douglas, 18

Z
721
A525
1978

SEP 19 1978

RAYMOND H. FOGLER LIBRARY